THE NORTON ANTHOLOGY OF

WORLD LITERATURE

FOURTH EDITION

VOLUME F

THE NORTON ANTHOLOGY OF

WORLD LITERATURE

FOURTH EDITION

MARTIN PUCHNER, *General Editor*
HARVARD UNIVERSITY

SUZANNE AKBARI
UNIVERSITY OF TORONTO

WIEBKE DENECKE
BOSTON UNIVERSITY

BARBARA FUCHS
UNIVERSITY OF CALIFORNIA, LOS ANGELES

CAROLINE LEVINE
CORNELL UNIVERSITY

PERICLES LEWIS
YALE UNIVERSITY

EMILY WILSON
UNIVERSITY OF PENNSYLVANIA

VOLUME F

W. W. NORTON & COMPANY | New York · London

W. W. Norton & Company has been independent since its founding in 1923, when William Warder Norton and Mary D. Herter Norton first published lectures delivered at the People's Institute, the adult education division of New York City's Cooper Union. The firm soon expanded its program beyond the Institute, publishing books by celebrated academics from America and abroad. By midcentury, the two major pillars of Norton's publishing program—trade books and college texts—were firmly established. In the 1950s, the Norton family transferred control of the company to its employees, and today—with a staff of four hundred and a comparable number of trade, college, and professional titles published each year—W. W. Norton & Company stands as the largest and oldest publishing house owned wholly by its employees.

Editor: Peter Simon
Associate Editor: Gerra Goff
Project Editor: Christine D'Antonio
Manuscript Editor: Mike Fleming
Managing Editor, College: Marian Johnson
Managing Editor, College Digital Media: Kim Yi
Production Manager: Sean Mintus
Media Editor: Carly Fraser-Doria
Media Project Editor: Cooper Wilhelm
Assistant Media Editor: Ava Bramson
Editorial Assistant, Media: Joshua Bianchi
Marketing Manager, Literature: Kimberly Bowers
Art Direction: Rubina Yeh
Book Design: Jo Anne Metsch
Permissions Manager: Megan Schindel
Permissions Clearer: Margaret Gorenstein
Photo Editor: Catherine Abelman
Composition: Westchester Book Services
Cartographer: Adrian Kitzinger
Manufacturing: LSC Communications—Crawfordsville

Permission to use copyrighted material is included in the backmatter of this book.

ISBN 978-0-393-60286-9 (pbk.)

W. W. Norton & Company, Inc., 500 Fifth Avenue, New York, NY 10110-0017
wwnorton.com
W. W. Norton & Company Ltd., 15 Carlisle Street, London W1D 3BS

1 2 3 4 5 6 7 8 9 0

Contents

Preface

They arrive in boats, men exhausted from years of warfare and travel. As they approach the shore, their leader spots signs of habitation: flocks of goats and sheep, smoke rising from dwellings. A natural harbor permits them to anchor their boats so that they will be safe from storms. The leader takes an advance team with him to explore the island. It is rich in soil and vegetation, and natural springs flow with cool, clear water. With luck, they will be able to replenish their provisions and be on their way.

In the world of these men, welcoming travelers is a sacred custom, sanctioned by the gods themselves. It is also good policy among seafaring people. Someday, the roles may very well be reversed: today's host may be tomorrow's guest. Yet the travelers can never be certain whether a particular people will honor this custom. Wondering what to expect, the thirteen men enter one of the caves dotting the coastline.

The owner isn't home, but the men enter anyway, without any compunction. There are pens for sheep and goats, and there is plenty of cheese and milk, so the men begin eating. When the owner returns, they are terrified, but their leader, boldly, asks for gifts. The owner is not pleased. Instead of giving the intruders what they demand, he kills two of them and eats them for dinner. And then two more the next day. All the while, he keeps the men trapped in his cave.

A wily man, the leader devises a scheme to escape. He offers the owner wine, enough to make him drunk and sleepy. Once he dozes off, the men take a staff that they have secretly sharpened and they plunge it into the owner's eye, blinding him. Without sight, he cannot see the men clinging to the undersides of his prized sheep as they stroll, one by one, out of the cave to graze, and cleverly the men cling only to the male sheep, not the females, which get milked.

* * *

This story of hospitality gone wrong comes from *The Odyssey*, one of the best-known works in all of world literature. We learn of this strange encounter of Greek soldiers with the one-eyed Cyclops named Polyphemus from Odysseus, the protagonist of the epic, when he recounts his exploits at the court of another host, the king of the Phaeacians. Unsurprisingly, Polyphemus isn't presented in the best light. Odysseus describes the Cyclopes as a people without a "proper" community, without agriculture, without hospitality. Is Odysseus, who has been wined and dined by his current host, trying to curry favor with the king of the Phaeacians by telling him how terribly he was treated by these non-Greek others? Reading the passage closely, we can see that Polyphemus and the other Cyclopes are adroit makers of cheese, so they can't be all that lazy. When the blinded Polyphemus cries out for help, his associates come to help him as a matter of course, so they don't live quite as isolated from one another as Odysseus claims. Even though Odysseus asserts that Polyphemus is godless, the land is blessed by the gods with fertility, and Polyphemus's divine father comes to his aid when he prays. Odysseus says that the Cyclopes lack laws and custom, yet we are also shown the careful, regular, customary way that Polyphemus takes care of his household. In a touching scene toward the end of his encounter with Odysseus, after he is blinded, Polyphemus speaks gently and respectfully to his favorite ram, so he can't be all that monstrous. The one-eyed giants assist one another, they are shepherds and artisans, and they are capable of kindness. The passage's ambiguities suggest that perhaps it was partly Odysseus's fault that this encounter between cultures went so badly. Were he and his companions simply travelers badly in need of food, or were they looters hoping to enrich themselves? The passage suggests that it's a matter of narrative perspective, from whose point of view the story is told.

Scenes of hospitality (or the lack thereof) are everywhere in world literature, and questions about hospitality, about the courtesies that we owe to strangers and that strangers owe to us (whether we are guests or hosts), are as important today as they were in the ancient world. Although many writers and thinkers today are fond of saying that our era is the first "truly global" one, stories such as this episode from Homer's *Odyssey* remind us that travel, trade, exile, migration, and cultural encounters of all kinds have been features of human experience for thousands of years.

The experience of reading world literature, too, is a form of travel—a mode of cultural encounter that presents us with languages, cultural norms, customs, and ideas that may be unfamiliar to us, even strange. As readers, each time we begin to read a new work, we put ourselves in the role of a traveler in a foreign land, trying to understand its practices and values and hoping to feel, to some degree and in some way, connected to and welcome among the people we meet there. *The Epic of Gilgamesh*, for example, takes its readers on a tour of Uruk, the first large city in human history, in today's Iraq, boasting of its city walls, its buildings and temples with their stairways and foundations, all made of clay bricks. Like a tour guide, the text even lets its readers inspect the city's clay pits, over one square mile large, that provided the material for this miraculous city made from clay. The greatest marvel of them all is of course *The Epic of Gilgamesh* itself, which was inscribed on clay tablets—the first monument of literature.

Foundational Texts

From its beginnings, *The Norton Anthology of World Literature* has been committed to offering students and teachers as many complete or substantially represented texts as possible. This Fourth Edition emphasizes the importance of *foundational* texts as never before by offering new translations of some of the best-known and most-loved works in the history of world literature. *The Epic of Gilgamesh* stands first in line of these foundational texts, which capture the story of an entire people, telling them where they came from and who they are. Some foundational texts become an object of worship and are deemed sacred, while others are revered as the most consequential story of an entire civilization. Because foundational texts inspire countless retellings—as Homer did for the Greek tragedians—these texts are reference points for the entire subsequent history of literature.

Perhaps no text is more foundational than the one with which we opened this preface: Homer's *Odyssey*. In this Fourth Edition, we feature *The Odyssey* in a new translation by our classics editor, Emily Wilson. This version captures the fast pace and rhythmic regularity of the original and offers a fresh perspective on cultural encounters such as the one between Odysseus and Polyphemus that is described above. Astonishingly, Wilson's translation is the first translation of *The Odyssey* into English by a woman. For centuries, commentators have remarked that *The Odyssey* is unusually attuned to the lives of women, especially in its portrait of Odysseus's wife, Penelope, a compelling and powerful character who cunningly holds a rowdy group of suitors at bay. Wilson's translation pays special attention to the poem's characterization of this remarkable woman, who is every bit as intriguing as the "complicated man" who is the eponymous hero of the tale. Other female characters, too, are given a new voice in this translation. For example, Helen, wife of the Greek king Menelaus and (according to legend) possessor of "the face that launched a thousand ships," is revealed through Wilson's translation to speak of herself not as a "whore" for whose sake so many young Greek men fought, suffered, and died (as she does in most other translations) but instead as a perceptive, clever person, onto whom the Greeks, already eager to fight the Trojans, projected their own aggressive impulses: "They made my face the cause that hounded them," she says. The central conflicts of the epic, the very origin of the Trojan War, appear here in a startling new light.

We are also delighted to feature a new translation of the great Indian epic *The Mahabharata* by Carole Satyamurti, whose modern retelling captures the careful, patterned language of the original by rendering it in a fluent blank verse, a form familiar in English literature from Shakespeare to Wordsworth and also used in Wilson's *Odyssey*, a form particularly suitable to narrative. Readers used to older prose versions will find that the quest for honor and fame at the heart of this epic comes across as never before.

These two examples highlight an exciting dimension of our emphasis on new translations. The first several volumes of this anthology have always been dominated by male voices because men enjoyed privileged access to literacy and cultural influence in the centuries prior to modernity. Our focus on new translations has allowed us to introduce into these volumes many female voices—the voices of translators. So, for example, we present Homer's *Iliad* in a new translation by Caroline Alexander, Sophocles' *Antigone* in a recent translation by Ruby Blondell, and Euripides' *Medea* in a new, specially commissioned translation by Sheila H. Murnaghan, and we continue to offer work in the first volumes translated by female translators such as Laura Gibbs (Aesop's *Fables*), Dorothy Gilbert (Marie de France's *Lais*), Sholeh Wolpé (*The Conference of the Birds*), Wendy Belcher (*Kebra Nagast*), Sheila Fisher (Chaucer's *Canterbury Tales*), Rosalind Brown-Grant (Christine de Pizan's *Book of the City of Ladies*), and Pauline Yu (Wang Wei's poetry), among others. This commitment to featuring the work of female translators extends beyond these early centuries as well, for example in the brilliant new translation by Susan Bernofsky of a foundational text of literary modernity—Kafka's *Metamorphosis*. The result throughout the anthology is that these works now speak to today's readers in new and sometimes surprising ways.

Our emphasis in this edition on new translations is based on and amplifies the conviction expressed by the original editors of this anthology over fifty years ago: that world literature gains its power when it travels from its place of origin and speaks to people in different places. While purists sometimes insist on studying literature only in the original language, a dogma that radically shrinks what one can read, world literature not only relies on translation but actually thrives on it. Translation is a necessity; it is what enables a worldwide circulation of literature. It also is an art. One need only think of the way in which translations of the Bible shaped the history of Latin or English or German. Translations are re-creations of works for new readers. This edition pays keen attention to translation, featuring dozens of new translations that make classic texts newly readable and capture the originals in compelling ways. With each choice of translation, we have sought a version that would spark a sense of wonder while still being accessible to a contemporary reader.

Among other foundational texts presented in new translations and selections is the Qur'an, in a verse translation that is the product of a collaboration between M. A. Rafey Habib, a poet, literary scholar, and Muslim, and Bruce Lawrence, a renowned scholar of Islam. Their team effort captures some of the beauty of this extraordinary, and extraordinarily influential, sacred text. Augustine's *Confessions* are newly presented in a version by Peter Constantine, and Dante's *Inferno* is featured in the long-respected and highly readable translation by the American poet John Ciardi.

We have also maintained our commitment to exciting epics that deserve wider recognition such as the Maya *Popol Vuh*, the East African *Kebra Nagast*, and the *Sunjata*, which commemorates the founding of a West African empire in the late Middle Ages. Like *The Odyssey* and *The Mahabharata*, *Sunjata* was transmitted for centuries in purely oral form. But while *The Odyssey* was written down around 800 B.C.E. and *The Mahabharata* several hundred years later, the *Sunjata* was written down only in the twentieth century. We feature it here in a new prose translation by David C. Conrad, who personally recorded this version from a Mande storyteller, Djanka Tassey Condé, in 1994. In this way, *Sunjata* speaks to the continuing importance of oral storytelling, the origin of all foundational epics, from South Asia via Greece and Africa to Central America. Throughout the anthology, we remind readers that writing has coexisted with oral storytelling since the invention of literature and that it will continue to do so in the future.

A Network of Stories

In addition to foundational texts, we include in this edition a great number of story collections. The origins of this form of literature reach deep into the ancient world, as scribes collected oral stories and assembled them in larger works. We've substantially increased our offerings from what is undoubtedly the most famous of these collections, *The Thousand and One Nights*, to give readers a better sense of the intricate structure of this work, with its stories within stories within stories, all neatly framed by the overarching narrative of Shahrazad, who is telling them to her sister and the king to avoid being put to death. What is most notable about these story collections is how interconnected they are. Stories travel with striking ease from one collection to the next, appearing in *The Jataka*, one of the oldest Indian story collections framed by the

Buddha, and the *Pañcatantra*, an Indian collection put together for the education of princes, to *The Thousand and One Nights*, and, in Greece, Aesop's *Fables*. There existed a continent-spanning network of stories that allowed storytellers and scribes to recycle and reframe what they learned in ever new ways; it proved so compelling that later writers, from Marie de France to Chaucer, borrowed from it frequently. To give readers a sense of these connections, we have rethought our selection of stories by including those that appear in different collections, allowing readers to track the changes that occur when a story is told by the Buddha, by Shahrazad, or on a pilgrimage to Canterbury Cathedral.

Expanded Selections

Along with our focus on making foundational texts and story collections fresh and accessible, we have pruned the overall number of authors and were therefore able to increase our offerings from major texts that feature in many world literature courses. *Don Quixote* now includes the compelling "Captive's Tale," in which Cervantes draws on his own experiences as a slave in Algiers, where he spent five years after having been captured by pirates. Sor Juana Inés de la Cruz, whose significance is steadily increasing, is now represented by an additional selection from her mystery play, *The Divine Narcissus*, in Edith Grossman's elegant translation. Other major texts with increased selections include Machiavelli's *Prince* and, in the twentieth century, Lu Xun, who now can be introduced to students as the author not only of *Diary of a Madman* but also of *Ah Q—The Real Story*.

Despite this focus on foundational texts, story collections, and other major works, there are plenty of entirely new texts in this Fourth Edition. The Spanish Renaissance tale *The Abencerraje* tells of a Moorish knight who is taken prisoner by a Christian on his wedding day. Ultimately his captor relents and allows the knight to marry his beloved. This enormously popular tale speaks of the complex relations between Christianity and Islam in the early modern era and is featured here in a new translation by our Renaissance editor, Barbara Fuchs. Equally exciting is our representation of Korean literature. The *Tale of Hong Kiltong*, a story of a Korean Robin Hood endowed with magical powers, is a classic that we paired with excerpts from Lady Hyegyŏng's memoirs, which chronicle with deep psychological insight the horror and violence at the Korean royal court. These older Korean texts are complemented by a modern writer, Park Wansuh, whose work reflects the upheavals of the twentieth century on the Korean peninsula, from Japanese occupation and the Korean War to economic development. One of the first women to achieve critical success in modern Korea, Park offers readers keen insight into Korea's modern struggles.

We are particularly excited to now close the anthology with a story by the Nigerian writer Chimamanda Ngozi Adichie called "The Headstrong Historian," which, since its publication in 2008, has already become a favorite in world literature classrooms. This compact work introduces us to three generations of Nigerians as they navigate a complicated series of personal and cultural displacements. A thought-provoking exploration of the complex results of cultural contact and influence, this probing, searching journey seemed to us the most fitting conclusion to the anthology's survey of 4,000 years of literature.

Cultural Contact

Odysseus's encounter with the Cyclopes speaks not only to hospitality but also to the theme of cultural contact more generally. The earliest civilizations—those that invented writing and hence literature—sprang up where they did because they were located along strategic trading and migration routes. Contact was not just something that happened between fully formed cultures but something that made these cultures possible in the first place.

Committed to presenting the anthology's riches in a way that conveys this central fact of world literature, we have created sections that encompass broad contact zones—areas of intense trade in peoples, goods, art, and ideas where the earliest literatures emerged and intermingled. One of these is the Mediterranean Sea, whose central importance we visualize with four new maps. It was not just a hostile environment that could derail a journey home, as it did for Odysseus, or where nontravelers, like Polyphemus, might encounter violent invaders willing to attack and steal; it was also a connecting tissue, allowing for intense contact around its harbors. Medieval maps of the Mediterranean pay tribute to this fact: so-called portolan charts show a veritable mesh of lines connecting hundreds of ports. For this edition, we have further emphasized these contact zones, the location of intense conflict (including Cervantes's experience as a slave in North Africa) as well as friendly exchange. In a similar manner, the two major traditions of East Asia—China and Japan—are presented in the context of the larger region, including our new emphasis on Korea.

The importance of cultural contact and encounter is expressed not just in the overall organization of the anthology and the selection of material; it is also made visible in clusters of texts on the theme of travel and conquest, giving students access to documents related to travel, contact, trade, and conflict. For not all travel was voluntary. People traveled to escape wars and famine, plagues and environmental disasters. They were abducted, enslaved, and trafficked. Beginning with the early modern era, European empires dominated global politics and economics and accelerated the pace of globalization by laying down worldwide trade routes and communication networks, but old empires, such as China, continued to be influential as well. We added more material to our cluster "At the Crossroads of Empire," including a letter by Machemba, a chief in East Africa under German colonial control, and Mark Twain's trenchant soliloquy of Belgian King Leopold defending his brutal rule in Congo.

To these expanded clusters, we added a new one, "Poetry and Politics," which includes the Polish national poet Adam Mickiewicz and Latin American poet Rubén Darío's *To Roosevelt*, a powerful reminder of the crucial role poetry played in the gaining of national independence across the world. Poets captured the aspirations of nations and often enshrined those aspirations in national anthems, which also led us to include the Puerto Rican national anthem (one poet included in our anthology, Rabindranath Tagore, wrote not one but two national anthems, of both India and Bangladesh).

In the same volume, we also enhanced our cluster "Realism across the Globe," which traces one of the most successful global literary movements, one that found expression in France, Britain, Russia, Brazil, Mexico, and Japan. In keeping with our commitment to frequently taught authors, we increased our selection of Chekhov and present Tolstoy's *Death of Ivan Ilyich* in a new, acclaimed translation by Peter Carson.

The Birth of World Literature

In 1827, a provincial German writer, living in small-town Weimar, recognized that he was in the privileged position of having access not only to European literature but also to literature from much further afield, including Persian poetry, Chinese novels, and Sanskrit drama. The writer was Johann Wolfgang von Goethe, and in 1827, he coined a term to capture this new force of globalization in literature: "world literature." (We now include the "prologue" to Goethe's play *Faust*, which he wrote after encountering a similar prologue in the classical Sanskrit play *Śhakuntalā*, also included in the anthology.)

Since 1827, for less than 200 years, we have been living in an era of world literature. This era has brought many lost masterpieces back to life, including *The Epic of Gilgamesh*, which was rediscovered in the nineteenth century, and the *Popol Vuh*, which languished in a library until well into the twentieth century. Other works of world literature weren't translated and therefore didn't begin to circulate outside their sphere of origin until the last 200 years, including *The Tale of Genji*. With more literature becoming more widely available than ever before, Goethe's vision of world literature has become a reality today.

In presenting world literature from the dawn of writing to the early twenty-first century, and from oral storytelling to literary experiments of the avant-garde, this anthology raises the question not only of what world literature is but also of the nature of literature itself. We call attention to the changing nature of literature with thematic clusters on literature in the early volumes, to give students and teachers access to how early writers from different cultures thought about literature. But the changing role and nature of literature are visible in the anthology as a whole. Greek tragedy and comedy are experienced by modern students as literary genres, encountered in written texts; but for the ancient Athenians, they were primarily dramas, experienced live in an outdoor theater in the context of a religious and civic ritual. Other texts, such as the Qur'an or the Bible, are sacred pieces of writing, central to many people's religious faith, while others appreciate them primarily or exclusively as literature. Some texts, such as those by Laozi or Plato or Kant, belong in philosophy, while others, such as the Declaration of Independence, are primarily political documents. Our modern conception of literature as imaginative literature, as fiction, is very recent, about 200 years old. We have therefore opted for a much-expanded conception of literature that includes creation myths, wisdom literature, religious texts, philosophy, political writing, and fairy tales in addition to poems, plays, and narrative fiction. This answers to an older definition of literature as writing of high quality or of great cultural significance. There are many texts of philosophy or religion or politics that are not remarkable or influential for their literary qualities and that would therefore have no place in an anthology of world literature. But the works presented here do: in addition to or as part of their other functions, they have acquired the status of literature.

This brings us to the last and perhaps most important question: When we study the world, why study it through its literature? Hasn't literature lost some of its luster for us, we who are faced with so many competing media and art forms? Like no other art form or medium, literature offers us a deep history of human thinking. As our illustration program shows, writing was invented not for the composition of literature but for much more mundane purposes, such as the recording of ownership, contracts, or astronomical observations. But literature is writing's most glorious by-product. Literature can be reactivated with each reading. Many of the great architectural monuments of the past are now in ruins. Literature, too, often has to be excavated, as with many classical texts. But once a text has been found or reconstructed it can be experienced as if for the first time by new readers. Even though many of the literary texts collected in this anthology are at first strange, because they originated so very long ago, they still speak to today's readers with great eloquence and freshness. No other art form can capture the human past with the precision and scope of literature because language expresses human consciousness. Language shapes our thinking, and literature, the highest expression of language, plays an important role in that process, pushing the boundaries of what we can think and how we think it. This is especially true with great, complex, and contradictory works that allow us to explore different narrative perspectives, different points of view.

Works of world literature continue to elicit strong emotions and investments. The epic *Rāmāyana*, for example, plays an important role in the politics of India, where it has been used to bolster Hindu nationalism, just as the *Bhagavad-Gītā* continues to be a moral touchstone in the ethical deliberation about war. The so-called religions of the book, Judaism, Christianity, and Islam, make our selections from their scriptures a more than historical exercise as well. China has recently elevated the sayings of Confucius, whose influence on Chinese attitudes about the state had waned in the twentieth century, creating Confucius Institutes all over the world to promote Chinese culture in what is now called New Confucianism. World literature is never neutral. We know its relevance precisely by the controversies it inspires.

There are many ways of studying other cultures and of understanding the place of our own culture in the world. Archaeologists can show us objects and buildings from the past and speculate, through material remains, how people in the past ate, fought, lived, died, and were buried; scientists can date layers of soil. Literature is capable of something much more extraordinary: it allows us a glimpse into the imaginative lives, the thoughts and feelings of humans from thousands of years ago or living halfway around the world. This is the true magic of world literature as captured in this anthology, our shared human inheritance.

About the Fourth Edition

New Selections and Translations

Following is a list of the new translations, selections, and works in the Fourth Edition, in order:

VOLUME A

A new translation of Homer's *The Iliad* by Caroline Alexander • A new translation of Homer's *The Odyssey* by Emily Wilson, complete • Six new Aesop's *Fables*: "The Onager, the Donkey and the Driver," "The Eagle and the Farmer," "The Dung Beetle and the Eagle," "The Fox, the Donkey, and the Lion Skin," "Aesop and His Lamp," and "The Lion, the Fox, and the Deer" • New translations of Sappho's poetry by Philip Freeman, including ten new poems • New translations of *Oedipus the King* by David Grene, *Antigone* by Ruby Blondell, *Medea* by Sheila H. Murnaghan, and *Lysistrata* by Jeffrey Henderson • Benjamin Jowett's translation of *Symposium*, new to this edition • New translations of Catullus's poetry by Charles Martin • A new selection from *The Aeneid* from "The Kingdom of the Dead" • A new translation of *The Mahabharata* by Carole Satyamurti, including new selections from "The Book of Drona" and "Books 17 and 18: The Books of the Final Journey and the Ascent to Heaven" • New selections from *Zhuangzi* from "The Way of Heaven," "Outer Things," and "Of Swords"

VOLUME B

A new translation of Augustine's *Confessions* by Peter Constantine with a new selection from "Book XI [Time]" • A new translation of the Qur'an by M. A. Rafey Habib and Bruce Lawrence with new selections from "Light," "Ya Sin," and "The Sun" • A new translation of Marie de France's *Lais* by Dorothy Gilbert, including the new selection "Bisclavret" • A selection from *Vis and Ramin* translated by Dick Davis • A new translation of *The Conference of the Birds* by Sholeh Wolpé • A new translation and selection of Rumi's poetry, including six new poems: "[The nights I spend with you]," "[Like blood beneath my skin]," "[Profession, profit, trade]," "[A rose is still a rose]," "[How marvelous, that moment]," and "[On death's day]," as well as selections from *The Masnavi* translated by Dick Davis: "[On the Prohibition of Wine]," "[This World as a Dream]," "[On Men's Behavior with Women]," "[Man's Life Compared to That of an Embryo in the Womb]," and "[Moses and the Shepherd]" • John Ciardi's translation of *The Divine Comedy*, newly included, supplemented by two additional translations from Canto 3 of *Inferno* by Clive James and Mark Musa • A new translation of *Kebra Nagast* by Wendy Belcher and Michael Kleiner, including a new chapter, "About How King Solomon Swore an Oath to the Queen" • Seven new tales from *The Thousand and One Nights*: "[The Story of the Porter and the Three Ladies]," "[The First Dervish's Tale]," "[The Second Dervish's Tale]," "[The Tale of the Envious and the Envied]," "[The Third Dervish's Tale]," "[The Tale of the First Lady]," and "[The Tale of the Second Lady]" • "The Nun's Priest's Tale" from *The Canterbury Tales* • Three new tales from the *Pañcatantra*: "The Bird with Golden Dung" and "The Ass in the Tiger Skin" translated by Arthur W. Ryder and "The Ass without Ears or a Heart" translated by Patrick Olivelle • New selections from *The Tale of Genji*: "Sakaki: A Branch of Sacred Evergreens," "Maboroshi: Spirit Summoner," "Hashihime: The Divine Princess at Uji Bridge," "Agemaki: A Bowknot Tied in Maiden's Loops," "Yadoriki: Trees Encoiled in Vines of Ivy," and "Tenarai: Practicing Calligraphy"

VOLUME C

A new prose translation of *Sunjata: A West African Epic of the Mande* by David C. Conrad • New selections from *The Prince*: "[Liberality and Parsimony]," "[Love and Fear]," "[Dissimulation]," "[Contempt and Hatred]," "[Princely Devices; Fortresses]," "[The Excellent Prince]," "[Flatterers]," and "[The Princes of Italy]" • "The Abencerraje" translated by Barbara Fuchs, Larissa Brewer-García, and Aaron J. Ilika • A new selection from *Don Quixote*, "[A Story of Captivity in North Africa, Told to Don Quixote at the Inn]" • A revised *Fuenteovejuna* translated by G. J. Racz

VOLUME D

A new translation of "What Is Enlightenment?" by Mary C. Smith • A new translation of Sor Juana Inés de la Cruz's work translated by Edith Grossman, including three new sonnets, "[O World, why do you wish to persecute me?]," "[I adore Lisi but do not pretend]," and "[Because you have died, Laura, let affections]," as well as *Loa* to the Mystery Play *The Divine Narcissus: An Allegory* translated by Edith Grossman • Hŏ Kyun's "The Tale of Hong Kiltong" translated by Marshall R. Pihl • A selection from Lady Hyegyŏng's *The Memoirs of Lady Hyegyŏng* translated by JaHyun Kim Haboush

VOLUME E

A new selection from *Faust*, "Prelude in the Theatre" • Machemba's "Letter to Major von Wissmann" translated by Robert Sullivan and Sarah Lawall • A selection from Mark Twain's "King Leopold's Soliloquy" • A new cluster, "Poetry and Politics," including four new works, Adam Mickiewicz's "The Prisoner's Return" translated by Jerzy Peterkiewicz and Burns Singer, Speranza's (Lady Jane Wilde's) "A Lament for the Potato" and "The Exodus," and Lola Rodríguez de Tió's "The Song of the Borinquen" translated by José Nieto, as well as the new translation of "Guantanamera" by Elinor Randall • A new translation of *The Death of Ivan Ilyich* by Peter Carson • A new translation of "The Cane" by Margaret Jull Costa • José López Portillo y Rojas's "Unclaimed Watch" translated by Roberta H. Kimble • Anton Chekhov's "The Lady with the Dog" translated by Ivy Litvinov

VOLUME F

A new translation of *The Metamorphosis* by Susan Bernofsky • Lu Xun's "Ah Q—The Real Story" translated by William A. Lyell • Eric Bentley's translation, new to this edition, of Pirandello's *Six Characters in Search of an Author* • A new translation of "The Dancing Girl of Izu" by J. Martin Homan • Jorge Luis Borges's "The Library of Babel" translated by James E. Irby • M. D. Herder Norton's translations of Rainer Maria Rilke's poems, newly included • A new translation of "Lament for Ignacio Sánchez Mejías" by Pablo Medina • A new translation of "Matryona's Home" by Michael Glenny • Derek Walcott's "Sea Grapes" • Park Wansuh's "Mother's Hitching Post, Part 2" • Yu Hua's "On the Road at Eighteen" • Chimamanda Ngozi Adichie's "The Headstrong Historian"

Resources for Students and Instructors

Norton is pleased to provide students and instructors with abundant resources to make the teaching and study of world literature an even more interesting and rewarding experience.

We are pleased to launch the new *Norton Anthology of World Literature* website, found at digital.wwnorton.com/worldlit4pre1650 (for volumes A, B, C) and digital.wwnorton.com/worldlit4post1650 (for volumes D, E, F). This searchable and sortable site contains thousands of resources for students and instructors in one centralized place at no additional cost. Following are some highlights:

- A series of eight brand-new video modules are designed to enhance classroom presentation and spark student interest in the anthology's works. These videos, conceived of and narrated by the anthology editors, ask students to consider why it is important for them to read and engage with this literature.
- Hundreds of images—maps, author portraits, literary places, and manuscripts—are available for student browsing or instructor download for in-class presentation.
- Several hours of audio recordings are available, including a 10,000-term audio glossary that helps students pronounce the character and place names in the anthologized works.

The site also provides a wealth of teaching resources that are unlocked with an instructor's log-in:

- "Quick read" summaries, teaching notes, discussion questions, and suggested resources for every work in the anthology, from the much-praised *Teaching with* The Norton Anthology of World Literature: *A Guide for Instructors*
- Downloadable Lecture PowerPoints featuring images, quotations from the texts, and lecture notes in the notes view for in-class presentation

In addition to the wealth of resources in *The Norton Anthology of World Literature* website, Norton offers a downloadable Coursepack that allows instructors to easily add high-quality Norton digital media to online, hybrid, or lecture courses—all at no cost. Norton Coursepacks work within existing learning management systems; there's no new system to learn, and access is free and easy. Content is customizable and includes over seventy reading-comprehension quizzes, short-answer questions, links to the videos, and more.

Acknowledgments

The editors would like to thank the following people, who have provided invaluable assistance by giving us sage advice, important encouragement, and help with the preparation of the manuscript: Sara Akbari, Alannah de Barra, Wendy Belcher, Jodi Bilinkoff, Daniel Boucher, Freya Brackett, Psyche Brackett, Michaela Bronstein, Rachel Carroll, Sookja Cho, Kyeong-Hee Choi, Amanda Claybaugh, Lewis Cook, David Damrosch, Dick Davis, Burghild Denecke, Amanda Detry, Anthony Domestico, Megan Eckerle, Marion Eggert, Merve Emre, Maria Fackler, Guillermina de Ferrari, Alyssa Findley, Karina Galperín, Stanton B. Garner, Kimberly Dara Gordon, Elyse Graham, Stephen Greenblatt, Sara Guyer, Langdon Hammer, Emily Hayman, Iain Higgins, Paulo Lemos Horta, Mohja Kahf, Peter Kornicki, Paul W. Kroll, Peter H. Lee, Sung-il Lee, Lydia Liu, Bala Venkat Mani, Ann Matter, Barry McCrea, Alexandra McCullough-Garcia, Rachel McGuiness, Jon McKenzie, Mary Mullen, Djibril Tamsir Niane, Johann Noh, Felicity Nussbaum, Andy Orchard, John Peters, Michael Pettid, Daniel Taro Poch, Daniel Potts, Megan Quigley, Payton Phillips Quintanilla, Catherine de Rose, Imogen Roth, Katherine Rupp, Ellen Sapega, Jesse Schotter, Stephen Scully, Kyung-ho Sim, Sarah Star, Brian Stock, Tomi Suzuki, Joshua Taft, Sara Torres, J. Keith Vincent, Lisa Voigt, Kristen Wanner, Emily Weissbourd, Karoline Xu, Yoon Sun Yang, and Catherine Vance Yeh.

All the editors would like to thank the wonderful people at Norton, principally our editor Pete Simon, the driving force behind this whole undertaking, as well as Marian Johnson (Managing Editor, College), Christine D'Antonio and Kurt Wildermuth (Project Editors), Michael Fleming (Copyeditor), Gerra Goff (Associate Editor), Megan Jackson (College Permissions Manager), Margaret Gorenstein (Permissions), Catherine Abelman (Photo Editor), Debra Morton Hoyt (Art Director; cover design), Rubina Yeh (Design Director), Jo Anne Metsch (Designer; interior text design), Adrian Kitzinger (cartography), Agnieszka Gasparska (timeline design), Carly Fraser-Doria (Media Editor), Ava Bramson (Assistant Editor, Media), Sean Mintus (Production Manager), and Kim Bowers (Marketing Manager, Literature). We'd also like to thank our Instructor's Guide authors: Colleen Clemens (Kutztown University), Elizabeth Watkins (Loyola University New Orleans), and Janet Zong (Harvard University).

This anthology represents a collaboration not only among the editors and their close advisers but also among the thousands of instructors who teach from the anthology and provide valuable and constructive guidance to the publisher and editors. *The Norton Anthology of World Literature* is as much their book as it is ours, and we are grateful to everyone who has cared enough about this anthology to help make it better. We're especially grateful to the professors of world literature who responded to an online survey in 2014, whom we have listed below. Thank you all.

Michelle Abbott (Georgia Highlands College), Elizabeth Ashworth (Castleton State College), Clinton Atchley (Henderson State University), Amber Barnes (Trinity Valley Community College), Rosemary Baxter (Clarendon College), Khani Begum (Bowling Green State University), Joyce Boss (Wartburg College), Floyd Brigdon (Trinity Valley Community College), James Bryant-Trerise (Clackamas Community College), Barbara Cade (Texas College), Kellie Cannon (Coastal Carolina Community College), Amee Carmines (Hampton University), Farrah Cato (University of Central Florida), Brandon Chitwood (Marquette University), Paul Cohen (Texas State University), Judith Cortelloni (Lincoln College), Randall Crump (Kennesaw State University), Sunni Davis (Cossatot Community College), Michael Demson (Sam Houston State University), Richard Diguette (Georgia Perimeter College, Dunwoody), Daniel Dooghan (University of Tampa), Jeff Doty (West Texas A&M University), Myrto Drizou (Valdosta State University), Ashley Dugas (Copiah-Lincoln Community College), Richmond Eustis (Nicholls State University), David Fell (Carroll Community College), Allison Fetters (Chattanooga State Community College), Francis Fletcher (Folsom Lake College), Kathleen D. Fowler (Surry Community College), Louisa Franklin (Young Harris College), James Gamble (University of Arkansas), Antoinette Gazda (Averett University), Adam Golaski (Central Connecticut State University), Anissa Graham (University of North Alabama), Eric Gray (St. Gregory's University), Jared Griffin (Kodiak College), Marne Griffin (Hilbert College), Frank Gruber (Bergen Community College), Laura Hammons (Hinds Community College), Nancy G. Hancock (Austin Peay State University), C. E. Harding (Western Oregon University), Leslie Harrelson (Dalton State College), Eleanor J. Harrington-Austin (North Carolina Central University), Matthew Hokom (Fairmont State University), Scott Hollifield (University of Nevada, Las Vegas), Catherine Howard (University of Houston, Downtown), Jack Kelnhofer (Ocean County College), Katherine King (University of California, Los Angeles), Pam Kingsbury (University of North Alabama), Sophia Kowalski (Hillsborough Community College), Roger Ladd (University of North Carolina at Pembroke), Jameela Lares (University of Southern Mississippi), Susan Lewis (Delaware Technical Community College), Christina Lovin (Eastern Kentucky University), Richard Mace (Pace University), Nicholas R. Marino (Borough of Manhattan Community College, CUNY), Brandi Martinez (Mountain Empire Community College), Kathy Martinez (Sandhills Community College), Matthew Masucci (State College of Florida), Kelli McBride (Seminole State College), Melissa McCoy (Clarendon College), Geoffrey McNeil (Notre Dame de Namur University), Renee Moore (Mississippi Delta Community College), Anna C. Oldfield (Coastal Carolina University), Keri Overall (Texas Woman's University), Maggie Piccolo (Rutgers University), Oana Popescu-Sandu (University of Southern Indiana), Jonathan Purkiss (Pulaski Technical College), Rocio Quispe-Agnoli (Michigan State University), Evan Radcliffe (Villanova University), Ken Raines (Eastern Arizona College), Jonathan Randle (Mississippi College), Kirk G. Rasmussen (Utah Valley University), Helaine Razovsky (Northwestern State University of Louisiana), Karin Rhodes (Salem State University), Stephanie Roberts (Georgia Military College), Allen Salerno (Auburn University), Shannin

Schroeder (Southern Arkansas University), Heather Seratt (University of Houston, Downtown), Conrad Shumaker (University of Central Arkansas), Edward Soloff (St. John's University), Eric Sterling (Auburn University Montgomery), Ron Stormer (Culver-Stockton College), Marianne Szlyk (Montgomery College), Tim Tarkington (Georgia Perimeter College), Allison Tharp (University of Southern Mississippi), Diane Thompson (Northern Virginia Community College), Sevinc Turkkan (College at Brockport, State University of New York), Verne Underwood (Rogue Community College), Patricia Vazquez (College of Southern Nevada), William Wallis (Los Angeles Valley College), Eric Weil (Elizabeth City State University), Denise C. White (Kennesaw State University), Tamora Whitney (Creighton University), Todd Williams (Kutztown University of Pennsylvania), Bertha Wise (Oklahoma City Community College), and Lindsey Zanchettin (Auburn University).

THE NORTON ANTHOLOGY OF

WORLD LITERATURE

FOURTH EDITION

VOLUME F

I

Modernity and Modernism, 1900–1945

At the beginning of the twentieth century, the world was interconnected as never before. New means of transportation, such as the steamship, the railroad, the automobile, and the airplane, allowed people in the industrialized West to cover vast distances quickly. Other technologies, such as the telegraph and the telephone, allowed them to communicate instantaneously. In the decades to come, such inventions, powered either by electricity or by the internal combustion engine, along with improvements in agriculture, nutrition, public health, and medical care, would foster remarkable growth in human health and material prosperity. Infant mortality declined and world population more than tripled, from under two billion to around six billion. In unprecedented numbers, people were living in large cities; correspondingly, the experience of urban life is one of the major themes of twentieth-century literature. Together, these vast transformations in human experience can be characterized as *modernization*.

Yet the technological advances that undeniably improved human life led, as well, to the production of weapons that were increasingly effective, and therefore increasingly destructive. As distant parts of the globe grew closer through trade, immigration,

"Books!" (1925), a promotional poster by the Russian artist Alexander Rodchenko (1891–1956).

and communications, they often came into deadly conflict. Indeed, the twentieth century was the bloodiest in human history: as many as 200 million died in wars, revolutions, genocides, and related famines. In response to the century's horrors, the old dream of a unified, peaceful world became ever more appealing; and to many, in the splendid light of new technologies and optimistic ideas of progress, it even seemed achievable as never before. Frequently, those who sought to end war looked to supranational bodies, such as the League of Nations, the United Nations, the European Community (later the European Union), the Organization of American States, and the Organization for African Unity, as the future guarantors of "peaceful coexistence," a term that gained currency during the Cold War to refer to the arms race between the United States and the Soviet Union.

A caricature of Cecil John Rhodes, perhaps the most famous supporter of British colonialism and imperialism in the late nineteenth century, here straddling the continent of Africa. The wires in his hands are telegraph cables. The cartoon was drawn soon after Rhodes announced his intention to connect Cape Town, South Africa, with Cairo, Egypt, by telegraph and rail.

MODERNITY AND CONFLICT IN WORLD HISTORY, 1900–1945

As Europe and North America became industrialized over the course of the nineteenth century, they extended their political power to cover most of the globe. By 1900, after centuries of European expansion, there were no longer, in the words of **Joseph Conrad**'s ***Heart of Darkness***, any "blank spaces" on the map. Within a few years, explorers would even reach the North and South Poles. At the 1884 Berlin Conference, the European powers had carved up Africa among themselves; they also controlled most of southern Asia. The remaining independent nations in the Americas and the antipodes maintained close ties with their former colonial masters—Britain, Spain, France, Portugal, and the Netherlands. The small kingdom of Belgium and the recently unified nations of Germany and Italy sought to acquire overseas empires of their own. The British Empire was still at its zenith, and since Britain retained colonial possessions in all parts of the world, it was known as "the empire on which the sun never sets."

Yet as the twentieth century advanced, the sun did set on the British Empire—and on every other European empire as well. During the first half of the century, the world system that the European powers dominated experienced massive crises in the forms of two world wars, the Russian Revolution, the Great Depression, and the Holocaust. These upheavals became central concerns for the literature of the period and contributed to a rethinking of traditional literary forms and techniques.

The First World War (1914–18) took place mainly in Europe; it was the most mechanized war to date and killed some 15 million people. Much of the war on the Western Front (in Belgium and France) was characterized by stale-

A large parade in support of women's suffrage, Manhattan, 1913.

mate, as each side ferociously defended entrenched positions with machine guns, resulting in massive battles over tiny slices of territory, as at Ypres, Vimy Ridge, and Verdun. It was only after the United States joined the war, in 1917, that the Allies (France, Britain and its colonies, Italy, and the United States) gained the initiative and were able to repel Germany.

In the East, Germany and Austria-Hungary drove deep into Russian territory. Russia's near-defeat contributed to the revolution of 1917, in which the Bolsheviks under V. I. Lenin sought to establish a communist "dictatorship of the proletariat," with a tiny vanguard of party members taking power in the name of the working classes. During the succeeding decades, forced collectivization of agriculture and enterprise (which led to widespread famine), as well as purges of people considered enemies of the Communist Party (especially under Lenin's successor, Joseph Stalin), caused tens of millions of deaths, both in Russia and in other former territories of the Russian Empire, such as the Ukraine. (They were united under the communist regime of the Soviet Union.) The communist movement, initially supportive of some literary experiments, increasingly restricted the scope of acceptable artistic expression in the countries where it gained control. In response, a dissident literature developed, published abroad or in informal, private editions that could circulate without being censored. Writers such as **Anna Akhmatova** and **Alexander Solzhenitsyn** had to work within these constraints.

The Treaty of Versailles (1919) formalized the end of the war, and of four great empires—the German, Austro-Hungarian, Russian, and Ottoman—dividing most of Central and Eastern Europe into a multitude of smaller nations (some of which would later be reabsorbed by the resurgent Soviet Union and Nazi Germany). The treaty also founded the first of the great international organizations, the League of Nations—which, despite its idealistic beginnings, proved incapable of enforcing the demilitarization of Germany.

MILES
0
1200
2400
3600
4800
AT THE EQUATOR
0
2400
4800
KILOMETERS
Arctic Ocean
Arctic Ocean
Greenland (Den.)
SIBERIA (Russia)
ALASKA (U.S.)
NORTH AMERICA
Dominion of Canada
North Pacific Ocean
Chicago
New York
United States of America
Bermuda (Br.)
North Atlantic
Los Angeles
Mexico
Gulf of Mexico
BAHAMAS (Br.)
Cuba
Haiti
Dominican Rep.
Puerto Rico (U.S.)
HAWAIIAN IS. (U.S.)
Mexico City
Jamaica (Br.)
Br. Honduras
VIRGIN IS. (Br. & Den.)
Guadeloupe (Fr.)
Guatemala
Honduras
Caribbean Sea
El Salvador
Nicaragua
Martinique (Fr.)
Barbados (Br.)
Trinidad & Tobago (Br.)
Costa Rica
Panama
Colombia
Venezuela
Br. Guiana
Dutch Guiana
French Guiana
GILBERT IS. (Br.)
Christmas I. (Br.)
Equator
GALAPAGOS IS. (Ecuador)
Ecuador
BISMARCK ARCH. (Ger.)
United States of Brazil
Peru
SOUTH AMERICA
SOLOMON IS. (Br. & Ger.)
FIJI IS. (Br.)
TONGA IS. (Br.)
Bolivia
Australia
New Caledonia (Fr.)
Paraguay
Rio de Janeiro
Chile
Tahiti (Fr.)
Argentina
South Pacific Ocean
Santiago
Buenos Aires
Uruguay
Sydney
New Zealand
South Atlantic
FALKLAND IS. (Br.)
S. Georgia (Br

THE WORLD
1913
The British Empire
Arctic Ocean
Spitsbergen (Nor.)
Iceland (Den.)
SIBERIA
Russian Empire
Norway
Sweden
St. Petersburg
Denmark
Netherlands
Great Britain
Dublin
London
Germany
Berlin
Warsaw
Moscow
Belgium
Lux.
Prague
Paris
France
Switz.
Vienna
Austro-Hungary
Venice
Romania
Serbia
Mont.
Alb.
Bulgaria
Black Sea
Greece
Istanbul
Portugal
Madrid
Spain
Rome
Italy
Ottoman Empire
ZORES (Port.)
Gibraltar (Br.)
Mediterranean Sea
Madeira (Port.)
Algeria
Tunisia
Malta (Br.)
Cyprus (Br.)
Beirut
Alexandria
Jerusalem
Cairo
Morocco
ANARIES (Sp.)
Rio de Oro
Libya (It.)
Egypt
AFRICA
Cape Verde (Port.)
French West Africa
Red Sea
Anglo-Egyptian Sudan
Eritrea (It.)
Persia
Bahrein (Br.)
Arabia
Aden
Oman
Fr. Somaliland
Socotra I. (Br.)
British Somaliland
Arabian Sea
Afghanistan
New Delhi
TIBET
Nepal
Bhutan
British India
Bombay (Mumbai)
Bay of Bengal
Burma
Gambia
Portuguese Guinea
Sierra Leone
Liberia
Togoland (Ger.)
Gold Coast
Nigeria
Ibadan
Cameroon (Ger.)
Abyssinia (It.)
Italian Somaliland
Uganda
Br. E. Africa (Kenya)
Nairobi
Sp. Guinea
Fr. Congo
Belgian Congo
Ascension I. (Br.)
Kabinda (Port.)
Zanzibar (Br.)
German E. Africa
SEYCHELLES (Br.)
LACCADIVES (Br.)
Ceylon
MALDIVES (Br.)
Equator
CHAGOS ARCH. (Br.)
ANDAMAN IS. (Br.)
Angola (Port.)
Nyasaland
Rhodesia
Mozambique (Port.)
St. Helena I. (Br.)
Ger. S.W. Africa
Walvis Bay (Br.)
Bechuanaland
Johannesburg
Swaziland
Basutoland
Union of South Africa
Madagascar (Fr.)
Mauritius (Br.)
Réunion (Fr.)
Tristan da Cunha I. (Br.)
Indian Ocean
Kerguélen I. (Fr.)
Ocean
ASIA
MONGOLIA
MANCHURIA
Chinese Republic
Peking (Beijing)
Korea (Jap.)
Seoul
Weihaiwei (Br.)
Tokyo
Japan
Shanghai
Okinawa (Japan)
Formosa (Jap.)
Hanoi
Hong Kong (Br.)
Macao (Port.)
Hainan
Siam
Fr. Indochina
PHILIPPINES (U.S.)
Pacific Ocean
Br. N. Borneo
Brunei
Malay States
Sarawak
Dutch East Indies
NEW GUINEA
Papua
COCOS IS. (Br.)
Christmas I. (Br.)
Commonwealth of Australia
TASMANIA
ANTARCTICA

Making matters worse, the Allies' demand for huge reparations contributed to the economic chaos in Germany that, in turn, furthered the cause of the National Socialists (Nazis). The party came to power under Adolf Hitler in 1933 with a program of national rearmament and authoritarian politics held together by the glue of anti-Semitism. The Nazis were unremittingly hostile to modern literature, and writers such as **Thomas Mann** and **Bertolt Brecht** went into exile.

Beginning on October 24, 1929, the liberal capitalist world also experienced financial disaster, with the stock market crash that heralded the Great Depression. Within a few years, a third of American workers were unemployed; hunger and joblessness spread throughout the industrialized world. Despite fears that radical parties like the Communists or the Nazis would emerge from the economic devastation in the United States, Franklin D. Roosevelt (president from 1933 to 1945) was able to reverse the worst effects of the Depression with the New Deal, which included public works spending and the introduction of Social Security and other forms of protection for the elderly and the unemployed. "The only thing we have to fear," the president told an anxious public, "is fear itself."

Germany annexed Austria and invaded Czechoslovakia in 1938. After Hitler's military forces invaded Poland in 1939, the Second World War began, with Germany rapidly conquering most of continental Europe. France fell in 1940, and the following year Germany invaded the Soviet Union. Germany allied itself with both Fascist Italy and authoritarian Japan, which had earlier conquered Korea and occupied China. The United States entered the war after the surprise Japanese attack on Pearl Harbor, Hawaii, on December 7, 1941. It took almost three years for the Allies to find a foothold in Western Europe; during that time, the most intense battles took place in the Soviet Union.

In November 1940, the Nazis closed off a portion of Warsaw, Poland, and designated it a Jewish ghetto—essentially condemning 400,000 people to an urban prison. Predictably, nearly 100,000 of the people in the ghetto died of disease and starvation over the next year and a half. Among those trapped behind the wall were these two children, begging for food.

Once Germany controlled much of Eastern Europe, Hitler, who had enforced anti-Semitic policies and encouraged persecution of the Jews on such occasions as *Kristallnacht,* or the Night of Broken Glass (on November 9, 1938), took even more extreme measures. His troops massacred large numbers of Jews (and also Poles) between 1939 and 1941, while others were either forced into ghettos or transported to concentration camps. Starting in 1941, Hitler authorized the so-called Final Solution, aimed at destroying the Jewish people. In the end, his death squads and camps would exterminate 6 million Jews (more than half the Jewish population of Europe), as well as several million Poles, Gypsies, homosexuals, and political enemies of the Nazis.

The war in Europe ended when the Soviets entered Berlin in May 1945; Hitler had committed suicide the previous month. Fighting still raged in the

Pacific, and the United States dropped atomic bombs on Hiroshima and on Nagasaki, obliterating those Japanese cities and starting the nuclear age. The cessation of the global hostilities, which had resulted in some 60 million deaths, took place on August 14, 1945. The return to peacetime brought much relief, but also the sense that a new era of conflict was at hand. The wartime British prime minister Winston Churchill spoke of an "iron curtain" that had "descended across the Continent." The aftermath of the Second World War led quickly to the Cold War, in which most nations aligned themselves with either the capitalist West or the communist East.

MODERNISM IN WORLD LITERATURE

Writers around the world responded to these cataclysmic events with an unprecedented wave of literary experimentation, known collectively as *modernism*, which linked the political crises with a crisis of representation—a sense that the old ways of portraying the human experience were no longer adequate. The modernists therefore broke away from such conventions as standard plots, verse forms, narrative techniques, and the boundaries of genre. They often grouped themselves in avant-garde movements with names like futurism, Dadaism, and surrealism, seeing their literary experiments in the context of a broader search for a type of society to replace the broken prewar consensus.

The modernist crisis of representation also reflected a broader "crisis of reason" that had begun in Europe in the late nineteenth century, as radical thinkers challenged the ability of human reason to understand the world. In the wake of Charles Darwin's discovery of the process of natural selection, human beings could no longer be so easily distinguished from the other animals; the animal nature of human existence was a crucial concept to three thinkers from the nineteenth century who wielded significant influence in the twentieth. Karl Marx saw the struggle between social classes for control of the means of economic production as the motor force of history; his thought inspired the communist revolutions in Russia and China during the twentieth century and also the more moderate Socialist and Communist Parties of Western Europe. Friedrich Nietzsche attacked both a belief in God and the conviction that humans are fundamentally rational. His emphasis on the variety of perspectives from which we shape our notions of truth would have a substantial affect on both modernists and postmodernists. Sigmund Freud published the first major work of psychoanalysis, *The Interpretation of Dreams*, in 1900. His exploration of the unconscious, the power of sexual and destructive instincts, the shaping force of early childhood, and the Oedipal conflict between fathers and sons led many writers to reimagine the wellsprings of family interactions. More specifically, Freud's stress on the hidden, or "latent," meanings contained in dreams, jokes, and slips of the tongue lent itself to creative wordplay.

While philosophers and psychologists were examining the dynamics of the human mind, scientists found that the natural world does not necessarily function in the way it appears to. The most famous of the scientific discoveries of the early twentieth century was Albert Einstein's theory of relativity (Special Theory, 1905; General Theory, 1915). Other discoveries around the turn of the century, such as radioactivity, X-rays, and quantum theory, presented counterintuitive understandings of the physical universe that conflicted with classical Newtonian physics and even with common sense.

Although Pablo Picasso's *Guernica* (1937) memorializes a historical event—the bombing of Guernica, in the Basque region of Spain, in April 1937, during the Spanish Civil War—the painting stresses the psychological horror, rather than the physical appearance, of the event.

Modernism began in Europe and can be traced both to these new currents of thought and to the experimental literature of the late nineteenth century, including the symbolist poets and the realist novelists. Like such symbolists as **Charles Baudelaire** and **Stéphane Mallarmé**, the modernist poets held a high conception of the power and significance of poetry. In their works, they often drew on symbolist techniques, such as ambiguous and esoteric meanings. **T. S. Eliot**'s ***The Waste Land*** (1922) responded to the prevalent sense of devastation after the First World War and was seen at the time as the high-water mark of modernism in the English language.

Modernist fiction followed the realists, especially **Gustave Flaubert**, in attempting to portray life "as it is" by using precise language. Modernists found, however, that in depicting characters, settings, and events with directness and without sentiment, they discovered mysteries that lay beyond language. The great modern novelists, including Conrad, **Marcel Proust**, Mann, **James Joyce**, and **Virginia Woolf**, all started out by writing realistic works in the manner of Flaubert or **Leo Tolstoy**. The great difference, which became more apparent as the modernists reached maturity, was that the realists tended to balance their attention between the objective, outside world and the inner world of their characters, whereas the modernists shifted the balance toward interiority. Thus, rather than offer objective descriptions of the outside world, they increasingly focused on the more limited perspective of an individual, often idiosyncratic, character. In this approach they were following the lead of another great nineteenth-century precursor, **Fyodor Dostoyevsky**.

It would be too simple to say that the modernists did away with the omniscient narrator. They might retain a narrator who seemed to be observing the characters and events with an objective, all-knowing eye, but the authors counterbalanced such narrators with storytellers like Conrad's Marlow or Proust's Marcel, who were themselves characters in the stories they related and whose reliability might therefore be in doubt. Joyce's story "**The Dead**," with its narrator who sees into the mind of the protagonist Gabriel Conroy, could easily belong to the nineteenth century, but Joyce later pioneered the move toward a deeper interiority in two novels, *A Portrait of the Artist as a Young Man* (1916) and *Ulysses* (1922)—the latter is, in fact, the most famous and influential of all modernist novels. The new method, called "the stream of consciousness," was well described by another of its great practitioners, Woolf, when she wrote: "Let us record the atoms as they fall upon the mind in the order in which they fall, let us trace the pattern, however disconnected and incoherent in appearance, which each sight or incident scores upon the consciousness."

A similar, possibly even farther-reaching transformation took place in the theater. Just as novelists questioned the role of an omniscient narrator, dramatists challenged the separation of the audience from the action of the play—specifically, the tradition of the "fourth wall." According to this concept, developed in realist and naturalist theater of the nineteenth century, the actors on stage went about their business as if they did not know that an audience was watching them. In different ways, the major modernist playwrights, represented in this section by **Luigi Pirandello**, broke down the fourth wall. Pirandello introduced a playful "metatheater," calling attention to the fictionality of his works by having his characters debate the nature of drama. In Brecht's Epic Theater, audience members were encouraged not to identify with the characters and be carried away by the drama but to think critically about the actions they were witnessing. The German writer's notion of an "estrangement effect" that would shock audiences out of their complacency was linked closely to broader modernist theories in which the task of art was to break through our habitual assumptions to make the world appear strange and new.

Many of these modernist experiments took place on the level of form; but modernism also entailed a change in the content of literature, specifically in the inclusion of previously taboo subject matter (especially sexuality), as well as greater attention to shifting social roles (often relating to the impact of feminism). Woolf was famous both as a novelist and as an essayist on feminist issues. Her work ***A Room of One's Own*** makes the case for women's writing and, more broadly, for women's admission into traditionally male professions and institutions of learning, which were gradually becoming more open to women during the first decades of the century. Feminism had won a major victory with the achievement of women's suffrage in 1918 in Britain; the United States would guarantee all women the vote in 1920. Conrad's novel *Heart of Darkness* criticizes the actions of European imperialists in Africa, although he seems to make an exception for the British Empire. Joyce addresses the political situation of Ireland in the midst of its quest for independence from Britain. **Franz Kafka**'s work has been seen as a commentary on the status of the Jews in a hostile world. Mann addresses homosexuality, which was becoming socially acceptable even though it remained illegal in many countries. **William Faulkner** documents the decline of an aristocratic South and the persistence of racial tensions. Even the seemingly most intimate of works, Proust's ***Swann's Way***, documents the social changes that France was undergoing in the late nineteenth century. (In subsequent volumes of his masterpiece, *Remembrance of Things Past*, Proust also treats both anti-Semitism and homosexuality at length.) In their later works, Mann and Proust were conscious of reconstructing the bygone Europe of the years before the First World War.

Modernist experimentation persisted in various forms throughout the century. Somewhat younger than the European novelists represented here, **Jorge Luis Borges** wrote short pieces that present alternative universes; in **"The**

Garden of the Forking Paths," the fictional universe he creates starts out as a commentary on a work of history. Whereas Pirandello's play with theatricality came to be known as "metatheater," Borges's games with the border between fact and fiction have been called "metafiction" or even "metahistory." Borges is also representative of the mobility of writers in the twentieth century: educated mostly in Europe, he returned home to Argentina and formed a bridge between European modernism and the significant expansion of Latin American fiction in the second half of the century.

Asian writers followed European and American developments with interest and typically responded in one of three ways. Some embraced modern Western themes and styles; others, while drawing on nineteenth-century European realist forms, tended to blend them with more traditional Asian subject matter or linguistic styles. Finally, a substantial number of Asian writers embraced communist or socialist politics and a related style of politically engaged fiction. Often, a single writer would combine more than one of these responses. For example, in Japan, **Akutagawa Ryūnosuke** draws on techniques of European modernism but also mines old Japanese tales for material. **Kushi Fusako** adopts the form of personal narrative popular in modern Japan but infuses it with political commentary critical of the Japanese annexation of Okinawa. In Korea, **Ch'ae Man-sik** uses modernist techniques to make a political statement about Japanese domination that could nonetheless pass muster with the censors. In China, **Lao She** infuses realist techniques with political allegory, while **Lu Xun** combines modernist techniques with a more satirical attitude to contemporary Chinese society.

In other parts of the world, nationalist movements against colonization were gathering force and would result in a wave of independence after the Second World War. The African American writer and activist W. E. B. Du Bois had said early in the century that "the problem of the Twentieth Century is the problem of the color line." Literature played a major role both in the articulation of this challenge and in the attempts to solve it. During the 1920s, when, in the words of Langston Hughes, "Harlem was in vogue," a group of African American intellectuals and writers enjoyed unprecedented success in what came to be known as the Harlem Renaissance. During the 1930s, a group of African and Caribbean intellectuals, led by Léopold Sédar Senghor and **Aimé Césaire**, met in Paris, where they had come to pursue higher education, and formed the Négritude movement. It would celebrate the culture of Africa and the African diaspora and provide intellectual support

A self-portrait, circa 1939, of Tsuguharu Foujita (1886–1968), a Tokyo-born artist who applied traditional Japanese printing, painting, and coloring techniques to works that were otherwise modernist in style.

and political leadership for decolonization movements after the war.

These developments pointed the way to a postwar and postcolonial literature that often rejected the formal experiments of the modernist generation and sought a more direct engagement with the pressing political issues of the day, such as decolonization, civil rights, and economic empowerment. The Holocaust also presented a distinct challenge to writers who sought to record the unspeakable: some took a straightforward, documentary style, while others turned to a minimalist, almost mystical language. While Europe, after 1945, set about rebuilding the cities destroyed in the war, much of the rest of the world entered a period of decolonization, establishing nation-states on the basis of the principles (democracy, equality) that the Allies had defended during the war and that they now had to acknowledge as the basis for their colonies' self-determination. The postwar world would inspire both avant-garde literary movements and a return to more traditional forms, but the literature of the twentieth century had been decisively marked by the experiments of the modernists, who created a diverse, remarkable range of masterpieces during a period of continual social crisis.

JOSEPH CONRAD

1857–1924

Born in Polish Ukraine, learning English at twenty-one, and then serving as a sailor for sixteen years, Joseph Conrad nonetheless became a prolific, innovative writer of English fiction. Works like *Heart of Darkness* and *Lord Jim* have influenced novelists throughout the twentieth century, because of Conrad's ability to evoke the feel and color of distant places as well as the complexity of human responses to moral crisis. Conrad's sense of separation and exile, his yearning for the kinship and solidarity of humanity, permeates these works, along with the despairing vision of a universe in which even the most ardent idealist finds no ultimate meaning or moral value.

He was born Jozef Teodor Konrad Korzeniowski on December 3, 1857, the only child of Polish patriots who were involved in resistance to Russian rule. (He changed his name to the more English-sounding Conrad for the publication of his first novel, in 1895.) Their country had been partitioned through most of the nineteenth century among Russia, Prussia, and Austria. The town where Conrad was born, now part of Ukraine, had traditionally been ruled by the Polish aristocracy, and Conrad's family bore a coat of arms. When his father was condemned for conspiracy in 1862, the family went into exile in northern Russia, where Conrad's mother died three years later from tuberculosis. Conrad's father, a poet and a translator, supported the small family by translating Shakespeare and Victor Hugo; Conrad himself read English novels by William Makepeace Thackeray, Walter Scott, and Charles Dickens in Polish and in French translation. When his father, too, succumbed to tuberculosis in 1869, the eleven-year-old orphan went to live with his maternal uncle, Tadeusz Bobrowski, who sent him to school in Cracow (in Austrian-ruled Poland) and Switzerland. Bobrowski supported his orphaned nephew both financially and emotionally, and, when Conrad asked to fulfill a long-standing dream of going to sea, he gave him an annual allowance (which Conrad consistently overspent) and helped him find a berth in the merchant marine. The decision to go to sea reflected the gallant and romantic aspirations of a child who had often been frail and sickly; it also marked a permanent departure from the nation that his parents had fought and, as Conrad saw it, died for.

During the next few years, he worked on French ships, traveling to the West Indies and participating in various activities—some of which, such as smuggling, were probably illegal—that would play a role in his novels of the sea. He also lost money at the casino in Monte Carlo, may have had an unhappy romance, and attempted suicide. Many events of these years are known only through the fictionalized versions Conrad used in short stories written years later. After signing onto a British ship in 1878 to avoid conscription by the French or the Russians (he had just turned twenty-one), Conrad visited England for the first time, speaking the language only haltingly. He served for sixteen years on British merchant ships, earning his Master's Certificate in 1886 (the same year that he became a British subject) and learning English fast and well. During this period, he made trips to the Far East and India that would provide material for his fiction throughout his writing career, including major works like *The Nigger of the "Narcissus"* (1897) and *Typhoon* (1903). When he married in 1896, he turned his back on the sea as a profession and, buoyed by the publication of his first novel, *Almayer's Folly* (1895), chose writing as his new career. His early novels, including *An Outcast of the Islands* (1896), established his initial literary reputation as an exotic storyteller and novelist of adventure at sea.

Among the many voyages that furnished material for his fiction, one stands out as the most emotional and intense: the trip up the Congo River that Conrad made in 1890, straight into the heart of King Leopold II's privately owned Congo Free State. Like many nineteenth-century explorers, Conrad was fascinated by the mystery of this "dark" (because uncharted by Europeans) continent, and he persuaded a relative to find him a job as pilot on a Belgian merchant steamer. The steamer that Conrad was supposed to pilot had been damaged, and while he waited for a replacement, his supervisors shifted him to another where he could help out and learn about the river. The boat traveled upstream to collect a seriously ill trader, Georges Antoine Klein (who died on the return trip), and Conrad, after speaking with Klein and observing the inhuman conditions imposed by slave labor and the ruthless search for ivory, returned seriously ill and traumatized by his journey. The experience marked Conrad both physically and mentally. After a few years, he began to write about it with a moral rage that emerged openly at first and subsequently in more complex, ironic form. *An Outpost of Progress*, a harshly satirical story of two murderous incompetents in a jungle trading post, was published in 1897, and Conrad wrote *Heart of Darkness* two years later; it appeared in *Blackwood's Magazine* in 1899 and in the volume *"Youth" and Other Stories* in 1902.

Along with *Lord Jim* (1900) and *Nostromo* (1904), this volume established him as one of the leading novelists of the day. He became friendly with other writers such as Henry James, Stephen Crane, H. G. Wells, John Galsworthy, and Ford Madox Ford. Yet he preferred a quiet life in the country to the attractions of literary London. From 1898 he lived on Pent Farm in Kent, near James, Wells, and Crane. He found writing difficult, often suffering from insomnia and physical ailments while trying to complete a novel (one biographer remarks that each of his later novels "cost him a tooth"). His novels from this period, *The Secret Agent* (1907) and *Under Western Eyes* (1911), revolve around political conflicts, but Conrad usually refrained from taking sides in politics—his interest lay in the effect that espionage and intrigue have on individual character. He hated autocratic rule but opposed revolution and was skeptical of social reform movements. His two abiding political commitments were to his adoptive homeland, England, and to the cause of Polish independence; he traveled to Poland on the eve of the First World War, returning with difficulty to England once war broke out. Although he had struggled financially throughout his writing life, Conrad had his first popular success with *Chance* (1913), which is now less highly regarded than his other works. His later works returned, typically with a more optimistic tone, to the Eastern settings with which he began. They have not received much appreciation from critics, although *The Shadow Line* (1917) recaptures some of the earlier works' appreciation of the moment of crisis in a youthful life.

HEART OF DARKNESS

Although the subject matter of *Heart of Darkness* is clearly one of the reasons for its continued influence, equally important is Conrad's introduction of many literary techniques that would be central to modern fiction. In the preface to *The Nigger of the "Narcissus,"* Conrad describes the task of the writer as "before all, to make you *see*," and his works stress the visual perception of reality. His technique of registering the way that a scene appears to an individual before explaining the scene's contents has been described as "delayed decoding"; it is an element of his literary impressionism, his emphasis on how the mind processes the information that the senses provide. In *Heart of Darkness*, Conrad records first the impressions that an event makes on Marlow and only later Marlow's arrival at an explanation of the event. The reader must continually decide when to accept Marlow's account as accurate and when to treat it as ironic and unreliable. Marlow describes his experiences in Africa from a position of experience, having contemplated the episode for many years, but the reader, like the narrator, may question some aspects of Marlow's story as self-justification. Conrad also uses symbolism in a distinctly modern way. As he later wrote, "a work of art is very seldom limited to one exclusive meaning and not necessarily tending to a definite conclusion. And this for the reason that the nearer it approaches art, the more it acquires a symbolic character." Frequently, Marlow's story seems to carry symbolic overtones that are not easily extracted from the story as a simple kernel of wisdom. This symbolic character has its exemplar in the primary narrator's comment that "the yarns of seamen have a direct simplicity, the whole meaning of which lies within the shell of a cracked nut. . . . [But to Marlow,] the meaning of an episode was not inside like a kernel but outside, enveloping the tale which brought it out only as a glow brings out a haze." *Heart of Darkness* does not reveal its meaning in digestible morsels, like the kernel of a nut. Rather, its meanings evade the interpreter; they are larger than the story itself. The story's hazy atmosphere, rich symbolic suggestiveness, and complex narrative structure have all appealed to later readers and writers. Although it was published at the end of the nineteenth century, *Heart of Darkness* became one of the most influential works of the twentieth century. It greatly influenced Nobel Prize winners **T. S. Eliot, William Faulkner, and Gabriel García Márquez**. In the second half of the century, the novella was seen as so relevant to the aftermath of imperialism that the filmmaker Francis Ford Coppola used it as the basis of his film about the Vietnam War, *Apocalypse Now*.

The "darkness" of the title exemplifies this symbolism. Although it is both a conventional metaphor for obscurity and evil and a cliché referring to Africa and the "unenlightened" state of its indigenous population, the story leaves it unclear where the heart of darkness is located: in the "uncivilized" jungle or in the hearts of the European imperialists. Leopold II of Belgium, who owned the trading company that effectively was the Congo Free State, gained a free hand in the area after calling an international conference in 1876 "to open to civilization the only part of our globe where Christianity has not penetrated and to pierce the darkness which envelops the entire population." Leopold had pledged to end the slave trade in central Africa, but his rule continued slavery under another guise, extracting forced labor for infrastructure projects, such as road building, that were poorly managed. Throughout the novella, Conrad plays on images of darkness and savagery and complicates any simple opposition by associating moral darkness—the evil that lurks within humans and underlies their predatory idealism—with a white exterior, beginning with the town (Brussels) that serves as the Belgian firm's headquarters and that Marlow describes as a "whited sepulchre."

Still, it is not surprising that later critics and writers, most notably the Nigerian novelist and essayist **Chinua Achebe**, would criticize *Heart of Darkness* for its racist portrayal of Africans. Marlow's words and behavior—indeed, the selectivity of his narrative—can be as distant and cruelly patronizing as those of any European colonialist. Yet he also recognizes his "kinship" with the Africans and often sees them as morally superior to the Europeans; Marlow's quiet critique of imperialism has inspired many postcolonial writers. For the most part, however, the Africans in his story constitute the background for the strange figure of Kurtz, the charismatic, once idealistic, now totally corrupt trader who becomes the destination of Marlow's journey. Marlow's strange bond with this maddened soul stems initially from a desire to see a man whom others have described to him as a universal genius—an "emissary of pity, and science, and progress" and part of the "gang of virtue." In time, though, it becomes a horrified fascination with someone who has explored moral extremes to their furthest end. Kurtz's famous judgment on what he has lived and seen—"The horror! The horror!"—speaks at once to personal despair, to the political realities of imperialism, and to a broader sense of the human condition.

Heart of Darkness

1

The *Nellie*, a cruising yawl,[1] swung to her anchor without a flutter of the sails, and was at rest. The flood had made, the wind was nearly calm, and being bound down the river, the only thing for it was to come to[2] and wait for the turn of the tide.

The sea-reach of the Thames stretched before us like the beginning of an interminable waterway. In the offing[3] the sea and the sky were welded together without a joint, and in the luminous space the tanned sails of the barges drifting up with the tide seemed to stand still in red clusters of canvas sharply peaked, with gleams of varnished sprits. A haze rested on the low shores that ran out to sea in vanishing flatness. The air was dark above Gravesend,[4] and farther back still seemed condensed into a mournful gloom, brooding motionless over the biggest, and the greatest, town on earth.

The Director of Companies was our captain and our host. We four affectionately watched his back as he stood in the bows looking to seaward. On the whole river there was nothing that looked half so nautical. He resembled a pilot, which to a seaman is trustworthiness personified. It was difficult to realise his work was not out there in the luminous estuary, but behind him, within the brooding gloom.

1. A two-masted boat.
2. To come to a standstill in a fixed position.
3. The part of the sea distant but visible from the shore.
4. A port on the Thames River, and the last major town in the estuary.

Between us there was, as I have already said somewhere, the bond of the sea.[5] Besides holding our hearts together through long periods of separation, it had the effect of making us tolerant of each other's yarns—and even convictions. The Lawyer—the best of old fellows—had, because of his many years and many virtues, the only cushion on deck, and was lying on the only rug. The Accountant had brought out already a box of dominoes, and was toying architecturally with the bones. Marlow sat cross-legged right aft, leaning against the mizzenmast.[6] He had sunken cheeks, a yellow complexion, a straight back, an ascetic aspect, and, with his arms dropped, the palms of hands outwards, resembled an idol. The Director, satisfied the anchor had good hold, made his way aft and sat down amongst us. We exchanged a few words lazily. Afterwards there was silence on board the yacht. For some reason or other we did not begin that game of dominoes. We felt meditative, and fit for nothing but placid staring. The day was ending in a serenity of still and exquisite brilliance. The water shone pacifically; the sky, without a speck, was a benign immensity of unstained light; the very mist on the Essex marshes was like a gauzy and radiant fabric, hung from the wooded rises inland, and draping the low shores in diaphanous folds. Only the gloom to the west, brooding over the upper reaches, became more sombre every minute, as if angered by the approach of the sun.

And at last, in its curved and imperceptible fall, the sun sank low, and from glowing white changed to a dull red without rays and without heat, as if about to go out suddenly, stricken to death by the touch of that gloom brooding over a crowd of men.

Forthwith a change came over the waters, and the serenity became less brilliant but more profound. The old river in its broad reach rested unruffled at the decline of day, after ages of good service done to the race that peopled its banks, spread out in the tranquil dignity of a waterway leading to the uttermost ends of the earth. We looked at the venerable stream not in the vivid flush of a short day that comes and departs for ever, but in the august light of abiding memories. And indeed nothing is easier for a man who has, as the phrase goes, "followed the sea" with reverence and affection, than to evoke the great spirit of the past upon the lower reaches of the Thames. The tidal current runs to and fro in its unceasing service, crowded with memories of men and ships it has borne to the rest of home or to the battles of the sea. It had known and served all the men of whom the nation is proud, from Sir Francis Drake to Sir John Franklin, knights all, titled and untitled—the great knights-errant of the sea. It had borne all the ships whose names are like jewels flashing in the night of time, from the *Golden Hind* returning with her round flanks full of treasure, to be visited by the Queen's Highness and thus pass out of the gigantic tale, to the *Erebus* and *Terror*,[7] bound on other conquests—and that never returned. It had known the ships and the men. They had sailed from Deptford, from Green-

5. "The bond of the sea" appears in "Youth," Conrad's first story to feature Marlow. "Youth" and *Heart of Darkness* were first published in book form as part of the same volume, with "Youth" immediately preceding *Heart of Darkness*.

6. The mast aft (to the rear) of the mainmast on any ship with two or more masts.

7. The *Erebus* and the *Terror* were ships commanded by Arctic explorer Sir John Franklin (1786–1847) and lost in an attempt to find a passage from the Atlantic Ocean to the Pacific. *Golden Hind:* the ship in which Elizabethan explorer Sir Francis Drake (1540–1596) sailed around the world.

wich, from Erith—the adventurers and the settlers; kings' ships and the ships of men on 'Change; captains, admirals, the dark "interlopers"[8] of the Eastern trade, and the commissioned "generals" of East India fleets. Hunters for gold or pursuers of fame, they all had gone out on that stream, bearing the sword, and often the torch, messengers of the might within the land, bearers of a spark from the sacred fire.[9] What greatness had not floated on the ebb of that river into the mystery of an unknown earth! . . . The dreams of men, the seed of commonwealths, the germs of empires.

The sun set; the dusk fell on the stream, and lights began to appear along the shore. The Chapman lighthouse, a three-legged thing erect on a mudflat, shone strongly. Lights of ships moved in the fairway[1]—a great stir of lights going up and going down. And farther west on the upper reaches the place of the monstrous town[2] was still marked ominously on the sky, a brooding gloom in sunshine, a lurid glare under the stars.

"And this also," said Marlow suddenly, "has been one of the dark places of the earth."

He was the only man of us who still "followed the sea." The worst that could be said of him was that he did not represent his class. He was a seaman, but he was a wanderer too, while most seamen lead, if one may so express it, a sedentary life. Their minds are of the stay-at-home order, and their home is always with them—the ship; and so is their country—the sea. One ship is very much like another, and the sea is always the same. In the immutability of their surroundings the foreign shores, the foreign faces, the changing immensity of life, glide past, veiled not by a sense of mystery but by a slightly disdainful ignorance; for there is nothing mysterious to a seaman unless it be the sea itself, which is the mistress of his existence and as inscrutable as Destiny. For the rest, after his hours of work, a casual stroll or a casual spree on shore suffices to unfold for him the secret of a whole continent, and generally he finds the secret not worth knowing. The yarns of seamen have a direct simplicity, the whole meaning of which lies within the shell of a cracked nut. But Marlow was not typical (if his propensity to spin yarns be excepted), and to him the meaning of an episode was not inside like a kernel but outside, enveloping the tale which brought it out only as a glow brings out a haze, in the likeness of one of these misty halos that sometimes are made visible by the spectral illumination of moonshine.

His remark did not seem at all surprising. It was just like Marlow. It was accepted in silence. No one took the trouble to grunt even; and presently he said, very slow:

"I was thinking of very old times, when the Romans first came here, nineteen hundred years ago[3]—the other day. . . . Light came out of this river since—you

8. Private ships intruding on the East India Company's legal trade monopoly. "Deptford, Greenwich, Erith": ports on the Thames between London and Gravesend. "'Change": the stock exchange.

9. An allusion to the myth of Prometheus, who stole fire from the gods to give to humankind; by extension, refers to civilization, human ingenuity, and adventurousness.

1. A navigable passage in a river between rocks or sandbanks; the usual route into or out of a port.

2. I.e., London.

3. Romans first invaded England under Julius Caesar, in 55 and 54 B.C.E. These attempts were unsuccessful; in 43 C.E. a lengthy and effective conquest began.

say Knights? Yes; but it is like a running blaze on a plain, like a flash of lightning in the clouds. We live in the flicker—may it last as long as the old earth keeps rolling! But darkness was here yesterday. Imagine the feelings of a commander of a fine—what d'ye call 'em?—trireme[4] in the Mediterranean, ordered suddenly to the north; run overland across the Gauls[5] in a hurry; put in charge of one of these craft the legionaries[6]—a wonderful lot of handy men they must have been too—used to build, apparently by the hundred, in a month or two, if we may believe what we read. Imagine him here—the very end of the world, a sea the colour of lead, a sky the colour of smoke, a kind of ship about as rigid as a concertina[7]—and going up this river with stores, or orders, or what you like. Sandbanks, marshes, forests, savages—precious little to eat fit for a civilised man, nothing but Thames water to drink. No Falernian wine[8] here, no going ashore. Here and there a military camp lost in a wilderness, like a needle in a bundle of hay—cold, fog, tempests, disease, exile, and death—death skulking in the air, in the water, in the bush. They must have been dying like flies here. Oh yes—he did it. Did it very well, too, no doubt, and without thinking much about it either, except afterwards to brag of what he had gone through in his time, perhaps. They were men enough to face the darkness. And perhaps he was cheered by keeping his eye on a chance of promotion to the fleet at Ravenna[9] by and by, if he had good friends in Rome and survived the awful climate. Or think of a decent young citizen in a toga—perhaps too much dice, you know—coming out here in the train of some prefect, or tax-gatherer, or trader, even, to mend his fortunes. Land in a swamp, march through the woods, and in some inland post feel the savagery, the utter savagery, had closed round him—all that mysterious life of the wilderness that stirs in the forest, in the jungles, in the hearts of wild men. There's no initiation either into such mysteries. He has to live in the midst of the incomprehensible, which is also detestable. And it has a fascination, too, that goes to work upon him. The fascination of the abomination—you know. Imagine the growing regrets, the longing to escape, the powerless disgust, the surrender, the hate."

He paused.

"Mind," he began again, lifting one arm from the elbow, the palm of the hand outwards, so that, with his legs folded before him, he had the pose of a Buddha preaching in European clothes and without a lotus-flower[1]—"Mind, none of us would feel exactly like this. What saves us is efficiency—the devotion to efficiency. But these chaps were not much account, really. They were no colonists; their administration was merely a squeeze, and nothing more, I suspect. They were conquerors, and for that you want only brute force—nothing to boast of, when you have it, since your strength is just an accident arising from the weakness of others. They grabbed what they could get for the sake of what was to be got. It was just robbery with violence, aggravated murder

4. A Roman galley with three banks of oars.
5. Name used by the Romans to refer to the three regions of what is now France.
6. The members of a legion, a unit of Roman infantrymen.
7. An instrument resembling an accordion, with a bellows and buttons on either end: hence, not rigid at all.
8. Wine from a famous wine-making district in southern Italy.
9. Once a major Roman port on the Adriatic Sea.
1. Siddhartha Gautama, founder of Buddhism, is traditionally portrayed seated cross-legged on a lotus flower.

on a great scale, and men going at it blind—as is very proper for those who tackle a darkness. The conquest of the earth, which mostly means the taking it away from those who have a different complexion or slightly flatter noses than ourselves, is not a pretty thing when you look into it too much. What redeems it is the idea only. An idea at the back of it; not a sentimental pretence but an idea; and an unselfish belief in the idea—something you can set up, and bow down before, and offer a sacrifice to. . . ."

He broke off. Flames glided in the river, small green flames, red flames, white flames, pursuing, overtaking, joining, crossing each other—then separating slowly or hastily. The traffic of the great city went on in the deepening night upon the sleepless river. We looked on, waiting patiently—there was nothing else to do till the end of the flood; but it was only after a long silence, when he said, in a hesitating voice, "I suppose you fellows remember I did once turn fresh-water sailor for a bit," that we knew we were fated, before the ebb began to run,[2] to hear about one of Marlow's inconclusive experiences.

"I don't want to bother you much with what happened to me personally," he began, showing in this remark the weakness of many tellers of tales who seem so often unaware of what their audience would best like to hear; "yet to understand the effect of it on me you ought to know how I got out there, what I saw, how I went up that river to the place where I first met the poor chap. It was the farthest point of navigation and the culminating point of my experience. It seemed somehow to throw a kind of light on everything about me—and into my thoughts. It was sombre enough too—and pitiful—not extraordinary in any way—not very clear either. No, not very clear. And yet it seemed to throw a kind of light.

"I had then, as you remember, just returned to London after a lot of Indian Ocean, Pacific, China Seas—a regular dose of the East—six years or so, and I was loafing about, hindering you fellows in your work and invading your homes, just as though I had got a heavenly mission to civilise you. It was very fine for a time, but after a bit I did get tired of resting. Then I began to look for a ship—I should think the hardest work on earth. But the ships wouldn't even look at me. And I got tired of that game too.

"Now when I was a little chap I had a passion for maps. I would look for hours at South America, or Africa, or Australia, and lose myself in all the glories of exploration. At that time there were many blank spaces[3] on the earth, and when I saw one that looked particularly inviting on a map (but they all look that) I would put my finger on it and say, When I grow up I will go there. The North Pole was one of these places, I remember. Well, I haven't been there yet, and shall not try now. The glamour's off. Other places were scattered about the Equator, and in every sort of latitude all over the two hemispheres. I have been in some of them, and . . . well, we won't talk about that. But there was one yet—the biggest, the most blank, so to speak—that I had a hankering after.

"True, by this time it was not a blank space any more. It had got filled since my boyhood with rivers and lakes and names. It had ceased to be a blank space of delightful mystery—a white patch for a boy to dream gloriously over. It had become a place of darkness. But there was in it one river especially, a mighty

2. "Flood" and "ebb": the rise and fall of the tide in the river.

3. I.e., regions unexplored by Europeans at the time and hence left blank on European maps.

big river,[4] that you could see on the map, resembling an immense snake uncoiled, with its head in the sea, its body at rest curving afar over a vast country, and its tail lost in the depths of the land. And as I looked at the map of it in a shop-window, it fascinated me as a snake would a bird—a silly little bird. Then I remembered there was a big concern, a Company for trade on that river. Dash it all! I thought to myself, they can't trade without using some kind of craft on that lot of fresh water—steamboats![5] Why shouldn't I try to get charge of one? I went on along Fleet Street,[6] but could not shake off the idea. The snake had charmed me.

"You understand it was a Continental concern, that Trading Society;[7] but I have a lot of relations living on the Continent, because it's cheap and not so nasty as it looks, they say.

"I am sorry to own I began to worry them. This was already a fresh departure for me. I was not used to get things that way, you know. I always went my own road and on my own legs where I had a mind to go. I wouldn't have believed it of myself; but, then—you see—I felt somehow I must get there by hook or by crook. So I worried them. The men said, 'My dear fellow,' and did nothing. Then—would you believe it?—I tried the women. I, Charlie Marlow, set the women to work—to get a job. Heavens! Well, you see, the notion drove me. I had an aunt, a dear enthusiastic soul. She wrote: 'It will be delightful. I am ready to do anything, anything for you. It is a glorious idea. I know the wife of a very high personage in the Administration, and also a man who has lots of influence with,' etc. etc. She was determined to make no end of fuss to get me appointed skipper of a river steamboat, if such was my fancy.

"I got my appointment—of course; and I got it very quick. It appears the Company had received news that one of their captains had been killed in a scuffle with the natives. This was my chance, and it made me the more anxious to go. It was only months and months afterwards, when I made the attempt to recover what was left of the body, that I heard the original quarrel arose from a misunderstanding about some hens. Yes, two black hens. Fresleven—that was the fellow's name, a Dane—thought himself wronged somehow in the bargain, so he went ashore and started to hammer the chief of the village with a stick. Oh, it didn't surprise me in the least to hear this, and at the same time to be told that Fresleven was the gentlest, quietest creature that ever walked on two legs. No doubt he was; but he had been a couple of years already out there engaged in the noble cause, you know, and he probably felt the need at last of asserting his self-respect in some way. Therefore he whacked the old nigger mercilessly, while a big crowd of his people watched him, thunderstruck, till some man—I was told the chief's son—in desperation at hearing the old chap yell, made a tentative jab with a spear at the white man—and of course it went quite easy between the shoulder-blades. Then the whole population cleared into the forest, expecting all kinds of calamities to happen, while, on the other hand, the steamer Fresleven commanded left also in a bad panic, in charge of

4. The Congo River.
5. Flat-bottomed steamboats were essential for navigating the shallow waters of the Congo.
6. A major street in central London, famous as a publishing center.
7. The trading company—specifically, a Belgian company that operated ships on the Congo River in the protectorate of King Leopold II of Belgium.

the engineer, I believe. Afterwards nobody seemed to trouble much about Fresleven's remains, till I got out and stepped into his shoes. I couldn't let it rest, though; but when an opportunity offered at last to meet my predecessor, the grass growing through his ribs was tall enough to hide his bones. They were all there. The supernatural being had not been touched after he fell. And the village was deserted, the huts gaped black, rotting, all askew within the fallen enclosures. A calamity had come to it, sure enough. The people had vanished. Mad terror had scattered them, men, women, and children, through the bush, and they had never returned. What became of the hens I don't know either. I should think the cause of progress got them, anyhow. However, through this glorious affair I got my appontment, before I had fairly begun to hope for it.

"I flew around like mad to get ready, and before forty-eight hours I was crossing the Channel to show myself to my employers, and sign the contract. In a very few hours I arrived in a city that always makes me think of a whited sepulchre.[8] Prejudice no doubt. I had no difficulty in finding the Company's offices. It was the biggest thing in the town, and everybody I met was full of it. They were going to run an overseas empire, and make no end of coin by trade.

"A narrow and deserted street in deep shadow, high houses, innumerable windows with venetian blinds, a dead silence, grass sprouting between the stones, imposing carriage archways right and left, immense double doors standing ponderously ajar. I slipped through one of these cracks, went up a swept and ungarnished staircase, as arid as a desert, and opened the first door I came to. Two women, one fat and the other slim, sat on straw-bottomed chairs, knitting black wool.[9] The slim one got up and walked straight at me—still knitting with downcast eyes—and only just as I began to think of getting out of her way, as you would for a somnambulist, stood still, and looked up. Her dress was as plain as an umbrella-cover, and she turned round without a word and preceded me into a waiting-room. I gave my name, and looked about. Deal table in the middle, plain chairs all round the walls, on one end a large shining map, marked with all the colours of a rainbow. There was a vast amount of red—good to see at any time, because one knows that some real work is done in there, a deuce of a lot of blue, a little green, smears of orange, and, on the East Coast, a purple patch, to show where the jolly pioneers of progress drink the jolly lager-beer.[1] However, I wasn't going into any of these. I was going into the yellow. Dead in the centre. And the river was there—fascinating—deadly—like a snake. Ough! A door opened, a white-haired secretarial head, but wearing a compassionate expression, appeared, and a skinny forefinger beckoned me into

8. The city is based on Brussels. "Whited sepulchre": a biblical allusion, Matthew 23.27: "Woe unto you, scribes and Pharisees, hypocrites! for ye are like unto whited sepulchres, which indeed appear beautiful outward, but are within full of dead men's bones, and of all uncleanness."

9. The knitters allude to at least two sources: in Charles Dickens's *Tale of Two Cities*, the villainous Madame Defarge knits the names of those she condemns to die. In Greek mythology, the Fates were usually three women spinning, measuring, and cutting the thread of life.

1. The map shows territories claimed by European nations in the aftermath of the Berlin Conference of 1884–85: red is England, Conrad's adopted nation; blue territories belonged to France; and purple, Germany. Although color schemes varied, in the map Marlow is looking at, orange presumably refers to Portugal and green to Italy, which also had holdings in Africa. Yellow stands for the Congo Free State, controlled by King Leopold II.

the sanctuary. Its light was dim, and a heavy writing desk squatted in the middle. From behind that structure came out an impression of pale plumpness in a frockcoat. The great man himself. He was five feet six, I should judge, and had his grip on the handle-end of ever so many millions. He shook hands, I fancy, murmured vaguely, was satisfied with my French. *Bon voyage*.[2]

"In about forty-five seconds I found myself again in the waiting-room with the compassionate secretary, who, full of desolation and sympathy, made me sign some document. I believe I undertook amongst other things not to disclose any trade secrets. Well, I am not going to.

"I began to feel slightly uneasy. You know I am not used to such ceremonies, and there was something ominous in the atmosphere. It was just as though I had been let into some conspiracy—I don't know—something not quite right; and I was glad to get out. In the outer room the two women knitted black wool feverishly. People were arriving, and the younger one was walking back and forth introducing them. The old one sat on her chair. Her flat cloth slippers were propped up on a foot-warmer, and a cat reposed on her lap. She wore a starched white affair on her head, had a wart on one cheek, and silver-rimmed spectacles hung on the tip of her nose. She glanced at me above the glasses. The swift and indifferent placidity of that look troubled me. Two youths with foolish and cheery countenances were being piloted over, and she threw at them the same quick glance of unconcerned wisdom. She seemed to know all about them and about me too. An eerie feeling came over me. She seemed uncanny and fateful. Often far away there I thought of these two, guarding the door of Darkness, knitting black wool as for a warm pall, one introducing, introducing continuously to the unknown, the other scrutinising the cheery and foolish faces with unconcerned old eyes. *Ave!* Old knitter of black wool. *Morituri te salutant.*[3] Not many of those she looked at ever saw her again—not half, by a long way.

"There was yet a visit to the doctor. 'A simple formality,' assured me the secretary, with an air of taking an immense part in all my sorrows. Accordingly a young chap wearing his hat over the left eyebrow, some clerk I suppose—there must have been clerks in the business, though the house was as still as a house in a city of the dead—came from somewhere upstairs, and led me forth. He was shabby and careless, with ink-stains on the sleeves of his jacket, and his cravat was large and billowy, under a chin shaped like the toe of an old boot. It was a little too early for the doctor, so I proposed a drink, and thereupon he developed a vein of joviality. As we sat over our vermuths[4] he glorified the Company's business, and by and by I expressed casually my surprise at him not going out there. He became very cool and collected all at once. 'I am not such a fool as I look, quoth Plato to his disciples,' he said sententiously, emptied his glass with great resolution, and we rose.

"The old doctor felt my pulse, evidently thinking of something else the while. 'Good, good for there,' he mumbled, and then with a certain eagerness asked me whether I would let him measure my head. Rather surprised, I said Yes, when he produced a thing like callipers and got the dimensions back and front

2. "Have a good trip" (French).
3. "Those who are about to die salute you" (Latin): the greeting of gladiators to the Roman emperor before beginning combat in the arena.
4. Vermuth, now known as vermouth, is wine fortified with alcohol and, usually, additional flavors.

and every way, taking notes carefully. He was an unshaven little man in a threadbare coat like a gaberdine, with his feet in slippers, and I thought him a harmless fool. 'I always ask leave, in the interests of science, to measure the crania of those going out there,'[5] he said. 'And when they come back too?' I asked. 'Oh, I never see them,' he remarked; 'and, moreover, the changes take place inside, you know.' He smiled, as if at some quiet joke. 'So you are going out there. Famous. Interesting too.' He gave me a searching glance, and made another note. 'Ever any madness in your family?' he asked, in a matter-of-fact tone. I felt very annoyed. 'Is that question in the interests of science too?' 'It would be,' he said, without taking notice of my irritation, 'interesting for science to watch the mental changes of individuals, on the spot, but . . .' 'Are you an alienist?' I interrupted. 'Every doctor should be—a little,' answered that original[6] imperturbably. 'I have a little theory which you Messieurs who go out there must help me to prove. This is my share in the advantages my country shall reap from the possession of such a magnificent dependency. The mere wealth I leave to others. Pardon my questions, but you are the first Englishman coming under my observation . . .' I hastened to assure him I was not in the least typical. 'If I were,' said I, 'I wouldn't be talking like this with you.' 'What you say is rather profound, and probably erroneous,' he said, with a laugh. 'Avoid irritation more than exposure to the sun. Adieu. How do you English say, eh? Good-bye. Ah! Good-bye. Adieu. In the tropics one must before everything keep calm.' . . . He lifted a warning forefinger. . . . '*Du calme, du calme. Adieu.*'[7]

"One thing more remained to do—say good-bye to my excellent aunt. I found her triumphant. I had a cup of tea—the last decent cup of tea for many days—and in a room that most soothingly looked just as you would expect a lady's drawing-room to look, we had a long quiet chat by the fireside. In the course of these confidences it became quite plain to me I had been represented to the wife of the high dignitary, and goodness knows to how many more people besides, as an exceptional and gifted creature—a piece of good fortune for the Company—a man you don't get hold of every day. Good heavens! and I was going to take charge of a two-penny-halfpenny river-steamboat with a penny whistle attached! It appeared, however, I was also one of the Workers, with a capital—you know. Something like an emissary of light, something like a lower sort of apostle. There had been a lot of such rot let loose in print and talk just about that time,[8] and the excellent woman, living right in the rush of all that humbug, got carried off her feet. She talked about 'weaning those ignorant millions from their horrid ways,' till, upon my word, she made me quite uncomfortable. I ventured to hint that the Company was run for profit.

"'You forget, dear Charlie, that the labourer is worthy of his hire,'[9] she said brightly. It's queer how out of touch with truth women are. They live in a world of their own, and there had never been anything like it, and never can be. It is

5. The doctor may practice some form of phrenology, a pseudoscience holding that personality traits could be determined by the shape and size of the skull.

6. Unusual or eccentric person. "Alienist": early term for a psychiatrist.

7. "Calm, calm. Goodbye" (French).

8. Initially, Leopold II was viewed as a philanthropist—bringing missionaries to pagans and, it was thought, using Belgian military forces to rescue the native people from homegrown slave traders.

9. The aunt quotes Luke 10.7, one of Christ's instructions to his disciples as they depart to proselytize: to make themselves welcome in the homes they visit.

too beautiful altogether, and if they were to set it up it would go to pieces before the first sunset. Some confounded fact we men have been living contentedly with ever since the day of creation would start up and knock the whole thing over.

"After this I got embraced, told to wear flannel, be sure to write often, and so on—and I left. In the street—I don't know why—a queer feeling came to me that I was an impostor. Odd thing that I, who used to clear out for any part of the world at twenty-four hours' notice, with less thought than most men give to the crossing of a street, had a moment—I won't say of hesitation, but of startled pause, before this commonplace affair. The best way I can explain it to you is by saying that, for a second or two, I felt as though, instead of going to the centre of a continent, I were about to set off for the centre of the earth.[1]

"I left in a French steamer, and she called in every blamed port they have out there, for, as far as I could see, the sole purpose of landing soldiers and custom-house officers.[2] I watched the coast. Watching a coast as it slips by the ship is like thinking about an enigma. There it is before you—smiling, frowning, inviting, grand, mean, insipid, or savage, and always mute with an air of whispering, Come and find out. This one was almost featureless, as if still in the making, with an aspect of monotonous grimness. The edge of a colossal jungle, so dark green as to be almost black, fringed with white surf, ran straight, like a ruled line, far, far away along a blue sea whose glitter was blurred by a creeping mist. The sun was fierce, the land seemed to glisten and drip with steam. Here and there greyish-whitish specks showed up clustered inside the white surf, with a flag flying above them perhaps—settlements some centuries old, and still no bigger than pin-heads on the untouched expanse of their background. We pounded along, stopped, landed soldiers; went on, landed custom-house clerks to levy toll in what looked like a God-forsaken wilderness, with a tin shed and a flag-pole lost in it; landed more soldiers—to take care of the custom-house clerks presumably. Some, I heard, got drowned in the surf; but whether they did or not, nobody seemed particularly to care. They were just flung out there, and on we went. Every day the coast looked the same, as though we had not moved; but we passed various places—trading places—with names like Gran' Bassam, Little Popo;[3] names that seemed to belong to some sordid farce acted in front of a sinister back-cloth. The idleness of a passenger, my isolation amongst all these men with whom I had no point of contact, the oily and languid sea, the uniform sombreness of the coast, seemed to keep me away from the truth of things, within the toil of a mournful and senseless delusion. The voice of the surf heard now and then was a positive pleasure, like the speech of a brother. It was something natural, that had its reason, that had a meaning. Now and then a boat from the shore gave one a momentary contact with reality. It was paddled by black fellows. You could see from afar the white of their eyeballs glistening. They shouted, sang; their bodies streamed with perspiration; they had faces like grotesque masks—these chaps; but they had bone, muscle, a wild vitality, an intense energy of movement, that was as

1. Jules Verne's science fiction novel *Journey to the Center of the Earth* (1864) featured characters encountering prehistoric animals of greater age in successive layers of the earth.
2. Colonial officials.
3. The former name of Aného, a coastal city in Togo, then under German control. "Gran' Bassam": Grand-Bassam, a city in Côte d'Ivoire, was then a French colony and a major seaport.

natural and true as the surf along their coast. They wanted no excuse for being there. They were a great comfort to look at. For a time I would feel I belonged still to a world of straightforward facts; but the feeling would not last long. Something would turn up to scare it away. Once, I remember, we came upon a man-of-war anchored off the coast. There wasn't even a shed there, and she was shelling the bush. It appears the French had one of their wars going on thereabouts. Her ensign dropped limp like a rag; the muzzles of the long six-inch guns stuck out all over the low hull; the greasy, slimy swell swung her up lazily and let her down, swaying her thin masts. In the empty immensity of earth, sky, and water, there she was, incomprehensible, firing into a continent. Pop, would go one of the six-inch guns; a small flame would dart and vanish, a little white smoke would disappear, a tiny projectile would give a feeble screech—and nothing happened. Nothing could happen. There was a touch of insanity in the proceeding, a sense of lugubrious drollery in the sight; and it was not dissipated by somebody on board assuring me earnestly there was a camp of natives—he called them enemies!—hidden out of sight somewhere.

"We gave her her letters (I heard the men in that lonely ship were dying of fever at the rate of three a day) and went on. We called at some more places with farcical names, where the merry dance of death and trade goes on in a still and earthy atmosphere as of an overheated catacomb; all along the formless coast bordered by dangerous surf, as if Nature herself had tried to ward off intruders; in and out of rivers, streams of death in life, whose banks were rotting into mud, whose waters, thickened into slime, invaded the contorted mangroves, that seemed to writhe at us in the extremity of an impotent despair. Nowhere did we stop long enough to get a particularised impression, but the general sense of vague and oppressive wonder grew upon me. It was like a weary pilgrimage amongst hints for nightmares.

"It was upward of thirty days before I saw the mouth of the big river. We anchored off the seat of the government.[4] But my work would not begin till some two hundred miles farther on. So as soon as I could I made a start for a place thirty miles higher up.

"I had my passage on a little sea-going steamer. Her captain was a Swede, and knowing me for a seaman, invited me on the bridge. He was a young man, lean, fair, and morose, with lanky hair and a shuffling gait. As we left the miserable little wharf, he tossed his head contemptuously at the shore. 'Been living there?' he asked. I said, 'Yes.' 'Fine lot these government chaps—are they not?' he went on, speaking English with great precision and considerable bitterness. 'It is funny what some people will do for a few francs a month. I wonder what becomes of that kind when it goes up country?' I said to him I expected to see that soon. 'So-o-o!' he exclaimed. He shuffled athwart, keeping one eye ahead vigilantly. 'Don't be too sure,' he continued. 'The other day I took up a man who hanged himself on the road. He was a Swede, too.' 'Hanged himself! Why, in God's name?' I cried. He kept on looking out watchfully. 'Who knows? The sun too much for him, or the country perhaps.'

"At last we opened a reach.[5] A rocky cliff appeared, mounds of turned-up earth by the shore, houses on a hill, others with iron roofs, amongst a waste of

4. The capital of the Congo Free State was Boma, a port at the mouth of the Congo.

5. Found an open, visible stretch of river.

excavations, or hanging to the declivity. A continuous noise of the rapids above hovered over this scene of inhabited devastation. A lot of people, mostly black and naked, moved about like ants. A jetty projected into the river. A blinding sunlight drowned all this at times in a sudden recrudescence of glare. 'There's your Company's station,' said the Swede, pointing to three wooden barrack-like structures on the rocky slope. 'I will send your things up. Four boxes did you say? So. Farewell.'

"I came upon a boiler[6] wallowing in the grass, then found a path leading up the hill. It turned aside for the boulders, and also for an undersized railway truck lying there on its back with its wheels in the air. One was off. The thing looked as dead as the carcass of some animal. I came upon more pieces of decaying machinery, a stack of rusty nails. To the left a clump of trees made a shady spot, where dark things seemed to stir feebly. I blinked, the path was steep. A horn tooted to the right, and I saw the black people run. A heavy and dull detonation shook the ground, a puff of smoke came out of the cliff, and that was all. No change appeared on the face of the rock. They were building a railway. The cliff was not in the way or anything; but this objectless blasting was all the work going on.

"A slight clinking behind me made me turn my head. Six black men advanced in a file, toiling up the path. They walked erect and slow, balancing small baskets full of earth on their heads, and the clink kept time with their footsteps. Black rags were wound round their loins, and the short ends behind waggled to and fro like tails. I could see every rib, the joints of their limbs were like knots in a rope; each had an iron collar on his neck, and all were connected together with a chain whose bights[7] swung between them, rhythmically clinking. Another report from the cliff made me think suddenly of that ship of war I had seen firing into a continent. It was the same kind of ominous voice; but these men could by no stretch of imagination be called enemies. They were called criminals, and the outraged law, like the bursting shells, had come to them, an insoluble mystery from the sea. All their meagre breasts panted together, the violently dilated nostrils quivered, the eyes stared stonily uphill. They passed me within six inches, without a glance, with that complete, deathlike indifference of unhappy savages. Behind this raw matter one of the reclaimed, the product of the new forces at work, strolled despondently, carrying a rifle by its middle. He had a uniform jacket with one button off, and seeing a white man on the path, hoisted his weapon to his shoulder with alacrity. This was simple prudence, white men being so much alike at a distance that he could not tell who I might be. He was speedily reassured, and with a large, white, rascally grin, and a glance at his charge, seemed to take me into partnership in his exalted trust. After all, I also was a part of the great cause of these high and just proceedings.

"Instead of going up, I turned and descended to the left. My idea was to let that chain-gang get out of sight before I climbed the hill. You know I am not particularly tender; I've had to strike and to fend off. I've had to resist and to attack sometimes—that's only one way of resisting—without counting the exact cost, according to the demands of such sort of life as I had blundered into. I've seen the devil of violence, and the devil of greed, and the devil of hot desire; but, by all the stars! these were strong, lusty, red-eyed devils, that

6. A machine for converting water into steam.

7. The dangling excess of chain.

swayed and drove men—men, I tell you. But as I stood on this hillside, I foresaw that in the blinding sunshine of that land I would become acquainted with a flabby, pretending, weak-eyed devil of a rapacious and pitiless folly. How insidious he could be, too, I was only to find out several months later and a thousand miles farther. For a moment I stood appalled, as though by a warning. Finally I descended the hill, obliquely, towards the trees I had seen.

"I avoided a vast artificial hole somebody had been digging on the slope, the purpose of which I found it impossible to divine. It wasn't a quarry or a sandpit, anyhow. It was just a hole. It might have been connected with the philanthropic desire of giving the criminals something to do. I don't know. Then I nearly fell into a very narrow ravine, almost no more than a scar in the hillside. I discovered that a lot of imported drainage-pipes for the settlement had been tumbled in there. There wasn't one that was not broken. It was a wanton smash-up. At last I got under the trees. My purpose was to stroll into the shade for a moment; but no sooner within than it seemed to me I had stepped into the gloomy circle of some Inferno.[8] The rapids were near, and an uninterrupted, uniform, headlong, rushing noise filled the mournful stillness of the grove, where not a breath stirred, not a leaf moved, with a mysterious sound—as though the tearing pace of the launched earth had suddenly become audible.

"Black shapes crouched, lay, sat between the trees, leaning against the trunks, clinging to the earth, half coming out, half effaced within the dim light, in all the attitudes of pain, abandonment, and despair. Another mine[9] on the cliff went off, followed by a slight shudder of the soil under my feet. The work was going on. The work! And this was the place where some of the helpers had withdrawn to die.

"They were dying slowly—it was very clear. They were not enemies, they were not criminals, they were nothing earthly now—nothing but black shadows of disease and starvation, lying confusedly in the greenish gloom. Brought from all the recesses of the coast in all the legality of time contracts, lost in uncongenial surroundings, fed on unfamiliar food, they sickened, became inefficient, and were then allowed to crawl away and rest.[1] These moribund shapes were free as air—and nearly as thin. I began to distinguish the gleam of eyes under the trees. Then, glancing down, I saw a face near my hand. The black bones reclined at full length with one shoulder against the tree, and slowly the eyelids rose and the sunken eyes looked up at me, enormous and vacant, a kind of blind, white flicker in the depths of the orbs, which died out slowly. The man seemed young—almost a boy—but you know with them it's hard to tell. I found nothing else to do but to offer him one of my good Swede's ship's biscuits I had in my pocket. The fingers closed slowly on it and held—there was no other movement and no other glance. He had tied a bit of white worsted[2] round his neck—Why? Where did he get it? Was it a badge—an ornament—a charm—a propitiatory act? Was there any idea at all connected with it? It looked startling round his black neck, this bit of white thread from beyond the seas.

8. Hell, often of fire. The term is associated with the portrayal of hell in the *Inferno*, the first section of the *Divine Comedy*, by Dante Alighieri (ca. 1265–1321).
9. Explosive charge.
1. The workers and porters who provided the infrastructure of the Congo Free State were often conscripts: overworked, underfed, and beaten, they died in enormous numbers.
2. Wool fabric.

"Near the same tree two more bundles of acute angles sat with their legs drawn up. One, with his chin propped on his knees, stared at nothing, in an intolerable and appalling manner: his brother phantom rested its forehead, as if overcome with a great weariness; and all about others were scattered in every pose of contorted collapse, as in some picture of a massacre or a pestilence. While I stood horror-struck, one of these creatures rose to his hands and knees, and went off on all-fours towards the river to drink. He lapped out of his hand, then sat up in the sunlight, crossing his shins in front of him, and after a time let his woolly head fall on his breastbone.

"I didn't want any more loitering in the shade, and I made haste towards the station. When near the buildings I met a white man, in such an unexpected elegance of get-up that in the first moment I took him for a sort of vision. I saw a high starched collar, white cuffs, a light alpaca[3] jacket, snowy trousers, a clear necktie, and varnished boots. No hat. Hair parted, brushed, oiled, under a green-lined parasol held in a big white hand. He was amazing, and had a penholder behind his ear.

"I shook hands with this miracle, and I learned he was the Company's chief accountant, and that all the book-keeping was done at this station. He had come out for a moment, he said, 'to get a breath of fresh air.' The expression sounded wonderfully odd, with its suggestion of sedentary desk-life. I wouldn't have mentioned the fellow to you at all, only it was from his lips that I first heard the name of the man who is so indissolubly connected with the memories of that time. Moreover, I respected the fellow. Yes; I respected his collars, his vast cuffs, his brushed hair. His appearance was certainly that of a hairdresser's dummy; but in the great demoralisation of the land he kept up his appearance. That's backbone. His starched collars and got-up shirt-fronts were achievements of character. He had been out nearly three years; and, later, I could not help asking him how he managed to sport such linen. He had just the faintest blush, and said modestly, 'I've been teaching one of the native women about the station. It was difficult. She had a distaste for the work.' Thus this man had verily accomplished something. And he was devoted to his books, which were in apple-pie order.

"Everything else in the station was in a muddle,—heads, things, buildings. Strings of dusty niggers with splay feet arrived and departed; a stream of manufactured goods, rubbishy cottons, beads, and brass-wire sent into the depths of darkness, and in return came a precious trickle of ivory.[4]

"I had to wait in the station for ten days—an eternity. I lived in a hut in the yard, but to be out of the chaos I would sometimes get into the accountant's office. It was built of horizontal planks, and so badly put together that, as he bent over his high desk, he was barred from neck to heels with narrow strips of sunlight. There was no need to open the big shutter to see. It was hot there too; big flies buzzed fiendishly, and did not sting, but stabbed. I sat generally on the floor, while, of faultless appearance (and even slightly scented), perching on a high stool, he wrote, he wrote. Sometimes he stood up for exercise.

3. An expensive fine wool that comes from a South American animal of the same name.

4. Congolese were not allowed currency, and the enormous disparity between the value of goods returning from the Congo and the value of goods being sent there eventually gave activists the first hint of the forced labor conditions that would turn public opinion against Leopold.

When a truckle-bed[5] with a sick man (some invalided agent from up country) was put in there, he exhibited a gentle annoyance. 'The groans of this sick person' he said, 'distract my attention. And without that it is extremely difficult to guard against clerical errors in this climate.'

"One day he remarked, without lifting his head, 'In the interior you will no doubt meet Mr Kurtz.' On my asking who Mr Kurtz was, he said he was a first-class agent; and seeing my disappointment at this information, he added slowly, laying down his pen, 'He is a very remarkable person.' Further questions elicited from him that Mr Kurtz was at present in charge of a trading-post, a very important one, in the true ivory-country, at 'the very bottom of there. Sends in as much ivory as all the others put together . . .' He began to write again. The sick man was too ill to groan. The flies buzzed in a great peace.

"Suddenly there was a growing murmur of voices and a great tramping of feet. A caravan had come in. A violent babble of uncouth sounds burst out on the other side of the planks. All the carriers were speaking together, and in the midst of the uproar the lamentable voice of the chief agent was heard 'giving it up' tearfully for the twentieth time that day. . . . He rose slowly. 'What a frightful row,' he said. He crossed the room gently to look at the sick man, and returning, said to me, 'He does not hear.' 'What! Dead?' I asked, startled. 'No, not yet,' he answered, with great composure. Then, alluding with a toss of the head to the tumult in the station-yard, 'When one has got to make correct entries, one comes to hate those savages—hate them to the death.' He remained thoughtful for a moment. 'When you see Mr Kurtz,' he went on, 'tell him from me that everything here'—he glanced at the desk—'is very satisfactory. I don't like to write to him—with those messengers of ours you never know who may get hold of your letter—at that Central Station.' He stared at me for a moment with his mild, bulging eyes. 'Oh, he will go far, very far,' he began again. 'He will be a somebody in the Administration before long. They, above—the Council in Europe, you know—mean him to be.'

"He turned to his work. The noise outside had ceased, and presently in going out I stopped at the door. In the steady buzz of flies the homeward-bound agent was lying flushed and insensible; the other, bent over his books, was making correct entries of perfectly correct transactions; and fifty feet below the doorstep I could see the still tree-tops of the grove of death.

"Next day I left that station at last, with a caravan of sixty men, for a two-hundred-mile tramp.

"No use telling you much about that. Paths, paths, everywhere; a stamped-in network of paths spreading over the empty land, through long grass, through burnt grass, through thickets, down and up chilly ravines, up and down stony hills ablaze with heat; and a solitude, a solitude, nobody, not a hut. The population had cleared out a long time ago. Well, if a lot of mysterious niggers armed with all kinds of fearful weapons suddenly took to travelling on the road between Deal and Gravesend,[6] catching the yokels right and left to carry heavy loads for them, I fancy every farm and cottage thereabouts would get empty very soon. Only here the dwellings were gone too. Still, I passed through several abandoned

5. I.e., trundle bed, a low portable bed that is on castors and that may be slid under a higher bed when not being used.

6. Deal, like Gravesend, is a coastal town in southeastern England.

villages. There's something pathetically childish in the ruins of grass walls. Day after day, with the stamp and shuffle of sixty pair of bare feet behind me, each pair under a 60-lb. load. Camp, cook, sleep, strike camp, march. Now and then a carrier dead in harness, at rest in the long grass near the path, with an empty water-gourd and his long staff lying by his side. A great silence around and above. Perhaps on some quiet night the tremor of far-off drums, sinking, swelling, a tremor vast, faint; a sound weird, appealing, suggestive, and wild—and perhaps with as profound a meaning as the sound of bells in a Christian country. Once a white man in an unbuttoned uniform, camping on the path with an armed escort of lank Zanzibaris,[7] very hospitable and festive—not to say drunk. Was looking after the upkeep of the road, he declared. Can't say I saw any road or any upkeep, unless the body of a middle-aged negro, with a bullet-hole in the forehead, upon which I absolutely stumbled three miles farther on, may be considered as a permanent improvement. I had a white companion too, not a bad chap, but rather too fleshy and with the exasperating habit of fainting on the hot hillsides, miles away from the least bit of shade and water. Annoying, you know, to hold your own coat like a parasol over a man's head while he is coming-to. I couldn't help asking him once what he meant by coming there at all. 'To make money, of course. What do you think?' he said scornfully. Then he got fever, and had to be carried in a hammock slung under a pole. As he weighed sixteen stone[8] I had no end of rows with the carriers. They jibbed, ran away, sneaked off with their loads in the night—quite a mutiny. So, one evening, I made a speech in English with gestures, not one of which was lost to the sixty pairs of eyes before me, and the next morning I started the hammock off in front all right. An hour afterwards I came upon the whole concern wrecked in a bush—man, hammock, groans, blankets, horrors. The heavy pole had skinned his poor nose. He was very anxious for me to kill somebody, but there wasn't the shadow of a carrier near. I remembered the old doctor—'It would be interesting for science to watch the mental changes of individuals, on the spot.' I felt I was becoming scientifically interesting. However, all that is to no purpose. On the fifteenth day I came in sight of the big river again, and hobbled into the Central Station. It was on a back water surrounded by scrub and forest, with a pretty border of smelly mud on one side, and on the three others enclosed by a crazy fence of rushes. A neglected gap was all the gate it had, and the first glance at the place was enough to let you see the flabby devil was running that show. White men with long staves in their hands appeared languidly from amongst the buildings, strolling up to take a look at me, and then retired out of sight somewhere. One of them, a stout, excitable chap with black moustaches, informed me with great volubility and many digressions, as soon as I told him who I was, that my steamer was at the bottom of the river. I was thunderstruck. What, how, why? Oh, it was 'all right.' The 'manager himself' was there. All quite correct. 'Everybody had behaved splendidly! splendidly!'—'You must,' he said in agitation, 'go and see the general manager at once. He is waiting!'

"I did not see the real significance of that wreck at once. I fancy I see it now, but I am not sure—not at all. Certainly the affair was too stupid—when I think of it—to be altogether natural. Still . . . But at the moment it presented itself

7. Mercenary soldiers from the island of Zanzibar, off the east African coast.

8. I.e., 224 pounds (1 stone equals 14 pounds).

simply as a confounded nuisance. The steamer was sunk. They had started two days before in a sudden hurry up the river with the manager on board, in charge of some volunteer skipper, and before they had been out three hours they tore the bottom out of her on stones, and she sank near the south bank. I asked myself what I was to do there, now my boat was lost. As a matter of fact, I had plenty to do in fishing my command out of the river. I had to set about it the very next day. That, and the repairs when I brought the pieces to the station, took some months.

"My first interview with the manager was curious. He did not ask me to sit down after my twenty-mile walk that morning. He was commonplace in complexion, in feature, in manners, and in voice. He was of middle size and of ordinary build. His eyes, of the usual blue, were perhaps remarkably cold, and he certainly could make his glance fall on one as trenchant and heavy as an axe. But even at these times the rest of his person seemed to disclaim the intention. Otherwise there was only an indefinable, faint expression of his lips, something stealthy—a smile—not a smile—I remember it, but I can't explain. It was unconscious, this smile was, though just after he had said something it got intensified for an instant. It came at the end of his speeches like a seal applied on the words to make the meaning of the commonest phrase appear absolutely inscrutable. He was a common trader, from his youth up employed in these parts—nothing more. He was obeyed, yet he inspired neither love nor fear, nor even respect. He inspired uneasiness. That was it! Uneasiness. Not a definite mistrust—just uneasiness—nothing more. You have no idea how effective such a . . . a . . . faculty can be. He had no genius for organising, for initiative, or for order even. That was evident in such things as the deplorable state of the station. He had no learning, and no intelligence. His position had come to him—why? Perhaps because he was never ill . . . He had served three terms of three years out there . . . Because triumphant health in the general rout of constitutions is a kind of power in itself. When he went home on leave he rioted on a large scale—pompously. Jack ashore[9]—with a difference—in externals only. This one could gather from his casual talk. He originated nothing, he could keep the routine going—that's all. But he was great. He was great by this little thing that it was impossible to tell what could control such a man. He never gave that secret away. Perhaps there was nothing within him. Such a suspicion made one pause—for out there there were no external checks. Once when various tropical diseases had laid low almost every 'agent' in the station, he was heard to say, 'Men who come out here should have no entrails.' He sealed the utterance with that smile of his, as though it had been a door opening into a darkness he had in his keeping. You fancied you had seen things—but the seal was on. When annoyed at meal-times by the constant quarrels of the white men about precedence, he ordered an immense round table[1] to be made, for which a special house had to be built. This was the station's mess-room. Where he sat was the first place—the rest were nowhere. One felt this to be his unalterable conviction. He was neither civil nor uncivil. He was quiet. He allowed his 'boy'—an overfed young negro from the coast—to treat the white men, under his very eyes, with provoking insolence.

9. The carousing of seamen ("Jack Tar") on shore leave was proverbial.

1. King Arthur, legendary ruler of England, seated his knights at a round table so that none would take precedence over any of the others.

"He began to speak as soon as he saw me. I had been very long on the road. He could not wait. Had to start without me. The up-river stations had to be relieved. There had been so many delays already that he did not know who was dead and who was alive, and how they got on—and so on, and so on. He paid no attention to my explanations, and, playing with a stick of sealing-wax, repeated several times that the situation was 'very grave, very grave.' There were rumours that a very important station was in jeopardy, and its chief, Mr Kurtz, was ill. Hoped it was not true. Mr Kurtz was . . . I felt weary and irritable. Hang Kurtz, I thought. I interrupted him by saying I had heard of Mr Kurtz on the coast. 'Ah! So they talk of him down there,' he murmured to himself. Then he began again, assuring me Mr Kurtz was the best agent he had, an exceptional man, of the greatest importance to the Company; therefore I could understand his anxiety. He was, he said, 'very, very uneasy.' Certainly he fidgeted on his chair a good deal, exclaimed, 'Ah, Mr Kurtz!' broke the stick of sealing-wax and seemed dumbfounded by the accident. Next thing he wanted to know 'how long it would take to' . . . I interrupted him again. Being hungry, you know, and kept on my feet too, I was getting savage. 'How can I tell?' I said, 'I haven't even seen the wreck yet—some months, no doubt.' All this talk seemed to me so futile. 'Some months,' he said. 'Well, let us say three months before we can make a start. Yes. That ought to do the affair.' I flung out of his hut (he lived all alone in a clay hut with a sort of verandah) muttering to myself my opinion of him. He was a chattering idiot. Afterwards I took it back when it was borne in upon me startlingly with what extreme nicety he had estimated the time requisite for the 'affair.'

"I went to work the next day, turning, so to speak, my back on that station. In that way only it seemed to me I could keep my hold on the redeeming facts of life. Still, one must look about sometimes; and then I saw this station, these men strolling aimlessly about in the sunshine of the yard. I asked myself sometimes what it all meant. They wandered here and there with their absurd long staves in their hands, like a lot of faithless pilgrims bewitched inside a rotten fence. The word 'ivory' rang in the air, was whispered, was sighed. You would think they were praying to it. A taint of imbecile rapacity blew through it all, like a whiff from some corpse. By Jove! I've never seen anything so unreal in my life. And outside, the silent wilderness surrounding this cleared speck on the earth struck me as something great and invincible, like evil or truth, waiting patiently for the passing away of this fantastic invasion.

"Oh, these months! Well, never mind. Various things happened. One evening a grass shed full of calico, cotton prints, beads, and I don't know what else, burst into a blaze so suddenly that you would have thought the earth had opened to let an avenging fire consume all that trash. I was smoking my pipe quietly by my dismantled steamer, and saw them all cutting capers[2] in the light, with their arms lifted high, when the stout man with moustaches came tearing down to the river, a tin pail in his hand, assured me that everybody was 'behaving splendidly, splendidly,' dipped about a quart of water and tore back again. I noticed there was a hole in the bottom of his pail.

"I strolled up. There was no hurry. You see the thing had gone off like a box of matches. It had been hopeless from the very first. The flame had leaped high,

2. Jumping, dancing.

driven everybody back, lighted up everything—and collapsed. The shed was already a heap of embers glowing fiercely. A nigger was being beaten near by. They said he had caused the fire in some way; be that as it may, he was screeching most horribly. I saw him, later, for several days, sitting in a bit of shade looking very sick and trying to recover himself: afterwards he arose and went out—and the wilderness without a sound took him into its bosom again. As I approached the glow from the dark I found myself at the back of two men, talking. I heard the name of Kurtz pronounced, then the words, 'take advantage of this unfortunate accident.' One of the men was the manager. I wished him a good evening. 'Did you ever see anything like it—eh? it is incredible,' he said, and walked off. The other man remained. He was a first-class agent, young, gentlemanly, a bit reserved, with a forked little beard and a hooked nose. He was standoffish with the other agents, and they on their side said he was the manager's spy upon them. As to me, I had hardly ever spoken to him before. We got into talk, and by and by we strolled away from the hissing ruins. Then he asked me to his room, which was in the main building of the station. He struck a match, and I perceived that this young aristocrat had not only a silver-mounted dressing-case but also a whole candle all to himself. Just at that time the manager was the only man supposed to have any right to candles. Native mats covered the clay walls; a collection of spears, assegais,[3] shields, knives, was hung up in trophies. The business entrusted to this fellow was the making of bricks—so I had been informed; but there wasn't a fragment of a brick anywhere in the station, and he had been there more than a year—waiting. It seems he could not make bricks without something, I don't know what—straw maybe. Anyway, it could not be found there, and as it was not likely to be sent from Europe, it did not appear clear to me what he was waiting for. An act of special creation[4] perhaps. However, they were all waiting—all the sixteen or twenty pilgrims of them—for something; and upon my word it did not seem an uncongenial occupation, from the way they took it, though the only thing that ever came to them was disease—as far as I could see. They beguiled the time by backbiting and intriguing against each other in a foolish kind of way. There was an air of plotting about that station, but nothing came of it, of course. It was as unreal as everything else—as the philanthropic pretence of the whole concern, as their talk, as their government, as their show of work. The only real feeling was a desire to get appointed to a trading-post where ivory was to be had, so that they could earn percentages. They intrigued and slandered and hated each other only on that account—but as to effectually lifting a little finger—oh no. By heavens! there is something after all in the world allowing one man to steal a horse while another must not look at a halter. Steal a horse straight out. Very well. He has done it. Perhaps he can ride. But there is a way of looking at a halter that would provoke the most charitable of saints into a kick.

"I had no idea why he wanted to be sociable, but as we chatted in there it suddenly occurred to me the fellow was trying to get at something—in fact, pumping me. He alluded constantly to Europe, to the people I was supposed to know there—putting leading questions as to my acquaintances in the sepulchral city,

3. Slender hardwood javelins used as weapons.

4. The religious doctrine of "special creation" referred to a literal interpretation of Genesis in which the universe came into being by instant divine decree.

and so on. His little eyes glittered like mica[5] discs—with curiosity—though he tried to keep up a bit of superciliousness. At first I was astonished, but very soon I became awfully curious to see what he would find out from me. I couldn't possibly imagine what I had in me to make it worth his while. It was very pretty to see how he baffled himself, for in truth my body was full only of chills, and my head had nothing in it but that wretched steamboat business. It was evident he took me for a perfectly shameless prevaricator. At last he got angry, and, to conceal a movement of furious annoyance, he yawned. I rose. Then I noticed a small sketch in oils, on a panel, representing a woman, draped and blindfolded, carrying a lighted torch.[6] The background was sombre—almost black. The movement of the woman was stately, and the effect of the torchlight on the face was sinister.

"It arrested me, and he stood by civilly, holding an empty half-pint champagne bottle (medical comforts) with the candle stuck in it. To my question he said Mr Kurtz had painted this—in this very station more than a year ago—while waiting for means to go to his trading-post. 'Tell me, pray,' said I, 'who is this Mr Kurtz?'

"'The chief of the Inner Station,' he answered in a short tone, looking away. 'Much obliged,' I said, laughing. 'And you are the brickmaker of the Central Station. Every one knows that.' He was silent for a while. 'He is a prodigy,' he said at last. 'He is an emissary of pity, and science, and progress, and devil knows what else. We want,' he began to declaim suddenly, 'for the guidance of the cause entrusted to us by Europe, so to speak, higher intelligence, wide sympathies, a singleness of purpose.' 'Who says that?' I asked. 'Lots of them,' he replied. 'Some even write that; and so *he* comes here, a special being, as you ought to know.' 'Why ought I to know?' I interrupted, really surprised. He paid no attention. 'Yes. To-day he is chief of the best station, next year he will be assistant-manager, two years more and . . . but I daresay you know what he will be in two years' time. You are of the new gang—the gang of virtue. The same people who sent him specially also recommended you. Oh, don't say no. I've my own eyes to trust.' Light dawned upon me. My dear aunt's influential acquaintances were producing an unexpected effect upon that young man. I nearly burst into a laugh. 'Do you read the Company's confidential correspondence?' I asked. He hadn't a word to say. It was great fun. 'When Mr Kurtz,' I continued severely, 'is General Manager, you won't have the opportunity.'

"He blew the candle out suddenly, and we went outside. The moon had risen. Black figures strolled about listlessly, pouring water on the glow, whence proceeded a sound of hissing; steam ascended in the moonlight; the beaten nigger groaned somewhere. 'What a row the brute makes!' said the indefatigable man with the moustaches, appearing near us. 'Serve him right. Transgression—punishment—bang! Pitiless, pitiless. That's the only way. This will prevent all conflagrations for the future. I was just telling the manager . . .' He noticed my companion, and became crestfallen all at once. 'Not in bed yet,' he said, with a kind of servile heartiness; 'it's so natural. Ha! Danger—agitation.' He vanished. I went on to the river-side, and the other followed me. I heard a scathing murmur

5. A mineral silicate that separates into glittering layers.
6. Justice was traditionally portrayed as a blindfolded woman, although usually bearing scales and a sword rather than a torch.

at my ear, 'Heap of muffs[7]—go to.' The pilgrims could be seen in knots gesticulating, discussing. Several had still their staves in their hands. I verily believe they took these sticks to bed with them. Beyond the fence the forest stood up spectrally in the moonlight, and through the dim stir, through the faint sounds of that lamentable courtyard, the silence of the land went home to one's very heart—its mystery, its greatness, the amazing reality of its concealed life. The hurt nigger moaned feebly somewhere near by, and then fetched a deep sigh that made me mend my pace away from there. I felt a hand introducing itself under my arm. 'My dear sir,' said the fellow, 'I don't want to be misunderstood, and especially by you, who will see Mr Kurtz long before I can have that pleasure. I wouldn't like him to get a false idea of my disposition. . . .'

"I let him run on, this papier-mâché Mephistopheles,[8] and it seemed to me that if I tried I could poke my forefinger through him, and would find nothing inside but a little loose dirt, maybe. He, don't you see, had been planning to be assistant-manager by and by under the present man, and I could see that the coming of that Kurtz had upset them both not a little. He talked precipitately, and I did not try to stop him. I had my shoulders against the wreck of my steamer, hauled up on the slope like a carcass of some big river animal. The smell of mud, of primeval mud, by Jove! was in my nostrils, the high stillness of primeval forest was before my eyes; there were shiny patches on the black creek. The moon had spread over everything a thin layer of silver—over the rank grass, over the mud, upon the wall of matted vegetation standing higher than the wall of a temple, over the great river I could see through a sombre gap glittering, glittering, as it flowed broadly by without a murmur. All this was great, expectant, mute, while the man jabbered about himself. I wondered whether the stillness on the face of the immensity looking at us two were meant as an appeal or as a menace. What were we who had strayed in here? Could we handle that dumb thing, or would it handle us? I felt how big, how confoundedly big, was that thing that couldn't talk and perhaps was deaf as well. What was in there? I could see a little ivory coming out from there, and I had heard Mr Kurtz was in there. I had heard enough about it too—God knows! Yet somehow it didn't bring any image with it—no more than if I had been told an angel or a fiend was in there. I believed it in the same way one of you might believe there are inhabitants in the planet Mars. I knew once a Scotch sailmaker who was certain, dead sure, there were people in Mars.[9] If you asked him for some idea how they looked and behaved, he would get shy and mutter something about 'walking on all-fours.' If you as much as smiled, he would—though a man of sixty—offer to fight you. I would not have gone so far as to fight for Kurtz, but I went for him near enough to a lie. You know I hate, detest, and can't bear a lie, not because I am straighter than the rest of us, but simply because it appals me. There is a taint of death, a flavour of mortality in lies—which is exactly what I hate and detest in the world—what I want to forget. It makes me miserable and sick, like biting something rotten would do.

7. A "muff" is a foolish, stupid, feeble, or incompetent person, especially in matters of physical skill.

8. A devil, associated with the legend of Faust, who sells his soul to Mephistopheles; in exchange, the devil is to do his bidding on earth. "Papier-mâché": method of constructing (e.g., masks, props, ornaments) using paper and glue; suggestive of fragility, pretension, illusoriness.

9. H. G. Wells's *The War of the Worlds*, about an invasion of Earth by aliens from Mars, was first serialized in 1897.

Temperament, I suppose. Well, I went near enough to it by letting the young fool there believe anything he liked to imagine as to my influence in Europe. I became in an instant as much of a pretence as the rest of the bewitched pilgrims. This simply because I had a notion it somehow would be of help to that Kurtz whom at the time I did not see—you understand. He was just a word for me. I did not see the man in the name any more than you do. Do you see him? Do you see the story? Do you see anything? It seems to me I am trying to tell you a dream—making a vain attempt, because no relation of a dream can convey the dream-sensation, that commingling of absurdity, surprise, and bewilderment in a tremor of struggling revolt, that notion of being captured by the incredible which is of the very essence of dreams. . . ."

He was silent for a while.

". . . No, it is impossible; it is impossible to convey the life-sensation of any given epoch of one's existence—that which makes its truth, its meaning—its subtle and penetrating essence. It is impossible. We live, as we dream—alone. . . ."

He paused again as if reflecting, then added:

"Of course in this you fellows see more than I could then. You see me, whom you know. . . ."

It had become so pitch dark that we listeners could hardly see one another. For a long time already he, sitting apart, had been no more to us than a voice. There was not a word from anybody. The others might have been asleep, but I was awake. I listened, I listened on the watch for the sentence, for the word, that would give me the clue to the faint uneasiness inspired by this narrative that seemed to shape itself without human lips in the heavy night-air of the river.

". . . Yes—I let him run on," Marlow began again, "and think what he pleased about the powers that were behind me. I did! And there was nothing behind me! There was nothing but that wretched, old, mangled steamboat I was leaning against, while he talked fluently about 'the necessity for every man to get on.' 'And when one comes out here, you conceive, it is not to gaze at the moon.' Mr Kurtz was a 'universal genius,' but even a genius would find it easier to work with 'adequate tools—intelligent men.' He did not make bricks—why, there was a physical impossibility in the way—as I was well aware; and if he did secretarial work for the manager, it was because 'no sensible man rejects wantonly the confidence of his superiors.' Did I see it? I saw it. What more did I want? What I really wanted was rivets, by heaven! Rivets. To get on with the work—to stop the hole. Rivets I wanted. There were cases of them down at the coast—cases—piled up—burst—split! You kicked a loose rivet at every second step in that station yard on the hillside. Rivets had rolled into the grove of death. You could fill your pockets with rivets for the trouble of stooping down—and there wasn't one rivet to be found where it was wanted. We had plates that would do, but nothing to fasten them with. And every week the messenger, a lone negro, letter-bag on shoulder and staff in hand, left our station for the coast. And several times a week a coast caravan came in with trade goods—ghastly glazed calico that made you shudder only to look at it, glass beads value about a penny a quart, confounded spotted cotton handkerchiefs. And no rivets. Three carriers could have brought all that was wanted to set that steamboat afloat.

"He was becoming confidential now, but I fancy my unresponsive attitude must have exasperated him at last, for he judged it necessary to inform me he feared neither God nor devil, let alone any mere man. I said I could see that very well, but what I wanted was a certain quantity of rivets—and rivets were what really Mr Kurtz wanted, if he had only known it. Now letters went to the coast every week. . . . 'My dear sir,' he cried, 'I write from dictation.' I demanded rivets. There was a way—for an intelligent man. He changed his manner; became very cold, and suddenly began to talk about a hippopotamus; wondered whether sleeping on board the steamer (I stuck to my salvage night and day) I wasn't disturbed. There was an old hippo that had the bad habit of getting out on the bank and roaming at night over the station grounds. The pilgrims used to turn out in a body and empty every rifle they could lay hands on at him. Some even had sat up o' nights for him. All this energy was wasted, though. 'That animal has a charmed life,' he said; 'but you can say this only of brutes in this country. No man—you apprehend me?—no man here bears a charmed life.' He stood there for a moment in the moonlight with his delicate hooked nose set a little askew, and his mica eyes glittering without a wink, then, with a curt Good-night, he strode off. I could see he was disturbed and considerably puzzled, which made me feel more hopeful than I had been for days. It was a great comfort to turn from that chap to my influential friend, the battered, twisted, ruined, tinpot steamboat. I clambered on board. She rang under my feet like an empty Huntley & Palmer biscuit-tin[1] kicked along a gutter; she was nothing so solid in make, and rather less pretty in shape, but I had expended enough hard work on her to make me love her. No influential friend would have served me better. She had given me a chance to come out a bit—to find out what I could do. No, I don't like work. I had rather laze about and think of all the fine things that can be done. I don't like work—no man does—but I like what is in the work—the chance to find yourself. Your own reality—for yourself, not for others—what no other man can ever know. They can only see the mere show, and never can tell what it really means.

"I was not surprised to see somebody sitting aft, on the deck, with his legs dangling over the mud. You see I rather chummed with the few mechanics there were in that station, whom the other pilgrims naturally despised—on account of their imperfect manners, I suppose. This was the foreman—a boiler-maker by trade—a good worker. He was a lank, bony, yellow-faced man, with big intense eyes. His aspect was worried, and his head was as bald as the palm of my hand; but his hair in falling seemed to have stuck to his chin, and had prospered in the new locality, for his beard hung down to his waist. He was a widower with six young children (he had left them in charge of a sister of his to come out there), and the passion of his life was pigeon-flying. He was an enthusiast and a connoisseur. He would rave about pigeons. After work hours he used to sometimes come over from his hut for a talk about his children and his pigeons; at work, when he had to crawl in the mud under the bottom of the steamboat, he would tie up that beard of his in a kind of white serviette[2] he brought for the purpose. It had loops to go over his ears. In the evening he

1. Huntley & Palmer biscuits were made in Reading, England, and exported throughout the British Empire; they came in a variety of collectible tins.

2. Table napkin (French).

could be seen squatted on the bank rinsing that wrapper in the creek with great care, then spreading it solemnly on a bush to dry.

"I slapped him on the back and shouted 'We shall have rivets!' He scrambled to his feet exclaiming 'No! Rivets!' as though he couldn't believe his ears. Then in a low voice, 'You . . . eh?' I don't know why we behaved like lunatics. I put my finger to the side of my nose and nodded mysteriously. 'Good for you!' he cried, snapped his fingers above his head, lifting one foot. I tried a jig. We capered on the iron deck. A frightful clatter came out of that hulk, and the virgin forest on the other bank of the creek sent it back in a thundering roll upon the sleeping station. It must have made some of the pilgrims sit up in their hovels. A dark figure obscured the lighted doorway of the manager's hut, vanished, then, a second or so after, the doorway itself vanished too. We stopped, and the silence driven away by the stamping of our feet flowed back again from the recesses of the land. The great wall of vegetation, an exuberant and entangled mass of trunks, branches, leaves, boughs, festoons, motionless in the moonlight, was like a rioting invasion of soundless life, a rolling wave of plants, piled up, crested, ready to topple over the creek, to sweep every little man of us out of his little existence. And it moved not. A deadened burst of mighty splashes and snorts reached us from afar, as though an ichthyosaurus[3] had been taking a bath of glitter in the great river. 'After all,' said the boiler-maker in a reasonable tone, 'why shouldn't we get the rivets?' Why not, indeed! I did not know of any reason why we shouldn't. 'They'll come in three weeks,' I said confidently.

"But they didn't. Instead of rivets there came an invasion, an infliction, a visitation. It came in sections during the next three weeks, each section headed by a donkey carrying a white man in new clothes and tan shoes, bowing from that elevation right and left to the impressed pilgrims. A quarrelsome band of footsore sulky niggers trod on the heels of the donkey; a lot of tents, camp-stools, tin boxes, white cases, brown bales would be shot down in the courtyard, and the air of mystery would deepen a little over the muddle of the station. Five such instalments came, with their absurd air of disorderly flight with the loot of innumerable outfit shops and provision stores, that, one would think, they were lugging, after a raid, into the wilderness for equitable division. It was an inextricable mess of things decent in themselves but that human folly made look like the spoils of thieving.

"This devoted band called itself the Eldorado[4] Exploring Expedition, and I believe they were sworn to secrecy. Their talk, however, was the talk of sordid buccaneers: it was reckless without hardihood, greedy without audacity, and cruel without courage; there was not an atom of foresight or of serious intention in the whole batch of them, and they did not seem aware these things are wanted for the work of the world. To tear treasure out of the bowels of the land was their desire, with no more moral purpose at the back of it than there is in burglars breaking into a safe. Who paid the expenses of the noble enterprise I don't know; but the uncle of our manager was leader of that lot.

"In exterior he resembled a butcher in a poor neighbourhood, and his eyes had a look of sleepy cunning. He carried his fat paunch with ostentation on his

3. An extinct prehistoric marine reptile resembling a fish or a dolphin.

4. *El Dorado* (literally, "the gilded one," Spanish); the mythical land of gold sought by the Spanish conquistadors in South America.

short legs, and during the time his gang infested the station spoke to no one but his nephew. You could see these two roaming about all day long with their heads close together in an everlasting confab.[5]

"I had given up worrying myself about the rivets. One's capacity for that kind of folly is more limited than you would suppose. I said Hang!—and let things slide. I had plenty of time for meditation, and now and then I would give some thought to Kurtz. I wasn't very interested in him. No. Still, I was curious to see whether this man, who had come out equipped with moral ideas of some sort, would climb to the top after all, and how he would set about his work when there."

2

"One evening as I was lying flat on the deck of my steamboat, I heard voices approaching—and there were the nephew and the uncle strolling along the bank. I laid my head on my arm again, and had nearly lost myself in a doze, when somebody said in my ear, as it were: 'I am as harmless as a little child, but I don't like to be dictated to. Am I the manager—or am I not? I was ordered to send him there. It's incredible.' . . . I became aware that the two were standing on the shore alongside the forepart of the steamboat, just below my head. I did not move; it did not occur to me to move: I was sleepy. 'It *is* unpleasant,' grunted the uncle. 'He has asked the Administration to be sent there,' said the other, 'with the idea of showing what he could do; and I was instructed accordingly. Look at the influence that man must have. Is it not frightful?' They both agreed it was frightful, then made several bizarre remarks: 'Make rain and fine weather—one man—the Council—by the nose'—bits of absurd sentences that got the better of my drowsiness, so that I had pretty near the whole of my wits about me when the uncle said, 'The climate may do away with this difficulty for you. Is he alone there?' 'Yes,' answered the manager; 'he sent his assistant down the river with a note to me in these terms: "Clear this poor devil out of the country, and don't bother sending more of that sort. I had rather be alone than have the kind of men you can dispose of with me." It was more than a year ago. Can you imagine such impudence?' 'Anything since then?' asked the other hoarsely. 'Ivory,' jerked the nephew; 'lots of it—prime sort—lots—most annoying, from him.' 'And with that?' questioned the heavy rumble. 'Invoice,' was the reply fired out, so to speak. Then silence. They had been talking about Kurtz.

"I was broad awake by this time, but, lying perfectly at ease, remained still, having no inducement to change my position. 'How did that ivory come all this way?' growled the elder man, who seemed very vexed. The other explained that it had come with a fleet of canoes in charge of an English half-caste[6] clerk Kurtz had with him; that Kurtz had apparently intended to return himself, the station being by that time bare of goods and stores, but after coming three hundred miles, had suddenly decided to go back, which he started to do alone in a small dugout with four paddlers, leaving the half-caste to continue down the river with the ivory. The two fellows there seemed astounded at anybody attempting such a thing. They were at a loss for an adequate motive. As for me, I seemed to see Kurtz for the first time. It was a distinct glimpse: the dugout, four paddling

5. Conversation.

6. Of mixed race.

savages, and the lone white man turning his back suddenly on the headquarters, on relief, on thoughts of home—perhaps; setting his face towards the depths of the wilderness, towards his empty and desolate station. I did not know the motive. Perhaps he was just simply a fine fellow who stuck to his work for its own sake. His name, you understand, had not been pronounced once. He was 'that man.' The half-caste, who, as far as I could see, had conducted a difficult trip with great prudence and pluck, was invariably alluded to as 'that scoundrel.' The 'scoundrel' had reported that the 'man' had been very ill—had recovered imperfectly. . . . The two below me moved away then a few paces, and strolled back and forth at some little distance. I heard: 'Military post—doctor—two hundred miles—quite alone now—unavoidable delays—nine months—no news—strange rumours.' They approached again, just as the manager was saying, 'No one, as far as I know, unless a species of wandering trader—a pestilential fellow, snapping ivory from the natives.' Who was it they were talking about now? I gathered in snatches that this was some man supposed to be in Kurtz's district, and of whom the manager did not approve. 'We will not be free from unfair competition till one of these fellows is hanged for an example,' he said. 'Certainly,' grunted the other; 'get him hanged! Why not? Anything—anything can be done in this country. That's what I say; nobody here, you understand, *here*, can endanger your position. And why? You stand the climate—you outlast them all. The danger is in Europe; but there before I left I took care to—' They moved off and whispered, then their voices rose again. 'The extraordinary series of delays is not my fault. I did my possible.' The fat man sighed, 'Very sad.' 'And the pestiferous absurdity of his talk,' continued the other; 'he bothered me enough when he was here. "Each station should be like a beacon on the road towards better things, a centre for trade of course, but also for humanising, improving, instructing." Conceive you[7]—that ass! And he wants to be manager! No, it's—' Here he got choked by excessive indignation, and I lifted my head the least bit. I was surprised to see how near they were—right under me. I could have spat upon their hats. They were looking on the ground, absorbed in thought. The manager was switching his leg with a slender twig: his sagacious relative lifted his head. 'You have been well since you came out this time?' he asked. The other gave a start. 'Who? I? Oh! Like a charm—like a charm. But the rest—oh, my goodness! All sick. They die so quick, too, that I haven't the time to send them out of the country—it's incredible!' 'H'm. Just so,' grunted the uncle. 'Ah! my boy, trust to this—I say, trust to this.' I saw him extend his short flipper of an arm for a gesture that took in the forest, the creek, the mud, the river—seemed to beckon with a dishonouring flourish before the sunlit face of the land a treacherous appeal to the lurking death, to the hidden evil, to the profound darkness of its heart. It was so startling that I leaped to my feet and looked back at the edge of the forest, as though I had expected an answer of some sort to that black display of confidence. You know the foolish notions that come to one sometimes. The high stillness confronted these two figures with its ominous patience, waiting for the passing away of a fantastic invasion.

"They swore aloud together—out of sheer fright, I believe—then, pretending not to know anything of my existence, turned back to the station. The sun was

7. "Just imagine." This phrase, like "I did my possible" (I did the best I could), above, and others throughout the novel, is a literal translation of the French spoken by Belgian traders.

low; and leaning forward side by side, they seemed to be tugging painfully uphill their two ridiculous shadows of unequal length, that trailed behind them slowly over the tall grass without bending a single blade.

"In a few days the Eldorado Expedition went into the patient wilderness, that closed upon it as the sea closes over a diver. Long afterwards the news came that all the donkeys were dead. I know nothing as to the fate of the less valuable animals.[8] They, no doubt, like the rest of us, found what they deserved. I did not inquire. I was then rather excited at the prospect of meeting Kurtz very soon. When I say very soon I mean it comparatively. It was just two months from the day we left the creek when we came to the bank below Kurtz's station.

"Going up that river was like travelling back to the earliest beginnings of the world, when vegetation rioted on the earth and the big trees were kings. An empty stream, a great silence, an impenetrable forest. The air was warm, thick, heavy, sluggish. There was no joy in the brilliance of sunshine. The long stretches of the waterway ran on, deserted, into the gloom of overshadowed distances. On silvery sandbanks hippos and alligators sunned themselves side by side. The broadening waters flowed through a mob of wooded islands; you lost your way on that river as you would in a desert, and butted all day long against shoals, trying to find the channel, till you thought yourself bewitched and cut off for ever from everything you had known once—somewhere—far away—in another existence perhaps. There were moments when one's past came back to one, as it will sometimes when you have not a moment to spare to yourself; but it came in the shape of an unrestful and noisy dream, remembered with wonder amongst the overwhelming realities of this strange world of plants, and water, and silence. And this stillness of life did not in the least resemble a peace. It was the stillness of an implacable force brooding over an inscrutable intention. It looked at you with a vengeful aspect. I got used to it afterwards; I did not see it any more; I had no time. I had to keep guessing at the channel; I had to discern, mostly by inspiration, the signs of hidden banks; I watched for sunken stones; I was learning to clap my teeth smartly before my heart flew out, when I shaved by a fluke some infernal sly old snag[9] that would have ripped the life out of the tin-pot steamboat and drowned all the pilgrims; I had to keep a look-out for the signs of dead wood we could cut up in the night for next day's steaming. When you have to attend to things of that sort, to the mere incidents of the surface, the reality—the reality, I tell you—fades. The inner truth is hidden—luckily, luckily. But I felt it all the same; I felt often its mysterious stillness watching me at my monkey tricks, just as it watches you fellows performing on your respective tight-ropes for—what is it? half a crown[1] a tumble—"

"Try to be civil, Marlow," growled a voice, and I knew there was at least one listener awake besides myself.

"I beg your pardon. I forgot the heartache which makes up the rest of the price. And indeed what does the price matter, if the trick be well done? You do your tricks very well. And I didn't do badly either, since I managed not to sink that steamboat on my first trip. It's a wonder to me yet. Imagine a blindfolded

8. I.e., humans.
9. A large branch or tree trunk embedded in the river bottom with one end pointing up.
1. British denomination of coin, equal to 2 shillings and 6 pence, or an eighth of a pound. Not much money: at the time, the value of a London cab fare or a generous tip.

man set to drive a van over a bad road. I sweated and shivered over that business considerably, I can tell you. After all, for a seaman, to scrape the bottom of the thing that's supposed to float all the time under his care is the unpardonable sin. No one may know of it, but you never forget the thump—eh? A blow on the very heart. You remember it, you dream of it, you wake up at night and think of it—years after—and go hot and cold all over. I don't pretend to say that steamboat floated all the time. More than once she had to wade for a bit, with twenty cannibals splashing around and pushing. We had enlisted some of these chaps on the way for a crew. Fine fellows—cannibals—in their place. They were men one could work with, and I am grateful to them. And, after all, they did not eat each other before my face: they had brought along a provision of hippo-meat which went rotten, and made the mystery of the wilderness stink in my nostrils. Phoo! I can sniff it now. I had the manager on board and three or four pilgrims with their staves—all complete. Sometimes we came upon a station close by the bank, clinging to the skirts of the unknown, and the white men rushing out of a tumble-down hovel, with great gestures of joy and surprise and welcome, seemed very strange—had the appearance of being held there captive by a spell. The word 'ivory' would ring in the air for a while—and on we went again into the silence, along empty reaches, round the still bends, between the high walls of our winding way, reverberating in hollow claps the ponderous beat of the stern-wheel.[2] Trees, trees, millions of trees, massive, immense, running up high; and at their foot, hugging the bank against the stream, crept the little begrimed steamboat, like a sluggish beetle crawling on the floor of a lofty portico. It made you feel very small, very lost, and yet it was not altogether depressing, that feeling. After all, if you were small, the grimy beetle crawled on—which was just what you wanted it to do. Where the pilgrims imagined it crawled to I don't know. To some place where they expected to get something, I bet! For me it crawled towards Kurtz—exclusively; but when the steam-pipes started leaking we crawled very slow. The reaches opened before us and closed behind, as if the forest had stepped leisurely across the water to bar the way for our return. We penetrated deeper and deeper into the heart of darkness. It was very quiet there. At night sometimes the roll of drums behind the curtain of trees would run up the river and remain sustained faintly, as if hovering in the air high over our heads, till the first break of day. Whether it meant war, peace, or prayer we could not tell. The dawns were heralded by the descent of a chill stillness; the woodcutters slept, their fires burned low; the snapping of a twig would make you start. We were wanderers on a prehistoric earth, on an earth that wore the aspect of an unknown planet. We could have fancied ourselves the first of men taking possession of an accursed inheritance, to be subdued at the cost of profound anguish and of excessive toil. But suddenly, as we struggled round a bend, there would be a glimpse of rush walls, of peaked grass-roofs, a burst of yells, a whirl of black limbs, a mass of hands clapping, of feet stamping, of bodies swaying, of eyes rolling, under the droop of heavy and motionless foliage. The steamer toiled along slowly on the edge of a black and incomprehensible frenzy. The prehistoric man was cursing us, praying to us, welcoming us—who could tell? We were cut off from the

2. The paddle wheel at the rear of the boat; the main source of propulsion on a steamboat.

comprehension of our surroundings; we glided past like phantoms, wondering and secretly appalled, as sane men would be before an enthusiastic outbreak in a madhouse. We could not understand because we were too far and could not remember, because we were travelling in the night of first ages, of those ages that are gone, leaving hardly a sign—and no memories.

"The earth seemed unearthly. We are accustomed to look upon the shackled form of a conquered monster, but there—there you could look at a thing monstrous and free. It was unearthly, and the men were—No, they were not inhuman. Well, you know, that was the worst of it—this suspicion of their not being inhuman. It would come slowly to one. They howled and leaped, and spun, and made horrid faces; but what thrilled you was just the thought of their humanity—like yours—the thought of your remote kinship with this wild and passionate uproar. Ugly. Yes, it was ugly enough; but if you were man enough you would admit to yourself that there was in you just the faintest trace of a response to the terrible frankness of that noise, a dim suspicion of there being a meaning in it which you—you so remote from the night of first ages—could comprehend. And why not? The mind of man is capable of anything—because everything is in it, all the past as well as all the future. What was there after all? Joy, fear, sorrow, devotion, valour, rage—who can tell?—but truth—truth stripped of its cloak of time. Let the fool gape and shudder—the man knows, and can look on without a wink. But he must at least be as much of a man as these on the shore. He must meet that truth with his own true stuff—with his own inborn strength. Principles? Principles won't do. Acquisitions, clothes, pretty rags—rags that would fly off at the first good shake. No; you want a deliberate belief. An appeal to me in this fiendish row—is there? Very well; I hear; I admit, but I have a voice too, and for good or evil mine is the speech that cannot be silenced. Of course, a fool, what with sheer fright and fine sentiments, is always safe. Who's that grunting? You wonder I didn't go ashore for a howl and a dance? Well, no—I didn't. Fine sentiments, you say? Fine sentiments be hanged! I had no time. I had to mess about with white-lead[3] and strips of woollen blanket helping to put bandages on those leaky steam-pipes—I tell you. I had to watch the steering, and circumvent those snags, and get the tin-pot along by hook or by crook. There was surface-truth enough in these things to save a wiser man. And between whiles I had to look after the savage who was fireman. He was an improved specimen; he could fire up a vertical boiler.[4] He was there below me, and, upon my word, to look at him was as edifying as seeing a dog in a parody of breeches and a feather hat, walking on his hind legs. A few months of training had done for that really fine chap. He squinted at the steam-gauge and at the water-gauge with an evident effort of intrepidity—and he had filed teeth too, the poor devil, and the wool of his pate shaved into queer patterns, and three ornamental scars on each of his cheeks. He ought to have been clapping his hands and stamping his feet on the bank, instead of which he was hard at work, a thrall to strange witchcraft, full of improving knowledge. He was useful because he had been instructed; and what he knew was this—that should the water in that transparent thing disappear, the evil spirit inside the boiler would get angry through the greatness of

3. Lead compound often used in white paint for caulking seams and waterproofing timber.

4. A simple and easily fired narrow boiler.

his thirst, and take a terrible vengeance. So he sweated and fired up and watched the glass fearfully (with an impromptu charm, made of rags, tied to his arm, and a piece of polished bone, as big as a watch, stuck flatways through his lower lip), while the wooded banks slipped past us slowly, the short noise was left behind, the interminable miles of silence—and we crept on, towards Kurtz. But the snags were thick, the water was treacherous and shallow, the boiler seemed indeed to have a sulky devil in it, and thus neither that fireman nor I had any time to peer into our creepy thoughts.

"Some fifty miles below the Inner Station we came upon a hut of reeds, an inclined and melancholy pole, with the unrecognisable tatters of what had been a flag of some sort flying from it, and a neatly stacked wood-pile. This was unexpected. We came to the bank, and on the stack of firewood found a flat piece of board with some faded pencil-writing on it. When deciphered it said: 'Wood for you. Hurry up. Approach cautiously.' There was a signature, but it was illegible—not Kurtz—a much longer word. Hurry up. Where? Up the river? 'Approach cautiously.' We had not done so. But the warning could not have been meant for the place where it could be only found after approach. Something was wrong above. But what—and how much? That was the question. We commented adversely upon the imbecility of that telegraphic style.[5] The bush around said nothing, and would not let us look very far, either. A torn curtain of red twill hung in the doorway of the hut, and flapped sadly in our faces. The dwelling was dismantled; but we could see a white man had lived there not very long ago. There remained a rude table—a plank on two posts; a heap of rubbish reposed in a dark corner, and by the door I picked up a book. It had lost its covers, and the pages had been thumbed into a state of extremely dirty softness; but the back had been lovingly stitched afresh with white cotton thread, which looked clean yet. It was an extraordinary find. Its title was, *An Inquiry into some Points of Seamanship*, by a man Towser, Towson—some such name—Master in His Majesty's Navy.[6] The matter looked dreary reading enough, with illustrative diagrams and repulsive tables of figures, and the copy was sixty years old. I handled this amazing antiquity with the greatest possible tenderness, lest it should dissolve in my hands. Within, Towson or Towser was inquiring earnestly into the breaking strain of ships' chains and tackle, and other such matters. Not a very enthralling book; but at the first glance you could see there a singleness of intention, an honest concern for the right way of going to work, which made these humble pages, thought out so many years ago, luminous with another than a professional light. The simple old sailor, with his talk of chains and purchases,[7] made me forget the jungle and the pilgrims in a delicious sensation of having come upon something unmistakably real. Such a book being there was wonderful enough; but still more astounding were the notes pencilled in the margin, and plainly referring to the text. I couldn't believe my eyes! They were in cipher! Yes, it looked like cipher. Fancy a man lugging with him a book of that description into this nowhere and studying it—and making notes—in cipher at that! It was an extravagant mystery.

5. Using as few words as possible, as in a telegram.
6. I.e., the British Navy.
7. Nautical terms. "Chains": contrivances for fastening ropes supporting the mast to the deck and the sides of a ship. "Purchases": devices for applying or increasing force: pulleys, windlasses, etc.

"I had been dimly aware for some time of a worrying noise, and when I lifted my eyes I saw the wood-pile was gone, and the manager, aided by all the pilgrims, was shouting at me from the river-side. I slipped the book into my pocket. I assure you to leave off reading was like tearing myself away from the shelter of an old and solid friendship.

"I started the lame engine ahead. 'It must be this miserable trader—this intruder,' exclaimed the manager, looking back malevolently at the place we had left. 'He must be English,' I said. 'It will not save him from getting into trouble if he is not careful,' muttered the manager darkly. I observed with assumed innocence that no man was safe from trouble in this world.

"The current was more rapid now, the steamer seemed at her last gasp, the stern-wheel flopped languidly, and I caught myself listening on tiptoe for the next beat of the float,[8] for in sober truth I expected the wretched thing to give up every moment. It was like watching the last flickers of a life. But still we crawled. Sometimes I would pick out a tree a little way head to measure our progress towards Kurtz by, but I lost it invariably before we got abreast. To keep the eyes so long on one thing was too much for human patience. The manager displayed a beautiful resignation. I fretted and fumed and took to arguing with myself whether or no I would talk openly with Kurtz; but before I could come to any conclusion it occurred to me that my speech or my silence, indeed any action of mine, would be a mere futility. What did it matter what any one knew or ignored? What did it matter who was manager? One gets sometimes such a flash of insight. The essentials of this affair lay deep under the surface, beyond my reach, and beyond my power of meddling.

"Towards the evening of the second day we judged ourselves about eight miles from Kurtz's station. I wanted to push on; but the manager looked grave, and told me the navigation up there was so dangerous that it would be advisable, the sun being very low already, to wait where we were till next morning. Moreover, he pointed out that if the warning to approach cautiously were to be followed, we must approach in daylight—not at dusk, or in the dark. This was sensible enough. Eight miles meant nearly three hours' steaming for us, and I could also see suspicious ripples at the upper end of the reach. Nevertheless, I was annoyed beyond expression at the delay, and most unreasonably too, since one night more could not matter much after so many months. As we had plenty of wood, and caution was the word, I brought up in the middle of the stream. The reach was narrow, straight, with high sides like a railway cutting. The dusk came gliding into it long before the sun had set. The current ran smooth and swift, but a dumb immobility sat on the banks. The living trees, lashed together by the creepers and every living bush of the undergrowth, might have been changed into stone, even to the slenderest twig, to the lightest leaf. It was not sleep—it seemed unnatural, like a state of trance. Not the faintest sound of any kind could be heard. You looked on amazed, and began to suspect yourself of being deaf—then the night came suddenly, and struck you blind as well. About three in the morning some large fish leaped, and the loud splash made me jump as though a gun had been fired. When the sun rose there was a white fog, very warm and clammy, and more blinding than the night. It did not shift or drive; it was just there, standing all round you like something

8. The sound of the paddle ("paddle float") as it hits the water.

solid. At eight or nine, perhaps, it lifted as a shutter lifts. We had a glimpse of the towering multitude of trees, of the immense matted jungle, with the blazing little ball of the sun hanging over it—all perfectly still—and then the white shutter came down again, smoothly, as if sliding in greased grooves. I ordered the chain, which we had begun to heave in, to be paid out again. Before it stopped running with a muffled rattle, a cry, a very loud cry, as of infinite desolation, soared slowly in the opaque air. It ceased. A complaining clamour, modulated in savage discords, filled our ears. The sheer unexpectedness of it made my hair stir under my cap. I don't know how it struck the others: to me it seemed as though the mist itself had screamed, so suddenly, and apparently from all sides at once, did this tumultuous and mournful uproar arise. It culminated in a hurried outbreak of almost intolerably excessive shrieking, which stopped short, leaving us stiffened in a variety of silly attitudes, and obstinately listening to the nearly as appalling and excessive silence. 'Good God! What is the meaning—?' stammered at my elbow one of the pilgrims—a little fat man, with sandy hair and red whiskers, who wore side-spring boots, and pink pyjamas tucked into his socks. Two others remained open-mouthed a whole minute, then dashed into the little cabin, to rush out incontinently and stand darting scared glances, with Winchesters[9] at 'ready' in their hands. What we could see was just the steamer we were on, her outlines blurred as though she had been on the point of dissolving, and a misty strip of water, perhaps two feet broad, around her—and that was all. The rest of the world was nowhere, as far as our eyes and ears were concerned. Just nowhere. Gone, disappeared; swept off without leaving a whisper or a shadow behind.

"I went forward, and ordered the chain to be hauled in short, so as to be ready to trip the anchor and move the steamboat at once if necessary. 'Will they attack?' whispered an awed voice. 'We will all be butchered in this fog,' murmured another. The faces twitched with the strain, the hands trembled slightly, the eyes forgot to wink. It was very curious to see the contrast of expressions of the white men and of the black fellows of our crew, who were as much strangers to that part of the river as we, though their homes were only eight hundred miles away. The whites, of course greatly discomposed, had besides a curious look of being painfully shocked by such an outrageous row. The others had an alert, naturally interested expression; but their faces were essentially quiet, even those of the one or two who grinned as they hauled at the chain. Several exchanged short, grunting phrases, which seemed to settle the matter to their satisfaction. Their headman, a young, broad-chested black, severely draped in dark-blue fringed cloths, with fierce nostrils and his hair all done up artfully in oily ringlets, stood near me. 'Aha!' I said, just for good fellowship's sake. 'Catch 'im,' he snapped, with a bloodshot widening of his eyes and a flash of sharp teeth—'catch 'im. Give 'im to us.' 'To you, eh?' I asked; 'what would you do with them?' 'Eat 'im!' he said curtly, and, leaning his elbow on the rail, looked out into the fog in a dignified and profoundly pensive attitude. I would no doubt have been properly horrified, had it not occurred to me that he and his chaps must be very hungry: that they must have been growing increasingly hungry for at least this month past. They had been engaged for six months (I don't think a

9. Lever-action repeating rifles.

single one of them had any clear idea of time, as we at the end of countless ages have. They still belonged to the beginnings of time—had no inherited experience to teach them, as it were), and of course, as long as there was a piece of paper written over in accordance with some farcical law or other made down the river, it didn't enter anybody's head to trouble how they would live. Certainly they had brought with them some rotten hippo-meat, which couldn't have lasted very long, anyway, even if the pilgrims hadn't, in the midst of a shocking hullabaloo, thrown a considerable quantity of it overboard. It looked like a high-handed proceeding; but it was really a case of legitimate self-defence. You can't breathe dead hippo waking, sleeping, and eating, and at the same time keep your precarious grip on existence. Besides that, they had given them every week three pieces of brass wire, each about nine inches long; and the theory was they were to buy their provisions with that currency in river-side villages. You can see how *that* worked. There were either no villages, or the people were hostile, or the director, who like the rest of us fed out of tins, with an occasional old he-goat thrown in, didn't want to stop the steamer for some more or less recondite reasons. So, unless they swallowed the wire itself, or made loops of it to snare the fishes with, I don't see what good their extravagant salary could be to them. I must say it was paid with a regularity worthy of a large and honourable trading company. For the rest, the only thing to eat—though it didn't look eatable in the least—I saw in their possession was a few lumps of some stuff like half-cooked dough, of a dirty lavender colour, they kept wrapped in leaves, and now and then swallowed a piece of, but so small that it seemed done more for the look of the thing than for any serious purpose of sustenance. Why in the name of all the gnawing devils of hunger they didn't go for us—they were thirty to five—and have a good tuck-in for once, amazes me now when I think of it. They were big powerful men, with not much capacity to weigh the consequences, with courage, with strength, even yet, though their skins were no longer glossy and their muscles no longer hard. And I saw that something restraining, one of those human secrets that baffle probability, had come into play there. I looked at them with a swift quickening of interest—not because it occurred to me I might be eaten by them before very long, though I own to you that just then I perceived—in a new light, as it were—how unwholesome the pilgrims looked, and I hoped, yes, I positively hoped, that my aspect was not so—what shall I say?—so—unappetising: a touch of fantastic vanity which fitted well with the dream-sensation that pervaded all my days at that time. Perhaps I had a little fever too. One can't live with one's finger everlastingly on one's pulse. I had often 'a little fever,' or a little touch of other things—the playful paw-strokes of the wilderness, the preliminary trifling before the more serious onslaught which came in due course. Yes; I looked at them as you would on any human being, with a curiosity of their impulses, motives, capacities, weaknesses, when brought to the test of an inexorable physical necessity. Restraint! What possible restraint? Was it superstition, disgust, patience, fear—or some kind of primitive honour? No fear can stand up to hunger, no patience can wear it out, disgust simply does not exist where hunger is; and as to superstition, beliefs, and what you may call principles, they are less than chaff in a breeze. Don't you know the devilry of lingering starvation, its exasperating torment, its black thoughts, its sombre and brooding ferocity? Well, I do. It takes a man all his inborn strength to fight hunger properly. It's really easier to face bereavement, dishonour, and the perdition of one's soul—than this kind of prolonged hunger. Sad, but true. And these chaps too had no earthly reason for any kind of scruple. Restraint! I would just as soon have expected restraint from a hyena prowling amongst the corpses of a battlefield. But there was the fact facing me—the fact dazzling, to be seen, like the foam on the depths of the sea, like a ripple on an unfathomable enigma, a mystery greater—when I thought of it—than the curious, inexplicable note of desperate grief in this savage clamour that had swept by us on the river-bank, behind the blind whiteness of the fog.

"Two pilgrims were quarrelling in hurried whispers as to which bank. 'Left.' 'No, no; how can you? Right, right, of course.' 'It is very serious,' said the manager's voice behind me; 'I would be desolated if anything should happen to Mr. Kurtz before we came up.' I looked at him, and had not the slightest doubt he was sincere. He was just the kind of man who would wish to preserve appearances. That was his restraint. But when he muttered something about going on at once, I did not even take the trouble to answer him. I knew, and he knew, that it was impossible. Were we to let go our hold of the bottom, we would be absolutely in the air—in space. We wouldn't be able to tell where we were going to—whether up or down stream, or across—till we fetched against one bank or the other—and then we wouldn't know at first which it was. Of course I made no move. I had no mind for a smashup. You couldn't imagine a more deadly place for a shipwreck. Whether drowned at once or not, we were sure to perish speedily in one way or another. 'I authorise you to take all the risks,' he said, after a short silence. 'I refuse to take any,' I said shortly; which was just the answer he expected, though its tone might have surprised him. 'Well, I must defer to your judgment. You are captain,' he said, with marked civility. I turned my shoulder to him in sign of my appreciation, and looked into the fog. How long would it last? It was the most hopeless look-out. The approach to this Kurtz grubbing for ivory in the wretched bush was beset by as many dangers as though he had been an enchanted princess sleeping in a fabulous castle. 'Will they attack, do you think?' asked the manager, in a confidential tone.

"I did not think they would attack, for several obvious reasons. The thick fog was one. If they left the bank in their canoes they would get lost in it, as we would be if we attempted to move. Still, I had also judged the jungle of both banks quite impenetrable—and yet eyes were in it, eyes that had seen us. The river-side bushes were certainly very thick; but the undergrowth behind was evidently penetrable. However, during the short lift I had seen no canoes anywhere in the reach—certainly not abreast of the steamer. But what made the idea of attack inconceivable to me was the nature of the noise—of the cries we had heard. They had not the fierce character boding of immediate hostile intention. Unexpected, wild, and violent as they had been, they had given me an irresistible impression of sorrow. The glimpse of the steamboat had for some reason filled those savages with unrestrained grief. The danger, if any, I expounded, was from our proximity to a great human passion let loose. Even extreme grief may ultimately vent itself in violence—but more generally takes the form of apathy. . . .

"You should have seen the pilgrims stare! They had no heart to grin, or even to revile me; but I believe they thought me gone mad—with fright, maybe. I delivered a regular lecture. My dear boys, it was no good bothering. Keep a look-out? Well, you may guess I watched the fog for the signs of lifting as a cat watches a mouse; but for anything else our eyes were of no more use to us than if we had been buried miles deep in a heap of cottonwool. It felt like it too—choking, warm, stifling. Besides, all I said, though it sounded extravagant, was absolutely true to fact. What we afterwards alluded to as an attack was really an attempt at repulse. The action was very far from being aggressive—it was not even defensive, in the usual sense: it was undertaken under the stress of desperation, and in its essence was purely protective.

"It developed itself, I should say, two hours after the fog lifted, and its commencement was at a spot, roughly speaking, about a mile and a half below Kurtz's station. We had just floundered and flopped round a bend, when I saw an islet, a mere grassy hummock of bright green, in the middle of the stream. It was the only thing of the kind; but as we opened the reach more, I perceived it was the head of a long sandbank, or rather of a chain of shallow patches stretching down the middle of the river. They were discoloured, just awash, and the whole lot was seen just under the water, exactly as a man's backbone is seen running down the middle of his back under the skin. Now, as far as I did see, I could go to the right or to the left of this. I didn't know either channel, of course. The banks looked pretty well alike, the depth appeared the same; but as I had been informed the station was on the west side, I naturally headed for the western passage.

"No sooner had we fairly entered it than I became aware it was much narrower than I had supposed. To the left of us there was the long uninterrupted shoal, and to the right a high steep bank heavily overgrown with bushes. Above the bush the trees stood in serried ranks. The twigs overhung the current thickly, and from distance to distance a large limb of some tree projected rigidly over the stream. It was then well on in the afternoon, the face of the forest was gloomy, and a broad strip of shadow had already fallen on the water. In this shadow we steamed up—very slowly, as you may imagine. I sheered her well inshore—the water being deepest near the bank, as the sounding-pole[1] informed me.

"One of my hungry and forbearing friends was sounding in the bows just below me. This steamboat was exactly like a decked scow.[2] On the deck there were two little teak-wood houses, with doors and windows. The boiler was in the fore-end, and the machinery right astern. Over the whole there was a light roof, supported on stanchions. The funnel projected through that roof, and in front of the funnel a small cabin built of light planks served for a pilot-house. It contained a couch, two camp-stools, a loaded Martini-Henry[3] leaning in one corner, a tiny table, and the steering-wheel. It had a wide door in front and a broad shutter at each side. All these were always thrown open, of course. I spent my days perched up there on the extreme fore-end of that roof, before the door. At night I slept, or tried to, on the couch. An athletic black belonging to some coast tribe, and educated by my poor predecessor, was the helmsman. He sported a pair of brass earrings, wore a blue cloth wrapper from the waist to the

1. A pole with measurements, stuck in the water until it hits bottom, to determine the depth of a shallow body of water. "Sheered her well inshore": i.e., steered so as to be going upriver while close to the bank.

2. A large, flat-bottomed boat for cargo; in this case, with the addition of a deck.

3. A lever-action rifle taking an especially powerful charge; standard British service weapon of the time.

ankles, and thought all the world of himself. He was the most unstable kind of fool I had ever seen. He steered with no end of a swagger while you were by; but if he lost sight of you, he became instantly the prey of an abject funk, and would let that cripple of a steamboat get the upper hand of him in a minute.

"I was looking down at the sounding-pole, and feeling much annoyed to see at each try a little more of it stick out of that river, when I saw my poleman give up the business suddenly, and stretch himself flat on the deck, without even taking the trouble to haul his pole in. He kept hold on it though, and it trailed in the water. At the same time the fireman, whom I could also see below me, sat down abruptly before his furnace and ducked his head. I was amazed. Then I had to look at the river mighty quick, because there was a snag in the fairway. Sticks, little sticks, were flying about—thick; they were whizzing before my nose, dropping below me, striking behind me against my pilot-house. All this time the river, the shore, the woods, were very quiet—perfectly quiet. I could only hear the heavy splashing thump of the stern-wheel and the patter of these things. We cleared the snag clumsily. Arrows, by Jove! We were being shot at! I stepped in quickly to close the shutter on the land-side. That fool-helmsman, his hands on the spokes, was lifting his knees high, stamping his feet, champing his mouth, like a reined-in horse. Confound him! And we were staggering within ten feet of the bank. I had to lean right out to swing the heavy shutter, and I saw a face amongst the leaves on the level with my own, looking at me very fierce and steady; and then suddenly, as though a veil had been removed from my eyes, I made out, deep in the tangled gloom, naked breasts, arms, legs, glaring eyes—the bush was swarming with human limbs in movement, glistening, of bronze colour. The twigs shook, swayed, and rustled, the arrows flew out of them, and then the shutter came to. 'Steer her straight,' I said to the helmsman. He held his head rigid, face forward; but his eyes rolled, he kept on lifting and setting down his feet gently, his mouth foamed a little. 'Keep quiet!' I said in a fury. I might just as well have ordered a tree not to sway in the wind. I darted out. Below me there was a great scuffle of feet on the iron deck; confused exclamations; a voice screamed, 'Can you turn back?' I caught sight of a V-shaped ripple on the water ahead. What? Another snag! A fusillade[4] burst out under my feet. The pilgrims had opened with their Winchesters, and were simply squirting lead into that bush. A deuce of a lot of smoke came up and drove slowly forward. I swore at it. Now I couldn't see the ripple or the snag either. I stood in the doorway, peering, and the arrows came in swarms. They might have been poisoned, but they looked as though they wouldn't kill a cat. The bush began to howl. Our wood-cutters raised a warlike whoop; the report of a rifle just at my back deafened me. I glanced over my shoulder, and the pilot-house was yet full of noise and smoke when I made a dash at the wheel. The fool-nigger had dropped everything, to throw the shutter open and let off that Martini-Henry. He stood before the wide opening, glaring, and I yelled at him to come back, while I straightened the sudden twist out of that steamboat. There was no room to turn even if I had wanted to, the snag was somewhere very near ahead in that confounded smoke, there was no time to lose, so I just crowded her into the bank—right into the bank, where I knew the water was deep.

4. The simultaneous discharge of many firearms.

"We tore slowly along the overhanging bushes in a whirl of broken twigs and flying leaves. The fusillade below stopped short, as I had foreseen it would when the squirts got empty. I threw my head back to a glinting whizz that traversed the pilot-house, in at one shutter-hole and out at the other. Looking past that mad helmsman, who was shaking the empty rifle and yelling at the shore, I saw vague forms of men running bent double, leaping, gliding, distinct, incomplete, evanescent. Something big appeared in the air before the shutter, the rifle went overboard, and the man stepped back swiftly, looked at me over his shoulder in an extraordinary, profound, familiar manner, and fell upon my feet. The side of his head hit the wheel twice, and the end of what appeared a long cane clattered round and knocked over a little camp-stool. It looked as though after wrenching that thing from somebody ashore he had lost his balance in the effort. The thin smoke had blown away, we were clear of the snag, and looking ahead I could see that in another hundred yards or so I would be free to sheer off, away from the bank; but my feet felt so very warm and wet that I had to look down. The man had rolled on his back and stared straight up at me; both his hands clutched that cane. It was the shaft of a spear that, either thrown or lunged through the opening, had caught him in the side just below the ribs; the blade had gone in out of sight, after making a frightful gash; my shoes were full; a pool of blood lay very still, gleaming dark-red under the wheel; his eyes shone with an amazing lustre. The fusillade burst out again. He looked at me anxiously, gripping the spear like something precious, with an air of being afraid I would try to take it away from him. I had to make an effort to free my eyes from his gaze and attend to the steering. With one hand I felt above my head for the line of the steam whistle, and jerked out screech after screech hurriedly. The tumult of angry and warlike yells was checked instantly, and then from the depths of the woods went out such a tremulous and prolonged wail of mournful fear and utter despair as may be imagined to follow the flight of the last hope from the earth. There was a great commotion in the bush; the shower of arrows stopped, a few dropping shots rang out sharply—then silence, in which the languid beat of the stern-wheel came plainly to my ears. I put the helm hard a-starboard at the moment when the pilgrim in pink pyjamas, very hot and agitated, appeared in the doorway. 'The manager sends me—' he began in an official tone, and stopped short. 'Good God!' he said, glaring at the wounded man.

"We two whites stood over him, and his lustrous and inquiring glance enveloped us both. I declare it looked as though he would presently put to us some question in an understandable language; but he died without uttering a sound, without moving a limb, without twitching a muscle. Only in the very last moment, as though in response to some sign we could not see, to some whisper we could not hear, he frowned heavily, and that frown gave to his black death-mask an inconceivably sombre, brooding, and menacing expression. The lustre of inquiring glance faded swiftly into vacant glassiness. 'Can you steer?' I asked the agent eagerly. He looked very dubious; but I made a grab at his arm, and he understood at once I meant him to steer whether or no. To tell you the truth, I was morbidly anxious to change my shoes and socks. 'He is dead,' murmured the fellow, immensely impressed. 'No doubt about it,' said I, tugging like mad at the shoelaces. 'And by the way, I suppose Mr Kurtz is dead as well by this time.'

"For the moment that was the dominant thought. There was a sense of extreme disappointment, as though I had found out I had been striving after something altogether without a substance. I couldn't have been more disgusted if I had travelled all this way for the sole purpose of talking with Mr Kurtz. Talking with . . . I flung one shoe overboard, and became aware that that was exactly what I had been looking forward to—a talk with Kurtz. I made the strange discovery that I had never imagined him as doing, you know, but as discoursing. I didn't say to myself, 'Now I will never see him,' or 'Now I will never shake him by the hand,' but, 'Now I will never hear him.' The man presented himself as a voice. Not of course that I did not connect him with some sort of action. Hadn't I been told in all the tones of jealousy and admiration that he had collected, bartered, swindled, or stolen more ivory than all the other agents together? That was not the point. The point was in his being a gifted creature, and that of all his gifts the one that stood out pre-eminently, that carried with it a sense of real presence, was his ability to talk, his words—the gift of expression, the bewildering, the illuminating, the most exalted and the most contemptible, the pulsating stream of light, or the deceitful flow from the heart of an impenetrable darkness.

"The other shoe went flying unto the devil-god of that river. I thought, By Jove! it's all over. We are too late; he has vanished—the gift has vanished, by means of some spear, arrow, or club. I will never hear that chap speak after all—and my sorrow had a startling extravagance of emotion, even such as I had noticed in the howling sorrow of these savages in the bush. I couldn't have felt more of lonely desolation somehow, had I been robbed of a belief or had missed my destiny in life. . . . Why do you sigh in this beastly way, somebody? Absurd? Well, absurd. Good Lord! mustn't a man ever—Here, give me some tobacco." . . .

There was a pause of profound stillness, then a match flared, and Marlow's lean face appeared, worn, hollow, with downward folds and dropped eyelids, with an aspect of concentrated attention; and as he took vigorous draws at his pipe, it seemed to retreat and advance out of the night in the regular flicker of the tiny flame. The match went out.

"Absurd!" he cried. "This is the worst of trying to tell . . . Here you all are, each moored with two good addresses, like a hulk with two anchors, a butcher round one corner, a policeman round another, excellent appetites, and temperature normal—you hear—normal from year's end to year's end. And you say, Absurd! Absurd be—exploded! Absurd! My dear boys, what can you expect from a man who out of sheer nervousness had just flung overboard a pair of new shoes? Now I think of it, it is amazing I did not shed tears. I am, upon the whole, proud of my fortitude. I was cut to the quick at the idea of having lost the inestimable privilege of listening to the gifted Kurtz. Of course I was wrong. The privilege was waiting for me. Oh yes, I heard more than enough. And I was right, too. A voice. He was very little more than a voice. And I heard—him—it—this voice—other voices—all of them were so little more than voices—and the memory of that time itself lingers around me, impalpable, like a dying vibration of one immense jabber, silly, atrocious, sordid, savage, or simply mean, without any kind of sense. Voices, voices—even the girl herself—now—"

He was silent for a long time.

"I laid the ghost of his gifts at last with a lie," he began suddenly. "Girl! What? Did I mention a girl? Oh, she is out of it—completely. They—the women I mean—are out of it—should be out of it. We must help them to stay in that beautiful world of their own, lest ours gets worse. Oh, she had to be ou of it. You should have heard the disinterred body of Mr Kurtz saying, 'My Intended.' You would have perceived directly then how completely she was out of it. And the lofty frontal bone of Mr Kurtz! They say the hair goes on growing sometimes, but this—ah—specimen was impressively bald. The wilderness had patted him on the head, and, behold, it was like a ball—an ivory ball; it had caressed him, and—lo!—he had withered; it had taken him, loved him, embraced him, got into his veins, consumed his flesh, and sealed his soul to its own by the inconceivable ceremonies of some devilish initiation. He was its spoiled and pampered favourite. Ivory? I should think so. Heaps of it, stacks of it. The old mud shanty was bursting with it. You would think there was not a single tusk left either above or below the ground in the whole country. 'Mostly fossil,' the manager had remarked disparagingly. It was no more fossil than I am; but they call it fossil when it is dug up. It appears these niggers do bury the tusks sometimes—but evidently they couldn't bury this parcel deep enough to save the gifted Mr Kurtz from his fate. We filled the steamboat with it, and had to pile a lot on the deck. Thus he could see and enjoy as long as he could see, because the appreciation of this favour had remained with him to the last. You should have heard him say, 'My ivory.' Oh yes, I heard him. 'My Intended, my ivory, my station, my river, my—' everything belonged to him. It made me hold my breath in expectation of hearing the wilderness burst into a prodigious peal of laughter that would shake the fixed stars in their places. Everything belonged to him—but that was a trifle. The thing was to know what he belonged to, how many powers of darkness claimed him for their own. That was the reflection that made you creepy all over. It was impossible—it was not good for one either—trying to imagine. He had taken a high seat amongst the devils of the land—I mean literally. You can't understand. How could you?—with solid pavement under your feet, surrounded by kind neighbours ready to cheer you or to fall on you, stepping delicately between the butcher and the policeman, in the holy terror of scandal and gallows and lunatic asylums—how can you imagine what particular region of the first ages a man's untrammelled feet may take him into by the way of solitude—utter solitude without a policeman—by the way of silence—utter silence, where no warning voice of a kind neighbour can be heard whispering of public opinion? These little things make all the great difference. When they are gone you must fall back upon your own innate strength, upon your own capacity for faithfulness. Of course you may be too much of a fool to go wrong—too dull even to know you are being assaulted by the powers of darkness. I take it, no fool ever made a bargain for his soul with the devil: the fool is too much of a fool, or the devil too much of a devil—I don't know which. Or you may be such a thunderingly exalted creature as to be altogether deaf and blind to anything but heavenly sights and sounds. Then the earth for you is only a standing place—and whether to be like this is your loss or your gain I won't pretend to say. But most of us are neither one nor the other. The earth for us is a place to live in, where we must put up with sights, with sounds, with smells, too, by Jove!—breathe dead hippo, so to speak, and not be contaminated. And there, don't you see? your strength comes in, the faith in your ability for the digging of unostentatious holes to bury the stuff in—your power of devotion, not to yourself, but to an obscure, back-breaking business. And that's difficult enough. Mind, I am not trying to excuse or even rying to account to myself for—for—Mr Kurtz—for the shade his initiated wraith[5] from the back of Nowhere honoured me confidence before it vanished altogether. This was because it speak English to me. The original Kurtz had been educated partly in England, and—as he was good enough to say himself—his sympathies were in the right place. His mother was half-English, his father was half-French. All Europe contributed to the making of Kurtz; and by and by I learned that, most appropriately, the International Society for the Suppression of Savage Customs[6] had entrusted him with the making of a report, for its future guidance. And he had written it too. I've seen it. I've read it. It was eloquent, vibrating with eloquence, but too high-strung, I think. Seventeen pages of close writing he had found time for! But this must have been before his—let us say—nerves went wrong, and caused him to preside at certain midnight dances ending with unspeakable rites, which—as far as I reluctantly gathered from what I heard at various times—were offered up to him—do you understand?—to Mr Kurtz himself. But it was a beautiful piece of writing. The opening paragraph, however, in the light of later information, strikes me now as ominous. He began with the argument that we whites, from the point of development we had arrived at, 'must necessarily appear to them [savages] in the nature of supernatural beings—we approach them with the might as of a deity,' and so on, and so on. 'By the simple exercise of our will we can exert a power for good practically unbounded,' etc. etc. From that point he soared and took me with him. The peroration was magnificent, though difficult to remember, you know. It gave me the notion of an exotic Immensity ruled by an august Benevolence. It made me tingle with enthusiasm. This was the unbounded power of eloquence—of words—of burning noble words. There were no practical hints to interrupt the magic current of phrases, unless a kind of note at the foot of the last page, scrawled evidently much later, in an unsteady hand, may be regarded as the exposition of a method. It was very simple, and at the end of that moving appeal to every altruistic sentiment it blazed at you, luminous and terrifying, like a flash of lightning in a serene sky: 'Exterminate all the brutes!' The curious part was that he had apparently forgotten all about that valuable postscriptum, because, later on, when he in a sense came to himself, he repeatedly entreated me to take good care of 'my pamphlet' (he called it), as it was sure to have in the future a good influence upon his career. I had full information about all these things, and, besides, as it turned out, I was to have the care of his memory. I've done enough for it to give me the indisputable right to lay it, if I choose, for an everlasting rest in the dust-bin of progress, amongst all the sweepings and, figuratively speaking, all the dead cats of civilisation. But then, you see, I can't choose. He won't be forgotten. Whatever he was, he was not common. He had the power to charm or frighten rudimentary souls into an aggravated witchdance in his honour; he could also fill the small souls of the pilgrims with bitter misgivings: he had one devoted friend at least, and he had conquered one soul in the world that was neither rudimentary nor tainted with

5. Either the spectral or immaterial appearance of a living being, often viewed as a portent of that person's death, or simply a ghost.

6. This society is fictional, but in 1889–90 the international Anti-Slavery Conference at Brussels in effect granted Leopold control of the Congo trade, ostensibly in return for his help in eliminating African slavers.

self-seeking. No; I can't forget him, though I am not prepared to affirm the fellow was exactly worth the life we lost in getting to him. I missed my late helmsman awfully—I missed him even while his body was still lying in the pilot-house. Perhaps you will think it passing strange this regret for a savage who was no more account than a grain of sand in a black Sahara. Well, don't you see, he had done something, he had steered; for months I had him at my back—a help—an instrument. It was a kind of partnership. He steered for me—I had to look after him, I worried about his deficiencies, and thus a subtle bond had been created, of which I only became aware when it was suddenly broken. And the intimate profundity of that look he gave me when he received his hurt remains to this day in my memory—like a claim of distant kinship affirmed in a supreme moment.

"Poor fool! If he had only left that shutter alone. He had no restraint, no restraint—just like Kurtz—a tree swayed by the wind. As soon as I had put on a dry pair of slippers, I dragged him out, after first jerking the spear out of his side, which operation I confess I performed with my eyes shut tight. His heels leaped together over the little doorstep; his shoulders were pressed to my breast; I hugged him from behind desperately. Oh! he was heavy, heavy; heavier than any man on earth, I should imagine. Then without more ado I tipped him overboard. The current snatched him as though he had been a wisp of grass, and I saw the body roll over twice before I lost sight of it for ever. All the pilgrims and the manager were then congregated on the awning-deck about the pilot-house, chattering at each other like a flock of excited magpies, and there was a scandalised murmur at my heartless promptitude. What they wanted to keep that body hanging about for I can't guess. Embalm it, maybe. But I had also heard another, and a very ominous, murmur on the deck below. My friends the wood-cutters were likewise scandalised, and with a better show of reason—though I admit that the reason itself was quite inadmissible. Oh, quite! I had made up my mind that if my late helmsman was to be eaten, the fishes alone should have him. He had been a very second-rate helmsman while alive, but now he was dead he might have become a first-class temptation, and possibly cause some startling trouble. Besides, I was anxious to take the wheel, the man in pink pyjamas showing himself a hopeless duffer at the business.

"This I did directly the simple funeral was over. We were going half-speed, keeping right in the middle of the stream, and I listened to the talk about me. They had given up Kurtz, they had given up the station; Kurtz was dead, and the station had been burnt—and so on—and so on. The red-haired pilgrim was beside himself with the thought that at least this poor Kurtz had been properly revenged. 'Say! We must have made a glorious slaughter of them in the bush. Eh? What do you think? Say?' He positively danced, the bloodthirsty little gingery beggar.[7] And he had nearly fainted when he saw the wounded man! I could not help saying, 'You made a glorious lot of smoke, anyhow.' I had seen, from the way the tops of the bushes rustled and flew, that almost all the shots had gone too high. You can't hit anything unless you take aim and fire from the shoulder; but these chaps fired from the hip with their eyes shut. The retreat, I maintained—and I was right—was caused by the screeching of the steam-whistle. Upon this they forgot Kurtz, and began to howl at me with indignant protests.

7. Red-haired rascal (British slang).

"The manager stood by the wheel murmuring confidentially about the necessity of getting well away down the river before dark at all events, when I saw in the distance a clearing on the river-side and the outlines of some sort of building. 'What's this?' I asked. He clapped his hands in wonder. 'The station!' he cried. I edged in at once, still going half-speed.

"Through my glasses I saw the slope of a hill interspersed with rare trees and perfectly free from undergrowth. A long decaying building on the summit was half buried in the high grass; the large holes in the peaked roof gaped black from afar; the jungle and the woods made a background. There was no enclosure or fence of any kind; but there had been one apparently, for near the house half a dozen slim posts remained in a row, roughly trimmed, and with their upper ends ornamented with round carved balls. The rails, or whatever there had been between, had disappeared. Of course the forest surrounded all that. The river-bank was clear, and on the water side I saw a white man under a hat like a cart-wheel beckoning persistently with his whole arm. Examining the edge of the forest above and below, I was almost certain I could see movements—human forms gliding here and there. I steamed past prudently, then stopped the engines and let her drift down. The man on the shore began to shout, urging us to land. 'We have been attacked,' screamed the manager. 'I know—I know. It's all right,' yelled back the other, as cheerful as you please. 'Come along. It's all right. I am glad.'

"His aspect reminded me of something I had seen—something funny I had seen somewhere. As I manœuvred to get alongside, I was asking myself, 'What does this fellow look like?' Suddenly I got it. He looked like a harlequin. His clothes had been made of some stuff that was brown holland[8] probably, but it was covered with patches all over, with bright patches, blue, red, and yellow—patches on the back, patches on the front, patches on elbows, on knees; coloured binding round his jacket, scarlet edging at the bottom of his trousers; and the sunshine made him look extremely gay and wonderfully neat withal, because you could see how beautifully all this patching had been done. A beardless, boyish face, very fair, no features to speak of, nose peeling, little blue eyes, smiles and frowns chasing each other over that open countenance like sunshine and shadow on a wind-swept plain. 'Look out, captain!' he cried; 'there's a snag lodged in here last night.' What! Another snag? I confess I swore shamefully. I had nearly holed my cripple, to finish off that charming trip. The harlequin on the bank turned his little pug nose up to me. 'You English?' he asked, all smiles. 'Are you?' I shouted from the wheel. The smiles vanished, and he shook his head as if sorry for my disappointment. Then he brightened up. 'Never mind!' he cried encouragingly. 'Are we in time?' I asked. 'He is up there,' he replied, with a toss of the head up the hill, and becoming gloomy all of a sudden. His face was like the autumn sky, overcast one moment and bright the next.

"When the manager, escorted by the pilgrims, all of them armed to the teeth, had gone to the house, this chap came on board. 'I say, I don't like this. These natives are in the bush,' I said. He assured me earnestly it was all right. 'They are simple people,' he added; 'well, I am glad you came. It took me all my time to keep them off.' 'But you said it was all right,' I cried. 'Oh, they meant no

8. Unbleached linen fabric. "Harlequin": a traditional clown figure known by his multicolored costume.

harm,' he said; and as I stared he corrected himself, 'Not exactly.' Then vivaciously, 'My faith, your pilot-house wants a clean up!' In the next breath he advised me to keep enough steam on the boiler to blow the whistle in case of any trouble. 'One good screech will do more for you than all your rifles. They are simple people,' he repeated. He rattled away at such a rate he quite overwhelmed me. He seemed to be trying to make up for lots of silence, and actually hinted, laughing, that such was the case. 'Don't you talk with Mr Kurtz?' I said. 'You don't talk with that man—you listen to him,' he exclaimed with severe exaltation. 'But now—' He waved his arm, and in the twinkling of an eye was in the uttermost depths of despondency. In a moment he came up again with a jump, possessed himself of both my hands, shook them continuously, while he gabbled: 'Brother sailor . . . honour . . . pleasure . . . delight . . . introduce myself . . . Russian . . . son of an arch-priest . . . Government of Tambov[9] . . . What? Tobacco! English tobacco; the excellent English tobacco! Now, that's brotherly. Smoke? Where's a sailor that does not smoke?'

"The pipe soothed him, and gradually I made out he had run away from school, had gone to sea in a Russian ship; ran away again; served some time in English ships; was now reconciled with the arch-priest. He made a point of that. 'But when one is young one must see things, gather experience, ideas; enlarge the mind.' 'Here!' I interrupted. 'You can never tell! Here I met Mr Kurtz,' he said, youthfully solemn and reproachful. I held my tongue after that. It appears he had persuaded a Dutch trading-house on the coast to fit him out with stores and goods, and had started for the interior with a light heart, and no more idea of what would happen to him than a baby. He had been wandering about that river for nearly two years alone, cut off from everybody and everything. 'I am not so young as I look. I am twenty-five,' he said. 'At first old Van Shuyten would tell me to go to the devil,' he narrated with keen enjoyment; 'but I stuck to him, and talked and talked, till at last he got afraid I would talk the hind-leg off his favourite dog, so he gave me some cheap things and a few guns, and told me he hoped he would never see my face again. Good old Dutchman, Van Shuyten. I sent him one small lot of ivory a year ago, so that he can't call me a little thief when I get back. I hope he got it. And for the rest I don't care. I had some wood stacked for you. That was my old house. Did you see?'

"I gave him Towson's book. He made as though he would kiss me, but restrained himself. 'The only book I had left, and I thought I had lost it,' he said, looking at it ecstatically. 'So many accidents happen to a man going about alone, you know. Canoes get upset sometimes—and sometimes you've got to clear out so quick when the people get angry.' He thumbed the pages. 'You made notes in Russian?' I asked. He nodded. 'I thought they were written in cipher,' I said. He laughed, then became serious. 'I had lots of trouble to keep these people off,' he said. 'Did they want to kill you?' I asked. 'Oh no!' he cried, and checked himself. 'Why did they attack us?' I pursued. He hesitated, then said shamefacedly, 'They don't want him to go.' 'Don't they?' I said curiously. He nodded a nod full of mystery and wisdom. 'I tell you,' he cried, 'this man has enlarged my mind.' He opened his arms wide, staring at me with his little blue eyes that were perfectly round."

9. A province in Russia, south of Moscow, a cultural center.

3

"I looked at him, lost in astonishment. There he was before me, in motley,[1] as though he had absconded from a troupe of mimes, enthusiastic, fabulous. His very existence was improbable, inexplicable, and altogether bewildering. He was an insoluble problem. It was inconceivable how he had existed, how he had succeeded in getting so far, how he had managed to remain—why he did not instantly disappear. 'I went a little farther,' he said, 'then still a little farther—till I had gone so far that I don't know how I'll ever get back. Never mind. Plenty time. I can manage. You take Kurtz away quick—quick—I tell you.' The glamour of youth enveloped his particoloured rags, his destitution, his loneliness, the essential desolation of his futile wanderings. For months—for years—his life hadn't been worth a day's purchase; and there he was gallantly, thoughtlessly alive, to all appearance indestructible solely by the virtue of his few years and of his unreflecting audacity. I was seduced into something like admiration—like envy. Glamour urged him on, glamour kept him unscathed. He surely wanted nothing from the wilderness but space to breathe in and to push on through. His need was to exist, and to move onwards at the greatest possible risk, and with a maximum of privation. If the absolutely pure, uncalculating, unpractical spirit of adventure had ever ruled a human being, it ruled this be-patched youth. I almost envied him the possession of this modest and clear flame. It seemed to have consumed all thought of self so completely, that, even while he was talking to you, you forgot that it was he—the man before your eyes—who had gone through these things. I did not envy him his devotion to Kurtz, though. He had not meditated over it. It came to him, and he accepted it with a sort of eager fatalism. I must say that to me it appeared about the most dangerous thing in every way he had come upon so far.

"They had come together unavoidably, like two ships becalmed near each other, and lay rubbing sides at last. I suppose Kurtz wanted an audience, because on a certain occasion, when encamped in the forest, they had talked all night, or more probably Kurtz had talked. 'We talked of everything,' he said, quite transported at the recollection. 'I forgot there was such a thing as sleep. The night did not seem to last an hour. Everything! Everything! . . . Of love too.' 'Ah, he talked to you of love!' I said, much amused. 'It isn't what you think,' he cried, almost passionately. 'It was in general. He made me see things—things.'

"He threw his arms up. We were on deck at the time, and the head-man of my wood-cutters, lounging near by, turned upon him his heavy and glittering eyes. I looked around, and I don't know why, but I assure you that never, never before, did this land, this river, this jungle, the very arch of this blazing sky, appear to me so hopeless and so dark, so impenetrable to human thought, so pitiless to human weakness. 'And, ever since, you have been with him, of course?' I said.

"On the contrary. It appears their intercourse had been very much broken by various causes. He had, as he informed me proudly, managed to nurse Kurtz through two illnesses (he alluded to it as you would to some risky feat), but as a rule Kurtz wandered alone, far in the depths of the forest. 'Very often coming to this station, I had to wait days and days before he would turn up,' he said. 'Ah, it was worth waiting for!—sometimes.' 'What was he doing? exploring or what?'

1. Like a jester, who wore a distinctive multicolored costume.

I asked. 'Oh yes, of course'; he had discovered lots of villages, a lake too—he did not know exactly in what direction; it was dangerous to inquire too much—but mostly his expeditions had been for ivory. 'But he had no goods to trade with by that time,' I objected. 'There's a good lot of cartridges left even yet,' he answered, looking away. 'To speak plainly, he raided the country,'[2] I said. He nodded. 'Not alone, surely!' He muttered something about the villages round that lake. 'Kurtz got the tribe to follow him, did he?' I suggested. He fidgeted a little. 'They adored[3] him,' he said. The tone of these words was so extraordinary that I looked at him searchingly. It was curious to see his mingled eagerness and reluctance to speak of Kurtz. The man filled his life, occupied his thoughts, swayed his emotions. 'What can you expect?' he burst out; 'he came to them with thunder and lightning, you know—and they had never seen anything like it—and very terrible. He could be very terrible. You can't judge Mr Kurtz as you would an ordinary man. No, no, no! Now—just to give you an idea—I don't mind telling you, he wanted to shoot me too one day—but I don't judge him.' 'Shoot you!' I cried. 'What for?' 'Well, I had a small lot of ivory the chief of that village near my house gave me. You see I used to shoot game for them. Well, he wanted it, and wouldn't hear reason. He declared he would shoot me unless I gave him the ivory and then cleared out of the country, because he could do so, and had a fancy for it, and there was nothing on earth to prevent him killing whom he jolly well pleased. And it was true too. I gave him the ivory. What did I care! But I didn't clear out. No, no. I couldn't leave him. I had to be careful, of course, till we got friendly again for a time. He had his second illness then. Afterwards I had to keep out of the way; but I didn't mind. He was living for the most part in those villages on the lake. When he came down to the river, sometimes he would take to me, and sometimes it was better for me to be careful. This man suffered too much. He hated all this, and somehow he couldn't get away. When I had a chance I begged him to try and leave while there was time; I offered to go back with him. And he would say yes, and then he would remain; go off on another ivory hunt; disappear for weeks; forget himself amongst these people—forget himself—you know.' 'Why! he's mad,' I said. He protested indignantly. Mr Kurtz couldn't be mad. If I had heard him talk, only two days ago, I wouldn't dare hint at such a thing. . . . I had taken up my binoculars while we talked, and was looking at the shore, sweeping the limit of the forest at each side and at the back of the house. The consciousness of there being people in that bush, so silent, so quiet—as silent and quiet as the ruined house on the hill—made me uneasy. There was no sign on the face of nature of this amazing tale that was not so much told as suggested to me in desolate exclamations, completed by shrugs, in interrupted phrases, in hints ending in deep sighs. The woods were unmoved, like a mask—heavy, like the closed door of a prison—they looked with their air of hidden knowledge, of patient expectation, of unapproachable silence. The Russian was explaining to me that it was only lately that Mr Kurtz had come down to the river, bringing along with him all the fighting men of that lake tribe. He had been absent for several months—getting himself adored, I suppose—and had come down unexpectedly, with the intention to all appearance of making a raid either across the river or down stream. Evidently

2. Raids for ivory were a common practice, with little or no attempt to compensate natives for the stolen goods.

3. Literally, worshipped as a deity.

the appetite for more ivory had got the better of the—what shall I say?—less material aspirations. However, he had got much worse suddenly. 'I heard he was lying helpless, and so I came up—took my chance,' said the Russian. 'Oh, he is bad, very bad.' I directed my glass to the house. There were no signs of life, but there was the ruined roof, the long mud wall peeping above the grass, with three little square window-holes, no two of the same size; all this brought within reach of my hand, as it were. And then I made a brusque movement, and one of the remaining posts of that vanished fence leaped up in the field of my glass. You remember I told you I had been struck at the distance by certain attempts at ornamentation, rather remarkable in the ruinous aspect of the place. Now I had suddenly a nearer view, and its first result was to make me throw my head back as if before a blow. Then I went carefully from post to post with my glass, and I saw my mistake. These round knobs were not ornamental but symbolic; they were expressive and puzzling, striking and disturbing—food for thought and also for the vultures if there had been any looking down from the sky; but at all events for such ants as were industrious enough to ascend the pole. They would have been even more impressive, those heads on the stakes, if their faces had not been turned to the house. Only one, the first I had made out, was facing my way. I was not so shocked as you may think. The start back I had given was really nothing but a movement of surprise. I had expected to see a knob of wood there, you know. I returned deliberately to the first I had seen—and there it was, black, dried, sunken, with closed eyelids—a head that seemed to sleep at the top of that pole, and, with the shrunken dry lips showing a narrow white line of the teeth, was smiling too, smiling continuously at some endless and jocose dream of that eternal slumber.

"I am not disclosing any trade secrets. In fact the manager said afterwards that Mr Kurtz's methods[4] had ruined the district. I have no opinion on that point, but I want you clearly to understand that there was nothing exactly profitable in these heads being there. They only show that Mr Kurtz lacked restraint in the gratification of his various lusts, that there was something wanting in him—some small matter which, when the pressing need arose, could not be found under his magnificent eloquence. Whether he knew of this deficiency himself I can't say. I think the knowledge came to him at last—only at the very last. But the wilderness had found him out early, and had taken on him a terrible vengeance for the fantastic invasion. I think it had whispered to him things about himself which he did not know, things of which he had no conception till he took counsel with this great solitude—and the whisper had proved irresistibly fascinating. It echoed loudly within him because he was hollow at the core. . . . I put down the glass, and the head that had appeared near enough to be spoken to seemed at once to have leaped away from me into inaccessible distance.

"The admirer of Mr Kurtz was a bit crestfallen. In a hurried, indistinct voice he began to assure me he had not dared to take these—say, symbols—down. He was not afraid of the natives; they would not stir till Mr Kurtz gave the word. His ascendancy was extraordinary. The camps of these people surrounded the place, and the chiefs came every day to see him. They would crawl . . . 'I don't

4. Perhaps an allusion to *Hamlet*, where Polonius comments on Hamlet's apparent insanity, "Though this be madness, yet there is method in 't."

want to know anything of the ceremonies used when approaching Mr Kurtz,' I shouted. Curious, this feeling that came over me that such details would be more intolerable than those heads drying on the stakes under Mr Kurtz's windows. After all, that was only a savage sight, while I seemed at one bound to have been transported into some lightless region of subtle horrors, where pure, uncomplicated savagery was a positive relief, being something that had a right to exist—obviously—in the sunshine. The young man looked at me with surprise. I suppose it did not occur to him that Mr Kurtz was no idol of mine. He forgot I hadn't heard any of these splendid monologues on, what was it? on love, justice, conduct of life—or what not. If it had come to crawling before Mr Kurtz, he crawled as much as the veriest savage of them all. I had no idea of the conditions, he said: these heads were the heads of rebels. I shocked him excessively by laughing. Rebels! What would be the next definition I was to hear? There had been enemies, criminals, workers—and these were rebels. Those rebellious heads looked very subdued to me on their sticks. 'You don't know how such a life tries a man like Kurtz,' cried Kurtz's last disciple. 'Well, and you?' I said. 'I! I! I am a simple man. I have no great thoughts. I want nothing from anybody. How can you compare me to . . .?' His feelings were too much for speech, and suddenly he broke down. 'I don't understand,' he groaned. 'I've been doing my best to keep him alive, and that's enough. I had no hand in all this. I have no abilities. There hasn't been a drop of medicine or a mouthful of invalid food for months here. He was shamefully abandoned. A man like this, with such ideas. Shamefully! Shamefully! I—I—haven't slept for the last ten nights. . . .'

"His voice lost itself in the calm of the evening. The long shadows of the forest had slipped down hill while we talked, had gone far beyond the ruined hovel, beyond the symbolic row of stakes. All this was in the gloom, while we down there were yet in the sunshine, and the stretch of the river abreast of the clearing glittered in a still and dazzling splendour, with a murky and overshadowed bend above and below. Not a living soul was seen on the shore. The bushes did not rustle.

"Suddenly round the corner of the house a group of men appeared, as though they had come up from the ground. They waded waist-deep in the grass, in a compact body, bearing an improvised stretcher in their midst. Instantly, in the emptiness of the landscape, a cry arose whose shrillness pierced the still air like a sharp arrow flying straight to the very heart of the land; and, as if by enchantment, streams of human beings—of naked human beings—with spears in their hands, with bows, with shields, with wild glances and savage movements, were poured into the clearing by the darkfaced and pensive forest. The bushes shook, the grass swayed for a time, and then everything stood still in attentive immobility.

"'Now, if he does not say the right thing to them we are all done for,' said the Russian at my elbow. The knot of men with the stretcher had stopped too, halfway to the steamer, as if petrified. I saw the man on the stretcher sit up, lank and with an uplifted arm, above the shoulders of the bearers. 'Let us hope that the man who can talk so well of love in general will find some particular reason to spare us this time,' I said. I resented bitterly the absurd danger of our situation, as if to be at the mercy of that atrocious phantom had been a dishonouring necessity. I could not hear a sound, but through my glasses I saw the thin arm extended commandingly, the lower jaw moving, the eyes of that apparition shining darkly far in its bony head that nodded with grotesque jerks. Kurtz—Kurtz—that means 'short' in German—don't it? Well, the name was as true as everything else in his life—and death. He looked at least seven feet long. His covering had fallen off, and his body emerged from it pitiful and appalling as from a winding-sheet. I could see the cage of his ribs all astir, the bones of his arm waving. It was as though an animated image of death carved out of old ivory had been shaking its hand with menaces at a motionless crowd of men made of dark and glittering bronze. I saw him open his mouth wide—it gave him a weirdly voracious aspect, as though he had wanted to swallow all the air, all the earth, all the men before him. A deep voice reached me faintly. He must have been shouting. He fell back suddenly. The stretcher shook as the bearers staggered forward again, and almost at the same time I noticed that the crowd of savages was vanishing without any perceptible movement of retreat, as if the forest that had ejected these beings so suddenly had drawn them in again as the breath is drawn in a long aspiration.

"Some of the pilgrims behind the stretcher carried his arms—two shotguns, a heavy rifle, and a light revolver-carbine[5]—the thunderbolts of that pitiful Jupiter.[6] The manager bent over him murmuring as he walked beside his head. They laid him down in one of the little cabins—just a room for a bedplace and a camp-stool or two, you know. We had brought his belated correspondence, and a lot of torn envelopes and open letters littered his bed. His hand roamed feebly amongst these papers. I was struck by the fire of his eyes and the composed languor of his expression. It was not so much the exhaustion of disease. He did not seem in pain. This shadow looked satiated and calm, as though for the moment it had had its fill of all the emotions.

"He rustled one of the letters, and looking straight in my face said, 'I am glad.' Somebody had been writing to him about me. These special recommendations were turning up again. The volume of tone he emitted without effort, almost without the trouble of moving his lips, amazed me. A voice! a voice! It was grave, profound, vibrating, while the man did not seem capable of a whisper. However, he had enough strength in him—factitious[7] no doubt—to very nearly make an end of us, as you shall hear directly.

"The manager appeared silently in the doorway; I stepped out at once and he drew the curtain after me. The Russian, eyed curiously by the pilgrims, was staring at the shore. I followed the direction of his glance.

"Dark human shapes could be made out in the distance, flitting indistinctly against the gloomy border of the forest, and near the river two bronze figures, leaning on tall spears, stood in the sunlight under fantastic head-dresses of spotted skins, warlike and still in statuesque repose. And from right to left along the lighted shore moved a wild and gorgeous apparition of a woman.

"She walked with measured steps, draped in striped and fringed cloths, treading the earth proudly, with a slight jingle and flash of barbarous ornaments. She carried her head high; her hair was done in the shape of a helmet; she had brass leggings to the knee,[8] brass wire gauntlets to the elbow, a crimson spot on her

5. A rifle with a revolving clip.
6. The Roman god of the sky, ruler over the other gods.
7. Not natural; got up for a particular purpose; artificial.
8. From the ankle to the knee.

tawny cheek, innumerable necklaces of glass beads on her neck; bizarre things, charms, gifts of witch-men, that hung about her, glittered and trembled at every step. She must have had the value of several elephant tusks upon her. She was savage and superb, wild-eyed and magnificent; there was something ominous and stately in her deliberate progress. And in the hush that had fallen suddenly upon the whole sorrowful land, the immense wilderness, the colossal body of the fecund and mysterious life seemed to look at her, pensive, as though it had been looking at the image of its own tenebrous[9] and passionate soul.

"She came abreast of the steamer, stood still, and faced us. Her long shadow fell to the water's edge. Her face had a tragic and fierce aspect of wild sorrow and of dumb pain mingled with the fear of some struggling, half-shaped resolve. She stood looking at us without a stir, and like the wilderness itself, with an air of brooding over an inscrutable purpose. A whole minute passed, and then she made a step forward. There was a low jingle, a glint of yellow metal, a sway of fringed draperies, and she stopped as if her heart had failed her. The young fellow by my side growled. The pilgrims murmured at my back. She looked at us all as if her life had depended upon the unswerving steadiness of her glance. Suddenly she opened her bared arms and threw them up rigid above her head, as though in an uncontrollable desire to touch the sky, and at the same time the swift shadows darted out on the earth, swept around on the river, gathering the steamer into a shadowy embrace. A formidable silence hung over the scene.

"She turned away slowly, walked on, following the bank, and passed into the bushes to the left. Once only her eyes gleamed back at us in the dusk of the thickets before she disappeared.

"'If she had offered to come aboard I really think I would have tried to shoot her,' said the man of patches nervously. 'I had been risking my life every day for the last fortnight to keep her out of the house. She got in one day and kicked up a row about those miserable rags I picked up in the storeroom to mend my clothes with. I wasn't decent. At least it must have been that, for she talked like a fury to Kurtz for an hour, pointing at me now and then. I don't understand the dialect of this tribe. Luckily for me, I fancy Kurtz felt too ill that day to care, or there would have been mischief. I don't understand. . . . No—it's too much for me. Ah, well, it's all over now.'

"At this moment I heard Kurtz's deep voice behind the curtain: 'Save me!—save the ivory, you mean. Don't tell me. Save *me*! Why, I've had to save you. You are interrupting my plans now. Sick! Sick! Not so sick as you would like to believe. Never mind. I'll carry my ideas out yet—I will return. I'll show you what can be done. You with your little peddling notions—you are interfering with me. I will return. I . . .'

"The manager came out. He did me the honour to take me under the arm and lead me aside. 'He is very low, very low,' he said. He considered it necessary to sigh, but neglected to be consistently sorrowful. 'We have done all we could for him—haven't we? But there is no disguising the fact, Mr Kurtz has done more harm than good to the Company. He did not see the time was not ripe for vigorous action. Cautiously, cautiously—that's my principle. We must be cautious yet. The district is closed to us for a time. Deplorable! Upon the whole, the trade will suffer. I don't deny there is a remarkable quantity of ivory—mostly

9. Full of darkness or shadows; obscure; gloomy.

fossil. We must save it, at all events—but look how precarious the position is—and why? Because the method is unsound.' 'Do you,' said I, looking at the shore, 'call it "unsound method"?' 'Without doubt,' he exclaimed hotly, 'Don't you?' . . . 'No method at all,' I murmured after a while. 'Exactly,' he exulted. 'I anticipated this. Shows a complete want of judgment. It is my duty to point it out in the proper quarter.' 'Oh,' said I, 'that fellow—what's his name?—the brickmaker, will make a readable report for you.' He appeared confounded for a moment. It seemed to me I had never breathed an atmosphere so vile, and I turned mentally to Kurtz for relief—positively for relief. 'Nevertheless, I think Mr Kurtz is a remarkable man,' I said with emphasis. He started, dropped on me a cold heavy glance, said very quietly, 'He *was*,' and turned his back on me. My hour of favour was over; I found myself lumped along with Kurtz as a partisan of methods for which the time was not ripe: I was unsound! Ah! but it was something to have at least a choice of nightmares.

"I had turned to the wilderness really, not to Mr Kurtz, who, I was ready to admit, was as good as buried. And for a moment it seemed to me as if I also were buried in a vast grave full of unspeakable secrets. I felt an intolerable weight oppressing my breast, the smell of the damp earth, the unseen presence of victorious corruption, the darkness of an impenetrable night. . . . The Russian tapped me on the shoulder. I heard him mumbling and stammering something about 'brother seaman—couldn't conceal—knowledge of matters that would affect Mr Kurtz's reputation.' I waited. For him evidently Mr Kurtz was not in his grave; I suspect that for him Mr Kurtz was one of the immortals. 'Well!' said I at last, 'speak out. As it happens, I am Mr Kurtz's friend—in a way.'

"He stated with a good deal of formality that had we not been 'of the same profession,' he would have kept the matter to himself without regard to consequences. He suspected 'there was an active ill-will towards him on the part of these white men that—' 'You are right,' I said, remembering a certain conversation I had overheard. 'The manager thinks you ought to be hanged.' He showed a concern at this intelligence which amused me at first. 'I had better get out of the way quietly,' he said earnestly. 'I can do no more for Kurtz now, and they would soon find some excuse. What's to stop them? There's a military post three hundred miles from here.' 'Well, upon my word,' said I, 'perhaps you had better go if you have any friends amongst the savages near by.' 'Plenty,' he said. 'They are simple people—and I want nothing, you know.' He stood biting his lip, then: 'I don't want any harm to happen to these whites here, but of course I was thinking of Mr Kurtz's reputation—but you are a brother seaman and—' 'All right,' said I, after a time. 'Mr Kurtz's reputation is safe with me.' I did not know how truly I spoke.

"He informed me, lowering his voice, that it was Kurtz who had ordered the attack to be made on the steamer. 'He hated sometimes the idea of being taken away—and then again . . . But I don't understand these matters. I am a simple man. He thought it would scare you away—that you would give it up, thinking him dead. I could not stop him. Oh, I had an awful time of it this last month.' 'Very well,' I said. 'He is all right now.' 'Ye-e-es,' he muttered, not very convinced apparently. 'Thanks,' said I; 'I shall keep my eyes open.' 'But quiet—eh?' he urged anxiously. 'It would be awful for his reputation if anybody here—' I promised a complete discretion with great gravity. 'I have a canoe and three black fellows waiting not very far. I am off. Could you give me a few Martini-Henry cartridges?' I could, and did, with proper secrecy. He helped himself, with a wink at me, to a handful of my tobacco. 'Between sailors—you know—good English tobacco.' At the door of the pilot-house he turned round—'I say, haven't you a pair of shoes you could spare?' He raised one leg. 'Look.' The soles were tied with knotted strings sandal-wise under his bare feet. I rooted out an old pair, at which he looked with admiration before tucking it under his left arm. One of his pockets (bright red) was bulging with cartridges, from the other (dark blue) peeped 'Towson's Inquiry,' etc. etc. He seemed to think himself excellently well equipped for a renewed encounter with the wilderness. 'Ah! I'll never, never meet such a man again. You ought to have heard him recite poetry—his own too it was, he told me. Poetry!' He rolled his eyes at the recollection of these delights. 'Oh, he enlarged my mind!' 'Good-bye,' said I. He shook hands and vanished in the night. Sometimes I ask myself whether I had ever really seen him—whether it was possible to meet such a phenomenon! . . .

"When I woke up shortly after midnight his warning came to my mind with its hint of danger that seemed, in the starred darkness, real enough to make me get up for the purpose of having a look round. On the hill a big fire burned, illuminating fitfully a crooked corner of the station-house. One of the agents with a picket of a few of our blacks, armed for the purpose, was keeping guard over the ivory; but deep within the forest, red gleams that wavered, that seemed to sink and rise from the ground amongst confused columnar shapes of intense blackness, showed the exact position of the camp where Mr Kurtz's adorers were keeping their uneasy vigil. The monotonous beating of a big drum filled the air with muffled shocks and a lingering vibration. A steady droning sound of many men chanting each to himself some weird incantation came out from the black, flat wall of the woods as the humming of bees comes out of a hive, and had a strange narcotic effect upon my half-awake senses. I believe I dozed off leaning over the rail, till an abrupt burst of yells, an overwhelming outbreak of a pent-up and mysterious frenzy, woke me up in a bewildered wonder. It was cut short all at once, and the low droning went on with an effect of audible and soothing silence. I glanced casually into the little cabin. A light was burning within, but Mr Kurtz was not there.

"I think I would have raised an outcry if I had believed my eyes. But I didn't believe them at first—the thing seemed so impossible. The fact is I was completely unnerved by a sheer blank fright, pure abstract terror, unconnected with any distinct shape of physical danger. What made this emotion so overpowering was—how shall I define it?—the moral shock I received, as if something altogether monstrous, intolerable to thought and odious to the soul, had been thrust upon me unexpectedly. This lasted of course the merest fraction of a second, and then the usual sense of commonplace, deadly danger, the possibility of a sudden onslaught and massacre, or something of the kind, which I saw impending, was positively welcome and composing. It pacified me, in fact, so much, that I did not raise an alarm.

"There was an agent buttoned up inside an ulster[1] and sleeping on a chair on deck within three feet of me. The yells had not awakened him; he snored very slightly; I left him to his slumbers and leaped ashore. I did not betray Mr Kurtz—it was ordered I should never betray him—it was written I should be loyal to the

1. A long, loose overcoat, often with a belt.

nightmare of my choice. I was anxious to deal with this shadow by myself alone—and to this day I don't know why I was so jealous of sharing with any one the peculiar blackness of that experience.

"As soon as I got on the bank I saw a trail—a broad trail through the grass. I remember the exultation with which I said to myself, 'He can't walk—he is crawling on all-fours—I've got him.' The grass was wet with dew. I strode rapidly with clenched fists. I fancy I had some vague notion of falling upon him and giving him a drubbing. I don't know. I had some imbecile thoughts. The knitting old woman with the cat obtruded herself upon my memory as a most improper person to be sitting at the other end of such an affair. I saw a row of pilgrims squirting lead in the air out of Winchesters held to the hip. I thought I would never get back to the steamer, and imagined myself living alone and unarmed in the woods to an advanced age. Such silly things—you know. And I remember I confounded the beat of the drum with the beating of my heart, and was pleased at its calm regularity.

"I kept to the track though—then stopped to listen. The night was very clear; a dark blue space, sparkling with dew and starlight, in which black things stood very still. I thought I could see a kind of motion ahead of me. I was strangely cocksure of everything that night. I actually left the track and ran in a wide semicircle (I verily believe chuckling to myself) so as to get in front of that stir, of that motion I had seen—if indeed I had seen anything. I was circumventing Kurtz as though it had been a boyish game.

"I came upon him, and, if he had not heard me coming, I would have fallen over him too, but he got up in time. He rose, unsteady, long, pale, indistinct, like a vapour exhaled by the earth, and swayed slightly, misty and silent before me; while at my back the fires loomed between the trees, and the murmur of many voices issued from the forest. I had cut him off cleverly; but when actually confronting him I seemed to come to my senses, I saw the danger in its right proportion. It was by no means over yet. Suppose he began to shout? Though he could hardly stand, there was still plenty of vigour in his voice. 'Go away—hide yourself,' he said, in that profound tone. It was very awful. I glanced back. We were within thirty yards of the nearest fire. A black figure stood up, strode on long black legs, waving long black arms, across the glow. It had horns—antelope horns, I think—on its head. Some sorcerer, some witch-man no doubt: it looked fiend-like enough. 'Do you know what you are doing?' I whispered. 'Perfectly,' he answered, raising his voice for that single word: it sounded to me far off and yet loud, like a hail through a speaking-trumpet. If he makes a row we are lost, I thought to myself. This clearly was not a case for fisticuffs, even apart from the very natural aversion I had to beat that Shadow—this wandering and tormented thing. 'You will be lost,' I said—'utterly lost.' One gets sometimes such a flash of inspiration, you know. I did say the right thing, though indeed he could not have been more irretrievably lost than he was at this very moment, when the foundations of our intimacy were being laid—to endure—to endure—even to the end—even beyond.

"'I had immense plans,' he muttered irresolutely. 'Yes,' said I; 'but if you try to shout I'll smash your head with—' There was not a stick or a stone near. 'I will throttle you for good,' I corrected myself. 'I was on the threshold of great things,' he pleaded, in a voice of longing, with a wistfulness of tone that made my blood run cold. 'And now for this stupid scoundrel—' 'Your success in

Europe is assured in any case,' I affirmed steadily. I did not want to have the throttling of him, you understand—and indeed it would have been very little use for any practical purpose. I tried to break the spell—the heavy, mute spell of the wilderness—that seemed to draw him to its pitiless breast by the awakening of forgotten and brutal instincts, by the memory of gratified and monstrous passions. This alone, I was convinced, had driven him out to the edge of the forest, to the bush, towards the gleam of fires, the throb of drums, the drone of weird incantations; this alone had beguiled his unlawful soul beyond the bounds of permitted aspirations. And, don't you see, the terror of the position was not in being knocked on the head—though I had a very lively sense of that danger too—but in this, that I had to deal with a being to whom I could not appeal in the name of anything high or low. I had, even like the niggers, to invoke him—himself—his own exalted and incredible degradation. There was nothing either above or below him, and I knew it. He had kicked himself loose of the earth. Confound the man! he had kicked the very earth to pieces. He was alone, and I before him did not know whether I stood on the ground or floated in the air. I've been telling you what we said—repeating the phrases we pronounced—but what's the good? They were common everyday words—the familiar, vague sounds exchanged on every waking day of life. But what of that? They had behind them, to my mind, the terrific suggestiveness of words heard in dreams, of phrases spoken in nightmares. Soul! If anybody had ever struggled with a soul, I am the man. And I wasn't arguing with a lunatic either. Believe me or not, his intelligence was perfectly clear—concentrated, it is true, upon himself with horrible intensity, yet clear; and therein was my only chance—barring, of course, the killing him there and then, which wasn't so good, on account of unavoidable noise. But his soul was mad. Being alone in the wilderness, it had looked within itself, and, by heavens! I tell you, it had gone mad. I had—for my sins, I suppose, to go through the ordeal of looking into it myself. No eloquence could have been so withering to one's belief in mankind as his final burst of sincerity. He struggled with himself too. I saw it—I heard it. I saw the inconceivable mystery of a soul that knew no restraint, no faith, and no fear, yet struggling blindly with itself. I kept my head pretty well; but when I had him at last stretched on the couch, I wiped my forehead, while my legs shook under me as though I had carried half a ton on my back down that hill. And yet I had only supported him, his bony arm clasped round my neck—and he was not much heavier than a child.

"When next day we left at noon, the crowd, of whose presence behind the curtain of trees I had been acutely conscious all the time, flowed out of the woods again, filled the clearing, covered the slope with a mass of naked, breathing, quivering, bronze bodies. I steamed up a bit, then swung downstream, and two thousand eyes followed the evolutions of the splashing, thumping, fierce river-demon beating the water with its terrible tail and breathing black smoke into the air. In front of the first rank, along the river, three men, plastered with bright red earth from head to foot, strutted to and fro restlessly. When we came abreast again, they faced the river, stamped their feet, nodded their horned heads, swayed their scarlet bodies; they shook towards the fierce river-demon a bunch of black feathers, a mangy skin with a pendent tail—something that looked like a dried gourd; they shouted periodically together strings of amazing words that resembled no sounds of human language; and the deep murmurs of the crowd, interrupted suddenly, were like the responses of some satanic litany.

"We had carried Kurtz into the pilot-house: there was more air there. Lying on the couch, he stared through the open shutter. There was an eddy in the mass of human bodies, and the woman with helmeted head and tawny cheeks rushed out to the very brink of the stream. She put out her hands, shouted something, and all that wild mob took up the shout in a roaring chorus of articulated, rapid, breathless utterance.

"'Do you understand this?' I asked.

"He kept on looking out past me with fiery, longing eyes, with a mingled expression of wistfulness and hate. He made no answer, but I saw a smile, a smile of indefinable meaning, appear on his colourless lips that a moment after twitched convulsively. 'Do I not?' he said slowly, gasping, as if the words had been torn out of him by a supernatural power.

"I pulled the string of the whistle, and I did this because I saw the pilgrims on deck getting out their rifles with an air of anticipating a jolly lark. At the sudden screech there was a movement of abject terror through that wedged mass of bodies. 'Don't! don't you frighten them away,' cried someone on deck disconsolately. I pulled the string time after time. They broke and ran, they leaped, they crouched, they swerved, they dodged the flying terror of the sound. The three red chaps had fallen flat, face down on the shore, as though they had been shot dead. Only the barbarous and superb woman did not so much as flinch, and stretched tragically her bare arms after us over the sombre and glittering river.

"And then that imbecile crowd down on the deck started their little fun, and I could see nothing more for smoke.

"The brown current ran swiftly out of the heart of darkness, bearing us down towards the sea with twice the speed of our upward progress; and Kurtz's life was running swiftly too, ebbing, ebbing out of his heart into the sea of inexorable time. The manager was very placid, he had no vital anxieties now, he took us both in with a comprehensive and satisfied glance: the 'affair' had come off as well as could be wished. I saw the time approaching when I would be left alone of the party of 'unsound method.' The pilgrims looked upon me with disfavour. I was, so to speak, numbered with the dead. It is strange how I accepted this unforeseen partnership, this choice of nightmares forced upon me in the tenebrous land invaded by these mean and greedy phantoms.

"Kurtz discoursed. A voice! a voice! It rang deep to the very last. It survived his strength to hide in the magnificent folds of eloquence the barren darkness of his heart. Oh, he struggled! he struggled! The wastes of his weary brain were haunted by shadowy images now—images of wealth and fame revolving obsequiously round his unextinguishable gift of noble and lofty expression. My Intended, my station, my career, my ideas—these were the subjects for the occasional utterances of elevated sentiments. The shade of the original Kurtz frequented the bedside of the hollow sham, whose fate it was to be buried presently in the mould of primeval earth. But both the diabolic love and the unearthly hate of the mysteries it had penetrated fought for the possession of that soul satiated with primitive emotions, avid of lying fame, of sham distinction, of all the appearances of success and power.

"Sometimes he was contemptibly childish. He desired to have kings meet him at railway stations on his return from some ghastly Nowhere, where he intended to accomplish great things. 'You show them you have in you something that is really profitable, and then there will be no limits to the recognition of your ability,' he would say. 'Of course you must take care of the motives—right motives—always.' The long reaches that were like one and the same reach, monotonous bends that were exactly alike, slipped past the steamer with their multitude of secular[2] trees looking patiently after this grimy fragment of another world, the forerunner of change, of conquest, of trade, of massacres, of blessings. I looked ahead—piloting. 'Close the shutter,' said Kurtz suddenly one day; 'I can't bear to look at this.' I did so. There was a silence. 'Oh, but I will wring your heart yet!' he cried at the invisible wilderness.

"We broke down—as I had expected—and had to lie up for repairs at the head of an island. This delay was the first thing that shook Kurtz's confidence. One morning he gave me a packet of papers and a photograph—the lot tied together with a shoe-string. 'Keep this for me,' he said. 'This noxious fool' (meaning the manager) 'is capable of prying into my boxes when I am not looking.' In the afternoon I saw him. He was lying on his back with closed eyes, and I withdrew quietly, but I heard him mutter, 'Live rightly, die, die . . .' I listened. There was nothing more. Was he rehearsing some speech in his sleep, or was it a fragment of a phrase from some newspaper article? He had been writing for the papers and meant to do so again, 'for the furthering of my ideas. It's a duty.'

"His was an impenetrable darkness. I looked at him as you peer down at a man who is lying at the bottom of a precipice where the sun never shines. But I had not much time to give him, because I was helping the engine-driver to take to pieces the leaky cylinders, to straighten a bent connecting-rod, and in other such matters. I lived in an infernal mess of rust, filings, nuts, bolts, spanners, hammers, ratchet-drills—things I abominate, because I don't get on with them. I tended the little forge we fortunately had aboard; I toiled wearily in a wretched scrap-heap—unless I had the shakes too bad to stand.

"One evening coming in with a candle I was startled to hear him say a little tremulously, 'I am lying here in the dark waiting for death.' The light was within a foot of his eyes. I forced myself to murmur, 'Oh, nonsense!' and stood over him as if transfixed.

"Anything approaching the change that came over his features I have never seen before, and hope never to see again. Oh, I wasn't touched. I was fascinated. It was as though a veil had been rent. I saw on that ivory face the expression of sombre pride, of ruthless power, of craven terror—of an intense and hopeless despair. Did he live his life again in every detail of desire, temptation, and surrender during that supreme moment of complete knowledge? He cried in a whisper at some image, at some vision—he cried out twice, a cry that was no more than a breath:

"'The horror! The horror!'

"I blew the candle out and left the cabin. The pilgrims were dining in the mess-room, and I took my place opposite the manager, who lifted his eyes to give me a questioning glance, which I successfully ignored. He leaned back,

2. Centuries old (from *séculaire*, French).

serene, with that peculiar smile of his sealing the unexpressed depths of his meanness. A continuous shower of small flies streamed upon the lamp, upon the cloth, upon our hands and faces. Suddenly the manager's boy put his insolent black head in the doorway, and said in a tone of scathing contempt:

"'Mistah Kurtz—he dead.'

"All the pilgrims rushed out to see. I remained, and went on with my dinner. I believe I was considered brutally callous. However, I did not eat much. There was a lamp in there—light, don't you know—and outside it was so beastly, beastly dark. I went no more near the remarkable man who had pronounced a judgement upon the adventures of his soul on this earth. The voice was gone. What else had been there? But I am of course aware that next day the pilgrims buried something in a muddy hole.

"And then they very nearly buried me.

"However, as you see, I did not go to join Kurtz there and then. I did not. I remained to dream the nightmare out to the end, and to show my loyalty to Kurtz once more. Destiny. My destiny! Droll thing life is—that mysterious arrangement of merciless logic for a futile purpose. The most you can hope from it is some knowledge of yourself—that comes too late—a crop of unextinguishable regrets. I have wrestled with death. It is the most unexciting contest you can imagine. It takes place in an impalpable greyness, with nothing underfoot, with nothing around, without spectators, without clamour, without glory, without the great desire of victory, without the great fear of defeat, in a sickly atmosphere of tepid scepticism, without much belief in your own right, and still less in that of your adversary. If such is the form of ultimate wisdom, then life is a greater riddle than some of us think it to be. I was within a hair's-breadth of the last opportunity for pronouncement, and I found with humiliation that probably I would have nothing to say. This is the reason why I affirm that Kurtz was a remarkable man. He had something to say. He said it. Since I had peeped over the edge myself, I understand better the meaning of his stare, that could not see the flame of the candle, but was wide enough to embrace the whole universe, piercing enough to penetrate all the hearts that beat in the darkness. He had summed up—he had judged. 'The horror!' He was a remarkable man. After all, this was the expression of some sort of belief; it had candour, it had conviction, it had a vibrating note of revolt in its whisper, it had the appalling face of a glimpsed truth—the strange commingling of desire and hate. And it is not my own extremity I remember best—a vision of greyness without form filled with physical pain, and a careless contempt for the evanescence of all things—even of this pain itself. No! It is his extremity that I seem to have lived through. True, he had made that last stride, he had stepped over the edge, while I had been permitted to draw back my hesitating foot. And perhaps in this is the whole difference; perhaps all the wisdom, and all truth, and all sincerity, are just compressed into that inappreciable moment of time in which we step over the threshold of the invisible. Perhaps! I like to think my summing-up would not have been a word of careless contempt. Better his cry—much better. It was an affirmation, a moral victory paid for by innumerable defeats, by abominable terrors, by abominable satisfactions. But it was a victory! That is why I have remained loyal to Kurtz to the last, and even beyond, when a long time after I heard once more, not his own voice, but the echo of his magnificent eloquence thrown to me from a soul as translucently pure as a cliff of crystal.

"No, they did not bury me, though there is a period of time which I remember mistily, with a shuddering wonder, like a passage through some inconceivable world that had no hope in it and no desire. I found myself back in the sepulchral city resenting the sight of people hurrying through the streets to filch a little money from each other, to devour their infamous cookery, to gulp their unwholesome beer, to dream their insignificant and silly dreams. They trespassed upon my thoughts. They were intruders whose knowledge of life was to me an irritating pretence, because I felt so sure they could not possibly know the things I knew. Their bearing, which was simply the bearing of commonplace individuals going about their business in the assurance of perfect safety, was offensive to me like the outrageous flauntings of folly in the face of a danger it is unable to comprehend. I had no particular desire to enlighten them, but I had some difficulty in restraining myself from laughing in their faces, so full of stupid importance. I daresay I was not very well at that time. I tottered about the streets—there were various affairs to settle—grinning bitterly at perfectly respectable persons. I admit my behaviour was inexcusable, but then my temperature was seldom normal in these days. My dear aunt's endeavours to 'nurse up my strength' seemed altogether beside the mark. It was not my strength that wanted nursing, it was my imagination that wanted soothing. I kept the bundle of papers given me by Kurtz, not knowing exactly what to do with it. His mother had died lately, watched over, as I was told, by his Intended. A clean-shaven man, with an official manner and wearing gold-rimmed spectacles, called on me one day and made inquiries, at first circuitous, afterwards suavely pressing, about what he was pleased to denominate certain 'documents.' I was not surprised, because I had had two rows with the manager on the subject out there. I had refused to give up the smallest scrap out of that package, and I took the same attitude with the spectacled man. He became darkly menacing at last, and with much heat argued that the Company had the right to every bit of information about its 'territories.' And, said he, 'Mr Kurtz's knowledge of unexplored regions must have been necessarily extensive and peculiar—owing to his great abilities and to the deplorable circumstances in which he had been placed: therefore—' I assured him Mr Kurtz's knowledge, however extensive, did not bear upon the problems of commerce or administration. He invoked then the name of science. 'It would be an incalculable loss if,' etc. etc. I offered him the report on the 'Suppression of Savage Customs,' with the postscriptum torn off. He took it up eagerly, but ended by sniffing at it with an air of contempt. 'This is not what we had a right to expect,' he remarked. 'Expect nothing else,' I said. 'There are only private letters.' He withdrew upon some threat of legal proceedings, and I saw him no more; but another fellow, calling himself Kurtz's cousin, appeared two days later, and was anxious to hear all the details about his dear relative's last moments. Incidentally he gave me to understand that Kurtz had been essentially a great musician. 'There was the making of an immense success,' said the man, who was an organist, I believe, with lank grey hair flowing over a greasy coat-collar. I had no reason to doubt his statement; and to this day I am unable to say what was Kurtz's profession, whether he ever had any—which was the greatest of his talents. I had taken him for a painter who wrote for the papers, or else for a journalist who could paint—but even the cousin (who took snuff during the interview) could not tell me what he had been—exactly. He was a universal genius—on that point I agreed with the old chap, who thereupon blew his nose noisily into a large cotton handkerchief and withdrew in senile agitation, bearing off some family letters and memoranda without importance. Ultimately a journalist anxious to know something of the fate of his 'dear colleague' turned up. This visitor informed me Kurtz's proper sphere ought to have been politics 'on the popular side.' He had furry straight eyebrows, bristly hair cropped short, an eyeglass on a broad ribbon, and, becoming expansive, confessed his opinion that Kurtz really couldn't write a bit—'but heavens! how that man could talk! He electrified large meetings. He had faith—don't you see?—he had the faith. He could get himself to believe anything—anything. He would have been a splendid leader of an extreme party.' 'What party?' I asked. 'Any party,' answered the other. 'He was an—an—extremist.' Did I not think so? I assented. Did I know, he asked, with a sudden flash of curiosity, 'what it was that had induced him to go out there?' 'Yes,' said I, and forthwith handed him the famous Report for publication, if he thought fit. He glanced through it hurriedly, mumbling all the time, judged 'it would do,' and took himself off with this plunder.

"Thus I was left at last with a slim packet of letters and the girl's portrait. She struck me as beautiful—I mean she had a beautiful expression. I know that the sunlight can be made to lie too, yet one felt that no manipulation of light and pose could have conveyed the delicate shade of truthfulness upon those features. She seemed ready to listen without mental reservation, without suspicion, without a thought for herself. I concluded I would go and give her back her portrait and those letters myself. Curiosity? Yes; and also some other feeling perhaps. All that had been Kurtz's had passed out of my hands: his soul, his body, his station, his plans, his ivory, his career. There remained only his memory and his Intended—and I wanted to give that up too to the past, in a way—to surrender personally all that remained of him with me to that oblivion which is the last word of our common fate. I don't defend myself. I had no clear perception of what it was I really wanted. Perhaps it was an impulse of unconscious loyalty, or the fulfilment of one of those ironic necessities that lurk in the facts of human existence. I don't know. I can't tell. But I went.

"I thought his memory was like the other memories of the dead that accumulate in every man's life—a vague impress on the brain of shadows that had fallen on it in their swift and final passage; but before the high and ponderous door, between the tall houses of a street as still and decorous as a well-kept alley in a cemetery, I had a vision of him on the stretcher, opening his mouth voraciously, as if to devour all the earth with all its mankind. He lived then before me; he lived as much as he had ever lived—a shadow insatiable of splendid appearances, of frightful realities; a shadow darker than the shadow of the night, and draped nobly in the folds of a gorgeous eloquence. The vision seemed to enter the house with me—the stretcher, the phantom-bearers, the wild crowd of obedient worshippers, the gloom of the forests, the glitter of the reach between the murky bends, the beat of the drum, regular and muffled like the beating of a heart—the heart of a conquering darkness. It was a moment of triumph for the wilderness, an invading and vengeful rush which, it seemed to me, I would have to keep back alone for the salvation of another soul. And the memory of what I had heard him say afar there, with the horned shapes stirring at my back, in the glow of fires, within the patient woods, those broken phrases came back to me, were heard again in their ominous and terrifying simplicity. I remembered his abject pleading, his abject threats, the colossal scale of his vile desires, the meanness, the torment, the tempestuous anguish of his soul. And later on I seemed to see his collected languid manner, when he said one day, 'This lot of ivory now is really mine. The Company did not pay for it. I collected it myself at a very great personal risk. I am afraid they will try to claim it as theirs though. H'm. It is a difficult case. What do you think I ought to do—resist? Eh? I want no more than justice.' . . . He wanted no more than justice—no more than justice. I rang the bell before a mahogany door on the first floor, and while I waited he seemed to stare at me out of the glossy panel—stare with that wide and immense stare embracing, condemning, loathing all the universe. I seemed to hear the whispered cry, 'The horror! The horror!'

"The dusk was falling. I had to wait in a lofty drawing room with three long windows from floor to ceiling that were like three luminous and bedraped columns. The bent gilt legs and backs of the furniture shone in indistinct curves. The tall marble fireplace had a cold and monumental whiteness. A grand piano stood massively in a corner; with dark gleams on the flat surfaces like a sombre and polished sarcophagus. A high door opened—closed. I rose.

"She came forward, all in black, with a pale head, floating towards me in the dusk. She was in mourning. It was more than a year since his death, more than a year since the news came; she seemed as though she would remember and mourn for ever. She took both my hands in hers and murmured, 'I had heard you were coming.' I noticed she was not very young—I mean not girlish. She had a mature capacity for fidelity, for belief, for suffering. The room seemed to have grown darker, as if all the sad light of the cloudy evening had taken refuge on her forehead. This fair hair, this pale visage, this pure brow, seemed surrounded by an ashy halo from which the dark eyes looked out at me. Their glance was guileless, profound, confident, and trustful. She carried her sorrowful head as though she were proud of that sorrow, as though she would say, I—I alone know how to mourn for him as he deserves. But while we were still shaking hands, such a look of awful desolation came upon her face that I perceived she was one of those creatures that are not the playthings of Time. For her he had died only yesterday. And, by Jove! the impression was so powerful that for me too he seemed to have died only yesterday—nay, this very minute. I saw her and him in the same instant of time—his death and her sorrow—I saw her sorrow in the very moment of his death. Do you understand? I saw them together—I heard them together. She had said, with a deep catch of the breath, 'I have survived'; while my strained ears seemed to hear distinctly, mingled with her tone of despairing regret, the summing-up whisper of his eternal condemnation. I asked myself what I was doing there, with a sensation of panic in my heart as though I had blundered into a place of cruel and absurd mysteries not fit for a human being to behold. She motioned me to a chair. We sat down. I laid the packet gently on the little table, and she put her hand over it. . . . 'You knew him well,' she murmured, after a moment of mourning silence.

"'Intimacy grows quickly out there,' I said. 'I knew him as well as it is possible for one man to know another.'

"'And you admired him,' she said. 'It was impossible to know him and not to admire him. Was it?'

"'He was a remarkable man,' I said unsteadily. Then before the appealing fixity of her gaze, that seemed to watch for more words on my lips, I went on, 'It was impossible not to—'

"'Love him,' she finished eagerly, silencing me into an appalled dumbness. 'How true! how true! But when you think that no one knew him so well as I! I had all his noble confidence. I knew him best.'

"'You knew him best,' I repeated. And perhaps she did. But with every word spoken the room was growing darker, and only her forehead, smooth and white, remained illumined by the unextinguishable light of belief and love.

"'You were his friend,' she went on. 'His friend,' she repeated, a little louder. 'You must have been, if he had given you this, and sent you to me. I feel I can speak to you—and oh! I must speak. I want you—you who have heard his last words—to know I have been worthy of him. . . . It is not pride. . . . Yes! I am proud to know I understood him better than any one on earth—he told me so himself. And since his mother died I have had no one—no one—to—to—'

"I listened. The darkness deepened. I was not even sure whether he had given me the right bundle. I rather suspect he wanted me to take care of another batch of his papers which, after his death, I saw the manager examining under the lamp. And the girl talked, easing her pain in the certitude of my sympathy; she talked as thirsty men drink. I had heard that her engagement with Kurtz had been disapproved by her people. He wasn't rich enough or something. And indeed I don't know whether he had not been a pauper all his life. He had given me some reason to infer that it was his impatience of comparative poverty that drove him out there.

"'. . . Who was not his friend who had heard him speak once?' she was saying. 'He drew men towards him by what was best in them.' She looked at me with intensity. 'It is the gift of the great,' she went on, and the sound of her low voice seemed to have the accompaniment of all the other sounds, full of mystery, desolation, and sorrow, I had ever heard—the ripple of the river, the soughing[3] of the trees swayed by the wind, the murmurs of the crowds, the faint ring of incomprehensible words cried from afar, the whisper of a voice speaking from beyond the threshold of an eternal darkness. 'But you have heard him! You know!' she cried.

"'Yes, I know,' I said with something like despair in my heart, but bowing my head before the faith that was in her, before that great and saving illusion that shone with an unearthly glow in the darkness, in the triumphant darkness from which I could not have defended her—from which I could not even defend myself.

"'What a loss to me—to us!'—she corrected herself with beautiful generosity; then added in a murmur, 'To the world.' By the last gleams of twilight I could see the glitter of her eyes, full of tears—of tears that would not fall.

"'I have been very happy—very fortunate—very proud,' she went on. 'Too fortunate. Too happy for a little while. And now I am unhappy for—for life.'

"She stood up; her fair hair seemed to catch all the remaining light in a glimmer of gold. I rose too.

3. A rushing or murmuring sound.

"'And of all this,' she went on mournfully, 'of all his promise, and of all his greatness, of his generous mind, of his noble heart, nothing remains—nothing but a memory. You and I—'

"'We shall always remember him,' I said hastily.

"'No!' she cried. 'It is impossible that all this should be lost—that such a life should be sacrificed to leave nothing—but sorrow. You know what vast plans he had. I knew of them too—I could not perhaps understand—but others knew of them. Something must remain. His words, at least, have not died.'

"'His words will remain,' I said.

"'And his example,' she whispered to herself. 'Men looked up to him—his goodness shone in every act. His example—'

"'True,' I said; 'his example too. Yes, his example. I forgot that.'

"'But I do not. I cannot—I cannot believe—not yet. I cannot believe that I shall never see him again, that nobody will see him again, never, never, never.'

"She put out her arms as if after a retreating figure, stretching them back and with clasped pale hands across the fading and narrow sheen of the window. Never see him! I saw him clearly enough then. I shall see this eloquent phantom as long as I live, and I shall see her too, a tragic and familiar Shade, resembling in this gesture another one, tragic also, and bedecked with powerless charms, stretching bare brown arms over the glitter of the infernal stream, the stream of darkness. She said suddenly very low, 'He died as he lived.'

"'His end,' said I, with dull anger stirring in me, 'was in every way worthy of his life.'

"'And I was not with him,' she murmured. My anger subsided before a feeling of infinite pity.

"'Everything that could be done—' I mumbled.

"'Ah, but I believed in him more than any one on earth—more than his own mother, more than—himself. He needed me! Me! I would have treasured every sigh, every word, every sign, every glance.'

"I felt like a chill grip on my chest. 'Don't,' I said, in a muffled voice.

"'Forgive me. I—I—have mourned so long in silence—in silence. . . . You were with him—to the last? I think of his loneliness. Nobody near to understand him as I would have understood. Perhaps no one to hear. . . .'

"'To the very end,' I said shakily. 'I heard his very last words. . . .' I stopped in a fright.

"'Repeat them,' she murmured in a heart-broken tone. 'I want—I want—something—something—to—to live with.'

"I was on the point of crying at her, 'Don't you hear them?' The dusk was repeating them in a persistent whisper all around us, in a whisper that seemed to swell menacingly like the first whisper of a rising wind. 'The horror! The horror!'

"'His last word—to live with,' she insisted. 'Don't you understand I loved him—I loved him—I loved him!'

"I pulled myself together and spoke slowly.

"'The last word he pronounced was—your name.'

"I heard a light sigh and then my heart stood still, stopped dead short by an exulting and terrible cry, by the cry of inconceivable triumph and of unspeakable pain. 'I knew it—I was sure!' . . . She knew. She was sure. I heard her weeping; she had hidden her face in her hands. It seemed to me that the house would collapse before I could escape, that the heavens would fall upon my head. But nothing happened. The heavens do not fall for such a trifle. Would they have fallen, I wonder, if I had rendered Kurtz that justice which was his due? Hadn't he said he wanted only justice? But I couldn't. I could not tell her. It would have been too dark—too dark altogether. . . ."

Marlow ceased, and sat apart, indistinct and silent, in the pose of a meditating Buddha. Nobody moved for a time. "We have lost the first of the ebb," said the Director suddenly. I raised my head. The offing was barred by a black bank of clouds, and the tranquil waterway leading to the uttermost ends of the earth flowed sombre under an overcast sky—seemed to lead into the heart of an immense darkness.

1899

THOMAS MANN

1875–1955

The greatest German novelist of the twentieth century, Thomas Mann also became an international figure to whom people looked for statements on art, modern society, and the human condition. Carrying on the nineteenth-century tradition of psychological realism, Mann took as his subject the cultural and spiritual crises of Europe at the turn of the century. His career spanned a time of great change, including the upheaval of two world wars and the disintegration of an entire society. Whereas other modern novelists such as **James Joyce**, **William Faulkner**, and **Virginia Woolf** stressed innovative language and style, Mann wrote in a more traditional, realistic style about the universal human conflicts between art and life, sensuality and intellect, individual and social will. Yet in his struggle with themes like time, subjectivity, and homosexuality, he too participated in the modernist movement that transformed the literature of the twentieth century.

Mann was born on June 6, 1875, in Lübeck, a historic seaport and commercial city in northern Germany. His father was a grain merchant and head of the family firm; his mother, who came from a German-Brazilian family, was known for her beauty and musical talent. The contrast between Nordic and Latin that plays such a large part in Mann's work began in his consciousness of his own heritage. Mann became acquainted with mortality early on: his father died when he was sixteen, and later both his sister and his son committed suicide. Although Thomas failed two years in school, he viewed the failure as liberating, since it relieved him of his parents' high expectations. He graduated from high school in 1894. Joining his family in Munich, where they had moved after his father's death, he worked as an unpaid apprentice in a fire insurance business, but was more interested in university lectures in history, political economy, and art. He decided against a business career after his first published story, *Fallen* (1896), received praise from the noted poet Richard Dehmel. He lived and wrote for two years in Italy before returning to Munich for a stint as manuscript reader for the satiric weekly *Simplicissimus*. In 1905 he married Katia Pringsheim, with whom he had six children. Yet as a young man he had experienced homosexual attractions, which continued throughout his life and became a recurring theme in his fiction. He recorded these attractions privately in his diary but never acted on them; he commented that "I would never have wanted to go to bed even with the Belvedere Apollo."

His first major work, *Buddenbrooks* (1901), describes the decline of a prosperous German family through four generations and is to some extent based on the history of the Mann family business. Nonetheless, the elements of autobiography are quickly absorbed into the universal themes of the inner decay of the German burgher ("bourgeois," or middle-class) tradition and its growing isolation from other segments of society—a decline paralleled in the portrait of a developing artistic sensitivity and its relation to death. Throughout his writings before and during the First World War, Mann established himself as an important spokesman for modern Germany. He argued with his brother Heinrich about politics; Heinrich was a passionate liberal, but Thomas defined freedom as "a moral, spiritual idea" and said that "for political freedom I've absolutely no interest." The political crises after the First World War shook Mann, however, and the subsequent rise of the Nazis changed his views. He rejected his early conservatism and defense of an authoritarian nationalist government (*Reflections of a Non-Political Man*, 1918) in favor of ardent support for democracy and liberal humanism.

One of the first signs of this new attitude was Mann's most famous novel, *The Magic Mountain* (1924), a bildungsroman (a novel of the protagonist's education and development) that uses the isolation of a mountaintop tuberculosis sanatorium to gain perspective on the philosophic issues of twentieth-century Europe. *The Magic Mountain* was immensely popular, and in 1929 its author received the Nobel Prize. As his international stature grew, Mann spoke out against the Nazis; his wife, Katia, came from a Jewish family, and when Hitler rose to power in 1933, the Manns went into voluntary exile in neutral Switzerland. Stung by Mann's criticism, the Nazis revoked his citizenship. Moving to the United States in 1938, he wrote and lectured against Nazism, and in 1944 he became an American citizen. After the Second World War, Mann refused to live in Germany, arguing that the country had not expiated its crimes. He became an active advocate for the cause of peace; criticized by the House Un-American Activities Committee for his support of allegedly communist peace organizations, Mann left the United States for Switzerland in 1952.

Mann's later works deal with the conflicts and interrelations between society and inspired individuals whose spiritual, intellectual, or artistic gifts set them apart. *Joseph and His Brothers* (1933–45) is a tetralogy that reimagines the biblical tale of Joseph, who, abandoned for dead by his brothers, survives and comes to power in Egypt. *Doctor Faustus* (1947), which Mann called "the novel of my epoch, dressed up in the story of a highly precarious and sinful artistic life," portrays the composer Adrian Leverkühn as a modern Faust who personifies the temptation and corruption of contemporary Germany. Well after the war, when Mann had moved to Zurich, he published a final, comic picture of the artist figure as a confidence man who uses his skill and ironic insight to manipulate society (*The Confessions of Felix Krull*, 1954). Mann's last work before his death, on August 12, 1955, the *Confessions* recapitulates his familiar themes, but in a lighthearted parody of the traditional bildungsroman that is a far cry from the moral seriousness of earlier tales.

Many of Mann's themes derive from the nineteenth-century German aesthetic tradition in which he grew up. The philosophers Schopenhauer and Nietzsche and the composer Wagner had the most influence on his work: Arthur Schopenhauer (1788–1860) for his vision of the artist's suffering and development; Friedrich Nietzsche (1844–1900) for his portrait of the diseased artist overcoming chaos and decay to produce, through discipline and will, works that justify existence; and Richard Wagner (1813–1883) for embodying the complete artist who controlled all aspects of his work: music, lyrics, the very staging of his operas. Mann's well-known use of the verbal leitmotif is also borrowed from Wagner, whose operas are notable for the recurrent musical theme (the leitmotif) associated with a particular person, thing, action, or state of being. In Mann's literary adaptation, evocative phrases, repeated almost without change, link memories throughout the text and establish a cumulative emotional resonance. Inside the tradition of realistic narration, Mann creates a highly organized literary structure with subtly interrelated themes and images that build up rich associations of ideas: in his own words, an "epic prose composition . . . understood by me as spiritual thematic pattern, as a musical complex of associations." At the same time, Mann's works cultivate objectivity, distance, and irony, and no character—including the narrator—is immune from the author's critical eye. Indeed, it is in his tendency to treat realist techniques with irony that Mann most reveals himself as a modern, unable to accept narrative convention at face value.

DEATH IN VENICE

The work presented here, *Death in Venice*, is Mann's most famous novella, published in 1912, shortly after the author's vacation in Venice and two years before the First World War. Its sense of impending doom involves the cultural disintegration of the "European soul" (soon to be expressed in the war), which has its symbol in the corruption and death of the writer Gustav von Aschenbach during an epidemic. The story portrays a loss of psychological balance, a sickness of the artistic soul to match that of plague-ridden Venice masking its true condition before unsuspecting tourists. Erotic and artistic themes mingle as the respected Aschenbach, escaping a lifetime of laborious creation and self-discipline, allows himself to be swept away by the classical beauty of a young boy until he becomes a grotesque figure, dyeing his hair and rouging his cheeks in a vain attempt to appear young. Aschenbach's fatal obsession with Tadzio casts light on the artist's whole career.

Aschenbach has laboriously repressed emotions and spontaneity to achieve the disciplined, classical style of a master—and also to earn fame. Plagued by nervous exhaustion at the beginning of the story, he reacts to the sight of a foreign traveler with a "sudden, strange expansion of his inner space" and starts dreaming of exotic, dangerous landscapes. From the tropical swampland and tigers of the Ganges delta to the mountains of a later dream's Dionysiac revels, these visionary landscapes become a metaphor for all the subterranean impulses he has rejected in himself and for his art. Enigmatic figures guide Aschenbach's adventure of the emotions: the traveler, the grotesque old man on the boat, the gondolier, the street singer, and Tadzio himself, interpreted as a godlike figure out of Greek myth. Indeed, allusions to ancient myth and literature multiply rapidly as Aschenbach falls under Tadzio's spell and begins to rationalize his fascination as the artist's pursuit of divine beauty. Turning to Plato's *Phaedrus*, a dialogue that combines themes of love with the search for absolute beauty and truth, Aschenbach sketches his own "Platonic" argument as a meditation on the dual nature of the artist. "Who can untangle the riddle of the artist's essence and character?" asks the narrator. *Death in Venice* is a crystallization of Mann's work at its best, displaying the penetrating detail of his social and psychological realism, the power of his tightly interwoven symbolic structure, and the tragic force of his artist-hero's crisis.

Death in Venice[1]

CHAPTER I

On a spring afternoon in 19—,[2] a year that for months glowered threateningly over our continent, Gustav Aschenbach—or von[3] Aschenbach, as he had been known officially since his fiftieth birthday—set off alone from his dwelling in Prinzregentenstrasse[4] in Munich on a rather long walk. He had been overstrained by the difficult and dangerous morning's work, which just now required particular discretion, caution, penetration, and precision of will: even after his midday meal the writer had not been able to halt the running on of the productive machinery within him, that "motus animi continuus" which Cicero[5] claims is the essence of eloquence, nor had he been able to obtain the relaxing slumber so necessary to him once a day to relieve the increasing demands on his resources. Thus, he sought the open air right after tea, hoping that fresh air and exercise would restore him and help him to have a profitable evening.

It was early May, and after weeks of cold, wet weather a premature summer had set in. The Englischer Garten,[6] although only beginning to come into leaf, was as muggy as in August and at the end near the city was full of vehicles and people out for a stroll. Increasingly quiet paths led Aschenbach toward

1. Translated by and some notes adapted from Clayton Koelb.
2. In 1911, when the story was written, the "Moroccan crisis" was precipitated when a German gunboat appeared off the coast of Agadir, prompting negotiations between France and Germany over their respective national interests. A series of similar diplomatic crises led to the outbreak of World War I in 1914.
3. From or of. "Von" appears only in the names of nobility. Aschenbach was made an honorary nobleman on his fiftieth birthday. Aschenbach: "stream of ashes" (German, literal translation).
4. A street in Munich that forms the southern boundary of the Englischer Garten (English Garden). Mann lived in various apartments in this neighborhood.
5. Marcus Tullius Cicero (106–43 B.C.E.), Roman orator. "Motus animi continuus": the continuous motion of the spirit (Latin, attributed to Cicero).
6. The English Garden, a 900-acre public park with diverse attractions that extended from the city to the water meadows of the Isar River.

Aumeister,[7] where he spent a moment surveying the lively crowd in the beer garden, next to which several hackneys and carriages were lingering; but then as the sun went down he took a route homeward outside the park over the open fields and, since he felt tired and thunder clouds now threatened over Föhring,[8] he waited at the North Cemetery stop for the tram that would take him directly back into the city.

As it happened he found the tram stop and the surrounding area deserted. Neither on the paved Ungererstrasse, whose streetcar-tracks stretched in glistening solitude toward Schwabing, nor on the Föhringer Chaussee[9] was there a vehicle to be seen, nothing stirred behind the fences of the stonemasons' shops, where the crosses, headstones, and monuments for sale formed a second, untenanted graveyard, and the Byzantine architecture of the mortuary chapel across the way lay silent in the glow of the departing day. Its facade was decorated with Greek crosses and hieratic paintings in soft colors; in addition it displayed symmetrically arranged scriptural quotations in gold letters, such as, "They are entering the house of God," or, "May the eternal light shine upon them." Waiting, he found a few moments' solemn diversion in reading these formulations and letting his mind's eye bask in their radiant mysticism, when, returning from his reveries, he noticed a man in the portico, above the two apocalyptic beasts guarding the front steps. The man's not altogether ordinary appearance took his thoughts in a completely different direction.

It was not clear whether the man had emerged from the chapel through the bronze door or had climbed the steps up to the entry from the outside without being noticed. Aschenbach, without entering too deeply into the question, inclined to the first assumption. Moderately tall, thin, clean-shaven, and strikingly snub-nosed, the man belonged to the red-haired type and possessed a redhead's milky and freckled complexion. He was clearly not of Bavarian stock, and in any case the wide and straight-brimmed straw hat that covered his head lent him the appearance of a foreigner, of a traveler from afar. To be sure, he also wore the familiar native rucksack strapped to his shoulders and a yellowish Norfolk suit[1] apparently of loden cloth. He had a gray mackintosh over his left forearm, which he held supported against his side, and in his right hand he held a stick with an iron tip, which he propped obliquely against the ground, leaning his hip against its handle and crossing his ankles. With his head held up, so that his Adam's apple protruded nakedly from the thin neck that emerged from his loose sport shirt, he gazed intently into the distance with colorless, red-lashed eyes, between which stood two stark vertical furrows that went rather oddly with his short, turned-up nose. It may be that his elevated and elevating location had something to do with it, but his posture conveyed an impression of imperious surveillance, fortitude, even wildness. His lips seemed insufficient, perhaps because he was squinting, blinded, toward the setting sun or maybe because he was afflicted by a facial deformity—in any case they were retracted to such an extent that his teeth, revealed as far as the gums, menacingly displayed their entire white length.

7. A beer garden in the northern section.
8. A district in Munich.
9. A street. Ungererstrasse is a street that borders the North Cemetery. Schwabing is another district in Munich.
1. A belted suit.

It is entirely possible that Aschenbach had been somewhat indiscreet in his half-distracted, half-inquisitive survey of the stranger, for he suddenly realized that his gaze was being returned, and indeed returned so belligerently, so directly eye to eye, with such a clear intent to bring matters to a head and force the other to avert his eyes, that Aschenbach, with an awkward sense of embarrassment, turned away and began to walk along the fence, intending for the time being to pay no more attention to the fellow. In a moment he had forgotten about him. But perhaps the man had the look of the traveler about him, or perhaps because he exercised some physical or spiritual influence, Aschenbach's imagination was set working. He felt a sudden, strange expansion of his inner space, a rambling unrest, a youthful thirst for faraway places, a feeling so intense, so new—or rather so long unused and forgotten—that he stood rooted to the spot, his hands behind his back and his gaze to the ground, pondering the essence and direction of his emotion.

It was wanderlust and nothing more, but it was an overwhelming wanderlust that rose to a passion and even to a delusion. His desire acquired vision, and his imagination, not yet calmed down from the morning's work, created its own version of the manifold marvels and terrors of the earth, all of them at once now seeking to take shape within him. He saw, saw a landscape, a tropical swamp under a vaporous sky, moist, luxuriant, and monstrous, a sort of primitive wilderness of islands, morasses, and alluvial estuaries; saw hairy palm trunks rise up near and far out of rank fern brakes, out of thick, swollen, wildly blooming vegetation; saw wondrously formless trees sink their aerial roots into the earth through stagnant, green-shadowed pools, where exotic birds, their shoulders high and their bills shaped weirdly, stood motionless in the shallows looking askance amidst floating flowers that were white as milk and big as platters; saw the eyes of a lurking tiger sparkle between the gnarled stems of a bamboo thicket; and felt his heart pound with horror and mysterious desire. Then the vision faded, and with a shake of his head Aschenbach resumed his promenade along the fences bordering the headstone-makers' yard.

He had regarded travel, at least since he had commanded the financial resources to enjoy the advantages of global transportation at will, as nothing more than a measure he had to take for his health, no matter how much it went against his inclination. Too much taken up with the tasks that his problematic self and the European soul posed for him, too burdened with the obligation of productivity, too averse to distraction to be a success as a lover of the world's motley show, he had quite contented himself with the view of the earth's surface anyone could get without stirring very far from home. He had never even been tempted to leave Europe. Especially now that his life was slowly waning, now that his artist's fear of never getting finished—his concern that the sands might run out of the glass before he had done his utmost and given his all—could no longer be dismissed as pure fancy, his external existence had confined itself almost exclusively to the lovely city that had become his home and to the rustic country house he had built in the mountains where he spent the rainy summers.

Besides, even this impulse that had come over him so suddenly and so late in life was quickly moderated and set right by reason and a self-discipline practiced since early youth. He had intended to keep at the work to which he now devoted his life until he reached a certain point and then move out to the country. The thought of sauntering about the world, of thereby being seduced away from months of work, seemed all too frivolous, too contrary to plan, and ultimately impermissible. And yet he knew all too well why this temptation had assailed him so unexpectedly. He had to admit it to himself: it was the urge to escape that was behind this yearning for the far away and the new, this desire for release, freedom, and forgetfulness. It was the urge to get away from his work, from the daily scene of an inflexible, cold, and passionate service. Of course he loved this service and almost loved the enervating struggle, renewed each day, between his stubborn, proud, so-often-tested will and his growing lassitude, about which no one could be allowed to know and which the product of his toil could not be permitted to reveal in any way, by any sign of failure or of negligence. Yet it seemed reasonable not to overbend the bow and not to stifle obstinately the outbreak of such a vital need. He thought about his work, thought about the place where once again, today as yesterday, he had been forced to abandon it, a passage that would submit, it seemed, neither to patient care nor to surprise attack. He considered it again, sought once more to break through or untangle the logjam, then broke off the effort with a shudder of repugnance. The passage presented no extraordinary difficulty; what disabled him was the malaise of scrupulousness confronting him in the guise of an insatiable perfectionism. Even as a young man, to be sure, he had considered perfectionism the basis and most intimate essence of his talent, and for its sake he had curbed and cooled his emotions, because he knew that emotion inclines one to satisfaction with a comfortable approximation, a half of perfection. Was his enslaved sensitivity now avenging itself by leaving him, refusing to advance his project and give wings to his art, taking with it all his joy, all his delight in form and expression? It was not that he was producing bad work—that at least was the advantage of his advanced years; he felt every moment comfortably secure in his mastery. But, though the nation honored it, he himself was not pleased with his mastery, and indeed it seemed to him that his work lacked those earmarks of a fiery, playful fancy that, stemming from joy, gave more joy to his appreciative audience than did any inner content or weighty excellence. He was fearful of the summer in the country, all alone in the little house with the maid who prepared his meals and the servant who waited on him at table, fearful too of the familiar mountaintops and mountainsides that once more would surround him in his discontented, slow progress. And so what he needed was a respite, a kind of spur-of-the-moment existence, a way to waste some time, foreign air and an infusion of new blood, to make the summer bearable and productive. Travel it would be then—it was all right with him. Not too far, though, not quite all the way to the tigers. One night in a sleeping car and a siesta for three or maybe four weeks in some fashionable vacation spot in the charming south . . .

Such were his thoughts as the noise of the electric tram approached along the Ungererstrasse, and he decided as he got on to devote this evening to studying maps and time tables. Once aboard it occurred to him to look around for the man in the straw hat, his comrade in this excursion that had been, in spite of all, so consequential. But he could get no clear idea of the man's whereabouts; neither his previous location, nor the next stop, nor the tram car itself revealed any signs of his presence.

CHAPTER 2

Gustav Aschenbach, the author of the clear and vigorous prose epic on the life of Frederick the Great;[2] the patient artist who wove together with enduring diligence the novelistic tapestry *Maia*,[3] a work rich in characters and eminently successful in gathering together many human destinies under the shadow of a single idea; the creator of that powerful story bearing the title "A Man of Misery," which had earned the gratitude of an entire young generation by showing it the possibility for a moral resolution that passed through and beyond the deepest knowledge; the author, finally (and this completes the short list of his mature works), of the passionate treatment of the topic "Art and Intellect,"[4] an essay whose power of organization and antithetical eloquence had prompted serious observers to rank it alongside Schiller's "On Naïve and Sentimental Poetry";[5] Gustav Aschenbach, then, was born the son of a career civil servant in the justice ministry in L., a district capital in the province of Silesia. His ancestors had been officers, judges, and government functionaries, men who had led upright lives of austere decency devoted to the service of king and country. A more ardent spirituality had expressed itself once among them in the person of a preacher; more impetuous and sensuous blood had entered the family line in the previous generation through the writer's mother, the daughter of a Bohemian music director. It was from her that he had in his features the traits of a foreign race. The marriage of sober conscientiousness devoted to service with darker, more fiery impulses engendered an artist and indeed this very special artist.

Since his entire being was bent on fame, he emerged early on as, perhaps not exactly precocious, but nonetheless, thanks to the decisiveness and peculiar terseness of his style, surprisingly mature and ready to go before the public. He was practically still in high school when he made a name for himself. Ten years later he learned how to keep up appearances, to manage his fame from his writing desk, to produce gracious and significant sentences for his necessarily brief letters (for many demands are made on such a successful and reliable man). By the age of forty, exhausted by the tortures and vicissitudes of his real work, he had to deal with a daily flood of mail bearing stamps from countries in every corner of the globe.

Tending neither to the banal nor to the eccentric, his talent was such as to win for his stories both the acceptance of the general public and an admiring, challenging interest from a more discerning audience. Thus he found himself even as a young man obliged in every way to achieve and indeed to achieve extraordinary things. He had therefore never known sloth, never known the carefree, laissez-faire attitude of youth. When he got sick in Vienna around the age of thirty-five, a canny observer remarked about him to friends, "You

2. King Frederick II (1712–1786) started Prussia on its rise to domination of Germany and made his court a prominent European cultural center.
3. In Hinduism, the illusory appearance of the world concealing a higher spiritual reality.
4. *Frederick, Maia, A Man of Misery*, and *Art and Intellect* are titles of projects Mann had worked on and abandoned.
5. An influential essay by the German Romantic writer Friedrich Schiller (1759–1805).

see, Aschenbach has always lived like this"—and the speaker closed the fingers of his left hand into a fist—"never like this"—and he let his open hand dangle comfortably from the arm of the chair. How right he was! And the morally courageous aspect of it was that, possessing anything but a naturally robust constitution, he was not so much born for constant exertion as he was called to it.

Medical concerns had prevented him from attending school as a child and compelled the employment of private instruction at home. He had grown up alone and without companions, and yet he must have realized early on that he belonged to a tribe in which talent was not so much a rarity as was the bodily frame talent needs to find its fulfillment, a tribe known for giving their best early in life but not for longevity. His watchword, however, was "Endure," and he saw in his novel about Frederick the Great precisely the apotheosis of this commandment, which seemed to him the essence of a selflessly active virtue. He harbored, moreover, a keen desire to live to a ripe old age, for he had long believed that an artistic career could be called truly great, encompassing, indeed truly worthy of honor only if the artist were allotted sufficient years to be fruitful in his own way at all stages of human life.

Since he thus bore the burdens of his talent on slender shoulders and wished to carry those burdens far, he was in great need of discipline. Fortunately for him discipline was his heritage at birth from his paternal side. At forty, at fifty, even at an age when others squander and stray, content to put their great plans aside for the time being, he started his day at an early hour by dousing his chest and back with cold water. Then, placing two tall wax candles in silver candlesticks at the head of his manuscript, he would spend two or three fervently conscientious morning hours sacrificing on the altar of art the powers he had assembled during his sleep. It was forgivable—indeed it even indicated the victory of his moral force—that uninformed readers mistook the Maia-world or the epic scroll on which unrolled Frederick's heroic life for the products of single sustained bursts of energy, whereas they actually grew into grandeur layer by layer, out of small daily doses of work and countless individual flashes of inspiration. These works were thoroughly excellent in every detail solely because their creator had endured for years under the pressure of a single project, bringing to bear a tenacity and perseverance similar to that which had conquered his home province,[6] and because he had devoted only his freshest and worthiest hours to actual composition.

If a work of the intellect is to have an immediate, broad, and deep effect, there must be a mysterious affinity, a correspondence between the personal fate of its originator and the more general fate of his contemporaries. People do not know why they accord fame to a particular work. Far from being experts, they suppose they see in it a hundred virtues that would justify their interest; but the real reason for their approval is something imponderable—it is sympathy. Aschenbach had actually stated forthrightly, though in a relatively inconspicuous passage, that nearly everyone achieving greatness did so under the banner of "Despite"—despite grief and suffering, despite poverty, destitution,

6. As a result of the Seven Years' War (1759–63), Frederick the Great wrested Silesia from Austria. Today, most of Silesia has become a region in southwestern Poland.

infirmity, affliction, passion, and a thousand obstacles. But this was more than an observation, it was the fruit of experience; no, it was the very formula for his life and his fame, the key to his work. Was it any wonder, then, that it was also the basis for the moral disposition and outward demeanor of his most original fictional characters?

Early on an observant critic had described the new type of hero that this writer preferred, a figure returning over and over again in manifold variation: it was based on the concept of "an intellectual and youthful manliness which grits its teeth in proud modesty and calmly endures the swords and spears as they pass through its body." It was a nice description, ingenious and precise, despite its seemingly excessive emphasis on passivity. For meeting one's fate with dignity, grace under pressure of pain, is not simply a matter of sufferance; it is an active achievement, a positive triumph, and the figure of St. Sebastian[7] is thus the most beautiful image, if not of art in general, then surely of the art under discussion here. Having looked at the characters in Aschenbach's narrated world, having seen the elegant self-discipline that managed right up to the last moment to hide from the eyes of the world the undermining process, the biological decline, taking place within; having seen the yellow, physically handicapped ugliness that nonetheless managed to kindle its smoldering ardor into a pure flame, managed even to catapult itself to mastery in the realm of beauty; or having seen the pale impotence that pulls out of the glowing depths of the spirit enough power to force a whole frivolous people to fall at the feet of the cross, at the feet of that very impotence; or the lovable charm that survives even the empty and rigorous service of pure form; or the false, dangerous life of the born deceiver, with the quick enervation of its longing and with its artfulness—having seen all these human destinies and many more besides, it was easy enough to doubt that there could be any other sort of heroism than that of weakness. In any case, what kind of heroism was more appropriate to the times than this? Gustav Aschenbach was the poet of all those who work on the edge of exhaustion, of the overburdened, worn down moralists of achievement who nonetheless still stand tall, those who, stunted in growth and short of means, use ecstatic feats of will and clever management to extract from themselves at least for a period of time the effects of greatness. Their names are legion, and they are the heroes of the age. And all of them recognized themselves in his work; they saw themselves justified, exalted, their praises sung. And they were grateful; they heralded his name.

He had been once as young and rough as the times and, seduced by them, had made public blunders and mistakes, had made himself vulnerable, had committed errors against tact and good sense in word and deed. But he had won the dignity toward which, in his opinion, every great talent feels an inborn urge and spur. One could say in fact that his entire development had been a conscious and defiant rise to dignity, beyond any twinge of doubt and of irony that might have stood in his way.

Pleasing the great mass of middle-class readers depends mainly on offering vividly depicted, intellectually undemanding characterizations, but passionately uncompromising youth is smitten only with what is problematic; and

7. A 3rd-century Roman martyr whose arrow-pierced body was a popular subject for Renaissance painters.

Aschenbach had been as problematic and uncompromising as any young man can be. He had pandered to the intellect, exhausted the soil of knowledge, milled flour from his seed corn, revealed secrets, put talent under suspicion, betrayed art. Indeed, while his portrayals entertained, elevated, invigorated the blissfully credulous among his readers, as a youthful artist it was his cynical observations on the questionable nature of art and of the artist's calling that had kept the twenty-year-old element fascinated.

But it seems that nothing so quickly or so thoroughly blunts a high-minded and capable spirit as the sharp and bitter charm of knowledge; and it is certain that the melancholy, scrupulous thoroughness characteristic of the young seems shallow in comparison with the solemn decision of masterful maturity to disavow knowledge, to reject it, to move beyond it with head held high, to forestall the least possibility that it could cripple, dishearten, or dishonor his will, his capacity for action and feeling, or even his passion. How else could one interpret the famous story "A Man of Misery" save as an outbreak of disgust at the indecent psychologism then current? This disgust was embodied in the figure of that soft and foolish semi-villain who, out of weakness, viciousness, and moral impotence, buys a black-market destiny for himself by driving his wife into the arms of a beardless boy, who imagines profundity can justify committing the basest acts. The weight of the words with which the writer of that work reviled the vile announced a decisive turn away from all moral skepticism, from all sympathy with the abyss, a rejection of the laxity inherent in the supposedly compassionate maxim that to understand everything is to forgive everything. What was coming into play here—or rather, what was already in full swing—was that "miracle of ingenuousness reborn" about which there was explicit discussion, not without a certain mysterious emphasis, in one of the author's dialogues published only slightly later. Strange relationships! Was it an intellectual consequence of this "rebirth," of this new dignity and rigor, that just then readers began to notice an almost excessive increase in his sense of beauty, a noble purity, simplicity, and sense of proportion that henceforth gave his works such a palpable, one might say deliberately classical and masterful quality? But moral determination that goes beyond knowledge, beyond analytic and inhibiting perception—would that not also be a reduction, a moral simplification of the world and of the human soul and therefore also a growing potential for what is evil, forbidden, and morally unacceptable? And does form not have two faces? Is it not moral and amoral at the same time—moral insofar as form is the product and expression of discipline, but amoral and indeed immoral insofar as it harbors within itself by nature a certain moral indifference and indeed is essentially bent on forcing the moral realm to stoop under its proud and absolute scepter?

That is as may be. Since human development is human destiny, how could a life led in public, accompanied by the accolades and confidence of thousands, develop as does one led without the glory and the obligations of fame? Only those committed to eternal bohemianism would be bored and inclined to ridicule when a great talent emerges from its libertine chrysalis, accustoms itself to recognizing emphatically the dignity of the spirit, takes on the courtly airs of solitude, a solitude full of unassisted, defiantly independent suffering and struggle, and ultimately achieves power and honor in the public sphere. And how much playfulness, defiance, and indulgence there is in the way talent develops! A kind of official, educative element began in time to appear in Aschenbach's productions. His style in later years dispensed with the sheer audacity, the subtle and innovative shadings of his younger days, and moved toward the paradigmatic, the polished and traditional, the conservative and formal, even formulaic. Like Louis XIV[8]—as report would have it—the aging writer banished from his vocabulary every base expression. About this time it came to pass that the educational authorities began using selected passages from his works in their prescribed textbooks.[9] He seemed to sense the inner appropriateness of it, and he did not refuse when a German prince, newly ascended to the throne, bestowed on the author of *Frederick*, on his fiftieth birthday, a nonhereditary title.

Relatively early on, after a few years of moving about, a few tries at living here and there, he chose Munich as his permanent residence and lived there in bourgeois respectability such as comes to intellectuals sometimes, in exceptional cases. His marriage to a girl from a learned family, entered upon when still a young man, was terminated after only a short term of happiness by her death. A daughter, already married, remained to him. He never had a son.

Gustav Aschenbach was a man of slightly less than middle height, dark-haired and clean shaven. His head seemed a little too big for a body that was almost dainty. His hair, combed back, receding at the top, still very full at the temples, though quite gray, framed a high, furrowed, and almost embossed-looking brow. The gold frame of his rimless glasses cut into the bridge of his full, nobly curved nose. His mouth was large, sometimes relaxed and full, sometimes thin and tense; his cheeks were lean and hollow, and his well-proportioned chin was marked by a slight cleft. Important destinies seemed to have played themselves out on this long-suffering face, which he often held tilted somewhat to one side. And yet it was art alone, not a difficult and troubled life, that had taken over the task of chiseling these features. Behind this brow was born the scintillating repartee between Voltaire and King Frederick on the subject of war; these eyes, looking tiredly but piercingly through the glasses, had seen the bloody inferno of the field hospitals during the Seven Years' War.[1] Indeed, even on the personal level art provides an intensified version of life. Art offers a deeper happiness, but it consumes one more quickly. It engraves upon the faces of its servants the traces of imaginary, mental adventures and over the long term, even given an external existence of cloistered quietude, engenders in them a nervous sensitivity, an over-refinement, a weariness and an inquisitiveness such as are scarcely ever produced by a life full of extravagant passions and pleasures.

8. King of France (1638–1715), the "great monarch" of the French classical period.

9. I.e., he received national recognition in the highly centralized German educational system.

1. A global war (1756–63) fought in Europe, North America, and India between European powers. François-Marie Arouet de Voltaire (1694–1778), French writer and philosopher, was a guest at the court of Frederick the Great from 1750 until 1753, when he found it wise to leave after a disagreement.

CHAPTER 3

Several obligations of both a practical and a literary nature forced the eager traveler to remain in Munich for about two weeks after his walk in the park. Finally he gave instructions for his country house to be prepared for his moving in within a month's time and, on a day sometime between the middle and end of May, he took the night train to Trieste, where he remained only twenty-four hours and where he boarded the boat to Pola[2] on the morning of the next day.

What he sought was someplace foreign, someplace isolated, but someplace nonetheless easy to get to. He thus took up residence on an Adriatic island, a destination that had been highly spoken of in recent years and lay not far from the Istrian coast. It was populated by locals dressed in colorful rags who spoke in wildly exotic accents, and the landscape was graced by rugged cliffs on the coast facing the open sea. But the rain and oppressive air, the provincial, exclusively Austrian clientele at the hotel, and the lack of the peaceful, intimate relation with the sea that only a soft sandy beach can offer—these things irritated him, denied him a sense of having found the place he was looking for; he was troubled by a pressure within him pushing in a direction he could not quite grasp; he studied ship schedules, he sought about for something; and suddenly the surprising but obvious destination came to him. If you wanted to reach in a single night someplace incomparable, someplace as out of the ordinary as a fairy tale, where did you go? The answer was clear. What was he doing here? He had gone astray. It was over there that he had wanted to go all along. He did not hesitate a moment in remedying his error and gave notice of his departure. A week and a half after his arrival on the island a swift motorboat carried him and his baggage through the early morning mist across the water to the military port, where he landed only long enough to find the gangway leading him onto the damp deck of a ship that was already getting up steam for a trip to Venice.[3]

It was an aged vessel, long past its prime, sooty, and gloomy, sailing under the Italian flag. In a cavernous, artificially lit cabin in the ship's interior—to which Aschenbach had been conducted with smirking politeness by a hunchbacked, scruffy sailor the moment he embarked—sat a goateed man behind a desk. With his hat cocked over his brow and a cigarette butt hanging from the corner of his mouth, his facial features were reminiscent of an old time ringmaster. He took down the passengers' personal information and doled out tickets with the grimacing, easy demeanor of the professional. "To Venice!" He repeated Aschenbach's request, stretching his arm to dip his pen in the congealed remains at the bottom of his slightly tilted inkwell. "To Venice, first class! There, sir, you're all taken care of." He inscribed great letters like crane's feet on a piece of paper, poured blue sand out of a box onto them, poured it back into an earthenware bowl, folded the paper with his yellow, bony fingers, and resumed writing. "What a fine choice for your destination!" he babbled in the meantime. "Ah, Venice, a wonderful city! A city that is irresistible to

2. Trieste (in Italy) and Pola (or Pula, in Croatia) are major ports at the head of the Adriatic Sea. Until 1919 they were Austrian possessions.

3. An ancient city whose network of bridges and canals links 118 islands in the Gulf of Venice. The Republic of Venice was headed by a doge (duke) and was a cultural, commercial, and political center in Europe from the 14th century.

cultured people both for its history and for its modern charm!" The smooth swiftness of his movements and the empty chatter with which he accompanied them had an anesthetic and diversionary effect, as if he were concerned that the traveler should change his mind about his decision to go to Venice. He hastily took the money and dropped the change on the stained cloth covering the table with the practiced swiftness of a croupier.[4] "Enjoy yourself, sir!" he said with a theatrical bow. "It is an honor to be of service to you. . . . Next, please!" he cried with his arm raised, acting as if he were still doing a brisk business, though in fact there was no one else there to do business with. Aschenbach returned above deck.

With one arm resting on the rail, he observed the passengers on board and the idle crowd loitering on the pier to watch the ship depart. The second-class passengers, both men and women, crouched on the forward deck using boxes and bundles as seats. A group of young people, apparently employees of businesses in Pola, who had banded together in great excitement for an excursion to Italy, formed the social set of the first upper deck. They made no little fuss over themselves and their plans, chattered, laughed, and took complacent enjoyment in their own continual gesturing. Leaning over the railing they called out in fluent and mocking phrases to various friends going about their business, briefcases under their arms, along the dockside street below, while the latter in turn made mock-threatening gestures with their walking sticks at the celebrants above. One of the merrymakers, wearing a bright yellow, overly fashionable summer suit, red tie, and a panama hat with a cockily turned-up brim, outdid all the others in his screeching gaiety. But scarcely had Aschenbach gotten a closer look at him when he realized with something like horror that this youth was not genuine. He was old, no doubt about it. There were wrinkles around his eyes and mouth. The faint carmine of his cheeks was rouge; the brown hair beneath the colorfully banded hat was a wig; his neck was shrunken and sinewy; his clipped mustache and goatee were dyed; the full, yellowish set of teeth he exposed when he laughed was a cheap set of dentures; and his hands, bedecked with signet rings on both forefingers, were those of an old man. With a shudder Aschenbach watched him and his interaction with his friends. Did they not know, had they not noticed that he was old, that he had no right to wear their foppish and colorful clothes, had no right to pretend to be one of their own? They apparently tolerated him in their midst as a matter of course, out of habit, and treated him as an equal, answering in kind without reluctance when he teasingly poked one of them in the ribs. But how could this be? Aschenbach covered his brow with his hand and closed his eyes, which were feeling inflamed from not getting enough sleep. It seemed to him that things were starting to take a turn away from the ordinary, as if a dreamy estrangement, a bizarre distortion of the world were setting in and would spread if he did not put a stop to it by shading his eyes a bit and taking another look around him. Just at this moment he experienced a sensation of motion and, looking up with an unreasoning terror, realized that the heavy and gloomy hulk of the ship was slowly parting company with the stone pier. The engines ran alternately forward and reverse, and inch by inch the band of oily, iridescent water between the pier and the hull of the ship widened. After a set of

4. Attendant at a gambling table who handles bets and money.

cumbersome maneuvers the steamer managed to point its bowsprit toward the open sea. Aschenbach went over to the starboard side, where the hunchback had set up a deck chair for him and a steward dressed in a stained tailcoat offered him service.

The sky was gray and the wind was moist. The harbor and the island were left behind, and soon all sight of land vanished beyond the misty horizon. Flakes of coal soot saturated with moisture fell on the scrubbed, never drying deck. No more than an hour later a canvas canopy was put up, since it had started to rain.

Wrapped in his cloak, a book on his lap, the traveler rested, and the hours passed by unnoticed. It stopped raining; the linen canopy was removed. The horizon was unobstructed. Beneath the overcast dome of the sky the immense disk of the desolate sea stretched into the distance all around. But in empty, undivided space our sense of time fails us, and we lose ourselves in the immeasurable. Strange and shadowy figures—the old fop, the goat-beard from below deck—invaded Aschenbach's mind as he rested. They gestured obscurely and spoke the confused speech of dreams. He fell asleep.

At noon they called him to lunch down in the corridorlike dining hall onto which opened the doors of all the sleeping quarters and in which stood a long table. He dined at one end, while at the other the business employees from Pola, including the old fop, had been carousing since ten o'clock with the jolly captain. The meal was wretched and he soon got up. He felt an urgent need to get out, to look at the sky, to see if it might not be brightening over Venice.

It had never occurred to him that anything else could happen, for the city had always received him in shining glory. But the sky and the sea remained overcast and leaden. From time to time a misty rain fell, and he came to the realization that he would approach a very different Venice by sea than the one he had previously reached by land. He stood by the foremast, gazing into the distance, awaiting the sight of land. He remembered the melancholy, enthusiastic poet of long ago who had furnished his dreams with the domes and bell towers rising from these waters. He softly repeated to himself some of those verses in which the awe, joy, and sadness of a former time had taken stately shape[5] and, easily moved by sensations thus already formed, looked into his earnest and weary heart to see if some new enthusiasm or entanglement, some late adventure of feeling might be in store for him, the idle traveler.

Then the flat coastline emerged on the right; the sea became populated with fishing boats; the barrier island with its beach appeared. The steamer soon left the island behind to the left, slipping at reduced speed through the narrow harbor named after it.[6] They came to a full stop in the lagoon in view of rows of colorfully wretched dwellings and awaited the arrival of the launch belonging to the health service.

An hour passed before it appeared. One had arrived and yet had not arrived; there was no great hurry and yet one felt driven by impatience. The young people from Pola had come up on deck, apparently yielding to a patriotic attraction to the military trumpet calls resounding across the water from the

5. The lines are probably from *Sonnets on Venice* (1825) by the German classical poet August Graf Platen (1796–1835): "My eye left the high seas behind / as the temples of [the architect Andrea] Palladio rose from the waters."

6. Both the barrier island and the harbor are called Lido. The island is the site of a famous resort.

public garden. Full of excitement and Asti, they shouted cheers at the *bersaglieri*[7] conducting drills over there. It was disgusting, however, to see the state into which the made-up old coot's false fellowship with the young people had brought him. His aged brain had not been able to put up the same resistance to the wine as the younger and more vigorous heads, and he was wretchedly drunk. His vision blurred; a cigarette dangled from his shaking fingers; he stood swaying tipsily in place, pulled to and fro by intoxication, barely able to maintain his balance. Since he would have fallen over at the first step, he dared not move from the spot. Yet he maintained a woeful bravado, buttonholing everyone who came near; he stammered, blinked, giggled, raised his beringed, wrinkled forefinger in fatuous banter, and ran the tip of his tongue around the corners of his mouth in an obscenely suggestive manner. Aschenbach watched him from under a darkened brow and was once again seized by a feeling of giddiness, as if the world were displaying a slight but uncontrollable tendency to distort, to take on a bizarre and sneering aspect. It was a feeling, to be sure, that conditions prevented him from indulging, for just then the engine began anew its pounding, and the ship, interrupted so close to its destination, resumed its course through the canal of San Marco.[8]

Once more, then, it lay before him, that most astounding of landing places, that dazzling grouping of fantastic buildings that the republic presented to the awed gaze of approaching mariners: the airy splendor of the palace and the Bridge of Sighs; the pillars on the water's edge bearing the lion and the saint; the showy projecting flank of the fairy tale cathedral; the view toward the gate and the great clock.[9] It occurred to him as he raised his eyes that to arrive in Venice by land, at the railway station, was like entering a palace by a back door; that one ought not to approach this most improbable of cities save as he now did, by ship, over the high seas.

The engine stopped, gondolas swarmed about, the gangway was lowered, customs officials boarded and haughtily went about their duties; disembarkation could begin. Aschenbach let it be known that he desired a gondola to take him and his luggage over to the landing where he could get one of the little steamboats that ran between the city and the Lido; for it was his intention to take up residence by the sea. His wishes met with acquiescence; a call went down with his request to the water's surface where the gondoliers were quarreling with each other in dialect. He was still prevented from disembarking; his trunk presented problems; only with considerable difficulty could it be pulled and tugged down the ladderlike gangway. He therefore found himself unable for several moments to escape from the importunities of the ghastly old impostor, who, driven by some dark drunken impulse, was determined to bid elaborate farewell to the foreign traveler. "We wish you the happiest of stays," he bleated, bowing and scraping. "Keeping a fond memory of us! Au revoir, excusez, and bonjour,[1] your excellency!" He drooled, he batted his eyes, he licked

7. Elite Italian troops. "Asti": or asti spumante, a sweet, sparkling Italian wine.
8. Saint Mark's Canal, named for the patron saint of Venice.
9. A large clock tower built in the late 15th century. "Bridge of Sighs": condemned prisoners walked over this bridge when proceeding to prison from the ducal palace. "Pillars": one is surmounted by a statue of St. Theodore stepping on a crocodile; the second, by a winged lion, emblem of St. Mark. "Cathedral": the Church of St. Mark.
1. "Goodbye, excuse me, and good-day" (French).

the corners of his mouth, and the dyed goatee on his elderly chin bristled. "Our compliments," he babbled, two fingertips at his mouth, "our compliments to your beloved, your dearly beloved, your lovely beloved . . ." And suddenly his uppers fell out of his jaw onto his lower lip. Aschenbach took his chance to escape. "Your beloved, your sweet beloved . . ." He heard the cooing, hollow, obstructed sounds behind his back as he descended the gangway, clutching at the rope handrail as he went.

Who would not need to fight off a fleeting shiver, a secret aversion and anxiety, at the prospect of boarding a Venetian gondola for the first time or after a long absence? This strange conveyance, surviving unchanged since legendary times and painted the particular sort of black[2] ordinarily reserved for coffins, makes one think of silent, criminal adventures in a darkness full of splashing sounds; makes one think even more of death itself, of biers and gloomy funerals, and of that final, silent journey. And has anyone noticed that the seat of one of these boats, this armchair painted coffin-black and upholstered in dull black cloth, is one of the softest, most luxurious, most sleep-inducing seats in the world? Aschenbach certainly realized this as he sat down at the gondolier's feet, opposite his luggage lying in a copious pile in the bow. The oarsmen were still quarreling in a rough, incomprehensible language punctuated by threatening gestures. The peculiar quiet of this city of water, however, seemed to soften their voices, to disembody them, to disperse them over the sea. It was warm here in the harbor. Stroked by the mild breath of the sirocco,[3] leaning back into the cushions as the yielding element carried him, the traveler closed his eyes in the pleasure of indulging in an indolence both unaccustomed and sweet. The trip will be short, he thought; if only it could last forever! The gondola rocked softly, and he felt himself slip away from the crowded ship and the clamoring voices.

How quiet, ever more quiet it grew around him! Nothing could be heard but the splashing of the oar, the hollow slap of the waves against the gondola's prow, rising rigid and black above the water with its halberdlike beak—and then a third thing, a voice, a whisper. It was the murmur of the gondolier, who was talking to himself through his clenched teeth in fits and starts, emitting sounds that were squeezed out of him by the labor of his arms. Aschenbach looked up and realized with some astonishment that the lagoon was widening about him and that he was traveling in the direction of the open sea. It seemed, then, that he ought not to rest quite so peacefully but instead make sure his wishes were carried out.

"I told you to take me to the steamer landing," he said with a half turn toward the stern. The murmur ceased. He received no answer.

"I told you to take me to the steamer landing!" he repeated, turning around completely and looking up into the face of the gondolier, whose figure, perched on the high deck and silhouetted against the dun sky, towered behind him. The man had a disagreeable, indeed brutal-looking appearance; he wore a blue sailor suit belted with a yellow sash, and a shapeless straw hat that was beginning to come unraveled and was tilted rakishly on his head. His facial features and the blond, curly mustache under his short, turned-up nose marked him as

2. Legend explains the gondolas' traditional black through an ancient law forbidding ostentation.

3. A hot wind originating in the Sahara, which becomes humid as it picks up moisture over the Mediterranean.

clearly not of Italian stock. Although rather slender of build, so that one would not have thought him particularly well suited to his profession, he plied his oar with great energy, putting his whole body into every stroke. Several times he pulled his lips back with the strain, baring his white teeth. His reddish eyebrows puckered, he looked out over his passenger's head and replied in a decisive, almost curt tone of voice: "You are going to the Lido."

Aschenbach responded, "Indeed. But I took the gondola only to get over to San Marco. I want to use the vaporetto."[4]

"You cannot use the vaporetto, sir."

"And why not?"

"Because the vaporetto does not accept luggage."

He was right about that; Aschenbach remembered. He said nothing. But the gruff, presumptuous manner of the man, so unlike the normal way of treating foreigners in this country, was not to be endured. He said, "That is my business. Perhaps I intend to put my luggage in storage. You will kindly turn back."

There was silence. The oar splashed, the waves slapped dully against the bow. And the murmuring and whispering began anew: the gondolier was talking to himself through his clenched teeth.

What to do? Alone at sea with this strangely insubordinate, uncannily resolute person, the traveler saw no way to enforce his wishes. And anyway, if he could just avoid getting angry, what a lovely rest he could have! Had he not wished the trip could last longer, could last forever? The smartest thing to do was to let matters take their course; more important, it was also the most pleasant thing to do. A magic circle of indolence seemed to surround the place where he sat, this low armchair upholstered in black, so gently rocked by the rowing of the autocratic gondolier behind him. The idea that he might have fallen into the hands of a criminal rambled about dreamily in Aschenbach's mind, but it was incapable of rousing his thoughts to active resistance. More annoying was the possibility that all this was simply a device by which to extort money from him. A sense of duty or of pride, the memory, as it were, that one must prevent such things, induced him once more to pull himself together. He asked, "What do you want for the trip?"

And the gondolier, looking out over him, answered, "You will pay."

It was clear what reply was necessary here. Aschenbach said mechanically, "I will pay nothing, absolutely nothing, if you take me where I do not want to go."

"You want to go to the Lido."

"But not with you."

"I row you well."

True enough, thought Aschenbach, and relaxed. True enough, you row me well. Even if you are just after my money, even if you send me to the house of Aides[5] with a stroke of your oar from behind, you will have rowed me well.

But no such thing occurred. In fact, some company even happened by in the form of a boat filled with musicians, both men and women, who waylaid the

4. Little steamboat (Italian); used for public transport.

5. A Greek spelling of "Hades," the ruler of the world of the dead in Greek and Roman mythology. The newly dead entered the underworld by paying a coin to the boatman, Charon, who then ferried them across the river Styx.

gondola, sailing obtrusively right alongside. They sang to the accompaniment of guitars and mandolins and filled the quiet air over the lagoon with the strains of their mercenary tourist lyrics. Aschenbach threw some money in the hat they held out to him, whereupon they fell silent and sailed off. The murmur of the gondolier became perceptible once again as he talked to himself in fits and starts.

And so they arrived, bobbing in the wake of a steamer sailing back to the city. Two municipal officials walked up and down along the landing, their hands behind their backs and their faces turned to the lagoon. Aschenbach stepped from the gondola onto the dock assisted by one of those old men who seemed on hand, armed with a boathook, at every pier in Venice. Since he had no small coins with him, he crossed over to the hotel next to the steamer wharf to get change with which to pay the boatman an appropriate fee. His needs met in the lobby, he returned to find his baggage stowed on a cart on the dock. Gondola and gondolier had disappeared.

"He took off," said the old man with the boathook. "A bad man he was, sir, a man without a license. He's the only gondolier who doesn't have a license. The others telephoned over. He saw that we were on the lookout for him, so he took off."

Aschenbach shrugged his shoulders.

"You had a free ride, sir," the old man said, holding out his hat. Aschenbach threw some coins in it. He gave instructions that his luggage be taken to the Hotel des Bains[6] and then followed the cart along the boulevard of white blossoms, lined on both sides by taverns, shops, and boarding houses, that runs straight across the island to the beach.

He entered the spacious hotel from behind, from the garden terrace, and crossed the great lobby to reach the vestibule where the office was. Since he had a reservation, he was received with officious courtesy. A manager, a quiet, flatteringly polite little man with a black mustache and a French-style frock coat, accompanied him in the elevator to the third floor and showed him to his room. It was a pleasant place, furnished in cherry wood, decorated with highly fragrant flowers, and offering a view of the open sea through a set of tall windows. After the manager had withdrawn and while his luggage was being brought up and put in place in his room, he went up to one of the windows and looked out on the beach. It was nearly deserted in the afternoon lull, and the ocean, at high tide and bereft of sunshine, was sending long, low waves against the shore in a peaceful rhythm.

A lonely, quiet person has observations and experiences that are at once both more indistinct and more penetrating than those of one more gregarious; his thoughts are weightier, stranger, and never without a tinge of sadness. Images and perceptions that others might shrug off with a glance, a laugh, or a brief conversation occupy him unduly, become profound in his silence, become significant, become experience, adventure, emotion. Loneliness fosters that which is original, daringly and bewilderingly beautiful, poetic. But loneliness also fosters that which is perverse, incongruous, absurd, forbidden. Thus the events of the journey that brought him here—the ghastly old fop with his drivel about a beloved, the outlaw gondolier who was cheated of his reward—

6. Hotel of the Baths (French, literal trans.); a famous seaside hotel.

continued to trouble the traveler's mind. Though they did not appear contrary to reason, did not really give cause for second thoughts, the paradox was that they were nonetheless fundamentally and essentially odd, or so it seemed to him, and therefore troubling precisely because of this paradox. In the meantime his eyes greeted the sea, and he felt joy in knowing Venice to be in such comfortable proximity. He turned away at last, went to wash his face, gave some instructions to the maid with regard to completing arrangements to insure his comfort, and then put himself in the hands of the green-uniformed elevator operator, who took him down to the ground floor.

He took his tea on the terrace facing the sea, then went down to the shore and walked along the boardwalk for a good distance toward the Hotel Excelsior. When he got back it seemed about time to change for dinner. He did so slowly and precisely, the way he did everything, because he was used to working as he got dressed. Still, he found himself in the lobby a bit on the early side for dinner. There he found many of the hotel's guests gathered, unfamiliar with and affecting indifference to each other, sharing only the wait for the dinner bell. He picked up a newspaper from a table, sat down in a leather chair, and looked over the assembled company. It differed from that of his previous sojourn in a way that pleased him.

A broad horizon, tolerant and comprehensive, opened up before him. All the great languages of Europe melded together in subdued tones. Evening dress, the universal uniform of cultured society, provided a decorous external unity to the variety of humanity assembled here. There was the dry, long face of an American, a Russian extended family, English ladies, German children with French nannies. The Slavic component seemed to predominate. Polish was being spoken nearby.

It came from a group of adolescents and young adults gathered around a little wicker table under the supervision of a governess or companion. There were three young girls who looked to be fifteen to seventeen years old and a long-haired boy of maybe fourteen. Aschenbach noted with astonishment that the boy was perfectly beautiful. His face, pale and gracefully reserved, was framed by honey-colored curls. He had a straight nose and a lovely mouth and wore an expression of exquisite, divine solemnity. It was a face reminiscent of Greek statues from the noblest period of antiquity; it combined perfection of form with a unique personal charm that caused the onlooker to doubt ever having met with anything in nature or in art that could match its perfection. One could not help noticing, furthermore, that widely differing views on child-rearing had evidently directed the dress and general treatment of the siblings. The three girls, the eldest of whom was for all intents an adult, were got up in a way that was almost disfiguringly chaste and austere. Every grace of figure was suppressed and obscured by their uniformly habitlike half-length dresses, sober and slate-gray in color, tailored as if to be deliberately unflattering, relieved by no decoration save white, turned-down collars. Their smooth hair, combed tightly against their heads, made their faces appear nunnishly vacant and expressionless. It could only be a mother who was in charge here, one who never once considered applying to the boy the severity of upbringing that seemed required of her when it came to the girls. Softness and tenderness were the obvious conditions of the boy's existence. No one had yet been so bold as to take the scissors to his lovely hair, which curled about his brows, over his ears, and even further down the back of his neck—as it does on the statue of the "Boy Pulling a Thorn from his Foot."[7] His English sailor suit had puffy sleeves that narrowed at the cuff to embrace snugly the delicate wrists of his still childlike yet delicate hands. The suit made his slim figure seem somehow opulent and pampered with all its decoration, its bow, braidwork, and embroidery. He sat so that the observer saw him in profile. His feet were clad in black patent leather and arranged one in front of the other; one elbow was propped on the arm of his wicker chair with his cheek resting on his closed hand; his demeanor was one of careless refinement, quite without the almost submissive stiffness that seemed to be the norm for his sisters. Was he in poor health? Perhaps, for the skin of his face was white as ivory and stood out in sharp contrast to the darker gold of the surrounding curls. Or was he simply a coddled favorite, the object of a biased and capricious affection? Aschenbach was inclined to suppose the latter. There is inborn in every artistic disposition an indulgent and treacherous tendency to accept injustice when it produces beauty and to respond with complicity and even admiration when the aristocrats of this world get preferential treatment.

A waiter went about and announced in English that dinner was ready. Most of the company gradually disappeared through the glass door into the dining room. Latecomers passed by, arriving from the vestibule or from the elevators. Dinner was beginning to be served inside, but the young Poles still lingered by their wicker table. Aschenbach, comfortably seated in his deep armchair, his eyes captivated by the beautiful vision before him, waited with them.

The governess, a short, corpulent, rather unladylike woman with a red face, finally gave the sign to get up. With her brows raised she pushed back her chair and bowed as a tall lady, dressed in gray and white and richly bejeweled with pearls, entered the lobby. The demeanor of this woman was cool and measured; the arrangement of her lightly powdered hair and the cut of her clothes displayed the taste for simplicity favored by those who regard piety as an essential component of good breeding. She could have been the wife of a highly placed German official. Her jewelry was the only thing about her appearance that suggested fabulous luxury; it was priceless, consisting of earrings and a very long, triple strand of softly shimmering pearls, each as big as a cherry.

The boy and the girls had risen quickly. They bent to kiss their mother's hand while she, with a restrained smile on her well-preserved but slightly tired and rather pointy-nosed face, looked across the tops of their heads at the governess, to whom she directed a few words in French. Then she walked to the glass door. The young ones followed her, the girls in the order of their ages, behind them the governess, the boy last of all. For some reason he turned around before crossing the threshold. Since there was no one else left in the lobby, his strangely misty gray eyes met those of Aschenbach, who was sunk deep in contemplation of the departing group, his newspaper on his knees.

What he had seen was, to be sure, in none of its particulars remarkable. They did not go in to dinner before their mother; they had waited for her, greeted her respectfully when she came, and then observed perfectly normal manners going into the dining room. It was just that it had all happened so

7. A bronze Greco-Roman statue admired for the graceful pose and handsome appearance of the boy it depicts.

deliberately, with such a sense of discipline, responsibility, and self-respect, that Aschenbach felt strangely moved. He lingered a few moments more, then went along into the dining room himself. He was shown to his table, which, he noted with a brief twinge of regret, was very far away from that of the Polish family.

Tired but nonetheless mentally stimulated, he entertained himself during the tedious meal with abstract, even transcendent matters. He pondered the mysterious combination of regularity and individuality that is necessary to produce human beauty; proceeded then to the general problem of form and of art; and ultimately concluded that his thoughts and discoveries resembled those inspirations that come in dreams: they seem wonderful at the time, but in the sober light of day they show up as utterly shallow and useless. After dinner he spent some time smoking, sitting, and wandering about in the park, which was fragrant in the evening air. He went to bed early and passed the night in a sleep uninterruptedly deep but frequently enlivened by all sorts of dreams.

The next day the weather had gotten no better. There was a steady wind off the land. Under a pale overcast sky the sea lay in a dull calm, almost as if it had shriveled up, with a soberingly contracted horizon; it had receded so far from the beach that it uncovered several rows of long sandbars. When Aschenbach opened his window, he thought he could detect the stagnant smell of the lagoon.

He was beset by ill humor. He was already having thoughts of leaving. Once years ago, after several lovely weeks here in springtime, just such weather had been visited upon him and had made him feel so poorly that he had had to take flight from Venice like a fugitive. Was he not feeling once again the onset of the feverish listlessness he had felt then, the throbbing of his temples, the heaviness in his eyelids? To change his vacation spot yet again would be a nuisance; but if the wind did not shift soon, he simply could not remain here. He did not unpack everything, just in case. He ate at nine in the special breakfast room between the lobby and the dining room.

In this room prevailed the solemn stillness that great hotels aspire to. The waiters went about on tip-toe. The clink of the tea service and a half-whispered word were all one could hear. Aschenbach noticed the Polish girls and their governess at a table in the corner diagonally across from the door, two tables away. They sat very straight, their ash-blond hair newly smoothed down flat, their eyes red. They wore starched blue linen dresses with little white turned-down collars and cuffs, and they passed a jar of preserves to each other. They had almost finished their breakfast. The boy was not there.

Aschenbach smiled. Well, little Phaeacian, he thought. It seems you, and not they, have the privilege of sleeping to your heart's content. Suddenly cheered, he recited to himself the line:

"Changes of dress, warm baths, and downy beds."[8]

He ate his breakfast at a leisurely pace, received some mail that had been forwarded—delivered personally by the doorman, who entered the room with his braided hat in hand—and opened a few letters while he smoked a cigarette.

8. A reference to Homer's *Odyssey* 8.249. The Phaeacians were a peaceful, happy people who showed hospitality to the shipwrecked Odysseus.

Thus it happened that he was present for the entrance of the late sleeper they were waiting for over there in the corner.

He came through the glass door and traversed the silent room diagonally over to the table where his sisters sat. His carriage was extraordinarily graceful, not only in the way he held his torso but also in the way he moved his knees and set one white-shod foot in front of the other. He moved lightly, in a manner both gentle and proud, made more lovely still by the childlike bashfulness with which he twice lifted and lowered his eyelids as he went by, turning his face out toward the room. Smiling, he murmured a word in his soft, indistinct speech and took his place, showing his full profile to the observer. The latter was once more, and now especially, struck with amazement, indeed even alarm, at the truly godlike beauty possessed by this mortal child. Today the boy wore a lightweight sailor suit of blue and white striped cotton with a red silk bow on the chest, finished at the neck with a simple white upright collar. And above this collar, which did not even fit in very elegantly with the character of the costume, rose up that blossom, his face, a sight unforgettably charming. It was the face of Eros, with the yellowish glaze of Parian marble,[9] with delicate and serious brows, the temples and ears richly and rectangularly framed by soft, dusky curls.

Fine, very fine, thought Aschenbach with that professional, cool air of appraisal artists sometimes use to cover their delight, their enthusiasm when they encounter a masterpiece. He thought further: Really, if the sea and the sand were not waiting for me, I would stay here as long as you stay. With that, however, he departed, walking past the attentive employees through the lobby, down the terrace steps, and straight across the wooden walkway to the hotel's private beach. There he let a barefoot old man in linen pants, sailor shirt, and straw hat who managed affairs on the beach show him to his rented beach cabana and arrange a table and chair on its sandy, wooden platform. Then he made himself comfortable in his beach chair, which he had pulled through the pale yellow sand closer to the sea.

The beach scene, this view of a carefree society engaged in purely sensual enjoyment on the edge of the watery element, entertained and cheered him as it always did. The gray, smooth ocean was already full of wading children, swimmers, and colorful figures lying on the sandbars with their arms crossed behind their heads. Others were rowing about in little flat-bottomed boats painted red and blue, capsizing to gales of laughter. People sat on the platforms of the cabanas, arranged in a long neat row along the beach, as if they were little verandas. In front of them people played games, lounged lazily, visited and chatted, some dressed in elegant morning clothes and others enjoying the nakedness sanctioned by the bold and easy freedom of the place. Down on the moist, hard sand there were a few individuals strolling about in white beach robes or in loose, brightly colored bathing dresses. To the right some children had built an elaborate sand castle and bedecked it with little flags in the colors of every country. Vendors of mussels, cakes, and fruit knelt and spread their wares before them. On the left, a Russian family was encamped in front of one of the cabanas that were set at a right angle between the others and the sea, thus closing that end of the beach. The family included men with beards and

9. White marble from the island of Paros was especially prized by sculptors in antiquity. Eros was the Greek god of love.

huge teeth; languid women past their prime; a young lady from a Baltic country, sitting at an easel and painting the ocean to the accompaniment of cries of frustration; two affable, ugly children; and an old maid in a babushka, displaying the affectionately servile demeanor of a slave. They resided there in grateful enjoyment, called out endlessly the names of their unruly, giddy children, exchanged pleasantries at surprising length in their few words of Italian with the jocular old man from whom they bought candy, kissed each other on the cheeks, and cared not a whit for anyone who might witness their scene of shared humanity.

Well, then, I will stay, thought Aschenbach. Where could things be better? His hands folded in his lap, he let his eyes roam the ocean's distances, let his gaze slip out of focus, grow hazy, blur in the uniform distances, mistiness of empty space. He loved the sea from the depth of his being: first of all because a hardworking artist needs his rest from the demanding variety of phenomena he works with and longs to take refuge in the bosom of simplicity and enormity; and, second, because he harbors an affinity for the undivided, the immeasurable, the eternal, the void. It was a forbidden affinity, directly contrary to his calling, and seductive precisely for that reason. To rest in the arms of perfection is what all those who struggle for excellence long to do; and is the void not a form of perfection? But while he was thus dreaming away toward the depths of emptiness, the horizontal line of the sea's edge was crossed by a human figure. When he had retrieved his gaze from the boundless realms and refocused his eyes, he saw it was the lovely boy who, coming from the left, was passing before him across the sand. He went barefoot, ready to go in wading, his slim legs bare from the knees down. He walked slowly but with a light, proud step, as if he were used to going about without shoes, and looked around at the row of cabanas that closed the end of the beach. The Russian family was still there, gratefully leading its harmonious existence, but no sooner had he laid eyes on them than a storm cloud of angry contempt crossed his face. His brow darkened, his lips began to curl, and from one side of his mouth emerged a bitter grimace that gouged a furrow in his cheek. He frowned so deeply that his eyes seemed pressed inward and sunken, seemed to speak dark and evil volumes of hatred from their depths. He looked down at the ground, cast one more threatening glance backward, and then, shrugging his shoulders as if to discard something and get away from it, he left his enemies behind.

A sort of delicacy or fright, something like a mixture of respect and shame, caused Aschenbach to turn away as if he had not seen anything; for it is repugnant to a chance witness, if he is a serious person, to make use of his observations, even to himself. But Aschenbach felt cheered and shaken at the same time—that is, happiness overwhelmed him. This childish fanaticism directed against the most harmless, good-natured target imaginable put into a human perspective something that otherwise seemed divinely indeterminate. It transformed a precious creation of nature that had before been no more than a feast for the eyes into a worthy object of deeper sympathy. It endowed the figure of the youngster, who had already shone with significance because of his beauty, with an aura that allowed him to be taken seriously beyond his years.

Still turned away, Aschenbach listened to the boy's voice, his clear, somewhat weak voice, by means of which he was trying to hail from afar his playmates at work on the sand castle. They answered him, calling again and again his name or an affectionate variation on his name. Aschenbach listened with a certain curiosity, unable to distinguish anything more than two melodious syllables—something like Adgio or more frequently Adgiu, with a drawn-out *u* at the end of the cry. The sound made him glad, it seemed to him that its harmony suited its object, and he repeated it softly to himself as he turned back with satisfaction to his letters and papers.

With his small traveling briefcase on his knees, he took his fountain pen and began to attend to various matters of correspondence. But after a mere quarter of an hour he was feeling regret that he should thus take leave in spirit and miss out on this, the most charming set of circumstances he knew of, for the sake of an activity he carried on with indifference. He cast his writing materials aside and turned his attention back to the sea; and not long after, distracted by the voices of the youngsters at the sand castle, he turned his head to the right and let it rest comfortably on the back of his chair, where he could once more observe the comings and goings of the exquisite Adgio.

His first glance found him; the red bow on his breast could not be missed. He was engaged with some others in setting up an old board as a bridge over the moat around the sand castle, calling out advice on proper procedure and nodding his head. There were about ten companions with him, boys and girls, most of an age with him but a few younger, chattering in a confusion of tongues—Polish, French, and even some Balkan languages. But it was his name that most often resounded through it all. He was evidently popular, sought after, admired. One companion, likewise a Pole, a sturdy boy called something like Yashu, who wore a belted linen suit and had black hair slicked down with pomade, seemed to be his closest friend and vassal. With the work on the sand castle finished for the time being, they went off together along the beach, arms about each other, and the one called Yashu gave his beautiful partner a kiss.

Aschenbach was tempted to shake his finger at him. "Let me give you a piece of advice, Kritobulos," he thought and smiled to himself. "Take a year's journey. You will need at least that much time for your recovery."[1] And then he breakfasted on large, fully ripe strawberries that he obtained from a peddler. It had gotten very warm, although the sun had not managed to pierce the layer of mist that covered the sky. Lassitude seized his spirit, while his senses enjoyed the enormous, lulling entertainment afforded by the quiet sea. The task of puzzling out what name it was that sounded like Adgio struck the serious man as a fitting, entirely satisfying occupation. With the help of a few Polish memories he determined that it was probably Tadzio he had heard, the nickname for Tadeusz. It was pronounced Tadziu in the form used for direct address.

Tadzio was taking a swim. Aschenbach, who had lost sight of him for a moment, spotted his head and then his arm, which rose as it stroked. He was very far out; the water apparently stayed shallow for a long way. But already his family seemed to be getting concerned about him, already women's voices were calling to him from the cabanas, shouting out once more this name that ruled over the beach almost like a watchword and that possessed something both sweet and wild in its soft consonants and drawnout cry of *uuu* at the end. "Tadziu! Tadziu!" He turned back; he ran through the sea with his head thrown

1. Recalling Socrates' advice to Kritoboulos when the latter kissed Alcibiades' handsome son (Xenophon's *Memorabilia* 1.3).

back, beating the resisting water into a foam with his legs. The sight of this lively adolescent figure, seductive and chaste, lovely as a tender young god, emerging from the depths of the sky and the sea with dripping locks and escaping the clutches of the elements—it all gave rise to mythic images. It was a sight belonging to poetic legends from the beginning of time that tell of the origins of form and of the birth of the gods. Aschenbach listened with his eyes closed to this mythic song reverberating within him, and once again he thought about how good it was here and how he wanted to stay.

Later on Tadzio lay on the sand, resting from his swim, wrapped in a white beach towel that was drawn up under his right shoulder, his head resting on his bare arm. Even when Aschenbach refrained from looking at him, instead reading a few pages in his book, he almost never forgot who was lying nearby or forgot that it would cost him only a slight turn of his head to the right to bring the adorable sight back into view. It almost seemed to him that he was sitting here with the express purpose of keeping watch over the resting boy. Busy as he might be with his own affairs, he maintained his vigilant care for the noble human figure not far away on his right. A paternal kindness, an emotional attachment filled and moved his heart, the attachment that someone who produces beauty at the cost of intellectual self-sacrifice feels toward someone who naturally possesses beauty.

After midday he left the beach, returned to the hotel, and took the elevator up to his room. There he spent a considerable length of time in front of the mirror looking at his gray hair and his severe, tired face. At the same time he thought about his fame and about the fact that many people recognized him on the street and looked at him with respect, all on account of those graceful, unerringly accurate words of his. He called the roll of the long list of successes his talent had brought him, as many as he could think of, and even recalled his elevation to the nobility. He then retired to the dining room for lunch and ate at his little table. As he was entering the elevator when the meal was over, a throng of young people likewise coming from lunch crowded him to the back of the swaying little chamber. Tadzio was among them. He stood very close by, so close in fact that for the first time Aschenbach had the opportunity to view him not from a distance like a picture but minutely, scrutinizing every detail of his human form. Someone was talking to the boy, and while he was answering with his indescribably sweet smile they reached the second floor, where he got off, backing out, his eyes cast down. Beauty breeds modesty, Aschenbach thought and gave urgent consideration as to why. He had had occasion to notice, however, that Tadzio's teeth were not a very pleasing sight. They were rather jagged and pale and had no luster of health but rather a peculiar brittle transparency such as one sometimes sees in anemics. He is very sensitive, he is sickly, thought Aschenbach. He will probably not live long. And he refrained from trying to account for the feeling of satisfaction and reassurance that accompanied this thought.

He passed a couple of hours in his room and in the afternoon took the vaporetto across the stagnant-smelling lagoon to Venice. He got off at San Marco, took tea in the piazza,[2] and then, following his habitual routine in Venice, set off on a walk through the streets. It was this walk, however, that initiated a complete reversal of his mood and his plans.

2. A famous public square in front of the church, lined by restaurants and cafés.

The air in the little streets was odiously oppressive, so thick that the smells surging out of the dwellings, shops, and restaurants, a suffocating vapor of oil, perfume, and more, all hung about and failed to disperse. Cigarette smoke hovered in place and only slowly disappeared. The press of people in the small spaces annoyed rather than entertained him as he walked. The longer he went on, the more it became a torture. He was overwhelmed by that horrible condition produced by the sea air in combination with the sirocco, a state of both nervousness and debility at once. He began to sweat uncomfortably. His eyes ceased to function, his breathing was labored, he felt feverish, the blood pounded in his head. He fled from the crowded shop-lined streets across bridges into the poor quarter. There beggars molested him, and the evil emanations from the canals hindered his breathing. In a quiet piazza, one of those forgotten, seemingly enchanted little places in the interior of the city, he rested on the edge of a well, dried his forehead, and reached the conclusion that he would have to leave Venice.

For the second time, and this time definitively, it became clear that this city in this weather was particularly harmful to his health. To remain stubbornly in place obviously went against all reason, and the prospect of a change in the direction of the wind was highly uncertain. A quick decision had to be made. To return home this soon was out of the question. Neither his summer nor his winter quarters were prepared for his arrival. But this was not the only place with beaches on the ocean, and those other places did not have the noxious extra of the lagoon and its fever-inducing vapors. He recalled a little beach resort not far from Trieste that had been enthusiastically recommended to him. Why not go there and, indeed, without delay, so that yet another change of location would still be worthwhile? He declared himself resolved and stood up. At the next gondola stop he boarded a boat to take him to San Marco through the dim labyrinth of canals, under graceful marble balconies flanked by stone lions, around corners of slippery masonry, past mournful palace facades affixed with business insignia[3] reflected in the garbage-strewn water. He had trouble getting to his destination, since the gondolier was in league with lace and glass factories and made constant efforts to induce him to stop at them to sightsee and buy; and so whenever the bizarre journey through Venice began to weave its magic, the mercenary lust for booty afflicting this sunken queen of cities[4] did what it could to bring the enchanted spirit back to unpleasant reality.

Upon returning to the hotel he did not even wait for dinner but went right to the office and declared that unforeseen circumstances compelled him to depart the next morning. With many expressions of regret the staff acknowledged the payment of his bill. He dined and then passed the mild evening reading magazines in a rocking chair on the rear terrace. Before going to bed he did all his packing for the morning's departure.

He did not sleep especially well, as the impending move made him restless. When he opened the windows the next morning the sky was still overcast, but the air seemed fresher and . . . he already started to have second thoughts. Had he been hasty or wrong to give notice thus? Was it a result of his sick and unreliable condition? If he had just put it off a bit, if he had just made an

3. Once-stately Renaissance homes that now house businesses.

4. A major sea power by the 15th century, Venice was called Queen of the Seas.

attempt to get used to the Venetian air or to hold out for an improvement in the weather instead of losing heart so quickly! Then, instead of this hustle and bustle, he would have a morning on the beach like the one yesterday to look forward to. Too late. Now he would have to go ahead with it, to wish today what he wished for yesterday. He got dressed and at eight o'clock took the elevator down to breakfast on the ground floor.

The breakfast room was still empty when he entered. A number of individual guests arrived while he sat waiting for his order. With his teacup at his lips he watched the Polish girls and their attendant come in. Severe and morning-fresh, eyes still red, they proceeded to their table in the corner by the window. Immediately thereafter the doorman approached him with hat in hand to tell him it was time to leave. The car was ready, he said, to take him and some other travelers to the Hotel Excelsior, and from there a motor boat would convey them through the company's private canal to the railroad station. Time was pressing, he said. Aschenbach found it not at all pressing. There was more than an hour until the departure of his train. He was annoyed at the habitual hotel practice of packing departing guests off earlier than necessary and informed the doorman that he wanted to finish his breakfast in peace. The man withdrew hesitatingly only to show up again five minutes later. The car simply could not wait longer, he said. Very well, let it go and take his trunks with it, Aschenbach replied with annoyance. As for himself, he preferred to take the public steamer at the proper time and asked that they let him take care of his own arrangements. The employee bowed. Aschenbach, happy to have fended off this nuisance, finished his meal without haste and even had the waiter bring him a newspaper. Time had become short indeed when at last he got up to leave. And it just so happened that at that very moment Tadzio came in through the glass door.

He crossed the path of the departing traveler on his way to his family's table. He lowered his eyes modestly before the gray-haired, high-browed gentleman, only to raise them again immediately in his own charming way, displaying their soft fullness to him. Then he was past. Adieu, Tadzio, thought Aschenbach. I saw you for such a short time. And enunciating his thought as it occurred to him, contrary to his every habit, he added under his breath the words: "Blessings on you." He then made his departure, dispensed tips, received a parting greeting from the quiet little manager in the French frock coat, and left the hotel on foot, as he had arrived. Followed by a servant with his hand luggage, he traversed the island along the boulevard, white with flowers, that led to the steamer landing. He arrived, he took his seat—and what followed was a journey of pain and sorrow through the uttermost depths of regret.

It was the familiar trip across the lagoon, past San Marco, up the Grand Canal. Aschenbach sat on the curved bench in the bow, his arm resting on the railing, his hand shading his eyes. They left the public gardens behind them; the Piazzetta once more revealed its princely splendor, and soon it too was left behind. Then came the great line of palaces, and as the waterway turned there appeared the magnificent marble arch of the Rialto.[5] The traveler looked, and his heart was torn. He breathed the atmosphere of the city, this slightly stagnant smell of sea and of swamp from which he had felt so strongly compelled to

5. A famous, highly arched bridge over the Grand Canal.

flee, breathed it now deeply, in tenderly painful draughts. Was it possible that he had not known, had not considered how desperately he was attached to all this? What this morning had been a partial regret, a slight doubt as to the rightness of his decision, now became affliction, genuine pain, a suffering in his soul so bitter that it brought tears to his eyes more than once. He told himself he could not possibly have foreseen such a reaction. What was so hard to take, actually sometimes down-right impossible to endure, was the thought that he would never see Venice again, that this was a parting forever. Since it had become evident for the second time that the city made him sick, since for the second time he had been forced to run head over heels away, he would have to regard it henceforth as an impossible destination, forbidden to him, something he simply was not up to, something it would be pointless for him to try for again. Yes, he felt that, should he go away now, shame and spite would certainly prevent him from ever seeing the beloved city again, now that it had twice forced him to admit physical defeat. This conflict between the inclination of his soul and the capacity of his body seemed to the aging traveler suddenly so weighty and so important, his physical defeat so ignominious, so much to be resisted at all cost, that he could no longer grasp the ease with which he had reached the decision yesterday, without serious struggle, to acquiesce.

Meanwhile, the steamer was approaching the railway station, and his pain and helplessness were rising to the level of total disorientation. His tortured mind found the thought of departure impossible, the thought of return no less so. In such a state of acute inner strife he entered the station. It was already very late, he had not a moment to lose if he was to catch his train. He wanted to, and he did not want to. But time was pressing, it goaded him onward; he made haste to obtain his ticket and looked about in the bustle of the station for the hotel employee stationed here. This person appeared and announced that the large trunk was already checked and on its way. Already on its way? Yes indeed—to Como.[6] To Como? After a frantic exchange, after angry questions and embarrassed answers, the fact emerged that the trunk had been put together with the baggage of other, unknown travelers in the luggage office at the Hotel Excelsior and sent off in precisely the wrong direction.

Aschenbach had difficulty maintaining the facial expression expected under such circumstances. An adventurous joy, an unbelievable cheerfulness seized his breast from within like a spasm. The hotel employee sped off to see if he could retrieve the trunk and returned, as one might have expected, with no success whatever. Only then did Aschenbach declare that he did not wish to travel without his luggage and that he had decided to return and await the recovery of the trunk at the Hotel des Bains. Was the company boat still here at the station? The man assured him it was waiting right at the door. With an impressive display of Italian cajolery he persuaded the agent to take back Aschenbach's ticket. He swore he would telegraph ahead, that no effort would be spared to get the trunk back with all due speed, and . . . thus came to pass something very odd indeed. The traveler, not twenty minutes after his arrival at the station, found himself once again on the Grand Canal on his way back to the Lido.

6. A large lake and resort area in northwest Italy.

What a wondrous, incredible, embarrassing, odd and dreamlike adventure! Thanks to a sudden reversal of destiny, he was to see once again, within the very hour, places that he had thought in deepest melancholy he was leaving forever. The speedy little vessel shot toward its destination, foam flying before its bow, maneuvering with droll agility between gondolas and steamers, while its single passenger hid beneath a mask of annoyed resignation the anxious excitement of a boy playing hooky. Still from time to time his frame was shaken with laughter over this mischance, which he told himself could not have worked out better for the luckiest person in the world. Explanations would have to be made, amazed faces confronted, but then—so he told himself—all would be well again, a great disaster averted, a terrible error made right, and everything he thought he had left behind would be open to him once more, would be his to enjoy at his leisure. . . . And by the way, was it just the rapid movement of the boat, or could it really be that he felt a strong breeze off the ocean to complete his bliss?

The waves slapped against the concrete walls of the narrow canal that cut through the island to the Hotel Excelsior. A motor bus was waiting there for the returning traveler and conveyed him alongside the curling waves down the straight road to the Hotel des Bains. The little manager with the mustache and the cutaway frock coat came down the broad flight of steps to meet him.

With quiet cajolery the manager expressed his regret over the incident, declared it extremely embarrassing for himself personally and for the establishment, but expressed his emphatic approval of Aschenbach's decision to wait here for the return of his luggage. To be sure, his room was already taken, but another, by no means worse, stood ready. "Pas de chance, monsieur,"[7] said the elevator man with a smile as they glided upwards. And so the fugitive was billeted once again, and in a room that matched almost exactly his previous one in orientation and furnishings.

Tired, numb from the whirl of this strange morning, he distributed the contents of his small suitcase in his room and then sank down in an armchair by the open window. The sea had taken on a light green coloration, the air seemed thinner and purer, the beach with its cabanas and boats seemed more colorful, although the sky was still gray. Aschenbach looked out, his hands folded in his lap, content to be here once more, but shaking his head in reproach at his own fickle mood, his lack of knowledge of his own desires. He sat thus for perhaps an hour, resting and thoughtlessly dreaming. At noon he spied Tadzio, dressed in his striped linen suit with red bow, returning from the shore through the beach barrier and along the wooden walkway to the hotel. Aschenbach recognized him at once from his high vantage point even before he got a good look at him, and he was just about to form a thought something like: Look, Tadzio, you too have returned! But at that very moment he felt the casual greeting collapse and fall silent before the truth of his heart. He felt the excitement in his blood, the joy and pain in his soul, and recognized that it was because of Tadzio that his departure had been so difficult.

He sat quite still, quite unseen in his elevated location and looked into himself. His features were active; his brows rose; an alert, curious, witty smile

7. "No luck, sir" (French).

crossed his lips. Then he raised his head and with both his arms, which were hanging limp over the arms of his chair, he made a slow circling and lifting movement that turned his palms forward, as if to signify an opening and extending of his embrace. It was a gesture of readiness, of welcome, and of relaxed acceptance.

CHAPTER 4

The god with fiery cheeks[8] now, naked, directed his horses, four-abreast, fire-breathing, day by day through the chambers of heaven, and his yellow curls fluttered along with the blast of the east wind. A silky-white sheen lay on the Pontos,[9] its broad stretches undulating languidly. The sands burned. Under the silvery shimmering blue of the ether there were rustcolored canvas awnings spread out in front of the beach cabanas, and one passed the morning hours in the sharply framed patch of shade they offered. But the evening was also delightful, when the plants in the park wafted balsamic perfumes, the stars above paced out their circuits, and the murmur of the nightshrouded sea, softly penetrating, cast a spell on the soul. Such an evening bore the joyful promise of another festive day of loosely ordered leisure, bejeweled with countless, thickly strewn possibilities of happy accidents.

The guest, whom accommodating mischance kept here, was far from disposed to see in the return of his belongings a reason to depart once more. He had been obliged to get along without a few things for a couple of days and to appear at meals in the great dining room wearing his traveling clothes. Then, when the errant baggage was finally set down once more in his room, he unpacked thoroughly and filled closets and drawers with his things, determined for the time being to stay indefinitely, happy to be able to pass the morning's hours on the beach in his silk suit and to present himself once more at his little table at dinner time wearing proper evening attire.

The benevolent regularity of this existence had at once drawn him into its power; the soft and splendid calm of this lifestyle had him quickly ensnared. What a fine place to stay, indeed, combining the charms of a refined southern beach resort with the cozy proximity of the wondrous, wonder-filled city! Aschenbach was no lover of pleasure. Whenever and wherever it seemed proper to celebrate, to take a rest, to take a few days off, he soon had to get back—it was especially so in his younger days—anxiously and reluctantly back to the affliction of his high calling, the sacred, sober service of his day-to-day life. This place alone enchanted him, relaxed his will, made him happy. Sometimes in the morning, under the canopy of his beach cabana, dreaming away across the blue of the southern sea, or sometimes as well on a balmy night, leaning back under the great starry sky on the cushions of a gondola taking him back home to the Lido from the Piazza San Marco, where he had tarried long—and the bright lights and the melting sounds of the serenade were left behind—he remembered his country home in the mountains, the site of his summertime struggles, where the clouds drifted through the garden, where in the evening fearful thunderstorms extinguished the lights in the house and the

8. Helios, Greek god of the sun (later equated with Apollo).

9. The sea (Greek, literal trans.); a figurative reference to the Adriatic Sea.

revens he fed soared to the tops of the spruce trees. Then it might seem to him that he had been transported to the land of Elysium[1] at the far ends of the earth, where a life of ease is bestowed upon mortals, where there is no snow, no winter, no storms or streaming rain, but rather always the cooling breath rising from Okeanos,[2] where the days run out in blissful leisure, trouble-free, struggle-free, dedicated only to the sun and its revels.

Aschenbach saw the boy Tadzio often, indeed almost continually; limited space and a regular schedule common to all the guests made it inevitable that the lovely boy was in his vicinity nearly all day, with brief interruptions. He saw, he met him everywhere: in the hotel's public places, on the cooling boat trips to the city and back, in the ostentation of the piazza itself; and often too in the streets and byways a chance encounter would take place. Chiefly, however, it was the mornings on the beach that offered him with delightful regularity an extended opportunity to study and worship the charming apparition. Yes, it was this narrow and constrained happiness, this regularly recurring good fortune that filled him with contentment and joy in life, that made his stay all the more dear to him and caused one sunny day after another to fall so agreeably in line.

He got up early, as he otherwise did under the relentless pressure of work, and was one of the first on the beach when the sun was still mild and the sea lay white in the glare of morning dreams. He gave a friendly greeting to the guard at the beach barrier, said a familiar hello to the barefoot old man who got his place ready, spreading the brown awning and arranging the cabana furniture on the platform, and settled in. Three hours or four were then his in which, as the sun rose to its zenith and grew fearsome in strength and the sea turned a deeper and deeper blue, he could watch Tadzio.

He would see him coming from the left along the edge of the sea, would see him from the back as he appeared from between the cabanas, or sometimes would suddenly discover, not without a happy shudder, that he had missed his arrival and that he was already there, already in the blue and white bathing suit that was now his only article of attire on the beach, that he was already up to his usual doings in sand and sun—his charmingly trivial, lazily irregular life that was both recreation and rest, filled with lounging, wading, digging, catching, resting, and swimming, watched over by the women on the platform who called to him, making his name resound with their high voices: "Tadziu! Tadziu!" He would come running to them gesturing excitedly and telling them what he had done, showing them what he had found or caught: mussels and sea horses, jelly fish, crabs that ran off going sideways. Aschenbach understood not a single word he said, and though it may have been the most ordinary thing in the world it was all a vague harmony to his ear. Thus, foreignness raised the boy's speech to the level of music, a wanton sun poured unstinting splendor over him, and the sublime perspectives of the sea always formed the background and aura that set off his appearance.

Soon the observer knew every line and pose of this noble body that displayed itself so freely; he exulted in greeting anew every beauty, familiar though it had

1. Located at the western edge of the earth, a pleasant otherworld for those heroes favored by the gods.

2. According to Greek mythology, a river encircling the world.

become, and his admiration, the discreet arousal of his senses, knew no end. They called the boy to pay his compliments to a guest who was attending the ladies at the cabana; he came running, still wet from the sea; he tossed his curls, and as he held out his hand he stood on one foot while holding the other up on tiptoe. His body was gracefully poised in the midst of a charming turning motion, while his face showed an embarrassed amiability, a desire to please that came from an aristocratic sense of duty. Sometimes he would lie stretched out with his beach towel wrapped about his chest, his delicately chiseled arm propped in the sand, his chin in the hollow of his hand. The one called Yashu sat crouching by him, playing up to him, and nothing could have been more enchanting than the smiling eyes and lips with which the object of this flattery looked upon his inferior, his vassal. Or he would stand at the edge of the sea, alone, separated from his friends, very near Aschenbach, erect, his hands clasped behind his neck, slowly rocking on the balls of his feet and dreaming off into the blue yonder, while little waves that rolled in bathed his toes. His honey-colored hair clung in circles to his temples and his neck; the sun made the down shine on his upper back; the subtle definition of the ribs and the symmetry of his chest stood out through the tight-fitting material covering his torso; his armpits were still as smooth as those of a statue, the hollows behind his knees shone likewise, and the blue veins showing through made his body seem to be made of translucent material. What discipline, what precision of thought was expressed in the stretch of this youthfully perfect body! But was not the rigorous and pure will that had been darkly active in bringing this divine form into the clear light of day entirely familiar to the artist in him? Was this same will not active in him, too, when he, full of sober passion, freed a slender form from the marble mass of language,[3] a form he had seen with his spiritual eye and that he presented to mortal men as image and mirror of spiritual beauty?

Image and mirror! His eyes embraced the noble figure there on the edge of the blue, and in a transport of delight he thought his gaze was grasping beauty itself, the pure form of divine thought, the universal and pure perfection that lives in the spirit and which here, graceful and lovely, presented itself for worship in the form of a human likeness and exemplar. Such was his intoxication; the aging artist welcomed the experience without reluctance, even greedily. His intellect was in labor, his educated mind set in motion. His memory dredged up ancient images passed on to him in the days of his youth, thoughts not until now touched by the spark of his personal involvement. Was it not written that the sun turns our attention from intellectual to sensuous matters?[4] It was said that the sun numbs and enchants our reason and memory to such an extent that the soul in its pleasure forgets its ordinary condition; its amazed admiration remains fixed on the loveliest of sun-drenched objects. Indeed, only with the help of a body can the soul rise to the contemplation of still higher things. Amor[5] truly did as mathematicians have always done by assisting slow-learning children with concrete pictures of pure forms: so, too, did the god like

3. The Italian artist Michelangelo Buonarroti (1475–1564) explained that he created his statues by carving away the marble block until the figure within was set free.

4. In section 764E of the *Erotikos* (Dialogue on love) by the Greek essayist Plutarch (46–120 C.E.).

5. The god of love (Latin).

to make use of the figure and coloration of human youth in order to make the spiritual visible to us, furnishing it with the reflected glory of beauty and thus making of it a tool of memory, so that seeing it we might then be set aflame with pain and hope.

Those, at any rate, were the thoughts of the impassioned onlooker. He was capable of sustaining just such a high pitch of emotion. He spun himself a charming tapestry out of the roar of the sea and the glare of the sun. He saw the ancient plane tree not far from the walls of Athens,[6] that sacred, shadowy place filled with the scent of willow blossoms, decorated with holy images and votive offerings in honor of the nymphs and of Achelous.[7] The stream flowed in crystal clarity over smooth pebbles past the foot of the wide-branched tree. The crickets sang. Two figures reclined on the grass that gently sloped so that you could lie with your head held up; they were sheltered here from the heat of the day—an older man and a younger, one ugly and one handsome, wisdom at the side of charm. Amidst polite banter and wooing wit Socrates taught Phaedrus about longing and virtue. He spoke to him of the searing terror that the sensitive man experiences when his eye lights on an image of eternal beauty; spoke to him of the appetites of the impious, bad man who cannot conceive of beauty when he sees beauty's image and is incapable of reverence; spoke of the holy fear that overcomes a noble heart when a godlike face or a perfect body appears before him—how he then trembles and is beside himself and scarcely dares turn his eyes upon the sight and honors him who has beauty, indeed would even sacrifice to him as to a holy image, if he did not fear looking foolish in the eyes of others. For beauty, my dear Phaedrus, beauty alone is both worthy of love and visible at the same time; beauty, mark me well, is the only form of spirit that our senses can both grasp and endure. For what should become of us if divinity itself, or reason and virtue and truth were to appear directly to our senses? Would we not be overcome and consumed in the flames of love, as Semele[8] was at the sight of Zeus? Thus beauty is the sensitive man's way to the spirit—just the way, just the means, little Phaedrus. . . . And then he said the subtlest thing of all, crafty wooer that he was: he said that the lover was more divine than the beloved, because the god was in the former and not in the latter—perhaps the tenderest, most mocking thought that ever was thought, a thought alive with all the guile and the most secret bliss of love's longing.

A writer's chief joy is that thought can become all feeling, that feeling can become all thought. The lonely author possessed and commanded at this moment just such a vibrant thought, such a precise feeling: namely, that nature herself would shiver with delight were intellect to bow in homage before beauty. He suddenly wanted to write. They say, to be sure, that Eros loves idleness; the god was made to engage in no other activity. But at this moment of crisis the excitement of the love-struck traveler drove him to productivity, and the occasion was almost a matter of indifference. The intellectual world had

6. A reference to the scene and some of the arguments in Plato's dialogue *Phaedrus*. Plato's school, or Academy, was located in a grove of plane trees outside Athens; in the dialogue, the young student Phaedrus tells Socrates of Lysias's speech on love, and Socrates responds with two speeches of his own.

7. A brook or small river in ancient Athens, here personified as a god.

8. The mortal mother of Zeus's son Dionysus. She perished in flames when the king of the gods appeared (at her request) in his divine glory.

been challenged to profess its views on a certain great and burning problem of culture and of taste, and the challenge had reached him. The problem was well known to him, was part of his experience; the desire to illuminate it with the splendor of his eloquence was suddenly irresistible. And what is more, he wanted to work here in the presence of Tadzio, to use the boy's physical frame as the model for his writing, to let his style follow the lines of that body that seemed to him divine, to carry his beauty into the realm of intellect as once the eagle carried the Trojan shepherd into the ethereal heavens.[9] Never had his pleasure in the word seemed sweeter to him, never had he known so surely that Eros dwelt in the word as now in the dangerous and delightful hours he spent at his rough table under the awning. There with his idol's image in full view, the music of his voice resounding in his ear, he formed his little essay after the image of Tadzio's beauty—composed that page-and-a-half of choice prose that soon would amaze many a reader with its purity, nobility, and surging depth of feeling. It is surely for the best that the world knows only the lovely work and not also its origins, not the conditions under which it came into being; for knowledge of the origins from which flowed the artist's inspiration would surely often confuse the world, repel it, and thus vitiate the effects of excellence. Strange hours! Strangely enervating effort! Strangely fertile intercourse between a mind and a body! When Aschenbach folded up his work and left the beach, he felt exhausted, even unhinged, as if his conscience were indicting him after a debauch.

The next morning as he was about to leave the hotel he chanced to notice from the steps that Tadzio was already on his way to the shore, alone; he was just approaching the beach barrier. He felt first a suggestion, then a compulsion: the wish, the simple thought that he might make use of the opportunity to strike up a casual, cheerful acquaintanceship with this boy who unwittingly had caused such a stir in his mind and heart, speak with him and enjoy his answer and his gaze. The lovely lad sauntered along; he could be easily caught up with; Aschenbach quickened his steps. He reached him on the walkway behind the cabanas, was about to put his hand on his head or on his shoulder, was about to let some word pass his lips, some friendly French phrase. But then he felt his heart beating like a hammer, perhaps only because of his rapid walk, so that he was short of breath and could only have spoken in a trembling gasp. He hesitated, tried to master himself, then suddenly feared he had been walking too long right behind the handsome boy, feared he might notice, might turn around with an inquiring look. He took one more run at him, but then he gave up, renounced his goal, and hung his head as he went by.

Too late! he thought at that moment. Too late! But was it really too late? This step he had failed to take might very possibly have led to something good, to something easy and happy, to a salutary return to reality. But it may have been that the aging traveler did not wish to return to reality, that he was too much in love with his own intoxication. Who can untangle the riddle of the artist's essence and character? Who can understand the deep instinctive fusion of discipline and a desire for licentiousness upon which that character is

9. The young Trojan prince Ganymede was tending flocks when Zeus, in the form of an eagle, carried him off to Olympus where he became Zeus's lover and the cupbearer to the gods.

based? For it is licentiousness to be unable to wish for a salutary return to reality. Aschenbach was no longer inclined to self-criticism. The taste, the intellectual constitution that came with his years, his self-esteem, maturity, and the simplicity of age made him disinclined to analyze the grounds for his behavior or to decide whether it was conscience or debauchery and weakness that caused him not to carry out his plan. He was confused; he feared that someone, if only the custodian on the beach, might have observed his accelerated gait and his defeat; he feared very much looking foolish. And all the while he made fun of himself, of his comically solemn anxiety. "We've been quite confounded," he thought, "and now we're as crestfallen as a gamecock that lets its wings droop during a fight.[1] It must surely be the god himself who thus destroys our courage at the very sight of loveliness, who crushes our proud spirit so deeply in the dust. . . ." His thoughts roamed playfully: he was far too arrogant to be fearful of a mere emotion.

He had already ceased to pay much attention to the extent of time he was allowing himself for his holiday; the thought of returning home did not even cross his mind. He had an ample amount of money sent to him by mail. His sole source of concern was the possible departure of the Polish family, but he had privately obtained information, thanks to casual inquiries at the hotel barber shop, that the Polish party had arrived only very shortly before he did. The sun tanned his face and hands, the bracing salt air stimulated his emotions. Just as he ordinarily used up all the resources he gathered from sleep, nourishment, or nature on literary work, so now he expended each contribution that sun, leisure, and sea air made to his daily increase in strength in a generous, extravagant burst of enthusiasm and sentiment.

He slept fitfully; the exquisitely uniform days were separated by short nights full of happy restlessness. To be sure he retired early, for at nine o'clock, when Tadzio had left the scene, the day was over as far as he was concerned. At the first glimmer of dawn, however, a softly penetrating pang of alarm awakened him, as his heart remembered its great adventure. No longer able to endure the pillow, he arose, wrapped himself in a light robe against the morning chill, and positioned himself at the open window to await the sunrise. This wonderful occurrence filled his sleep-blessed soul with reverence. Heaven, earth, and sea still lay in the ghostly, glassy pallor of dawn; a fading star still floated in the insubstantial distance. Then a breath of wind arose, a winged message from unapproachable abodes announcing that Eos was arising from the side of her spouse. There became visible on the furthest boundary between sea and sky that first sweet blush of red that reveals creation assuming perceptible form. The goddess was approaching, she who seduced young men, she who had stolen Kleitos and Kephalos and enjoyed the love of handsome Orion in defiance of all the envious Olympians.[2] A strewing of roses began there on the edge of the world, where all shone and blossomed in unspeakable purity. Childlike clouds, transfigured and luminous, hovered like attending Cupids in the rosy bluish fragrance. Purple light fell on the sea, then washed forward in waves.

1. From the Greek tragedian Phrynichus (512–476 B.C.E.), quoted in Plutarch's *Erotikos* (762E).
2. Eos, the Greek goddess of dawn, was known for seducing handsome young men, including Kleitos and Kephalos. When she took the hunter Orion for her lover, Artemis, the jealous goddess of the hunt, killed him with her arrows.

Golden spears shot up from below to the heights of the heavens, and the brilliance began to burn. Silently, with divine ascendancy, glow and heat and blazing flames spun upwards, as the brother-god's sacred chargers, hooves beating, mounted the heavens. The lonely, wakeful watcher sat bathed in the splendor of the god's rays; he closed his eyes and let the glory kiss his eyelids. With a confused, wondering smile on his lips he recognized feelings from long ago, early, exquisite afflictions of the heart that had withered in the severe service that his life had become and now returned so strangely transformed. He meditated, he dreamed. Slowly his lips formed a name, and still smiling, his face turned upward, his hands folded in his lap, he fell asleep once more in his armchair.

The whole day that had thus began in fiery celebration was strangely heightened and mythically transformed. Where did that breath of air come from, the one that suddenly played about his temples and ears so softly and significantly like a whisper from a higher realm? White feathery clouds stood in scattered flocks in the heavens like grazing herds that the gods tend. A stronger wind blew up; Poseidon's[3] steeds reared and ran, and the bulls obedient to the god with the blue-green locks lowered their horns and bellowed as they charged. But amid the boulders on the distant beach the waves hopped up like leaping goats. A magical world, sacred and animated by the spirit of Pan,[4] surrounded the beguiled traveler, and his heart dreamed tender fables. Often, as the sun set behind Venice, he would sit on a bench in the park to watch Tadzio, dressed in white with a colorful sash, delight in playing ball on the smooth, rolled gravel; and it was as if he were watching Hyacinthos, who had to die because two gods loved him.[5] Indeed he felt the painful envy Zephyros felt toward his rival in love, the god who abandoned his oracle, his bow, and his cithara to spend all his time playing with the beautiful boy. He saw the discus, directed by cruel jealousy, strike the lovely head; he too, turned pale as he received the stricken body; and the flower that sprang from that sweet blood bore the inscription of his unending lament. . . .

There is nothing stranger or more precarious than the relationship between people who know each other only by sight, who meet and watch each other every day, even every hour, yet are compelled by convention or their own whim to maintain the appearance of indifference and unfamiliarity, to avoid any word or greeting. There arises between them a certain restlessness and frustrated curiosity, the hysteria of an unsatisfied, unnaturally suppressed urge for acquaintanceship and mutual exchange, and in point of fact also a kind of tense respect. For people tend to love and honor other people so long as they are not in a position to pass judgment on them; and longing is the result of insufficient knowledge.

Some sort of relationship or acquaintance necessarily had to develop between Aschenbach and the young Tadzio, and with a pang of joy the older man was

3. God of the sea and brother of Zeus in Greek mythology, associated with the horse and the bull.

4. A Greek demigod, half man and half goat, associated with fertility and sexuality.

5. Apollo and Zephyr, god of the west wind, both loved the youth Hyacinthos. When Apollo accidentally killed him in a discus game—Zephyr blew the discus off course—a flower marked with the Greek syllables "ai ai" ("alas!") sprang from the boy's blood. Apollo is an archer and musician as well as the god of the Delphic oracle.

able to ascertain that his involvement and attentions were not altogether unrequited. For example, what impelled the lovely boy no longer to use the boardwalk behind the cabanas when he appeared on the beach in the morning but instead to saunter by toward his family's cabana on the front path, through the sand, past Aschenbach's customary spot, sometimes unnecessarily close by him, almost touching his table, his chair? Did Aschenbach's superior emotional energy exercise such an attraction, such a fascination on the tender, unreflecting object of those emotions? The writer waited daily for Tadzio's appearance; sometimes he would act as if he were busy when this event took place and let the lovely one pass by without seeming to notice. Sometimes, though, he would look up, and their eyes would meet. Both of them were gravely serious when it happened. In the refined and respectable bearing of the older man nothing betrayed his inner tumult; but in Tadzio's eyes there was the hint of an inquiry, of a thoughtful question. A hesitation became visible in his gait, he looked at the ground, he looked up again in his charming way, and when he was past there seemed to be something in his demeanor saying that only his good breeding prevented him from turning around.

One evening, however, something quite different happened. The Polish children and their governess were missing at the main meal in the large dining room. Aschenbach had taken note of it with alarm. Concerned about their absence, he was strolling in front of the hotel at the bottom of the terrace after dinner, dressed in his evening clothes and a straw hat, when he suddenly saw appear in the light of the arc lamps the nunlike sisters and their attendant, with Tadzio four steps behind. They were apparently returning from the steamer landing after having taken their meal for some reason in the city. It must have been cool on the water: Tadzio wore a dark blue sailor's coat with gold buttons and a sailor's hat to go with it. The sun and sea air had not browned him. His skin was the same marble-like yellow color it had been from the beginning. But today he seemed paler than usual, whether because of the cool temperature or because of the pallid moonglow cast by the lamps. His even brows showed in starker contrast, his eyes darkened to an even deeper tone. He was more beautiful than words could ever tell, and Aschenbach felt as he often had before the painful truth that words are capable only of praising physical beauty, not of rendering it visible.

He had not been expecting the exquisite apparition: it had come on unhoped for. He had not had time to fortify himself in a peaceful, respectable demeanor. Joy, surprise, and admiration might have been clearly displayed in the gaze that met that of the one he had so missed—and in that very second, it came to pass that Tadzio smiled. He smiled at Aschenbach, smiled eloquently, intimately, charmingly, and without disguise, with lips that began to open only as he smiled. It was the smile of Narcissus[6] leaning over the mirroring water, that deep, beguiled, unresisting smile that comes as he extends his arm toward the reflection of his own beauty—a very slightly distorted smile, distorted by the

6. A beautiful Greek youth who fell in love with his own image in a pool and drowned trying to reach it. "Tadzio's smile is Narcissus', who sees his own reflection—he sees it in the face of another / he sees his beauty in its effects. Coquettishness and tenderness are also in this smile" [Mann's note].

hopelessness of his desire to kiss the lovely lips of his shadow—a coquettish smile, curious and faintly pained, infatuated and infatuating.

He who had been the recipient of this smile rushed away with it as if it were a gift heavy with destiny. He was so thoroughly shaken that he was forced to flee the light of the terrace and the front garden and to seek with a hasty tread the darkness of the park in the rear. Strangely indignant and tender exhortations broke forth from him: "You must not smile so! Listen, no one is allowed to smile that way at anyone!" He threw himself on a bench; he breathed in the nocturnal fragrance of the plants, beside himself. Leaning back with his arms hanging at his sides, overpowered and shivering uncontrollably, he whispered the eternal formula of longing—impossible under these conditions, absurd, reviled, ridiculous, and yet holy and venerable even under these conditions—"I love you!"

CHAPTER 5

In the fourth week of his stay on the Lido Gustav Aschenbach made a number of disturbing discoveries regarding events in the outside world. In the first place it seemed to him that as the season progressed toward its height the number of guests at the hotel declined rather than increased. In particular it seemed that the German language ceased to be heard around him: lately his ear could detect only foreign sounds in the dining room and on the beach. He had taken to visiting the barbershop frequently, and in a conversation there one day he heard something that startled him. The barber had mentioned a German family that had just left after staying only a short time; then he added by way of flattering small talk, "But you're staying, sir, aren't you. You're not afraid of the disease." Aschenbach looked at him. "The disease?" he repeated. The man broke off his chatter, acted busy, ignored the question. When Aschenbach pressed the issue, he explained that he knew nothing and tried to change the subject with a stream of embarrassed eloquence.

That was at noon. In the afternoon Aschenbach sailed across to Venice in a dead calm and under a burning sun. He was driven by his mania to pursue the Polish children, whom he had seen making for the steamer landing along with their attendant. He did not find his idol at San Marco. But at tea, sitting at his round wrought-iron table on the shady side of the piazza, he suddenly smelled a peculiar aroma in the air, one that he now felt had been lurking at the edge of his consciousness for several days without his becoming fully aware of it. It was a medicinally sweet smell that put in mind thoughts of misery and wounds and ominous cleanliness. After a few moments' reflection he recognized it; then he finished his snack and left the piazza on the side opposite the cathedral. The odor became stronger in the narrow streets. At the street corners there were affixed printed posters in which the city fathers warned the population about certain illnesses of the gastric system that could be expected under these atmospheric conditions, advising that they should not eat oysters and mussels or use the water in the canals. The euphemistic nature of the announcement was obvious. Groups of local people stood together silently on the bridges and in the piazzas, and the foreign traveler stood among them, sniffing and musing.

There was a shopkeeper leaning in the doorway of his little vaulted quarters among coral necklaces and imitation amethyst trinkets, and Aschenbach asked him for some information about the ominous odor. The man took his measure with a heavy-lidded stare and then hastily put on a cheerful expression. "A precautionary measure, sir," he answered with many a gesture. "A police regulation that we must accept. The weather is oppressive, the sirocco is not conductive to good health. In short, you understand—perhaps they're being too careful. . . ." Aschenbach thanked him and went on. Even on the steamer that took him back to the Lido he could now detect the odor of disinfectant.

Once back at the hotel he went directly to the lobby to have a look at the newspapers. In the ones in foreign languages he found nothing. The German papers mentioned rumors, cited highly varying figures, quoted official denials, and offered doubts about their veracity. This explained the departure of the German and Austrian element. The citizens of other nations apparently knew nothing, suspected nothing, and were not yet concerned. "Best to keep quiet," thought Aschenbach anxiously, as he threw the papers back on the table. "Best to keep it under wraps." But at the same time his heart filled with a feeling of satisfaction over this adventure in which the outside world was becoming involved. For passion, like crime, does not sit well with the sure order and even course of everyday life; it welcomes every loosening of the social fabric, every confusion and affliction visited upon the world, for passion sees in such disorder a vague hope of finding an advantage for itself. Thus Aschenbach felt a dark satisfaction over the official cover-up of events in the dirty alleys of Venice. This heinous secret belonging to the city fused and became one with his own innermost secret, which he was likewise intent upon keeping. For the lovesick traveler had no concern other than that Tadzio might depart, and he recognized, not without a certain horror, that he would not know how to go on living were that to happen.

Recently he had not contented himself with allowing chance and the daily routine to determine his opportunities to see and be near the lovely lad; he pursued him, he lay in wait for him. On Sundays, for example, the Polish family never went to the beach. He guessed that they went to mass at San Marco. He followed speedily, entered the golden twilight of the sanctuary from the heat of the piazza, and found him, the one he had missed so, bent over a prie-dieu[7] taking part in the holy service. He stood in the background on the fissured mosaic floor, in the midst of a kneeling, murmuring crowd of people who kept crossing themselves, and felt the condensed grandeur of the oriental temple weigh voluptuously on his senses. Up in front the priest moved about, conducted his ritual, and chanted away, while incense billowed up and enshrouded the feeble flames of the altar candles. Mixed in with the sweet, heavy, ceremonial fragrance seemed to be another: the smell of the diseased city. But through all the haze and glitter Aschenbach saw how the lovely one up in front turned his head, looked for him, and found him.

When at last the crowd streamed out of the open portals into the shining piazza with its flocks of pigeons, the infatuated lover hid in the vestibule where

7. Pray God (French, literal trans.); a low bench on which to kneel during prayers, with a raised shelf for elbows or book.

he lay in wait, staking out his quarry. He saw the Polish family leave the church, saw the children take leave of their mother with great ceremony, saw her make for the Piazzetta on her way home. He ascertained that the lovely one, his cloisterly sisters, and the governess were on their way off to the right, through the clock tower gate, and into the Merceria,[8] and after giving them a reasonable head start he followed. He followed like a thief as they strolled through Venice. He had to stop when they lingered somewhere, had to flee into restaurants or courtyards to avoid them when they turned back. He lost them, got hot and tired as he searched for them over bridges and in dirty cul-de-sacs, and suffered long moments of mortal pain when he saw them coming toward him in a narrow passage where no escape was possible. And yet one cannot really say he suffered. He was intoxicated in head and heart, and his steps followed the instructions of the demon whose pleasure it is to crush under foot human reason and dignity.[9]

At some point or other Tadzio and his party would take a gondola, and Aschenbach, remaining hidden behind a portico or a fountain while they got in, did likewise shortly after they pulled away from the bank. He spoke quickly and in subdued tones to the gondolier, instructing him that a generous tip was in store for him if he would follow that gondola just now rounding the corner—but not too close, as unobtrusively as possible. Sweat trickled over his body as the gondolier, with the roguish willingness of a procurer, assured him in the same lowered tones that he would get service, that he would get conscientious service.

He leaned back in the soft black cushions and glided and rocked in pursuit of the other black, beak-prowed bark, to which his passion held him fastened as if by a chain. Sometimes he lost sight of it, and at those times he would feel worried and restless. But his boatman seemed entirely familiar with such assignments and always knew just how to bring the object of his desire back into view by means of clever maneuvers and quick passages and shortcuts. The air was still, and it smelled. The sun burned heavily through a haze that gave the sky the color of slate. Water gurgled against wood and stone. The cry of the gondolier, half warning and half greeting, received distant answer from out of the silent labyrinth as if by mysterious arrangement. Umbels of flowers hung down over crumbling walls from small gardens on higher ground. They were white and purple and smelled like almonds. Moorish window casings showed their forms in the haze. The marble steps of a church descended into the waters; a beggar crouching there and asserting his misery held out his hat and showed the whites of his eyes as if he were blind; a dealer in antiques stood before his cavelike shop and with fawning gestures invited the passerby to stop, hoping for a chance to swindle him. That was Venice, that coquettish, dubious beauty of a city, half fairy tale and half tourist trap, in whose noisome air the fine arts once thrived luxuriantly and where musicians were inspired to create sounds that cradle the listener and seductively rock him to sleep. To the traveler in the midst of his adventure it seemed as if his eyes were drinking in just this luxury, as if his ears were wooed by just such melodies. He remembered, too, that the city was sick and was keeping its secret out of pure greed, and he

8. Commercial district north of the Piazza San Marco.

9. Dionysus, originally an Eastern fertility god, worshipped with wild dances in ecstatic rites.

cast an even more licentious leer toward the gondola floating in the distance before him.

Entangled and besotted as he was, he no longer wished for anything else than to pursue the beloved object that inflamed him, to dream about him when he was absent and to speak amorous phrases, after the manner of lovers, to his mere shadow. His solitary life, the foreign locale, and his late but deep transport of ecstasy encouraged and persuaded him to allow himself the most bewildering transgressions without timidity or embarrassment. That is how it happened that on his return from Venice late in the evening he had stopped on the second floor of the hotel in front of the lovely one's door, leaned his brow against the hinge in complete intoxication, unable for a protracted period to drag himself away, heedless of the danger of being caught in such an outrageous position.

Still, there were moments when he paused and half came to his senses. How has this come to pass? he wondered in alarm. How did I come to this? Like everyone who has achieved something thanks to his natural talents, he had an aristocratic interest in his family background. At times when his life brought him recognition and success he would think about his ancestors and try to reassure himself that they would approve, that they would be pleased, that they would have had to admire him. Even here and now he thought about them, entangled as he was in such an illicit experience, seized by such exotic emotional aberrations. He thought about their rigorous self-possession, their manly respectability, and he smiled a melancholy smile. What would they say? But then what would they have said about his whole life, a life that had so diverged, one might say degenerated, from theirs, a life under the spell of art that he himself had mocked in the precocity of his youth, this life that yet so fundamentally resembled theirs? He too had done his service, he too had practiced a strict discipline; he too had been a soldier and a man of war, like many of them. For art was a war, a grinding battle that one was just no longer up to fighting for very long these days. It was a life of self-control and a life lived in despite, a harsh, steadfast, abstemious existence that he had made the symbol of a tender and timely heroism. He had every right to call it manly, call it courageous, and he wondered if the love-god who had taken possession of him might be particularly inclined and partial somehow to those who lived such a life. Had not that very god enjoyed the highest respect among the bravest nations of the earth? Did they not say that it was because of their courage that he had flourished in their cities? Numerous war heroes of ages past had willingly borne the yoke imposed by the god, for a humiliation imposed by the god did not count. Acts that would have been denounced as signs of cowardice when done in other circumstances and for other ends—prostrations, oaths, urgent pleas, and fawning behavior—none redounded to the shame of the lover, but rather he more likely reaped praise for them.[1]

Such was the infatuated thinker's train of thought; thus he sought to offer himself support; thus he attempted to preserve his dignity. But at the same time he stubbornly kept on the track of the dirty doings in the city's interior, that adventure of the outside world that darkly joined together with his heart's

1. A reference to the Athenian code of love as described by Pausanias in Plato's *Symposium*, sections 182d–e and 183b.

adventure and nourished his passion with vague, lawless hopes. Obsessed with finding out the latest and most reliable news about the status and progress of the disease, he went to the city's coffee houses and leafed through the German newspapers, which had long since disappeared from the table in the hotel lobby. He read alternating assertions and denials. The number of illnesses and deaths might be as high as twenty, forty, even a hundred or more; but then in the next article or next issue any outbreak of the epidemic, if not categorically denied, would be reported as limited to a few isolated cases brought in by foreigners. There were periodic doubts, warnings, and protests against the dangerous game being played by the Italian authorities. Reliable information was simply not available.

The solitary guest was nonetheless conscious of having a special claim on his share in the secret. Though he was excluded, he took a bizarre pleasure in pressing knowledgeable people with insidious questions and forcing those who were part of the conspiracy of silence to utter explicit lies. At breakfast one day in the main dining room, for example, he engaged the manager in conversation. This unobtrusive little person in his French frock coat was going about between the tables greeting everyone and supervising the help. He made a brief stop at Aschenbach's table, too, for a casual chat. Now then why, the guest just happened to ask very casually, why in the world had they been disinfecting Venice for all this time? "It's a police matter," the toady answered, "a measure intended to stop in due and timely fashion any and all unwholesome conditions, any disturbance of the public health that might come about owing to the brooding heat of this exceptionally warm weather." "The police are to be commended," replied Aschenbach. After the exchange of a few more meteorological observations the manager took his leave.

On that very same day, in the evening after dinner, it happened that a little band of street singers from the city performed in the hotel's front garden. They stood, two men and two women, next to the iron lamppost of an arc light and raised their faces, shining in the white illumination, toward the great terrace, where the guests were enjoying this traditional popular entertainment while drinking coffee and cooling beverages. Hotel employees—elevator boys, waiters, and office personnel—stood by listening at the entrances to the lobby. The Russian family, zealous and precise in taking their pleasure, had wicker chairs moved down into the garden so as to be nearer the performers. There they sat in a semi-circle, in their characteristically grateful attitude. Behind the ladies and gentlemen stood the old slave woman in her turbanlike headdress.

The low-life virtuosos were extracting sounds from a mandolin, a guitar, a harmonica, and a squeaky violin. Interspersed among the instrumental numbers were vocals in which the younger of the women blended her sharp, quavering voice with the sweet falsetto of the tenor in a love duet full of yearning. But the chief talent and real leader of the group was clearly the other man, the guitar player, who sang a kind of buffo[2] baritone while he played. Though his voice was weak, he was a gifted mime and projected remarkable comic energy. Often he would move away from the group, his great instrument under his arm, and advance toward the terrace with many a flourish. The audience rewarded his

2. Comic.

antics with rousing laughter. The Russians in particular, ensconced in their orchestra seats, displayed particular delight over all this southern vivacity and encouraged him with applause and cheers to ever bolder and more brazen behavior.

Aschenbach sat at the balustrade, cooling his lips from time to time with a mixture of pomegranate[3] juice and soda that sparkled ruby-red in his glass. His nerves greedily consumed the piping sounds, the vulgar, pining melodies; for passion numbs good taste and succumbs in all seriousness to enticements that a sober spirit would receive with humor or even reject scornfully. His features, reacting to the antics of the buffoon, had become fixed in a rigid and almost painful smile. He sat in an apparently relaxed attitude, and all the while he was internally tense and sharply attentive, for Tadzio stood no more than six paces away, leaning against the stone railing.

He stood there in the white belted suit that he sometimes wore to dinner, a figure of inevitable and innate grace, his left forearm on the railing, his ankles crossed, his right hand supported on his hip. He wore an expression that was not quite a smile but more an air of distant curiosity or polite receptivity as he looked down toward the street musicians. Sometimes he straightened up and, with a lovely movement of both arms that lifted his chest, he would pull his white blouse down through his leather belt. Occasionally, though—as the aging observer noted with triumph and even with horror, his reason staggering—Tadzio would turn his head to look across his left shoulder in the direction of the one who loved him, sometimes with deliberate hesitation, sometimes with sudden swiftness as if to catch him unawares. Their eyes never met, for an ignominious caution forced the errant lover to keep his gaze fearfully in check. The women guarding Tadzio were sitting in the back of the terrace, and things had reached the point that the smitten traveler had to take care lest his behavior should become noticeable and he fall under suspicion. Indeed his blood had nearly frozen on a number of occasions when he had been compelled to notice on the beach, in the hotel lobby, or in the Piazza San Marco that Tadzio was called away from his vicinity, that they were intent on keeping the boy away from him. He felt horribly insulted, and his pride flinched from unfamiliar tortures that his conscience prevented him from dismissing.

In the meantime the guitar player had begun singing a solo to his own accompaniment, a popular ditty in many verses that was quite the hit just then all over Italy. He was adept at performing it in a highly histrionic manner, and his band joined in the refrain each time, both with their voices and all their instruments. He was of a lean build, and even his face was thin to the point of emaciation. He stood there on the gravel in an attitude of impertinent bravura, apart from his fellow performers, his shabby felt hat so far back on his head that a roll of red hair surged forth from beneath the brim, and as he thumped the guitar strings, he hurled his buffooneries toward the terrace above in an insistent recitative. The veins on his brow swelled in response to his exertions. He seemed not to be of Venetian stock, more likely a member of the race of Neapolitan comics, half pimp, half actor, brutal and daring, dangerous and entertaining. The lyrics of his song were as banal as could be, but in his mouth

3. A tropical fruit with many seeds, associated in Greek mythology both with Persephone, the queen of Hades, and with the world of the dead.

they acquired an ambiguous, vaguely offensive quality because of his facial expressions and his gestures, his suggestive winks and his manner of letting his tongue play lasciviously at the corner of his mouth. His strikingly large Adam's apple protruded nakedly from his scrawny neck, which emerged from the soft collar of a sport shirt worn in incongruous combination with more formal city clothes. His pale, snubnosed face was beardless and did not permit an easy reckoning of his age; it seemed ravaged by grimaces and by vice. The two defiant, imperious, even wild-looking furrows that stood between his reddish eyebrows went rather oddly with the grin on his mobile lips. What particularly drew the attention of the lonely spectator, however, was his observation that this questionable figure seemed to carry with it its own questionable atmosphere. For every time the refrain began again the singer would commence a grotesque circular march, clowning and shaking the hands of his audience; every time his path would bring him directly underneath Aschenbach's spot, and every time that happened there wafted up to the terrace from his clothes and from his body a choking stench of carbolic acid.[4]

His song finished, he began collecting money. He started with the Russians, who produced a generous offering, and then ascended the steps. As bold as he had been during the performance, just so obsequious was he now. Bowing and scraping, he slithered about between the tables, a smile of crafty submissiveness laying bare his large teeth, and all the while the two furrows between his red eyebrows stood forth menacingly. The guests surveyed with curiosity and some revulsion this strange being who was gathering in his livelihood. They threw coins in his hat from a distance and were careful not to touch him. The elimination of the physical separation between the performer and his respectable audience always tends to produce a certain embarrassment, no matter how pleasurable the performance. The singer felt it and sought to excuse himself by acting servile. He came up to Aschenbach, and with him came the smell, though no one else in the vicinity seemed concerned about it.

"Listen," the lonely traveler said in lowered tones, almost mechanically. "They are disinfecting Venice. Why?" The jester answered hoarsely: "Because of the police. That, sir, is the procedure when it gets hot like this and when the sirocco comes. The sirocco is oppressive. It's not conducive to good health. . . ." He spoke as if he were amazed that anyone could ask such questions, and he demonstrated by pushing with his open palm just how oppressive the sirocco was. "So there is no disease in Venice?" Aschenbach asked very quietly through his closed teeth. The tense muscles in the comedian's face produced a grimace of comic perplexity. "A disease? What sort of disease? Is the sirocco a disease? Do you suppose our police force is a disease? You like to make fun, don't you? A disease! Why on earth? Some preventive measures, you understand. A police regulation to minimize the effects of the oppressive weather . . . ," he gesticulated. "Very well," Aschenbach said once again, briefly and quietly, and he dropped an indecently large coin into the hat. Then he indicated with a look that the man should go. He obeyed with a grin and a bow. But even before he reached the steps two hotel employees intercepted him and, putting their faces very close to his, cross-examined him in whispers. He shrugged, he protested, he swore that he had been circumspect. You could tell. Dismissed, he returned

4. A chemical used as a disinfectant.

to the garden and, after making a few arrangements with his group by the light of the arc lamp, he stepped forward to offer one parting song.

It was a song the solitary traveler could not remember ever having heard before, an impudent Italian hit in an incomprehensible dialect embellished with a laughing refrain in which the whole group regularly joined, fortissimo. The refrain had neither words nor instrumental accompaniment; nothing was left but a certain rhythmically structured but still very natural-sounding laughter, which the soloist in particular was capable of producing with great talent and deceptive realism. Having reestablished a proper artistic distance between himself and his audience, he had regained all his former impudence. His artfully artificial laughter, directed impertinently up to the terrace, was the laughter of scorn. Even before the part of the song with actual lyrics had come to a close, one could see him begin to battle an irresistible itch. He would hiccup, his voice would catch, he would put his hand up to his mouth, he would twist his shoulders, and at the proper moment the unruly laughter would break forth, exploding in a hoot, but with such realism that it was infectious. It spread among the listeners so that even on the terrace an unfounded mirth set in, feeding on nothing but itself. This appeared only to double the singer's exuberance. He bent his knees, slapped his thighs, held his sides, fairly split with laughter; but he was no longer laughing, he was howling. He pointed his finger upwards, as if to say that there could be nothing funnier than the laughing audience up there, and soon everyone in the garden and on the veranda was laughing, including the waiters, elevator boys, and servants lingering in the doorways.

Aschenbach no longer reclined in his chair; he sat upright as if trying to defend himself or to flee. But the laughter, the rising smell of hospital sanitation, and the nearness of the lovely boy—all blended to cast a dreamy spell about him that held his mind and his senses in an unbreakable, inescapable embrace. In the general confusion of the moment he made so bold as to cast a glance at Tadzio, and when he did so he was granted the opportunity to see that the lovely lad answered his gaze with a seriousness equal to his own. It was as if the boy were regulating his behavior and attitude according to that of the man, as if the general mood of gaiety had no power over the boy so long as the man kept apart from it. This childlike and meaningful docility was so disarming, so overwhelming, that the gray-haired traveler could only with difficulty refrain from hiding his face in his hands. It had also seemed to him that Tadzio's habit of straightening up and taking a deep sighing breath suggested an obstruction in his breathing. "He is sickly; he will probably not live long," he thought once again with that sobriety that sometimes frees itself in some strange manner from intoxication and longing. Ingenuous solicitude mixed with a dissolute satisfaction filled his heart.

The Venetian singers had meanwhile finished their number and left, accompanied by applause. Their leader did not fail to adorn even his departure with jests. He bowed and scraped and blew kisses so that everyone laughed, which made him redouble his efforts. When his fellow performers were already gone, he pretended to back hard into a lamppost at full speed, then crept toward the gate bent over in mock pain. There at last he cast off the mask of the comic loser, unbent or rather snapped up straight, stuck his tongue out impudently at the guests on the terrace, and slipped into the darkness. The audience dispersed; Tadzio was already long gone from his place at the balustrade. But the lonely traveler remained sitting for a long time at his little table, nursing his pomegranate drink much to the annoyance of the waiters. The night progressed; time crumbled away. Many years ago in his parents' house there had been an hourglass. He suddenly could see the fragile and portentous little device once more, as though it were standing right in front of him. The rust-colored fine sand ran silently through the glass neck, and as it began to run out of the upper vessel a rapid little vortex formed.

In the afternoon of the very next day the obstinate visitor took a further step in his probing of the outside world, and this time he met with all possible success. What he did was to enter the English travel agency in the Piazza San Marco and, having changed some money at the cash register and having assumed the demeanor of a diffident foreigner, he directed his fateful question to the clerk who was taking care of him. The clerk was a wool-clad Briton, still young, his hair parted in the middle and eyes set close together, possessed of that steady, trustworthy bearing that stands out as so foreign and so remarkable among the roguishly nimble southerners. He began: "No cause for concern, sir. A measure of no serious importance. Such regulations are frequently imposed to ward off the ill effects of the heat and the sirocco. . . ." But when he raised his blue eyes he met the foreigner's gaze. It was a tired and rather sad gaze, and it was directed with an air of mild contempt toward his lips. The Englishman blushed. "That is," he continued in a low voice, somewhat discomfited, "the official explanation, which they see fit to stick to hereabouts. I can tell you, though, that there's a good deal more to it." And then, in his candid and comfortable language, he told the truth.

For some years now Asiatic cholera had shown an increasing tendency to spread and roam. The pestilence originated in the warm swamps of the Ganges delta,[5] rising on the foul-smelling air of that lushly uninhabitable primeval world, that wilderness of islands avoided by humankind where tigers lurk in bamboo thickets. It had raged persistently and with unusual ferocity throughout Hindustan; then it had spread eastwards to China and westwards to Afghanistan and Persia; and, following the great caravan routes, it had brought its horrors as far as Astrakhan and even Moscow. But while Europe was shaking in fear lest the specter should progress by land from Russia westward, it had emerged simultaneously in several Mediterranean port cities, having been carried in on Syrian merchant ships. It had raised its grisly head in Toulon and Malaga, shown its grim mask several times in Palermo and Naples, and seemed now firmly ensconced throughout Calabria and Apulia.[6] The northern half of the peninsula had so far been spared. On a single day in mid-May of this year, however, the terrible vibrioid[7] bacteria had been found on two emaciated, blackening corpses, that of a ship's hand and that of a woman who sold vegetables. These cases were hushed up. A week later, though, there were ten more, twenty more, thirty more, not localized but spread through various parts of the city. A man from the Austrian hinterlands who had come for a pleasant holiday of a few days in Venice died upon returning to his home town, exhibiting

5. In India.
6. Regions in southern Italy. Astrakhan, Toulon, Málaga, Palermo, and Naples are seaports in Russia, France, Spain, Sicily, and southern Italy, respectively.
7. Belonging to a class of comma-shaped bacteria.

unmistakable symptoms. Thus it was that the first rumors of the affliction visited upon the city on the lagoon appeared in German newspapers. In response the Venetian authorities promulgated the assertion that matters of health had never been better in the city. They also immediately instituted the most urgent measures to counter the disease. But apparently the food supply—vegetables, meat, and milk—had been infected, for death, though denied and hushed up, devoured its way through the narrow streets. The early arrival of summer's heat made a lukewarm broth of the water in the canals and thus made conditions for the disease's spread particularly favorable. It almost seemed as though the pestilence had been reinvigorated, as if the tenacity and fecundity of its microscopic agitators had been redoubled. Cures were rare; out of a hundred infected eighty died, and in a particularly gruesome fashion, for the evil raged here with extreme ferocity. Often it took on its most dangerous form, commonly known as the "dry type." In such cases the body is unable to rid itself of the massive amounts of water secreted by the blood-vessels. In a few hours' time the patient dries up and suffocates, his blood as viscous as pitch, crying out hoarsely in his convulsions. It sometimes happened that a few lucky ones suffered only a mild discomfort followed by a loss of consciousness from which they would never again, or only rarely, awaken. At the beginning of June the quarantine wards of the Ospedale Civico quietly filled up, space became scarce in both of the orphanages, and a horrifyingly brisk traffic clogged the routes between the docks at the Fondamenta Nuove[8] and San Michele, the cemetery island. But the fear of adverse consequences to the city, concern for the newly opened exhibit of paintings in the public gardens, for the losses that the hotels, businesses, and the whole tourist industry would suffer in case of a panic or a boycott—these matters proved weightier in the city than the love of truth or respect for international agreements. They prompted the authorities stubbornly to maintain their policy of concealment and denial. The highest medical official in Venice, a man of considerable attainments, had angrily resigned his post and was surreptitiously replaced by a more pliable individual. The citizenry knew all about it, and the combination of corruption in high places with the prevailing uncertainty, the state of emergency in which the city was placed when death was striking all about, caused a certain demoralization of the lower levels of society. It encouraged those antisocial forces that shun the light, and they manifested themselves as immoderate, shameless, and increasingly criminal behavior. Contrary to the norm, one saw many drunks at evening time; people said that gangs of rogues made the streets unsafe at night; muggings and even murders multiplied. Already on two occasions it had come to light that alleged victims of the plague had in fact been robbed of their lives by their own relatives who administered poison. Prostitution and lasciviousness took on brazen and extravagant forms never before seen here and thought to be at home only in the southern parts of the country and in the seraglios of the orient.

The Englishman explained the salient points of these developments. "You would do well," he concluded, "to depart today rather than tomorrow. The imposition of a quarantine cannot be more than a few days off." "Thank you," said Aschenbach and left the agency.

8. New footings (Italian, literal trans.); the new piers. "Ospedale Civico": city hospital.

The piazza was sunless and sultry. Unsuspecting foreigners sat in the sidewalk cafes or stood in front of the cathedral completely covered with pigeons. They watched as the swarming birds beat their wings and jostled each other for their chance to pick at the kernels of corn offered to them in an open palm. In feverish excitement, triumphant in his possession of the truth, but with a taste of gall in his mouth and a fantastic horror in his heart, the lonely traveler paced back and forth over the flagstones of the magnificent plaza. He considered doing the decent thing, the thing that would cleanse him. Tonight after dinner he could go up to the lady with the pearls and speak to her. He planned exactly what he would say: "Permit me, Madame, stranger though I may be, to be of service to you with a piece of advice, a word of warning concerning a matter that has been withheld from you by self-serving people. Depart at once, taking Tadzio and your daughters with you. There is an epidemic in Venice." He could then lay his hand in farewell on the head of that instrument of a scornful deity, turn away, and flee this swamp. But at the same time he sensed that he was infinitely far from seriously wanting to take such a step. It would bring him back to his senses, would make him himself again; but when one is beside oneself there is nothing more abhorrent than returning to one's senses. He remembered a white building decorated with inscriptions that gleamed in the evening light, inscriptions in whose radiant mysticism his mind's eye had become lost. He remembered too that strange figure of the wanderer who had awakened in the aging man a young man's longing to roam in faraway and exotic places. The thought of returning home, of returning to prudence and sobriety, toil and mastery, was so repugnant to him that his face broke out in an expression of physical disgust. "Let them keep quiet," he whispered vehemently. And: "I will keep quiet!" The consciousness of his guilty complicity intoxicated him, just as small amounts of wine will intoxicate a weary brain. The image of the afflicted and ravaged city hovered chaotically in his imagination, incited in him inconceivable hopes, beyond all reason, monstrously sweet. How could that tender happiness he had dreamed of a moment earlier compare with these expectations? What value did art and virtue hold for him when he could have chaos? He held his peace and stayed.

That night he had a terrifying dream—if indeed one can call "dream" an experience that was both physical and mental, one that visited him in the depths of his sleep, in complete isolation as well as sensuous immediacy, but yet such that he did not see himself as physically and spatially present apart from its action. Instead, its setting was in his soul itself, and its events burst in upon him from outside, violently crushing his resistance, his deep, intellectual resistance, passing through easily and leaving his whole being, the culmination of a lifetime of effort, ravaged and annihilated.

It began with fear, fear and desire and a horrified curiosity about what was to come. Night ruled, and his senses were attentive; for from afar there approached a tumult, a turmoil, a mixture of noises: rattling, clarion calls and muffled thunder, shrill cheering on top of it all, and a certain howl with a drawn-out *uuu* sound at the end. All this was accompanied and drowned out by the gruesomely sweet tones of a flute playing a cooing, recklessly persistent tune that penetrated to the very bowels, where it cast a shameless enchantment. But there was a phrase, darkly familiar, that named what was coming: "*The stranger god!*"[9] A smoky glow welled up, and he recognized a mountain landscape like the one around his summer house. And in the fragmented light he could see people, animals, a swarm, a roaring mob, all rolling and plunging and whirling down from the forested heights, past tree-trunks and great moss-covered fragments of rock, overflowing the slope with their bodies, flames, tumult, and reeling circular dance. Women, stumbling over the fur skirts that hung too long from their belts, moaned, threw their heads back, shook their tambourines on high, brandished naked daggers and torches that threw off sparks, held serpents with flickering tongues by the middle of their bodies, or cried out, lifting their breasts in both hands. Men with horns on their brows, girdled with hides, their own skins shaggy, bent their necks and raised their arms and thighs, clashed brazen cymbals and beat furiously on drums, while smooth-skinned boys used garlanded staves to prod their goats, clinging to the horns so they could be dragged along, shouting with joy, when the goats sprang. And the ecstatic band howled the cry with soft consonants in the middle and a drawn-out *uuu* sound on the end, a cry that was sweet and wild at the same time, like none ever heard before: here it rang in the air like the bellowing of stags in rut; and there many voices echoed it back in anarchic triumph, using it to goad each other to dance and shake their limbs, never letting it fall silent. But it was all suffused and dominated by the deep, beckoning melody of the flute. Was it not also beckoning him, the resisting dreamer, with shameless persistence to the festival, to its excesses, and to its ultimate sacrifice? Great was his loathing, great his fear, sincere his resolve to defend his own against the foreign invader, the enemy of self-controlled and dignified intellect. But the noise and the howling, multiplied by the echoing mountainsides, grew, gained the upper hand, swelled to a madness that swept everything along with it. Fumes oppressed the senses: the acrid scent of the goats, the emanation of panting human bodies, a whiff as of stagnant water—and another smell perceptible through it all, a familiar reek of wounds and raging sickness. His heart pounded with the rhythm of the drum beats, his mind whirled, rage took hold of him and blinded him, he was overcome by a numbing lust, and his soul longed to join in the reeling dance of the god. Their obscene symbol,[1] gigantic, wooden, was uncovered and raised on high, and they howled out their watchword all the more licentiously. With foam on their lips they raved; they stimulated each other with lewd gestures and fondling hands; laughing and wheezing, they pierced each other's flesh with their pointed staves and then licked the bleeding limbs. Now among them, now a part of them, the dreamer belonged to the stranger god. Yes, they were he, and he was they, when they threw themselves on the animals, tearing and killing, devouring steaming gobbets of flesh, when on the trampled moss-covered ground there began an unfettered rite of copulation in sacrifice to the god. His soul tasted the lewdness and frenzy of surrender.

The afflicted dreamer awoke unnerved, shattered, a powerless victim of the demon. He no longer shunned the observant glances of people about him; he no longer cared if he was making himself a target of their suspicions. And in any case they were all departing, fleeing the sickness. Many cabanas now stood

9. Dionysus (also Bacchus), whose cult was brought to Greece from Thrace and Phrygia. The dream describes the orgiastic rites of his worship.

1. The phallus.

empty, the population of the dining room was seriously depleted, and in the city one only rarely saw a foreigner. The truth seemed to have leaked out, and in spite of the stubborn conniving of those with vested interests at stake, panic could no longer be averted. The lady with the pearls nonetheless remained with her family, perhaps because the rumors did not reach her or perhaps because she was too proud and fearless to succumb to them. Tadzio remained, and to Aschenbach, blind to all but his own concerns, it seemed at times that death and departure might very well remove all the distracting human life around them and leave him alone with the lovely one on this island. Indeed, in the mornings on the beach when his gaze would rest heavily, irresponsibly, fixedly on the object of his desire; or at the close of day when he would take up his shameful pursuit of the boy through narrow streets where loathsome death did its hushed-up business; then everything monstrous seemed to him to have a prosperous future, the moral law to have none.

He wished, like any other lover, to please his beloved and felt a bitter concern that it would not be possible. He added youthfully cheerful touches to his dress, took to using jewelry and perfume. Several times a day he took lengthy care getting dressed and then came down to the dining room all bedecked, excited and expectant. His aging body disgusted him when he looked at the sweet youth with whom he was smitten; the sight of his gray hair and his sharp facial features overwhelmed him with shame and hopelessness. He felt a need to restore and revive his body. He visited the barbershop more and more frequently.

Leaning back in the chair under the protective cloth, letting the manicured hands of the chattering barber care for him, he confronted the tortured gaze of his image in the mirror.

"Gray," he said with his mouth twisted.

"A bit," the man replied. "It's all because of a slight neglect, an indifference to externals—quite understandable in the case of important people, but still not altogether praiseworthy, all the less so since just such people ought not to harbor prejudices in matters of the natural and the artificial. If certain people were to extend the moral qualms they have about the cosmetic arts to their teeth, as logic compels, they would give no little offense. And anyway, we're only as old we feel in our hearts and minds. Gray hair can in certain circumstances give more of a false impression than the dye that some would scorn. In your case, sir, you have a right to your natural hair color. Will you allow me to give you back what is rightfully yours?"

"How?" Aschenbach inquired.

So the glib barber washed his customer's hair with two liquids, one clear and one dark, and it turned as black as it had been in youth. Then he rolled it with the curling iron into soft waves, stepped back and admired his handiwork.

"All that's left," he said, "is to freshen up the complexion a bit."

He went about, with ever renewed solicitude, moving from one task to another the way a person does who can never finish anything and is never satisfied. Aschenbach, resting comfortably, was in any case quite incapable of fending him off. Actually he was rather excited about what was happening, watching in the mirror as his brows took on a more decisive and symmetrical arch and his eyes grew in width and brilliance with the addition of a little shadow on the lids. A little further down he could see his skin, previously brown and leathery, perk up with a light application of delicate carmine rouge, his lips, pale and bloodless only a moment a ago, swell like raspberries, the furrows in his cheeks and mouth, the wrinkles around his eyes give way to a dab of cream and the glow of youth. His heart pounded as he saw in the mirror a young man in full bloom. The cosmetic artist finally pronounced himself satisfied and thanked the object of his ministrations with fawning politeness, the way such people do. "A minor repair job," he said as he put a final touch to Aschenbach's appearance. "Now, sir, you can go and fall in love without second thoughts." The beguiled lover went out, happy as in a dream, yet confused and timid. His tie was red, and his broad-brimmed straw hat was encircled by a band of many colors.

A tepid breeze had come up; it rained only seldom and then not hard, but the air was humid, thick, and full of the stench of decay. Rustling, rushing, and flapping sounds filled his ears. He burned with fever beneath his makeup, and it seemed to him that the air was filled with vile, evil windspirits, impure winged sea creatures who raked over, gnawed over, and defiled with garbage the meals of their victim.[2] For the sultry weather ruined one's appetite, and one could not suppress the idea that all the food was poisoned with infection.

Trailing the lovely boy one afternoon, Aschenbach had penetrated deep into the maze in the heart of the diseased city. He had lost his sense of direction, for the little streets, canals, bridges, and piazzas in the labyrinth all looked alike. He could no longer even tell east from west, since his only concern had been not to lose sight of the figure he pursued so ardently. He was compelled to a disgraceful sort of discretion that involved clinging to walls and seeking protection behind the backs of passersby, and so he did not for some time become conscious of the fatigue, the exhaustion which a high pitch of emotion and continual tension had inflicted on his body and spirit. Tadzio walked behind the rest of his family. In these narrow streets he would generally let the governess and the nunlike sisters go first, while he sauntered along by himself, occasionally turning his head to assure himself with a quick glance of his extraordinary dawn-gray eyes over his shoulder that his lover was still following. He saw him, and he did not betray him. Intoxicated by this discovery, lured onward by those eyes, tied to the apron string of his own passion, the lovesick traveler stole forth in pursuit of his unseemly hope—but ultimately found himself disappointed. The Polish family had gone across a tightly arched bridge, and the height of the arch had hidden them from their pursuer. When he was at last able to cross, he could no longer find them. He searched for them in three directions—straight ahead and to both sides along the narrow, dirty landing—but in vain. He finally had to give up, too debilitated and unnerved to go on.

His head was burning hot, his body was sticky with sweat, the scruff of his neck was tingling, an unbearable thirst assaulted him, and he looked about for immediate refreshment of any sort. In front of a small greengrocer's shop he bought some fruit, strawberries that were overripe and soft, and he ate them while he walked. A little piazza that was quite deserted and seemed enchanted

2. "Harpies: hideously thin, they flew swiftly in, fell with insatiable greed on whatever food was there, ate without being satisfied, and *befouled* whatever they left with their filth" [Mann's note]. See Virgil's *Aeneid* 3.210–62.

opened out before him. He recognized it, for it was here that weeks ago he had made his thwarted plan to flee the city. He collapsed on the steps of the well in the very middle of the plaza and rested his head on the stone rim. It was quiet, grass grew between the paving stones, refuse lay strewn about. Among the weathered buildings of varying heights around the periphery was one that looked rather palatial. It had Gothic-arched windows, now gaping emptily, and little balconies decorated with lions. On the ground floor of another there was a pharmacy. Warm gusts of wind from time to time carried the smell of carbolic acid.

He sat there, the master, the artist who had attained to dignity, the author of the "Man of Misery," that exemplary work which had with clarity of form renounced bohemianism and the gloomy murky depths, had condemned sympathy for the abyss, reviled the vile. There he sat, the great success who had overcome knowledge and outgrown every sort of irony, who had accustomed himself to the obligations imposed by the confidence of his large audience. There he sat, the author whose greatness had been officially recognized and whose name bore the title of nobility, the author whose style children were encouraged to emulate—sat there with his eyes shut, though from time to time a mocking and embarrassed look would slip sidelong out from underneath his lids, only to conceal itself again swiftly; and his slack, cosmetically enhanced lips formed occasional words that emerged out of the strange dream-logic engendered in his half-dozing brain.[3]

"For beauty, Phaedrus—mark me well—only beauty is both divine and visible at the same time, and thus it is the way of the senses, the way of the artist, little Phaedrus, to the spirit. But do you suppose, my dear boy, that anyone could ever attain to wisdom and genuine manly honor by taking a path to the spirit that leads through the senses? Or do you rather suppose (I leave the decision entirely up to you) that this is a dangerously delightful path, really a path of error and sin that necessarily leads astray? For you must know that we poets cannot walk the path of beauty without Eros joining our company and even making himself our leader; indeed, heroes though we may be after our own fashion, disciplined warriors though we may be, still we are as women, for passion is our exaltation, and our longing must ever be for love. That is our bliss and our shame. Do you see, then, that we poets can be neither wise nor honorable, that we necessarily go astray, that we necessarily remain dissolute adventurers of emotion? The masterly demeanor of our style is a lie and a folly, our fame and our honor a sham, the confidence accorded us by our public utterly ridiculous, the education of the populace and of the young by means of art a risky enterprise that ought not to be allowed. For how can a person succeed in educating others who has an inborn, irremediable, and natural affinity for the abyss? We may well deny it and achieve a certain dignity, but wherever we may turn that affinity abides. Let us say we renounce analytical knowledge; for knowledge, Phaedrus, has neither dignity nor discipline; it is knowing, understanding, forgiving, formless and unrestrained; it has sympathy for the abyss; it *is* the abyss. Let us therefore resolutely reject it, and henceforth our efforts will

3. Aschenbach adopts the role of Socrates in Plato's *Phaedrus* to examine the role of the artist. Although the Platonic dialogue briefly contrasts inspired art with mere technical perfection, it is chiefly concerned with moral choices and absolute beauty.

be directed only toward beauty, that is to say toward simplicity, grandeur, and a new discipline, toward reborn ingenuousness and toward form. But form and ingenuousness, Phaedrus, lead to intoxication and to desire, might lead the noble soul to horrible emotional outrages that his own lovely discipline would reject as infamous, lead him to the abyss. Yes, they too lead to the abyss. They lead us poets there, I say, because we are capable not of resolution but only of dissolution. And now I shall depart, Phaedrus; but you stay here until you can no longer see me, and then you depart as well."

A few days afterwards Gustav von Aschenbach left the hotel at a later hour than usual, since he was feeling unwell. He was struggling with certain attacks of dizziness that were only partly physical and were accompanied by a powerfully escalating sense of anxiety and indecision, a feeling of having no prospects and no way out. He was not at all sure whether these feelings concerned the outside world or his own existence. He noticed in the lobby a great pile of luggage prepared for departure, and when he asked the doorman who was leaving, he received for an answer the aristocratic Polish name he had in his heart been expecting to hear all along. He took it in with no change in the expression on his ravaged face, briefly raising his head as people do to acknowledge casually the receipt of a piece of information they do not need, and asked, "When?" The answer came: "After lunch." He nodded and went to the beach.

It was dreary there. Rippling tremors crossed from near to far on the wide, flat stretch of water between the beach and the first extended sandbar. Where so recently there had been color, life, and joy, it was now almost deserted, and an autumnal mood prevailed, a feeling that the season was past its prime. The sand was no longer kept clean. A camera with no photographer to operate it stood on its tripod at the edge of the sea, a black cloth that covered it fluttering with a snapping noise in a wind that now blew colder.

Tadzio and three or four playmates that still remained were active in front of his family's cabana to Aschenbach's right; and, resting in his beach chair approximately halfway between the ocean and the row of cabanas, with a blanket over his legs, Aschenbach watched him once more. Their play was unsupervised, since the women must have been busy with preparations for their departure. The game seemed to have no rules and quickly degenerated. The sturdy boy with the belted suit and the black, slicked-down hair who was called Yashu, angered and blinded by sand thrown in his face, forced Tadzio into a wrestling match, which ended swiftly with the defeat of the weaker, lovely boy. It seemed as if in the last moments before leave-taking the subservient feelings of the underling turned to vindictive cruelty as he sought to take revenge for a long period of slavery. The winner would not release his defeated opponent but instead kneeled on his back and pushed his face in the sand, persisting for so long that Tadzio, already out of breath from the fight, seemed in danger of suffocating. He made spasmodic attempts to shake off his oppressor, lay still for whole moments, then tried again with no more than a twitch. Horrified, Aschenbach wanted to spring to the rescue, but then the bully finally released his victim. Tadzio was very pale; he got up halfway and sat motionless for several minutes supported on one arm, his hair disheveled and his eyes darkening. Then he rose to his feet and slowly walked away. They called to him, cheerfully at first but then with pleading timidity. He paid no attention. The black-haired boy, apparently instantly regretting his transgression, caught up with him and tried to make up. A jerk of a lovely shoulder put him off. Tadzio crossed diagonally down to the water. He was barefoot and wore his striped linen suit with the red bow.

He lingered at the edge of the sea with his head hung down, drawing figures in the wet sand with his toe. Then he went into the shallows, which at their deepest point did not wet his knees, strode through them, and progressed idly to the sandbar. Upon reaching it he stood for a moment, his face turned to the open sea, then began to walk slowly to the left along the narrow stretch of uncovered ground. Separated from the mainland by the broad expanse of water, separated from his mates by a proud mood, he strode forth, a highly remote and isolated apparition with wind-blown hair, wandering about out there in the sea, in the wind, on the edge of the misty boundlessness. Once more he stopped to gaze outward. Suddenly, as if prompted by a memory or an impulse, he rotated his upper body in a lovely turn out of its basic posture, his hand resting on his hip, and looked over his shoulder toward the shore. The observer sat there as he had sat once before, when for the first time he had met the gaze of those dawn-gray eyes cast back at him from that threshold. His head, resting on the back of the chair, had slowly followed the movements of the one who was striding about out there; now his head rose as if returning the gaze, then sank on his chest so that his eyes looked out from beneath. His face took on the slack, intimately absorbed expression of deep sleep. It seemed to him, though, as if the pale and charming psychagogue[4] out there were smiling at him, beckoning to him; as if, lifting his hand from his hip, he were pointing outwards, hovering before him in an immensity full of promise. And, as so often before, he arose to follow him.

Minutes passed before anyone rushed to the aid of the man who had collapsed to one side in his chair. They carried him to his room. And later that same day a respectfully shaken world received the news of his death.

1912

4. Leader of souls to the underworld (Greek); a title of the god Hermes.

MARCEL PROUST

1871–1922

Marcel Proust's influence on twentieth-century literature is unequaled by that of any other writer, except **James Joyce**. Known primarily as a minor essayist until the age of forty, Proust devoted the last decade of his life to a massive sequence—*In Search of Lost Time* (*À la recherche du temps perdu,* 1913–27), also known in English as *Remembrance of Things Past*—that transformed the way writers and readers think about the novel as a form. It is a monumental construction coordinated down to its smallest part not by the progress of a traditional plot but by the narrator's intuition and "involuntary memory," and all external events are presented through the prism of the narrator's experience.

Proust was born on July 10, 1871, the older of two sons in a wealthy middle-class Parisian family. His father was a well-known doctor and professor of medicine, a Catholic from a small town outside Paris. His mother, a sensitive, scrupulous, and highly educated woman to whom Marcel was devoted, came from an urban Jewish family. When he was nine, Proust fell ill with severe asthma; thereafter, he spent his childhood holidays at a seaside resort in Normandy that became the model for the fictional Balbec, the setting for a portion of *In Search of Lost Time*. His asthma interfered with his favorite pastimes: walking in the country and smelling the flowering hawthorns near his aunt's home in Illiers (the fictional Combray, where the novel's protagonist grows up). In spite of his illness, which limited what he could do, Marcel graduated with honors from the Lycée Condorcet in Paris in 1889. He then did a year's military service at Orléans, which provided more material for his later novel. He went on to attend law school briefly and graduated with a degree in philosophy from the Sorbonne. As a student, Proust met many young writers and composers, and he frequented the salons of the wealthy bourgeoisie and the aristocracy of the Faubourg Saint-Germain (an elegant area of Paris), from which he drew much of the material for his portraits of society. He wrote for symbolist magazines, such as *Le Banquet* and *La Revue blanche*, and published a collection of essays, poems, and stories in an elegant book, *Pleasures and Days* (1896), but his work received relatively little attention from readers or critics. In 1899 (with his mother's help, since he knew little English), he began to translate the English social and art critic John Ruskin. He did not need to work, since his parents supported him, but he did briefly have a volunteer position at one of France's national libraries; after a few days' work, he went on permanent sick leave.

Proust is known as the author of one novel: the enormous, seven-volume exploration of time and consciousness called *In Search of Lost Time*. As early as 1895, he embarked on a shorter novel that traced the same themes and autobiographical awareness as his masterwork would, but *Jean Santeuil* (published posthumously in 1952) never found a coherent structure for its numerous episodes, and Proust abandoned it in 1899. Themes, ideas, and some episodes from the earlier novel were absorbed into *In Search of Lost Time;* the major difference (aside from length) between the two works is simply the highly sophisticated and subtle structure that Proust devised for the later one.

Proust's parents both died in 1905. The following year, his asthma worsening, he moved into a cork-lined, fumigated room in Paris, where he stayed until forced to move in 1919. From 1907 to 1914, he spent summers in the seacoast town of Cabourg (another source of material for the fictional Balbec), but when in Paris he emerged rarely from his apartment and then only late at night for dinners with friends. Proust was, he later said, "from the medical point of view, many different things, though in fact no one has ever known exactly what. But I am above all, and indisputably, an asthmatic." In an effort to control his symptoms, which he believed were exacerbated by drafts, sunlight, smells, noises, and digestive discomfort, he developed a number of rituals. For example, he ate only once a day, ordering in from high-end restaurants. He slept during the daylight hours, rising around eight in the evening and working through the night. He insisted that everything that touched his skin—bathwater, changes of clothes—had to be just his temperature, so his housekeeper kept extra shirts and long underwear in the oven.

While considering what to write next, Proust improved his style by creating a series of pastiches of great French writers. In 1909 he conceived the structure of his novel as a whole and wrote its first and last chapters together. A first draft was finished by September 1912, but Proust had difficulty finding a publisher and finally published the first volume, *Swann's Way (Du côté de chez Swann)*, at his own expense, in 1913. Though this volume was a success, the First World War delayed publication of subsequent volumes, and Proust began the painstaking revision and enlargement of the whole manuscript (from fifteen hundred to four thousand pages, and three to seven parts) that was to occupy him until his death. He continually added material, even as his health deteriorated, often pasting strips onto earlier pages of the manuscript so that he could present a more detailed account of a particular incident or memory. *Within a Budding Grove (À l'ombre des jeunes filles en fleurs,* or "In the shadow of young girls in flower") won the prestigious Goncourt Prize in 1919, and *The Guermantes Way (Le Côté de Guermantes)* followed, in 1920–21. The last volume published in Proust's lifetime was *Sodom and Gomorrah (Sodome et Gomorrhe II,* 1922), and the remaining volumes—*The Captive (La Prisonnière,* 1923), *The Fugitive (Albertine disparue,* or "Albertine disappeared," 1925), and *Time Regained (Le Temps retrouvé,* 1927)—were released posthumously from manuscripts on which he had been working.

Throughout 1922, Proust's symptoms, particularly nausea, vomiting, and occasional delirium, grew more and more perilous. On November 18, after an especially bad week, his housekeeper, already alarmed by his deterioration, noticed the normally untidy Proust "pulling up the sheet and picking up the papers strewn over the bed." "I'd never been at a deathbed before," she later wrote, "but in our village I'd heard people say that dying men gather things." By that afternoon three doctors, including the patient's brother, Robert Proust, had determined that he had only a few hours to live. Proust died before nightfall. A man who had always looked eerily young, he preserved enough of a glow in death to allow friends and colleagues to visit the bedroom over the weekend to pay their respects. When the writer Jean Cocteau visited, he remarked on the tall stacks of notebooks near the bed: "That pile of paper on his left was still alive, like watches ticking on the wrists of dead soldiers." Proust had achieved fame and was buried with military honors as a knight of the French Legion of Honor.

The selection presented here, from "Combray," is the first section of the first volume of *In Search of Lost Time*. Written almost completely in the first person and based on events in the author's life (although by no means purely autobiographical), the novel is famous both for its evocation of the closed world of Parisian society at the turn of the century and as a meditation on time. Proust was homosexual, and homosexuality eventually became a major theme in his writing. He once told another gay French writer, André Gide, that in a novel or short story one could say whatever one wanted about sexuality as long as the words were those of a fictional character: "never say I." Although the first-person pronoun appears on most pages of his novel, homosexuality is attributed to many characters but never to the narrator; likewise, in a novel with a number of Jewish characters, the narrator does not share Proust's religious heritage. Indeed, Proust took the events of his life and the traits of people he knew and rearranged them, combining them into fictional composites.

When *Swann's Way* appeared, in 1913, it was immediately seen as a new kind of fiction. Unlike nineteenth-century novels such as **Flaubert**'s *Madame Bovary, In Search of Lost Time* has no clear and continuous plotline building to a denouement, nor (until the final volume, published in 1927) could the reader detect a consistent development of the central character, Marcel. Proust's plot acquires purpose only gradually, through the interconnection of several themes. Likewise, the characters, Marcel included, are not sketched in fully from the beginning, but rather are revealed piece by piece, evolving within the distinctive perspectives of individual chapters. Only at the end does the narrator recognize the meaning and value of what has preceded, and when he retells his story, he does so not from an omniscient, explanatory point of view but as the reliving and gradual assessment of Marcel's lifelong experience. Most of the novel sets forth a roughly chronological sequence of events, yet its opening pages swing through recollections of times and places before settling on the narrator's childhood in Combray. The second section, *Swann in Love (Un Amour de Swann)*, recounts the story of the title character in the third person. Thus the novel proceeds by apparently discontinuous blocks of recollection, bound together by the central consciousness of the narrator. This was always Proust's plan: he insisted that, from the beginning, he had in mind a fixed structure and a goal for the novel in its entirety that would reach down to the "solidity of the smallest parts." Still, his substantial revisions and expansion of the first draft enriched the existing structure; and as he was writing, history intruded: he moved the location of the fictional Combary to the front lines in order to include the war.

The overall theme of the novel is suggested by the translation of its title: "In Search of Lost Time." The narrator, "Marcel," who suggests but is not identical to the author, is an old man, weakened by a long illness, who puzzles over the events of his past, trying to find in them a significant pattern. He begins with his childhood, orderly and comfortable in the security of accepted manners and ideals in the family home at Combray. In succeeding volumes Marcel goes out into the world, experiences love and disappointment, discovers the disparity between idealized images of places and their crude, sometimes banal reality, and is increasingly overcome by disillusionment with himself and with society.

In the short ending chapter, things suddenly come into focus as Marcel reaches an understanding of the role of time. Abruptly reliving a childhood experience when he sees a familiar book and recognizing the ravages of time in the aged and enfeebled figures of his old friends, Marcel faces the approach of death with a sense of existential continuity and realizes that his vocation as an artist lies in giving form to this buried existence. Apparently lost, the past is still alive within us, a part of our being, and memory can recapture it to give coherence and depth to present identity. By the end of the last volume, *Time Regained*, Marcel has not yet begun to write, but paradoxically the book that he plans to write is already there: Proust's *In Search of Lost Time*.

"Swann's Way" is one of the two directions in which Marcel's family took walks from their home in Combray, toward Tansonville, home of Charles Swann, and is associated with various scenes and anecdotes of love and private life. The longer walk toward the estate of the Guermantes (*The Guermantes Way*), a fictional family of the highest aristocracy appearing frequently in the novel, evokes an aura of high society and French history, a more public sphere. Fictional people and places mingle throughout with the real; here, names that are not annotated are Proust's inventions. The narrator of "Combray" is Marcel as an old man, and the French verb tense used in his recollections (here and throughout all but the final volume) is appropriately the imperfect, a tense of uncompleted action ("I used to . . . I would ask myself"). The famous first sentence points to a period in the narrator's life that is both private and somehow universal: "For a long time, I went to bed early." He would often wake up unsure where he was, what year it was, and even who he was. Proust then presents a kaleidoscopic vision of the many bedrooms where his narrator will sleep during the course of the novel, thus plunging the reader into the fictional world and demonstrating the instability of time and space.

The first chapter of "Combray" introduces the work's themes and methods, rather like the overture of an opera. All but one of the main characters appear or are mentioned, and the patterns of future encounters are set. Marcel, waiting anxiously for his beloved mother's response to a note sent down to her during dinner, suffers the same agony of separation as does Swann in his love for the promiscuous Odette, or the older Marcel himself for Albertine. The strange world of half-sleep, half-waking with which the novel begins prefigures later awakenings of memory. Long passages of intricate introspection, and sudden shifts of time and space, introduce us to the style and point of view of the rest of the book.

The selection ends with Proust's most famous image, summing up for many readers the world, the style, and the process of discovery of the author's vision. Nibbling at a madeleine (a small, rich cookielike pastry) that he has dipped in lime-blossom tea, Marcel suddenly has an overwhelming feeling of happiness. He soon associates this tantalizing, puzzling phenomenon with the memory of earlier times when he sipped tea with his aunt Leonie. He realizes that there is something valuable about such passive, spontaneous, and sensuous memory, quite different from the abstract operations of reason. Although the Marcel of "Combray" does not yet know it, he will pursue the elusive significance of this moment of happiness until, in *Time Regained,* he can, as a complete artist, bring it to the surface and link past and present in a fuller and richer vision.

Proust's novel has a unique architectural design that integrates large blocks of material: themes, situations, places, and events recur and are transformed across time. His long sentences and mammoth paragraphs reflect the slow, careful progression of thought among the changing objects of its perception. The ending paragraph of the "overture" is composed of two long sentences that encompass a wide range of meditative detail as the narrator not only recalls his childhood world—the old gray house, garden, public square and country roads, Swann's park, the river, the villagers, and indeed the whole town of Combray—but simultaneously compares the sudden recollection of the house to a stage set, and the unfolding village itself to the twists and turns of a Japanese paper flower expanding inside a bowl of water: here, inside the narrator's cup of lime-blossom tea. Characters are remembered in shifting settings and perspectives, creating a "multiple self" that is free to change and still remain the same.

Swann's Way[1]

Part 1. Combray

I

For a long time, I went to bed early. Sometimes, my candle scarcely out, my eyes would close so quickly that I did not have time to say to myself: "I'm falling asleep." And, half an hour later, the thought that it was time to try to sleep would wake me; I wanted to put down the book I thought I still had in my hands and blow out my light; I had not ceased while sleeping to form reflections on what I had just read, but these reflections had taken a rather peculiar turn; it seemed to me that I myself was what the book was talking about: a church, a quartet, the rivalry between François I and Charles V.[2] This belief lived on for a few seconds after my waking; it did not shock my reason but lay heavy like scales on my eyes and kept them from realizing that the candlestick was no longer lit. Then it began to grow unintelligible to me, as after metempsychosis do the thoughts of an earlier existence; the subject of the book detached itself from me, I was free to apply myself to it or not; immediately I recovered my sight and I was amazed to find a darkness around me soft and restful for my eyes, but perhaps even more so for my mind, to which it appeared a thing without cause, incomprehensible, a thing truly dark. I would ask myself what time it might be; I could hear the whistling of the trains which, remote or nearby, like the singing of a bird in a forest, plotting the distances, described to me the extent of the deserted countryside where the traveler hastens toward the nearest station; and the little road he is following will be engraved on his memory by the excitement he owes to new places, to unaccustomed activities, to the recent conversation and the farewells under the unfamiliar lamp that follow him still through the silence of the night, to the imminent sweetness of his return.

I would rest my cheeks tenderly against the lovely cheeks of the pillow, which, full and fresh, are like the cheeks of our childhood. I would strike a match to look at my watch. Nearly midnight. This is the hour when the invalid who has been obliged to go off on a journey and has had to sleep in an unfamiliar hotel, wakened by an attack, is cheered to see a ray of light under the door. How fortunate, it's already morning! In a moment the servants will be up, he will be able to ring, someone will come help him. The hope of being relieved gives him the courage to suffer. In fact he thought he heard footsteps; the steps approach, then recede. And the ray of light that was under his door has disappeared. It is midnight; they have just turned off the gas; the last servant has gone and he will have to suffer the whole night through without remedy.

I would go back to sleep, and would sometimes afterward wake again for brief moments only, long enough to hear the organic creak of the woodwork, open my eyes and stare at the kaleidoscope of the darkness, savor in a momentary glimmer of consciousness the sleep into which were plunged the furniture, the room, that whole of which I was only a small part and whose insensibility I

1. Translated by Lydia Davis.
2. Francis I (1496–1567), king of France, and Charles V (1500–1558), Holy Roman emperor and king of Spain, fought four wars over the empire's expansion in Europe.

would soon return to share. Or else while sleeping I had effortlessly returned to a period of my early life that had ended forever, rediscovered one of my childish terrors such as my great-uncle pulling me by my curls, a terror dispelled on the day—the dawn for me of a new era—when they were cut off. I had forgotten that event during my sleep, I recovered its memory as soon as I managed to wake myself up to escape the hands of my great-uncle, but as a precautionary measure I would completely surround my head with my pillow before returning to the world of dreams.

Sometimes, as Eve was born from one of Adam's ribs, a woman was born during my sleep from a cramped position of my thigh. Formed from the pleasure I was on the point of enjoying, she, I imagined, was the one offering it to me. My body, which felt in hers my own warmth, would try to find itself inside her, I would wake up. The rest of humanity seemed very remote compared with this woman I had left scarcely a few moments before; my cheek was still warm from her kiss, my body aching from the weight of hers. If, as sometimes happened, she had the features of a woman I had known in life, I would devote myself entirely to this end: to finding her again, like those who go off on a journey to see a longed-for city with their own eyes and imagine that one can enjoy in reality the charm of a dream. Little by little the memory of her would fade, I had forgotten the girl of my dream.

A sleeping man holds in a circle around him the sequence of the hours, the order of the years and worlds. He consults them instinctively as he wakes and reads in a second the point on the earth he occupies, the time that has elapsed before his waking; but their ranks can be mixed up, broken. If toward morning, after a bout of insomnia, sleep overcomes him as he is reading, in a position quite different from the one in which he usually sleeps, his raised arm alone is enough to stop the sun and make it retreat,[3] and, in the first minute of his waking, he will no longer know what time it is, he will think he has only just gone to bed. If he dozes off in a position still more displaced and divergent, after dinner sitting in an armchair for instance, then the confusion among the disordered worlds will be complete, the magic armchair will send him traveling at top speed through time and space, and, at the moment of opening his eyelids, he will believe he went to bed several months earlier in another country. But it was enough if, in my own bed, my sleep was deep and allowed my mind to relax entirely; then it would let go of the map of the place where I had fallen asleep and, when I woke in the middle of the night, since I did not know where I was, I did not even understand in the first moment who I was; I had only, in its original simplicity, the sense of existence as it may quiver in the depths of an animal; I was more destitute than a cave dweller; but then the memory—not yet of the place where I was, but of several of those where I had lived and where I might have been—would come to me like help from on high to pull me out of the void from which I could not have got out on my own; I crossed centuries of civilization in one second, and the image confusedly glimpsed of oil lamps, then of wingcollar shirts, gradually recomposed my self's original features.

Perhaps the immobility of the things around us is imposed on them by our certainty that they are themselves and not anything else, by the immobility of

3. If his uplifted arm prevents him from seeing the sunlight, he will think it is still night.

our mind confronting them. However that may be, when I woke thus, my mind restlessly attempting, without success, to discover where I was, everything revolved around me in the darkness, things, countries, years. My body, too benumbed to move, would try to locate, according to the form of its fatigue, the position of its limbs so as to deduce from this the direction of the wall, the placement of the furniture, so as to reconstruct and name the dwelling in which it found itself. Its memory, the memory of its ribs, its knees, its shoulders, offered in succession several of the rooms where it had slept, while around it the invisible walls, changing place according to the shape of the imagined room, spun through the shadows. And even before my mind, hesitating on the thresholds of times and shapes, had identified the house by reassembling the circumstances, it—my body—would recall the kind of bed in each one, the location of the doors, the angle at which the light came in through the windows, the existence of a hallway, along with the thought I had had as I fell asleep and that I had recovered upon waking. My stiffened side, trying to guess its orientation, would imagine, for instance, that it lay facing the wall in a big canopied bed and immediately I would say to myself: "Why, I went to sleep in the end even though Mama didn't come to say goodnight to me," I was in the country in the home of my grandfather, dead for many years; and my body, the side on which I was resting, faithful guardians of a past my mind ought never to have forgotten, recalled to me the flame of the night-light of Bohemian glass, in the shape of an urn, which hung from the ceiling by little chains, the mantelpiece of Siena marble,[4] in my bedroom at Combray, at my grandparents' house, in faraway days which at this moment I imagined were present without picturing them to myself exactly and which I would see more clearly in a little while when I was fully awake.

Then the memory of a new position would reappear; the wall would slip away in another direction: I was in my room at Mme. de Saint-Loup's,[5] in the country; good Lord! It's ten o'clock or even later, they will have finished dinner! I must have overslept during the nap I take every evening when I come back from my walk with Mme. de Saint-Loup, before putting on my evening clothes. For many years have passed since Combray, where, however late we returned, it was the sunset's red reflections I saw in the panes of my window. It is another sort of life one leads at Tansonville, at Mme. de Saint-Loup's, another sort of pleasure I take in going out only at night, in following by moonlight those lanes where I used to play in the sun; and the room where I fell asleep instead of dressing for dinner—from far off I can see it, as we come back, pierced by the flares of the lamp, a lone beacon in the night.

These revolving, confused evocations never lasted for more than a few seconds; often, in my brief uncertainty about where I was, I did not distinguish the various suppositions of which it was composed any better than we isolate, when we see a horse run, the successive positions shown to us by a kinetoscope.[6] But

4. Marble from central Italy, mottled and reddish in color. "Bohemian glass": likely to have been ornately engraved. Bohemia (now part of the Czech Republic) was a major center of the glass industry.

5. Charles Swann's daughter, Gilberte, who has married Robert de Saint-Loup, a nephew of the Guermantes.

6. An early moving-picture machine that showed photographs in rapid succession, giving the illusion of motion.

I had seen sometimes one, sometimes another, of the bedrooms I had inhabited in my life, and in the end I would recall them all in the long reveries that followed my waking: winter bedrooms in which, as soon as you are in bed, you bury your head in a nest braided of the most disparate things: a corner of the pillow, the top of the covers, a bit of shawl, the side of the bed and an issue of the *Débats roses*,[7] which you end by cementing together using the birds' technique of pressing down on it indefinitely; where in icy weather the pleasure you enjoy is the feeling that you are separated from the outdoors (like the sea swallow which makes its nest deep in an underground passage in the warmth of the earth) and where, since the fire is kept burning all night in the fireplace, you sleep in a great cloak of warm, smoky air, shot with the glimmers from the logs breaking into flame again, a sort of immaterial alcove, a warm cave dug out of the heart of the room itself, a zone of heat with shifting thermal contours, aerated by drafts which cool your face and come from the corners, from the parts close to the window or far from the hearth, and which have grown cold again: summer bedrooms where you delight in becoming one with the soft night, where the moonlight leaning against the half-open shutters casts its enchanted ladder to the foot of the bed, where you sleep almost in the open air, like a titmouse rocked by the breeze on the tip of a ray of light; sometimes the Louis XVI[8] bedroom, so cheerful that even on the first night I had not been too unhappy there and where the slender columns that lightly supported the ceiling stood aside with such grace to show and reserve the place where the bed was; at other times, the small bedroom with the very high ceiling, hollowed out in the form of a pyramid two stories high and partly paneled in mahogany, where from the first second I had been mentally poisoned by the unfamiliar odor of the vetiver,[9] convinced of the hostility of the violet curtains and the insolent indifference of the clock chattering loudly as though I were not there; where a strange and pitiless quadrangular cheval glass, barring obliquely one of the corners of the room, carved from deep inside the soft fullness of my usual field of vision a site for itself which I had not expected; where my mind, struggling for hours to dislodge itself, to stretch upward so as to assume the exact shape of the room and succeed in filling its gigantic funnel to the very top, had suffered many hard nights, while I lay stretched out in my bed, my eyes lifted, my ear anxious, my nostril restive, my heart pounding, until habit had changed the color of the curtains, silenced the clock, taught pity to the cruel oblique mirror, concealed, if not driven out completely, the smell of the vetiver and appreciably diminished the apparent height of the ceiling. Habit! That skillful but very slow housekeeper who begins by letting our mind suffer for weeks in a temporary arrangement; but whom we are nevertheless truly happy to discover, for without habit our mind, reduced to no more than its own resources, would be powerless to make a lodging habitable.

Certainly I was now wide-awake, my body had veered around one last time and the good angel of certainty had brought everything around me to a standstill, laid me down under my covers, in my bedroom, and put approximately

7. The evening edition of the daily newspaper *Le Journal des Débats*.
8. Furnished in late 18th-century style, named for the French king of the time and marked by great elegance.
9. The aromatic root of a tropical grass packaged as a moth repellent.

where they belonged in the darkness my chest of drawers, my desk, my fireplace, the window onto the street and the two doors. But even though I knew I was not in any of the houses of which my ignorance upon waking had instantly, if not presented me with the distinct picture, at least made me believe the presence possible, my memory had been stirred; generally I would not try to go back to sleep right away; I would spend the greater part of the night remembering our life in the old days, in Combray at my great-aunt's house, in Balbec,[1] in Paris, in Doncières, in Venice, elsewhere still, remembering the places, the people I had known there, what I had seen of them, what I had been told about them.

At Combray, every day, in the late afternoon, long before the moment when I would have to go to bed and stay there, without sleeping, far away from my mother and grandmother, my bedroom again became the fixed and painful focus of my preoccupations. They had indeed hit upon the idea, to distract me on the evenings when they found me looking too unhappy, of giving me a magic lantern,[2] which, while awaiting the dinner hour, they would set on top of my lamp; and, after the fashion of the first architects and master glaziers of the Gothic age, it replaced the opacity of the walls with impalpable iridescences, supernatural multicolored apparitions, where legends were depicted as in a wavering, momentary stained-glass window. But my sadness was only increased by this since the mere change in lighting destroyed the familiarity which my bedroom had acquired for me and which, except for the torment of going to bed, had made it tolerable to me. Now I no longer recognized it and I was uneasy there, as in a room in some hotel or "chalet" to which I had come for the first time straight from the railway train.

Moving at the jerky pace of his horse, and filled with a hideous design, Golo[3] would come out of the small triangular forest that velveted the hillside with dark green and advance jolting toward the castle of poor Geneviève de Brabant. This castle was cut off along a curved line that was actually the edge of one of the glass ovals arranged in the frame which you slipped between the grooves of the lantern. It was only a section of castle and it had a moor in front of it where Geneviève stood dreaming, wearing a blue belt. The castle and the moor were yellow, and I had not had to wait to see them to find out their color since, before the glasses of the frame did so, the bronze sonority of the name Brabant had shown it to me clearly. Golo would stop for a moment to listen sadly to the patter read out loud by my great-aunt,[4] which he seemed to understand perfectly, modifying his posture, with a meekness that did not exclude a certain majesty, to conform to the directions of the text; then he moved off at the same jerky pace. And nothing could stop his slow ride. If the lantern was moved, I could make out Golo's horse continuing to advance over the window curtains, swelling out with their folds, descending into their fissures. The body of Golo himself, in its essence as supernatural as that of his steed, accommodated every material obstacle, every hindersome object that he encountered by

1. The narrator's room at the fictional seaside resort of Balbec, a setting in the later novel *Within a Budding Grove*.
2. A kind of slide projector.
3. Villain of a 5th-century legend. He falsely accuses Geneviève de Brabant of adultery. Brabant was a principality in what is now Belgium.
4. Marcel's great-aunt is reading the story to him as they wait for dinner.

taking it as his skeleton and absorbing it into himself, even the doorknob he immediately adapted to and floated invincibly over with his red robe or his pale face as noble and as melancholy as ever, but revealing no disturbance at this transvertebration.

Certainly I found some charm in these brilliant projections, which seemed to emanate from a Merovingian[5] past and send out around me such ancient reflections of history. But I cannot express the uneasiness caused in me by this intrusion of mystery and beauty into a room I had at last filled with myself to the point of paying no more attention to the room than to that self. The anesthetizing influence of habit having ceased, I would begin to have thoughts, and feelings, and they are such sad things. That doorknob of my room, which differed for me from all other doorknobs in the world in that it seemed to open of its own accord, without my having to turn it, so unconscious had its handling become for me, was now serving as an astral body[6] for Golo. And as soon as they rang for dinner, I hastened to run to the dining room where the big hanging lamp, ignorant of Golo and Bluebeard,[7] and well acquainted with my family and beef casserole, shed the same light as on every other evening; and to fall into the arms of Mama, whom Geneviève de Brabant's misfortunes made all the dearer to me, while Golo's crimes drove me to examine my own conscience more scrupulously.

After dinner, alas, I soon had to leave Mama, who stayed there talking with the others, in the garden if the weather was fine, in the little drawing room to which everyone withdrew if the weather was bad. Everyone, except my grandmother, who felt that "it's a pity to shut oneself indoors in the country" and who had endless arguments with my father on days when it rained too heavily, because he sent me to read in my room instead of having me stay outdoors. "That's no way to make him strong and active," she would say sadly, "especially that boy, who so needs to build up his endurance and willpower." My father would shrug his shoulders and study the barometer, for he liked meteorology, while my mother, making no noise so as not to disturb him, watched him with a tender respect, but not so intently as to try to penetrate the mystery of his superior qualities. But as for my grandmother, in all weathers, even in a downpour when Françoise had rushed the precious wicker armchairs indoors so that they would not get wet, we would see her in the empty, rain-lashed garden, pushing back her disordered gray locks so that her forehead could more freely drink in the salubriousness of the wind and rain. She would say: "At last, one can breathe!" and would roam the soaked paths—too symmetrically aligned for her liking by the new gardener, who lacked all feeling for nature and whom my father had been asking since morning if the weather would clear—with her jerky, enthusiastic little step, regulated by the various emotions excited in her soul by the intoxication of the storm, the power of good health, the stupidity of my upbringing, and the symmetry of the gardens, rather than by the desire, quite unknown to her, to spare her plum-colored skirt the spots of mud under

5. The first dynasty of French kings (ca. 500–751).

6. Spiritual counterpart of the physical body. According to the doctrine of Theosophy (a spiritualist movement originating in 1875), the astral body survives the death of the physical body.

7. The legendary wife murderer, presumably shown on another set of slides.

which it would disappear up to a height that was always, for her maid, a source of despair and a problem.

When these garden walks of my grandmother's took place after dinner, one thing had the power to make her come inside again: this was—at one of the periodic intervals when her circular itinerary brought her back, like an insect, in front of the lights of the little drawing room where the liqueurs were set out on the card table—if my great-aunt called out to her: "Bathilde! Come and stop your husband from drinking cognac!" To tease her, in fact (she had brought into my father's family so different a mentality that everyone poked fun at her and tormented her), since liqueurs were forbidden to my grandfather, my great-aunt would make him drink a few drops. My poor grandmother would come in, fervently beg her husband not to taste the cognac; he would become angry, drink his mouthful despite her, and my grandmother would go off again, sad, discouraged, yet smiling, for she was so humble at heart and so gentle that her tenderness for others, and the lack of fuss she made over her own person and her sufferings, came together in her gaze in a smile in which, unlike what one sees in the faces of so many people, there was irony only for herself, and for all of us a sort of kiss from her eyes, which could not see those she cherished without caressing them passionately with her gaze. This torture which my great-aunt inflicted on her, the spectacle of my grandmother's vain entreaties and of her weakness, defeated in advance, trying uselessly to take the liqueur glass away from my grandfather, were the kinds of things which you later become so accustomed to seeing that you smile as you contemplate them and take the part of the persecutor resolutely and gaily enough to persuade yourself privately that no persecution is involved; at that time they filled me with such horror that I would have liked to hit my great-aunt. But as soon as I heard: "Bathilde, come and stop your husband from drinking cognac!," already a man in my cowardice, I did what we all do, once we are grown up, when confronted with sufferings and injustices: I did not want to see them; I went up to sob at the very top of the house next to the schoolroom,[8] under the roofs, in a little room that smelled of orris root[9] and was also perfumed by a wild black-currant bush which had sprouted outside between the stones of the wall and extended a branch of flowers through the half-open window. Intended for a more specialized and more vulgar use, this room, from which during the day you could see all the way to the keep[1] of Roussainville-le-Pin, for a long time served me as a refuge, no doubt because it was the only one I was permitted to lock, for all those occupations of mine that demanded an inviolable solitude: reading, reverie, tears, and sensuous pleasure. Alas! I did not know that, much more than her husband's little deviations from his regimen, it was my weak will, my delicate health, the uncertainty they cast on my future that so sadly preoccupied my grandmother in the course of those incessant perambulations, afternoon and evening, when we would see, as it passed and then passed again, lifted slantwise toward the sky, her beautiful face with its brown furrowed cheeks, which with age had become almost mauve like the plowed fields in autumn, crossed, if she was

8. A room in the house dedicated to the children's schoolwork.
9. A powder then used as a room deodorizer.
1. The best-fortified tower of a medieval castle. "Vulgar use": it was used as a toilet.

going out, by a veil half raised, while upon them, brought there by the cold or some sad thought, an involuntary tear was always drying.

My sole consolation, when I went upstairs for the night, was that Mama would come and kiss me once I was in bed. But this goodnight lasted so short a time, she went down again so soon, that the moment when I heard her coming up, then the soft sound of her garden dress of blue muslin, hung with little cords of plaited straw, passing along the hallway with its double doors, was for me a painful one. It heralded the moment that was to follow it, when she had left me, when she had gone down again. So that I came to wish that this goodnight I loved so much would take place as late as possible, so as to prolong the time of respite in which Mama had not yet come. Sometimes when, after kissing me, she opened the door to go, I wanted to call her back, to say "kiss me one more time," but I knew that immediately her face would look vexed, because the concession she was making to my sadness and agitation by coming up to kiss me, by bringing me this kiss of peace, irritated my father, who found these rituals absurd, and she would have liked to try to induce me to lose the need for it, the habit of it, far indeed from allowing me to acquire that of asking her, when she was already on the doorstep, for one kiss more. And to see her vexed destroyed all the calm she had brought me a moment before, when she had bent her loving face down over my bed and held it out to me like a host[2] for a communion of peace from which my lips would draw her real presence and the power to fall asleep. But those evenings, when Mama stayed so short a time in my room, were still sweet compared to the ones when there was company for dinner and when, because of that, she did not come up to say goodnight to me. That company was usually limited to M. Swann, who, apart from a few acquaintances passing through, was almost the only person who came to our house at Combray, sometimes for a neighborly dinner (more rarely after that unfortunate marriage of his, because my parents did not want to receive his wife), sometimes after dinner, unexpectedly. On those evenings when, as we sat in front of the house under the large chestnut tree, around the iron table, we heard at the far end of the garden, not the copious high-pitched bell that drenched, that deafened in passing with its ferruginous,[3] icy, inexhaustible noise any person in the household who set it off by coming in "without ringing," but the shy, oval, golden double tinkling of the little visitors' bell, everyone would immediately wonder: "A visitor—now who can that be?" but we knew very well it could only be M. Swann; my great-aunt speaking loudly, to set an example, in a tone of voice that she strained to make natural, said not to whisper that way; that nothing is more disagreeable for a visitor just coming in who is led to think that people are saying things he should not hear; and they would send as a scout my grandmother, who was always glad to have a pretext for taking one more walk around the garden and who would profit from it by surreptitiously pulling up a few rose stakes on the way so as to make the roses look a little more natural, like a mother who runs her hand through her son's hair to fluff it up after the barber has flattened it too much.

We would all remain hanging on the news my grandmother was going to bring us of the enemy, as though there had been a great number of possible

2. Communion wafer.

3. Ironlike.

assailants to choose among, and soon afterward my grandfather would say: "I recognize Swann's voice." In fact one could recognize him only by his voice, it was difficult to make out his face, his aquiline nose, his green eyes under a high forehead framed by blond, almost red hair, cut Bressant-style,[4] because we kept as little light as possible in the garden so as not to attract mosquitoes, and I would go off, as though not going for that reason, to say that the syrups should be brought out; my grandmother placed a great deal of importance, considering it more amiable, on the idea that they should not seem anything exceptional, and for visitors only. M. Swann, though much younger, was very attached to my grandfather, who had been one of the closest friends of his father, an excellent man but peculiar, in whom, apparently, a trifle was sometimes enough to interrupt the ardor of his feelings, to change the course of his thinking. Several times a year I would hear my grandfather at the table telling anecdotes, always the same ones, about the behavior of old M. Swann upon the death of his wife, over whom he had watched day and night. My grandfather, who had not seen him for a long time, had rushed to his side at the estate the Swanns owned in the vicinity of Combray and, so that he would not be present at the coffining, managed to entice him for a while, all in tears, out of the death chamber. They walked a short way in the park, where there was a little sunshine. Suddenly M. Swann, taking my grandfather by the arm, cried out: "Oh, my old friend, what a joy it is to be walking here together in such fine weather! Don't you think it's pretty, all these trees, these hawthorns! And my pond—which you've never congratulated me on! You look as sad as an old nightcap. Feel that little breeze? Oh, say what you like, life has something to offer despite everything, my dear Amédée!" Suddenly the memory of his dead wife came back to him and, no doubt feeling it would be too complicated to try to understand how he could have yielded to an impulse of happiness at such a time, he confined himself, in a habitual gesture of his whenever a difficult question came into his mind, to passing his hand over his forehead, wiping his eyes and the lenses of his lorgnon. Yet he could not be consoled for the death of his wife, but, during the two years he survived her, would say to my grandfather: "It's odd, I think of my poor wife often, but I can't think of her for long at a time." "Often, but only a little at a time, like poor old Swann," had become one of my grandfather's favorite phrases, which he uttered apropos of the most different sorts of things. I would have thought Swann's father was a monster, if my grandfather, whom I considered a better judge and whose pronouncement, forming a legal precedent for me, often allowed me later to dismiss offenses I might have been inclined to condemn, had not exclaimed: "What! He had a heart of gold!"

For many years, even though, especially before his marriage, the younger M. Swann often came to see them at Combray, my great-aunt and my grandparents did not suspect that he had entirely ceased to live in the kind of society his family had frequented and that, under the sort of incognito which this name Swann gave him among us, they were harboring—with the perfect innocence of honest innkeepers who have under their roof, without knowing it, some celebrated highwayman—one of the most elegant members of the Jockey

4. Crew cut in front and longer in back: a hair style popularized by the actor Jean-Baptiste Bressant (1815–1886).

Club, a favorite friend of the Comte de Paris and the Prince of Wales, one of the men most sought after by the high society of the Faubourg Saint-Germain.[5]

Our ignorance of this brilliant social life that Swann led was obviously due in part to the reserve and discretion of his character, but also to the fact that bourgeois people in those days formed for themselves a rather Hindu notion of society and considered it to be made up of closed castes, in which each person, from birth, found himself placed in the station which his family occupied and from which nothing, except the accidents of an exceptional career or an unhoped-for marriage, could withdraw him in order to move him into a higher caste. M. Swann, the father, was a stockbroker; "Swann the son" would find he belonged for his entire life to a caste in which fortunes varied, as in a tax bracket, between such and such fixed incomes. One knew which had been his father's associations, one therefore knew which were his own, with which people he was "in a position" to consort. If he knew others, these were bachelor acquaintances on whom old friends of the family, such as my relatives, would close their eyes all the more benignly because he continued, after losing his parents, to come faithfully to see us; but we would have been ready to wager that these people he saw, who were unknown to us, were the sort he would not have dared greet had he encountered them when he was with us. If you were determined to assign Swann a social coefficient that was his alone, among the other sons of stockbrokers in a position equal to that of his parents, this coefficient would have been a little lower for him because, very simple in his manner and with a long-standing "craze" for antiques and painting, he now lived and amassed his collections in an old town house which my grandmother dreamed of visiting, but which was situated on the quai d'Orléans,[6] a part of town where my great-aunt felt it was ignominious to live. "But are you a connoisseur? I ask for your own sake, because you're likely to let the dealers unload some awful daubs on you," my great-aunt would say to him; in fact she did not assume he had any competence and even from an intellectual point of view had no great opinion of a man who in conversation avoided serious subjects and showed a most prosaic preciseness not only when he gave us cooking recipes, entering into the smallest details, but even when my grandmother's sisters talked about artistic subjects. Challenged by them to give his opinion, to express his admiration for a painting, he would maintain an almost ungracious silence and then, on the other hand, redeem himself if he could provide, about the museum in which it was to be found, about the date at which it had been painted, a pertinent piece of information. But usually he would content himself with trying to entertain us by telling a new story each time about something that had just happened to him involving people selected from among those we knew, the Combray pharmacist, our cook, our coachman. Certainly these tales made my great-aunt laugh, but she could not distinguish clearly if this was because of the absurd role Swann always assigned himself or because of the

5. A fashionable area of Paris on the left bank of the Seine; many of the French aristocracy lived there. "Jockey Club": an exclusive men's club devoted to horse racing, opera, and other diversions. Louis-Philippe-Albert d'Orléans, comte de Paris (1838–1894), was the heir apparent to the French throne, should the monarchy ever be restored; the Prince of Wales became, in 1901, King Edward VII of England.

6. A beautiful though less fashionable section in the heart of Paris, along the Seine.

wit he showed in telling them: "You are quite a character, Monsieur Swann!" Being the only rather vulgar person in our family, she took care to point out to strangers, when they were talking about Swann, that, had he wanted to, he could have lived on the boulevard Haussmann or the avenue de l'Opéra, that he was the son of M. Swann, who must have left four or five million,[7] but that this was his whim. One that she felt moreover must be so amusing to others that in Paris, when M. Swann came on New Year's Day to bring her her bag of marrons glacés,[8] she never failed, if there was company, to say to him: "Well, Monsieur Swann! Do you still live next door to the wine warehouse, so as to be sure of not missing the train when you go to Lyon?"[9] And she would look out of the corner of her eye, over her lorgnon, at the other visitors.

But if anyone had told my great-aunt that this same Swann, who, as the son of old M. Swann, was perfectly "qualified" to be received by all the "best of the bourgeoisie," by the most respected notaries or lawyers of Paris (a hereditary privilege he seemed to make little use of), had, as though in secret, quite a different life; that on leaving our house, in Paris, after telling us he was going home to bed, he retraced his steps as soon as he had turned the corner and went to a certain drawing room that no eye of any broker or broker's associate would ever contemplate, this would have seemed to my aunt as extraordinary as might to a better-educated lady the thought of being personally on close terms with Aristaeus[1] and learning that, after having a chat with her, he would go deep into the heart of the realms of Thetis, into an empire hidden from mortal eyes, where Virgil shows him being received with open arms; or—to be content with an image that had more chance of occurring to her, for she had seen it painted on our petits-fours plates at Combray—of having had as a dinner guest Ali Baba,[2] who, as soon as he knows he is alone, will enter the cave dazzling with unsuspected treasure.

One day when he had come to see us in Paris after dinner apologizing for being in evening clothes, Françoise having said, after he left, that she had learned from the coachman that he had dined "at the home of a princess," "Yes, a princess of the demimonde!"[3] my aunt had responded, shrugging her shoulders without raising her eyes from her knitting, with serene irony.

Thus, my great-aunt was cavalier in her treatment of him. Since she believed he must be flattered by our invitations, she found it quite natural that he never came to see us in the summertime without having in his hand a basket of peaches or raspberries from his garden and that from each of his trips to Italy he would bring me back photographs of masterpieces.

7. I.e., francs—nearly $1 million in the currency of the day, about $19 million in 2011. (The franc has since been replaced by the euro.) "Boulevard Haussmann" and "avenue de l'Opéra": large modern avenues where the wealthy bourgeoisie liked to live.
8. Candied chestnuts, a traditional Parisian New Year's gift.
9. The wine warehouse was close to the Gare de Lyon, the terminal from which trains left for the industrial city of Lyon and other destinations in southeastern France.
1. Son of the Greek god Apollo. In Virgil's *Fourth Georgic,* Aristaeus seeks help from the sea nymph Thetis.
2. Hero of an *Arabian Nights* tale, a poor youth who discovers a robbers' cave filled with treasure.
3. Literally, "half-world" (French): women of questionable reputation, not quite members of society.

They did not hesitate to send him off in search of it when they needed a recipe for gribiche sauce[4] or pineapple salad for large dinners to which they had not invited him, believing he did not have sufficient prestige for one to be able to serve him up to acquaintances who were coming for the first time. If the conversation turned to the princes of the House of France:[5] "people you and I will never know, will we, and we can manage quite well without that, can't we," my great-aunt would say to Swann, who had, perhaps, a letter from Twickenham[6] in his pocket; she had him push the piano around and turn the pages on the evenings when my grandmother's sister sang, handling this creature, who was elsewhere so sought after, with the naive roughness of a child who plays with a collector's curio no more carefully than with some object of little value. No doubt the Swann who was known at the same time to so many clubmen was quite different from the one created by my great-aunt, when in the evening, in the little garden at Combray, after the two hesitant rings of the bell had sounded, she injected and invigorated with all that she knew about the Swann family the dark and uncertain figure who emerged, followed by my grandmother, from a background of shadows, and whom we recognized by his voice. But even with respect to the most insignificant things in life, none of us constitutes a material whole, identical for everyone, which a person has only to go look up as though we were a book of specifications or a last testament; our social personality is a creation of the minds of others. Even the very simple act that we call "seeing a person we know" is in part an intellectual one. We fill the physical appearance of the individual we see with all the notions we have about him, and of the total picture that we form for ourselves, these notions certainly occupy the greater part. In the end they swell his cheeks so perfectly, follow the line of his nose in an adherence so exact, they do so well at nuancing the sonority of his voice as though the latter were only a transparent envelope that each time we see this face and hear this voice, it is these notions that we encounter again, that we hear. No doubt, in the Swann they had formed for themselves, my family had failed out of ignorance to include a host of details from his life in the fashionable world that caused other people, when they were in his presence, to see refinements rule his face and stop at his aquiline nose as though at their natural frontier; but they had also been able to garner in this face disaffected of its prestige, vacant and spacious, in the depths of these depreciated eyes, the vague, sweet residue—half memory, half forgetfulness—of the idle hours spent together after our weekly dinners, around the card table or in the garden, during our life of good country neighborliness. The corporeal envelope of our friend had been so well stuffed with all this, as well as with a few memories relating to his parents, that this particular Swann had become a complete and living being, and I have the impression of leaving one person to go to another distinct from him, when, in my memory, I pass from the Swann I knew later with accuracy to that first Swann—to that first Swann in whom I rediscover the charming mistakes of my youth and who in fact resembles less

4. A seasoned mayonnaise that includes chopped hard-boiled eggs.

5. The French royal family, headed by the comte de Paris. The political climate was anti-royalist, and all claimants to the French throne and their heirs were banished from France by law in 1886.

6. Fashionable London suburb. The French royal family had a house there, which was, for some time, the residence of the exiled comte de Paris.

the other Swann than he resembles the other people I knew at the time, as though one's life were like a museum in which all the portraits from one period have a family look about them, a single tonality—to that first Swann abounding in leisure, fragrant with the smell of the tall chestnut tree, the baskets of raspberries, and a sprig of tarragon.

Yet one day when my grandmother had gone to ask a favor from a lady she had known at the Sacré-Coeur[7] (and with whom, because of our notion of the castes, she had not wished to remain in close contact despite a reciprocal congeniality), this lady, the Marquise de Villeparisis of the famous de Bouillon family, had said to her: "I believe you know M. Swann very well; he is a great friend of my nephew and niece, the des Laumes."[8] My grandmother had returned from her visit full of enthusiasm for the house, which overlooked some gardens and in which Mme. de Villeparisis had advised her to rent a flat, and also for a waistcoat maker and his daughter, who kept a shop in the courtyard where she had gone to ask them to put a stitch in her skirt, which she had torn in the stairwell. My grandmother had found these people wonderful, she declared that the girl was a gem and the waistcoat maker was most distinguished, the finest man she had ever seen. Because for her, distinction was something absolutely independent of social position. She went into ecstasies over an answer the waistcoat maker had given her, saying to Mama: "Sévigné[9] couldn't have said it any better!" and, in contrast, of a nephew of Mme. de Villeparisis whom she had met at the house: "Oh, my dear daughter, how common he is!"

Now the remark about Swann had had the effect, not of raising him in my great-aunt's estimation, but of lowering Mme. de Villeparisis. It seemed that the respect which, on my grandmother's faith, we accorded Mme. de Villeparisis created a duty on her part to do nothing that would make her less worthy, a duty in which she had failed by learning of Swann's existence, by permitting relatives of hers to associate with him. "What! She knows Swann? A person you claim is a relation of the Maréchal de MacMahon?"[1] My family's opinion regarding Swann's associations seemed confirmed later by his marriage to a woman of the worst social station, practically a cocotte, whom, what was more, he never attempted to introduce, continuing to come to our house alone, though less and less, but from whom they believed they could judge—assuming it was there that he had found her—the social circle, unknown to them, that he habitually frequented.

But one time, my grandfather read in a newspaper that M. Swann was one of the most faithful guests at the Sunday lunches given by the Duc de X . . ., whose father and uncle had been the most prominent statesmen in the reign of Louis-Philippe.[2] Now, my grandfather was interested in all the little facts that

7. A convent school in Paris, attended by daughters of the aristocracy and the wealthy bourgeoisie.

8. A fictional family, like the Guermantes. Proust strengthens the apparent reality of the Guermantes family, including the marquise de Villeparisis, by relating them to the historical house of Bouillon, a famous aristocratic family that could trace its descent from the Middle Ages.

9. The marquise de Sévigné (1626–1696), known for her lively style in letters that described contemporary events and the life of the aristocracy.

1. Marshal of France (1808–1893), elected president of the French Republic in 1873.

2. King of France from 1830 to 1848, father of the comte de Paris.

could help him enter imaginatively into the private lives of men like Molé, the Duc Pasquier, the Duc de Broglie.[3] He was delighted to learn that Swann associated with people who had known them. My great-aunt, however, interpreted this news in a sense unfavorable to Swann: anyone who chose his associations outside the caste into which he had been born, outside his social "class," suffered in her eyes a regrettable lowering of his social position. It seemed to her that he gave up forthwith the fruit of all the good relations with well-placed people so honorably preserved and stored away for their children by foresightful families (my great-aunt had even stopped seeing the son of a lawyer we knew because he had married royalty and was therefore in her opinion demoted from the respected rank of lawyer's son to that of one of those adventurers, former valets or stableboys, on whom they say that queens sometimes bestowed their favors). She disapproved of my grandfather's plan to question Swann, the next evening he was to come to dinner, about these friends of his we had discovered. At the same time my grandmother's two sisters, old maids who shared her nobility of character, but not her sort of mind, declared that they could not understand what pleasure their brother-in-law could find in talking about such foolishness. They were women of lofty aspirations, who for that very reason were incapable of taking an interest in what is known as tittle-tattle, even if it had some historic interest, and more generally in anything that was not directly connected to an aesthetic or moral subject. The disinterestedness of their minds was such, with respect to all that, closely or distantly, seemed connected with worldly matters, that their sense of hearing—having finally understood its temporary uselessness when the conversation at dinner assumed a tone that was frivolous or merely pedestrian without these two old spinsters being able to lead it back to the subjects dear to them—would suspend the functioning of its receptive organs and allow them to begin to atrophy. If my grandfather needed to attract the two sisters' attention at such times, he had to resort to those bodily signals used by alienists with certain lunatics suffering from distraction: striking a glass repeatedly with the blade of a knife while speaking to them sharply and looking them suddenly in the eye, violent methods which these psychiatrists often bring with them into their ordinary relations with healthy people, either from professional habit or because they believe everyone is a little crazy.

They were more interested when, the day before Swann was to come to dinner, and had personally sent them a case of Asti wine, my aunt, holding a copy of the *Figaro*[4] in which next to the title of a painting in an exhibition of Corot,[5] these words appeared: "From the collection of M. Charles Swann," said: "Did you see this? Swann is 'front page news' in the *Figaro*." "But I've always told you he had a great deal of taste," said my grandmother. "Of course you would! Anything so long as your opinion is not the same as *ours*," answered my great-

3. Achille-Charles-Léon-Victor, duc de Broglie (1785–1870) had a busy public career that ended in 1851. Louis-Mathieu, comte Molé (1781–1855) held various cabinet positions before becoming premier of France in 1836. Duc Etienne-Denis Pasquier (1767–1862) also held important public positions up to 1837. All three were active during the reign of Louis-Philippe.

4. A leading Parisian newspaper. "Asti": an Italian white wine.

5. Jean-Baptiste-Camille Corot (1796–1875), a popular French landscape painter.

aunt, who, knowing that my grandmother was never of the same opinion as she, and not being quite sure that she herself was the one we always declared was right, wanted to extract from us a general condemnation of my grandmother's convictions against which she was trying to force us into solidarity with her own. But we remained silent. When my grandmother's sisters expressed their intention of speaking to Swann about this mention in the *Figaro,* my great-aunt advised them against it. Whenever she saw in others an advantage, however small, that she did not have, she persuaded herself that it was not an advantage but a detriment and she pitied them so as not to have to envy them. "I believe you would not be pleasing him at all; I am quite sure I would find it very unpleasant to see my name printed boldly like that in the newspaper, and I would not be at all gratified if someone spoke to me about it." But she did not persist in trying to convince my grandmother's sisters; for they in their horror of vulgarity had made such a fine art of concealing a personal allusion beneath ingenious circumlocutions that it often went unnoticed even by the person to whom it was addressed. As for my mother, she thought only of trying to persuade my father to agree to talk to Swann not about his wife but about his daughter, whom he adored and because of whom it was said he had finally entered into this marriage. "You might just say a word to him; just ask how she is: It must be so hard for him." But my father would become annoyed: "No, no; you have the most absurd ideas. It would be ridiculous."

But the only one of us for whom Swann's arrival became the object of a painful preoccupation was I. This was because on the evenings when strangers, or merely M. Swann, were present, Mama did not come up to my room. I had dinner before everyone else and afterward I came and sat at the table, until eight o'clock when it was understood that I had to go upstairs; the precious and fragile kiss that Mama usually entrusted to me in my bed when I was going to sleep I would have to convey from the dining room to my bedroom and protect during the whole time I undressed, so that its sweetness would not shatter, so that its volatile essence would not disperse and evaporate, and on precisely those evenings when I needed to receive it with more care, I had to take it, I had to snatch it brusquely, publicly, without even having the time and the freedom of mind necessary to bring to what I was doing the attention of those individuals controlled by some mania, who do their utmost not to think of anything else while they are shutting a door, so as to be able, when the morbid uncertainty returns to them, to confront it victoriously with the memory of the moment when they did shut the door. We were all in the garden when the two hesitant rings of the little bell sounded. We knew it was Swann; even so we all looked at one another questioningly and my grandmother was sent on reconnaissance. "Remember to thank him intelligibly for the wine, you know how delicious it is and the case is enormous," my grandfather exhorted his two sisters-in-law. "Don't start whispering," said my great-aunt. "How comfortable would you feel arriving at a house where everyone is speaking so quietly!" "Ah! Here's M. Swann. Let's ask him if he thinks the weather will be good tomorrow," said my father. My mother thought that one word from her would wipe out all the pain that we in our family might have caused Swann since his marriage. She found an opportunity to take him aside. But I followed her; I could not bring myself to part from her by even one step while thinking that very soon I would have to leave her in the dining room and that I would have to go up to my room without having the consolation I had on the other evenings, that she would come kiss me. "Now, M. Swann," she said to him, "do tell me about your daughter; I'm sure she already has a taste for beautiful things like her papa." "Here, come and sit with the rest of us on the veranda," said my grandfather, coming up to them. My mother was obliged to stop, but she derived from this very constraint one more delicate thought, like good poets forced by the tyranny of rhyme to find their most beautiful lines: "We can talk about her again when we're by ourselves," she said softly to Swann. "Only a mother is capable of understanding you. I'm sure her own mother would agree with me." We all sat down around the iron table. I would have preferred not to think about the hours of anguish I was going to endure that evening alone in my room without being able to go to sleep; I tried to persuade myself they were not at all important, since I would have forgotten them by tomorrow morning, and to fix my mind on ideas of the future that should have led me as though across a bridge beyond the imminent abyss that frightened me so. But my mind, strained by my preoccupation, convex like the glance which I shot at my mother, would not allow itself to be penetrated by any foreign impressions. Thoughts certainly entered it, but only on condition that they left outside every element of beauty or simply of playfulness that could have moved or distracted me. Just as a patient, by means of an anesthetic, can watch with complete lucidity the operation being performed on him, but without feeling anything, I could recite to myself some lines that I loved or observe the efforts my grandfather made to talk to Swann about the Duc d'Audiffret-Pasquier,[6] without the former making me feel any emotion, the latter any hilarity. Those efforts were fruitless. Scarcely had my grandfather asked Swann a question relating to that orator than one of my grandmother's sisters, in whose ears the question was resonating like a profound but untimely silence that should be broken for the sake of politeness, would address the other: "Just imagine, Céline,[7] I've met a young Swedish governess who has been telling me about cooperatives in the Scandinavian countries; the details are most interesting. We really must have her here for dinner one evening." "Certainly!" answered her sister Flora, "but I haven't been wasting my time either. At M. Vinteuil's I met a learned old man who knows Maubant[8] very well, and Maubant has explained to him in the greatest detail how he creates his parts. It's most interesting. He's a neighbor of M. Vinteuil's, I had no idea; and he's very nice." "M. Vinteuil isn't the only one who has nice neighbors," exclaimed my aunt Céline in a voice amplified by her shyness and given an artificial tone by her premeditation, while casting at Swann what she called a meaningful look. At the same time my aunt Flora, who had understood that this phrase was Céline's way of thanking Swann for the Asti, was also looking at Swann with an expression that combined congratulation and irony, either simply to emphasize her sister's witticism, or because she envied Swann for having inspired it, or because she could not help making fun of him since she thought he was being put on the spot. "I think we can manage to persuade the old gentleman to come for dinner," continued

6. The duc d'Audiffret-Pasquier (1823–1905) was president of the Chamber of Peers during the reign of Louis-Philippe.
7. A misprint—as the context makes clear, it is Céline who speaks and Flora who responds.
8. Henri-Polydore Maubant (1823–1902), an actor at the Comédie Française. "Vinteuil": a fictitious composer.

Flora; "when you get him started on Maubant or Mme. Materna,[9] he talks for hours without stopping." "That must be delightful," sighed my grandfather, in whose mind, unfortunately, nature had as completely failed to include the possibility of taking a passionate interest in Swedish cooperatives or the creation of Maubant's parts as it had forgotten to furnish those of my grandmother's sisters with the little grain of salt one must add oneself, in order to find some savor in it, to a story about the private life of Molé or the Comte de Paris. "Now, then," said Swann to my grandfather, "what I'm going to say has more to do than it might appear with what you were asking me, because in certain respects things haven't changed enormously. This morning I was rereading something in Saint-Simon[1] that would have amused you. It's in the volume about his mission to Spain; it's not one of the best, hardly more than a journal, but at least it's a marvelously well written one, which already makes it rather fundamentally different from the deadly boring journals we think we have to read every morning and evening." "I don't agree, there are days when reading the papers seems to me very pleasant indeed . . ." my aunt Flora interrupted, to show that she had read the sentence about Swann's Corot in *Le Figaro*. "When they talk about things or people that interest us!" said my aunt Céline, going one better. "I don't deny it," answered Swann with surprise. "What I fault the newspapers for is that day after day they draw our attention to insignificant things whereas only three or four times in our lives do we read a book in which there is something really essential. Since we tear the band off the newspaper so feverishly every morning, they ought to change things and put into the newspaper, oh, I don't know, perhaps . . . Pascal's *Pensées*![2] (He isolated this word with an ironic emphasis so as not to seem pedantic.) "And then, in the gilt-edged volume that we open only once in ten years," he added, showing the disdain for worldly matters affected by certain worldly men, "we would read that the Queen of Greece has gone to Cannes or that the Princesse de Léon has given a costume ball. This way, the proper proportions would be reestablished." But, feeling sorry he had gone so far as to speak even lightly of serious things: "What a lofty conversation we're having," he said ironically; "I don't know why we're climbing to such 'heights' "—and turning to my grandfather: "Well, Saint-Simon describes how Maulévrier[3] had the audacity to offer to shake hands with Saint-Simon's sons. You know, this is the same Maulévrier of whom he says: 'Never did I see in that thick bottle anything but ill-humor, vulgarity, and foolishness.'" "Thick or not, I know some bottles in which there is something quite different," said Flora vivaciously, determined that she too should thank Swann, because the gift of Asti was addressed to both of them. Céline laughed. Swann, disconcerted, went on: "'I cannot say whether it was

9. Amalie Materna (1845–1918), Austrian soprano who took part in the premiere of Wagner's *Ring* cycle at Bayreuth in 1876.
1. The memoirs of the duc de Saint-Simon (1675–1755) describe court life and intrigue during the reigns of Louis XIV and Louis XV. He was sent to Spain in 1721 to arrange the marriage of Louis XV to the daughter of the king of Spain.
2. The *Thoughts* of the religious philosopher Blaise Pascal (1623–1662) are comments on the human condition and one of the major works of French classicism.
3. Jean-Baptiste-Louis Andrault, marquis de Maulévrier-Langeron (1677–1754), the French ambassador to Spain. Saint-Simon considered him of inferior birth and would not let his own children shake Maulévrier's hand (*Memoirs*, vol. 39).

ignorance or a trap,' wrote Saint-Simon. 'He tried to shake hands with my children. I noticed it in time to prevent him.'" My grandfather was already in ecstasies over "ignorance or a trap," but Mlle. Céline, in whom the name of Saint-Simon—a literary man—had prevented the complete anesthesia of her auditory faculties, was already growing indignant: "What? You admire that? Well, that's a fine thing! But what can it mean; isn't one man as good as the next? What difference does it make whether he's a duke or a coachman, if he's intelligent and good-hearted? Your Saint-Simon had a fine way of raising his children, if he didn't teach them to offer their hands to all decent people. Why, it's quite abominable. And you dare to quote that?" And my grandfather, terribly upset and sensing how impossible it would be, in the face of this obstruction, to try to get Swann to tell the stories that would have amused him, said quietly to Mama: "Now remind me of the line you taught me that comforts me so much at times like this. Oh, yes! 'What virtues, Lord, Thou makest us abhor![4] Oh, how good that is!"

I did not take my eyes off my mother, I knew that when we were at the table, they would not let me stay during the entire dinner and that, in order not to annoy my father, Mama would not let me kiss her several times in front of the guests as though we were in my room. And so I promised myself that in the dining room, as they were beginning dinner and I felt the hour approaching, I would do everything I could do alone in advance of this kiss which would be so brief and furtive, choose with my eyes the place on her cheek that I would kiss, prepare my thoughts so as to be able, by means of this mental beginning of the kiss, to devote the whole of the minute Mama would grant me to feeling her cheek against my lips, as a painter who can obtain only short sittings prepares his palette and, guided by his notes, does in advance from memory everything for which he could if necessary manage without the presence of the model. But now before the dinner bell rang my grandfather had the unwitting brutality to say: "The boy looks tired, he ought to go up to bed. We're dining late tonight anyway." And my father, who was not as scrupulous as my grandmother and my mother about honoring treaties, said: "Yes, go on now, up to bed with you." I tried to kiss Mama, at that moment we heard the dinner bell. "No, really, leave your mother alone, you've already said goodnight to each other as it is, these demonstrations are ridiculous. Go on now, upstairs!" And I had to leave without my viaticum;[5] I had to climb each step of the staircase, as the popular expression has it, "against my heart,"[6] climbing against my heart which wanted to go back to my mother because she had not, by kissing me, given it license to go with me. That detested staircase which I always entered with such gloom exhaled an odor of varnish that had in some sense absorbed, fixated, the particular sort of sorrow I felt every evening and made it perhaps even crueler to my sensibility because, when it took that olfactory form, my intelligence could no longer share in it. When we are asleep and a raging toothache is as yet perceived by us only in the form of a girl whom we attempt two hundred times to pull out of the water or a line by Molière[7] that we repeat to ourselves incessantly, it is a great relief to wake up so that our intelli-

4. Adaptation of a line from *Pompey's Death* (III.4), a tragedy by the French classical dramatist Pierre Corneille (1606–1684).
5. The communion wafer and wine given to the dying in Catholic rites.
6. The literal translation of a common phrase meaning "reluctantly" (French).
7. Jean-Baptiste Poquelin Molière (1622–1673), French classical dramatist.

gence can divest the idea of raging toothache of its disguise of heroism or cadence. It was the opposite of this relief that I experienced when my sorrow at going up to my room entered me in a manner infinitely swifter, almost instantaneous, at once insidious and abrupt, through the inhalation—far more toxic than the intellectual penetration—of the smell of varnish peculiar to that staircase. Once in my room, I had to stop up all the exits, close the shutters, dig my own grave by undoing my covers, put on the shroud of my nightshirt. But before burying myself in the iron bed which they had added to the room because I was too hot in the summer under the rep curtains of the big bed, I had a fit of rebelliousness, I wanted to attempt the ruse of a condemned man. I wrote to my mother begging her to come upstairs for something serious that I could not tell her in my letter. My fear was that Françoise, my aunt's cook who was charged with looking after me when I was at Combray, would refuse to convey my note. I suspected that, for her, delivering a message to my mother when there was company would seem as impossible as for a porter to hand a letter to an actor while he was onstage. With respect to things that could or could not be done she possessed a code at once imperious, extensive, subtle, and intransigent about distinctions that were impalpable or otiose[8] (which made it resemble those ancient laws which, alongside such fierce prescriptions as the massacre of children at the breast, forbid one with an exaggerated delicacy to boil a kid in its mother's milk, or to eat the sinew from an animal's thigh).[9] This code, to judge from her sudden obstinacy when she did not wish to do certain errands that we gave her, seemed to have anticipated social complexities and worldly refinements that nothing in Françoise's associations or her life as a village domestic could have suggested to her; and we had to say to ourselves that in her there was a very old French past, noble and ill understood, as in those manufacturing towns where elegant old houses testify that there was once a court life, and where the employees of a factory for chemical products work surrounded by delicate sculptures representing the miracle of Saint Théophile or the four sons of Aymon.[1] In this particular case, the article of the code which made it unlikely that except in case of fire Françoise would go bother Mama in the presence of M. Swann for so small a personage as myself simply betokened the respect she professed not only for the family—as for the dead, for priests, and for kings—but also for the visitor to whom one was offering one's hospitality, a respect that would perhaps have touched me in a book but that always irritated me on her lips, because of the solemn and tender tones she adopted in speaking of it, and especially so this evening when the sacred character she conferred on the dinner might have the effect of making her refuse to disturb its ceremonial. But to give myself a better chance, I did not hesitate to lie and tell her that it was not in the least I who had wanted to write to Mama, but that it was Mama who, as she said goodnight to me, had exhorted me not to forget to send her an answer concerning something she had asked me to look for; and she would certainly be very annoyed if this note was not delivered to her. I think Françoise did not believe me, for, like those

8. Serving no practical purpose.
9. References to the strict dietary laws of Deuteronomy 14.21 and Genesis 31.32, respectively.
1. The four sons of Aymon, heroic knights who together rode the magic horse Bayard. "Théophile": a cleric who was saved from damnation by the Virgin Mary after he repented for having signed a pact with the devil.

primitive men whose senses were so much more powerful than ours, she could immediately discern, from signs imperceptible to us, any truth that we wanted to hide from her; she looked at the envelope for five minutes as if the examination of the paper and the appearance of the writing would inform her about the nature of the contents or tell her which article of her code she ought to apply. Then she went out with an air of resignation that seemed to signify: "If it isn't a misfortune for parents to have a child like that!" She came back after a moment to tell me that they were still only at the ice stage, that it was impossible for the butler to deliver the letter right away in front of everyone, but that, when the mouth-rinsing bowls[2] were put round, they would find a way to hand it to Mama. Instantly my anxiety subsided; it was now no longer, as it had been only a moment ago, until tomorrow that I had left my mother, since my little note, no doubt annoying her (and doubly because this stratagem would make me ridiculous in Swann's eyes), would at least allow me, invisible and enraptured, to enter the same room as she, would whisper about me in her ear; since that forbidden, hostile dining room, where, just a moment before, the ice itself—the "*granité*"[3]—and the rinsing bowls seemed to me to contain pleasures noxious and mortally sad because Mama was enjoying them far away from me, was opening itself to me and, like a fruit that has turned sweet and bursts its skin, was about to propel, to project, all the way to my intoxicated heart, Mama's attention as she read my lines. Now I was no longer separated from her; the barriers were down, an exquisite thread joined us. And that was not all: Mama would probably come!

I thought Swann would surely have laughed at the anguish I had just suffered if he had read my letter and guessed its purpose; yet, on the contrary, as I learned later, a similar anguish[4] was the torment of long years of his life and no one, perhaps, could have understood me as well as he; in his case, the anguish that comes from feeling that the person you love is in a place of amusement where you are not, where you cannot join her, came to him through love, to which it is in some sense predestined, by which it will be hoarded, appropriated; but when, as in my case, this anguish enters us before love has made its appearance in our life, it drifts as it waits for it, vague and free, without a particular assignment, at the service of one feeling one day, of another the next, sometimes of filial tenderness or affection for a friend. And the joy with which I served my first apprenticeship when Françoise came back to tell me my letter would be delivered Swann too had known well, that deceptive joy given to us by some friend, some relative of the woman we love when, arriving at the house or theater where she is, for some dance, gala evening, or premiere at which he is going to see her, this friend notices us wandering outside, desperately awaiting some opportunity to communicate with her. He recognizes us, speaks to us familiarly, asks us what we are doing there. And when we invent the story that we have something urgent to say to his relative or friend, he assures us that nothing could be simpler, leads us into the hall, and promises to send her to us in five minutes. How we love him, as at that moment I loved Françoise—the well-intentioned intermediary who with a single word has just made tolerable, human, and almost propitious the unimaginable, infernal festivity into the thick

2. Bowls with warm water for rinsing were passed around at the end of the meal.
3. A sherbetlike ice served as a separate course or after dinner.
4. I.e., his unhappy love for Odette de Crécy, described later in *Swann in Love*.

of which we had been imagining that hostile, perverse, and exquisite vortices of pleasure were carrying away from us and inspiring with derisive laughter the woman we love! If we are to judge by him, the relative who has come up to us and is himself also one of the initiates in the cruel mysteries, the other guests at the party cannot have anything very demoniacal about them. Those inaccessible and excruciating hours during which she was about to enjoy unknown pleasures—now, through an unexpected breach, we are entering them; now, one of the moments which, in succession, would have composed those hours, a moment as real as the others, perhaps even more important to us, because our mistress is more involved in it, we can picture to ourselves, we possess it, we are taking part in it, we have created it, almost: the moment in which he will tell her we are here, downstairs. And no doubt the other moments of the party would not have been essentially very different from this one, would not have had anything more delectable about them that should make us suffer so, since the kind friend has said to us: "Why, she'll be delighted to come down! It'll be much nicer for her to chat with you than to be bored up there." Alas! Swann had learned by experience that the good intentions of a third person have no power over a woman who is annoyed to find herself pursued even into a party by someone she does not love. Often, the friend comes back down alone.

My mother did not come, and with no consideration for my pride (which was invested in her not denying the story that she was supposed to have asked me to let her know the results of some search) asked Françoise to say these words to me: "There is no answer," words I have so often since then heard the doormen in grand hotels or the footmen in bawdy houses bring back to some poor girl who exclaims in surprise: "What, he said nothing? Why, that's impossible! Did you really give him my note? All right, I'll go on waiting." And—just as she invariably assures him she does not need the extra gas jet which the doorman wants to light for her, and remains there, hearing nothing further but the few remarks about the weather exchanged by the doorman and a lackey whom he sends off suddenly, when he notices the time, to put a customer's drink on ice—having declined Françoise's offer to make me some tea or to stay with me, I let her return to the servant's hall, I went to bed and closed my eyes, trying not to hear the voices of my family, who were having their coffee in the garden. But after a few seconds, I became aware that, by writing that note to Mama, by approaching, at the risk of angering her, so close to her that I thought I could touch the moment when I would see her again, I had shut off from myself the possibility of falling asleep without seeing her again, and the beating of my heart grew more painful each minute because I was increasing my agitation by telling myself to be calm, to accept my misfortune. Suddenly my anxiety subsided, a happiness invaded me as when a powerful medicine begins to take effect and our pain vanishes: I had just formed the resolution not to continue trying to fall asleep without seeing Mama again, to kiss her at all costs even though it was with the certainty of being on bad terms with her for a long time after, when she came up to bed. The calm that came with the end of my distress filled me with an extraordinary joy, quite as much as did my expectation, my thirst for and my fear of danger. I opened the window noiselessly and sat down on the foot of my bed; I hardly moved so that I would not be heard from below. Outdoors, too, things seemed frozen in silent attention so as not to disturb the moonlight which, duplicating and distancing each thing by extending its shadow before it, denser and more concrete than itself, had at once thinned and enlarged the landscape like a map that had been folded and was now opened out. What needed to move, some foliage of the chestnut tree, moved. But its quivering, minute, complete, executed even in its slightest nuances and ultimate refinements, did not spill over onto the rest, did not merge with it, remained circumscribed. Exposed against this silence, which absorbed nothing of them, the most distant noises, those that must have come from gardens that lay at the other end of town, could be perceived detailed with such "finish" that they seemed to owe this effect of remoteness only to their pianissimo, like those muted motifs so well executed by the orchestra of the Conservatoire[5] that, although you do not lose a single note, you nonetheless think you are hearing them far away from the concert hall and all the old subscribers—my grandmother's sisters too, when Swann had given them his seats—strained their ears as if they were listening to the distant advances of an army on the march that had not yet turned the corner of the rue de Trévise.[6]

I knew that the situation I was now placing myself in was the one that could provoke the gravest consequences of all for me, coming from my parents, much graver in truth than a stranger would have supposed, the sort he would have believed could be produced only by truly shameful misdeeds. But in my upbringing, the order of misdeeds was not the same as in that of other children, and I had become accustomed to placing before all the rest (because there were probably no others from which I needed to be more carefully protected) those whose common characteristic I now understand was that you lapse into them by yielding to a nervous impulse. But at the time no one uttered these words, no one revealed this cause, which might have made me believe I was excusable for succumbing to them or even perhaps incapable of resisting them. But I recognized them clearly from the anguish that preceded them as well as from the rigor of the punishment that followed them; and I knew that the one I had just committed was in the same family as others for which I had been severely punished, though infinitely graver. When I went and placed myself in my mother's path at the moment she was going up to bed, and when she saw that I had stayed up to say goodnight to her again in the hallway, they would not let me continue to live at home, they would send me away to school the next day, that much was certain. Well! Even if I had had to throw myself out of the window five minutes later, I still preferred this. What I wanted now was Mama, to say goodnight to her, I had gone too far along the road that led to the fulfillment of that desire to be able to turn back now.

I heard the footsteps of my family, who were seeing Swann out; and when the bell on the gate told me he had left, I went to the window. Mama was asking my father if he had thought the lobster was good and if M. Swann had had more coffee-and-pistachio ice. "I found it quite ordinary," said my mother; "I think next time we'll have to try another flavor." "I can't tell you how changed I find Swann," said my great-aunt, "he has aged so!" My great-aunt was so used to seeing Swann always as the same adolescent that she was surprised to find him suddenly not as young as the age she continued to attribute to him. And my family was also beginning to feel that in him this aging was abnormal, exces-

5. The national music conservatory (academy) in Paris.
6. A street in Combray.

sive, shameful, and more deserved by the unmarried, by all those for whom it seems that the great day that has no tomorrow is longer than for others, because for them it is empty and the moments in it add up from morning on without then being divided among children. "I think he has no end of worries with that wretched wife of his who is living with a certain Monsieur de Charlus,[7] as all of Combray knows. It's the talk of the town." My mother pointed out that in spite of this he had been looking much less sad for some time now. "He also doesn't make that gesture of his as often, so like his father, of wiping his eyes and running his hand across his forehead. I myself think that in his heart of hearts he no longer loves that woman." "Why, naturally he doesn't love her anymore," answered my grandfather. "I received a letter from him about it a long time ago, by now, a letter with which I hastened not to comply and which leaves no doubt about his feelings, at least his feelings of love, for his wife. Well now! You see, you didn't thank him for the Asti," added my grandfather, turning to his two sisters-in-law. "What? We didn't thank him? I think, just between you and me, that I put it quite delicately," answered my aunt Flora. "Yes, you managed it very well: quite admirable," said my aunt Céline. "But you were very good too." "Yes, I was rather proud of my remark about kind neighbors." "What? Is that what you call thanking him?" exclaimed my grandfather. "I certainly heard that, but devil take me if I thought it was directed at Swann. You can be sure he never noticed." "But see here, Swann isn't stupid, I'm sure he appreciated it. After all, I couldn't tell him how many bottles there were and what the wine cost!" My father and mother were left alone there, and sat down for a moment; then my father said: "Well, shall we go up to bed?" "If you like, my dear, even though I'm not the least bit sleepy; yet it couldn't be that perfectly harmless coffee ice that's keeping me so wide-awake; but I can see a light in the servants' hall, and since poor Françoise has waited up for me, I'll go and ask her to unhook my bodice while you're getting undressed." And my mother opened the latticed door that led from the vestibule to the staircase. Soon, I heard her coming upstairs to close her window. I went without a sound into the hallway; my heart was beating so hard I had trouble walking, but at least it was no longer pounding from anxiety, but from terror and joy. I saw the light cast in the stairwell by Mama's candle. Then I saw Mama herself; I threw myself forward. In the first second, she looked at me with astonishment, not understanding what could have happened. Then an expression of anger came over her face, she did not say a single word to me, and indeed for much less than this they would go several days without speaking to me. If Mama had said one word to me, it would have been an admission that they could talk to me again and in any case it would perhaps have seemed to me even more terrible, as a sign that, given the gravity of the punishment that was going to be prepared for me, silence, and estrangement, would have been childish. A word would have been like the calm with which you answer a servant when you have just decided to dismiss him; the kiss you give a son you are sending off to enlist, whereas you would have refused it if you were simply going to be annoyed with him for a few days. But she heard my father coming up from the dressing room where he had gone to undress and, to avoid the scene he would make over me, she said to me in a

7. The brother of the duc de Guermantes.

voice choked with anger: "Run, run, so at least your father won't see you waiting like this as if you were out of your mind!" But I repeated to her: "Come say goodnight to me," terrified as I saw the gleam from my father's candle already rising up the wall, but also using his approach as a means of blackmail and hoping that Mama, to avoid my father's finding me there still if she continued to refuse, would say: "Go back to your room, I'll come." It was too late, my father was there in front of us. Involuntarily, though no one heard, I murmured these words: "I'm done for!"

It was not so. My father was constantly refusing me permission for things that had been authorized in the more generous covenants granted by my mother and grandmother because he did not bother about "principles" and for him there was no "rule of law."[8] For a completely contingent reason, or even for no reason at all, he would at the last minute deny me a certain walk that was so customary, so consecrated that to deprive me of it was a violation, or, as he had done once again this evening, long before the ritual hour he would say to me: "Go on now, up to bed, no arguments!" But also, because he had no principles (in my grandmother's sense), he was not strictly speaking intransigent. He looked at me for a moment with an expression of surprise and annoyance, then as soon as Mama had explained to him with a few embarrassed words what had happened, he said to her: "Go along with him, then. You were just saying you didn't feel very sleepy, stay in his room for a little while, I don't need anything." "But my dear," answered my mother timidly, "whether I'm sleepy or not doesn't change anything, we can't let the child get into the habit . . ." "But it isn't a question of habit," said my father, shrugging his shoulders, "you can see the boy is upset, he seems very sad; look, we're not executioners! You'll end by making him ill, and that won't do us much good! There are two beds in his room; go tell Françoise to prepare the big one for you and sleep there with him tonight. Now then, goodnight, I'm not as high-strung as the two of you, I'm going to bed."

It was impossible to thank my father; he would have been irritated by what he called mawkishness. I stood there not daring to move; he was still there in front of us, tall in his white nightshirt, under the pink and violet Indian cashmere shawl that he tied around his head now that he had attacks of neuralgia, with the gesture of Abraham in the engraving after Benozzo Gozzoli[9] that M. Swann had given me, as he told Sarah she must leave Isaac's side. This was many years ago. The staircase wall on which I saw the rising glimmer of his candle has long since ceased to exist. In me, too, many things have been destroyed that I thought were bound to last forever and new ones have formed that have given birth to new sorrows and joys which I could not have foreseen then, just as the old ones have become difficult for me to understand. It was a very long time ago, too, that my father ceased to be able to say to Mama: "Go with the boy." The possibility of such hours will never be reborn for me. But for a little while now, I have begun to hear again very clearly, if I take care to listen, the sobs that I was strong enough to contain in front of my father and that broke out only when I found myself alone again with Mama. They have never

8. Natural law, supposed to govern international and public relations. Marcel sees his relationship with his mother and grandmother as a social contract; his father, who does not respect the rules, becomes the unpredictable tyrant.

9. Florentine painter (1420–1497) whose frescoes at Pisa contain scenes from the life of the biblical patriarch Abraham.

really stopped; and it is only because life is now becoming quieter around me that I can hear them again, like those convent bells covered so well by the clamor of the town during the day that one would think they had ceased altogether but which begin sounding again in the silence of the evening.

Mama spent that night in my room; when I had just committed such a misdeed that I expected to have to leave the house, my parents granted me more than I could ever have won from them as a reward for any good deed. Even at the moment when it manifested itself through this pardon, my father's conduct toward me retained that arbitrary and undeserved quality that characterized it and was due to the fact that it generally resulted from fortuitous convenience rather than a premeditated plan. It may even be that what I called his severity, when he sent me to bed, deserved that name less than my mother's or my grandmother's, for his nature, in certain respects more different from mine than theirs was, had probably kept him from discovering until now how very unhappy I was every evening, something my mother and my grandmother knew well; but they loved me enough not to consent to spare me my suffering, they wanted to teach me to master it in order to reduce my nervous sensitivity and strengthen my will. As for my father, whose affection for me was of another sort, I do not know if he would have been courageous enough for that: the one time he realized that I was upset, he had said to my mother: "Go and comfort him." Mama stayed in my room that night and, as though not to allow any remorse to spoil those hours which were so different from what I had had any right to expect, when Françoise, realizing that something extraordinary was happening when she saw Mama sitting next to me, holding my hand and letting me cry without scolding me, asked her: "Why, madame, now what's wrong with Monsieur that he's crying so?" Mama answered her: "Why, even he doesn't know, Françoise, he's in a state; prepare the big bed for me quickly and then go on up to bed yourself." And so, for the first time, my sadness was regarded no longer as a punishable offense but as an involuntary ailment that had just been officially recognized, a nervous condition for which I was not responsible; I had the relief of no longer having to mingle qualms of conscience with the bitterness of my tears, I could cry without sin. I was also not a little proud, with respect to Françoise, of this turnabout in human affairs which, an hour after Mama had refused to come up to my room and had sent the disdainful answer that I should go to sleep, raised me to the dignity of a grown-up and brought me suddenly to a sort of puberty of grief, of emancipation from tears. I ought to have been happy: I was not. It seemed to me that my mother had just made me a first concession which must have been painful to her, that this was a first abdication on her part from the ideal she had conceived for me, and that for the first time she, who was so courageous, had to confess herself beaten. It seemed to me that, if I had just gained a victory, it was over her, that I had succeeded, as illness, affliction, or age might have done, in relaxing her will, in weakening her judgment, and that this evening was the beginning of a new era, would remain as a sad date. If I had dared, now, I would have said to Mama: "No, I don't want you to do this, don't sleep here." But I was aware of the practical wisdom, the realism as it would be called now, which in her tempered my grandmother's ardently idealistic nature, and I knew that, now that the harm was done, she would prefer to let me at least enjoy the soothing pleasure of it and not disturb my father. To be sure, my mother's lovely face still shone with youth that evening when she so gently held my hands and tried to stop my tears; but it seemed to me that this was precisely what should not have been, her anger would have saddened me less than this new gentleness which my childhood had not known before; it seemed to me that with an impious and secret hand I had just traced in her soul a first wrinkle and caused a first white hair to appear. At the thought of this my sobs redoubled, and then I saw that Mama, who never let herself give way to any emotion with me, was suddenly overcome by my own and was trying to suppress a desire to cry. When she saw that I had noticed, she said to me with a smile: "There now, my little chick, my little canary, he's going to make his mama as silly as himself if this continues. Look, since you're not sleepy and your mama isn't either, let's not go on upsetting each other, let's do something, let's get one of your books." But I had none there. "Would you enjoy it less if I took out the books your grandmother will be giving you on your saint's day? Think about it carefully: you mustn't be disappointed not to have anything the day after tomorrow." On the contrary, I was delighted, and Mama went to get a packet of books, of which I could not distinguish, through the paper in which they were wrapped, more than their shape, short and thick, but which, in this first guise, though summary and veiled, already eclipsed the box of colors from New Year's Day and the silkworms from last year. They were *La Mare au Diable, François le Champi, La Petite Fadette*, and *Les Maîtres Sonneurs*.[1] My grandmother, as I learned afterward, had first chosen the poems of Musset, a volume of Rousseau, and *Indiana*;[2] for though she judged frivolous reading to be as unhealthy as sweets and pastries, it did not occur to her that a great breath of genius might have a more dangerous and less invigorating influence on the mind even of a child than would the open air and the sea breeze on his body. But as my father had nearly called her mad when he learned which books she wanted to give me, she had returned to the bookstore, in Jouy-le-Vicomte herself, so that I would not risk not having my present (it was a burning-hot day and she had come home so indisposed that the doctor had warned my mother not to let her tire herself out that way again) and she had resorted to the four pastoral novels of George Sand. "My dear daughter," she said to Mama, "I could not bring myself to give the boy something badly written."

In fact, she could never resign herself to buying anything from which one could not derive an intellectual profit, and especially that which beautiful things afford us by teaching us to seek our pleasure elsewhere than in the satisfactions of material comfort and vanity. Even when she had to make someone a present of the kind called "useful," when she had to give an armchair, silverware, a walking stick, she looked for "old" ones, as though, now that long desuetude had effaced their character of usefulness, they would appear more disposed to tell us about the life of people of other times than to serve the needs of our own life. She would have liked me to have in my room photographs of the most

1. *The Devil's Pool, François the Foundling Discovered in the Fields, Little Fadette,* and *The Master Bellringers,* all novels of idealized country life by the French woman writer George Sand (1806–1876).

2. The works of Alfred de Musset (1810–1857) and Jean-Jacques Rousseau (1712–1778), often romantic and sometimes confessional, and George Sand's *Indiana* (1832), a novel of free love, would be thought unsuitable reading for a young child.

beautiful monuments or landscapes. But at the moment of buying them, and even though the thing represented had an aesthetic value, she would find that vulgarity and utility too quickly resumed their places in that mechanical mode of representation, the photograph. She would try to use cunning and, if not to eliminate commercial banality entirely, at least to reduce it, to substitute for the greater part of it more art, to introduce into it in a sense several "layers" of art: instead of photographs of Chartres Cathedral, the Fountains of Saint-Cloud, or Mount Vesuvius, she would make inquiries of Swann as to whether some great painter had not depicted them, and preferred to give me photographs of Chartres Cathedral by Corot, of the Fountains of Saint-Cloud by Hubert Robert, of Mount Vesuvius by Turner,[3] which made one further degree of art. But if the photographer had been removed from the representation of the masterpiece or of nature and replaced by a great artist, he still reclaimed his rights to reproduce that very interpretation. Having deferred vulgarity as far as possible, my grandmother would try to move it back still further. She would ask Swann if the work had not been engraved, preferring, whenever possible, old engravings that also had an interest beyond themselves, such as those that represent a masterpiece in a state in which we can no longer see it today (like the engraving by Morghen of Leonardo's *Last Supper* before its deterioration).[4] It must be said that the results of this interpretation of the art of gift giving were not always brilliant. The idea I formed of Venice from a drawing by Titian[5] that is supposed to have the lagoon in the background was certainly far less accurate than the one I would have derived from simple photographs. We could no longer keep count, at home, when my great-aunt wanted to draw up an indictment against my grandmother, of the armchairs she had presented to young couples engaged to be married or old married couples which, at the first attempt to make use of them, had immediately collapsed under the weight of one of the recipients. But my grandmother would have believed it petty to be overly concerned about the solidity of a piece of wood in which one could still distinguish a small flower, a smile, sometimes a lovely invention from the past. Even what might, in these pieces of furniture, answer a need, since it did so in a manner to which we are no longer accustomed, charmed her like the old ways of speaking in which we see a metaphor that is obliterated, in our modern language, by the abrasion of habit. Now, in fact, the pastoral novels of George Sand that she was giving me for my saint's day were, like an old piece of furniture, full of expressions that had fallen into disuse and turned figurative again, the sort you no longer find anywhere but in the country. And my grandmother had bought them in preference to others just as she would sooner have rented an estate on which there was a Gothic dovecote or another of those old things that exercise such a happy influence on the mind by filling it with longing for impossible voyages through time.

3. All photographs of paintings: the cathedral at Chartres, painted in 1830 by Corot; the fountains in the old park at Saint-Cloud, outside Paris, painted by Hubert Robert (1733–1809); and Vesuvius, a famous volcano near Naples, painted by J. M. W. Turner (1775–1851).
4. Leonardo da Vinci's *Last Supper* was the subject of a famous engraving by Raphael Morghen (1758–1833). The paints in the original fresco had deteriorated rapidly, and a major restoration took place only in the 19th century.
5. Tiziano Vecellio (1488?–1576), Renaissance painter of the Venetian school.

Mama sat down by my bed; she had picked up *François le Champi*, whose reddish cover and incomprehensible title[6] gave it, in my eyes, a distinct personality and a mysterious attraction. I had not yet read a real novel. I had heard people say that George Sand was an exemplary novelist. This already predisposed me to imagine something indefinable and delicious in *François le Champi*. Narrative devices intended to arouse curiosity or emotion, certain modes of expression that make one uneasy or melancholy, and that a reader with some education will recognize as common to many novels, appeared to me—who considered a new book not as a thing having many counterparts, but as a unique person, having no reason for existing but in itself—simply as a disturbing emanation of *François le Champi*'s peculiar essence. Behind those events so ordinary, those things so common, those words so current, I sensed a strange sort of intonation, accentuation. The action began; it seemed to me all the more obscure because in those days, when I read, I often daydreamed, for entire pages, of something quite different. And in addition to the lacunae that this distraction left in the story, there was the fact, when Mama was the one reading aloud to me, that she skipped all the love scenes. Thus, all the bizarre changes that take place in the respective attitudes of the miller's wife and the child and that can be explained only by the progress of a nascent love seemed to me marked by a profound mystery whose source I readily imagined must be in that strange and sweet name "Champi," which gave the child, who bore it without my knowing why, its vivid, charming purplish color. If my mother was an unfaithful reader she was also, in the case of books in which she found the inflection of true feeling, a wonderful reader for the respect and simplicity of her interpretation, the beauty and gentleness of the sound of her voice. Even in real life, when it was people and not works of art which moved her to compassion or admiration, it was touching to see with what deference she removed from her voice, from her motions, from her words, any spark of gaiety that might hurt some mother who had once lost a child, any recollection of a saint's day or birthday that might remind some old man of his advanced age, any remark about housekeeping that might seem tedious to some young scholar. In the same way, when she was reading George Sand's prose, which always breathes that goodness, that moral distinction which Mama had learned from my grandmother to consider superior to all else in life, and which I was to teach her only much later not to consider superior to all else in books too, taking care to banish from her voice any pettiness, any affectation which might have prevented it from receiving that powerful torrent, she imparted all the natural tenderness, all the ample sweetness they demanded to those sentences which seemed written for her voice and which remained, so to speak, entirely within the register of her sensibility. She found, to attack them in the necessary tone, the warm inflection that preexists them and that dictated them, but that the words do not indicate; with this inflection she softened as she went along any crudeness in the tenses of the verbs, gave the imperfect and the past historic the sweetness that lies in goodness, the melancholy that lies in tenderness, directed the sentence that was ending toward the one that was about to begin, sometimes hurrying, sometimes slowing down the pace of the syllables so as to bring them, though their quantities were different, into one uniform rhythm, she breathed into this very common prose a sort of continuous emotional life.

6. *Champi* ("foundling") is an old French word that the child Marcel would not have known.

My remorse was quieted, I gave in to the sweetness of that night in which I had my mother close to me. I knew that such a night could not be repeated; that the greatest desire I had in the world, to keep my mother in my room during those sad hours of darkness, was too contrary to the necessities of life and the wishes of others for its fulfillment, granted this night, to be anything other than artificial and exceptional. Tomorrow my anxieties would reawaken and Mama would not stay here. But when my anxieties were soothed, I no longer understood them; and then tomorrow night was still far away; I told myself I would have time to think of what to do, even though that time could not bring me any access of power, since these things did not depend on my will and seemed more avoidable to me only because of the interval that still separated them from me.

So it was that, for a long time, when, awakened at night, I remembered Combray again, I saw nothing of it but this sort of luminous panel, cut out among indistinct shadows, like those panels which the glow of a Bengal light[7] or some electric projection will cut out and illuminate in a building whose other parts remain plunged in darkness: at the rather broad base, the small parlor, the dining room, the opening of the dark path by which M. Swann, the unconscious author of my sufferings, would arrive, the front hall where I would head toward the first step of the staircase, so painful to climb, that formed, by itself, the very narrow trunk of this irregular pyramid; and, at the top, my bedroom with the little hallway and its glass-paned door for Mama's entrance; in a word, always seen at the same hour, isolated from everything that might surround it, standing out alone against the darkness, the bare minimum of scenery (such as one sees prescribed at the beginnings of the old plays for performances in the provinces) needed for the drama of my undressing; as though Combray had consisted only of two floors connected by a slender staircase and as though it had always been seven o'clock in the evening there. The fact is, I could have answered anyone who asked me that Combray also included other things and existed at other times of day. But since what I recalled would have been supplied to me only by my voluntary memory, the memory of the intelligence, and since the information it gives about the past preserves nothing of the past itself, I would never have had any desire to think about the rest of Combray. It was all really quite dead for me.

Dead forever? Possibly.

There is a great deal of chance in all this, and a second sort of chance event, that of our own death, often does not allow us to wait long for the favors of the first.

I find the Celtic belief very reasonable, that the souls of those we have lost are held captive in some inferior creature, in an animal, in a plant, in some inanimate object, effectively lost to us until the day, which for many never comes, when we happen to pass close to the tree, come into possession of the object that is their prison.[8] Then they quiver, they call out to us, and as soon as we have recognized them, the spell is broken. Delivered by us, they have overcome death and they return to live with us.

7. A steady, blue-colored firework often used for signals.

8. A belief attributed to Druids, the priests of the ancient Celtic peoples.

It is the same with our past. It is a waste of effort for us to try to summon it, all the exertions of our intelligence are useless. The past is hidden outside the realm of our intelligence and beyond its reach, in some material object (in the sensation that this material object would give us) which we do not suspect. It depends on chance whether we encounter this object before we die, or do not encounter it.

For many years, already, everything about Combray that was not the theater and drama of my bedtime had ceased to exist for me, when one day in winter, as I returned home, my mother, seeing that I was cold, suggested that, contrary to my habit, I have a little tea. I refused at first and then, I do not know why, changed my mind. She sent for one of those squat, plump cakes called *petites madeleines* that look as though they have been molded in the grooved valve of a scallop shell. And soon, mechanically, oppressed by the gloomy day and the prospect of another sad day to follow, I carried to my lips a spoonful of the tea in which I had let soften a bit of madeleine. But at the very instant when the mouthful of tea mixed with cake crumbs touched my palate, I quivered, attentive to the extraordinary thing that was happening inside me. A delicious pleasure had invaded me, isolated me, without my having any notion as to its cause. It had immediately rendered the vicissitudes of life unimportant to me, its disasters innocuous, its brevity illusory, acting in the same way that love acts, by filling me with a precious essence: or rather this essence was not merely inside me, it was me. I had ceased to feel mediocre, contingent, mortal. Where could it have come to me from—this powerful joy? I sensed that it was connected to the taste of the tea and the cake, but that it went infinitely far beyond it, could not be of the same nature. Where did it come from? What did it mean? How could I grasp it? I drink a second mouthful, in which I find nothing more than in the first, a third that gives me a little less than the second. It is time for me to stop, the virtue of the drink seems to be diminishing. Clearly, the truth I am seeking is not in the drink, but in me. The drink has awoken it in me, but does not know this truth, and can do no more than repeat indefinitely, with less and less force, this same testimony which I do not know how to interpret and which I want at least to be able to ask of it again and find again, intact, available to me, soon, for a decisive clarification. I put down the cup and turn to my mind. It is up to my mind to find the truth. But how? Such grave uncertainty, whenever the mind feels overtaken by itself; when it, the seeker, is also the obscure country where it must seek and where all its baggage will be nothing to it. Seek? Not only that: create. It is face-to-face with something that does not yet exist and that only it can accomplish, then bring into its light.

And I begin asking myself again what it could be, this unknown state which brought with it no logical proof, but only the evidence of its felicity, its reality, and in whose presence the other states of consciousness faded away. I want to try to make it reappear. I return in my thoughts to the moment when I took the first spoonful of tea. I find the same state again, without any new clarity. I ask my mind to make another effort, to bring back once more the sensation that is slipping away. And, so that nothing may interrupt the thrust with which it will try to grasp it again, I clear away every obstacle, every foreign idea, I protect my ears and my attention from the noises in the next room. But feeling my mind grow tired without succeeding, I now compel it to accept the very distraction I was denying it, to think of something else, to recover its strength before a supreme attempt. Then for a second time I create an empty space before it, I confront it again with the still recent taste of that first mouthful, and I feel something quiver in me, shift, try to rise, something that seems to have been unanchored at a great depth; I do not know what it is, but it comes up slowly; I feel the resistance and I hear the murmur of the distances traversed.

Undoubtedly what is palpitating thus, deep inside me, must be the image, the visual memory which is attached to this taste and is trying to follow it to me. But it is struggling too far away, too confusedly; I can just barely perceive the neutral glimmer in which the elusive eddying of stirred-up colors is blended; but I cannot distinguish the form, cannot ask it, as the one possible interpreter, to translate for me the evidence of its contemporary, its inseparable companion, the taste, ask it to tell me what particular circumstance is involved, what period of the past.

Will it reach the clear surface of my consciousness—this memory, this old moment which the attraction of an identical moment has come from so far to invite, to move, to raise up from the deepest part of me? I don't know. Now I no longer feel anything, it has stopped, gone back down perhaps; who knows if it will ever rise up from its darkness again? Ten times I must begin again, lean down toward it. And each time, the laziness that deters us from every difficult task, every work of importance, has counseled me to leave it, to drink my tea and think only about my worries of today, my desires for tomorrow, upon which I may ruminate effortlessly.

And suddenly the memory appeared. That taste was the taste of the little piece of madeleine which on Sunday mornings at Combray (because that day I did not go out before it was time for Mass), when I went to say good morning to her in her bedroom, my aunt Léonie would give me after dipping it in her infusion of tea or lime blossom. The sight of the little madeleine had not reminded me of anything before I tasted it; perhaps because I had often seen them since, without eating them, on the shelves of the pastry shops, and their image had therefore left those days of Combray and attached itself to others more recent; perhaps because of these recollections abandoned so long outside my memory, nothing survived, everything had come apart; the forms and the form, too, of the little shell made of cake, so fatly sensual within its severe and pious pleating—had been destroyed, or, still half asleep, had lost the force of expansion that would have allowed them to rejoin my consciousness. But, when nothing subsists of an old past, after the death of people, after the destruction of things, alone, frailer but more enduring, more immaterial, more persistent, more faithful, smell and taste still remain for a long time, like souls, remembering, waiting, hoping, upon the ruins of all the rest, bearing without giving way, on their almost impalpable droplet, the immense edifice of memory.

And as soon as I had recognized the taste of the piece of madeleine dipped in lime-blossom tea that my aunt used to give me (though I did not yet know and had to put off to much later discovering why this memory made me so happy), immediately the old gray house on the street, where her bedroom was, came like a stage set to attach itself to the little wing opening onto the garden that had been built for my parents behind it (that truncated section which was all I had seen before then); and with the house the town, from morning to night and in all weathers, the Square, where they sent me before lunch, the streets where I went on errands, the paths we took if the weather was fine. And as in that game in which the Japanese amuse themselves by filling a porcelain bowl with water and steeping in it little pieces of paper until then undifferentiated which, the moment they are immersed in it, stretch and bend, take color and distinctive shape, turn into flowers, houses, human figures, firm and recognizable, so now all the flowers in our garden and in M. Swann's park, and the water lilies on the Vivonne,[9] and the good people of the village and their little dwellings and the church and all of Combray and its surroundings, all of this, acquiring form and solidity, emerged, town and gardens alike, from my cup of tea.

1913

9. The local river.

JAMES JOYCE

1882–1941

More than any other writer of the twentieth century, James Joyce shaped modern literature. His experiments with narrative form helped to define the major literary movements of the century, from modernism to postmodernism. By developing methods of tracing individual consciousness, Joyce, along with **Marcel Proust** and **Virginia Woolf**, helped us to understand the functioning of the human mind. Equally capable of realistic portrayal of urban life in Dublin and playful deformations of the English language, Joyce expanded the possibilities of the novel—as a record of intimate human experiences, as a massive encyclopedia of human culture, and as a funhouse mirror that shows the world a transformed image of itself.

Joyce left Ireland as a young man but made his native country the subject of all his works. Born in Dublin on February 2, 1882, to May Murray and John Stanislaus Joyce, he was given the impressive name James Augustine Aloysius Joyce; he was the eldest surviving child of what would soon be a large family (ten children plus three who died in infancy). His father held a well-paid and undemanding post in the civil service, and the family was comfortable until 1891, when his job was eliminated. John received a small pension and declined to take up more demanding work elsewhere. The Joyce family moved steadily down the social and economic scale, and life became difficult under the improvident guidance of a man whom Joyce later portrayed as "a drinker, a good fellow, a storyteller, somebody's secretary, something in a distillery, a tax-gatherer, a bankrupt, and at present a praiser of his own past."

Joyce attended the well-known Catholic preparatory school of Clongowes Wood College from the ages of six to nine, leaving when his family could no longer afford the tuition. Two years later, he was admitted as a scholarship student to Belvedere College in Dublin. Both were Jesuit schools and provided a rigorous Catholic training against which Joyce violently rebelled but which he never forgot. In Belvedere College, shaken by a dramatic hell-fire sermon shortly after his first experience with sex, he even seriously considered becoming a priest; in the end, the life of the senses and his sense of vocation as an artist won out. After graduating from Belvedere in 1898, Joyce entered another Catholic institution—University College, Dublin—where he rejected Irish tradition and looked abroad for new values. Teaching himself Norwegian in order to read **Henrik Ibsen** in the original, he criticized the writers of the Irish Literary Renaissance as provincial and showed no interest in joining their ranks. His first published piece was an essay on Ibsen, to which the great playwright responded in a brief note of thanks. Like Stephen Dedalus, the hero, of his autobiographical novel, *A Portrait of the Artist as a Young Man* (1916), Joyce decided (in 1902) to escape the stifling conventions of his native country and leave for the Continent.

This trip did not last long. He studied medicine briefly, then for six months supported himself in Paris by giving English lessons, but when his mother became seriously ill, he was called home. After her death, he taught school for a time in Dublin and then returned to the Continent with Nora Barnacle, a country woman from western Ireland with whom he had two children and whom he married (after twenty-seven years of cohabitation) in 1931. The young couple moved to Trieste, where Joyce taught English in a Berlitz school and started writing both the short stories collected as *Dubliners* (1914) and an early version, partially published as *Stephen Hero* in 1944, of *A Portrait of the Artist as a Young Man*. He also wrote some mostly forgettable poetry and a play, *Exiles* (1918), that he had trouble getting produced. The couple remained poor for much of Joyce's life and relied on grants from the British government and gifts from wealthy patrons to allow Joyce to complete his literary projects. Joyce made a few brief business trips to Dublin, but, after 1912, never returned to the city.

When the First World War broke out, the Joyces moved to neutral Zurich, then after the war to Paris, where Joyce completed his most famous work, *Ulysses* (1922). In Paris he briefly met the other great novelist of the day, Marcel Proust, but claimed never to have read his work. He did, however, attend Proust's funeral. By now, Joyce was a celebrity and developed a circle of literary friends who supported and publicized his work. Throughout his life Joyce was a heavy drinker, and his conversation was legendary. His eyesight deteriorated as he devoted himself to the project he called *Work in Progress* (completed as *Finnegans Wake* in 1939). He sometimes relied on others, including the young Irish writer **Samuel Beckett**, to take dictation. These years were blighted by the mental illness of Joyce's daughter, Lucia, who ended up institutionalized for most of her life. The Joyces remained in Paris until the German occupation during the Second World War, when Joyce and his wife returned to Zurich, where Joyce died in 1941 after an operation for a perforated ulcer.

From *Dubliners* to *Ulysses* and *Finnegans Wake*, Joyce developed ways of exploring the lives and dreams of characters, including his youthful self, from the parochial Dublin society he had fled. Each of the major works presents innovative literary approaches that were to have a substantial impact on later writers. *A Portrait of the Artist as a Young Man* introduced into English the technique of stream of consciousness, as a means of capturing thoughts and emotions. Because it suggests the seemingly arbitrary manner in which thoughts and feelings often arise and then dissipate, stream-of-conscious writing may sound illogical or confusing; nevertheless it can indeed be convincing, since it gives the reader apparent access to the workings of a character's mind. The author's aim in employing the technique is to achieve a deeper understanding of human experience by displaying subconscious associations along with conscious thoughts. *Portrait* is based on Joyce's life until 1902, but the novel is clearly not a conventional autobiography and the reader recognizes in the first pages a radical experiment in fictional language. The novel's sophisticated symbolism and stress on dramatic dialogue hint at the radical break with narrative tradition that Joyce was preparing in *Ulysses*.

While introducing a host of stylistic devices to English, including an expanded form of stream of consciousness, a complex set of mythic parallels, and a series of literary parodies, *Ulysses* also provided one of the most celebrated instances of modern literary censorship. Its serial publication in the New York *Little Review* (from 1918 to 1920) was halted by the U.S. Post Office after a complaint, from the New York Society for the Prevention of Vice, that the work was obscene. The novel was outlawed and all available copies were actually burned in England and in America, until a 1933 decision by Judge Woolsey in federal district court lifted the ban in the United States. Although Joyce's descriptions have lost none of their pungency, it is hard to imagine a reader who would not be struck by another element—the density and mythic scope of this complex, symbolic, and linguistically innovative novel. Openly referring to an ancient predecessor, the *Odyssey* of Homer ("Ulysses" is the Latin name for the hero Odysseus), *Ulysses* structures numerous episodes to suggest parallels with the Greek epic, and transforms the twenty-year Homeric journey home into the daylong wanderings through Dublin of an unheroic advertising man, Leopold Bloom, and a rebellious young teacher and writer from *Portrait*, Stephen Dedalus. **T. S. Eliot** saw Joyce's use of ancient myth to explore modern life as "a way of controlling, of ordering, of giving a shape and significance to the immense panorama of futility and anarchy which is contemporary history." The first half of *Ulysses* uses stream-of-consciousness technique to explore Bloom's and Stephen's thoughts through the course of the day. By the second half of the novel, however, a number of intrusive and parodic narrators intervene in the action; Joyce's games with language and representation in this section were prime influences on postmodernism.

After the publication of *Ulysses*, Joyce spent the next seventeen years writing an even more complex work: *Finnegans Wake* (1939). Despite the title, a reference to a balled in which the bricklayer Tim Finnegan is brought back to life at his wake when somebody spills whiskey on him, the novel is the multivoiced, multidimensional dream of Humphrey Chimpden Earwicker. *Finnegans Wake* expands on the encyclopedic series of literary and cultural references underlying *Ulysses*, in language that has been even more radically broken apart and reassembled than that of *Ulysses*. Digressing exuberantly in all directions at once, with complex puns and hybrid words that mix languages, *Finnegans Wake* is—in spite of its cosmic symbolism—a game of language and reference by an artist "hoppy on akkant of his joyicity."

"THE DEAD"

These influential literary experiments had their roots in Joyce's command of more traditional narrative technique. "The Dead," presented here, was the last and greatest story in Joyce's first published volume, *Dubliners*. The collection as a whole sketches aspects of life in the Irish capital as Joyce knew it, in which the parochialism, piety, and repressive conventions of life are shown stifling artistic and psychological development. Whether it is the young boy who arrives too late at the fair in "Araby," the poor-aunt laundress of "Clay," or the frustrated writer Gabriel Conroy of "The Dead," the characters in *Dubliners* dream of a better life against a dismal, impoverishing background whose cumulative effect is of despair. The style of *Dubliners* is more realistic than in Joyce's later fiction, but he already employs a structure of symbolic meanings and revelatory moments he called "epiphanies." Joyce wrote to his publisher that the collection would be "a chapter of the moral history of my country," and he further explained that he had chosen Dublin because it was the "centre of paralysis" in Ireland—a city of blunted hopes and lost dreams: desperately poor, with large slums and more people than jobs, it stagnated in political, religious, and cultural divisions that color the lives of the characters in the stories. The book is arranged, Joyce noted, in an order that represents four aspects of life in the city: "childhood, adolescence, maturity and public life." Individual stories focus on one or a few characters, who may dream of a better life but are eventually frustrated by, or sink voluntarily back into, their shabby reality. Stories often end with a moment of special insight (epiphany), evident to the reader but not always to the protagonist, that puts events into sharp and illuminating perspective.

Several aspects of "The Dead" recall—and transmute—elements in Joyce's life. As in other stories, the neighborhood setting is familiar from his youth. The real-life models for Miss Kate and Miss Julia were indeed music teachers. Mr. Bartell D'Arcy evokes a contemporary tenor who performed under a similar name. The figure of Gabriel Conroy—who writes reviews for local journals, dislikes Irish nationalism, and prefers European culture—physically resembles Joyce—a lesser Joyce who might never have had the courage to leave home for Europe. The tale that Gretta tells Gabriel at the end of the story echoes Nora's experience.

"The Dead" is divided into three parts, chronicling the stages of the Misses Morkan's party and also the stages by which Gabriel Conroy moves from the rather pompous, insecure, and externally oriented figure of the beginning to a man who has been forced to reassess himself and human relationships at the end. The party is an annual dinner dance that takes place after the New Year, probably on January 6, the Catholic Feast of the Epiphany (which many have connected with Gabriel's personal epiphany at the end of the story). A jovial occasion, it brings together friends and acquaintances for an evening of music, dancing, sumptuous food, and a formal after-dinner speech that Gabriel delivers. The undercurrents are not always harmonious, however, for small anxieties and personal frictions crop up that both create a realistic picture and suggest tensions in contemporary Irish society: nationalism, religion, poverty, and class differences. Gabriel has a position to maintain, and he is determined to live up to his responsibilities: he is at once cultured speaker and intellectual, carver and master of ceremonies, and the man whom the Misses Morkan expect to take care of occasional problems like alcoholic guests. He is a complex character, both a writer of real imagination and a narcissistic figure who is so used to focusing on himself that he has drawn apart from other people.

Joyce's method in "The Dead" relies heavily on free indirect discourse, the presentation of a character's thoughts (without quotation marks) by the narrator. Joyce drew this style partly from **Flaubert**—in *Portrait*, Stephen Dedalus quotes Flaubert's idea of the artist who "like the God of the creation, remains within or behind or beyond or above his handiwork, invisible, refined out of existence, indifferent, paring his fingernails." Joyce's later development of stream of consciousness would allow the character's thoughts to be presented directly to the reader, sometimes without the intervention of a narrator, but in "The Dead" the narrator unobtrusively filters Gabriel's thoughts for us, allowing us to sympathize with Gabriel in his insecurity but also inviting us to judge him in his complacency.

The Dead

Lily, the caretaker's daughter, was literally run off her feet. Hardly had she brought one gentleman into the little pantry behind the office on the ground floor and helped him off with his overcoat than the wheezy hall-door bell clanged again and she had to scamper along the bare hallway to let in another guest. It was well for her she had not to attend to the ladies also. But Miss Kate and Miss Julia had thought of that and had converted the bathroom upstairs into a ladies' dressing-room. Miss Kate and Miss Julia were there, gossiping and laughing and fussing, walking after each other to the head of the stairs, peering down over the banisters and calling down to Lily to ask her who had come.

It was always a great affair, the Misses Morkan's annual dance. Everybody who knew them came to it, members of the family, old friends of the family, the members of Julia's choir, any of Kate's pupils that were grown up enough and even some of Mary Jane's pupils too. Never once had it fallen flat. For years and years it had gone off in splendid style as long as anyone could remember; ever since Kate and Julia, after the death of their brother Pat, had left the house in Stoney Batter and taken Mary Jane, their only niece, to live with them in the dark gaunt house on Usher's Island,[1] the upper part of which they had rented from Mr. Fulham, the cornfactor[2] on the ground floor. That was a good thirty years ago if it was a day. Mary Jane, who was then a little girl in short clothes, was now the main prop of the household for she had the organ[3] in Haddington Road. She had been through the Academy[4] and gave a pupils' concert every year in the upper room of the Antient Concert Rooms. Many of her pupils belonged to better-class families on the Kingstown and Dalkey line.[5] Old as they were, her aunts also did their share. Julia, though she was quite grey, was still the leading soprano in Adam and Eve's, and Kate, being too feeble to go about much, gave music lessons to beginners on the old square[6] piano in the back room. Lily, the caretaker's daughter, did housemaid's work for them. Though their life was modest they believed in eating well; the best of everything: diamond-bone sirloins, three-shilling tea and the best bottled stout.[7] But Lily seldom made a mistake in the orders so that she got on well with her three mistresses. They were fussy, that was all. But the only thing they would not stand was back answers.

1. Not an island, but an area in western Dublin on the south bank of the River Liffey. Stoney Batter is a street of small shops and a few houses in Dublin.
2. Dealer in grain.
3. I.e., earned money by playing the organ at church.
4. The Royal Academy of Music.
5. Railway to a fashionable section of Dublin.
6. I.e., upright. "Adam and Eve's": popular name (taken from a nearby inn) for a Dublin Catholic church.
7. Strong beer.

Of course they had good reason to be fussy on such a night. And then it was long after ten o'clock and yet there was no sign of Gabriel and his wife. Besides they were dreadfully afraid that Freddy Malins might turn up screwed.[8] They would not wish for worlds that any of Mary Jane's pupils should see him under the influence; and when he was like that it was sometimes very hard to manage him. Freddy Malins always came late but they wondered what could be keeping Gabriel: and that was what brought them every two minutes to the banisters to ask Lily had Gabriel or Freddy come.

—O, Mr. Conroy, said Lily to Gabriel when she opened the door for him, Miss Kate and Miss Julia thought you were never coming. Good-night, Mrs. Conroy.

—I'll engage they did, said Gabriel, but they forgot that my wife here takes three mortal hours to dress herself.

He stood on the mat, scraping the snow from his goloshes, while Lily led his wife to the foot of the stairs and called out:

—Miss Kate, here's Mrs. Conroy.

Kate and Julia came toddling down the dark stairs at once. Both of them kissed Gabriel's wife, said she must be perished alive and asked was Gabriel with her.

—Here I am as right as the mail,[9] Aunt Kate! Go on up. I'll follow, called out Gabriel from the dark.

He continued scraping his feet vigorously while the three women went upstairs, laughing, to the ladies' dressing-room. A light fringe of snow lay like a cape on the shoulders of his overcoat and like toecaps on the toes of his goloshes: and, as the buttons of his overcoat slipped with a squeaking noise through the snow-stiffened frieze, a cold fragrant air from out-of-doors escaped from crevices and folds.

—Is it snowing again, Mr. Conroy? asked Lily.

She had preceded him into the pantry to help him off with his overcoat. Gabriel smiled at the three syllables she had given his surname and glanced at her. She was a slim, growing girl, pale in complexion and with hay-coloured hair. The gas in the pantry made her look still paler. Gabriel had known her when she was a child and used to sit on the lowest step nursing a rag doll.

—Yes, Lily, he answered, and I think we're in for a night of it.

He looked up at the pantry ceiling, which was shaking with the stamping and shuffling of feet on the floor above, listened for a moment to the piano and then glanced at the girl, who was folding his overcoat carefully at the end of a shelf.

—Tell me, Lily, he said in a friendly tone, do you still go to school?

—O no, sir, she answered. I'm done schooling this year and more.

—O, then, said Gabriel gaily, I suppose we'll be going to your wedding one of these fine days with your young man, eh?

The girl glanced back at him over her shoulder and said with great bitterness:

—The men that is now is only all palaver[1] and what they can get out of you.

Gabriel coloured as if he felt he had made a mistake and, without looking at her, kicked off his goloshes and flicked actively with his muffler at his patent-leather shoes.

8. Drunk.
9. Reliable as mail delivery.
1. Fancy talk.

He was a stout tallish young man. The high colour of his cheeks pushed upwards even to his forehead where it scattered itself in a few formless patches of pale red; and on his hairless face there scintillated restlessly the polished lenses and the bright gilt rims of the glasses which screened his delicate and restless eyes. His glossy black hair was parted in the middle and brushed in a long curve behind his ears where it curled slightly beneath the groove left by his hat.

When he had flicked lustre into his shoes he stood up and pulled his waistcoat down more tightly on his plump body. Then he took a coin rapidly from his pocket.

—O Lily, he said, thrusting it into her hands, it's Christmastime, isn't it? Just . . . here's a little. . . .

He walked rapidly towards the door.

—O no, sir! cried the girl, following him. Really, sir, I wouldn't take it.

—Christmas-time! Christmas-time! said Gabriel, almost trotting to the stairs and waving his hand to her in deprecation.

The girl, seeing that he had gained the stairs, called out after him:

—Well, thank you, sir.

He waited outside the drawing-room door until the waltz should finish, listening to the skirts that swept against it and to the shuffling of feet. He was still discomposed by the girl's bitter and sudden retort. It had cast a gloom over him which he tried to dispel by arranging his cuffs and the bows of his tie. Then he took from his waistcoat pocket a little paper and glanced at the headings he had made for his speech. He was undecided about the lines from Robert Browning[2] for he feared they would be above the heads of his hearers. Some quotation that they could recognise from Shakespeare or from the Melodies[3] would be better. The indelicate clacking of the men's heels and the shuffling of their soles reminded him that their grade of culture differed from his. He would only make himself ridiculous by quoting poetry to them which they could not understand. They would think that he was airing his superior education. He would fail with them just as he had failed with the girl in the pantry. He had taken up a wrong tone. His whole speech was a mistake from first to last, an utter failure.

Just then his aunts and his wife came out of the ladies' dressing-room. His aunts were two small plainly dressed old women. Aunt Julia was an inch or so the taller. Her hair, drawn low over the tops of her ears, was grey; and grey also, with darker shadows, was her large flaccid face. Though she was stout in build and stood erect her slow eyes and parted lips gave her the appearance of a woman who did not know where she was or where she was going. Aunt Kate was more vivacious. Her face, healthier than her sister's, was all puckers and creases, like a shrivelled red apple, and her hair, braided in the same old-fashioned way, had not lost its ripe nut colour.

They both kissed Gabriel frankly. He was their favourite nephew, the son of their dead elder sister, Ellen, who had married T. J. Conroy of the Port and Docks.[4]

2. English poet (1812–1889) who had a contemporary reputation for obscurity.
3. Thomas Moore's (1779–1852) immensely popular *Irish Melodies*, a collection of poems with many set to old Irish melodies.
4. The Dublin Port and Docks Board, which regulated customs and shipping.

—Gretta tells me you're not going to take a cab back to Monkstown[5] tonight, Gabriel, said Aunt Kate.

—No, said Gabriel, turning to his wife, we had quite enough of that last year, hadn't we? Don't you remember, Aunt Kate, what a cold Gretta got out of it? Cab windows rattling all the way, and the east wind blowing in after we passed Merrion.[6] Very jolly it was. Gretta caught a dreadful cold.

Aunt Kate frowned severely and nodded her head at every word.

—Quite right, Gabriel, quite right, she said. You can't be too careful.

—But as for Gretta there, said Gabriel, she'd walk home in the snow if she were let.

Mrs. Conroy laughed.

—Don't mind him, Aunt Kate, she said. He's really an awful bother, what with green shades for Tom's eyes at night and making him do the dumb-bells, and forcing Eva to eat the stirabout.[7] The poor child! And she simply hates the sight of it! . . . O, but you'll never guess what he makes me wear now!

She broke out into a peal of laughter and glanced at her husband, whose admiring and happy eyes had been wandering from her dress to her face and hair. The two aunts laughed heartily too, for Gabriel's solicitude was a standing joke with them.

—Goloshes! said Mrs. Conroy. That's the latest. Whenever it's wet underfoot I must put on my goloshes. To-night even he wanted me to put them on, but I wouldn't. The next thing he'll buy me will be a diving suit.

Gabriel laughed nervously and patted his tie reassuringly while Aunt Kate nearly doubled herself, so heartily did she enjoy the joke. The smile soon faded from Aunt Julia's face and her mirthless eyes were directed towards her nephew's face. After a pause she asked:

—And what are goloshes, Gabriel?

—Goloshes, Julia! exclaimed her sister. Goodness me, don't you know what goloshes are? You wear them over your . . . over your boots, Gretta, isn't it?

—Yes, said Mrs. Conroy. Guttapercha[8] things. We both have a pair now. Gabriel says everyone wears them on the continent.

—O, on the continent, murmured Aunt Julia, nodding her head slowly.

Gabriel knitted his brows and said, as if he were slightly angered:

—It's nothing very wonderful but Gretta thinks it very funny because she says the word reminds her of Christy Minstrels.[9]

—But tell me, Gabriel, said Aunt Kate, with brisk tact. Of course, you've seen about the room. Gretta was saying . . .

—O, the room is all right, replied Gabriel. I've taken one in the Gresham.[1]

—To be sure, said Aunt Kate, by far the best thing to do. And the children, Gretta, you're not anxious about them?

—O, for one night, said Mrs. Conroy. Besides, Bessie will look after them.

—To be sure, said Aunt Kate again. What a comfort it is to have a girl like that, one you can depend on! There's that Lily, I'm sure I don't know what has come over her lately. She's not the girl she was at all.

5. Well-to-do suburb of Dublin.
6. Village on Dublin Bay.
7. Porridge.
8. A rubberlike substance.
9. "Goloshes" sounds like "golly shoes," which reminds Gretta of the Christy Minstrels, a popular blackface minstrel show.
1. Fashionable hotel in central Dublin.

Gabriel was about to ask his aunt some questions on this point but she broke off suddenly to gaze after her sister who had wandered down the stairs and was craning her neck over the banisters.

—Now, I ask you, she said, almost testily, where is Julia going? Julia! Julia! Where are you going?

Julia, who had gone halfway down one flight, came back and announced blandly:

—Here's Freddy.

At the same moment a clapping of hands and a final flourish of the pianist told that the waltz had ended. The drawing-room door was opened from within and some couples came out. Aunt Kate drew Gabriel aside hurriedly and whispered into his ear:

—Slip down, Gabriel, like a good fellow and see if he's all right, and don't let him up if he's screwed. I'm sure he's screwed. I'm sure he is.

Gabriel went to the stairs and listened over the banisters. He could hear two persons talking in the pantry. Then he recognised Freddy Malins' laugh. He went down the stairs noisily.

—It's such a relief, said Aunt Kate to Mrs. Conroy, that Gabriel is here. I always feel easier in my mind when he's here. . . . Julia, there's Miss Daly and Miss Power will take some refreshment. Thanks for your beautiful waltz, Miss Daly. It made lovely time.

A tall wizen-faced man, with a stiff grizzled moustache and swarthy skin, who was passing out with his partner said:

—And may we have some refreshment, too, Miss Morkan?

—Julia, said Aunt Kate summarily, and here's Mr. Browne and Miss Furlong. Take them in, Julia, with Miss Daly and Miss Power.

—I'm the man for the ladies, said Mr. Browne, pursing his lips until his moustache bristled and smiling in all his wrinkles. You know, Miss Morkan, the reason they are so fond of me is—

He did not finish his sentence, but, seeing that Aunt Kate was out of earshot, at once led the three young ladies into the back room. The middle of the room was occupied by two square tables placed end to end, and on these Aunt Julia and the caretaker were straightening and smoothing a large cloth. On the sideboard were arrayed dishes and plates, and glasses and bundles of knives and forks and spoons. The top of the closed square piano served also as a sideboard for viands and sweets. At a smaller sideboard in one corner two young men were standing, drinking hop-bitters.[2]

Mr. Browne led his charges thither and invited them all, in jest, to some ladies' punch, hot, strong and sweet. As they said they never took anything strong he opened three bottles of lemonade for them. Then he asked one of the young men to move aside, and, taking hold of the decanter, filled out for himself a goodly measure of whiskey. The young men eyed him respectfully while he took a trial sip.

—God help me, he said, smiling, it's the doctor's orders.

His wizened face broke into a broader smile, and the three young ladies laughed in musical echo to his pleasantry, swaying their bodies to and fro, with nervous jerks of their shoulders. The boldest said:

2. Unfermented beer.

—O, now, Mr. Browne, I'm sure the doctor never ordered anything of the kind.

Mr. Browne took another sip of his whiskey and said, with sidling mimicry:

—Well, you see, I'm like the famous Mrs. Cassidy, who is reported to have said: *Now, Mary Grimes, if I don't take it, make me take it, for I feel I want it.*

His hot face had leaned forward a little too confidentially and he had assumed a very low Dublin accent so that the young ladies, with one instinct, received his speech in silence. Miss Furlong, who was one of Mary Jane's pupils, asked Miss Daly what was the name of the pretty waltz she had played; and Mr. Browne, seeing that he was ignored, turned promptly to the two young men who were more appreciative.

A red-faced young woman, dressed in pansy,[3] came into the room, excitedly clapping her hands and crying:

—Quadrilles![4] Quadrilles!

Close on her heels came Aunt Kate, crying:

—Two gentlemen and three ladies, Mary Jane!

—O, here's Mr. Bergin and Mr. Kerrigan, said Mary Jane. Mr. Kerrigan, will you take Miss Power? Miss Furlong, may I get you a partner, Mr. Bergin. O, that'll just do now.

—Three ladies, Mary Jane, said Aunt Kate.

The two young gentlemen asked the ladies if they might have the pleasure, and Mary Jane turned to Miss Daly.

—O, Miss Daly, you're really awfully good, after playing for the last two dances, but really we're so short of ladies to-night.

—I don't mind in the least, Miss Morkan.

—But I've a nice partner for you, Mr. Bartell D'Arcy, the tenor. I'll get him to sing later on. All Dublin is raving about him.

—Lovely voice, lovely voice! said Aunt Kate.

As the piano had twice begun the prelude to the first figure Mary Jane led her recruits quickly from the room. They had hardly gone when Aunt Julia wandered slowly into the room, looking behind her at something.

—What is the matter, Julia? asked Aunt Kate anxiously. Who is it?

Julia, who was carrying in a column of table-napkins, turned to her sister and said, simply, as if the question had surprised her:

—It's only Freddy, Kate, and Gabriel with him.

In fact right behind her Gabriel could be seen piloting Freddy Malins across the landing. The latter, a young man of forty, was of Gabriel's size and build, with very round shoulders. His face was fleshy and pallid, touched with colour only at the thick hanging lobes of his ears and at the wide wings of his nose. He had coarse features, a blunt nose, a convex and receding brow, tumid and protruded lips. His heavy-lidded eyes and the disorder of his scanty hair made him look sleepy. He was laughing heartily in a high key at a story which he had been telling Gabriel on the stairs and at the same time rubbing the knuckles of his left fist backwards and forwards into his left eye.

—Good-evening, Freddy, said Aunt Julia.

3. Violet.

4. An intricate square dance for four couples.

Freddy Malins bade the Misses Morkan good-evening in what seemed an offhand fashion by reason of the habitual catch in his voice and then, seeing that Mr. Browne was grinning at him from the sideboard, crossed the room on rather shaky legs and began to repeat in an undertone the story he had just told to Gabriel.

—He's not so bad, is he? said Aunt Kate to Gabriel.

Gabriel's brows were dark but he raised them quickly and answered:

—O no, hardly noticeable.

—Now, isn't he a terrible fellow! she said. And his poor mother made him take the pledge on New Year's Eve. But come on, Gabriel, into the drawing-room.

Before leaving the room with Gabriel she signalled to Mr. Browne by frowning and shaking her forefinger in warning to and fro. Mr. Browne nodded in answer and, when she had gone, said to Freddy Malins:

—Now, then, Teddy, I'm going to fill you out a good glass of lemonade just to buck you up.

Freddy Malins, who was nearing the climax of his story, waved the offer aside impatiently but Mr. Browne, having first called Freddy Malins' attention to a disarray in his dress,[5] filled out and handed him a full glass of lemonade. Freddy Malins' left hand accepted the glass mechanically, his right hand being engaged in the mechanical readjustment of his dress. Mr. Browne, whose face was once more wrinkling with mirth, poured out for himself a glass of whisky while Freddy Malins exploded, before he had well reached the climax of his story, in a kink of high-pitched bronchitic laughter and, setting down his untasted and overflowing glass, began to rub the knuckles of his left fist backwards and forwards into his left eye, repeating words of his last phrase as well as his fit of laughter would allow him.

Gabriel could not listen while Mary Jane was playing her Academy piece, full of runs and difficult passages, to the hushed drawing-room. He liked music but the piece she was playing had no melody for him and he doubted whether it had any melody for the other listeners, though they had begged Mary Jane to play something. Four young men, who had come from the refreshment-room to stand in the doorway at the sound of the piano, had gone away quietly in couples after a few minutes. The only persons who seemed to follow the music were Mary Jane herself, her hands racing along the key-board or lifted from it at the pauses like those of a priestess in momentary imprecation, and Aunt Kate standing at her elbow to turn the page.

Gabriel's eyes, irritated by the floor, which glittered with beeswax under the heavy chandelier, wandered to the wall above the piano. A picture of the balcony scene in *Romeo and Juliet* hung there and beside it was a picture of the two murdered princes[6] in the Tower which Aunt Julia had worked in red, blue and brown wools when she was a girl. Probably in the school they had gone to as girls that kind of work had been taught, for one year his mother had worked for him as a birthday present a waistcoat of purple tabinet,[7] with little foxes'

5. That his fly was open.
6. According to Shakespeare's *Richard III*, the young heirs to the British throne were murdered in the Tower of London by order of their uncle, King Richard III. Balcony scene: Shakespeare's *Romeo and Juliet* 2.2.
7. A damasklike fabric.

heads upon it, lined with brown satin and having round mulberry buttons. It was strange that his mother had had no musical talent though Aunt Kate used to call her the brains carrier of the Morkan family. Both she and Julia had always seemed a little proud of their serious and matronly sister. Her photograph stood before the pierglass.[8] She held an open book on her knees and was pointing out something in it to Constantine who, dressed in a man-o'-war suit,[9] lay at her feet. It was she who had chosen the names for her sons for she was very sensible of the dignity of family life. Thanks to her, Constantine was now senior curate in Balbriggan and, thanks to her, Gabriel himself had taken his degree in the Royal University. A shadow passed over his face as he remembered her sullen opposition to his marriage. Some slighting phrases she had used still rankled in his memory; she had once spoken of Gretta as being country cute[1] and that was not true of Gretta at all. It was Gretta who had nursed her during all her last long illness in their house at Monkstown.

He knew that Mary Jane must be near the end of her piece for she was playing again the opening melody with runs of scales after every bar and while he waited for the end the resentment died down in his heart. The piece ended with a trill of octaves in the treble and a final deep octave in the bass. Great applause greeted Mary Jane as, blushing and rolling up her music nervously, she escaped from the room. The most vigorous clapping came from the four young men in the doorway who had gone away to the refreshment-room at the beginning of the piece but had come back when the piano had stopped.

Lancers were arranged. Gabriel found himself partnered with Miss Ivors. She was a frank-mannered talkative young lady, with a freckled face and prominent brown eyes. She did not wear a low-cut bodice and the large brooch which was fixed in the front of her collar bore on it an Irish device.

When they had taken their places she said abruptly:

—I have a crow to pluck[2] with you.

—With me? said Gabriel.

She nodded her head gravely.

—What is it? asked Gabriel, smiling at her solemn manner.

—Who is G. C.? answered Miss Ivors, turning her eyes upon him.

Gabriel coloured and was about to knit his brows, as if he did not understand, when she said bluntly:

—O, innocent Amy! I have found out that you write for *The Daily Express*.[3] Now, aren't you ashamed of yourself?

—Why should I be ashamed of myself? asked Gabriel, blinking his eyes and trying to smile.

—Well, I'm ashamed of you, said Miss Ivors frankly. To say you'd write for a rag like that. I didn't think you were a West Briton.[4]

A look of perplexity appeared on Gabriel's face. It was true that he wrote a literary column every Wednesday in *The Daily Express*, for which he was paid fifteen shillings. But that did not make him a West Briton surely. The books he received for review were almost more welcome than the paltry cheque. He

8. A large mirror.
9. A sailor suit.
1. Unintelligent (not acute).
2. A bone to pick; an argument.
3. Conservative Dublin newspaper opposed to Irish independence.
4. An Irishman who supports union with Britain (an insult).

loved to feel the covers and turn over the pages of newly printed books. Nearly every day when his teaching in the college was ended he used to wander down the quays to the second-hand booksellers, to Hickey's on Bachelor's Walk, to Webb's or Massey's on Aston's Quay, or to O'Clohissey's in the by-street. He did not know how to meet her charge. He wanted to say that literature was above politics. But they were friends of many years' standing and their careers had been parallel, first at the University and then as teachers: he could not risk a grandiose phrase with her. He continued blinking his eyes and trying to smile and murmured lamely that he saw nothing political in writing reviews of books.

When their turn to cross[5] had come he was still perplexed and inattentive. Miss Ivors promptly took his hand in a warm grasp and said in a soft friendly tone:

—Of course, I was only joking. Come, we cross now.

When they were together again she spoke of the University question,[6] and Gabriel felt more at ease. A friend of hers had shown her his review of Browning's poems. That was how she had found out the secret: but she liked the review immensely. Then she said suddenly:

—O, Mr. Conroy, will you come for an excursion to the Aran Isles[7] this summer? We're going to stay there a whole month. It will be splendid out in the Atlantic. You ought to come. Mr. Clancy is coming, and Mr. Kilkelly and Kathleen Kearney. It would be splendid for Gretta too if she'd come. She's from Connacht,[8] isn't she?

—Her people are, said Gabriel shortly.

—But you will come, won't you? said Miss Ivors, laying her warm hand eagerly on his arm.

—The fact is, said Gabriel, I have already arranged to go—

—Go where? asked Miss Ivors.

—Well, you know, every year I go for a cycling tour with some fellows and so—

—But where? asked Miss Ivors.

—Well, we usually go to France or Belgium or perhaps Germany, said Gabriel awkwardly.

—And why do you go to France and Belgium, said Miss Ivors, instead of visiting your own land?

—Well, said Gabriel, it's partly to keep in touch with the languages and partly for a change.

—And haven't you your own language to keep in touch with—Irish? asked Miss Ivors.

—Well, said Gabriel, if it comes to that, you know, Irish is not my language.

Their neighbours had turned to listen to the cross-examination. Gabriel glanced right and left nervously and tried to keep his good humour under the ordeal which was making a blush invade his forehead.

5. A step in the square dance.
6. Controversy over the establishment of Irish Catholic universities to rival the dominant Protestant tradition of Oxford and Cambridge in England, and Trinity College in Dublin.
7. Off the west coast of Ireland, idealized by the nationalists as an example of unspoiled Irish culture and language.
8. The westernmost province of Ireland.

—And haven't you your own land to visit, continued Miss Ivors, that you know nothing of, your own people, and your own country?

—O, to tell you the truth, retorted Gabriel suddenly, I'm sick of my own country, sick of it!

—Why? asked Miss Ivors.

Gabriel did not answer for his retort had heated him.

—Why? repeated Miss Ivors.

They had to go visiting together[9] and, as he had not answered her, Miss Ivors said warmly:

—Of course, you've no answer.

Gabriel tried to cover his agitation by taking part in the dance with great energy. He avoided her eyes for he had seen a sour expression on her face. But when they met in the long chain[1] he was surprised to feel his hand firmly pressed. She looked at him from under her brows for a moment quizzically until he smiled. Then, just as the chain was about to start again, she stood on tiptoe and whispered into his ear:

—West Briton!

When the lancers were over Gabriel went away to a remote corner of the room where Freddy Malins' mother was sitting. She was a stout feeble old woman with white hair. Her voice had a catch in it like her son's and she stuttered slightly. She had been told that Freddy had come and that he was nearly all right. Gabriel asked her whether she had had a good crossing. She lived with her married daughter in Glasgow and came to Dublin on a visit once a year. She answered placidly that she had had a beautiful crossing and that the captain had been most attentive to her. She spoke also of the beautiful house her daughter kept in Glasgow, and of all the nice friends they had there. While her tongue rambled on Gabriel tried to banish from his mind all memory of the unpleasant incident with Miss Ivors. Of course the girl or woman, or whatever she was, was an enthusiast but there was a time for all things. Perhaps he ought not to have answered her like that. But she had no right to call him a West Briton before people, even in joke. She had tried to make him ridiculous before people, heckling him and staring at him with her rabbit's eyes.

He saw his wife making her way towards him through the waltzing couples. When she reached him she said into his ear:

—Gabriel, Aunt Kate wants to know won't you carve the goose as usual. Miss Daly will carve the ham and I'll do the pudding.

—All right, said Gabriel.

—She's sending in the younger ones first as soon as this waltz is over so that we'll have the table to ourselves.

—Were you dancing? asked Gabriel.

—Of course I was. Didn't you see me? What words had you with Molly Ivors?

—No words. Why? Did she say so?

—Something like that. I'm trying to get that Mr. D'Arcy to sing. He's full of conceit, I think.

9. A square-dance step.

1. Another square-dance step.

—There were no words, said Gabriel moodily, only she wanted me to go for a trip to the west of Ireland and I said I wouldn't.

His wife clasped her hands excitedly and gave a little jump.

—O, do go, Gabriel, she cried. I'd love to see Galway again.

—You can go if you like, said Gabriel coldly.

She looked at him for a moment, then turned to Mrs. Malins and said:

—There's a nice husband for you, Mrs. Malins.

While she was threading her way back across the room Mrs. Malins, without adverting to the interruption, went on to tell Gabriel what beautiful places there were in Scotland and beautiful scenery. Her son-in-law brought them every year to the lakes and they used to go fishing. Her son-in-law was a splendid fisher. One day he caught a fish, a beautiful big big fish, and the man in the hotel boiled it for their dinner.

Gabriel hardly heard what she said. Now that supper was coming near he began to think again about his speech and about the quotation. When he saw Freddy Malins coming across the room to visit his mother Gabriel left the chair free for him and retired into the embrasure[2] of the window. The room had already cleared and from the back room came the clatter of plates and knives. Those who still remained in the drawing-room seemed tired of dancing and were conversing quietly in little groups. Gabriel's warm trembling fingers tapped the cold pane of the window. How cool it must be outside! How pleasant it would be to walk out alone, first along by the river and then through the park! The snow would be lying on the branches of the trees and forming a bright cap on the top of the Wellington Monument.[3] How much more pleasant it would be there than at the supper-table!

He ran over the headings of his speech: Irish hospitality, sad memories, the Three Graces, Paris,[4] the quotation from Browning. He repeated to himself a phrase he had written in his review: *One feels that one is listening to a thought-tormented music*. Miss Ivors had praised the review. Was she sincere? Had she really any life of her own behind all her propagandism? There had never been any ill-feeling between them until that night. It unnerved him to think that she would be at the supper-table, looking up at him while he spoke with her critical quizzing eyes. Perhaps she would not be sorry to see him fail in his speech. An idea came into his mind and gave him courage. He would say, alluding to Aunt Kate and Aunt Julia: *Ladies and Gentlemen, the generation which is now on the wane among us may have had its faults but for my part I think it had certain qualities of hospitality, of humour, of humanity, which the new and very serious and hypereducated generation that is growing up around us seems to me to lack.* Very good: that was one for Miss Ivors. What did he care that his aunts were only two ignorant old women?

A murmur in the room attracted his attention. Mr. Browne was advancing from the door, gallantly escorting Aunt Julia, who leaned upon his arm, smiling and hanging her head. An irregular musketry of applause escorted her also as

2. Window nook.
3. A tall obelisk in Phoenix Park, celebrating the duke of Wellington (1769–1852), an Anglo-Irish statesman and general, who served as British prime minister and commander-in-chief of the army.
4. The Trojan prince of Homer's *Iliad*. "Three Graces": daughters of Zeus and Eurynome in Greek mythology; they embodied (and bestowed) charm.

far as the piano and then, as Mary Jane seated herself on the stool, and Aunt Julia, no longer smiling, half turned so as to pitch her voice fairly into the room, gradually ceased. Gabriel recognized the prelude. It was that of an old song of Aunt Julia's—*Arrayed for the Bridal.*[5] Her voice, strong and clear in tone, attacked with great spirit the runs which embellish the air and though she sang very rapidly she did not miss even the smallest of the grace notes. To follow the voice, without looking at the singer's face, was to feel and share the excitement of swift and secure flight. Gabriel applauded loudly with all the others at the close of the song and loud applause was borne in from the invisible supper-table. It sounded so genuine that a little colour struggled into Aunt Julia's face as she bent to replace in the music-stand the old leather-bound song-book that had her initials on the cover. Freddy Malins, who had listened with his head perched sideways to hear her better, was still applauding when everyone else had ceased and talking animatedly to his mother who nodded her head gravely and slowly in acquiescence. At last, when he could clap no more, he stood up suddenly and hurried across the room to Aunt Julia whose hand he seized and held in both his hands, shaking it when words failed him or the catch in his voice proved too much for him.

—I was just telling my mother, he said, I never heard you sing so well, never. No, I never heard your voice so good as it is to-night. Now! Would you believe that now? That's the truth. Upon my word and honour that's the truth. I never heard your voice sound so fresh and so . . . so clear and fresh, never.

Aunt Julia smiled broadly and murmured something about compliments as she released her hand from his grasp. Mr. Browne extended his open hand towards her and said to those who were near him in the manner of a showman introducing a prodigy to an audience:

—Miss Julia Morkan, my latest discovery!

—He was laughing very heartily at this himself when Freddy Malins turned to him and said:

—Well, Browne, if you're serious you might make a worse discovery. All I can say is I never heard her sing half so well as long as I am coming here. And that's the honest truth.

—Neither did I, said Mr. Browne. I think her voice has greatly improved.

Aunt Julia shrugged her shoulders and said with meek pride:

—Thirty years ago I hadn't a bad voice as voices go.

—I often told Julia, said Aunt Kate emphatically, that she was simply thrown away in that choir. But she never would be said by me.

She turned as if to appeal to the good sense of the others against a refractory child while Aunt Julia gazed in front of her, a vague smile of reminiscence playing on her face.

—No, continued Aunt Kate, she wouldn't be said or led by anyone, slaving there in that choir night and day, night and day. Six o'clock on Christmas morning! And all for what?

—Well, isn't it for the honour of God, Aunt Kate? asked Mary Jane, twisting round on the piano-stool and smiling.

Aunt Kate turned fiercely on her niece and said:

5. An English lyric by George Linley; from the first act of Vincenzo Bellini's 1835 opera *I Puritani* (The Puritans).

—I know all about the honour of God, Mary Jane, but I think it's not at all honourable for the pope to turn out the women out of the choirs that have slaved there all their lives and put little whipper-snappers of boys over their heads.[6] I suppose it is for the good of the Church if the pope does it. But it's not just, Mary Jane, and it's not right.

She had worked herself into a passion and would have continued in defence of her sister for it was a sore subject with her but Mary Jane, seeing that all the dancers had come back, intervened pacifically:

—Now, Aunt Kate, you're giving scandal to Mr. Browne who is of the other persuasion.

Aunt Kate turned to Mr. Browne, who was grinning at this allusion to his religion, and said hastily:

—O, I don't question the pope's being right. I'm only a stupid old woman and I wouldn't presume to do such a thing. But there's such a thing as common everyday politeness and gratitude. And if I were in Julia's place I'd tell that Father Healy straight up to his face . . .

—And besides, Aunt Kate, said Mary Jane, we really are all hungry and when we are hungry we are all very quarrelsome.

—And when we are thirsty we are also quarrelsome, added Mr. Browne.

—So that we had better go to supper, said Mary Jane, and finish the discussion afterwards.

On the landing outside the drawing-room Gabriel found his wife and Mary Jane trying to persuade Miss Ivors to stay for supper. But Miss Ivors, who had put on her hat and was buttoning her cloak, would not stay. She did not feel in the least hungry and she had already overstayed her time.

—But only for ten minutes, Molly, said Mrs. Conroy. That won't delay you.

—To take a pick itself, said Mary Jane, after all your dancing.

—I really couldn't, said Miss Ivors.

—I am afraid you didn't enjoy yourself at all, said Mary Jane hopelessly.

—Ever so much, I assure you, said Miss Ivors, but you really must let me run off now.

—But how can you get home? asked Mrs. Conroy.

—O, it's only two steps up the quay.

Gabriel hesitated a moment and said:

—If you will allow me, Miss Ivors, I'll see you home if you really are obliged to go.

But Miss Ivors broke away from them.

—I won't hear of it, she cried. For goodness sake go in to your suppers and don't mind me. I'm quite well able to take care of myself.

—Well, you're the comical girl, Molly, said Mrs. Conroy frankly.

—*Beannacht libh*,[7] cried Miss Ivors, with a laugh, as she ran down the staircase.

Mary Jane gazed after her, a moody puzzled expression on her face, while Mrs. Conroy leaned over the banisters to listen for the hall-door. Gabriel asked himself was he the cause of her abrupt departure. But she did not seem to be in ill humour: she had gone away laughing. He stared blankly down the staircase.

6. In 1903, Pope Pius X decreed that all church singers be male.

7. Farewell: blessings on you (Irish).

At that moment Aunt Kate came toddling out of the supper-room, almost wringing her hands in despair.

—Where is Gabriel? she cried. Where on earth is Gabriel? There's everyone waiting in there, stage to let, and nobody to carve the goose!

—Here I am, Aunt Kate! cried Gabriel, with sudden animation, ready to carve a flock of geese, if necessary.

A fat brown goose lay at one end of the table and at the other end, on a bed of creased paper strewn with sprigs of parsley, lay a great ham, stripped of its outer skin and peppered over with crust crumbs, a neat paper frill round its shin and beside this was a round of spiced beef. Between these rival ends ran parallel lines of side-dishes: two little minsters[8] of jelly, red and yellow; a shallow dish full of blocks of blancmange and red jam, a large green leaf-shaped dish with a stalk-shaped handle, on which lay bunches of purple raisins and peeled almonds, a companion dish on which lay a solid rectangle of Smyrna figs, a dish of custard topped with grated nutmeg, a small bowl full of chocolates and sweets wrapped in gold and silver papers and a glass vase in which stood some tall celery stalks. In the center of the table there stood, as sentries to a fruit-stand which upheld a pyramid of oranges and American apples, two squat old-fashioned decanters of cut glass, one containing port and the other dark sherry. On the closed square piano a pudding in a huge yellow dish lay in waiting and behind it were three squads of bottles of stout and ale and minerals,[9] drawn up according to the colours of their uniforms, the first two black, with brown and red labels, the third and smallest squad white, with transverse green sashes.

Gabriel took his seat boldly at the head of the table and, having looked to the edge of the carver, plunged his fork firmly into the goose. He felt quite at ease now for he was an expert carver and liked nothing better than to find himself at the head of a well-laden table.

—Miss Furlong, what shall I send you? he asked. A wing or a slice of the breast?

—Just a small slice of the breast.

—Miss Higgins, what for you?

—O, anything at all, Mr. Conroy.

While Gabriel and Miss Daly exchanged plates of goose and plates of ham and spiced beef Lily went from guest to guest with a dish of hot floury potatoes wrapped in a white napkin. This was Mary Jane's idea and she had also suggested apple sauce for the goose but Aunt Kate had said that plain roast goose without apple sauce had always been good enough for her and she hoped she might never eat worse. Mary Jane waited on her pupils and saw that they got the best slices and Aunt Kate and Aunt Julia opened and carried across from the piano bottles of stout and ale for the gentlemen and bottles of minerals for the ladies. There was a great deal of confusion and laughter and noise, the noise of orders and counter-orders, of knives and forks, of corks and glass-stoppers. Gabriel began to carve second helpings as soon as he had finished the first round without serving himself. Everyone protested loudly so that he compromised by taking a long draught of stout for he had found the carving hot

8. Confectioneries shaped to look like cathedrals.

9. Carbonated drinks.

work. Mary Jane settled down quietly to her supper but Aunt Kate and Aunt Julia were still toddling round the table, walking on each other's heels, getting in each other's way and giving each other unheeded orders. Mr. Browne begged of them to sit down and eat their suppers and so did Gabriel but they said there was time enough so that, at last, Freddy Malins stood up and, capturing Aunt Kate, plumped her down on her chair amid general laughter.

When everyone had been well served Gabriel said, smiling:

—Now, if anyone wants a little more of what vulgar people call stuffing let him or her speak.

A chorus of voices invited him to begin his own supper and Lily came forward with three potatoes which she had reserved for him.

—Very well, said Gabriel amiably, as he took another preparatory draught, kindly forget my existence, ladies and gentlemen, for a few minutes.

He sat to his supper and took no part in the conversation with which the table covered Lily's removal of the plates. The subject of talk was the opera company which was then at the Theatre Royal. Mr. Bartell D'Arcy, the tenor, a dark-complexioned young man with a smart moustache, praised very highly the leading contralto of the company but Miss Furlong thought she had a rather vulgar style of production. Freddy Malins said there was a negro chieftain[1] singing in the second part of the Gaiety pantomime who had one of the finest tenor voices he had ever heard.

—Have you heard him? he asked Mr. Bartell D'Arcy across the table.

—No, answered Mr. Bartell D'Arcy carelessly.

—Because, Freddy Malins explained, now I'd be curious to hear your opinion of him. I think he has a grand voice.

—It takes Teddy to find out the really good things, said Mr. Browne familiarly to the table.

—And why couldn't he have a voice too? asked Freddy Malins sharply. Is it because he's only a black?

Nobody answered this question and Mary Jane led the table back to the legitimate opera. One of her pupils had given her a pass for *Mignon*.[2] Of course it was very fine, she said, but it made her think of poor Georgina Burns. Mr. Browne could go back farther still, to the old Italian companies that used to come to Dublin—Tietjens, Ilma de Murzka, Campanini, the great Trebelli, Giuglini, Ravelli, Aramburo.[3] Those were the days, he said, when there was something like singing to be heard in Dublin. He told too of how the top gallery of the old Royal used to be packed night after night, of how one night an Italian tenor had sung five encores to *Let Me Like a Soldier Fall*,[4] introducing a high C every time, and of how the gallery boys would sometimes in their enthusiasm unyoke the horses from the carriage of some great *prima donna* and pull her themselves through the streets to her hotel. Why did they never play the grand old operas now, he asked, *Dinorah, Lucrezia Borgia*?[5] Because they could not get the voices to sing them: that was why.

1. Actually, a blackface performer.
2. Popular French opera (1866) by Ambroise Thomas.
3. Famous opera singers.
4. From William V. Wallace's romantic light opera *Maritana* (1845).
5. Operas by Giacomo Meyerbeer (1859) and Gaetano Donizetti (1833), respectively.

—O, well, said Mr. Bartell D'Arcy, I presume there are as good singers today as there were then.

—Where are they? asked Mr. Browne defiantly.

—In London, Paris, Milan, said Mr. Bartell D'Arcy warmly. I suppose Caruso,[6] for example, is quite as good, if not better than any of the men you have mentioned.

—Maybe so, said Mr. Browne. But I may tell you I doubt it strongly.

—O, I'd give anything to hear Caruso sing, said Mary Jane.

—For me, said Aunt Kate, who had been picking a bone, there was only one tenor. To please me, I mean. But I suppose none of you ever heard of him.

—Who was he, Miss Morkan? asked Mr. Bartell D'Arcy politely.

—His name, said Aunt Kate, was Parkinson. I heard him when he was in his prime and I think he had then the purest tenor voice that was ever put into a man's throat.

—Strange, said Mr. Bartell D'Arcy. I never even heard of him.

—Yes, yes, Miss Morkan is right, said Mr. Browne. I remember hearing of old Parkinson but he's too far back for me.

—A beautiful pure sweet mellow English tenor, said Aunt Kate with enthusiasm.

Gabriel having finished, the huge pudding was transferred to the table. The clatter of forks and spoons began again. Gabriel's wife served out spoonfuls of the pudding and passed the plates down the table. Midway down they were held up by Mary Jane, who replenished them with raspberry or orange jelly or with blancmange and jam. The pudding was of Aunt Julia's making and she received praises for it from all quarters. She herself said that it was not quite brown enough.

—Well, I hope, Miss Morkan, said Mr. Browne, that I'm brown enough for you because, you know, I'm all brown.

All the gentlemen, except Gabriel, ate some of the pudding out of compliment to Aunt Julia. As Gabriel never ate sweets the celery had been left for him. Freddy Malins also took a stalk of celery and ate it with his pudding. He had been told that celery was a capital thing for the blood and he was just then under doctor's care. Mrs. Malins, who had been silent all through the supper, said that her son was going down to Mount Melleray[7] in a week or so. The table then spoke of Mount Melleray, how bracing the air was down there, how hospitable the monks were and how they never asked for a penny-piece from their guests.

—And do you mean to say, asked Mr. Browne incredulously, that a chap can go down there and put up there as if it were a hotel and live on the fat of the land and then come away without paying a farthing?

—O, most people give some donation to the monastery when they leave, said Mary Jane.

—I wish we had an institution like that in our Church, said Mr. Browne candidly.

He was astonished to hear that the monks never spoke, got up at two in the morning and slept in their coffins.[8] He asked what they did it for.

6. Enrico Caruso (1873–1921).
7. A Trappist abbey whose hospitality included the treatment of wealthy alcoholics.
8. The coffin story is a popular fiction.

—That's the rule of the order, said Aunt Kate firmly.

—Yes, but why? asked Mr. Browne.

Aunt Kate repeated that it was the rule, that was all. Mr. Browne still seemed not to understand. Freddy Malins explained to him, as best he could, that the monks were trying to make up for the sins committed by all the sinners in the outside world. The explanation was not very clear for Mr. Browne grinned and said:

—I like that idea very much but wouldn't a comfortable spring bed do them as well as a coffin?

—The coffin, said Mary Jane, is to remind them of their last end.

As the subject had grown lugubrious it was buried in a silence of the table during which Mrs. Malins could be heard saying to her neighbour in an indistinct undertone:

—They are very good men, the monks, very pious men.

The raisins and almonds and figs and apples and oranges and chocolates and sweets were now passed about the table and Aunt Julia invited all the guests to have either port or sherry. At first Mr. Bartell D'Arcy refused to take either but one of his neighbours nudged him and whispered something to him upon which he allowed his glass to be filled. Gradually as the last glasses were being filled the conversation ceased. A pause followed, broken only by the noise of the wine and by unsettlings of chairs. The Misses Morkan, all three, looked down at the tablecloth. Someone coughed once or twice and then a few gentlemen patted the table gently as a signal for silence. The silence came and Gabriel pushed back his chair and stood up.

The patting at once grew louder in encouragement and then ceased altogether. Gabriel leaned his ten trembling fingers on the tablecloth and smiled nervously at the company. Meeting a row of upturned faces he raised his eyes to the chandelier. The piano was playing a waltz tune and he could hear the skirts sweeping against the drawing-room door. People, perhaps, were standing in the snow on the quay outside, gazing up at the lighted windows and listening to the waltz music. The air was pure there. In the distance lay the park where the trees were weighted with snow. The Wellington Monument wore a gleaming cap of snow that flashed westward over the white field of Fifteen Acres.[9]

He began:

—Ladies and Gentlemen.

—It has fallen to my lot this evening, as in years past, to perform a very pleasing task but a task for which I am afraid my poor powers as a speaker are all too inadequate.

—No, no! said Mr. Browne.

—But, however that may be, I can only ask you to-night to take the will for the deed and to lend me your attention for a few moments while I endeavour to express to you in words what my feelings are on this occasion.

—Ladies and Gentlemen. It is not the first time that we have gathered together under this hospitable roof, around this hospitable board. It is not the first time that we have been the recipients—or perhaps, I had better say, the victims—of the hospitality of certain good ladies.

9. A section of Phoenix Park used for British military reviews.

He made a circle in the air with his arm and paused. Everyone laughed or smiled at Aunt Kate and Aunt Julia and Mary Jane who all turned crimson with pleasure. Gabriel went on more boldly:

—I feel more strongly with every recurring year that our country has no tradition which does it so much honour and which it should guard so jealously as that of its hospitality. It is a tradition that is unique as far as my experience goes (and I have visited not a few places abroad) among the modern nations. Some would say, perhaps, that with us it is rather a failing than anything to be boasted of. But granted even that, it is, to my mind, a princely failing, and one that I trust will long be cultivated among us. Of one thing, at least, I am sure. As long as this one roof shelters the good ladies aforesaid—and I wish from my heart it may do so for many and many a long year to come—the tradition of genuine warm-hearted courteous Irish hospitality, which our forefathers have handed down to us and which we in turn must hand down to our descendants, is still alive among us.

A hearty murmur of assent ran around the table. It shot through Gabriel's mind that Miss Ivors was not there and that she had gone away discourteously: and he said with confidence in himself:

—Ladies and Gentlemen.

—A new generation is growing up in our midst, a generation actuated by new ideas and new principles. It is serious and enthusiastic for these new ideas and its enthusiasm, even when it is misdirected, is, I believe, in the main sincere. But we are living in a skeptical and, if I may use the phrase, a thought-tormented age: and sometimes I fear that this new generation, educated or hypereducated as it is, will lack those qualities of humanity, of hospitality, of kindly humour which belonged to an older day. Listening tonight to the names of all those great singers of the past it seemed to me, I must confess, that we were living in a less spacious age. Those days might, without exaggeration, be called spacious days: and if they are gone beyond recall let us hope, at least, that in gatherings such as this we shall still speak of them with pride and affection, still cherish in our hearts the memory of those dead and gone great ones whose fame the world will not willingly let die.

—Hear, hear! said Mr. Browne loudly.

—But yet, continued Gabriel, his voice falling into a softer inflection, there are always in gatherings such as this sadder thoughts that will recur to our minds: thoughts of the past, of youth, of changes, of absent faces that we miss here tonight. Our path through life is strewn with many such sad memories: and were we to brood upon them always we could not find the heart to go on bravely with our work among the living. We have all of us living duties and living affections which claim, and rightly claim, our strenuous endeavours.

—Therefore, I will not linger on the past. I will not let any gloomy moralising intrude upon us here to-night. Here we are gathered together for a brief moment from the bustle and rush of our everyday routine. We are met here as friends, in the spirit of good-fellowship, as colleagues, also to a certain extent, in the true spirit of *camaraderie*, and as the guests of—what shall I call them?—the Three Graces of the Dublin musical world.

The table burst into applause and laughter at this sally. Aunt Julia vainly asked each of her neighbours in turn to tell her what Gabriel had said.

—He says we are the Three Graces, Aunt Julia, said Mary Jane.

Aunt Julia did not understand but she looked up, smiling, at Gabriel, who continued in the same vein:

—Ladies and Gentlemen.

—I will not attempt to play to-night the part that Paris played on another occasion.[1] I will not attempt to choose between them. The task would be an invidious one and one beyond my poor powers. For when I view them in turn, whether it be our chief hostess herself, whose good heart, whose too good heart, has become a byword with all who know her, or her sister, who seems to be gifted with perennial youth and whose singing must have been a surprise and a revelation to us all to-night, or, last but not least, when I consider our youngest hostess, talented, cheerful, hard-working and the best of nieces, I confess, Ladies and Gentlemen, that I do not know to which of them I should award the prize.

Gabriel glanced down at his aunts and, seeing the large smile on Aunt Julia's face and the tears which had risen to Aunt Kate's eyes, hastened to his close. He raised his glass of port gallantly, while every member of the company fingered a glass expectantly, and said loudly:

—Let us toast them all three together. Let us drink to their health, wealth, long life, happiness and prosperity and may they long continue to hold the proud and self-won position which they hold in their profession and the position of honour and affection which they hold in our hearts.

All the guests stood up, glass in hand, and, turning towards the three seated ladies, sang in unison, with Mr. Browne as leader:

For they are jolly gay fellows,
For they are jolly gay fellows,
For they are jolly gay fellows,
Which nobody can deny.

Aunt Kate was making frank use of her handkerchief and even Aunt Julia seemed moved. Freddy Malins beat time with his pudding-fork and the singers turned towards one another, as if in melodious conference, while they sang, with emphasis:

Unless he tells a lie,
Unless he tells a lie,

Then, turning once more towards their hostesses, they sang:

For they are jolly gay fellows,
For they are jolly gay fellows,
For they are jolly gay fellows,
Which nobody can deny.

The acclamation which followed was taken up beyond the door of the supper-room by many of the other guests and renewed time after time, Freddy Malins acting as officer with his fork on high.

---

1. Paris was required to judge a beauty contest between the Greek goddesses Hera, Athena, and Aphrodite; see p. 182, n. 34.

The piercing morning air came into the hall where they were standing so that Aunt Kate said:

—Close the door, somebody. Mrs. Malins will get her death of cold.

—Browne is out there, Aunt Kate, said Mary Jane.

—Browne is everywhere, said Aunt Kate, lowering her voice.

Mary Jane laughed at her tone.

—Really, she said archly, he is very attentive.

—He has been laid on here like the gas, said Aunt Kate in the same tone, all during the Christmas.

She laughed herself this time good-humouredly and then added quickly:

—But tell him to come in, Mary Jane, and close the door. I hope to goodness he didn't hear me.

At that moment the hall-door was opened and Mr. Browne came in from the doorstep, laughing as if his heart would break. He was dressed in a long green overcoat with mock astrakhan[2] cuffs and collar and wore on his head an oval fur cap. He pointed down the snow-covered quay from where the sound of shrill prolonged whistling was borne in.

—Teddy will have all the cabs in Dublin out, he said.

Gabriel advanced from the little pantry behind the office, struggling into his overcoat and, looking round the hall, said:

—Gretta not down yet?

—She's getting on her things, Gabriel, said Aunt Kate.

—Who's playing up there? asked Gabriel.

—Nobody. They're all gone.

—O no, Aunt Kate, said Mary Jane. Bartell D'Arcy and Miss O'Callaghan aren't gone yet.

—Someone is strumming at the piano, anyhow, said Gabriel.

Mary Jane glanced at Gabriel and Mr. Browne and said with a shiver:

—It makes me feel cold to look at you two gentlemen muffled up like that. I wouldn't like to face your journey home at this hour.

—I'd like nothing better this minute, said Mr. Browne stoutly, than a rattling fine walk in the country or a fast drive with a good spanking goer between the shafts.

—We used to have a very good horse and trap at home, said Aunt Julia sadly.

—The never-to-be-forgotten Johnny, said Mary Jane, laughing.

Aunt Kate and Gabriel laughed too.

—Why, what was wonderful about Johnny? asked Mr. Browne.

—The late lamented Patrick Morkan, our grandfather, that is, explained Gabriel, commonly known in his later years as the old gentleman, was a glue-boiler.

—O, now, Gabriel, said Aunt Kate, laughing, he had a starch mill.

—Well, glue or starch, said Gabriel, the old gentleman had a horse by the name of Johnny. And Johnny used to work in the old gentleman's mill, walking round and round in order to drive the mill. That was all very well; but now comes the tragic part about Johnny. One fine day the old gentleman thought he'd like to drive out with the quality[3] to a military review in the park.

2. Tight, curly-haired lambswool.

3. Social eliter.

—The Lord have mercy on his soul, said Aunt Kate compassionately.

—Amen, said Gabriel. So the old gentleman, as I said, harnessed Johnny and put on his very best tall hat and his very best stock collar and drove out in grand style from his ancestral mansion somewhere near Back Lane,[4] I think.

Everyone laughed, even Mrs. Malins, at Gabriel's manner and Aunt Kate said:

—O now, Gabriel, he didn't live in Back Lane, really. Only the mill was there.

—Out from the mansion of his forefathers, continued Gabriel, he drove with Johnny. And everything went on beautifully until Johnny came in sight of King Billy's[5] statue: and whether he fell in love with the horse King Billy sits on or whether he thought he was back again in the mill, anyhow he began to walk round the statue.

Gabriel paced in a circle round the hall in his goloshes amid the laughter of the others.

—Round and round he went, said Gabriel, and the old gentleman, who was a very pompous old gentleman, was highly indignant. *Go on, sir! What do you mean, sir? Johnny! Johnny! Most extraordinary conduct! Can't understand the horse!*

The peals of laughter which followed Gabriel's imitation of the incident were interrupted by a resounding knock at the hall-door. Mary Jane ran to open it and let in Freddy Malins. Freddy Malins, with his hat well back on his head and his shoulders humped with cold, was puffing and steaming after his exertions.

—I could only get one cab, he said.

—O, we'll find another along the quay, said Gabriel.

—Yes, said Aunt Kate. Better not keep Mrs. Malins standing in the draught.

Mrs. Malins was helped down the front steps by her son and Mr. Browne and, after many manœuvres, hoisted into the cab. Freddy Malins clambered in after her and spent a long time settling her on the seat, Mr. Browne helping him with advice. At last she was settled comfortably and Freddy Malins invited Mr. Browne into the cab. There was a good deal of confused talk, and then Mr. Browne got into the cab. The cabman settled his rug over his knees, and bent down for the address. The confusion grew greater and the cabman was directed differently by Freddy Malins and Mr. Browne, each of whom had his head out through a window of the cab. The difficulty was to know where to drop Mr. Browne along the route and Aunt Kate, Aunt Julia and Mary Jane helped the discussion from the doorstep with cross-directions and contradictions and abundance of laughter. As for Freddy Malins he was speechless with laughter. He popped his head in and out of the window every moment, to the great danger of his hat, and told his mother how the discussion was progressing till at last Mr. Browne shouted to the bewildered cabman above the din of everybody's laughter:

—Do you know Trinity College?

—Yes, sir, said the cabman.

—Well, drive bang up against Trinity College gates, said Mr. Browne, and then we'll tell you where to go. You understand now?

4. A shabby street in a run-down area of Dublin.

5. William III, king of England from 1689 to 1702, defeated the Irish nationalists at the Battle of the Boyne.

—Yes, sir, said the cabman.

—Make like a bird for Trinity College.

—Right, sir, cried the cabman.

The horse was whipped up and the cab rattled off along the quay amid a chorus of laughter and adieus.

Gabriel had not gone to the door with the others. He was in a dark part of the hall gazing up the staircase. A woman was standing near the top of the first flight, in the shadow also. He could not see her face but he could see the terracotta and salmonpink panels of her skirt which the shadow made appear black and white. It was his wife. She was leaning on the banisters, listening to something. Gabriel was surprised at her stillness and strained his ear to listen also. But he could hear little save the noise of laughter and dispute on the front steps, a few chords struck on the piano and a few notes of a man's voice singing.

He stood still in the gloom of the hall, trying to catch the air that the voice was singing and gazing up at his wife. There was grace and mystery in her attitude as if she were a symbol of something. He asked himself what is a woman standing on the stairs in the shadow, listening to distant music, a symbol of. If he were a painter he would paint her in that attitude. Her blue felt hat would show off the bronze of her hair against the darkness and the dark panels of her skirt would show off the light ones. *Distant Music* he would call the picture if he were a painter.

The hall-door was closed; and Aunt Kate, Aunt Julia and Mary Jane came down the hall, still laughing.

—Well, isn't Freddy terrible? said Mary Jane. He's really terrible.

Gabriel said nothing but pointed up the stairs towards where his wife was standing. Now that the hall-door was closed the voice and the piano could be heard more clearly. Gabriel held up his hand for them to be silent. The song seemed to be in the old Irish tonality[6] and the singer seemed uncertain both of his words and of his voice. The voice, made plaintive by distance and by the singer's hoarseness, faintly illuminated the cadence of the air with words expressing grief:

O, the rain falls on my heavy locks
And the dew wets my skin,
My babe lies cold[7] . . .

—O, exclaimed Mary Jane. It's Bartell D'Arcy singing and he wouldn't sing all the night. O, I'll get him to sing a song before he goes.

—O do, Mary Jane, said Aunt Kate.

Mary Jane brushed past the others and ran to the staircase but before she reached it the singing stopped and the piano was closed abruptly.

—O, what a pity! she cried. Is he coming down, Gretta?

Gabriel heard his wife answer yes and saw her come down towards them. A few steps behind her were Mr. Bartell D'Arcy and Miss O'Callaghan.

6. Based on five (and later seven) tones rather than the modern eight-tone scale.

7. From "The Lass of Aughrim," a ballad about a peasant girl seduced by a lord; when she brings her baby to the castle door, the lord's mother imitates his voice and sends her away. Mother and child are drowned at sea, and the repentant lord curses his mother.

—O, Mr. D'Arcy, cried Mary Jane, it's downright mean of you to break off like that when we were all in raptures listening to you.

—I have been at him all the evening, said Miss O'Callaghan, and Mrs. Conroy too and he told us he had a dreadful cold and couldn't sing.

—O, Mr. D'Arcy, said Aunt Kate, now that was a great fib to tell.

—Can't you see that I'm as hoarse as a crow? said Mr. D'Arcy roughly.

He went into the pantry hastily and put on his overcoat. The others, taken aback by his rude speech, could find nothing to say. Aunt Kate wrinkled her brows and made signs to the others to drop the subject. Mr. D'Arcy stood swathing his neck carefully and frowning.

—It's the weather, said Aunt Julia, after a pause.

—Yes, everybody has colds, said Aunt Kate readily, everybody.

—They say, said Mary Jane, we haven't had snow like it for thirty years; and I read this morning in the newspapers that the snow is general all over Ireland.

—I love the look of snow, said Aunt Julia sadly.

—So do I, said Miss O'Callaghan. I think Christmas is never really Christmas unless we have the snow on the ground.

—But poor Mr. D'Arcy doesn't like the snow, said Aunt Kate, smiling.

Mr. D'Arcy came from the pantry, fully swathed and buttoned, and in a repentant tone told them the history of his cold. Everyone gave him advice and said it was a great pity and urged him to be very careful of his throat in the night air. Gabriel watched his wife who did not join in the conversation. She was standing right under the dusty fanlight and the flame of the gas lit up the rich bronze of her hair which he had seen her drying at the fire a few days before. She was in the same attitude and seemed unaware of the talk about her. At last she turned towards them and Gabriel saw that there was colour on her cheeks and that her eyes were shining. A sudden tide of joy went leaping out of his heart.

—Mr. D'Arcy, she said, what is the name of that song you were singing?

—It's called *The Lass of Aughrim*, said Mr. D'Arcy, but I couldn't remember it properly. Why? Do you know it?

—*The Lass of Aughrim*, she repeated. I couldn't think of the name.

—It's a very nice air, said Mary Jane. I'm sorry you were not in voice to-night.

—Now, Mary Jane, said Aunt Kate, don't annoy Mr. D'Arcy. I won't have him annoyed.

Seeing that all were ready to start she shepherded them to the door where good-night was said:

—Well, good-night, Aunt Kate, and thanks for the pleasant evening.

—Good-night, Gabriel. Good-night, Gretta!

—Good-night, Aunt Kate, and thanks ever so much. Good-night, Aunt Julia.

—O, good-night, Gretta, I didn't see you.

—Good-night, Mr. D'Arcy. Good-night, Miss O'Callaghan.

—Good-night, Miss Morkan.

—Good-night, again.

—Good-night, all. Safe home.

—Good-night. Good-night.

The morning was still dark. A dull yellow light brooded over the houses and the river; and the sky seemed to be descending. It was slushy underfoot; and only streaks and patches of snow lay on the roofs, on the parapets of the quay and on the area railings. The lamps were still burning redly in the murky air and, across the river, the palace of the Four Courts[8] stood out menacingly against the heavy sky.

She was walking on before him with Mr. Bartell D'Arcy, her shoes in a brown parcel tucked under one arm and her hands holding her skirt up from the slush. She had no longer any grace of attitude but Gabriel's eyes were still bright with happiness. The blood went bounding along his veins; and the thoughts went rioting through his brain, proud, joyful, tender, valorous.

She was walking on before him so lightly and so erect that he longed to run after her noiselessly, catch her by the shoulders and say something foolish and affectionate into her ear. She seemed to him so frail that he longed to defend her against something and then to be alone with her. Moments of their secret life together burst like stars upon his memory. A heliotrope envelope was lying beside his breakfast-cup and he was caressing it with his hand. Birds were twittering in the ivy and the sunny web of the curtain was shimmering along the floor: he could not eat for happiness. They were standing on the crowded platform and he was placing a ticket inside the warm palm of her glove. He was standing with her in the cold, looking in through a grated window at a man making bottles in a roaring furnace. It was very cold. Her face, fragrant in the cold air, was quite close to his; and suddenly she called out to the man at the furnace:

—Is the fire hot, sir?

But the man could not hear her with the noise of the furnace. It was just as well. He might have answered rudely.

A wave of yet more tender joy escaped from his heart and went coursing in warm flood along his arteries. Like the tender fires of stars moments of their life together, that no one knew of or would ever know of, broke upon and illumined his memory. He longed to recall to her those moments, to make her forget the years of their dull existence together and remember only their moments of ecstasy. For the years, he felt, had not quenched his soul or hers. Their children, his writing, her household cares had not quenched all their souls' tender fire. In one letter that he had written to her then he had said: *Why is it that words like these seem to me so dull and cold? Is it because there is no word tender enough to be your name?*

Like distant music these words that he had written years before were borne towards him from the past. He longed to be alone with her. When the others had gone away, when he and she were in their room in the hotel, then they would be alone together. He would call her softly:

—Gretta!

Perhaps she would not hear at once: she would be undressing. Then something in his voice would strike her. She would turn and look at him.

At the corner of Winetavern Street they met a cab. He was glad of its rattling noise as it saved him from conversation. She was looking out of the window and seemed tired. The others spoke only a few words, pointing out some building or street. The horse galloped along wearily under the murky morning sky, dragging his old rattling box after his heels, and Gabriel was again in a cab with her, galloping to catch the boat, galloping to their honeymoon.

8. The Irish law courts building.

As the cab drove across O'Connell Bridge Miss O'Callaghan said:

—They say you never cross O'Connell Bridge without seeing a white horse.

—I see a white man this time, said Gabriel.

—Where? asked Mr. Bartell D'Arcy.

Gabriel pointed to the statue,[9] on which lay patches of snow. Then he nodded familiarly to it and waved his hand.

—Good-night, Dan, he said gaily.

When the cab drew up before the hotel Gabriel jumped out and, in spite of Mr. Bartell D'Arcy's protest, paid the driver. He gave the man a shilling over his fare. The man saluted and said:

—A prosperous New Year to you, sir.

—The same to you, said Gabriel cordially.

She leaned for a moment on his arm in getting out of the cab and while standing at the curbstone, bidding the others good-night. She leaned lightly on his arm, as lightly as when she had danced with him a few hours before. He had felt proud and happy then, happy that she was his, proud of her grace and wifely carriage. But now, after the kindling again of so many memories, the first touch of her body, musical and strange and perfumed, sent through him a keen pang of lust. Under cover of her silence he pressed her arm closely to his side; and, as they stood at the hotel door, he felt that they had escaped from their lives and duties, escaped from home and friends and run away together with wild and radiant hearts to a new adventure.

An old man was dozing in a great hooded chair in the hall. He lit a candle in the office and went before them to the stairs. They followed him in silence, their feet falling in soft thuds on the thickly carpeted stairs. She mounted the stairs behind the porter, her head bowed in the ascent, her frail shoulders curved as with a burden, her skirt girt tightly about her. He could have flung his arms about her hips and held her still for his arms were trembling with desire to seize her and only the stress of his nails against the palms of his hands held the wild impulse of his body in check. The porter halted on the stairs to settle his guttering candle. They halted too on the steps below him. In the silence Gabriel could hear the falling of the molten wax into the tray and the thumping of his own heart against his ribs.

The porter led them along a corridor and opened a door. Then he set his unstable candle down on a toilet-table and asked at what hour they were to be called in the morning.

—Eight, said Gabriel.

The porter pointed to the tap of the electric-light and began a muttered apology but Gabriel cut him short.

—We don't want any light. We have light enough from the street. And I say, he added, pointing to the candle, you might remove that handsome article, like a good man.

The porter took up his candle again, but slowly for he was surprised by such a novel idea. Then he mumbled good-night and went out. Gabriel shot the lock to.

9. Of Daniel O'Connell (1775–1847), called "The Liberator" by the Irish independence movement.

A ghostly light from the street lamp lay in a long shaft from one window to the door. Gabriel threw his overcoat and hat on a couch and crossed the room towards the window. He looked down into the street in order that his emotion might calm a little. Then he turned and leaned against a chest of drawers with his back to the light. She had taken off her hat and cloak and was standing before a large swinging mirror, unhooking her waist.[1] Gabriel paused for a few moments, watching her, and then said:

—Gretta!

She turned away from the mirror slowly and walked along the shaft of light towards him. Her face looked so serious and weary that the words would not pass Gabriel's lips. No, it was not the moment yet.

—You looked tired, he said.

—I am a little, she answered.

—You don't feel ill or weak?

—No, tired: that's all.

She went on to the window and stood there, looking out. Gabriel waited again and then, fearing that diffidence was about to conquer him, he said abruptly:

—By the way, Gretta!

—What is it?

—You know that poor fellow Malins? he said quickly.

—Yes. What about him?

—Well, poor fellow, he's a decent sort of chap after all, continued Gabriel in a false voice. He gave me back that sovereign I lent him and I didn't expect it really. It's a pity he wouldn't keep away from that Browne, because he's not a bad fellow at heart.

He was trembling now with annoyance. Why did she seem so abstracted? He did not know how he could begin. Was she annoyed, too, about something? If she would only turn to him or come to him of her own accord! To take her as she was would be brutal. No, he must see some ardour in her eyes first. He longed to be master of her strange mood.

—When did you lend him the pound? she asked, after a pause.

Gabriel strove to restrain himself from breaking out into brutal language about the sottish Malins and his pound. He longed to cry to her from his soul, to crush her body against his, to overmaster her. But he said:

—O, at Christmas, when he opened that little Christmas-card shop in Henry Street.

He was in such a fever of rage and desire that he did not hear her come from the window. She stood before him for an instant, looking at him strangely. Then, suddenly raising herself on tiptoe and resting her hands lightly on his shoulders, she kissed him.

—You are a very generous person, Gabriel, she said.

Gabriel, trembling with delight at her sudden kiss and at the quaintness of her phrase, put his hands on her hair and began smoothing it back, scarcely touching it with his fingers. The washing had made it fine and brilliant. His heart was brimming over with happiness. Just when he was wishing for it she had come to him of her own accord. Perhaps her thoughts had been running

1. I.e., loosening her waistband.

with his. Perhaps she had felt the impetuous desire that was in him and then the yielding mood had come upon her. Now that she had fallen to him so easily he wondered why he had been so diffident.

He stood, holding her head between his hands. Then, slipping one arm swiftly about her body and drawing her towards him, he said softly:

—Gretta dear, what are you thinking about?

She did not answer nor yield wholly to his arm. He said again, softly:

—Tell me what it is, Gretta. I think I know what is the matter. Do I know?

She did not answer at once. Then she said in an outburst of tears:

—O, I am thinking about that song, *The Lass of Aughrim*.

She broke loose from him and ran to the bed and, throwing her arms across the bed-rail, hid her face. Gabriel stood stock-still for a moment in astonishment and then followed her. As he passed in the way of the cheval-glass he caught sight of himself in full length, his broad, well-filled shirt-front, the face whose expression always puzzled him when he saw it in a mirror and his glimmering gilt-rimmed eyeglasses. He halted a few paces from her and said:

—What about the song? Why does that make you cry?

She raised her head from her arms and dried her eyes with the back of her hand like a child. A kinder note than he had intended went into his voice.

—Why, Gretta? he asked.

—I am thinking about a person long ago who used to sing that song.

—And who was the person long ago? asked Gabriel, smiling.

—It was a person I used to know in Galway when I was living with my grandmother, she said.

The smile passed away from Gabriel's face. A dull anger began to gather again at the back of his mind and the dull fires of his lust began to glow angrily in his veins.

—Someone you were in love with? he asked ironically.

—It was a young boy I used to know, she answered, named Michael Furey. He used to sing that song, *The Lass of Aughrim*. He was very delicate.

Gabriel was silent. He did not wish her to think that he was interested in this delicate boy.

—I can see him so plainly, she said after a moment. Such eyes as he had: big dark eyes! And such an expression in them—an expression!

—O then, you were in love with him? said Gabriel.

—I used to go out walking with him,[2] she said, when I was in Galway. A thought flew across Gabriel's mind.

—Perhaps that was why you wanted to go to Galway with that Ivors girl? he said coldly.

She looked at him and asked in surprise:

—What for?

Her eyes made Gabriel feel awkward. He shrugged his shoulders and said:

—How do I know? To see him perhaps.

She looked away from him along the shaft of light towards the window in silence.

—He is dead, she said at length. He died when he was only seventeen. Isn't it a terrible thing to die so young as that?

—What was he? asked Gabriel, still ironically.

2. I.e., she dated him.

—He was in the gasworks,[3] she said.

Gabriel felt humiliated by the failure of his irony and by the evocation of this figure from the dead, a boy in the gasworks. While he had been full of memories of their secret life together, full of tenderness and joy and desire, she had been comparing him in her mind with another. A shameful consciousness of his own person assailed him. He saw himself as a ludicrous figure, acting as a pennyboy[4] for his aunts, a nervous well-meaning sentimentalist, orating to vulgarians and idealising his own clownish lusts, the pitiable fatuous fellow he had caught a glimpse of in the mirror. Instinctively he turned his back more to the light lest she might see the shame that burned upon his forehead.

He tried to keep up his tone of cold interrogation but his voice when he spoke was humble and indifferent.

—I suppose you were in love with this Michael Furey, Gretta, he said.

—I was great[5] with him at that time, she said.

Her voice was veiled and sad. Gabriel, feeling now how vain it would be to try to lead her whither he had purposed, caressed one of her hands and said, also sadly:

—And what did he die of so young, Gretta? Consumption, was it?

—I think he died for me, she answered.

A vague terror seized Gabriel at this answer as if, at that hour when he had hoped to triumph, some impalpable and vindictive being was coming against him, gathering forces against him in its vague world. But he shook himself free of it with an effort of reason and continued to caress her hand. He did not question her again for he felt that she would tell him of herself. Her hand was warm and moist: it did not respond to his touch but he continued to caress it just as he had caressed her first letter to him that spring morning.

—It was in the winter, she said, about the beginning of the winter when I was going to leave my grandmother's and come up here to the convent. And he was ill at the time in his lodgings in Galway and wouldn't be let out and his people in Oughterard[6] were written to. He was in decline, they said, or something like that. I never knew rightly.

She paused for a moment and sighed.

—Poor fellow, she said. He was very fond of me and he was such a gentle boy. We used to go out together, walking, you know, Gabriel, like the way they do in the country. He was going to study singing only for his health. He had a very good voice, poor Michael Furey.

—Well; and then? asked Gabriel.

—And then when it came to the time for me to leave Galway and come up to the convent he was much worse and I wouldn't be let see him so I wrote a letter saying I was going up to Dublin and would be back in the summer and hoping he would be better then.

She paused for a moment to get her voice under control and then went on:

—Then the night before I left I was in my grandmother's house in Nun's Island,[7] packing up, and I heard gravel thrown up against the window. The window was so wet I couldn't see so I ran downstairs as I was and slipped out

3. A utilities plant that manufactured coal gas. Working there was an unhealthy occupation.
4. Errand boy.
5. Close friends.
6. A small village in western Ireland.
7. An island in the western city of Galway, on which is located the Convent of Poor Clares.

the back into the garden and there was the poor fellow at the end of the garden, shivering.

—And did you not tell him to go back? asked Gabriel.

—I implored of him to go home at once and told him he would get his death in the rain. But he said he did not want to live. I can see his eyes as well as well! He was standing at the end of the wall where there was a tree.

—And did he go home? asked Gabriel.

—Yes, he went home. And when I was only a week in the convent he died and he was buried in Oughterard where his people came from. O, the day I heard that, that he was dead!

She stopped, choking with sobs, and, overcome by emotion, flung herself face downward on the bed, sobbing in the quilt. Gabriel held her hand for a moment longer, irresolutely, and then, shy of intruding on her grief, let it fall gently and walked quietly to the window.

She was fast asleep.

Gabriel, leaning on his elbow, looked for a few moments unresentfully on her tangled hair and half-open mouth, listening to her deep-drawn breath. So she had that romance in her life: a man had died for her sake. It hardly pained him now to think how poor a part he, her husband, had played in her life. He watched her while she slept as though he and she had never lived together as man and wife. His curious eyes rested long upon her face and on her hair: and, as he thought of what she must have been then, in that time of her first girlish beauty, a strange friendly pity for her entered his soul. He did not like to say even to himself that her face was no longer beautiful but he knew that it was no longer the face for which Michael Furey had braved death.

Perhaps she had not told him all the story. His eyes moved to the chair over which she had thrown some of her clothes. A petticoat string dangled to the floor. One boot stood upright, its limp upper fallen down: the fellow of it lay upon its side. He wondered at his riot of emotions of an hour before. From what had it proceeded? From his aunt's supper, from his own foolish speech, from the wine and dancing, the merrymaking when saying goodnight in the hall, the pleasure of the walk along the river in the snow. Poor Aunt Julia! She, too, would soon be a shade with the shade of Patrick Morkan and his horse. He had caught that haggard look upon her face for a moment when she was singing *Arrayed for the Bridal*. Soon, perhaps, he would be sitting in that same drawing-room, dressed in black, his silk hat on his knees. The blinds would be drawn down and Aunt Kate would be sitting beside him, crying and blowing her nose and telling him how Julia had died. He would cast about in his mind for some words that might console her, and would find only lame and useless ones. Yes, yes: that would happen very soon.

The air of the room chilled his shoulders. He stretched himself cautiously along under the sheets and lay down beside his wife. One by one they were all becoming shades. Better pass boldly into that other world, in the full glory of some passion, than fade and wither dismally with age. He thought of how she who lay beside him had locked in her heart for so many years that image of her lover's eyes when he had told her that he did not wish to live.

Generous tears filled Gabriel's eyes. He had never felt like that himself towards any woman but he knew that such a feeling must be love. The tears gathered more thickly in his eyes and in the partial darkness he imagined he saw the form of a young man standing under a dripping tree. Other forms were near. His soul had approached that region where dwell the vast hosts of the dead. He was conscious of, but could not apprehend, their wayward and flickering existence. His own identity was fading out into a grey impalpable world: the solid world itself which these dead had one time reared and lived in was dissolving and dwindling.

A few light taps upon the pane made him turn to the window. It had begun to snow again. He watched sleepily the flakes, silver and dark, falling obliquely against the lamplight. The time had come for him to set out on his journey westward. Yes, the newspapers were right: snow was general all over Ireland. It was falling on every part of the dark central plain, on the treeless hills, falling softly upon the Bog of Allen and, farther westward, softly falling into the dark mutinous Shannon[8] waves. It was falling, too, upon every part of the lonely churchyard on the hill where Michael Furey lay buried. It lay thickly drifted on the crooked crosses and headstones, on the spears of the little gate, on the barren thorns. His soul swooned slowly as he heard the snow falling faintly through the universe and faintly falling, like the descent of their last end, upon all the living and the dead.

1914

8. An estuary of the Shannon River, west-southwest of Dublin. The Bog of Allen is southwest of Dublin.

FRANZ KAFKA

1883–1924

Franz Kafka's stories and novels contain such nightmarish scenarios that the word *Kafkaesque* has been coined to describe the most unpleasant and bizarre aspects of modern life, especially when it comes to bureaucracy. Despite the bleakness of the world he depicted, Kafka was in fact a highly amusing writer who, when reading his work to friends, would sometimes leave them laughing out loud. A master of dark humor and an artist of unique vision, Kafka captures perfectly the anxiety and absurdity of contemporary urban society.

Born in Prague, a majority Catholic, Czech-speaking city in the Austro-Hungarian Empire, to a nonobservant Jewish, German-speaking family, Kafka trained as a lawyer and went to work for an insurance company, while still living at home with his parents. He began writing in his twenties and published his first short prose works in 1908. Around the same time, he developed a renewed interest in Judaism, which he had mostly ignored as a child. Although he was an attractive and popular person—in this respect not much like his character Gregor Samsa—he was never quite satisfied with his relationships with women or with his family. He was engaged three times, twice to the same woman, and broke off all three engagements. Kafka had a difficult relationship with his father, a self-made man who could not take his son's writing seriously. Having learned from friends about the psychoanalytic theories of Sigmund Freud, Kafka recognized the oedipal tension in aspects of his family life and expressed uneasiness with authority, especially parental authority, in his fiction. He also kept extensive diaries about his dissatisfaction with his personal and work life and, in his late thirties, wrote a long letter to his father harshly criticizing his upbringing.

Most of Kafka's writing published during his life consisted of short stories, parables, and two novellas, including *The Metamorphosis*, the selection here, which were released in six slim volumes. Kafka did not believe himself to be a successful author, although he had won a prestigious literary award, the Fontane Prize of the City of Berlin, for one of his early stories, "The Stoker." He wrote three long novels, *The Trial, The Castle*, and *Amerika*, but completed none of them. In despair, he asked his friend and executor, Max Brod, to have them all burned at his death. Brod disobeyed Kafka's instructions and instead had the three novels published posthumously. Apparently reflecting the guilt their author experienced over his relations with women, and his failure to get married, the three novels are haunted by regret and a sense of culpability, although the source of the characters' disquiet can never be identified with certainty.

Unlike some of his characters—resentful employees of large bureaucracies—Kafka was a successful senior executive who handled an array of business matters. Nonetheless, he was unhappy with his day job and blamed the hours he spent at work for his inability to complete the novels: in his mind, he was a failure both in life and in art. After developing tuberculosis in his mid-thirties, Kafka quit his job, at age thirty-nine, in 1922. He published a number of stories, collected in *The Hunger Artist*, and traveled extensively, spending a year in Berlin; but as his health deteriorated, he eventually moved to a sanatorium outside Vienna, where he died. Once Brod released the novels and unfinished stories, the author's fame grew quickly. During the Great Depression and the political crises of the 1930s, Kafka became popular in the English-speaking world. Readers viewed his work as demonstrating the anxiety and isolation of modern life, particularly the problem of living in alienation from God, a major theme of existentialist philosophers after World War II. More recently, however, critics have emphasized Kafka's humor and the social contexts of his work, including his experiences in his native Prague.

Until the middle of the nineteenth century, Jews had been excluded from most aspects of Austro-Hungarian society. Kafka and his family felt a strong affinity for the emperor, who represented for them German high culture and whose family had emancipated the Jews. The old city of Prague, with its narrow streets, crowded apartment houses, Gothic cathedral, and huge medieval castle, was cosmopolitan for a small town. After 1918, Czechoslovakia became an independent republic, and Czech replaced German as the official language. Kafka was able to adapt—he knew Czech well—and in fact was one of the few "German" business executives who were retained after Czech independence. And yet he felt himself to be an outsider—a German-speaking Jew among Czech-speaking Christians. This feeling was no doubt reinforced by a resurgent anti-Semitism that coincided with the rise of Czech nationalism and that threatened the Jews' relatively recent emancipation. (Kafka didn't live to see the final confirmation of his sense of alienation and isolation, but his three sisters would later die in Nazi concentration camps.) In his thirties, Kafka studied Hebrew and Yiddish and became interested in the Yiddish theater; the Jewish Enlightenment of his friend Martin Buber (Austrian philosopher, 1878–1965); Jewish folklore; and the philosophical writings of Søren Kierkegaard (1813–1855). Kafka's work seldom discusses Judaism directly, but the sense of exclusion and persecution that underlies much of his writing may spring in part from his experience of anti-Semitism; certainly his interest in interpretation and the nature of language owes much to his understanding of Jewish thought.

THE METAMORPHOSIS

Written in 1912 and published in 1915, *The Metamorphosis*, Kafka's longest work published in his lifetime, was, as well, his most famous work released before his death. It is a consummate narrative: from the moment Gregor Samsa wakes up to find himself transformed into a "monstrous insect," the reader asks, "What happens next?" Although the events seem dreamlike, the narrator assures us "it was no dream," no nightmarish fantasy in which Gregor temporarily identified himself with other downtrodden vermin of society. Instead, this grotesque transformation is permanent, a single, unshakable fact that renders almost comic his family's calculations and attempts to adjust. Indeed, the events of the story are described in great detail, often with an emphasis on the kind of concrete, vivid imagery that plays a prominent role in dreams and in Freud's interpretations of them: the father's fist, the bug's blood, the sister's violin playing.

When the novella begins, Gregor seems to be simply a man in a bug suit, but as the tale progresses, his thinking becomes increasingly buglike, and he loses touch with the people around him. A major theme of the work is the meaning of humanity, and Gregor experiences a sense of exclusion from what Kafka calls the "circle of humankind." As the author relays the protagonist's thoughts, the reader gets the impression that Gregor considers himself to be put upon: he has taken a job he dislikes in order to pay off his parents' debt. Yet even before his transformation, he felt that his family misunderstood him. Once he becomes a bug, he loses the power of speech: although he continues to think, he cannot express his thoughts. Thus, when he turns into a despised species, the lack of communication Gregor perceived as a man becomes an actuality.

"The terror of art," said Kafka in a conversation about *The Metamorphosis*, is that "the dream reveals the reality." This dream, which in the novella becomes Gregor's reality, sheds light on the intolerable nature of his former existence. Another aspect of his professional life is its mechanical rigidity, personal rivalries, and threatening suspicion of any deviation from the norm. Gregor himself is part of this world, as he shows when he fawns on the chief clerk and tries to manipulate him by criticizing their boss.

More disturbing is the transformation that takes place in Gregor's family, where the expected love and support turn into shamed resignation and animal resentment now that Gregor has let the family down. Mother and sister are ineffectual, and their sympathy is slowly replaced by disgust. Gregor's father quickly reassumes his position of authority and beats the vermin back into his room: first with the newspaper and chief clerk's cane, and later with a barrage of apples from the family table. Gregor eventually becomes an "it" for whom the family feels no affection. Even before his transformation, Gregor seems to have lost all purpose in life except earning money to repay his parents' debts.

These frustrated desires contribute to the central conflict: whether Gregor can ever emerge from his bedroom and become part of the family again. The slapstick-like comedy of Gregor's attempts to use his insect body underlines the sense of frustration and exclusion. This, indeed, may lie at the heart of the novella's appeal; perhaps everyone has, occasionally, felt like an outsider. Gregor's metamorphosis, though, makes him an alien of a literal sort. His attitude at times reflects the sullenness of an unhappy teenager; at other times, he seems more like a terminal patient who fears placing an undue burden on his family. The theme of transformation goes back to Ovid's *Metamorphoses*, in which frustrated sexual desire often plays a role in turning people into plants or animals. The dark humor and uncanniness of Kafka's work links it to fantastic works by authors such as Edgar Allan Poe (American, 1809–1849) and Heinrich Wilhelm Kleist (German, 1771–1811) and to the analysis of the psyche conducted, during Kafka's lifetime, by Sigmund Freud. Without directly blaming Gregor, Kafka sometimes seems to hint that his transformation results in part from the protagonist's desire to escape from human interaction.

Kafka exposes both the pathos and the humor of the situation, and for this reason the story retains its attraction today. He has been recognized as an important influence by a range of modern writers, including **Samuel Beckett**, Harold Pinter (English playwright, 1930–2008), and many Latin Americans, including **Jorge Luis Borges** and **Gabriel García Márquez**. Kafka was one of the great storytellers of modern life, capable of revealing the lonely emptiness of even a busy life in a crowded city apartment.

The Metamorphosis[1]

I

When Gregor Samsa woke one morning from troubled dreams, he found himself transformed right there in his bed into some sort of monstrous insect.[2] He was lying on his back—which was hard, like a carapace—and when he raised his head a little he saw his curved brown belly segmented by rigid arches atop which the blanket, already slipping, was just barely managing to cling. His many legs, pitifully thin compared to the rest of him, waved helplessly before his eyes.

"What in the world has happened to me?" he thought. It was no dream. His room, a proper human room, if admittedly rather too small, lay peacefully between the four familiar walls. Above the table, where an unpacked collection of cloth samples was arranged (Samsa was a traveling salesman), hung the picture he had recently clipped from a glossy magazine and placed in an attractive gilt frame. This picture showed a lady in a fur hat and fur boa who sat erect, holding out to the viewer a heavy fur muff in which her entire forearm had vanished.

Gregor's gaze then shifted to the window, where the bleak weather—raindrops could be heard striking the metal sill—made him feel quite melan-

1. Translated by Susan Bernofsky.
2. Kafka uses the adjective *ungeheuer* (monstrous) and the noun *Ungeziefer* (in Old High German, an unclean animal unfit for sacrifice). In his *Essays on Literature*, Russian novelist (and entomologist) Vladimir Nabokov identifies the insect simply as a "big beetle" about three feet long.

choly. "What if I just go back to sleep for a little while and forget all this foolishness," he thought, but this proved utterly impossible, for it was his habit to sleep on his right side, and in his present state he was unable to assume this position. No matter how forcefully he thrust himself onto his side, he kept rolling back. Perhaps a hundred times he attempted it, closing his eyes so as not to have to see those struggling legs, and relented only when he began to feel a faint dull ache in his side, unlike anything he'd ever felt before.

"Good Lord," he thought, "what an exhausting profession I've chosen. Day in and day out on the road. Work like this is far more unsettling than business conducted at home, and then I have the agony of traveling itself to contend with: worrying about train connections, the irregular, unpalatable meals, and human intercourse that is constantly changing, never developing the least constancy or warmth. Devil take it all!" He felt a faint itch high up on his belly; still on his back, he laboriously edged himself over to the bedpost so he could raise his head more easily; identified the site of the itch: a cluster of tiny white dots he was unable to judge; and wanted to probe the spot with a leg, but drew it back again at once, for the touch sent cold shivers rippling through him.

He slid back into his earlier position. "All this early rising," he thought, "it's enough to make one soft in the head. Human beings need their sleep. Other traveling salesmen live like harem girls. When I go back to the boardinghouse, for example, to copy out the morning's commissions: why, these gentlemen may still be sitting at breakfast. I'd like to see my boss's face if I tried that some time; he'd can me on the spot. Although who knows, maybe that would be the best thing for me. If I didn't have to hold back for my parents' sake, I'd have given notice long ago—I'd have marched right up to him and given him a piece of my mind. He'd have fallen right off his desk! And what an odd custom that is: perching high up atop one's elevated desk and from this considerable height addressing one's employee down below, especially as the latter is obliged to stand quite close because his boss is hard of hearing. Well, all hope is not yet lost; as soon as I've saved up enough money to pay back what my parents owe him—another five or six years ought to be enough—I'll most definitely do just that. This will be the great parting of ways. For the time being, though, I've got to get up, my train leaves at five."

And he glanced over at the alarm clock ticking away atop the wardrobe. "Heavenly Father!" he thought. It was half past six, and the clock's hands kept shifting calmly forward, in fact the half-hour had already passed, it was getting on toward six forty-five. Could the alarm have failed to ring? Even from the bed one could see it was properly set for four o'clock; it must have rung. Yes, but was it possible to sleep tranquilly through this furniture-shaking racket? Well, his sleep hadn't been exactly tranquil, but no doubt that's why it had been so sound. But what should he do now? The next train was at seven o'clock; to catch it, he would have to rush like a madman, and his sample case wasn't even packed yet, and he himself felt far from agile or alert. And even if he managed to catch this train, his boss was certain to unleash a thunderstorm of invective upon his head, for the clerk who met the five o'clock train had no doubt long since reported Gregor's absence. This clerk was the boss's underling, a creature devoid of backbone and wit. What if he called in sick? But that would be mortifying and also suspicious, since Gregor had never once been ill in all his five years of service. No doubt his boss would come calling with the company doctor, would reproach Gregor's parents for their son's laziness, silencing all objections by referring them to this doctor, in whose opinion there existed only healthy individuals unwilling to work. And would the doctor be so terribly wrong in this instance? Aside from a mild drowsiness that was certainly superfluous after so many hours of sleep, Gregor felt perfectly fine; in fact, he was ravenous.

While he was considering these matters with the greatest possible speed, yet still without managing to make up his mind to leave the bed (the clock was just striking a quarter to seven), a timid knock came at the door at the head of his bed. "Gregor," the voice called—it was his mother—"it's a quarter to seven. Didn't you want to catch your train?" That gentle voice! Gregor flinched when he heard his own in response: it was unmistakably his old voice, but now it had been infiltrated as if from below by a tortured peeping sound that was impossible to suppress—leaving each word intact, comprehensible, but only for an instant before so completely annihilating it as it continued to reverberate that a person could not tell for sure whether his ears were deceiving him. Gregor had meant to give a proper response explaining everything, but under the circumstances he limited himself to saying, "Yes, thank you, Mother, I'm just getting up." Because of the wooden door, the change in Gregor's voice appeared not to be noticeable from the other side, for his mother was reassured by his response and shuffled off. But their brief conversation had alerted the other family members that Gregor was unexpectedly still at home, and already his father was knocking at one of the room's side doors, softly, but with his fist: "Gregor, Gregor," he called. "What's the problem?" And after a short while he repeated his question in a deeper register: "Gregor! Gregor!" Meanwhile, at the other side door came his sister's faint lament: "Gregor? Are you unwell? Do you need anything?" "Just a second," Gregor answered in both directions at once, making an effort, by enunciating as clearly as possible and inserting long pauses between the individual words, to remove anything conspicuous from his voice. And in fact his father returned to his breakfast, but his sister whispered: "Gregor, open the door, I implore you." But Gregor had no intention of opening the door; he praised the cautious habit he had acquired while traveling of locking all his doors at night, even at home.

First he would get up calmly and undisturbed, he would get dressed and above all have breakfast, and only then would he consider his next steps, for all these supine contemplations, he suddenly realized, would yield no useful results. He recalled often having felt mild aches and pains in bed, caused perhaps by lying in an awkward position, and this pain had then proven to be a figment of his imagination the moment he got up; he was curious to see how this morning's imaginings would gradually fade. The change in his voice was nothing more than the harbinger of a proper head cold, an occupational hazard among traveling salesmen; this he doubted not in the least.

It was simple enough to rid himself of the blanket; he needed only puff himself up a bit, and it fell right off. But the rest proved difficult, not least because he was so exceedingly wide. He would have needed arms and hands to prop himself up; but instead all he had were these many little legs, variously in motion, that he was unable to control. If he tried to bend one leg, it would be the first to straighten; and when he finally succeeded in getting one leg to do his bidding, all the others went flailing about in an unnerving frenzy. "Enough of this lying about uselessly in bed," Gregor said to himself.

At first he tried to maneuver the lower part of his body out of the bed, but this lower part—which, by the way, he had not yet seen and couldn't properly imagine—proved too unwieldy; it all went so slowly; and when at last, half-mad with impatience, he thrust himself recklessly forward with all his strength, it was in the wrong direction, and he slammed against the lower bedpost; the throbbing pain he felt instructed him that for now at least the lower part of his body was perhaps the most sensitive.

So he decided to try leading instead with his upper body and carefully twisted his head toward the edge of the bed. This was easily accomplished, and in the end, despite his width and weight, the mass of his body slowly followed the turning of his head. But once his head was dangling in midair outside the bed, he was afraid to keep shifting forward like this, since if eventually he had to let himself fall in this position, it would be practically a miracle if his head escaped injury. And right now he had to keep his wits about him at all costs, even if it meant staying where he was.

But when, sighing after redoubled efforts, he found himself lying there as before, watching his little legs engaged in their struggles, perhaps more flailingly now, and seeing no possible way to bring calm or order to this chaos, he told himself once more that he could not possibly remain lying here any longer and that the most sensible thing would be to sacrifice anything and everything as long as there remained even the slightest hope of liberating himself from the bed. Simultaneously, though, he continued to remind himself that calm consideration—indeed, the calmest consideration—was far preferable to resolutions seized on in despair. At such moments he fixed his eyes as sharply as possible on the window, but regrettably the view of the morning fog, which veiled even the far side of the narrow street, offered little by way of optimism and good spirits. "Seven o'clock already," he said to himself as the clock struck once more, "already seven and still such dense fog." And for a little while he lay there quietly, his breathing shallow, in the expectation, perhaps, that this perfect silence might possibly restore the real and ordinary state of things.

Then he said to himself: "Before it strikes a quarter past seven, I must absolutely have gotten myself completely out of bed. Besides, by then someone will have come from the office to inquire after me, as the office opens before seven." And he now set himself to rocking his body out of the bed as evenly as possible along his entire length. If he allowed himself to fall from the bed like this, his head—which he intended to lift up cleanly as he fell—would in all likelihood remain unharmed. His back seemed to be hard; surely it would sustain no damage as he fell to the rug. His greatest concern was what to do about the loud crash that would clearly result, no doubt calling forth not terror perhaps but certainly alarm behind each door. Nonetheless it would have to be ventured.

By the time Gregor was already protruding halfway out of bed—this new method was more a game than a struggle, all he had to do was keep rocking sideways a little at a time—it occurred to him how simple things would be if only someone came to his aid. Two strong individuals—he was thinking of his father and the maidservant—would suffice; all they'd have to do was slip their arms beneath his curved back to scoop him out of bed, then crouch down with their burden and wait patiently for him to flip himself over onto the floor, where he hoped those tiny legs of his would take on some meaning. But even aside from the fact that the doors were locked, should he really call for help? Despite his distress, he couldn't help smiling at the thought.

Already he'd reached the point where the vigorous rocking motion was making it almost impossible for him to keep his balance, and soon he would have to make up his mind and take the plunge, for a quarter after seven was only five minutes away—when the front doorbell rang. "It's someone from the office," he said to himself and nearly froze while his little legs went on scrabbling all the more frenetically. For a moment all was still. "They won't answer," Gregor said to himself, caught up in some deluded hope. But then of course, as always, the maid strode resolutely to the door and opened it.

Gregor needed only hear the visitor's first words of greeting to know who it was: the general manager himself. Why oh why was Gregor condemned to serve in a firm where even the most negligible falling short was enough to arouse the greatest possible suspicion? Was every last one of the firm's employees a scoundrel, was there not a single loyal, devoted soul among them who would be driven mad by pangs of conscience should he fail to make the best possible use of even just a few morning hours for his employer's benefit, such that his guilt would render him virtually incapable of rising from his bed? Would it really not have sufficed to send an apprentice to inquire—if indeed such inquiries were necessary at all—did the general manager have to come in person, and was it necessary to demonstrate to the entire innocent family that the investigation of this suspicious matter could be entrusted only to the general manager's sharp intellect? And more because of the agitation aroused in Gregor by this train of thought than because of some proper resolution on his part, he swung himself out of bed with all his might. There was a loud thud, you couldn't really call it a crash. The rug cushioned the impact a little, and since his back was more elastic than he'd thought, the resulting sound was muffled and not so obvious. But he hadn't managed to hold his head up carefully enough and had bumped it; he turned it this way and that, pressing it against the rug in his vexation and pain.

"Something just fell in there," the general manager now said in the room on the left. Gregor tried to imagine whether anything like what he was now experiencing could ever befall the general manager; the possibility must certainly be admitted. But as if brusquely dismissing the question, the manager now took a few purposeful steps in the next room, making his patent leather boots creak. From the room on the right came the whisper of Gregor's sister informing him: "Gregor, the general manager is here." "I know," Gregor murmured; but he didn't dare raise his voice high enough for his sister to hear.

"Gregor," his father now said from the room on the left, "the general manager has come to inquire why you failed to depart by the early train. We don't know what to tell him. Besides, he'd like to have a word with you in person. So please open the door. I'm sure he'll be kind enough not to take offense at the untidiness of your room." "Good morning, Herr Samsa," the general manager now cried out in a friendly tone. "He isn't well," Gregor's mother said to the general manager while his father was still having his say beside the door, "not well at all, take my word for it, sir. Why else would Gregor miss his train! The office is the only thing that boy ever thinks of. It really bothers me that he never goes out in the evening; he's been back in the city an entire week now, but he's spent every last evening at home. He just sits at the table with us, quietly reading the newspaper, or else studies the timetables. Even just doing woodworking projects seems to entertain him. He carved a little picture frame, for example, did it in two or three evenings with his fretsaw; you'll be amazed how pretty it is; it's hanging there in his room; you'll see it in a minute when Gregor opens the door. Oh, and I'm so glad you paid us a visit, sir; on our own we'd never have managed to persuade Gregor to open up; he's so stubborn; and surely he isn't well, even though he denied it this morning." "Be . . . right . . . there," Gregor said, not moving, so as not to miss a single word of their conversation. "No other explanation, madam, is conceivable to me," the general manager said. "Let us hope it is nothing grave. Though on the other hand I would note that, as businessmen—fortunately or unfortunately, as one will—we are very often obliged to suppress indispositions out of consideration for the firm." "So are you ready to let the general manager in?" Gregor's impatient father asked, knocking again at the door. "No," Gregor responded. In the left-hand room horrified silence, while in the room on the right Gregor's sister began to sob.

Why didn't his sister go to join the others? She must have just gotten out of bed and not yet begun to dress. And why was she crying? Because he wasn't getting up and opening his door to the general manager, because he was in danger of losing his position, and because his boss would then start hounding his parents once more over their ancient debt? For the time being, all such worries were assuredly unnecessary. Gregor was still here, and abandoning his family was the farthest thing from his thoughts. At the moment, to be sure, he was lying on the rug, and no one familiar with his current state would seriously expect him to let the general manager in. But surely he wouldn't be sent packing just like that because of so trivial an act of discourtesy, for which it would be simple enough to find an appropriate excuse later on. And it seemed to Gregor it would be far more sensible to just leave him in peace rather than disturbing him with all this weeping and cajoling. But the others were distressed by the uncertainty of it all; their behavior was understandable.

"Herr Samsa," the general manager now called out, raising his voice. "What has come over you? You barricade yourself in your room, you reply to queries only with yes and no, you cause your parents onerous, unnecessary worries, and you are neglecting—let me permit myself to note—your professional responsibilities in a truly unprecedented manner. I speak here in the name of your parents as well as your employer and in all seriousness must ask you for a clear and immediate explanation. I am astonished, utterly astonished. I have always known you as a calm, sensible person, and now it seems you've begun to permit yourself the most whimsical extravagances. To be sure, the boss did suggest one possible explanation for your absence this morning—it concerns the cash payments recently entrusted to your care—and truthfully, I all but gave him my word of honor that this explanation could not be correct. But confronted here with your incomprehensible obstinacy, I find myself losing any desire I might have had to come to your defense. And your position is anything but secure. It was originally my intention to discuss all this with you in a private conversation, but since you compel me to waste my time here, I do not know why your esteemed parents should not hear of it as well. In short: your productivity of late has been highly unsatisfactory; admittedly this is not the best season for drumming up business, we do acknowledge this; but a season in which no business at all is drummed up is something that does not, and indeed may not exist, Herr Samsa."

"But sir," Gregor cried out, beside himself and forgetting all else in his agitation, "I shall open the door at once, this very instant. A slight indisposition, a fit of dizziness kept me from getting up. Even now I'm still in bed. But already I am feeling very much refreshed. Here, I'm getting up. Just a moment's patience! It's a bit more difficult than I thought. But already I'm feeling quite fine. How odd, the way such a thing can suddenly come over one. Yesterday evening I felt perfectly all right, my parents can attest to this, or rather: I did in fact feel a mild foreboding yesterday evening already. Surely it was noticeable to anyone looking at me. Why didn't I send word to the office? But we always just assume we'll be able to overcome these illnesses without staying home. Sir! Do be gentle with my parents. The allegations you make are unfounded, and no one has ever mentioned anything of the sort to me. Perhaps you haven't yet looked over the most recent commissions I sent in. In any case, I'll be back on the road in time for the eight o'clock train; these additional hours of rest have fortified me. Please do not allow me to detain you any longer, sir; I shall be at the office myself in no time; do be so good as to say I'm on my way and give my regards to the boss."

And while Gregor was hastily blurting out all of this, scarcely knowing what he said, he edged closer to the wardrobe with minimal effort, no doubt thanks to the practice he had already acquired while still in bed, and now he did his best to haul himself upright. Indeed, he really did want to open the door, to show himself and speak with the general manager; he was eager to learn what the others, who were so anxious to see him, would say when they finally laid eyes on him. If they recoiled in horror, Gregor could surrender all responsibility and rest easy. But if they accepted it all calmly, that meant he too had no reason to get himself worked up, and if he hurried, he could still make it to the station by eight. At first he couldn't get a grip on the wardrobe's smooth surface, but finally he gave a great heave and found himself standing upright; he no longer paid any heed to the pain in his lower body, ache as it might. Now he let himself drop against the back of a nearby chair, clinging to its edges with his little legs. And having thus attained control over himself, he fell silent, for now he could listen to the general manager.

"Did you understand a single word?" the manager was asking Gregor's parents. "Surely he isn't trying to make fools of us?" "For heaven's sake," Gregor's mother cried, already weeping, "he might be gravely ill, and here we are tormenting him. Grete! Grete!" she cried out. "Mother?" Gregor's sister called from the other side. They were communicating through Gregor's room. "You must go for the doctor at once. Gregor is ill. Quick, fetch the doctor. Did you hear him speaking just now?" "That was an animal's voice," the general manager said, speaking in noticeably subdued tones compared to the cries of Gregor's mother. "Anna! Anna!" the father shouted into the kitchen through the vestibule, clapping his hands. "Run and fetch a locksmith, hurry!" And already the two girls were racing through the vestibule, their skirts rustling (how had Gregor's sister possibly gotten dressed so quickly?), and flung open the front door. There was no sound of the door closing again; no doubt they had left it standing open, as one sees with apartments in which a great calamity has occurred.

But Gregor was far less troubled now. Even though the others were no longer able to understand his words—though they had seemed to him clear enough, clearer than in the past, perhaps because his ear had grown accustomed to their sound—they were now convinced that things were not right with him and were prepared to offer help. The confidence and conviction with which these first arrangements had been made comforted him. He felt drawn once more into the circle of humankind and was expecting both the doctor and the locksmith—without properly differentiating between the two—to perform magnificent, astounding feats. So as to have as intelligible a voice as possible for the crucial discussions that lay ahead, he cleared his throat a little, making an effort to do this as discreetly as possible, since even this sound might differ from human throat-clearing, which he no longer trusted himself to judge. In the next room, meanwhile, all was quiet. Perhaps his parents sat whispering at the table with the general manager, or perhaps all of them were leaning against the door, listening.

Gregor slowly pushed himself over to the door using the armchair, then let go and allowed himself to fall against the door, propping himself upright—the pads of his little legs turned out to be slightly sticky—and there he rested briefly from his exertions. Then he set about turning the key in the lock using his mouth. Unfortunately it seemed he had no real teeth—so how was he supposed to grasp the key?—but his jaws turned out to be surprisingly strong; and with their help he actually succeeded in causing the key to move, paying no heed to the fact that he was no doubt injuring himself in the process, for a brown fluid ran out of his mouth and down the key, dripping onto the floor. "Listen to that," the general manager said in the next room, "he's turning the key in the lock." Gregor found these words most encouraging; but all of them should have been cheering him on, including his father and mother: "Come on, Gregor!" they should have shouted, "just keep at it, keep working on that lock!" And now, imagining all of them following his efforts with great suspense, he bit down on the key uncomprehendingly, with all the force he could muster. With each revolution of the key, he danced about the lock, holding himself upright using only his mouth and, as needed, either clinging to the key or using the entire weight of his body to press it down. The brighter sound of the lock finally springing open positively revived him. Sighing in relief, he said to himself: "I guess I didn't need the locksmith after all," and he laid his head upon the handle of the door to press it open.

But he remained hidden from view as the door swung toward him, even after it was wide open. To be seen, he had to work his way slowly around one of the wings of the double door, a delicate operation if he wanted to avoid plopping down awkwardly on his back before he'd even entered the room. He was still occupied with this difficult maneuver and had no leisure to attend to anything else when he heard the general manager utter a loud "Oh!"—it sounded like wind howling—and now he saw him too, saw how the general manager, who was standing closest to the door, pressed his hand to his open mouth, slowly retreating, as though being driven back by an invisible, steady force. Gregor's mother—who despite the general manager's presence stood with her hair still undone from the night, wildly bristling—first looked over at his father, her hands clasped, then took two steps in Gregor's direction before falling down in the midst of all her billowing skirts, her face vanishing completely where it sank to her bosom. Gregor's father clenched his fist with a hostile grimace, as if he intended to thrust Gregor back into his room, then glanced uncertainly about the living room, shaded his eyes with his hands, and wept until his mighty chest shook.

Gregor made no move to enter the room, instead he leaned from the inside against the wing of the door that was bolted fast, so that only half his body and the head inclined sideways above it could be seen as he peered across at the others. Meanwhile it had grown much lighter out; on the far side of the street, a section of the infinitely long, dark gray building opposite—a hospital—came into view with its regular windows punched into the facade; rain was still falling, but only in large drops that were separately visible and seemed to have been hurled one by one to the ground. An inordinate number of breakfast dishes crowded the table, for Gregor's father considered breakfast the most important meal of the day and would drag it out for hours reading various newspapers. Straight ahead, on the opposite wall, hung a photograph of Gregor from his time in the military, showing him as a second lieutenant whose carefree smile as he rested his hand on his dagger commanded respect for his bearing and his uniform. The door to the vestibule was open, and since the front door was open as well, one could see all the way out to the landing and the head of the stairs leading down.

"Well," Gregor said, quite conscious of the fact that he was the only one who had retained his composure, "I shall get dressed at once, pack up my samples and be on my way. As for the rest of you, are you prepared to let me do so? You can see, sir"—he said, addressing the general manager—"I am not obstinate, nor a shirker; traveling is burdensome, but without it I could not live. Where are you going now, sir? To the office? Yes? Will you report all these things truthfully? A person can be incapable of working at the moment, but this is precisely the right time to recall his earlier accomplishments and consider that he will later, once the hindrance has been overcome, work all the more industriously and with greater focus. I am so dreadfully indebted to the boss, surely you're aware of this. On the other hand, I have my parents and sister to think of. Truly I'm in a bind, but I shall work my way out of it. Don't make things more difficult for me than they already are. Take my side at the office! No one loves us drummers,[3] I know. Everyone thinks the salesmen rake in a king's ransom while enjoying life's pleasures. And there's never any particular cause to reconsider this prejudice. But you, sir, have a far better grasp of the general circumstances than the rest of the staff, better even—if I may speak confidentially—than the boss himself, who in his role as businessman can easily err in his opinion to an employee's disadvantage. And you no doubt know quite well that a drummer, who spends almost the entire year away from the office, can easily become the victim of gossip, happenstance and groundless complaints against which he cannot possibly defend himself, as he usually never even learns of them, or only when he has completed one of his journeys, exhausted, and then back at home is forced to observe the dire physical effects of causes that can no longer be identified. Please, sir, do not leave without saying something to show you agree with me at least to some small extent!"

But the general manager had already turned away as soon as Gregor began to speak, and merely glanced back at him over a hunched shoulder, his mouth contorted. And during Gregor's speech he did not stand still for a moment but instead continued to retreat—not letting Gregor out of his sight—in the direc-

3. Traveling salesmen.

tion of the door, but only gradually, as though it were secretly prohibited to exit this room. Already he was in the vestibule, and to judge by the abrupt motion with which he withdrew his foot from the living room for the last time, one might have supposed he'd just burned it. Having reached the vestibule, however, he stretched out his right hand, gesturing broadly in the direction of the stairs, as if some all but supernatural salvation awaited him there.

Gregor realized he could not possibly allow the general manager to depart in his present frame of mind if his own position at the firm was not to be put in the gravest jeopardy. His parents didn't fully comprehend his situation: over these long years they had formed the conviction that Gregor was provided for in this office for life, and besides they were so preoccupied with their present worries that they were bereft of all foresight. But Gregor had this foresight. The general manager would have to be detained, reasoned with, convinced and finally won over; after all, Gregor's future and that of his family depended on it. If only his sister were here! She was clever; she had already begun to weep while Gregor was still lying quietly on his back. And surely the general manager, ever the ladies' man, would have let himself be assuaged by her; she would have closed the front door of the apartment and talked him out of his fear in the vestibule. But his sister was not there, so Gregor himself would have to act. And without stopping to consider that he was not yet familiar with his current abilities with respect to locomotion, nor even taking into account the fact that this last speech of his had quite possibly—indeed probably—eluded comprehension, he let go of the door; forced his way through the opening; meant to walk over to where the general manager, already out on the landing, was foolishly clutching at the banister with both hands; but right away, groping in vain for something to catch hold of, he fell with a faint shriek upon his many little legs. No sooner had this occurred than he felt—for the first time all morning—a sense of physical well-being; his legs had solid ground beneath them; they obeyed his will perfectly, as he noted to his delight; they even strove to bear him wherever he wished; and already it seemed to him he would soon be delivered from all his sufferings. But as he lay there on the floor directly in front of his mother and not far from her, swaying with mobility held in check, she suddenly leapt up—rapt as she had appeared within her own contemplations—leapt high up into the air, her arms thrust wide, fingers spread, crying out: "Help me, for God's sake, help!" her head cocked at an angle, as if to see Gregor better, but then, contradicting this, she senselessly retreated; but she had forgotten the table set for breakfast just behind her; sat down hurriedly upon it as soon as she reached it, as if absent-mindedly; and didn't seem to notice that the big overturned coffeepot beside her was pouring a thick stream of coffee on the rug.

"Mother, Mother," Gregor said softly, gazing up at her. For a moment he had forgotten all about the general manager; on the other hand, he could not restrain himself, when he beheld this flowing coffee, from snapping his jaws several times. At this, the mother gave another shriek and fled from the table into the arms of Gregor's father as he rushed to her aid. But Gregor had no time for his parents now; the general manager was already on the stairs; his chin propped on the banister, he looked back on the scene one last time. Gregor was just preparing to dash after him to be sure of catching up with him; but the manager must have sensed something, for he leapt down several steps at once and vanished; and the cry of horror he gave as he fled resounded through the stairwell. Unfortunately the manager's flight now appeared to utterly discombobulate Gregor's father, who up till then had been relatively composed, for instead of running after the manager himself or at least not hindering Gregor in his own pursuit, he seized the manager's walking stick in one hand—it had been left lying on an armchair along with his overcoat and hat—with the other took up a large newspaper from the table, and set about driving Gregor back into his room with a great stamping of feet, brandishing both newspaper and stick. All Gregor's entreaties were in vain, nor were they even understood, for as submissively as he might swivel his head, his father only stamped his feet all the more ferociously. Across the room, his mother had flung open a window despite the chilly weather, and, leaning out, she pressed her face into her hands far outside the window frame. Between street and stairwell, a powerful draft arose, the window curtains flew into the air, the newspapers on the table rustled, and a few pages scudded across the floor. Inexorably Gregor's father drove him backward, uttering hissing sounds like a wild man. But Gregor had no practice at all in reverse locomotion, and his progress was very slow. If only he'd been permitted to turn around, he'd have been back in his room at once, but he was afraid of provoking his father's fury with this time-consuming maneuver, and at any moment a fatal blow from the stick in his father's hand might come crashing down on his back or head. In the end, though, he had no alternative: horrified, he realized he was incapable of controlling his direction; and so he began, with constant anxious glances back at his father, to turn around as quickly as he could, which in fact was rather slowly. Perhaps his father discerned his good intentions, for he did not hinder him in this operation but instead even guided his rotation here and there from a distance, using the tip of his stick. If only his father were not making that unbearable hissing noise! It made Gregor lose his head completely. He had already turned almost all the way around when—still with this hissing in his ear—he became confused and started turning back in the wrong direction. But when finally he succeeded in positioning his head in front of the doorway, it turned out that his body was too wide to fit through the opening. And of course in his father's current state it could not possibly have occurred to him to open the door's other wing to create an adequate passage. He was fixated on the notion that Gregor must disappear into his room as quickly as possible. Never would he have tolerated the complicated preparations necessary for Gregor to prop himself up so as possibly to pass through the door in an upright position. Instead, as though there were no obstacle at all, he now drove Gregor before him, raising a great din: what Gregor heard at his back no longer resembled the voice of merely a single father; it was do or die, and Gregor thrust himself—come what would—into the doorway. One side of his body tilted up, rising at an angle as he pressed forward, scraping his one flank raw and leaving ugly stains behind on the white door, and soon he was wedged tight, unable to move on his own; on one side, his little legs dangled trembling in midair, while on the other they were crushed painfully beneath him—then his father administered a powerful shove from behind, a genuinely liberating thrust that sent him flying, bleeding profusely, into the far reaches of his room. The door was banged shut with the stick, and then at last all was still.

II

Only as dusk was falling did Gregor wake from his heavy, faintlike sleep. He probably wouldn't have slept much longer even without a disturbance, for he felt sufficiently rested and restored, but it seemed to him he had been woken by a fleeting step and the careful shutting of the door to the vestibule. The pallid gleam of the electric streetlamps touched the ceiling here and there and the upper edges of the furniture, but down where Gregor lay, all was dark. Slowly, groping awkwardly with his feelers, which he was only now learning to appreciate, he dragged himself toward the door, wanting to see what had happened. His left side felt like one long unpleasantly contracting scar, and he was forced to limp outright on his two rows of legs. One of these diminutive legs, incidentally, had suffered grievous injuries in the course of the morning's events—it was almost miraculous only one had been injured—and now trailed lifelessly behind him.

Not until he reached the door did he realize what in fact had lured him there: it was the smell of something edible. There stood a bowl filled with sweet milk in which little pieces of white bread were floating. He almost laughed with delight, for his hunger was now even more powerful than in the morning, and right away he dunked his head in the milk almost up to his eyes. But he quickly drew it out again in disappointment; it wasn't just that eating was difficult thanks to his tender left side—and he couldn't eat at all without his entire body becoming gaspingly involved—but beyond that: even though milk had always been his favorite drink, which is no doubt why his sister had brought him some, now it didn't taste good to him at all, indeed it was almost with revulsion that he turned away from the bowl and crept back to the center of the room.

In the living room, as Gregor saw through the crack, the gas had been lit, but while usually at this hour his father liked to read aloud from the afternoon paper to Gregor's mother and sometimes his sister as well in a dramatic voice, now there was not a sound to be heard. Well, perhaps this customary reading aloud that his sister had often told and written him about had recently fallen out of practice. But even in the other rooms everything was so still, even though the apartment was surely not empty. "What a quiet life my family has been leading," Gregor said to himself, and as he gazed fixedly into the darkness before him, he felt great pride at having been able to give his parents and sister a life like this in such a beautiful apartment. But what if all this tranquility, all this prosperity and contentment were now coming to a horrific end? So as not to get lost in such contemplations, Gregor set himself in motion, crawling back and forth across the room.

Once in the course of this long evening one of the side doors was opened a tiny crack and then quickly shut again, and once the other one; someone must have felt an urge to enter and then been overcome by misgivings. Gregor now stationed himself just in front of the living room door, determined to somehow coax the hesitant visitor inside or at least find out who it was; but the door did not open again, and Gregor waited in vain. Before, when all the doors were locked, everyone kept trying to come in, and now that he had opened the one door and the others had apparently been opened during the day, no one came, and the keys were sticking in their locks from the outside.

It was late at night by the time the light in the living room went out, and now it was easy to ascertain that Gregor's parents and sister had remained awake all this time, for all three of them could clearly be heard departing on tiptoe. Now it was unlikely anyone would come into Gregor's room before morning; so he had plenty of time to ponder how best to reorder his life. But this high open room in which he was forced to lie flat on the floor distressed him, without his being able to determine the cause—after all, it was his room, which he had been living in for five years now—and with a half-unconscious motion, and not without a twinge of shame, he scurried beneath the settee, where even though his back was a bit cramped and he could no longer raise his head, he at once felt right at home, his only regret being that his body was too wide across to be accommodated entirely beneath this piece of furniture.

Here he remained the entire night, which he spent by turns dozing—though he was woken again and again by his hunger—and mulling over his worries and indistinct hopes, which however all led to the conclusion that, for the time being, he should behave calmly and, by employing patience and the utmost consideration, assist his family in enduring the inconveniences his current state inevitably forced him to impose on them.

Early the next morning already, so early it was almost still night, Gregor had the opportunity to test the strength of these resolutions he had made, for from the vestibule his sister, almost completely clothed, opened his door and cast an anxious glance into the room. She didn't immediately spot him, but when she noticed him beneath the settee—well, goodness, he had to be somewhere, it's not as if he might have flown away—the sight so alarmed her that, unable to control herself, she slammed the door from the outside. But as if regretting this conduct, she opened it again at once and came in, walking on tiptoe as though she were entering the room of a gravely ill patient or even a stranger. Gregor, having slid his head to just beneath the edge of the settee, observed her. Would she see that he had left the milk standing, and not because of a lack of hunger, and would she bring him some other food more to his liking? If she failed to do so of her own accord, he would sooner starve than call this to her attention, though in fact he felt a nearly monstrous urge to scoot out from beneath the settee, throw himself at his sister's feet, and beg her for something good to eat. But his sister immediately remarked with surprise that the bowl was still full, with just a little of its milk spilled on the floor around it, and she picked it up right away—not with her bare hands, to be sure, but with a rag—and carried it out of the room. Gregor was exceptionally curious to see what she would bring in its stead and mulled over various possibilities. But never would he have been able to predict what his sister in her kindness proceeded to do. To gauge his tastes, she brought him an entire assortment of foodstuffs, all spread out on an old newspaper. There were old, half-rotten vegetables; bones from the family supper the night before caked in a congealed white sauce; a few raisins and almonds; a piece of cheese Gregor had declared inedible two days before; a dry piece of bread; a slice of buttered bread; and a slice of bread with butter and salt. In addition, she placed beside this feast the bowl that apparently had been reserved for Gregor once and for all; it was now filled with water. And out of delicacy, since she knew Gregor would not eat in front of her, she quickly withdrew and even turned the key in the lock so that Gregor would understand he could make himself at home. Gregor's little legs whirred as he now went to take his meal. His wounds, incidentally, seemed to have healed entirely in the meantime, for he no longer felt the least impairment; this was astonishing, for more than a month ago he had cut his finger just a tiny bit with a knife, and this wound had still been painful enough just the day before yesterday. "Might I be less fastidious than before?" he thought, already sucking greedily at the cheese, to which he'd found himself immediately, inexorably drawn, more than to any of the other items. Quickly, his eyes shedding tears of gratification, he devoured in swift succession: the cheese, the vegetables, and the sauce; the fresh food, by contrast, did not taste good to him, in fact he could not even stand the smell of it and so dragged the things he wished to eat a little to one side. He had long since finished everything and was just lying indolently where he was when his sister slowly turned the key in the lock as a signal for him to withdraw. At once he gave a start, though he'd been on the point of nodding off, and he hurried back under the settee. But it cost him a great deal of willpower to remain there even for the short period of time his sister spent in the room, for the hearty meal he'd enjoyed had caused his abdomen to swell, and he could scarcely breathe in his confinement. In between little attacks of suffocation, he peered out with slightly bulging eyes as his sister, oblivious, used a broom to sweep up not only the remains of his meal but also the food he hadn't even touched, as if these items too were no longer fit for consumption, then she hastily dumped everything in a bucket that she covered with a wooden lid before carrying it all out of the room again. She had scarcely turned her back when Gregor hauled himself out from under the settee, stretching and puffing up his body.

This was how Gregor now received his food each day, once in the morning, when his parents and the maid were still asleep, and the second time after everyone had eaten lunch, for his parents would always nap a little afterward, and his sister would send the maid out on some errand or other. Surely they didn't want Gregor to starve either, but perhaps it would have been too much for them to experience his meals through more than hearsay, or perhaps his sister wanted to spare them even this modest sorrow, for Lord knows they were suffering enough.

Gregor never learned on what pretext the doctor and locksmith had been sent away that first morning, for since he himself could not be understood, it occurred to no one, not even his sister, that he could understand the others, so when his sister came to his room, he had to be content merely with hearing the sighs she heaved now and then and her words of supplication addressed to the saints. Only later, when she had started to grow accustomed to all of this—though of course it was impossible to become fully accustomed to circumstances like these—would Gregor sometimes catch a remark that was meant in a friendly way or could be interpreted as such. "He tucked right in today," she would say when Gregor had found the food she left him particularly tasty, while in the opposite case, which gradually began to occur more and more often, she was in the habit of saying almost mournfully: "This time he didn't touch a thing."

But while no news reached Gregor directly, he sometimes was able to overhear this and that from the rooms to either side of his, and whenever he heard voices, he would immediately run over to the door in question and press his entire body against it. Especially in the early days there was rarely a conversation that did not somehow, if only indirectly, refer to him. For two days, every mealtime was spent deliberating how the family should now comport itself; but even between meals this same discussion continued, for at least two members of the household were present at all times, since apparently no one wanted to remain at home alone, and of course leaving the apartment unattended was out of the question. What's more, the maid had fallen on her knees before Gregor's mother that very first day—it was not entirely clear what and how much she knew of what had occurred—begging to be released from the family's service, and when she took her leave a quarter of an hour later, she tearfully thanked them for dismissing her, as though this were the greatest benefaction she had experienced at their hands, and without anyone asking this of her, she swore a solemn oath never to reveal anything at all to anyone.

Now Gregor's sister was forced to do the cooking in concert with his mother; to be sure, not much effort was involved, as no one did much eating. Again and again Gregor would hear one of them pressing the others to eat—always in vain, and never with any other response than "Thank you, I've had all I want," or similar words. Perhaps they didn't drink anything either. Often Gregor's sister would ask her father if he wouldn't like a beer, affectionately offering to fetch it herself, and when he did not respond, she would say, wishing to relieve him of all scruples, that she could send the porter's wife for it as well, but then the father would utter a great "No," and no one spoke of it any longer.

Already in the course of the first day, Gregor's father explained the family's finances and prospects not only to Gregor's mother but to his sister as well. Now and then he would get up from the table and, from his small Wertheim safe,[4] which he had salvaged when his business collapsed five years before, extract some receipt or memorandum book. One could hear him opening the complicated lock and then bolting it shut again after removing the desired item. These explanations on his father's part included the first bits of heartening news Gregor had heard since his captivity began. He had been under the impression that his father had retained nothing at all of his former firm's holdings, or at least his father had never said anything to the contrary, and admittedly Gregor himself had never asked him about this. At the time, his only concern had been to do everything in his power to let the family forget, as quickly as possible, the mercantile catastrophe that had plunged all of them into a state of utter hopelessness. And so he had set to work with particular zeal and risen almost overnight from petty clerk to salesman, in which capacity of course he had a quite different earning potential, and his professional accomplishments, in the form of commissions, were immediately transformed into cash that could be plunked down on the table at home, before the eyes of his astonished, delighted family. Those had been lovely times, and never since had they been repeated, at least not with such glory, although Gregor later earned so much money that he was in a position to cover the expenses for the entire family, which he then did. All had grown accustomed to this arrangement, not just the family but Gregor as well: they gratefully accepted the money, and he was happy to provide it, but the exchange no longer felt particularly warm. Only Gregor's sister had remained close to him all this time, and it was his secret plan to send her off to study at the Conservatory next year (unlike

4. Safe manufactured by the German firm Wertheim, founded in 1852 and still in operation today.

Gregor, she dearly loved music and could play the violin quite movingly), despite the considerable costs this would no doubt entail, money that could surely be brought in by other means. Often during the brief periods of time Gregor spent in town, the Conservatory would come up in his conversations with his sister, but only ever as a lovely dream whose realization was unthinkable, and their parents did not like to hear it mentioned even in this innocuous way; but Gregor was thinking the matter over with great determination and intended to make a formal announcement on Christmas Eve.

Thoughts like these, utterly futile in his current state, passed through his head as he stood pressed against the door, eavesdropping. Sometimes general exhaustion made it impossible for him to go on listening, and he would carelessly let his head bump against the door, but then he would immediately hold his head still again, for even the faint sound this produced had been heard in the next room, causing everyone to fall silent. "I wonder what he's getting up to now," his father would say after a while, apparently facing the door, and only then would the interrupted conversation resume.

Gregor now learned, and learned quite well (his father tended to repeat himself in his explanations, in part because it had been so long since he'd last concerned himself with such matters, in part because Gregor's mother did not always understand everything the first time), that despite all their misfortunes, a small nest egg—really only a tiny one—still remained to them from before, and had even grown a little thanks to the untouched interest that had accumulated meanwhile. In addition, the money Gregor had brought home each month—he only ever kept a few gulden[5] for himself—had not yet been entirely used up and had grown into a small capital. Behind his door, Gregor nodded eagerly, delighted at this unexpected prudence and thrift. To be sure, he might have used this surplus to pay off more of his father's debts with his boss, and the day on which he would have been able to divest himself of his post would no longer have been nearly so far off, but as things stood, his father's arrangements were no doubt for the best.

Now this money was by no means sufficient to allow the family to live off the interest or anything of that sort; it might possibly have been enough to sustain the family for a year, two at most, but that's all there was. So in fact it was the kind of sum one really shouldn't touch, one to be set aside in case of emergency; the money to live on would have to be earned. Gregor's father was admittedly in good health, but he was old and hadn't worked in a full five years, and in any case he was supposed to avoid overtaxing himself; in those five years—the first holiday in his strenuous and yet unsuccessful life—he had put on a lot of weight and now lumbered as he walked. And was Gregor's old mother now supposed to hold down a job, despite her asthma and the fact that it was already an exertion for her to cross from one end of the apartment to the other, for which reason she spent every second day gasping for breath on the sofa beside the open window? And was his sister to go out working, this child of seventeen whose lifestyle no one would begrudge her: dressing nicely, sleeping late, helping out around the house, taking part in a few modest entertainments, and above all, playing the violin? Whenever the family came to speak of the necessity of

5. Guilders, a unit of currency, worth somewhat less than a dollar.

someone earning money, Gregor would let go of the door and throw himself down upon the cool leather sofa beside it, burning with shame and sorrow.

Often he would lie there the entire long night, not sleeping for a moment, just scrabbling for hours against the leather. Or, not shunning the great effort it cost him to push an armchair over to the window, he would climb up the sill and, propped in the armchair, lean against the window, apparently lost in some sort of reverie of how liberating he'd always found it to gaze outside. For in truth he saw even the objects that were quite near at hand less and less clearly as the days progressed; the hospital across the way whose all too constant sight he had earlier reviled was now no longer even visible to him, and if he had not known perfectly well that he was a resident of Charlottenstrasse, a quiet but perfectly urban street, he might have imagined he was gazing out his window onto a desert in which the gray sky and the gray earth were indistinguishably conjoined. His attentive sister only had to see the armchair standing beside the window twice before she started pushing it back to its place there each time she tidied his room; indeed she even began leaving the window's inner sash open.

If only Gregor had been able to speak to his sister and thank her for all she was compelled to do for him, he would have found her ministrations easier to bear; as it was, he suffered beneath them. His sister, to be sure, did all she could to obscure the awkwardness of the situation, and the more time passed, the better she succeeded, of course, but Gregor came to see it all more and more clearly. Even the way she made her entrance jangled his nerves. The moment she came in, without even pausing to shut the door—although she always took such pains to shield the others from the sight of Gregor's room—she would race straight away to the window and fling it open with hasty hands as though she were on the point of suffocating, then remain standing there, however cold it might be, gulping in the air. All this racing and racket was inflicted on Gregor twice a day; he would be trembling beneath the settee, painfully aware that she would no doubt have willingly spared him this disruption if it were possible for her to endure being in the same room as Gregor with the window closed.

Once—it must have been a month since Gregor's metamorphosis, so there was no particular call for his sister to be startled by his appearance—she came into his room a little earlier than usual and discovered him, motionless and propped upright as if for horrific effect, gazing out the window. Gregor would not have found it surprising if she had chosen not to enter, since his position prevented her from opening the window right away, but she didn't just not enter: she started in alarm and shut the door; a stranger might have thought Gregor had been lying in wait, meaning to bite her. Gregor naturally went and hid himself away beneath the settee, but he had to wait there until noon before his sister returned, and she seemed far more agitated than usual. From this he understood that his appearance was still unbearable to her and would remain so, and that she no doubt had to struggle to force herself not to run away at the sight of even the small part of his body that protruded from beneath the settee. In order to spare her even this sight, one day he carried the bedsheet over to the settee on his back—this labor cost him four hours—and arranged it in such a way that he was now completely covered, so that his sister would not be able to see him even if she bent down. If she considered the sheet unnecessary, she could have removed it, since it was clear enough that it could not possibly be considered a pleasure for Gregor to shut himself off so completely, but she left the sheet where it was, and Gregor even thought he glimpsed a grateful look when at one point he carefully lifted the sheet just a little with his head to see how his sister liked the new arrangement.

During the first fortnight, Gregor's parents could not bring themselves to enter his room, and often he heard them expressing their heartfelt appreciation of his sister's labors, whereas earlier they had often been annoyed with her, since she had seemed to them a rather useless girl. But now both of them, father and mother alike, would often be waiting just outside Gregor's door while his sister tidied up his room, and as soon as she emerged, she had to give a full report on what things looked like in the room, what Gregor had eaten, how he had behaved this time, and whether perhaps any modest improvement could be seen. His mother, incidentally, had wanted to visit him relatively soon, but his father and sister held her back, appealing at first to her sense of reason as Gregor listened attentively, wholeheartedly approving. Later, though, she had to be held back by force, and when she then cried out: "Let me go to Gregor, he is my unhappy son! Can't you understand that I must go to him?" then Gregor thought it would perhaps be good for his mother to visit him, not every day of course, but perhaps once a week; after all, she had a far better grasp of things than his sister, who despite her courage was still a child and, when it came right down to it, had perhaps only taken on this difficult task out of childish frivolity.

Gregor's wish to see his mother was soon fulfilled. During the day, Gregor avoided showing himself at the window, if only out of consideration for his parents, but there wasn't much crawling he could do in the few square meters of space the floor provided, lying still was already difficult for him to endure during the night, eating had soon ceased to give him even the slightest pleasure, and so to divert himself he took up the habit of crawling back and forth across the walls and ceiling. He particularly liked hanging from the ceiling high above the room; it was completely different from lying on the floor; one could breathe more freely there; a gentle swaying motion rocked the body; and in the almost happy absentmindedness Gregor experienced, it might happen, to his own astonishment, that he would let go and crash to the floor. But now, of course, he had his body far better under control than before, and even as great a fall as this did him no harm. His sister immediately noticed the new entertainment Gregor had devised for himself—his peregrinations left behind sticky trails here and there—and she got it into her head to make it possible for Gregor to range as widely as possible by removing the furniture that impeded his movement, above all the wardrobe and desk. But she wasn't able to do so on her own; she didn't dare ask her father for help; the maid most certainly would not have helped her, for this girl of sixteen or so, though she had courageously remained in the household after the departure of the former cook, had at the same time requested the privilege of keeping the kitchen locked at all times and only opening the door upon particular request; and so the sister had no choice but to summon her mother one day when her father was out. The mother arrived with exclamations of feverish joy but fell silent at the door to Gregor's room. At first, of course, Gregor's sister checked to confirm that all in the room was as it should be; only then did she allow her mother to enter. With the utmost haste, Gregor had tugged the sheet down lower and in looser folds so that it really did look as if a bedsheet just happened to have been tossed over the settee. He also refrained from peering out from beneath the sheet this time; for the moment, he would resign himself to not seeing his mother and just be glad she had come. "It's all right, come in, you won't see him," Gregor's sister said, apparently leading her mother by the hand. Gregor now heard the sounds of these two weak women grappling with this in fact quite heavy old wardrobe, with his sister laying claim to the bulk of the work, not listening to the admonitions of her mother, who was afraid she would overtax herself. It took a very long time. After perhaps a quarter of an hour's labor, Gregor's mother said they should leave the wardrobe where it was after all; in the first place, it was too heavy—they would not finish before Gregor's father came home, and by leaving the wardrobe in the middle of the room, they would prevent Gregor from moving around at all—and secondly, it wasn't even clear they were doing him a favor by taking away the furniture. To her, it seemed the opposite was true: the sight of the empty wall positively oppressed her heart; and why should Gregor not experience this same sentiment, since after all he was long accustomed to having this furniture around him—wouldn't he feel abandoned in an emptied-out room? "And is it not as if," his mother concluded in a low voice—in fact, she had been whispering all along, as though she wished to avoid letting Gregor, whose exact whereabouts she did not know, hear so much as the sound of her voice, for she was convinced he could not understand her words—"and is it not as if by removing the furniture we would be showing that we are giving up all hope of a cure and are ruthlessly abandoning him to his own devices? I think it would be best if we try to keep the room in precisely the same state it was in before, so that when Gregor returns to us he will find everything unchanged, which will make it that much easier for him to forget all that has happened in the meantime."

Hearing his mother's words, Gregor realized that the absence of all direct human address, combined with the monotony of life in his family's midst, must have muddled his understanding over the course of these two months, for he could not otherwise explain to himself how he could seriously have wished to have his room emptied out. Did he really want to have this warm room, comfortably furnished with family heirlooms, transformed into a cave or den—in which, to be sure, he would be able to crawl about unhindered in every direction, but at the price of simultaneously swiftly and completely forgetting his human past? He was already on the verge of forgetting, and only his mother's voice, which he had gone so long now without hearing, had shaken him awake. Nothing should be removed; everything must remain; he was unwilling to forego the good influence this furniture had on his condition; and if the furniture got in the way of his practicing this mindless crawling about, this was by no means to his detriment, in fact, it was a great advantage.

Unfortunately his sister was of a different opinion; she had developed the habit—not entirely without cause, to be sure—of presenting herself as the holder of particular expertise when discussing Gregor with her parents, and so now too her mother's counsel was reason enough for her to insist on the removal not only of the wardrobe and desk, as she had originally been intending, but of every last bit of the room's furnishings, with the exception of the indispensable settee. Naturally, it was not simply childish defiance and the hard-won self-assurance she had so unexpectedly acquired in recent weeks that dictated this demand; she had, in fact, observed that Gregor needed a great deal of space to crawl around in, while as far as anyone could see, he made no use whatever of the furniture.

But perhaps the fanciful imagination of a girl of her age played a role as well, a sensibility always seeking its own gratification, and one which Grete now allowed to persuade her to render Gregor's situation even more horrific than before, so as to be able to do even more for him than she had hitherto. For a room in which Gregor held sole dominion over empty walls was a place where no one other than Grete would ever dare to set foot.

And so she held fast to her resolve despite the protests of her mother, who appeared troubled to the point of indecision even by the room in its present state; she soon fell silent and helped Gregor's sister remove the wardrobe as best she could. Well, the wardrobe was something Gregor could do without if need be, but the desk would certainly have to stay. And no sooner had the women left the room with the cabinet, groaning as they pressed against its weight, than Gregor poked out his head from beneath the settee to see how he might, cautiously and as considerately as possible, intervene. But unfortunately his mother was the first to return while Grete was still in the next room, clasping the wardrobe in her arms and tipping it back and forth on her own—without, of course, moving it from the spot. But Gregor's mother was unaccustomed to his appearance, it might have made her ill to catch a glimpse of him, and so Gregor in alarm withdrew as fast as he could to the far end of the settee, but it was too late to prevent the front edge of the bedsheet from stirring a little. This was enough to attract his mother's notice. Startled, she froze for a moment, then went back to where Grete was.

Although Gregor kept telling himself that nothing extraordinary was happening, just a few sticks of furniture being shifted about, he was soon forced to admit that all this coming and going on the part of the women, their little exclamations, the furniture scraping against the floor, had the combined effect of a tumultuous hubbub intensifying all around him, and no matter how tightly he drew his head and legs in and pressed his body against the floor, he soon was forced to consider that he would not be able to endure this much longer. They were clearing out his room; taking from him all that was dear to him; they had already borne away the cabinet in which lay his fretsaw and other tools; and now they were prying loose the desk that had dug itself firmly into the floorboards, this desk at which he had written his homework assignments as a student at the commercial academy, and as a secondary and even primary school pupil—truly there was no time left to explore the good intentions of these two women, whose existence, by the way, he had almost forgotten, for their exhaustion was now making them labor in silence, and one heard only their heavy footsteps.

And so he burst out of hiding—the women in the next room were just leaning on the desk to catch their breath—changing direction four times as he raced about, for he really didn't know what to save first, but then his eyes lit on the picture of the lady clad all in furs, conspicuous now on the otherwise empty wall, and quickly he made his way up to it and pressed himself against the glass, which adhered to him, pleasantly cool against his hot belly. At least this picture, which Gregor's body now covered up completely, was absolutely certain not to be taken away from him. He swiveled his head toward the living room door to observe the women as they returned.

They hadn't permitted themselves much rest at all and were already on their way back; Grete had slung one arm about her mother and was nearly carrying her. "So what should we take next?" Grete said, looking around. Then her eyes met those of Gregor where he clung to the wall. It was no doubt only because of her mother's presence that she kept her composure; bowing her face toward her mother to prevent her from glancing about, she said—hastily and trembling, to be sure—"Let's go back to the living room for a moment, shall we?" Grete's intentions were perfectly clear to Gregor: she meant to bring their mother to safety and then chase him from the wall. Well, let her try! He sat there on his picture and would not give it up. He'd sooner leap right in her face.

But Grete's words succeeded in unsettling her mother even more: taking one step to the side, she saw the huge brown blotch on the flowered wallpaper, and before she was even able to realize that what she saw there was Gregor, she cried out in a hoarse, shrieking voice, "Oh God, oh God!" and fell back upon the settee, her arms spread wide as though she were giving up everything, and lay there without moving. "Gregor!" his sister shouted, raising her fist with a threatening glower. It was the first time she had addressed him directly since his metamorphosis. She ran into the next room to fetch some sort of essence that could be used to awaken her mother from her faint; Gregor wanted to help as well—there would be time enough to save the picture later—but he stuck fast to the glass and had to tear himself away by force; he too then ran into the next room as if he might offer his sister advice of some sort, like in the old days; but then could only stand idly behind her as she rummaged among various little bottles, and scared her out of her wits when she turned around; one bottle flew to the floor and shattered; a shard of glass scratched Gregor's face, and some sort of corrosive medicine engulfed him; without further delay, Grete took up as many bottles as she could hold and ran with them to her mother, slamming the door behind her with her foot. Gregor was now cut off from his mother, who was possibly on the brink of death, for which he himself was to blame; he could not open the door if he didn't want to drive away his sister, who had to stay there with his mother; there was nothing for him to do but wait; and tormented by his worries and self-reproach, he began to crawl about, crawling over everything, walls, furniture, the ceiling, and finally in his despair, as the entire room began to spin around him, he fell smack in the middle of the big table.

A short while passed. Gregor lay there, spent, and around him all was still, possibly a good sign. Then the bell rang. The maid was naturally locked up in her kitchen and so Grete had to open the door. Their father was back. "What happened?" were his first words; the look on Grete's face had no doubt revealed all. Grete's voice as she responded was muffled, apparently she was pressing her face against his chest: "Mother fainted, but she's better already. Gregor has broken out." "That's just what I expected," the father said. "I kept telling you, but you women refused to listen." To Gregor it was clear his father had misinterpreted Grete's all too brief pronouncement to assume him guilty of some act of violence. So it behooved Gregor to try to pacify his father, as he was lacking both the time and means to enlighten him. With this in mind, he fled to the door of his room and pressed himself against it, so that the moment his father came into the living room from the vestibule he would see that Gregor had every intention of returning at once to his room, that it was unnecessary to drive him back inside, and that one had merely to open the door, and he would disappear at once.

But his father was in no mood to take note of subtleties. "Ah!" he exclaimed upon entering, in a tone of voice suggesting he was at once furious and glad.

Gregor pulled his head back from the door and turned it toward his father. He had truly not expected to see his father looking as he looked now standing before him; though to be sure the novelty of crawling about had distracted him recently from paying as much attention as before to the goings-on in the rest of the apartment, and really he ought to have been prepared to find a changed set of circumstances. Even so, even so: was this still his father? The same man who used to lie wearily entombed in his bed when Gregor set off on a business trip; who would greet him on the evening of his return sitting in an armchair in his nightshirt; who, incapable of rising, would merely raise his arms to signify his delight, and on the rare walks they still shared, a few Sundays each year and on major holidays, would trudge between Gregor and his mother, who themselves were already walking rather slowly, moving even a bit slower than they, bundled up in his old overcoat, always with his gingerly advancing cane and almost invariably coming to a halt and collecting his companions around him whenever he had something to say? Now he was standing properly erect; dressed in a smart blue uniform with gold buttons of the sort worn by porters in banking establishments; above the jacket's tall, stiff collar his powerful double chin unfurled; beneath bushy eyebrows, his black eyes peered out acutely and attentively; his once disheveled white hair had been painstakingly combed and parted until it gleamed. He tossed his cap, to which a gold monogram was affixed, probably that of a bank, across the entire room in a wide arc to land on the settee, then advanced grim-faced upon Gregor with the tips of his long uniform jacket flung back and his hands in his trouser pockets. He himself probably had no idea what he intended to do; at any rate, he raised up each foot unusually high, and Gregor marveled at the gigantic dimensions of his bootsoles. But he did not lose any time over them, having learned on the very first day of his new life that his father considered only the utmost severity appropriate for him. And so he fled from his father, hesitating whenever his father stopped short, and then rushing forward again as soon as he stirred. They circled the room several times in this manner without anything decisive occurring, and indeed, given the slow speed at which this interaction was taking place, without its even having the appearance of a chase. For this reason Gregor remained at floor level for the time being, especially as he feared his father might consider it particular wickedness on his part if he were to take refuge on the walls or ceiling. To be sure, he was forced to realize he would not be able to keep up even this pace for long, since each time his father took a step, he himself had to execute any number of motions. A shortness of breath began to set in—even in his earlier life his lungs had been none too reliable. As he now lurched along, reserving all his strength for this continued flight, his eyes barely open (and not thinking, in his stupefaction, that there might be other ways of saving himself than running across the floor, indeed he had almost forgotten he also had the walls at his disposal, though here, to be sure, they were obstructed by delicately carved furniture full of jagged, pointy edges), all at once something flew to the rug beside him, casually flung, and rolled across his path. It was an apple; and already a second one came flying after it; in horror, Gregor stopped in his tracks; there was no point continuing to run now that his father had decided to bombard him. He had filled his pockets from the fruit bowl on the sideboard and now was tossing apple after apple in Gregor's direction, for the moment not even bothering to take particular aim. The petite red apples rolled around the floor as if electrified, knocking into each other. One lightly lobbed apple grazed Gregor's back and slid off again harmlessly. But it was immediately followed by another that embedded itself in his back. Gregor tried to drag himself forward, as if this sudden shocking pain might vanish with a change of place; but he felt nailed to the spot and collapsed there, his legs splaying out, all his senses in a state of utter bewilderment. He caught only a last glimpse of the door to his room flying open, his shrieking sister, and his mother running out of the room before her wearing only a chemise, for his sister had undressed the unconscious woman to let her breathe more freely, then he saw his mother rush to his father's side, her unfastened skirts slipping one by one from about her waist as she ran, saw her stumble across these skirts as she threw herself at his father and, embracing him, in perfect union with him—but now Gregor's vision began to fail him—she clasped her hands at the back of his father's head and pleaded with him to spare Gregor's life.

III

The grievous wound Gregor had received, which plagued him for over a month—the apple remained lodged there in his flesh, a visible memento, since no one dared to remove it—seemed to have reminded even his father that Gregor, despite his current lamentable, repulsive form, was a member of the family who should not be treated like an enemy, for family duty dictated that the others swallow down the disgust he aroused in them and show him tolerance, only tolerance.

And even though this wound cost Gregor some of his mobility, probably for good, and for the time being he required many, many minutes to hobble across his room like an old invalid—crawling up the walls was out of the question now—he was compensated for this worsening of his condition by what seemed to him a perfectly adequate substitute: as evening approached, the door to the living room, on which he would start keeping a sharp eye an hour or two beforehand, would always be opened so as to permit him, lying in his own dark room and invisible from the living room, to watch the entire family sitting at the brightly lit table and listen to their conversations now, as it were, in an officially sanctioned capacity and thus quite differently than before.

To be sure, these were no longer the animated conversations of earlier times that Gregor used to think back on with a certain longing from various cramped hotel rooms when it was time to throw himself, exhausted, into the damp bedding. Now everything was fairly quiet. Gregor's father would fall asleep in his armchair soon after supper; his mother and sister would admonish one another to silence; his mother, bent far over beneath the light, would be sewing ladies' underthings for a dress shop; his sister, who had taken a job as a salesgirl, was studying stenography and French in the evenings so as possibly to move to a better position later on. Sometimes Gregor's father would wake up and, as if unaware he had been sleeping, would say to Gregor's mother: "How long you've been sewing again today!" and then go right back to sleep, which would prompt Gregor's mother and sister to exchange weary smiles.

In a peculiar form of stubbornness, Gregor's father refused to take off his porter's uniform even at home; and while his nightshirt hung uselessly on its hook, he would slumber where he sat, fully clothed, as though he remained ready for service at all times and even here was awaiting his supervisor's call. As a result, his uniform, which had not been new to start with, soon forfeited much of its cleanliness, despite the care lavished on it by mother and sister, and Gregor would sometimes gaze for an entire evening at this stain-covered jacket resplendent with gold buttons, always highly polished, in which the old man slept in considerable discomfort but nonetheless soundly.

The moment the clock struck ten, Gregor's mother would attempt to rouse his father with a few hushed words and then persuade him to go to bed, for he would get no proper sleep sitting here, and sleep was something Gregor's father—who had to report for duty at six in the morning—desperately needed. But in keeping with the stubbornness that had taken hold of him when he started working as a porter, he always insisted on continuing to sit there at the table, even though he kept falling asleep, and then it was only with the greatest effort that he could be persuaded to exchange armchair for bed. Gregor's mother and sister could persist in their little admonishments as doggedly as they liked; for a quarter of an hour, he would just shake his head slowly, his eyes closed, without getting up. Gregor's mother would pluck at his sleeve, whispering cajoling words in his ear, and his sister would set aside her studies to come to her mother's aid, but to no avail. Gregor's father only settled deeper into his armchair. Only when the women gripped him beneath the arms would he open his eyes, looking by turns at mother and sister and saying: "What sort of life is this? Is this the peace and quiet of my old age?" Then, supported by the two women, he would rise, laboriously, as though he himself were receiving the brunt of this burden, and allow the women to escort him to the doorway, where he would shoo them away and continue on his own, while Gregor's mother hastily threw down her sewing and his sister her pen so they could run after him to offer further assistance. The household was ever further reduced; the maid was now let go after all; a bony giant of a charwoman with white hair flapping about her head came by in the morning and evening to perform the heaviest labors; everything else was handled by Gregor's mother along with all her sewing. It even came to pass that several pieces of jewelry that had been in the family—jewels Gregor's mother and sister had delighted in wearing at entertainments and festivities—were sold, as Gregor would learn in the evening when the price each piece had brought would be discussed. But their greatest lament was always that they were unable to leave this apartment, which was far too large for their current circumstances, since no one could imagine how Gregor might be moved. But Gregor understood that it was not only out of consideration for him that a move was being ruled out, since he could easily enough have been transported in a crate of appropriate size with a few air holes; the main thing keeping the family from moving to a new apartment was their complete sense of hopelessness and the thought that they had been struck with a misfortune such as no one else in their entire circle of relations and friends had ever experienced. They were fulfilling to the utmost the demands the world makes on the poor: Gregor's father fetched breakfast for the petty employees at the bank, his mother sacrificed herself for the underclothes of strangers, his sister ran back and forth behind the shop counter at her customers' behest, but this was all the strength they had. And the wound in Gregor's back would begin to ache anew when mother and sister, having brought his father to bed, would now return and, leaving their work where it lay, huddle close beside one another pressing their cheeks together; when Gregor's mother, gesturing toward his room, would say: "Shut the door now, Grete"; and when Gregor was left in the dark again while next door the two women intermingled their tears or else sat there tearless, staring down at the table.

Gregor spent his nights and days almost entirely without sleeping. Sometimes he thought about taking the family's affairs in hand again, just as he used to, the next time his door was opened; once more his boss and the general manager would appear before his mind's eye after all this time, the clerks and apprentices, the dull-witted hired man, two or three friends from other firms, a chambermaid from a provincial hotel (a sweet, fleeting specter), the shopgirl from a haberdashery whom he had courted earnestly but too slowly—all of these now appeared to him, interspersed with strangers or people already forgotten, but instead of coming to his aid and that of his family, every last one of them was unapproachable, and he was glad when they disappeared. At other times he would be not at all in a frame of mind to look after his family; instead he was filled with rage at how poorly he was attended to, and although he could not imagine anything he would have liked to eat, he plotted how he might gain access to the pantry so as to help himself to what—despite his total absence of hunger—was his due. Without bothering to consider how she might give Gregor particular pleasure, his sister would quickly thrust some randomly chosen foodstuff into his room with her foot on her way to work in the morning or at midday, only to sweep it out again at night with a quick swipe of the broom, paying no heed if the food had been only barely nibbled at or—as was most often the case now—not touched at all. Setting Gregor's room to rights, a task she now saved for the evenings, could not possibly have been done any more perfunctorily. Great streaks of dirt extended across the walls, with balls of dust and rubbish lying scattered about. At first when Gregor's sister came into his room he would position himself in corners particularly indicative of this problem—to reproach her, as it were, by his presence there. But he could just as well have spent entire weeks sitting there without any improvement on his sister's part; after all, she saw the dirt as plainly as he did, but had made up her mind to leave it be. At the same time, with a sensitivity that was new in her, one that had now taken hold of the family as a whole, she was on her guard to make sure the task of tidying Gregor's room was reserved for her. Once Gregor's mother had subjected his room to a thorough scrubbing, which she accomplished only after using up several buckets of water—admittedly, all this moisture was itself an affront to Gregor, who lay stretched out, bitter and immobile, upon the settee—but his mother did not escape punishment. For no sooner had his sister remarked the change in Gregor's room that evening than she ran into the living room, grievously insulted, and ignoring her mother's imploringly raised hands, set to weeping so violently that her parents—naturally her father was startled out of his chair—at first stood by helpless and astonished; until they too began to stir; on the right, Gregor's father reproached his mother for not having left the cleaning of Gregor's room to his sister; while on the left he shouted at Gregor's sister, threatening that she would never again be permitted to clean Gregor's room; while his mother attempted to drag his father, now so agitated he hardly recognized himself, into the bedroom; Gregor's sister, shaking with sobs, pummeled the table with her tiny fists; and Gregor hissed loudly in fury because it had occurred to no one to shut the door of his room to spare him this sight and commotion.

But even if Gregor's sister, who was exhausted by her professional work, had wearied of caring for Gregor as she'd previously done, there was absolutely no need for his mother to fill her shoes, and Gregor needn't have suffered neglect. For now the charwoman was here. This old widow—who had seen and survived the worst in her long life with the help of her sturdy bones—felt no particular repugnance toward Gregor. Without being at all inquisitive, she had once chanced to open the door to his room and, seeing Gregor, who had begun to run back and forth although no one was chasing him, she stood there staring in astonishment, her hands clasped across her lap. Ever since, she never failed to open the door a crack for a moment every morning and evening to look in on him. At the beginning she would call him over to her, saying things that were probably intended to sound friendly, like "Hey, over here, you old dung beetle!" or "Just look at the old dung beetle!" Thus addressed, Gregor gave no reply but instead remained where he was, immobile, as if the door had never been opened. If only this charwoman, instead of being allowed to disturb him uselessly at whim, had been given instructions to clean his room daily! Once, early in the morning—a heavy rain, perhaps already a portent of the coming spring, was beating against the windowpanes—Gregor became so infuriated when the charwoman started up again with her quips that he turned on her as if to attack, if admittedly slowly and decrepitly. But instead of being frightened, the charwoman just picked up a chair that was standing beside the door and held it high in the air; and as she stood there, her mouth gaping wide, her intention was clear: not to close her mouth again until the chair in her hand had come crashing down upon Gregor's back. "Aha, so that's as far as it goes?" she asked as Gregor turned around again, and she placed the chair calmly back in its corner.

Gregor now ate almost nothing at all. Only if he happened by chance to wander past the food that had been prepared for him might he playfully take a bite of something into his mouth, where he would hold it for hours and then usually spit it out again later. At first he thought it was his sorrow at the state of his room that prevented him from eating, but in fact he had resigned himself very quickly to the changes there. Everyone had gotten into the habit of using his room to store things there was no space for in other parts of the apartment, and now there were many such things, since one room of the apartment had been rented out to three lodgers. These solemn gentlemen—all three of them were bearded, as Gregor once noted, peering through the crack of the door—were scrupulously intent on having everything tidy, not just in their room but also, since they were now paying rent here, in the entire household, particularly the kitchen. They could not bear the presence of unnecessary, much less dirty items. Moreover, they had brought most of their own furnishings with them. For this reason, many things had become superfluous, things that could not be sold but were still too valuable to throw out. All of this found its way into Gregor's room. As did the ash box and the garbage pail from the kitchen. The charwoman, always in a great hurry, would simply fling any unserviceable item into Gregor's room; mercifully, Gregor generally saw only the object in question and the hand that held it. The charwoman may have intended at some point, when she had occasion or a free minute, to come collect these things, or else throw all of them out at once, but as it was they remained wherever they first landed, except when Gregor made his way through the refuse, stirring it around—at first out of necessity, since there was no room left for him to crawl about, but later with ever-increasing pleasure, though after these wanderings, which left him mortally exhausted and sad, he would spend hours without moving.

Since the lodgers sometimes also took their supper at home in the shared living room, the living room door remained shut on some evenings, but Gregor was happy to forgo having the door open; in fact, even when it was open, he sometimes failed to take advantage of it and instead, unbeknownst to his family, would remain lying in the darkest corner of his room. Once, however, the charwoman had left the door to the living room slightly ajar, and ajar it remained even when the lodgers came in that evening and struck a light. They sat down at the head of the table where in earlier times Gregor had sat with his father and mother, unfolded the napkins and took up their knives and forks. At once Gregor's mother appeared in the doorway with a serving dish filled with meat, and right behind her came his sister bearing a plate piled high with potatoes. A heavy vapor rose from the steaming food. The lodgers bent over the dishes that had been placed before them, as though wishing to inspect them before beginning their meal, and in fact the one who sat in the middle and appeared to be an authority figure to the other two cut off a piece of meat right there on the platter to check whether it was tender enough and didn't have to be sent back to the kitchen. He was satisfied, and Gregor's mother and sister, who had been watching nervously, now smiled with relief.

The family members themselves ate in the kitchen. Nonetheless Gregor's father visited the living room on his way to the kitchen and with a single bow, cap in hand, took a tour around the table. The lodgers all rose from their seats and mumbled into their beards. Left alone again, they ate in almost perfect silence. It struck Gregor as peculiar that amid all the various sounds of this meal, one could also make out their champing teeth, as if to demonstrate to Gregor that a person needs teeth to eat and that even the most splendid jaws, if toothless, can accomplish nothing at all. "I'm hungry," Gregor said sorrowfully to himself, "but not for these things. Just look how these lodgers take their nourishment while I am wasting away!"

On this very evening—Gregor couldn't remember having heard the violin once in all this time—the sound of it was heard coming from the kitchen. The lodgers had already finished their evening meal, the one in the middle had pulled out a newspaper, giving each of the others a page, and now the three of them were reading, leaning back in their chairs and smoking. When the violin began to play, their interest was piqued, they got up from their chairs and tiptoed over to the doorway leading to the vestibule, where they stood in a tight cluster. The sounds of this activity must have traveled to the kitchen, for Gregor's father now called out: "Are the gentlemen disturbed by this playing? It can be silenced at once." "On the contrary," said the one in the middle, "would the young lady care to join us and play here in the living room, where it is much more comfortable and pleasant?" "Why, of course," Gregor's father exclaimed, as though he were the violinist. The gentlemen went back into the room and waited. Soon Gregor's father arrived with the music stand, his mother with the sheet music and his sister with the violin. His sister calmly prepared to play; his parents, who never rented out rooms in earlier days and therefore were treating these lodgers with exaggerated deference, did not even dare to sit in their own armchairs; his father leaned against the door, his right hand tucked between two buttons of his closed livery jacket; his mother, meanwhile, was offered an armchair by one of the lodgers, and since she left the chair where he had happened to place it, she sat off to one side in a corner.

Gregor's sister began to play; on either side, his father and mother attentively followed each movement of her hands. Attracted by her playing, Gregor had ventured a bit further than usual and was already sticking his head into the living room. It scarcely surprised him that he had become so inconsiderate of the others; earlier on, his considerateness had been a source of pride. And he had all the more reason to keep himself hidden away now: thanks to the dust that lay everywhere in his room and would swirl up at the slightest motion, he too was covered in dust; he dragged around threads, hair and food scraps clinging to his back and sides; his general indifference was far too great now for him to keep up with a habit he'd once practiced several times a day: flipping over so as to scrub his back against the rug. And despite his condition, he did not hesitate now to continue his advance a little way out onto the immaculate floor of the living room.

To be sure, no one paid him the slightest heed. The family was completely absorbed in the violin playing; the lodgers, on the other hand, having at first positioned themselves, hands in their trouser pockets, much too close behind his sister's music stand, so that they could all look at the sheet music, which surely must have distracted her, soon withdrew to the window, conversing in an undertone, and remained there, anxiously observed by Gregor's father. It appeared more than clear they had been disappointed in their expectation of hearing beautiful or entertaining violin music and now, tired of the whole performance, were continuing to tolerate this disturbance of their peace only out of politeness. Particularly the way in which all of them were blowing the smoke of their cigars high into the air from their noses and mouths suggested extreme agitation. And yet his sister's playing was so lovely. Her face was tilted to one side; searchingly, sadly, her eyes followed the lines of notes. Gregor crept a bit farther forward and ducked his head down close to the floor so as perhaps to catch her eye. Was he a beast, that music so moved him? He felt as if he were being shown the way to that unknown nourishment he craved. He was determined to creep all the way up to his sister, to pluck at her skirt and in this way indicate to her that she should come to his room with her violin, for no one here was rewarding her playing as he meant to reward her. He would not allow her to leave his room ever again, at least as long as he was alive; his horrific figure would, for the first time ever, be useful to him; he would be at all the doors of his room at once, growling at his attackers; but his sister should remain with him not by force but of her own free will; she should sit beside him on the settee, bend down, the better to hear, and he would confess to her that he'd had the firm intention of sending her to the Conservatory and that if the disaster had not disrupted his plans, he would have made a general announcement last Christmas—Christmas had passed now, hadn't it?—without letting himself be swayed by objections of any sort. After this declaration, his sister would be moved to the point of tears, and Gregor would raise himself to the height of her armpit and kiss her throat, which, now that she went to the office every day, she wore free of ribbon or collar.

"Herr Samsa!" the gentleman in the middle shouted at Gregor's father, and without wasting a single word, pointed his finger at Gregor, who was slowly advancing. The violin fell silent, the middle lodger at first just smiled and shook his head, turning toward his friends, then looked again at Gregor. Gregor's father apparently found the task of driving Gregor back into his room less urgent than that of calming the lodgers, despite the fact that they did not appear particularly worked up and seemed to be finding Gregor more entertaining than the music. He hurried over to them and tried with outspread arms to herd them back into their room, at the same time using his body to shield Gregor from their view. And now they did in fact become a little angry, though it was no longer clear whether this was on account of Gregor's father's behavior or the realization dawning on them that without their knowledge they had been sharing their home with a roommate of this sort. They demanded explanations of Gregor's father; now it was their turn to throw their arms into the air; they plucked uneasily at their beards and only slowly withdrew in the direction of their room. Meanwhile Gregor's sister, who had been standing there at a loss since her playing had been so unexpectedly interrupted—she still held violin and bow in her carelessly dangling hands, looking over at the notes as though she were continuing to play—all at once pulled herself together, laid her instrument in the lap of her mother, who still sat there in her armchair, her lungs heaving as she fought for breath, and ran into the next room, toward which the lodgers were now moving somewhat more quickly as Gregor's father urged them on. One saw how, beneath his sister's practiced hands, the beds' blankets and pillows flew into the air and into orderliness. Even before the lodgers reached the room, she had finished making up the beds and slipped out. Gregor's father appeared to be once more so firmly in the grip of his own stubbornness that he forgot the basic respect that, after all, he owed his tenants. He kept up his pressing and urging until, already standing in the doorway, the middle lodger thunderously stamped his foot, causing Gregor's father to stop short. "I hereby declare," he said, raising his hand and seeking out Gregor's mother and sister too as he glanced about, "that in consideration of the reprehensible circumstances prevailing in this apartment and family"—and here he spat on the floor without forethought—"I give notice on my room effective immediately. It goes without saying that I will not pay a penny for the days I have spent here; on the contrary, I shall consider whether or not to pursue you with—please believe me—easily justifiable claims." He fell silent and went on looking straight before him expectantly. And indeed his two friends at once chimed in with the words, "We too give notice effective immediately." Hereupon he seized the door handle and with a great crash slammed the door.

Gregor's father staggered to his armchair with groping hands and let himself fall into it; it looked as though he was stretching out for his customary evening nap, but the violent nodding of his anchorless head showed that he was absolutely not sleeping. Gregor had gone on lying quietly on the spot where the lodgers had espied him. His disappointment at the failure of his plan and perhaps also the weakness caused by starvation rendered him incapable of moving. With a certain definitiveness he sensed, terrified, that everything was about to collapse all around him, and so he waited. Not even the violin startled him when it fell from his mother's lap beneath her trembling fingers, giving off a note that echoed in the air.

"Dear parents," his sister said, striking the table by way of preamble, "things cannot go on like this. Even if you two perhaps do not realize it, I most certainly do. I am unwilling to utter my brother's name before this creature, and therefore will say only: we have to try to get rid of it. We have done everything humanly possible to care for it and show it tolerance, I don't think anyone would reproach us on this account."

"She is right a thousand times over," Gregor's father murmured under his breath. His mother, still incapable of breathing freely, began to cough dully into her lifted hand, a lunatic expression in her eyes.

Gregor's sister hurried over to her mother and held her forehead. Her words seemed to have given her father an idea, for he now sat up straight, playing with his uniform cap between the plates left behind on the table from the lodgers' supper and glancing over from time to time at a quiet Gregor.

"We have to try to get rid of it," his sister said, addressing her words exclusively to Gregor's father this time, for his mother was coughing too hard to hear anything. "It'll be the death of you two, I can see it now. When people have to work as hard as all of us have been doing, it just isn't possible to endure these endless torments at home. I cannot bear it anymore either." And she burst into sobs, weeping so forcefully that her tears flowed down upon her mother's face, from which the girl wiped them with a mechanical gesture.

"Child," her father said sympathetically and with noticeable compassion, "but what can we do?"

Gregor's sister just shrugged her shoulders as a sign of the helplessness that had come over her while she was weeping, in contrast to the confidence she'd displayed a moment before.

"If he understood us," Gregor's father said, half-questioning; his sister, still caught up in her weeping, shook one hand vehemently as a sign of how unthinkable she found this.

"If he understood us," his father repeated, closing his eyes to absorb her conviction that this was utterly out of the question, "then it might be possible to come to an agreement with him. But as things stand—"

"It has to go," Gregor's sister cried out, "that's the only way, Father. You just have to try to let go of the notion that this thing is Gregor. The real disaster is that we believed this for so long. But how could it be Gregor? If it were Gregor, it would have realized a long time ago that it just isn't possible for human beings to live beside such a creature, and it would have gone away on its own. We still would have been lacking a brother but we would have been able to go on living and honoring his memory. But now we have this beast tormenting us; it drives away our lodgers and apparently intends to take over the entire apartment and have us sleep in the gutter. Just look, Father," she suddenly shrieked, "he's starting again!" And in a fright that Gregor found bewildering, she now went so far as to leave her mother behind, launching herself from her chair as if she would rather sacrifice her mother than remain in Gregor's proximity, and ran to take cover behind her father who, agitated by the way she was carrying on, rose from his own chair and half-raised his arms as if to shield her.

But Gregor was far from wanting to frighten anyone, above all his sister. All he'd done was start to turn around to make his way back to his room, and admittedly this operation would have been hard not to notice, since in his current injured state he was obliged to use his head to help with this difficult maneuver;

he kept raising it up and then thumping it against the floor. Pausing, he glanced around. His good intentions seemed to have been recognized; it had been only a momentary fright. Now all of them gazed at him sadly and in silence. His mother lay in her armchair, her extended legs pressed together, barely able to keep her eyes open in her exhaustion; his father and sister sat side by side, and his sister had draped one hand across her father's neck.

"Perhaps I'll be allowed to turn around now," Gregor thought and resumed his labors. He could not entirely suppress the wheezing this exertion produced, and now and then he had to rest. Otherwise no one was harassing him, he had been left to attend to matters on his own. When he had completed this rotation, he immediately made straight for the door to his room. He was astonished at how great a distance separated him from his destination, and he didn't understand how, weak as he was, he had been able to traverse the same distance just a little while before almost without noticing. Steadfastly concentrating only on crawling as quickly as possible, he scarcely paid any heed to the fact that not a word, not a cry came from his family to disturb him. Only when he was already in the doorway did he turn his head—not all the way around, as he felt his neck growing stiff, but even so he was able to see that all was unchanged behind him, except that his sister had risen to her feet. The last thing he saw was a glimpse of his mother, who had now fallen entirely asleep.

No sooner was he in his room again than the door was hastily pressed shut, locked and bolted. The sudden commotion at his back gave him such a frightful start that his little legs gave way beneath him. It was his sister who had hurried thus. She had already been standing there upright and waiting, then pounced so lightfootedly Gregor didn't hear her approach, and she cried out, "Finally!" to her parents as she turned the key in the lock.

"And now?" Gregor wondered, looking around in the dark. He soon made the discovery that he was no longer capable of moving at all. He wasn't surprised at this; on the contrary, it struck him as unnatural that he had actually until now been able to support himself on those thin little legs. As for the rest, he felt relatively at ease. Admittedly his entire body was racked with pain, but it seemed to him as if it was gradually becoming weaker and weaker and in the end would fade away altogether. Already he could scarcely feel the rotting apple in his back, nor the inflamed area surrounding it, both now enveloped in soft dust. He thought back on his family with tenderness and love. His opinion that he must by all means disappear was possibly even more emphatic than that of his sister. He remained in this state of empty, peaceful reflection until the clock-tower struck the third hour of morning. He watched as everything began to lighten outside his window. Then his head sank all the way to the floor without volition and from his nostrils his last breath faintly streamed.

When the charwoman arrived early the next morning, slamming the doors so loudly in her strength and haste—often as she'd been asked to avoid this—that sleep was out of the question anywhere in the apartment after her arrival, her usual cursory visit to Gregor's room revealed at first nothing out of the ordinary. She thought he was lying there so motionless on purpose, feigning indignation; she considered him perfectly capable of rational thought. Since she happened to be holding the long broom in her hand, she tried tickling Gregor with it from the doorway. When even this had no effect, she grew vexed and began to poke Gregor a little, and only when she had actually shifted him from the spot where he lay with no resistance at all were her suspicions roused.

When soon thereafter the facts of the matter became clear to her, she gawked in surprise, gave a low whistle, then without further delay flung open the door of the bedroom and in a loud voice shouted into the darkness: "Come have a look, it's gone and croaked—just lying there, dead as a doornail!"

The Samsa couple shot upright in their marital bed and first had to struggle to recover from their shock at the charwoman's conduct before they were able to grasp her words. But then Herr and Frau Samsa hurriedly got out of bed, one on either side, Herr Samsa threw the blanket about his shoulders while Frau Samsa emerged wearing only her nightdress; in this state, they entered Gregor's room. Meanwhile the door to the living room, where Grete had been sleeping since the lodgers' arrival, had opened as well; she was fully dressed, as though she had not slept at all, as even the pallor of her cheeks seemed to prove. "Dead?" Frau Samsa asked, looking questioningly up at the charwoman, although she herself was free to investigate and, indeed, could see how things stood even without investigation. "I should say so," the charwoman said, and by way of proof, pushed Gregor's corpse quite some way to the side with her broom. Frau Samsa made a gesture as though she wanted to hold back the broom but didn't. "Well," Herr Samsa said, "now we can thank God." He crossed himself, and the three women followed his example. Grete, who did not take her eyes off the corpse for a moment, said: "Just look how skinny he was. He went such a long time without eating anything at all. All the food that went into his room would come out again just as before." And indeed Gregor's body was completely flat and dry, which hadn't really been noticeable until now when he was no longer raised up on those little legs and nothing else remained to distract the gaze.

"Grete, come sit with us for a bit," Frau Samsa said with a melancholy smile, and Grete, glancing back at the corpse, followed her parents into their bedroom. The charwoman shut the door and opened the window wide. Despite the early morning, the crisp air was already tempered by a certain mildness: after all, it was already the end of March.

The three lodgers now emerged from their room and looked about in astonishment for their breakfast; they had been forgotten. "Where's breakfast?" the one in the middle asked the charwoman peevishly. But she just put a finger to her lips and then quickly, without a word, beckoned the lodgers into Gregor's room. They did as she bade them and with their hands in the pockets of their slightly threadbare little jackets, they surrounded Gregor's corpse in the room that had meanwhile become quite bright.

Then the bedroom door opened, and Herr Samsa appeared wearing his livery, with his wife on one arm, his daughter on the other. All three looked as if they'd been weeping; Grete kept pressing her face against her father's arm.

"Leave my home at once!" Herr Samsa said, pointing at the door without letting go of the womenfolk. "What do you mean?" the gentleman in the middle inquired, dumbfounded, and gave a saccharine smile. The two others held their hands at their backs and kept rubbing them together uninterruptedly, as if in gleeful expectation of a fight that was certain to be decided in their favor. "I mean exactly what I say," Herr Samsa replied, now advancing on the lodger flanked by his two companions. The lodger just stood there at first, looking at the ground, as if things were just rearranging themselves in his head into a new order. "So we'll be leaving," he said then, looking up at Herr Samsa as if this new humility that had suddenly come over him required him to petition for the approval of even this decision. Herr Samsa merely nodded curtly in his direction a few times, goggle-eyed. At this, the gentleman did, in fact, make haste to stride back out to the vestibule, where his two friends had been listening attentively for some moments, their hands at rest, and now they practically hopped and skipped in their hurry to follow, as if worried Herr Samsa might somehow precede them into the vestibule, cutting off their line of communication with their leader.

In the vestibule, all three of them took their hats from the coat rack, withdrew their walking sticks from the cane stand, made a silent bow and left the apartment. Displaying what soon proved to be an utterly unfounded mistrustfulness, Herr Samsa stepped out onto the landing with the two women; leaning against the banister, they watched as the three gentlemen descended the long staircase, moving slowly but at a steady pace and disappearing on each floor at a certain bend of the stairwell only to appear again a few moments later; the farther down they went, the more the Samsa family's interest in them faded, and when a butcher's apprentice came toward and then passed them on his way up, proudly bearing his tray upon his head, Herr Samsa and the women abandoned the banister, and all of them returned, seemingly relieved, to their apartment.

They decided to spend the day resting and to go out for a stroll; they had not only earned this respite from their work, but were desperately in need of it. And so they all sat down at the table and wrote three letters of excuse: Herr Samsa to his supervisor, Frau Samsa to her employer, and Grete to her superior. While they were writing, the charwoman came in to say she was leaving, as her morning's work was completed. The three scribes at first merely nodded without looking up, and only when the charwoman failed to go on her way did they glance up in annoyance. "Well?" Herr Samsa asked. The charwoman stood smiling in the doorway as if she had some splendid good fortune to announce to the family but would not do so until she was properly questioned. The nearly vertical little ostrich feathers on her hat, which had annoyed Herr Samsa for as long as she had been in the family's service, bobbed gently in all directions. "So what is it you want?" she was asked now by Frau Samsa, the member of the family for whom the charwoman still had the most respect. "Well," the charwoman replied, her own good-natured laughter making it impossible at first for her to go on speaking, "there's no need for you to go worrying about how to get rid of that mess in there. It's already taken care of." Frau Samsa and Grete bent down over their letters as if they meant to go on writing; Herr Samsa, who saw that the charwoman was about to start describing everything in detail, summarily silenced her with an outstretched hand. And since she was not permitted to say what she wished, she suddenly remembered the great hurry she was in, and so with an insulted air she cried, "So long, everyone," turned wildly on her heel, and with the most excruciating slamming of doors left the apartment.

"Tonight she'll be let go," Herr Samsa said, but received an answer neither from his wife nor his daughter, for the charwoman seemed to have disturbed the equanimity they had only just attained. They rose from their seats, went to the window, and remained there with their arms about each other. Herr Samsa turned in his chair to look at them and observed them quietly for a little while. Then he cried out: "So come here already. Let these old matters rest. And show a little consideration for me as well." At once the women obeyed, hurried over to him, caressed him and quickly finished their letters.

Then all three of them left the apartment together, something they had not done for months, and took the electric tram all the way to the open countryside at the edge of town. The car in which they sat all alone was entirely suffused with warm sunlight. Cozily leaning back in their seats, they discussed their future prospects, and on closer investigation it appeared that these prospects were not bad at all, for all three of their positions—something they had never before properly discussed—were in fact quite advantageous and above all offered promising opportunities for advancement. The greatest immediate improvement in their situation, of course, would be easily achieved by moving to a new apartment; they now wished to take a smaller and cheaper but more convenient and above all more practical flat than their current one, which had been picked out for them by Gregor. As they were conversing in this way, Herr and Frau Samsa were struck almost as one while observing their daughter, who was growing ever more vivacious, by the thought that despite all the torments that had made her cheeks grow pale, she had recently blossomed into a beautiful, voluptuous girl. Growing quieter now and communicating with one another almost unconsciously by an exchange of glances, they thought about how it would soon be time to find her a good husband. And when they arrived at their destination, it seemed to them almost a confirmation of their new dreams and good intentions when their daughter swiftly sprang to her feet and stretched her young body.

1915

LU XUN

1881–1936

Modern China has produced many talented writers, with the usual division of critical opinion concerning them. There is, however, almost universal agreement on one authentic genius: Lu Xun (also Romanized Lu Hsün), the pen name of Zhou Shuren. Few writers of fiction have gained so much fame for such a small oeuvre. His reputation rests mostly on twenty-five stories released between 1918 and 1926, gathered into two collections: *Cheering from the Sidelines* and *Wondering Where to Turn*. In addition to his fiction, he published a collection of prose poems, *Wild Grass*, and a number of literary and political essays. His small body of stories offers a bleak portrayal of a culture that, despite its failures, continues to capture the modern Chinese imagination. Whether the older culture had indeed failed is less important here than Lu Xun's powerful representation of it and the deep chord of response that his work has touched in Chinese readers. Lu Xun was a controlled ironist and a craftsman whose narrative skill far exceeded that of most of his contemporaries; yet beneath his stylistic mastery the reader senses the depth of his anger at traditional culture.

Born into a Shaoxing family of Confucian scholar-officials, Lu Xun had a traditional education and became a classical scholar of considerable erudition, as well as a writer of poetry in the classical language. Sometimes he displays this learning in his fiction, where it is always undercut with irony. He grew up at a time when the traditional education system, based on the Confucian classics, was giving way, to the approval of Lu Xun and others, to a more modern one; and after the early death of his father in 1896, he joined the many young Chinese intellectuals of the era in traveling abroad for higher education—first in Tokyo, then in Sendai, where he attended a Japanese medical school. (Because it was successfully modernizing a traditional culture, Japan attracted young Chinese intellectuals who wished the same for their own society.) During the period of his studies, the Russians and Japanese were at war in the former Chinese territory of Manchuria. In a famous anecdote describing his decision to become a writer, Lu Xun tells of seeing a classroom slide of a Chinese prisoner about to be decapitated as a Russian spy. What shocked the young medical student was the apathetic crowd of Chinese onlookers, gathered around to watch the execution. At that moment, he decided that what truly needed healing were not their bodies but their dulled spirits.

Returning to Tokyo, Lu Xun founded a journal in which he published literary essays and Western works of fiction in translation. In 1909, financial difficulties drove him back to China, where he worked as a teacher in Hangzhou and his native Shaoxing. With the arrival of the Republican Revolution of 1911, which overthrew the Qing, or Manchu, dynasty, he joined the ministry of education, moving north to Beijing, where he also taught at various universities. The Republican government was soon at the mercy of the powerful armies competing for regional power; during this period, perhaps for self-protection, Lu Xun devoted himself to traditional scholarship. One might have expected this revolutionary to write, as Lu Xun did, a groundbreaking work of scholarship, the first history of Chinese fiction; but he also produced an erudite textual study of the third-century writer Xi Kang, which is still used.

On May 4, 1919, a massive student strike forced the Chinese government not to sign the Versailles Peace Treaty, which would have given Japan effective control over the province of Shandong. The date gave its name to the May Fourth Movement, led by a group of young intellectuals who advocated the use of vernacular Chinese in all writing and the repudiation of classical Chinese literature. Though Lu Xun himself was not an active participant in the political side of the May Fourth Movement, it was during this period (1918–26) that he wrote all but one of his short stories. In the final decade of his life, he became a political activist and put his satirical talents at the service of the left, becoming one of the favorite writers of the Communist Party leader Mao Zedong.

"Diary of a Madman" (1918), Lu Xun's earliest story in modern Chinese, opens with a preface in mannered classical Chinese, giving an account of the discovery of the diary. Such ironic use of classical Chinese to suggest a falsely polite world of social appearances had been common in traditional Chinese fiction. Usually its presence suggested, however, the alternative possibility, of immediate, direct, and genuine language, a language of the heart that shows up the language of society. Here, the diary that follows the preface is indeed immediate, direct, and genuine, but it is also deluded and twisted. The diarist becomes increasingly convinced that everyone around him wants to eat him; after observing this growing circle of cannibals in the present, the diarist then turns to examine old texts, where he discovers that the history of the culture has been one of secret cannibalism. Beneath society's false politeness, the veneer of such decorous forms as the voice in the preface, he detects a brutality lurking, a hunger to assimilate others, to "eat men."

As the diary progresses, it becomes increasingly clear that the diarist, who sees himself as a potential victim, recapitulates the flaws and dangers of the society he describes, assimilating everyone around him into his fixed view of the world. His reading of ancient texts to discover evidence of cannibalism, with its distorting discovery of "secret meanings" that only serve to confirm beliefs already held, works in part as a parody of traditional Confucian scholarship. His is a world closed in on itself, one that survives by feeding on itself and its young. Yet the story opens itself to other interpretations: some see the madman as understanding the truth to which everyone else in the tale is blind, while others have noted that the madman's possible cannibalism undermines his apparent vision and that in any case his account is suspect because he is awaiting appointment to an official position.

The novella *Ah Q* was published in weekly and sometimes biweekly installments from 1920 to 1921. In writing about *Ah Q*, Lu Xun stated: "My method is to make the reader unable to tell who this character can be apart from himself, so that he cannot back away to become a bystander but rather suspects that this is a portrait of himself as well as everyone." Lu Xun's skillful choice of the name "Ah Q" both reflects and reinforces this intent. The narrator claims not to remember Ah Q's correct name. *Ah* in Chinese is a diminutive prefix for names. *Q* is short for *Quei*, but as many characters are pronounced "quei," the narrator says he does not know which character he should use, and therefore shortens it to the Roman letter *Q*, which is phonetic only (every Chinese character not only denotes sound but also connotes meaning). The reader is left with a sound that could have any number of meanings and thus refer to a large number of people. In the same way that Lu Xun became a writer after viewing the slide of the apathetic Chinese bystanders surrounding the prisoner about to be executed, Lu Xun's selection of a ubiquitous name urges his readers to become active critics of themselves and their society—to see themselves in Ah Q. Lu Xun fought against what he saw as a human inclination toward self-deception and narcissism. Mao Zedong's selective use of Lu Xun's writings for propaganda is in this respect ironic. As he passed away at the young age of only fifty-five, Lu Xun did not live to witness this perversion of his work. In Chinese today, the term "Ah Q mentality" refers to people who deny reality, especially in their refusal to recognize their sycophantic behavior toward the strong and their lack of empathy for or outright aggression toward the weak.

In the original Chinese, "Q" stands out in great contrast to the surrounding Chinese characters. This use of a letter from the Roman alphabet is a reference to the 1919 May Fourth Movement, led by intellectuals who embraced some aspects of Western learning. They sought to create new values for a modern China. These included writing in vernacular rather than classical Chinese. Classical Chinese was the province of Confucian scholars, who occupied positions of power and authority in part based on their mastery of this ancient language and its accompanying literature, philosophy, and history. The participants of the May Fourth Movement sought to question traditional Confucian authority, especially as they felt betrayed by a political elite that did not stand up for China in its Versailles treaty negotiations. *Ah Q—The Real Story* is the first work in vernacular Chinese published after the May Fourth Movement and is a significant foundational text of modern Chinese literature.

Diary of a Madman[1]

There was once a pair of male siblings whose actual names I beg your indulgence to withhold. Suffice it to say that we three were boon companions during our school years. Subsequently, circumstances contrived to rend us asunder so that we were gradually bereft of knowledge regarding each other's activities.

Not too long ago, however, I chanced to hear that one of them had been hard afflicted with a dread disease. I obtained this intelligence at a time when I happened to be returning to my native haunts and, hence, made so bold as to detour somewhat from my normal course in order to visit them. I encountered but one of the siblings. He apprised me that it had been his younger brother who had suffered the dire illness. By now, however, he had long since become sound and fit again; in fact he had already repaired to other parts to await a substantive official appointment.[2]

The elder brother apologized for having needlessly put me to the inconvenience of this visitation, and concluding his disquisition with a hearty smile, showed me two volumes of diaries which, he assured me, would reveal the nature of his brother's disorder during those fearful days.

As to the lapsus calami[3] *that occur in the course of the diaries, I have altered not a word. Nonetheless, I have changed all the names, despite the fact that their publication would be of no great consequence since they are all humble villagers unknown to the world at large.*

Recorded this 2nd day in the 7th year of the Republic.[4]

1

Moonlight's really nice tonight. Haven't seen it in over thirty years. Seeing it today, I feel like a new man. I know now that I've been completely out of things for the last three decades or more. But I've still got to be *very* careful. Otherwise, how do you explain those dirty looks the Zhao family's dog gave me?

I've got good reason for my fears.

2

No moonlight at all tonight—something's not quite right. When I made my way out the front gate this morning—ever so carefully—there was something funny about the way the Venerable Old Zhao looked at me: seemed as though he was afraid of me and yet, at the same time, looked as though he had it in for me. There were seven or eight other people who had their heads together whispering about me. They were afraid I'd see them too! All up and down the street people acted the same way. The meanest looking one of all spread his lips out

1. Both Lu Xun selections translated by and with notes adapted from William A. Lyell.

2. When there were too many officials for the number of offices to be filled, a man might well be appointed to an office that was already occupied. The new appointee would go to his post and wait until the office was vacated. Sometimes there would be a number of such appointees waiting their turns.

3. "The fall of the reed [writing instrument]" (Latin, literal trans.); hence, lapses in writing.

4. The Qing Dynasty was overthrown and the Republic of China was established in 1911; thus it is April 2, 1918. The introduction is written in classical Chinese, whereas the diary entries that follow are all in the colloquial language.

wide and actually *smiled* at me! A shiver ran from the top of my head clear down to the tips of my toes, for I realized that meant they already had their henchmen well deployed, and were ready to strike.

But I wasn't going to let that intimidate *me*. I kept right on walking. There was a group of children up ahead and they were talking about me too. The expressions in their eyes were just like the Venerable Old Zhao's, and their faces were iron gray. I wondered what grudge the children had against me that they were acting this way too. I couldn't contain myself any longer and shouted, "Tell me, tell me!" But they just ran away.

Let's see now, what grudge can there be between me and the Venerable Old Zhao, or the people on the street for that matter? The only thing I can think of is that twenty years ago I trampled the account books kept by Mr. Antiquity, and he was hopping mad about it too. Though the Venerable Old Zhao doesn't know him, he must have gotten wind of it somehow. Probably decided to right the injustice I had done Mr. Antiquity by getting all those people on the street to gang up on me. But the children? Back then they hadn't even come into the world yet. Why should they have given me those funny looks today? Seemed as though they were afraid of me and yet, at the same time, looked as though they would like to do me some harm. That really frightens me. Bewilders me. Hurts me.

I have it! Their fathers and mothers have *taught* them to be like that!

3

I can never get to sleep at night. You really have to study something before you can understand it.

Take all those people: some have worn the cangue on the district magistrate's order, some have had their faces slapped by the gentry, some have had their wives ravished by *yamen*[5] clerks, some have had their dads and moms dunned to death by creditors; and yet, right at the time when all those terrible things were taking place, the expressions on their faces were never as frightened, or as savage, as the ones they wore yesterday.

Strangest of all was that woman on the street. She slapped her son and said: "Damn it all, you've got me so riled up I could take a good bite right out of your hide!" She was talking to him, but she was looking at me! I tried, but couldn't conceal a shudder of fright. That's when that ghastly crew of people, with their green faces and protruding fangs, began to roar with laughter. Old Fifth Chen[6] ran up, took me firmly in tow, and dragged me away.

When we got back, the people at home all pretended not to know me. The expressions in their eyes were just like all the others too. After he got me into the study, Old Fifth Chen bolted the door from the outside—just the way you would pen up a chicken or a duck! That made figuring out what was at the bottom of it all harder than ever.

5. Local government offices. The petty clerks who worked in them were notorious for relying on their proximity to power to bully and abuse the common people. "Cangue": a split board, hinged at one end and locked at the other; holes were cut out to accommodate the prisoner's neck and wrists.

6. People were often referred to by their hierarchical position within their extended family.

A few days back one of our tenant farmers came in from Wolf Cub Village to report a famine. Told my elder brother the villagers had all ganged up on a "bad" man and beaten him to death. Even gouged out his heart and liver. Fried them up and ate them to bolster their own courage! When I tried to horn in on the conversation, Elder Brother and the tenant farmer both gave me sinister looks. I realized for the first time today that the expression in their eyes was just the same as what I saw in those people on the street.

As I think of it now, a shiver's running from the top of my head clear down to the tips of my toes.

If they're capable of eating people, then who's to say they won't eat *me*?

Don't you see? That woman's words about "taking a good bite," and the laughter of that ghastly crew with their green faces and protruding fangs, and the words of our tenant farmer a few days back—it's perfectly clear to me now that all that talk and all that laughter were really a set of secret signals. Those words were poison! That laughter, a knife! Their teeth are bared and waiting—white and razor sharp! Those people are cannibals!

As I see it myself, though I'm not what you'd call an evil man, still, ever since I trampled the Antiquity family's account books, it's hard to say *what* they'll do. They seem to have something in mind, but I can't begin to guess what. What's more, as soon as they turn against someone, they'll *say* he's evil anyway. I can still remember how it was when Elder Brother was teaching me composition.[7] No matter how good a man was, if I could find a few things wrong with him he would approvingly underline my words; on the other hand, if I made a few allowances for a bad man, he'd say I was "an extraordinary student, an absolute genius." When all is said and done, how can I possibly guess what people like *that* have in mind, especially when they're getting ready for a cannibals' feast?

You have to *really* go into something before you can understand it. I seemed to remember, though not too clearly, that from ancient times on people have often been eaten, and so I started leafing through a history book to look it up. There were no dates in this history, but scrawled this way and that across every page were the words BENEVOLENCE, RIGHTEOUSNESS, and MORALITY. Since I couldn't get to sleep anyway, I read that history very carefully for most of the night, and finally I began to make out what was written *between* the lines; the whole volume was filled with a single phrase: EAT PEOPLE!

The words written in the history book, the things the tenant farmer said—all of it began to stare at me with hideous eyes, began to snarl and growl at me from behind bared teeth!

Why sure, *I'm* a person too, and they want to eat *me*!

4

In the morning I sat in the study for a while, calm and collected. Old Fifth Chen brought in some food—vegetables and a steamed fish. The fish's eyes were white and hard. Its mouth was wide open, just like the mouths of those people who wanted to eat human flesh. After I'd taken a few bites, the meat felt so smooth and slippery in my mouth that I couldn't tell whether it was fish or human flesh. I vomited.

7. That is, to compose essays in the classical style.

"Old Fifth," I said, "tell Elder Brother that it's absolutely stifling in here and that I'd like to take a walk in the garden." He left without answering, but sure enough, after a while the door opened. I didn't even budge—just sat there waiting to see what they'd do to me. I *knew* that they wouldn't be willing to set me loose.

Just as I expected! Elder Brother came in with an old man in tow and walked slowly toward me. There was a savage glint in the old man's eyes. He was afraid I'd see it and kept his head tilted toward the floor while stealing sidewise glances at me over the temples of his glasses. "You seem to be fine today," said Elder Brother.

"You bet!" I replied.

"I've asked Dr. He to come and examine your pulse today."

"He's welcome!" I said. But don't think for one moment that I didn't know the old geezer was an executioner in disguise! Taking my pulse was nothing but a ruse; he wanted to feel my flesh and decide if I was fat enough to butcher yet. He'd probably even get a share of the meat for his troubles. I wasn't a *bit* afraid. Even though I don't eat human flesh, I still have a lot more courage than those who do. I thrust both hands out to see how the old buzzard would make his move. Sitting down, he closed his eyes and felt my pulse[8] for a good long while. Then he froze. Just sat there without moving a muscle for another good long while. Finally he opened his spooky eyes and said: "Don't let your thoughts run away with you. Just convalesce in peace and quiet for a few days and you'll be all right."

Don't let my thoughts run away with me? Convalesce in peace and quiet? If I convalesce till I'm good and fat, they get more to eat, but what do *I* get out of it? How can I possibly be *all right*? What a bunch! All they think about is eating human flesh, and then they go sneaking around, thinking up every which way they can to camouflage their real intentions. They were comical enough to crack *anybody* up. I couldn't hold it in any longer and let out a good loud laugh. Now *that* really felt good. I knew in my heart of hearts that my laughter was *packed* with courage and righteousness. And do you know what? They were so completely subdued by it that the old man and my elder brother both went pale!

But the more *courage* I had, the more that made them want to eat me so that they could get a little of it for free. The old man walked out. Before he had taken many steps, he lowered his head and told Elder Brother, "To be eaten as soon as possible!" He nodded understandingly. So, Elder Brother, you're in it too! Although that discovery seemed unforeseen, it really wasn't, either. My own elder brother had thrown in with the very people who wanted to eat me!

My elder brother is a cannibal!

I'm brother to a cannibal.

Even though I'm to be the victim of cannibalism, I'm *brother* to a cannibal all the same!

5

During the past few days I've taken a step back in my thinking. Supposing that old man wasn't an executioner in disguise but really was a doctor—well, he'd still be a cannibal just the same. In *Medicinal . . . something or other* by Li

8. In Chinese medicine, the pulse is taken at both wrists.

Shizhen,[9] the grandfather of the doctor's trade, it says quite clearly that human flesh can be eaten, so how can that old man say that *he's* not a cannibal too?

And as for my own elder brother, I'm not being the least bit unfair to him. When he was explaining the classics to me, he said with his very own tongue that it was all right to *exchange children and eat them*. And then there was another time when he happened to start in on an evil man and said that not only should the man be killed, but his *flesh should be eaten* and *his skin used as a sleeping mat*[1] as well.

When our tenant farmer came in from Wolf Cub Village a few days back and talked about eating a man's heart and liver, Elder Brother didn't seem to see anything out of the way in that either—just kept nodding his head. You can tell from that alone that his present way of thinking is every bit as malicious as it was when I was a child. If it's all right to exchange *children* and eat them, then *anyone* can be exchanged, anyone can be eaten. Back then I just took what he said as explanation of the classics and let it go at that, but now I realize that while he was explaining, the grease of human flesh was smeared all over his lips, and what's more, his mind was filled with plans for further cannibalism.

6

Pitch black out. Can't tell if it's day or night. The Zhao family's dog has started barking again.

Savage as a lion, timid as a rabbit, crafty as a fox . . .

7

I'm on to the way they operate. They'll never be willing to come straight out and kill me. Besides, they wouldn't dare. They'd be afraid of all the bad luck it might bring down on them if they did. And so, they've gotten everyone into cahoots with them and have set traps all over the place so that I'll do *myself* in. When I think back on the looks of those men and women on the streets a few days ago, coupled with the things my elder brother's been up to recently, I can figure out eight or nine tenths of it. From their point of view, the best thing of all would be for me to take off my belt, fasten it around a beam, and hang myself. They wouldn't be guilty of murder, and yet they'd still get everything they're after. Why, they'd be so beside themselves with joy, they'd sob with laughter. Or if they couldn't get me to do that, maybe they could torment me until I died of fright and worry. Even though I'd come out a bit leaner that way, they'd still nod their heads in approval.

9. Lived from 1518 to 1593. *Taxonomy of Medicinal Herbs*, a gigantic work, was the most important pharmacopoeia in traditional China.

1. Both italicized expressions are from the *Zuozhuan* (Zuo commentary to the *Spring and Summer Annals*, a historical work that dates from the 3rd century B.C.E.). In 448 B.C.E., an officer who was exhorting his own side not to surrender is recorded as having said, "When the army of Chu besieged the capital of Song [in 603 B.C.E.], the people exchanged their children and ate them, and used the bones for fuel; and still they would not submit to a covenant at the foot of their walls. For us who have sustained no great loss, to do so is to cast our state away" (translated by James Legge, 5.817). It is also recorded that in 551 B.C.E. an officer boasting of his own prowess before his ruler pointed to two men whom his ruler considered brave and said, "As to those two, they are like beasts, whose flesh I will eat, and then sleep upon their skins" (Legge 5.492).

Their kind only know how to eat dead meat. I remember reading in a book somewhere about something called the *hai-yi-na*.[2] Its general appearance is said to be hideous, and the expression in its eyes particularly ugly and malicious. Often eats carrion, too. Even chews the bones to a pulp and swallows them down. Just thinking about it's enough to frighten a man.

The *hai-yi-na* is kin to the wolf. The wolf's a relative of the dog, and just a few days ago the Zhao family dog gave me a funny look. It's easy to see that he's in on it too. How did that old man expect to fool *me* by staring at the floor?

My elder brother's the most pathetic of the whole lot. Since he's a human being too, how can he manage to be so totally without qualms, and what's more, even gang up with them to eat me? Could it be that he's been used to this sort of thing all along and sees nothing wrong with it? Or could it be that he's lost all conscience and just goes ahead and does it even though he knows it's wrong?

If I'm going to curse cannibals, I'll have to start with him. And if I'm going to *convert* cannibals, I'll have to start with him too.

8

Actually, by now even they should long since have understood the truth of this . . .

Someone came in. Couldn't have been more than twenty or so. I wasn't able to make out what he looked like too clearly, but he was all smiles. He nodded at me. His smile didn't look like the real thing either. And so I asked him, "Is this business of eating people right?"

He just kept right on smiling and said, "Except perhaps in a famine year, how could anyone get eaten?" I knew right off that he was one of them—one of those monsters who devour people!

At that point my own courage increased a hundredfold and I asked him, "Is it right?"

"Why are you talking about this kind of thing anyway? You really know how to . . . uh . . . how to pull a fellow's leg. Nice weather we're having."

"The weather *is* nice. There's a nice moon out, too, but I *still* want to know if it's right."

He seemed quite put out with me and began to mumble, "It's not—"

"Not right? Then how come they're still eating people?"

"No one's eating anyone."

"No one's *eating* anyone? They're eating people in Wolf Cub Village this very minute. And it's written in all the books, too, written in bright red blood!"

His expression changed and his face went gray like a slab of iron. His eyes started out from their sockets as he said, "Maybe they are, but it's always been that way, it's—"

"Just because it's always been that way, does that make it *right*?"

"I'm not going to discuss such things with you. If you insist on talking about that, then *you're* the one who's in the wrong!"

I leaped from my chair, opened my eyes, and looked around—but the fellow was nowhere to be seen. He was far younger than my elder brother, and yet he

2. Three Chinese characters are used here for phonetic value only; that is, *hai yi na* is a transliteration into Chinese of the English word *hyena*.

was actually one of them. It must be because his mom and dad taught him to be that way. And he's probably already passed it on to his own son. No wonder that even the children give me murderous looks.

9

They want to eat others and at the same time they're afraid that other people are going to eat them. That's why they're always watching each other with such suspicious looks in their eyes.

But all they'd have to do is give up that way of thinking, and then they could travel about, work, eat, and sleep in perfect security. Think how happy they'd feel! It's only a threshold, a pass. But what do they do instead? What is it that these fathers, sons, brothers, husbands, wives, friends, teachers, students, enemies, and even people who don't know each other *really* do? Why they all join together to hold each other back, and talk each other out of it!

That's it! They'd rather *die* than take that one little step.

10

I went to see Elder Brother bright and early. He was standing in the courtyard looking at the sky. I went up behind him so as to cut him off from the door back into the house. In the calmest and friendliest of tones, I said, "Elder Brother, there's something I'd like to tell you."

"Go right ahead." He immediately turned and nodded his head.

"It's only a few words, really, but it's hard to get them out. Elder Brother, way back in the beginning, it's probably the case that primitive peoples *all* ate some human flesh. But later on, because their ways of thinking changed, some gave up the practice and tried their level best to improve themselves; they kept on changing until they became human beings, *real* human beings. But the others didn't; they just kept right on with their cannibalism and stayed at that primitive level.

"You have the same sort of thing with evolution[3] in the animal world. Some reptiles, for instance, changed into fish, and then they evolved into birds, then into apes, and then into human beings. But the others didn't want to improve themselves and just kept right on being reptiles down to this very day.

"Think how ashamed those primitive men who have remained cannibals must feel when they stand before *real* human beings. They must feel even more ashamed than reptiles do when confronted with their brethren who have evolved into apes.

"There's an old story from ancient times about Yi Ya boiling his son and serving him up to Jie Zhou.[4] But if the truth be known, people have *always* prac-

3. Charles Darwin's (1809–1892) theory of evolution was immensely important to Chinese intellectuals during Lu's lifetime and the common coin of much discourse.

4. An early philosophical text, *Guan Zi*, reports that the famous cook Yi Ya boiled his son and served him to his ruler, Duke Huan of Qi (685–643 B.C.E.), because the meat of a human infant was one of the few delicacies the duke had never tasted. Ji and Zhou were the last evil rulers of the Sang (1776–1122 B.C.E.) and Zhou (1122–221 B.C.E.) dynasties. The madman has mixed up some facts here.

ticed cannibalism, all the way from the time when Pan Gu separated heaven and earth down to Yi Ya's son, down to Xu Xilin,[5] and on down to the man they killed in Wolf Cub Village. And just last year when they executed a criminal in town, there was even someone with T.B. who dunked a steamed bread roll in his blood and then licked it off.

"When they decided to eat me, by yourself, of course, you couldn't do much to prevent it, but why did you have to go and *join* them? Cannibals are capable of anything! If they're capable of eating me, then they're capable of eating *you* too! Even within their own group, they think nothing of devouring each other. And yet all they'd have to do is turn back—*change*—and then everything would be fine. Even though people may say, 'It's always been like this,' we can still do our best to improve. And we can start today!

"You're going to tell me it can't be done! Elder Brother, I think you're very likely to say that. When that tenant wanted to reduce his rent the day before yesterday, wasn't it you who said it couldn't be done?"

At first he just stood there with a cold smile, but then his eyes took on a murderous gleam. (I had exposed their innermost secrets.) His whole face had gone pale. Some people were standing outside the front gate. The Venerable Old Zhao and his dog were among them. Stealthily peering this way and that, they began to crowd through the open gate. Some I couldn't make out too well—their faces seemed covered with cloth. Some looked the same as ever—smiling green faces with protruding fangs. I could tell at a glance that they all belonged to the same gang, that they were all cannibals. But at the same time I also realized that they didn't all think the same way. Some thought *it's always been like this* and that they really should eat human flesh. Others knew they shouldn't but went right on doing it anyway, always on the lookout for fear someone might give them away. And since that's exactly what I had just done, I knew they must be furious. But they were all *smiling* at me—cold little smiles!

At this point Elder Brother suddenly took on an ugly look and barked, "Get out of here! All of you! What's so funny about a madman?"

Now I'm on to *another* of their tricks: not only are they unwilling to change, but they're already setting me up for their next cannibalistic feast by labeling me a "madman." That way, they'll be able to eat me without getting into the slightest trouble. Some people will even be grateful to them. Wasn't that the very trick used in the case that the tenant reported? Everybody ganged up on a "bad" man and ate him. It's the same old thing.

Old Fifth Chen came in and made straight for me, looking mad as could be. But he wasn't going to shut *me* up! I was going to tell that bunch of cannibals off, and no two ways about it!

5. From Lu's hometown, Shaoxing (1873–1907). After studies in Japan, he returned to China and served as head of the Anhui Police Academy. When a high Qing official, En Ming, participated in a graduation ceremony at the academy, Xu assassinated him, hoping that this would touch off the revolution. After the assassination, he and some of his students at the academy occupied the police armory and managed, for a while, to hold off En Ming's troops. When Xu was finally captured, En Ming's personal body guards dug out his heart and liver and ate them. Pan Gu (literally, "Coiled-up Antiquity") was born out of an egg. As he stood up, he separated heaven and earth. The world as we know it was formed from his body.

"You can change! You can change from the bottom of your hearts! You ought to know that in the future they're not going to allow cannibalism in the world anymore. If you don't change, you're going to devour each other anyway. And even if a lot of you *are* left, a real human being's going to come along and eradicate the lot of you, just like a hunter getting rid of wolves—or reptiles!"

Old Fifth Chen chased them all out. I don't know where Elder Brother disappeared to. Old Fifth talked me into going back to my room.

It was pitch black inside. The beams and rafters started trembling overhead. They shook for a bit, and then they started getting bigger and bigger. They piled themselves up into a great heap on top of my body!

The weight was incredibly heavy and I couldn't even budge—they were trying to kill me! But I knew their weight was an illusion, and I struggled out from under them, my body bathed in sweat. I was still going to have my say. "Change this minute! Change from the bottom of your hearts! You ought to know that in the future they're not going to allow cannibals in the world anymore . . ."

11

The sun doesn't come out. The door doesn't open. It's two meals a day.

I picked up my chopsticks and that got me thinking about Elder Brother. I realized that the reason for my younger sister's death lay entirely with him. I can see her now—such a lovable and helpless little thing, only five at the time. Mother couldn't stop crying, but *he* urged her to stop, probably because he'd eaten sister's flesh himself and hearing mother cry over her like that shamed him! But if he's still capable of feeling shame, then maybe . . .

Younger Sister was eaten by Elder Brother. I have no way of knowing whether Mother knew about it or not.

I think she *did* know, but while she was crying she didn't say anything about it. She probably thought it was all right, too. I can remember once when I was four or five, I was sitting out in the courtyard taking in a cool breeze when Elder Brother told me that when parents are ill, a son, in order to be counted as a really good person, should slice off a piece of his own flesh, boil it, and let them eat it.[6] At the time Mother didn't come out and say there was anything wrong with that. But if it was all right to eat one piece, then there certainly wouldn't be anything wrong with her eating the whole body. And yet when I think back to the way she cried and cried that day, it's enough to break my heart. It's all strange—very, very strange.

12

Can't think about it anymore. I just realized today that I too have muddled around for a good many years in a place where they've been continually eating people for four thousand years. Younger Sister happened to die at just the time when Elder Brother was in charge of the house. Who's to say he didn't slip some of her meat into the food we ate?

Who's to say I didn't eat a few pieces of my younger sister's flesh without knowing it? And now it's my turn . . .

6. In traditional literature, stories about such gruesome acts of filial piety were not unusual.

Although I wasn't aware of it in the beginning, now that I *know* I'm someone with four thousand years' experience of cannibalism behind me, how hard it is to look real human beings in the eye!

13

Maybe there are some children around who still haven't eaten human flesh. Save the children . . .

1918

Ah Q—The Real Story

Chapter I. An Introduction

For at least a couple of years now, I've had it in the back of my mind to do a biography of Ah Q, but whenever it's come right down to it, I've always had second thoughts. Goes to show I'm not the kind of writer who *Forgeth words of immortalitie / For generations yet to be.*[1] Besides, if you're going to get your words to last all that long, they've got to be about someone worth remembering all that long in the first place. Then the man gets remembered because of the words, and the words because of the man. And then after a while people gradually lose track of which one's remembered because of which. Knowing all of this, why did I finally settle on the likes of Ah Q for a biography? Guess the devil made me do it.

No sooner did I take up my writing brush to begin this very *un*immortal work of mine than I ran into a horrendous host of difficulties.

One. The question of a title. What *kind* of biography was it to be? As Confucius once said, *"Be the title not just so / Then the words refuse to flow."*[2] You really *do* have to be pretty darned careful about titles. But there are so many! Why, just for biographies alone there are enough titles hanging around to make your head swim: *narrative biography, autobiography, private biography, public biography, supplementary biography, family biography, biographical sketch.* Trouble is—not one of them fits.

Narrative biography? That's the kind done for well-heeled people rich enough to make it into the official histories, and Ah Q certainly wouldn't be at home in that crowd. *Autobiography?* But I'm not Ah Q. *Public biography?* Okay then, where's the *private* one? Or, why not just make this one the *private* one? But then *private biography* is the term they use for accounts of Daoist monks who live forever, and Ah Q doesn't fit in with that crew either. *Supplementary biography?* But then there'd have to be a *basic biography* for this to be supplementary to, and the president of our republic has yet to order the National Historical Institute to do the basic one. Still and all, that didn't stop Charles Dickens. You

1. The *Zuo Zhuan*, a historical work dating from the third or fourth century B.C.E., lists three immortal accomplishments of the virtuous man: establishing virtue, establishing civil or military merit, and establishing words.

2. *The Analects of Confucius* 13.3.

won't find any section entitled "Narrative Biographies of Gamblers" in the standard English histories, but he went right ahead and called one of his works *Alternate Biographies of Gamblers* just the same, even though there were no standard ones for them to be alternate to.[3] Well, a literary giant like Dickens might get away with something like that, but I certainly wouldn't be able to pull it off.

How about *family biography*? Yes, but I'm not part of his family, nor has any of his descendants come by to commission me to do it. *Abbreviated biography* won't work either because there's no full one around. When you come right down to it, what I'm writing here is going to be the only standard biography of Ah Q you'll find anywhere. Of course I don't dare forget my place and call it that, for the style is "vulgar" and the language I've cast it in is not the language of the classics but rather the "vile vernacular of mere rickshaw boys and peddlers."[4] And so in the end I've taken my title from a phrase that's popular among the storytellers, those lowly souls who have always been beyond the pale of the Three Doctrines and Nine Schools.[5] Storytellers often end a long digression with the cliché, "Enough of this idle chatter, let's get back to the *real story*." That's where I got my title from. And if "real story" in this context gets mixed up with the "real story" in that book left to us by the ancients, *The Real Story of Calligraphy*—well, sorry, I just don't have the time to worry about all that.[6]

Two. The standard format for biographies requires that you begin with something like: "So-and-so, whose courtesy name was this-or-that, was a native of such-and-such." The trouble is I don't know what Ah Q's family name was. There was once a day when it *seemed* to be Zhao, but then the very next morning it wasn't all that clear anymore. That was the day Old Master Zhao's son passed the *Budding Talent* exam.

With a *clang-clang* of gongs and all the usual pomp, the good news arrived in the village. As luck would have it, Ah Q had just downed a bowl of wine or two. Soon as he heard the news, he danced for joy and told everyone what a great honor this was to him *personally* because he belonged to the same clan as Old Master Zhao. As a matter of fact, the way Ah Q had it worked out, he even came out three notches above the *Budding Talent* in the clan's generational pecking order! The people who were standing around when Ah Q announced this actually began to treat him with more respect too.

Who could have foreseen that the very next day the local sheriff would order Ah Q to hightail it on out to the Zhaos' place? As soon as Old Master Zhao clapped eyes on Ah Q, the old fellow's face flushed scarlet. "Ah Q, you miserable bastard," he bellowed, "did you say you're a clansman of mine?"

3. Lu Xun, as he himself recognized a few years later, is mistaken here. *Alternate Biographies of Gamblers (Botu biezhuan)* is the Chinese title of Sir Arthur Conan Doyle's *Rodney Stone*.

4. A sarcastic reference to Lin Shu (1852–1924). A prolific and respected translator of foreign fiction, Lin always wrote in the literary language.

5. The three doctrines are Confucianism, Buddhism, and Daoism. The nine schools are (1) Confucian, (2) Daoist, (3) Yin-yang, (4) Legalist, (5) School of Names, (6) Mohist, (7) Alliances and Strategies, (8) Miscellaneous Writers, and (9) Agriculturalist.

6. A Qing dynasty (1644–1911) work by Feng Wu. The Chinese expression translated as "real story" *(zheng zhuan)* may be alternately read as *zheng chuan*, meaning "orthodox transmission." Thus the title of Feng Wu's work might be more accurately translated as *Passing On the Correct Way of Doing Calligraphy*.

Ah Q didn't let out a peep. The more the old man looked at him, the madder he got. He bore in a few steps closer: "How dare you talk such rubbish? How could *I* possibly have a clansman like *you*?"

Still not a peep. Just as Ah Q was about to beat a hasty retreat, Old Master Zhao bolted forward and slapped him across the face. "How could *you* be named Zhao? How could you even *deserve* to be named Zhao?"

Instead of offering any argument to prove that he was an honest-to-goodness Zhao, Ah Q simply retreated on out through the gate, putting his hand to his cheek as he went. The sheriff escorted him and gave him another good bawling out once they were outside. Only after Ah Q had greased that notable's palm with two hundred coppers was he free of him. Everybody who heard about this agreed that Ah Q had been too reckless, that he had gone *looking* for a beating, for more than likely he wasn't named Zhao in the first place. And supposing he was? What with Master Zhao living right there in the area, he shouldn't have been dumb enough to say so. After that, nobody ever mentioned Ah Q's family background again. And so—to make a long story short—I have no idea what his family name was.

Three. I don't know how to write his *given* name either. While he was alive everybody called him Ah-QUEI,[7] but after he died, even the man on the street never thought of mentioning his name again. Much less did any scholar-official take it into his head to *inscribe it on bamboo and silk for generations yet to be.*[8] And so it is that I lead the way in facing up to a linguistic crisis: should the QUEI be written with the character meaning "laurel" or with the one meaning "high rank"?

If Ah Q had used the character meaning "moon pavilion" as his courtesy name, or if he had been born in the eighth lunar month, then his given name would certainly be written with the QUEI meaning "laurel."[9] But he didn't *have* a courtesy name. Or if he did, nobody knew it. If only at some point in his career he had sent out invitations soliciting eulogies on the grand occasion of his fiftieth or sixtieth birthday, the way scholar-officials do, then I could check "laurel" against those. But since Ah Q never sent out any such invitations, it would be downright dogmatic of me to insist on "laurel."

Again, if he'd had an elder or younger brother named Ah Fu, written with the *fu* that means "riches," then Ah Q's QUEI would certainly be written with the character meaning "high rank" so as to balance it. But Ah Q was a loner, and so I've got no evidence in favor of the word meaning "high rank" either. I have even less of a case for any of the other relatively obscure characters pronounced "QUEI." I once tried asking Old Master Zhao's son, his nibs the *Budding Talent*.[1] You can imagine my surprise when I ended up drawing a blank from someone as learned and cultivated as Mister *Budding Talent* himself. But the upshot of what little he *did* have to say was that there was no longer any way of telling what character "QUEI" should

7. The "Ah" of Ah Q is a common prefix for given names, especially in south China, and is always written with the same Chinese character.

8. The *locus classicus* for this phrase is a work of the third century B.C.E. entitled *Historical Anecdotes of Mr. Lü* (*Lü shi chun qiu*).

9. The eighth lunar month is also known as the Laurel Month.

1. Here the original text calls him *maocai*. "*Maocai*" was used at one point during the Han Dynasty (206 B.C.E.–220 C.E.) to avoid the given name of an emperor, Liu Xiu.

be, because ever since Chen Duxiu[2] had put out that radical magazine *New Youth* and advocated scrapping the Chinese characters altogether in favor of spelling with a foreign alphabet, our "national heritage" had sunk into utter oblivion.

The only thing I hadn't tried was writing to a certain friend back home. And so I got off a letter to him asking him to look up Ah Q's police record. Didn't get a reply for eight months. When it did come, my friend said he hadn't been able to find any name that sounded even remotely like Ah-QUEI. I still don't know if that was really the case or whether he just hadn't bothered to look it up in the first place. At any rate, I was at a dead end.

I'm afraid the Chinese phonetic symbols[3] aren't all that popular yet, and so I've had to resort to a foreign word to represent the second character in my hero's given name. According to the popular English way of spelling Chinese it would be QUEI, or just "Q" for short.[4] Now I'll grant you this comes perilously close to blindly following *New Youth*—and I am terribly sorry about that—but when even a wise and learned *Budding Talent* doesn't know what character to use, what can you expect from the likes of me?

Four. The question of his native place. If his family name were definitely Zhao then I could follow the custom, so popular in present-day biographical writing, of naming the ancient district from whence his family hailed. That way, basing myself on the standard reference, *The Hundred Surnames and Their Places of Origin*, I could assert with confidence that our Ah Q *doth a Tianshui man of Longxi be*.[5] Trouble is, since it's somewhat doubtful that Zhao was his family name in the first place, how can I assert with any degree of certainty *where* his family came from? Granted, he lived mostly in Wei Village, but he often spent time in other places too. And so if I wrote that Ah Q *doth a Tianshui man of Longxi be*, I'd be downright guilty of violating the hallowed principles of historiography.

There's one thing I do pride myself on: when you take the "Q" away from "Ah Q," you've still got an "Ah" there, and I'm positive I haven't mixed that character up with any other. I could show that one off to anybody, no matter how learned.[6] As to the rest, well, that's beyond the scope of a man of shallow scholarship like myself. I can only hope that the disciples of Mr. Hu Shi,[7] who describes himself

2. Chen Duxiu (1879–1942) began to publish *Youth Magazine* (*Qingnian zazhi*) in 1915; its title was changed to *New Youth* (*Xin Qingnian*) the following year. Beginning in 1918 this influential organ of the New Culture movement was published entirely in the vernacular language. Chen was also one of the founders of the Chinese Communist Party.

3. A set of symbols that was widely used before 1949 to represent the pronunciation of Chinese characters.

4. According to his younger brother, Zhou Zuoren, Lu Xun was intrigued by the letter Q because it resembled a man's head with a queue at the back.

5. *The Hundred Surnames* was a school primer in which common Chinese family names were grouped together into twenty-five rhyming lines of four characters each. The edition mentioned here also had a commentary that gave the name of the ancient administrative district where each family was thought to have originated. Tianshui is a city in present-day Shaanxi Province.

6. Since "Ah" is such a common prefix in given names, this is somewhat like saying, "I may have gotten the 'Smith,' 'Smithe,' or 'Smythe' wrong, but I'm certain I've spelled the 'John' right."

7. A frequent target of Lu Xun's satire, Hu Shi (1891–1962) was the earliest and most influential advocate of abolishing classical Chinese altogether and replacing it with the vernacular language.

as having a "weakness for historical research coupled with an addiction to textual criticism," will be able to ferret out new clues at some time in the future. But by that time I'm afraid my "Ah Q—The Real Story" will have long since passed out of existence.

What I've written up to here may be taken as a preface.

Chapter 2. A Brief Account of His Victories

Not only is there a certain vagueness surrounding Ah Q's given name, family name, and place of origin, but there is also a great deal of uncertainty regarding his "official resumé."[8] Since the people in Wei Village were only interested in Ah Q for his labor—or to serve as the butt of their jokes—they had never paid any attention to what "positions" he had held in the past. Nor did Ah Q himself ever throw any light on his background, except when in the course of a squabble he would occasionally glower at someone and say, "We used to be much richer than you! Who the hell do you think you are anyway?"

Having no family, Ah Q lived at the local Land-and-Grain Temple, and having no fixed occupation, he did odd jobs. When there was wheat to be harvested, he harvested it; when there was rice to be hulled, he did that; and if there was a boat to be poled, he'd turn his hand to that too. When a job lasted a bit longer than the usual, he might temporarily put up at the home of his employer, but once the work was done, he'd move out.

When the busy season came, to be sure, people's minds would turn to Ah Q, but what they would think about was his ability to work and not the particulars of his "resumé." Once the busy season was over they would have forgotten his very *existence*, not to mention the details of his past career. There was only a single instance when anyone had ever praised him, and that was when an old man had said, "That Ah Q's *some* worker!" Bare-chested at the time and standing right in front of the old man, Ah Q looked so scrawny and worn-out that one couldn't tell whether the old fellow had really meant it or was simply making fun of him. Nonetheless, Ah Q had been pleased as punch.

Since he thought so well of *himself*, Ah Q considered the other villagers simply beneath his notice. He went so far with this that he even looked down his nose at the village's two *Young Literati*.[9] He didn't realize, of course, that up there in the rarefied world of scholar-officialdom *those whom one doth Young Literati name* can darn well get to be *those whom one must Budding Talents proclaim*—if you don't keep an eye on them. That's why Old Master Qian and Old Master Zhao were so all-fired respected in the village: they were daddies to those two *Young Literati*—and rich to boot. Ah Q, however, was less than impressed. "My son's gonna be a lot richer." On top of that, Ah Q had been to town a couple of times and that made him even more full of himself. Yet he could

8. *Xingzhuang*, translated here as "resumé," actually refers to the posthumous account of a deceased official's career put together by his relatives.

9. *Wentong*, translated here as "literati," referred specifically to young men in preparation for the *Budding Talent* examination.

be contemptuous of townsfolk too. For instance, Wei Villagers called a seat made from a three-foot plank a *longbench* and so did Ah Q, but the townsfolk called it a *stickbench*. "That's not right, that's flatass dumb!" he thought to himself. And how about fish? When frying bigheads, Wei Villagers would toss chopped scallions into the pan, but the townsfolk always used *shredded* ones. "That's not right, that's flatass stupid!" he thought to himself. "On the other hand, I gotta remember that next to me, Wei Villagers are just a bunch of hicks. They've never even *seen* how bigheads are fried in town."

So Ah Q used to be rich, had seen a thing or two, and was "some" worker—in sum, he came very close to being the perfect man. Unfortunately, however, he had a few physical shortcomings, the most annoying of which was an assortment of shiny scars that had been left on his scalp by an attack of scabies. Despite the undeniable fact that those scars had the good fortune to be attached to Ah Q's body, strange to say, he didn't seem to think them particularly worth bragging about. And so it was that he shunned the word "scabies" and any other word sounding even remotely like it.

He later expanded the scope of this taboo until it included words like "bright" and "shiny" and—still later—even "lamp" and "candle." Whether it was intentional or not, if anyone should violate this taboo, Ah Q would seethe with anger until every last one of his scabies scars would flush its deepest red. Then he would size up his opponent: if it happened to be someone who stuttered so badly that he couldn't get the second word out after the first, Ah Q would curse him up one side and down the other; if it was someone so puny and weak that he could hardly stand, Ah Q would start a fight. And yet, strange to tell, in all such encounters Ah Q somehow still managed to come out the loser more often than not. After some time, he modified his plan of battle and for the most part simply gave his opponent a dirty look.

Who would have expected that after Ah Q adopted his policy of dirtylookism, the Wei Village idlers would take even greater pleasure in taunting him? As soon as they set eyes on him, they would draw back in feigned surprise and say, "Hey, it's getting lighter out!"

As usual, Ah Q would start to go into a slow boil.

"Oh, so that's it, there's a kerosene lamp here—no wonder!" They weren't about to be intimidated by any dirty look from the likes of Ah Q.

Since a dirty look didn't seem to do it, he would try a snappy comeback: "Why you guys don't even deserve to gaze on . . ." At this point it usually seemed as if those whatchamacallits up there on his head had been transformed into grand and glorious *Scars de Scabie*, not at all to be confused with the ordinary variety. But as I have said before, our Ah Q was a man of keen insight, and therefore he would realize immediately that he was on the verge of violating his own taboo and would catch himself up in midsentence.

Not content to let it go at that, the Wei Village idlers would keep right on baiting him until it all ended up in a fight anyway. From a purely formal point of view, Ah Q would be defeated: he would be grabbed by his discolored queue, and would have his head given four or five resounding thumps against a wall. Then the idlers would walk away, fully satisfied and fully victorious. Ah Q would stand there for a bit and then think to himself, "It's just as though I'd been beaten up by my own sons! What's the world coming to, anyway, when sons . . ." At this point Ah Q too would walk away, fully satisfied and fully victorious.[1]

Later on Ah Q took to saying out loud the various things he thought to himself. And so it was that before long every Ah-Q-baiter in the village was onto his schemes for winning psychological victories. From then on, whenever Ah Q's discolored queue was grabbed, his tormentor would steal a march on him as well: "Ah Q, this isn't a son beatin' up on his old man, it's a human being beatin' up on an *animal!* Let's hear *you* say it now, 'A human being beatin' up on an animal'!"

Holding fast to the base of his queue with both hands, Ali Q would cock his head to one side and rejoin: "Beatin' up on a *bug*, does that make you happy? Now give a guy a break, huh?"

But even though he was only a "bug," the idlers still wouldn't let him off the hook. In the time-honored fashion, they would seek out the nearest wall and give his head four or five resounding thumps before walking away, fully satisfied and fully victorious—and convinced that *this* time they had done him in once and for all. But before ten seconds were out, Ah Q would also walk away, fully satisfied and fully victorious, for he was convinced that of all the "self-putdown artists" this old world has seen, he was number one. Take away "self-putdown artist" and what did you have left? *Number one*—that's what! What was a *Metropolitan Graduate*?[2] *Number one*—that's all. "Who the hell do these jerks think they are anyway!" Having subdued his foes with such ingenious strategems, Ah Q would go happily off to the wineshop and down a few bowls. He would banter with some, squabble with others, and then on the crest of fresh victories, would make his way happily back to the Land-and-Grain Temple, put his head down on his pillow, and go to sleep.

If he happened to have money, he'd go and play a round of *Pickaside*.[3] As people crowded around the gambling stand, Ah Q would sandwich his way in among them, his face bathed in sweat. Of all the voices his would be the loudest.

"Four hundred on *Green Dragon!*"

"Oh-kay, off with the cover and let's see which side has turned up!" His face bathed in sweat, the stakeholder would take off the cover. "*Heaven's Gate* gets the money! *In-the-Corner* splits even! Nobody on *White Tiger* or *Through-the-Hall!* Pass Ah Q's dough over here!"

"One hundred on *Through-the-Hall*—make it a hundred and fifty!"

In the midst of the stakeholder's incantations, Ah Q's money would gradually make its way into the pockets of other people whose faces, like his own, were also bathed in sweat. Finally Ah Q would have to squeeze his way back through the crowd and stand on the sidelines, now reduced to becoming excited or disappointed on someone else's behalf. He would continue to watch until the

1. Contemporary readers saw Ah Q as representing China in miniature: continually humiliated by the imperialist powers, China had gained "psychological victories" by boasting about the superiority of her ancient civilization.

2. "Metropolitan Graduate" was a title given to the examinee who had, in effect, the highest "pass" of all those who had competed for the *Advanced Scholar* degree.

3. The *Pickaside* stakeholder would set up a square gambling stand with four sides.

game broke up and then reluctantly make his way back to the Land-and-Grain Temple. Next day, with swollen eyes, Ah Q would go to work.

It is true, however, that losing can sometimes be a blessing in disguise, for once when Ah Q *did* actually win, he came very close to losing.

It was on a night when Wei Village was holding a festival of thanksgiving to the gods. As usual, a religious opera was performed. As usual again, a number of gambling stands were set up close to the stage. So as far as Ah Q was concerned, the orchestra's crashing cymbals and pounding drums might just as well have been miles away, for he heard nothing but the singsong chant of the stake-holder. Ah Q won! He won again! And then again he won some more! Copper pennies turned into silver dollars, and the dollars piled up into a tall stack. Ah Q was beside himself. "Two dollars on *Heaven's Gate!*"

He never found out who started the fight or why, but at any rate he suddenly found himself buried under a pandemonium of curses, blows, and kicks. No sooner had he struggled to his feet than he discovered that the gambling stand was gone, and the people who had been surrounding it were nowhere to be seen. His body seemed to hurt in a couple of spots, as though he too had taken a few punches and kicks. One or two people looked at him in surprise. Looking somewhat lost, he made his way back to the Land-and-Grain Temple. After collecting himself a bit, he realized that his pile of silver dollars had disappeared. Since most people who set up gambling stands at festivals like this didn't come from the village themselves, there was no possible way of ever finding out what actually had happened.

What a bright and glittering pile of dollars that had been, too. And now they were gone. Gone! He tried to write the whole thing off by telling himself that he'd been robbed by his own sons, but somehow or other he still felt disappointed and depressed. Then he considered dismissing it by calling himself a bug, but somehow or other that left him feeling just as depressed and disappointed as ever. For the first time in Ah Q's life, he tasted something like the real bitterness of defeat.

But then, in the twinkling of an eye, he transformed that defeat into victory! He raised his right hand and, one after the other, gave himself two sharp slaps across the mouth. His face burned with a prickly pain. After those slaps, however, he began to feel at peace with himself. It was as though Ah Q had done the slapping and the person he had slapped was some *other* Ah Q. And before too long it actually seemed as though he had slapped someone else altogether—though he had to admit that his own face still stung a bit. Complacent and content, Ah Q now lay down—victorious.

He slept.

Chapter 3. A Brief Account of His Victories (cont.)

Although Ah Q was indeed often victorious, it wasn't until he had been graced with a slap across the mouth from Old Master Zhao—for his temerity in laying claim to the Zhao family name—that he finally became famous.

That day, after he had greased the sheriff's palm to the tune of two hundred coppers, Ah Q went home and lay down fuming with anger. But before very long, he began to think, "What's the world coming to when a son strikes his own father?" And then his thoughts turned another corner as he considered the great prestige that Old Master Zhao enjoyed in the village. Gradually Ah Q began feeling quite pleased with himself that such a prestigious man was now his son. He got up and headed off to the wineshop, singing the strains of *The Young Widow Visits Her Husband's Grave* as he went.[4] At this juncture, Ah Q truly felt that Old Master Zhao really *was* a cut above everyone else.

Strange to tell, after the slapping incident everyone did in fact seem to treat Ah Q with unusual respect. The way Ah Q saw it, this was probably because he was Old Master Zhao's father. But if the truth be known, that wasn't it at all. Instead it was the result of a Wei Village precedent that ran something like this: if Ah-seven slugged Ah-eight, or if Li-four clobbered Zhang-three, no one thought anything of it.[5] But if such an incident was connected to some eminent personage like his nibs Old Master Zhao, then it would be permanently recorded on the lips of the people. And after that, because the man who had done the striking was already famous, the man who had been hit would ride to renown on his coattails.

It goes without saying, of course, that everyone laid the blame for the incident on Ah Q. Now, here one might be tempted to ask, *"Pray tell wherein lieth the why and the wherefore of that?"* Simple. His nibs Old Master Zhao *couldn't* be wrong! But if Ah Q *was* the one at fault, then why should everyone treat him with such respect? Well, that's a tough one. A rough answer might go something like this: though it's true that Ah Q got slapped for claiming to be a clansman of Old Master Zhao, who's to say that there might not be some truth to it? On the off chance that there was, it would still be prudent to treat Ah Q with respect. Or perhaps it may have been related to the example of the Sacrificial Ox in the Confucian Temple. Although the ox is just as much a domestic animal as the pig or sheep, Confucian scholars would not dare commit the blasphemy of eating its meat once the spirit of Confucius had set his chopsticks to it during the sacrifice. And in point of fact, for several years after the slapping incident things went swimmingly for Ah Q.

In the spring of one year, a pleasantly inebriated Ah Q was walking down the street when he chanced upon Bearded Wang. Chest bared, Wang sat in the sunlight at the base of a wall, picking lice out of his jacket. Ah Q suddenly became aware of an itching sensation on his own body too. Now this Bearded Wang was not only bearded, but boasted a set of scabies scars as well, and so everyone else called him *Scabby* Bearded Wang. Ah Q, on the other hand, edited out the "scabby" but disdained the man completely nonetheless. It wasn't that Ah Q saw anything all that unusual in being scabby, but that beard of Wang's was going just a bit too far—what an eyesore! But now Ah Q sat down right next to him. Had it been any other villager, he wouldn't have been so bold, but what did he have to fear from the likes of Bearded Wang? As a matter of fact, he was doing Bearded Wang an honor by being willing to sit down with him in the first place.

4. A Shaoxing opera that was popular at the time this story was written.
5. These are, of course, Chinese equivalents for such expressions as Tom, Dick, and Harry; or John Smith and Jane Doe.

Ah Q peeled off his raggedy old jacket and turned it inside out. But a prolonged search yielded—perhaps because the jacket had recently been washed, or perhaps because Ah Q didn't look carefully enough—only three or four lice. He looked over and saw that Bearded Wang was picking them out one after the other and sometimes even two or three at a time. What's more, those lice kept going *pow pow pow*, as loud as you please, when Bearded Wang popped them between his teeth.

At first Ah Q felt merely disappointed, but after a while he began to resent the downright injustice of it all—to think that even the low-life likes of Bearded Wang could come up with all those nice lice while he, on the other hand, could find only a paltry few. Why it was nothing short of a social disgrace! How he longed to find a couple of good big ones. But he simply couldn't. It was all he could do to come up with even one *medium* louse. He angrily thrust that one between his teeth and bit down with all his might—only a piddling little *pop*, nothing to compare with Bearded Wang's loud and lusty *pows*. Now every last scabies scar on Ah Q's head flushed scarlet. He hurled his jacket to the ground and spat with disgust. "Hairy beast!"

"Who are you cursin' out, you mangy dog?" Bearded Wang raised his eyes and gave Ah Q a contemptuous glance.

Although people had treated Ah Q a bit more respectfully of late, making him more full of himself than ever, still he was always cautious in the presence of the Wei Village idlers, all of whom would just as soon fight as have breakfast. In fact this was the first time he had dared to put on such a martial display before one of them. Did this hairy-faced beast actually have the gall to use intemperate language within Ah Q's hearing?

"If the shoe fits!" Ah Q got up and put his hands on his waist.

"Are your bones itchin' for a good trouncin'?" Bearded Wang stood up and threw his jacket across his shoulders.

Thinking that Bearded Wang was getting ready to make a run for it, Ah Q sprang forward and threw a punch. But before his fist had reached its mark, Bearded Wang grabbed it and gave it such a yank that Ah Q went stumbling forward completely off balance. At the same time, with his free hand, Bearded Wang grabbed Ah Q's queue, twisted it fast, and prepared to drag him over to the wall and smack his head against it in the time-honored fashion.

"His fists need never be swung, for the gentleman useth his tongue," quoted Ah Q, head cocked to one side.

It would appear, however, that Bearded Wang was no gentleman, for ignoring this classical lore, he slammed Ah Q's head against the wall five times in succession, and then gave him a good hard shove that sent Ah Q staggering away, fighting to regain his balance. Thoroughly satisfied then, Bearded Wang strode away.[6]

In Ah Q's memory, this could probably be reckoned as the first real disgrace of an entire lifetime, for Bearded Wang—flawed by a beard growing rampant all over his face—had always been the object of Ah Q's taunts, and had cer-

6. Some contemporary readers drew an analogy between this encounter and the Sino-Japanese War of 1894. China had been accustomed to looking down on Japan as a cultural stepchild and was rudely surprised when a modernized Japan defeated China quite handily.

tainly never before made light of Ah Q, much less dared to lay hands on him. Thus the event that had just transpired was something totally unexpected. Could it possibly be true, as people were saying in town, that the emperor had put an end to the civil service examinations and did not need *Budding Talents* anymore? Could it be that the Zhao family's prestige had consequently declined and that people now felt free to look down on Ah Q as a result?[7]

Thrown for a loss, Ah Q just stood there.

Out of the distance, someone else was coming toward him—another enemy had arrived. This too was one of the people whom Ah Q most detested, the son of Old Master Qian. Some time back, this lad had gone off to town and attended one of those new fangled academies where they taught foreign things along with Chinese subjects. After that, somehow or other, he'd sailed off to Japan. By the time he came back half a year later he was walking stiff-legged, just the way foreigners do, and his queue was gone! That was enough to send his mother into a good dozen fits of wailing and his dear wife had thrice tried to drown herself in the well. Later on his mother went around saying: "Some hoodlums got him drunk and cut it off. He could have been an important official, but now we can't make any plans until it grows back again." Ah Q, however, did not buy a word of it and made a point of calling him "fake foreign devil" or "foreign sellout," cursing him under his breath the moment he set eyes on him.

But the thing that Ah Q, in the tradition of all the doughty heroes of yore, did *shunneth full well and righteously repel* was that fake queue. To have a queue and sink so low as to let it be a *fake* one was clear proof that the man had lost all claim to humanity, and since that wife of his hadn't taken a fourth dive into the well, she obviously couldn't be a good woman either.

This Fake Foreign Devil came closer.

"Baldy! Jackass!" Now, previously Ah Q had always said that kind of thing under his breath, but today after his defeat at the hands of Bearded Wang, he was seething with fury and hungry for revenge. Lightly, yet quite audibly, the words escaped his lips before even *he* knew they were out.

To Ah Q's surprise, "Baldy" started moving directly toward him, a yellow-lacquered cane—what Ah Q called a *wailing stick*—in his hand.[8] In that split second Ah Q realized he was probably in for a drubbing. Pulling his head down between his shoulders, he braced himself for the worst. *WHACK!* Sure enough, there was the right sound, and it felt as though a blow had landed on his head, too. Ah Q pointed to a child nearby and offered defensively, "I was talking about *him!*"

WHACK! WHACK-WHACK!

In Ah Q's memory, this could probably be reckoned as the *second* real disgrace of an entire lifetime. Fortunately, however, by the time the whacking

7. In one of the most drastic moves of modern Chinese history, the Manchu government announced the abolition of the civil service examinations in 1905. The examination system had existed in some form ever since 136 B.C.E. All through that long period, knowledge of the classics had provided virtually the only access to the Confucian ladder of success. Now that ladder was gone.

8. Young foreign gentlemen of the time often carried canes, and young Chinese who had studied abroad often emulated them even after returning home. The "wailing stick" (*kusang bang*) had been traditionally carried by filial sons in funeral processions; the idea it represented was that the son was so overwhelmed with grief he would have been otherwise unable to walk.

sounds had subsided, he had begun to feel somewhat relaxed. It was rather as if he'd just completed some pressing task that had to be done. What was more, "forgetfulness"—that priceless medicine handed down to us by our ancestors—began to take its effect too. He headed away toward the wineshop and by the time he drew near the door he had long since begun to feel quite happy again.

But walking straight toward him was a young Buddhist nun from the Convent of Silent Cultivation. Even in ordinary times, Ah Q would always have spit whenever he ran across a nun and now, having just been humiliated, he had all the more reason. At this point he began to think back over his day and once again began itching for revenge. He walked straight toward her and spat on the ground.

"*Aaaaaaawk . . . tuh!*"

Doing her best to ignore him, the young nun lowered her head and kept on her way. Ah Q fell in step beside her. Suddenly he reached over and fondled the skin of her shaved head. "Hey Baldy, better hurry on back—your monk's waitin' for ya," he said with an inane smile.

"What's gotten into you? Get your filthy paws off me!" Her face flushing scarlet, the nun hurried onward.

The patrons of the wineshop roared with laughter. Seeing that his meritorious service to the court had gained such great favor with these tippling nobles, Ah Q felt his spirits soar ever higher. "If the monk can fondle you, then why can't I?" He pinched her cheek between his thumb and forefinger.

Once again the patrons of the wineshop roared with laughter, and Ah Q was even more elated. Then, so as to fully satisfy these courtly connoisseurs of his martial performance, he gave the nun's cheek a final pinch before letting her go.

Because of this encounter with the nun, Ah Q had long since forgotten Bearded Wang and the Fake Foreign Devil as well. It was as if he'd avenged himself for all the bad luck he'd had that day. Strange to tell, his whole body seemed to feel relaxed, too, even more relaxed than after the echoes of the Fake Foreign Devil's *WHACK! WHACK-WHACK!* had died away. Walking on air, Ah Q seemed ready to take off and soar away at any minute.

"May you never have a son, Ah Q!" He heard the sound of the nun's sobbing voice in the distance.

"Hah, hah, hah!" One hundred percent elated, Ah Q laughed.

"Hah, hah!" Ninety percent elated, the patrons of the wineshop laughed too.

Chapter 4. The Tragedy of Love

It has long been noted that some conquerors prefer enemies as fierce as tigers and brave as eagles, for only then can they savor the true joy of victory. If, on the other hand, their foes are as tame as sheep or timid as chickens, then they find no pleasure in their triumph.

Then too, you have the conqueror who overcomes all opposition, sees his enemies die or surrender, and finally reports his victory back to the throne: "*In fear and trembling; thy servant draws his breath, who, in addressing you, deser-*

veth only death."[9] Such a conqueror has no enemies, no rivals, and no friends—he has nothing left except himself, standing there in utter isolation at the very apex of his triumph, lonely and forlorn. At such a time the hero experiences not the joy of victory, but rather its poignant melancholy.

Rest assured, dear reader, that our Ah Q was not so feckless as any of the above. No, he was *always* full of himself. Perhaps we have here yet another proof that the spiritual civilization of China is superior to any other on the face of the earth.

Why just look at him! Tripping along on air like that, he might well soar skyward and fly away at any moment!

And yet there was something about this *particular* victory that made Ah Q feel somehow—different. After tripping along on air for quite some time, he finally floated back to the Land-and-Grain Temple. Now ordinarily at this point he would have flopped down and begun to snore. Who would have thought that tonight he wouldn't even be able to get his eyes shut? There was something very strange—he could feel it—going on in the index finger and thumb of one hand. Could it be that there was something soft and smooth on that young nun's face that had somehow rubbed off on them? Or could it be that he had somehow rubbed his finger and thumb smooth on her face?

"May you never have a son, Ah Q!"

The nun's curse echoed in his ears again and set Ah Q to thinking, "That's right, oughta have a woman! If I die with no son, who's gonna sacrifice a bowl of rice now and then for my ghost to eat? Yeah, gotta get me a woman!"

Now bear in mind, gentle reader, *Of three things which do unfilial be / The worst is to lack posteritie.*[1] And then too, if you also remember how the classics tell of the exemplary concern of Ziwen, in those days of yore, lest *the ghosts of the Ruo'ao clan go hungry, woman and man*—a great human tragedy, indeed!—then you'll see right off quick that Ah Q's thinking was, as a matter of fact, thoroughly in accord with the sagacious morality of our classical tradition.[2] Unfortunately, however, after his thoughts started galloping off in this direction, Ah Q *completely lacked the art to rein in his unbridled heart.*[3]

"Woman, woman!" Ah Q thought to himself.

And then Ah Q thought to himself again, ". . . if the monk can fondle you . . . woman . . . woman!"

There is no way of telling when it was that Ah Q finally began to snore that night. What is certain, however, is that from that time forward his index finger and

9. "Deserving only death" in that he has taken the liberty of addressing the throne directly. This stock phrase is an example of the exaggerated politeness that was the norm in framing memorials to the emperor.

1. The other two are following parents' orders when one knows that such a course will sink them into unrighteousness and refusing to become an official when one's parents are old and poor.

2. The story of Ruo'ao Ziwen is recorded under the fourth year of Duke Xuan (604 B.C.E.) in the historical classic *Zuo Zhuan*; see n. 1, p. 249 above. Observing the inauspicious countenance of his younger brother's baby son, Ziwen exhorted the father to kill the boy lest he bring down destruction on the entire clan. The father did not heed his elder brother's advice, and when the boy grew up he fulfilled his uncle's prophecy, so that, with no posterity to sacrifice to them, *the ghosts of the Ruo'ao'clan* did in fact end up going hungry.

3. Based on a passage in the Bi Ming chapter of the *History Classic*, an ancient anthology (author unknown).

thumb always had a certain smooth feel to them, and so it was that from that time forward, too, he was always walking on air. "Woman!!!" Ah Q thought to himself.

From this instance alone, you can see what baleful creatures women be. Now by rights most Chinese men could have become saints or sages a long time back—trouble is, they were all done in by women. The Shang dynasty [1766–1122 B.C.E.] was brought down by the enticing Da Ji, and the captivating Bao Si destroyed the Zhou [1122–221 B.C.E.][4] As for the Qin dynasty [221–206 B.C.E.], though we can't find any clear statement as to exactly what happened, we probably wouldn't be one hundred percent wrong if we assumed that a female had put that one on the skids, too. And we know for an undeniable fact that it was because of the singsong girl Diao Chan that Dong Zhuo [d. 192 C.E.] was killed.[5]

Now our Ah Q started out as an upright man too. Though we don't know if this was because he had been shown the way by some enlightened teacher, we do know that he rigorously observed *the great barrier that should be 'twixt the he and the she* and was well endowed with a sense of moral uprightness that made him despise heretical behavior such as that of the young nun or the Fake Foreign Devil.[6] Ah Q's philosophy ran like this: Any nun is bound to be secretly shacked up with a monk. If a woman is out walking on the street, she's certainly trying to seduce a man or two. If a man and woman are talking to each other, they're sure to be arranging a tryst. He often employed his dirtylookism to punish such miscreants. Occasionally he would voice a loud comment to show that *he* knew what a couple was "really up to," no matter how innocent their behavior might seem on the surface. And occasionally—if the place was isolated—he'd throw a pebble at them from behind.

Who could possibly have foreseen that just as he was approaching the age when, like Confucius, he should have "stood firm,"[7] Ah Q would be so subverted by a young Buddhist nun that he would go around walking on air. Now according to the tenets of Confucian morality, the kinds of feelings engendered by airwalking are *not* the kinds of feelings one should have in the first place. So we can readily see what utterly despicable creatures females really are. If the young nun's face had not been so smooth, Ah Q would not have fallen, or had there been a veil between her face and his fingers, things would never have gone so far either. As a matter of fact, five or six years back he'd even pinched a girl's thigh once while watching an opera, but in that case her trousers had separated his fingers from her skin, so that the experience had not been enough to set him

4. The women mentioned here were concubines to the last rulers of their respective dynastic periods. According to the paternalistic views of traditional Chinese historiography, they beguiled their royal consorts into debauchery and ruin.

5. During the decline of the Han (206 B.C.E.–220 C.E.), Wang Yun (a minister of the dynasty) presented the singsong girl Diao Chan to a subordinate of Dong Zhuo (a contemporary warlord). Later the crafty Wang spirited the girl away and presented her to Dong Zhuo himself. He then told the subordinate that Dong had taken her by force. As Wang had anticipated, the subordinate then assassinated the much-despised minister.

6. According to the puritanical ethics of traditional Confucian morality, any contact between an unrelated man and woman was potentially, if not actually, immoral. A popular proverb decreed that "a man and woman, unless related, should not touch hands when giving or receiving things" (*nan nü shoushou buqin*).

7. In a well-known passage of the *Analects* Confucius says, "At thirty, I stood firm."

airwalking afterwards. In the case of the young nun, however, things had been entirely different. Goes to show you what a detestable and heretical doctrine Buddhism really is, too.

"Woman!" thought Ah Q.

He constantly kept an eye out for women who were "trying to seduce a man or two," but none of them so much as smiled at him. Whenever a woman talked with him, Ah Q kept a close ear to everything that was said but still he heard nothing that was even vaguely related to "having an affair." Why of course! That's partly what made women so rotten in the first place—the hypocrites all *pretended* to be straight!

After supper one evening, Ah Q sat in Old Master Zhao's kitchen having a leisurely smoke on his pipe. He had just put in a full day of hulling rice. If it had been at anyone else's place, he would have gone right home after supper, but here the situation was somewhat different. Ordinarily the Zhao family ate quite early, for it was an established item of family protocol that no one was allowed to waste good money lighting a lamp. People simply went straight to bed after supper. There were, however, certain exceptions to the rule: Old Master Zhao's young hopeful had been permitted to burn the midnight oil while preparing for his *Budding Talent* exam, and Ah Q was allowed to hull rice by lamplight whenever he came to help out during the busy season. Indeed, that's why he could not afford to sit and dawdle over his pipe like this.

Having finished the dishes, Amah Wu, the one and only maid in Old Master Zhao's household, sat down on the *longbench* next to Ah Q and began to chat. "The Old Missus hasn't eaten a thing for days now. It's all because the Old Master's going to buy a concubine."

"Woman . . . Amah Wu . . . this nice young widow," Ah Q thought to himself.

"Our Young Missus is going to have a baby in August and . . ."

"WOMAN," thought Ah Q to himself. He put down his pipe and stood up.

". . . the Young Missus says . . ." Amah Wu prattled on.

Now Ah Q moved directly in front of her and knelt at her feet. "Sleep with me! Sleep with me!"

For a brief instant you could have heard a pin drop.

"AIYA!!!" Amah Wu had been stunned speechless at first. And then quite suddenly, she had begun to tremble, and then she had let out that big aiya-scream. Now she bolted for the door and ran outside, screaming as she went. It sounded as if she was crying, too.

Ah Q found himself kneeling before a blank wall. He too was stunned for a moment. Placing his hands on the *longbench*, he slowly dragged himself to his feet, barely conscious that he'd probably gotten himself into some kind of mess. Heart pounding, he hastily thrust his pipe into his belt and made ready to go back to his hulling when *BONG!* a good solid blow landed on his head. He turned and saw the young *Budding Talent* standing before him, a heavy staff in hand.

"Rebellious wretch, why you . . ."

The heavy pole clove the air again. Ah Q grabbed the top of his head with both hands. *WHACK!* The blow landed on his knuckles and hurt more than a little. As he burst through the kitchen door, he seemed to feel yet another hard blow land on his back.

"Turtle's egg!" the *Budding Talent* cursed from behind.[8]

Ah Q ran to the hulling shed as fast as his legs would carry him. He stood there alone. Pain lingered in his fingers, and the expression "turtle's egg" in his mind, for that was one locution that the countryfolk of Wei Village never used. Only rich people who rubbed noses with officials said fancy things like that, and thus it made a deep impression on Ah Q and gave him quite a fright to boot. By now, all those "woman" thoughts had left him. What was more, having taken a good cursing and beating, he felt as though he had actually accomplished something, gotten it over and done with. And so before long, without a care in the world, Ah Q set himself to hulling rice again. He worked up a sweat and paused to strip down.

While taking off his shirt, Ah Q heard a loud commotion somewhere outside. Now Ah Q had never liked anything better than a bit of excitement, and so without a second thought he headed off in the direction of the noise. Little by little, the sounds led him to the inner courtyard outside Old Master Zhao's rooms. Although it was dusk, Ah Q was able to make out several of the people: Old Master Zhao's wife—the one who hadn't eaten for two days in a row—Seventh Sister Zou from next door, and two honest-to-goodness Zhao clansmen, Zhao Baiyan and Zhao Sichen.

The Young Missus was leading Amah Wu out of the servants' quarters. "Come on outside. Don't hole up in your room and brood like that."

"Everyone knows what a virtuous woman you are. Don't go looking on the short side of things, no matter what!" said Seventh Sister Zou from the sidelines.[9]

Amah Wu went right on with her wailing. She sandwiched in some words too, but they weren't all that easy to make out. "Now that's interesting," thought Ah Q. "Wonder what kind of tricks this Young Widow's been up to anyway?" He moved in closer and stood next to Zhao Sichen to find out what was going on.

Suddenly Ah Q caught sight of the *Budding Talent* bearing down on him. What's more, there was a large bamboo pole in his hands. As Ah Q looked at the pole, it suddenly occurred to him that he had recently been whacked with just such a pole, and that the commotion in progress somehow or other seemed to have something to do with him personally. Ah Q turned, intending to hightail it back to the hulling shed, but found himself cut off by the pole. He backtracked, went the other way, and made it safely out the rear gate. Before long he was back inside the Land-and-Grain Temple.

After Ah Q had sat there for a while, his skin started to break out in goosebumps—he was cold. Though it was spring, the nights were still quite chilly and it was certainly no time to be going around bare-chested. Now he remembered, he had left his cotton jacket back at the Zhaos' place. Fear of the *Budding Talent*'s bamboo pole, however, kept him from going to get the jacket. At this impasse, the sheriff entered.

"You motherfucker, Ah Q! Even tryin' to make out with the Zhao servants. You're a rebel, pure and simple! You've screwed up my sleep too, mother!" On

8. Cuckolds were called turtles, and thus "turtle's egg" comes close to "S.O.B." in English.

9. Seventh Sister Zou is afraid Amah Wu will commit suicide.

and on in this vein, the sheriff gave Ah Q a good tongue-lashing, and there was, of course, no reasonable defense that Ah Q could offer. Toward the end of this harangue, the sheriff demanded a four-dollar tip (twice the usual amount because he had been forced to come out at night). Since Ah Q had no ready cash, the sheriff took his old felt hat as security. Then he laid down the law:

(1) Ah Q was to take a pair of candles (one catty apiece) along with a packet of incense to the Zhao residence and apologize.

(2) The Zhao family was to hire Daoist priests to exorcise the ghosts of people who had hanged themselves—cost to be borne by Ah Q.

(3) Henceforth Ah Q was never to darken the Zhao family's door again.

(4) Should anything at all *ever* befall Amah Wu, Ah Q would be held responsible.

(5) Ah Q would not be allowed to ask the Zhao family for his back wages or his jacket.

Ah Q, of course, agreed to all these conditions—trouble was he didn't have the money to make good on them. Fortunately, since it was already spring, he didn't need his cotton quilt all that much anymore, and so he hocked it for two thousand coppers so as to fulfill the five conditions.

After a bare-chested Ah Q had kowtowed his apology to the Zhaos, he even had a few coppers left over. But instead of redeeming his felt hat, he simply bought some wine and drank them up. The Zhao family didn't actually light the candles or burn the incense he had bought either, but since the Old Missus could make good use of them when she worshipped Buddha, they kept them all the same. The best part of Ah Q's raggedy old jacket went into making diapers for the baby born to the Young Missus in August. The rest of it was converted into liners for Amah Wu's shoes.

Chapter 5. The Problem of Livelihood

Having complied with the five conditions laid down by the sheriff, Ah Q went back to the Land-and-Grain Temple just as he always did. But after the sun went down that night, he gradually became aware that something was not quite right in this world of his. He wracked his brains for a good long while and then finally figured it out: the reason for his not-quite-right feeling probably had something to do with his being bare-chested. Remembering that he still had a tattered old winter jacket, he threw that across his shoulders and lay down. When he opened his eyes again, the rays of the rising sun were already falling on top of the west wall. He sat up straight and declared, "Shit!"

After rising, he went out and wandered around the streets just as he always did. Although this time it wasn't any physical discomfort that bothered him—as had his bare-chested state the previous night—once again Ah Q began to feel that there was something not quite right in this world of his, for it seemed that from this day forward all the women of Wei Village began turning shy on him. As soon as they saw Ah Q approaching, they'd scurry into their houses. Even Seventh Sister Zou, who was fast approaching fifty, scurried inside like all the others and called her eleven-year-old daughter inside after her. Ah Q was puzzled. "The bitches have started actin' like high-class young ladies all of a sudden—sluts!" But it wasn't until several days later that this not-quite-right feeling took on a critical intensity. First off, the wineshop wouldn't extend him any more credit. In the second place, the old man who took care of the temple started running off at the mouth with the obvious intention of running him off. In the third place, it had been quite some time—though he couldn't remember exactly how long—since anyone had asked Ah Q to do any odd jobs. No credit at the wineshop? He could deal with that. And so what if the caretaker did try to run him off? He could handle that one too. But if no one gave him any work to do, his stomach would be empty in short order and that would truly constitute an extraordinarily "shitty" state of affairs.

At the end of his rope, he went to hunt up the people who used to hire him to see what was going on. Of course the one place he couldn't go was to the Zhaos' house, because he'd been enjoined never to darken their door again. But it turned out that even at his former employers' places the situation had changed radically too. Everywhere he went, a man would walk out looking quite put out at his intrusion and shoo him away like a beggar. "We don't have anything for you. Now scram!"

At this point Ah Q was more confused than ever. "Always used to be that these folks couldn't do without me," he thought to himself. "Doesn't make any sense that they just don't have any more work all of a sudden. There's gotta be more to this than meets the eye." Only after carefully asking around did he discover that *now* whenever people had any work, they all went to a certain Young Don.[1] Now in Ah Q's eyes, this Young D was a miserable little critter, all skinny and weak as could be. Why he was even lower than Bearded Wang! Who would ever have dreamt that a young nobody like that would actually do him out of his ricebowl?

In light of all the above, Ah Q's present fury was not to be compared with any of his ordinary rages. As he walked along, seething with resentment, Ah Q suddenly raised a fist and belted out a line of local opera: *"My mace of steel I grasp full tight / And with it I shall now thee smite!"*[2]

A few days later he finally came across Young D in front of the short stretch of wall that protected the Qian family compound from prying eyes. As the saying goes, *"When met by chance, foe spots foe at one fell glance."* Ah Q immediately moved in on Young D and the latter stopped dead in his tracks.

"Animal!" shouted Ah Q, giving him his dirtiest look as spittle shot from the corners of his mouth.

"I'm a bug—does that make you happy?" responded Young D.

Such modesty only served to intensify Ah Q's ire. Since he had no steel mace handy, however, he was forced to join battle barehanded. He reached out and grabbed Young D by the queue. Young D defended himself by holding tight to the root of his own queue with one hand while grabbing Ah Q's with the other. In like fashion, Ah Q used *his* free hand to protect himself by holding fast, too, to

1. In the original text, "Don" is printed in English. In a letter to the editor of *Theatre*, Lu Xun wrote that the Chinese word he had in mind was *tong* (this word, meaning "alike, identical," sounds something like "don" in Lu Xun's native dialect). The idea behind this is that when Young D grows up, he will turn out just like Ah Q.

2. A line from a local Shaoxing opera, *Battle of the Dragon and Tiger Generals*, which recreates an epic battle fought by Zhao Guangyin, founder of the Song dynasty (960–1269).

the root of his own queue. The old Ah Q had never considered Young D's martial skills to be worthy of mention, but the new Ah Q hadn't had anything to eat recently and by now yielded nothing to Young D in miserable-little-critterliness himself. It was an even match. As Young D and Ah Q bent toward each other, four hands grasped two heads. The blue shadow that was cast by the two men on the Qian family's whitewashed wall was shaped like a rainbow, a rainbow that froze and then remained motionless for a good half hour.

"Okay now, okay!" said some of the people who had gathered round to watch—they were probably trying to break up the fight. "All right now, *all right!*" said some others. One couldn't tell whether they were simply expressing admiration or were urging the combatants to show greater animation. But whatever the case, neither Ah Q nor Young D was paying any attention to the crowd.

When Ah Q advanced three steps, Young D retreated three steps and they both stood still. When Young D advanced three steps, Ah Q retreated three steps and they both stood still. After approximately half an hour of this—it's really hard to tell because there were very few clocks in Wei Village that struck the hours, so maybe it was only twenty minutes—both their heads were steaming and their faces were bathed in sweat. Finally Ah Q's hands released their hold; at precisely the same moment Young D's hands released their hold, too. Simultaneously the two men straightened up; simultaneously they backed away from each other and elbowed their separate ways out through the ring of spectators.

"Let that be a lesson, you fucker!" said Ah Q, turning his head back to Young D.

"Let that be a lesson, you fucker!" said Young D, turning his head back to Ah Q.

So it would seem that there was no victory or defeat in the epic battle that was mounted by these two renowned warriors, nor is it known whether the spectators were satisfied with the show. At any rate, Ah Q came out of it in the same fix he had been in before—no one came to offer him work.

One day when it was quite warm and a gentle breeze was just bringing the first hint of summer into the village, quite incongruously Ah Q started to feel cold. This he could put up with. The first order of business was that hungry stomach of his. His cotton quilt, felt hat, and cotton shirt had long since disappeared, and after that he'd even sold his padded-cotton winter jacket. Now he was left with nothing but a pair of pants—he couldn't part with those no matter what—and a raggedy unlined jacket. He might have been able to *give* that away for somebody to make shoe soles with, but he certainly wouldn't be able to turn a profit on it.

For quite some time now he had fantasized about *finding* some money on the street someplace, but so far he hadn't seen any lying around. Okay then, why not find some money right here in this dilapidated room of his at the Land-and-Grain Temple? Eagerly he searched his quarters over. His room was empty, so empty that he could see at a glance there was nothing to be found in it. At this point, Ah Q decided to go out and scare up something to eat.

Although his intention in going out was to "scare up something to eat," yet when he saw the familiar wineshop, the familiar steamed breadrolls, strange to tell, he walked right on by. Not only did he fail to stop, but what's more, he didn't even want the bread or wine. That's not what he was really looking for.

Then, exactly what was it that he *was* looking for? Even Ah Q himself couldn't have told you.

Now Wei Village wasn't very large to begin with, and before too long Ah Q had walked clear through the place. Then he came to a sea of rice paddies covered with fresh green sprouts and extending as far as the eye could see. It was animated here and there by bobbing dots of black—peasants working in the fields. But Ah Q did not take time to stop and savor the rustic charm of such a scene; he kept right on walking, for he knew instinctively that all of that was far removed from his basic concern of "scaring up something to eat." Finally he came to the walls of the Convent of Silent Cultivation.

The whitewashed walls rose abruptly out of the green sea surrounding them. The low earthen wall behind the convent enclosed a vegetable garden. Ah Q hesitated for a moment, but looking around and seeing no one in sight, he grabbed the blackhair vines that covered the wall and started to climb.[3] Everyplace he managed to get a toehold, the dirt of the wall crumbled and *whooshed* down through the leaves while the trembling of his feet rustled the vines. Availing himself of a nearby mulberry limb, he finally made it over the wall and jumped down into the garden. There was a profusion of things growing there but there didn't seem to be any wine or steamed breadrolls handy, or anything else you could readily sink your teeth into. There was a copse of bamboo over by the western wall with lots of sprouts growing below. As luck would have it, though, none of them were steamed and ready to eat. There was also some rape, but it had long since gone to seed. There was some mustard, too, but it was about to flower, and the little cabbages were also long past ripe.

Feeling every bit as wronged as a Young Literatus who had just failed the civil service examinations, Ah Q slowly walked through a gate into the rear courtyard. He was suddenly greeted by an extraordinarily pleasant surprise, for what met his eyes could be nothing else but a turnip patch. He squatted down and started pulling them up when suddenly a very round head thrust itself out of a door and then shrank back as quickly as it had emerged. Now *that* could be nothing else but a young Buddhist nun. Ah Q thought young Buddhist nuns were worthless to begin with and was not about to be intimidated by the likes of them, but still, men of the world have always appreciated the wisdom of "playing it safe," and so he stripped the leaves from four turnips without further delay and hastily stuffed them into the front of his shirt. By that time, the old abbess herself had already come out.

"Buddha preserve us, what do you think you're doing climbing into our garden to steal turnips, Ah Q? Aiya! Such a sin! Buddha preserve us!"

"When did *I* ever climb into *your* garden to steal turnips?" Ah Q asked, walking away but keeping an eye on the nun too.

"Just now . . . aren't those . . ." The old nun pointed to his bulging shirt.

"Oh, you think these are yours, huh? Can you call 'em by name and make 'em come to you? Why you don't even—"

Before he could finish, a black dog was lunging toward him and Ah Q broke into a run. The dog had been at the front gate but somehow or other had come

3. "Blackhair" refers to *Polygonum multiforum*, known popularly in Chinese as *heshouwu:* so powerful in its rejuvenative function that it turned a certain Mr. He's head (*shou*) of hair black (*wu*) overnight.

around to the back. It was right on Ah Q's heels and about to grab his leg when, as luck would have it, a turnip dropped out of his shirt, startling the animal long enough to give Ah Q time to climb the mulberry tree and vault over the wall. Outside, both Ah Q and turnips went spilling all over the ground; inside, the black dog kept barking at the mulberry tree while the old abbess continued to invoke the name of Buddha.

Afraid lest the abbess might let the dog out after him, Ah Q quickly gathered up the turnips and hurried on his way. He picked up a few pebbles at the side of the road just in case, but since the black dog did not reappear, he finally threw them away and began eating the turnips as he walked along. "Not gonna find anything to eat around here," he thought to himself. "I could always go to town." By the time he had finished the third turnip, he was already quite firm in his decision to head for town.

Chapter 6. From Dynastic Revival to the Fading Days of Empire

It was just past the Mid-Autumn Festival that year when Wei Village caught sight of Ah Q again.[4] "Ah Q's back." All who heard the news were surprised and forthwith rolled back their minds to ponder: "Wonder where he went?" The last few times he went to town, Ah Q had been bursting with news when he got back and had wasted no time telling everyone about his trip. But this time—nary a word. No one had even noticed that he was gone, although it is possible he may have told the old man who looked after the Land-and-Grain Temple that he was going. According to old established Wei Village precedent, however, going to town was no big thing unless it was Old Master Zhao or Old Master Qian who did the going. Even a trip to town by the Fake Foreign Devil was nothing to get worked up about, much less a trip by the likes of Ah Q. Thus the old caretaker at the temple hadn't bothered to spread word of our hero's departure for town, and consequently the inhabitants of Wei Village had been ignorant of the event.

The circumstances of his return this time were rather different too—to tell the truth, they were downright odd. The sky was almost black when Ah Q appeared, all sleepy-eyed, at the door of the wineshop. He shuffled up to the counter, extended a hand from his waist, and threw down a whole fistful of silver and copper coins. "Hard cash! Bring on the wine!" He was sporting a brand new unlined jacket and a money pouch weighed his belt down into an arc. According to old established Wei Village precedent, should one chance to meet a presentable personage with anything about him that caught the eye, then *Come what may, sweet courtesie / Should be the order of the day*. Now there was no mistaking that it really *was* Ah Q they were dealing with, but this Ah Q was entirely different from the raggedy-jacket Ah Q they were accustomed to, and thus they treated him with deference. This was an instance of what the ancients had in mind when they advised: *After an absence of even three days / A scholar-official rates a fresh gaze.*[5]

4. The Mid-Autumn Festival falls on the fifteenth day of the eighth lunar month.
5. Who could tell what examinations had been passed, what fresh honors attained in the interim?

Thus, from the manager to the waiters, and from patrons on down to mere passers-by, everyone quite naturally assumed a respectful, albeit inquisitive, air. *Behold how yon manager doth begin, with a nod to which he now appendeth some words:* "Hey, it's Ah Q! You're back!"

"I'm back."

"Looks like you've done pretty well for yourself. Let's see, you were at . . . uh . . . at . . ."

"Went to town."

This momentous item of intelligence had blanketed all of Wei Village by the very next day.

Everyone wanted to hear the saga of Ah Q's "dynastic restoration" to his present ready-cash and new-lined-jacket level of affluence. In the wineshop, in the teashop, and under the eaves of the temple, bit by bit people ferreted out the details. And as a consequence of all this, Ah Q was treated with new respect.

The way Ah Q told it, he had been working for an Old Master in town—a *Selectman*, no less. All who heard this chapter and verse looked impressed. This *Selectman*'s last name was Bai, but since he was the only *Selectman* in the whole town, there was no reason to use it. Whenever a *Selectman* was spoken of, it would have had to be Bai. This was true not only in the town but also in every place within a hundred miles around. It was as if people actually thought this man's family name was *Selectman*, and his given name, Old Master. To have been employed in the residence of such a man was, of course, impressive enough. But according to what Ah Q further revealed, he had not deemed it appropriate to remain in Bai's employ, for he considered the Old Master *Selectman* a bit too "fuckin'" this and a mite too "fuckin'" that. All who heard this sighed, but they were secretly pleased as well. They sighed because Ah Q had thrown away such a good job, but they were secretly pleased because they felt he hadn't deserved it to begin with.

The way Ah Q told it, the main reason for his return to Wei Village was his general dissatisfaction with the townsfolk. They called a *longbench* a *stickbench* and used shredded leeks—yes, *shredded*—when frying fish. And as if that weren't enough, he'd recently discovered an even greater shortcoming among them: when the women walked, their fannies didn't have much wiggle. Despite all that, however, here and there one did find things in town worthy of admiration. For instance, when it came to gambling, the Wei Village bumpkins couldn't manage anything better than a simple game played with thirty-two bamboo counters. Here only the Fake Foreign Devil knew how to play Ma John, but in town every little shitkicker on the block knew it up one side and down the other.[6] If the Fake Foreign Devil ever fell into the clutches of one of those little bastards, it'd be like some two-for-a-nickel ghost coming up against the King of Hell! All who heard this chapter and verse took on an embarrassed air.[7]

"Have you ever seen a de-capi-tation?" Ah Q asked. "Wow! Is that ever somethin' to see! Killin' the revolutionaries—yup, that's a real sight!" He shook his head with such appreciative enthusiasm that spittle flew from his mouth and

6. In the original text, Ah Q hears *majiang* (the game of mah-jongg) as two other characters, pronounced the same way but with a completely different meaning.

7. Presumably, embarrassed at the provincialism of their own village.

landed on the face of Zhao Sichen, seated directly opposite him. All who heard this chapter and verse assumed an air of solemnity. Once more Ah Q looked all around and surveyed his audience. Listening with rapt attention, Bearded Wang had stretched out his neck, the better to hear Ah Q's rendition. Suddenly Ah Q raised his right arm, took aim at the nape of Bearded Wang's neck, clove the air with his hand, and shouted, "*ZAP!*"

Fairly jumping out of his skin with fright, Bearded Wang jerked his head in as quick as lightning. All who heard this chapter and verse of Ah Q's story took on a frightened—albeit appreciative—air. For several days afterward, Bearded Wang wandered around in a daze, no longer daring even to come near to Ah Q. And the others who had listened to Ah Q that day were similarly wary.

Although I dare not make so bold as to say that at this point Ah Q's standing in the eyes of the Wei Villagers was actually higher than that of Old Master Zhao, still if I were to characterize it as almost equivalent, I should probably not be guilty of any great linguistic lapse.

This being the case, it was not long before the great name of Ah Q was bruited about in the boudoirs of Wei Village for a second time. Actually only the Qians and Zhaos lived in households large enough to boast "boudoirs." Nine out of ten families had only ordinary bedrooms at best. But be they boudoirs or bedrooms, women's quarters are women's quarters and it was something of a miracle that Ah Q's name should ever be heard in such precincts at all. Yet it seemed that of late, whenever the village women met, conversation would invariably turn to Ah Q. How about that blue silk skirt Seventh Sister Zou had bought of him! Secondhand, to be sure, but for ninety cents who could complain? And what about the red calico shirt Zhao Baiyan's mother had bought—seven-tenths new and it had only cost her three strings of cash, at ninety-two to the string.[8] (One authority states that it was actually Zhao Sichen's mother. Pending further research, however, this identification can only be regarded as tentative.)[9]

And now all the women's eyes throughout the village were hanging out: they all wanted to see Ah Q. In the market for a silk skirt? See Ah Q. Need a calico shirt? Go look up Ah Q. Not only did they no longer avoid him, but occasionally they would even hunt him down. "Any more silk skirts, Ah Q? No? How about calico then? You've gotta have some calico ones left." News of all this excitement eventually made its way from the shallows of ordinary village bedrooms into the depths of the Zhao and Qian boudoirs, carried thence by Seventh Sister Zou, who in an excess of smug satisfaction had taken the blue skirt and shown it off to Mrs. Zhao. That lady had, in her turn, told Old Master Zhao about Seventh Sister's purchase in terms of highest approbation. That gentleman, in his turn, had discussed it with Young Master Zhao, his *Budding Talent* son, at a dinner-table conclave that very evening, opining that there was

8. Supposedly, a string of cash consisted of one hundred round coins with square holes through the middle. The string was threaded through the holes, and its two ends tied together so as to form a loop. However, such strings seldom carried a full hundred coins.

9. Lu Xun is having fun at the expense of contemporary Chinese scholars who, returning from sojourns in foreign universities, attempted to apply Western academic methodology to every problem and seemed to value research over action; cf. Lu Xun's remark about Hu Shi in the introduction to this story (chap. 1).

something suspicious about Ah Q. "We had better be a bit more careful about locking our windows and doors at night. Wonder what kind of stuff he has left? We might be able to get some real bargains."

At just that time, Mrs. Zhao happened to be in the market for a good sleeveless fur jacket—if the price was right. That did it. The clan conclave approved a resolution that called for one of their number to prevail upon the good offices of Seventh Sister Zou to seek out Ah Q on that very night. Furthermore, in order that the resolution might be carried out, an exception to family protocol was also passed: an oil lamp would be lit after sunset.

The lamp burned and burned, but Ah Q was nowhere to be seen. The entire Zhao household was thrown out of kilter. Forever yawning, some faulted Ah Q's fly-by-night character, while others blamed Seventh Sister Zou for lack of diligence. Mrs. Zhao was of the opinion that Ah Q was afraid to come because of the restrictions imposed on him by the sheriff back in the spring. Old Master Zhao, on the other hand, believed that this wouldn't have made any difference because "I am the one who sent for him." In the end, it was Old Master Zhao who proved best at predicting the ways of the world, for Seventh Sister finally arrived with Ah Q in tow.

"He kept telling me . . . he didn't have anything left, but I told . . . I told him to come and tell you that to your face. He even said . . . even said . . ." Still trying to catch her breath, Seventh Sister Zou wheezed heavily.

"Old Master!" Ah Q hailed, stopping dead in his tracks under the eaves and smiling a smile that didn't look like a smile.

"Ah Q, I hear that you prospered while you were away," offered Old Master Zhao, who strode forward in greeting, his eyes busy with a head-to-toe inventory of Ah Q. "Glad to hear it, very glad. Now . . . uh . . . I hear you have a few secondhand items for sale. Why not bring over whatever you've got and let us have a look. The only reason I'm interested is that I just happen to be in the market for—"

"I've already told Seventh Sister Zou, stuff's all gone."

"Gone?" The plaintive note slipped out before Old Master Zhao had time to catch it. "How could they all go so quickly?"

"It was only some stuff a buddy of mine let me have. Wasn't much to begin with. Sold some to—"

"Surely you must have something left."

"All I've got now is a door curtain."

"All right then, bring *that* over," said Mrs. Zhao excitedly.

"In that case, we'll see you again tomorrow," said Old Master Zhao without much enthusiasm. "Ah Q, whenever you have anything from now on, be sure to bring it to our place first."

"We would certainly offer you better prices than anyone else around," added the *Budding Talent*. Mrs. *Budding Talent* stole a furtive glance at Ah Q to see if her husband's words had had any effect.

"I need a sleeveless fur jacket!" Mrs. Zhao came right out with it.

Although Ah Q had promised to do as they said, he sauntered out in such a lackadaisical way that it was hard to tell if he really meant it. This whole business proved a great disappointment to Old Master Zhao. In fact he was so vexed that he stopped yawning. The *Budding Talent* was quite put out with Ah

Q as well. "Have to keep a sharp eye on that turtle's egg. Maybe we ought to have the sheriff drive him out of town and be done with it."

Old Master Zhao, however, did not see things the same way and opined that such a course would only serve to turn Ah Q into a lifelong enemy. Besides, people in that line of work were likely to bear out the truth of the saying *The hawk is always a pest, but never 'round its own nest*, and hence there was no need for concern around Wei Village. "As long as we keep a little more alert nights, we should be all right." The beneficiary of this "courtyard guidance" promptly decided that his father couldn't be more correct and immediately tabled the resolution calling for exile.[1] Furthermore, he enjoined Seventh Sister Zou to refrain from telling anyone that such a possibility had even been entertained. The following day Seventh Sister Zou took the blue silk skirt she had bought from Ah Q and dyed it black. Then, far and wide, she broadcast all the Zhaos' suspicions regarding Ah Q—though she did not, in good faith, touch on that particular chapter and verse having to do with the *Budding Talent*'s suggestion about exile. Nonetheless, what she did say proved quite damaging to Ah Q.

First off, the sheriff hunted him down and made off with the door curtain, steadfastly refusing to return it despite Ah Q's protestation that Mrs. Zhao was anxious to see it. Worse yet, the sheriff even tried to press Ah Q into making a monthly "filial donation."[2] Second, there was a sudden transformation in the form of respect that Wei Villagers showed Ah Q. The expressions they wore now announced that although they still weren't about to take any liberties with him, they would just as soon give him a wide berth. These expressions were by no means identical to the ones they had worn earlier when guarding against a surprise *"ZAP!"* either. No, there was now an element of the attitude that Confucius recommended one should take with regard to ghosts and spirits: *"Respectful you may be, but keep some distance 'twixt them and thee."*

Only the village roustabouts had the temerity to get close to Ah Q. They moved in and subjected him to an unrelenting barrage of questions, hoping to find out exactly what he'd been up to in town. For his part, Ah Q didn't hold anything back either. On the contrary, he related his urban experiences with a real touch of pride. It was now they learned that, in the brief course of his criminal career, Ah Q's role had been little more than that of an extra. He had neither *scaled walls* nor had he *tunneled through barriers* the way real burglars are supposed to do. In fact, he had merely waited outside to receive the stolen goods as they were passed to him from inside. One night, just after the head of the gang had handed him a sack of stuff and headed back for more, Ah Q heard a great commotion break out on the inside. He had immediately taken to his heels, climbed over the city wall, and fled back to Wei Village, no longer possessing the nerve to continue in his new calling.[3]

1. "Courtyard guidance" alludes to Confucius' education of his own son; see *The Analects of Confucius* 16.13.

2. Many Chinese expressions acknowledge the superior status of another person by referring to him as father, or even grandfather. Protection money that was extorted by gangsters (or as in this case, hush money extorted by the sheriff) could thus be spoken of as a sum of money offered out of filial respect.

3. The gates of the city wall would have been locked for the night.

Strange to say, these revelations had a remarkably adverse effect on Ah Q. The Wei Villagers' *respectful-be* attitude had been sustained by fear, pure and simple. Who would ever have guessed that in point of fact Ah Q was nothing more than a burglar who no longer dared to burgle? It was truly a case of *He whose years bring nought of fame / To our respect can lay no claim.*[4]

Chapter 7. Revolution

On the Fourteenth Day of the Ninth Month of the Third Year of the Xuantong Reign—in other words, on the day Ah Q sold his money pouch to Zhao Baiyan—on the Fourth Stroke of the Third Watch,[5] a large black-canopied boat tied up at the Zhao family wharf. Since it had been poled in during the middle of the night, the villagers were sound asleep and unaware of its arrival. When they left their homes before dawn next morning, however, quite a few of them caught sight of it. After some quick nosing around, they discovered it belonged to none other than Old Master *Selectman.*

That boat carried a cargo of unrest into Wei Village. Well before noon, everyone had heard about it and was quite worried. The Zhaos, of course, were secretive as to the boat's real mission, but out on the street word had it that the Revolutionary Party was about to occupy the town and that Old Master *Selectman* had come out to Wei Village to hole up until things blew over. The sole dissenting opinion was offered by Seventh Sister Zou. The way she told it, the boat only carried a few battered old trunks that Old Master *Selectman* wanted to store at the Zhaos' place, but Old Master Zhao had refused and the trunks had been sent back to town. If you stopped to think about it, she probably had something there, for despite their both being members of the educated scholar-official class, *Budding Talent* Zhao and Old Master *Selectman* had never hit it off very well and it would seem unlikely that there could be any "brothers-in-adversity" relationship between them. What was more, since Seventh Sister Zou was a *neighbor* of the Zhaos, her view of things ought to be closer to the mark. And so people decided that, more likely than not, Seventh Sister Zou had the right of it.

Nevertheless rumors continued to fly. One of them went like this: although, to be sure, Old Master *Selectman* had probably not come in person, he *had* sent along a lengthy letter in which, after many a twist and turn through the maze of kith and kin, he had established himself as at least a "kissin' cousin" to the Zhaos. After reading the said letter, Old Master Zhao had given that possibility a quick roll around his brain and concluded that such a relationship could certainly do him no harm. He had therefore kept the battered old trunks, which were at this very moment stuffed under his wife's bed. And as to the Revolutionary Party, there were those who held that it had occupied the town that

4. The reference is to *Analects* 9.22. "The Master said: Those who are born after us merit our respect. How do we know that in the future they will not be equal to what we are now? If, on the other hand, by the age of forty or fifty a man has done nothing to make his name known in the world, then such a common lout merits not our respect."

5. Xuantong was the reign title of the last Qing emperor. The lunar date given here corresponds to November 4, 1911, the day Lu Xun's own hometown was "liberated." The time given is about midnight.

very night, every soldier wearing a white helmet—obviously in mourning for the Emperor Chong Zhen.[6]

Ah Q's ear had long since been exposed to the expression "Revolutionary Party." What was more, only this year he had seen members of that same party being executed. His idea of the whole thing—though he wouldn't have been able to tell you exactly how he came by it—had always been that "revolutionaries" were troublemakers, hell-bent on turning the world upside down, and that meant giving Ah Q a hard time personally. Hence his own attitude toward such mischief makers had been one of *antipathy most intense* and *abhorrence most immense*. But who could ever have guessed that Old Master *Selectman*—respected and feared as he was for miles and miles around—would be utterly terrified by this Revolutionary Party? It was a sweet thought and it made Ah Q lean their way. Furthermore, with all the "cocksuckin' villagers" running around like chickens with their heads cut off, how could Ah Q help but be pleased?

"Why *not* be a revolutionary?" he asked himself. "There's a whole bunch of fuckers I'd like to revolution clear out of this world and into the next, the sorry bastards! I just might throw in with that Revolution Party myself!"

Ah Q had been a bit hard up lately and that probably helped put him out of sorts to begin with. On top of that, he'd had two bowls of wine on an empty stomach that very afternoon. He thought as he walked; and he walked as he thought. And then he began to walk an inch or so above the ground. Thoughts and wine had suddenly transformed his single person into an entire revolutionary army! Everyone in Wei Village was now his prisoner. Everyone! He was soon so full of himself he could no longer contain it.

"On with the rebellion!" shouted Ah Q.

The Wei Villagers watched him with a look that bordered on a look of terror, a look that made Ah Q feel as comfortable as a man drinking melted snow in the middle of June. Now he was full to the point of overflowing. "Whatever Ah Q wants, Ah Q gets! Whatever *woman* Ah Q wants, Ah Q gets!" he shouted happily and then began to sing.

Da-da dum-dum!
In my cups, would that I had ne'er . . .
Da-da dum-dum!
. . . taken the head of my brother-in-arms,
Brother Zheng.
Would that I had ne'er . . .
Ah . . . ah-ah . . . ah . . .
Da-da dum-dum, da dum-ya-dum!
My mace of steel I grasp full tight,
And with it I shall now thee smite . . .

6. White was the traditional color of mourning. Chong Zhen was the last Ming emperor before the Manchu invasion that established the Qing dynasty (1644–1912). Many peasant rebel groups that tried to overthrow the Manchus did so under the slogan "Destroy the Qing, restore the Ming." So it is natural for the Wei Villagers to assume that the Revolutionary Party, which has just established a new republic, is just one more of these restorationist groups.

Two Zhaos were standing at the front gate of their family compound discussing the implications of the revolution with two honest-to-goodness relatives. Head held jauntily aloft, Ah Q cruised on past without deigning to notice them.

"Da-da . . ."

"Q, my friend," hailed Old Master Zhao somewhat diffidently.

"Dum-dum!" Never dreaming that his own name could possibly be linked with "friend," it did not occur to Ah Q that these words had anything to do with him, and so he kept right on singing: *"Da-dum . . . dum-ya-dum . . . dum!"*

"Old friend, Q!"

"Would that I had ne'er—"

"AH Q!" The *Budding Talent* was forced to shout out the name they usually used on him.

Ah Q stopped dead in his tracks, cocked his head to one side, and inquired, "What?"

"Q, my friend. Now . . . uh . . ." Old Gentleman Zhao seemed at a loss for words. "Uh . . . you've gotten rich, huh?"

"Rich? You betcha! From here on out, whatever Ah Q wants, Ah Q gets!"

"Ah Q . . . I mean, Elder Brother Q. Poor folks like us won't be in any trouble, will they?" Zhao Baiyan asked anxiously in an attempt to determine which way the revolutionary winds were blowing.

"Poor, my foot! You sure as hell have a lot more dough than I do." Ah Q turned and walked away, bringing all conversation to a disappointing halt.

Old Master Zhao and son went back inside and discussed everything that had transpired until it was time to light—or time not to light—their lamps. Zhao Baiyan went back home, undid his moneybelt, and ordered his wife to hide it at the bottom of the family trunk.

Walking on air, Ah Q continued floating hither and yon for quite a while so that by the time he got back to the Land-and-Grain Temple, he was thoroughly sober. Tonight even the caretaker turned affable and invited him in for tea. Ah Q asked him for two crackers, and after finishing them, even managed to hit him up for a four-ounce candle and candlestick. Alone in his little room at last, luxuriating, Ah Q lit the candle and lay down. He was indescribably happy.

The flames shimmered and danced as if it were New Year's Eve, and Ah Q's thoughts began to do some high stepping too. "Throw in with the troublemakers? Yeah, that would be fun. I can see it now. A bunch of those Revolution Party guys'll come by the temple here, all decked out in white armor and white helmets, wearin' sabers too! They'll come marchin' right in and shout: 'Let's go, Ah Q, come with us!' And I'll go with them too! Steel maces, bombs, foreign rifles, spears, knives—they'll have it all. Then those cock-suckin' villagers will find out how pitiful they really are. I can see 'em kneelin' on the ground and beggin' me to spare 'em. Fat chance! Young D and Old Master Zhao'll be the first to go. I'll get the *Budding Talent* too, and then I'll do in the Fake Foreign Devil. Wonder if I should let any of 'em live? Well by rights I suppose I could spare Bearded Wang—but no, I'm not gonna.

"And think of all the stuff I'll get, too. March right into their houses and rip open their trunks—gold, silver, foreign money, foreign calico shirts! For starters I'll take that Ningbo bed the *Budding Talent*'s wife has and move it over here to the temple. The Qians' tables and chairs will do just fine, thank you—maybe I'll take some from the Zhaos, too. Won't even have to lift a finger. Get Young D to do all the heavy work. Better step lively too, if he doesn't want a good belt or two.

"Let's see. Zhao Sichen's sister is a real dog, and there's not much point in talkin' about Seventh Sister Zou's daughter for a couple of years yet. Fake Foreign Devil's wife is willin' to sleep with a husband that's got no queue—she can't be any damn good! If only *Budding Talent*'s old lady didn't have that mole on her eyelid. Haven't seen Amah Wu in a while, wonder where she is? But then she's got those big-ass feet."

Before he had time to arrange all the pieces just right, Ah Q was already snoring. The four-ounce candle had burned down less than half an inch and its bright rays shone warm and red on his open mouth. And then all of a sudden he screamed, raised his head, and looked around in panic. Finally his gaze came to rest on the four-ounce candle. He put his head back down and went to sleep.

Ah Q didn't get out of bed until quite late the next day. He went out on the street and did a quick survey—everything was exactly as it had always been. His stomach was exactly as it had always been too—empty. He thought about what he should do next but failed to come up with anything. And then suddenly he seemed to have hit on something, for his body gradually began to move. Thinking more with his feet than with anything else, Ah Q finally arrived at the Convent of Silent Cultivation.

It was every bit as quiet as he remembered it from the previous spring. He knocked on the gate. A dog began to bark inside. Ah Q hastily picked out a large piece of brick and approached the gate again. He began knocking with the brick, much harder than before, but it was not until many a pockmark had appeared on the surface of the big black gate that he heard someone coming out.

Ah Q immediately secured a better hold on the brick, spread his feet wide, and prepared to do battle with the dog. The gate opened no more than a crack, however, and no guardian canine burst forth. Peeking in through that crack, Ah Q saw nothing but an elderly nun.

"What are *you* doing here again?" she asked in alarm.

"There's been a revolution, haven't you heard?"

"Revolution? Haven't we had just about enough revolution for one day?"

"Huh?" Ah Q was puzzled.

"Don't you know? The revolutionists have already been here."

"*What* revolutionists?" Ah Q was more puzzled than ever.

"The *Budding Talent* and Fake Foreign Devil!"

Ah Q was stunned by the news. The elderly nun, sensing his loss of momentum, quickly shut the gate. By the time he realized what had happened, the gate was locked tighter than a drum. Ah Q pounded on it once again, but this time there was no response.

It had all happened that very morning. Always right on top of things, *Budding Talent* Zhao learned that the revolutionaries had taken the town during the night. He responded by coiling his queue up on top of his head and heading out bright and early to pay his respects to the Fake Foreign Devil, a man with whom he had never been on good terms heretofore. However, since this was "a time for people from all walks of life to unite in national renewal,"[7] they now hit it off just fine, quickly became the comradeliest of comrades-in-arms, and joined together to undertake the task of revolution.

But where to begin? After wracking their brains at great length, they finally remembered that there was a "Long Live the Emperor" tablet over at the Convent of Silent Cultivation. They righteously decided that this tablet would have to go, and set out forthwith for the convent. Giving the two a good piece of her mind, the elderly nun had tried to stop them. Thereupon, taking her as a symbol of the entire Manchu establishment, they gave her a sound thrashing. After they left, the old nun had collected herself enough to survey the damage. The objectionable tablet, of course, lay shattered on the ground. She also discovered that an extremely valuable antique censer that had stood before a statue of the Bodhisattva Guanyin[8] was nowhere to be seen.

It was only much later that day that Ah Q found out about all this. He was more than a little sorry that he had been asleep during the foray and was also quite put out that they hadn't come to get him. He backed up another step in his thoughts and wondered: "Do you suppose they don't know I've already thrown in with the Revolution Party?"

Chapter 8. Request to Revolt Denied

The Wei Villagers felt more reassured with every passing day. The word from town was that although the Revolutionary Party had indeed taken over, it hadn't made any changes to speak of. His honor the county magistrate was still the same man, though they called him something else now. Old Master *Selectman* had also acquired some sort of new label (the Wei Villagers couldn't keep track of all these new revolutionary titles). And the same old lieutenant was in charge of the soldiers, too.[9]

The only worrisome thing about this whole business was that some bad elements had slipped into the Revolutionary Party and started lopping queues off the day after they arrived in town. The boatman from over in the next village, Sevenpounder, had fallen into their clutches and had been so transformed that he no longer looked even human.[1] The incident occasioned but little anxiety among the Wei Villagers, however, because few of them ever ventured into town in the first place, and the one or two who were thinking of making the trek immediately changed their plans. Why risk ending up like Sevenpounder if you didn't have to? At first, Ah Q had considered going into town to look up some old friends, but on hearing of Sevenpounder's tragic fate, he too had no choice but to cancel his trip.

And yet you couldn't say that the revolution hadn't triggered any reforms in Wei Village, either. Within a few days after the revolutionaries took the town, for

7. This slogan (*xian yü wei xin*) is quoted from the *History Classic*, an ancient anthology (author unknown), and was widely popular around the beginning of the republic.

8. The Goddess of Mercy, better known to Western readers by her Japanese name, Kannon.

9. As Lu Xun saw it, the 1911 Republican Revolution had done nothing to alter the basic power structure of Chinese society.

1. A reference to the protagonist of "A Passing Storm" (published under the pen name Lu Xun) and another clue to the identity of Ba Ren, the pseudonym under which Lu Xun first published the present story.

instance, the number of people with queues coiled up on top of their heads gradually began to increase. As I have reported earlier, it was his nibs the *Budding Talent* who led the way; next came Zhao Sichen and Zhao Baiyan; and after that Ah Q also joined the parade. During the summer, of course, it was not uncommon for people in Wei Village to coil their queues up on top of their heads, or even to do them up in knots. But this was late autumn, not summer. And so, from the point of view of those who did the coiling, one cannot maintain that this "autumn practice of summer etiquette" demonstrated anything less than a magnificent decisiveness worthy of the doughtiest heroes. And once that's granted, one cannot say that the revolution didn't trigger any reforms in Wei Village either.

When Zhao Sichen came walking down the street with the back of his head scandalously bared, people would look at him and then warn each other: "Look out, here comes a revolutionary!" When Ah Q heard of this, he was quite envious. Although Ah Q had long since gotten wind of the momentous news about the *Budding Talent*'s coiling his queue up, the idea that *he* might do the same had never crossed his mind. It was only when he saw Zhao Sichen do it that Ah Q gave a thought to imitating this new fashion. Having resolved to put that thought into practice, and using a chopstick for hairpin, Ah Q coiled up his queue too. After some hesitation, he even got up the nerve to go out on the street looking like that.

People actually did give him a second look, but they didn't warn each other about a revolutionary coming. At first, Ah Q merely felt displeased, but later on he began to resent the injustice of it all. He got so worked up that he began flying off the handle at the least provocation. In point of fact, however, he wasn't any worse off now than he had been before he revolted. People were passably polite to him and the stores didn't insist on cash every time he bought anything, yet somehow or other Ah Q felt that this whole revolution business was a big disappointment. Since there really *had* been a revolution, there ought to be more to it than just this.

Later on he ran into Young D. That was the straw that broke the camel's back—Young D had coiled up his queue too! What was more, he'd had the gall to use a chopstick! Never in his wildest dreams had Ah Q expected that someone the likes of Young D would have the nerve to join in on the queue-coiling and he was simply not going to have it! Just who the hell did Young D think he was anyway? Ah Q felt like seizing him on the spot, breaking that chopstick, putting that queue back down, and slapping him across the mouth a few times as punishment for forgetting his place. In the end, however, Ah Q let him off with a contemptuous "*Aaaaaaawk . . . tuh!*" accompanied by a dirty look.

During these parlous times, the Fake Foreign Devil was the only one who ventured into town. *Budding Talent* Zhao had briefly considered going in to visit Old Master *Selectman* in order to cash in on the goodwill the Zhaos had earned by hiding the *Selectman*'s trunks. But the *Budding Talent* was also mindful of the risk he would bring to bear on his queue and decided against it. Instead, he wrote a yellow-umbrella letter[2] and prevailed upon the Fake

2. Yellow umbrellas had been a distinctive part of the emperor's regalia. In a "yellow-umbrella letter" the Chinese characters were so arranged that the middle vertical line (the text was written from top to bottom, starting at the right-hand side of the page) was much longer than those on either side, in a form suggesting the stem of the umbrella, while the lines of characters to the right and left (lines of varying lengths) suggested the umbrella covering.

Foreign Devil to take it into town and show it around in the right places, so that he might gain entry to the Revolutionary Party. When the Fake Foreign Devil returned, he promptly relieved the *Budding Talent* of four dollars, in exchange for which the latter received a Silver Peach to pin onto his lapel. That peach bowled the villagers over. Everyone said it was the symbol of the "Persimmon Oil Party"[3] and worth at least an Imperial Academy Button.[4] Old Master Zhao's prestige soared to even greater heights than it had reached when his son won the *Budding Talent*. The upshot was that Old Master Zhao began lording it over everyone again and even started getting uppity with Ah Q.

Ah Q, in turn, felt he wasn't getting a square deal. He was left out of things at every turn. But as soon as he heard about the Silver Peach business, he realized why this was so. If you're going to revolt, just *saying* so isn't enough. And coiling your queue won't cut it either. The first order of business is to get in touch with the revolutionaries.

Now Ah Q had known only two revolutionaries in his entire life. The one in town had gotten his head *ZAPPED!* off a good while back. The other one was the Fake Foreign Devil. That settled it. Like it or not, Ah Q would have to get in touch with him.

The front gate at the Qians' stood wide open. Ah Q skulked inside and was somewhat startled by the sight that greeted him. There in the middle of the courtyard stood the Fake Foreign Devil, decked out from stem to stern in solid black—foreign clothes, it looked like—and sporting a Silver Peach too! His hand grasped the cane from whose instruction Ah Q had so often profited in the past. His queue, grown out to a good foot and a half by now, was all undone. The freed hair cascaded down over his shoulders, making him look for all the world like some kind of Daoist Immortal. Standing just opposite this apparition, at straight-arrow attention, were Zhao Baiyan and a trio of Wei Villagers. Making a great show of deference, they hung on the Fake Foreign Devil's every word.

Quietly Ah Q made his way in, taking up a position behind Zhao Baiyan. He wanted to say something to the black-garbed star of the show but couldn't figure out what to call him. "Fake Foreign Devil" obviously wouldn't do. "Foreigner" was no better. And "Revolutionary" didn't quite do it either. Maybe he just ought to call him *Mr.* Foreigner.

"Mr. Foreigner" hadn't even noticed Ah Q. Eyes rolled skyward, he was just now hitting his stride: "I'm an impatient sort myself, and so whenever I met him, I'd always say, 'Brother Hong, let's get on with it.' But he would reply, '*Mais non,*

To send such a letter expressed profound respect on the part of the sender. It is ironic here that a letter whose form calls to mind the old imperial court is sent to the Revolutionary Party, presumably a petition for membership.

3. Unfamiliar with the concept of "freedom" (*ziyou*), the villagers hear the name of the party in question as "persimmon oil" (*shiyou*).

4. Qing dynasty officials wore buttons on their ceremonial hats. Oval in shape, the buttons varied in color according to the rank of the wearer. An Imperial Academy Button was the most prestigious. After passing the first two levels of the civil service examinations (*Budding Talent* and *Selectman*), a candidate receiving a "high pass" on the third exam (*Advanced Scholar*) might then sit for an additional examination over which the emperor himself presided. A "pass" on this one entitled the candidate to join the Imperial Academy and to wear the corresponding button.

mon ami!'—that's a foreign expression for 'no.'[5] If he hadn't kept 'no-ing' me like that, the revolution would have come off a long time ago, but it goes to show you how carefully he proceeds in everything. He's tried to get me to take a post up there in Hubei I don't know how many times, but I've never agreed. After all, who wants a post in some insignificant county seat?"

"Ahem . . . Mr. . . ." Ah Q took advantage of a momentary pause in the Fake Foreign Devil's monologue to say his piece. It had taken all the courage he could muster, and then some, to even open his mouth.

But for some reason or other his intended form of address, "Mr. Foreigner," stuck in his throat.

"Out with it! What is it?"

"I . . . I . . ."

"Get out of here!"

"I want to throw in with . . ."

"Beat it!" Mr. Foreigner raised his *wailing stick* ominously high.

Then Zhao Baiyan and the village idlers began to bark at him too. "The gentleman has told you to beat it. That should be enough!"

Letting his feet do the thinking, Ah Q escaped through the gate, one hand shielding his head. To his surprise, however, Mr. Foreigner didn't bother to come after him. Nonetheless Ah Q hightailed it some sixty paces or so before gradually slowing down to a walk. He was heartbroken. If Mr. Foreigner wouldn't give him permission to revolt, he was done for. Never again could he look forward to having men in white helmets and white armor come by and ask him to join up. The idlers back there at Mr. Foreigner's place would waste no time in spreading word of what had just taken place, and Ah Q would become a laughingstock to the likes of Young D and Bearded Wang. That was bad enough. But the worst of it was that all his ambitions, hopes, and plans for the future had been wiped out at a single stroke.

In his entire life, Ah Q had never before experienced such a feeling of utter aimlessness. He felt that even coiling up his queue was pointless and briefly considered letting it down again just to get even. In the end, however, he didn't. With no particular goal in mind, Ah Q loafed around until nightfall. Then he put two bowls of wine on his tab and promptly drank them down. Gradually his spirits began to rise and glimpses of white helmets and white armor began to flicker across his brain once again.

One night, as had become his habit of late, Ah Q dawdled around in the wineshop till closing time and then started to trudge on back to the temple. *BIFF BANG BAM BOOM*—an odd kind of racket. Didn't sound like firecrackers either. Always a lover of excitement, Ah Q liked nothing better than minding everyone else's business. So he made a beeline through the darkness to the source of the noise. Hearing some footsteps, he stopped and cocked his head, the better to listen. A man hurtled past him in full retreat from something or

5. "Brother Hong" is a pretentious reference to Li Yuanhong (1864–1928), the Qing commander who reluctantly took charge of the revolutionary government in Hubei (at the behest of his own troops) following the 1911 Wuchang uprising. Subsequently he served twice as president of the republic. The italicized French expression in the translation appears as English "No!" in the original Chinese text.

other. Ah Q reversed his own course and fell in beside him. When he made a turn, Ah Q made a turn. When he stopped, Ah Q also stopped. Seeing there was no one behind them, Ah Q took a closer look—Young D!

"What's goin' on?" Ah Q felt left out again.

"The Zhaos . . . the Zhaos . . . got robbed!" Young D tried to catch his breath. The news made Ah Q's heart *thump thump* all the faster. Having caught his breath, Young D continued to make his escape under the eaves of the houses and so, at first, did Ah Q. Having had some experience in "this line of work," however, Ah Q was the bolder of the two and finally headed back up the street to see what was really going on. He stopped and watched while a steady line of white helmets and white jackets came out of the Zhaos' place—with trunks, furniture, even the stylish Ningbo bed that belonged to the *Budding Talent*'s old lady. He wanted to get closer for a better look, but his feet simply wouldn't move.

Wei Village lay very quiet in the darkness, as quiet as it might have lain during the reign of Fu Xi.[6] Ah Q stood and watched until he was tired of watching, but there was still no end in sight. A steady stream of people went back and forth moving things out, so many things that Ah Q could scarcely believe his eyes. He decided against getting any closer and headed back to the temple.

It was pitch black in the Land-and-Grain Temple. Closing the main gate behind him, Ah Q groped his way back into his room. He lay there for a long time before he was finally able to collect his thoughts enough to assess his own situation. Quite clearly the white-helmet white-armor people had arrived, but also just as clearly, they had not invited him to join them. And so no matter how much loot they made off with at the Zhaos' place, he didn't stand to get any share of it. "It's all because that Fake Foreign Devil wouldn't let me revolt, otherwise I'd sure as hell have gotten some of that stuff." The more he thought, the madder he got, until at last he could contain himself no longer. "Won't let me revolt, huh? You're the only one allowed to revolt, fuckin' Fake Foreign Devil! Okay, go right ahead and revolt to your heart's content. Revolt's a crime you can get your head chopped off for. Just watch and see if I don't turn your ass in! I'll just sit back and watch 'em haul you into town and lop off your head! They'll do in your whole family—*ZAP! ZAP! ZAP!*"

Chapter 9. The Grand Reunion

After the burglary at Old Master Zhao's the villagers were, for the most part, quite pleased—and frightened too; Ah Q was, for the most part, quite pleased—and frightened as well. Four days later he was arrested in the middle of the night and hauled off to town.

As luck would have it, there was no moon that night and taking full advantage of the darkness, one squad of soldiers, one squad of militia, and five detectives slipped into the village to surround the Land-and-Grain Temple. Expectantly, they set up a machine gun opposite the temple gate. Ah Q, however, failed to

6. Legendary ruler of high antiquity under whose idyllic reign China prospered in peace and tranquility.

come roaring out on cue. They waited and waited, but there was nary a peep within the temple compound. Unable to stand the suspense, the lieutenant persuaded two of his bravos—for a reward of twenty strings of cash, one full thousand to the string—to scale the temple wall. Once inside they let their cohorts in through the gate, and together they all thundered onward to Ah Q's room and took him captive there. When they had dragged him out to the machine gun emplacement, he was beginning to wake up.

And by the time they entered the town with Ah Q in tow, it was already high noon. He watched himself supported under the arms and escorted into a rundown *yamen*[7] where, after five or six shifts in direction, he was finally shoved into a cell. A big barred door slammed shut at his heels as he stumbled inside. The other three sides of the cell were bare walls. Upon closer inspection he discovered two other men over in one corner.

Although somewhat upset, Ah Q was not particularly dissatisfied with his present accommodations, for his own room back at the temple was certainly no more elegantly appointed than this cell. The other two men, it turned out, were country people like himself, and it wasn't too long before he had struck up a conversation with them. One said he was there because Old Master *Selectman* was dunning him for rents owed by his dead grandfather. The other had no idea why he had been arrested. When they asked Ah Q what he was in for, he replied without the slightest hesitation: "Cause I wanna revolt."

During the second half of the day, the big barred door opened once again. Ah Q was hauled out and taken to the courtroom. Up front an old man, head shaved clean, sat on a dais. Ah Q thought he must be some kind of monk at first, but then he noticed a line of soldiers standing below the old fellow and many long-gowned gentry types on either side of him as well. Some of these long-gowns had their heads shaved clean just like the old geezer, but one had hair that was a good foot and a half long and fanned out all over his shoulders just like the Fake Foreign Devil's. Every mother's son of them looked mean and ugly. What was more, they nailed Ah Q with dirty looks. At this juncture, it occurred to Ah Q that there must be something more to the bald old geezer than met the eye. Ah Q's knees instantly loosened of their own accord and he sank to a kneeling position.

"Stand! Stand while addressing this court! No kneeling!" barked the long-gowned types virtually in unison.

Ah Q appeared to understand, but didn't seem able to stay on his feet. As if of its own accord, his body collapsed into a squat and then, capitalizing on the momentum already built up, continued right on down into a full-fledged kneel.

"A born slave!" observed the long-gowned types with contempt, but they didn't try to get him to stand up again either.

"Why not come right out and confess it all now, and spare yourself a lot of needless suffering later on. We know exactly what happened anyway." The bald-headed old man's gaze never left Ah Q's face. His voice was kindly—calm and clear. "Just fess up and we'll let you go."

7. The seat of a local government.

"Confess!" bellowed the long-gowns.

"Well, to tell the truth . . . I was gonna . . . gonna come and throw—"[8]

"Then why *didn't* you come?" asked the old man in the sweetest of tones.

"Fake Foreign Devil wouldn't let me!"

"Nonsense! Too late to talk about that now anyway. Where are your confederates?"

"My what?"

"The bunch that burglarized the Zhaos' place with you?"

"Those guys didn't even come by to get me! Carted all that stuff off for themselves!" Ah Q waxed indignant at the very thought of it.

"Where did they cart it off to? If you tell, I can let you walk out of here." The old man's voice was more mellifluous than ever.

"How should I know? They didn't come by to get me!"

At this juncture the old man gave a wink, and Ah Q was once again shoved through the big barred door.

The next morning he was hauled out a second time. The courtroom was exactly as it had been yesterday—the bald-headed old man sitting on the dais while Ah Q knelt on the floor before him. "Do you have anything to say to this court?" asked the old man, voice dripping with compassion.

Ah Q thought for a bit. He didn't, and said no.

Then one of the long-gowns presented him with a sheet of paper and a writing brush. When the said personage thrust the brush into the prisoner's hand, Ah Q was so terrified that it was almost a case of *the heavenly part of the soul took to wing, and the earthly part to heel*, for this was the first time in his whole life that any relationship had ever been established between his hand and a writing brush. Just as he was wondering how you were supposed to hold the thing, the long-gown pointed to a place on the paper and told him to sign.

Ah Q's fingers tightened around the brush. In a voice that echoed with fear and shame he confessed: "Don't . . . don't know how to write."

"In that case we'll go easy on you. Just draw a circle."

Ah Q tried to compose himself enough to make the circle, but the hand that held the brush refused to stop trembling. The long-gowns carefully spread the paper out flat on the floor before him. Ah Q leaned forward over it, and marshaling all the strength and concentration at his command, approached the task at hand. Dreadfully concerned lest someone laugh at him, he was determined to make that circle a nice round one, but that damned brush lay heavy in his hand and turned out to be disobedient as well. Tremble after tremble, he traced the circle around and was on the point of closing it up when suddenly the brush shrugged off to one side, producing something that looked more like a watermelon seed than a circle.

Just as Ah Q was starting to feel conscience stricken at not being able to make a nice round circle, one of the long-gowns, not seeming to mind in the least, made off with both brush and paper.

The second time Ah Q was shoved into the cell, it didn't seem to bother him much at all, for he had come to the conclusion that in this old world of ours

8. Ah Q is about to say "throw in with the Revolutionaries." The judge, however, thinks he is going to say "throw in the towel" or surrender (*touxiang*).

there must be times when a man is supposed to get hauled in and out of cells, and times when he's supposed to draw circles on a sheet of paper too. "It would take a real jackass to draw a nice *round* circle anyway," he told himself and then promptly fell asleep.

Old Master *Selectman*, on the other hand, didn't get a single wink that whole night, for he'd had a good go-round with the lieutenant during the day. The *Selectman* had maintained that the first order of business was recovery of the stolen property, but the lieutenant had insisted that the most important thing was to make a public example of Ah Q. The lieutenant, who had only recently stopped giving a hoot *what* Old Master *Selectman* thought, had slammed his fist hard on the table and quoted: "*Make an example of only one / And a hundred crimes will go undone*. Put yourself in my shoes. I've been a lieutenant in the Revolutionary Party for less than three weeks and we've already had a dozen cases of burglary. Not a single one solved, either. Now what kind of face does that give me? When I finally do figure one out, you have to come along and start acting like some old fuddy-duddy scholar. Well I won't have it! *I'm* the one in charge of this case!" But Old Master *Selectman* held his ground. He even threatened to resign his new position as deputy in the Revolutionary Government if the lieutenant didn't do his best to recover the stolen property. "Be my guest!" had been the lieutenant's only response. And so it was that Old Master *Selectman* didn't get a single wink that whole night. We can thank our lucky stars, however, that he did not actually resign the next day.

The third time Ah Q was hauled out through the big barred door was on the morrow of the entire night during which Old Master *Selectman* didn't get a single wink.

Ah Q entered the courtroom once again. Just as before, the bald-headed old man sat on the dais while Ah Q knelt on the floor before him.

"Do you have anything more to tell the court?" asked the old man in kindly tones.

Ah Q thought for a bit. He didn't, and said no.

And then all of a sudden some of the long-gowned and short-gowned types put a white cotton vest on him, a vest with words written all over it.[9]

Now a very queasy feeling came over Ah Q, for such an outfit was like unto the *mourning clothes* that people wore when their parents died—and mourning clothes were definitely unlucky.[1]

Hands tied behind him, Ah Q was hauled out through the front gate of the *yamen* and lifted up onto an open cart. Two men in short jackets seated themselves on either side of him. The cart lurched into motion.

Ah Q saw that there were some militiamen and a squad of soldiers marching in front of the cart. The soldiers were shouldering foreign rifles. Mouths agape, spectators lined both sides of the road. He couldn't see, of course, whatever it was that was bringing up the rear. Suddenly it dawned on him. It couldn't be anything else—this was an execution!

Ah Q panicked. Everything went black. There was a loud ringing in his ears and he slipped to the edge of unconsciousness. But rather than falling in, he stayed there teetering on the brink. Remaining in this state, he was by turns

9. The words give details of his crimes.

1. White, not black, is the color of mourning.

terror-stricken and perfectly at ease. As his mind flickered on and off, Ah Q concluded that in this old world of ours there must be times when a man is supposed to get hauled away and have his head chopped off.

He recognized their route of march. He was puzzled—why weren't they headed to the execution ground? Ah Q didn't realize that he was first being paraded through the streets as "a warning to the people." But even if he had known, it would have made no difference. He would simply have concluded that in this old world of ours there must be times when a man is supposed to be paraded through the streets as a warning to the people. Then he solved the puzzle—yes, he was in fact headed toward the execution ground, but they were taking the long way around.

There was no longer even the slightest doubt. He was going to be beheaded—*ZAP!* In a daze, he turned his head first to one side and then the other. Everywhere he looked people were following along behind him just like ants. Then he just so happened to catch sight of Amah Wu standing in the midst of a group over by the roadside. Because she had been working in town, he had not been able to pay his respects to her in a long, long time.

Ah Q was suddenly gripped by shame at his own lack of pluck—all this time and he still hadn't sung a single line of opera.[2] Thoughts began to swirl around like a cyclone in his brain. *The Young Widow Visits Her Husband's Grave* was not stirring enough. *"Would that I had not . . ."* from *Battle of the Dragon and Tiger Generals* did not have any real, wallop either. Better stick to that old reliable: *"My mace of steel I grasp full tight / And with it I shall now thee smite!"* Having made his selection and suiting gesture to word, he started to raise his hand, but it wouldn't go up. Then he remembered—it was tied behind him. Couldn't sing that one either.

"Twenty years from now . . ." Ah Q shouted the first half of the sentence, a sentence he had never used before, one he had never been taught but which he seemed to have mastered on his own nonetheless.[3]

"Bravo! Bravo!" Shouts rose from the crowd like the howls of so many wolves.

The cart continued relentlessly forward. Amid all the cheering, Ah Q turned and looked at Amah Wu once again. It was apparent, however, that she had not even noticed him, for she was lost in contemplation of the novel-looking foreign rifles the soldiers were carrying. So he turned back and looked again at the people who had just cheered.

Once again thoughts began to swirl around like a cyclone in his brain. He was taken back to a time four years earlier when he had encountered a hungry wolf at the foot of a mountain. It had stalked him with persistent tenacity, neither closing in nor dropping back by so much as half a step, patiently awaiting its chance to tear into his flesh. Ah Q had been terrified and it was only because he happened to be carrying a small hatchet at the time that he had mustered the courage to make it back to Wei Village. He had never forgotten that wolf's

2. Defiant lines quoted from popular heroic operas are the stuff of melodramatic execution scenes.

3. To show contempt for authority and indifference to death, condemned criminals would often shout just before execution, "Twenty years from now I'll come back as big and bad as ever." The idea, based on the Buddhist doctrine of rebirth, was that the criminal's spirit would enter a fetus lodged inside a pregnant mother's womb at the moment of his death.

eyes—ferocious and timid at the same time and glowing like two fiendish flames that might, at any moment, burn through his body from afar.[4]

But now he saw eyes that were even more terrible, eyes such as he had never seen before. Sharp and dull at the same time, these eyes had already devoured his words and now sought to tear into something beyond mere flesh and bone. Neither closing in nor dropping back by so much as half a step, they stalked him with persistent tenacity. And then they all merged into a single set of fangs that ripped and tore at Ah Q's soul.

"Help . . ."

But before Ah Q could get it out, everything went black before his eyes, there was a loud ringing in his ears, and he felt his entire being crumble like so much dust.

As for the impact of his death, the greatest was on Old Master *Selectman*, for he was thus unable to recover any of the stolen property. Hence his entire family took to wailing. Next came the Zhao family. Some Revolutionaries cut the *Budding Talent*'s queue off when he went into town to report the burglary. On top of that, they forced him to tip them twenty strings of cash for their services. Thus the entire Zhao family took to wailing, too.

As to public opinion, the inhabitants of Wei Village were unanimous. Everyone agreed that Ah Q had indeed been an evil man, the clear proof of which could be found in the fact that he had in truth been executed. If he hadn't been bad, then how could he have gone and gotten himself executed?

Public opinion in town was something less than favorable too. Most townsfolk were disappointed—a shooting had not proved nearly so much fun as a good old-fashioned beheading. Worse yet, in his role as condemned criminal Ah Q had given a miserable performance—paraded through the streets all that time and not a single line of opera! They had followed him in vain.

DECEMBER 1921

4. Cf. the sixth entry in "Diary of a Madman."

LUIGI PIRANDELLO

1867–1936

"Who am I?" and "What is real?" are the persistent questions that underlie Luigi Pirandello's novels, short stories, and plays. Sometimes in a playful mood, sometimes more anxiously, Pirandello toys with these questions but refuses to answer them definitively. In fact, the term *Pirandellismo*, or "Pirandellism"—coined from the author's name—has come to stand in for the idea that there are as many truths as there are points of view. Yet Pirandello treats such weighty philosophical issues with a combination of humor and pathos that makes them highly entertaining.

Pirandello's great fame came late in life, as a result of his experimental dramas, but he had been an active writer for decades. Born in Girgenti (now Agrigento), Sicily, on June 28, 1867, Pirandello was the son of a sulfur merchant who intended his son to follow him into business. Pirandello preferred language and literature. After studying in Palermo and at the University of Rome, he traveled to the University of Bonn, where he received a doctorate in romance philology with a dissertation on the dialect of his hometown. Soon after completing his doctorate, Pirandello agreed to an arranged marriage with the daughter of a rich sulfur merchant, although he had never met her. They lived for ten years in Rome, where he wrote poetry and short stories, until flooding of the sulfur mines destroyed the fortunes of both families, and he was suddenly forced to earn a living. To add to their misfortune, his wife developed a jealous paranoia that grew so severe she had to be committed to an insane asylum in 1919; she remained institutionalized until her death four decades later.

Pirandello's early work included short stories and novellas written under the influence of the narrative style *verismo* (realism or naturalism) that he found exemplified in the work of the Sicilian writer Giovanni Verga (1840–1922). Pirandello wrote hundreds of stories of all lengths. He is recognized—in his clarity, realism, and psychological acuteness (often including a taste for the grotesque)—as an Italian master of the story form. His anthology of 1922, *A Year's Worth of Stories*, remains hugely popular in Italy. Not until he was in his fifties, however, did Pirandello write the more experimental plays, such as *Six Characters in Search of an Author* (1921) and *Henry IV* (1922), that established him as a major dramatist.

Despite the intellectualism of his plays, in politics Pirandello favored the irrational appeal of a strong leader. He was drawn to the fascist dictator Benito Mussolini and supported his regime at key moments—for example, in the wake of the murder by fascists of a socialist member of Parliament, Giacomo Matteotti. As Pirandello's fame spread, he directed his own company (Il Teatro d'Arte di Roma) with support from Mussolini's government and toured Europe with his plays. In 1934 he received the Nobel Prize for Literature. His later plays, featuring fantastic and grotesque elements, did not achieve the wide popularity of their predecessors.

Pirandello's plays turn the trappings of the theater itself—the stage, the producer, the author, the actors—into the material for comedy and invention. In their manipulation of ambiguous appearances and tragicomic effects, these plays foreshadow the absurdist theater of **Samuel Beckett** and others. Above all, they insist that "real" life is that which changes from moment to moment, exhibiting a fluidity that renders difficult and perhaps impossible any single formulation of either character or situation. Pirandello's playful treatment of the theatrical enterprise has been dubbed "metatheater," or theater about theater.

SIX CHARACTERS IN SEARCH OF AN AUTHOR

Six Characters in Search of an Author, the selection below, combines the elements of "metatheater" in an extraordinary self-reflexive style. At the beginning of the play, the Technician's interrupted hammering suggests that the audience has chanced on a rehearsal—of still another play by Pirandello—instead of coming to an actual performance. Concurrently, Pirandello's stage dialogue pokes fun at his reputation for obscurity. Just as the Actors are apparently set to rehearse *The Game of Role Playing*, six unexpected persons come down the aisle seeking an author: they are Characters from an unwritten novel who demand to be given dramatic existence. The play *Six Characters* is continually in the process of being composed: composed as the interwoven double plot we see on stage, composed by the Prompter writing a script in shorthand for the Actors to reproduce, and composed as the inner drama of the Characters finally achieves its rightful existence as a work of art.

The play's initial absurdity emerges when the six fictional Characters arrive with their claim to be "truer and more real" than the "real" Actors who seek to impersonate them. (Of course, to the audience all the figures onstage are equally real—or unreal.) Each Character represents a particular identity created by the author. Pirandello later had the Characters wear masks to distinguish them from the Actors—not the conventional masks of ancient Greek drama or of the Japanese *Noh* theater that identify the characters' roles, nor the ceremonial masks, representing spirits in African ritual, that temporarily invest the wearer with the spirit's identity and authority. Instead, they are a theatrical device, a symbol and visual reminder of each Character's unchanging being. The six Characters are incapable of developing outside their roles and are condemned, in their search for existence, painfully to reenact their essential roles.

Conversely, the fictional Characters have more stable personalities than "real" people, including the Actors, who are still "no one," incomplete, open to change and misinterpretation. Characters can claim to be "someone" because their natures have been decided once and for all. Yet further complications attend this contrast between fictional characters and real actors: for instance, the Characters feel the urge to play their own roles and are disturbed at the prospect of having the Actors misrepresent them. All human beings, asserts Pirandello, whether fictional or real, are subject to being misunderstood; we even misunderstand ourselves when we think our identities are constant in all situations. We always have "the illusion of being always one thing for all men," says the Father, but "It's not true!"

Pirandello does not hold his audience's attention simply by uttering grand philosophical truths, however. *Six Characters* hums with suspense and discovery, from the moment that the Characters interrupt the rehearsal with its complaining Actors and Stage Manager. The story that the Characters tell about themselves hints of melodrama and family scandal, like attention-grabbing headlines from a sensationalist newspaper. Indeed, Pirandello plays with the risqué element by focusing on the Characters' repeated attempts to portray one emotionally fraught scene. Eventually, the pathos of this play within the play comes to overwhelm the more philosophical metatheatrical frame.

Six Characters in Search of an Author underwent an interesting evolution to become the play that we see today. First performed in 1921 in Rome, where its unsettling plot and characters scandalized a traditionalist audience, it was reshaped in more radical form after the remarkable performance produced by Georges Pitoëff in 1923. Pirandello, who came to Paris wary of Pitoëff's innovations (for instance, he had the Characters arrive in a green-lit stage elevator), was soon convinced that the Russian director's stagecraft enhanced the original text. Pitoëff used his knowledge of technical effects to accentuate the relationship of appearance and reality: he extended the stage with several steps leading down to the auditorium (a break from the conventional "fourth wall" concept, in which the actors on stage proceed as if unaware of the audience); underscored the play within a play with rehearsal effects, showing the Technician hammering and the Director arranging suitable props and lighting; he emphasized the division between Characters and Actors by separating the groups on stage and dressing all the Characters (except the Little Girl) in black. Pirandello welcomed these changes and expanded on many of them. To distinguish the Characters even further from the Actors, he proposed contrasting clothing in addition to masks, black for the former and pale for the latter. Most striking, however, is his transformation of Pitoëff's steps into an actual bridge between the world of the stage and the auditorium, a strategy that allows the Actors (and Characters) to come and go in the "real world" of the audience.

In breaking down comfortable illusions of compartmentalized, stable reality, Pirandello revolutionized European stage techniques. In place of the nineteenth century's "well-made play"—with its neatly constructed plot that boxes real life into a conventional beginning, middle, and end, and its safely inaccessible characters on the other side of the footlights—he offers unpredictable plots and ambiguous roles. It is not easy to know the truth about others, he suggests, or to make ourselves known behind the "mask" that each of us wears.

Readers might enjoy testing the enduring liveliness of Pirandello's dialogue by rehearsing their own selection of scenes—or perhaps by relocating them in a contemporary setting. According to the director Robert Brustein, whose 1988 production of *Six Characters in Search of an Author* set the action in New York and replaced Madam Pace with a pimp, "Pirandello both encourages and stimulates a pluralism in theater because there can be dozens, hundreds, thousands of productions of *Six Characters*, and every one of them is going to be different."

Six Characters in Search of an Author[1]

Characters of the Play-in-the-Making

The FATHER
The MOTHER
The SON, *aged 22*
The STEPDAUGHTER, *18*
The BOY, *14*
The LITTLE GIRL, *4*
(these two last do not speak)
Then, called into being: MADAM PACE

Actors in the Company

The DIRECTOR *(direttore-capocomico)*
LEADING LADY
LEADING MAN
SECOND ACTRESS
INGENUE
JUVENILE LEAD
Other actors and actresses
STAGE MANAGER
PROMPTER
PROPERTY MAN
TECHNICIAN
Director's SECRETARY
STAGE DOOR MAN
STAGE CREW

THE PLACE: *The stage of a playhouse.*

When the audience arrives in the theater, the curtain is raised; and the stage, as normally in the daytime, is without wings or scenery and almost completely dark and empty. From the beginning we are to receive the impression of an unrehearsed performance.

Two stairways, left and right respectively, connect the stage with the auditorium.

Onstage the dome of the prompter's box has been placed on one side of the box itself. On the other side, at the front of the stage, a small table and an armchair with its back to the audience, for the DIRETTORE-CAPOCOMICO [DIRECTOR].

Two other small tables of different sizes with several chairs around them have also been placed at the front of the stage, ready as needed for the rehearsal. Other chairs here and there, left and right, for the actors, and at the back, a piano, on one side and almost hidden.

As soon as the houselights dim, the TECHNICIAN *is seen entering at the door onstage. He is wearing a blue shirt, and a tool bag hangs from his belt. From a corner at the back he takes several stage braces, then arranges them on the floor downstage, and kneels down to hammer some nails in. At the sound of the hammering, the* STAGE MANAGER *comes running from the door that leads to the dressing rooms.*

STAGE MANAGER Oh! What are you doing?

TECHNICIAN What am I doing? Hammering.

1. Translated by Eric Bentley. In the Italian editions, Pirandello notes that he did not divide the play into formal acts or scenes. The translator has marked the divisions for clarity, however, according to the stage directions.

STAGE MANAGER At this hour? [*He looks at the clock.*] It's ten-thirty already. The Director will be here any moment. For the rehearsal.

TECHNICIAN I gotta have time to work, too, see.

STAGE MANAGER You will have. But not now.

TECHNICIAN When?

STAGE MANAGER Not during rehearsal hours. Now move along, take all this stuff away, and let me set the stage for the second act of, um, *The Game of Role Playing.*[2]

[*Muttering, grumbling, the* TECHNICIAN *picks up the stage braces and goes away. Meanwhile, from the door onstage, the actors of the company start coming in, both men and women, one at a time at first, then in twos, at random, nine or ten of them, the number one would expect as the cast in rehearsals of Pirandello's play* The Game of Role Playing, *which is the order of the day. They enter, greet the* STAGE MANAGER *and each other, all saying good-morning to all. Several go to their dressing rooms. Others, among them the* PROMPTER, *who has a copy of the script rolled up under his arm, stay onstage, waiting for the* DIRECTOR *to begin the rehearsal. Meanwhile, either seated in conversational groups, or standing, they exchange a few words among themselves. One lights a cigarette, one complains about the part he has been assigned, one reads aloud to his companions items of news from a theater journal. It would be well if both the Actresses and the Actors wore rather gay and brightly colored clothes and if this first improvised scene* [scena a soggetto] *combined vivacity with naturalness. At a certain point, one of the actors can sit down at the piano and strike up a dance tune. The younger actors and actresses start dancing.*]

STAGE MANAGER [*clapping his hands to call them to order*] All right, that's enough of that. The Director's here.

[*The noise and the dancing stop at once. The Actors turn and look toward the auditorium from the door of which the* DIRECTOR *is now seen coming. A bowler hat on his head, a walking stick under his arm, and a big cigar in his mouth, he walks down the aisle and, greeted by the Actors, goes onstage by one of the two stairways. The* SECRETARY *hands him his mail: several newspapers and a script in a wrapper.*]

DIRECTOR Letters?

SECRETARY None. That's all the mail there is.

DIRECTOR [*handing him the script*] Take this to my room. [*Then, looking around and addressing himself to the* STAGE MANAGER] We can't see each other in here. Want to give us a little light?

STAGE MANAGER OK.

[*He goes to give the order, and shortly afterward, the whole left side of the stage where the Actors are is lit by a vivid white light. Meanwhile, the* PROMPTER *has taken up his position in his box. He uses a small lamp and has the script open in front of him.*]

DIRECTOR [*clapping his hands*] Very well, let's start. [*To the* STAGE MANAGER] Someone missing?

2. *Il Giuoco delle Parti* (1918), a stage adaptation of Pirandello's own novella. The hero, Leone Gala, pretends to ignore his wife Silia's infidelity until the end, when he takes revenge by tricking her lover, Guido Venanzi, into taking his place in a fatal duel she had engineered to get rid of her husband.

STAGE MANAGER The Leading Lady.

DIRECTOR As usual! [*He looks at the clock.*] We're ten minutes late already. Fine her for that, would you, please? Then she'll learn to be on time.

[*He has not completed his rebuke when the voice of the* LEADING LADY *is heard from the back of the auditorium.*]

LEADING LADY No, no, for heaven's sake! I'm here! I'm here! [*She is dressed all in white with a big, impudent hat on her head and a cute little dog in her arms. She runs down the aisle and climbs one of the sets of stairs in great haste.*]

DIRECTOR You've sworn an oath always to keep people waiting.

LEADING LADY You must excuse me. Just couldn't find a taxi. But you haven't even begun, I see. And I'm not on right away. [*Then, calling the* STAGE MANAGER *by name, and handing the little dog over to him*] Would you please shut him in my dressing room?

DIRECTOR [*grumbling*] And the little dog to boot! As if there weren't enough dogs around here. [*He claps his hands again and turns to the* PROMPTER.] Now then, the second act of *The Game of Role Playing*. [*As he sits down in his armchair*] Quiet, gentlemen. Who's onstage?

[*The Actresses and Actors clear the front of the stage and go and sit on one side, except for the three who will start the rehearsal and the* LEADING LADY *who, disregarding the* DIRECTOR'S *request, sits herself down at one of the two small tables.*]

DIRECTOR [*to the* LEADING LADY] You're in this scene, are you?

LEADING LADY Me? No, no.

DIRECTOR [*irritated*] Then how about getting up, for Heaven's sake?

[*The* LEADING LADY *rises and goes and sits beside the other Actors who have already gone to one side.*]

DIRECTOR [*to the* PROMPTER] Start, start.

PROMPTER [*reading from the script*] "In the house of Leone Gala. A strange room, combined study and dining room."

DIRECTOR [*turning to the* STAGE MANAGER] We'll use the red room.

STAGE MANAGER [*making a note on a piece of paper*] Red room. Very good.

PROMPTER [*continuing to read from the script*] "The table is set and the desk has books and papers on it. Shelves with books on them, and cupboards with lavish tableware. Door in the rear through which one goes to Leone's bedroom. Side door on the left through which one goes to the kitchen. The main entrance is on the right."

DIRECTOR [*rising and pointing*] All right, now listen carefully. That's the main door. This is the way to the kitchen. [*Addressing himself to the Actor playing the part of Socrates*[3]] You will come on and go out on this side. [*To the* STAGE MANAGER] The compass at the back. And curtains. [*He sits down again.*]

STAGE MANAGER [*making a note*] Very good.

3. Nickname given to Gala's servant, Filippo, in *The Game of Role Playing*, the play they are rehearsing.

PROMPTER [*reading as before*] "Scene One. Leone Gala, Guido Venanzi, Filippo called Socrates." [*To the* DIRECTOR] Am I supposed to read the stage directions, too?

DIRECTOR Yes, yes, yes! I've told you that a hundred times!

PROMPTER [*reading as before*] "At the rise of the curtain, Leone Gala, wearing a chef's hat and apron, is intent on beating an egg in a saucepan with a wooden spoon. Filippo, also dressed as a cook, is beating another egg. Guido Venanzi, seated, is listening."

LEADING ACTOR [*to the* DIRECTOR] Excuse me, but do I really have to wear a chef's hat?

DIRECTOR [*annoyed by this observation*] I should say so! It's in the script. [*And he points at it.*]

LEADING ACTOR But it's ridiculous, if I may say so.

DIRECTOR [*leaping to his feet, furious*] "Ridiculous, ridiculous!" What do you want me to do? We never get a good play from France any more,[4] so we're reduced to producing plays by Pirandello, a fine man and all that, but neither the actors, the critics, nor the audience are ever happy with his plays, and if you ask me, he does it all on purpose. [*The Actors laugh. And now he rises and coming over to the* LEADING ACTOR *shouts.*] A cook's hat, yes, my dear man! And you beat eggs. And you think you have nothing more on your hands than the beating of eggs? Guess again. You symbolize the shell of those eggs. [*The Actors resume their laughing, and start making ironical comments among themselves.*] Silence! And pay attention while I explain. [*Again addressing himself to the* LEADING ACTOR] Yes, the shell: that is to say, the empty *form* of reason without the *content* of instinct, which is blind. You are reason, and your wife is instinct in the game of role playing. You play the part assigned you, and you're your own puppet—of your own free will.[5] Understand?

LEADING ACTOR [*extending his arms, palms upward*] Me? No.

DIRECTOR [*returning to his place*] Nor do I. Let's go on. Wait and see what I do with the ending. [*In a confidential tone*] I suggest you face three-quarters front. Otherwise, what with the abstruseness of the dialogue, and an audience that can't hear you, good-bye play! [*Again clapping*] Now, again, order! Let's go.

PROMPTER Excuse me, sir, may I put the top back on the prompter's box? There's rather a draft.

DIRECTOR Yes, yes, do that.

[*The* STAGE DOOR MAN *has entered the auditorium in the meanwhile, his braided cap on his head. Proceeding down the aisle, he goes up onstage to announce to the* DIRECTOR *the arrival of the Six Characters, who have also entered the auditorium, and have started following him at a certain distance, a little lost and perplexed, looking around them.*

4. The producer refers to the realistic, tightly constructed plays (often French) that were internationally popular in the late 19th century and a staple of Italian theaters at the beginning of the 20th.

5. Leone Gala is a rationalist and an aesthete—the opposite of his impulsive, passionate wife, Silia. By masking his feelings and constantly playing the role of gourmet cook, he chooses his own role and thus becomes his own "puppet."

Whoever is going to try and translate this play into scenic terms must take all possible measures not to let these Six Characters get confused with the Actors of the Company. Placing both groups correctly, in accordance with the stage directions, once the Six are onstage, will certainly help, as will lighting the two groups in contrasting colors. But the most suitable and effective means to be suggested here is the use of special masks for the Characters: masks specially made of material which doesn't go limp when sweaty and yet masks which are not too heavy for the Actors wearing them, cut out and worked over so they leave eyes, nostrils, and mouth free. This will also bring out the inner significance of the play. The Characters in fact should not be presented as ghosts but as created realities, unchanging constructs of the imagination, and therefore more solidly real than the Actors with their fluid naturalness. The masks will help to give the impression of figures constructed by art, each one unchangeably fixed in the expression of its own fundamental sentiment, thus:

remorse *in the case of the* FATHER; revenge *in the case of the* STEPDAUGHTER; disdain *in the case of the* SON; grief *in the case of the* MOTHER, *who should have wax tears fixed in the rings under her eyes and on her cheeks, as with the sculpted and painted images of the* mater dolorosa[6] *in church. Their clothes should be of special material and design, without extravagance, with rigid, full folds like a statue, in short not suggesting a material you might buy at any store in town, cut out and tailored at any dressmaker's.*

The FATHER *is a man of about fifty, hair thin at the temples, but not bald, thick mustache coiled round a still youthful mouth that is often open in an uncertain, pointless smile. Pale, most notably on his broad forehead: blue eyes, oval, very clear and piercing; dark jacket and light trousers: at times gentle and smooth, at times he has hard, harsh outbursts.*

The MOTHER *seems scared and crushed by an intolerable weight of shame and self-abasement. Wearing a thick black crepe widow's veil, she is modestly dressed in black, and when she lifts the veil, the face does not show signs of suffering, and yet seems made of wax. Her eyes are always on the ground.*

The STEPDAUGHTER, *eighteen, is impudent, almost insolent. Very beautiful, and also in mourning, but mourning of a showy elegance. She shows contempt for the timid, afflicted, almost humiliated manner of her little brother, rather a mess of a* BOY, *fourteen, also dressed in black, but a lively tenderness for her little sister, a* LITTLE GIRL *of around four, dressed in white with a black silk sash round her waist.*

The SON, *twenty-two, tall, almost rigid with contained disdain for the* FATHER *and supercilious indifference toward the* MOTHER, *wears a mauve topcoat and a long green scarf wound round his neck.*]

STAGE DOOR MAN [*beret in hand*] Excuse me, your honor.

DIRECTOR [*rudely jumping on him*] What is it now?

STAGE DOOR MAN [*timidly*] There are some people here asking for you.

[*The* DIRECTOR *and the Actors turn in astonishment to look down into the auditorium.*]

DIRECTOR [*furious again*] But I'm rehearsing here! And you know perfectly well no one can come in during rehearsal! [*Turning again toward the house*] Who are these people? What do they want?

6. Mother of Sorrows (Latin), a traditional representation of Mary, mother of Jesus.

THE FATHER [*stepping forward, followed by the others, to one of the two little stairways to the stage*] We're here in search of an author.

DIRECTOR [*half angry, half astounded*] An author? What author?

FATHER Any author, sir.

DIRECTOR There's no author here at all. It's not a new play we're rehearsing.

STEPDAUGHTER [*very vivaciously as she rushes up the stairs*] Then so much the better, sir! *We* can be your new play!

ONE OF THE ACTORS [*among the racy comments and laughs of the others*] Did you hear that?

FATHER [*following the* STEPDAUGHTER *onstage*] Certainly, but if the author's not here . . . [*To the* DIRECTOR] Unless *you'd* like to be the author?

[*The* MOTHER, *holding the* LITTLE GIRL *by the hand, and the* BOY *climb the first steps of the stairway and remain there waiting. The* SON *stays morosely below.*]

DIRECTOR Is this your idea of a joke?

FATHER Heavens, no! Oh, sir, on the contrary: we bring you a painful drama.

STEPDAUGHTER We can make your fortune for you.

DIRECTOR Do me a favor, and leave. We have no time to waste on madmen.

FATHER [*wounded, smoothly*] Oh, sir, you surely know that life is full of infinite absurdities which, brazenly enough, do not need to appear probable, because they're true.

DIRECTOR What in God's name are you saying?

FATHER I'm saying it can actually be considered madness, sir, to force oneself to do the opposite: that is, to give probability to things so they will seem true. But permit me to observe that, if this is madness, it is also the *raison d'être*[7] of your profession.

[*The Actors become agitated and indignant.*]

DIRECTOR [*rising and looking him over*] It is, is it? It seems to you an affair for madmen, our profession?

FATHER Well, to make something seem true which is not true . . . without any need, sir: just for fun . . . Isn't it your job to give life onstage to creatures of fantasy?

DIRECTOR [*immediately, making himself spokesman for the growing indignation of his Actors*] Let me tell you something, my good sir. The actor's profession is a very noble one. If, as things go nowadays, our new playwrights give us nothing but stupid plays, with puppets in them instead of men, it is our boast, I'd have you know, to have given life—on these very boards—to immortal works of art.

[*Satisfied, the Actors approve and applaud their* DIRECTOR.]

FATHER [*interrupting and bearing down hard*] Exactly! That's just it. You have created living beings—*more* alive than those that breathe and wear clothes! Less real, perhaps; but more true! We agree completely!

[*The Actors look at each other, astounded.*]

DIRECTOR What? You were saying just now . . .

7. Reason for being (French).

FATHER No, no, don't misunderstand me. You shouted that you hadn't time to waste on madmen. So I wanted to tell you that no one knows better than you that Nature employs the human imagination to carry her work of creation on to a higher plane!

DIRECTOR All right, all right. But what are you getting at, exactly?

FATHER Nothing, sir. I only wanted to show that one may be born to this life in many modes, in many forms: as tree, as rock, water or butterfly . . . or woman. And that . . . characters are born too.

DIRECTOR [*his amazement ironically feigned*] And you—with these companions of yours—were born a character?

FATHER Right, sir. And alive, as you see.

[*The* DIRECTOR *and the Actors burst out laughing as at a joke.*]

FATHER [*wounded*] I'm sorry to hear you laugh, because, I repeat, we carry a painful drama within us, as you all might deduce from the sight of that lady there, veiled in black.

[*As he says this, he gives his hand to the* MOTHER *to help her up the last steps and, still holding her by the hand, he leads her with a certain tragic solemnity to the other side of the stage, which is suddenly bathed in fantastic light. The* LITTLE GIRL *and the* BOY *follow the* MOTHER; *then the* SON, *who stands on one side at the back; then the* STEPDAUGHTER *who also detaches herself from the others—downstage and leaning against the proscenium arch. At first astonished at this development, then overcome with admiration, the Actors now burst into applause as at a show performed for their benefit.*]

DIRECTOR [*bowled over at first, then indignant*] Oh, stop this! Silence please! [*Then, turning to the Characters*] And you, leave! Get out of here! [*To the* STAGE MANAGER] For God's sake, get them out!

STAGE MANAGER [*stepping forward but then stopping, as if held back by a strange dismay*] Go! Go!

FATHER [*to the* DIRECTOR] No, look, we, um—

DIRECTOR [*shouting*] I tell you we've got to work!

LEADING MAN It's not right to fool around like this . . .

FATHER [*resolute, stepping forward*] I'm amazed at your incredulity! You're accustomed to seeing the created characters of an author spring to life, aren't you, right here on this stage, the one confronting the other? Perhaps the trouble is there's no script *there* [*Pointing to the* PROMPTER'S *box*] with us in it?

STEPDAUGHTER [*going right up to the* DIRECTOR, *smiling, coquettish*] Believe me, we really are six characters, sir. Very interesting ones at that. But lost. Adrift.

FATHER [*brushing her aside*] Very well: lost, adrift. [*Going right on*] In the sense, that is, that the author who created us, made us live, did not wish, or simply and materially was not able, to place us in the world of art.[8] And that was a real crime, sir, because whoever has the luck to be born a living character can also laugh at death. He will never die! The man will die, the writer, the instrument of creation; the creature will never die! And to have

8. In the 1925 preface to *Six Characters*, Pirandello explains that these characters came to him first as characters for a novel that he later abandoned. Haunted by their half-realized personalities, he decided to use the situation in a play.

eternal life it doesn't even take extraordinary gifts, nor the performance of miracles. Who was Sancho Panza? Who was Don Abbondio?[9] But they live forever because, as live germs, they have the luck to find a fertile matrix, an imagination which knew how to raise and nourish them, make them live through all eternity!

DIRECTOR That's all well and good. But what do you people want here?

FATHER We want to live, sir.

DIRECTOR [*ironically*] Through all eternity?

FATHER No, sir. But for a moment at least. In you.

AN ACTOR Well, well, well!

LEADING LADY They want to live in us.

JUVENILE LEAD [*pointing to the* STEPDAUGHTER] Well, I've no objection, so long as I get that one.

FATHER Now look, look. The play is still in the making. [*To the* DIRECTOR] But if you wish, and your actors wish, we can make it right away. Acting in concert.

LEADING MAN [*annoyed*] Concert? We don't put on concerts! We do plays, dramas, comedies!

FATHER Very good. That's why we came.

DIRECTOR Well, where's the script?

FATHER Inside us, sir. [*The Actors laugh.*] The drama is inside us. It *is* us. And we're impatient to perform it. According to the dictates of the passion within us.

STEPDAUGHTER [*scornful, with treacherous grace, deliberate impudence*] My passion—if you only knew, sir! My passion—for him! [*She points to the* FATHER *and makes as if to embrace him but then breaks into a strident laugh.*]

FATHER [*an angry interjection*] You keep out of this now. And please don't laugh that way!

STEPDAUGHTER No? Then, ladies and gentlemen, permit me. A two months' orphan, I shall dance and sing for you all. Watch how! [*She mischievously starts to sing "Beware of Chu Chin Chow" by Dave Stamper, reduced to fox-trot or slow one-step by Francis Salabert: the first verse, accompanied by a step or two of dancing.*[1] *While she sings and dances, the Actors, especially the young ones, as if drawn by some strange fascination, move toward her and half raise their hands as if to take hold of her. She runs away and when the Actors burst into applause she just stands there, remote, abstracted, while the* DIRECTOR *protests.*]

ACTORS and ACTRESSES [*laughing and clapping*] Brava! Fine! Splendid!

DIRECTOR [*annoyed*] Silence! What do you think this is, a night spot? [*Taking the* FATHER *a step or two to one side, with a certain amount of consternation*] Tell me something. Is she crazy?

FATHER Crazy? Of course not. It's much worse than that.

9. A rural priest in Alessandro Manzoni's novel *I Promessi sposi* (*The Betrothed*, 1825–27). Sancho Panza was Don Quixote's servant in Cervantes' novel *Don Quixote* (1605–15).

1. "Chu-Chin-Chow" was a contemporary popular song from the Ziegfeld Follies of 1917.

STEPDAUGHTER [*running over at once to the* DIRECTOR] Worse! Worse! Not crazy but worse! Just listen: I'll play it for you right now, this drama, and at a certain point you'll see me—when this dear little thing—[*She takes the* LITTLE GIRL *who is beside the* MOTHER *by the hand and leads her to the* DIRECTOR.]—isn't she darling? [*Takes her in her arms and kisses her.*] Sweetie! Sweetie! [*Puts her down again and adds with almost involuntary emotion.*] Well, when God suddenly takes this little sweetheart away from her poor mother, and that idiot there—[*Thrusting the* BOY *forward, rudely seizing him by a sleeve*] does the stupidest of things, like the nitwit that he is, [*With a shove she drives him back toward the* MOTHER] then you will see me take to my heels. Yes, ladies and gentlemen, take to my heels! I can hardly wait for that moment. For after what happened between him and me—[*She points to the* FATHER *with a horrible wink.*] something very intimate, you understand—I can't stay in such company any longer, witnessing the anguish of our mother on account of that fool there—[*She points to the* SON.] Just look at him, look at him!—how indifferent, how frozen, because he is the legitimate son, that's what he is, full of contempt for me, for him [*the* BOY], and for that little creature [*the* LITTLE GIRL], because we three are bastards, d'you see? Bastards. [*Goes to the* MOTHER *and embraces her.*] And this poor mother, the common mother of us all, he—well, he doesn't want to acknowledge her as *his* mother too, and he looks down on her, that's what he does, looks on her as only the mother of us three bastards, the wretch! [*She says this rapidly in a state of extreme excitement. Her voice swells to the word: "bastards!" and descends again to the final "wretch," almost spitting it out.*]

MOTHER [*to the* DIRECTOR, *with infinite anguish*] In the name of these two small children, sir, I implore you . . . [*She grows faint and sways.*] Oh, heavens . . .

FATHER [*rushing over to support her with almost all the Actors, who are astonished and scared*] Please! Please, a chair, a chair for this poor widow!

ACTORS [*rushing over*] —Is it true then?—She's *really* fainting?

DIRECTOR A chair!

[*One of the Actors proffers a chair. The others stand around, ready to help. The* MOTHER, *seated, tries to stop the* FATHER *from lifting the veil that hides her face.*]

FATHER [*to the* DIRECTOR] Look at her, look at her . . .

MOTHER Heavens, no, stop it!

FATHER Let them see you. [*He lifts her veil.*]

MOTHER [*rising and covering her face with her hands, desperate*] Oh, sir, please stop this man from carrying out his plan. It's horrible for me!

DIRECTOR [*surprised, stunned*] I don't know where we're at! What's this all about? [*To the* FATHER] Is this your wife?

FATHER [*at once*] Yes, sir, my wife.

DIRECTOR Then how is she a widow, if you're alive?

[*The Actors relieve their astonishment in a loud burst of laughter.*]

FATHER [*wounded, with bitter resentment*] Don't laugh! Don't laugh like that! Please! Just that is her drama, sir. She had another man. Another man who should be here!

MOTHER [*with a shout*] No! No!

STEPDAUGHTER He had the good luck to die. Two months ago, as I told you. We're still in mourning as you see.

FATHER But he's absent, you see, not just because he's dead. He's absent—take a look at her, sir, and you will understand at once!—Her drama wasn't in the love of two men for whom she was incapable of feeling anything—except maybe a little gratitude [not to me, but to him]—She is not a woman, she is a mother!—And her drama—a powerful one, very powerful—is in fact all in those four children which she bore to her two men.

MOTHER *My* men? Have you the gall to say I wanted two men? It was him, sir. He forced the other man on me. Compelled—yes, compelled—me to go off with him!

STEPDAUGHTER [*cutting in, roused*] It's not true!

MOTHER [*astounded*] How d'you mean, not true?

STEPDAUGHTER It's not true! It's not true!

MOTHER And what can you know about it?

STEPDAUGHTER It's not true. [*To the* DIRECTOR] Don't believe it. Know why she says it? For his sake. [*Pointing to the* SON] His indifference tortures her, destroys her. She wants him to believe that, if she abandoned him when he was two, it was because he [*the* FATHER] compelled her to.

MOTHER [*with violence*] He did compel me, he did compel me, as God is my witness! [*To the* DIRECTOR] Ask him if that isn't true. [*Her husband*] Make him tell him. [*The* SON] She couldn't know anything about it.

STEPDAUGHTER With my father, while he lived, I know you were always happy and content. Deny it if you can.

MOTHER I don't deny it, I don't . . .

STEPDAUGHTER He loved you, he cared for you! [*To the* BOY, *with rage*] Isn't that so? Say it! Why don't you speak, you dope?

MOTHER Leave the poor boy alone. Why d'you want to make me out ungrateful, daughter? I have no wish to offend your father! I told him [*the* FATHER] I didn't abandon my son and my home for my own pleasure. It wasn't my fault.

FATHER That's true, sir. It was mine.

[*Pause.*]

LEADING MAN [*to his companions*] What a show!

LEADING LADY And *they* put it on—for us.

JUVENILE LEAD Quite a change!

DIRECTOR [*who is now beginning to get very interested*] Let's listen to this, let's listen! [*And saying this, he goes down one of the stairways into the auditorium, and stands in front of the stage, as if to receive a spectator's impression of the show.*]

SON [*without moving from his position, cold, quiet, ironic*] Oh yes, you can now listen to the philosophy lecture. He will tell you about the Demon of Experiment.

FATHER You are a cynical idiot, as I've told you a hundred times. [*To the* DIRECTOR, *now in the auditorium*] He mocks me, sir, on account of that phrase I found to excuse myself with.

SON [*contemptuously*] Phrases!

FATHER Phrases! Phrases! As if they were not a comfort to everyone: in the face of some unexplained fact, in the face of an evil that eats into us, to find a word that says nothing but at least quiets us down!

STEPDAUGHTER Quiets our guilt feelings too. That above all.

FATHER Our guilt feelings? Not so. I have never quieted my guilt feelings with words alone.

STEPDAUGHTER It took a little money as well, didn't it, it took a little dough! The hundred lire[2] he was going to pay me, ladies and gentlemen!

[*Movement of horror among the Actors.*]

SON [*with contempt toward the* STEPDAUGHTER] That's filthy.

STEPDAUGHTER Filthy? The dough was there. In a small pale blue envelope on the mahogany table in the room behind the shop. Madam Pace's [*she pronounces it "Pah-chay"*] shop. One of those Madams who lure us poor girls from good families into their *ateliers* under the pretext of selling *Robes et Manteaux*.[3]

SON And with those hundred lire he was going to pay she has bought the right to tyrannize over us all. Only it so happens—I'd have you know—that he never actually incurred the debt.

STEPDAUGHTER Oh, oh, but we were really going to it, I assure you! [*She bursts out laughing.*]

MOTHER [*rising in protest*] Shame, daughter! Shame!

STEPDAUGHTER [*quickly*] Shame? It's my revenge! I am frantic, sir, frantic to live it, live that scene! The room . . . here's the shop window with the coats in it; there's the bed-sofa; the mirror; a screen; and in front of the window the little mahogany table with the hundred lire in the pale blue envelope. I can see it. I could take it. But you men should turn away now: I'm almost naked. I don't blush anymore. It's he that blushes now. [*Points to the* FATHER.] But I assure you he was very pale, very pale, at that moment. [*To the* DIRECTOR] You must believe me, sir.

DIRECTOR You lost me some time ago.

FATHER Of course! Getting it thrown at you like that! Restore a little order, sir, and let *me* speak. And never mind this ferocious girl. She's trying to heap opprobrium on me by withholding the relevant explanations!

STEPDAUGHTER This is no place for long-winded narratives!

FATHER I said—explanations.

STEPDAUGHTER Oh, certainly. Those that suit your turn.

[*At this point, the* DIRECTOR *returns to the stage to restore order.*]

FATHER But that's the whole root of the evil. Words. Each of us has, inside him, a world of things—to everyone, his world of things. And how can we understand each other, sir, if, in the words I speak, I put the sense and value of things as they are inside me, whereas the man who hears them inevitably receives them in the sense and with the value they have for him,

2. About $40 in today's U.S. currency.

3. The implication is that Madam Pace (Italian for "peace") runs a call-girl operation under the guise of selling fashionable *Robes et Manteaux*, or dressing gowns and coats (French). *Ateliers*: workshops (French).

the sense and value of the world inside him? We think we understand each other but we never do. Consider: the compassion, all the compassion I feel for this woman [*the* MOTHER] has been received by her as the most ferocious of cruelties!

MOTHER You ran me out of the house.

FATHER Hear that? Ran her out. It *seemed to her* that I ran her out.

MOTHER You can talk; I can't . . . But, look, sir, after he married me . . . and who knows why he did? I was poor, of humble birth . . .

FATHER And that's why I married you for your . . . humility. I loved you for it, believing . . . [*He breaks off, seeing her gestured denials; seeing the impossibility of making himself understood by her, he opens his arms wide in a gesture of despair, and turns to the* DIRECTOR.] See that? She says No. It's scarifying, isn't it, sir, scarifying, this deafness of hers, this mental deafness! She has a heart, oh yes, where her children are concerned! But she's deaf, deaf in the brain, deaf, sir, to the point of desperation!

STEPDAUGHTER [*to the* DIRECTOR] All right, but now make him tell you what his intelligence has ever done for us.

FATHER If we could only foresee all the evil that can result from the good we believe we're doing!

[*At this point, the* LEADING LADY, *who has been on hot coals seeing the* LEADING MAN *flirt with the* STEPDAUGHTER, *steps forward and asks of the* DIRECTOR:]

LEADING LADY Excuse me, is the rehearsal continuing?

DIRECTOR Yes, of course! But let me listen a moment.

JUVENILE LEAD This is something quite new.

INGENUE Very interesting!

LEADING LADY If that sort of thing interests you. [*And she darts a look at the* LEADING MAN.]

DIRECTOR [*to the* FATHER] But you must give us *clear* explanations. [*He goes and sits down.*]

FATHER Right. Yes. Listen. There was a man working for me. A poor man. As my secretary. Very devoted to me. Understood *her* [*the* MOTHER] very well. There was mutual understanding between them. Nothing wrong in it. They thought no harm at all. Nothing off-color about it. No, no, he knew his place, as she did. They didn't do anything wrong. Didn't even think it.

STEPDAUGHTER So he thought it *for* them. And did it.

FATHER It's not true! I wanted to do them some good. And myself too, oh yes, I admit. I'd got to this point, sir: I couldn't say a word to either of them but they would exchange a significant look. The one would consult the eyes of the other, asking how what I had said should be taken, if they didn't want to put me in a rage. That sufficed, you will understand, to keep me continually in a rage, in a state of unbearable exasperation.

DIRECTOR Excuse me, why didn't you fire him, this secretary?

FATHER Good question! That's what I did do, sir. But then I had to see that poor woman remain in my house, a lost soul. Like an animal without a master that one takes pity on and carries home.

MOTHER No, no, it's—

FATHER [*at once, turning to her to get it in first*] Your son? Right?

MOTHER He'd already snatched my son from me.

FATHER But not from cruelty. Just so he'd grow up strong and healthy. In touch with the soil.

STEPDAUGHTER [*pointing at the latter, ironic*] And just look at him!

FATHER [*at once*] Uh? Is it also my fault if he then grew up this way? I sent him to a wet nurse, sir, in the country, a peasant woman. I didn't find her [*the* MOTHER] strong enough, despite her humble origin. I'd married her for similar reasons, as I said. All nonsense maybe, but there we are. I always had these confounded aspirations toward a certain solidity, toward what is morally sound. [*Here the* STEPDAUGHTER *bursts out laughing.*] Make her stop that! It's unbearable!

DIRECTOR Stop it. I can't hear, for Heaven's sake!

[*Suddenly, again, as the* DIRECTOR *rebukes her, she is withdrawn and remote, her laughter cut off in the middle. The* DIRECTOR *goes down again from the stage to get an impression of the scene.*]

FATHER I couldn't bear to be with that woman anymore. [*Points to the* MOTHER] Not so much, believe me, because she irritated me, and even made me feel physically ill, as because of the pain—a veritable anguish—that I felt on her account.

MOTHER And he sent me away!

FATHER. Well provided for. And to that man. Yes, sir. So she could be free of me.

MOTHER And so *he* could be free.

FATHER That, too. I admit it. And much evil resulted. But I intended good. And more for her than for me, I swear it! [*He folds his arms across his chest. Then, suddenly, turning to the* MOTHER] I never lost sight of you, never lost sight of you till, from one day to the next, unbeknown to me, he carried you off to another town. He noticed I was interested in her, you see, but that was silly, because my interest was absolutely pure, absolutely without ulterior motive. The interest I took in her new family, as it grew up, had an unbelievable tenderness to it. Even she should bear witness to that! [*He points to the* STEPDAUGHTER.]

STEPDAUGHTER Oh, very much so! I was a little sweetie. Pigtails over my shoulders. Panties coming down a little bit below my skirt. A little sweetie. He would see me coming out of school, at the gate. He would come and see me as I grew up . . .

FATHER This is outrageous. You're betraying me!

STEPDAUGHTER I'm not! What do you mean?

FATHER Outrageous. Outrageous. [*Immediately, still excited, he continues in a tone of explanation, to the* DIRECTOR.] My house, sir, when she had left it, at once seemed empty. [*Points to the* MOTHER.] She was an incubus. But she filled my house for me. Left alone, I wandered through these rooms like a fly without a head. This fellow here [*the* SON] was raised away from home. Somehow, when he got back, he didn't seem mine anymore. Without a mother between me and him, he grew up on his own, apart, without any relationship to me, emotional or intellectual. And then—strange, sir, but true—first I grew curious, then I was gradually attracted toward *her* family, which I had brought into being. The thought of *this* family began to fill the void around me. I had to—really had to—believe she was at peace, absorbed in the simplest cares of life, lucky to be away and far removed from the complicated torments of my spirit. And to have proof of this, I would go and see that little girl at the school gate.

STEPDAUGHTER Correct! He followed me home, smiled at me and, when I was home, waved to me, like this! I would open my eyes wide and look at him suspiciously. I didn't know who it was. I told mother. And she guessed right away it was him. [*The* MOTHER *nods.*] At first she didn't want to send me back to school for several days. When I did go, I saw him again at the gate—the clown!—with a brown paper bag in his hand. He came up to me, caressed me, and took from the bag a lovely big Florentine straw hat with a ring of little May roses round it—for me!

DIRECTOR You're making too long a story of this.

SON [*contemptuously*] Story is right! Fiction! Literature!

FATHER Literature? This is life, sir. Passion!

DIRECTOR Maybe! But not actable!

FATHER I agree. This is all preliminary. I wouldn't *want* you to act it. As you see, in fact, she [*the* STEPDAUGHTER] is no longer that little girl with pigtails—

STEPDAUGHTER —and the panties showing below her skirt!

FATHER The drama comes now, sir. Novel, complex—

STEPDAUGHTER [*gloomy, fierce, steps forward*] —What my father's death meant for us was—

FATHER [*not giving her time to continue*] —poverty, sir. They returned, unbeknownst to me. She's so thickheaded. [*Pointing to the* MOTHER] It's true she can hardly write herself, but she could have had her daughter write, or her son, telling me they were in need!

MOTHER But, sir, how could I have guessed he felt the way he did?

FATHER Which is just where you always went wrong. You could never guess how I felt about anything!

MOTHER After so many years of separation, with all that had happened . . .

FATHER And is it my fault if that fellow carried you off as he did? [*Turning to the* DIRECTOR] From one day to the next, as I say. He'd found some job someplace. I couldn't even trace them. Necessarily, then, my interest dwindled, with the years. The drama breaks out, sir, unforeseen and violent, at their return. When I, alas, was impelled by the misery of my still-living flesh . . . Oh, and what misery that is for a man who is alone, who has not wanted to form debasing relationships, not yet old enough to do without a woman, and no longer young enough to go and look for one without shame! Misery? It's horror, horror, because no woman can give him love anymore.—Knowing this, one should go without! Well, sir, on the outside, when other people are watching, each man is clothed in dignity: but, on the inside, he knows what unconfessable things are going on within him. One gives way, gives way to temptation, to rise again, right afterward, of course, in a great hurry to put our dignity together again, complete, solid, a stone on a grave that hides and buries from our eyes every sign of our shame and even the very memory of it! It's like that with everybody. Only the courage to say it is lacking—to say certain things.

STEPDAUGHTER The courage to do them, though—everybody's got that.

FATHER Everybody. But in secret. That's why it takes more courage to say them. A man only has to say them and it's all over: he's labeled a cynic. But, sir, he isn't! He's just like everybody else. Better! He's better because he's not afraid to reveal, by the light of intelligence, the red stain of shame, there, in the human beast, which closes its eyes to it. Woman—yes, woman—what is she like, actually? She looks at us, inviting, tantalizing. You take hold of her. She's no sooner in your arms than she shuts her eyes. It is the sign of her submission. The sign with which she tells the man: Blind yourself for I am blind.

STEPDAUGHTER How about when she no longer keeps them shut? When she no longer feels the need to hide the red stain of shame from herself by closing her eyes, and instead, her eyes now dry and impassive, sees the shame of the man, who has blinded himself even without love? They make me vomit, all those intellectual elaborations, this philosophy that begins by revealing the beast and then goes on to excuse it and save its soul . . . I can't bear to hear about it! Because when a man feels obliged to *reduce* life this way, reduce it all to "the beast," throwing overboard every vestige of the truly human, every aspiration after chastity, all feelings of purity, of the ideal, of duties, of modesty, of shame, then nothing is more contemptible, more nauseating than his wretched guilt feelings! Crocodile tears!

DIRECTOR Let's get to the facts, to the facts! This is just discussion.

FATHER Very well. But a fact is like a sack. When it's empty, it won't stand up. To make it stand up you must first pour into it the reasons and feelings by which it exists. I couldn't know that—when that man died and they returned here in poverty—she went out to work as a dressmaker to support the children, nor that the person she went to work for was that . . . that Madam Pace!

STEPDAUGHTER A high-class dressmaker, if you'd all like to know! To all appearances, she serves fine ladies, but then she arranges things so that the fine ladies serve *her* . . . without prejudice to ladies not so fine!

MOTHER Believe me, sir, I never had the slightest suspicion that that old witch hired me because she had her eye on my daughter . . .

STEPDAUGHTER Poor mama! Do you know, sir, what the woman did when I brought her my mother's work? She would point out to me the material she'd ruined by giving it to my mother to sew. And she deducted for that, she deducted. And so, you understand, *I* paid, while that poor creature thought she was making sacrifices for me and those two by sewing, even at night, Madam Pace's material!

[*Indignant movements and exclamations from the Actors.*]

DIRECTOR [*without pause*] And there, one day, you met—

STEPDAUGHTER [*pointing to the* FATHER] —him, him, yes sir! An old client! Now there's a scene for you to put on! Superb!

FATHER Interrupted by her—the mother—

STEPDAUGHTER [*without pause, treacherously*] —almost in time!—

FATHER [*shouting*] No, no, *in* time! Because, luckily, I recognized the girl in time. And I took them all back, sir, into my home. Now try to visualize my situation and hers, the one confronting the other—she as you see her now, myself unable to look her in the face anymore.

STEPDAUGHTER It's too absurd! But—afterward—was it possible for me to be a modest little miss, virtuous and well-bred, in accordance with those confounded aspirations toward a certain solidity, toward what is morally sound?

FATHER And therein lies the drama, sir, as far as I'm concerned: in my awareness that each of us thinks of himself as *one* but that, well, it's not true, each of us is many, oh so many, sir, according to the possibilities of being that are in us. We are one thing for this person, another for that! Already *two* utterly different things! And with it all, the illusion of being always one thing for all men, and always this one thing in every single action. It's not true! Not true! We realize as much when, by some unfortunate chance, in one or another of our acts, we find ourselves suspended, hooked. We see, I mean, that we are not wholly in that act, and that therefore it would be abominably unjust to judge us by that act alone, to hold us suspended, hooked, in the pillory, our whole life long, as if our life were summed up in that act! Now do you understand this girl's treachery? She surprised me in a place, in an act, in which she should never have had to know me—I couldn't be that way for her. And she wants to give me a reality such as I could never had expected I would have to assume for her, the reality of a fleeting moment, a shameful one, in my life! This, sir, this is what I feel most strongly. And you will see that the drama will derive tremendous value from this. But now add the situation of the others! His . . . [*He points to the* SON.]

SON [*shrugging contemptuously*] Leave me out of this! It's none of my business.

FATHER What? None of your business?

SON None. And I *want* to be left out. I wasn't made to be one of you, and you know it.

STEPDAUGHTER We're common, aren't we?—And he's so refined.—But from time to time I give him a hard, contemptuous look, and he looks down at the ground. You may have noticed that, sir. He looks down at the ground. For he knows the wrong he's done me.

SON [*hardly looking at her*] Me?

STEPDAUGHTER You! You! I'm on the streets because of you! [*A movement of horror from the Actors*] Did you or did you not, by your attitude, deny us—I won't say the intimacy of home but even the hospitality which puts guests at their ease? We were the intruders, coming to invade the kingdom of your legitimacy! I'd like to have you see, sir, certain little scenes between just him and me! He says I tyrannized over them all. But it was entirely because of his attitude that I started to exploit the situation he calls filthy, a situation which had brought me into his home with my mother, who is also *his* mother, *as its mistress!*

SON [*coming slowly forward*] They can't lose, sir, three against one, an easy game. But figure to yourself a son, sitting quietly at home, who one fine day sees a young woman arrive, an impudent type with her nose in the air, asking for his father, with whom she has heaven knows what business; and then he sees her return, in the same style, accompanied by that little girl over there; and finally he sees her treat his father—who can say why?—in a very ambiguous and cool manner, demanding money, in a tone that takes for granted that he *has* to give it, has to, is obligated—

FATHER —but I *am* obligated: it's for your mother!

SON How would I know? When, sir, [*To the* DIRECTOR] have I ever seen her? When have I ever heard her spoken of? One day I see her arrive with her [*the* STEPDAUGHTER], with that boy, with that little girl. They say to me: "It's your mother too, know that?" I manage to figure out from her carryings-on [*Pointing at the* STEPDAUGHTER] why they arrived in our home from one day to the next . . . What I'm feeling and experiencing I can't put into words, and wouldn't want to. I wouldn't want to confess it, even to myself. It cannot therefore result in any action on my part. You can see that. Believe me, sir, I'm a character that, dramatically speaking, remains unrealized. I'm out of place in their company. So please leave me out of it all!

FATHER What? But it's just because you're so—

SON [*in violent exasperation*] —I'm so what? How would *you* know? When did you ever care about me?

FATHER *Touché! Touché!*[4] But isn't even that a dramatic situation? This withdrawnness of yours, so cruel to me, and to your mother who, on her return home is seeing you almost for the first time, a grown man she doesn't recognize, though she knows you're her son . . . [*Pointing out the* MOTHER *to the* DIRECTOR] Just look at her, she's crying.

STEPDAUGHTER [*angrily, stamping her foot*] Like the fool she is!

FATHER [*pointing her out to the* DIRECTOR] And she can't abide him, you know. [*Again referring to the* SON]—He says it's none of his business. The truth is he's almost the pivot of the action. Look at that little boy, clinging to his mother all the time, scared, humiliated . . . It's all because of *him* [*the* SON]. Perhaps the most painful situation of all is that little boy's: he feels alien, more than all the others, and the poor little thing is so mortified, so anguished at being taken into our home—out of charity, as it were . . . [*Confidentially*] He's just like his father: humble, doesn't say anything . . .

DIRECTOR He won't fit anyway. You've no idea what a nuisance children are onstage.

FATHER But he wouldn't be a nuisance for long. Nor would the little girl, no, she's the first to go . . .

DIRECTOR Very good, yes! The whole thing interests me very much indeed. I have a hunch, a definite hunch, that there's material here for a fine play!

STEPDAUGHTER [*trying to inject herself*] With a character like me in it!

FATHER [*pushing her to one side in his anxiety to know what the* DIRECTOR *will decide*] You be quiet!

4. Literally "touched" (French), a term in fencing to acknowledge a hit by an opponent; here used ironically.

DIRECTOR [*going right on, ignoring the interruption*] Yes, it's new stuff . . .

FATHER Very new!

DIRECTOR You had some gall, though, to come and throw it at me this way . . .

FATHER Well, you see, sir, born as we are to the stage . . .

DIRECTOR You're amateurs, are you?

FATHER No. I say: "born to the stage" because . . .

DIRECTOR Oh, come on, you must have done some acting!

FATHER No, no, sir, only as every man acts the part assigned to him—by himself or others—in this life. In me you see passion itself, which—in almost all people, as it rises—invariably becomes a bit theatrical . . .

DIRECTOR Well, never mind! Never mind about that!—You see, my dear sir, without the author . . . I could direct you to an author . . .

FATHER No, no, look: you be the author!

DIRECTOR Me? What are you talking about?

FATHER Yes, you. You. Why not?

DIRECTOR Because I've never been an author, that's why not!

FATHER Couldn't you be one now, hm? There's nothing to it. Everyone's doing it. And your job is made all the easier by the fact that you have us—here—alive—right in front of your nose!

DIRECTOR It wouldn't be enough.

FATHER Not enough? Seeing us live our own drama . . .

DIRECTOR I know, but you always need someone to write it!

FATHER No. Just someone to take it down, maybe, since you have us here—in action—scene by scene. It'll be enough if we piece together a rough sketch for you, then you can rehearse it.

DIRECTOR [*tempted, goes up onstage again*] Well, I'm almost, almost tempted . . . Just for kicks . . . We could actually rehearse . . .

FATHER Of course you could! What scenes you'll see emerge! I can list them for you right away.

DIRECTOR I'm tempted . . . I'm tempted . . . Let's give it a try . . . Come to my office. [*Turns to the Actors.*] Take a break, will you? But don't go away. We'll be back in fifteen or twenty minutes. [*To the* FATHER] Let's see what we can do . . . Maybe we can get something very extraordinary out of all this . . .

FATHER We certainly can. Wouldn't it be better to take *them* along? [*He points to the Characters.*]

DIRECTOR Yes, let them all come. [*Starts going off, then comes back to address the Actors.*] Now don't forget. Everyone on time. Fifteen minutes.

[DIRECTOR *and Six Characters cross the stage and disappear. The Actors stay there and look at one another in amazement.*]

LEADING MAN Is he serious? What's he going to do?

JUVENILE This is outright insanity.

A THIRD ACTOR We have to improvise a drama right off the bat?

JUVENILE LEAD That's right. Like Commedia dell'Arte.[5]

LEADING LADY Well, if he thinks *I'm* going to lend myself to that sort of thing . . .

5. A form of popular theater beginning in 16th-century Italy; the actors improvised dialogue according to basic comic or dramatic plots and in response to the audience's reaction.

INGENUE Count me out.

A FOURTH ACTOR [*alluding to the Characters*] I'd like to know who those people are.

THE THIRD ACTOR Who would they be? Madmen or crooks!

JUVENILE LEAD And he's going to pay attention to them?

INGENUE Carried away by vanity! Wants to be an author now . . .

LEADING MAN It's out of this world. If this is what the theater is coming to, my friends . . .

A FIFTH ACTOR I think it's rather fun.

THE THIRD ACTOR Well! We shall see. We shall see. [*And chatting thus among themselves, the Actors leave the stage, some using the little door at the back, others returning to their dressing rooms.*]

The curtain remains raised. The performance is interrupted by a twenty-minute intermission.

Bells ring. The performance is resumed.

[*From dressing rooms, from the door, and also from the house, the Actors, the* STAGE MANAGER, *the* TECHNICIAN, *the* PROMPTER, *the* PROPERTY MAN *return to the stage; at the same time the* DIRECTOR *and the Six Characters emerge from the office.*

As soon as the house lights are out, the stage lighting is as before.]

DIRECTOR Let's go, everybody! Is everyone here? Quiet! We're beginning. [*Calls the* TECHNICIAN *by name.*]

TECHNICIAN Here!

DIRECTOR Set the stage for the parlor scene. Two wings and a backdrop with a door in it will do, quickly please!

[*The* TECHNICIAN *at once runs to do the job, and does it while the* DIRECTOR *works things out with the* STAGE MANAGER, *the* PROPERTY MAN, *the* PROMPTER, *and the Actors. This indication of a set consists of two wings, a drop with a door in it, all in pink and gold stripes.*]

DIRECTOR [*to the* PROPERTY MAN] See if we have some sort of bed-sofa in the prop room.

PROPERTY MAN Yes, sir, there's the green one.

STEPDAUGHTER No, no, not green! It was yellow, flowered, plush, and very big. Extremely comfortable.

PROPERTY MAN Well, we have nothing like that.

DIRECTOR But it doesn't matter. Bring the one you have.

STEPDAUGHTER Doesn't matter? Madam Pace's famous chaise longue!

DIRECTOR This is just for rehearsal. Please don't meddle! [*To the* STAGE MANAGER] See if we have a display case—long and rather narrow.

STEPDAUGHTER The table, the little mahogany table for the pale blue envelope!

STAGE MANAGER [*to the* DIRECTOR] There's the small one. Gilded.

DIRECTOR All right. Get that one.

FATHER A large mirror.

STEPDAUGHTER And the screen. A screen, please, or what'll I do?

STAGE MANAGER Yes, ma'am, we have lots of screens, don't worry.

DIRECTOR [*to the* STEPDAUGHTER] A few coat hangers?

STEPDAUGHTER A great many, yes.

DIRECTOR [*to the* STAGE MANAGER] See how many we've got, and have them brought on.

STAGE MANAGER Right, sir, I'll see to it.

[*The* STAGE MANAGER *also hurries to do his job and while the* DIRECTOR *goes on talking with the* PROMPTER *and then with the Characters and the Actors, has the furniture carried on by stagehands and arranges it as he thinks fit.*]

DIRECTOR [*to the* PROMPTER] Meanwhile you can get into position. Look: this is the outline of the scenes, act by act. [*He gives him several sheets of paper.*] You'll have to be a bit of a virtuoso today.

PROMPTER Shorthand?

DIRECTOR [*pleasantly surprised*] Oh, good! You know shorthand?

PROMPTER I may not know prompting, but shorthand . . . [*Turning to a stagehand*] Get me some paper from my room—quite a lot—all you can find!

[*The stagehand runs off and returns a little later with a wad of paper which he gives to the* PROMPTER.]

DIRECTOR [*going right on, to the* PROMPTER] Follow the scenes line by line as we play them, and try to pin down the speeches, at least the most important ones. [*Then, turning to the Actors*] Clear the stage please, everyone! Yes, come over to this side and pay close attention. [*He indicates the left.*]

LEADING LADY Excuse me but—

DIRECTOR [*forestalling*] There'll be no improvising, don't fret.

LEADING MAN Then what are we to do?

DIRECTOR Nothing. For now, just stop, look, and listen. Afterward you'll be given written parts. Right now we'll rehearse. As best we can. With them doing the rehearsing for us. [*He points to the Characters.*]

FATHER [*amid all the confusion onstage, as if he'd fallen from the clouds*] *We're* rehearsing? How d'you mean?

DIRECTOR Yes, for them. You rehearse for them. [*Indicates the Actors.*]

FATHER But if we are the characters . . .

DIRECTOR All right, you're characters, but, my dear sir, characters don't perform here, actors perform here. The characters are there, in the script [*He points to the* PROMPTER'S *box.*]—when there *is* a script!

FATHER Exactly! Since there isn't, and you gentlemen have the luck to have them right here, alive in front of you, those characters . . .

DIRECTOR Oh, great! Want to do it all yourselves? Appear before the public, do the acting yourselves?

FATHER Of course. Just as we are.

DIRECTOR [*ironically*] I'll bet you'd put on a splendid show!

LEADING MAN Then what's the use of staying?

DIRECTOR [*without irony, to the Characters*] Don't run away with the idea that you can act! That's laughable . . . [*And in fact the Actors laugh.*] Hear that? They're laughing. [*Coming back to the point*] I was forgetting. I must cast the show. It's quite easy. It casts itself. [*To the* SECOND ACTRESS] You, ma'am, will play the Mother. [*To the* FATHER] You'll have to find her a name.

FATHER Amalia, sir.

DIRECTOR But that's this lady's real name. We wouldn't want to call her by her real name!

FATHER Why not? If that is her name . . . But of course, if it's to be this lady . . . [*He indicates the* SECOND ACTRESS *with a vague gesture.*] To me *she* [*the* MOTHER] is Amalia. But suit yourself . . . [*He is getting more and more confused.*] I don't know what to tell you . . . I'm beginning to . . . oh, I don't know . . . to find my own words ringing false, they sound different somehow.

DIRECTOR Don't bother about that, just don't bother about it. We can always find the right sound. As for the name, if you say Amalia, Amalia it shall be; or we'll find another. For now, we'll designate the characters thus: [*To the* JUVENILE LEAD] You're the Son. [*To the* LEADING LADY] You, ma'am, are of course the Stepdaughter.

STEPDAUGHTER [*excitedly*] What, what? That one there is me? [*She bursts out laughing.*]

DIRECTOR [*mad*] What is there to laugh at?

LEADING LADY [*aroused*] No one has ever dared laugh at me! I insist on respect—or I quit!

STEPDAUGHTER But, excuse me, I'm not laughing at you.

DIRECTOR [*to the* STEPDAUGHTER] You should consider yourself honored to be played by . . .

LEADING LADY [*without pause, contemptuously*] —"That one there!"

STEPDAUGHTER But I wasn't speaking of you, believe me. I was speaking of me. I don't see me in you, that's all. I don't know why . . . I guess you're just not like me!

FATHER That's it, exactly, my dear sir! What is *expressed* in us . . .

DIRECTOR Expression, expression! You think that's your business? Not at all!

FATHER Well, but what *we* express . . .

DIRECTOR But you don't. You don't express. You provide us with raw material. The actors give it body and face, voice and gesture. They've given expression to much loftier material, let me tell you. Yours is on such a small scale that, if it stands up onstage at all, the credit, believe me, should all go to my actors.

FATHER I don't dare contradict you, sir, but it's terribly painful for us who are as you see us—with these bodies, these faces—

DIRECTOR [*cutting in, out of patience*] —that's where makeup comes in, my dear sir, for whatever concerns the face, the remedy is makeup!

FATHER Yes. But the voice, gesture—

DIRECTOR Oh, for Heaven's sake! You can't exist here! Here the actor acts you, and that's that!

FATHER I understand, sir. But now perhaps I begin to guess also why our author who saw us, alive as we are, did not want to put us onstage. I don't want to offend your actors. God forbid! But I feel that seeing myself acted . . . I don't know by whom . . .

LEADING MAN [*rising with dignity and coming over, followed by the gay young Actresses who laugh*] By me, if you've no objection.

FATHER [*humble, smooth*] I'm very honored, sir. [*He bows.*] But however much art and willpower the gentleman puts into absorbing me into himself . . . [*He is bewildered now.*]

LEADING MAN Finish. Finish.

[*The Actresses laugh.*]

FATHER Well, the performance he will give, even forcing himself with makeup to resemble me, well, with that figure [*All the Actors laugh.*] he can hardly play me as I am. I shall rather be—even apart from the face—what he interprets me to be, as he feels I am—if he feels I am anything—and not as I feel myself inside myself. And it seems to me that whoever is called upon to judge us should take this into account.

DIRECTOR So now you're thinking of what the critics will say? And I was still listening! Let the critics say what they want. We will concentrate on putting on your play! [*He walks away a little, and looks around.*] Come on, come on. Is the set ready? [*To the Actors and the Characters*] Don't clutter up the stage, I want to be able to see! [*He goes down from the stage.*] Let's not lose any more time! [*To the* STEPDAUGHTER] Does the set seem pretty good to you?

STEPDAUGHTER Oh! But I can't recognize it!

DIRECTOR Oh my God, don't tell me we should reconstruct Madam Pace's back room for you! [*To the* FATHER] Didn't you say a parlor with flowered wallpaper?

FATHER Yes, sir. White.

DIRECTOR It's not white. Stripes. But it doesn't matter. As for furniture we're in pretty good shape. That little table—bring it forward a bit! [*Stagehands do this. To the* PROPERTY MAN] Meanwhile you get an envelope, possibly a light blue one, and give it to the gentleman. [*Indicating the* FATHER]

PROPERTY MAN A letter envelope?

DIRECTOR and FATHER Yes, a letter envelope.

PROPERTY MAN I'll be right back.

[*He exits.*]

DIRECTOR Come on, come on. It's the young lady's scene first. [*The* LEADING LADY *comes forward.*] No, no, wait. I said the young lady. [*Indicating the* STEPDAUGHTER] You will just watch—

STEPDAUGHTER [*adding, without pause*] —watch me live it!

LEADING LADY [*resenting this*] I'll know how to live it, too, don't worry, once I put myself in the role!

DIRECTOR [*raising his hands to his head*] Please! No more chatter! Now, scene one. The Young Lady with Madam Pace. Oh, and how about this Madam Pace? [*Bewildered, looking around him, he climbs back onstage.*]

FATHER She isn't with us, sir.

DIRECTOR Then what do we do?

FATHER But she's alive. She's alive too.

DIRECTOR Fine. But where?

FATHER I'll tell you. [*Turning to the Actresses*] If you ladies will do me the favor of giving me your hats for a moment.

THE ACTRESSES [*surprised a little, laughing a little, in chorus*] —What?—Our hats?—What does he say?—Why?—Oh, dear!

DIRECTOR What are you going to do with the ladies' hats?

[*The Actors laugh.*]

FATHER Oh, nothing. Just put them on these coathooks for a minute. And would some of you be so kind as to take your coats off too?

ACTORS [*as before*] Their coats too?—And then?—He's nuts!

AN ACTRESS OR TWO [*as above*] —But why?—Just the coats?

FATHER Just so they can be hung there for a moment. Do me this favor. Will you?

ACTRESSES [*taking their hats off, and one or two of them their coats, too, continuing to laugh, and going to hang the hats here and there on the coathooks*] —Well, why not?—There!—This is getting to be really funny!—Are we to put them on display?

FATHER Exactly! That's just right, ma'am: on display!

DIRECTOR May one inquire *why* you are doing this?

FATHER Yes, sir. If we set the stage better, who knows but she may come to us, drawn by the objects of her trade . . . [*Inviting them to look toward the entrance at the back*] Look! Look!

[*The entrance at the back opens, and* MADAM PACE *walks a few paces downstage, a hag of enormous fatness with a pompous wig of carrot-colored wool and a fiery red rose on one side of it,* à l'espagnole,[6] *heavily made up, dressed with gauche elegance in garish red silk, a feathered fan in one hand and the other hand raised to hold a lighted cigarette between two fingers. At the sight of this apparition, the* DIRECTOR *and the Actors at once dash off the stage with a yell of terror, rushing down the stairs and making as if to flee up the aisle. The* STEPDAUGHTER, *on the other hand runs to* MADAM PACE*—deferentially, as to her boss.*]

STEPDAUGHTER [*running to her*] Here she is, here she is!

FATHER [*beaming*] It's she! What did I tell you? Here she is!

DIRECTOR [*overcoming his first astonishment, and incensed now*] What tricks are these?

[*The next four speeches are more or less simultaneous.*]

LEADING MAN What goes on around here?

JUVENILE LEAD Where on earth did she come from?

INGENUE They must have been holding her in reserve.

LEADING LADY Hocus pocus! Hocus pocus!

FATHER [*dominating these protests*] Excuse me, though! Why, actually, would you want to destroy this prodigy in the name of vulgar truth, this miracle of a reality that is born of the stage itself—called into being by the stage, drawn here by the stage, and shaped by the stage—and which has more right to live on the stage than you have because it is much truer? Which of you actresses will later re-create Madam Pace? This lady *is* Madam Pace. You must admit that the actress who re-creates her will be less true than this lady—who is Madam Pace. Look: my daughter recognized her, and went right over to her. Stand and watch the scene!

[*Hesitantly, the* DIRECTOR *and the Actors climb back onstage. But the scene between the* STEPDAUGHTER *and* MADAM PACE *has begun during the protest of the Actors and the* FATHER*'s answer:* sotto voce,[7] *very quietly, in short naturally—as would never be possible on a stage. When, called to order by the* FATHER, *the Actors turn again to watch, they hear* MADAM PACE, *who has just placed her hand under the* STEPDAUGHTER*'s chin in order to raise*

6. In the Spanish manner.

7. In a low voice (Italian).

her head, talk unintelligibly. After trying to hear for a moment, they just give up.]

DIRECTOR Well?

LEADING MAN What's she saying?

LEADING LADY One can't hear a thing.

JUVENILE LEAD Louder!

STEPDAUGHTER [*leaving* MADAM PACE, *who smiles a priceless smile, and walking down toward the Actors*] Louder, huh? How d'you mean: louder? These aren't things that can be said louder. *I* was able to say them loudly—to shame him [*Indicating the* FATHER]—that was my revenge. For Madam, it's different, my friends: it would mean—jail.

DIRECTOR Oh my God! It's like that, is it? But, my dear young lady, in the theater one must be heard. And even we couldn't hear you, right here on the stage. How about an audience out front? There's a scene to be done. And anyway you *can* speak loudly—it's just between yourselves, we won't be standing here listening like now. Pretend you're alone. In a room. The back room of the shop. No one can hear you. [*The* STEPDAUGHTER *charmingly and with a mischievous smile tells him No with a repeated movement of the finger.*] Why not?

STEPDAUGHTER [*sotto voce, mysteriously*] There's someone who'll hear if she [MADAM PACE] speaks loudly.

DIRECTOR [*in consternation*] Is someone else going to pop up now?

[*The Actors make as if to quit the stage again.*]

FATHER No, no, sir. She means me. I'm to be there—behind the door—waiting. And Madam knows. So if you'll excuse me. I must be ready for my entrance. [*He starts to move.*]

DIRECTOR [*stopping him*] No, wait. We must respect the exigencies of the theater. Before you get ready—

STEPDAUGHTER [*interrupting him*] Let's get on with it! I tell you I'm dying with desire to live it, to live that scene! If he's ready, I'm more than ready!

DIRECTOR [*shouting*] But first we have to get that scene out of you and her! [*Indicating* MADAM PACE] Do you follow me?

STEPDAUGHTER Oh dear, oh dear, she was telling me things you already know—that my mother's work had been badly done once again, the material is ruined, and I'm going to have to bear with her if I want her to go on helping us in our misery.

MADAM PACE [*coming forward with a great air of importance*] Sí, sí, señor, porque yo[8] no want profit. No advantage, no.

DIRECTOR [*almost scared*] What, what? She talks like *that?!*

[*All the Actors loudly burst out laughing.*]

STEPDAUGHTER [*also laughing*] Yes, sir, she talks like that—halfway between Spanish and English—very funny, isn't it?

MADAM PACE Now that is not good manners, no, that you laugh at me! Yo hablo[9] the English as good I can, señor!

8. Yes, yes, Mister, because I (broken Spanish). 9. I speak (Spanish).

DIRECTOR And it *is* good! Yes! Do talk that way, ma'am! It's a surefire effect! There couldn't be anything better to, um, soften the crudity of the situation! Do talk that way! It's fine!

STEPDAUGHTER Fine! Of course! To have certain propositions put to you in a lingo like that. Surefire, isn't it? Because, sir, it seems almost a joke. When I hear there's "an old señor" who wants to "have good time conmigo," I start to laugh—don't I, Madam Pace?

MADAM PACE Old, viejo, no. Viejito—leetle beet old, sí, darling? Better like that: if he no give you fun, he bring you prudencia.[1]

MOTHER [*jumping up, to the stupefaction and consternation of all the Actors, who had been taking no notice of her, and who now respond to her shouts with a start and, smiling, try to restrain her, because she has grabbed* MADAM PACE*'s wig and thrown it on the floor*] Witch! Witch! Murderess! My daughter!

STEPDAUGHTER [*running over to restrain her* MOTHER] No, no, mama, no, please!

FATHER [*running over too at the same time*] Calm down, calm down! Sit here.

MOTHER Then send that woman away!

STEPDAUGHTER [*to the* DIRECTOR, *who also has run over*] It's not possible, not possible that my mother should be here!

FATHER [*also to the* DIRECTOR] They can't be together. That's why, you see, the woman wasn't with us when we came. Their being together would spoil it, you understand.

DIRECTOR It doesn't matter, doesn't matter at all. This is just a preliminary sketch. Everything helps. However confusing the elements, I'll piece them together somehow. [*Turning to the* MOTHER *and sitting her down again in her place*] Come along, come along, ma'am, calm down: sit down again.

STEPDAUGHTER [*who meanwhile has moved center stage again. Turning to* MADAM PACE] All right, let's go!

MADAM PACE Ah, no! No thank you! Yo aquí no do nada[2] with your mother present.

STEPDAUGHTER Oh, come on! Bring in that old señor who wants to have good time conmigo! [*Turning imperiously to all the others*] Yes, we've got to have it, this scene!—Come on, let's go! [*To* MADAM PACE] You may leave.

MADAM PACE Ah sí, I go, I go, go seguramente[3] . . . [*She makes her exit furiously, putting her wig back on, and looking haughtily at the Actors who applaud mockingly.*]

STEPDAUGHTER [*to the* FATHER] And you can make your entrance. No need to go out and come in again. Come here. Pretend, you're already in. Right. Now I'm here with bowed head, modest, huh? Let's go! Speak up! With a different voice, the voice of someone just in off the street: "Hello, miss."

DIRECTOR [*by this time out front again*] Now look: are you directing this, or am I? [*To the* FATHER *who looks undecided and perplexed.*] Do it, yes. Go to the back. Don't leave the stage, though. And then come forward.

1. Discretion (Spanish). *Viejo*: old man (Spanish). *Viejito*: little old man (Spanish).
2. Here I don't do anything (broken Spanish).
3. Certainly (Spanish).

[*The* FATHER *does it, almost dismayed. Very pale; but already clothed in the reality of his created life, he smiles as he approaches from the back, as if still alien to the drama which will break upon him. The Actors now pay attention to the scene which is beginning.*]

DIRECTOR [*softly, in haste, to the* PROMPTER *in the box*] And you, be ready now, ready to write!

THE SCENE

FATHER [*coming forward, with a different voice*] Hello, miss.

STEPDAUGHTER [*with bowed head and contained disgust*] Hello.

FATHER [*scrutinizing her under her hat which almost hides her face and noting that she is very young, exclaims, almost to himself, a little out of complaisance and a little out of fear of compromising himself in a risky adventure*] Oh . . . —Well, I was thinking, it wouldn't be the first time, hm? The first time you came here.

STEPDAUGHTER [*as above*] No, sir.

FATHER You've been here other times? [*And when the* STEPDAUGHTER *nods*] More than once? [*He waits a moment for her to answer, then again scrutinizes her under her hat; smiles; then says*] Well then, hm . . . it shouldn't any longer be so . . . May I take this hat off for you?

STEPDAUGHTER [*without pause, to forestall him, not now containing her disgust*] No, sir, *I* will take it off! [*And she does so in haste, convulsed.*]

[*The* MOTHER, *watching the scene with the* SON *and with the two others, smaller and more her own, who are close to her all the time, forming a group at the opposite side of the stage from the Actors, is on tenterhooks as she follows the words and actions of* FATHER *and* STEPDAUGHTER *with varied expression: grief, disdain, anxiety, horror, now hiding her face, now emitting a moan.*]

MOTHER Oh God! My God!

FATHER [*is momentarily turned to stone by the moaning; then he reassumes the previous tone*] Now give it to me: I'll hang it up for you. [*He takes the hat from her hands.*] But I could wish for a little hat worthier of such a dear, lovely little head! Would you like to help me choose one? From the many Madam has?—You wouldn't?

INGENUE [*interrupting*] Oh now, come on, those are *our* hats!

DIRECTOR [*without pause, very angry*] Silence, for Heaven's sake, don't try to be funny!—This is the stage. [*Turning back to the* STEPDAUGHTER] Would you begin again, please?

STEPDAUGHTER [*beginning again*] No, thank you, sir.

FATHER Oh, come on now, don't say no. Accept one from me. To please me . . . There are some lovely ones you know. And we would make Madam happy. Why else does she put them on display?

STEPDAUGHTER No, no, sir, look: I wouldn't even be able to wear it.

FATHER You mean because of what the family would think when they saw you come home with a new hat on? Think nothing of it. Know how to handle that? What to tell them at home?

STEPDAUGHTER [*breaking out, at the end of her rope*] But that's not why, sir. I couldn't wear it because I'm . . . as you see me. You might surely have noticed! [*Points to her black attire.*]

FATHER In mourning, yes. Excuse me. It's true: I do see it. I beg your pardon. I'm absolutely mortified, believe me.

STEPDAUGHTER [*forcing herself and plucking up courage to conquer her contempt and nausea*] Enough! Enough! It's for me to thank you, it is not for you to be mortified or afflicted. Please pay no more attention to what I said. Even for me, you understand . . . [*She forces herself to smile and adds*] I need to forget I am dressed like this.

DIRECTOR [*interrupting, addressing himself to the* PROMPTER *in his box, and going up onstage again*] Wait! Wait! Don't write. Leave that last sentence out, leave it out! [*Turning to the* FATHER *and* STEPDAUGHTER] It's going very well indeed. [*Then to the* FATHER *alone*] This is where you go into the part we prepared. [*To the Actors*] Enchanting, that little hat scene, don't you agree?

STEPDAUGHTER Oh, but the best is just coming. Why aren't we continuing?

DIRECTOR Patience one moment. [*Again addressing himself to the Actors*] Needs rather delicate handling, of course . . .

LEADING MAN —With a certain *ease*—

LEADING LADY Obviously. But there's nothing to it. [*To the* LEADING MAN] We can rehearse it at once, can't we?

LEADING MAN As far as I'm . . . Very well, I'll go out and make my entrance. [*And he does go out by the back door, ready to reenter.*]

DIRECTOR [*to the* LEADING LADY] And so, look, your scene with that Madam Pace is over. I'll write it up later. You are standing . . . Hey, where are you going?

LEADING LADY Wait. I'm putting my hat back on . . . [*She does so, taking the hat from the hook.*]

DIRECTOR Oh yes, good.—Now, you're standing here with your head bowed.

STEPDAUGHTER [*amused*] But she's not wearing black!

LEADING LADY *I shall* wear black! And I'll carry it better than you!

DIRECTOR [*to the* STEPDAUGHTER] Keep quiet, please! Just watch. You can learn something. [*Claps his hands.*] Get going, get going! The entrance! [*And he goes back out front to get an impression of the stage.*]

[*The door at the back opens, and the* LEADING MAN *comes forward, with the relaxed, waggish manner of an elderly Don Juan.*[4] *From the first speeches, the performance of the scene by the Actors is quite a different thing, without, however, having any element of parody in it—rather, it seems corrected, set to rights. Naturally, the* STEPDAUGHTER *and the* FATHER, *being quite unable to recognize themselves in this* LEADING LADY *and* LEADING MAN *but hearing them speak their own words, express in various ways, now with gestures, now with smiles, now with open protests, their surprise, their wonderment, their suffering, etc., as will be seen forthwith.*

The PROMPTER*'s voice is clearly heard from the box.*]

LEADING MAN Hello, miss.

FATHER [*without pause, unable to contain himself*] No, no!

[*The* STEPDAUGHTER, *seeing how the* LEADING MAN *makes his entrance, has burst out laughing.*]

4. Stereotypical Spanish lover.

DIRECTOR [*coming from the proscenium, furious*] Silence here! And stop that laughing at once! We can't go ahead till it stops.

STEPDAUGHTER [*coming from the proscenium*] How can I help it? This lady [*the* LEADING LADY] just stands there. If she's supposed to be me, let me tell you that if anyone said hello to me in that manner and that tone of voice, I'd burst out laughing just as I actually did!

FATHER [*coming forward a little too*] That's right . . . the manner, the tone . . .

DIRECTOR Manner! Tone! Stand to one side now, and let me see the rehearsal.

LEADING MAN [*coming forward*] If I'm to play an old man entering a house of ill—

DIRECTOR Oh, pay no attention, please. Just begin again. It was going fine. [*Waiting for the Actor to resume*] Now then . . .

LEADING MAN Hello, miss.

LEADING LADY Hello.

LEADING MAN [*re-creating the* FATHER'*s gesture of scrutinizing her under her hat, but then expressing very distinctly first the complaisance and then the fear*] Oh . . . Well . . . I was thinking it wouldn't be the first time, I hope . . .

FATHER [*unable to help correcting him*] Not "I hope." "Would it?" "Would it?"

DIRECTOR He says: "would it?" A question.

LEADING MAN [*pointing to the* PROMPTER] I heard: "I hope."

DIRECTOR Same thing! "Would it." Or: "I hope." Continue, continue.—Now, maybe a bit less affected . . . Look, I'll do it for you. Watch me . . . [*Returns to the stage, then repeats the bit since the entrance*]—Hello, miss.

LEADING LADY Hello.

DIRECTOR Oh, well . . . I was thinking . . . [*Turning to the* LEADING MAN *to have him note how he has looked at the* LEADING LADY *under her hat*] Surprise . . . fear and complaisance. [*Then, going on, and turning to the* LEADING LADY] It wouldn't be the first time, would it? The first time you came here. [*Again turning to the* LEADING MAN *with an inquiring look*] Clear? [*To the* LEADING LADY] Then you say: No, sir. [*Back to the* LEADING MAN] How shall I put it? Plasticity! [*Goes back out front.*]

LEADING LADY No, sir.

LEADING MAN You came here other times? More than once?

DIRECTOR No, no, wait. [*Indicating the* LEADING LADY] First let her nod. "You came here other times?"

> [*The* LEADING LADY *raises her head a little, closes her eyes painfully as if in disgust, then nods twice at the word "Down" from the* DIRECTOR.]

STEPDAUGHTER [*involuntarily*] Oh, my God! [*And she at once puts her hand on her mouth to keep the laughter in.*]

DIRECTOR [*turning round*] What is it?

STEPDAUGHTER [*without pause*] Nothing, nothing.

DIRECTOR [*to the* LEADING MAN That's your cue. Go straight on.

LEADING MAN More than once? Well then, hm . . . it shouldn't any longer be so . . . May I take this little hat off for you?

[*The* LEADING MAN *says this last speech in such a tone and accompanies it with such a gesture that the* STEPDAUGHTER, *her hands on her mouth, much as she wants to hold herself in, cannot contain her laughter, which comes bursting out through her fingers irresistibly and very loud.*]

LEADING LADY [*returning to her place, enraged*] Now look, I'm not going to be made a clown of by that person!

LEADING MAN Nor am I. Let's stop.

DIRECTOR [*to the* STEPDAUGHTER, *roaring*] Stop it! Stop it!

STEPDAUGHTER Yes, yes. Forgive me, forgive me . . .

DIRECTOR You have no manners! You're presumptuous! So there!

FATHER [*seeking to intervene*] That's true, yes, that's true, sir, but forgive . . .

DIRECTOR [*onstage again*] Forgive nothing! It's disgusting!

FATHER Yes, sir. But believe me, it has such a strange effect—

DIRECTOR Strange? Strange? What's strange about it?

FATHER I admire your actors, sir, I really admire them, this gentleman [LEADING MAN] and that lady [LEADING LADY] but assuredly . . . well, they're not us . . .

DIRECTOR So what? How *could* they be you, if they're the actors?

FATHER Exactly, the actors! And they play our parts well, both of them. But of course, to us, they seem something else—that tries to be the same but simply isn't!

DIRECTOR How d'you mean: isn't? What is it then?

FATHER Something that . . . becomes theirs. And stops being ours.

DIRECTOR Necessarily! I explained that to you!

FATHER Yes. I understand, I do under—

DIRECTOR Then that will be enough! [*Turning to the Actors*] We'll be rehearsing by ourselves as we usually do. Rehearsing with authors present has always been hell, in my experience. There's no satisfying them. [*Turning to the* FATHER and the STEPDAUGHTER] Come along then. Let's resume. And let's hope you find it possible not to laugh this time.

STEPDAUGHTER Oh, no, I won't be laughing this time around. My big moment comes up now. Don't worry!

DIRECTOR Very well, when she says: "Please pay no more attention to what I said . . . Even for me—you understand . . ." [*Turning to the* FATHER] You'll have to cut right in with: "I understand, oh yes, I understand . . ." and ask her right away—

STEPDAUGHTER [*interrupting*] Oh? Ask me what?

DIRECTOR —why she is in mourning.

STEPDAUGHTER No, no, look: when I told him I needed to forget I was dressed like this, do you know what his answer was? "Oh, good! Then let's take that little dress right off, shall we?"

DIRECTOR Great! Terrific! It'll knock 'em right out of their seats!

STEPDAUGHTER But it's the truth.

DIRECTOR Truth, is it? Well, well, well. This is the theater! Our motto is: truth up to a certain point!

STEPDAUGHTER Then what would you propose?

DIRECTOR You'll see. You'll see it. Just leave me alone.

STEPDAUGHTER Certainly not. From my nausea—from all the reasons one more cruel than another why I am what I am, why I am "that one there"—you'd like to cook up some romantic, sentimental concoction, wouldn't you? He asks me why I'm in mourning, and I tell him, through my tears, that Papa died two months ago! No, my dear sir! He has to say what he did say: "Then let's take that little dress right off, shall we?" And I, with my two-months mourning in my heart, went back there—you see? behind that screen—and—my fingers quivering with shame, with loathing—I took off my dress, took off my corset . . .

DIRECTOR [*running his hands through his hair*] Good God, what are you saying?

STEPDAUGHTER [*shouting frantically*] The truth, sir, the truth!

DIRECTOR Well, yes, of course, that must be the truth . . . and I quite understand your horror, young lady. Would you try to understand that all that is impossible *on the stage*?

STEPDAUGHTER Impossible? Then, thanks very much, I'm leaving.

DIRECTOR No, no, look . . .

STEPDAUGHTER I'm leaving, I'm leaving! You went in that room, you two, didn't you, and figured out "what is possible on the stage"? Thanks very much. I see it all. He wants to skip to the point where he can act out his [*Exaggerating*] spiritual travail! But I want to play *my* drama. Mine!

DIRECTOR [*annoyed, and shrugging haughtily*] Oh well, *your* drama. This is not just your drama, if I may say so. How about the drama of the others? His drama [*the* FATHER], hers [*the* MOTHER]? We can't let one character hog the limelight, just taking the whole stage over, and overshadowing all the others! Everything must be placed within the frame of one harmonious picture! We must perform only what is performable! I know as well as you do that each of us has a whole life of his own inside him and would like to bring it all out. But the difficult thing is this: to bring out only as much as is needed—in relation to the others—and in this to *imply* all the rest, *suggest* what remains inside! Oh, it would be nice if every character could come down to the footlights and tell the audience just what is brewing inside him—in a fine monologue or, if you will, a lecture! [*Good-natured, conciliatory*] Miss, you will have to *contain yourself*. And it will be in your interest. It could make a bad impression—let me warn you—this tearing fury, this desperate disgust—since, if I may say so, you confessed having been with others at Madam Pace's—before him—more than once!

STEPDAUGHTER [*lowering her head, pausing to recollect, a deeper note in her voice*] It's true. But to me the others are also *him*, all of them equally!

DIRECTOR [*not getting it*] The others? How d'you mean?

STEPDAUGHTER People "go wrong." And wrong follows on the heels of wrong. Who is responsible, if not whoever it was who first brought them down? Isn't that always the case? And for me that is him. Even before I was born. Look at him, and see if it isn't so.

DIRECTOR Very good. And if he has so much to feel guilty about, can't you appreciate how it must weigh him down? So let's at least permit him to act it out.

STEPDAUGHTER And how, may I ask, how could he act out all that "noble" guilt, all those so "moral" torments, if you propose to spare him the horror of one day finding in his arms—after having bade her take off the black clothes that marked her recent loss—a woman now, and already gone wrong—that little girl, sir, that little girl whom he used to go watch coming out of school?

[*She says these last words in a voice trembling with emotion. The* MOTHER, *hearing her say this, overcome with uncontrollable anguish, which comes out first in suffocated moans and subsequently bursts out in bitter weeping. The emotion takes hold of everyone. Long pause.*]

STEPDAUGHTER [*as soon as the* MOTHER *gives signs of calming down, somber, determined*] We're just among ourselves now. Still unknown to the public. Tomorrow you will make of us the show you have in mind. You will put it together in your way. But would you like to really see—our drama? Have it explode—the real thing?

DIRECTOR Of course. Nothing I'd like better. And I'll use as much of it as I possibly can!

STEPDAUGHTER Very well. Have this Mother here go out.

MOTHER [*ceasing to weep, with a loud cry*] No, no! Don't allow this, don't allow it!

DIRECTOR I only want to take a look, ma'am.

MOTHER I can't, I just can't!

DIRECTOR But if it's already happened? Excuse me but I just don't get it.

MOTHER No, no, it's happening now. It's always happening. My torment is not a pretense! I am alive and present—always, in every moment of my torment—it keeps renewing itself, it too is alive and always present. But those two little ones over there—have you heard them speak? They cannot speak, sir, not anymore! They still keep clinging to me—to keep my torment alive and present. For themselves they don't exist, don't exist any longer. And she [*the* STEPDAUGHTER], she just fled, ran away from me, she's lost, lost . . . If I see her before me now, it's for the same reason: to renew the torment, keep it always alive and present forever—the torment I've suffered on her account too—forever!

FATHER [*solemn*] The eternal moment, sir, as I told you. She [*the* STEPDAUGHTER] is here to catch me, fix me, hold me there in the pillory, hanging there forever, hooked, in that single fleeting shameful moment of my life! She cannot give it up. And, actually, sir, *you* cannot spare me.

DIRECTOR But I didn't say I wouldn't use that. On the contrary, it will be the nucleus of the whole first act. To the point where she [*the* MOTHER] surprises you.

FATHER Yes, exactly. Because that is the sentence passed upon me: all our passion which has to culminate in her [*the* MOTHER's] final cry!

STEPDAUGHTER It still rings in my ears. It's driven me out of my mind, that cry!—You can present me as you wish, sir, it doesn't matter. Even dressed. As long as at least my arms—just my arms—are bare. Because it was like this. [*She goes to the* FATHER *and rests her head on his chest.*] I was standing like this with my head on his chest and my arms round his neck like this.

Then I saw something throbbing right here on my arm. A vein. Then, as if it was just this living vein that disgusted me, I jammed my eyes shut, like this, d'you see? and buried my head on his chest. [*Turning to the* MOTHER] Scream, scream, mama! [*Buries her head on the* FATHER*'s chest and with her shoulders raised as if to avoid hearing the scream she adds in a voice stifled with torment.*] Scream as you screamed then!

MOTHER [*rushing forward to part them*] No! My daughter! My daughter! [*Having pulled her from him*] Brute! Brute! It's my daughter, don't you see—my daughter!

DIRECTOR [*the outburst having sent him reeling to the footlights, while the Actors show dismay*] Fine! Splendid! And now: curtain, curtain!

FATHER [*running to him, convulsed*] Right! Yes! Because that, sir, is how it actually was!

DIRECTOR [*in admiration and conviction*] Yes, yes, of course! Curtain! Curtain!

[*Hearing this repeated cry of the* DIRECTOR, *the* TECHNICIAN *lets down the curtain, trapping the* DIRECTOR *and the* FATHER *between curtain and footlights.*]

DIRECTOR [*looking up, with raised arms*] What an idiot! I say Curtain, meaning that's how the act should end, and they let down the actual curtain! [*He lifts a corner of the curtain so he can get back onstage. To the* FATHER] Yes, yes, fine, splendid! Absolutely surefire! Has to end that way. I can vouch for the first act. [*Goes behind the curtain with the* FATHER.]

[*When the curtain rises we see that the stagehands have struck that first "indication of a set," and have put onstage in its stead a small garden fountain. On one side of the stage, the Actors are sitting in a row, and on the other are the Characters. The* DIRECTOR *is standing in the middle of the stage, in the act of meditating with one hand, fist clenched, on his mouth.*]

DIRECTOR [*shrugging after a short pause*] Yes, well then, let's get to the second act. Just leave it to me as we agreed beforehand and everything will be all right.

STEPDAUGHTER Our entrance into his house [*the* FATHER] in spite of him [*the* SON].

DIRECTOR [*losing patience*] Very well. But leave it all to me, I say.

STEPDAUGHTER In spite of him. Just let that be clear.

MOTHER [*shaking her head from her corner*] For all the good that's come out of it . . .

STEPDAUGHTER [*turning quickly on her*] It doesn't matter. The more damage to us, the more guilt feelings for him.

DIRECTOR [*still out of patience*] I understand, I understand. All this will be taken into account, especially at the beginning. Rest assured.

MOTHER [*supplicatingly*] Do make them understand, I beg you, sir, for my conscience's sake, for I tried in every possible way—

STEPDAUGHTER [*continuing her* MOTHER*'s speech, contemptuously*] To placate me, to advise me not to give him trouble. [*To the* DIRECTOR] Do what she wants, do it because it's true. I enjoy the whole thing very much because, look: the more she plays the suppliant and tries to gain entrance into his heart, the more he holds himself aloof: he's an absentee! How I relish this!

DIRECTOR We want to get going—on the second act, don't we?

STEPDAUGHTER I won't say another word. But to play it all in the garden, as you want to, won't be possible.

DIRECTOR Why won't it be possible?

STEPDAUGHTER Because he [*the* SON] stays shut up in his room, on his own. Then again we need the house for the part about this poor bewildered little boy, as I told you.

DIRECTOR Quite right. But on the other hand, we can't change the scenery in view of the audience three or four times in one act, nor can we stick up signs—

LEADING MAN They used to at one time . . .

DIRECTOR Yes, when the audiences were about as mature as that little girl.

LEADING LADY They got the illusion more easily.

FATHER [*suddenly, rising*] The illusion, please don't say illusion! Don't use that word! It's especially cruel to us.

DIRECTOR [*astonished*] And why, if I may ask?

FATHER Oh yes, cruel, cruel! You should understand that.

DIRECTOR What word would you have us use anyway? The illusion of creating here for our spectators—

LEADING MAN —By our performance—

DIRECTOR —the illusion of a reality.

FATHER I understand, sir, but perhaps you do not understand us. Because, you see, for you and for your actors all this—quite rightly—is a game—

LEADING LADY [*indignantly interrupting*] Game! We are not children, sir. We act in earnest.

FATHER I don't deny it. I just mean the game of your art which, as this gentleman rightly says, must provide a perfect illusion of reality.

DIRECTOR Yes, exactly.

FATHER But consider this. We [*He quickly indicates himself and the other five Characters.*], we have no reality outside this illusion.

DIRECTOR [*astonished, looking at his Actors who remain bewildered and lost*] And that means?

FATHER [*after observing them briefly, with a pale smile*] Just that, ladies and gentlemen. How should we have any other reality? What for you is an illusion, to be created, is for us our unique reality. [*Short pause. He takes several short steps toward the* DIRECTOR, *and adds*] But not for us alone, of course. Think a moment. [*He looks into his eyes.*] Can you tell me who you are? [*And he stands there pointing his first finger at him.*]

DIRECTOR [*upset, with a half-smile*] How do you mean, who I am? I am I.

FATHER And if I told you that wasn't true because you are me?

DIRECTOR I would reply that you are out of your mind. [*The Actors laugh.*]

FATHER You are right to laugh: because this is a game. [*To the* DIRECTOR] And you can object that it's only in a game that that gentleman there [LEADING MAN], who is himself, must be me, who am *my*self. I've caught you in a trap, do you see that?

[*Actors start laughing again.*]

DIRECTOR [*annoyed*] You said all this before. Why repeat it?

FATHER I won't—I didn't intend to say that. I'm inviting you to emerge from this game. [*He looks at the* LEADING LADY *as if to forestall what she might say.*] This game of art which you are accustomed to play here with your actors. Let me again ask quite seriously: Who are you?

DIRECTOR [*turning to the Actors, amazed and at the same time irritated*] The gall of this fellow! Calls himself a character and comes here to ask me who I am!

FATHER [*dignified, but not haughty*] A character, sir, can always ask a man who he is. Because a character really has his own life, marked with his own characteristics, by virtue of which he is always someone. Whereas, a man—I'm not speaking of you now—*a man* can be no one.

DIRECTOR Oh sure. But you are asking me! And I am the manager, understand?

FATHER [*quite softly with mellifluous modesty*] Only in order to know, sir, if you as you now are see yourself . . . for example, at a distance in time. Do you see the man you once were, with all the illusions you had then, with everything, inside you and outside, as it seemed then—as it was then for you?—Well sir, thinking back to those illusions which you don't have anymore, to all those things which no longer seem to be what at one time they were for you, don't you feel, not just the boards of this stage, but the very earth beneath slipping away from you? For will not all that you feel yourself to be now, your whole reality of today, as it is now, inevitably seem an illusion tomorrow?

DIRECTOR [*who has not followed exactly, but has been staggered by the plausibilities of the argument*] Well, well, what do you want to prove?

FATHER Oh nothing, sir. I just wanted to make you see that if *we* [*pointing again at himself and the other Characters*] have no reality outside of illusion, it would be well if you should distrust your reality because, though you breathe it and touch it today, it is destined like that of yesterday to stand revealed to you tomorrow as illusion.

DIRECTOR [*deciding to mock him*] Oh splendid! And you'll be telling me next that you and this play that you have come to perform for me are truer and more real than I am.

FATHER [*quite seriously*] There can be no doubt of that, sir.

DIRECTOR Really?

FATHER I thought you had understood that from the start.

DIRECTOR More real than me?

FATHER If your reality can change overnight . . .

DIRECTOR Of course it can, it changes all the time, like everyone else's.

FATHER [*with a cry*] But ours does not, sir. You see, that is the difference. It does not change, it cannot ever change or be otherwise because it is already fixed, it is what is, just that, forever—a terrible thing, sir!—an immutable reality. You should shudder to come near us.

DIRECTOR [*suddenly struck by a new idea, he steps in front of the* FATHER] I should like to know, however, when anyone ever saw a character get out of his part and set about expounding and explicating it, delivering lectures on it. Can you tell me? I have never seen anything like that.

FATHER You have never seen it, sir, because authors generally hide the travail of their creations. When characters are alive and turn up, living, before their author, all that author does is follow the words and gestures which they propose to him. He has to want them to be as they themselves want to be. Woe betide him if he doesn't! When a character is born, he at once acquires such an independence, even of his own author, that the whole world can imagine him in innumerable situations other than those the author thought to place him in. At times he acquires a meaning that the author never dreamt of giving him.

DIRECTOR Certainly, I know that.

FATHER Then why all this astonishment at us? Imagine what a misfortune it is for a character such as I described to you—given life in the imagination of an author who then wished to deny him life—and tell me frankly: isn't such a character, given life and left without life, isn't he right to set about doing just what we are doing now as we stand here before you, after having done just the same—for a very long time, believe me—before *him,* trying to persuade him, trying to push him . . . I would appear before him sometimes, sometimes she [*looks at* STEPDAUGHTER] would go to him, sometimes that poor mother . . .

STEPDAUGHTER [*coming forward as if in a trance*] It's true. I too went there, sir, to tempt him, many times, in the melancholy of that study of his, at the twilight hour, when he would sit stretched out in his armchair, unable to make up his mind to switch the light on, and letting the evening shadows invade the room, knowing that these shadows were alive with us and that we were coming to tempt him . . . [*As if she saw herself still in that study and felt only annoyance at the presence of all of these Actors*] Oh, if only you would all go away! Leave us alone! My mother there with her son—I with this little girl—the boy there always alone—then I with him [*the* FATHER]—then I by myself, I by myself . . . in those shadows. [*Suddenly she jumps up as if she wished to take hold of herself in the vision she has of herself lighting up the shadows and alive.*] Ah, my life! What scenes, what scenes we went there to propose to him: I, I tempted him more than the others.

FATHER Right, but perhaps that was the trouble: you insisted too much. You thought you could seduce him.

STEPDAUGHTER Nonsense. He wanted me that way. [*She comes up to the* DIRECTOR *to tell him as in confidence.*] If you ask me, sir, it was because he was so depressed, or because he despised the theater the public knows and wants . . .

DIRECTOR Let's continue. Let's continue, for heaven's sake. Enough theories, I'd like some facts. Give me some facts.

STEPDAUGHTER It seems to me that we have already given you more facts than you can handle—with our entry into his [*the* FATHER*'s*] house! You said you couldn't change the scene every five minutes or start hanging signs.

DIRECTOR Nor can we, of course not, we have to combine the scenes and group them in one simultaneous close-knit action. Not your idea at all. You'd like to see your brother come home from school and wander through the house like a ghost, hiding behind the doors, and brooding on a plan which—how did you put it—?

STEPDAUGHTER —shrivels him up, sir, completely shrivels him up, sir.

DIRECTOR "Shrivels!" What a word! All right then: his growth was stunted except for his eyes. Is that what you said?

STEPDAUGHTER Yes, sir. Just look at him. [*She points him out next to the* MOTHER.]

DIRECTOR Good girl. And then at the same time you want this little girl to be playing in the garden, dead to the world. Now, the boy in the house, the girl in the garden, is that possible?

STEPDAUGHTER Happy in the sunshine! Yes, that is my only reward, her pleasure, her joy in that garden! After the misery, the squalor of a horrible room where we slept, all four of us, she with me: just think, of the horror of my contaminated body next to hers! She held me tight, oh so tight with her loving innocent little arms! In the garden she would run and take my hand as soon as she saw me. She did not see the big flowers, she ran around looking for the teeny ones and wanted to show them to me, oh the joy of it!

[*Saying this and tortured by the memory she breaks into prolonged desperate sobbing, dropping her head onto her arms which are spread out on the work table. Everyone is overcome by her emotion. The* DIRECTOR *goes to her almost paternally and says to comfort her*]

DIRECTOR We'll do the garden. We'll do the garden, don't worry, and you'll be very happy about it. We'll bring all the scenes together in the garden. [*Calling a* STAGEHAND *by name*] Hey, drop me a couple of trees, will you, two small cypress trees, here in front of the fountain.

[*Two small cypress trees are seen descending from the flies. A* STAGEHAND *runs on to secure them with nails and a couple of braces.*]

DIRECTOR [*to the* STEPDAUGHTER] Something to go on with anyway. Gives us an idea. [*Again calling the* STAGEHAND *by name*] Hey, give me a bit of sky.

STAGEHAND [*from above*] What?

DIRECTOR Bit of sky, a backcloth, to go behind that fountain. [*A white backdrop is seen descending from the flies.*] Not white, I said sky. It doesn't matter, leave it, I'll take care of it. [*Shouting*] Hey, Electrician, put these lights out. Let's have a bit of atmosphere, lunar atmosphere, blue background, and give me a blue spot on that backcloth. That's right. That's enough. [*At his command a mysterious lunar scene is created which induces the Actors to talk and move as they would on an evening in the garden beneath the moon.*] [*To* STEPDAUGHTER] You see? And now instead of hiding behind doors in the house the boy could move around here in the garden and hide behind trees. But it will be difficult, you know, to find a little girl to play the scene where she shows you the flowers. [*Turning to the* BOY] Come down this way a bit. Let's see how this can be worked out. [*And when the* BOY *doesn't move*] Come on, come on. [*Then dragging him forward he tries to make him hold his head up but it falls down again every time.*] Oh dear, another problem, this boy . . . What *is* it? . . . My God, he'll have to say something . . . [*He goes up to him, puts a hand on his shoulder and leads him behind one of the tree drops.*] Come on. Come on. Let me see. You can hide a bit here . . . Like this . . . You can stick your head out a bit to look . . . [*He goes to one side to see the effect. The* BOY *has scarcely run through the actions when the Actors are deeply affected; and they remain quite overwhelmed.*] Ah! Fine!

Splendid! [*He turns again to the* STEPDAUGHTER.] If the little girl surprises him looking out and runs over to him, don't you think she might drag a few words out of him too?

STEPDAUGHTER [*jumping to her feet*] Don't expect him to speak while *he's* here. [*She points to the* SON.] You have to send *him* away first.

SON [*going resolutely toward one of the two stairways*] Suits me. Glad to go. Nothing I want more.

DIRECTOR [*immediately calling him*] No. Where are you going? Wait.

[*The* MOTHER *rises, deeply moved, in anguish at the thought that he is really going. She instinctively raises her arms as if to halt him, yet without moving away from her position.*]

SON [*arriving at the footlights, where the* DIRECTOR *stops him*] I have absolutely nothing to do here. So let me go please. Just let me go.

DIRECTOR How do you mean, you have nothing to do?

STEPDAUGHTER [*placidly, with irony*] Don't hold him! He won't go.

FATHER He has to play the terrible scene in the garden with his mother.

SON [*unhesitating, resolute, proud*] I play nothing. I said so from the start. [*To the* DIRECTOR] Let me go.

STEPDAUGHTER [*running to the* DIRECTOR *to get him to lower his arms so that he is no longer holding the* SON *back*] Let him go. [*Then turning to the* SON *as soon as the* DIRECTOR *has let him go*] Very well, go. [*The* SON *is all set to move toward the stairs but, as if held by some occult power, he cannot go down the steps. While the Actors are both astounded and deeply troubled, he moves slowly across the footlights straight to the other stairway. But having arrived there he remains poised for the descent but unable to descend. The* STEPDAUGHTER, *who has followed him with her eyes in an attitude of defiance, bursts out laughing.*] He can't, you see. He can't. He has to stay here, has to. Bound by a chain, indissolubly. But if I who do take flight, sir, when that happens which has to happen, and precisely because of the hatred I feel for him, precisely so as not to see him again—very well, if *I* am still here and can bear the sight of him and his company—you can imagine whether *he* can go away. He who really must, must remain here with that fine father of his and that mother there who no longer has any other children. [*Turning again to the* MOTHER] Come on, Mother, come on. [*Turning again to the* DIRECTOR *and pointing to the* MOTHER] Look, she got up to hold him back. [*To the* MOTHER, *as if exerting a magical power over her*] Come. Come . . . [*Then to the* DIRECTOR] You can imagine how little she wants to display her love in front of your actors. But so great is her desire to get at him that—look, you see—she is even prepared to live her scene.

[*In fact the* MOTHER *has approached and no sooner has the* STEPDAUGHTER *spoken her last words than she spreads her arms to signify consent.*]

SON [*without pause*] But *I* am not, *I* am not. If I cannot go I will stay here, but I repeat: I will play nothing.

FATHER [*to the* DIRECTOR, *enraged*] You can force him, sir.

SON No one can force me.

FATHER I will force you.

STEPDAUGHTER Wait, wait. First the little girl must be at the fountain. [*She runs to take the* LITTLE GIRL, *drops on her knees in front of her, takes her little face in her hands.*] My poor little darling, you look bewildered with those lovely big eyes of yours. Who knows where you think you are? We are on a stage, my dear. What is a stage? It is a place where you play at being serious, a place for playacting, where we will now playact. But seriously! For real! You too . . . [*She embraces her, presses her to her bosom, and rocks her a little.*] Oh, little darling, little darling, what an ugly play you will enact! What a horrible thing has been planned for you, the garden, the fountain . . . All pretense, of course, that's the trouble, my sweet, everything is make-believe here, but perhaps for you, my child, a make-believe fountain is nicer than a real one for playing in, hmm? It will be a game for the others, but not for you, alas, because you are real, my darling, and are actually playing in a fountain that is real, beautiful, big, green with many bamboo plants reflected in it and giving it shade. Many, many ducklings can swim in it, breaking the shade to bits. You want to take hold of one of these ducklings . . . [*With a shout that fills everyone with dismay*] No! No, my Rosetta! Your mother is not looking after you because of that beast of a son. A thousand devils are loose in my head . . . and *he* . . . [*She leaves the* LITTLE GIRL *and turns with her usual hostility to the* BOY.] And what are you doing here, always looking like a beggar child? It will be your fault too if this little girl drowns—with all your standing around like that. As if I hadn't paid for everybody when I got you all into this house. [*Grabbing one of his arms to force him to take a hand out of his pocket*] What have you got there? What are you hiding? Let's see this hand. [*Tears his hand out of his pocket, and to the horror of everyone discovers that it holds a small revolver. She looks at it for a moment as if satisfied and then says*] Ah! Where did you get that and how? [*And as the* BOY *in his confusion, with his eyes staring and vacant all the time, does not answer her*] Idiot, if I were you I wouldn't have killed myself, I would have killed one of those two—or both of them—the father and the son! [*She hides him behind the small cypress tree from which he had been looking out, and she takes the* LITTLE GIRL *and hides her in the fountain, having her lie down in it in such a way as to be quite hidden. Finally, the* STEPDAUGHTER *goes down on her knees with her face in her hands, which are resting on the rim of the fountain.*]

DIRECTOR Splendid! [*Turning to the* SON] And at the same time . . .

SON [*with contempt*] And at the same time, nothing. It is not true, sir. There was never any scene between me and her. [*He points to the* MOTHER.] Let her tell you herself how it was.

[*Meanwhile the* SECOND ACTRESS *and the* JUVENILE LEAD *have detached themselves from the group of Actors. The former has started to observe the* MOTHER, *who is opposite her, very closely. And the other has started to observe the* SON. *Both are planning how they will re-create the roles.*]

MOTHER Yes, it is true, sir. I had gone to his room.

SON My room, did you hear that? Not the garden.

DIRECTOR That is of no importance. We have to rearrange the action, I told you that.

SON [*noticing that the* JUVENILE LEAD *is observing him*] What do *you* want?

JUVENILE LEAD Nothing. I am observing you.

SON [*turning to the other side where the* SECOND ACTRESS *is*] Ah, and here we have you to re-create the role, eh? [*He points to the* MOTHER.]

DIRECTOR Exactly, exactly. You should be grateful, it seems to me, for the attention they are giving you.

SON Oh yes, thank you. But you still haven't understood that you cannot do this drama. We are not inside you, not in the least, and your actors are looking at us from the outside. Do you think it's possible for us to live before a mirror which, not content to freeze us in the fixed image it provides of our expression, also throws back at us an unrecognizable grimace purporting to be ourselves?

FATHER That is true. That is true. You must see that.

DIRECTOR [*to the* JUVENILE LEAD *and the* SECOND ACTRESS] Very well, get away from here.

SON No good. I won't cooperate.

DIRECTOR Just be quiet a minute and let me hear your mother. [*To the* MOTHER] Well? You went into his room?

MOTHER Yes sir, into his room. I was at the end of my tether. I wanted to pour out all of the anguish which was oppressing me. But as soon as he saw me come in—

SON —There was no scene. I went away. I went away so there would be no scene. Because I have never made scenes, never, understand?

MOTHER That's true. That's how it was. Yes.

DIRECTOR But now there's got to be a scene between you and him. It is indispensable.

MOTHER As for me, sir, I am ready. If only you could find some way to have me speak to him for one moment, to have me say what is in my heart.

FATHER [*going right up to the* SON, *very violent*] You will do it! For your mother! For your mother!

SON [*more decisively than ever*] I will do nothing!

FATHER [*grabbing him by the chest and shaking him*] By God, you will obey! Can't you hear how she is talking to you? Aren't you her son?

SON [*grabbing his* FATHER] No! No! Once and for all let's have done with it!

[*General agitation. The* MOTHER, *terrified, tries to get between them to separate them.*]

MOTHER [*as before*] Please, please!

FATHER [*without letting go of the* SON] You must obey, you must obey!

SON [*wrestling with his* FATHER *and in the end throwing him to the ground beside the little stairway, to the horror of everyone*] What's this frenzy that's taken hold of you? To show your shame and ours to everyone? Have you no restraint? I won't cooperate, I won't cooperate! And that is how I interpret the wishes of the man who did not choose to put us onstage.

DIRECTOR But you came here.

SON [*pointing to his* FATHER] He came here—not me!

DIRECTOR But aren't you here too?

SON It was he who wanted to come, dragging the rest of us with him, and then getting together with you to plot not only what really happened, but also—as if that did not suffice—*what did not happen*.

DIRECTOR Then tell me. Tell me what did happen. Just tell me. You came out of your room without saying a thing?

SON [*after a moment of hesitation*] Without saying a thing. In order not to make a scene.

DIRECTOR [*driving him on*] Very well, and then, what did you do then?

SON [*while everyone looks on in anguished attention, he moves a few steps on the front part of the stage*] Nothing . . . crossing the garden . . . [*He stops, gloomy, withdrawn.*]

DIRECTOR [*always driving him on to speak, impressed by his reticence*] Very well, crossing the garden?

SON [*desperate, hiding his face with one arm*] Why do you want to make me say it, sir? It is horrible.

[*The* MOTHER *trembles all over, and stifles groans, looking toward the fountain.*]

DIRECTOR [*softly, noticing this look of hers, turning to the* SON, *with growing apprehension*] The little girl?

SON [*looking out into the auditorium*] Over there—in the fountain . . .

FATHER [*on the ground, pointing compassionately toward the* MOTHER] And she followed him, sir.

DIRECTOR [*to the* SON, *anxiously*] And then you . . .

SON [*slowly, looking straight ahead all the time*] I ran out. I started to fish her out . . . but all of a sudden I stopped. Behind those trees I saw something that froze me: the boy, the boy was standing there, quite still. There was madness in the eyes. He was looking at his drowned sister in the fountain. [*The* STEPDAUGHTER, *who has been bent over the fountain, hiding the* LITTLE GIRL, *is sobbing desperately, like an echo from the bottom. Pause.*] I started to approach and then . . .

[*From behind the trees where the* BOY *has been hiding, a revolver shot rings out.*]

MOTHER [*running up with a tormented shout, accompanied by the* SON *and all the Actors in a general tumult*] Son! My son! [*And then amid the hubbub and the disconnected shouts of the others*] Help! Help!

DIRECTOR [*amid the shouting, trying to clear a space while the* BOY *is lifted by his head and feet and carried away behind the backcloth*] Is he wounded, is he wounded, really?

[*Everyone except the* DIRECTOR *and the* FATHER, *who has remained on the ground beside the steps, has disappeared behind the backcloth which has served for a sky, where they can still be heard for a while whispering anxiously. Then from one side and the other of this curtain, the Actors come back onstage.*]

LEADING LADY [*reentering from the right, very much upset*] He's dead! Poor boy! He's dead! What a terrible thing!

LEADING MAN [*reentering from the left, laughing*] How do you mean, dead? Fiction, fiction, one doesn't believe such things.

OTHER ACTORS [*on the right*] Fiction? Reality! Reality! He is dead!

OTHER ACTORS [*on the left*] No! Fiction! Fiction!

FATHER [*rising, and crying out to them*] Fiction indeed! Reality, reality, gentlemen, reality! [*Desperate, he too disappears at the back.*]

DIRECTOR [*at the end of his rope*] Fiction! Reality! To hell with all of you! Lights, lights, lights![5] [*At a single stroke the whole stage and auditorium is flooded with very bright light. The* DIRECTOR *breathes again, as if freed from an incubus, and they all look each other in the eyes, bewildered and lost.*] Things like this don't happen to me, they've made me lose a whole day. [*He looks at his watch.*] Go, you can all go. What could we do now anyway? It is too late to pick up the rehearsal where we left off. See you this evening. [*As soon as the Actors have gone he talks to the* ELECTRICIAN *by name.*] Hey, Electrician, lights out. [*He has hardly said the words when the theater is plunged for a moment into complete darkness.*] Hey, for God's sake, leave me at least one light! I like to see where I am going!

[*Immediately, from behind the backcloth, as if the wrong switch had been pulled, a green light comes on which projects the silhouettes, clear-cut and large, of the Characters, minus the* BOY *and the* LITTLE GIRL. *Seeing the silhouettes, the* DIRECTOR, *terrified, rushes from the stage. At the same time the light behind the backcloth goes out and the stage is again lit in nocturnal blue as before.*

Slowly, from the right side of the curtain, the SON *comes forward first, followed by the* MOTHER *with her arms stretched out toward him; then from the left side, the* FATHER. *They stop in the middle of the stage and stay there as if in a trance. Last of all from the right, the* STEPDAUGHTER *comes out and runs toward the two stairways. She stops on the first step, to look for a moment at the other three, and then breaks into a harsh laugh before throwing herself down the steps; she runs down the aisle between the rows of seats; she stops one more time and again laughs, looking at the three who are still onstage; she disappears from the auditorium, and from the lobby her laughter is still heard. Shortly thereafter the curtain falls.*]

5. I.e., house lights as well as onstage working lights.

AKUTAGAWA RYŪNOSUKE

1892–1927

Despite his short career—he committed suicide at thirty-five—Akutagawa is considered one of the major writers of early twentieth-century Japan. Most of his work consists of short stories, in both historical and contemporary settings, as well as stories based on his experiences. Marked by literary inventiveness, his work reflects the energy and the anxieties of modern Japan but has also come to epitomize the postmodern questioning of absolute truth and certainty.

From the time he was an infant, Akutagawa's mother suffered from a crippling mental illness; she died when he was ten. In later years he admitted to a lasting fear that he would inherit the disease. Meanwhile, he was raised in the family of his maternal uncle, in a cultivated household that encouraged his youthful passion for literature. His reading included Japanese and Chinese classics, Japanese writers from the 1880s to the turn of the century, especially Natsume Sōseki and Mori Ōgai, and European writers including Guy de Maupassant, Anatole France, August Strindberg, and **Fyodor Dostoyevsky**. Traces of these influences can be found throughout Akutagawa's works. In 1913 he entered the English department of Tokyo Imperial University (now the University of Tokyo), and his translations and original works soon appeared in campus literary magazines.

From the start of his career, Akutagawa set most of his stories in the past, favoring three eras: the twelfth century, a time of widespread strife and disorder when the capital city, Kyoto, was wracked by disasters ranging from epidemics to massive fires; the late sixteenth century, when Christianity was exerting a disruptive force over parts of Japan, contributing to a century of civil war; and the 1870s and 1880s, when Japan's intellectual classes were eager to learn about the cultures of Europe and North America. His interest in the latter two periods may in part reflect his far-flung literary tastes, which likewise combined the East Asian classics, modern Japanese fiction, and the literary and philosophical traditions of Europe. Yet however distant his settings, his characters often suffer from distinctly twentieth-century feelings of social dislocation and individual desperation.

As a writer, Akutagawa is known for drawing upon the works of others. The story that launched his career, "The Nose" (1916), about a Buddhist priest with a fantastically large nose, was inspired partly by a story in a classical collection, and possibly also by "The Nose" (1836), a story by the Russian author Nicolay Gogol (1809–1852). Here and elsewhere, we find Akutagawa stitching together material from sources whose juxtaposition seems unlikely: the unifying element comes from Akutagawa's distinctive sensibilities, which include a fascination with the absurd and grotesque, the contradictions of human motivation, social decay, and Modernist narrative techniques.

Starting in the early 1920s, as his reputation grew, Akutagawa labored under the strain of editors' requests for new manuscripts; increasingly he complained of nervous exhaustion and insomnia. Yet he continued to make demands on himself to produce stories displaying a virtuosic manipulation of setting and narrative, to be found in works of the period such as "In a Bamboo Grove" (1921), the selection here. Even the publication of this story showed virtuosity: it was one of four stories that appeared, almost simultaneously, in the prestigious New Year's issues of four magazines in 1922.

The period in which Akutagawa achieved fame was the Taishō era, in the late 1910s and the 1920s, in many ways a time of high cultural play and experimentation, not unlike the Roaring Twenties in the United States. During these years a tide of mass culture that included recorded music, cinema, mass-circulation magazines, and cheap editions of popular fiction swept aside more traditional forms. The triumph of mass culture prompted writers with literary ambitions to set themselves apart as visibly as they could from popular fiction. Taking up the position of an embattled minority, many serious writers, including Akutagawa, portrayed the pursuit of true art as a sacred but dangerous calling, even demonic in its unworldliness and the force of its demands.

"In a Bamboo Grove" incorporates themes and techniques typical of Akutagawa's work. As popular fiction settled into established genres such as the detective novel, Japanese Modernists pushed language and narrative form in unknown directions. Their experiments included the creation of fiction composed solely of sensory perceptions and the use of "concrete" prose styles stressing nouns over verbs as well as shifting points of view, such as those in the selection here. Like so many of Akutagawa's works, this story draws upon others: the situation derives from a vignette in a twelfth-century collection, *Tales of Times Now Past*, about a murder and rape. Akutagawa transforms the source, however, by recounting the central crimes from seven points of view. Rather than present the events from the perspective of an omniscient narrator, he provides transcripts of police interviews and other conversations, from which the reader tries to assemble the truth.

The story's reputation as a touchstone in the use of narrative perspective was secured in 1950 with the premiere of Kurosawa Akira's film *Rashōmon*, which won the first prize at the 1951 Venice film festival. The film uses scenes set at the Rashōmon gate from Akutagawa's story of the same name but is mainly based on "In a Bamboo Grove." It became an example of postmodern questioning of the way that the truth varies according to viewers' perspectives. In the story the classic problem of detective fiction—"Who done it?"—leads not only to the mutual recriminations of the three primary witnesses to the event but also to surprising forms of self-revelation.

In a Bamboo Grove[1]

The Testimony of a Woodcutter under Questioning by the Magistrate

That is true, Your Honor. I am the one who found the body. I went out as usual this morning to cut cedar in the hills behind my place. The body was in a bamboo grove on the other side of the mountain. Its exact location? A few hundred yards off the Yamashina post road. A deserted place where a few scrub cedar trees are mixed in with the bamboo.

The man was lying on his back in his pale blue robe with the sleeves tied up and one of those fancy Kyoto-style[2] black hats with the sharp creases. He had only one stab wound, but it was right in the middle of his chest; the bamboo leaves around the body were soaked with dark red blood. No, the bleeding had stopped. The wound looked dry, and I remember it had a big horsefly sucking on it so hard the thing didn't even notice my footsteps.

Did I see a sword or anything? No, Sir, not a thing. Just a length of rope by the cedar tree next to the body. And—oh yes, there was a comb there, too. Just the rope and the comb is all. But the weeds and the bamboo leaves on the ground were pretty trampled down: he must have put up a tremendous fight

1. Translated by, and with some notes adapted from, Jay Rubin.

2. In the fashion of Kyoto, the Japanese capital at the time of the story.

before they killed him. How's that, Sir—a horse? No, a horse could never have gotten into that place. It's all bamboo thicket between there and the road.

The Testimony of a Traveling Priest under Questioning by the Magistrate

I'm sure I passed the man yesterday, Your Honor. Yesterday at—about noon, I'd say. Near Checkpoint Hill on the way to Yamashina. He was walking toward the checkpoint with a woman on horseback. She wore a stiff, round straw hat with a long veil hanging down around the brim; I couldn't see her face, just her robe. I think it had a kind of dark-red outer layer with a blue-green lining. The horse was a dappled gray with a tinge of red, and I'm fairly sure it had a clipped mane. Was it a big horse? I'd say it was a few inches taller than most, but I'm a priest after all. I don't know much about horses. The man? No, Sir, he had a good-sized sword, and he was equipped with a bow and arrows. I can still see that black-lacquered quiver of his: he must have had twenty arrows in it, maybe more. I would never have dreamt that a thing like this could happen to such a man. Ah, what is the life of a human being—a drop of dew, a flash of lightning? This is so sad, so sad. What can I say?

The Testimony of a Policeman under Questioning by the Magistrate

The man I captured, Your Honor? I am certain he is the famous bandit, Tajōmaru. True, when I caught him he had fallen off his horse, and he was moaning and groaning on the stone bridge at Awataguchi. The time, Sir? It was last night at the first watch.[3] He was wearing the same dark blue robe and carrying the same long sword he used the time I almost captured him before. You can see he also has a bow and arrows now. Oh, is that so, Sir? The dead man, too? That settles it, then: I'm sure this Tajōmaru fellow is the murderer. A leather-wrapped bow, a quiver in black lacquer, seventeen hawk-feather arrows—they must have belonged to the victim. And yes, as you say, Sir, the horse is a dappled gray with a touch of red, and it has a clipped mane. It's only a dumb animal, but it gave that bandit just what he deserved, throwing him like that. It was a short way beyond the bridge, trailing its reins on the ground and eating plume grass by the road.

Of all the bandits prowling around Kyoto, this Tajōmaru is known as a fellow who likes the women. Last fall, people at Toribe Temple found a pair of worshippers murdered—a woman and a child—on the hill behind the statue of Binzuru.[4] Everybody said Tajōmaru must have done it. If it turns out he killed the man, there's no telling what he might have done to the woman who was on the horse. I don't mean to meddle, Sir, but I do think you ought to question him about that.

The Testimony of an Old Woman under Questioning by the Magistrate

Yes, Your Honor, my daughter was married to the dead man. He is not from the capital, though. He was a samurai serving in the Wakasa provincial office. His name was Kanazawa no Takehiro, and he was twenty-six years old. No, Sir,

3. 8:00 P.M.

4. One of the Buddha's disciples.

he was a very kind man. I can't believe anyone would have hated him enough to do this.

My daughter, Sir? Her name is Masago, and she is nineteen years old. She's as bold as any man, but the only man she has ever known is Takehiro. Her complexion is a little on the dark side, and she has a mole by the outside corner of her left eye, but her face is a tiny, perfect oval.

Takehiro left for Wakasa yesterday with my daughter, but what turn of fate could have led to this? There's nothing I can do for my son-in-law anymore, but what could have happened to my daughter? I'm worried sick about her. Oh please, Sir, do everything you can to find her, leave no stone unturned: I have lived a long time, but I have never wanted anything so badly in my life. Oh how I hate that bandit—that, that Tajōmaru! Not only my son-in-law, but my daughter . . . (Here the old woman broke down and was unable to go on speaking.)

Tajōmaru's Confession

Sure, I killed the man. But I didn't kill the woman. So, where did she go? I don't know any better than you do. Now, wait just a minute—you can torture me all you want, but I can't tell you what I don't know. And besides, now that you've got me, I'm not going to hide anything. I'm no coward.

I met that couple yesterday, a little after noon. The second I saw them, a puff of wind lifted her veil and I caught a peek at her. Just a peek: that's maybe why she looked so perfect to me—an absolute bodhisattva[5] of a woman. I made up my mind right then to take her even if I had to kill the man.

Oh come on, killing a man is not as big a thing as people like you seem to think. If you're going to take somebody's woman, a man has to die. When *I* kill a man, I do it with my sword, but people like you don't use swords. You gentlemen kill with your power, with your money, and sometimes just with your words: you tell people you're doing them a favor. True, no blood flows, the man is still alive, but you've killed him all the same. I don't know whose sin is greater—yours or mine. (A sarcastic smile.)

Of course, if you can take the woman without killing the man, all the better. Which is exactly what I was hoping to do yesterday. It would have been impossible on the Yamashina post road, of course, so I thought of a way to lure them into the hills.

It was easy. I fell in with them on the road and made up a story. I told them I had found an old burial mound in the hills, and when I opened it it was full of swords and mirrors and things. I said I had buried the stuff in a bamboo grove on the other side of the mountain to keep anyone from finding out about it, and I'd sell it cheap to the right buyer. He started getting interested soon enough. It's scary what greed can do to people, don't you think? In less than an hour, I was leading that couple and their horse up a mountain trail.

When we reached the grove, I told them the treasure was buried in there and they should come inside with me and look at it. The man was so hungry for the

5. Someone who has attained Buddhist enlightenment but remains in the world to help others; here, a woman whose beauty blesses the world.

stuff by then, he couldn't refuse, but the woman said she'd wait there on the horse. I figured that would happen—the woods are so thick. They fell right into my trap. We left the woman alone and went into the grove.

It was all bamboo at first. Fifty yards or so inside, there was a sort of open clump of cedars—the perfect place for what I was going to do. I pushed through the thicket and made up some nonsense about how the treasure was buried under one of them. When he heard that, the man charged toward some scrawny cedars visible up ahead. The bamboo thinned out, and the trees were standing there in a row. As soon as we got to them, I grabbed him and pinned him down. I could see he was a strong man—he carried a sword—but I took him by surprise, and he couldn't do a thing. I had him tied to the base of a tree in no time. Where did I get the rope? Well, I'm a thief, you know—I might have to scale a wall at any time—so I've always got a piece of rope in my belt. I stuffed his mouth full of bamboo leaves to keep him quiet. That's all there was to it.

Once I finished with the man, I went and told the woman that her husband had suddenly been taken ill and she should come and have a look at him. This was another bull's-eye, of course. She took off her hat and let me lead her by the hand into the grove. As soon as she saw the man tied to the tree, though, she whipped a dagger out of her breast. I never saw a woman with such fire! If I'd been off my guard, she'd have stuck that thing in my gut. And the way she kept coming, she would have done me some damage eventually no matter how much I dodged. Still, I *am* Tajōmaru. One way or another, I managed to knock the knife out of her hand without drawing my sword. Even the most spirited woman is going to be helpless if she hasn't got a weapon. And so I was able to make the woman mine without taking her husband's life.

Yes, you heard me: without taking her husband's life. I wasn't planning to kill him on top of everything else. The woman was on the ground, crying, and I was getting ready to run out of the grove and leave her there when all of a sudden she grabbed my arm like some kind of crazy person. And then I heard what she was shouting between sobs. She could hardly catch her breath: "Either you die or my husband dies. It has to be one of you. It's worse than death for me to have two men see my shame. I want to stay with the one left alive, whether it's you or him." That gave me a wild desire to kill her husband. (Sullen excitement.)

When I say this, you probably think I'm crueler than you are. But that's because you didn't see the look on her face—and especially, you never saw the way her eyes were burning at that moment. When those eyes met mine, I knew I wanted to make her my wife. Let the thunder god kill me, I'd make her my wife—that was the only thought in my head. And no, not just from lust. I know that's what you gentlemen are thinking. If lust was all I felt for her, I'd already taken care of that. I could've just kicked her down and gotten out of there. And the man wouldn't have stained my sword with his blood. But the moment my eyes locked onto hers in that dark grove, I knew I couldn't leave there until I had killed him.

Still, I didn't want to kill him in a cowardly way. I untied him and challenged him to a sword fight. (That piece of rope they found was the one I threw aside then.) The man looked furious as he drew his big sword, and without a word he sprang at me in a rage. I don't have to tell you the outcome of the fight. My sword pierced his breast on the twenty-third thrust. Not till the twenty-third: I want you to keep that in mind. I still admire him for that. He's the only man who ever lasted even twenty thrusts with me. (Cheerful grin.)

As he went down, I lowered my bloody sword and turned toward the woman. But she was gone! I looked for her among the cedars, but the bamboo leaves on the ground showed no sign she'd ever been there. I cocked my ear for any sound of her, but all I could hear was the man's death rattle.

Maybe she had run through the underbrush to call for help when the sword fight started. The thought made me fear for my life. I grabbed the man's sword and his bow and arrows and headed straight for the mountain road. The woman's horse was still there, just chewing on grass. Anything else I could tell you after that would be a waste of breath. I got rid of his sword before coming to Kyoto, though.

So that's my confession. I always knew my head would end up hanging in the tree outside the prison some day, so let me have the ultimate punishment. (Defiant attitude.)

Penitent Confession of a Woman in the Kiyomizu Temple

After the man in the dark blue robe had his way with me, he looked at my husband, all tied up, and taunted him with laughter. How humiliated my husband must have felt! He squirmed and twisted in the ropes that covered his body, but the knots ate all the deeper into his flesh. Stumbling, I ran to his side. No—I *tried* to run to him, but instantly the man kicked me down. And that was when it happened: that was when I saw the indescribable glint in my husband's eyes. Truly, it was indescribable. It makes me shudder to recall it even now. My husband was unable to speak a word, and yet, in that moment, his eyes conveyed his whole heart to me. What I saw shining there was neither anger nor sorrow. It was the cold flash of contempt—contempt for *me*. This struck me more painfully than the bandit's kick. I let out a cry and collapsed on the spot.

When I regained consciousness, the man in blue was gone. The only one there in the grove was my husband, still tied to the cedar tree. I just barely managed to raise myself on the carpet of dead bamboo leaves, and look into my husband's face. His eyes were exactly as they had been before, with that same cold look of contempt and hatred. How can I describe the emotion that filled my heart then? Shame . . . sorrow . . . anger . . . I staggered over to him.

"Oh, my husband! Now that this has happened, I cannot go on living with you. I am prepared to die here and now. But you—yes, I want you to die as well. You witnessed my shame. I cannot leave you behind with that knowledge."

I struggled to say everything I needed to say, but my husband simply went on staring at me in disgust. I felt as if my breast would burst open at any moment, but holding my feelings in check, I began to search the bamboo thicket for his sword. The bandit must have taken it—I couldn't find it anywhere—and my husband's bow and arrows were gone as well. But then I had the good luck to find the dagger at my feet. I brandished it before my husband and spoke to him once again.

"This is the end, then. Please be so good as to allow me to take your life. I will quickly follow you in death."

When he heard this, my husband finally began moving his lips. Of course his mouth was stuffed with bamboo leaves, so he couldn't make a sound, but I knew immediately what he was saying. With total contempt for me, he said only, "Do it." Drifting somewhere between dream and reality, I thrust the dagger through the chest of his pale blue robe.

Then I lost consciousness again. When I was able to look around me at last, my husband, still tied to the tree, was no longer breathing. Across his ashen face shone a streak of light from the setting sun, filtered through the bamboo and cedar. Gulping back my tears, I untied him and cast the rope aside. And then—and then what happened to me? I no longer have the strength to tell it. That I failed to kill myself is obvious. I tried to stab myself in the throat. I threw myself in a pond at the foot of the mountain. Nothing worked. I am still here, by no means proud of my inability to die. (Forlorn smile.) Perhaps even Kanzeon,[6] bodhisattva of compassion, has turned away from me for being so weak. But now—now that I have killed my husband, now that I have been violated by a bandit—what am I to do? Tell me, what am I to . . . (Sudden violent sobbing.)

The Testimony of the Dead Man's Spirit Told through a Medium

After the bandit had his way with my wife, he sat there on the ground, trying to comfort her. I could say nothing, of course, and I was bound to the cedar tree. But I kept trying to signal her with my eyes: *Don't believe anything he tells you. He's lying, no matter what he says.* I tried to convey my meaning to her, but she just went on cringing there on the fallen bamboo leaves, staring at her knees. And, you know, I could see she was listening to him. I writhed with jealousy, but the bandit kept his smooth talk going from one point to the next. "Now that your flesh has been sullied, things will never be the same with your husband. Don't stay with him—come and be my wife! It's because I love you so much that I was so wild with you." The bandit had the gall to speak to her like that!

When my wife raised her face in response to him, she seemed almost spellbound. I had never seen her look so beautiful as she did at that moment. And what do you think this beautiful wife of mine said to the bandit, in my presence—in the presence of her husband bound hand and foot? My spirit may be wandering now between one life and the next, but every time I recall her answer, I burn with indignation. "All right," she told him, "take me anywhere you like." (Long silence.)

And that was not her only crime against me. If that were all she did, I would not be suffering so here in the darkness. With him leading her by the hand, she was stepping out of the bamboo grove as if in a dream, when suddenly the color drained from her face and she pointed back to me. "Kill him!" she screamed. "Kill him! I can't be with you as long as he is alive!" Again and again she screamed, as if she had lost her mind, "Kill him!" Even now her words like a windstorm threaten to blow me headlong into the darkest depths. Have such hateful words ever come from the mouth of a human being before? Have such damnable words ever reached the ears of a human being before? Have such—(An explosion of derisive laughter.) Even the bandit went pale when he heard her. She clung to his arm and screamed again, "Kill him!" The bandit stared at her, say-

6. Also known as Kannon.

ing neither that he would kill me nor that he would not. The next thing I knew, however, he sent my wife sprawling on the bamboo leaves with a single kick. (Another explosion of derisive laughter.) The bandit calmly folded his arms and turned to look at me.

"What do you want me to do with her?" he asked. "Kill her or let her go? Just nod to answer. Kill her?" For this if for nothing else, I am ready to forgive the bandit his crimes. (Second long silence.)

When I hesitated with my answer, my wife let out a scream and darted into the depths of the bamboo thicket. He sprang after her, but I don't think he even managed to lay a hand on her sleeve. I watched the spectacle as if it were some kind of vision.

After my wife ran off, the bandit picked up my sword and bow and arrows, and he cut my ropes at one place. "Now it's my turn to run," I remember hearing him mutter as he disappeared from the thicket. Then the whole area was quiet. No—I could hear someone weeping. While I was untying myself, I listened to the sound, until I realized—I realized that I was the one crying. (Another long silence.)

I finally raised myself, exhausted, from the foot of the tree. Lying there before me was the dagger that my wife had dropped. I picked it up and shoved it into my chest. Some kind of bloody mass rose to my mouth, but I felt no pain at all. My chest grew cold, and then everything sank into stillness. What perfect silence! In the skies above that grove on the hidden side of the mountain, not a single bird came to sing. The lonely glow of the sun lingered among the high branches of cedar and bamboo. The sun—but gradually, even that began to fade, and with it the cedars and bamboo. I lay there wrapped in a deep silence.

Then stealthy footsteps came up to me. I tried to see who it was, but the darkness had closed in all around me. Someone—that someone gently pulled the dagger from my chest with an invisible hand. Again a rush of blood filled my mouth, but then I sank once and for all into the darkness between lives.

1921

KAWABATA YASUNARI

1899–1972

At the time he was awarded the Nobel Prize in 1968, Kawabata Yasunari was the patriarch of Japanese letters. One of Japan's most frequently translated novelists, he served as a literary godfather to the country's aspiring writers, both in his official capacity as president of the Japan P.E.N. Club (part of an international organization of poets, essayists, and novelists) and through countless book reviews and an active interest in fostering new talent.

Kawabata was only the second literary Nobel laureate in all of Asia (Rabindranath Tagore of India having received the prize in 1913); not until twenty-six years later would he be joined by another Japanese novelist, Ōe Kenzaburō, who received the Nobel Prize in 1994.

Kawabata was born in Osaka in 1899 and was orphaned by the age of three. Childhood for him meant becoming "an expert in funerals": his grandmother died when he was seven, his only sister when he was nine, his grandfather when he was fifteen. Bereft of close relations and living mainly in school dormitories, Kawabata had a largely solitary youth, which may help to account for the rootlessness and melancholy that would color his fiction.

While studying Japanese literature as an undergraduate at the University of Tokyo, Kawabata joined up with twenty or so other literary youths to form a group that called itself the "New Sensibilities" (or "New Perception") school. The group's readings in avant-garde European literature, which its members explored for inspiration in their budding careers as writers, supplemented his formal studies of Japanese literature. The group took as its mission the redirection of contemporary Japanese literature away from naturalistic confessional fiction and politically engaged proletarian fiction, both widespread movements at the time, and toward more esoteric aesthetic principles of "art for art's sake." Just as the European school known as Modernism might be better described in the plural, multiple modernisms influenced the New Sensibilities writers, with the Western movements of futurism, cubism, expressionism, and Dadaism commanding the strongest attention.

Yet following his New Sensibilities phase, after the mid-1920s Kawabata turned to works that placed a stronger emphasis on a simple, if poetic, realistic style. Though the prose is deceptively straightforward, it features arresting images that appear suddenly, almost offhandedly, but burn in the memory afterward. Often the characters in these works are distilled to the few traits needed to establish them: languor, desperation, loneliness. The characters depicted most warmly tend to be those who possess a purity of emotion that heightens their perception of beauty. (Kawabata considered "little children, young women, and dying men" to live closest to such a state.)

In its citation in 1968, the Swedish Academy (the organization that awards the Nobel Prize) commended Kawabata's mastery in illuminating what it called, using language that seems slightly outdated today, "the essence of the Japanese mind." Indeed, Kawabata was acutely aware of "the old Japan's beauty." He spoke of it in his acceptance speech in Stockholm, and he writes of it frequently in his novels, which take as their backdrop such traditions as the tea ceremony, the *geisha* house, and *go*, the ancient board game. At the root of this beauty is the Buddhist notion of *mu* (emptiness) that pervades Kawabata's writing, and that he explains in his Nobel Prize acceptance speech in great detail.

In this speech, Kawabata quotes the writings of many famous Zen priests, especially Dogen, a Rinzai Zen master who lived from 1200 to 1253. In referring to Dogen's poetry, Kawabata states: "Here we have the emptiness, the nothingness, of the Orient. My own works have been described as works of emptiness, but it is not to be taken for the nihilism of the West. The spiritual foundation would seem to be quite different. Dogen entitled his poem about the seasons 'Innate Reality,' and even as he sang of the beauty of the seasons he was deeply immersed in Zen." This notion of emptiness means in part that the bough with withered flowers or the single bud is more beautiful than flowers at their peak of bloom. What Kawabata refers to as "the transience of things" is the Buddhist principle of emptiness, of longing, of unconsummated relationships, of falling leaves, fading flowers, buds that have yet to bloom. In accordance with this Buddhist sensibility, strains of bitterness and even ugliness run through Kawabata's writing: beauty is seldom present without aspects of sadness and decay. Critics see in the complex and nuanced joining of these elements one of Kawabata's sources of mastery.

Another great strength is his magician's ability to fashion weightless texts. Ungrounded by anything but the most elemental structure, his narratives seem to levitate and float—between past and present, action and setting, oblique depiction of character and a mystical sense of unity in humanity and nature—until at last they turn and descend to their "conclusion." To some, this will appear the badge of Modernism, to others, classic Japanese style: it is the joining of the two that makes Kawabata interesting.

"The Dancing Girl of Izu" (1925), the story presented here, is an early piece that foreshadows much of Kawabata's later work. It relies on a limpid prose style that is all the more poetic for its deceptive simplicity. The story is set on the Izu Peninsula, a mountainous area west of Tokyo on the largest Japanese island, Honshū. The peninsula is known for its hot springs and its striking coastline. Because of its mountainous terrain, it was popular for walking tours like the one the narrator undertakes; at the time, such tourism was still mainly an activity for the well-to-do. As a student at a state-run high school (where pupils study up through the age of about twenty), the narrator belongs to an elite social class, and in the first pages of the story he meets a troupe of traveling dancers, who have a very low social status. A deeply felt longing, partly erotic but partly a simple need for human connection, draws him to the group, and particularly to its youngest member, a dancing girl on the cusp of adolescence.

The dancers come from Oshima, an island near the tip of the Izu Peninsula but remote in the narrator's metropolitan perspective. The narrator accompanies the troupe to their mutual destination of Shimoda and along the way they achieve the intimacy of social equals, although the dancers remind him in subtle ways of the differences between them. Through his encounters with the dancers, he experiences an intensity of emotion that seems new to him. At the same time, however, he gains a kind of distance from his own feelings by reflecting on them after they have passed. The interplay of feeling and reflection is clearest in the story's final scenes, where the narrator is able to observe himself experiencing emotions that overwhelm his very sense of self.

The Dancing Girl of Izu[1]

1

About the time the road began to wind and I realized that I was finally near Amagi Pass,[2] a curtain of rain swept up after me at a terrific speed from the foot of the mountain, painting the dense cedar forests white.

1. Translated by J. Martin Holman.
2. An ancient mountain pass about 800 meters (2,600 feet) above sea level. Located in the center of the Izu Peninsula, a mountainous region west of Tokyo, the pass leads through forests of beautiful cedar and cypress trees.

I was twenty years old. I wore my school cap, *hakama*[3] over my indigo-dyed kimono, and carried a student's bag over my shoulder. It was the fourth day of my solitary journey down the Izu Peninsula. I had stayed at Shuzenji[4] Hot Spring one night, then two nights at Yugashima. And now, wearing high clogs, I was climbing Amagi. Although I had been enchanted by the layers upon layers of mountains, the virgin forests, and the shades of autumn in the deep valleys, I was hurrying along this road, my chest pounding with a certain expectation. Before long, great drops of rain began to pelt me, and I bolted up the steep, twisted road. I was relieved to reach the teahouse on the north side of the pass at last, but stopped short in the doorway. My expectation had been realized all too splendidly. The troupe of itinerant performers was inside, taking a rest.

As soon as the dancing girl noticed me standing there, she pulled out the cushion she had been kneeling on, turned it over, and placed it near her.

"Yes." That's all I said before I sat down. The words "thank you" stuck in my throat. I was out of breath from running up the road and from my astonishment.

Sitting so close, facing the dancing girl, I fumbled to pull a cigarette from my kimono sleeve. The girl took the ashtray sitting in front of her female companion and placed it near me. Naturally, I did not speak.

The dancing girl looked to be about seventeen years old. Her hair was arranged elaborately in an unusual old style unfamiliar to me. Although it made her striking oval face look quite small, it created a beautiful harmony. She gave the impression of the girls from illustrations in old romances who were depicted with an emphasis on their extravagant hair. The dancing girl was accompanied by a woman in her forties, two older girls, and a man of about twenty-five, who was wearing a jacket with the insignia of Nagaoka Hot Springs on it.

I had seen this troupe twice previously. The first time I encountered them, near Yugawa Bridge, I was on my way to Yugashima Hot Springs while they were going to Shuzenji. There were three girls in the group. The dancing girl was carrying a drum. After we passed, I looked back at them again and again. I had finally experienced the romance of travel. Then, my second night at Yugashima, the entertainers had come to the inn to perform. Sitting halfway down the ladderlike stairs, I had gazed intently at the girl as she danced on the wooden floor of the entryway.

"If they were at Shuzenji the other day and Yugashima tonight, then they would probably go to Yugano Springs on the south side of Amagi Pass tomorrow. Surely I could catch up with them along the fifteen miles of mountain road over Amagi." Thus I had been daydreaming as I hastened along the road that day. Now we had ended up taking shelter from the rain at the same teahouse. My heart was pounding.

In a moment the old woman who ran the teahouse led me to another room. It appeared it was not used regularly and had no sliding paper doors. When I

3. A kind of loose trousers worn over a kimono; formerly a required part of men's clothing, nowadays *hakama* are worn by most Japanese men only on extremely formal occasions, or for practicing martial arts.

4. Shuzenji and Yugashima are famous open-air hot springs in a spa area of the southern portion of the Izu Peninsula. At this time in Japanese history, male and female spa guests would bathe nude in the same hot spring.

peered down into the magnificent valley outside the window, I could scarcely see the bottom. It gave me goose bumps. My teeth chattered and I shivered. The old woman came back to serve tea. I told her I felt cold.

"You're all wet, aren't you, sir?" She spoke with great deference. "Come in here for a while. Dry your clothes." Reaching for my hand, she led me into her own parlor.

There was a hearth in the middle of the floor of her room. When she opened the sliding door, the hot air flowed out. I stood at the threshold, hesitating. An old man sat cross-legged by the fire, his body pale and swollen like a drowning victim. He turned his languid eyes toward me. They were yellowed to the pupils as if putrefied. Around him lay piles of old letters and scraps of paper. They almost buried him. I stood stiff, staring at him, wondering how he could be alive, this mystery in the mountains.

"I'm embarrassed to have you see him this way. Don't worry. This is my old husband. He may be unsightly, but he can't move. Please be patient with him."

After thus apologizing, the old woman explained that her husband had suffered from palsy for many years and now his whole body was almost paralyzed. The mountains of papers were actually correspondence from every possible source describing treatments for palsy and packets of medicine the old man had ordered from throughout the country. Whenever he heard of a treatment from travelers who came over the pass or saw an advertisement in the newspaper, he never failed to send for it. He kept the papers around him in heaps, staring at them, never disposing of a single one. Through the years he had accumulated mountains of aging scraps of paper.

Without a word to the old woman, I bent over the hearth. An automobile navigating the pass rattled the house. I wondered why the old man did not move down to a lower elevation, with the autumn already this cold and snow soon to cover the pass. Steam rose from my kimono. The fire was hot enough to scorch my face. The old woman went back out to the shop, commenting to one of the female entertainers.

"So this is the little girl you had with you before. She's turned out to be such a nice girl. That's good for you. How pretty she's become. Girls grow up so fast."

About an hour later, I heard the entertainers preparing to leave. I had not settled in to stay either, but I was so anxious that I did not have the courage to stand up. Although they were seasoned travelers, they would be walking at a woman's pace, so I was certain I could catch up even if I left a mile or so behind them. Still, I grew impatient sitting by the hearth. Once the entertainers had left, my daydreams began a vivid, reckless dance. The old woman returned from seeing the entertainers off.

"Where are they staying tonight?" I asked.

"There's no way to tell where people like that are going to stay, is there, young man? Wherever they can attract an audience, that's where they stay. It doesn't matter where it might be. I don't think the likes of them would have a place already planned."

The scorn that lurked in the woman's words so stirred me, I thought to myself: If that is true, then I'll have the dancing girl stay in my room tonight.

The rain abated and the mountain peak cleared. The old woman tried to detain me longer, telling me the sky would be completely cloudless if only I would wait ten more minutes. But I just could not remain sitting there.

"Please take care of yourself," I said to the old man. "It's going to get colder." I spoke from my heart as I stood up. His yellow eyes lolled in his head, and he gave a slight nod.

"Sir! Sir!" The old woman followed me outside. "This is far too much money. I just can't accept it." She picked up my bag in both hands and refused to give it to me. She would not listen, no matter how much I tried to dissuade her. The old woman told me she would accompany me up the road a bit. She repeated the same words as she tottered along behind me for a hundred yards.

"This is much too generous. I'm sorry we didn't serve you better. I'll make certain to remember your face. When you pass this way again, we'll do something special for you. Be sure to stop by next time. I won't forget you."

She seemed so overwhelmed, as if she were on the verge of tears, just because I had left a fifty-sen coin.[5] But I was eager to catch up with the dancers, and the old woman's doddering pace hindered me. At last we reached the tunnel at the pass.

"Thank you very much," I said. "You'd better go back now. Your husband is there all alone." The old woman finally released my bag.

Cold drops of water plopped inside the dark tunnel. Up ahead, the tiny portal to southern Izu grew brighter.

2

The mountain road, stitched on one side with whitewashed pickets, coursed down from the mouth of the tunnel like a jagged lightning bolt. The scene resembled a landscape in miniature. I could make out the itinerant entertainers down at the bottom. Before I had walked half a mile, I overtook them. It would be too obvious were I to slacken my pace too abruptly, so I nonchalantly passed the women. When the man, who was walking about twenty yards ahead of the others, noticed me, he paused.

"You walk fast. . . . We're lucky the weather cleared up," he said.

Relieved, I fell into step with the man. He asked me all kinds of questions. Seeing the two of us talking, the women scurried to join us.

The man was carrying a large wicker trunk on his back. The woman in her forties was holding a puppy. The oldest girl was toting a cloth bundle. The middle girl also had a wicker trunk. Everyone carried something. The dancing girl had a drum and frame on her back. Little by little, the woman, who seemed to be in her forties, began to talk to me.

"He's an upper-school student," the oldest girl whispered to the dancing girl. When I looked around she smiled. "That's right, isn't it? I know that much. Students are always coming down to the island."

They were from the harbor town of Habu on Oshima, the largest island off the southern tip of the Izu Peninsula. They had been on the road since leaving the island in the spring, but it was turning cold and they had not yet made preparations for winter. They said they were planning to stay in Shimoda for

5. Half a yen, approximately 25 US cents (a few dollars in today's currency).

just ten days, then cross over to the island from Ito Hot Springs. At the mention of Oshima, I felt even more the poetry of the situation. Again I glanced at the dancing girl's lovely hair. I asked questions about Oshima.

"A lot of students come to the island to swim, don't they?" the dancing girl said to the girl with her.

I turned back toward them. "In the summer, right?"

The dancing girl was flustered. "In the winter, too," I thought I heard her answer softly.

"In the winter, too?" I asked.

The dancing girl simply looked at her companion and giggled.

"You can swim in the winter, too?" I asked again. The dancing girl blushed. She nodded, with a serious look.

"This girl is such a silly one," the older woman laughed.

The road to Yugano ran about eight miles down through the valley of the Kawazu River. On this side of the pass, even the mountains and the color of the sky began to look more southern. As the man and I continued our conversation, we took a liking to each other. We passed tiny villages with names like Oginori and Nashimoto. About the time the thatched roofs of Yugano came into view at the foot of the mountain, I ventured to tell the man that I wanted to travel with them to Shimoda. He seemed delighted.

When we arrived at a cheap lodging house in Yugano, the older woman nodded as if to say good-bye. But the man spoke for me: "This young gentleman has kindly offered to accompany us."

"Well, well. As the old saying goes, 'On the road, a traveling companion; and in the world, kindness.' Even boring people like us will help you pass the time. Come on in and take a rest." She spoke without formality. The girls all glanced at me at the same time. They stopped talking, their faces seemingly indifferent. Then their gaze turned to embarrassment.

I went upstairs with them and put down my bag. The woven floor mats and sliding panel doors were old and dirty. The dancing girl brought us some tea from downstairs. Kneeling in front of me, she blushed bright red. Her hands were trembling. The teacup almost tumbled off the saucer. She set it down on the mat to keep it from falling but spilled the whole cup of tea. I was amazed at her bashfulness.

"My goodness. She's started thinking about the opposite sex. How disgusting! Look at that!" The older woman furrowed her brow in dismay and threw a hand towel at the girl, who picked it up and wiped the mat, looking ill at ease.

Caught off guard by the woman's words, I reconsidered my feelings. The daydream that the old woman at the pass had sparked in me had been dashed.

"The young student's indigo kimono certainly is nice," the woman remarked, her eyes fixed on me. "The pattern is the same as Tamiji's. Isn't it? Isn't it the same?"

After pressing the girls several times, she spoke to me. "We have another child at home still in school. I was thinking of him. He has the same kind of kimono as yours. These days indigo kimonos are so expensive, I just don't know what to do."

"What kind of school?"

"Elementary school, fifth grade."

"Oh, you have a fifth grader? . . ."

"His school is not on Oshima. It's in Kofu.[6] We've been on Oshima for a long time, but Kofu is our original home."

After we rested for an hour, the man led me to another hot spring inn. Until then I had assumed I would be staying at the same lodging house with the entertainers. We walked about one hundred yards along a gravel road and down some stone steps, then crossed a bridge near a public bath beside a stream. The garden of the inn was on the other side of the bridge.[7]

I stepped into the bath and the man got in after me. He told me he was twenty-four. His wife had lost two children, one by miscarriage and one that was born prematurely.[8] I assumed he was from Nagaoka,[9] since his jacket bore a Nagaoka Hot Springs emblem. His intellectual manner of speaking and his facial expressions made me wonder if he had been following the entertainers and carrying their luggage simply out of curiosity, or perhaps because he had fallen in love with one of them.

I ate lunch as soon as I got out of the bath. I had left Yugashima at eight o'clock in the morning, but it was not yet three o'clock now.

As the man made his way to the inn gate, he looked up at my window to say good-bye.

"Buy yourself some persimmons or something. I'm sorry. This is such a rude way to give this to you, from the second floor." I tossed down a packet of money. The man refused it and turned to go, but he couldn't leave the money lying in the garden so he returned and picked it up.

"You shouldn't do things like this,"[1] he said, tossing the packet back up at me. It landed on the thatched roof. When I threw it down a second time, he took it with him.

Rain started pouring around sunset. The mountains turned colorless and lost their depth. The small stream in front of the inn ran yellow as I watched it. The sound of rushing water grew louder. Thinking that the dancers would never come looking for customers in this torrent, I could not sit still, so I went to the bath two or three more times. My room was dismal. An electric light hung in a square hole cut in the wall between my room and the next, where it could illuminate both rooms.

"Ton, ton, ton, ton." In the distance beyond the clamor of the rain, the vague reverberations of a drum arose. I shoved open one of the shutters and hung out the window. The drum seemed to be getting closer. The rain and wind lashed my head. Closing my eyes and straining to hear, I tried to determine the path of the drum as it approached. A moment later I heard the sound of a samisen.[2] I heard a woman's long scream. I heard boisterous laughter. I surmised that the entertainers had been called to the banquet room at the inn across from their own. I could distinguish two or three women's voices and three or four men's. I expected them to travel in my direction once the party broke up, but it

6. An inland city, also famous for hot springs, about 60 miles from the Izu penisula.

7. Communal bathing requires ritualized steps, including disrobing, scrubbing, rinsing, and then entering the hot spring to relax.

8. Japanese refer to "naked communion" for breaking down barriers and getting to know people intimately on an emotional level when bathing together.

9. A town in the northern part of the Izu Peninsula.

1. This way of giving money is against proper etiquette; perhaps the narrator is deliberately informal to lessen the recipient's social obligation.

2. A three-stringed musical instrument.

seemed the party would pass the point of merry drinking and dissolve into riotous nonsense. Occasionally a woman's high, piercing voice rent the night like a thunderbolt. My nerves were on edge. I left the shutter open and just sat by the window. I felt some consolation every time I heard the drum.

"Oh, the dancing girl is still at the party. She's sitting, playing the drum."

I could not bear the silences when the drum stopped. I sank down into the depths of the sound of the rain.

At length I could hear the noise of confused footsteps—were they playing tag or dancing in circles? Then all fell silent. I opened my eyes wide, trying to peer through the darkness. What was this stillness? I was tormented, wondering if the dancing girl's night might be sullied.

I closed the shutters and crawled into bed, but my chest felt heavy. I went down again for a bath. I thrashed the water. The rain stopped and the moon came out. The autumn night was bright, washed clean by the rain. I slipped out of the bathhouse barefoot, but I could not do anything. It was past two o'clock.

3

After nine o'clock the next morning, the man from the troupe called on me at my inn. I had just awakened, so I invited him along to the bath. It was a cloudless, almost springlike day in southern Izu. The water had risen in the stream beside the inn and reflected the warm sun. My previous night's anguish seemed like a dream. Still, I broached the subject with the man.

"You were having quite a time last night. The drum was going until late."

"What? You could hear it?"

"Yes, I could."

"It was for some local folks. They make such a racket. It's not much fun."

He appeared unconcerned, so I said no more.

"Look. They're over at the other bath. I think they've noticed us. They're laughing."

He pointed across the stream toward the public bath on the other side. I could distinguish seven or eight bodies through the steam.

Suddenly a naked woman ran out from the rear of the dark bathhouse. She stood at the edge of the changing area as if she might come flying down the bank. She was shouting with her arms outstretched. She was stark naked, without even a towel.[3] It was the dancing girl. When I gazed at her white body, legs stretched, standing like a young paulownia tree, I felt pure water flowing through my heart. I breathed a sigh of relief and laughed out loud. She's a child—a child who can run out naked in broad daylight, overcome with joy at finding me, and stand tall on her tiptoes. I kept laughing with delight. My head was clear as though wiped clean. I could not stop smiling.

The dancing girl's hair had been arranged too elaborately for her age. She had looked seventeen or eighteen. What's more, she had been dressed like a young woman in her prime. I had made a ridiculous mistake.

3. According to public bath etiquette, adults cover their genitals with small thin towels when entering or exiting the hot spring.

After I returned to my room with the man, the oldest girl came to the garden at my inn and stood looking at the chrysanthemum bed. The dancing girl had stopped halfway across the bridge. The older woman came out of the public bath and glanced over at the two of them. The dancing girl smiled and shrugged her shoulders at me as if to indicate that she would be scolded if she didn't go back. She hurried away.

The older woman walked out as far as the bridge and called to me. "Please come visit us."

"Please come visit us," the oldest girl repeated. Then they left. However, the man stayed until late afternoon.

That evening I was playing go with a traveling paper wholesaler when I heard a drum in the garden. I started to get up. "Some entertainers have come looking for customers."

"What? Them? They're nothing. Well, then it's your turn. I put my stone here." The paper seller pointed at the board, intent on the game. But now I was restless. It sounded as though the entertainers were leaving. The man called from the garden.

"Good night."

I went out to the window in the hall and motioned for them to come up. The entertainers whispered among themselves in the garden, then walked around to the entrance.

"Good evening." After the man, the three girls each bowed to the two of us, kneeling on the floor like geisha. It suddenly became apparent that I had lost the go game.

"There doesn't appear to be any way out. I give up."

"You think so? I think I'm the one who's on the short side. Either way, it's close."

The paper dealer kept playing, studying the board and counting points without even a glance at the entertainers. The girls placed their drums and samisen in the corner of the room, then started playing a game of "five-in-a-row" on a Chinese chess board. Meanwhile, I indeed lost the go game that I had previously been winning.

"How about it? One more round, just one more round," the paper dealer pleaded. He was persistent, but I just smiled vacantly. He gave up and left the room.

The girls came over to the go board.

"Are you making the rounds again this evening?" I asked.

"Yes, we are, but . . ." The man looked toward the girls. "What do you think? Shall we just forget about it and have a good time instead?"

"That would be wonderful."

"Won't you get in trouble?"

"What do you mean? We wouldn't find any customers anyway, even if we did make the rounds."

We played "five-in-a-row" and enjoyed ourselves until past midnight.

After the entertainers left, I could not get to sleep. My mind was so keen. I stepped into the hall and called out, "Hey, Mr. Paper Dealer!"

The man, who was about sixty, sprang out of his room, elated. "It's all night tonight! We're going to play until morning."

Now I, too, felt ready for a good battle.

4

We had agreed to leave Yugano at eight o'clock the next morning. Wearing a hunting cap I had bought at a shop beside the public bath, I stuffed my school cap into the bottom of my bag and walked over to the cheap lodging house on the roadside. The sliding doors were all open on the second floor, so I casually went upstairs. The entertainers were still in bed. I stood in the hall, confused.

Lying at my feet, the dancing girl blushed and quickly covered her face with her hands. She was sharing a futon with the middle girl. She still had on her heavy makeup from the night before. The rouge on her lips and the corners of her eyes was slightly smudged. Her emotional appearance as she lay there touched my heart. She turned away as if to avoid the light. Hiding her face with her hands, she slid out of the covers and knelt in the hall.

"Thank you for last night." She gave a pretty bow. I felt awkward standing over her.

The man was sleeping with the oldest girl. Until then I had had no idea they were a couple.

"Oh, I'm sorry." The older woman spoke, sitting up halfway. "I know we had planned to leave today, but we were told there's to be a big party this evening where we can perform, so we decided to stay one more night. If you have to move on today, we could meet in Shimoda. We've already decided to stay at an inn there called Koshuya. It's easy to find." I felt as though I had been dismissed.

"Why don't you wait and leave tomorrow?" the man spoke up. "As she said, we're staying an extra day. I'm sorry. We'd like to keep you on as a traveling companion. Why don't you go with us tomorrow?"

"Yes. Let's do that," the woman added. "After all, you've come with us this far. I'm sorry we're being so selfish. We'll leave tomorrow, even if it's raining spears outside. The day after tomorrow is the forty-ninth[4] day since the baby died. Since it died while we were on the road, we've been planning all along that we should commemorate the forty-ninth day in Shimoda. We've been hurrying to get there by tomorrow. It's probably not proper for me to tell you so much, but it's like we have some kind of connection to you from a previous life. Would you offer devotions with us the day after tomorrow?"

I decided to delay my departure. I went downstairs and talked with the clerk in the dirty office of the lodging house while I waited for the entertainers. The man came down and invited me to go for a walk with him. Along the road to the south was a beautiful bridge. Leaning against the railing, the man began to tell me more about himself. He had acted in a new-style Kabuki troupe in Tokyo for a time and said he still performed occasionally at the port on Oshima. That explained the sword sheath that stuck out of their luggage like an appendage. He told me he also performed when they entertained at gatherings. The wicker trunk held the costumes they used, as well as pots, dishes, and other household effects.

"It's wretched, the mess I've made of my life. But my older brother in Kofu is doing fine as family heir, keeping up the reputation of the family. So, I would be of no use anyway."

4. In East Asian Buddhism, the soul of the deceased separates from this world in seven-day increments. The 49th day (7×7) is an especially important rite of passage in which the soul completely detaches from this world. Prayers and offerings are made to the departed spirit.

"All along I thought you were from Nagaoka Hot Springs."

"Did you? The oldest girl there with us, she's my wife. She's a year younger than you—nineteen. Our second baby was born prematurely, on the road. It lived just a week. My wife still hasn't recovered her full health. The older woman is her mother. The dancing girl is my own little sister."

"So the fourteen-year-old sister you told me about is? . . ."

"She's the one. Actually, it bothers me; I didn't want my sister to have to live like this, but it's a long story."

Then he told me his name was Eikichi, his wife's was Chiyoko, and his sister's was Kaoru. The other girl, Yuriko, seventeen years old, was the only native of Oshima. She was employed by them. Eikichi stared down at the river shallows. He became sentimental and appeared to be on the brink of tears.

As we walked back, we found the dancing girl, her face washed clean of the white makeup, crouching by the road, petting the puppy on the head. I spoke to her as I started back to my room alone.

"Come on over," I said.

"But, by myself, I . . ."

"So, come with your brother."

"We'll be right there."

Before long Eikichi came to my room.

"Where is everyone?" I asked.

"The old lady is so strict with the girls."

However, we had been playing "five-in-a-row" only a short while when the girls came across the bridge and upstairs. They bowed politely as always and hesitated,[5] kneeling in the hallway. First, Chiyoko, the oldest, stood up.

"This is my room. Don't be so formal. Come on in," I said.

The entertainers stayed about an hour, then went down to the inn bath. They begged me to come along, but I put them off. I said I would go later since there would be three girls in the bath. Shortly, the dancing girl came back upstairs alone to relay a message from Chiyoko.

"She said to come on down. She'll rinse your shoulders for you."

I did not go. Instead I played "five-in-a-row" with the dancing girl. She was surprisingly good. Earlier, when she had played "winner-stays" against Eikichi and the other girls, she had defeated them all handily. I usually win at "five-in-a-row," but I needed all my skill with her. It was refreshing not to have to make easy moves for her. With just the two of us there, the dancing girl initially sat back, playing her stones from a distance with her arm outstretched. But gradually she forgot herself and hunched over the board, absorbed in the game. Her unnaturally beautiful black hair almost touched my chest. Without warning, she blushed. "Please forgive me. I'll get in trouble." Tossing down her stones, she fled the room. The older woman was standing outside the public bath. Chiyoko and Yuriko rushed out of the bath at my inn and hurried back to their lodging house without coming upstairs.

Again Eikichi stayed at the inn with me from morning until late afternoon. The proprietress, a simple, honest woman, warned me against keeping his company, saying it was a waste to feed a fellow like him.

5. It is proper etiquette to bow and hesitate before crossing a threshold, especially if it is into a space belonging to another person.

That evening, when I went to the entertainers' lodging house, I found the dancing girl receiving a samisen lesson from the older woman. She stopped playing when she saw me but resumed after the woman said something to her. Whenever the girl's voice rose as she was singing, the woman reprimanded her. "I told you not so loud."

Eikichi had been called over to the banquet room of the inn on the other side of the road. I could see him across the way. From where I watched, it looked as though he were groaning.

"What's he doing?"

"That? . . . It's chanting from a Noh[6] drama."

"Noh drama? It sounds strange."

"He's a jack-of-all-trades. You never know what he'll do."

A man of about forty who said he was a poulterer was also staying at the lodging house. He opened the partition between the rooms and invited the girls to have dinner with him. The dancing girl took her chopsticks and went over with Yuriko. They picked through the chicken stew that remained after the man had ravaged the pot. As the girls were returning to their own room, the man patted the dancing girl's shoulder. The woman glared at him.

"Hey, don't touch her. She's an innocent virgin."

The dancing girl addressed the man as "uncle" and asked him to read "The Story of the Lord of Mito" to her, but he left immediately. She did not want to ask me directly, so she told the woman that she would like me to read the rest of "The Story of the Lord of Mito" for her. I picked up the book, with a certain expectation in my heart. Just as I hoped, the dancing girl scooted over beside me. Once I began reading, she brought her face close enough to touch my shoulder, her expression serious. Her eyes sparkled as she gazed at my forehead without blinking. It seemed to be her habit when she was being read to. Earlier, I had noticed that she had held her face right beside the poulterer. The dancing girl's most beautiful feature was her sparkling big dark eyes. The curve of her double eyelids was unspeakably lovely. Next was her flowerlike smile. In her case, the word "flowerlike" was absolutely accurate.

A moment later, the maid from the inn came to call for the dancing girl. She put on her costume.

"I'll be back soon, so please wait. And read the rest to me."

Out in the hallway she bowed low.

"I'll return soon."

"Don't sing," the woman said. The dancing girl picked up her drum and nodded slightly. The woman turned back to me. "Her voice is changing now."

The dancing girl knelt properly in the second floor of the restaurant, beating the drum. I could watch her back from the window as though she were in the next room. The sound of the drum set my heart dancing.

"When the drum enters, the party certainly does liven up." The woman was also looking across the way.

Chiyoko and Yuriko went to the same gathering.

About an hour later all four returned.

"This is all we got." The dancing girl dropped some fifty-sen coins from her fist into the older woman's palm. I read "The Story of the Lord of Mito" out

6. A type of classical Japanese musical play.

loud for a while. Then they talked about the baby that had died while they were on the road. They said the baby was almost as transparent as water at birth and did not even have the strength to cry. Nevertheless, it lived for a week.

My common goodwill—which neither was mere curiosity nor bore any trace of contempt for their status as itinerant entertainers—seemed to have touched their hearts. Before I knew it, they had decided that I should accompany them to their place on Oshima.

"The house where Grandpa lives would be good. It's big, and it would be quiet if we chased Grandpa out. You could stay as long as you wanted. And you could study." They made this announcement to me after conferring among themselves.

"We have two small houses. The one in the mountains is usually empty."

Moreover, I was to help out during new year holidays when they performed at the port in Habu.

I realized that their sense of the road was not so hardened as I had first supposed. Rather, it was more of a lighthearted attitude that had not lost the scent of the fields. They were bound together by the familial affection you would expect between parent and child or brother and sister. The hired girl, Yuriko, was the only one who was sullen around me. Perhaps she was at the age when a girl is most bashful.

I left their lodging house halfway through the night. The girls came downstairs to see me off. The dancing girl placed my clogs at the door so I could step into them easily.[7] She stuck her head out the gate and looked up at the bright sky.

"Oh, the moon! We'll be in Shimoda tomorrow. How wonderful. We'll have the baby's forty-ninth-day services. Mother will buy me a comb. We'll do all kinds of things! Would you take me to see a movie?"

The port of Shimoda—it had the air of a hometown that the itinerant entertainers who traveled around the hot springs in Izu and Sagami longed for when they were on the road.

5

The entertainers were carrying the same luggage they had hauled through Amagi Pass. The puppy rested his paws on the woman's arm, looking like a seasoned traveler. Just outside Yugano we found ourselves again in the mountains. The sun hanging over the sea warmed the slopes. We gazed toward the morning sun. Kawazu Beach spread wide in the sunlight out where the Kawazu River flowed.

"That's Oshima over there, isn't it?" I said.

"Of course it is. See how big it looks. Please do come," the dancing girl said.

Perhaps the autumn sky was too dazzling; the sea near the sun looked misted over as it is in the spring. It was another twelve-mile walk from there to Shimoda. For a while the ocean was blocked from view. Chiyoko began to sing a carefree song.

Along the way I was asked whether I preferred to take the main road, which was easier, or a steep path over the mountains that was well over a mile shorter. Naturally I chose the shortcut.

7. Etiquette requires removal of shoes in the entry way before stepping up into a dwelling. Turning shoes so that a person can easily step down into them is an act of respect and politeness.

It was an abrupt climb through the trees. I feared we would slip on the fallen leaves. I got so winded that, half in desperation, I pressed down on my knees with the palms of my hands to pick up my pace. Every time I glanced back, the others had fallen farther behind until I could only hear their voices among the trees, except for the dancing girl, who was holding up her skirts and trudging along behind me. She was trailing me by about two yards, neither trying to close the distance between us nor dropping farther back. When I turned and spoke to her, she paused as if startled, then smiled and replied. When she spoke to me, I waited, to give her a chance to catch up. But I should have known that she would stop short and refuse to take a step until I did. When the path twisted and grew even steeper, I quickened my pace again and found the dancing girl climbing intently, as always, just a couple of yards behind me. The mountains were still. The rest of the group was so far behind I could no longer hear them talking.

"Where is your house in Tokyo?"

"My home isn't Tokyo. I live in the school dormitory there."

"I know about Tokyo. I went there to dance during the cherry blossom season. . . . I was little then, so I don't remember anything about it." Then she went on. "Do you have a father?" "Have you ever been to Kofu?" She asked all kinds of questions. We talked about going to see a movie when we got to Shimoda, and again about the dead baby.

We emerged at the mountaintop. The dancing girl placed her drum on a bench in the dry grass and wiped the perspiration from her face with a handkerchief. She started to brush the dust from her legs, then suddenly crouched at my feet and began to brush the hem of my *hakama*. I jerked away, and she dropped to her knees with a thud. She brushed the dust all the way around my kimono, then dropped the hem. I stood there breathing deeply.

"Sit down," she said.

A flock of small birds appeared beside the bench. It was so still I could hear the dry leaves on the branches rustle when they alighted.

"Why do you walk so fast?"

She looked flushed. I thumped the drum with my fingers and the birds flew away.

"I'm thirsty," I said.

"I'll go see if I can find some water."

But shortly the girl came back empty-handed through the grove of yellow trees.

"What do you do on Oshima?"

The dancing girl mentioned two or three girl's names and began talking about something I could not follow. She seemed to be describing Kofu, not Oshima. Apparently the names were her friends at the elementary school she had attended until second grade. The dancing girl just rambled on.

We had waited about ten minutes when the three younger people reached the top. The older woman arrived another ten minutes after them.

On the way down, Eikichi and I purposely hung back, talking at leisure. When we had walked about two hundred yards, the dancing girl came back up from below.

"There's a spring further down. They said you should hurry down. They're waiting until you get there to take a drink."

When I heard they had found water, I ran. Fresh water sprang from between some large rocks in the shade of the trees. The girls stood waiting around the spring.

"Please, you go first," the woman said. "The water will get all cloudy if we put our hands in. You'd think it was too dirty after us women."

I scooped up the cold water in my hands and drank. The women lingered. They wrung out some damp hand towels and wiped themselves.

When we rejoined the Shimoda Highway at the foot of the mountain, we saw several threads of smoke from charcoal-burning huts. We sat down to rest on some timber stacked by the roadside. The dancing girl crouched on the road combing the puppy's shaggy fur with her pink comb.

"The teeth will break," the woman warned her.

"It's okay. I'll get a new one in Shimoda."

Ever since our stay in Yugano, I had been hoping to be given the comb she wore in the front of her hair as a memento, so I did not want her using it on the dog, either.

Eikichi and I spotted bundles of thin bamboo piled by the roadside. Remarking that it would be perfect for walking sticks, we reached them ahead of the others. Following on our heels, the dancing girl located a thick piece taller than she was.

"What are you going to do with it?" Eikichi asked.

She seemed puzzled for a moment, then held it out to me. "Here. It's a walking stick. I pulled out the thickest one."

"You can't do that. If someone sees him with the thickest one, they'll know we stole it. We don't want to get caught. Put it back," Eikichi said.

The dancing girl returned the bamboo pole and caught up with us. This time she handed me a piece of bamboo about the size of my middle finger. Then she threw herself flat on her back on the path between the rice paddies beside the road. Breathing heavily, she waited for the other women.

Eikichi and I walked together as before, this time ten or twelve yards ahead.

"It wouldn't be hard to pull them and replace them with gold teeth."

I turned around when I overheard the dancing girl's voice. She was walking with Chiyoko. The older woman and Yuriko were a short distance behind them. The dancing girl did not appear to notice me looking back.

I heard Chiyoko reply. "That's right. Why don't you tell him."

I gathered they were talking about me. Chiyoko had probably commented that my teeth were crooked, so the dancing girl had suggested gold teeth. They were discussing my looks, yet it did not bother me. I felt so close to them that I did not even care to eavesdrop. They continued their conversation for a time. Then I caught the dancing girl's voice again.

"He's a nice person."

"You're right. He seems like a nice person."

"He really is nice. It's good to have such a nice person around."

This exchange had an echo of simplicity and frankness. Hers was a child's voice expressing her sentiments without censure. I, too, was able to meekly consider myself a nice person. Refreshed, I lifted my eyes and surveyed the brilliant mountains. I felt a vague pain behind my eyelids. Twenty years old, I had embarked on this trip to Izu heavy with resentment that my personality had been permanently warped by my orphan's complex and that I would never be able to overcome a stifling melancholy. So I was inexpressibly grateful to find that I looked like a nice person as the world defines the word. The mountains looked bright because we were by the ocean near Shimoda. I swung my bamboo walking stick back and forth, lopping off the heads of the autumn grasses.

Here and there along the way stood signs as we entered villages.

"Beggars and itinerant entertainers—KEEP OUT."

6

Koshuya, a cheap lodging house, was located just within Shimoda on the north side. I followed the entertainers into a second-floor room that had all the appearances of an attic. There was no ceiling, and when I sat near the windowsill, facing the road, my head almost touched the roof.

"Do your shoulders hurt?" the woman kept asking the dancing girl. "Do your hands hurt?"

The dancing girl moved her hands in the graceful gestures she used when playing the drum. "No, they don't. I can play. I can."

"Well, I'm glad to hear that."

I hefted her drum. "Hey, that's heavy."

"It's heavier than you thought, . . . heavier than that bag of yours." The dancing girl laughed.

The entertainers heartily greeted the other people staying at the inn. Naturally, they were all entertainers and carnival people. Shimoda appeared to be a temporary roost for these birds of passage. The dancing girl gave a copper coin to one of the innkeeper's children who came toddling into the room. When I stood up to leave Koshuya, the dancing girl hurried down ahead of me to the entryway and set my clogs out for me.

"Please be sure to take me to a movie," she whispered, as though to herself.

A man who was likely a day laborer guided us halfway to our destination. Eikichi and I went on to an inn where, he said, the former district mayor was the innkeeper. We bathed, then ate a lunch of fresh fish.

"Please use this to buy some flowers[8] for tomorrow's services." I gave Eikichi a small packet of money before he returned to his lodging house. I had to return to Tokyo on the morning boat the next day because I had no more money with which to travel. I told Eikichi that school was about to start, so I could not stay with them any longer.

I ate dinner less than three hours after lunch. Alone, I crossed the bridge to the north of Shimoda and climbed the hill Shimoda Fuji to view the harbor. When I called at Koshuya on my way back, the entertainers were eating a dinner of chicken stew.

"Won't you at least have a bite with us? It's not very appetizing now that we women have put in our chopsticks, but maybe this could be the makings of a funny story." The woman took a bowl and chopsticks out of the wicker basket and asked Yuriko to wash them.

They pleaded with me to delay my departure at least one more day, as tomorrow would be the forty-ninth day since the baby's death. But again I used school as an excuse and declined their invitation.

8. Flowers to be offered to the baby's departed spirit.

The woman spoke again. "Well, then, during winter vacation, we'll all come out to meet your boat. Just let us know what day you'll arrive. We'll be waiting. Now don't try staying at an inn or anything. We'll meet you at the boat."

When only Chiyoko and Yuriko were in the room, I invited them to a movie. Chiyoko held her stomach saying, "I don't feel well. I'm too weak to walk that far." She slumped down, her face pale. Yuriko stiffened and hung her head. The dancing girl was playing with the innkeeper's children on the stairs. When she heard me, she clung to the woman, begging for permission to go to a movie with me. She returned crestfallen. She set out my clogs.

"What do you mean? There's no harm in letting him take her by himself," Eikichi interjected. But the woman would not assent. I thought it indeed strange that she would not let us go together. As I went out the door, the dancing girl was stroking the puppy's head. The atmosphere was so restrained that I could not speak a word. The dancing girl lacked the vitality even to lift her face and look at me.

I went to the movie alone. The woman narrator read the script of the silent movie by the light of a tiny lamp. I left as soon as it ended and returned to my inn. Resting my elbows on the windowsill, I stared out into the night town for a long time. It was a dark town. I thought I might hear a faint drum sounding far away. Inexplicably my tears fell.

7

While I was eating breakfast the next morning, Eikichi called to me from the street. He was wearing a crested black *haori*.[9] Apparently, he had dressed formally to send me off. There was no sign of the women. I felt sad. Eikichi came up to my room.

"Everyone else wanted to come see you off, but they went to bed so late, they couldn't get up. They won't be coming. They said they'll be waiting for you this winter, so please do come."

The morning autumn breeze blew chill in the town. Along the way Eikichi bought four packs of Shikishima cigarettes, some persimmons, and a mouthwash called "Kaoru" for me. "Because my sister's name is Kaoru." He smiled faintly. "Mandarin oranges aren't the best thing to eat on a boat, but persimmons are good for seasickness, so you can have these."

"Here. You take this." I pulled off my hunting cap and placed it on Eikichi's head. Then I dug my school cap out of my bag, and we laughed as I smoothed the wrinkles.

As we approached the dock, I was struck by the sight of the dancing girl crouching near the water. She remained motionless until I reached her. Silently, she lowered her head. Her makeup, the same this morning as it was the previous night, made me feel even more sentimental. The rouge at the corners of her eyes bestowed a youthful strength, as though she might even be angry.

"Are the others coming?" Eikichi asked.

She shook her head.

"Are they still asleep?"

She nodded.

9. Formal kimono jacket.

Eikichi went to buy my ticket for the boat to Tokyo and our passes for the launch. While he was gone, I tried to make small talk, but the dancing girl said nothing. She just stared down at the water pouring from a drain-pipe into the sea. She just kept nodding over and over before I even finished speaking.

"Granny, this fellow looks nice." A man approached who looked like a laborer.

"You're a student, aren't you? Going back to Tokyo? I think I can trust you. Would you accompany this old lady to Tokyo? She's had some hard times. Her son was working at the silver mine at Rendaiji. But he and his wife both died in the flu epidemic. They left three children behind. We couldn't think of anything else to do, so we talked it over, and we're sending them back to their old hometown. That's Mito in Ibaraki Prefecture. But this old woman doesn't understand anything, so when the boat gets to Reiganjima in Tokyo, would you put her on a train to Ueno.[1] I know it's a lot of trouble, but we're begging you. Just look at her. Don't you think it's pitiful?"

The old woman stood there with a blank expression, an infant strapped to her back. Two girls, about three and five, held her hands. I could see big rice balls and pickled plums in her dirty bundle. Five or six miners were looking after the old woman. I was pleased to accept the task.

"Thank you. We're counting on you."

"Thank you. We really should see her all the way to Mito, but we can't." The miners expressed their gratitude.

The launch rocked violently. The dancing girl kept her mouth shut tight, staring at the same spot. When I grabbed the rope ladder and looked back, she tried to say good-bye but gave up and merely nodded one last time. The launch headed back to the wharf. Again and again Eikichi waved the hunting cap I had just given him. As the launch receded in the distance, the dancing girl began to wave something white.

The steamship left Shimoda. I leaned against the railing and gazed at Oshima in the offing until the southern tip of the Izu Peninsula vanished behind me. It already seemed long ago that I parted from the dancing girl. When I glanced into the cabin to check on the old woman, I saw a group of people gathered around her in a circle, consoling her. I felt relieved. I entered the cabin next door. The waves were choppy on Sagami Bay. I was tossed left and right as I sat. A crewman passed out small metal bowls. I lay down, using my bag as a pillow. My head felt empty, and I had no sense of time. My tears spilled onto my bag. My cheeks were so cold I turned my bag over. There was a boy lying next to me. He was the son of a factory owner in Kawazu and was on his way to Tokyo to prepare to enter school. The sight of me in my First Upper School cap seemed to elicit his goodwill.

After we talked for a while, he asked, "Have you had a death in your family?"

"No, I just left someone."

I spoke meekly. I did not mind that he had seen me crying. I was not thinking about anything. I simply felt as though I were sleeping quietly, soothed and contented.

1. Major train station in Tokyo. Reiganjima: wharf district on Tokyo Bay.

I was not aware that darkness had settled on the ocean, but now lights glimmered on the shores of Ajiro and Atam.[2] My skin was chilled and my stomach empty. The boy took out some sushi wrapped in bamboo leaves. I ate his food, forgetting it belonged to someone else. Then I nestled inside his school coat. I felt a lovely hollow sensation, as if I could accept any sort of kindness and it would be only right. It was utterly natural that I should accompany the old woman to Ueno Station early the next morning and buy her a ticket to Mito. Everything seemed to melt together into one.

The lamp in the cabin went out. The smell of the tide and the fresh fish loaded in the hold grew stronger. In the darkness, warmed by the boy beside me, I let my tears flow unrestrained. My head had become clear water, dripping away drop by drop. It was a sweet, pleasant feeling, as though nothing would remain.

2. Coastal towns north of the Izu Peninsula.

VIRGINIA WOOLF

1882–1941

Virginia Woolf was one of the great modern novelists, known for her precise evocations of states of mind—or of mind and body, since she refused to separate the two. She was an ardent feminist who explored—directly in her essays and indirectly in her novels and short stories—the situation of women in society, the construction of gender identity, and the predicament of the woman writer.

Born Adeline Virginia Stephen on January 25, 1882, she was one of the four children of the eminent Victorian editor and historian Leslie Stephen and his wife, Julia, both of whom also had children from earlier marriages. The family actively pursued intellectual and artistic interests, and Julia was admired and sketched by some of the most famous Pre-Raphaelite artists. Following the customs of the day, only the sons, Adrian and Thoby, were sent to boarding school and university; Virginia and her sister, Vanessa (the painter Vanessa Bell), were instructed at home by their parents and depended for further education on their father's immense library. Woolf bitterly resented this unequal treatment and the systematic discouragement of women's intellectual development that it implied.

After her mother's death in 1895, Woolf was expected to take over the supervision of the household, which she did until her father's death in 1904. She worried that women in literary families like hers were expected to write memoirs of their fathers or to edit their correspondence. Woolf did in fact write a memoir of her father, but she later noted that if he had not died when she was relatively young, she never would have become an author. Of fragile physical health after an attack of whooping cough when she was six, Woolf suffered psychological breakdowns after the death of each parent and was frequently hospitalized, especially after a number of suicide attempts. During her lifetime Woolf consulted at least twelve doctors and, consequently, experienced firsthand the developments in medicine for treating the mentally ill, from the Victorian era to the shell shock of the First World War.

Woolf moved to central London with her sister and brother Adrian after their father's death and took a house in the Bloomsbury district. It was a time of shifting social and cultural mores, of which Woolf later claimed: "on or about December, 1910, human character changed." She and her sister, though unmarried, lived with several men (some of them openly homosexual), challenging the social conventions that respectable unmarried women were expected to follow. She and her friends soon became the focus of what was later called the Bloomsbury Group, a gathering of writers, artists, and intellectuals impatient with conservative Edwardian society who met regularly to discuss ideas and to promote a freer view of culture. This eclectic group included the novelist E. M. Forster, the historian Lytton Strachey, the economist John Maynard Keynes, and the art critics Clive Bell (who married Vanessa) and Roger Fry (who introduced the group to the work of French painters Édouard Manet and Paul Cézanne).

Woolf was not yet writing fiction but contributed reviews to the *Times Literary Supplement*, taught literature and composition at Morley College (an institution with a volunteer faculty that provided educational opportunities for workers), and participated in the adult suffrage movement and a feminist group. In 1912 she married Leonard Woolf, who encouraged her to write and with whom she founded the Hogarth Press in 1917. One of the most respected of the small literary presses, it published works by such major authors as **T. S. Eliot**, Katherine Mansfield, Strachey, Forster, Maxim Gorky, and John Middleton Murry, as well as Woolf's own novels and translations of Sigmund Freud's most significant output. Over the next two decades she produced her best-known work while coping with frequent bouts of physical and mental illness. Already depressed during World War II and exhausted after the completion of her final novel, *Between the Acts* (1941), Woolf sensed the approach of a serious attack of psychosis and the confinement it would entail: in such situations, she was obliged to "rest" and forbidden to read or write. In March 1941 she drowned herself in a river close to her Sussex home.

Woolf is admired for her poetic evocations of the way we think and feel. Like Proust and Joyce, she brings to life the concrete, sensuous details of everyday experience; like them, she explores the structures of consciousness. Championing modern fiction as an alternative to the realism of the preceding generation, she proposed a more subjective and, therefore, more accurate account of experience. Her focus was not so much on the object under observation as on the observers' perception of it: "Let us record the atoms as they fall upon the mind in the order in which they fall, let us trace the pattern, however disconnected and incoherent in appearance, which sight or incident scores upon the consciousness." Such writing, undertaken with a woman's creative vision, would open avenues for literature. Although she was dismayed by what she saw as Joyce's vulgarity, she recognized him as one of the few living writers who achieved the successful rendering of stream of consciousness.

Woolf's writing has been compared with modern painting in its emphasis on the abstract arrangement of perspectives to suggest networks of meaning. After two relatively traditional novels, she developed a more flexible approach that manipulated fictional structure. The unfolding plot gave way to an organization by juxtaposed points of view; the experience of "real," or chronological, time was partially displaced by a mind ranging ambiguously among its memories; and an intricate pattern of symbolic themes connected otherwise unrelated characters. These techniques made unfamiliar demands on the reader's ability to synthesize and re-create a complete picture. In *Jacob's Room* (1922), an understanding of the hero must be assembled from a series of partial points of view. In *The Waves* (1931), the multiple perspectives of several characters soliloquizing on their relationship to the dead Percival are broken by ten interludes that together construct an additional, interacting perspective as they describe the passage of a single day from dawn to dusk. Woolf's novels may expand or telescope the passage of time: *Mrs. Dalloway* (1925) seems to focus on Clarissa Dalloway's preparations for a party that evening, but at the same time calls up—at different times, and according to different contexts—her entire life, from childhood to her present age of fifty. Woolf also concerned herself with the question of women's equality with men in marriage, and she brilliantly evoked the inequality in her parents' marriage in her novel *To the Lighthouse* (1927).

A ROOM OF ONE'S OWN

One of Woolf's major themes is society's different attitudes toward men and toward women. The work presented here, *A Room of One's Own* (1929), examines the history of literature written by women and offers an impassioned plea that women writers be given conditions equal to those available for men: specifically, the privacy of a room in which to write and economic independence. (At the time Woolf wrote, it was unusual for women to have money of their own or to be able to devote themselves to a career.) *A Room of One's Own* does not conform to any fixed form. At once lecture and essay, autobiography and fiction, it originated in a pair of lectures on women and fiction that the author gave at Newnham and Girton Colleges (for women) at Cambridge University in 1928. Woolf warns her audience that, instead of defining either women or fiction, she will use "all the liberties and licenses of a novelist" to approach the matter obliquely and leave her auditors to sort out the truth from the "lies [that] will flow from my lips." She will, she claims, retrace the days (that is, the narrator's days) preceding her visit, and lay bare the thought processes leading up to the lecture itself.

The lecture (or, in its written form, Chapter 1), continues as a meditative ramble through various parts of Oxbridge (an informal verbal linking of *Oxford* and *Cambridge* universities) and London. It includes the famous, and apparently true, anecdote in which Woolf is warned off the university lawn and forbidden entrance to the library because she is a woman, as well as a vivid description of the differences between the food and the living quarters for women and those for men at Oxbridge. By the end of her visit, frustrated, furious, and puzzled, she decides that the subject needs research—and London's British Museum, at least, is open to all.

In Chapter 2 the narrator heads for the British Museum to locate a comprehensive definition of femininity. To her surprise and mounting anger, she discovers that the thousands of books on the subject written by men all define women as inferior animals, useful but somewhat alien in nature. Moreover, those very definitions have become prescriptions for generations of young women who learn to see themselves and their place in life accordingly. Raised in poverty and dependence, such women have neither the material means nor the self-confidence to write seriously or to become anything other than the Victorian "Angel in the House." What they require, asserts the narrator, is the self-sufficiency brought by an annual income of five hundred pounds. (Woolf had recently inherited such a sum.)

Chapter 3 pursues similar themes, adding to the five hundred pounds the need for "a room of one's own" and the privacy necessary to follow out an idea. Moving to history and focusing on the Elizabethan Age, after a discouraging inspection of the well-known *History of England* by George Macaulay Trevelyan (1876–1962), Woolf evokes the career of the "wonderfully gifted" Judith Shakespeare, William's imaginary sister (his actual sister was named Joan). Judith has the same literary and dramatic ambitions as her brother, and she too finds her way to London, but she is blocked at each turn by her identity as a woman. Woolf does not belittle William Shakespeare with this contrast; instead, her narrator remarks meaningfully that his work reveals an "incandescent, unimpeded mind."

The bleak portrayals in these chapters are lightened by satirical wit and humor, often conveyed by calculated historical distortion. Woolf uses her novelist's license to subvert and criticize the patriarchal message she describes. The Reading Room of the British Museum, august repository of masculine knowledge about women, is seen as a (bald-foreheaded) dome crowned with the names of famous men. The narrator's scholarly-seeming list of feminine characteristics is not only amusingly biased but contradictory and incoherent; it implies that the "masculine" passion for lists and documentation is not the best way to learn about human nature. Professor von X.'s portrait is an open caricature linked to suggestions that his scientific disdain hides repressed fear and anger. *A Room of One's Own* is still famous for its vivid, scathing, and occasionally humorous portrayal of women as objects of male definition and disapproval. Its model of a feminine literary history and its hypothesis of a separate feminine consciousness and manner of writing had substantial influence on writers and literary theory in the latter half of the twentieth century.

From A Room of One's Own[1]

CHAPTER 1

But, you may say, we asked you to speak about women and fiction—what has that got to do with a room of one's own? I will try to explain. When you asked me to speak about women and fiction I sat down on the banks of a river and began to wonder what the words meant. They might mean simply a few remarks about Fanny Burney; a few more about Jane Austen; a tribute to the Brontës and a sketch of Haworth Parsonage under snow; some witticisms if possible

1. This essay is based upon two papers read to the Arts Society at Newnham and the Odtaa at Girton in October 1928. The papers were too long to be read in full, and have since been altered and expanded [Woolf's note]. Newnham and Girton are women's colleges at Cambridge University, and Odtaa ("One damn thing after another") is the acronym of a literary society. Woolf's talk was entitled *Women and Fiction*.

about Miss Mitford; a respectful allusion to George Eliot; a reference to Mrs. Gaskell[2] and one would have done. But at second sight the words seemed not so simple. The title women and fiction might mean, and you may have meant it to mean, women and what they are like; or it might mean women and the fiction that they write; or it might mean women and the fiction that is written about them; or it might mean that somehow all three are inextricably mixed together and you want me to consider them in that light. But when I began to consider the subject in this last way, which seemed the most interesting, I soon saw that it had one fatal drawback. I should never be able to come to a conclusion. I should never be able to fulfil what is, I understand, the first duty of a lecturer—to hand you after an hour's discourse a nugget of pure truth to wrap up between the pages of your notebooks and keep on the mantelpiece for ever. All I could do was to offer you an opinion upon one minor point—a woman must have money and a room of her own if she is to write fiction; and that, as you will see, leaves the great problem of the true nature of woman and the true nature of fiction unsolved. I have shirked the duty of coming to a conclusion upon these two questions—women and fiction remain, so far as I am concerned, unsolved problems. But in order to make some amends I am going to do what I can to show you how I arrived at this opinion about the room and the money. I am going to develop in your presence as fully and freely as I can the train of thought which led me to think this. Perhaps if I lay bare the ideas, the prejudices, that lie behind this statement you will find that they have some bearing upon women and some upon fiction. At any rate, when a subject is highly controversial—and any question about sex is that—one cannot hope to tell the truth. One can only show how one came to hold whatever opinion one does hold. One can only give one's audience the chance of drawing their own conclusions as they observe the limitations, the prejudices, the idiosyncrasies of the speaker. Fiction here is likely to contain more truth than fact. Therefore I propose, making use of all the liberties and licences of a novelist, to tell you the story of the two days that preceded my coming here—how, bowed down by the weight of the subject which you have laid upon my shoulders, I pondered it, and made it work in and out of my daily life. I need not say that what I am about to describe has no existence; Oxbridge[3] is an invention; so is Fernham; "I" is only a convenient term for somebody who has no real being. Lies will flow from my lips, but there may perhaps be some truth mixed up with them; it is for you to seek out this truth and to decide whether any part of it is worth keeping. If not, you will of course throw the whole of it into the waste-paper basket and forget all about it.

Here then was I (call me Mary Beton, Mary Seton, Mary Carmichael or by any name you please—it is not a matter of any importance) sitting on the banks of a river a week or two ago in fine October weather, lost in thought. That collar I have

2. English novelist Elizabeth Gaskell (1810–1865) was the author of *Cranford* (1853). British writers: Fanny (Frances) Burney (1752–1840), author of *Evelina* (1778); Jane Austen (1775–1817), author of *Pride and Prejudice* (1813); the three Brontë sisters, who were raised in the Yorkshire parsonage of Haworth—Charlotte (1816–1855), author of *Jane Eyre* (1847); Emily (1818–1848), author of *Wuthering Heights* (1847); and Anne (1820–1849), author of *Agnes Grey* (1847); Mary Russell Mitford (1787–1855), author of the blank-verse tragedy *Rienzi* (1828); George Eliot (pen name of Mary Ann Evans; 1819–1880), author of *Middlemarch* (1871–72).

3. A fictional university combining the names of Oxford and Cambridge.

spoken of, women and fiction, the need of coming to some conclusion on a subject that raises all sorts of prejudices and passions, bowed my head to the ground. To the right and left bushes of some sort, golden and crimson, glowed with the colour, even it seemed burnt with the heat, of fire. On the further bank the willows wept in perpetual lamentation, their hair about their shoulders. The river reflected whatever it chose of sky and bridge and burning tree, and when the undergraduate had oared his boat through the reflections they closed again, completely, as if he had never been. There one might have sat the clock round lost in thought. Thought—to call it by a prouder name than it deserved—had let its line down into the stream. It swayed, minute after minute, hither and thither among the reflections and the weeds, letting the water lift it and sink it, until—you know the little tug—the sudden conglomeration of an idea at the end of one's line: and then the cautious hauling of it in, and the careful laying of it out? Alas, laid on the grass how small, how insignificant this thought of mine looked; the sort of fish that a good fisherman puts back into the water so that it may grow fatter and be one day worth cooking and eating. I will not trouble you with that thought now, though if you look carefully you may find it for yourselves in the course of what I am going to say.

But however small it was, it had, nevertheless, the mysterious property of its kind—put back into the mind, it became at once very exciting, and important; and as it darted and sank, and flashed hither and thither, set up such a wash and tumult of ideas that it was impossible to sit still. It was thus that I found myself walking with extreme rapidity across a grass plot. Instantly a man's figure rose to intercept me. Nor did I at first understand that the gesticulations of a curious-looking object, in a cut-away coat and evening shirt, were aimed at me. His face expressed horror and indignation. Instinct rather than reason came to my help; he was a Beadle;[4] I was a woman. This was the turf; there was the path. Only the Fellows and Scholars are allowed here; the gravel is the place for me. Such thoughts were the work of a moment. As I regained the path the arms of the Beadle sank, his face assumed its usual repose, and though turf is better walking than gravel, no very great harm was done. The only charge I could bring against the Fellows and Scholars of whatever the college might happen to be was that in protection of their turf, which has been rolled for 300 years in succession, they had sent my little fish into hiding.

What idea it had been that had sent me so audaciously trespassing I could not now remember. The spirit of peace descended like a cloud from heaven, for if the spirit of peace dwells anywhere, it is in the courts and quadrangles of Oxbridge on a fine October morning. Strolling through those colleges past those ancient halls the roughness of the present seemed smoothed away; the body seemed contained in a miraculous glass cabinet through which no sound could penetrate, and the mind, freed from any contact with facts (unless one trespassed on the turf again), was at liberty to settle down upon whatever meditation was in harmony with the moment. As chance would have it, some stray memory of some old essay about revisiting Oxbridge in the long vacation brought Charles Lamb to mind—Saint Charles, said Thackeray,[5] putting a letter of Lamb's to his forehead. Indeed,

4. A lower-ranked university officer, assistant to authority.

5. I.e., William Makepeace Thackeray (1811–1863), whose novels include *Vanity Fair* (1847–1848) and *The History of Henry Esmond, Esq.* (1852). Charles Lamb (1775–1834): English essayist and letter writer, author of *Essays of Elia* (1823), which contains *Oxford in the Vacation*, mentioned in Woolf's text.

among all the dead (I give you my thoughts as they came to me), Lamb is one of the most congenial; one to whom one would have liked to say, Tell me then how you wrote your essays? For his essays are superior even to Max Beerbohm's,[6] I thought, with all their perfection, because of that wild flash of imagination, that lightning crack of genius in the middle of them which leaves them flawed and imperfect, but starred with poetry. Lamb then came to Oxbridge perhaps a hundred years ago. Certainly he wrote an essay—the name escapes me—about the manuscript of one of Milton's poems which he saw here. It was *Lycidas* perhaps, and Lamb wrote how it shocked him to think it possible that any word in *Lycidas* could have been different from what it is. To think of Milton changing the words in that poem seemed to him a sort of sacrilege. This led me to remember what I could of *Lycidas* and to amuse myself with guessing which word it could have been that Milton had altered, and why. It then occurred to me that the very manuscript itself which Lamb had looked at was only a few hundred yards away, so that one could follow Lamb's footsteps across the quadrangle to that famous library[7] where the treasure is kept. Moreover, I recollected, as I put this plan into execution, it is in this famous library that the manuscript of Thackeray's *Esmond* is also preserved. The critics often say that *Esmond* is Thackeray's most perfect novel. But the affectation of the style, with its imitation of the eighteenth century, hampers one, so far as I remember; unless indeed the eighteenth-century style was natural to Thackeray—a fact that one might prove by looking at the manuscript and seeing whether the alterations were for the benefit of the style or of the sense. But then one would have to decide what is style and what is meaning, a question which—but here I was actually at the door which leads into the library itself. I must have opened it, for instantly there issued, like a guardian angel barring the way with a flutter of black gown instead of white wings, a deprecating, silvery, kindly gentleman, who regretted in a low voice as he waved me back that ladies are only admitted to the library if accompanied by a Fellow of the College or furnished with a letter of introduction.

That a famous library has been cursed by a woman is a matter of complete indifference to a famous library. Venerable and calm, with all its treasures safe locked within its breast, it sleeps complacently and will, so far as I am concerned, so sleep for ever. Never will I wake those echoes, never will I ask for that hospitality again, I vowed as I descended the steps in anger. Still an hour remained before luncheon, and what was one to do? Stroll on the meadows? sit by the river? Certainly it was a lovely autumn morning; the leaves were fluttering red to the ground; there was no great hardship in doing either. But the sound of music reached my ear. Some service or celebration was going forward. The organ complained magnificently as I passed the chapel door. Even the sorrow of Christianity sounded in that serene air more like the recollection of sorrow than sorrow itself; even the groanings of the ancient organ seemed lapped in peace. I had no wish to enter had I the right, and this time the verger might have stopped me, demanding perhaps my baptismal certificate, or a letter of introduction from the Dean. But the outside of these magnificent buildings is often as beautiful as the inside. Moreover, it was amusing enough to watch the congregation assembling, coming in and going out again, busying themselves at the door of the chapel like bees at the mouth of a

6. English caricaturist and writer (1872–1956).
7. Trinity College Library, in Cambridge, designed by Sir Christopher Wren and built from 1676 to 1684.

hive. Many were in cap and gown; some had tufts of fur on their shoulders; others were wheeled in bath-chairs; others, though not past middle age, seemed creased and crushed into shapes so singular that one was reminded of those giant crabs and crayfish who heave with difficulty across the sand of an aquarium. As I leant against the wall the University indeed seemed a sanctuary in which are preserved rare types which would soon be obsolete if left to fight for existence on the pavement of the Strand.[8] Old stories of old deans and old dons came back to mind, but before I had summoned up courage to whistle—it used to be said that at the sound of a whistle old Professor —— instantly broke into a gallop—the venerable congregation had gone inside. The outside of the chapel remained. As you know, its high domes and pinnacles can be seen, like a sailing-ship always voyaging never arriving, lit up at night and visible for miles, far away across the hills. Once, presumably, this quadrangle with its smooth lawns, its massive buildings, and the chapel itself was marsh too, where the grasses waved and the swine rootled. Teams of horses and oxen, I thought, must have hauled the stone in wagons from far countries, and then with infinite labour the grey blocks in whose shade I was now standing were poised in order one on top of another, and then the painters brought their glass for the windows, and the masons were busy for centuries[9] up on that roof with putty and cement, spade and trowel. Every Saturday somebody must have poured gold and silver out of a leathern purse into their ancient fists, for they had their beer and skittles presumably of an evening. An unending stream of gold and silver, I thought, must have flowed into this court perpetually to keep the stones coming and the masons working; to level, to ditch, to dig and to drain. But it was then the age of faith, and money was poured liberally to set these stones on a deep foundation, and when the stones were raised, still more money was poured in from the coffers of kings and queens and great nobles to ensure that hymns should be sung here and scholars taught. Lands were granted; tithes were paid. And when the age of faith was over and the age of reason had come, still the same flow of gold and silver went on; fellowships were founded; lectureships endowed; only the gold and silver flowed now, not from the coffers of the king, but from the chests of merchants and manufacturers, from the purses of men who had made, say, a fortune from industry, and returned, in their wills, a bounteous share of it to endow more chairs, more lectureships, more fellowships in the university where they had learnt their craft. Hence the libraries and laboratories; the observatories; the splendid equipment of costly and delicate instruments which now stands on glass shelves, where centuries ago the grasses waved and the swine rootled. Certainly, as I strolled round the court, the foundation of gold and silver seemed deep enough; the pavement laid solidly over the wild grasses. Men with trays on their heads went busily from staircase to staircase. Gaudy blossoms flowered in window-boxes. The strains of the gramophone blared out from the rooms within. It was impossible not to reflect—the reflection whatever it may have been was cut short. The clock struck. It was time to find one's way to luncheon.

It is a curious fact that novelists have a way of making us believe that luncheon parties are invariably memorable for something very witty that was said, or for

8. One of the busiest streets in London, the main artery between the city and the West End.
9. Just over one century: King's College Chapel at Cambridge was built from 1446 to 1547. The college guidebook attributes its superb craftsmanship to the work of four master masons: Reginald Ely, John Wolrich, Simon Clerk, and John Wastell.

something very wise that was done. But they seldom spare a word for what was eaten. It is part of the novelist's convention not to mention soup and salmon and ducklings, as if soup and salmon and ducklings were of no importance whatsoever, as if nobody ever smoked a cigar or drank a glass of wine. Here, however, I shall take the liberty to defy that convention and to tell you that the lunch on this occasion began with soles, sunk in a deep dish, over which the college cook had spread a counterpane of the whitest cream, save that it was branded here and there with brown spots like the spots on the flanks of a doe. After that came the partridges, but if this suggests a couple of bald, brown birds on a plate you are mistaken. The partridges, many and various, came with all their retinue of sauces and salads, the sharp and the sweet, each in its order; their potatoes, thin as coins but not so hard; their sprouts, foliated as rosebuds but more succulent. And no sooner had the roast and its retinue been done with than the silent serving-man, the Beadle himself perhaps in a milder manifestation, set before us, wreathed in napkins, a confection which rose all sugar from the waves. To call it pudding and so relate it to rice and tapioca would be an insult. Meanwhile the wineglasses had flushed yellow and flushed crimson; had been emptied; had been filled. And thus by degrees was lit, halfway down the spine, which is the seat of the soul, not that hard little electric light which we call brilliance, as it pops in and out upon our lips, but the more profound, subtle and subterranean glow, which is the rich yellow flame of rational intercourse. No need to hurry. No need to sparkle. No need to be anybody but oneself. We are all going to heaven and Vandyck[1] is of the company—in other words, how good life seemed, how sweet its rewards, how trivial this grudge or that grievance, how admirable friendship and the society of one's kind, as, lighting a good cigarette, one sunk among the cushions in the window-seat.

If by good luck there had been an ash-tray handy, if one had not knocked the ash out of the window in default, if things had been a little different from what they were, one would not have seen, presumably, a cat without a tail. The sight of that abrupt and truncated animal padding softly across the quadrangle changed by some fluke of the subconscious intelligence the emotional light for me. It was as if some one had let fall a shade. Perhaps the excellent hock was relinquishing its hold. Certainly, as I watched the Manx cat pause in the middle of the lawn as if it too questioned the universe, something seemed lacking, something seemed different. But what was lacking, what was different, I asked myself, listening to the talk. And to answer that question I had to think myself out of the room, back into the past, before the war indeed, and to set before my eyes the model of another luncheon party held in rooms not very far distant from these; but different. Everything was different. Meanwhile the talk went on among the guests, who were many and young, some of this sex, some of that; it went on swimmingly, it went on agreeably, freely, amusingly. And as it went on I set it against the background of that other talk, and as I matched the two together I had no doubt that one was the descendant, the legitimate heir of the other. Nothing was changed; nothing was different save only—here I listened with all my ears not entirely to what was being said, but to the murmur or current behind it. Yes, that was it—the change was there. Before the war at a luncheon party

1. The Flemish portrait painter Sir Anthony Van Dyck (1599–1641), who was appointed court painter by Charles I of England in 1632 and painted many portraits of the royal family and the nobility.

like this people would have said precisely the same things but they would have sounded different, because in those days they were accompanied by a sort of humming noise, not articulate, but musical, exciting, which changed the value of the words themselves. Could one set that humming noise to words? Perhaps with the help of the poets one could. A book lay beside me and, opening it, I turned casually enough to Tennyson.[2] And here I found Tennyson was singing:

There has fallen a splendid tear
From the passion-flower at the gate.
She is coming, my dove, my dear;
She is coming, my life, my fate;
The red rose cries, "She is near, she is near";
And the white rose weeps, "She is late";
The larkspur listens, "I hear, I hear";
And the lily whispers, "I wait."

Was that what men hummed at luncheon parties before the war? And the women?

My heart is like a singing bird
Whose nest is in a water'd shoot;
My heart is like an apple tree
Whose boughs are bent with thick-set fruit;
My heart is like a rainbow shell
That paddles in a halcyon sea;
My heart is gladder than all these
Because my love is come to me.[3]

Was that what women hummed at luncheon parties before the war?

There was something so ludicrous in thinking of people humming such things even under their breath at luncheon parties before the war that I burst out laughing, and had to explain my laughter by pointing at the Manx cat, who did look a little absurd, poor beast, without a tail, in the middle of the lawn. Was he really born so, or had he lost his tail in an accident? The tailless cat, though some are said to exist in the Isle of Man, is rarer than one thinks. It is a queer animal, quaint rather than beautiful. It is strange what a difference a tail makes—you know the sort of things one says as a lunch party breaks up and people are finding their coats and hats.

This one, thanks to the hospitality of the host, had lasted far into the afternoon. The beautiful October day was fading and the leaves were falling from the trees in the avenue as I walked through it. Gate after gate seemed to close with gentle finality behind me. Innumerable beadles were fitting innumerable keys into well-oiled locks; the treasure-house was being made secure for another night. After the avenue one comes out upon a road—I forget its name—which leads you, if you take the right turning, along to Fernham. But there was plenty of time. Dinner was not till half-past seven. One could almost do without dinner after such a luncheon. It is strange how a scrap of poetry works in the mind and makes the legs move in time to it along the road. Those words—

2. Alfred, Lord Tennyson (1809–1892); a passage from his long poem *Maud* (1855) follows.

3. The first stanza of "A Birthday," a short poem by Christina Rossetti (1830–1894).

There has fallen a splendid tear
From the passion-flower at the gate.
She is coming, my dove, my dear—

sang in my blood as I stepped quickly along towards Headingley.[4] And then, switching off into the other measure, I sang, where the waters are churned up by the weir:

My heart is like a singing bird
Whose nest is in a water'd shoot;
My heart is like an apple tree . . .

What poets, I cried aloud, as one does in the dusk, what poets they were!

In a sort of jealousy, I suppose, for our own age, silly and absurd though these comparisons are, I went on to wonder if honestly one could name two living poets now as great as Tennyson and Christina Rossetti were then. Obviously it is impossible, I thought, looking into those foaming waters, to compare them. The very reason why the poetry excites one to such abandonment, such rapture, is that it celebrates some feeling that one used to have (at luncheon parties before the war perhaps), so that one responds easily, familiarly, without troubling to check the feeling, or to compare it with any that one has now. But the living poets express a feeling that is actually being made and torn out of us at the moment. One does not recognize it in the first place; often for some reason one fears it; one watches it with keenness and compares it jealously and suspiciously with the old feeling that one knew. Hence the difficulty of modern poetry; and it is because of this difficulty that one cannot remember more than two consecutive lines of any good modern poet. For this reason—that my memory failed me—the argument flagged for want of material. But why, I continued, moving on towards Headingley, have we stopped humming under our breath at luncheon parties? Why has Alfred ceased to sing

She is coming, my dove, my dear?

Why has Christina ceased to respond

My heart is gladder than all these
Because my love is come to me?

Shall we lay the blame on the war? When the guns fired in August 1914, did the faces of men and women show so plain in each other's eyes that romance was killed? Certainly it was a shock (to women in particular with their illusions about education, and so on) to see the faces of our rulers in the light of the shell-fire. So ugly they looked—German, English, French—so stupid. But lay the blame where one will, on whom one will, the illusion which inspired Tennyson and Christina Rossetti to sing so passionately about the coming of their loves is far rarer now than then. One has only to read, to look, to listen, to remember. But why say "blame"? Why, if it was an illusion, not praise the catastrophe, whatever it was, that destroyed illusion and put truth in its place? For truth . . . those dots mark the spot where, in search of truth, I missed the

4. In Leeds (Yorkshire).

turning up to Fernham. Yes indeed, which was truth and which was illusion, I asked myself. What was the truth about these houses, for example, dim and festive now with their red windows in the dusk, but raw and red and squalid, with their sweets and their boot-laces, at nine o'clock in the morning? And the willows and the river and the gardens that run down to the river, vague now with the mist stealing over them, but gold and red in the sunlight—which was the truth, which was the illusion about them? I spare you the twists and turns of my cogitations, for no conclusion was found on the road to Headingley, and I ask you to suppose that I soon found out my mistake about the turning and retraced my steps to Fernham.

As I have said already that it was an October day, I dare not forfeit your respect and imperil the fair name of fiction by changing the season and describing lilacs hanging over garden walls, crocuses, tulips and other flowers of spring. Fiction must stick to facts, and the truer the facts the better the fiction—so we are told. Therefore it was still autumn and the leaves were still yellow and falling, if anything, a little faster than before, because it was now evening (seven twenty-three to be precise) and a breeze (from the southwest to be exact) had risen. But for all that there was something odd at work:

My heart is like a singing bird
Whose nest is in a water'd shoot;
My heart is like an apple tree
Whose boughs are bent with thick-set fruit—

perhaps the words of Christina Rossetti were partly responsible for the folly of the fancy—it was nothing of course but a fancy—that the lilac was shaking its flowers over the garden walls, and the brimstone butterflies were scudding hither and thither, and the dust of the pollen was in the air. A wind blew, from what quarter I know not, but it lifted the half-grown leaves so that there was a flash of silver grey in the air. It was the time between the lights when colours undergo their intensification and purples and golds burn in window-panes like the beat of an excitable heart; when for some reason the beauty of the world revealed and yet soon to perish (here I pushed into the garden, for, unwisely, the door was left open and no beadles seemed about), the beauty of the world which is so soon to perish, has two edges, one of laughter, one of anguish, cutting the heart asunder. The gardens of Fernham lay before me in the spring twilight, wild and open, and in the long grass, sprinkled and carelessly flung, were daffodils and bluebells, not orderly perhaps at the best of times, and now wind-blown and waving as they tugged at their roots. The windows of the building, curved like ships' windows among generous waves of red brick, changed from lemon to silver under the flight of the quick spring clouds. Somebody was in a hammock, somebody, but in this light they were phantoms only, half guessed, half seen, raced across the grass—would no one stop her?—and then on the terrace, as if popping out to breathe the air, to glance at the garden, came a bent figure, formidable yet humble, with her great forehead and her shabby dress—could it be the famous scholar, could it be J—— H—— herself?[5]

5. Jane Harrison (1850–1928), English classical scholar, fellow, and lecturer at Newnham College, and author of *Prolegomena to the Study of Greek Religion* (1903) and *Ancient Art and Ritual* (1913).

All was dim, yet intense too, as if the scarf which the dusk had flung over the garden were torn asunder by star or sword—the flash of some terrible reality leaping, as its way is, out of the heart of the spring. For youth——

Here was my soup. Dinner was being served in the great dining-hall. Far from being spring it was in fact an evening in October. Everybody was assembled in the big dining-room. Dinner was ready. Here was the soup. It was a plain gravy soup. There was nothing to stir the fancy in that. One could have seen through the transparent liquid any pattern that there might have been on the plate itself. But there was no pattern. The plate was plain. Next came beef with its attendant greens and potatoes—a homely trinity, suggesting the rumps of cattle in a muddy market, and sprouts curled and yellowed at the edge, and bargaining and cheapening, and women with string bags on Monday morning. There was no reason to complain of human nature's daily food, seeing that the supply was sufficient and coal-miners doubtless were sitting down to less. Prunes and custard followed. And if any one complains that prunes, even when mitigated by custard, are an uncharitable vegetable (fruit they are not), stringy as a miser's heart and exuding a fluid such as might run in misers' veins who have denied themselves wine and warmth for eighty years and yet not given to the poor, he should reflect that there are people whose charity embraces even the prune. Biscuits and cheese came next, and here the water-jug was liberally passed round, for it is the nature of biscuits to be dry, and these were biscuits to the core. That was all. The meal was over. Everybody scraped their chairs back; the swing-doors swung violently to and fro; soon the hall was emptied of every sign of food and made ready no doubt for breakfast next morning. Down corridors and up staircases the youth of England went banging and singing. And was it for a guest, a stranger (for I had no more right here in Fernham than in Trinity or Somerville or Girton or Newnham or Christchurch), to say, "The dinner was not good," or to say (we were now, Mary Seton and I, in her sitting-room), "Could we not have dined up here alone?" for if I had said anything of the kind I should have been prying and searching into the secret economies of a house which to the stranger wears so fine a front of gaiety and courage. No, one could say nothing of the sort. Indeed, conversation for a moment flagged. The human frame being what it is, heart, body and brain all mixed together, and not contained in separate compartments as they will be no doubt in another million years, a good dinner is of great importance to good talk. One cannot think well, love well, sleep well, if one has not dined well. The lamp in the spine does not light on beef and prunes. We are all *probably* going to heaven, and Vandyck is, we *hope*, to meet us round the next corner—that is the dubious and qualifying state of mind that beef and prunes at the end of the day's work breed between them. Happily my friend, who taught science, had a cupboard where there was a squat bottle and little glasses—(but there should have been sole and partridge to begin with)—so that we were able to draw up to the fire and repair some of the damages of the day's living. In a minute or so we were slipping freely in and out among all those objects of curiosity and interest which form in the mind in the absence of a particular person, and are naturally to be discussed on coming together again—how somebody has married, another has not; one thinks this, another that; one has improved out of all knowledge, the other most amazingly gone to the bad—with all those speculations upon human nature and the character of the amazing world we live in which spring naturally from such beginnings. While these things were being said, however, I became shamefacedly aware of a current setting in of its own accord and carrying everything forward to an end of its own. One might be talking of Spain or Portugal, of book or racehorse, but the real interest of whatever was said was none of those things, but a scene of masons on a high roof some five centuries ago. Kings and nobles brought treasure in huge sacks and poured it under the earth. This scene was for ever coming alive in my mind and placing itself by another of lean cows and a muddy market and withered greens and the stringy hearts of old men—these two pictures, disjointed and disconnected and nonsensical as they were, were for ever coming together and combating each other and had me entirely at their mercy. The best course, unless the whole talk was to be distorted, was to expose what was in my mind to the air, when with good luck it would fade and crumble like the head of the dead king when they opened the coffin at Windsor.[6] Briefly, then, I told Miss Seton about the masons who had been all those years on the roof of the chapel, and about the kings and queens and nobles bearing sacks of gold and silver on their shoulders, which they shovelled into the earth; and then how the great financial magnates of our own time came and laid cheques and bonds, I suppose, where the others had laid ingots and rough lumps of gold. All that lies beneath the colleges down there, I said; but this college, where we are now sitting, what lies beneath its gallant red brick and the wild unkempt grasses of the garden? What force is behind the plain china off which we dined, and (here it popped out of my mouth before I could stop it) the beef, the custard and the prunes?

Well, said Mary Seton, about the year 1860—Oh, but you know the story, she said, bored, I suppose, by the recital. And she told me—rooms were hired. Committees met. Envelopes were addressed. Circulars were drawn up. Meetings were held; letters were read out; so-and-so has promised so much; on the contrary, Mr. —— won't give a penny. The *Saturday Review* has been very rude. How can we raise a fund to pay for offices? Shall we hold a bazaar? Can't we find a pretty girl to sit in the front row? Let us look up what John Stuart Mill said on the subject. Can any one persuade the editor of the —— to print a letter? Can we get Lady —— to sign it? Lady —— is out of town. That was the way it was done, presumably, sixty years ago, and it was a prodigious effort, and a great deal of time was spent on it. And it was only after a long struggle and with the utmost difficulty that they got thirty thousand pounds together.[7] So obviously we cannot have wine and partridges and servants carrying tin dishes on their heads, she said. We cannot have sofas and separate rooms. "The amenities," she said, quoting from some book or other, "will have to wait."[8]

At the thought of all those women working year after year and finding it hard to get two thousand pounds together, and as much as they could do to get thirty thousand pounds, we burst out in scorn at the reprehensible poverty of

6. At the royal residence of Windsor Castle, nine English kings are buried in two chapels serving as royal mausoleums.
7. "We are told that we ought to ask for £30,000 at least. . . . It is not a large sum, considering that there is to be but one college of this sort for Great Britain, Ireland and the Colonies, and considering how easy it is to raise immense sums for boys' schools. But considering how few people really wish women to be educated, it is a good deal."—Lady Stephen, *Life of Miss Emily Davies* [Woolf's note].
8. "Every penny which could be scraped together was set aside for building, and the amenities had to be postponed."—R. Strachey, *The Cause* [Woolf's note].

our sex. What had our mothers been doing then that they had no wealth to leave us? Powdering their noses? Looking in at shop windows? Flaunting in the sun at Monte Carlo? There were some photographs on the mantel-piece. Mary's mother—if that was her picture—may have been a wastrel in her spare time (she had thirteen children by a minister of the church), but if so her gay and dissipated life had left too few traces of its pleasures on her face. She was a homely body; an old lady in a plaid shawl which was fastened by a large cameo; and she sat in a basket-chair, encouraging a spaniel to look at the camera, with the amused, yet strained expression of one who is sure that the dog will move directly the bulb is pressed. Now if she had gone into business; had become a manufacturer of artificial silk or a magnate on the Stock Exchange; if she had left two or three hundred thousand pounds to Fernham, we could have been sitting at our ease tonight and the subject of our talk might have been archaeology, botany, anthropology, physics, the nature of the atom, mathematics, astronomy, relativity, geography. If only Mrs Seton and her mother and her mother before her had learnt the great art of making money and had left their money, like their fathers and their grandfathers before them, to found fellowships and lectureships and prizes and scholarships appropriated to the use of their own sex, we might have dined very tolerably up here alone off a bird and a bottle of wine; we might have looked forward without undue confidence to a pleasant and honourable lifetime spent in the shelter of one of the liberally endowed professions. We might have been exploring or writing; mooning about the venerable places of the earth; sitting contemplative on the steps of the Parthenon, or going at ten to an office and coming home comfortably at half-past four to write a little poetry. Only, if Mrs Seton and her like had gone into business at the age of fifteen, there would have been—that was the snag in the argument—no Mary. What, I asked, did Mary think of that? There between the curtains was the October night, calm and lovely, with a star or two caught in the yellowing trees. Was she ready to resign her share of it and her memories (for they had been a happy family, though a large one) of games and quarrels up in Scotland, which she is never tired of praising for the fineness of its air and the quality of its cakes, in order that Fernham might have been endowed with fifty thousand pounds or so by a stroke of the pen? For, to endow a college would necessitate the suppression of families altogether. Making a fortune and bearing thirteen children—no human being could stand it. Consider the facts, we said. First there are nine months before the baby is born. Then the baby is born. Then there are three or four months spent in feeding the baby. After the baby is fed there are certainly five years spent in playing with the baby. You cannot, it seems, let children run about the streets. People who have seen them running wild in Russia say that the sight is not a pleasant one. People say, too, that human nature takes its shape in the years between one and five. If Mrs Seton, I said, had been making money, what sort of memories would you have had of games and quarrels? What would you have known of Scotland, and its fine air and cakes and all the rest of it? But it is useless to ask these questions, because you would never have come into existence at all. Moreover, it is equally useless to ask what might have happened if Mrs Seton and her mother and her mother before her had amassed great wealth and laid it under the foundations of college and library, because, in the first place, to earn money was impossible for them, and in the second, had it been possible, the law denied them the right to possess what money they earned. It is only for the last forty-eight years that Mrs Seton has had a penny of her own. For all the centuries before that it would have been her husband's property—a thought which, perhaps, may have had its share in keeping Mrs Seton and her mothers off the Stock Exchange. Every penny I earn, they may have said, will be taken from me and disposed of according to my husband's wisdom—perhaps to found a scholarship or to endow a fellowship in Balliol or Kings,[9] so that to earn money, even if I could earn money, is not a matter that interests me very greatly. I had better leave it to my husband.

At any rate, whether or not the blame rested on the old lady who was looking at the spaniel, there could be no doubt that for some reason or other our mothers had mismanaged their affairs very gravely. Not a penny could be spared for "amenities"; for partridges and wine, beadles and turf, books and cigars, libraries and leisure. To raise bare walls out of the bare earth was the utmost they could do.

So we talked standing at the window and looking, as so many thousands look every night, down on the domes and towers of the famous city beneath us. It was very beautiful, very mysterious in the autumn moonlight. The old stone looked very white and venerable. One thought of all the books that were assembled down there; of the pictures of old prelates and worthies hanging in the panelled rooms; of the painted windows that would be throwing strange globes and crescents on the pavement; of the tablets and memorials and inscriptions; of the fountains and the grass; of the quiet rooms looking across the quiet quadrangles. And (pardon me the thought) I thought, too, of the admirable smoke and drink and the deep armchairs and the pleasant carpets: of the urbanity, the geniality, the dignity which are the offspring of luxury and privacy and space. Certainly our mothers had not provided us with anything comparable to all this—our mothers who found it difficult to scrape together thirty thousand pounds, our mothers who bore thirteen children to ministers of religion at St Andrews.[1]

So I went back to my inn, and as I walked through the dark streets I pondered this and that, as one does at the end of the day's work. I pondered why it was that Mrs Seton had no money to leave us; and what effect poverty has on the mind; and what effect wealth has on the mind; and I thought of the queer old gentlemen I had seen that morning with tufts of fur upon their shoulders; and I remembered how if one whistled one of them ran; and I thought of the organ booming in the chapel and of the shut doors of the library; and I thought how unpleasant it is to be locked out; and I thought how it is worse perhaps to be locked in; and, thinking of the safety and prosperity of the one sex and of the poverty and insecurity of the other and of the effect of tradition and of the lack of tradition upon the mind of a writer, I thought at last that it was time to roll up the crumpled skin of the day, with its arguments and its impressions and its anger and its laughter, and cast it into the hedge. A thousand stars were flashing across the blue wastes of the sky. One seemed alone with an inscrutable society. All human beings were laid asleep—prone, horizontal, dumb.

9. I.e., King's College, Cambridge. Balliol: Balliol College, Oxford.

1. Probably St. Andrew's in Holborn, an old London church rebuilt under the famous architect Sir Christopher Wren during 1683–1695.

Nobody seemed stirring in the streets of Oxbridge. Even the door of the hotel sprang open at the touch of an invisible hand—not a boots was sitting up to light me to bed, it was so late.

CHAPTER 2

The scene, if I may ask you to follow me, was now changed. The leaves were still falling, but in London now, not Oxbridge; and I must ask you to imagine a room, like many thousands, with a window looking across people's hats and vans and motor-cars to other windows, and on the table inside the room a blank sheet of paper on which was written in large letters WOMEN AND FICTION, but no more. The inevitable sequel to lunching and dining at Oxbridge seemed, unfortunately, to be a visit to the British Museum. One must strain off what was personal and accidental in all these impressions and so reach the pure fluid, the essential oil of truth. For that visit to Oxbridge and the luncheon and the dinner had started a swarm of questions. Why did men drink wine and women water? Why was one sex so prosperous and the other so poor? What effect has poverty on fiction? What conditions are necessary for the creation of works of art?—a thousand questions at once suggested themselves. But one needed answers, not questions; and an answer was only to be had by consulting the learned and the unprejudiced, who have removed themselves above the strife of tongue and the confusion of body and issued the result of their reasoning and research in books which are to be found in the British Museum. If truth is not to be found on the shelves of the British Museum, where, I asked myself, picking up a notebook and a pencil, is truth?

Thus provided, thus confident and enquiring, I set out in the pursuit of truth. The day, though not actually wet, was dismal, and the streets in the neighborhood of the Museum were full of open coal-holes, down which sacks were showering; four-wheeled cabs were drawing up and depositing on the pavement corded boxes containing, presumably, the entire wardrobe of some Swiss or Italian family seeking fortune or refuge or some other desirable commodity which is to be found in the boarding-houses of Bloomsbury[2] in the winter. The usual hoarse-voiced men paraded the streets with plants on barrows. Some shouted; others sang. London was like a workshop. London was like a machine. We were all being shot backwards and forwards on this plain foundation to make some pattern. The British Museum was another department of the factory. The swing-doors swung open; and there one stood under the vast dome, as if one were a thought in the huge bald forehead which is so splendidly encircled by a band of famous names.[3] One went to the counter; one took a slip of paper; one opened a volume of the catalogue, and . . . . . the five dots here indicate five separate minutes of stupefaction, wonder and bewilderment. Have you any notion how many books are written about women in the course of one year? Have you any notion how many are written by men?

2. A residential and academic borough in London, site of the British Museum and various educational institutions.
3. The names of famous men, including Chaucer, Spenser, Shakespeare, Milton, Pope, Wordsworth, Byron, Carlyle, and Tennyson, are painted in a circle around the dome of the Reading Room at the British Museum.

Are you aware that you are, perhaps, the most discussed animal in the universe? Here had I come with a notebook and a pencil proposing to spend a morning reading, supposing that at the end of the morning I should have transferred the truth to my notebook. But I should need to be a herd of elephants, I thought, and a wilderness of spiders, desperately referring to the animals that are reputed longest lived and most multitudinously eyed, to cope with all this. I should need claws of steel and beak of brass even to penetrate the husk. How shall I ever find the grains of truth embedded in all this mass of paper, I asked myself, and in despair began running my eye up and down the long list of titles. Even the names of the books gave me food for thought. Sex and its nature might well attract doctors and biologists; but what was surprising and difficult of explanation was the fact that sex—woman, that is to say—also attracts agreeable essayists, light-fingered novelists, young men who have taken the M.A. degree; men who have taken no degree; men who have no apparent qualification save that they are not women. Some of these books were, on the face of it, frivolous and facetious; but many, on the other hand, were serious and prophetic, moral and hortatory. Merely to read the titles suggested innumerable schoolmasters, innumerable clergymen mounting their platforms and pulpits and holding forth with a loquacity which far exceeded the hour usually allotted to such discourse on this one subject. It was a most strange phenomenon; and apparently—here I consulted the letter M—one confined to male sex. Women do not write books about men—a fact that I could not help welcoming with relief, for if I had first to read all that men have written about women, then all that women have written about men, the aloe that flowers once in a hundred years would flower twice before I could set pen to paper. So, making a perfectly arbitrary choice of a dozen volumes or so, I sent my slips of paper to lie in the wire tray, and waited in my stall, among the other seekers for the essential oil of truth.

What could be the reason, then, of this curious disparity, I wondered, drawing cart-wheels on the slips of paper provided by the British taxpayer for other purposes. Why are women, judging from this catalogue, so much more interesting to men than men are to women? A very curious fact it seemed, and my mind wandered to picture the lives of men who spend their time in writing books about women; whether they were old or young, married or unmarried, red-nosed or humpbacked—anyhow, it was flattering, vaguely, to feel oneself the object of such attention, provided that it was not entirely bestowed by the crippled and the infirm—so I pondered until all such frivolous thoughts were ended by an avalanche of books sliding down on to the desk in front of me. Now the trouble began. The student who has been trained in research at Oxbridge has no doubt some method of shepherding his question past all distractions till it runs into its answer as a sheep runs into its pen. The student by my side, for instance, who was copying assiduously from a scientific manual was, I felt sure, extracting pure nuggets of the essential ore every ten minutes or so. His little grunts of satisfaction indicated so much. But if, unfortunately, one has had no training in a university, the question far from being shepherded to its pen flies like a frightened flock hither and thither, helter-skelter, pursued by a whole pack of hounds. Professors, schoolmasters, sociologists, clergymen, novelists, essayists, journalists, men who had no qualification save that they were not women, chased my simple and single question—Why are women poor?—until it became fifty questions; until the fifty questions leapt frantically into mid-stream and were carried away. Every page in my notebook was scribbled over with notes. To show the state of mind I was in, I will read you a few of them, explaining that the page was headed quite simply, WOMEN AND POVERTY, in block letters; but what followed was something like this:

Condition in Middle Ages of,
Habits in the Fiji Islands of,
Worshipped as goddesses by,
Weaker in moral sense than,
Idealism of,
Greater conscientiousness of,
South Sea Islanders, age of puberty among,
Attractiveness of,
Offered as sacrifice to,
Small size of brain of,
Profounder sub-consciousness of,
Less hair on the body of,
Mental, moral and physical inferiority of,
Love of children of,
Greater length of life of,
Weaker muscles of,
Strength of affections of,
Vanity of,
Higher education of,
Shakespeare's opinion of,
Lord Birkenhead's opinion of,
Dean Inge's opinion of,
La Bruyère's opinion of,
Dr. Johnson's opinion of,
Mr. Oscar Browning's[4] *opinion of, . . .*

Here I drew breath and added, indeed, in the margin, Why does Samuel Butler[5] say, "Wise men never say what they think of women"? Wise men never say anything else apparently. But, I continued, leaning back in my chair and looking at the vast dome in which I was a single but by now somewhat harassed thought, what is so unfortunate is that wise men never think the same thing about women. Here is Pope:[6]

4. A schoolmaster and later fellow of King's College, Cambridge (1837–1923); anecdotes about his strong opinions (see p. 391) were published in a 1927 biography. The first earl of Birkenhead, F. E. Smith (1872–1930), a conservative politician who opposed women's suffrage and praised the domestic "true functions of womanhood." William Ralph Inge (1860–1954), dean of St. Paul's Cathedral in London and a religious writer. Jean de La Bruyère (1645–1696), French moralist and author of satirical *Characters* (1688), imitating the Greek writer Theophrastus. Samuel Johnson (1709–1784), author of moral essays and of the famous *A Dictionary of the English Language* (1747).

5. Satirical author (1835–1902) who wrote *Erewhon* (1872) and *The Way of All Flesh* (1903); his *Notebooks* are the source of this statement.

6. Alexander Pope (1688–1744), translator of Homer and author of *An Essay on Man* (1733–34) and the satirical *The Rape of the Lock* (1712–14).

Most women have no character at all.

And here is La Bruyère:

> Les femmes sont extrêmes; elles sont meilleures ou pires que les hommes—[7]

a direct contradiction by keen observers who were contemporary. Are they capable of education or incapable? Napoleon thought them incapable.[8] Dr. Johnson thought the opposite.[9] Have they souls or have they not souls? Some savages say they have none. Others, on the contrary, maintain that women are half divine and worship them on that account.[1] Some sages hold that they are shallower in the brain; others that they are deeper in the consciousness. Goethe honoured them; Mussolini[2] despises them. Wherever one looked men thought about women and thought differently. It was impossible to make head or tail of it all, I decided, glancing with envy at the reader next door who was making the neatest abstracts, headed often with an A or a B or a C, while my own notebook rioted with the wildest scribble of contradictory jottings. It was distressing, it was bewildering, it was humiliating. Truth had run through my fingers. Every drop had escaped.

I could not possibly go home, I reflected, and add as a serious contribution to the study of women and fiction that women have less hair on their bodies than men, or that the age of puberty among the South Sea Islanders[3] is nine—or is it ninety?—even the handwriting had become in its distraction indecipherable. It was disgraceful to have nothing more weighty or respectable to show after a whole morning's work. And if I could not grasp the truth about W. (as for brevity's sake I had come to call her) in the past, why bother about W. in the future? It seemed pure waste of time to consult all those gentlemen who specialise in woman and her effect on whatever it may be—politics, children, wages, morality—numerous and learned as they are. One might as well leave their books unopened.

But while I pondered I had unconsciously, in my listlessness, in my desperation, been drawing a picture where I should, like my neighbour, have been writing a conclusion. I had been drawing a face, a figure. It was the face and

7. Women are extreme; they are better or worse than men (French).
8. Napoleon wrote: "What we ask of education is not that girls should think, but that they should believe. The weakness of women's brains, the instability of their ideas, the place they will fill in society, their need for perpetual resignation, and for an easy and generous type of charity—all this can only be met by religion" (notes written on May 15, 1807, concerning the establishment of a girl's school at Écouen).
9. "'Men know that women are an overmatch for them, and therefore they choose the weakest or the most ignorant. If they did not think so, they never could be afraid of women knowing as much as themselves.'. . . In justice to the sex, I think it but candid to acknowledge that, in a subsequent conversation, he told me that he was serious in what he said."—BOSWELL, *The Journal of a Tour to the Hebrides* [Woolf's note].
1. "The ancient Germans believed that there was something holy in women, and accordingly consulted them as oracles."—FRAZER, *Golden Bough* [Woolf's note].
2. Benito Mussolini (1883–1945), fascist dictator of Italy between 1922 and 1943. Johann Wolfgang von Goethe (1749–1832), German author of *Faust*. "The eternal feminine draws us along" is the last line of *Faust*, Part 2.
3. The native peoples of the islands in the south-central Pacific Ocean were the subject of several anthropological studies in the early 20th century, including Margaret Mead's widely read *Coming of Age in Samoa* (1928).

the figure of Professor von X. engaged in writing his monumental work entitled *The Mental, Moral, and Physical Inferiority of the Female Sex*.[4] He was not in my picture a man attractive to women. He was heavily built; he had a great jowl; to balance that he had very small eyes; he was very red in the face. His expression suggested that he was labouring under some emotion that made him jab his pen on the paper as if he were killing some noxious insect as he wrote, but even when he had killed it that did not satisfy him; he must go on killing it; and even so, some cause for anger and irritation remained. Could it be his wife, I asked, looking at my picture. Was she in love with a cavalry officer? Was the cavalry officer slim and elegant and dressed in astrachan?[5] Had he been laughed at, to adopt the Freudian theory, in his cradle by a pretty girl? For even in his cradle the professor, I thought, could not have been an attractive child. Whatever the reason, the professor was made to look very angry and very ugly in my sketch, as he wrote his great book upon the mental, moral and physical inferiority of women. Drawing pictures was an idle way of finishing an unprofitable morning's work. Yet it is in our idleness, in our dreams, that the submerged truth sometimes comes to the top. A very elementary exercise in psychology, not to be dignified by the name of psycho-analysis, showed me, on looking at my notebook, that the sketch of the angry professor had been made in anger. Anger had snatched my pencil while I dreamt. But what was anger doing there? Interest, confusion, amusement, boredom—all these emotions I could trace and name as they succeeded each other throughout the morning. Had anger, the black snake, been lurking among them? Yes, said the sketch, anger had. It referred me unmistakably to the one book, to the one phrase, which had roused the demon; it was the professor's statement about the mental, moral and physical inferiority of women. My heart had leapt. My cheeks had burnt. I had flushed with anger. There was nothing specially remarkable, however foolish, in that. One does not like to be told that one is naturally the inferior of a little man—I looked at the student next me—who breathes hard, wears a ready-made tie, and has not shaved this fortnight. One has certain foolish vanities. It is only human nature, I reflected, and began drawing cart-wheels and circles over the angry professor's face till he looked like a burning bush or a flaming comet—anyhow, an apparition without human semblance or significance. The professor was nothing now but a faggot burning on the top of Hampstead Heath.[6] Soon my own anger was explained and done with; but curiosity remained. How explain the anger of the professors? Why were they angry? For when it came to analysing the impression left by these books there was always an element of heat. This heat took many forms; it showed itself in satire, in sentiment, in curiosity, in reprobation. But there was another element which was often present and could not immediately be identified. Anger, I called it. But it was anger that had gone underground and mixed itself with all kinds of other emotions. To judge from its odd effects, it was anger disguised and complex, not anger simple and open.

4. A fictional portrait, probably based on Otto Weininger's *Sex and Character* (1906), that distinguished between male (productive and moral) and female (negative and amoral) characteristics.

5. Curly lambskin.

6. A public open space in the village of Hampstead, in London. Faggot: a bundle of sticks.

Whatever the reason, all these books,[7] I thought, surveying the pile on the desk, are worthless for my purposes. They were worthless scientifically, that is to say, though humanly they were full of instruction, interest, boredom, and very queer facts about the habits of the Fiji Islanders. They had been written in the red light of emotion and not in the white light of truth. Therefore they must be returned to the central desk and restored each to his own cell in the enormous honeycomb. All that I had retrieved from that morning's work had been the one fact of anger. The professors—I lumped them together thus—were angry. But why, I asked myself, having returned the books, why, I repeated, standing under the colonnade among the pigeons and the prehistoric canoes, why are they angry? And, asking myself this question, I strolled off to find a place for luncheon. What is the real nature of what I call for the moment their anger? I asked. Here was a puzzle that would last all the time that it takes to be served with food in a small restaurant somewhere near the British Museum. Some previous luncher had left the lunch edition of the evening paper on a chair, and, waiting to be served, I began idly reading the headlines. A ribbon of very large letters ran across the page. Somebody had made a big score in South Africa. Lesser ribbons announced that Sir Austen Chamberlain was at Geneva.[8] A meat axe with human hair on it had been found in a cellar. Mr. Justice —— commented in the Divorce Courts upon the Shamelessness of Women. Sprinkled about the paper were other pieces of news. A film actress had been lowered from a peak in California and hung suspended in mid-air. The weather was going to be foggy. The most transient visitor to this planet, I thought, who picked up this paper could not fail to be aware, even from this scattered testimony, that England is under the rule of a patriarchy. Nobody in their senses could fail to detect the dominance of the professor. His was the power and the money and the influence. He was the proprietor of the paper and its editor and sub-editor. He was the Foreign Secretary and the Judge. He was the cricketer; he owned the race-horses and the yachts. He was the director of the company that pays two hundred per cent to its shareholders. He left millions to charities and colleges that were ruled by himself. He suspended the film actress in mid-air. He will decide if the hair on the meat axe is human; he it is who will acquit or convict the murderer, and hang him, or let him go free. With the exception of the fog he seemed to control everything. Yet he was angry. I knew that he was angry by this token. When I read what he wrote about women I thought, not of what he was saying, but of himself. When an arguer argues dispassionately he thinks only of the argument; and the reader cannot help thinking of the argument too. If he had written dispassionately about women, had used indisputable proofs to establish his argument and had shown no trace of wishing that the result should be one thing rather than another, one would not have been angry either. One would have accepted the fact, as one accepts the fact that a pea is green or a canary yellow. So be it, I should have said. But I

7. E.g., *Fijian Society, or the Sociology and Psychology of the Fijians* (1921), by Reverend W. Deane, principal of a teachers' training college in Ndávuilévu, Fiji; and *The Hill Tribes of Fiji* (1922), by A. B. Brewster, a colonial functionary, mixed facts with interpretation. Reverend Deane remarks that "the amount of sexual immorality and promiscuous intercourse during the past forty years is appalling." Fiji is an island in the South Pacific (see n. 3, p. 377).

8. The site of the League of Nations. Chamberlain was the British foreign secretary between 1924 and 1929.

had been angry because he was angry. Yet it seemed absurd, I thought, turning over the evening paper, that a man with all this power should be angry. Or is anger, I wondered, somehow, the familiar, the attendant sprite on power? Rich people, for example, are often angry because they suspect that the poor want to seize their wealth. The professors, or patriarchs, as it might be more accurate to call them, might be angry for that reason partly, but partly for one that lies a little less obviously on the surface. Possibly they were not "angry" at all; often, indeed, they were admiring, devoted, exemplary in the relations of private life. Possibly when the professor insisted a little too emphatically upon the inferiority of women, he was concerned not with their inferiority, but with his own superiority. That was what he was protecting rather hot-headedly and with too much emphasis, because it was a jewel to him of the rarest price. Life for both sexes—and I looked at them, shouldering their way along the pavement—is arduous, difficult, a perpetual struggle. It calls for gigantic courage and strength. More than anything, perhaps, creatures of illusion as we are, it calls for confidence in oneself. Without self-confidence we are as babes in the cradle. And how can we generate this imponderable quality, which is yet so invaluable, most quickly? By thinking that other people are inferior to oneself. By feeling that one has some innate superiority—it may be wealth, or rank, a straight nose, or the portrait of a grandfather by Romney[9]—for there is no end to the pathetic devices of the human imagination—over other people. Hence the enormous importance to a patriarch who has to conquer, who has to rule, of feeling that great numbers of people, half the human race indeed, are by nature inferior to himself. It must indeed be one of the chief sources of his power. But let me turn the light of this observation on to real life, I thought. Does it help to explain some of those psychological puzzles that one notes in the margin of daily life? Does it explain my astonishment the other day when Z, most humane, most modest of men, taking up some book by Rebecca West[1] and reading a passage in it, exclaimed, "The arrant feminist! She says that men are snobs!" The exclamation, to me so surprising—for why was Miss West an arrant feminist for making a possibly true if uncomplimentary statement about the other sex?—was not merely the cry of wounded vanity; it was a protest against some infringement of his power to believe in himself. Women have served all these centuries as looking-glasses possessing the magic and delicious power of reflecting the figure of man at twice its natural size. Without that power probably the earth would still be swamp and jungle. The glories of all our wars would be unknown. We should still be scratching the outlines of deer on the remains of mutton bones and bartering flints for sheepskins or whatever simple ornament took our unsophisticated taste. Supermen[2] and Fingers of Destiny would never have existed. The Czar and the Kaiser would never have worn their crowns or lost them. Whatever may be their use in civilized societies, mirrors are essential to all violent and heroic action. That is why Napoleon and Mussolini both insist so emphatically upon the inferiority of women, for if

9. George Romney (1734–1802), portrait painter of 18th-century British society.
1. Pseudonym of Cicely Isabel Andrews (1892–1983), British novelist and journalist.
2. Fascist politicians, such as Adolf Hitler (1889–1945) in Germany and Mussolini (1883–1945) in Italy, rationalized their aggressive policies by exploiting and distorting Friedrich Nietzsche's (1844–1900) concept of the *Übermensch*, or superior being (in *Thus Spake Zarathustra*, 1883–85).

they were not inferior, they would cease to enlarge. That serves to explain in part the necessity that women so often are to men. And it serves to explain how restless they are under her criticism; how impossible it is for her to say to them this book is bad, this picture is feeble, or whatever it may be, without giving far more pain and rousing far more anger than a man would do who gave the same criticism. For if she begins to tell the truth, the figure in the looking-glass shrinks; his fitness for life is diminished. How is he to go on giving judgment, civilising natives, making laws, writing books, dressing up and speechifying at banquets, unless he can see himself at breakfast and at dinner at least twice the size he really is? So I reflected, crumbling my bread and stirring my coffee and now and again looking at the people in the street. The looking-glass vision is of supreme importance because it charges the vitality; it stimulates the nervous system. Take it away and man may die, like the drug fiend deprived of his cocaine. Under the spell of that illusion, I thought, looking out of the window, half the people on the pavement are striding to work. They put on their hats and coats in the morning under its agreeable rays. They start the day confident, braced, believing themselves desired at Miss Smith's tea party; they say to themselves as they go into the room, I am the superior of half the people here, and it is thus that they speak with that self-confidence, that self-assurance, which have had such profound consequences in public life and lead to such curious notes in the margin of the private mind.

But these contributions to the dangerous and fascinating subject of the psychology of the other sex—it is one, I hope, that you will investigate when you have five hundred a year of your own—were interrupted by the necessity of paying the bill. It came to five shillings and ninepence. I gave the waiter a ten-shilling note and he went to bring me change. There was another ten-shilling note in my purse; I noticed it, because it is a fact that still takes my breath away—the power of my purse to breed ten-shilling notes automatically. I open it and there they are. Society gives me chicken and coffee, bed and lodging, in return for a certain number of pieces of paper which were left me by an aunt, for no other reason than that I share her name.

My aunt, Mary Beton, I must tell you, died by a fall from her horse when she was riding out to take the air in Bombay. The news of my legacy reached me one night about the same time that the act was passed that gave votes to women.[3] A solicitor's letter fell into the post-box and when I opened it I found that she had left me five hundred pounds[4] a year for ever. Of the two—the vote and the money—the money, I own, seemed infinitely the more important. Before that I had made my living by cadging odd jobs from newspapers, by reporting a donkey show here or a wedding there; I had earned a few pounds by addressing envelopes, reading to old ladies, making artificial flowers, teaching the alphabet to small children in a kindergarten. Such were the chief occupations that were open to women before 1918. I need not, I am afraid, describe in any detail the hardness of the work, for you know perhaps women who have done it; nor the difficulty of living on the money when it was earned, for you may have tried. But what still remains with me as a worse infliction than either was the poison of fear and bitterness which those days bred in me. To begin with, always to be

3. Women were given the vote in 1918; the voting age for women was lowered from thirty to twenty-one in 1928.

4. Roughly $30,000 today.

doing work that one did not wish to do, and to do it like a slave, flattering and fawning, not always necessarily perhaps, but it seemed necessary and the stakes were too great to run risks; and then the thought of that one gift which it was death to hide[5]—a small one but dear to the possessor—perishing and with it myself, my soul—all this became like a rust eating away the bloom of the spring, destroying the tree at its heart. However, as I say, my aunt died; and whenever I change a ten-shilling note a little of that rust and corrosion is rubbed off; fear and bitterness go. Indeed, I thought, slipping the silver into my purse, it is remarkable, remembering the bitterness of those days, what a change of temper a fixed income will bring about. No force in the world can take from me my five hundred pounds. Food, house and clothing are mine for ever. Therefore not merely do effort and labour cease, but also hatred and bitterness. I need not hate any man; he cannot hurt me. I need not flatter any man; he has nothing to give me. So imperceptibly I found myself adopting a new attitude towards the other half of the human race. It was absurd to blame any class or any sex, as a whole. Great bodies of people are never responsible for what they do. They are driven by instincts which are not within their control. They too, the patriarchs, the professors, had endless difficulties, terrible drawbacks to contend with. Their education had been in some ways as faulty as my own. It had bred in them defects as great. True, they had money and power, but only at the cost of harbouring in their breasts an eagle, a vulture, for ever tearing the liver out and plucking at the lungs—the instinct for possession, the rage for acquisition which drives them to desire other people's fields and goods perpetually; to make frontiers and flags; battleships and poison gas; to offer up their own lives and their children's lives. Walk through the Admiralty Arch[6] (I had reached that monument), or any other avenue given up to trophies and cannon, and reflect upon the kind of glory celebrated there. Or watch in the spring sunshine the stockbroker and the great barrister going indoors to make money and more money and more money when it is a fact that five hundred pounds a year will keep one alive in the sunshine. These are unpleasant instincts to harbour, I reflected. They are bred of the conditions of life; of the lack of civilisation, I thought, looking at the statue of the Duke of Cambridge,[7] and in particular at the feathers in his cocked hat, with a fixity that they have scarcely ever received before. And, as I realised these drawbacks, by degrees fear and bitterness modified themselves into pity and toleration; and then in a year or two, pity and toleration went, and the greatest release of all came, which is freedom to think of things in themselves. That building, for example, do I like it or not? Is that picture beautiful or not? Is that in my opinion a good book or a bad? Indeed my aunt's legacy unveiled the sky to me, and substituted for the large and imposing figure of a gentleman, which Milton recommended for my perpetual adoration, a view of the open sky.

So thinking, so speculating, I found my way back to my house by the river. Lamps were being lit and an indescribable change had come over London since

5. From "When I Consider How My Light Is Spent" by John Milton (1608–1673): "And that one talent which is death to hide, / Lodged with me useless."

6. A triple arch in Trafalgar Square (London) at the entrance to the Mall, erected in 1910.

7. An equestrian statue of the second duke of Cambridge (1819–1904), cousin of Queen Victoria, in the full dress uniform of a field marshal.

the morning hour. It was as if the great machine after labouring all day had made with our help a few yards of something very exciting and beautiful—a fiery fabric flashing with red eyes, a tawny monster roaring with hot breath. Even the wind seemed flung like a flag as it lashed the houses and rattled the hoardings.

In my little street, however, domesticity prevailed. The house painter was descending his ladder; the nursemaid was wheeling the perambulator carefully in and out back to nursery tea; the coal-heaver was folding his empty sacks on top of each other; the woman who keeps the green-grocer's shop was adding up the day's takings with her hands in red mittens. But so engrossed was I with the problem you have laid upon my shoulders that I could not see even these usual sights without referring them to one centre. I thought how much harder it is now than it must have been even a century ago to say which of these employments is the higher, the more necessary. Is it better to be a coal-heaver or a nursemaid; is the charwoman who has brought up eight children of less value to the world than the barrister who has made a hundred thousand pounds? It is useless to ask such questions; for nobody can answer them. Not only do the comparative values of charwomen and lawyers rise and fall from decade to decade, but we have no rods with which to measure them even as they are at the moment. I had been foolish to ask my professor to furnish me with "indisputable proofs" of this or that in his argument about women. Even if one could state the value of any one gift at the moment, those values will change; in a century's time very possibly they will have changed completely. Moreover, in a hundred years, I thought, reaching my own doorstep, women will have ceased to be the protected sex. Logically they will take part in all the activities and exertions that were once denied them. The nursemaid will heave coal. The shop-woman will drive an engine. All assumptions founded on the facts observed when women were the protected sex will have disappeared—as, for example (here a squad of soldiers marched down the street), that women and clergymen and gardeners live longer than other people. Remove that protection, expose them to the same exertions and activities, make them soldiers and sailors and engine-drivers and dock labourers, and will not women die off so much younger, so much quicker, than men that one will say, "I saw a woman today," as one used to say, "I saw an aeroplane." Anything may happen when womanhood has ceased to be a protected occupation, I thought, opening the door. But what bearing has all this upon the subject of my paper, Women and Fiction? I asked, going indoors.

CHAPTER 3

It was disappointing not to have brought back in the evening some important statement, some authentic fact. Women are poorer than men because—this or that. Perhaps now it would be better to give up seeking for the truth, and receiving on one's head an avalanche of opinion hot as lava, discoloured as dish-water. It would be better to draw the curtains; to shut out distractions; to light the lamp; to narrow the enquiry and to ask the historian, who records not opinions but facts, to describe under what conditions women lived, not throughout the ages, but in England, say in the time of Elizabeth.[8]

8. Queen of England from 1558 to 1603.

For it is a perennial puzzle why no woman wrote a word of that extraordinary literature when every other man, it seemed, was capable of song or sonnet. What were the conditions in which women lived, I asked myself; for fiction, imaginative work that is, is not dropped like a pebble upon the ground, as science may be; fiction is like a spider's web, attached ever so lightly perhaps, but still attached to life at all four corners. Often the attachment is scarcely perceptible; Shakespeare's plays, for instance, seem to hang there complete by themselves. But when the web is pulled askew, hooked up at the edge, torn in the middle, one remembers that these webs are not spun in mid-air by incorporeal creatures, but are the work of suffering human beings, and are attached to grossly material things, like health and money and the houses we live in.

I went, therefore, to the shelf where the histories stand and took down one of the latest, Professor Trevelyan's *History of England*.[9] Once more I looked up Women, found "position of," and turned to the pages indicated. "Wife-beating," I read, "was a recognised right of man, and was practised without shame by high as well as low. . . . Similarly," the historian goes on, "the daughter who refused to marry the gentleman of her parents' choice was liable to be locked up, beaten and flung about the room, without any shock being inflicted on public opinion. Marriage was not an affair of personal affection, but of family avarice, particularly in the 'chivalrous' upper classes. . . . Betrothal often took place while one or both of the parties was in the cradle, and marriage when they were scarcely out of the nurses' charge." That was about 1470, soon after Chaucer's[1] time. The next reference to the position of women is some two hundred years later, in the time of the Stuarts.[2] "It was still the exception for women of the upper and middle class to choose their own husbands, and when the husband had been assigned, he was lord and master, so far at least as law and custom could make him. Yet even so," Professor Trevelyan concludes, "neither Shakespeare's women nor those of authentic seventeenth-century memoirs, like the Verneys and the Hutchinsons,[3] seem wanting in personality and character." Certainly, if we consider it, Cleopatra must have had a way with her; Lady Macbeth,[4] one would suppose, had a will of her own; Rosalind, one might conclude, was an attractive girl. Professor Trevelyan is speaking no more than the truth when he remarks that Shakespeare's women do not seem wanting in personality and character. Not being a historian, one might go even further and say that women have burnt like beacons in all the works of all the poets from the beginning of time—Clytemnestra, Antigone, Cleopatra, Lady Macbeth, Phèdre, Cressida, Rosalind, Desdemona, the Duchess of Malfi,[5]

9. Published in London in 1926. References are to pages 260–61 and, later, to pages 436–37.
1. Geoffrey Chaucer (1340?–1400), author of *The Canterbury Tales* (1390–1400).
2. The British royal house from 1603 to 1714 (except for the Commonwealth interregnum of 1649–60).
3. F. P. Verney compiled *The Memoirs of the Verney Family during the Seventeenth Century* (1892–1899), and Lucy Hutchinson recounted her husband's life in *Memoirs of the Life of Colonel Hutchinson* (1806).
4. Heroine of Shakespeare's *Macbeth*. Cleopatra (69–30 B.C.E.), queen of Egypt and heroine of Shakespeare's *Antony and Cleopatra*.
5. Doomed heroine of John Webster's *The Duchess of Malfi* (ca. 1613). Clytemnestra is the heroine of Aeschylus's *Agamemnon* (458 B.C.E.). Antigone is the eponymous heroine of a 442 B.C.E. play by Sophocles. Phèdre is the heroine of Jean Racine's *Phèdre* (1677). Cressida, Rosalind, and Desdemona are heroines of Shakespeare's *Troilus and Cressida*, *As You Like It*, and *Othello*, respectively.

among the dramatists; then among the prose writers: Millamant, Clarissa, Becky Sharp, Anna Karenina, Emma Bovary, Madame de Guermantes[6]—the names flock to mind, nor do they recall women "lacking in personality and character." Indeed, if woman had no existence save in the fiction written by men, one would imagine her a person of the utmost importance; very various; heroic and mean; splendid and sordid; infinitely beautiful and hideous in the extreme; as great as a man, some think even greater.[7] But this is woman in fiction. In fact, as Professor Trevelyan points out, she was locked up, beaten and flung about the room.

A very queer, composite being thus emerges. Imaginatively she is of the highest importance; practically she is completely insignificant. She pervades poetry from cover to cover; she is all but absent from history. She dominates the lives of kings and conquerors in fiction; in fact she was the slave of any boy whose parents forced a ring upon her finger. Some of the most inspired words, some of the most profound thoughts in literature fall from her lips; in real life she could hardly read, could scarcely spell, and was the property of her husband.

It was certainly an odd monster that one made up by reading the historians first and the poets afterwards—a worm winged like an eagle; the spirit of life and beauty in a kitchen chopping up suet. But these monsters, however amusing to the imagination, have no existence in fact. What one must do to bring her to life was to think poetically and prosaically at one and the same moment, thus keeping in touch with fact—that she is Mrs. Martin, aged thirty-six, dressed in blue, wearing a black hat and brown shoes; but not losing sight of fiction either—that she is a vessel in which all sorts of spirits and forces are coursing and flashing perpetually. The moment, however, that one tries this method with the Elizabethan woman, one branch of illumination fails; one is held up by the scarcity of facts. One knows nothing detailed, nothing perfectly true and substantial about her. History scarcely mentions her. And I turned to Professor Trevelyan again to see what history meant to him. I found by looking at his chapter headings that it meant—

"The Manor Court and the Methods of Open-field Agriculture . . . The Cistercians and Sheep-farming . . . The Crusades . . . The University . . . The

6. A character in Marcel Proust's *Remembrance of Things Past* (*The Guermantes Way*, 1920–21). Millamant is the heroine of William Congreve's satirical comedy *The Way of the World* (1700). Clarissa is the eponymous heroine of Samuel Richardson's seven-volume epistolary novel (1747–48). Becky Sharp appears in William Thackeray's *Vanity Fair* (1847–48). Anna Karenina is the title character in a Leo Tolstoy novel (1875–77). Emma Bovary is the heroine of Gustave Flaubert's *Madame Bovary* (1856).

7. "It remains a strange and almost inexplicable fact that in Athena's city, where women were kept in almost Oriental suppression as odalisques or drudges, the stage should yet have produced figures like Clytemnestra and Cassandra, Atossa and Antigone, Phèdre and Medea, and all the other heroines who dominate play after play of the 'misogynist' Euripides. But the paradox of this world where in real life a respectable woman could hardly show her face alone in the street, and yet on the stage woman equals or surpasses man, has never been satisfactorily explained. In modern tragedy the same predominance exists. At all events, a very cursory survey of Shakespeare's work (similarly with Webster, though not with Marlowe or Jonson) suffices to reveal how this dominance, this initiative of women, persists from Rosalind to Lady Macbeth. So too in Racine; six of his tragedies bear their heroines' names; and what male characters of his shall we set against Hermione and Andromaque, Bérénice and Roxane, Phèdre and Athalie? So again with Ibsen; what men shall we match with Solveig and Nora, Hedda and Hilda Wangel and Rebecca West?"—F. L. LUCAS, *Tragedy*, pp. 114–15 [Woolf's note].

House of Commons . . . The Hundred Years' War . . . The Wars of the Roses . . . The Renaissance Scholars . . . The Dissolution of the Monasteries . . . Agrarian and Religious Strife . . . The Origin of English Sea-power . . . The Armada . . ." and so on. Occasionally an individual woman is mentioned, an Elizabeth, or a Mary; a queen or a great lady. But by no possible means could middle-class women with nothing but brains and character at their command have taken part in any one of the great movements which, brought together, constitute the historian's view of the past. Nor shall we find her in any collection of anecdotes. Aubrey[8] hardly mentions her. She never writes her own life and scarcely keeps a diary; there are only a handful of her letters in existence. She left no plays or poems by which we can judge her. What one wants, I thought—and why does not some brilliant student at Newnham or Girton[9] supply it?—is a mass of information; at what age did she marry; how many children had she as a rule; what was her house like; had she a room to herself; did she do the cooking; would she be likely to have a servant? All these facts lie somewhere, presumably, in parish registers and account books; the life of the average Elizabethan woman must be scattered about somewhere, could one collect it and make a book of it. It would be ambitious beyond my daring, I thought, looking about the shelves for books that were not there, to suggest to the students of those famous colleges that they should re-write history, though I own that it often seems a little queer as it is, unreal, lop-sided; but why should they not add a supplement to history? calling it, of course, by some inconspicuous name so that women might figure there without impropriety? For one often catches a glimpse of them in the lives of the great, whisking away into the background, concealing, I sometimes think, a wink, a laugh, perhaps a tear. And, after all, we have lives enough of Jane Austen; it scarcely seems necessary to consider again the influence of the tragedies of Joanna Baillie[1] upon the poetry of Edgar Allan Poe; as for myself, I should not mind if the homes and haunts of Mary Russell Mitford were closed to the public for a century at least. But what I find deplorable, I continued, looking about the bookshelves again, is that nothing is known about women before the eighteenth century. I have no model in my mind to turn about this way and that. Here am I asking why women did not write poetry in the Elizabethan age, and I am not sure how they were educated; whether they were taught to write; whether they had sitting-rooms to themselves; how many women had children before they were twenty-one; what, in short, they did from eight in the morning till eight at night. They had no money evidently; according to Professor Trevelyan they were married whether they liked it or not before they were out of the nursery, at fifteen or sixteen very likely. It would have been extremely odd, even upon this showing, had one of them suddenly written the plays of Shakespeare, I concluded, and I thought of that old gentleman, who is dead now, but was a bishop, I think, who declared that it was impossible for any woman, past, present, or to come, to have the genius of Shakespeare. He wrote to the papers about it. He also told a lady who

8. John Aubrey (1626–1697), author of *Brief Lives*, which includes sketches of his famous contemporaries.

9. Woolf delivered her lectures at Newnham and Girton Colleges for women, part of Cambridge University since 1880 and 1873, respectively.

1. Joanna Baillie (1762–1851) was a poet and dramatist whose *Plays on the Passions* (1798–1812) were famous in her day.

applied to him for information that cats do not as a matter of fact go to heaven, though they have, he added, souls of a sort. How much thinking those old gentlemen used to save one! How the borders of ignorance shrank back at their approach! Cats do not go to heaven. Women cannot write the plays of Shakespeare.

Be that as it may, I could not help thinking, as I looked at the works of Shakespeare on the shelf, that the bishop was right at least in this; it would have been impossible, completely and entirely, for any woman to have written the plays of Shakespeare in the age of Shakespeare. Let me imagine, since facts are so hard to come by, what would have happened had Shakespeare had a wonderfully gifted sister, called Judith,[2] let us say. Shakespeare himself went, very probably—his mother was an heiress—to the grammar school, where he may have learnt Latin—Ovid, Virgil and Horace[3]—and the elements of grammar and logic. He was, it is well known, a wild boy who poached rabbits, perhaps shot a deer, and had, rather sooner than he should have done, to marry a woman in the neighbourhood, who bore him a child rather quicker than was right. That escapade sent him to seek his fortune in London. He had, it seemed, a taste for the theatre; he began by holding horses at the stage door. Very soon he got work in the theatre, became a successful actor, and lived at the hub of the universe, meeting everybody, knowing everybody, practising his art on the boards, exercising his wits in the streets, and even getting access to the palace of the queen. Meanwhile his extraordinarily gifted sister, let us suppose, remained at home. She was as adventurous, as imaginative, as agog to see the world as he was. But she was not sent to school. She had no chance of learning grammar and logic, let alone of reading Horace and Virgil. She picked up a book now and then, one of her brother's perhaps, and read a few pages. But then her parents came in and told her to mend the stockings or mind the stew and not moon about with books and papers. They would have spoken sharply but kindly, for they were substantial people who knew the conditions of life for a woman and loved their daughter—indeed, more likely than not she was the apple of her father's eye. Perhaps she scribbled some pages up in an apple loft on the sly, but was careful to hide them or set fire to them. Soon, however, before she was out of her teens, she was to be betrothed to the son of a neighbouring wool-stapler.[4] She cried out that marriage was hateful to her, and for that she was severely beaten by her father. Then he ceased to scold her. He begged her instead not to hurt him, not to shame him in this matter of her marriage. He would give her a chain of beads or a fine petticoat, he said; and there were tears in his eyes. How could she disobey him? How could she break his heart? The force of her own gift alone drove her to it. She made up a small parcel of her belongings, let herself down by a rope one summer's night and took the road to London. She was not seventeen. The birds that sang in the hedge were not more musical than she was. She had the quickest fancy, a gift like her brother's, for the tune of words. Like him, she had a taste for the theatre. She stood at the stage door; she wanted to act, she said. Men laughed in her face. The manager—a fat,

2. The name of Shakespeare's younger daughter.
3. Roman authors. Publius Ovidius Naso (43 B.C.E.–17 C.E.), author of the *Metamorphoses*. Publius Vergilius Maro (70–19 B.C.E.), author of the *Aeneid*. Quintus Horatius Flaccus (65–8 B.C.E.), author of *Odes* and satires.
4. A dealer in woolen goods, which were a "staple" or established type of merchandise.

loose-lipped man—guffawed. He bellowed something about poodles dancing and women acting—no woman, he said, could possibly be an actress. He hinted—you can imagine what. She could get no training in her craft. Could she even seek her dinner in a tavern or roam the streets at midnight? Yet her genius was for fiction and lusted to feed abundantly upon the lives of men and women and the study of their ways. At last—for she was very young, oddly like Shakespeare the poet in her face, with the same grey eyes and rounded brows—at last Nick Greene[5] the actor-manager took pity on her; she found herself with child by that gentleman and so—who shall measure the heat and violence of the poet's heart when caught and tangled in a woman's body?—killed herself one winter's night and lies buried at some cross-roads where the omnibuses now stop outside the Elephant and Castle.[6]

That, more or less, is how the story would run, I think, if a woman in Shakespeare's day had had Shakespeare's genius. But for my part, I agree with the deceased bishop, if such he was—it is unthinkable that any woman in Shakespeare's day should have had Shakespeare's genius. For genius like Shakespeare's is not born among labouring, uneducated, servile people. It was not born in England among the Saxons and the Britons. It is not born today among the working classes. How, then, could it have been born among women whose work began, according to Professor Trevelyan, almost before they were out of the nursery, who were forced to it by their parents and held to it by all the power of law and custom? Yet genius of a sort must have existed among women as it must have existed among the working classes. Now and again an Emily Brontë or a Robert Burns[7] blazes out and proves its presence. But certainly it never got itself on to paper. When, however, one reads of a witch being ducked, of a woman possessed by devils, of a wise woman selling herbs, or even of a very remarkable man who had a mother, then I think we are on the track of a lost novelist, a suppressed poet, of some mute and inglorious[8] Jane Austen, some Emily Brontë who dashed her brains out on the moor or mopped and mowed about the highways crazed with the torture that her gift had put her to. Indeed, I would venture to guess that Anon, who wrote so many poems without signing them, was often a woman. It was a woman Edward Fitzgerald,[9] I think, suggested who made the ballads and the folk-songs, crooning them to her children, beguiling her spinning with them, or the length of the winter's night.

This may be true or it may be false—who can say?—but what is true in it, so it seemed to me, reviewing the story of Shakespeare's sister as I had made it, is that any woman born with a great gift in the sixteenth century would certainly have gone crazed, shot herself, or ended her days in some lonely cottage outside the village, half witch, half wizard, feared and mocked at. For it needs little skill in psychology to be sure that a highly gifted girl who had tried to use her gift for poetry would have been so thwarted and hindered by other people, so tortured and pulled asunder by her own contrary instincts, that she must

5. A fictional character based on Shakespeare's contemporary Robert Greene (1558–1592) and appearing in Woolf's *Orlando*.
6. A popular London pub. "Cross-roads": suicides were commonly buried at crossroads.
7. Scottish poet (1759–1796).
8. A reference to Thomas Gray's line in *Elegy Written in a Country Churchyard* (1751): "Some mute inglorious Milton here may rest."
9. British author (1809–1883), known for his translation from the Persian of *The Rubáiyát of Omar Khayyám* (1859).

have lost her health and sanity to a certainty. No girl could have walked to London and stood at a stage door and forced her way into the presence of actor-managers without doing herself a violence and suffering an anguish which may have been irrational—for chastity may be a fetish invented by certain societies for unknown reasons—but were none the less inevitable. Chastity had then, it has even now, a religious importance in a woman's life, and has so wrapped itself round with nerves and instincts that to cut it free and bring it to the light of day demands courage of the rarest. To have lived a free life in London in the sixteenth century would have meant for a woman who was poet and playwright a nervous stress and dilemma which might well have killed her. Had she survived, whatever she had written would have been twisted and deformed, issuing from a strained and morbid imagination. And undoubtedly, I thought, looking at the shelf where there are no plays by women, her work would have gone unsigned. That refuge she would have sought certainly. It was the relic of the sense of chastity that dictated anonymity to women even so late as the nineteenth century. Currer Bell, George Eliot, George Sand,[1] all the victims of inner strife as their writings prove, sought ineffectively to veil themselves by using the name of a man. Thus they did homage to the convention, which if not implanted by the other sex was liberally encouraged by them (the chief glory of a woman is not to be talked of, said Pericles,[2] himself a much-talked-of man), that publicity in women is detestable. Anonymity runs in their blood. The desire to be veiled still possesses them. They are not even now as concerned about the health of their fame as men are, and, speaking generally, will pass a tombstone or a signpost without feeling an irresistible desire to cut their names on it, as Alf, Bert or Chas. must do in obedience to their instinct, which murmurs if it sees a fine woman go by, or even a dog, Ce chien est à moi.[3] And, of course, it may not be a dog, I thought, remembering Parliament Square, the Sièges Allée[4] and other avenues; it may be a piece of land or a man with curly black hair. It is one of the great advantages of being a woman that one can pass even a very fine negress without wishing to make an Englishwoman of her.

That woman, then, who was born with a gift of poetry in the sixteenth century, was an unhappy woman, a woman at strife against herself. All the conditions of her life, all her own instincts, were hostile to the state of mind which is needed to set free whatever is in the brain. But what is the state of mind that is most propitious to the act of creation, I asked. Can one come by any notion of the state that furthers and makes possible that strange activity? Here I opened the volume containing the Tragedies of Shakespeare. What was Shakespeare's state of mind, for instance, when he wrote *Lear* and *Antony and Cleopatra*? It was certainly the state of mind most favourable to poetry that there has ever existed. But Shakespeare himself said nothing about it. We only

1. Pseudonyms of Charlotte Brontë, Mary Ann Evans (1819–1880), and Lucile-Aurore Dupin (1804–1876), author of *Lélia* (1833), respectively.
2. From the Greek leader Pericles' funeral oration (431 B.C.E.) as reported in Thucydides' history of the Peloponnesian War (2.35–46).
3. This dog is mine (French); from the philosopher Blaise Pascal's *Thoughts* (1657–58). He uses an anecdote about poor children to illustrate what he considers a universal impulse to assert property claims.
4. An avenue in Berlin containing statues of Hohenzollern rulers. Parliament Square is in London next to the Houses of Parliament and Westminster Abbey.

know casually and by chance that he "never blotted a line."[5] Nothing indeed was ever said by the artist himself about his state of mind until the eighteenth century perhaps. Rousseau[6] perhaps began it. At any rate, by the nineteenth century self-consciousness had developed so far that it was the habit for men of letters to describe their minds in confessions and autobiographies. Their lives also were written, and their letters were printed after their deaths. Thus, though we do not know what Shakespeare went through when he wrote *Lear*, we do know what Carlyle went through when he wrote the *French Revolution*; what Flaubert went through when he wrote *Madame Bovary*; what Keats[7] was going through when he tried to write poetry against the coming of death and the indifference of the world.

And one gathers from this enormous modern literature of confession and self-analysis that to write a work of genius is almost always a feat of prodigious difficulty. Everything is against the likelihood that it will come from the writer's mind whole and entire. Generally material circumstances are against it. Dogs will bark; people will interrupt; money must be made; health will break down. Further, accentuating all these difficulties and making them harder to bear is the world's notorious indifference. It does not ask people to write poems and novels and histories; it does not need them. It does not care whether Flaubert finds the right word or whether Carlyle scrupulously verifies this or that fact. Naturally, it will not pay for what it does not want. And so the writer, Keats, Flaubert, Carlyle, suffers, especially in the creative years of youth, every form of distraction and discouragement. A curse, a cry of agony, rises from those books of analysis and confession. "Mighty poets in their misery dead"[8]—that is the burden of their song. If anything comes through in spite of all this, it is a miracle, and probably no book is born entire and uncrippled as it was conceived.

But for women, I thought, looking at the empty shelves, these difficulties were infinitely more formidable. In the first place, to have a room of her own, let alone a quiet room or a sound-proof room, was out of the question, unless her parents were exceptionally rich or very noble, even up to the beginning of the nineteenth century. Since her pin money, which depended on the good will of her father, was only enough to keep her clothed, she was debarred from such alleviations as came even to Keats or Tennyson or Carlyle, all poor men, from a walking tour, a little journey to France, from the separate lodging which, even if it were miserable enough, sheltered them from the claims and tyrannies of their families. Such material difficulties were formidable; but much worse were the immaterial. The indifference of the world which Keats and Flaubert and other men of genius have found so hard to bear was in her case not indifference but hostility. The world did not say to her as it said to them, Write if you choose; it makes no difference to me. The world said with a guffaw, Write? What's the good of your writing? Here the psychologists of Newnham and Girton might come to our help, I thought, looking again at the blank spaces on the shelves. For surely it is time that the effect of discouragement upon the

5. Ben Jonson's (1572–1637) description of Shakespeare.
6. Jean-Jacques Rousseau (1712–1778), French author of the *Confessions* (1781).
7. John Keats (1795–1821), British poet. Thomas Carlyle (1795–1881), essayist and historian, translator of Goethe and author of *The French Revolution* (1837).
8. From Wordsworth's "Resolution and Independence" (1807).

mind of the artist should be measured, as I have seen a dairy company measure the effect of ordinary milk and Grade A milk upon the body of the rat. They set two rats in cages side by side, and of the two one was furtive, timid and small, and the other was glossy, bold and big. Now what food do we feed women as artists upon? I asked, remembering, I suppose, that dinner of prunes and custard. To answer that question I had only to open the evening paper and to read that Lord Birkenhead is of opinion—but really I am not going to trouble to copy out Lord Birkenhead's opinion upon the writing of women. What Dean Inge says I will leave in peace. The Harley Street specialist may be allowed to rouse the echoes of Harley Street[9] with his vociferations without raising a hair on my head. I will quote, however, Mr. Oscar Browning, because Mr. Oscar Browning was a great figure in Cambridge at one time, and used to examine the students at Girton and Newnham. Mr. Oscar Browning was wont to declare "that the impression left on his mind, after looking over any set of examination papers, was that, irrespective of the marks he might give, the best woman was intellectually the inferior of the worst man." After saying that Mr. Browning went back to his rooms—and it is this sequel that endears him and makes him a human figure of some bulk and majesty—he went back to his rooms and found a stable-boy lying on the sofa—"a mere skeleton, his cheeks were cavernous and sallow, his teeth were black, and he did not appear to have the full use of his limbs. . . . 'That's Arthur' [said Mr. Browning]. 'He's a dear boy really and most high-minded.'" The two pictures always seem to me to complete each other. And happily in this age of biography the two pictures often do complete each other, so that we are able to interpret the opinions of great men not only by what they say, but by what they do.

But though this is possible now, such opinions coming from the lips of important people must have been formidable enough even fifty years ago. Let us suppose that a father from the highest motives did not wish his daughter to leave home and become writer, painter or scholar. "See what Mr. Oscar Browning says," he would say; and there was not only Mr. Oscar Browning; there was the *Saturday Review*; there was Mr. Greg[1]—the "essentials of a woman's being," said Mr. Greg emphatically, "are that *they are supported by, and they minister to, men*"—there was an enormous body of masculine opinion to the effect that nothing could be expected of women intellectually. Even if her father did not read out loud these opinions, any girl could read them for herself; and the reading, even in the nineteenth century, must have lowered her vitality, and told profoundly upon her work. There would always have been that assertion—you cannot do this, you are incapable of doing that—to protest against, to overcome. Probably for a novelist this germ is no longer of much effect; for there have been women novelists of merit. But for painters it must still have some sting in it; and for musicians, I imagine, is even now active and poisonous in the extreme. The woman composer stands where the actress stood in the time of Shakespeare. Nick Greene, I thought, remembering the story I had made about Shakespeare's sister, said that a woman acting put him in mind of a dog dancing. Johnson repeated the phrase two hundred years later of women

9. A London street known for its many prominent physicians' offices.
1. William Rathbone Greg (1809–1891), cited from a *Saturday Review* essay entitled "Why Are Women Redundant?" (1873).

preaching. And here, I said, opening a book about music, we have the very words used again in this year of grace, 1928, of women who try to write music. "Of Mlle. Germaine Tailleferre one can only repeat Dr. Johnson's dictum concerning a woman preacher, transposed into terms of music. 'Sir, a woman's composing is like a dog's walking on his hind legs. It is not done well, but you are surprised to find it done at all.' "[2] So accurately does history repeat itself.

Thus, I concluded, shutting Mr. Oscar Browning's life and pushing away the rest, it is fairly evident that even in the nineteenth century a woman was not encouraged to be an artist. On the contrary, she was snubbed, slapped, lectured and exhorted. Her mind must have been strained and her vitality lowered by the need of opposing this, of disproving that. For here again we come within range of that very interesting and obscure masculine complex which has had so much influence upon the woman's movement; that deep-seated desire, not so much that *she* shall be inferior as that *he* shall be superior, which plants him wherever one looks, not only in front of the arts, but barring the way to politics too, even when the risk to himself seems infinitesimal and the suppliant humble and devoted. Even Lady Bessborough,[3] I remembered, with all her passion for politics, must humbly bow herself and write to Lord Granville Leveson-Gower: ". . . notwithstanding all my violence in politics and talking so much on that subject, I perfectly agree with you that no woman has any business to meddle with that or any other serious business, farther than giving her opinion (if she is ask'd)." And so she goes on to spend her enthusiasm where it meets with no obstacle whatsoever upon that immensely important subject, Lord Granville's maiden speech in the House of Commons. The spectacle is certainly a strange one, I thought. The history of men's opposition to women's emancipation is more interesting perhaps than the story of that emancipation itself. An amusing book might be made of it if some young student at Girton or Newnham would collect examples and deduce a theory—but she would need thick gloves on her hands, and bars to protect her of solid gold.

But what is amusing now, I recollected, shutting Lady Bessborough, had to be taken in desperate earnest once. Opinions that one now pastes in a book labelled cock-a-doodle-dum and keeps for reading to select audiences on summer nights once drew tears, I can assure you. Among your grandmothers and great-grandmothers there were many that wept their eyes out. Florence Nightingale shrieked aloud in her agony.[4] Moreover, it is all very well for you, who have got yourselves to college and enjoy sitting-rooms—or is it only bed-sitting-rooms?—of your own to say that genius should disregard such opinions; that genius should be above caring what is said of it. Unfortunately, it is precisely the men or women of genius who mind most what is said of them. Remember Keats. Remember the words he had cut on his tombstone.[5] Think of Tennyson;

2. *A Survey of Contemporary Music*, Cecil Gray, p. 246 [Woolf's note]. The statement is originally found in James Boswell's *Life of Johnson* (1791).

3. Henrietta, Countess of Bessborough (1761–1821), who corresponded with Lord Granville George Leveson-Gower (1815–1891), British foreign secretary in William Gladstone's administrations and after him the leader of the Liberal Party.

4. See *Cassandra*, by Florence Nightingale, printed in *The Cause*, by R. Strachey [Woolf's note]. Nightingale (1820–1910) was an English nurse and founder of nursing as a profession for women.

5. "Here lies one whose name was writ in water."

think—but I need hardly multiply instances of the undeniable, if very unfortunate, fact that it is the nature of the artist to mind excessively what is said about him. Literature is strewn with the wreckage of men who have minded beyond reason the opinions of others.

And this susceptibility of theirs is doubly unfortunate, I thought, returning again to my original enquiry into what state of mind is most propitious for creative work, because the mind of an artist, in order to achieve the prodigious effort of freeing whole and entire the work that is in him, must be incandescent, like Shakespeare's mind, I conjectured, looking at the book which lay open at *Antony and Cleopatra*. There must be no obstacle in it, no foreign matter unconsumed.

For though we say that we know nothing about Shakespeare's state of mind, even as we say that, we are saying something about Shakespeare's state of mind. The reason perhaps why we know so little of Shakespeare—compared with Donne or Ben Jonson or Milton—is that his grudges and spites and antipathies are hidden from us. We are not held up by some "revelation" which reminds us of the writer. All desire to protest, to preach, to proclaim an injury, to pay off a score, to make the world the witness of some hardship or grievance was fired out of him and consumed. Therefore his poetry flows from him free and unimpeded. If ever a human being got his work expressed completely, it was Shakespeare. If ever a mind was incandescent, unimpeded, I thought, turning again to the bookcase, it was Shakespeare's mind.

1929

WILLIAM FAULKNER

1897–1962

Chronicler of the American South, William Faulkner gained an international reputation for his vivid imagination and innovative use of language. His account of the historical change between the Old and the New South transcends regional issues or the mythical community of Yoknapatawpha (*yok-na-pa-taw'-pha*), Mississippi, where most of his work is situated; it came to influence writers in societies undergoing transition in Europe, Latin America, and China. Although his canvas is a single region, Faulkner encompasses broad themes: the clash of generations and ways of life, racial and family tragedies, and, in almost archetypal terms, the opposition of good and evil.

William Cuthbert Falkner was born on September 25, 1897, in New Albany, Mississippi, to a prosperous family with many ties to Southern history; their prosperity, however, was on the wane. The eldest of four sons, Faulkner (he adopted this spelling as a young man) was named for a great-grandfather who commanded a Confederate regiment in the Civil War, built railroads, and wrote novels. When asked as a child, "What do you want to be when you grow up?" William would reply, "I want to be a writer like my great-granddaddy." Faulkner's father worked for the family railroad enterprise until it was sold in 1902, afterward moving the family to Oxford and eventually becoming business manager of the University of Mississippi. The writer's close acquaintance with Southern customs and attitudes, his experience as the descendant of a once-prosperous and influential family, and his attachment to Lafayette County and the town of Oxford (Yoknapatawpha County and Jefferson in the novels) helped shape themes and setting in his fiction.

Young Faulkner read widely in his grandfather's library and borrowed books from an older friend, Philip Stone. Leaving high school after two years to work as a bookkeeper in his grandfather's bank, he continued reading and discussing literature with Stone, who encouraged his writing and introduced him to novels of the nineteenth-century French realist writer Honoré de Balzac (1799–1850). In his own novels, Faulkner would transform the Balzacian tradition of the human comedy—the novel as a panorama of society—by giving it a vocabulary drawn from the American South and a renewed place in literary history.

In the last six months of the First World War, Faulkner trained in Canada as a fighter pilot—then a common way of getting more quickly into combat—but the hostilities ended before he actually flew any missions; he returned to Oxford to enroll at the university (all the while claiming to have been shot down over France). By this time, Faulkner was known as a heavy drinker and teller of tall tales. Leaving the university in 1920 to work in a New York bookstore, he returned in 1921 and became postmaster for three years at the university. During this period he wrote poetry and seems to have been influenced by the French symbolists: his first published poem, *L'Après-midi d'un faune*, takes its title from **Stéphane Mallarmé**; he also admired the poetry of **T. S. Eliot**. Faulkner's first book, a collection of lyrics called *The Marble Faun*, appeared in 1924.

In 1925 the young writer spent six months in New Orleans, where he was attracted to a literary group associated with *The Double Dealer*, a magazine in which his poems, essays, and prose sketches appeared. The group's chief figure was Sherwood Anderson, author of a series of regional stories published as *Winesburg, Ohio* (1919), who encouraged Faulkner to make fictional use of his Southern background and who recommended Faulkner's first novel to his New York publisher. After completing *Soldier's Pay* (1926), Faulkner took a freighter to Europe, bicycling and hiking through Italy and France and living for a short while in Paris. At the end of the year, he returned to Mississippi, where he wrote his second novel, *Mosquitoes* (1927), a satire on the New Orleans group.

Taking up Anderson's earlier suggestion, Faulkner embarked on the regional Yoknapatawpha series with *Sartoris* (1929), an account of the return home, marriage, and death of a wounded First World War veteran, Bayard Sartoris. In *The Sound and the Fury* (1929), Faulkner experimented with the stream-of-consciousness technique pioneered by other modernists. Adapting **James Joyce**'s methods, Faulkner developed distinct literary styles, from brief fragments to the elaborate, lengthy sentences that have become famous as "Faulknerian," to represent the minds of the various characters. Both *Sartoris* and *The Sound and the Fury* were rejected several times before being published, and Faulkner supported himself, in the late 1920s, by working at odd jobs (on a shrimp trawler, in a lumber mill and a power plant, and as a carpenter, painter, and paperhanger) and then, between 1930 and 1932, from the sale of thirty short stories. One of his major experimental novels, *As I Lay Dying* (1930), was written in six weeks during his night shifts at the power plant. In 1929, Faulkner married Estelle Oldham Franklin, with whom he had two daughters; their first child died in infancy in 1931, and their second, Jill, was born two years later. Around this time he purchased an antebellum mansion, which he called Rowan Oak, that allowed him to establish a life akin to that of an impoverished Southern gentleman, a status he had known years before when his family lost the railroad.

Irritated by the difficulty of finding publishers for his serious or experimental works, the novelist set out to write a best seller—and succeeded. *Sanctuary* (1931), a novel of the Deep South that described the rape and prostitution of a schoolgirl as well as murder, perjury, and the lynching of an innocent man, was made into a movie (*The Story of Temple Drake*, 1933) and brought its author invitations to work on movie scripts for a variety of Hollywood studios. From 1932 to 1955, Faulkner added to his income by working as a film doctor, revising and collaborating on scripts for films such as *To Have and Have Not* and *The Big Sleep*. In Hollywood the movie star Clark Gable once asked him what modern books to read. Faulkner suggested his own works. When Gable asked, "Do you write?" Faulkner replied, "Yes, Mr. Gable. What do you do?"

Although his works continued to receive critical praise, Faulkner had no commercial successes after *Sanctuary*. In 1945, when he was, according to the French writer and philosopher Jean-Paul Sartre, the idol of young French readers, most of his novels were out of print. It took an anthology, *The Portable Faulkner* (1946), to reintroduce the author to a wider audience. In 1950 he won the Nobel Prize for Literature; five years later he received the Pulitzer Prize and the National Book Award for *A Fable* (1954). He used the Nobel Prize money to establish the William Faulkner Foundation to assist Latin American writers and to award educational scholarships to Mississippi blacks. His fantastic, sometimes allegorical depictions of events influenced the development of "magical realism" in Latin America, while his forthright treatment of race relations inspired African American writers, including **James Baldwin** and **Toni Morrison**. In later years, Faulkner supported civil rights for African Americans but aroused controversy by suggesting that they "go slow, now." He died of a heart attack in Oxford, Mississippi, on July 6, 1962.

In setting many of his works in Yoknapatawpha County, Faulkner created a fictional world, with characters who reappear from novel to novel. Here imaginary families such as the Sartorises, Compsons, Sutpens, McCaslins, and Snopeses rise to prosperity or descend into weakness, degradation, and death. Individual characters may believe they have control of their lives but they work out destinies that are already half-shaped by family tradition and invisible community pressures. Caught in close, often incestuous relationships, they make their way in a world in which the values, traditions, and privileges of the old plantation society are yielding to those of an emerging mercantile class. A network of dynasties illustrates the picture of a changing society: the decaying and impoverished Compson family (*The Sound and the Fury*); two generations of Sutpens rising to great wealth and dying in madness and isolation (*Absalom, Absalom!*, 1936); and the McCaslin family, with its history of incest, miscegenation, and guilt (*Go Down, Moses*, 1942). *Light in August* (1932) shows the force of history and family tradition by having the central character, Joe Christmas, engage in a catastrophic struggle with his heritage without even knowing what it is. "The past is never dead. It's not even past," wrote Faulkner: his characters constantly struggle with the ambiguous legacies of history, family, and their personal traumas.

These are violent works, and the murders, lynchings, and bestialities that appear in them account for Faulkner's early reputation, in the United States, as a lurid local writer. European critics, however, especially the French, who recognized his ability as early as 1931, were quick to identify mythic overtones and classical, even biblical prototypes in these tales of twisted family relationships. Faulkner himself described his approach as follows: "There's always a moment in experience—a thought—an incident—that's there. Then all I do is work up to that moment. I figure what must have happened before to lead people to that particular moment, and I work away from it, finding out how people act after the moment."

The stories paired here are early versions of material alluded to and incorporated into *The Hamlet* (1940), which tells of the rise of Flem Snopes (the unnamed brother in "Barn Burning"). These stories exhibit the range of Faulkner's art: "Spotted Horses" (1931), one of Faulkner's first portrayals of the Snopes family, is a comic tall tale about Flem's trickery of his community, while "Barn Burning" (1938) unearths Snopes family history through its presentation of Abner Snopes's dehumanized menace. "Barn Burning" appears here first because it is set earlier. The viciously grasping ambitious "Snopes family" rises and falls over the course of three novels (*The Hamlet*; *The Town*, 1957; and *The Mansion*, 1959). Both Flem Snopes and his victims are socially and geographically distant from the wealthy Compsons, Sartorises, and Sutpens, whose lives take them to the center of Jefferson; the residents of Frenchman's Bend are rural, white, and poor, like the Bundren family of *As I Lay Dying*, whose trip to town to bury their mother becomes an arduous journey fit for a novel. Just as the Sartoris family represents Southern aristocratic tradition in all its romanticism and humanity, the Snopeses originate as the shiftless "poor whites" and come to embody the cold, calculating, exploitative side of human nature that is working its way to the fore in an industrializing, commercially oriented age. Although, when described separately, members of the Snopes family take on individuality and human traits (generally perverse), together they turn into "Snopesism," a vision of evil that is openly diabolical. In Faulkner's view of the eternal battle between good and evil, "There is always someone that will never stop trying to cope with Snopes, that will never stop trying to get rid of Snopes."

These stories connect a local, isolated setting, with its colloquialisms and dialect speech, with grandiose convictions about human nature and society, often expressed in Latinate rhetoric. In "Barn Burning," Abner Snopes, father of Flem (unnamed in this story) and Colonel Sartoris Snopes, is a personification of inhuman, two-dimensional evil: "without face or depth—a shape black, flat, and bloodless as though cut from tin . . . , the voice harsh like tin and without heat like tin." His human qualities are purely destructive: a ferocious independence and a conviction of his own rectitude, linked to deep jealousy and rage against others' prosperity or authority; a vicious paranoia that creates opportunities for revenge; an arsonist's love for the destructive element of fire that speaks to "some deep mainspring" of his being. Young Colonel Sartoris Snopes is torn between two loyalties, as his name implies. To the psychological realism of individual portraits, and the conflict between father and son, Faulkner adds a struggle between right and wrong—two sides inextricably related to each other and, at the end, both left with an unknown future.

The picture of pure destruction that

plays such a significant role in "Barn Burning" returns in comic vein in "Spotted Horses," as the animals bursting out of their pen run wild over the countryside and defy their new owners' best attempts to catch them. Literally an unbridled force of nature (spotted horses are often demonic in folklore), they upset the normal order of things. V. K. Ratliff, the sewing-machine agent who narrates the story, cannot help but admire the craftiness with which Snopes manipulates events for his own profit, although Ratliff opposes everything that Snopes stands for and tries to shame him into returning some of his ill-gotten money. For this comedy has somber overtones as well: for some members of the community, the consequences of the action are severe. The farce ends with bitter irony, showing the hopelessness of its defeated characters against the legalistic precision and economic forces Flem represents.

Barn Burning

The store in which the Justice of the Peace's court was sitting smelled of cheese. The boy, crouched on his nail keg at the back of the crowded room, knew he smelled cheese, and more: from where he sat he could see the ranked shelves close-packed with the solid, squat, dynamic shapes of tin cans whose labels his stomach read, not from the lettering which meant nothing to his mind but from the scarlet devils and the silver curve of fish—this, the cheese which he knew he smelled and the hermetic[1] meat which his intestines believed he smelled coming in intermittent gusts momentary and brief between the other constant one, the smell and sense just a little of fear because mostly of despair and grief, the old fierce pull of blood. He could not see the table where the Justice sat and before which his father and his father's enemy (*our enemy* he thought in that despair; *ourn! mine and hisn both! He's my father!*) stood, but he could hear them, the two of them that is, because his father had said no word yet:

"But what proof have you, Mr. Harris?"

"I told you. The hog got into my corn. I caught it up and sent it back to him. He had no fence that would hold it. I told him so, warned him. The next time I put the hog in my pen. When he came to get it I gave him enough wire to patch up his pen. The next time I put the hog up and kept it. I rode down to his house and saw the wire I gave him still rolled on to the spool in his yard. I told him he could have the hog when he paid me a dollar pound fee. That evening a nigger came with the dollar and got the hog. He was a strange nigger. He said, 'He say to tell you wood and hay kin burn.' I said, 'What?' 'That whut he say to tell you,' the nigger said. 'Wood and hay kin burn.' That night my barn burned. I got the stock out but I lost the barn."

"Where is the nigger? Have you got him?"

"He was a strange nigger, I tell you. I don't know what became of him."

"But that's not proof. Don't you see that's not proof?"

"Get that boy up here. He knows." For a moment the boy thought too that the man meant his older brother until Harris said, "Not him. The little one. The boy," and, crouching, small for his age, small and wiry like his father, in

1. Canned, sealed in airtight tins.

patched and faded jeans even too small for him, with straight, uncombed, brown hair and eyes gray and wild as storm scud, he saw the men between himself and the table part and become a lane of grim faces, at the end of which he saw the Justice, a shabby, collarless, graying man in spectacles, beckoning him. He felt no floor under his bare feet; he seemed to walk beneath the palpable weight of the grim turning faces. His father, stiff in his black Sunday coat donned not for the trial but for the moving, did not even look at him. *He aims for me to lie,* he thought, again with that frantic grief and despair. *And I will have to do hit.*

"What's your name, boy?" the Justice said.

"Colonel Sartoris Snopes,"[2] the boy whispered.

"Hey?" the Justice said. "Talk louder. Colonel Sartoris? I reckon anybody named for Colonel Sartoris in this country can't help but tell the truth, can they?" The boy said nothing. *Enemy! Enemy!* he thought; for a moment he could not even see, could not see that the Justice's face was kindly nor discern that his voice was troubled when he spoke to the man named Harris: "Do you want me to question this boy?" But he could hear, and during those subsequent long seconds while there was absolutely no sound in the crowded little room save that of quiet and intent breathing it was as if he had swung outward at the end of a grape vine, over a ravine, and at the top of the swing had been caught in a prolonged instant of mesmerized gravity, weightless in time.

"No!" Harris said violently, explosively. "Damnation! Send him out of here!" Now time, the fluid world, rushed beneath him again, the voices coming to him again through the smell of cheese and sealed meat, the fear and despair and the old grief of blood:

"This case is closed. I can't find against you, Snopes, but I can give you advice. Leave this country and don't come back to it."

His father spoke for the first time, his voice cold and harsh, level, without emphasis: "I aim to. I don't figure to stay in a country among people who . . ." he said something unprintable and vile, addressed to no one.

"That'll do," the Justice said. "Take your wagon and get out of this country before dark. Case dismissed."

His father turned, and he followed the stiff black coat, the wiry figure walking a little stiffly from where a Confederate provost's man's[3] musket ball had taken him in the heel on a stolen horse thirty years ago, followed the two backs now, since his older brother had appeared from somewhere in the crowd, no taller than the father but thicker, chewing tobacco steadily, between the two lines of grim-faced men and out of the store and across the worn gallery and down the sagging steps and among the dogs and half-grown boys in the mild May dust, where as he passed a voice hissed:

"Barn burner!"

Again he could not see, whirling; there was a face in a red haze, moonlike, bigger than the full moon, the owner of it half again his size, he leaping in the red haze toward the face, feeling no blow, feeling no shock when his head struck the earth, scrabbling up and leaping again, feeling no blow this time either and tasting no blood, scrabbling up to see the other boy in full flight and himself already

2. The Snopes boy is named for Colonel John Sartoris, legendary founder of the aristocratic Sartoris family.

3. Military policeman.

leaping into pursuit as his father's hand jerked him back, the harsh, cold voice speaking above him: "Go get in the wagon."

It stood in a grove of locusts and mulberries across the road. His two hulking sisters in their Sunday dresses and his mother and her sister in calico and sunbonnets were already in it, sitting on and among the sorry residue of the dozen and more movings which even the boy could remember—the battered stove, the broken beds and chairs, the clock inlaid with mother-of-pearl, which would not run, stopped at some fourteen minutes past two o'clock of a dead and forgotten day and time, which had been his mother's dowry. She was crying, though when she saw him she drew her sleeve across her face and began to descend from the wagon. "Get back," the father said.

"He's hurt. I got to get some water and wash his . . ."

"Get back in the wagon," his father said. He got in too, over the tailgate. His father mounted to the seat where the older brother already sat and struck the gaunt mules two savage blows with the peeled willow, but without heat. It was not even sadistic; it was exactly that same quality which in later years would cause his descendants to over-run the engine before putting a motor car into motion, striking and reining back in the same movement. The wagon went on, the store with its quiet crowd of grimly watching men dropped behind; a curve in the road hid it. *Forever* he thought. *Maybe he's done satisfied now, now that he has* . . . stopping himself, not to say it aloud even to himself. His mother's hand touched his shoulder.

"Does hit hurt?" she said.

"Naw," he said. "Hit don't hurt. Lemme be."

"Can't you wipe some of the blood off before hit dries?"

"I'll wash to-night," he said. "Lemme be, I tell you."

The wagon went on. He did not know where they were going. None of them ever did or ever asked, because it was always somewhere, always a house of sorts waiting for them a day or two days or even three days away. Likely his father had already arranged to make a crop on another farm before he . . . Again he had to stop himself. He (the father) always did. There was something about his wolflike independence and even courage when the advantage was at least neutral which impressed strangers, as if they got from his latent ravening ferocity not so much a sense of dependability as a feeling that his ferocious conviction in the rightness of his own actions would be of advantage to all whose interest lay with his.

That night they camped, in a grove of oaks and beeches where a spring ran. The nights were still cool and they had a fire against it, of a rail lifted from a nearby fence and cut into lengths—a small fire, neat, niggard almost, a shrewd fire; such fires were his father's habit and custom always, even in freezing weather. Older, the boy might have remarked this and wondered why not a big one; why should not a man who had not only seen the waste and extravagance of war, but who had in his blood an inherent voracious prodigality with material not his own, have burned everything in sight? Then he might have gone a step farther and thought that that was the reason: that niggard blaze was the living fruit of nights passed during those four years in the woods hiding from all men, blue or gray,[4] with his strings of horses (captured horses, he called them). And older still, he might have divined the true reason: that the element of fire spoke

4. In the Civil War (1861–65), Union soldiers wore blue and Confederate soldiers gray uniforms.

to some deep mainspring of his father's being, as the element of steel or of powder spoke to other men, as the one weapon for the preservation of integrity, else breath were not worth the breathing, and hence to be regarded with respect and used with discretion.

But he did not think this now and he had seen those same niggard blazes all his life. He merely ate his supper beside it and was already half asleep over his iron plate when his father called him, and once more he followed the stiff back, the stiff and ruthless limp, up the slope and on to the starlit road where, turning, he could see his father against the stars but without face or depth—a shape black, flat, and bloodless as though cut from tin in the iron folds of the frockcoat which had not been made for him, the voice harsh like tin and without heat like tin:

"You were fixing to tell them. You would have told him." He didn't answer. His father struck him with the flat of his hand on the side of the head, hard but without heat, exactly as he had struck the two mules at the store, exactly as he would strike either of them with any stick in order to kill a horse fly, his voice still without heat or anger: "You're getting to be a man. You got to learn. You got to learn to stick to your own blood or you ain't going to have any blood to stick to you. Do you think either of them, any man there this morning, would? Don't you know all they wanted was a chance to get at me because they knew I had them beat? Eh?" Later, twenty years later, he was to tell himself, "If I had said they wanted only truth, justice, he would have hit me again." But now he said nothing. He was not crying. He just stood there. "Answer me," his father said.

"Yes," he whispered. His father turned.

"Get on to bed. We'll be there to-morrow."

To-morrow they were there. In the early afternoon the wagon stopped before a paintless two-room house identical almost with the dozen others it had stopped before even in the boy's ten years, and again, as on the other dozen occasions, his mother and aunt got down and began to unload the wagon, although his two sisters and his father and brother had not moved.

"Likely hit ain't fitten for hawgs," one of the sisters said.

"Nevertheless, fit it will and you'll hog it and like it," his father said. "Get out of them chairs and help your Ma unload."

The two sisters got down, big, bovine, in a flutter of cheap ribbons; one of them drew from the jumbled wagon bed a battered lantern, the other a worn broom. His father handed the reins to the older son and began to climb stiffly over the wheel. "When they get unloaded, take the team to the barn and feed them." Then he said, and at first the boy thought he was still speaking to his brother: "Come with me."

"Me?" he said.

"Yes," his father said. "You."

"Abner," his mother said. His father paused and looked back—the harsh level stare beneath the shaggy, graying, irascible brows.

"I reckon I'll have a word with the man that aims to begin to-morrow owning me body and soul for the next eight months."

They went back up the road. A week ago—or before last night, that is—he would have asked where they were going, but not now. His father had struck him before last night but never before had he paused afterward to explain why; it was as if the blow and the following calm, outrageous voice still rang, repercussed, divulging nothing to him save the terrible handicap of being young, the light weight of his few years, just heavy enough to prevent his soaring free of the world as it seemed to be ordered but not heavy enough to keep him footed solid in it, to resist it and try to change the course of its events.

Presently he could see the grove of oaks and cedars and the other flowering trees and shrubs where the house would be, though not the house yet. They walked beside a fence massed with honeysuckle and Cherokee roses[5] and came to a gate swinging open between two brick pillars, and now, beyond a sweep of drive, he saw the house for the first time and at that instant he forgot his father and the terror and despair both, and even when he remembered his father again (who had not stopped) the terror and despair did not return. Because, for all the twelve movings, they had sojourned until now in a poor country, a land of small farms and fields and houses, and he had never seen a house like this before. *Hit's big as a courthouse* he thought quietly, with a surge of peace and joy whose reason he could not have thought into words, being too young for that: *They are safe from him. People whose lives are a part of this peace and dignity are beyond his touch, he no more to them than a buzzing wasp: capable of stinging for a little moment but that's all; the spell of this peace and dignity rendering even the barns and stable and cribs which belong to it impervious to the puny flames he might contrive* . . . this, the peace and joy, ebbing for an instant as he looked again at the stiff black back, the stiff and implacable limp of the figure which was not dwarfed by the house, for the reason that it had never looked big anywhere and which now, against the serene columned backdrop, had more than ever that impervious quality of something cut ruthlessly from tin, depthless, as though, sidewise to the sun, it would cast no shadow. Watching him, the boy remarked the absolutely undeviating course which his father held and saw the stiff foot come squarely down in a pile of fresh droppings where a horse had stood in the drive and which his father could have avoided by a simple change of stride. But it ebbed only for a moment, though he could not have thought this into words either, walking on in the spell of the house, which he could even want but without envy, without sorrow, certainly never with that ravening and jealous rage which unknown to him walked in the ironlike black coat before him: *Maybe he will feel it too. Maybe it will even change him now from what maybe he couldn't help but be.*

They crossed the portico. Now he could hear his father's stiff foot as it came down on the boards with clocklike finality, a sound out of all proportion to the displacement of the body it bore and which was not dwarfed either by the white door before it, as though it had attained to a sort of vicious and ravening minimum not to be dwarfed by anything—the flat, wide, black hat, the formal coat of broadcloth which had once been black but which had now that friction-glazed greenish cast of the bodies of old house flies, the lifted sleeve which was too large, the lifted hand like a curled claw. The door opened so promptly that the boy knew the Negro must have been watching them all the time, an old man with neat grizzled hair, in a linen jacket, who stood barring the door with his body, saying, "Wipe you foots, white man, fo you come in here. Major ain't home nohow."

"Get out of my way, nigger," his father said, without heat too, flinging the door back and the Negro also and entering, his hat still on his head. And now the boy saw the prints of the stiff foot on the doorjamb and saw them appear on the pale rug behind the machinelike deliberation of the foot which seemed

5. An evergreen climbing rose with white flowers.

to bear (or transmit) twice the weight which the body compassed. The Negro was shouting "Miss Lula! Miss Lula!"[6] somewhere behind them, then the boy, deluged as though by a warm wave by a suave turn of carpeted stair and a pendant glitter of chandeliers and a mute gleam of gold frames, heard the swift feet and saw her too, a lady—perhaps he had never seen her like before either—in a gray, smooth gown with lace at the throat and an apron tied at the waist and the sleeves turned back, wiping cake or biscuit dough from her hands with a towel as she came up the hall, looking not at his father at all but at the tracks on the blond rug with an expression of incredulous amazement.

"I tried," the Negro cried. "I tole him to . . ."

"Will you please go away?" she said in a shaking voice. "Major de Spain is not at home. Will you please go away?"

His father had not spoken again. He did not speak again. He did not even look at her. He just stood stiff in the center of the rug, in his hat, the shaggy iron-gray brows twitching slightly above the pebble-colored eyes as he appeared to examine the house with brief deliberation. Then with the same deliberation he turned; the boy watched him pivot on the good leg and saw the stiff foot drag round the arc of the turning, leaving a final long and fading smear. His father never looked at it, he never once looked down at the rug. The Negro held the door. It closed behind them, upon the hysteric and indistinguishable woman-wail. His father stopped at the top of the steps and scraped his boot clean on the edge of it. At the gate he stopped again. He stood for a moment, planted stiffly on the stiff foot, looking back at the house. "Pretty and white, ain't it?" he said. "That's sweat. Nigger sweat. Maybe it ain't white enough yet to suit him. Maybe he wants to mix some white sweat with it."

Two hours later the boy was chopping wood behind the house within which his mother and aunt and the two sisters (the mother and aunt, not the two girls, he knew that; even at this distance and muffled by walls the flat loud voices of the two girls emanated an incorrigible idle inertia) were setting up the stove to prepare a meal, when he heard the hooves and saw the linen-clad man on a fine sorrel mare, whom he recognized even before he saw the rolled rug in front of the Negro youth following on a fat bay carriage horse—a suffused, angry face vanishing, still at full gallop, beyond the corner of the house where his father and brother were sitting in the two tilted chairs; and a moment later, almost before he could have put the axe down, he heard the hooves again and watched the sorrel mare go back out of the yard, already galloping again. Then his father began to shout one of the sisters' names, who presently emerged backward from the kitchen door dragging the rolled rug along the ground by one end while the other sister walked behind it.

"If you ain't going to tote, go on and set up the wash pot," the first said.

"You, Sarty!" the second shouted. "Set up the wash pot!" His father appeared at the door, framed against that shabbiness, as he had been against that other bland perfection, impervious to either, the mother's anxious face at his shoulder.

"Go on," the father said. "Pick it up." The two sisters stooped, broad, lethargic; stooping, they presented an incredible expanse of pale cloth and a flutter of tawdry ribbons.

6. "Miss" is a traditional southern form of respectful address used also for married women.

"If I thought enough of a rug to have to git hit all the way from France I wouldn't keep hit where folks coming in would have to tromp on hit," the first said. They raised the rug.

"Abner," the mother said. "Let me do it."

"You go back and git dinner," his father said. "I'll tend to this."

From the woodpile through the rest of the afternoon the boy watched them, the rug spread flat in the dust beside the bubbling wash-pot, the two sisters stooping over it with that profound and lethargic reluctance, while the father stood over them in turn, implacable and grim, driving them though never raising his voice again. He could smell the harsh homemade lye[7] they were using; he saw his mother come to the door once and look toward them with an expression not anxious now but very like despair; he saw his father turn, and he fell to with the axe and saw from the corner of his eye his father raise from the ground a flattish fragment of field stone and examine it and return to the pot, and this time his mother actually spoke: "Abner. Abner. Please don't. Please, Abner."

Then he was done too. It was dusk; the whippoorwills had already begun. He could smell coffee from the room where they would presently eat the cold food remaining from the mid-afternoon meal, though when he entered the house he realized they were having coffee again probably because there was a fire on the hearth, before which the rug now lay spread over the backs of the two chairs. The tracks of his father's foot were gone. Where they had been were now long, water-cloudy scoriations resembling the sporadic course of a lilliputian[8] mowing machine.

It still hung there while they ate the cold food and then went to bed, scattered without order or claim up and down the two rooms, his mother in one bed, where his father would later lie, the older brother in the other, himself, the aunt, and the two sisters on pallets on the floor. But his father was not in bed yet. The last thing the boy remembered was the depthless, harsh silhouette of the hat and coat bending over the rug and it seemed to him that he had not even closed his eyes when the silhouette was standing over him, the fire almost dead behind it, the stiff foot prodding him awake. "Catch up the mule," his father said.

When he returned with the mule his father was standing in the black door, the rolled rug over his shoulder. "Ain't you going to ride?" he said.

"No. Give me your foot."

He bent his knee into his father's hand, the wiry, surprising power flowed smoothly, rising, he rising with it, on to the mule's bare back (they had owned a saddle once; the boy could remember it though not when or where) and with the same effortlessness his father swung the rug up in front of him. Now in the starlight they retraced the afternoon's path, up the dusty road rife with honeysuckle, through the gate and up the black tunnel of the drive to the lightless house, where he sat on the mule and felt the rough warp of the rug drag across his thighs and vanish.

"Don't you want me to help?" he whispered. His father did not answer and now he heard again that stiff foot striking the hollow portico with that wooden and clocklike deliberation, that outrageous overstatement of the weight it carried. The rug, hunched, not flung (the boy could tell that even in the darkness)

7. A caustic cleanser made from leaching ashes, certain to damage any delicate material.
8. Miniature, after the tiny inhabitants of Lilliput described in Jonathan Swift's *Gulliver's Travels* (1726).

from his father's shoulder struck the angle of wall and floor with a sound unbelievably loud, thunderous, then the foot again, unhurried and enormous; a light came on in the house and the boy sat, tense, breathing steadily and quietly and just a little fast, though the foot itself did not increase its beat at all, descending the steps now; now the boy could see him.

"Don't you want to ride now?" he whispered. "We kin both ride now," the light within the house altering now, flaring up and sinking. *He's coming down the stairs now*, he thought. He had already ridden the mule up beside the horse block; presently his father was up behind him and he doubled the reins over and slashed the mule across the neck, but before the animal could begin to trot the hard, thin arm came round him, the hard, knotted hand jerking the mule back to a walk.

In the first red rays of the sun they were in the lot, putting plow gear on the mules. This time the sorrel mare was in the lot before he heard it at all, the rider collarless and even bareheaded, trembling, speaking in a shaking voice as the woman in the house had done, his father merely looking up once before stooping again to the hame he was buckling, so that the man on the mare spoke to his stooping back:

"You must realize you have ruined that rug. Wasn't there anybody here, any of your women . . ." he ceased, shaking, the boy watching him, the older brother leaning now in the stable door, chewing, blinking slowly and steadily at nothing apparently. "It cost a hundred dollars. But you never had a hundred dollars. You never will. So I'm going to charge you twenty bushels of corn against your crop. I'll add it in your contract and when you come to the commissary you can sign it. That won't keep Mrs. de Spain quiet but maybe it will teach you to wipe your feet off before you enter her house again."

Then he was gone. The boy looked at his father, who still had not spoken or even looked up again, who was now adjusting the logger-head in the hame.

"Pap," he said. His father looked at him—the inscrutable face, the shaggy brows beneath which the gray eyes glinted coldly. Suddenly the boy went toward him, fast, stopping as suddenly. "You done the best you could!" he cried. "If he wanted hit done different why didn't he wait and tell you how? He won't git no twenty bushels! He won't git none! We'll gether hit and hide hit! I kin watch . . ."

"Did you put the cutter back in that straight stock like I told you?"

"No, sir," he said.

"Then go do it."

That was Wednesday. During the rest of that week he worked steadily, at what was within his scope and some which was beyond it, with an industry that did not need to be driven nor even commanded twice; he had this from his mother, with the difference that some at least of what he did he liked to do, such as splitting wood with the half-size axe which his mother and aunt had earned, or saved money somehow, to present him with at Christmas. In company with the two older women (and on one afternoon, even one of the sisters), he built pens for the shoat and the cow which were a part of his father's contract with the landlord, and one afternoon, his father being absent, gone somewhere on one of the mules, he went to the field.

They were running a middle buster[9] now, his brother holding the plow straight while he handled the reins, and walking beside the straining mule, the

9. A double moldboard plow that throws a ridge of earth both ways.

rich black soil shearing cool and damp against his bare ankles, he thought *Maybe this is the end of it. Maybe even that twenty bushels that seems hard to have to pay for just a rug will be a cheap price for him to stop forever and always from being what he used to be*; thinking, dreaming now, so that his brother had to speak sharply to him to mind the mule: *Maybe he even won't collect the twenty bushels. Maybe it will all add up and balance and vanish—corn, rug, fire; the terror and grief, the being pulled two ways like between two teams of horses—gone, done with for ever and ever.*

Then it was Saturday; he looked up from beneath the mule he was harnessing and saw his father in the black coat and hat. "Not that," his father said. "The wagon gear." And then, two hours later, sitting in the wagon bed behind his father and brother on the seat, the wagon accomplished a final curve, and he saw the weathered paintless store with its tattered tobacco- and patent-medicine posters and the tethered wagons and saddle animals below the gallery. He mounted the gnawed steps behind his father and brother, and there again was the lane of quiet, watching faces for the three of them to walk through. He saw the man in spectacles sitting at the plank table and he did not need to be told this was a Justice of the Peace; he sent one glare of fierce, exultant, partisan defiance at the man in collar and cravat now, whom he had seen but twice before in his life, and that on a galloping horse, who now wore on his face an expression not of rage but of amazed unbelief which the boy could not have known was at the incredible circumstance of being used by one of his own tenants, and came and stood against his father and cried at the Justice: "He ain't done it! He ain't burnt . . ."

"Go back to the wagon," his father said.

"Burnt?" the Justice said. "Do I understand this rug was burned too?"

"Does anybody here claim it was?" his father said. "Go back to the wagon." But he did not, he merely retreated to the rear of the room, crowded as that other had been, but not to sit down this time, instead, to stand pressing among the motionless bodies, listening to the voices:

"And you claim twenty bushels of corn is too high for the damage you did to the rug?"

"He brought the rug to me and said he wanted the tracks washed out of it. I washed the tracks out and took the rug back to him."

"But you didn't carry the rug back to him in the same condition it was in before you made the tracks on it."

His father did not answer, and now for perhaps half a minute there was no sound at all save that of breathing, the faint, steady suspiration of complete and intent listening.

"You decline to answer that, Mr. Snopes?" Again his father did not answer. "I'm going to find against you, Mr. Snopes. I'm going to find that you were responsible for the injury to Major de Spain's rug and hold you liable for it. But twenty bushels of corn seems a little high for a man in your circumstances to have to pay. Major de Spain claims it cost a hundred dollars. October corn will be worth about fifty cents. I figure that if Major de Spain can stand a ninety-five dollar loss on something he paid cash for, you can stand a five-dollar loss you haven't earned yet. I hold you in damages to Major de Spain to the amount of ten bushels of corn over and above your contract with him, to be paid to him out of your crop at gathering time. Court adjourned."

It had taken no time hardly, the morning was but half begun. He thought they would return home and perhaps back to the field, since they were late, far behind all other farmers. But instead his father passed on behind the wagon, merely indicating with his hand for the older brother to follow with it, and crossed the road toward the blacksmith shop opposite, pressing on after his father, overtaking him, speaking, whispering up at the harsh, calm face beneath the weathered hat: "He won't git no ten bushels neither. He won't git one. We'll . . ." until his father glanced for an instant down at him, the face absolutely calm, the grizzled eyebrows tangled above the cold eyes, the voice almost pleasant, almost gentle:

"You think so? Well, we'll wait till October anyway."

The matter of the wagon—the setting of a spoke or two and the tightening of the tires—did not take long either, the business of the tires accomplished by driving the wagon into the spring branch behind the shop and letting it stand there, the mules nuzzling into the water from time to time, and the boy on the seat with the idle reins, looking up the slope and through the sooty tunnel of the shed where the slow hammer rang and where his father sat on an upended cypress bolt, easily, either talking or listening, still sitting there when the boy brought the dripping wagon up out of the branch and halted it before the door.

"Take them on to the shade and hitch," his father said. He did so and returned. His father and the smith and a third man squatting on his heels inside the door were talking, about crops and animals; the boy, squatting too in the ammoniac dust and hoof-parings and scales of rust, heard his father tell a long and unhurried story out of the time before the birth of the older brother even when he had been a professional horsetrader. And then his father came up beside him where he stood before a tattered last year's circus poster on the other side of the store, gazing rapt and quiet at the scarlet horses, the incredible poisings and convolutions of tulle and tights and the painted leers of comedians, and said, "It's time to eat."

But not at home. Squatting beside his brother against the front wall, he watched his father emerge from the store and produce from a paper sack a segment of cheese and divide it carefully and deliberately into three with his pocket knife and produce crackers from the same sack. They all three squatted on the gallery and ate, slowly, without talking; then in the store again, they drank from a tin dipper tepid water smelling of the cedar bucket and of living beech trees. And still they did not go home. It was a horse lot this time, a tall rail fence upon and along which men stood and sat and out of which one by one horses were led, to be walked and trotted and then cantered back and forth along the road while the slow swapping and buying went on and the sun began to slant westward, they—the three of them—watching and listening, the older brother with his muddy eyes and his steady, inevitable tobacco, the father commenting now and then on certain of the animals, to no one in particular.

It was after sundown when they reached home. They ate supper by lamplight, then, sitting on the doorstep, the boy watched the night fully accomplish, listening to the whippoorwills and the frogs, when he heard his mother's voice: "Abner! No! No! Oh, God. Oh, God. Abner!" and he rose, whirled, and saw the altered light through the door where a candle stub now burned in a bottle neck on the table and his father, still in the hat and coat, at once formal and burlesque as though dressed carefully for some shabby and ceremonial violence, emptying the reservoir of the lamp back into the five-gallon kerosene can from which it had been filled, while the mother tugged at his arm until he shifted the lamp to the other hand and flung her back, not savagely or viciously, just hard, into the wall, her hands flung out against the wall for balance, her mouth open and in her face the same quality of hopeless despair as had been in her voice. Then his father saw him standing in the door.

"Go to the barn and get that can of oil we were oiling the wagon with," he said. The boy did not move. Then he could speak.

"What . . ." he cried. "What are you . . ."

"Go get that oil," his father said. "Go."

Then he was moving, running, outside the house, toward the stable: this the old habit, the old blood which he had not been permitted to choose for himself, which had been bequeathed him willy nilly and which had run for so long (and who knew where, battening on what of outrage and savagery and lust) before it came to him. *I could keep on,* he thought. *I could run on and on and never look back, never need to see his face again. Only I can't I can't,* the rusted can in his hand now, the liquid sploshing in it as he ran back to the house and into it, into the sound of his mother's weeping in the next room, and handed the can to his father.

"Ain't you going to even send a nigger?" he cried. "At least you sent a nigger before!"

This time his father didn't strike him. The hand came even faster than the blow had, the same hand which had set the can on the table with almost excruciating care flashing from the can toward him too quick for him to follow it, gripping him by the back of his shirt and on to tiptoe before he had seen it quit the can, the face stooping at him in breathless and frozen ferocity, the cold, dead voice speaking over him to the older brother, who leaned against the table, chewing with that steady, curious, sidewise motion of cows:

"Empty the can into the big one and go on. I'll catch up with you."

"Better tie him up to the bedpost," the brother said.

"Do like I told you," the father said. Then the boy was moving, his bunched shirt and the hard, bony hand between his shoulder-blades, his toes just touching the floor, across the room and into the other one, past the sisters sitting with spread heavy thighs in the two chairs over the cold hearth, and to where his mother and aunt sat side by side on the bed, the aunt's arms about his mother's shoulders.

"Hold him," the father said. The aunt made a startled movement. "Not you," the father said. "Lennie. Take hold of him. You'll hold him better than that. If he gets loose don't you know what he is going to do? He will go up yonder." He jerked his head toward the road. "Maybe I'd better tie him."

"I'll hold him," his mother whispered.

"See you do then." Then his father was gone, the stiff foot heavy and measured upon the boards, ceasing at last.

Then he began to struggle. His mother caught him in both arms, he jerking and wrenching at them. He would be stronger in the end, he knew that. But he had no time to wait for it. "Lemme go!" he cried. "I don't want to have to hit you!"

"Let him go!" the aunt said. "If he don't go, before God, I am going up there myself!"

"Don't you see I can't?" his mother cried. "Sarty! Sarty! No! No! Help me, Lizzie!"

Then he was free. His aunt grasped at him but it was too late. He whirled, running, his mother stumbled forward on to her knees behind him, crying to the nearer sister: "Catch him, Net! Catch him!" But that was too late too, the sister (the sisters were twins, born at the same time, yet either of them now gave the impression of being, encompassing as much living meat and volume and weight as any other two of the family) not yet having begun to rise from the chair, her head, face, alone merely turned, presenting to him in the flying instant an astonishing expanse of young female features untroubled by any surprise even, wearing only an expression of bovine interest. Then he was out of the room, out of the house, in the mild dust of the starlit road and the heavy rifeness of honeysuckle, the pale ribbon unspooling with terrific slowness under his running feet, reaching the gate at last and turning in, running, his heart and lungs drumming, on up the drive toward the lighted house, the lighted door. He did not knock, he burst in, sobbing for breath, incapable for the moment of speech; he saw the astonished face of the Negro in the linen jacket without knowing when the Negro had appeared.

"De Spain!" he cried, panted. "Where's . . ." then he saw the white man too emerging from a white door down the hall. "Barn!" he cried. "Barn!"

"What?" the white man said. "Barn?"

"Yes!" the boy cried. "Barn!"

"Catch him!" the white man shouted.

But it was too late this time too. The Negro grasped his shirt, but the entire sleeve, rotten with washing, carried away, and he was out that door too and in the drive again, and had actually never ceased to run even while he was screaming into the white man's face.

Behind him the white man was shouting, "My horse! Fetch my horse!" and he thought for an instant of cutting across the park and climbing the fence into the road, but he did not know the park nor how high the vine-massed fence might be and he dared not risk it. So he ran on down the drive, blood and breath roaring; presently he was in the road again though he could not see it. He could not hear either: the galloping mare was almost upon him before he heard her, and even then he held his course, as if the very urgency of his wild grief and need must in a moment more find his wings, waiting until the ultimate instant to hurl himself aside and into the weed-choked roadside ditch as the horse thundered past and on, for an instant in furious silhouette against the stars, the tranquil early summer night sky which, even before the shape of the horse and rider vanished, stained abruptly and violently upward: a long, swirling roar incredible and soundless, blotting the stars, and he springing up and into the road again, running again, knowing it was too late yet still running even after he heard the shot and, an instant later, two shots, pausing now without knowing he had ceased to run, crying "Pap! Pap!", running again before he knew he had begun to run, stumbling, tripping over something and scrabbling up again without ceasing to run, looking backward over his shoulder at the glare as he got up, running on among the invisible trees, panting, sobbing, "Father! Father!"

At midnight he was sitting on the crest of a hill. He did not know it was midnight and he did not know how far he had come. But there was no glare behind him now and he sat now, his back toward what he had called home for four days anyhow, his face toward the dark woods which he would enter when breath was strong again, small, shaking steadily in the chill darkness, hugging himself into the remainder of his thin, rotten shirt, the grief and despair now no longer terror and fear but just grief and despair. *Father. My father*, he thought. "He was brave!" he cried suddenly, aloud but not loud, no more than a whisper: "He was! He was in the war! He was in Colonel Sartoris' cav'ry!" not knowing that his father had gone to that war a private in the fine old European sense, wearing no uniform, admitting the authority of and giving fidelity to no man or army or flag, going to war as Malbrouck[1] himself did: for booty—it meant nothing and less than nothing to him if it were enemy booty or his own.

The slow constellations wheeled on. It would be dawn and then sun-up after a while and he would be hungry. But that would be to-morrow and now he was only cold, and walking would cure that. His breathing was easier now and he decided to get up and go on, and then he found that he had been asleep because he knew it was almost dawn, the night almost over. He could tell that from the whippoorwills. They were everywhere now among the dark trees below him, constant and inflectioned and ceaseless, so that, as the instant for giving over to the day birds drew nearer and nearer, there was no interval at all between them. He got up. He was a little stiff, but walking would cure that too as it would the cold, and soon there would be the sun. He went on down the hill, toward the dark woods within which the liquid silver voices of the birds called unceasing—the rapid and urgent beating of the urgent and quiring heart of the late spring night. He did not look back.

1938

Spotted Horses

I

Yes, sir. Flem Snopes[1] has filled that whole country full of spotted horses. You can hear folks running them all day and all night, whooping and hollering, and the horses running back and forth across them little wooden bridges ever now and then kind of like thunder. Here I was this morning pretty near halfway to town, with the team ambling along and me setting in the buckboard about half asleep, when all of a sudden something come swurging up outen the bushes and jumped the road clean, without touching hoof to it. It flew right over my team, big as a billboard and flying through the air like a hawk. It taken me thirty minutes to stop my team and untangle the harness and the buckboard and hitch them up again.

That Flem Snopes. I be dog[2] if he ain't a case, now. One morning about ten years ago, the boys was just getting settled down on Varner's porch for a little talk and tobacco, when here come Flem out from behind the counter, with his

1. The Duke of Marlborough (1650–1722), an English general whose name became distorted as Malbrouch and Malbrouck in English and French popular songs celebrating his exploits.

1. The now older brother from "Barn Burning."
2. "I'll be darned."

coat off and his hair all parted like he might have been clerking for Varner for ten years already. Folks all knowed him; it was a big family of them about five miles down the bottom. That year, at least. Sharecropping. They never stayed on any place over a year. Then they would move on to another place, with the chap or maybe the twins of that year's litter. It was a regular nest of them. But Flem. The rest of them stayed tenant farmers, moving ever year, but here come Flem one day, walking out from behind Jody Varner's counter like he owned it. And he wasn't there but a year or two before folks knowed that, if him and Jody was both still in that store in ten years more, it would be Jody clerking for Flem Snopes. Why, that fellow could make a nickel where it wasn't but four cents to begin with. He skun me in two trades, myself, and the fellow that can do that, I just hope he'll get rich before I do; that's all.

All right. So here Flem was, clerking at Varner's, making a nickel here and there and not telling nobody about it. No, sir. Folks never knowed when Flem got the better of somebody lessen the fellow he beat told it. He'd just set there in the store-chair, chewing his tobacco and keeping his own business to hisself, until about a week later we'd find out it was somebody else's business he was keeping to hisself—provided the fellow he trimmed was mad enough to tell it. That's Flem.

We give him ten years to own everything Jody Varner had. But he never waited no ten years. I reckon you-all know that gal of Uncle Billy Varner's, the youngest one; Eula. Jody's sister. Ever Sunday ever yellow-wheeled buggy and curried riding horse in that country would be hitched to Bill Varner's fence, and the young bucks setting on the porch, swarming around Eula like bees around a honey pot. One of these here kind of big, soft-looking gals that could giggle richer than plowed newground. Wouldn't none of them leave before the others, and so they would set there on the porch until time to go home, with some of them with nine and ten miles to ride and then get up tomorrow and go back to the field. So they would all leave together and they would ride in a clump down to the creek ford and hitch them curried horses and yellow-wheeled buggies and get out and fight one another. Then they would get in the buggies again and go on home.

Well, one day about a year ago, one of them yellow-wheeled buggies and one of them curried saddle-horses quit this country. We heard they was heading for Texas. The next day Uncle Billy and Eula and Flem come into town in Uncle Bill's surrey, and when they come back, Flem and Eula was married. And on the next day we heard that two more of them yellow-wheeled buggies had left the country. They mought have gone to Texas, too. It's a big place.

Anyway, about a month after the wedding, Flem and Eula went to Texas, too. They was gone pretty near a year. Then one day last month, Eula come back, with a baby. We figgered up, and we decided that it was as well-growed a three-months-old baby as we ever see. It can already pull up on a chair. I reckon Texas makes big men quick, being a big place. Anyway, if it keeps on like it started, it'll be chewing tobacco and voting time it's eight years old.

And so last Friday here come Flem himself. He was on a wagon with another fellow. The other fellow had one of these two-gallon hats and a ivory-handled pistol and a box of gingersnaps sticking out of his hind pocket, and tied to the tailgate of the wagon was about two dozen of them Texas ponies, hitched to one another with barbed wire. They was colored like parrots and they was quiet as doves, and ere[3] a one of them would kill you quick as a rattlesnake. Nere a one of them had two eyes the same color, and nere a one of them had ever see a bridle, I reckon; and when that Texas man got down offen the wagon and walked up to them to show how gentle they was, one of them cut his vest clean offen him, same as with a razor.

Flem had done already disappeared; he had went on to see his wife, I reckon, and to see if that ere baby had done gone on to the field to help Uncle Billy plow, maybe. It was the Texas man that taken the horses on to Mrs. Littlejohn's lot. He had a little trouble at first, when they come to the gate, because they hadn't never see a fence before, and when he finally got them in and taken a pair of wire cutters and unhitched them and got them into the barn and poured some shell corn into the trough, they durn nigh tore down the barn. I reckon they thought that shell corn was bugs, maybe. So he left them in the lot and he announced that the auction would begin at sunup tomorrow.

That night we was setting on Mrs. Littlejohn's porch. You-all mind the moon was nigh full that night, and we would watch them spotted varmints swirling along the fence and back and forth across the lot same as minnows in a pond. And then now and then they would all kind of huddle up against the barn and rest themselves by biting and kicking one another. We would hear a squeal, and then a set of hoofs would go Bam! against the barn, like a pistol. It sounded just like a fellow with a pistol, in a nest of cattymounts,[4] taking his time.

II

It wasn't ere a man knowed yet if Flem owned them things or not. They just knowed one thing: that they wasn't never going to know for sho if Flem did or not, or if maybe he didn't just get on that wagon at the edge of town, for the ride or not. Even Eck Snopes didn't know, Flem's own cousin. But wasn't nobody surprised at that. We knowed that Flem would skin Eck quick as he would ere a one of us.

They was there by sunup next morning, some of them come twelve and sixteen miles, with seed-money tied up in tobacco sacks in their overalls, standing along the fence, when the Texas man come out of Mrs. Littlejohn's after breakfast and clumb onto the gate post with that ere white pistol butt sticking outen his hind pocket. He taken a new box of gingersnaps outen his pocket and bit the end offen it like a cigar and spit out the paper, and said the auction was open. And still they was coming up in wagons and a horse-and-mule-back and hitching the teams across the road and coming to the fence. Flem wasn't nowhere in sight.

But he couldn't get them started. He begun to work on Eck, because Eck holp him last night to get them into the barn and feed them that shell corn. Eck got out just in time. He come outen that barn like a chip of the crest on a busted dam of water, and clumb into the wagon just in time.

He was working on Eck when Henry Armstid come up in his wagon. Eck was saying he was skeered to bid on one of them, because he might get it, and the Texas man says, "Them ponies? Them little horses?" He clumb down offen the

3. Any.

4. Catamounts, wildcats.

gate post and went toward the horses. They broke and run, and him following them, kind of chirping to them, with his hand out like he was fixing to catch a fly, until he got three or four of them cornered. Then he jumped into them, and then we couldn't see nothing for a while because of the dust. It was a big cloud of it, and them blare-eyed, spotted things swoaring outen it twenty foot to a jump, in forty directions without counting up. Then the dust settled and there they was, that Texas man and the horse. He had its head twisted clean around like a owl's head. Its legs was braced and it was trembling like a new bride and groaning like a saw mill, and him holding its head wrung clean around on its neck so it was snuffing sky. "Look it over," he says, with his heels dug too and that white pistol sticking outen his pocket and his neck swole up like a spreading adder's until you could just tell what he was saying, cussing the horse and talking to us all at once: "Look him over, the fiddle-headed son of fourteen fathers. Try him, buy him; you will get the best—" Then it was all dust again, and we couldn't see nothing but spotted hide and mane, and that ere Texas man's boot-heels like a couple of walnuts on two strings, and after a while that two-gallon hat come sailing out like a fat old hen crossing a fence.

When the dust settled again, he was just getting outen the far fence corner, brushing himself off. He come and got his hat and brushed it off and come and clumb onto the gate post again. He was breathing hard. He taken the ginger-snap box outen his pocket and et one, breathing hard. The hammerhead horse was still running round and round the lot like a merry-go-round at a fair. That was when Henry Armstid come shoving up to the gate in them patched overalls and one of them dangle-armed shirts of hisn. Hadn't nobody noticed him until then. We was all watching the Texas man and the horses. Even Mrs. Littlejohn; she had done come out and built a fire under the washpot in her back yard, and she would stand at the fence a while and then go back into the house and come out again with a armful of wash and stand at the fence again. Well, here come Henry shoving up, and then we see Mrs. Armstid right behind him, in that ere faded wrapper and sunbonnet and them tennis shoes. "Git on back to that wagon," Henry says.

"Henry," she says.

"Here, boys," the Texas man says; "make room for missus to git up and see. Come on, Henry," he says; "here's your chance to buy that saddle-horse missus has been wanting. What about ten dollars, Henry?"

"Henry," Mrs. Armstid says. She put her hand on Henry's arm. Henry knocked her hand down.

"Git on back to that wagon, like I told you," he says.

Mrs. Armstid never moved. She stood behind Henry, with her hands rolled into her dress, not looking at nothing. "He hain't no more despair[5] than to buy one of them things," she says. "And us not five dollars ahead of the porehouse, he hain't no more despair." It was the truth, too. They ain't never made more than a bare living offen that place of theirs, and them with four chaps and the very clothes they wears she earns by weaving by the firelight at night while Henry's asleep.

"Shut your mouth and git on back to that wagon," Henry says. "Do you want I taken a wagon stake to you here in the big road?"

5. To spare.

Well, that Texas man taken one look at her. Then he begun on Eck again, like Henry wasn't even there. But Eck was skeered. "I can git me a snapping turtle or a water moccasin for nothing. I ain't going to buy none."

So the Texas man said he would give Eck a horse. "To start the auction, and because you holp me last night. If you'll start the bidding on the next horse," he says, "I'll give you that fiddle-head horse."

I wish you could have seen them, standing there with their seed-money in their pockets, watching that Texas man give Eck Snopes a live horse, all fixed to call him a fool if he taken it or not. Finally Eck says he'll take it. "Only I just starts the bidding," he says. "I don't have to buy the next one lessen I ain't overtopped." The Texas man said all right, and Eck bid a dollar on the next one, with Henry Armstid standing there with his mouth already open, watching Eck and the Texas man like a mad dog or something. "A dollar," Eck says.

The Texas man looked at Eck. His mouth was already open too, like he had started to say something and what he was going to say had up and died on him. "A dollar?" he says. "One dollar? You mean, *one* dollar, Eck?"

"Durn it," Eck says; "Two dollars, then."

Well, sir, I wish you could a seen that Texas man. He taken out that gingersnap box and held it up and looked into it, careful, like it might have been a diamond ring in it, or a spider. Then he throwed it away and wiped his face with a bandanna. "Well," he says. "Well. Two dollars. Two dollars. Is your pulse all right, Eck?" he says. "Do you have ager-sweats[6] at night, maybe?" he says. "Well," he says, "I got to take it. But are you boys going to stand there and see Eck get two horses at a dollar a head?"

That done it. I be dog if he wasn't nigh as smart as Flem Snopes. He hadn't no more than got the words outen his mouth before here was Henry Armstid, waving his hand. "Three dollars," Henry says. Mrs. Armstid tried to hold him again. He knocked her hand off, shoving up to the gate post.

"Mister," Mrs. Armstid says, "we got chaps in the house and not corn to feed the stock. We got five dollars I earned my chaps a-weaving after dark, and him snoring in the bed. And he hain't no more despair."

"Henry bids three dollars," the Texas man says. "Raise him a dollar, Eck, and the horse is yours."

"Henry," Mrs. Armstid says.

"Raise him, Eck," the Texas man says.

"Four dollars," Eck says.

"Five dollars," Henry says, shaking his fist. He shoved up right under the gate post. Mrs. Armstid was looking at the Texas man too.

"Mister," she says, "if you take that five dollars I earned my chaps a-weaving for one of them things, it'll be a curse onto you and yourn during all the time of man."

But it wasn't no stopping Henry. He had shoved up, waving his first at the Texas man. He opened it; the money was in nickels and quarters, and one dollar bill that looked like a cow's cud. "Five dollars," he says. "And the man that raises it'll have to beat my head off, or I'll beat hisn."

"All right," the Texas man says. "Five dollars is bid. But don't you shake your hand at me."

6. Ague; chills and fever with sweating.

III

It taken till nigh sundown before the last one was sold. He got them hotted up once and the bidding got up to seven dollars and a quarter, but most of them went around three or four dollars, him setting on the gate post and picking the horses out one at a time by mouthword, and Mrs. Littlejohn pumping up and down at the tub and stopping and coming to the fence for a while and going back to the tub again. She had done got done too, and the wash was hung on the line in the back yard, and we could smell supper cooking. Finally they was all sold; he swapped the last two and the wagon for a buckboard.

We was all kind of tired, but Henry Armstid looked more like a mad dog than ever. When he bought, Mrs. Armstid had went back to the wagon, setting in it behind them two rabbit-sized, bone-pore mules, and the wagon itself looking like it would fall all to pieces soon as the mules moved. Henry hadn't even waited to pull it outen the road; it was still in the middle of the road and her setting in it, not looking at nothing, ever since this morning.

Henry was right up against the gate. He went up to the Texas man. "I bought a horse and I paid cash," Henry says. "And yet you expect me to stand around here until they are all sold before I can get my horse. I'm going to take my horse outen that lot."

The Texas man looked at Henry. He talked like he might have been asking for a cup of coffee at the table. "Take your horse," he says.

Then Henry quit looking at the Texas man. He begun to swallow, holding onto the gate. "Ain't you going to help me?" he says.

"It ain't my horse," the Texas man says.

Henry never looked at the Texas man again, he never looked at nobody. "Who'll help me catch my horse?" he says. Never nobody said nothing. "Bring the plowline," Henry says. Mrs. Armstid got outen the wagon and brought the plowline. The Texas man got down offen the post. The woman made to pass him, carrying the rope.

"Don't you go in there, missus," the Texas man says.

Henry opened the gate. He didn't look back. "Come on here," he says.

"Don't you go in there, missus," the Texas man says.

Mrs. Armstid wasn't looking at nobody, neither, with her hands across her middle, holding the rope. "I reckon I better," she says. Her and Henry went into the lot. The horses broke and run. Henry and Mrs. Armstid followed.

"Get him into the corner," Henry says. They got Henry's horse cornered finally, and Henry taken the rope, but Mrs. Armstid let the horse get out. They hemmed it up again, but Mrs. Armstid let it get out again, and Henry turned and hit her with the rope. "Why didn't you head him back?" Henry says. He hit her again. "Why didn't you?" It was about that time I looked around and see Flem Snopes standing there.

It was the Texas man that done something. He moved fast for a big man. He caught the rope before Henry could hit the third time, and Henry whirled and made like he would jump at the Texas man. But he never jumped. The Texas man went and taken Henry's arm and led him outen the lot. Mrs. Armstid come behind them and the Texas man taken some money outen his pocket and he give it into Mrs. Armstid's hand. "Get him into the wagon and take him on home," the Texas man says, like he might have been telling them he enjoyed his supper.

Then here comes Flem. "What's that for, Buck?" Flem says.

"Thinks he bought one of them ponies," the Texas man says. "Get him on away, missus."

But Henry wouldn't go. "Give him back that money," he says. "I bought that horse and I aim to have him if I have to shoot him."

And there was Flem, standing there with his hands in his pockets, chewing, like he had just happened to be passing.

"You take your money and I take my horse," Henry says. "Give it back to him," he says to Mrs. Armstid.

"You don't own no horse of mine," the Texas man says. "Get him on home, missus."

Then Henry seen Flem. "You got something to do with these horses," he says. "I bought one. Here's the money for it." He taken the bill outen Mrs. Armstid's hand. He offered it to Flem. "I bought one. Ask him. Here. Here's the money," he says, giving the bill to Flem.

When Flem taken the money, the Texas man dropped the rope he had snatched outen Henry's hand. He had done sent Eck Snopes's boy up to the store for another box of gingersnaps, and he taken the box of gingersnaps, and he taken the box outen his pocket and looked into it. It was empty and he dropped it on the ground. "Mr. Snopes will have your money for you tomorrow," he says to Mrs. Armstid. "You can get it from him tomorrow. He don't own no horse. You get him into the wagon and get him on home." Mrs. Armstid went back to the wagon and got in. "Where's that ere buckboard I bought?" the Texas man says. It was after sundown then. And then Mrs. Littlejohn come out on the porch and rung the supper bell.

IV

I come on in and et supper. Mrs. Littlejohn would bring in a pan of bread or something, then she would go out to the porch a minute and come back and tell us. The Texas man had hitched his team to the buckboard he had swapped them last two horses for, and him and Flem had gone, and then she told that the rest of them that never had ropes had went back to the store with I. O. Snopes to get some ropes, and wasn't nobody at the gate but Henry Armstid, and Mrs. Armstid setting in the wagon in the road, and Eck Snopes and that boy of hisn. "I don't care how many of them fool men gets killed by them things," Mrs. Littlejohn says, "but I ain't going to let Eck Snopes take that boy into that lot again." So she went down to the gate, but she come back without the boy or Eck neither.

"It ain't no need to worry about that boy," I says. "He's charmed." He was right behind Eck last night when Eck went to help feed them. The whole drove of them jumped clean over that boy's head and never touched him. It was Eck that touched him. Eck snatched him into the wagon and taken a rope and frailed the tar outen him.

So I had done et and went to my room and was undressing, long as I had a long trip to make next day; I was trying to sell a machine[7] to Mrs. Bundren up past Whiteleaf; when Henry Armstid opened that gate and went in by hisself.

7. The narrator, V. K. Ratliff, is a traveling salesman who sells sewing machines.

They couldn't make him wait for the balance of them to get back with their ropes. Eck Snopes said he tried to make Henry wait, but Henry wouldn't do it. Eck said Henry walked right up to them and that when they broke, they run clean over Henry like a hay-mow breaking down. Eck said he snatched that boy of hisn out of the way just in time and that them things went through that gate like a creek flood and into the wagons and teams hitched side the road, busting wagon tongues and snapping harness like it was fishing line, with Mrs. Armstid still setting in their wagon in the middle of it like something carved outen wood. Then they scattered, wild horses and tame mules with pieces of harness and single trees dangling offen them, both ways up and down the road.

"There goes ourn, paw!" Eck says his boy said. "There it goes, into Mrs. Littlejohn's house." Eck says it run right up the steps and into the house like a boarder late for supper. I reckon so. Anyway, I was in my room, in my underclothes, with one sock on and one sock in my hand, leaning out the window when the commotion busted out, when I heard something run into the melodeon[8] in the hall; it sounded like a railroad engine. Then the door to my room come sailing in like when you throw a tin bucket top into the wind and I looked over my shoulder and see something that looked like a fourteen-foot pinwheel a-blaring its eyes at me. It had to blare them fast, because I was already done jumped out the window.

I reckon it was anxious, too. I reckon it hadn't never seen barbed wire or shell corn before, but I know it hadn't never seen underclothes before, or maybe it was a sewing-machine agent it hadn't never seen. Anyway, it swirled and turned to run back up the hall and outen the house, when it met Eck Snopes and that boy just coming in, carrying a rope. It swirled again and run down the hall and out the back door just in time to meet Mrs. Littlejohn. She had just gathered up the clothes she had washed, and she was coming onto the back porch with a armful of washing on one hand and a scrubbing board in the other, when the horse skidded up to her, trying to stop and swirl again. It never taken Mrs. Littlejohn no time a-tall.

"Git outen here, you son," she says. She hit it across the face with the scrubbing board; that ere scrubbing board split as neat as ere a axe could have done it, and when the horse swirled to run back up the hall, she hit it again with what was left of the scrubbing board, not on the head this time. "And stay out," she says.

Eck and that boy was halfway down the hall by this time. I reckon that horse looked like a pinwheel to Eck too. "Git to hell outen here, Ad!" Eck says. Only there wasn't time. Eck dropped flat on his face, but the boy never moved. The boy was about a yard tall maybe, in overhalls just like Eck's; that horse swoared over his head without touching a hair. I saw that, because I was just coming back up the front steps, still carrying that ere sock and still in my underclothes, when the horse come onto the porch again. It taken one look at me and swirled again and run to the end of the porch and jumped the banisters and the lot fence like a hen-hawk and lit in the lot running and went out the gate again and jumped eight or ten upside-down wagons and went on down the road. It was a full moon then. Mrs. Armstid was still setting in the wagon like she had done been carved outen wood and left there and forgot.

8. A small keyboard organ.

That horse. It ain't never missed a lick. It was going about forty miles a hour when it come to the bridge over the creek. It would have had a clear road, but it so happened that Vernon Tull was already using the bridge when it got there. He was coming back from town; he hadn't heard about the auction; him and his wife and three daughters and Mrs. Tull's aunt, all setting in chairs in the wagon bed, and all asleep, including the mules. They waked up when the horse hit the bridge one time, but Tull said the first he knew was when the mules tried to turn the wagon around in the middle of the bridge and he seen that spotted varmint run right twixt the mules and run up the wagon tongue like a squirrel. He said he just had time to hit it across the face with his whip-stock, because about that time the mules turned the wagon around on that ere one-way bridge and that horse clumb across one of the mules and jumped down onto the bridge again and went on, with Vernon standing up in the wagon and kicking at it.

Tull said the mules turned in the harness and clumb back into the wagon too, with Tull trying to beat them out again, with the reins wrapped around his wrist. After that he says all he seen was over-turned chairs and womenfolks' legs and white drawers shining in the moonlight, and his mules and that spotted horse going on up the road like a ghost.

The mules jerked Tull outen the wagon and drug him a spell on the bridge before the reins broke. They thought at first that he was dead, and while they was kneeling around him, picking the bridge splinters outen him, here comes Eck and that boy, still carrying the rope. They was running and breathing a little hard. "Where'd he go?" Eck says.

V

I went back and got my pants and shirt and shoes on just in time to go and help get Henry Armstid outen the trash in the lot. I be dog if he didn't look like he was dead, with his head hanging back and his teeth showing in the moonlight, and a little rim of white under his eyelids. He could still hear them horses, here and there; hadn't none of them got more than four-five miles away yet, not knowing the country, I reckon. So we could hear them and folks yelling now and then: "Whooey. Head him!"

We toted Henry into Mrs. Littlejohn's. She was in the hall; she hadn't put down the armful of clothes. She taken one look at us, and she laid down the busted scrubbing board and taken up the lamp and opened a empty door. "Bring him in here," she says.

We toted him in and laid him on the bed. Mrs. Littlejohn set the lamp on the dresser, still carrying the clothes. "I'll declare, you men," she says. Our shadows was way up the wall, tiptoeing too; we could hear ourselves breathing. "Better get his wife," Mrs. Littlejohn says. She went out, carrying the clothes.

"I reckon we had," Quick says. "Go get her, somebody."

"Whyn't you go?" Winterbottom says.

"Let Ernest git her," Durley says. "He lives neighbors with them."

Ernest went to fetch her. I be dog if Henry didn't look like he was dead. Mrs. Littlejohn come back, with a kettle and some towels. She went to work on Henry, and then Mrs. Armstid and Ernest come in. Mrs. Armstid come to the foot of the bed and stood there, with her hands rolled into her apron, watching what Mrs. Littlejohn was doing, I reckon.

"You men get outen the way," Mrs. Littlejohn says. "Git outside," she says. "See if you can't find something else to play with that will kill some more of you."

"Is he dead?" Winterbottom says.

"It ain't your fault if he ain't," Mrs. Littlejohn says. "Go tell Will Varner to come up here. I reckon a man ain't so different from a mule, come long come short. Except maybe a mule's got more sense."

We went to get Uncle Billy. It was a full moon. We could hear them, now and then, four mile away: "Whooey. Head him." The country was full of them, one on ever wooden bridge in the land, running across it like thunder: "Whooey. There he goes. Head him."

We hadn't got far before Henry begun to scream. I reckon Mrs. Littlejohn's water had brung him to; anyway, he wasn't dead. We went on to Uncle Billy's. The house was dark. We called to him, and after a while the window opened and Uncle Billy put his head out, peart as a peckerwood,[9] listening. "Are they still trying to catch them durn rabbits?" he says.

He come down, with his britches on over his nightshirt, and his suspenders dangling, carrying his horse-doctoring grip. "Yes, sir," he says, cocking his head like a woodpecker; "they're still a-trying."

We could hear Henry before we reached Mrs. Littlejohn's. He was going Ah-Ah-Ah. We stopped in the yard. Uncle Billy went on in. We could hear Henry. We stood in the yard, hearing them on the bridges, this-a-way and that: "Whooey. Whooey."

"Eck Snopes ought to caught hisn," Ernest says.

"Looks like he ought," Winterbottom said.

Henry was going Ah-Ah-Ah steady in the house; then he begun to scream. "Uncle Billy's started," Quick says. We looked into the hall. We could see the light where the door was. Then Mrs. Littlejohn come out.

"Will needs some help," she says. "You, Ernest. You'll do." Ernest went into the house.

"Hear them?" Quick said. "That one was on Four Mile bridge." We could hear them; it sounded like thunder a long way off; it didn't last long:

"Whooey."

We could hear Henry: "Ah-Ah-Ah-Ah-Ah."

"They are both started now," Winterbottom says. "Ernest too."

That was early in the night. Which was a good thing, because it taken a long night for folks to chase them things right and for Henry to lay there and holler, being as Uncle Billy never had none of this here chloryfoam to set Henry's leg with. So it was considerate in Flem to get them started early. And what do you reckon Flem's comment was?

That's right. Nothing. Because he wasn't there. Hadn't nobody see him since that Texas man left.

VI

That was Saturday night. I reckon Mrs. Armstid got home about daylight, to see about the chaps. I don't know where they thought her and Henry was. But

9. Pert as a woodpecker.

lucky the oldest one was a gal, about twelve, big enough to take care of the little ones. Which she did for the next two days. Mrs. Armstid would nurse Henry all night and work in the kitchen for hern and Henry's keep, and in the afternoon she would drive home (it was about four miles) to see to the chaps. She would cook up a pot of victuals and leave it on the stove, and the gal would bar the house and keep the little ones quiet. I would hear Mrs. Littlejohn and Mrs. Armstid talking in the kitchen. "How are the chaps making out?" Mrs. Littlejohn says.

"All right," Mrs. Armstid says.

"Don't they git skeered at night?" Mrs. Littlejohn says.

"Ina May bars the door when I leave," Mrs. Armstid says. "She's got the axe in bed with her. I reckon she can make out."

I reckon they did. And I reckon Mrs. Armstid was waiting for Flem to come back to town; hadn't nobody seen him until this morning; to get her money the Texas man said Flem was keeping for her. Sho. I reckon she was.

Anyway, I heard Mrs. Armstid and Mrs. Littlejohn talking in the kitchen this morning while I was eating breakfast. Mrs. Littlejohn had just told Mrs. Armstid that Flem was in town. "You can ask him for that five dollars," Mrs. Littlejohn says.

"You reckon he'll give it to me?" Mrs. Armstid says.

Mrs. Littlejohn was washing dishes, washing them like a man, like they was made out of iron. "No," she says. "But asking him won't do no hurt. It might shame him. I don't reckon it will, but it might."

"If he wouldn't give it back, it ain't no use to ask," Mrs. Armstid says.

"Suit yourself," Mrs. Littlejohn says. "It's your money."

I could hear the dishes.

"Do you reckon he might give it back to me?" Mrs. Armstid says. "That Texas man said he would. He said I could get it from Mr. Snopes later."

"Then go and ask him for it," Mrs. Littlejohn says.

I could hear the dishes.

"He won't give it back to me," Mrs. Armstid says.

"All right," Mrs. Littlejohn says. "Don't ask him for it, then."

I could hear the dishes; Mrs. Armstid was helping. "You don't reckon he would, do you?" she says. Mrs. Littlejohn never said nothing. It sounded like she was throwing the dishes at one another. "Maybe I better go and talk to Henry about it," Mrs. Armstid says.

"I would," Mrs. Littlejohn says. I be dog if it didn't sound like she had two plates in her hands, beating them together. "Then Henry can buy another five-dollar horse with it. Maybe he'll buy one next time that will out and out kill him. If I thought that, I'd give you back the money, myself."

"I reckon I better talk to him first," Mrs. Armstid said. Then it sounded like Mrs. Littlejohn taken up all the dishes and throwed them at the cookstove, and I come away.

That was this morning. I had been up to Bundren's and back, and I thought that things would have kind of settled down. So after breakfast, I went up to the store. And there was Flem, setting in the store chair and whittling, like he might not have ever moved since he come to clerk for Jody Varner. I. O. was leaning in the door, in his shirt sleeves and with his hair parted too, same as Flem was before he turned the clerking job over to I. O. It's a funny thing about them Snopes: they all looks alike, yet there ain't ere a two of them that claims brothers. They're always just cousins, like Flem and Eck and Flem and I. O. Eck was there too, squatting against the wall, him and that boy, eating cheese and crackers outen a sack; they told me that Eck hadn't been home a-tall. And that Lon Quick hadn't got back to town, even. He followed his horse clean down to Samson's Bridge, with a wagon and a camp outfit. Eck finally caught one of hisn. It run into a blind lane at Freeman's and Eck and the boy taken and tied their rope across the end of the lane, about three foot high. The horse come to the end of the lane and whirled and run back without ever stopping. Eck says it never seen the rope a-tall. He says it looked just like one of these here Christmas pinwheels. "Didn't it try to run again?" I says.

"No," Eck says, eating a bit of cheese often his knife blade. "Just kicked some."

"Kicked some?" I says.

"It broke its neck," Eck says.

Well, they was squatting there, about six of them, talking, talking at Flem; never nobody knowed yet if Flem had ere a interest in them horses or not. So finally I come right out and asked him. "Flem's done skun all of us so much," I says, "that we're proud of him. Come on, Flem," I says, "how much did you and that Texas man make offen them horses? You can tell us. Ain't nobody here but Eck that bought one of them; the others ain't got back to town yet, and Eck's your own cousin; he'll be proud to hear, too. How much did you-all make?"

They was all whittling, not looking at Flem, making like they was studying. But you could a heard a pin drop. And I. O. He had been rubbing his back up and down on the door, but he stopped now, watching Flem like a pointing dog. Flem finished cutting the sliver offen his stick. He spit across the porch, into the road. "'Twarn't none of my horses," he says.

I. O. cackled, like a hen, slapping his legs with both hands. "You boys might just as well quit trying to get ahead of Flem," he said.

Well, about that time I see Mrs. Armstid come outen Mrs. Littlejohn's gate, coming up the road. I never said nothing. I says, "Well, if a man can't take care of himself in a trade, he can't blame the man that trims him."

Flem never said nothing, trimming at the stick. He hadn't seen Mrs. Armstid. "Yes, sir," I says. "A fellow like Henry Armstid ain't got nobody but hisself to blame."

"Course he ain't," I. O. says. He ain't seen her, neither. "Henry Armstid's a born fool. Always is been. If Flem hadn't a got his money, somebody else would."

We looked at Flem. He never moved. Mrs. Armstid come on up the road.

"That's right," I says. "But, come to think of it, Henry never bought no horse." We looked at Flem; you could a heard a match drop. "That Texas man told her to get that five dollars back from Flem next day. I reckon Flem's done already taken that money to Mrs. Littlejohn's and give it to Mrs. Armstid."

We watched Flem. I. O. quit rubbing his back against the door again. After a while Flem raised his head and spit across the porch, into the dust. I. O. cackled, just like a hen. "Ain't he a beating fellow, now?" I. O. says.

Mrs. Armstid was getting closer, so I kept on talking, watching to see if Flem would look up and see her. But he never looked up. I went on talking about Tull, about how he was going to sue Flem, and Flem setting there, whittling his stick, not saying nothing else after he said they wasn't none of his horses.

Then I. O. happened to look around. He seen Mrs. Armstid. "Psssst!" he says. Flem looked up. "Here she comes!" I. O. says. "Go out the back. I'll tell her you done went in to town today."

But Flem never moved. He just set there, whittling, and we watched Mrs. Armstid come up onto the porch, in that ere faded sunbonnet and wrapper and them tennis shoes that made a kind of hissing noise on the porch. She come onto the porch and stopped, her hands rolled into her dress in front, not looking at nothing.

"He said Saturday," she says, "that he wouldn't sell Henry no horse. He said I could get the money from you."

Flem looked up. The knife never stopped. It went on trimming off a sliver same as if he was watching it. "He taken that money off with him when he left," Flem says.

Mrs. Armstid never looked at nothing. We never looked at her, neither, except the boy of Eck's. He had a half-et cracker in his hand, watching her, chewing.

"He said Henry hadn't bought no horse," Mrs. Armstid says. "He said for me to get the money from you today."

"I reckon he forgot about it," Flem said. "He taken that money off with him Saturday." He whittled again. I. O. kept on rubbing his back, slow. He licked his lips. After a while the woman looked up the road, where it went on up the hill, toward the graveyard. She looked up that way for a while, with that boy of Eck's watching her and I. O. rubbing his back slow against the door. Then she turned back toward the steps.

"I reckon it's time to get dinner started," she says.

"How's Henry this morning, Mrs. Armstid?" Winterbottom says.

She looked at Winterbottom; she almost stopped. "He's resting, I thank you kindly," she says.

Flem got up, outen the chair, putting his knife away. He spit across the porch. "Wait a minute, Mrs. Armstid," he says. She stopped again. She didn't look at him. Flem went on into the store, with I. O. done quit rubbing his back now, with his head craned after Flem, and Mrs. Armstid standing there with her hands rolled into her dress, not looking at nothing. A wagon come up the road and passes; it was Freeman, on the way to town. Then Flem come out again, with I. O. still watching him. Flem had one of these little striped sacks of Jody Varner's candy; I bet he still owes Jody that nickel, too. He put the sack into Mrs. Armstid's hand, like he would have put it into a hollow stump. He spit again across the porch. "A little sweetening for the chaps," he says.

"You're right kind," Mrs. Armstid says. She held the sack of candy in her hand, not looking at nothing. Eck's boy was watching the sack, the half-et cracker in his hand; he wasn't chewing now. He watched Mrs. Armstid roll the sack into her apron. "I reckon I better get on back and help with dinner," she says. She turned and went back across the porch. Flem set down in the chair again and opened his knife. He spit across the porch again, past Mrs. Armstid where she hadn't went down the steps yet. Then she went on, in that ere sunbonnet and wrapper all the same color, back down the road toward Mrs. Littlejohn's. You couldn't see her dress move, like a natural woman walking. She looked like a old snag[1] still standing up and moving along on a high water. We

1. Drifting tree.

watched her turn in at Mrs. Littlejohn's and go outen sight. Flem was whittling. I. O. begun to rub his back on the door. Then he begun to cackle, just like a durn hen.

"You boys might just as well quit trying," I. O. says. "You can't git ahead of Flem. You can't touch him. Ain't he a sight, now?"

I be dog if he ain't. If I had brung a herd of wild cattymounts into town and sold them to my neighbors and kinfolks, they would have lynched me. Yes, sir.

1931

KUSHI FUSAKO

1903–1986

Kushi Fusako is known for a single classic story, "Memoirs of a Declining Ryukyuan Woman" (1932), her only work. After graduating from high school, she taught for a time in Okinawa, an island chain under Japanese rule, then moved to Tokyo to pursue writing. Her famous story gives a memorable depiction of the life of minorities in modern Japan.

Kushi was one of only a few Okinawan women who published fiction in the early twentieth century. She intended the story as the first installment in a serial; when it appeared, many critics in Okinawa hailed it as the beginning of a promising career. It came to a sudden and memorable end, however, after the Okinawa Prefecture Student Association, a group based in Tokyo, criticized the author harshly for portraying Okinawans in what they considered a negative light. Although Kushi responded by publishing a strong-willed defense, the Student Association persuaded the magazine in which the story appeared to suspend publication of further installments. After this, Kushi renounced writing. She avoided the public eye from then on, and little is known of her later life.

The island chain of Okinawa belongs to the Ryuku islands, which extend about 700 miles, from the southern tip of Kyushu, the southernmost island of the Japanese "mainland," to northern Taiwan. Naha, the capital of Okinawa, is some 750 miles from Osaka. While the main "Okinawan" dialect is related to Japanese, the islands have many other dialects, some of which are mutually unintelligible. The two societies have interpenetrated for centuries, although since the late nineteenth century, Japan's influence on Okinawa has become more dominant than the reverse. In Japan, Okinawan literature retains a distinct regional voice.

Until 1600, Okinawa had been an independent kingdom with a vassal relationship to the Chinese court. There followed a period of dual loyalties, as the kingdom came under the partial domination of Japan; in the 1870s the Japanese state formally annexed the islands as a prefecture. The new government instituted assimilation campaigns to bring the supposedly backward Okinawan society in line with the civilized culture of Japan: its targets included the communal landholding system, the use of dialects, women's fashions, and the custom of tattooing the backs of women's hands, which is mentioned in "Memoirs of a Declining Ryukyuan Woman." Elite groups in Okinawa embraced some of these reforms and endorsed the use of standard (Tokyo) Japanese. Nonetheless, policymakers in Tokyo as well as the prefectural government at home (which mainlanders staffed) generally regarded Okinawans of all social levels as second-class citizens.

Desperate economic conditions prompted many Okinawans to migrate to the mainland in search of work, a trend that accelerated during the 1920s, when the islands' finances were wracked by a decline in the market for sugar. Because of prejudice against Okinawans in the main Japanese islands, many migrants tried to pass as Japanese. The uncle in "Memoirs," who has hidden his identity from his company and even from his wife and daughter, would have been a familiar type. (The scandal that the Student Association responded to was not the practice of "passing" but the fact that Kushi spoke openly about it.)

"Memoirs" first appeared in June 1932 in *Fujin kōron (Women's Forum)*, a large-circulation Japanese women's magazine. The story's form draws on a genre of autobiographical fiction that emerged in Japan during the 1910s and remains influential today. The narrator's life resembles the author's own, including the move from Okinawa to Tokyo to pursue a literary career. While "Memoirs" dwells at length on her friend, her uncle, and the poverty of her relatives, it is the narrator's attitudes toward these people and situations, the deeply introspective first-person voice, that give the story its core. It is therefore fitting that the story ends with the narrator's own meditation on Okinawa.

The uproar the story caused was probably unexpected. The month after the Student Association attacked the story for presenting Okinawans in a demeaning light, Kushi published, in *Fujin kōron*, a terse response to her critics, "In Defense of 'Memoirs of a Declining Ryukyuan Woman.'" As one can gather from this essay, the Student Association objected not only to Kushi's unsparing depiction of poverty and dissection of the uncle's motives but also to specific phrases in the story. At the time, the adjective *declining* was often used prejudicially to characterize the Ainu, an indigenous people who originally lived in northern portions of the main Japanese islands. The term *people*, which appears in the story, was potentially prejudicial as well, for it implied—the Student Association said—that Okinawans were not Japanese but rather like the Ainu or like Koreans, whose country Japan had annexed in 1910.

These objections were ironic, since the magazine's editors had selected both titles. Rather than fall back on this defense, however, in her reply Kushi probes her critics' preoccupations. The complaint that she has exposed embarrassing aspects of Okinawan life, she says, shows the critics' unreflective acceptance of the key idea behind the government's assimilation campaigns: that Okinawan culture is backward and shameful. Seeking to feel superior, they strive to elevate Okinawans above Koreans and the Ainu. Their intentness on assimilation reveals a malady of self-loathing that Japanese domination of the islands has created.

Kushi's response had the potential to be more controversial than her original story, since it challenged the orthodox hierarchy that placed Okinawans above the Ainu and the Koreans. Yet the "Defense" did not receive much of a response. Perhaps Kushi's critics were satisfied that she said she would never write again. Her literary style, though, proved to be influential; in particular, the evocative portrayal of nature that closes the story, which seems unrelated to the action but nonetheless conveys the narrator's intense emotions, became a familiar trope in the works of other writers.

Memoirs of a Declining Ryukyuan Woman[1]

I was visiting a friend who had just returned from a family funeral on our home island. I expected to hear from her about my mother but was afraid of what she might say. It was hard for me to imagine my mother surviving this winter with her failing health, and I listened to my friend, feeling as if I had walked out onto thin ice. But she spoke only of my mother's unflagging endurance, and I could detect no sign of concealment on her face, which looked as if it had been freshly swept by the salt sea breeze of our island. Then, sighing deeply, she began to talk about the state of total exhaustion in Ryukyu.

"It's pitch-black at night in S City. I heard that all the rich folks there want desperately to move to N to avoid high taxes. The stone hedges in front of the houses are all crumbling now, and most of the yards inside have been turned into farm fields. Can you believe that S is still Ryukyu's second largest city? To make matters worse, emigration abroad has been banned. People can barely make a living these days by going to work on the mainland."[2]

"I know."

For a time we forgot everything else as we talked of our homeland. My friend, looking worried, explained how she wanted to bring her mother up to Tokyo and help her start a business selling Oshima *tsumugi* cloth.[3]

"The problem is her tattoo."

Tattoos have caused suffering in almost every Ryukyuan family. Even if a woman can save enough money to send several sons to higher school, she is destined to be left behind in her hometown until she dies, thanks to those tattoos on the back of her hands. In the worst cases, mothers have died without ever knowing the names of their grandchildren. The more their sons succeed, the more strictly the mothers have to be confined to their "homes," where they are given a tiny bit of freedom and supported by whatever petty allowance their sons care to provide. Of course, there have been a few exceptions.

Ryukyuan intellectuals are not nearly so bold as those Koreans or Taiwanese who live in mainland Japan. While they openly maintain their customs and manners, we tend to form hidden clusters, like mushrooms, even in this vast metropolis of Tokyo. Though individuals, we can't help but share the loneliness of being Ryukyuan, a loneliness that echoes in our hearts like the sound of the *sanshin*.[4] Yet we never speak of this plaintive sound. If one of us broaches the subject, we avert our eyes, coldly, like two cripples passing on the sidewalk.

We are a people in desperate need of some rapid awakening, but only live from day to day mired in vacillation and pretense, blinded by the deep-rooted mentality of petite bourgeoisie. We always seem to be at the tail end of history, dragged along roads already ruined by others.

Now other dark thoughts filled my mind as I walked along beside the bergamot orange hedges on the way home from my friend's place. I remembered that I was supposed to meet my uncle at a certain train station. He was another

1. Translated by Kimiko Miyagi.
2. The main Japanese islands. Kushi's references to "S City" and "N" at the beginning of the story reflect the common practice in Japanese literature of using letters from the Roman alphabet to mask references to real places and people. "S City": probably Shuri. "N": probably Naha, the capital of Okinawa.
3. Silk fabric made from yarns of uneven thicknesses.
4. A type of samisen, a three-stringed instrument resembling a banjo.

of our people who could not reveal the truth about himself for all the twenty years he had lived in the middle of Tokyo. He managed several branches of a company, supervised university and technical school graduates, and lived in a spacious apartment with a bossy wife and a daughter in her prime who was soon to be married. Yet he had never disclosed the slightest hint to any of them that he was Ryukyuan.

Before I knew it, the faded green train had carried me to X Station, where I went to meet him, as usual, in the third-class waiting room, covering my face with a shawl. Only a few hours remained before New Year's Eve,[5] and there was a tension in the room that reminded me of a tightly wound spring. Everyone looked nervous. Only the young women, with their hair done up for the occasion in traditional Japanese style, basked in the calm afternoon sunlight and seemed to glow in anticipation. Watching them, I felt like some alien creature, constantly scratching my dandruff-filled hair. My body and spirit had all the vitality of a dead cat.

In one corner of the waiting room, a man in an old padded kimono, dirty and worn, was being interrogated by a policeman. The only reason seemed to be that he'd been lying on the floor. Why are the poor always the first to be regarded as criminals? Though this seemed to be someone else's problem, for some reason it disturbed me almost more than I could bear.

"Hello."

All at once I noticed my uncle standing in front of me. Without returning my silent bow, he sat down next to me, clenching a cigar between his teeth. Our awkward conversation lasted about two minutes.

"I've just been too busy," he said brusquely in what sounded like an excuse. "Please send this as usual." He took a ten-yen bill out of his wallet and put it down beside me.

"Certainly." My answer was also curt, as usual.

Our talks always ended quickly.

I gazed after him until his bulky figure had crossed the station square and was swallowed up in the crowd. It occurred to me that his body blended in well with the city buildings and with his large office desk, which was piled high with business letters. It was an even more perfect match, I thought, than the plum trees and bush warblers often portrayed together in traditional Japanese paintings. He was typical of that corporate breed of men who look as if they were born for these surroundings. Watching his back as he moved away, I felt only a machine-like precision, power, and coldness. The last fading rays of sunset that hovered over the layers of buildings seemed to reflect the gloom in my heart.

Though I had never met his wife or daughter, from what my uncle said, I had a general picture of how he lived. Of course, I do not know his home address. I once visited his office after finding that address in the telephone directory, but he had politely forbidden me to come again. This didn't really bother me, though, since I had no intention of relying on him for anything.

At home he kept three maids, an elderly handyman, and a piano. This is the story of how he started sending three yen every month to his stepmother at his other "home."

5. A busy time for travel, with many people returning home for the three-day New Year holiday.

One day five years ago he suddenly returned to Ryukyu. Thirty years had passed since he disappeared shortly after being discharged from the army somewhere in Kyushu,[6] and people even suspected he had died.

Apparently, he thought my family was still prospering. After giving our name to a ricksha man, he looked all over town for our house and finally arrived that evening at our wretched little shop, which sat behind a mailbox in a yard barely ten feet square. My mother bowed down almost to the ground, all in a fluster because she had mistaken this arrogant-looking man in a Western suit for the tax collector who always scolded her for the way she kept accounts on items like cigarettes and salt.

My uncle's own family and relatives, too, had all fallen on hard times. The mistress who had become his father's wife was reduced to wearing patched kimonos and lived with his grandmother, now hard of hearing, in a house with no floor padding under the tatami mats. His grandmother had come to resemble a child fearful of strangers as she sat facing the wall all day long silently spinning jute yarn. His father's wife, whose hair had turned white on top, eked out a living doing errands and washing clothes.

Despite her circumstances, this woman seemed to be the picture of trust and devotion, maybe in part because his father had so cherished her when he was young. Yet his affection waned after a few years, and his later profligacy threw her into the depths of despair. It wasn't long before he lost his head over some woman from the demimonde and, drawn by lust and her modest fortune, brought her into the house. Now his wife again fell to the status of maidservant. She slept curled up on the kitchen floor and did all the housework, washing everyone's clothes by hand and cooking for all of them. Yet she suppressed the urge to complain, never protesting to anyone. This was probably why she always looked as if she had just been crying.

It was during this time that my uncle's younger brother suddenly died, and the young, widowed wife and their three-year-old boy were added to the impoverished household. His father's wife, unbearably lonely, welcomed these new family members. And, while the widow weaved, the wife kept busy doing errands for people and cooking meals as before, along with baby-sitting for her grandson-in-law. Meanwhile, her estranged husband tried to make money in the fortune-telling business, but he failed miserably and soon returned to a life of dissipation with his mistress.

Poverty constantly threatened this complicated family. The mistress' meager savings were soon exhausted, and harsh reality was forced upon these two middle-aged voluptuaries. Then one morning, people were astonished to learn that the young widow had run away. And, less than half a year later, the wayward husband was confined to bed with tuberculosis. Now they were truly destitute.

After a time, the mistress also ran away, leaving in this ravaged family only a small boy, a tuberculosis patient, the patient's senile mother, nearing ninety, and the wife, who was also entering old age. Though she worked to the very limits of her strength, it was like sprinkling drops of water on parched soil. With that tearful expression on her face, she made the rounds of every relative

6. The southernmost of the main islands, nearest Okinawa.

she knew, begging for help, but found them all in similar straits. Occasionally, they would give her twenty or thirty sen, which she spent on sweets for the boy or medicine for her husband, never thinking of herself. All her clothes were threadbare hand-me-downs from relatives, and the hems and sleeves would soon be drooping like rags until a sympathetic family member gave her another piece of cast-off clothing. Having lost all pride, she received anything they gave her with a childlike delight that had, pitifully, become second nature by now.

She boiled foreign-grown rice into gruel for her mother-in-law, her sick husband, and the boy; but for herself she cooked only a few sweet potatoes that would comprise her meals over the next five or six days. She carried the boy on her back wherever she went. When he cried for a piece of brown sugar, pressing his head against her back, she felt her heart would break. "Poor thing. Please don't cry," she would say in her faltering voice, trying to comfort him, but she only ended up bursting into tears herself. It hurt her even more to think that he had given up on real sweets and just asked for brown sugar. Yet only during the days she spent with the boy did her face, which always had that tearful look, recover the tiny trace of a smile.

It was on one of those days that her husband finally died, leaving them nothing. Fate is like a rolling stone, and only God knows where it will stop. With her husband's death, at least she felt relieved of the burden to support him. But now the boy, who, though not related to her by blood, had become her only hope in life, came down with acute intestinal fever, and her world was plunged into total darkness. Like a woman gone mad, she wandered from doctor to doctor; then, having lost her powers of reason, she went on to try any superstitious remedy anyone suggested. She even began feeding this seriously ill child huge portions of candy, hoping to make up for his past malnutrition. Yet no one could stop her from following this blind impulse, for she couldn't bear the thought of allowing him to die without eating the sweets he loved.

In the end, his death left her insane with grief. She would gaze into space like an idiot for hours at a time and walk the streets with lowered eyes, the strands of her disheveled chignon dangling down her back. The little band of music makers that marched through town one day each week to advertise the movies had once brought the boy bounding out into the dusty street, but now it came only as a dreadful reminder of him, driving her again to bitter weeping. The tearful expression on her face grew even more sorrowful, and she seemed to be struggling constantly against the lure of death.

Yet there was one person who had been utterly indifferent to all these misfortunes: my uncle's grandmother. She appeared to accept the deaths of her own son and grandson with equanimity and even grinned when her great-grandson died. The only noticeable change in her was such an enormous increase in her appetite that she would ask for breakfast again four or five minutes after finishing it.

This was the state of my uncle's "home" when he returned after his long absence.

Since my uncle hated to stay in his own house, he lodged with my family. Our home consisted only of the dilapidated store, that ten-foot yard, and a small room of six tatami mats. We could let him use the room, though, because I had gone to live in the countryside, where I worked as an elementary school teacher.

When my mother took him around to the relatives announcing his return, he was welcomed everywhere with stained, sagging tatami and chipped teacups. Each family's conversation, gloomy as the rainy season, was all about the troubles that weighed down on them. The stone hedges were crumbling, the weeds were growing, and there were too many old people in the family. Yet instead of sympathy for the miserable state of his homeland, my uncle seemed to feel only disgust. And, after less than three weeks, he abandoned it again without telling anyone that he was leaving or where he was going.

"I've already transferred my family register to X Prefecture on the mainland," he explained to someone just before he left. "In fact, nobody in Tokyo knows I'm from Ryukyu. I do a good business with prestigious companies and have lots of university graduates working for me. You have to understand that if people found out I was Ryukyuan, it would cause me all kinds of trouble. To be honest, I even lied to my wife, telling her I was going to visit Beppu City in Kyushu."

At first his relatives had been captivated by his success in life and eagerly sought his company, only to have him reject them, refusing in his disgust even to let them see him off at the pier. He'd acted as if he wanted only to slice off these creatures that clung to him like octopus legs and get away as fast as he could.

I had known neither of his return nor of his departure until I heard my mother complaining about him. Yet I could truly sympathize with my uncle, who had only finished elementary school and was struggling to keep up this pretense to protect the business he had built with his sweat and blood. As I sat in the dirty, horse-drawn wagon, which bounced and jolted me on the ride back from my mother's house to the village where I worked, I could not help reflecting on the decline of our isolated homeland, Ryukyu.

The scenery all around me at dusk evoked poignantly the essence of these islands: sweet-potato vines trailing on the craggy soil, groves of lanky sugarcane plants, rows of red pine trees, clusters of fern palms, banyan trees with their aerial roots hanging down in thick strands like an old man's beard, and the sun setting radiantly in a shimmer of deep red behind the ridge of hills. It all flowed deep into my heart like the tide that rises to fill the bay.

The sounds of the horse trotting in choppy rhythms along the road and the coachman singing in a low, wailing voice seemed perfectly suited to our homeland's decline, as did the coachman's song in Ryukyuan dialect.

Who are you blaming
with your cries, oh plover?
My heart weeps, too,
when I hear your sad song.
The moon in the sky
is the same old moon as before.
What has changed
are the hearts of men and women.

With its sorrowful strains so common in Ryukyuan lyrics, the song reminded me of a poem by Karl Busse.[7] Even our songs that aren't sad often have rhyth-

7. German poet (1872–1918).

mic chants of nonsense syllables and melodies of passionate abandon like those heard in American jazz.

Such music was probably born of the smoldering emotions in a people oppressed for hundreds of years. Yet I loved this scenery at sunset and yearned for something in myself to compare with its declining beauty.

1932

In Defense of "Memoirs of a Declining Ryukyuan Woman"[1]

The current and former presidents of the Okinawa Student Association visited the other day to denounce me for what I wrote in the June issue of *Fujin kōron*[2] and to demand an apology. I am taking this opportunity to publish a defense.

First of all, these two men insisted that I stop writing because they found my revealing portrayal of our homeland extremely embarrassing. In addition, they ordered me to apologize for my depiction of one character in the story, my uncle, so that readers would not get the mistaken impression that all Okinawan men are like him. Yet in this story I wrote neither anything distorted about my uncle nor any suggestion that all successful Okinawans are like him. So I regret that I can find no suitable words of apology to satisfy these men.

Listening to them, I sensed that they were particularly upset by one phrase I used in the story: "the Okinawan people." It annoyed them, they said, to have Okinawans put in the same category as "the Ainu people"[3] or "the Korean people," minorities with which this word is often associated in Japan. Yet are we not living in modern times? I have no sympathy for their efforts to construct racial hierarchies of Ainu, Korean, and so-called "pure Japanese," or for their desire to feel some kind of superiority by placing themselves in the "highest" category. (I know, of course, that their views are not shared by everyone.)

Their outraged claims that what I wrote "demeans" and "discriminates against" Okinawans reveal, paradoxically, their own racial prejudice toward Ainu and Koreans. I don't care whether Okinawans are identified with Ainu or with "pure Japanese" because I firmly believe that, despite superficial differences resulting from environmental conditions, we are all Asians and equal as human beings. It was in this sense that I used the word "people," and certainly not to insult the Okinawan people of whom I myself am one.

I cannot deny that I have also felt the loneliness of being Okinawan as described in this story and that, in the past, I have struggled to hide my identity. However, I now realize the futility of this effort, for the constant fear of exposure leads only to the loss of dignity and to the weakening of one's spirit. I believe that we no longer need to demean ourselves by pandering to those who are ignorant about us. Truth is our only alternative, no matter how desperately we might wish to conceal it. (At this point, I planned to give some examples of

1. Translated by Kimiko Miyagi.
2. Monthly women's magazine in which "Memoirs of a Declining Ryukyuan Woman" appeared.
3. Original inhabitants of Hokkaido and parts of northern Honshu who had been subject to assimilation campaigns since the late 19th century.

our traditional folk practices from recent publications but will refrain because I would only be denounced again for revealing too much about Okinawan customs.)

These men told me of their painstaking efforts to camouflage the manners and customs of our islands from outsiders and of their vigorous exhortations for our people to reform. Yet I do not believe that our customs that differ from those on the mainland should necessarily be despised and discarded. Since such practices have deep roots in our culture, our natural environment, and especially our economic circumstances, obviously our ancestors were not so narrow-minded as these college men of today.

The representatives of the Student Association claim that my writing damages Okinawans' prospects for jobs and marriage on the mainland, but isn't it really their own servile attitude that is damaging our prospects? In this modern age even most capitalists are well aware of the evils wrought by discrimination. These men should aim their protests at those capitalists who still discriminate against Okinawans instead of trying so hard to silence a voice from the heart of one uneducated woman.

Like mainlanders, Okinawans serve in the military and perform their other duties as citizens. So why must Okinawan men hide their origins when they marry mainland women, which prevents them from ever visiting their families again? Or why don't successful Okinawan men marry Okinawan women, who are ready to be their devoted wives, instead of chasing after mainland women who would never accept an Okinawan husband?

I want my readers to understand that I never intended to write ill of my homeland; I only wished to show the pure heart of Ryukyuans, who remain largely untainted by modern culture. I was shocked to learn that my story, written so candidly, has disturbed men who have attained such high social status. I do apologize for their hurt feelings. I can well imagine how angry they are at me, an Okinawan woman with no higher education. It is the rule in Okinawa that only men with power are supposed to express their opinions, while people without power and formal education have no alternative but to follow behind them. As long as those with power control us, we who are powerless have no hope of salvation.

I also ask readers to note that all times and places in my story have been changed to avoid embarrassing anyone who might be regarded as a model for its characters.

1932

LAO SHE

1899–1966

One of China's most influential modern writers, Lao She captures the unique character of Beijing, with its small alleyways, courtyard homes, and imperial landmarks, as well as its culture and language. He renders the dialect of the nation's capital with a faithful ear. In focusing his works on his native Beijing, Lao She depicts a once-glorious imperial city in a period of decline, suffering from the corrosive effects of modernization and taking second seat to the new center of power, the cosmopolitan Shanghai.

Lao She was born to poor parents who had migrated to Beijing from Manchuria. His father, a Manchu soldier, died when Western European forces invaded Beijing to suppress the Boxer Rebellion (1899–1901), in which Chinese nationalists had attacked foreign settlements there. Unlike many other intellectuals of the day who scorned religion, Lao She became a Christian. Later, he participated in the nationalist May Fourth Movement, which protested Chinese concessions to Japan after the First World War. He traveled abroad to teach Chinese in London and Singapore before returning to China, where he taught at a number of universities.

Lao She began his career as a writer of comic novels; the best known are *Old Zhang's Philosophy* (1926), *Two Mas* (1931), and *Divorce* (1933), in which he uses farce and melodrama to reveal social abuses. By the mid-1930s his works, exemplified by his most famous novel, *Rickshaw Boy* (1936–37), about a greenhorn who comes to Beijing full of hope and experiences one tragedy after another, turned toward the tragic. A prolific short story writer, Lao She was also a playwright, whose drama *Teahouse* (1958) is regarded as a classic. During the war with Japan (1937–45), he promoted the use of traditional "national forms" as a means of anti-Japanese propaganda. He is the author of *City of Cats* (1933), sometimes considered a work of science fiction, although it is more obviously a satirical allegory about the impending war with Japan and political infighting within China that impeded a unified response to Japanese aggression. Lao She suffered during Mao Zedong's Cultural Revolution in the mid-1960s, when Communist China turned against its artists and intellectuals. After being beaten and humiliated by Red Guards, the writer committed suicide.

"An Old and Established Name" (1936), the story here, demonstrates Lao She's use of a realistic narrative mode to depict Chinese political and social life. The Fortune Silk Store, an "old and established" firm in Beijing, suddenly changes managers from Qian to Zhou. Xin Dezhi, who has worked there for sixteen years, is appalled at the transformation toward vulgarity (promotional discounts, undignified attempts to steal business, and so on) that the store undergoes. While he eventually comes to respect Zhou for the success at reviving the old store, Xin Dezhi cannot bring himself to approve of Zhou's commercialism.

The story is an allegory for the central conflict in twentieth-century China, between modernity and tradition. As China modernized in the first half of the century, replacing its emperor with a republic (and later the

Communist People's Republic), the country grappled with a major issue: whether to embrace capitalism or cling to older values, such as the Confucian emphasis on human relations as the key to a harmonious community, and its disdain for profit as a social goal. In the story the management of the store must choose between capitalist business techniques and old-style practices; the former are effective but alienating, vulgar, and undignified; the latter, based on ethical human relations, may not be effective. Although the story presents the choice in stark terms, Lao She does not obviously side with one or the other approach; rather, he focuses on the psychological and cultural difficulty Xin Dezhi has in negotiating his way through the conflict. Few writers have depicted the clash between the contemporary and the traditional as sympathetically or with such richly observed detail as Lao She.

An Old and Established Name[1]

After Manager Qian left, Xin Dezhi—the senior apprentice who now had quite a hand in the operation of the Fortune Silk Store—went for several days without eating a decent meal. Manager Qian had been universally recognized as a skilled old hand in the silk business just as the Fortune Silk Store was universally recognized as an old and established name. Xin Dezhi had been trained for the business under the hands of Manager Qian. However, it wasn't solely personal feeling that made Xin Dezhi take it so hard when Manager Qian left, nor was his agitation due to any personal ambition that might have been stimulated by the vague possibility that he himself might become the new manager. He really couldn't put his finger on the reason for all the anxiety that he felt; it was as though Manager Qian had taken away with him something or other that would be forever difficult to recover.

When Manager Zhou arrived to take things over, Xin Dezhi realized that his anxiety had not been unfounded. Previously he had only felt *sorrow* at the departure of the old manager, but now he felt downright *fury* at the arrival of the new one. Manager Zhou was a hustler. The Fortune Silk Store—an old and established name of years standing!—now demeaned itself into employing every kind of trick to rope in customers. Xin Dezhi's mouth hung so far open in dismay that his face began to look like a dumpling that had split apart while boiling. An old hand, an old and established name, old rules—all had vanished along with Manager Qian, perhaps never to return again. Manager Qian had been very honest and gentlemanly, so much so, in fact, that the Fortune Silk Store lost money. The owners, for their part, weren't all that impressed by Manager Qian's upright demeanor; they were only concerned with having dividends to split up at the end of the year. Hence, they had let him go.

For as long as anyone could remember, the Fortune Silk Store had maintained an air of cultured elegance—a simple sign with the name of the store in black characters against a gold background, green fittings in the shop itself, a black counter with blue cloth cover, large square stools sheathed in blue woolen cloth, and fresh flowers always set out on the tea table. For as long as anyone could remember, except for hanging out four lanterns with big red

1. Translated by William A. Lyell.

tassels upon the occasion of the Lantern Festival,[2] the Fortune Silk Store had never exhibited a trace of that vulgar ostentation so prevalent among ordinary merchants. For as long as anyone could remember, the Fortune had never engaged in such base practices as haggling with customers, letting the customer pay to the nearest dollar, pasting advertisements all over the place, or running two-week sales. What the Fortune Silk Store sold was its old and established name. For as long as anyone could remember, the Fortune had never set free cigarettes out on the counter as a come-on to customers; nor had any of the apprentices in the shop ever spoken in loud tones; the only sound in the store had been the gentle gurgle of the manager's water pipe intermingled with his occasional coughing.

As soon as Manager Zhou walked through the door, Xin Dezhi saw only too clearly that these precedents, as well as many other old and valuable customs, were all going to come to an end. There was something improper about the new manager's eyes. He never lowered his eyelids, but rather swept the whole world with his vision as if he were searching out a thief. Manager Qian, on the other hand, had always sat on a stool with his eyes closed, and yet if any of the apprentices did the slightest thing wrong, he knew about it immediately.

Just as Xin Dezhi had feared, within a few days Manager Zhou had transformed the Fortune into something akin to a carnival sideshow. In front of the main entrance the new manager set up a garish sign bearing the words GIANT SALE. Each word was five feet square! Then he installed two bright gaslights whose flames lit up faces in such a way as to turn them green. As if all this weren't enough, he had a drum and bugle set up by the main entrance, which made a din from dawn until the third watch at night. Four apprentices in red hats stood at the door and roamed up and down the sidewalk passing out handbills to anyone who came within their reach.

But Manager Zhou still wasn't satisfied. He appointed two clerks to the specific task of providing customers with cigarettes and tea; even someone who was buying only half a foot of plain cloth would be dragged to the back counter and given a cigarette. Soldiers, street-cleaners, and waitresses stood about firing up their tobacco until the shop was so smoked up that it looked like a Buddhist temple lost in incense fumes.[3] Manager Zhou even went a step further; if a customer bought one foot of material, he'd give him an extra one free and throw in a foreign doll for the kids. And now all the apprentices were expected to joke and make small talk with the customers. If the customer wanted something that the store didn't have, then the apprentice wasn't to tell him right out that the store didn't have it, but was rather expected to drag out something else and force the customer to take a look at it. Any order over ten dollars would be delivered by one of the apprentices, and Manager Zhou bought two broken-down bicycles for that purpose.

Xin Dezhi longed to find some place where he could have a good cry. In fifteen or sixteen years of faithful service he had never even imagined (much less expected to see) the Fortune Silk Store coming to such a pass. How could he look people in the face? In the past who on the whole street had not held the Fortune Silk Store in great respect? When an apprentice hung out the lantern

2. A festival marking the first full moon of the lunar new year.

3. Buddhists burn sticks of incense as part of their devotions.

which served as the store's sign at night, even the policemen on the beat would treat him with special regard. And remember that year when the soldiers came![4] To be sure, during the pillaging, the Fortune had been cleaned out just like the other stores, but the doors and the signs saying *We Never Go Back on Our Prices* had not been torn away, as had been the case with some of the neighboring shops. Yes, that golden plaque bearing the inscription *Fortune Silk Store* had a certain awe-inspiring dignity about it.

Xin Dezhi had already lived in the city now for twenty-some years and fifteen or sixteen of them had been spent in the Fortune. In fact, it was his second home. His way of speaking, his very cough, and the style of his long blue gown had all been given to him by the Fortune Silk Store. The store had given him his personal pride and he, in turn, was proud of the store. Whenever he went out to collect bills, people would invite him in for a cup of tea. For although the store was a business, it treated its steady customers as friends. Often Manager Qian would even participate in the weddings and funerals of his regular customers. The Fortune Silk Store was a business conducted with "gentlemanly style." The more prestigious people in the neighborhood could often be found sitting and chatting on the bench in front of the main entrance. Whenever there were parades or any lively doings on the streets, the women in his customers' families would contact Manager Qian and he would arrange good seats at his store from which they could observe all of the excitement. This past glorious history of the shop was ever in Xin Dezhi's heart. And now?

It wasn't that he didn't know that the times had changed. For instance, a number of old and established shops on both sides of the Fortune had already tossed their rules to the winds (the newer shops were not worth worrying about because they had never had any traditions to begin with). He realized all this. But it was precisely because the Fortune had remained doggedly faithful to its traditions that he loved it all the more, was all the more proud of it. It was as though the Fortune Silk Store were the only bolt of real silk in a pile of synthetics. If even the Fortune hit the skids, then the world would surely come to an end. Damn! He had to admit it—now the Fortune was just like all the others, if not worse.

In the past, his favorite object of contempt had always been the Village Silk Shop across the street. The manager over there was always shuffling around with a cigarette dangling from lips that occasionally opened wide enough to reveal gold-capped front teeth. The manager's wife was forever carrying little children on her back, in her arms, and seemingly even in her pockets. She scurried in and out of the shop all day clucking and cackling in a southern dialect so that Xin Dezhi couldn't make out what she was jabbering about. When the couple had a good spat, they always picked the shop to have it in; when they beat the children or breast-fed a baby, they always picked the shop to do it in. You couldn't tell whether they were doing business or putting on a circus over there. However, one thing was certain: the manager's wife had her breasts forever on display in the shop with a baby or two hanging from them. He had no idea as to where in the world they had dug up the clerks that worked

4. Soldiers might have pillaged the store during conflicts between Chinese Communists and Nationalists in 1925 or during the Nationalist takeover of Beijing in 1927, at the beginning of a decade of civil war.

there. They all wore shoddy shoes, but for the most part dressed in silk. Some of them had Sun-Brand Headache Salve plastered conspicuously on their temples; some had their hair so slicked down that the tops of their heads looked like the bottoms of large lacquerware spoons; and some of them wore gold-rimmed glasses. Besides all these specifics, the place had a generally contemptible air about it: they had GIANT SALES from one end of the year to the other; they always had gaudy gaslights hung out in front of the store; and they were forever playing a phonograph full blast in order to attract business. Whenever a customer bought two dollars' worth of goods, the manager would, with his own hands, offer him a sweet sesame cake; if the customer didn't accept it, he might even shove it right into his mouth. Nothing in the shop had a fixed price and the rate of exchange that was given for foreign currency often fluctuated. Xin Dezhi had never deigned to look directly at the three words on the shop's sign; moreover, he had never gone over there to buy anything. He had never imagined that such a business firm could even exist on this earth, much less have the nerve to be located right across the street from the Fortune Silk Store! But strange to say, the Village Silk Shop had prospered, while the Fortune had gone downhill day after day. He hadn't been able to figure out what the reason was. It certainly couldn't be that there was an inexorable law that required that a business be run completely divorced from any code of ethics before it could make money. If this were really the case, then why should stores bother to train apprentices? Couldn't any old lout do business just as long as he were alive and kicking? It couldn't be this way! It just couldn't! At least he had always been sure that the Fortune would never be like that.

How could he have foreseen that after Manager Zhou's arrival, his beloved Fortune would also hang out gaslights so that its lights combined with those of the Village Silk Shop lit up more than half the block? Yes, they were two of a kind now! The Fortune and the Village a pair!—he must be dreaming! But it wasn't a dream and even Xin Dezhi had to learn to do things in Manager Zhou's way. He had to chitchat with the customers, offer them cigarettes, and then inveigle them into going to the back counter for a cup of tea. He was forced to haul out ersatz goods and pass them off as genuine; he had to learn to wait until a customer became insistent before giving him an honest length of material. He had to learn tricks to be employed in measuring the cloth—he was even expected to use his finger on the sly to pinch back a bit of the cloth before cutting it! How much more could he take?

But most of the apprentices seemed happy with doing things the new way. If a woman came in, it was all they could do to keep themselves from completely surrounding her; they just itched to haul out every piece of goods in the store for her inspection. Even if she bought only two feet of dust-cloth it was all they could do to keep themselves from escorting her home. The manager loved this kind of thing. He wanted to see the clerks turn head over heels and do acrobatics when the customers came in; he would have liked it even better if they had been able to fly around the customers in midair.

Manager Zhou and the boss of the Village Silk Shop became fast friends. Sometimes the two of them would even make up a foursome with the people from the Heaven Silk Store and have a round of mahjong. The Heaven was another silk store on the same street that had been in business now for four or five years. In times gone by, Manager Qian had always ignored the Heaven;

hence the Heaven had made it a point to go into direct competition with the Fortune and even boasted that they wouldn't be satisfied until they had put it out of business. Manager Qian had never picked up the gauntlet, but occasionally he used to observe: "We do business on our old and established name." The Heaven was the kind of store that had a Giant Anniversary Sale three hundred and sixty-five days a year. And now even the people from the Heaven were coming over to play mahjong! When they did, Xin Dezhi, of course, utterly ignored them.

Whenever he had a little spare time, he would sit behind the counter and stare vacantly at the racks of materials. Originally all the goods on the racks had been covered up with white cloth. Now, ceiling to floor, all the rolls of material were exposed to full view in all their varied colors so that they might serve as an attraction to the customers. It was such a dazzling sight that it made one's eyes blur just to look at it. In his heart, Xin Dezhi knew that the Fortune Silk Store had already ceased to exist. And yet, after the first business third[5] had passed, he could not help but admire Manager Zhou. Because when it came time to balance the books, although Zhou hadn't made a great deal of money, yet he hadn't lost any either. He had pulled the Fortune out of the red. Manager Zhou smiled at everyone and explained: "You have to bear in mind that this is only my first third. I still have a lot of plans up my sleeve for the future that I haven't even tried yet. Furthermore, think of my initial outlay in advertising displays and gas lights. All of that took money, you know. So . . ." (Whenever he felt full of himself in conversation, he'd take a *so* . . . and tack it on the end of whatever he was saying.) "Later on we won't even have to use those advertising displays. We'll have newer and more economical ways of making ourselves known. Then there'll be a profit to show. So. . ." Xin Dezhi could plainly see that there was no turning back for Manager Zhou. The world had really changed. After all, Manager Zhou was on very good terms with people from the Heaven and the Village, and both of those businesses had prospered.

Just after the books were balanced, there was a great deal of commotion in town about searching out and boycotting Japanese goods.[6] And yet, as if possessed, Manager Zhou started laying in all the Japanese goods he could get his hands on, and even though student investigating teams were already on the streets, he displayed Japanese goods right out in the open. Then he issued an order: "When a customer comes in, show him the Japanese goods first. None of the other places dare to sell them, so we might as well make hay while the sun shines. If a farmer comes in, tell him straight out that it is Japanese cloth; they'll buy it anyway. But if someone from the city comes in, then say it's German material."

When the investigating students[7] arrived, Manager Zhou's face butterflied into smiles as he offered them cigarettes and tea. "The Fortune Silk Store swears by its good name that it will not sell Japanese goods. Look over there, gentlemen. Those goods by the door are German materials along with some

5. The books in Chinese shops are balanced every four months.
6. Chinese Nationalists frequently proposed boycotts of Japanese goods, particularly after Japanese troops, which had occupied portions of northern China, came into conflict with the Nationalists. The full-scale Sino-Japanese War broke out in 1937, the year after this story was written.
7. Nationalist students who are enforcing the boycott.

local products. Inside the store we have nothing but Chinese silks and satins. Our branch store in the south sends them up to us."

The students began to eye some of the printed materials with suspicion. Manager Zhou smiled and shouted, "Bring me that piece of leftover Japanese material that we have in back." When the cloth had been brought to him, he grabbed the leader of the investigating students by the sleeve and said, "Sir, I swear that this is the only piece of Japanese goods that we have left. It's the same material that the shirt you're wearing is made from. So . . ." He turned his head around and ordered, "All right, let's throw this piece of Japanese material out into the street." The leader of the investigating students looked at his own shirt and, not daring to raise his head, led the rest of the students out the door.

Manager Zhou made quite a bit of money from these Japanese materials, which could at any time turn into German, Chinese, or English goods. If a customer who knew his materials threw a piece of goods right down on the floor in front of Manager Zhou's face, the latter would issue an order to one of the apprentices: "Bring out the *real* Western goods. Can't you tell we have an intelligent man here who knows his materials?" Then he'd say to the customer: "You know what you want. You wouldn't take that even if I gave it to you free! So . . ." Thus he'd tie up another sale. By the time that the whole transaction was completed, it would be all the customer could do to tear himself away from the congenial company of Manager Zhou. Xin Dezhi came to the realization that if you plan to make money in business, you have to be a combination magician and burlesque comedian. Manager Zhou was really something, all right. And yet, Xin Dezhi didn't feel like working at the Fortune anymore. For the more he came to admire Manager Zhou, the worse he felt. Lately even his food all seemed to go down the wrong way. If he were ever again to enjoy a good night's sleep, he would have to leave his beloved Fortune Silk Store.

But before he had found a good position someplace else, Manager Zhou left. The Heaven Silk Store had need of just such talents, and Manager Zhou himself was anxious to make the change: he felt that the stick-in-the-mud traditions of the Fortune were so deeply rooted that he would never really be able to display his talents fully here.

When Xin Dezhi saw Manager Zhou off, it was as though he were seeing away a great burden that had been pressing on his heart. On the basis of his fifteen or sixteen years of service, Xin Dezhi felt that he had the right to talk things over with the owners of the store, although he could not be sure that his words would carry any real weight. However, he did know which of them were basically conservative and had a good idea as to how to influence them. He began to propagandize for Manager Qian's return and even got Qian's old friends to help. He didn't say that everything that Manager Qian had done was right, but would merely observe that each of the two managers had his good points and that these points ought to be combined harmoniously. One could not rigidly stick to old customs, but neither would it do to change too radically. An old and established name was worth preserving, but new business methods ought also be studied and applied. One ought to lay equal emphasis upon preserving the name *and* making a profit—he knew that this line of argument would be potent in persuading the owners.

But in his heart of hearts, he really had something quite different in mind. He hoped that when Manager Qian returned, everything that had been lost would come back with him and the Fortune Silk Store would once again be the *old* Fortune Silk Store; otherwise, as far as he was concerned, it would be nothing. He had it all figured out: they would get rid of the gaslights, the drum and bugle, the advertisements, handbills, and cigarettes; they would cut down on personnel as much as possible, and thus possibly save quite a bit on operating expenses. Moreover, without advertising the fact, they would sell low,[8] use a long foot in measuring, and stock honest-to-goodness materials. Could the customers all be such asses that they wouldn't see the advantages of doing business at the Fortune?

And in the end Manager Qian actually did return. Now the only gaslights left on the street were those of the Village Silk Shop. The Fortune had recovered its former air of austere simplicity—although, in order to welcome Manager Qian back, they had gone so far as to hang out four lanterns decorated with tassels.

The day that the Fortune put out its lanterns of welcome, two camels appeared before the door of the Heaven Silk Store. The camels' bodies were completely draped in satin sash, and flashing, colored electric lights were installed on the humps. On both sides of the camels, stands were set up to sell chances at ten cents each. Whenever at least ten people had bought tickets, a drawing would be held. If lucky, one had hopes of winning a fashionable piece of silk. With this sort of thing going on the area around the Heaven Silk Store soon became something of a country fair, so crowded you could scarcely budge in the press. Because, you see, it *was* true that every once in a while somebody really *did* emerge from the crowd, all smiles, with a piece of fashionable silk tucked under his arm.

Once again the bench in front of the Fortune was covered with a piece of blue woolen cloth. Once again Manager Qian sat within the shop, eyelids drooping. Once again the clerks sat quietly behind the counters. Some of them toyed quietly with the beads of an abacus; others yawned leisurely. Xin Dezhi didn't say anything, but in his heart he was really worried. Sometimes it would seem ages and ages before a single customer appeared. Occasionally someone would glance in from the outside as if he were about to enter, but then he would glance at the small golden plaque and head over in the direction of the Heaven Silk Store. Sometimes a customer would actually come in and look at materials, but upon discovering that one couldn't bargain over the price, would walk out again empty-handed. There were still a few of the old reliables who came regularly to buy a little something or other, but sometimes they merely stopped by to have a chat with Manager Qian. They'd usually sigh a bit over the poverty of the times, have a few cups of tea, and then leave without buying anything. Xin Dezhi loved to listen to them talk, for it would remind him of the good times the store had once known in the past. But even he knew that the past cannot be easily recovered. The Heaven Silk Store was the only one on the whole street that was really doing any business.

At the end of a season, the Fortune had to cut back again on personnel. With tears in his eyes, Xin Dezhi told Manager Qian: "I can do five clerks' work all by myself. What's there to worry about?" Manager Qian took courage and chimed in: "What do we have to be afraid of?" And that night Xin Dezhi

8. At reasonable prices.

slept a very sweet sleep, fully prepared to do the work of five clerks on the very next day.

Yet after a year, the Fortune Silk Store was bought out by the Heaven.

1936

CH'AE MAN-SIK

1902–1950

A master storyteller, Ch'ae Man-sik took his material from everyday life but blended the sardonic wit and humor of traditional oral narratives with a skillful use of irony and unreliable narrators to create some of the most memorable, innovative stories in Korean literature.

Ch'ae Man-sik was born into a wealthy farming family in Chŏlla Province, Korea. Like many of his generation, he attended schools in both Korea and Japan. Ch'ae's study at Japan's Waseda University was interrupted by the Great Kantō Earthquake of 1923; he returned home and began working as a newspaper reporter. Although Ch'ae published a number of short stories in the 1920s, it was his satirical stories of the mid-1930s that first brought him literary fame. Ch'ae had a gift for exposing the contradictions of contemporary colonial Korean society, particularly those embodied in the nouveau riche, as seen in his masterpiece *Peace Under Heaven* (1938), a novel that lays bare the foibles of a wealthy family in the late 1930s and the accommodations its members make to colonial rule. He published many short stories, novels, essays, and plays in the period of Japanese rule, as well as in the tumultuous period immediately following Korea's liberation in 1945.

Japan had ruled Korea as a colony since 1910. Following the March 1, 1919, Movement, in which millions of Koreans demonstrated against Japan, restrictions on publication permits were eased; soon Korean newspapers and journals were flourishing. From the early 1920s onward, a native literary scene emerged: leftist literature, especially, rose to prominence, with the literati embroiled in contentious debates between an internationalist working-class movement (the Korean Artists Proletarian Federation, or KAPF) and a cultural nationalist movement. While working as a reporter in 1920s' Seoul, Ch'ae became familiar with the debates, finding himself at once concerned with the plight of the poor and intrigued by the emergence of an urban middle and upper class. In many of his stories, the latter would serve as the target of satire.

In the mid-1930s a new literary movement, modernism, emerged. Its writers diverged from both the KAPF and the cultural nationalists by calling attention to literary form and by portraying the fragmentation and alienation of urban life. The Seoul cityscape had been dramatically transformed by this time, and Ch'ae, while not himself a modernist, was influenced by attempts to depict the changing society. Nonetheless, as a writer, Ch'ae charted a stubbornly independent course; and while he has sometimes been described as sympathetic to the proletarian camp, he was never a member of any literary group, including KAPF. Ch'ae is, in fact, one of the few colonial writers to cross post-1945 Cold War borders, appearing in anthologies of twentieth-century Korean literature published in both North and South Korea.

By the time Ch'ae wrote "My Innocent Uncle," the story presented here, in 1938, Japan was becoming increasingly militarist. It had invaded Manchuria in 1931 and escalated to full-scale war with China in 1937. In Korea the Japanese colonial state was intensifying its repression of artists and writers. KAPF was forcibly disbanded in 1935, and many leftist authors were jailed and later forced to recant their views. Even the modernists were suppressed, with one of the greatest of that group, Yi Sang, jailed in 1936; he would die shortly afterward in a Japanese prison. In the late 1930s and early 1940s, as the colonial state stepped up its enforcement of Japanese-language–only policies in Korea, writers were having more and more difficulty in publishing in their native language. It is in this context that "My Innocent Uncle" appeared.

To avoid censorship, while Japan was mobilizing its colonies to participate in the war effort, Ch'ae and other writers had to tread lightly by avoiding overt social commentary. "My Innocent Uncle" makes brilliant use of irony and an unreliable narrator—a young man fully assimilated as an imperial Japanese subject—to slyly but subtly expose the workings of colonial rule, particularly its impact on a younger generation of Koreans who have grown up under the empire, openly criticizing the Japanese administration. Meanwhile, through his portrayal of the narrator's left-leaning uncle, imprisoned for many years by the state, Ch'ae casts an ambivalent glance, both sympathetic and critical, at the possibilities socialism holds for anticolonial resistance. The long dialogue between the narrator and his uncle questions the narrator's naive belief in the benefits of Japanese rule even as it undercuts the uncle's adherence to proletarian ideals. With its cutting examination of everyday life in twentieth-century colonial society, "My Innocent Uncle" stands as one of the masterpieces of Korean literature and the global literatures of colonialism.

My Innocent Uncle[1]

My uncle? You mean that fine gentleman who married my father's cousin, the man they put in jail when he was younger on account of that darned socialism, or scotchalism, or whatever you call it, the one who's laid up with tuberculosis?

Don't get me started on him. It's beyond me how a man like that can . . . Brother!

He's got himself a fine row to hoe!

Sure, he had all those years of schooling, college too, but what's he got to show for it? He idled away his shining youth, his reputation's ruined because he's an ex-con, god-awful disease inside him, stretched out eyes shut night and day year round in a tiny rented room that's dark as a cave.

A house? Land of his own? No way! He's so poor you could wave a three-fathom stick around him and not a straw would catch on it.

1. Translated from Korean by Bruce Fulton and Ju-Chan Fulton.

Thank God for my aunt. She's so kind and gentle. She does piecework sewing, goes to other people's houses and does their wash, sells cosmetics—all so she can serve her dear husband. But what she makes from such miserable work is barely enough for them to scrape by.

However you look at it, the gentleman would be better off dead. But no, he's not about to die off.

My poor aunt. She should have turned her life around when she was younger. God only knows why she puts up with these troubles—must be she's hoping that after all the damned suffering she's gone through she'll have better luck later on.

She's been neglected by him going on twenty years now.

Sighed away twenty years of her sorrowful youth, and now it's too late. She sits at the bedside of that living corpse, caring for that fine gentleman just because he's her husband, wearing herself out going around trying to make a living—it's just plain pathetic.

And what did she do to deserve it? Everybody talks about fate—well, why don't they do something about it? Old-fashioned Chosŏn women![2] When are they going to wise up?

My aunt would be a lot better off if that fine gentleman would just up and die.

She's good-hearted and has a nice touch at what she sets her hand to, and I imagine she could take care of herself and live comfortably just about anywhere.

Let's see, she says she got married when she was sixteen, and that's when I was three, which means it's been a good eighteen years she's been neglected. Well, eighteen years, twenty—what's the difference?

My uncle was young when they got married and he spent a good ten years knocking around Seoul and Tokyo—"studying," you know—and when he was grown up enough to develop a taste for women he asked my aunt for a divorce, sent her packing to her family, and turned his back on her. . . . How generous of him.

No sooner did he finish his studies and come home than he went nuts over that damned scotchalism and got himself another woman, one of those "educated women," you know? I've seen her a few times and that puss of hers is not about to catch anyone's attention. Beats me how a woman who looks like that can be someone's mistress. They say pretty women are jilted but ugly women aren't, and it's a fact that if you stack up my aunt against that woman, then my aunt is prettier by a long shot.

Well, eventually that fine gentleman got nailed by the police and was a jailbird for five years. During that time my aunt's family and her in-laws were completely ruined and she had no one to depend on.

What was she supposed to do? It was just a matter of time till she starved.

Well, she ended up with me, though she said she didn't much like the idea, but she needed someone to provide for her, and she had to wait for Uncle's release, and I was the only one she had in Seoul. That was—let me see—the year before Uncle got out.

2. Chosŏn was the name used for Korea during the Japanese colonial period (1910–45).

I was just a kid then, but I played all the angles right and soon I had myself a job at Mr. Kurada's.

I wish I could count all the times I told my aunt she ought to remarry. Even to a young guy like me, it was pitiful and embarrassing to see her like this.

While all this was happening a better opportunity came my way. I knew a man named Mr. Mine who sold bananas cheap in front of the Mitsukoshi Department Store,[3] and he was a good person all right. My Japanese boss knew him well, too. This Mr. Mine was always telling me he'd like to live with a "Chosŏn *okam*,"[4] and he kept asking me to fix him up.

Mr. Mine didn't have much in the way of savings, but he was capable of supporting a family. And so I asked my aunt if she wouldn't be more comfortable living with such a person. I asked her more than that, but darned if she didn't turn a deaf ear and tell me to stop coming out with such unseemly talk.

That aside, I've done more than my fair share behind the scenes to take care of Aunt, right up to the present day, and that's no lie. Besides, I was kind of obligated to her.

You see, when I was seven I lost my parents. I had no place to go, but fortunately my aunt took me in and brought me up. This was after my uncle turned her loose and she went back to live with her parents.

Because back then, at least, they weren't so hard up. My aunt thought I was the most precious thing, but so did my great-aunt and great-uncle—they didn't have any other children.

I lived there till I was twelve.

Went through fourth grade, too.

Who knows, maybe if those three hadn't had such sour luck I'd have stuck around and maybe I'd be in college now.

I didn't forget that obligation, but I reckon I've paid it off.

Still, my aunt comes by from time to time and tells me she's bad off, out of food. To be honest, I find it kind of aggravating.

If I cave in to her every time, how am I supposed to get on with my life? So most times I just tell her flat out no.

But there are times, Western New Year for example, when the least I can do is send her a pound of meat, or else drop by her place for a chat—things like that.

In any event, for one whole year my aunt worked as a maid for Mr. Kurada's family and got five *wŏn* a month.[5] That's not much, but she managed to save it all, and in her spare time she took in sewing and earned a little money on the side, and by the time she left the Kuradas, the mister and missus were impressed enough with her to give her a seven-*wŏn* bonus, and in these various ways she put together close to a hundred *wŏn*.

With that money she took out a small room and bought a few household items, and then it happened that her dear former hubby-poo was set free and she took him in.

I went with Aunt the day he was let out, and—I can hardly believe this myself—the moment he came out from his cage the sight of her waiting for him brought tears to my eyes.

3. The Seoul branch of a Japanese chain, opened in 1930.

4. Woman (Japanese).

5. About $1 at the time.

And that bitch of a mistress he used to dote on—you suppose she showed her mug? Hell, no. What do you expect? They're all like that.

My uncle looked every which way, wondering if the other woman had come. That's how little sense he has. There was no woman, not even her shadow—just Aunt and me.

As he climbed into the taxi he spit up blood. Seems he started doing that about a month and a half ago in his cage.

After the taxi dropped us off we practically had to carry him piggyback the rest of the way home, the guy being half dead and all. But from the moment we laid him down inside, Aunt looked after him around the clock, and what with all her bustling and attentiveness he showed a gradual improvement until now he's got his life back. What a makeover, I'll tell you—like a toad turning into a dragon!

You can never underestimate a wife's devotion.

And that's the way it's been for a good three years now. But if someone had said to me, "Be nice to your uncle and I'll bring your parents back to life," I would have said, "No thanks!"

And now, you know what? If that fine gentleman my uncle had any kind of a conscience, don't you think he'd say to himself, "Well now, I ought to get myself back into condition real quick, make me some money fast, make my wife nice and comfortable, and repay her for all she's done for me, to atone for my sins"?

Thing is, he won't ever be able to make it up to her, even if he carried her around on his back all day long so her feet wouldn't get dirty.

It's time for him to come to his senses. Whatever it takes. And if he can't get a government job or work for a company because of his prison record, well, he's got no one to blame except himself, so he ought to roll up his sleeves and do some manual labor—that's the least he could do.

Now that would be worth seeing—a college graduate doing drudge work. But what else can he do, you know?

All of which makes me shudder to think what might have happened if my great-uncle's family hadn't gone under and I'd graduated from technical school or college and ended up like my uncle. Good thing I went the way I'm going now, without spending all that time studying.

Fact is, that fine gentleman with all his education, the best he can do now is day labor. Look at me, though—I barely made it through fourth grade but my future's bright. Compared with me, he's worse than an errand boy.

But drudge work's the last thing on his mind. Now that he's showing some signs of life, you wouldn't believe the nonsense that fine gentleman's cooking up.

That damned scotchalism is his worst enemy, and yet he can't give it up. He's nuts about it.

Is it supposed to put food on your table? Is it supposed to make you famous? Or maybe in the end it just makes a jailbird out of you.

Damned scotchalism, it's just like opium. Once you get a taste of it you're hooked.

But once you figure out what it really is, it's not very exciting, not much flavor to it. The ones who do it are a bunch of crooks. A bunch of crooks up to no good.

Now somewhere in the West, some lazybones who didn't like to work got together in a nice sunny place and figured out ways to goof around and still make a living. My landlord gave me a detailed explanation.

"What it is, these rascals get together and debate. One of 'em will say, 'Well, in this world there are rich people and poor people, and it's just not fair. Everyone's born with eyes, a nose, a mouth, and a throat, and with two arms and two legs, and yet this person is rich and lives well and that person is poor—what kind of nonsense is that? It's only right that the rich ought to share and share alike with us poor folks.'

"And someone else says, 'Yeah, that's the ticket! Yeah, that's telling 'em! Share and share alike.'"

Hey now, that's a pretty persuasive message. I'll bet it gets a lot of people worked up.

With that kind of nonsense you can see why I think those people are out-and-out crooks.

Some people get rich because they're born in the right place at the right time, or else they work hard. And some people are poor because they were born in the wrong place at the wrong time, or else they're lazy. That's the way things are—the way the world turns. Where do people get off saying it's unfair? Those that figure on stealing what's someone else's are crooks pure and simple.

But it's more than that. If those crooks make good on what they say, then the lazybones will only get lazier; they'll take what belongs to the rich folks and live off that, and then the world will be full of thieves. Tell me, though—what happens when the rich people have had everything taken away from them and there's nothing more to eat? It's doomsday, that's what.

If farmers sit around doing nothing and rob what other farmers have harvested, and if weavers sit around doing nothing and rob what other weavers have woven, then where's the grain and fabric supposed to come from? The world's doomed!

And you know darn well they don't realize that damned scotchalism's sending the world to ruin. Some of those poverty-stricken suckers—the lazy ones that don't like to work—got blinded right off the bat by the idea of robbing what they need from the rich, and then every Yi, Kim, and Pak of 'em joined in.

That's exactly what happened to the Russkies.

You want to know how? Simple: the farmers stopped producing grain and tens of thousands of people are starving to death. Well, any fool could have predicted that.

What did they expect! That's what happens when people go *yippie!* thinking they got themselves a quick fix.

Heck—in no time those worthless practices spread practically around the world, made waves in the home country too. Then a bunch of Chosŏn guys who don't know any better got carried away and tried to jump on the bandwagon.

But now it's strictly prohibited here, so it's been pretty much reined in and there's hardly anyone left who's committed to it.

And I say well done. If it's such a great thing, then tell me, why is it prohibited here and why do those fellows get pinched and locked up as if they're mortal enemies of the state?

If it's good and beneficial, then of course the government's going to promote it. And if you do well at it you'll get an award, right?[6]

Take motion pictures; sumo wrestling; comedy shows; Japanese festivals; the All Souls ceremony; doing calisthenics to the radio, things like that—all of them are beneficial and so they're encouraged by the government, right?

6. An award from the Japanese colonial government in Korea.

What's a government for, anyway? Well, it tells us what's good and bad and what's right and wrong, and it directs us to do this or that, and so it tries to help each of us live comfortably according to our lot.

Now what would happen if their damned scotchalism wasn't prohibited and they could do whatever they wanted? Can you imagine the state of the world now?

I'll bet a lot of people have gotten screwed over. Good thing it didn't happen to me. I can just imagine everything getting totally messed up.

Now here's my idea. My boss has taken a shine to me, and because he trusts me it looks like in just ten years or so he'll stake me a considerable amount of money and set me up in a different business. Based on that, in just thirty years' time, when I've reached the big six-oh, I'll have put together a good hundred thousand *wŏn* from my business. With that much money I'll be as rich as a thousand-sack-of-rice-a-year man—that's rich even by Chosŏn standards. I'll be living high on the hog and you better believe it.

And there's something else my boss said. You see, I'm going to take a young lady from the home country for my wife. My boss said he'd take care of everything—he'll pick out a nice, well-behaved one and fix me up with her. Women from the home country[7] sure are swell.

Me, I wouldn't take a Chosŏn woman if you *gave* me one.

The old-fashioned ones, even though they're well behaved, are ignorant, and people from the home country won't keep company with them. And the modern ones are all full of themselves just because they've had some schooling, so they won't do. So, old-fashioned, modern, doesn't matter—when it comes to Chosŏn women, forget it!

A wife from the home country—that's only for starters. I'll change my name to home-country style, same with house, clothes, food, I'll give my children Japanese names and send them to a Japanese school here.

Japanese schools, they're the thing. Chosŏn schools are dirty—just perfect for turning out rotten kids.

And I'm going to kiss the Chosŏn language goodbye and use only the national language.

Because once I've taken up home-country manners I'll be able to put together a lot of money, just like a home-country man.

That's my plan, and a road's going to open wide to me. At the end of that road I'll be a two-hundred-thousand-*wŏn* rich man, and I'm working hard to follow that road. Heck, is it any wonder I get the creeps from those bloodthirsty lunatic scotchalists who are going to be the ruin of the world? It's awful just to hear about them.

What do you expect me to do about something that's going to screw up the world? All my efforts'll go down the drain. And you call that justice?

You know, everything my boss says makes sense.

If you figure that common theft, extortion, or swindling is a form of robbery, then the only thing you lose is money, so these aren't such serious crimes. But that damned scotchalism or whatever you call it is going to mess up the world and throw the whole country into chaos—it's simply unforgivable, he said.

Forgiveness! If it was me, I'd sweep up the whole lot of 'em and show 'em no mercy. . . .

7. Japan.

Frankly, when I think about this, that fine gentleman my uncle is a very wicked man. You think I'd visit him if it wasn't for my aunt? No I wouldn't, even if he didn't have that bad disease—I'm no Catholic, you know. And I'm not about to get choked up when he dies.

It would be one thing if he'd repented for his sins and washed his dirty mind clean, but he'll always be like that—can't expect a tiger to change his stripes.

He really gets my dander up, and the occasional times I drop by, if I happen to be sitting across from him I'll make a point of attacking him with spiteful words; I'll pick on something he says and drive him into a corner.

I sure taught him a lesson last time. But get a load of what he told my aunt afterward: that rascal—meaning me—has fallen into bad habits and gone completely bad and turned into a good-for-nothing!

Brother! To hear that made me speechless!

People sure are different, but where does he get off saying I've gone bad and turned into a good-for-nothing! You could give that gentleman ten mouths and still he'd come up with something like that!

If I was him I'd wait until all the mutes of Chosŏn could talk before I said a word. He must think that what he says actually makes sense!

So that's his excuse for a lecture, huh? I'll bet he figured that if he told me that to my face I'd turn the tables on him and give him a hard time, so he decided to be sly about it and go through my aunt instead.

Amazing, isn't it? Good thing God made people's noses with two holes, so we can snort at stuff like that!

So what if I didn't get nice and educated like him? So what if I bounced around running errands and working as a clerk? I may not look like much, but I've gotten two commendations for being a model worker, and people praise me to the skies, saying I'm intelligent, skillful, and well mannered. I'm a young man with a bright, shining future, and in his eyes I've turned into a good-for-nothing rascal?

Yeah, right! Let me see if I've got this straight. He's saying that since he's right in what he does, then I'm all wrong?

And so if I was like him and got involved in that damned scotchalism and dropped dead, or became a jailbird and an ex-con and got tuberculosis, then I could practically say I didn't go bad and didn't turn into a good-for-nothing!

Huh! The very idea . . .

There's a saying that the man who doesn't know his rear end stinks blames others, and guess which fine gentleman that seems to fit?

And in fact that's how it was the day I taught him a lesson and then he said those things to my aunt.

It happened to be my day off, and I had something to talk about with my aunt, so I dropped by, but my aunt had left to do some sewing for a wedding. That fine gentleman my uncle was the only one home, and as usual he had found his way to the warm spot on the heated floor to lie down.

I found him thumbing through a big stack of Korean-language magazines he dug up from God knows where.

Well, just for fun I picked up one myself and started poking through it, but it was pretty dull stuff.

For the life of me I wish I knew why every magazine that Chosŏn people put out is like that one. No pictures, no comics. And they've all got those complicated Chinese characters stuck in there—who are they supposed to be for anyway?[8] Plus, for guys like us, even when you wade through the Korean in there, it's god-awful difficult to understand.

So when they combine difficult Korean with complicated Chinese, you can't make out the meaning and so you don't read it. There are these stupid stories written in Korean; they're hard to read, and what's more, stories written by Chosŏn people put me to sleep. Me, I gave up on Chosŏn newspapers and magazines a long time ago.

As far as magazines are concerned, you can't beat *King* and *Shonen Club*.[9] They're top-notch! Every time there's a Chinese character it has *kana*[1] tacked on to it, and wherever you open it up you can cruise right through it and know clearly what's going on.

And wherever you read, there's something to learn from it or else an interesting story.

The stories sure are fun! Especially the ones by Kan Kikuchi . . . nice entertainment, and they've got feeling too! And those swashbuckling epics by Yoshikawa Eiji—I just can't sit still when I read them.

The stories are all fun like that, there's a lot of comics, lots of photos too, and considering all that, the price is on the cheap side. You can get last month's issue for 15 *chŏn*,[2] and after you read it you can sell it back for 5 *chŏn*.

As long as you're going to make a magazine, that's how it ought to be, but for all their bullshit Chosŏn people haven't come up with one presentable magazine yet!

But heck, I wasn't going to find anything nifty to read in that crummy magazine, so I tried to find some comics or photos, and what do you know, I came across an article with my uncle's name on it! I was amazed, and I held it up to take a look. The title had something to do with economy and the characters it was written in were as big as cows' eyes. Next to it was a smaller line that included the word *society*.

I knew what was what just from seeing that much. Economy was what my uncle had studied in college, so he knew about that, and society, well, he was involved with scotchalism, so he knew about society too. So it was obvious he was writing about how economy and scotchalism were related, and which side he was on, and which side was right—stuff like that.

I didn't have to read that article to figure it out. I mean, this fine gentleman went to college and studied economy and wasn't interested in making money so he got mixed up with scotchalism, and so he probably swears up and down the whole article through that economy is wrong and scotchalism is right.

Anyway, I was impressed to see he'd actually written something, so I figured I'd give it a try. But when I glanced through it—no way did I have the brains for it.

I could have gotten a rough idea if the words weren't so hard, but when I pieced together what I could, not for the life of me could I figure out what he was trying to say.

I was kind of irritated so I said to myself, *ah, the hell with this*, and instead I decided to corner him and give him a hard time, and I spread out the article in front of him.

8. Korean was written in a mixed script, making use of both phonetic Korean and Chinese characters.

9. Japanese magazines.

1. Characters from the Japanese phonetic alphabet, sometimes written under Chinese characters for less educated readers.

2. About ten cents.

"Uncle?"

"What is it?"

"You're writing something here about economy and society—are you telling people to do economy, or are you telling them to do scotchalism?"

"What?"

He didn't understand. My question threw him off. This article must have been something he wrote a long time ago and forgot about, or else I was being too direct and he didn't know how to handle that. So I tried to be a little more precise.

"Uncle—doesn't *economy* mean making money and getting rich? And doesn't *scotchalism* mean taking money that rich folks have saved up and spending it yourself?"

"What are you trying to say, boy!"

"Hold on and please listen to me."

"Where did you come up with the notion that economics and socialism are like that?"

"It's common sense: doesn't *economy* mean making a lot of money, spending just a little, and saving the rest?"

"That's usually what people mean by *economizing*, and that's different from the study of economics and the word *economic*."

"Difference? I don't get it. If economy is all about making money, then economics must be the study of how to make money."

"No. There's something called finance, and I guess you could think of it as the study of making money, but that's not what economics is about."

"Well, if that's the case, then you made a mistake going to college. You spent five or six years studying economics that didn't teach you how to economize—what's the use? I always wondered how come you went to college and studied economy but didn't make any money. Now I see it's because you didn't study economy the right way."

"I didn't? Well, well, maybe so. You're right, yes, you are!"

Doggone, I got him now! I said to myself. *So what if he went to college and knows all sorts of obscure stuff? See, didn't I tell you—doggone!*

"Uncle?"

"What is it now?"

"You mean you went to college and studied scotchalism, not economy? You studied how to take money from rich people and spend it, instead of making it yourself?"

"What do you know about socialism, talking like that?"

"Well, I know something about that stuff."

And I proceeded to give it to him straight.

He looks right into my face from where he's lying and gives me a little smirk. And then listen to what this fine gentleman had to say.

"So that's socialism, eh? Well, I'd call it thuggery."

"Well now, so you know scotchalism is thuggery too."

"I didn't say that."

"Did too! Just now."

"What *you're* talking about is thuggery, not socialism."

"There you go! Scotchalism is highway robbery—didn't you say so yourself?"

"Listen to you, boy—carrying on just for the sake of argument."

There! Got him again. Now he's showing his true colors.

"Uncle?"

"What now?"

"You should straighten out your thinking."

"What's that supposed to mean?"

"Aren't you worried?"

"Someone like me, what's there to worry about? *I* worry about *you*."

"But I've got a plan and I think it makes sense."

"How so?"

"You really want to hear it?"

And once again I gave it to him straight. That fine gentleman heard me out, and you should have heard what he had to say.

"You're pitiful."

"How come?"

But he didn't say anything.

"How do you mean, I'm pitiful?"

He still didn't say anything.

"Uncle?"

"What?"

"You said I was pitiful?"

"No, I was only talking to myself."

"Still—"

"Listen, you!"

"Yes?"

"No matter who you are, nothing's so disgusting as kissing up to someone."

"Kissing up to someone?"

"Well . . . in this world there's a structure. The emperors are at the top and the beggars are at the bottom and everybody lives according to his means. There's nothing so disgusting as kissing up to someone for your livelihood, and going so far as to lose your individuality in the process. There's nobody as pathetic as such a person. Why does a person need a second bowl of rice if the first one fills him up?"

"What's that supposed to mean?"

"You want to marry a Japanese, you even want a Japanese name, you want your whole lifestyle to be Japanese."

"What's wrong with that?"

"That's just the point. It would be one thing if what you say comes from profound cultivation and sound judgment. But it would seem from what you say that you have something else in mind."

"Like what?"

"You want to cozy up to your boss, and your neighbors too—"

"You bet I do! My boss has to trust me, and I have to be on good terms with the neighbors from the home country."

My uncle didn't have any answer for that.

"Uncle, you still don't know the way of the world. You're older than I am and you went to college, but I got out there at an early age and took some hard knocks, and you don't know as much about the world as me. Do you have any idea what's going on out there?"

"Boy!"

"Yes?"

"Just now you mentioned the ways of the world."

"Yes."

"And you have a bright, shining future."

"Yes."

"And you're going to make a hundred thousand *wŏn* by the time you're sixty."

"Yes."

"The ways of the world as you would describe it and the ways of the world as I would describe it are different, but the fact is, they're quite complicated."

"I don't get it."

"No matter how a person tries, he ends up being controlled by powerful forces he isn't even aware of—the ways of the world, as you put it—and there's nothing he can do about it."

"What do you mean?"

"To put it simply, we can manufacture all the plans and opportunities we want, but things don't work out that way."

"Aw hell, Uncle, don't tell me . . . You know, there's an article on Napoleon in a recent issue of *King*. According to him, a man makes his own opportunities and *impossibility* is a word that's found in a fool's dictionary. If you keep planning and finding opportunities, there's nothing in this world you can't do as long as you fight for it. If you fail at something, then you pick yourself up and have at it again with twice as much courage. Haven't you ever heard the saying 'Seven times defeated, eighth time victory'?"

"Napoleon was successful as long as he adapted to the ways of the world. When he opposed them he failed. You talk about 'Seven times defeated, eighth time victory,' but you've only seen a few people who succeeded that way. Don't you realize how many people there are who succeed the eighth time, then fail the ninth time and can't get up anymore?"

"Well, you just wait. I'm going to succeed and nothing'll stop me. . . . You're even worse than I thought. You lose heart even before you try something because you're convinced you're going to fail."

"That's like saying a person has to go up in the sky before he can tell for sure it's high."

Brother, when the stakes are down he doesn't have anything to say, so he tries to get by with a completely irrelevant comparison. Is there anyone on earth who's dumb enough not to know that the sky is high? Where did he come up with that one?

I felt like dropping it right there. But then what? Well, I just had to start in again.

"Uncle?"

"Yes?"

"What are you going to do once you're all better again?"

"What do you mean?"

"I mean your future . . ."

"My future?"

"Don't you have any plans?"

"At this point, what's the use of making plans?"

"So, no plans? Just live from day to day?"

"I didn't say I didn't have plans."

"You do, then?"

"Sure I do."

"What are they?"

"Continue on like I've been doing . . ."

"You mean you're going back to that whatchamacallit?"

"Probably."

"Uncle?"

He didn't answer.

"Uncle?"

"What?"

"Why don't you give it up?"

"Just give it up?"

"Yes."

"You think I've just been killing time all along?"

"Well, haven't you?"

No response.

"Uncle?"

He still didn't answer.

"Uncle?"

"Yes?"

"How old are you?"

"Thirty-three."

"Aren't you old enough to turn over a new leaf and start taking care of family matters?"

"Take care of family matters, and then what?"

"If you're going to put it that way, then let's assume you take care of that whatchamacallit business—then what?"

"It's not a matter of 'then what.'"

"You mean you don't have any hopes or objectives when you do that other business?"

"Hopes? Objectives?"

"Yes."

"That's a different matter. One person's hopes and objectives—that's not the issue."

"That's a new one on me!"

"Really?"

"Yes, really!"

"Well, I'll be . . ."

"Uncle?"

"Yes?"

"Aren't you grateful to have Aunt?"

"Yes, I am."

"Isn't she pitiful?"

"Pitiful? If you put it like that, then, yes, she is indeed."

"So, you know that."

"Yes, I do."

"And still you act like you do."

"There are people who keep tasting bitterness and eventually they find some sweetness there—the joy you get from hardship. We're not born that way, but that's what happens when you put your heart and soul into something. And at that point hardship becomes joy. Now in your aunt's case, sure, hardship is hardship, but at the same time she finds joy in it."

"And you consider that a blessing?"

"No, I don't."

"Then, shouldn't you try to make it up to her?"

"Well, I'm not unaware of what she's done for me . . ."

"So, once you're all better, you'll—"

"Right, along with everything else."

Heck, can you believe that! There he is lying down, talking about "everything else" he has to do. What a bald-faced crock!

There's no hope for him. Look at him anyway you want, he's about as useful as a fingernail, he's a nuisance to others, a canker on the world. He'd be better off dead, and the sooner the better. He deserves to die, he has it coming.

But heck, he doesn't die, he just keeps twitching. It vexes me to no end. . . .

1938

JORGE LUIS BORGES

1899–1986

In the briefest of short stories, Jorge Luis Borges created convincing fictional worlds: alternate universes that obey their own laws of time and causation and shed light on the peculiarities of our own world. Borges's favorite symbol of these imaginary settings was the labyrinth, and readers the world over have enjoyed being lost in the mazes Borges built from his thought experiments. To read one of Borges's stories is to enter a new reality, imagined with great concreteness as an extension of our own world yet bearing distinctive features of the universes of fantasy and science fiction.

Born in Buenos Aires, Argentina, on August 24, 1899, Borges grew up in a large house whose library and garden were to form an essential part of his imagination. His father, who was half-English, was an unsuccessful lawyer with philosophical and literary interests; he spent much of his son's childhood working on a novel that he eventually published in middle age. Borges's mother also had literary ambitions; she translated works by **William Faulkner**, **Franz Kafka**, and D. H. Lawrence into Spanish. Her family, which the young Borges idealized, included Argentine patriots who had fought for independence from Spain and in the civil wars of the nineteenth century. At home Borges spoke English with his father, his paternal grandmother, and his tutor. He read widely in English as well as Spanish; his first publication was a Spanish translation of a children's story by Oscar Wilde, which a Buenos Aires newspaper published when he was only nine years old. Later he would translate works by **Walt Whitman**, **James Joyce**, and others. He remained close to his mother all his life and lived with her until her death, when she was ninety-nine and he was seventy-five.

Borges's father suffered from eye troubles and traveled to Europe with his family in 1914 for an operation. The family was caught in Geneva at the outbreak of World War I. Borges attended secondary school in Switzerland, learning French, German, and Latin. After the war the family moved to Spain, where he associated with a group of young experimental poets known as the Ultraists. When he returned to his homeland in 1921, Borges founded the Argentinian Ultraists, and befriended and collaborated with other intellectuals and artists, including the philosopher Macedonio Fernandez and a younger writer, Adolfo Bioy Casares.

Around the time of his father's death, in 1938, Borges got his first job, as a librarian in a small municipal library. His workplace served as the basis for one of the first, and most famous, of his stories, partly inspired by Kafka, "The Library of Babel." Taking the format of an academic essay, it tells of an endless library whose mazelike, interlocking galleries contain not only all books ever written but all possible combinations of letters. Although the library is infinite, the books, many of them meaningless, are shelved at random and therefore useless.

Early in the twentieth century, Argentina was among the wealthiest Latin American countries, but it suffered during the Great Depression and the years of Juan Perón's military dictatorship that followed. Borges openly opposed the Perón regime and its fascist tendencies, making his political views plain in his speeches and nonliterary writings, some of which circulated privately and were not published until after his death. His political leanings did not go unnoticed. When Perón became president in 1946, his government removed Borges from the librarian's post that he had held since 1938 and offered him a job as a chicken inspector. Borges refused the position and instead began teaching English and North American literature at the University of Buenos Aires. Having inherited weak eyes from his father, Borges suffered from increasingly poor vision in middle age; despite undergoing eight operations, he was forced eventually to dictate his work and to rely on his prodigious memory.

After the fall of Perón's regime in 1955, Borges was given the prestigious post of director of the National Library—in the same year that he became almost totally blind. When Perón's party returned to power, Borges opposed him, eventually supporting the military coup that overthrew the Peronists in 1976. His failure to recognize the autocratic character of the military government was a misjudgment that tarnished his image in his final years. Until his death, Borges lived in his beloved Buenos Aires, the city he had celebrated in his first volume of poetry.

The Garden of Forking Paths (1941), his first major collection, introduced Borges to a wider public as an idealist writer whose short stories subordinate character, scene, plot, and narration to a central concept, which is often a philosophical premise. Borges uses these ideas not didactically but as the starting point of fantastic elaborations that entertain and perplex readers—much like a challenging game or puzzle. In the immense labyrinth, or "garden of forking paths," that is Borges's world, images of mazes and infinite mirroring, of cyclical repetition and recall, leave the reader in a sort of hall of mirrors, unsure of what is reality and what is illusion. In *Borges and I* the author commented on the parallel existence of two Borgeses: the one who exists in his work (the one his readers know) and the warm, living identity felt by the man who sets pen to paper. "Little by little, I am giving over everything to him. . . . I do not know which one of us has written this page." Borges elaborated this notion by spinning out fictional identities and alternate realities. Disdaining the "psychological fakery" of realistic novels (the "draggy novel of characters"), he preferred art that calls attention to its own artificiality. He wrote many of his stories in the style of encyclopedia entries or historical essays, as in "The Garden of Forking Paths." Borges was fond, too, of detective stories (and wrote several of them), in which the search for an elusive explanation, the pursuit of intricately planted clues, matters more than the characters' recognizability. The author contrives an art of puzzles and discovery.

"The Garden of Forking Paths," the first selection below, begins as a simple spy story purporting to reveal the hidden truth about a German bombing raid during World War I. Borges alludes to documented facts: the geographic setting of the town of Albert and the Ancre River; a famous Chinese novel that serves as Ts'ui Pên's proposed model; the *History of the World War (1914–1918)* published by B. H. Liddell Hart in 1934. Official history is undermined on the first page, however, both by the recently discovered confession of Dr. Yu Tsun and by his editor's suspiciously defensive footnote, which calls into question the work we are about to read. Although Borges presents the story as a historical document, he warns his readers that it contains interpretive traps. In fact, the story is far from simple—it is a complex labyrinth in which the reader may easily be misled.

Borges executes his detective story with the carefully planted clues traditional to the genre, such as the need to convey the name of a bombing target and the presence of a single bullet in a revolver. Yet halfway through, what started as a conventional spy story takes on bizarre spatial and temporal dimensions. Coincidences—those chance relationships that might well have had different outcomes—introduce the idea of forking paths, or choice between two routes, for history. By inventing an ancient Chinese text modeled on a labyrinth, Borges portrays the universe as a series of alternative versions of experience. An infinite number of worlds opens up—but only one is embodied in this particular story: Yu Tsun faces a dilemma that places his personal loyalties at odds with his military duty. Both the personal and the philosophical ramifications of this choice are at the center of Borges's story.

Just as the "forking paths" present alternative versions of experience, so too has Borges's reputation and influence led in various directions. Perceived by outsiders as a major Argentine writer and a forerunner of the magical realism of successive Latin American generations, he is seen by many Latin Americans as a primarily European writer, a precursor to postmodernism. A favorite of literary intellectuals, he has influenced the development of science fiction. In the labyrinth of contemporary literature, Borges's fictions open up many paths for later writers.

In "The Library of Babel," also published in 1941, Borges seems to have envisioned the development of the information age. The narrator, in the style of an essayist, describes a library that is infinite and coextensive with the fictional universe of the story. The books, each of the same length, arranged on shelves in chambers of identical size and layout, contain "all that it is given to express, in all languages," as well as a great deal of nonsense. Although the number of possible combinations is not infinite, the library itself is infinite because it repeats itself continuously, thus creating a sort of order out of the vast disorder of books both meaningful and meaningless. Much of the story presents itself as a history of theories and beliefs held by residents of this universal library: the Vindicators who search for the one book that will vindicate their existence, the Inquisitors who try to catalogue the library's contents, the Purifiers who destroy meaningless books. To the narrator, "it does not seem unlikely that on some shelf of the universe there lies a total book," one that would explain all the mysteries of the universe. Having spent his whole life in search of it, however, his simple prayer is that someone someday may find this book.

The name Babel comes from the Bible, where it is the location of a tower created by humans who seek to rival God and ascend to heaven. In the Bible, God creates multiple languages to ensure that the builders of the tower cannot understand each other and therefore cannot complete their tower. This biblical story is said to explain the origin of multiple human languages. Borges's Library of Babel has become an irresistible metaphor for the internet, which was invented half a century after the story was written. Borges describes both a world with a seemingly inexhaustible store of information, much of which is unreliable, and also the challenges of finding what one really needs within it. But even if the internet had never been invented, Borges's story would stand as a meditation on the infinity of space and time, the complexities of language, and the limitations of human understanding.

The Garden of Forking Paths[1]

On page 22 of Liddell Hart's *History of World War I* you will read that an attack against the Serre-Montauban line by thirteen British divisions (supported by 1,400 artillery pieces), planned for the 24th of July, 1916, had to be postponed until the morning of the 29th. The torrential rains, Captain Liddell Hart comments, caused this delay, an insignificant one, to be sure.

The following statement, dictated, reread and signed by Dr. Yu Tsun, former professor of English at the *Hochschule* at Tsingtao,[2] throws an unsuspected light over the whole affair. The first two pages of the document are missing.

". . . and I hung up the receiver. Immediately afterwards, I recognized the voice that had answered in German. It was that of Captain Richard Madden. Madden's presence in Viktor Runeberg's apartment meant the end of our anxieties and—but this seemed, *or should have seemed*, very secondary to me—also the end of our lives. It meant that Runeberg had been arrested or murdered.[3] Before the sun set on that day, I would encounter the same fate. Madden was implacable. Or rather, he was obliged to be so. An Irishman at the service of England, a man accused of laxity and perhaps of treason, how could he fail to seize and be thankful for such a miraculous opportunity: the discovery, capture, maybe even the death of two agents of the German Reich?[4] I went up to my room; absurdly I locked the door and threw myself on my back on the narrow iron cot. Through the window I saw the familiar roofs and the cloud-shaded six o'clock sun. It seemed incredible to me that that day without premonitions or symbols should be the one of my inexorable death. In spite of

1. Translated by Donald A. Yates.
2. Or Ch'ing-tao; a major port in east China, part of territory leased to (and developed by) Germany in 1898. "Hochschule": university (German).
3. "A hypothesis both hateful and odd. The Prussian spy Hans Rabener, alias Viktor Runeberg, attacked with drawn automatic the bearer of the warrant for his arrest, Captain Richard Madden. The latter, in self-defense, inflicted the wound which brought about Runeberg's death [Editor's note]." This entire note is by Borges as "Editor."
4. Empire (German).

my dead father, in spite of having been a child in a symmetrical garden of Hai Feng, was I—now—going to die? Then I reflected that everything happens to a man precisely, precisely *now.* Centuries of centuries and only in the present do things happen; countless men in the air, on the face of the earth and the sea, and all that really is happening is happening to me . . . The almost intolerable recollection of Madden's horselike face banished these wanderings. In the midst of my hatred and terror (it means nothing to me now to speak of terror, now that I have mocked Richard Madden, now that my throat yearns for the noose) it occurred to me that that tumultuous and doubtless happy warrior did not suspect that I possessed the Secret. The name of the exact location of the new British artillery park on the River Ancre. A bird streaked across the gray sky and blindly I translated it into an airplane and that airplane into many (against the French sky) annihilating the artillery station with vertical bombs. If only my mouth, before a bullet shattered it, could cry out that secret name so it could be heard in Germany . . . My human voice was very weak. How might I make it carry to the ear of the Chief? To the ear of that sick and hateful man who knew nothing of Runeberg and me save that we were in Staffordshire[5] and who was waiting in vain for our report in his arid office in Berlin, endlessly examining newspapers . . . I said out loud: *I must flee.* I sat up noiselessly, in a useless perfection of silence, as if Madden were already lying in wait for me. Something—perhaps the mere vain ostentation of proving my resources were nil—made me look through my pockets. I found what I knew I would find. The American watch, the nickel chain and the square coin, the key ring with the incriminating useless keys to Runeberg's apartment, the notebook, a letter which I resolved to destroy immediately (and which I did not destroy), a crown, two shillings and a few pence, the red and blue pencil, the handkerchief, the revolver with one bullet. Absurdly, I took it in my hand and weighed it in order to inspire courage within myself. Vaguely I thought that a pistol report can be heard at a great distance. In ten minutes my plan was perfected. The telephone book listed the name of the only person capable of transmitting the message; he lived in a suburb of Fenton,[6] less than a half hour's train ride away.

I am a cowardly man. I say it now, now that I have carried to its end a plan whose perilous nature no one can deny. I know its execution was terrible. I didn't do it for Germany, no. I care nothing for a barbarous country which imposed upon me the abjection of being a spy. Besides, I know of a man from England—a modest man—who for me is no less great than Goethe.[7] I talked with him for scarcely an hour, but during that hour he was Goethe . . . I did it because I sensed that the Chief somehow feared people of my race—for the innumerable ancestors who merge within me. I wanted to prove to him that a yellow man could save his armies. Besides, I had to flee from Captain Madden. His hands and his voice could call at my door at any moment. I dressed silently, bade farewell to myself in the mirror, went downstairs, scrutinized the peaceful street and went out. The station was not far from my home, but I judged it wise to take a cab. I argued that in this way I ran less risk of being recognized; the fact is that in the deserted street I felt myself visible and vulnerable, infinitely

5. County in west-central England.
6. In Lincolnshire, a county in east England.
7. Johann Wolfgang von Goethe (1749–1832), German poet, novelist, and dramatist; author of *Faust*; often taken as representing the peak of German cultural achievement.

so. I remember that I told the cab driver to stop a short distance before the main entrance. I got out with voluntary, almost painful slowness; I was going to the village of Ashgrove but I bought a ticket for a more distant station. The train left within a very few minutes, at eight-fifty. I hurried; the next one would leave at nine-thirty. There was hardly a soul on the platform. I went through the coaches; I remember a few farmers, a woman dressed in mourning, a young boy who was reading with fervor the *Annals* of Tacitus,[8] a wounded and happy soldier. The coaches jerked forward at last. A man whom I recognized ran in vain to the end of the platform. It was Captain Richard Madden. Shattered, trembling, I shrank into the far corner of the seat, away from the dreaded window.

From this broken state I passed into an almost abject felicity. I told myself that the duel had already begun and that I had won the first encounter by frustrating, even if for forty minutes, even if by a stroke of fate, the attack of my adversary. I argued that this slightest of victories foreshadowed a total victory. I argued (no less fallaciously) that my cowardly felicity proved that I was a man capable of carrying out the adventure successfully. From this weakness I took strength that did not abandon me. I foresee that man will resign himself each day to more atrocious undertakings; soon there will be no one but warriors and brigands; I give them this counsel: *The author of an atrocious undertaking ought to imagine that he has already accomplished it, ought to impose upon himself a future as irrevocable as the past.* Thus I proceeded as my eyes of a man already dead registered the elapsing of that day, which was perhaps the last, and the diffusion of the night. The train ran gently along, amid ash trees. It stopped, almost in the middle of the fields. No one announced the name of the station. "Ashgrove?" I asked a few lads on the platform. "Ashgrove," they replied. I got off.

A lamp enlightened the platform but the faces of the boys were in shadow. One questioned me, "Are you going to Dr. Stephen Albert's house?" Without waiting for my answer, another said, "The house is a long way from here, but you won't get lost if you take this road to the left and at every crossroads turn again to your left." I tossed them a coin (my last), descended a few stone steps and started down the solitary road. It went downhill, slowly. It was of elemental earth; overhead the branches were tangled; the low, full moon seemed to accompany me.

For an instant, I thought that Richard Madden in some way had penetrated my desperate plan. Very quickly, I understood that that was impossible. The instructions to turn always to the left reminded me that such was the common procedure for discovering the central point of certain labyrinths. I have some understanding of labyrinths: not for nothing am I the great grandson of that Ts'ui Pên who was governor of Yunnan and who renounced worldly power in order to write a novel that might be even more populous than the *Hung Lu Meng*[9] and to construct a labyrinth in which all men would become lost. Thirteen years he dedicated to these heterogeneous tasks, but the hand of a stranger murdered him—and his novel was incoherent and no one found the labyrinth. Beneath English trees I meditated on that lost maze: I imagined it inviolate and perfect at the secret crest of a mountain; I imagined it erased by rice fields or

8. Cornelius Tacitus (55–117), Roman historian whose *Annals* give a vivid picture of the decadence and corruption of the Roman Empire under Tiberius, Claudius, and Nero.

9. *The Dream of the Red Chamber* (1791) by Ts'ao Hsüeh-ch'in; the most famous Chinese novel, a love story and panorama of Chinese family life involving more than 430 characters.

beneath the water; I imagined it infinite, no longer composed of octagonal kiosks and returning paths, but of rivers and provinces and kingdoms . . . I thought of a labyrinth of labyrinths, of one sinuous spreading labyrinth that would encompass the past and the future and in some way involve the stars. Absorbed in these illusory images, I forgot my destiny of one pursued. I felt myself to be, for an unknown period of time, an abstract perceiver of the world. The vague, living countryside, the moon, the remains of the day worked on me, as well as the slope of the road which eliminated any possibility of weariness. The afternoon was intimate, infinite. The road descended and forked among the now confused meadows. A high-pitched, almost syllabic music approached and receded in the shifting of the wind, dimmed by leaves and distance. I thought that a man can be an enemy of other men, of the moments of other men, but not of a country: not of fireflies, words, gardens, streams of water, sunsets. Thus I arrived before a tall, rusty gate. Between the iron bars I made out a poplar grove and a pavilion. I understood suddenly two things, the first trivial, the second almost unbelievable: the music came from the pavilion, and the music was Chinese. For precisely that reason I had openly accepted it without paying it any heed. I do not remember whether there was a bell or whether I knocked with my hand. The sparkling of the music continued.

From the rear of the house within a lantern approached: a lantern that the trees sometimes striped and sometimes eclipsed, a paper lantern that had the form of a drum and the color of the moon. A tall man bore it. I didn't see his face for the light blinded me. He opened the door and said slowly, in my own language: "I see that the pious Hsi P'êng persists in correcting my solitude. You no doubt wish to see the garden?"

I recognized the name of one of our consuls and I replied, disconcerted, "The garden?"

"The garden of forking paths."

Something stirred in my memory and I uttered with incomprehensible certainty, "The garden of my ancestor Ts'ui Pên."

"Your ancestor? Your illustrious ancestor? Come in."

The damp path zigzagged like those of my childhood. We came to a library of Eastern and Western books. I recognized bound in yellow silk several volumes of the Lost Encyclopedia, edited by the Third Emperor of the Luminous Dynasty but never printed.[1] The record on the phonograph revolved next to a bronze phoenix. I also recall a *famille rose*[2] vase and another, many centuries older, of that shade of blue which our craftsmen copied from the potters of Persia . . .

Stephen Albert observed me with a smile. He was, as I have said, very tall, sharp-featured, with gray eyes and a gray beard. He told me that he had been a missionary in Tientsin "before aspiring to become a Sinologist."

We sat down—I on a long, low divan, he with his back to the window and a tall circular clock. I calculated that my pursuer, Richard Madden, could not arrive for at least an hour. My irrevocable determination could wait.

1. The Yung-lo emperor of the Ming ("bright") Dynasty commissioned a massive encyclopedia between 1403 and 1408. A single copy of the 11,095 manuscript volumes was made in the mid-1500s; the original was later destroyed, and only 370 volumes of the copy remain today.

2. Pink family (French); refers to a Chinese decorative enamel ranging in color from an opaque pink to purplish rose. *Famille rose* pottery was at its best during the reign of Yung Chên (1723–1735).

"An astounding fate, that of Ts'ui Pên," Stephen Albert said. "Governor of his native province, learned in astronomy, in astrology and in the tireless interpretation of the canonical books, chess player, famous poet and calligrapher—he abandoned all this in order to compose a book and a maze. He renounced the pleasures of both tyranny and justice, of his populous couch, of his banquets and even of erudition—all to close himself up for thirteen years in the Pavilion of the Limpid Solitude. When he died, his heirs found nothing save chaotic manuscripts. His family, as you may be aware, wished to condemn them to the fire; but his executor—a Taoist or Buddhist monk—insisted on their publication."

"We descendants of Ts'ui Pên," I replied, "continue to curse that monk. Their publication was senseless. The book is an indeterminate heap of contradictory drafts. I examined it once: in the third chapter the hero dies, in the fourth he is alive. As for the other undertaking of Ts'ui Pên, his labyrinth . . ."

"Here is Ts'ui Pên's labyrinth," he said, indicating a tall lacquered desk.

"An ivory labyrinth!" I exclaimed. "A minimum labyrinth."

"A labyrinth of symbols," he corrected. "An invisible labyrinth of time. To me, a barbarous Englishman, has been entrusted the revelation of this diaphanous mystery. After more than a hundred years, the details are irretrievable; but it is not hard to conjecture what happened. Ts'ui Pên must have said once: *I am withdrawing to write a book.* And another time: *I am withdrawing to construct a labyrinth.* Every one imagined two works; to no one did it occur that the book and the maze were one and the same thing. The Pavilion of the Limpid Solitude stood in the center of a garden that was perhaps intricate; that circumstance could have suggested to the heirs a physical labyrinth. Ts'ui Pên died; no one in the vast territories that were his came upon the labyrinth; the confusion of the novel suggested to me that *it* was the maze. Two circumstances gave me the correct solution of the problem. One: the curious legend that Ts'ui Pên had planned to create a labyrinth which would be strictly infinite. The other: a fragment of a letter I discovered."

Albert rose. He turned his back on me for a moment; he opened a drawer of the black and gold desk. He faced me and in his hands he held a sheet of paper that had once been crimson, but was now pink and tenuous and cross-sectioned. The fame of Ts'ui Pên as a calligrapher had been justly won. I read, uncomprehendingly and with fervor, these words written with a minute brush by a man of my blood: *I leave to the various futures (not to all) my garden of forking paths.* Wordlessly, I returned the sheet. Albert continued:

"Before unearthing this letter, I had questioned myself about the ways in which a book can be infinite. I could think of nothing other than a cyclic volume, a circular one. A book whose last page was identical with the first, a book which had the possibility of continuing indefinitely. I remembered too that night which is at the middle of the Thousand and One Nights when Scheherazade[3] (through a magical oversight of the copyist) begins to relate word for word the story of the Thousand and One Nights, establishing the risk of coming once again to the night when she must repeat it, and thus on to

3. The narrator of the collection also known as the *Arabian Nights*, a thousand and one tales supposedly told by Scheherazade to her husband, Shahrayar, king of Samarkand, to postpone her execution.

infinity. I imagined as well a Platonic, hereditary work, transmitted from father to son, in which each new individual adds a chapter or corrects with pious care the pages of his elders. These conjectures diverted me; but none seemed to correspond, not even remotely, to the contradictory chapters of Ts'ui Pên. In the midst of this perplexity, I received from Oxford the manuscript you have examined. I lingered, naturally, on the sentence: *I leave to the various futures (not to all) my garden of forking paths.* Almost instantly, I understood: 'The garden of forking paths' was the chaotic novel; the phrase 'the various futures (not to all)' suggested to me the forking in time, not in space. A broad rereading of the work confirmed the theory. In all fictional works, each time a man is confronted with several alternatives, he chooses one and eliminates the others; in the fiction of Ts'ui Pên, he chooses—simultaneously—all of them. *He creates*, in this way, diverse futures, diverse times which themselves also proliferate and fork. Here, then, is the explanation of the novel's contradictions. Fang, let us say, has a secret; a stranger calls at his door; Fang resolves to kill him. Naturally, there are several possible outcomes: Fang can kill the intruder, the intruder can kill Fang, they both can escape, they both can die, and so forth. In the work of Ts'ui Pên, all possible outcomes occur; each one is the point of departure for other forkings. Sometimes, the paths of this labyrinth converge: for example, you arrive at this house, but in one of the possible pasts you are my enemy, in another, my friend. If you will resign yourself to my incurable pronunciation, we shall read a few pages."

His face, within the vivid circle of the lamplight, was unquestionably that of an old man, but with something unalterable about it, even immortal. He read with slow precision two versions of the same epic chapter. In the first, an army marches to a battle across a lonely mountain; the horror of the rocks and shadows makes the men undervalue their lives and they gain an easy victory. In the second, the same army traverses a palace where a great festival is taking place; the resplendent battle seems to them a continuation of the celebration and they win the victory. I listened with proper veneration to these ancient narratives, perhaps less admirable in themselves than the fact that they had been created by my blood and were being restored to me by a man of a remote empire, in the course of a desperate adventure, on a Western isle. I remember the last words, repeated in each version like a secret commandment: *Thus fought the heroes, tranquil their admirable hearts, violent their swords, resigned to kill and to die.*

From that moment on, I felt about me and within my dark body an invisible, intangible swarming. Not the swarming of the divergent, parallel and finally coalescent armies, but a more inaccessible, more intimate agitation that they in some manner prefigured. Stephen Albert continued:

"I don't believe that your illustrious ancestor played idly with these variations. I don't consider it credible that he would sacrifice thirteen years to the infinite execution of a rhetorical experiment. In your country, the novel is a subsidiary form of literature; in Ts'ui Pên's time it was a despicable form. Ts'ui Pên was a brilliant novelist, but he was also a man of letters who doubtless did not consider himself a mere novelist. The testimony of his contemporaries proclaims—and his life fully confirms—his metaphysical and mystical interests. Philosophic controversy usurps a good part of the novel. I know that of all problems, none disturbed him so greatly nor worked upon him so much as the abysmal problem of time. Now then, the latter is the only problem that does not figure in the pages of the *Garden*. He does not even use the word that signifies *time*. How do you explain this voluntary omission?"

I proposed several solutions—all unsatisfactory. We discussed them. Finally, Stephen Albert said to me:

"In a riddle whose answer is chess, what is the only prohibited word?"

I thought a moment and replied, "The word *chess*."

"Precisely," said Albert. "*The Garden of Forking Paths* is an enormous riddle, or parable, whose theme is time; this recondite cause prohibits its mention. To omit a word always, to resort to inept metaphors and obvious periphrases, is perhaps the most emphatic way of stressing it. That is the tortuous method preferred, in each of the meanderings of his indefatigable novel, by the oblique Ts'ui Pên. I have compared hundreds of manuscripts, I have corrected the errors that the negligence of the copyists has introduced, I have guessed the plan of this chaos, I have re-established—I believe I have re-established—the primordial organization, I have translated the entire work: it is clear to me that not once does he employ the word 'time.' The explanation is obvious: *The Garden of Forking Paths* is an incomplete, but not false, image of the universe as Ts'ui Pên conceived it. In contrast to Newton and Schopenhauer,[4] your ancestor did not believe in a uniform, absolute time. He believed in an infinite series of times, in a growing, dizzying net of divergent, convergent and parallel times. This network of times which approached one another, forked, broke off, or were unaware of one another for centuries, embraces *all* possibilities of time. We do not exist in the majority of these times; in some you exist, and not I; in others I, and not you; in others, both of us. In the present one, which a favorable fate has granted me, you have arrived at my house; in another, while crossing the garden, you found me dead; in still another, I utter these same words, but I am a mistake, a ghost."

"In every one," I pronounced, not without a tremble to my voice, "I am grateful to you and revere you for your re-creation of the garden of Ts'ui Pên."

"Not in all," he murmured with a smile. "Time forks perpetually toward innumerable futures. In one of them I am your enemy."

Once again I felt the swarming sensation of which I have spoken. It seemed to me that the humid garden that surrounded the house was infinitely saturated with invisible persons. Those persons were Albert and I, secret, busy and multiform in other dimensions of time. I raised my eyes and the tenuous nightmare dissolved. In the yellow and black garden there was only one man; but this man was as strong as a statue . . . this man was approaching along the path and he was Captain Richard Madden.

"The future already exists," I replied, "but I am your friend. Could I see the letter again?"

Albert rose. Standing tall, he opened the drawer of the tall desk; for the moment his back was to me. I had readied the revolver. I fired with extreme caution. Albert

4. Arthur Schopenhauer (1788–1860), German philosopher whose concept of will proceeded from a concept of the self as enduring through time. In *Seven Conversations with Jorge Luis Borges*, Borges also comments on Schopenhauer's interest in the "oneiric [dreamlike] essence of life." Isaac Newton (1642–1727), English mathematician and philosopher best known for his formulation of laws of gravitation and motion.

fell uncomplainingly, immediately. I swear his death was instantaneous—a lightning stroke.

The rest is unreal, insignificant. Madden broke in, arrested me. I have been condemned to the gallows. I have won out abominably; I have communicated to Berlin the secret name of the city they must attack. They bombed it yesterday; I read it in the same papers that offered to England the mystery of the learned Sinologist Stephen Albert who was murdered by a stranger, one Yu Tsun. The Chief had deciphered this mystery. He knew my problem was to indicate (through the uproar of the war) the city called Albert, and that I had found no other means to do so than to kill a man of that name. He does not know (no one can know) my innumerable contrition and weariness.

For Victoria Ocampo

1941

The Library of Babel[1]

By this art you may contemplate the variation of the 23 letters . . .
The Anatomy of Melancholy,[2] part 2, sect. II, mem. IV

The universe (which others call the Library) is composed of an indefinite and perhaps infinite number of hexagonal galleries, with vast air shafts between, surrounded by very low railings. From any of the hexagons one can see, interminably, the upper and lower floors. The distribution of the galleries is invariable. Twenty shelves, five long shelves per side, cover all the sides except two; their height, which is the distance from floor to ceiling, scarcely exceeds that of a normal bookcase. One of the free sides leads to a narrow hallway which opens onto another gallery, identical to the first and to all the rest. To the left and right of the hallway there are two very small closets. In the first, one may sleep standing up; in the other, satisfy one's fecal necessities. Also through here passes a spiral stairway, which sinks abysmally and soars upwards to remote distances. In the hallway there is a mirror which faithfully duplicates all appearances. Men usually infer from this mirror that the Library is not infinite (if it really were, why this illusory duplication?); I prefer to dream that its polished surfaces represent and promise the infinite . . . Light is provided by some spherical fruit which bear the name of lamps. There are two, transversally placed, in each hexagon. The light they emit is insufficient, incessant.

Like all men of the Library, I have traveled in my youth; I have wandered in search of a book, perhaps the catalogue of catalogues; now that my eyes can hardly decipher what I write, I am preparing to die just a few leagues from the hexagon in which I was born. Once I am dead, there will be no lack of pious hands to throw me over the railing; my grave will be the fathomless air; my

1. Translated by James E. Irby. "Babel": in Genesis 11, city whose inhabitants tried to build a tower that would reach heaven. God is said to have created multiple languages in order to prevent the inhabitants of Babel from understanding each other and completing their tower.
2. Philosophical work (1638) by English scholar Robert Burton (1577–1640).

body will sink endlessly and decay and dissolve in the wind generated by the fall, which is infinite. I say that the Library is unending. The idealists argue that the hexagonal rooms are a necessary form of absolute space or, at least, of our intuition of space. They reason that a triangular or pentagonal room is inconceivable. (The mystics claim that their ecstasy reveals to them a circular chamber containing a great circular book, whose spine is continuous and which follows the complete circle of the walls; but their testimony is suspect; their words, obscure. This cyclical book is God.) Let it suffice now for me to repeat the classic dictum: *The Library is a sphere whose exact center is any one of its hexagons and whose circumference is inaccessible.*

There are five shelves for each of the hexagon's walls; each shelf contains thirty-five books of uniform format; each book is of four hundred and ten pages; each page, of forty lines, each line, of some eighty letters which are black in color. There are also letters on the spine of each book; these letters do not indicate or prefigure what the pages will say. I know that this incoherence at one time seemed mysterious. Before summarizing the solution (whose discovery, in spite of its tragic projections, is perhaps the capital fact in history) I wish to recall a few axioms.

First: The Library exists *ab aeterno*.[3] This truth, whose immediate corollary is the future eternity of the world, cannot be placed in doubt by any reasonable mind. Man, the imperfect librarian, may be the product of chance or of malevolent demiurgi;[4] the universe, with its elegant endowment of shelves, of enigmatical volumes, of inexhaustible stairways for the traveler and latrines for the seated librarian, can only be the work of a god. To perceive the distance between the divine and the human, it is enough to compare these crude wavering symbols which my fallible hand scrawls on the cover of a book, with the organic letters inside: punctual, delicate, perfectly black, inimitably symmetrical.

Second: *The orthographical symbols are twenty-five in number*.[5] This finding made it possible, three hundred years ago, to formulate a general theory of the Library and solve satisfactorily the problem which no conjecture had deciphered: the formless and chaotic nature of almost all the books. One which my father saw in a hexagon on circuit fifteen ninety-four was made up of the letters MCV, perversely repeated from the first line to the last. Another (very much consulted in this area) is a mere labyrinth of letters, but the next-to-last page says *Oh time thy pyramids*. This much is already known: for every sensible line of straightforward statement, there are leagues of senseless cacophonies, verbal jumbles and incoherences. (I know of an uncouth region whose librarians repudiate the vain and superstitious custom of finding a meaning in books and equate it with that of finding a meaning in dreams or in the chaotic lines of one's palm . . . They admit that the inventors of this writing imitated the twenty-five natural symbols, but maintain that this application is accidental and that the books signify nothing in themselves. This dictum, we shall see, is not entirely fallacious.)

For a long time it was believed that these impenetrable books corresponded to past or remote languages. It is true that the most ancient men, the first

3. From the beginning of time (Latin).
4. Heavenly beings said in some Gnostic religions to have created the universe.
5. The original manuscript does not contain digits or capital letters. The punctuation has been limited to the comma and the period. These two signs, the space and the twenty-two letters of the alphabet are the twenty-five symbols considered sufficient by this unknown author [Borges's note].

librarians, used a language quite different from the one we now speak; it is true that a few miles to the right the tongue is dialectal and that ninety floors farther up, it is incomprehensible. All this, I repeat, is true, but four hundred and ten pages of inalterable MCV's cannot correspond to any language, no matter how dialectal or rudimentary it may be. Some insinuated that each letter could influence the following one and that the value of MCV in the third line of page 71 was not the one the same series may have in another position on another page, but this vague thesis did not prevail. Others thought of cryptographs; generally, this conjecture has been accepted, though not in the sense in which it was formulated by its originators.

Five hundred years ago, the chief of an upper hexagon[6] came upon a book as confusing as the others, but which had nearly two pages of homogeneous lines. He showed his find to a wandering decoder who told him the lines were written in Portuguese; others said they were Yiddish. Within a century, the language was established: a Samoyedic Lithuanian dialect of Guarani,[7] with classical Arabian inflections. The content was also deciphered: some notions of combinative analysis, illustrated with examples of variation with unlimited repetition. These examples made it possible for a librarian of genius to discover the fundamental law of the Library. This thinker observed that all the books, no matter how diverse they might be, are made up of the same elements: the space, the period, the comma, the twenty-two letters of the alphabet. He also alleged a fact which travelers have confirmed: *In the vast Library there are no two identical books*. From these two incontrovertible premises he deduced that the Library is total and that its shelves register all the possible combinations of the twenty-odd orthographical symbols (a number which, though extremely vast, is not infinite): in other words, all that it is given to express, in all languages. Everything: the minutely detailed history of the future, the archangels' autobiographies, the faithful catalogue of the Library, thousands and thousands of false catalogues, the demonstration of the fallacy of those catalogues, the demonstration of the fallacy of the true catalogue, the Gnostic gospel of Basilides,[8] the commentary on that gospel, the commentary on the commentary on that gospel, the true story of your death, the translation of every book in all languages, the interpolations of every book in all books.

When it was proclaimed that the Library contained all books, the first impression was one of extravagant happiness. All men felt themselves to be the masters of an intact and secret treasure. There was no personal or world problem whose eloquent solution did not exist in some hexagon. The universe was justified, the universe suddenly usurped the unlimited dimensions of hope. At that time a great deal was said about the Vindications: books of apology and prophecy which vindicated for all time the acts of every man in the universe and retained prodigious arcana for his future. Thousands of the greedy abandoned their sweet native hexagons and rushed up the stairways, urged on by the vain intention of

6. Before, there was a man for every three hexagons. Suicide and pulmonary diseases have destroyed that proportion. A memory of unspeakable melancholy: at times I have traveled for many nights through corridors and along polished stairways without finding a single librarian [Borges's note].

7. A native South American language. "Samoyedic": from a language group native to northern Eurasia. (There is, of course, no such dialect.)

8. A religious leader in Alexandria, Egypt, in the second century C.E.

finding their Vindication. These pilgrims disputed in the narrow corridors, proffered dark curses, strangled each other on the divine stairways, flung the deceptive books into the air shafts, met their death cast down in a similar fashion by the inhabitants of remote regions. Others went mad . . . The Vindications exist (I have seen two which refer to persons of the future, to persons who perhaps are not imaginary) but the searchers did not remember that the possibility of a man's finding his Vindication, or some treacherous variation thereof, can be computed as zero.

At that time it was also hoped that a clarification of humanity's basic mysteries—the origin of the Library and of time—might be found. It is verisimilar that these grave mysteries could be explained in words: if the language of philosophers is not sufficient, the multiform Library will have produced the unprecedented language required, with its vocabularies and grammars. For four centuries now men have exhausted the hexagons . . . There are official searchers, *inquisitors*. I have seen them in the performance of their function: they always arrive extremely tired from their journeys; they speak of a broken stairway which almost killed them; they talk with the librarian of galleries and stairs; sometimes they pick up the nearest volume and leaf through it, looking for infamous words. Obviously, no one expects to discover anything.

As was natural, this inordinate hope was followed by an excessive depression. The certitude that some shelf in some hexagon held precious books and that these precious books were inaccessible, seemed almost intolerable. A blasphemous sect suggested that the searches should cease and that all men should juggle letters and symbols until they constructed, by an improbable gift of chance, these canonical books. The authorities were obliged to issue severe orders. The sect disappeared, but in my childhood I have seen old men who, for long periods of time, would hide in the latrines with some metal disks in a forbidden dice cup and feebly mimic the divine disorder.

Others, inversely, believed that it was fundamental to eliminate useless works. They invaded the hexagons, showed credentials which were not always false, leafed through a volume with displeasure and condemned whole shelves: their hygienic, ascetic furor caused the senseless perdition of millions of books. Their name is execrated, but those who deplore the "treasures" destroyed by this frenzy neglect two notable facts. One: the Library is so enormous that any reduction of human origin is infinitesimal. The other: every copy is unique, irreplaceable, but (since the Library is total) there are always several hundred thousand imperfect facsimiles: works which differ only in a letter or a comma. Counter to general opinion, I venture to suppose that the consequences of the Purifiers' depredations have been exaggerated by the horror these fanatics produced. They were urged on by the delirium of trying to reach the books in the Crimson Hexagon: books whose format is smaller than usual, all-powerful, illustrated and magical.

We also know of another superstition of that time: that of the Man of the Book. On some shelf in some hexagon (men reasoned) there must exist a book which is the formula and perfect compendium *of all the rest*: some librarian has gone through it and he is analogous to a god. In the language of this zone vestiges of this remote functionary's cult still persist. Many wandered in search of Him. For a century they exhausted in vain the most varied areas. How could one locate the venerated and secret hexagon which housed Him? Someone proposed a regressive method: To locate book A, consult first a book B which indicates A's position; to locate book B, consult first a book C, and so on to infinity . . . In adventures such as these, I have squandered and wasted my years. It does not seem unlikely to me that there is a total book on some shelf of the universe;[9] I pray to the unknown gods that a man—just one, even though it were thousands of years ago!—may have examined and read it. If honor and wisdom and happiness are not for me, let them be for others. Let heaven exist, though my place be in hell. Let me be outraged and annihilated, but for one instant, in one being, let Your enormous Library be justified. The impious maintain that nonsense is normal in the Library and that the reasonable (and even humble and pure coherence) is an almost miraculous exception. They speak (I know) of the "feverish Library whose chance volumes are constantly in danger of changing into others and affirm, negate and confuse everything like a delirious divinity." These words, which not only denounce the disorder but exemplify it as well, notoriously prove their authors' abominable taste and desperate ignorance. In truth, the Library includes all verbal structures, all variations permitted by the twenty-five orthographical symbols, but not a single example of absolute nonsense. It is useless to observe that the best volume of the many hexagons under my administration is entitled *The Combed Thunderclap* and another *The Plaster Cramp* and another *Axaxaxas mlö*. These phrases, at first glance incoherent, can no doubt be justified in a cryptographical or allegorical manner; such a justification is verbal and, *ex hypothesi*,[1] already figures in the Library. I cannot combine some characters

dhcmrlchtdj

which the divine Library has not foreseen and which in one of its secret tongues do not contain a terrible meaning. No one can articulate a syllable which is not filled with tenderness and fear, which is not, in one of these languages, the powerful name of a god. To speak is to fall into tautology. This wordy and useless epistle already exists in one of the thirty volumes of the five shelves of one of the innumerable hexagons—and its refutation as well. (An *n* number of possible languages use the same vocabulary; in some of them, the symbol *library* allows the correct definition *a ubiquitous and lasting system of hexagonal galleries*, but *library* is *bread* or *pyramid* or anything else, and these seven words which define it have another value. You who read me, are You sure of understanding my language?)

The methodical task of writing distracts me from the present state of men. The certitude that everything has been written negates us or turns us into phantoms. I know of districts in which the young men prostrate themselves before books and kiss their pages in a barbarous manner, but they do not know how to decipher a single letter. Epidemics, heretical conflicts, peregrinations which inevitably degenerate into banditry, have decimated the population. I believe I have mentioned the suicides, more and more frequent with the years. Perhaps my old

9. I repeat: it suffices that a book be possible for it to exist. Only the impossible is excluded. For example: no book can be a ladder, although no doubt there are books which discuss and negate and demonstrate this possibility and others whose structure corresponds to that of a ladder [Borges's note].

1. According to the assumptions of the theory (Latin).

age and fearfulness deceive me, but I suspect that the human species—the unique species—is about to be extinguished, but the Library will endure: illuminated, solitary, infinite, perfectly motionless, equipped with precious volumes, useless, incorruptible, secret.

I have just written the word "infinite." I have not interpolated this adjective out of rhetorical habit; I say that it is not illogical to think that the world is infinite. Those who judge it to be limited postulate that in remote places the corridors and stairways and hexagons can conceivably come to an end—which is absurd. Those who imagine it to be without limit forget that the possible number of books does have such a limit. I venture to suggest this solution to the ancient problem: *The Library is unlimited and cyclical.* If an eternal traveler were to cross it in any direction, after centuries he would see that the same volumes were repeated in the same disorder (which, thus repeated, would be an order: the Order). My solitude is gladdened by this elegant hope.[2]

2. Letizia Álvarez de Toledo has observed that this vast Library is useless: rigorously speaking, *a single volume* would be sufficient, a volume of ordinary format, printed in nine or ten point type, containing an infinite number of infinitely thin leaves. (In the early seventeenth century, Cavalieri said that all solid bodies are the superimposition of an infinite number of planes.) The handling of this silky vade mecum would not be convenient: each apparent page would unfold into other analogous ones; the inconceivable middle page would have no reverse [Borges's note]. "Letizia Álvarez de Toledo": Argentine writer, socialite, and contemporary of Borges. "Cavalieri": Bonaventura Cavalieri, Italian mathematician (1598–1647). "Vade mecum": literally, "go with me" (Latin), a handbook or guidebook.

BERTOLT BRECHT

1898–1956

Bertolt Brecht wrote several plays that became modern classics; perhaps just as important, he introduced a radical concept of theater that would have a profound impact on contemporary playwrights and producers. Dissatisfied with the traditional notion, derived from Aristotle's *Poetics*, that drama should draw its spectators into sympathy for the characters, Brecht proposed the idea of the "Epic Theater," which would alienate the audience from the action of the play, making the familiar appear strange. Inspired by Marxist theory, Brecht hoped that his spectators would be more critical than traditional theater audiences—would not just enjoy a play but think critically about it and then take steps to transform the society from which the drama had sprung.

Eugen Berthold Brecht was born in the medieval town of Augsburg, Bavaria, on February 10, 1898. His father was a respected citizen, director of a paper mill, and a Catholic. His mother, the daughter of a civil servant from the Black Forest region, was a Protestant who raised young Berthold in her faith. (The spelling *Bertolt* was adopted later.) Brecht attended local schools until 1917, when he enrolled in Munich University to study natural science and medicine. He continued his studies while acting as drama critic for an Augsburg newspaper and writing plays: *Drums in the Night* (1918) won the Kleist Prize in 1922. Toward the end of the First World War, Brecht was mobilized for a year as an orderly in a military hospital, and he pursued medical studies in Munich until 1921. Several years later he married Helene Weigel, an actress and director who worked closely with him and for whom he wrote many leading roles.

Moving to Berlin in 1924, Brecht worked briefly with the directors Max Reinhardt and Erwin Piscator but was chiefly interested in writing: he was especially concerned with the plight of ordinary men and women, buffeted by social and economic forces beyond their control until they lose both identity and humanity. After Brecht became a fervent Marxist in the mid-1920s, he felt even more strongly that he had a moral and artistic duty to encourage the audience to remedy social ills. *The Threepenny Opera* (1928), a work sung in ballads, was written with composer Kurt Weill (1900–1950) and modeled on John Gay's *The Beggar's Opera* (1728). It satirizes capitalist society from the point of view of outcasts and romanticizes thieves. It is probably Brecht's most popular play, largely because of Weill's music, including the song of the gangster Macheath, "Mack the Knife," which became an American standard when it was recorded by Louis Armstrong, Frank Sinatra, and others. Moreover, Brecht wrote a number of "teaching" plays intended to set forth communist doctrine and instruct German workers in the meaning of social revolution. The lesson is particularly harsh in *The Measures Taken* (1930), which describes the necessary execution of a young party member who has broken discipline by helping the local poor, thus postponing the revolution. Such drama, however doctrinally pure, was not likely to win adherents to the cause, and the communist press in Berlin and Moscow condemned the teaching plays as unattractive and "intellectualist."

Brecht's desire to create an activist theater embodying a Marxist view of art put him at odds with the rise of Hitler's National Socialism. He fled Germany for Denmark in 1933, before the Nazis could include him in their purge of left-wing intellectuals; in 1935 he was deprived of his German citizenship. Brecht would flee several more times as the Nazi invasions expanded throughout Europe: in 1939 to Sweden, in 1940 to Finland, and in 1941 to the United States, where he joined a colony of German expatriates in Santa Monica, California, working for the film industry. This was the period of some of his greatest plays. *The Life of Galileo* (1938–39) attacks society for suppressing the Italian astronomer's discovery, in the seventeenth century, that Earth revolves around the sun (the traditional belief was in the opposite phenomenon), but the drama also condemns the scientist for not insisting on the truth. *Mother Courage and Her Children* (1939) portrays an avaricious peddler who doggedly pursues the profits to be made from war even though her three children are victims of it. *The Good Woman of Setzuan* (1938–40) shows how an instinctively generous person can survive only by putting on a mask of hardness and calculation. In *The Caucasian Chalk Circle* (1944–45), an adaptation of the story of the Judgment of Solomon, the child is given to the servant girl rather than to the governor's wife (the implied comparison is between those who do the work of society and those who merely profit from their possessions). Brecht arranged for the translation of his work into English, and *Galileo*, with Charles Laughton in the title role, was produced in 1947. That same year Brecht was questioned by the House Un-American Activities Committee as part of a wide-ranging inquiry into possible communist activity in the entertainment business. No charges were filed against Brecht, but he left for Europe the day after being brought before the committee.

After leaving the United States, Brecht worked for a year in Zurich before going to Berlin with his wife to stage *Mother Courage*. The East Berlin government offered the couple positions as directors of their own troupe, the Berliner Ensemble, and Brecht—who had just finished a theoretical treatise, *A Little Organon for the Theater* (1949)—turned his attention to the professional role of director. (Throughout his life, Brecht had often collaborated with other authors, notably Elisabeth Hauptmann, who was also his mistress.) Although the East Berliners subsidized Brecht's work and advertised his presence as a tribute to their economic system, Brecht was forced to defend some of his plays against charges of political unorthodoxy and indeed to revise them. After 1934 the Communist Party generally advocated "socialist realism," an approach to the humanities in which the goal was to offer simple messages and to foster identification with revolutionary heroes. Brecht's mind was too keen and questioning, too attracted by irony and paradox, for him to provide simplistic dramas or to have a comfortable relation with authority, either on the right or on the left. After settling in East Berlin, he wrote no major plays but only minor propaganda pieces and adaptations of classical works such as **Molière**'s *Don Juan*, Shakespeare's *Coriolanus*, and Sophocles' *Antigone*. As an additional measure of protection, he took out Austrian citizenship through his wife's nationality. Brecht died in Berlin on August 14, 1956.

The epic theater movement, born in the 1920s, suited Brecht's needs, and through his plays, theoretical writings, and dramatic productions, he developed its basic ideas into one of the most powerful theatrical styles of the twentieth century. Brecht rejected the aesthetic of naturalness and psychological credibility that created an illusion of reality on the stage. Like **Luigi Pirandello**, Brecht believed that the stage should break through the closed world that playwrights such as the Norwegian **Henrik Ibsen** (1828–1906) and the Russian **Anton Chekhov** (1860–1904) had established as a dramatic convention: audiences were to look at the action from outside, as if the play were a slice of life going on behind the invisible "fourth wall." Unlike Pirandello, however, Brecht did not stress the anguish of individuals lacking self-awareness; his focus was on social responsibility and the community at large. For Brecht the audience must not be allowed to indulge in passive empathy or in the subjective whirlpool of existential identity crises. His characters are to be seen as members of society, and his audience should be educated and moved to action.

The epic theater derives its name from a famous essay, *On Epic and Dramatic Poetry* (1797), by **Johann Wolfgang von Goethe** and Friedrich Schiller, who described *dramatic* poetry as pulling the audience into emotional identification, in contrast to *epic* poetry, which, distanced in the time, place, and nature of the action, can be absorbed in calm contemplation. The idea of an epic theater is a paradox: how can a play engage an audience that is held at a distance? Brecht's solution was to employ "estrangement effects" to encourage spectators to think critically about what is taking place. Here Brecht echoed the work of the revolutionary Soviet director Vsevolod Meyerhold, whose antirealistic use of masks, pantomime, posters and film projections, song interludes, and direct address to the audience was well known to German audiences in the 1920s. He also drew on the tradition of vaudeville theater. Despite Brecht's intentions and frequent revisions, however, the characters and situations of his plays remain emotionally engrossing, especially in his best-known works, such as *The Good Woman of Setzuan*. As for the estrangement effects themselves, they have become standard production techniques in contemporary theater.

Brecht's concept of epic theater encompasses dramatic structure, stage setting, music, and performance. Episodes may be performed independently as self-contained dramatic parables, rather than tied to a developing plot. Songs break dramatic action and yet crystallize themes. Sometimes a narrator comments on the action. The estrangement effects are heightened by setting most of the plays in distant times or faraway lands, such as China in *The Good Woman of Setzuan*.

Events on stage may be announced beforehand by signs or accompanied by projected images during the action. Place-names printed on signs are suspended over the actors, and footlights and stage machinery are displayed. Masks identify wicked people; soldiers' faces are chalked white to suggest a stylized fear. Songs that interrupt the dramatic action are addressed directly to the audience, sometimes heralded by a sign. In addition, actors should "demonstrate" their parts instead of being submerged in them. At rehearsals Brecht often asked actors to speak their parts in the third person instead of the first. Such artificiality makes it difficult for the audience to identify unself-consciously with the characters on stage; instead spectators maintain, ideally, the impartiality of a jury.

The Good Woman of Setzuan, printed here, was written between 1938 and 1940, with the collaboration of Margarete Steffin and Ruth Berlau, and with music by Paul Dessau. Painfully drafted while Brecht, his family, Steffin, and Berlau sought refuge in Scandinavia from the Nazis, the play is stamped with disillusionment with a world in which it is impossible to be good and survive. The "good woman," Shen Te, must save herself from a swarm of parasites and opportunists. The split that develops stands for the broader gulf between the intimate sphere in which moral action is possible and the social world in which one must struggle for survival. The play's setting in China was probably suggested by a 1935 visit to Moscow, where Brecht was impressed by the highly stylized performances of the Chinese actor Mei Lanfang. (He also admired Japanese Noh and Kabuki theater.)

Shen Te's story reflects a larger thematic concern: the state of the universe or, more mundanely, whether the world is so corrupt that drastic intervention is needed. Her situation arises from a good deed that has counterparts in world mythologies and also in the Bible: hospitality offered to disguised divine messengers, who reward the giver accordingly. Three Chinese gods visiting Earth in search of good people give Shen Te, a penniless prostitute, a thousand silver dollars in recompense for being the only person in Setzuan to provide them with lodging. Brecht borrows from the Old Testament story of Sodom and Gomorrah, in which God sends angels down to find ten good people in the debauched city of Sodom so that it may be saved from destruction. But these modern gods are comic and certainly ineffectual. Wearing old-fashioned clothes and dusty shoes, they have been delegated by a bureaucratic resolution on high (whose terms they debate); they ignore inconvenient questions and merely repeat the inapplicable regulations; and they are terrified of complications that would disturb the status quo. Their refusal to be involved reinforces Brecht's underlying thesis that "good" and "evil" are not divine entities but rather social issues, and that the way to reform a corrupt world is for people to unite in action focused on the common good.

The Good Woman of Setzuan[1]

CHARACTERS

WONG, *a water seller*
THREE GODS
SHEN TE, *a prostitute, later a shopkeeper*
MRS. SHIN, *former owner of Shen Te's shop*
A family of eight (HUSBAND, WIFE, BROTHER, SISTER-IN-LAW, GRANDFATHER, NEPHEW, NIECE, BOY)
An UNEMPLOYED MAN
A CARPENTER
MRS. MI TZU, *Shen Te's landlady*
MR. SHUI TA
YANG SUN, *an unemployed pilot, later a factory manager*
An OLD WHORE
A POLICEMAN
An OLD MAN
An OLD WOMAN, *his wife*
MR. SHU FU, *a barber*
MRS. YANG, *mother of Yang Sun*
GENTLEMEN, VOICES, PRIEST, WAITER, *children (three), etc.*

Prologue

At the gates of the half-Westernized city of Setzuan. Evening. WONG *the water seller*[2] *introduces himself to the audience.*

WONG I sell water here in the city of Setzuan. It isn't easy. When water is scarce, I have long distances to go in search of it, and when it is plentiful, I have no income. But in our part of the world there is nothing unusual about poverty. Many people think only the gods can save the situation. And I hear from a cattle merchant—who travels a lot—that some of the highest gods are on their way here at this very moment. Informed sources have it that heaven is quite disturbed at all the complaining.[3] I've been coming out here to the city gates for three days now to bid these gods welcome. I want to be the first to greet them. What about those fellows over there? No, no, they *work.* And that one there has ink on his fingers, he's no god, he must be a clerk from the cement factory. *Those* two are another story. They look as though they'd like to beat you. But gods don't need to beat you, do they? [THREE GODS *appear.*] What about those three? Old-fashioned clothes—dust on their feet—they *must* be gods! [*He throws himself at their feet.*] Do with me what you will, illustrious ones!

1. Translated by Eric Bentley. Setzuan is a province in China; the play's setting is both the capital of Setzuan and, according to a later statement in the play, a generalized location: "wherever man is exploited by man."
2. Water peddlers were common in ancient China.
3. Heaven, in Chinese philosophy, was identical with absolute and transcendental order.

FIRST GOD [*With an ear trumpet.*] Ah! [*He is pleased.*] So we were expected?

WONG [*Giving them water.*] Oh, yes. And I *knew* you'd come.

FIRST GOD We need somewhere to stay the night. You know of a place?

WONG The whole town is at your service, illustrious ones! What sort of a place would you like?

[*The* GODS *eye each other.*]

FIRST GOD Just try the first house you come to, my son.

WONG That would be Mr. Fo's place.

FIRST GOD Mr. Fo.

WONG One moment! [*He knocks at the first house.*]

VOICE FROM MR. FO'S. No!

[WONG *returns a little nervously.*]

WONG It's too bad. Mr. Fo isn't in. And his servants don't dare do a thing without his consent. He'll have a fit when he finds out who they turned away, won't he?

FIRST GOD [*Smiling.*] He will, won't he?

WONG One moment! The next house is Mr. Cheng's. Won't he be thrilled!

FIRST GOD Mr. Cheng.

[WONG *knocks.*]

VOICE FROM MR. CHENG'S Keep your gods. We have our own troubles!

WONG [*Back with the* GODS.] Mr. Cheng is very sorry, but he has a houseful of relations. I think some of them are a bad lot, and naturally, he wouldn't like you to see them.

THIRD GOD Are we so terrible?

WONG Well, only with bad people, of course. Everyone knows the province of Kwan is always having floods.

SECOND GOD Really? How's that?

WONG Why, because they're so irreligious.

SECOND GOD Rubbish. It's because they neglected the dam.

FIRST GOD [*To* SECOND.] Sh! [*To* WONG.] You're still in hopes, aren't you, my son?

WONG Certainly. All Setzuan is competing for the honor! What happened up to now is pure coincidence. I'll be back. [*He walks away, but then stands undecided.*]

SECOND GOD What did I tell you?

THIRD GOD It *could* be pure coincidence.

SECOND GOD The same coincidence in Shun, Kwan, and Setzuan? People just aren't religious any more, let's face the fact. Our mission has failed!

FIRST GOD Oh come, we might run into a good person any minute.

THIRD GOD How did the resolution read? [*Unrolling a scroll and reading from it.*] "The world can stay as it is if enough people are found [*At the word "found" he unrolls it a little more*] living lives worthy of human beings." Good people, that is. Well, what about this water seller himself? *He's* good, or I'm very much mistaken.

SECOND GOD You're very much mistaken. When he gave us a drink, I had the impression there was something odd about the cup. Well, look! [*He shows the cup to the* FIRST GOD.]

FIRST GOD A false bottom!

SECOND GOD The man is a swindler.

FIRST GOD Very well, count *him* out. That's one man among millions. And as a matter of fact, we only need one on *our* side. These atheists are saying, "The world must be changed because no one can *be* good and *stay* good." No one, eh? I say: let us find one—just one—and we have those fellows where we want them!

THIRD GOD [*To* WONG.] Water seller, is it so hard to find a place to stay?

WONG Nothing could be easier. It's just me. I don't go about it right.

THIRD GOD Really?

[*He returns to the others. A* GENTLEMAN *passes by.*]

WONG Oh dear, they're catching on. [*He accosts the* GENTLEMAN.] Excuse the intrusion, dear sir, but three gods have just turned up. Three of the very highest. They need a place for the night. Seize this rare opportunity—to have real gods as your guests!

GENTLEMAN [*laughing*]. A new way of finding free rooms for a gang of crooks. [*Exit* GENTLEMAN.]

WONG [*shouting at him.*] Godless rascal! Have you no religion, gentlemen of Setzuan? [*Pause*]. Patience, illustrious ones! [*Pause.*] There's only one person left. Shen Te, the prostitute. She *can't* say no. [*Calls up to a window.*] Shen Te!

[SHEN TE *opens the shutters and looks out.*]

WONG Shen Te, it's Wong. *They're* here, and nobody wants them. Will you take them?

SHEN TE Oh, no, Wong, I'm expecting a gentleman.

WONG Can't you forget about him for tonight?

SHEN TE The rent has to be paid by tomorrow or I'll be out on the street.

WONG This is no time for calculation, Shen Te.

SHEN TE Stomachs rumble even on the Emperor's birthday, Wong.

WONG Setzuan is one big dung hill!

SHEN TE Oh, very well! I'll hide till my gentleman has come and gone. Then I'll take them. [*She disappears.*]

WONG They mustn't see her gentleman or they'll know what she is.

FIRST GOD [*Who hasn't heard any of this.*] I think it's hopeless.

[*They approach* WONG.]

WONG [*Jumping, as he finds them behind him*]. A room has been found, illustrious ones! [*He wipes sweat off his brow.*]

SECOND GOD Oh, good.

THIRD GOD Let's see it.

WONG [*Nervously.*] Just a minute. It has to be tidied up a bit.

THIRD GOD Then we'll sit down here and wait.

WONG [*Still more nervous.*] No, no! [*Holding himself back.*] Too much traffic, you know.

THIRD GOD [*With a smile.*] Of course, if you *want* us to move.

[*They retire a little. They sit on a doorstep.* WONG *sits on the ground.*]

WONG [*After a deep breath.*] You'll be staying with a single girl—the finest human being in Setzuan!

THIRD GOD That's nice.

WONG [*To the audience.*] They gave me such a look when I picked up my cup just now.

THIRD GOD You're worn out, Wong.

WONG A little, maybe.

FIRST GOD Do people here have a hard time of it?

WONG The good ones do.

FIRST GOD What about yourself!

WONG You mean I'm not good. That's true. And I don't have an easy time either!

[*During this dialogue, a* GENTLEMAN *has turned up in front of Shen Te's House, and has whistled several times. Each time* WONG *has given a start.*]

THIRD GOD [*To* WONG, *softly.*] Psst! I think he's gone now.

WONG [*Confused and surprised.*] Ye-e-es.

[*The* GENTLEMAN *has left now, and* SHEN TE *has come down to the street.*]

SHEN TE [*softly.*] Wong!

[*Getting no answer, she goes off down the street.* WONG *arrives just too late, forgetting his carrying pole.*]

WONG [*Softly.*] Shen Te! Shen Te! [*To himself.*] So she's gone off to earn the rent. Oh dear, I can't go to the gods *again* with no room to offer them. Having failed in the service of the gods, I shall run to my den in the sewer pipe down by the river and hide from their sight!

[*He rushes off.* SHEN TE *returns, looking for him, but finding the* GODS. *She stops in confusion.*]

SHEN TE You are the illustrious ones? My name is Shen Te. It would please me very much if my simple room could be of use to you.

THIRD GOD Where is the water seller, Miss . . . Shen Te?

SHEN TE I missed him, somehow.

FIRST GOD Oh, he probably thought you weren't coming, and was afraid of telling us.

THIRD GOD [*Picking up the carrying pole.*] We'll leave this with you. He'll be needing it.

[*Led by* SHEN TE, *they go into the house. It grows dark, then light. Dawn. Again escorted by* SHEN TE, *who leads them through the half-light with a little lamp, the* GODS *take their leave.*]

FIRST GOD Thank you, thank you, dear Shen Te, for your elegant hospitality! We shall not forget! And give our thanks to the water seller—he showed us a good human being.

SHEN TE Oh, *I'm* not good. Let me tell you something: when Wong asked me to put you up, I hesitated.

FIRST GOD It's all right to hesitate if you then go ahead! And in giving us that room you did much more than you knew. You proved that good people still exist, a point that has been disputed of late—even in heaven. Farewell!

SECOND GOD Farewell!

THIRD GOD Farewell!

SHEN TE Stop, illustrious ones! I'm not sure you're right. I'd like to be good, it's true, but there's the rent to pay. And that's not all: I sell myself for a living. Even so I can't make ends meet, there's too much competition. I'd like to honor my father and mother and speak nothing but the truth and not covet my neighbor's house. I should love to stay with one man. But how?

How is it done? Even breaking a few of your commandments,[4] I can hardly manage.

FIRST GOD [*Clearing his throat.*] These thoughts are but, um, the misgivings of an unusually good woman!

THIRD GOD Good-bye, Shen Te! Give our regards to the water seller!

SECOND GOD And above all: be good! Farewell!

FIRST GOD Farewell!

THIRD GOD Farewell!

[*They start to wave good-bye.*]

SHEN TE But everything is so expensive, I don't feel sure I can do it!

SECOND GOD That's not in our sphere. We never meddle with economics.

THIRD GOD One moment. [*They stop.*] Isn't it true she might do better if she had more money?

SECOND GOD Come, come! How could we ever account for it Up Above?

FIRST GOD Oh, there are ways. [*They put their heads together and confer in dumb show. To* SHEN TE, *with embarrassment.*] As you say you can't pay your rent, well, um, we're not paupers, so of course we *insist* on paying for our room. [*Awkwardly thrusting money into her hands.*] There! [*Quickly.*] But don't tell anyone! The incident is open to misinterpretation.

SECOND GOD It certainly is!

FIRST GOD [*Defensively.*] But there's no law against it! It was never decreed that a god mustn't pay hotel bills!

[*The* GODS *leave.*]

1

A small tobacco shop. The shop is not as yet completely furnished and hasn't started doing business.

SHEN TE [*To the audience.*] It's three days now since the gods left. When they said they wanted to pay for the room, I looked down at my hand, and there was more than a thousand silver dollars![5] I bought a tobacco shop with the money, and moved in yesterday. I don't own the building, of course, but I can pay the rent, and I hope to do a lot of good here. Beginning with Mrs. Shin, who's just coming across the square with her pot. She had the shop before me, and yesterday she dropped in to ask for rice for her children. [*Enter* MRS. SHIN. *Both women bow.*] How do you do, Mrs. Shin.

MRS. SHIN How do you do, Miss Shen Te. You like your new home?

SHEN TE Indeed, yes. Did your children have a good night?

MRS. SHIN In that hovel? The youngest is coughing already.

SHEN TE Oh, dear!

MRS. SHIN You're going to learn a thing or two in these slums.

SHEN TE Slums? That's not what you said when you sold me the shop!

MRS. SHIN Now don't start nagging! Robbing me and my innocent children of their home and then calling it a slum! That's the limit!

[*She weeps.*]

4. An allusion to the Decalogue of the Old Testament and specifically to Commandments 4, 6, 8, 9, and 10 (Exodus 20).

5. Either official Chinese silver dollars (yuan) or coins from one of the foreign currencies in circulation.

SHEN TE [*Tactfully.*] I'll get your rice.

MRS. SHIN And a little cash while you're at it.

SHEN TE I'm afraid I haven't sold anything yet.

MRS. SHIN [*Screeching.*] I've got to have it. Strip the clothes from my back and then cut my throat, will you? I know what I'll do: I'll dump my children on your doorstep! [*She snatches the pot out of* SHEN TE*'s hands.*]

SHEN TE Please don't be angry. You'll spill the rice.

[*Enter an elderly* HUSBAND *and* WIFE *with their shabbily dressed* NEPHEW.]

WIFE Shen Te, dear! You've come into money, they tell me. And we haven't a roof over our heads! A tobacco shop. We had one too. But it's gone. Could we spend the night here, do you think?

NEPHEW [*Appraising the shop.*] Not bad!

WIFE He's our nephew. We're inseparable!

MRS. SHIN And who are these . . . ladies and gentlemen?

SHEN TE They put me up when I first came in from the country. [*To the audience.*] Of course, when my small purse was empty, they put me out on the street, and they may be afraid I'll do the same to them [*To the newcomers, kindly.*] Come in, and welcome, though I've only one little room for you—it's behind the shop.

HUSBAND That'll do. Don't worry.

WIFE [*Bringing* SHEN TE *some tea.*] We'll stay over here, so we won't be in your way. Did you make it a tobacco shop in memory of your first real home? We can certainly give you a hint or two! That's one reason we came.

MRS SHIN [*To* SHEN TE.] Very nice! As long as you have a few customers too!

HUSBAND Sh! A customer!

[*Enter an* UNEMPLOYED MAN, *in rags.*]

UNEMPLOYED MAN Excuse me. I'm unemployed.

[MRS. SHIN *laughs.*]

SHEN TE Can I help you?

UNEMPLOYED MAN Have you any damaged cigarettes? I thought there might be some damage when you're unpacking.

WIFE What nerve, begging for tobacco! [*Rhetorically.*] Why don't they ask for bread?

UNEMPLOYED MAN Bread is expensive. One cigarette butt and I'll be a new man.

SHEN TE [*Giving him cigarettes.*] That's very important—to be a new man. You'll be my first customer and bring me luck.

[*The* UNEMPLOYED MAN *quickly lights a cigarette, inhales, and goes off, coughing.*]

WIFE Was that right, Shen Te, dear?

MRS. SHIN If this is the opening of a shop, you can hold the closing at the end of the week.

HUSBAND I bet he had money on him.

SHEN TE Oh, no, he said he hadn't!

NEPHEW How d'you know he wasn't lying?

SHEN TE [*Angrily.*] How do you know he was?

WIFE [*Wagging her head.*] You're too good, Shen Te, dear. If you're going to keep this shop, you'll have to learn to say no.

HUSBAND Tell them the place isn't yours to dispose of. Belongs to . . . some relative who insists on all accounts being strictly in order . . .

MRS. SHIN That's right! What do you think you are—a philanthropist?

SHEN TE [*Laughing.*] Very well, suppose I ask you for my rice back, Mrs. Shin?

WIFE [*Combatively, at* MRS. SHIN.] So that's *her* rice?

[*Enter the* CARPENTER, *a small man.*]

MRS. SHIN [*Who, at the sight of him, starts to hurry away.*] See you tomorrow, Miss Shen Te! [*Exit* MRS. SHIN.]

CARPENTER Mrs. Shin, it's you I want!

WIFE [*To* SHEN TE.] Has she some claim on you?

SHEN TE She's hungry. That's a claim.

CARPENTER Are you the new tenant? And filling up the shelves already? Well, they're not yours till they're paid for, ma'am. I'm the carpenter, so I should know.

SHEN TE I took the shop "furnishings included."

CARPENTER You're in league with that Mrs. Shin, of course. All right. I demand my hundred silver dollars.

SHEN TE I'm afraid I haven't got a hundred silver dollars.

CARPENTER Then you'll find it. Or I'll have you arrested.

WIFE [*Whispering to* SHEN TE.] That relative: make it a cousin.

SHEN TE Can't it wait till next month?

CARPENTER No!

SHEN TE Be a little patient, Mr. Carpenter, I can't settle all claims at once.

CARPENTER Who's patient with me? [*He grabs a shelf from the wall.*] Pay up—or I take the shelves back!

WIFE Shen Te! Dear! Why don't you let your . . . cousin settle this affair? [*To* CARPENTER.] Put your claim in writing. Shen Te's cousin will see you get paid.

CARPENTER [*Derisively.*] Cousin, eh?

HUSBAND Cousin, yes.

CARPENTER I know these cousins!

NEPHEW Don't be silly. He's a personal friend of mine.

HUSBAND What a man! Sharp as a razor!

CARPENTER All right. I'll put my claim in writing. [*Puts shelf on floor, sits on it, writes out bill.*]

WIFE [*To* SHEN TE.] He'd tear the dress off your back to get his shelves. Never recognize a claim! That's my motto.

SHEN TE He's done a job, and wants something in return. It's shameful that I can't give it to him. What will the gods say?

HUSBAND You did your bit when you took *us* in.

[*Enter the* BROTHER, *limping, and the* SISTER-IN-LAW, *pregnant.*]

BROTHER [*To* HUSBAND *and* WIFE.] So this is where you're hiding out! There's family feeling for you! Leaving us on the corner!

WIFE [*Embarrassed, to* SHEN TE.] It's my brother and his wife. [*To them.*] Now stop grumbling, and sit quietly in that corner. [*To* SHEN TE.] It can't be helped. She's in her fifth month.

SHEN TE Oh yes. Welcome!

WIFE [*To the couple.*] Say thank you. [*They mutter something.*] The cups are there. [*To* SHEN TE.] Lucky you bought this shop when you did!

SHEN TE [*Laughing and bringing tea.*] Lucky indeed!

[*Enter* MRS. MI TZU, *the landlady.*]

MRS. MI TZU Miss Shen Te? I am Mrs. Mi Tzu, your landlady. I hope our relationship will be a happy one. I like to think I give my tenants modern, personalized service. Here is your lease. [*To the others, as* SHEN TE *reads the lease.*] There's nothing like the opening of a little shop, is there? A moment of true beauty! [*She is looking around.*] Not very much on the shelves, of course. But everything in the gods' good time! Where are your references, Miss Shen Te?

SHEN TE Do I *have* to have references?

MRS. MI TZU After all, I haven't a notion who you are!

HUSBAND Oh, *we'd* be glad to vouch for Miss Shen Te! We'd go through fire for her!

MRS. MI TZU And who may *you* be?

HUSBAND [*Stammering.*] Ma Fu, tobacco dealer.

MRS. MI TZU Where is your shop, Mr. . . . Ma Fu?

HUSBAND Well, um, I haven't got a shop—I've just sold it.

MRS. MI TZU I see. [*To* SHEN TE.] Is there no one else that knows you?

WIFE [*Whispering to* SHEN TE.] Your cousin! Your cousin!

MRS. MI TZU This is a respectable house, Miss Shen Te. I never sign a lease without certain assurances.

SHEN TE [*Slowly, her eyes downcast.*] I have . . . a cousin.

MRS. MI TZU On the square? Let's go over and see him. What does he do?

SHEN TE [*As before.*] He lives . . . in another city.

WIFE [*Prompting.*] Didn't you say he was in Shung?

SHEN TE That's right. Shung.

HUSBAND [*Prompting.*] I had his name on the tip of my tongue, Mr. . . .

SHEN TE [*With an effort.*] Mr. . . . Shui . . . Ta.

HUSBAND That's it! Tall, skinny fellow!

SHEN TE Shui Ta!

NEPHEW [*To* CARPENTER.] *You* were in touch with him, weren't you? About the shelves?

CARPENTER [*Surlily.*] Give him this bill. [*He hands it over.*] I'll be back in the morning. [*Exit* CARPENTER.]

NEPHEW [*Calling after him, but with his eyes on* MRS. MI TZU.] Don't worry! Mr. Shui Ta pays on the nail!

MRS. MI TZU [*Looking closely at* SHEN TE.] I'll be happy to make his acquaintance, Miss Shen Te. [*Exit* MRS. MI TZU.]

[*Pause.*]

WIFE By tomorrow morning she'll know more about you than you do yourself.

SISTER-IN-LAW [*To* NEPHEW.] This thing isn't built to last.

[*Enter* GRANDFATHER.]

WIFE It's Grandfather! [*To* SHEN TE.] Such a good old soul!

[*The* BOY *enters.*]

BOY [*Over his shoulder.*] Here they are!

WIFE And the boy, how he's grown! But he always could eat enough for ten.

[*Enter the* NIECE.]

WIFE [*To* SHEN TE.] Our little niece from the country. There are more of us now than in your time. The less we had, the more there were of us; the more there were of us, the less we had. Give me the key. We must protect ourselves from unwanted guests. [*She takes the key and locks the door.*] Just make yourself at home. I'll light the little lamp.

NEPHEW [*A big joke.*] I hope her cousin doesn't drop in tonight! The strict Mr. Shui Ta!

[SISTER-IN-LAW *laughs.*]

BROTHER [*Reaching for a cigarette.*] One cigarette more or less . . .

HUSBAND One cigarette more or less.

[*They pile into the cigarettes. The* BROTHER *hands a jug of wine round.*]

NEPHEW Mr. Shui Ta'll pay for it!

GRANDFATHER [*Gravely, to* SHEN TE.] How do you do?

[SHEN TE, *a little taken aback by the belatedness of the greeting, bows. She has the carpenter's bill in one hand, the landlady's lease in the other.*]

WIFE How about a bit of a song? To keep Shen Te's spirits up?

NEPHEW Good idea. Grandfather: you start!

SONG OF THE SMOKE

GRANDFATHER

I used to think (before old age beset me)
That brains could fill the pantry of the poor.
But where did all my cerebration get me?
I'm just as hungry as I was before.
So what's the use?
See the smoke float free
Into ever colder coldness!
It's the same with me.[6]

HUSBAND

The straight and narrow path leads to disaster
And so the crooked path I tried to tread.
That got me to disaster even faster.
(They say we shall be happy when we're dead.)
So what's the use?
See the smoke float free
Into ever colder coldness!
It's the same with me

NIECE

You older people, full of expectation,
At any moment now you'll walk the plank!
The future's for the younger generation!
Yes, even if that future is a blank.
So what's the use?
See the smoke float free
Into ever colder coldness!
It's the same with me.

NEPHEW [*To the* BROTHER.] Where'd you get that wine?

SISTER-IN-LAW [*Answering for the* BROTHER.] He pawned the sack of tobacco.

HUSBAND [*Stepping in.*] What? That tobacco was all we had to fall back on! You pig!

6. The refrain in this song is taken from a poem Brecht wrote in the 1920s entitled "The Song of the Opium Den."

BROTHER *You'd* call a man a pig because your wife was frigid! Did you refuse to drink it?

[*They fight. The shelves fall over.*]

SHEN TE [*Imploringly.*] Oh don't! Don't break everything! Take it, take it all, but don't destroy a gift from the gods!

WIFE [*Disparagingly.*] This shop isn't big enough. I should never have mentioned it to Uncle and the others. When *they* arrive, it's going to be disgustingly overcrowded.

SISTER-IN-LAW And did you hear our gracious hostess? She cools off quick!

[*Voices outside. Knocking at the door.*]

UNCLE'S VOICE Open the door!

WIFE Uncle? Is that you, Uncle?

UNCLE'S VOICE Certainly, it's me. Auntie says to tell you she'll have the children here in ten minutes.

WIFE [*To* SHEN TE.] I'll have to let him in.

SHEN TE [*Who scarcely hears her.*]

The little lifeboat is swiftly sent down
Too many men too greedily
Hold on to it as they drown.

1a

WONG'S *den in a sewer pipe.*

WONG [*Crouching there.*] All quiet! It's four days now since I left the city. The gods passed this way on the second day. I heard their steps on the bridge over there. They must be a long way off by this time, so I'm safe. [*Breathing a sigh of relief, he curls up and goes to sleep. In his dream the pipe becomes transparent, and the* GODS *appear. Raising an arm, as if in self-defense.*] I know, I know, illustrious ones! I found no one to give you a room—not in all Setzuan! There, it's out. Please continue on your way!

FIRST GOD [*Mildly.*] But you did find someone. Someone who took us in for the night, watched over us in our sleep, and in the early morning lighted us down to the street with a lamp.

WONG It was . . . Shen Te that took you in?

THIRD GOD Who else?

WONG And I ran away! "She isn't coming," I thought, "she just can't afford it."

GODS [*Singing.*]

O you feeble, well-intentioned, and yet feeble chap
Where there's need the fellow thinks there is no goodness!
When there's danger he thinks courage starts to ebb away!
Some people only see the seamy side!
What hasty judgment! What premature desperation!

WONG I'm *very* ashamed, illustrious ones.

FIRST GOD Do us a favor, water seller. Go back to Setzuan. Find Shen Te, and give us a report on her. We hear that she's come into a little money. Show interest in her goodness—for no one can be good for long if goodness is not in demand. Meanwhile we shall continue the search, and find other good people. After which, the idle chatter about the impossibility of goodness will stop!

[*The* GODS *vanish.*]

2

A knocking.

WIFE Shen Te! Someone at the door. Where is she anyway?

NEPHEW She must be getting the breakfast. Mr. Shui Ta will pay for it.

[*The* WIFE *laughs and shuffles to the door. Enter Mr.* SHUI TA *and the* CARPENTER.]

WIFE Who is it?

SHUI TA I am Miss Shen Te's cousin.

WIFE What??

SHUI TA My name is Shui Ta.

WIFE Her cousin?

NEPHEW Her cousin?

NIECE But that was a joke. She hasn't got a cousin.

HUSBAND So early in the morning?

BROTHER What's all the noise?

SISTER-IN-LAW This fellow says he's her cousin.

BROTHER Tell him to prove it.

NEPHEW Right. If you're Shen Te's cousin, prove it by getting the breakfast.

SHUI TA [*Whose regime begins as he puts out the lamp to save oil; loudly, to all present, asleep or awake.*] Would you all please get dressed! Customers will be coming! I wish to open my shop!

HUSBAND *Your* shop? Doesn't it belong to our good friend Shen Te?

[SHUI TA *shakes his head.*]

SISTER-IN-LAW So we've been cheated. Where *is* the little liar?

SHUI TA Miss Shen Te has been delayed. She wishes me to tell you there will be nothing she can do—now I am here.

WIFE [*Bowled over.*] I thought she was good!

NEPHEW Do you have to believe *him*?

HUSBAND I don't.

NEPHEW Then do something.

HUSBAND Certainly! I'll send out a search party at once. You, you, you, and you, go out and look for Shen Te. [*As the* GRANDFATHER *rises and makes for the door*] Not you, Grandfather, you and I will hold the fort.

SHUI TA You won't find Miss Shen Te. She has suspended her hospitable activity for an unlimited period. There are too many of you. She asked me to say: this is a tobacco shop, not a gold mine.

HUSBAND Shen Te never said a thing like that. Boy, food! There's a bakery on the corner. Stuff your shirt full when they're not looking!

SISTER-IN-LAW Don't overlook the raspberry tarts.

HUSBAND And don't let the policeman see you.

[*The* BOY *leaves.*]

SHUI TA Don't you depend on this shop now? Then why give it a bad name by stealing from the bakery?

NEPHEW Don't listen to him. Let's find Shen Te. She'll give him a piece of her mind.

SISTER-IN-LAW Don't forget to leave us some breakfast.

[BROTHER, SISTER-IN-LAW *and* NEPHEW *leave.*]

SHUI TA [*To the* CARPENTER.] You see, Mr. Carpenter, nothing has changed since the poet, eleven hundred years ago, penned these lines:

A governor was asked what was needed
To save the freezing people in the city.
He replied:
"A blanket ten thousand feet long
To cover the city and all its suburbs."[7]

[*He starts to tidy up the shop.*]

CARPENTER Your cousin owes me money. I've got witnesses. For the shelves.

SHUI TA Yes, I have your bill. [*He takes it out of his pocket.*] Isn't a hundred silver dollars rather a lot?

CARPENTER No deductions! I have a wife and children.

SHUI TA How many children?

CARPENTER Three.

SHUI TA I'll make you an offer. Twenty silver dollars.

[*The* HUSBAND *laughs.*]

CARPENTER You're crazy. Those shelves are real walnut.

SHUI TA Very well, take them away.

CARPENTER What?

SHUI TA They cost too much. Please take them away.

WIFE Not bad! [*And she, too, is laughing.*]

CARPENTER [*A little bewildered.*] Call Shen Te, someone! [*To* SHUI TA.] She's good!

SHUI TA Certainly. She's ruined.

CARPENTER [*Provoked into taking some of the shelves.*] All right, you can keep your tobacco on the floor.

SHUI TA [*to the* HUSBAND.] Help him with the shelves.

HUSBAND [*Grins and carries one shelf over to the door where the* CARPENTER *now is.*] Good-bye, shelves!

CARPENTER [*To the* HUSBAND.] You dog! You want my family to starve?

SHUI TA I repeat my offer. I have no desire to keep my tobacco on the floor. Twenty silver dollars.

CARPENTER [*With desperate aggressiveness.*] One hundred!

[SHUI TA *shows indifference, looks through the window. The* HUSBAND *picks up several shelves.*]

CARPENTER [*To* HUSBAND.] You needn't smash them against the doorpost, you idiot! [*To* SHUI TA.] These shelves were made to measure. They're no use anywhere else!

SHUI TA Precisely.

[*The* WIFE *squeals with pleasure.*]

CARPENTER [*Giving up, sullenly.*] Take the shelves. Pay what you want to pay.

7. Reference to a poem, "The Big Rug," by the classical Chinese poet Po Chü-i (772–846 C.E.).

SHUI TA [*Smoothly.*] Twenty silver dollars.

[*He places two large coins on the table. The* CARPENTER *picks them up.*]

HUSBAND [*Brings the shelves back in.*] And quite enough too!

CARPENTER [*Slinking off.*] Quite enough to get drunk on.

HUSBAND [*Happily.*] Well, we got rid of *him*!

WIFE [*Weeping with fun, gives a rendition of the dialogue just spoken.*] "Real walnut," says he. "Very well, take them away," says his lordship. "I have three children," says he. "Twenty silver dollars," says his lordship. "They're no use anywhere else," says he. "Pre-cisely," said his lordship! [*She dissolves into shrieks of merriment.*]

SHUI TA And now: go!

HUSBAND What's that?

SHUI TA You're thieves, parasites. I'm giving you this chance. Go!

HUSBAND [*Summoning all his ancestral dignity.*] That sort deserves no answer. Besides, one should never shout on an empty stomach.

WIFE Where's that boy?

SHUI TA Exactly. The boy. I want no stolen goods in this shop. [*Very loudly.*] I strongly advise you to leave! [*But they remain seated, noses in the air. Quietly.*] As you wish. [SHUI TA *goes to the door. A* POLICEMAN *appears.* SHUI TA *bows.*] I am addressing the officer in charge of this precinct?

POLICEMAN That's right, Mr., um, what was the name, sir?

SHUI TA Mr. Shui Ta.

POLICEMAN Yes, of course, sir.

[*They exchange a smile.*]

SHUI TA Nice weather we're having.

POLICEMAN A little on the warm side, sir.

SHUI TA Oh, a little on the warm side.

HUSBAND [*Whispering to the* WIFE.] If he keeps it up till the boy's back, we're done for. [*Tries to signal* SHUI TA.]

SHUI TA [*Ignoring the signal.*] Weather, of course, is one thing indoors, another out on the dusty street!

POLICEMAN Oh, quite another, sir!

WIFE [*To the* HUSBAND.] It's all right as long as he's standing in the doorway—the boy will see him.

SHUI TA Step inside for a moment! It's quite cool indoors. My cousin and I have just opened the place. And we attach the greatest importance to being on good terms with the, um, authorities.

POLICEMAN [*Entering.*] Thank you, Mr. Shui Ta. It *is* cool!

HUSBAND [*Whispering to the* WIFE.] And now the boy *won't* see him.

SHUI TA [*Showing* HUSBAND *and* WIFE *to the* POLICEMAN.] Visitors, I think my cousin knows them. They were just leaving.

HUSBAND [*Defeated.*] Ye-e-es, we were . . . just leaving.

SHUI TA I'll tell my cousin you couldn't wait.

[*Noise from the street. Shouts of* "Stop, Thief!"]

POLICEMAN What's that?

[*The* BOY *is in the doorway with cakes and buns and rolls spilling out of his shirt. The* WIFE *signals desperately to him to leave. He gets the idea.*]

POLICEMAN No, you don't. [*He grabs the* BOY *by the collar.*] Where's all this from?

BOY [*Vaguely pointing.*] Down the street.

POLICEMAN [*Grimly.*] So that's it. [*Prepares to arrest the* BOY.]

WIFE [*Stepping in.*] And *we* knew nothing about it. [*To the* BOY.] Nasty little thief!

POLICEMAN [*Dryly.*] Can you clarify the situation, Mr. Shui Ta?

[SHUI TA *is silent.*]

POLICEMAN [*Who understands silence.*] Aha. You're all coming with me—to the station.

SHUI TA I can hardly say how sorry I am that *my* establishment . . .

WIFE Oh, he saw the boy leave not ten minutes ago!

SHUI TA And to conceal the theft asked a policeman in?

POLICEMAN Don't listen to her, Mr. Shui Ta, I'll be happy to relieve you of their presence one and all! [*To all three.*] Out!

[*He drives them before him.*]

GRANDFATHER [*Leaving last, gravely.*] Good morning!

POLICEMAN Good morning!

[SHUI TA, *left alone, continues to tidy up.* MRS. MI TZU *breezes in.*]

MRS. MI TZU *You're* her cousin, are you? Then have the goodness to explain what all this means—police dragging people from a respectable house! By what right does your Miss Shen Te turn my property into a house of assignation?—Well, as you see, I know all!

SHUI TA Yes. My cousin has the worst possible reputation: that of being poor.

MRS. MI TZU No sentimental rubbish, Mr. Shui Ta. Your cousin was a common . . .

SHUI TA Pauper. Let's use the uglier word.

MRS. MI TZU I'm speaking of her conduct, not her earnings. But there must have *been* earnings, or how did she buy all this? Several elderly gentlemen took care of it, I suppose. I repeat: this is a respectable house! I have tenants who prefer not to live under the same roof with such a person.

SHUI TA [*Quietly.*] How much do you want?

MRS. MI TZU [*He is ahead of her now.*] I beg your pardon.

SHUI TA To reassure yourself. To reassure your tenants. How much will it cost?

MRS. MI TZU You're a cool customer

SHUI TA [*Picking up the lease.*] The rent is high. [*He reads on.*] I assume it's payable by the month?

MRS. MI TZU Not in her case.

SHUI TA [*Looking up.*] What?

MRS. MI TZU Six months' rent payable in advance. Two hundred silver dollars.

SHUI TA Six . . . ! Sheer usury! And where am I to find it?

MRS. MI TZU You should have thought of that before.

SHUI TA Have you no heart, Mrs. Mi Tzu? It's true Shen Te acted foolishly, being kind to all those people, but she'll improve with time. I'll see to it she does. She'll work her fingers to the bone to pay her rent, and all the time be as quiet as a mouse, as humble as a fly.

MRS. MI TZU Her social background . . .

SHUI TA Out of the depths! She came out of the depths! And before she'll go back there, she'll work, sacrifice, shrink from nothing. . . . Such a tenant is worth her weight in gold, Mrs. Mi Tzu.

MRS. MI TZU It's silver we were talking about, Mr. Shui Ta. Two hundred silver dollars or . . .

[*Enter the* POLICEMAN.]

POLICEMAN Am I intruding, Mr. Shui Ta?

MRS. MI TZU This tobacco shop is well known to the police, I see.

POLICEMAN Mr. Shui Ta has done us a service, Mrs. Mi Tzu. I am here to present our official felicitations!

MRS. MI TZU That means less than nothing to me, sir. Mr. Shui Ta, all I can say is: I hope your cousin will find my terms acceptable. Good day, gentlemen. [*Exit.*]

SHUI TA Good day, ma'am.

[*Pause.*]

POLICEMAN Mrs. Mi Tzu a bit of a stumbling block, sir?

SHUI TA She wants six months' rent in advance.

POLICEMAN And you haven't got it, eh? [SHUI TA *is silent.*] But surely you can get it, sir? A man like you?

SHUI TA What about a woman like Shen Te?

POLICEMAN You're not staying, sir?

SHUI TA No, and I won't be back. Do you smoke?

POLICEMAN [*Taking two cigars, and placing them both in his pocket.*] Thank you, sir—I see your point, Miss Shen Te—let's mince no words—Miss Shen Te lived by selling herself. "What else could she have done?" you ask. "How else was she to pay the rent?" True. But the fact remains, Mr. Shui Ta, it is not respectable. Why not? A very deep question. But, in the first place, love—love isn't bought and sold like cigars, Mr. Shui Ta. In the second place, it isn't respectable to go waltzing off with someone that's paying his way, so to speak—it must be for love! Thirdly and lastly, as the proverb has it: not for a handful of rice but for love! [*Pause. He is thinking hard.*] "Well," you may say, "and what good is all this wisdom if the milk's already spilt?" Miss Shen Te is what she is. Is *where* she is. We have to face the fact that if she doesn't get hold of six months' rent pronto, she'll be back on the streets. The question then as I see it—everything in this world is a matter of opinion—the question as I see it is: *how* is she to get hold of this rent? How? Mr. Shui Ta: I don't know. [*Pause.*] I take that back, sir. It's just come to me. A husband. We must find her a husband!

[*Enter a little* OLD WOMAN.]

OLD WOMAN A good cheap cigar for my husband, we'll have been married forty years tomorrow and we're having a little celebration.

SHUI TA Forty years? And you still want to celebrate?

OLD WOMAN As much as we can afford to. We have the carpet shop across the square. We'll be good neighbors, I hope?

SHUI TA I hope so too.

POLICEMAN [*Who keeps making discoveries.*] Mr. Shui Ta, you know what we need? We need capital. And how do we acquire capital? We get married.

SHUI TA [*To* OLD WOMAN.] I'm afraid I've been pestering this gentleman with my personal worries.

POLICEMAN [*Lyrically.*] We can't pay six months' rent, so what do we do? We marry money.

SHUI TA That might not be easy.

POLICEMAN Oh, I don't know. She's a good match. Has a nice, growing business. [*To the* OLD WOMAN.] What do you think?

OLD WOMAN [*Undecided.*] Well—

POLICEMAN Should she put an ad in the paper?

OLD WOMAN [*Not eager to commit herself.*] Well, if *she* agrees—

POLICEMAN I'll write it for her. *You* lend us a hand, and *we* write an ad for you! [*He chuckles away to himself, takes out his notebook, wets the stump of a pencil between his lips, and writes away.*]

SHUI TA [*Slowly.*] Not a bad idea.

POLICEMAN "What . . . *respectable* . . . man . . . with small capital . . . widower . . . not excluded . . . desires . . . marriage . . . into flourishing . . . tobacco shop?" And now let's add: "Am . . . pretty . . ." No! . . . "Prepossessing appearance."

SHUI TA If you don't think that's an exaggeration?

OLD WOMAN Oh, not a bit. I've seen her.

[*The* POLICEMAN *tears the page out of his notebook, and hands it over to* SHUI TA.]

SHUI TA [*With horror in his voice.*] How much luck we need to keep our heads above water! How many ideas! How many friends! [*To the* POLICEMAN.] Thank you, sir, I think I see my way clear.

3

Evening in the municipal park. Noise of a plane overhead. YANG SUN, *a young man in rags, is following the plane with his eyes: one can tell that the machine is describing a curve above the park.* YANG SUN *then takes a rope out of his pocket, looking anxiously about him as he does so. He moves toward a large willow. Enter two prostitutes, one old, the other the* NIECE *whom we have already met.*

NIECE Hello. Coming with me?

YANG SUN [*Taken aback.*] If you'd like to buy me a dinner.

OLD WHORE Buy you a dinner! [*To the* NIECE.] Oh, we know him—it's the unemployed pilot. Waste no time on him!

NIECE But he's the only man left in the park. And it's going to rain.

OLD WHORE Oh, how do you know?

[*And they pass by.* YANG SUN *again looks about him, again takes his rope, and this time throws it round a branch of the willow tree. Again he is interrupted. It is the two prostitutes returning—and in such a hurry they don't notice him.*]

NIECE It's going to pour!

[*Enter* SHEN TE.]

OLD WHORE There's that *gorgon* Shen Te! That *drove* your family out into the cold!

NIECE It wasn't her. It was that cousin of hers. She offered to pay for the cakes. I've nothing against her.

OLD WHORE I have, though. [*So that* SHEN TE *can hear.*] Now where could the little lady be off to? She may be rich now but that won't stop her snatching our young men, will it?

SHEN TE I'm going to the tearoom by the pond.

NIECE Is it true what they say? You're marrying a widower—with three children?

SHEN TE Yes. I'm just going to see him.

YANG SUN [*His patience at breaking point.*] Move on there! This is a park, not a whorehouse!

OLD WHORE Shut your mouth!

[*But the two prostitutes leave.*]

YANG SUN Even in the farthest corner of the park, even when it's raining, you can't get rid of them! [*He spits.*]

SHEN TE [*Overhearing this.*] And what right have you to scold them? [*But at this point she sees the rope.*] Oh!

YANG SUN Well, what are you staring at?

SHEN TE That rope. What is it for?

YANG SUN Think! Think! I haven't a penny. Even if I had, I wouldn't spend it on you. I'd buy a drink of water.

[*The rain starts.*]

SHEN TE [*Still looking at the rope.*] What is the rope for? You mustn't!

YANG SUN What's it to you? Clear out!

SHEN TE [*Irrelevantly.*] It's raining.

YANG SUN Well, don't try to come under this tree.

SHEN TE Oh, no. [*She stays in the rain.*]

YANG SUN Now go away. [*Pause.*] For one thing, I don't like your looks, you're bowlegged.

SHEN TE [*Indignantly.*] That's not true!

YANG SUN Well, don't show 'em to me. Look, it's raining. You better come under this tree.

[*Slowly, she takes shelter under the tree.*]

SHEN TE Why did you want to do it?

YANG SUN You really want to know? [*Pause.*] To get rid of you! [*Pause.*] You know what a flyer is?

SHEN TE Oh yes, I've met a lot of pilots. At the tearoom.

YANG SUN You call *them* flyers? Think they know what a machine is? Just 'cause they have leather helmets? They gave the airfield director a bribe, that's the way *those* fellows got up in the air! Try one of them out sometime. "Go up to two thousand feet," tell him, "then let it fall, then pick it up again with a flick of the wrist at the last moment." Know what he'll say to that? "It's not in my contract." Then again, there's the landing problem. It's like landing on your own backside. It's no different, planes are human. Those fools don't understand. [*Pause.*] And I'm the biggest fool for reading the book on flying in the Peking school and skipping the page where it says: "We've got enough flyers and we don't need you." I'm a mail pilot with no mail. You understand that?

SHEN TE [*Shyly.*] Yes, I do.

YANG SUN No, you don't. You'd never understand that.

SHEN TE When we were little we had a crane with a broken wing. He made friends with us and was very good-natured about our jokes. He would strut along behind us and call out to stop us going too fast for him. But every spring and autumn when the cranes flew over the villages in great swarms, he got quite restless. [*Pause.*] I understand that.

[*She bursts out crying.*]

YANG SUN Don't!

SHEN TE [*Quieting down.*] No.

YANG SUN It's bad for the complexion.

SHEN TE [*Sniffing.*] I've stopped.

[*She dries her tears on her big sleeve. Leaning against the tree, but not looking at her, he reaches for her face.*]

YANG SUN You can't even wipe your own face. [*He is wiping it for her with his handkerchief. Pause.*]

SHEN TE [*Still sobbing.*] I don't know *anything*!

YANG SUN You interrupted me! What for?

SHEN TE It's such a rainy day. You only wanted to do . . . *that* because it's such a rainy day. [*To the audience.*]

In our country
The evenings should never be somber
High bridges over rivers
The gray hour between night and morning
And the long, long winter:
Such things are dangerous
For, with all the misery,
A very little is enough
And men throw away an unbearable life.

[*Pause.*]

YANG SUN Talk about yourself for a change.

SHEN TE What about me? I have a shop.

YANG SUN [*Incredulous.*] You have a shop, have you? Never thought of walking the streets?

SHEN TE I did walk the streets. Now I have a shop.

YANG SUN [*Ironically.*] A gift of the gods, I suppose!

SHEN TE How did you know?

YANG SUN [*Even more ironical.*] One fine evening the gods turned up saying: here's some money!

SHEN TE [*Quickly.*] One fine morning.

YANG SUN [*Fed up.*] This isn't much of an entertainment.

[*Pause.*]

SHEN TE I can play the zither a little. [*Pause.*] And I can mimic men. [*Pause.*] I got the shop, so the first thing I did was to give my zither away. I can be as stupid as a fish now, I said to myself, and it won't matter.

I'm rich now, I said
I walk alone, I sleep alone
For a whole year, I said
I'll have nothing to do with a man.

YANG SUN And now you're marrying one! The one at the tearoom by the pond?

[SHEN TE *is silent.*]

YANG SUN What do you know about love?

SHEN TE Everything.

YANG SUN Nothing. [*Pause.*] Or d'you just mean you enjoyed it?

SHEN TE No.

YANG SUN [*Again without turning to look at her, he strokes her cheek with his hand.*] You like that?

SHEN TE Yes.

YANG SUN [*Breaking off.*] You're easily satisfied, I must say. [*Pause.*] What a town!

SHEN TE You have no friends?

YANG SUN [*Defensively.*] Yes, I have! [*Change of tone.*] But they don't want to hear I'm still unemployed. "What?" they ask. "Is there still water in the sea?" You have friends?

SHEN TE [*Hesitating.*] Just a . . . cousin.

YANG SUN Watch him carefully.

SHEN TE He only came once. Then he went away. He won't be back. [YANG SUN *is looking away.*] But to be without hope, they say, is to be without goodness!

[*Pause.*]

YANG SUN Go on talking. A voice is a voice.

SHEN TE Once, when I was a little girl, I fell, with a load of brushwood. An old man picked me up. He gave me a penny too. Isn't it funny how people who don't have very much like to give some of it away? They must like to show what they can do, and how could they show it better than by being kind? Being wicked is just like being clumsy. When we sing a song, or build a machine, or plant some rice, we're being kind. You're kind.

YANG SUN You make it sound easy.

SHEN TE Oh, no. [*Little pause.*] Oh! A drop of rain!

YANG SUN Where'd you feel it?

SHEN TE Between the eyes.

YANG SUN Near the right eye? Or the left?

SHEN TE Near the left eye.

YANG SUN Oh, good. [*He is getting sleepy.*] So you're through with men, eh?

SHEN TE [*With a smile.*] But I'm not bowlegged.

YANG SUN Perhaps not.

SHEN TE Definitely not.

[*Pause.*]

YANG SUN [*Leaning wearily against the willow.*] I haven't had a drop to drink all day, I haven't eaten anything for *two* days. I couldn't love you if I tried.

[*Pause.*]

SHEN TE I like it in the rain.

[*Enter* WONG *the water seller, singing.*]

THE SONG OF THE WATER SELLER IN THE RAIN

"Buy my water," I am yelling
And my fury restraining
For no water I'm selling
'Cause it's raining, 'cause it's raining!
  I keep yelling: "Buy my water!"
  But no one's buying
  Athirst and dying
  And drinking and paying!
  Buy water!
  Buy water, you dogs!

Nice to dream of lovely weather!
Think of all the consternation
Were there no precipitation

Half a dozen years together!
Can't you hear them shrieking: "Water!"
Pretending they adore me?
They all would go down on their knees before me!
Down on your knees!
Go down on your knees, you dogs!

What are lawns and hedges thinking?
What are fields and forests saying?
"At the cloud's breast we are drinking!
And we've no idea who's paying!"
I keep yelling: "Buy my water!"
But no one's buying
Athirst and dying
And drinking and paying!
Buy water!
Buy water, you dogs!

[*The rain has stopped now.* SHEN TE *sees* WONG *and runs toward him.*]

SHEN TE Wong! You're back! Your carrying pole's at the shop.

WONG Oh, thank you, Shen Te. And how is life treating *you*?

SHEN TE I've just met a brave and clever man. And I want to buy him a cup of your water.

WONG [*Bitterly.*] Throw back your head and open your mouth and you'll have all the water you need—

SHEN TE [*Tenderly.*]
I want *your* water, Wong
The water that has tired you so
The water that you carried all this way
The water that is hard to sell because it's been raining.
I need it for the young man over there—he's a flyer!
A flyer is a bold man:
Braving the storms
In company with the clouds
He crosses the heavens
And brings to friends in faraway lands
The friendly mail!

[*She pays* WONG, *and runs over to* YANG SUN *with the cup. But* YANG SUN *is fast asleep.*]

SHEN TE [*Calling to* WONG, *with a laugh.*] He's fallen asleep! Despair and rain and I have worn him out!

3a

WONG'S *den. The sewer pipe is transparent, and the* GODS *again appear to* WONG *in a dream.*

WONG [*Radiant*] I've seen her, illustrious ones! And she hasn't changed!

FIRST GOD That's good to hear.

WONG She loves someone.

FIRST GOD Let's hope the experience gives her the strength to stay good!

WONG It does. She's doing good deeds all the time.

FIRST GOD Ah? What sort? What sort of good deeds, Wong?

WONG Well, she has a kind word for everybody.

FIRST GOD [*Eagerly.*] And then?

WONG Hardly anyone leaves her shop without tobacco in his pocket—even if he can't pay for it.

FIRST GOD Not bad at all. Next?

WONG She's putting up a family of eight.

FIRST GOD [*Gleefully, to the* SECOND GOD.] Eight! [*To* WONG.] And that's not all, of course!

WONG She bought a cup of water from me even though it was raining.

FIRST GOD Yes, yes, yes, all these smaller good deeds!

WONG Even they run into money. A little tobacco shop doesn't make so much.

FIRST GOD [*Sententiously.*] A prudent gardener works miracles on the smallest plot.

WONG She hands out rice every morning. That eats up half her earnings.

FIRST GOD [*A little disappointed.*] Well, as a beginning . . .

WONG They call her the Angel of the Slums—whatever the carpenter may say!

FIRST GOD What's this? A carpenter speaks ill of her?

WONG Oh, he only says her shelves weren't paid for in full.

SECOND GOD [*Who has a bad cold and can't pronounce his n's and m's.*] What's this? Not paying a carpenter? Why was that?

WONG I suppose she didn't have the money.

SECOND GOD [*Severely.*] One pays what one owes, that's in our book of rules! First the letter of the law, then the spirit.

WONG But it wasn't Shen Te, illustrious ones, it was her cousin. She called *him* in to help.

SECOND GOD Then her cousin must never darken her threshold again!

WONG Very well, illustrious ones! But in fairness to Shen Te, let me say that her cousin is a businessman.

FIRST GOD Perhaps we should inquire what is customary? I find business quite unintelligible. But everybody's doing it. Business! Did the Seven Good Kings do business? Did Kung the Just[8] sell fish?

SECOND GOD In any case, such a thing must not occur again!

[*The* GODS *start to leave.*]

THIRD GOD Forgive us for taking this tone with you, Wong, we haven't been getting enough sleep. The rich recommend us to the poor, and the poor tell us they haven't enough room.

SECOND GOD Feeble, feeble, the best of them!

FIRST GOD No great deeds! No heroic daring!

THIRD GOD On such a *small* scale!

SECOND GOD Sincere, yes, but what is actually *achieved*?

[*One can no longer hear them.*]

WONG [*Calling after them.*] I've thought of something, illustrious ones: Perhaps you shouldn't ask—too—much—all—at—once!

8. The philosopher Confucius (551–479 B.C.E.). "Seven Good Kings": legendary wise kings who personified the old order and traditional values.

4

The square in front of Shen Te's tobacco shop. Besides Shen Te's place, two other shops are seen: the carpet shop and a barber's. Morning. Outside Shen Te's the GRANDFATHER, *the* SISTER-IN-LAW, *the* UNEMPLOYED MAN, *and* MRS. SHIN *stand waiting.*

SISTER-IN-LAW She's been out all night again.

MRS. SHIN No sooner did we get rid of that crazy cousin of hers than Shen Te herself starts carrying on! Maybe she does give us an ounce of rice now and then, but can you depend on her? Can you depend on her?

[*Loud voices from the barber's.*]

VOICE OF SHU FU What are you doing in my shop? Get out—at once!

VOICE OF WONG But sir. They all let me sell . . .

[WONG *comes staggering out of the barber's shop pursued by Mr.* SHU FU, *the barber, a fat man carrying a heavy curling iron.*]

SHU FU Get out, I said! Pestering my customers with your slimy old water! Get out! Take your cup!

[*He holds out the cup.* WONG *reaches out for it. Mr.* SHU FU *strikes his hand with the curling iron, which is hot.* WONG *howls.*]

SHU FU You had it coming, my man!

[*Puffing, he returns to his shop. The* UNEMPLOYED MAN *picks up the cup and gives it to* WONG.]

UNEMPLOYED MAN You can report that to the police.

WONG My hand! It's smashed up!

UNEMPLOYED MAN Any bones broken?

WONG I can't move my fingers.

UNEMPLOYED MAN Sit down. I'll put some water on it.

[WONG *sits.*]

MRS. SHIN The water won't cost you anything.

SISTER-IN-LAW You might have got a bandage from Miss Shen Te till she took to staying out all night. It's a scandal.

MRS. SHIN [*Despondently.*] If you ask me, she's forgotten we ever existed!

[*Enter* SHEN TE *down the street, with a dish of rice.*]

SHEN TE [*To the audience.*] How wonderful to see Setzuan in the early morning! I always used to stay in bed with my dirty blanket over my head afraid to wake up. This morning I saw the newspapers being delivered by little boys, the streets being washed by strong men, and fresh vegetables coming in from the country on ox carts. It's a long walk from where Yang Sun lives, but I feel lighter at every step. They say you walk on air when you're in love, but it's even better walking on the rough earth, on the hard cement. In the early morning, the old city looks like a great heap of rubbish! Nice, though, with all its little lights. And the sky, so pink, so transparent, before the dust comes and muddies it! What a lot you miss if you never see your city rising from its slumbers like an honest old craftsman pumping his lungs full of air and reaching for his tools, as the poet says! [*Cheerfully, to her waiting guests.*] Good morning, everyone, here's your rice! [*Distributing the rice, she comes upon* WONG.] Good morning, Wong, I'm quite lightheaded today. On my way over, I looked at myself in all the shop windows. I'd love to be beautiful.

[*She slips into the carpet shop. Mr.* SHU FU *has just emerged from his shop.*]

SHU FU [*To the audience.*] It surprises me how beautiful Miss Shen Te is looking today! I never gave her a passing thought before. But now I've been gazing upon her comely form for exactly three minutes! I begin to suspect I am in love with her. She is overpoweringly attractive! [*Crossly, to* WONG.] Be off with you, rascal!

[*He returns to his shop.* SHEN TE *comes back out of the carpet shop with the* OLD MAN, *its proprietor, and his wife—whom we have already met—the* OLD WOMAN. SHEN TE *is wearing a shawl. The* OLD MAN *is holding up a looking glass for her.*]

OLD WOMAN Isn't it lovely? We'll give you a reduction because there's a little hole in it.

SHEN TE [*Looking at another shawl on the old woman's arm.*] The other one's nice too.

OLD WOMAN [*Smiling.*] Too bad there's no hole in that!

SHEN TE That's right. My shop doesn't make very much.

OLD WOMAN And your deeds eat it all up! Be more careful, my dear . . .

SHEN TE [*Trying on the shawl with the hole.*] Just now, I'm lightheaded! Does the color suit me?

OLD WOMAN You'd better ask a man.

SHEN TE [*To the* OLD MAN.] Does the color suit me?

OLD MAN You'd better ask your young friend.

SHEN TE I'd like to have your opinion.

OLD MAN It suits you very well. But wear it this way: the dull side out.

[SHEN TE *pays up.*]

OLD WOMAN If you decide you don't like it, you can exchange it. [*She pulls* SHEN TE *to one side.*] Has he got money?

SHEN TE [*With a laugh*] Yang Sun? Oh, no.

OLD WOMAN Then how're you going to pay your rent?

SHEN TE I'd forgotten about that.

OLD WOMAN And next Monday is the first of the month! Miss Shen Te, I've got something to say to you. After we [*Indicating her husband.*] got to know you, we had our doubts about that marriage ad. We thought it would be better if you'd let *us* help you. Out of our savings. We reckon we could lend you two hundred silver dollars. We don't need anything in writing—you could pledge us your tobacco stock.

SHEN TE You're prepared to lend money to a person like me?

OLD WOMAN It's folks like you that need it. We'd think twice about lending anything to your cousin.

OLD MAN [*Coming up.*] All settled, my dear?

SHEN TE I wish the gods could have heard what your wife was just saying, Mr. Ma. They're looking for good people who're happy—and helping me makes you happy because you know it was love that got me into difficulties!

[*The old couple smile knowingly at each other.*]

OLD MAN And here's the money, Miss Shen Te.

[*He hands her an envelope.* SHEN TE *takes it. She bows. They bow back. They return to their shop.*]

SHEN TE [*Holding up her envelope.*] Look, Wong, here's six months' rent! Don't you believe in miracles now? And how do you like my new shawl?

WONG For the young fellow I saw you with in the park?

[SHEN TE *nods.*]

MRS. SHIN Never mind all that. It's time you took a look at this hand!

SHEN TE Have you hurt your hand?

MRS. SHIN That barber smashed it with his hot curling iron. Right in front of our eyes.

SHEN TE [*Shocked at herself.*] And I never noticed! We must get you to a doctor this minute or who knows what will happen?

UNEMPLOYED MAN It's not a doctor he should see, it's a judge. He can ask for compensation. The barber's filthy rich.

WONG You think I have a chance?

MRS. SHIN [*With relish.*] If it's really good and smashed. But is it?

WONG I think so. It's very swollen. Could I get a pension?

MRS. SHIN You'd need a witness.

WONG Well, you all saw it. You could all testify.

[*He looks round. The* UNEMPLOYED MAN, *the* GRANDFATHER, *and the* SISTER-IN-LAW *are all sitting against the wall of the shop eating rice. Their concentration on eating is complete.*]

SHEN TE [*To* MRS. SHIN.] You saw it yourself.

MRS. SHIN I want nothing to do with the police. It's against my principles.

SHEN TE [*To* SISTER-IN-LAW.] What about you?

SISTER-IN-LAW Me? I wasn't looking.

SHEN TE [*To the* GRANDFATHER, *coaxingly.*] Grandfather, *you'll* testify, won't you?

SISTER-IN-LAW And a lot of good that will do. He's simple-minded.

SHEN TE [*To the* UNEMPLOYED MAN.] You seem to be the only witness left.

UNEMPLOYED MAN My testimony would only hurt him. I've been picked up twice for begging.

SHEN TE

Your brother is assaulted, and you shut your eyes?
He is hit, cries out in pain, and you are silent?
The beast prowls, chooses and seizes his victim, and you say:
"Because we showed no displeasure, he has spared us."

If no one present will be a witness, I will. I'll say *I* saw it.

MRS. SHIN [*Solemnly.*] The name for that is perjury.

WONG I don't know if I can accept that. Though maybe I'll have to. [*Looking at his hand.*] Is it swollen enough, do you think? The swelling's not going down.

UNEMPLOYED MAN No, no, the swelling's holding up well.

WONG Yes. It's *more* swollen if anything. Maybe my wrist is broken after all. I'd better see a judge at once.

[*Holding his hand very carefully, and fixing his eyes on it, he runs off.* MRS. SHIN *goes quickly into the barber's shop.*]

UNEMPLOYED MAN [*Seeing her.*] She is getting on the right side of Mr. Shu Fu.

SISTER-IN-LAW You and I can't change the world, Shen Te.

SHEN TE Go away! Go away all of you! [*The* UNEMPLOYED MAN, *the* SISTER-IN-LAW, *and the* GRANDFATHER *stalk off, eating and sulking. To the audience.*]

They've stopped answering
They stay put
They do as they're told
They don't care
Nothing can make them look up
But the smell of food.

[*Enter* MRS. YANG, *Yang Sun's mother, out of breath.*]

MRS. YANG Miss Shen Te. My son has told me everything. I am Mrs. Yang, Sun's mother. Just think. He's got an offer. Of a job as a pilot. A letter has just come. From the director of the airfield in Peking!

SHEN TE So he can fly again! Isn't that wonderful!

MRS. YANG [*Less breathlessly all the time.*] They won't give him the job for nothing. They want five hundred silver dollars.

SHEN TE We can't let money stand in his way, Mrs. Yang!

MRS. YANG If only you could help him out!

SHEN TE I have the shop. I can try! [*She embraces* MRS. YANG.] I happen to have two hundred with me now. Take it. [*She gives her the old couple's money.*] It was a loan but they said I could repay it with my tobacco stock.

MRS. YANG And they were calling Sun the Dead Pilot of Setzuan! A friend in need!

SHEN TE We must find another three hundred.

MRS. YANG How?

SHEN TE Let me think. [*Slowly.*] I know someone who can help. I didn't want to call on his services again, he's hard and cunning. But a flyer must fly. And I'll make this the last time.

[*Distant sound of a plane.*]

MRS. YANG If the man you mentioned can do it . . . Oh, look, there's the morning mail plane, heading for Peking!

SHEN TE The pilot can see us, let's wave!

[*They wave. The noise of the engine is louder.*]

MRS. YANG You know that pilot up there?

SHEN TE Wave, Mrs. Yang! I know the pilot who will be up there. He gave up hope. But he'll do it now. One man to raise himself above the misery, above us all. [*To the audience.*]

Yang Sun, my lover:
Braving the storms
In company with the clouds
Crossing the heavens
And bringing to friends in faraway lands
The friendly mail!

4a

In front of the inner curtain. Enter SHEN TE, *carrying* SHUI TA*'s mask. She sings.*

THE SONG OF DEFENSELESSNESS

In our country
A useful man needs luck
Only if he finds strong backers
Can he prove himself useful.
The good can't defend themselves and
Even the gods are defenseless.

Oh, why don't the gods have their own ammunition
And launch against badness their own expedition
Enthroning the good and preventing sedition
And bringing the world to a peaceful condition?

Oh, why don't the gods do the buying and selling
Injustice forbidding, starvation dispelling
Give bread to each city and joy to each dwelling?
Oh, why don't the gods do the buying and selling?

[*She puts on* SHUI TA*'s mask and sings in his voice.*]

You can only help one of your luckless brothers
By trampling down a dozen others.

Why is it the gods do not feel indignation
And come down in fury to end exploitation
Defeat all defeat and forbid desperation
Refusing to tolerate such toleration?

Why is it?

5

SHEN TE*'s tobacco shop. Behind the counter, Mr.* SHUI TA, *reading the paper.* MRS. SHIN *is cleaning up. She talks and he takes no notice.*

MRS. SHIN And when certain rumors get about, what *happens* to a little place like this? It goes to pot. *I* know. So, if you want my advice, Mr. Shui Ta, find out just what has been going on between Miss Shen Te and that Yang Sun from Yellow Street. And remember: a certain interest in Miss Shen Te has been expressed by the barber next door, a man with twelve houses and only one wife,[9] who, for that matter, is likely to drop off at any time. A certain interest has been expressed. He was even inquiring about her means and, if *that* doesn't prove a man is getting serious, what would?

[*Still getting no response, she leaves with her bucket.*]

YANG SUN'S VOICE Is that Miss Shen Te's tobacco shop?

MRS. SHIN'S VOICE Yes, it is, but it's Mr. Shui Ta who's here today.

[SHUI TA *runs to the mirror with the short, light steps of* SHEN TE, *and is just about to start primping, when he realizes his mistake, and turns away, with a short laugh. Enter* YANG SUN. MRS. SHIN *enters behind him and slips into the back room to eavesdrop.*]

YANG SUN I am Yang Sun. [SHUI TA *bows.*] Is Shen Te in?

SHUI TA No.

YANG SUN I guess you know our relationship? [*He is inspecting the stock.*] Quite a place! And I thought she was just talking big. I'll be flying again, all right. [*He takes a cigar, solicits and receives a light from* SHUI TA.] You think we can squeeze the other three hundred out of the tobacco stock?

SHUI TA May I ask if it is your intention to sell at once?

YANG SUN It was decent of her to come out with the two hundred but they aren't much use with the other three hundred still missing.

9. Ancient Chinese law permitted a man to have more than one wife.

SHUI TA Shen Te was overhasty promising so much. She might have to sell the shop itself to raise it. Haste, they say, is the wind that blows the house down.

YANG SUN Oh, she isn't a girl to keep a man waiting. For one thing or the other, if you take my meaning.

SHUI TA I take your meaning

YANG SUN [*Leering.*] Uh, huh.

SHUI TA Would you explain what the five hundred silver dollars are for?

YANG SUN Want to sound me out? Very well. The director of the Peking airfield is a friend of mine from flying school. I give him five hundred: he gets me the job.

SHUI TA The price is high.

YANG SUN Not as these things go. He'll have to fire one of the present pilots—for negligence. Only the man he has in mind isn't negligent. Not easy, you understand. You needn't mention that part of it to Shen Te.

SHUI TA [*Looking intently at* YANG SUN.] Mr. Yang Sun, you are asking my cousin to give up her possessions, leave her friends, and place her entire fate in your hands. I presume you intend to marry her?

YANG SUN I'd be prepared to.

[*Slight pause.*]

SHUI TA Those two hundred silver dollars would pay the rent here for six months. If you were Shen Te wouldn't you be tempted to continue in business?

YANG SUN What? Can you imagine Yang Sun the flyer behind a counter? [*In an oily voice.*] "A strong cigar or a mild one, worthy sir?" Not in this century!

SHUI TA My cousin wishes to follow the promptings of her heart, and, from her own point of view, she may even have what is called the right to love. Accordingly, she has commissioned me to help you to this post. There is nothing here that I am not empowered to turn immediately into cash. Mrs. Mi Tzu, the landlady, will advise me about the sale.

[*Enter* MRS. MI TZU.]

MRS. MI TZU Good morning, Mr. Shui Ta, you wish to see me about the rent? As you know it falls due the day after tomorrow.

SHUI TA Circumstances have changed, Mrs. Mi Tzu: my cousin is getting married. Her future husband here, Mr. Yang Sun, will be taking her to Peking. I am interested in selling the tobacco stock.

MRS. MI TZU How much are you asking, Mr. Shui Ta?

YANG SUN Three hundred sil—

SHUI TA Five hundred silver dollars.

MRS. MI TZU How much did she pay for it, Mr. Shui Ta?

SHUI TA A thousand. And very little has been sold.

MRS. MI TZU She was robbed. But I'll make you a special offer if you'll promise to be out by the day after tomorrow. Three hundred silver dollars.

YANG SUN [*Shrugging.*] Take it, man, take it.

SHUI TA It is not enough.

YANG SUN Why not? Why not? Certainly, it's enough.

SHUI TA Five hundred silver dollars.

YANG SUN But why? We only need three!

SHUI TA [*To* MRS. MI TZU.] Excuse me. [*Takes* YANG SUN *on one side.*] The tobacco stock is pledged to the old couple who gave my cousin the two hundred.

YANG SUN Is it in writing?

SHUI TA No.

YANG SUN [*To* MRS. MI TZU.] Three hundred will do.

MRS. MI TZU Of course, I need an assurance that Miss Shen Te is not in debt.

YANG SUN Mr. Shui Ta?

SHUI TA She is not in debt.

YANG SUN When can you let us have the money?

MRS. MI TZU The day after tomorrow. And remember: I'm doing this because I have a soft spot in my heart for young lovers! [*Exit.*]

YANG SUN [*Calling after her.*] Boxes, jars and sacks—three hundred for the lot and the pain's over! [*To* SHUI TA.] Where else can we raise money by the day after tomorrow?

SHUI TA Nowhere. Haven't you enough for the trip and the first few weeks?

YANG SUN Oh, certainly.

SHUI TA How much, exactly.

YANG SUN Oh, I'll dig it up, even if I have to steal it.

SHUI TA I see.

YANG SUN Well, don't fall off the roof. I'll get to Peking somehow.

SHUI TA Two people can't travel for nothing.

YANG SUN [*Not giving* SHUI TA *a chance to answer.*] I'm leaving *her* behind. No millstones round *my* neck!

SHUI TA Oh.

YANG SUN Don't look at me like that!

SHUI TA How precisely is my cousin to live?

YANG SUN Oh, you'll think of something.

SHUI TA A small request, Mr. Yang Sun. Leave the two hundred silver dollars here until you can show me two tickets for Peking.

YANG SUN You learn to mind your own business, Mr. Shui Ta.

SHUI TA I'm afraid Miss Shen Te may not wish to sell the shop when she discovers that . . .

YANG SUN You don't know women. She'll want to. Even then.

SHUI TA [*A slight outburst.*] She is a human being, sir! And not devoid of common sense!

YANG SUN Shen Te is a woman: she *is* devoid of common sense. I only have to lay my hand on her shoulder, and church bells ring.

SHUI TA [*With difficulty.*] Mr. Yang Sun!

YANG SUN Mr. Shui Whatever-it-is!

SHUI TA My cousin is devoted to you . . . because . . .

YANG SUN Because I have my hands on her breasts. Give me a cigar. [*He takes one for himself, stuffs a few more in his pocket, then changes his mind and takes the whole box.*] Tell her I'll marry her, then bring me the three hundred. Or let her bring it. One or the other. [*Exit.*]

MRS. SHIN [*Sticking her head out of the back room.*] Well, he has your cousin under his thumb, and doesn't care if all Yellow Street knows it!

SHUI TA [*Crying out.*] I've lost my shop! And he doesn't love me! [*He runs berserk through the room, repeating these lines incoherently. Then stops suddenly, and addresses* MRS. SHIN.] Mrs. Shin, you grew up in the gutter, like me. Are we lacking in hardness? I doubt it. If you steal a penny from me, I'll take you by the throat till you spit it out! You'd do the same to me. The times are bad, this city is hell, but we're like ants, we keep coming, up and up the walls, however smooth! Till bad luck comes. Being in love, for instance. One weakness is enough, and love is the deadliest.

MRS. SHIN [*Emerging from the back room.*] You should have a little talk with Mr. Shu Fu, the barber. He's a real gentleman and just the thing for your cousin. [*She runs off.*]

SHUI TA

A caress becomes a stranglehold
A sigh of love turns to a cry of fear
Why are there vultures circling in the air?
A girl is going to meet her lover.

[SHUI TA *sits down and Mr.* SHU FU *enters with* MRS. SHIN.]

SHUI TA Mr. Shu Fu?

SHU FU Mr. Shui Ta.

[*They both bow.*]

SHUI TA I am told that you have expressed a certain interest in my cousin Shen Te. Let me set aside all propriety and confess: she is at this moment in grave danger.

SHU FU Oh, dear!

SHUI TA She has lost her shop, Mr. Shu Fu.

SHU FU The charm of Miss Shen Te, Mr. Shui Ta, derives from the goodness, not of her shop, but of her heart. Men call her the Angel of the Slums.

SHUI TA Yet her goodness has cost her two hundred silver dollars in a single day: we must put a stop to it.

SHU FU Permit me to differ, Mr. Shui Ta. Let us, rather, open wide the gates to such goodness! Every morning, with pleasure tinged by affection, I watch her charitable ministrations. For they are hungry, and she giveth them to eat! Four of them, to be precise. Why only four? I ask. Why not four hundred?[1] I hear she has been seeking shelter for the homeless. What about my humble cabins behind the cattle run? They are at her disposal. And so forth. And so on. Mr. Shui Ta, do you think Miss Shen Te could be persuaded to listen to certain ideas of mine? Ideas like these?

SHUI TA Mr. Shu Fu, she would be honored.

[*Enter* WONG *and the* POLICEMAN. *Mr.* SHU FU *turns abruptly away and studies the shelves.*]

WONG Is Miss Shen Te here?

SHUI TA No.

WONG I am Wong the water seller. You are Mr. Shui Ta?

SHUI TA I am.

WONG I am a friend of Shen Te's.

1. An allusion to the biblical miracle of loaves and fishes, when Christ fed five thousand people (Matthew 14.13–21).

SHUI TA An intimate friend, I hear.

WONG [*To the* POLICEMAN.] You see? [*To* SHUI TA.] It's because of my hand.

POLICEMAN He hurt his hand, sir, that's a fact.

SHUI TA [*Quickly.*] You need a sling, I see. [*He takes a shawl from the back room, and throws it to* WONG.]

WONG But that's her new shawl!

SHUI TA She has no more use for it.

WONG But she bought it to please someone!

SHUI TA It happens to be no longer necessary.

WONG [*Making the sling.*] She is my only witness.

POLICEMAN Mr. Shui Ta, your cousin is supposed to have seen the barber hit the water seller with a curling iron.

SHUI TA I'm afraid my cousin was not present at the time.

WONG But she was, sir! Just ask her! Isn't she in?

SHUI TA [*Gravely.*] Mr. Wong, my cousin has her own troubles. You wouldn't wish her to add to them by committing perjury?

WONG But it was she that told me to go to the judge!

SHUI TA Was the judge supposed to heal your hand?

[*Mr.* SHU FU *turns quickly around.* SHUI TA *bows to* SHU FU, *and vice versa.*]

WONG [*Taking the sling off, and putting it back.*] I see how it is.

POLICEMAN Well, I'll be on my way. [*To* WONG.] And you be careful. If Mr. Shu Fu wasn't a man who tempers justice with mercy, as the saying is, you'd be in jail for libel. Be off with you!

[*Exit* WONG *followed by* POLICEMAN.]

SHUI TA Profound apologies, Mr. Shu Fu.

SHU FU Not at all, Mr. Shui Ta. [*Pointing to the shawl.*] The episode is over?

SHUI TA It may take her time to recover. There are some fresh wounds.

SHU FU We shall be discreet. Delicate. A short vacation could be arranged . . .

SHUI TA First of course, you and she would have to talk things over.

SHU FU At a small supper in a small, but high-class, restaurant.

SHUI TA I'll go and find her. [*Exit into back room.*]

MRS. SHIN [*Sticking her head in again.*] Time for congratulations, Mr. Shu Fu?

SHU FU Ah, Mrs. Shin! Please inform Miss Shen Te's guests they may take shelter in the cabins behind the cattle run!

[MRS. SHIN *nods, grinning.*]

SHU FU [*To the audience.*] Well? What do you think of me, ladies and gentlemen? What could a man do more? Could he be less selfish? More farsighted? A small supper in a small but . . . Does that bring rather vulgar and clumsy thoughts into your mind? Ts, ts, ts. Nothing of the sort will occur. She won't even be touched. Not even accidentally while passing the salt. An exchange of ideas only. Over the flowers on the table—white chrysanthemums, by the way [*He writes down a note of this.*]—yes, over the white chrysanthemums, two young souls will . . . shall I say "find each other"? We shall NOT exploit the misfortune of others. Understanding? Yes. An offer of assistance? Certainly. But quietly. Almost inaudibly. Perhaps with a single glance. A glance that could also—mean more.

MRS. SHIN [*Coming forward.*] Everything under control, Mr. Shu Fu?

SHU FU Oh, Mrs. Shin, what do you know about this worthless rascal Yang Sun?

MRS. SHIN Why, he's the most worthless rascal . . .

SHU FU Is he really? You're sure? [*As she opens her mouth.*] From now on, he doesn't exist! Can't be found anywhere!

[*Enter* YANG SUN.]

YANG SUN What's been going on here?

MRS. SHIN Shall I call Mr. Shui Ta, Mr. Shu Fu? He wouldn't want strangers in here!

SHU FU Mr. Shui Ta is in conference with Miss Shen Te. Not to be disturbed!

YANG SUN Shen Te here? I didn't see her come in. What kind of conference?

SHU FU [*Not letting him enter the back room.*] Patience, dear sir! And if by chance I have an inkling who you are, pray take note that Miss Shen Te and I are about to announce our engagement.

YANG SUN What?

MRS. SHIN You didn't expect that, did you?

[YANG SUN *is trying to push past the barber into the back room when* SHEN TE *comes out.*]

SHU FU My dear Shen Te, ten thousand apologies! Perhaps you . . .

YANG SUN What is it, Shen Te? Have you gone crazy?

SHEN TE [*Breathless.*] My cousin and Mr. Shu Fu have come to an understanding. They wish me to hear Mr. Shu Fu's plans for helping the poor.

YANG SUN Your cousin wants to part us.

SHEN TE Yes.

YANG SUN And you've agreed to it?

SHEN TE Yes.

YANG SUN They told you I was bad. [SHEN TE *is silent.*] And suppose I am. Does that make me need you less? I'm low, Shen Te, I have no money, I don't do the right thing but at least I put up a fight! [*He is near her now, and speaks in an undertone.*] Have you no eyes? Look at him. Have you forgotten already?

SHEN TE No.

YANG SUN How it was raining?

SHEN TE No.

YANG SUN How you cut me down from the willow tree? Bought me water? Promised me money to fly with?

SHEN TE [*Shakily.*] Yang Sun, what do you want?

YANG SUN I want you to come with me.

SHEN TE [*In a small voice.*] Forgive me, Mr. Shu Fu, I want to go with Mr. Yang Sun.

YANG SUN We're lovers, you know. Give me the key to the shop. [SHEN TE *takes the key from around her neck.* YANG SUN *puts it on the counter. To* MRS. SHIN.] Leave it under the mat when you're through. Let's go, Shen Te.

SHU FU But this is rape! Mr. Shui Ta!!

YANG SUN [*To* SHEN TE.] Tell him not to shout.

SHEN TE Please don't shout for my cousin, Mr. Shu Fu. He doesn't agree with me, I know, but he's wrong. [*To the audience.*]

I want to go with the man I love
I don't want to count the cost
I don't want to consider if it's wise
I don't want to know if he loves me
I want to go with the man I love.

YANG SUN That's the spirit.

[*And the couple leave.*]

5*a*

In front of the inner curtain. SHEN TE *in her wedding clothes, on the way to her wedding.*

SHEN TE Something terrible has happened. As I left the shop with Yang Sun, I found the old carpet dealer's wife waiting on the street, trembling all over. She told me her husband had taken to his bed—sick with all the worry and excitement over the two hundred silver dollars they lent me. She said it would be best if I gave it back now. Of course, I had to say I would. She said she couldn't quite trust my cousin Shui Ta or even my fiancé, Yang Sun. There were tears in her eyes. With my emotions in an uproar, I threw myself into Yang Sun's arms, I couldn't resist him. The things he'd said to Shui Ta had taught Shen Te nothing. Sinking into his arms, I said to myself:

To let no one perish, not even oneself
To fill everyone with happiness, even oneself
Is so good

How could I have forgotten those two old people? Yang Sun swept me away like a small hurricane. But he's not a bad man, and he loves me. He'd rather work in the cement factory than owe his flying to a crime. Though, of course, flying *is* a great passion with Sun. Now, on the way to my wedding, I waver between fear and joy.

6

The "private dining room" on the upper floor of a cheap restaurant in a poor section of town. With SHEN TE: *the* GRANDFATHER, *the* SISTER-IN-LAW, THE NIECE, MRS. SHIN, *the* UNEMPLOYED MAN. *In a corner, alone, a* PRIEST.[2] *A* WAITER *pouring wine. Downstage,* YANG SUN *talking to his mother. He wears a dinner jacket.*

YANG SUN Bad news, Mamma. She came right out and told me she can't sell the shop for me. Some idiot is bringing a claim because he lent her the two hundred she gave you.

MRS. YANG What did you say? Of course, you can't marry her now.

YANG SUN It's no use saying anything to *her*. I've sent for her cousin, Mr. Shui Ta. He said there was nothing in writing.

MRS. YANG Good idea. I'll go out and look for him. Keep an eye on things.

[*Exit* MRS. YANG. SHEN TE *has been pouring wine.*]

2. A Buddhist monk or priest.

SHEN TE [*To the audience, pitcher in hand.*] I wasn't mistaken in him. He's bearing up well. Though it must have been an awful blow—giving up flying. I do love him so. [*Calling across the room to him.*] Sun, you haven't drunk a toast with the bride!

YANG SUN What do we drink to?

SHEN TE Why, to the future!

YANG SUN When the bridegroom's dinner jacket won't be a hired one!

SHEN TE But when the bride's dress will still get rained on sometimes!

YANG SUN To everything we ever wished for!

SHEN TE May all our dreams come true!

[*They drink.*]

YANG SUN [*With loud conviviality.*] And now, friends, before the wedding gets under way, I have to ask the bride a few questions. I've no idea what kind of a wife she'll make, and it worries me. [*Wheeling on* SHEN TE.] For example. Can you make five cups of tea with three tea leaves?

SHEN TE No.

YANG SUN So I won't be getting very much tea. Can you sleep on a straw mattress the size of that book? [*He points to the large volume the* PRIEST *is reading.*]

SHEN TE The two of us?

YANG SUN The one of you.

SHEN TE In that case, no.

YANG SUN What a wife! I'm shocked!

[*While the audience is laughing, his mother returns. With a shrug of her shoulders, she tells* SUN *the expected guest hasn't arrived. The* PRIEST *shuts the book with a bang, and makes for the door.*]

MRS. YANG Where are *you* off to? It's only a matter of minutes.

PRIEST [*Watch in hand.*] Time goes on, Mrs. Yang, and I've another wedding to attend to. Also a funeral.

MRS. YANG [*Irately.*] D'you think we planned it this way? I was hoping to manage with one pitcher of wine, and we've run through two already. [*Points to empty pitcher. Loudly.*] My dear Shen Te, I don't know where your cousin can be keeping himself!

SHEN TE My cousin?!

MRS. YANG Certainly. I'm old-fashioned enough to think such a close relative should attend the wedding.

SHEN TE Oh, Sun, is it the three hundred silver dollars?

YANG SUN [*Not looking her in the eye.*] Are you deaf? Mother says she's old-fashioned. And I say I'm considerate. We'll wait another fifteen minutes.

HUSBAND Another fifteen minutes.

MRS. YANG [*Addressing the company.*] Now you all know, don't you, that my son is getting a job as a mail pilot?

SISTER-IN-LAW In Peking, too, isn't it?

MRS. YANG In Peking, too! The two of us are moving to Peking!

SHEN TE Sun, tell your mother Peking is out of the question now.

YANG SUN Your cousin'll tell her. If he agrees. I don't agree.

SHEN TE [*Amazed, and dismayed.*] Sun!

YANG SUN I hate this godforsaken Setzuan. What people! Know what they look like when I half close my eyes? Horses! Whinnying, fretting, stamping, screwing their necks up! [*Loudly.*] And what is it the thunder says? They are su-per-flu-ous! [*He hammers out the syllables.*] They've run their last race! They can go trample themselves to death! [*Pause.*] I've got to get out of here.

SHEN TE But I've promised the money to the old couple.

YANG SUN And since you always do the wrong thing, it's lucky your cousin's coming. Have another drink.

SHEN TE [*Quietly.*] My cousin can't be coming.

YANG SUN How d'you mean?

SHEN TE My cousin can't be where I am.

YANG SUN Quite a conundrum!

SHEN TE [*Desperately.*] Sun, I'm the one that loves you. Not my cousin. He was thinking of the job in Peking when he promised you the old couple's money—

YANG SUN Right. And that's why he's bringing the three hundred silver dollars. Here—to my wedding.

SHEN TE He is not bringing the three hundred silver dollars.

YANG SUN Huh? What makes you think that?

SHEN TE [*Looking into his eyes.*] He says you only bought one ticket to Peking.

[*Short pause.*]

YANG SUN That was yesterday. [*He pulls two tickets part way out of his inside pocket, making her look under his coat.*] Two tickets. I don't want Mother to know. She'll get left behind. I sold her furniture to buy these tickets, so you see . . .

SHEN TE But what's to become of the old couple?

YANG SUN What's to become of me? Have another drink. Or do you believe in moderation? If I drink, I fly again. And if you drink, you may learn to understand me.

SHEN TE You want to fly. But I can't help you.

YANG SUN "Here's a plane, my darling—but it's only got one wing!"

[*The* WAITER *enters.*]

WAITER Mrs. Yang!

MRS. YANG Yes?

WAITER Another pitcher of wine, ma'am?

MRS. YANG We have enough, thanks. Drinking makes me sweat.

WAITER Would you mind paying, ma'am?

MRS. YANG [*To everyone.*] Just be patient a few moments longer, everyone, Mr. Shui Ta is on his way over! [*To the* WAITER.] Don't be a spoilsport.

WAITER I can't let you leave till you've paid your bill, ma'am.

MRS. YANG But they know me here!

WAITER That's just it.

PRIEST [*Ponderously getting up.*] I humbly take my leave. [*And he does.*]

MRS. YANG [*To the others, desperately.*] Stay where you are, everybody! The priest says he'll be back in two minutes!

YANG SUN It's no good, Mamma. Ladies and gentlemen, Mr. Shui Ta still hasn't arrived and the priest has gone home. We won't detain you any longer.

[*They are leaving now.*]

GRANDFATHER [*In the doorway, having forgotten to put his glass down.*] To the bride! [*He drinks, puts down the glass, and follows the others.*]

[*Pause.*]

SHEN TE Shall I go too?

YANG SUN You? Aren't you the bride? Isn't this your wedding? [*He drags her across the room, tearing her wedding dress.*] If we can wait, you can wait. Mother calls me her falcon. She wants to see me in the clouds. But I think it may be St. Nevercome's Day before she'll go to the door and see my plane thunder by. [*Pause. He pretends the guests are still present.*] Why such a lull in the conversation, ladies and gentlemen? Don't you like it here? The ceremony is only slightly postponed—because an important guest is expected at any moment. Also because the bride doesn't know what love is. While we're waiting, the bridegroom will sing a little song. [*He does so.*]

THE SONG OF ST. NEVERCOME'S DAY

On a certain day, as is generally known,
  One and all will be shouting: Hooray, hooray!
For the beggar maid's son has a solid-gold throne
  And the day is St. Nevercome's Day
On St. Nevercome's, Nevercome's, Nevercome's Day
  He'll sit on his solid-gold throne

Oh, hooray, hooray! That day goodness will pay!
  That day badness will cost you your head!
And merit and money will smile and be funny
  While exchanging salt and bread
On St. Nevercome's, Nevercome's, Nevercome's Day
  While exchanging salt and bread

And the grass, oh, the grass will look down at the sky
  And the pebbles will roll up the stream
And all men will be good without batting an eye
  They will make of our earth a dream
On St. Nevercome's, Nevercome's, Nevercome's Day
  They will make of our earth a dream

And as for me, that's the day I shall be
  A flyer and one of the best
Unemployed man, you will have work to do
  Washerwoman, you'll get your rest
On St. Nevercome's, Nevercome's, Nevercome's Day
  Washerwoman, you'll get your rest

MRS. YANG It looks like he's not coming.
[*The three of them sit looking at the door.*]

6a

WONG'*s den. The sewer pipe is again transparent and again the* GODS *appear to* WONG *in a dream.*

WONG I'm so glad you've come, illustrious ones. It's Shen Te. She's in great trouble from following the rule about loving thy neighbor. Perhaps she's *too* good for this world!

FIRST GOD Nonsense! You are eaten up by lice and doubts!

WONG Forgive me, illustrious one, I only meant you might deign to intervene.

FIRST GOD Out of the question! My colleague here intervened in some squabble or other only yesterday. [*He points to the* THIRD GOD, *who has a black eye.*] The results are before us!

WONG She had to call on her cousin again. But not even he could help. I'm afraid the shop is done for.

THIRD GOD [*A little concerned.*] Perhaps we should help after all?

FIRST GOD The gods help those that help themselves.

WONG What if we *can't* help ourselves, illustrious ones?

[*Slight pause.*]

SECOND GOD Try, anyway! Suffering ennobles!

FIRST GOD Our faith in Shen Te is unshaken!

THIRD GOD We certainly haven't found any *other* good people. You can see where we spend our nights from the straw on our clothes.

WONG You might help her find her way by—

FIRST GOD The good man finds his own way here below!

SECOND GOD The good woman too.

FIRST GOD The heavier the burden, the greater her strength!

THIRD GOD We're only onlookers, you know.

FIRST GOD And everything will be all right in the end, O ye of little faith!

[*They are gradually disappearing through these last lines.*]

7

The yard behind SHEN TE*'s shop. A few articles of furniture on a cart.* SHEN TE *and* MRS. SHIN *are taking the washing off the line.*

MRS. SHIN If you ask me, you should fight tooth and nail to keep the shop.

SHEN TE How can I? I have to sell the tobacco to pay back the two hundred silver dollars today.

MRS. SHIN No husband, no tobacco, no house and home! What are you going to live on?

SHEN TE I can work. I can sort tobacco.

MRS. SHIN Hey, look, Mr. Shui Ta's trousers! He must have left here stark naked!

SHEN TE Oh, he may have another pair, Mrs. Shin.

MRS. SHIN But if he's gone for good as you say, why has he left his pants behind?

SHEN TE Maybe he's thrown them away.

MRS. SHIN Can I take them?

SHEN TE Oh, no.

[*Enter Mr.* SHU FU, *running.*]

SHU FU Not a word! Total silence! I know all. You have sacrificed your own love and happiness so as not to hurt a dear old couple who had put their trust in you! Not in vain does this district—for all its malevolent tongues—call you the Angel of the Slums! That young man couldn't rise to your level, so you left him. And now, when I see you closing up the little shop, that veritable haven of rest for the multitude, well, I cannot, I cannot let it pass. Morning after morning I have stood watching in the doorway not unmoved—while you graciously handed out rice to the wretched. Is that never to happen again? Is the good woman of Setzuan to disappear? If only you would allow *me* to assist you! Now don't say anything! No assurances, no exclamations of gratitude! [*He has taken out his checkbook.*] Here! A blank check. [*He places it on the cart.*] Just my signature. Fill it out as you wish. Any sum in the world. I herewith retire from the scene, quietly, unobtrusively, making no claims, on tiptoe, full of veneration, absolutely selflessly . . . [*He has gone.*]

MRS. SHIN Well! You're saved. There's always some idiot of a man. . . . Now hurry! Put down a thousand silver dollars and let me fly to the bank before he comes to his senses.

SHEN TE I can pay you for the washing without any check.

MRS. SHIN What? You're not going to cash it just because you might have to marry him? Are you crazy? Men like him *want* to be led by the nose! Are you still thinking of that flyer? All Yellow Street knows how he treated you!

SHEN TE

When I heard his cunning laugh, I was afraid
But when I saw the holes in his shoes, I loved him dearly.

MRS. SHIN Defending that good-for-nothing after all that's happened!

SHEN TE [*Staggering as she holds some of the washing.*] Oh!

MRS. SHIN [*Taking the washing from her, dryly.*] So you feel dizzy when you stretch and bend? There couldn't be a little visitor on the way? If that's it, you can forget Mr. Shu Fu's blank check: it wasn't meant for a christening present!

[*She goes to the back with a basket.* SHEN TE*'s eyes follow* MRS. SHIN *for a moment. Then she looks down at her own body, feels her stomach, and a great joy comes into her eyes.*]

SHEN TE O joy! A new human being is on the way. The world awaits him. In the cities the people say: he's got to be reckoned with, this new human being! [*She imagines a little boy to be present, and introduces him to the audience.*] This is my son, the well-known flyer!

Say: Welcome
To the conqueror of unknown mountains and unreachable regions
Who brings us our mail across the impassable deserts!

[*She leads him up and down by the hand.*]

Take a look at the world, my son. That's a tree. Tree, yes. Say: "Hello, tree!" And bow. Like this. [*She bows.*] Now you know each other. And, look, here comes the water seller. He's a friend, give him your hand. A cup of fresh water for my little son, please. Yes, it *is* a warm day. [*Handing the cup.*] Oh dear, a policeman, we'll have to make a circle round *him.* Perhaps we can pick a few cherries over there in the rich Mr. Pung's garden. But we mustn't be seen. You want cherries? Just like children with fathers. No, no, you can't go straight at them like that. Don't pull. We must learn to be reasonable. Well, have it your own way. [*She has let him make for the cherries.*] Can you reach? Where to put them? Your mouth is the best place. [*She tries one herself.*] Mmm, they're good. But the policeman, we must run! [*They run.*] Yes, back to the street. Calm now, so no one will notice us. [*Walking the street with her child, she sings.*]

Once a plum—'twas in Japan—
Made a conquest of a man
But the man's turn soon did come
For he gobbled up the plum

[*Enter* WONG, *with a child by the hand. He coughs.*]

SHEN TE Wong!

WONG It's about the carpenter, Shen Te. He's lost his shop, and he's been drinking. His children are on the streets. This is one. Can you help?

SHEN TE [*To the child.*] Come here, little man. [*Takes him down to the footlights. To the audience.*]

You there! A man is asking you for shelter!
A man of tomorrow says: what about today?
His friend the conqueror, whom you know,
Is his advocate!

[*To* WONG.] He can live in Mr. Shu Fu's cabins. I may have to go there myself. I'm going to have a baby. That's a secret—don't tell Yang Sun—we'd only be in his way. Can you find the carpenter for me?

WONG I knew you'd think of something. [*To the child.*] Good-bye, son, I'm going for your father.

SHEN TE What about your hand, Wong? I wanted to help, but my cousin . . .

WONG Oh, I can get along with one hand, don't worry. [*He shows how he can handle his pole with his left hand alone.*]

SHEN TE But your right hand! Look, take this cart, sell everything that's on it, and go to the doctor with the money . . .

WONG She's still good. But first I'll bring the carpenter. I'll pick up the cart when I get back [*Exit* WONG.]

SHEN TE [*To the child.*] Sit down over here, son, till your father comes.

[*The child sits crosslegged on the ground. Enter the* HUSBAND *and* WIFE, *each dragging a large, full sack.*]

WIFE [*Furtively.*] You're alone, Shen Te, dear?

[SHEN TE *nods. The* WIFE *beckons to the* NEPHEW *offstage. He comes on with another sack.*]

WIFE Your cousin's away? [SHEN TE *nods.*] He's not coming back?

SHEN TE No. I'm giving up the shop.

WIFE That's why we're here. We want to know if we can leave these things in your new home. Will you do us this favor?

SHEN TE Why, yes, I'd be glad to.

HUSBAND [*Cryptically.*] And if anyone asks about them, say they're yours.

SHEN TE Would anyone ask?

WIFE [*With a glance back at her husband.*] Oh, someone might. The police, for instance. They don't seem to like us. Where can we put it?

SHEN TE Well, I'd rather not get in any more trouble . . .

WIFE Listen to her! The good woman of Setzuan!

[SHEN TE *is silent.*]

HUSBAND There's enough tobacco in those sacks to give us a new start in life. We could have our own tobacco factory!

SHEN TE [*Slowly.*] You'll have to put them in the back room.

[*The sacks are taken offstage, while the child is alone. Shyly glancing about him, he goes to the garbage can, starts playing with the contents, and eating some of the scraps. The others return.*]

WIFE We're counting on you, Shen Te!

SHEN TE Yes. [*She sees the child and is shocked.*]

HUSBAND We'll see you in Mr. Shu Fu's cabins.

NEPHEW The day after tomorrow.

SHEN TE Yes. Now, go. Go! I'm not feeling well.

[*Exeunt all three, virtually pushed off.*]

He is eating the refuse in the garbage can!
Only look at his little gray mouth!

[*Pause. Music.*]

As this is the world *my* son will enter
I will study to defend him.
To be good to you, my son,
I shall be a tigress to all others
If I have to.
And I shall have to.

[*She starts to go*]

One more time, then. I hope really the last.

[*Exit* SHEN TE, *taking* SHUI TA*'s trousers.* MRS. SHIN *enters and watches her with marked interest. Enter the* SISTER-IN-LAW *and the* GRANDFATHER.]

SISTER-IN-LAW So it's true, the shop has closed down. And the furniture's in the back yard. It's the end of the road!

MRS. SHIN [*Pompously.*] The fruit of high living, selfishness, and sensuality! Down the primrose path to Mr. Shu Fu's cabins—with you!

SISTER-IN-LAW Cabins? Rat holes! He gave them to us because his soap supplies only went moldy there!

[*Enter the* UNEMPLOYED MAN.]

UNEMPLOYED MAN Shen Te is moving?

SISTER-IN-LAW Yes, she was sneaking away.

MRS. SHIN She's ashamed of herself, and no wonder!

UNEMPLOYED MAN Tell her to call Mr. Shui Ta or she's done for this time!

[*Enter* WONG *and* CARPENTER, *the latter with a child on each hand.*]

CARPENTER So we'll have a roof over our heads for a change!

MRS. SHIN Roof? Whose roof?

CARPENTER Mr. Shu Fu's cabins. And we have little Feng to thank for it. [*Feng, we find, is the name of the child already there; his father now takes him. To the other two.*] Bow to your little brother, you two!

[*The* CARPENTER *and the two new arrivals bow to Feng. Enter* SHUI TA.]

UNEMPLOYED MAN Sst! Mr. Shui Ta!

[*Pause.*]

SHUI TA And what is this crowd here for, may I ask?

WONG How do you do, Mr. Shui Ta. This is the carpenter. Miss Shen Te promised him space in Mr. Shu Fu's cabins.

SHUI TA That will not be possible.

CARPENTER We can't go there after all?

SHUI TA All the space is needed for other purposes.

SISTER-IN-LAW You mean we have to get out? But we've got nowhere to go.

SHUI TA Miss Shen Te finds it possible to provide employment. If the proposition interests you, you may stay in the cabins.

SISTER-IN-LAW [*With distaste.*] You mean *work*? Work for Miss Shen Te?

SHUI TA Making tobacco, yes. There are three bales here already. Would you like to get them?

SISTER-IN-LAW [*Trying to bluster.*] We have our own tobacco! We were in the tobacco business before you were born!

SHUI TA [*To the* CARPENTER *and the* UNEMPLOYED MAN.] You *don't* have your own tobacco. What about you?

[*The* CARPENTER *and the* UNEMPLOYED MAN *get the point, and go for the sacks. Enter* MRS. MI TZU.]

MRS. MI TZU Mr. Shui Ta? I've brought you your three hundred silver dollars.

SHUI TA I'll sign your lease instead. I've decided not to sell.

MRS. MI TZU What? You don't need the money for that flyer?

SHUI TA No.

MRS. MI TZU And you can pay six months' rent?

SHUI TA [*Takes the barber's blank check from the cart and fills it out.*] Here is a check for ten thousand silver dollars. On Mr. Shu Fu's account. Look. [*He shows her the signature on the check.*] Your six months' rent will be in your hands by seven this evening. And now, if you'll excuse me.

MRS. MI TZU So it's Mr. Shu Fu now. The flyer has been given his walking papers. These modern girls! In my day they'd have said she was flighty. That poor, deserted Mr. Yang Sun!

[*Exit* MRS. MI TZU. *The* CARPENTER *and the* UNEMPLOYED MAN *drag the three sacks back on the stage.*]

CARPENTER [*To* SHUI TA.] I don't know why I'm doing this for you.

SHUI TA Perhaps your children want to eat, Mr. Carpenter.

SISTER-IN-LAW [*Catching sight of the sacks.*] Was my brother-in-law here?

MRS. SHIN Yes, he was.

SISTER-IN-LAW I thought as much. I know those sacks! That's our tobacco!

SHUI TA Really? I thought it came from my back room! Shall we consult the police on the point?

SISTER-IN-LAW [*Defeated.*] No.

SHUI TA Perhaps you will show me the way to Mr. Shu Fu's cabins?

[*Taking Feng by the hand,* SHUI TA *goes off, followed by the* CARPENTER *and his two older children, the* SISTER-IN-LAW, *the* GRANDFATHER, *and the* UNEMPLOYED MAN. *Each of the last three drags a sack. Enter* OLD MAN *and* OLD WOMAN.]

MRS. SHIN A pair of pants—missing from the clothes line one minute—and next minute on the honorable backside of Mr. Shui Ta.

OLD WOMAN We thought Miss Shen Te was here.

MRS. SHIN [*Preoccupied.*] Well, she's not.

OLD MAN There was something she was going to give us.

WONG She was going to help me too. [*Looking at his hand.*] It'll be too late soon. But she'll be back. This cousin has never stayed long.

MRS. SHIN [*Approaching a conclusion.*] No, he hasn't, has he?

7a

The Sewer Pipe: WONG *asleep. In his dream, he tells the* GODS *his fears. The* GODS *seem tired from all their travels. They stop for a moment and look over their shoulders at the water seller.*

WONG Illustrious ones. I've been having a bad dream. Our beloved Shen Te was in great distress in the rushes down by the river—the spot where the bodies of suicides are washed up. She kept staggering and holding her head down as if she was carrying something and it was dragging her down into the mud. When I called out to her, she said she had to take your Book of

Rules[3] to the other side, and not get it wet, or the ink would all come off. You had talked to her about the virtues, you know, the time she gave you shelter in Setzuan.

THIRD GOD Well, but what do you suggest, my dear Wong?

WONG Maybe a little relaxation of the rules, Benevolent One, in view of the bad times.

THIRD GOD As for instance?

WONG Well, um, good-will, for instance, might do instead of love?

THIRD GOD I'm afraid that would create new problems.

WONG Or, instead of justice, good sportsmanship?

THIRD GOD That would only mean more work.

WONG Instead of honor, outward propriety?

THIRD GOD Still more work! No, no! The rules will have to stand, my dear Wong!

[*Wearily shaking their heads, all three journey on.*]

8

SHUI TA'*s tobacco factory in* SHU FU'*s cabins. Huddled together behind bars, several families, mostly women and children. Among these people the* SISTER-IN-LAW, *the* GRANDFATHER, *the* CARPENTER, *and his three children. Enter* MRS. YANG *followed by* YANG SUN.

MRS. YANG [*To the audience.*] There's something I just *have* to tell you: strength and wisdom are wonderful things. The strong and wise Mr. Shui Ta has transformed my son from a dissipated good-for-nothing into a model citizen. As you may have heard, Mr. Shui Ta opened a small tobacco factory near the cattle runs. It flourished. Three months ago—I shall never forget it—I asked for an appointment, and Mr. Shui Ta agree to see us—me and my son. I can see him now as he came through the door to meet us. . . .

[*Enter* SHUI TA, *from a door.*]

SHUI TA What can I do for you, Mrs. Yang?

MRS. YANG This morning the police came to the house. We find you've brought an action for breach of promise of marriage. In the name of Shen Te. You also claim that Sun came by two hundred silver dollars by improper means.

SHUI TA That is correct.

MRS. YANG Mr. Shui Ta, the money's all gone. When the Peking job didn't materialize, he ran through it all in three days. I know he's a good-for-nothing. He sold my furniture. He was moving to Peking without me. Miss Shen Te thought highly of him at one time.

SHUI TA What do *you* say, Mr. Yang Sun?

YANG SUN The money's gone.

SHUI TA [*To* MRS. YANG.] Mrs. Yang, in consideration of my cousin's incomprehensible weakness for your son, I am prepared to give him another chance. He can have a job—here. The two hundred silver dollars will be taken out of his wages.

3. Reference to neo-Confucianist commentators' rigid and prescriptive interpretation of Confucius's *Analects*, especially regarding the role of women.

YANG SUN So it's the factory or jail?

SHUI TA Take your choice.

YANG SUN May I speak with Shen Te?

SHUI TA You may not.

[*Pause.*]

YANG SUN [*Sullenly.*] Show me where to go.

MRS. YANG Mr. Shui Ta, you are kindness itself: the gods will reward you! [*To* YANG SUN.] And honest work will make a man of you, my boy. [YANG SUN *follows* SHUI TA *into the factory.* MRS. YANG *comes down again to the footlights.*] Actually, honest work didn't agree with him—at first. And he got no opportunity to distinguish himself till—in the third week—when the wages were being paid . . .

[SHUI TA *has a bag of money. Standing next to his foreman—the former* UNEMPLOYED MAN*—he counts out the wages. It is* YANG SUN*'s turn.*]

UNEMPLOYED MAN [*Reading.*] Carpenter, six silver dollars. Yang Sun, six silver dollars.

YANG SUN [*Quietly.*] Excuse me, sir. I don't think it can be more than five. May I see? [*He takes the foreman's list.*] It says six working days. But that's a mistake, sir. I took a day off for court business. And I won't take what I haven't earned, however miserable the pay is!

UNEMPLOYED MAN Yang Sun. Five silver dollars. [*To* SHUI TA.] A rare case, Mr. Shui Ta!

SHUI TA How is it the book says six when it should say five?

UNEMPLOYED MAN I must've made a mistake, Mr. Shui Ta. [*With a look at* YANG SUN.] It won't happen again.

SHUI TA [*Taking* YANG SUN *aside.*] You don't hold back, do you? You give your all to the firm. You're even honest. Do the foreman's mistakes always favor the workers?

YANG SUN He does have . . . friends.

SHUI TA Thank you. May I offer you any little recompense?

YANG SUN Give me a trial period of one week, and I'll prove my intelligence is worth more to you than my strength.

MRS. YANG [*Still down at the footlights.*] Fighting words, fighting words! That evening, I said to Sun: "If you're a flyer, then fly, my falcon! Rise in the world!" And he got to be foreman. Yes, in Mr. Shui Ta's tobacco factory, he worked real miracles.

[*We see* YANG SUN *with his legs apart standing behind the workers, who are handing along a basket of raw tobacco above their heads.*]

YANG SUN Faster! Faster! You, there, d'you think you can just stand around, now you're not foreman any more? It'll be your job to lead us in song. Sing!

[UNEMPLOYED MAN *starts singing. The others join in the refrain.*]

SONG OF THE EIGHTH ELEPHANT

Chang had seven elephants—all much the same—
  But then there was Little Brother
The seven, they were wild, Little Brother, he was tame
  And to guard them Chang chose Little Brother
    Run faster!
    Mr. Chang has a forest park

Which must be cleared before tonight
And already it's growing dark!

When the seven elephants cleared that forest park
Mr. Chang rode high on Little Brother
While the seven toiled and moiled till dark
On his big behind sat Little Brother
Dig faster!
Mr. Chang has a forest park
Which must be cleared before tonight
And already it's growing dark!

And the seven elephants worked many an hour
Till none of them could work another
Old Chang, he looked sour, on the seven he did glower
But gave a pound of rice to Little Brother
What was that?
Mr. Chang has a forest park
Which must be cleared before tonight
And already it's growing dark!

And the seven elephants hadn't any tusks
The one that had the tusks was Little Brother
Seven are no match for one, if the one has a gun!
How old Chang did laugh at Little Brother!
Keep on digging!
Mr. Chang has a forest park
Which must be cleared before tonight
And already it's growing dark!

[*Smoking a cigar,* SHUI TA *strolls by.* YANG SUN, *laughing, has joined in the refrain of the third stanza and speeded up the tempo of the last stanza by clapping his hands.*]

MRS. YANG And that's why I say: strength and wisdom are wonderful things. It took the strong and wise Mr. Shui Ta to bring out the best in Yang Sun. A real superior man is like a bell. If you ring it, it rings, and if you don't, it don't, as the saying is.[4]

9

SHEN TE*'s shop, now an office with club chairs and fine carpets. It is raining.* SHUI TA, *now fat, is just dismissing the* OLD MAN *and* OLD WOMAN. MRS. SHIN, *in obviously new clothes, looks on, smirking.*

SHUI TA No! I canNOT tell you when we expect her back.

OLD WOMAN The two hundred silver dollars came today. In an envelope. There was no letter, but it must be from Shen Te. We want to write and thank her. May we have her address?

4. A saying by the Chinese philosopher Mo-tzu (470–391 B.C.E.).

SHUI TA I'm afraid I haven't got it.

OLD MAN [*Pulling Old Woman's sleeve.*] Let's be going.

OLD WOMAN She's got to come back some time!

[*They move off, uncertainly, worried.* SHUI TA *bows.*]

MRS. SHIN They lost the carpet shop because they couldn't pay their taxes. The money arrived too late.

SHUI TA They could have come to me.

MRS. SHIN People don't like coming to you.

SHUI TA [*Sits suddenly, one hand to his head.*] I'm dizzy.

MRS. SHIN After all, you *are* in your seventh month. But old Mrs. Shin will be there in your hour of trial! [*She cackles feebly.*]

SHUI TA [*In a stifled voice.*] Can I count on that?

MRS. SHIN We all have our price, and mine won't be too high for the great Mr. Shui Ta! [*She opens* SHUI TA*'s collar.*]

SHUI TA It's for the child's sake. All of this.

MRS. SHIN "All for the child," of course.

SHUI TA I'm so fat. People must notice.

MRS. SHIN Oh no, they think it's 'cause you're rich.

SHUI TA [*More feelingly.*] What will happen to the child?

MRS. SHIN You ask that nine times a day. Why, it'll have the best that money can buy!

SHUI TA He must never see Shui Ta.

MRS. SHIN Oh, no. Always Shen Te.

SHUI TA What about the neighbors? There are rumors, aren't there?

MRS. SHIN As long as Mr. Shu Fu doesn't find out, there's nothing to worry about. Drink this.

[*Enter* YANG SUN *in a smart business suit, and carrying a businessman's briefcase.* SHUI TA *is more or less in* MRS. SHIN*'s arms.*]

YANG SUN [*Surprised.*] I guess I'm in the way.

SHUI TA [*Ignoring this, rises with an effort.*] Till tomorrow, Mrs. Shin.

[MRS. SHIN *leaves with a smile, putting on her new gloves.*]

YANG SUN Gloves now! She couldn't be fleecing you? And since when did *you* have a private life? [*Taking a paper from the briefcase.*] You haven't been at your best lately, and things are getting out of hand. The police want to close us down. They say that at the most they can only permit twice the lawful number of workers.

SHUI TA [*Evasively.*] The cabins are quite good enough.

YANG SUN For the workers maybe, not for the tobacco. They're too damp. We must take over some of Mrs. Mi Tzu's buildings.

SHUI TA Her price is double what I can pay.

YANG SUN Not unconditionally. If she has me to stroke her knees she'll come down.

SHUI TA I'll never agree to that.

YANG SUN What's wrong? Is it the rain? You get so irritable whenever it rains.

SHUI TA Never! I will never . . .

YANG SUN Mrs. Mi Tzu'll be here in five minutes. *You* fix it. And Shu Fu will be with her. . . . What's all that noise?

[*During the above dialogue,* WONG *is heard offstage, calling:* "The good Shen Te, where is she? Which of you has seen Shen Te, good people? Where is Shen Te?" *A knock. Enter* WONG.]

WONG Mr. Shui Ta, I've come to ask when Miss Shen Te will be back, it's six months now. . . . There are rumors. People say something's happened to her.

SHUI TA I'm busy. Come back next week.

WONG [*Excited.*] In the morning there was always rice on her doorstep—for the needy. It's been there again lately!

SHUI TA And what do people conclude from this?

WONG That Shen Te is still in Setzuan! She's been . . . [*He breaks off.*]

SHUI TA She's been what? Mr. Wong, if you're Shen Te's friend, talk a little less about her, that's my advice to you.

WONG I don't want your advice! Before she disappeared, Miss Shen Te told me something very important—she's pregnant!

YANG SUN What? What was that?

SHUI TA [*Quickly.*] The man is lying.

WONG A good woman isn't so easily forgotten, Mr. Shui Ta.

[*He leaves.* SHUI TA *goes quickly into the back room.*]

YANG SUN [*To the audience.*] Shen Te pregnant? So that's why. Her cousin sent her away, so I wouldn't get wind of it. I have a son, a Yang appears on the scene, and what happens? Mother and child vanish into thin air! That scoundrel, that unspeakable . . . [*The sound of sobbing is heard from the back room.*] What was that? Someone sobbing? Who was it? Mr. Shui Ta the Tobacco King doesn't weep his heart out. And where does the rice come from that's on the doorstep in the morning? [SHUI TA *returns. He goes to the door and looks out into the rain.*] Where is she?

SHUI TA Sh! It's nine o'clock. But the rain's so heavy, you can't hear a thing.

YANG SUN What do you want to hear?

SHUI TA The mail plane.

YANG SUN What?!

SHUI TA I've been told *you* wanted to fly at one time. Is that all forgotten?

YANG SUN Flying mail is night work. I prefer the daytime. And the firm is very dear to me—after all it belongs to my ex-fiancée, even if she's not around. And she's not, is she?

SHUI TA What do you mean by that?

YANG SUN Oh, well, let's say I haven't altogether—lost interest.

SHUI TA My cousin might like to know that.

YANG SUN I might not be indifferent—if I found she was being kept under lock and key.

SHUI TA By whom?

YANG SUN By you.

SHUI TA What could you do about it?

YANG SUN I could submit for discussion—my position in the firm.

SHUI TA You are now my manager. In return for a more . . . appropriate position, you might agree to drop the inquiry into your ex-fiancée's whereabouts?

YANG SUN I might.

SHUI TA What position *would* be more appropriate?

YANG SUN The one at the top.

SHUI TA My own? [*Silence.*] And if I preferred to throw you out on your neck?

YANG SUN I'd come back on my feet. With suitable escort.

SHUI TA The police?

YANG SUN The police.

SHUI TA And when the police found no one?

YANG SUN I might ask them not to overlook the back room. [*Ending the pretense.*] In short, Mr. Shui Ta, my interest in this young woman has not been officially terminated. I should like to see more of her. [*Into* SHUI TA*'s face.*] Besides, she's pregnant and needs a friend. [*He moves to the door.*] I shall talk about it with the water seller.

[*Exit.* SHUI TA *is rigid for a moment, then he quickly goes into the back room. He returns with* SHEN TE*'s belongings: underwear, etc. He takes a long look at the shawl of the previous scene. He then wraps the things in a bundle, which, upon hearing a noise, he hides under the table. Enter* MRS. MI TZU *and Mr.* SHU FU. *They put away their umbrellas and galoshes.*]

MRS. MI TZU I thought your manager was here, Mr. Shui Ta. He combines charm with business in a way that can only be to the advantage of all of us.

SHU FU You sent for us, Mr. Shui Ta?

SHUI TA The factory is in trouble.

SHU FU It always is.

SHUI TA The police are threatening to close us down unless I can show that the extension of our facilities is imminent.

SHU FU Mr. Shui Ta, I'm sick and tired of your constantly expanding projects. I place cabins at your cousin's disposal; you make a factory of them. I hand your cousin a check; you present it. Your cousin disappears; you find the cabins too small and start talking of yet more—

SHUI TA Mr. Shu Fu, I'm authorized to inform you that Miss Shen Te's return is now imminent.

SHU FU Imminent? It's becoming his favorite word.

MRS. MI TZU Yes, what does it mean?

SHUI TA Mrs. Mi Tzu, I can pay you exactly half what you asked for your buildings. Are you ready to inform the police that I am taking them over?

MRS. MI TZU Certainly, if I can take over your manager.

SHU FU What?

MRS. MI TZU He's so efficient.

SHUI TA I'm afraid I need Mr. Yang Sun.

MRS. MI TZU So do I.

SHUI TA He will call on you tomorrow.

SHU FU So much the better. With Shen Te likely to turn up at any moment, the presence of that young man is hardly in good taste.

SHUI TA So we have reached a settlement. In what was once the good Shen Te's little shop we are laying the foundations for the great Mr. Shui Ta's twelve magnificent super tobacco markets. You will bear in mind that though they call me the Tobacco King of Setzuan, it is my cousin's interests that have been served . . .

VOICES [*Off.*] The police, the police! Going to the tobacco shop! Something must have happened!

[*Enter* YANG SUN, WONG, *and the* POLICEMAN.]

POLICEMAN Quiet there, quiet, quiet! [*They quiet down.*] I'm sorry, Mr. Shui Ta, but there's a report that you've been depriving Miss Shen Te of her freedom. Not that I believe all I hear, but the whole city's in an uproar.

SHUI TA That's a lie.

POLICEMAN Mr. Yang Sun has testified that he heard someone sobbing in the back room.

SHU FU Mrs. Mi Tzu and myself will testify that no one here has been sobbing.

MRS. MI TZU We have been quietly smoking our cigars.

POLICEMAN Mr. Shui Ta, I'm afraid I shall have to take a look at that room. [*He does so. The room is empty.*] No one there, of course, sir.

YANG SUN But I heard sobbing. What's that?

[*He finds the clothes.*]

WONG Those are Shen Te's things. [*To crowd.*] Shen Te's clothes are here!

VOICES [*Off, in sequence.*] Shen Te's clothes!
—They've been found under the table!
—Body of murdered girl still missing!
—Tobacco King suspected!

POLICEMAN Mr. Shui Ta, unless you can tell us where the girl is, I'll have to ask you to come along.

SHUI TA I do not know.

POLICEMAN I can't say how sorry I am, Mr. Shui Ta. [*He shows him the door.*]

SHUI TA Everything will be cleared up in no time. There are still judges in Setzuan.

YANG SUN I heard sobbing!

9a

WONG's den. For the last time, the GODS appear to the water seller in his dream. They have changed and show signs of a long journey, extreme fatigue, and plenty of mishaps. The FIRST no longer has a hat; the THIRD has lost a leg; all three are barefoot.

WONG Illustrious ones, at last you're here. Shen Te's been gone for months and today her cousin's been arrested. They think he murdered her to get the shop. But I had a dream and in this dream Shen Te said her cousin was keeping her prisoner. You must find her for us, illustrious ones!

FIRST GOD We've found very few good people anywhere, and even they didn't keep it up. Shen Te is still the only one that stayed good.

SECOND GOD If she *has* stayed good.

WONG Certainly she has. But she's vanished.

FIRST GOD That's the last straw. All is lost!

SECOND GOD A little moderation, dear colleague!

FIRST GOD [*Plaintively.*] What's the good of moderation now? If she can't be found, we'll have to resign! The world is a terrible place! Nothing but misery, vulgarity, and waste! Even the countryside isn't what it used to be. The trees are getting their heads chopped off by telephone wires, and there's such a noise from all the gunfire, and I can't stand those heavy clouds of smoke, and—

THIRD GOD The place is absolutely unlivable! Good intentions bring people to the brink of the abyss, and good deeds push them over the edge. I'm afraid our book of rules is destined for the scrap heap—

SECOND GOD It's people! They're a worthless lot!

THIRD GOD The world is too cold!

SECOND GOD It's people! They're too weak!

FIRST GOD Dignity, dear colleagues, dignity! Never despair! As for this world, didn't we agree that we only have to find one human being who can stand the place? Well, we found her. True, we lost her again. We must find her again, that's all! And at once!

[*They disappear.*]

10

Courtroom. Groups: SHU FU *and* MRS. MI TZU; YANG SUN *and* MRS. YANG; WONG, *the* CARPENTER, *the* GRANDFATHER, *the* NIECE, *the* OLD MAN, *the* OLD WOMAN; MRS. SHIN, *the* POLICEMAN; *the* UNEMPLOYED MAN, *the* SISTER-IN-LAW.

OLD MAN So much power isn't good for one man.

UNEMPLOYED MAN And he's going to open twelve super tobacco markets!

WIFE One of the judges is a friend of Mr. Shu Fu's.

SISTER-IN-LAW Another one accepted a present from Mr. Shui Ta only last night. A great fat goose.

OLD WOMAN [*To* WONG] And Shen Te is nowhere to be found.

WONG Only the gods will ever know the truth.

POLICEMAN Order in the court! My lords the judges!

[*Enter the* THREE GODS *in judges' robes. We overhear their conversation as they pass along the footlights to their bench.*]

THIRD GOD We'll never get away with it, our certificates were so badly forged.

SECOND GOD My predecessor's "sudden indigestion" will certainly cause comment.

FIRST GOD But he *had* just eaten a whole goose.

UNEMPLOYED MAN Look at that! *New* judges.

WONG New judges. And what good ones!

[*The* THIRD GOD *hears this, and turns to smile at* WONG. *The* GODS *sit. The* FIRST GOD *beats on the bench with his gavel. The* POLICEMAN *brings in* SHUI TA, *who walks with lordly steps. He is whistled*[5] *at.*]

POLICEMAN [*To* SHUI TA.] Be prepared for a surprise. The judges have been changed.

[SHUI TA *turns quickly round, looks at them, and staggers.*]

NIECE What's the matter now?

5. Hissed.

WIFE The great Tobacco King nearly fainted.

HUSBAND Yes, as soon as he saw the new judges.

WONG Does *he* know who they are?

[SHUI TA *picks himself up, and the proceedings open.*]

FIRST GOD Defendant Shui Ta, you are accused of doing away with your cousin Shen Te in order to take possession of her business. Do you plead guilty or not guilty?

SHUI TA Not guilty, my lord.

FIRST GOD [*Thumbing through the documents of the case.*] The first witness is the policeman. I shall ask him to tell us something of the respective reputations of Miss Shen Te and Mr. Shui Ta.

POLICEMAN Miss Shen Te was a young lady who aimed to please, my lord. She liked to live and let live, as the saying goes. Mr. Shui Ta, on the other hand, is a man of principle. Though the generosity of Miss Shen Te forced him at times to abandon half measures, unlike the girl he was always on the side of the law, my lord. One time, he even unmasked a gang of thieves to whom his too trustful cousin had given shelter. The evidence, in short, my lord, proves that Mr. Shui Ta was *incapable* of the crime of which he stands accused!

FIRST GOD I see. And are there others who could testify along, shall we say, the same lines?

[SHU FU *rises.*]

POLICEMAN [*Whispering to* GODS.] Mr. Shu Fu—a very important person.

FIRST GOD [*Inviting him to speak.*] Mr. Shu Fu!

SHU FU Mr. Shui Ta is a businessman, my lord. Need I say more?

FIRST GOD Yes.

SHU FU Very well, I will. He is Vice President of the Council of Commerce and is about to be elected a Justice of the Peace. [*He returns to his seat.* MRS. MI TZU *rises.*]

WONG Elected! *He* gave him the job!

[*With a gesture the* FIRST GOD *asks who* MRS. MI TZU *is.*]

POLICEMAN Another very important person. Mrs. Mi Tzu.

FIRST GOD [*Inviting her to speak.*] Mrs. Mi Tzu!

MRS. MI TZU My lord, as Chairman of the Committee on Social Work, I wish to call attention to just a couple of eloquent facts: Mr. Shui Ta not only has erected a model factory with model housing in our city, he is a regular contributor to our home for the disabled. [*She returns to her seat.*]

POLICEMAN [*Whispering.*] And she's a great friend of the judge that ate the goose!

FIRST GOD [*To the* POLICEMAN.] Oh, thank you. What next? [*To the Court, genially.*] Oh, yes. We should find out if any of the evidence is less favorable to the defendant.

[WONG, *the* CARPENTER, *the* OLD MAN, *the* OLD WOMAN, *the* UNEMPLOYED MAN, *the* SISTER-IN-LAW, *and the* NIECE *come forward.*]

POLICEMAN [*Whispering.*] Just the riffraff, my lord.

FIRST GOD [*Addressing the "riffraff."*] Well, um, riffraff—do you know anything of the defendant, Mr. Shui Ta?

WONG Too much, my lord.

UNEMPLOYED MAN What don't we know, my lord.
CARPENTER He ruined us.
SISTER-IN-LAW He's a cheat.
NIECE Liar.
WIFE Thief.
BOY Blackmailer.
BROTHER Murderer.
FIRST GOD Thank you. We should now let the defendant state his point of view.
SHUI TA I only came on the scene when Shen Te was in danger of losing what I had understood was a gift from the gods. Because I did the filthy jobs which someone had to do, they hate me. My activities were restricted to the minimum, my lord.
SISTER-IN-LAW He had us arrested!
SHUI TA Certainly. You stole from the bakery!
SISTER-IN-LAW Such concern for the bakery! You didn't want the shop for yourself, I suppose!
SHUI TA I didn't want the shop overrun with parasites.
SISTER-IN-LAW We had nowhere else to go.
SHUI TA There were too many of you.
WONG What about this old couple: Were *they* parasites?
OLD MAN We lost our shop because of you!
OLD WOMAN And we gave your cousin money!
SHUI TA My cousin's fiancé was a flyer. The money had to go to *him.*
WONG Did you care whether he flew or not? Did you care whether she married him or not? You wanted her to marry someone else!
[*He points to* SHU FU.]
SHUI TA The flyer unexpectedly turned out to be a scoundrel.
YANG SUN [*Jumping up.*] Which was the reason you made him your manager?
SHUI TA Later on he improved.
WONG And when he improved, you sold him to her? [*He points out* MRS. MI TZU.]
SHUI TA She wouldn't let me have her premises unless she had him to stroke her knees!
MRS. MI TZU What? The man's a pathological liar. [*To him.*] Don't mention my property to me as long as you live! Murderer! [*She rustles off, in high dudgeon.*]
YANG SUN [*Pushing in.*] My lord, I wish to speak for the defendant.
SISTER-IN-LAW Naturally. He's your employer.
UNEMPLOYED MAN And the worst slave driver in the country.
MRS. YANG That's a lie! My lord, Mr. Shui Ta is a great man. He . . .
YANG SUN He's this and he's that, but he is not a murderer, my lord. Just fifteen minutes before his arrest I heard Shen Te's voice in his own back room.
FIRST GOD Oh? Tell us more!
YANG SUN I heard sobbing, my lord!
FIRST GOD But lots of women sob, we've been finding.
YANG SUN Could I fail to recognize her voice?

SHU FU No, you made her sob so often yourself, young man!
YANG SUN Yes. But I also made her happy. Till he [*Pointing at* SHUI TA.] decided to sell her to you!
SHUI TA Because you didn't love her.
WONG Oh, no: it was for the money, my lord!
SHUI TA And what was the money for, my lord? For the poor! And for Shen Te so she could go on being good!
WONG For the poor? That he sent to his sweatshops? And why didn't you let Shen Te be good when you signed the big check?
SHUI TA For the child's sake, my lord.
CARPENTER What about *my* children? What did he do about them?

[SHUI TA *is silent.*]

WONG The shop was to be a fountain of goodness. That was the gods' idea. You came and spoiled it!
SHUI TA If I hadn't, it would have run dry!
MRS. SHIN There's a lot in that, my lord.
WONG What have you done with the good Shen Te, bad man? She *was* good, my lords, she was, I swear it! [*He raises his hand in an oath.*]
THIRD GOD What's happened to your hand, water seller?
WONG [*Pointing to* SHUI TA.] It's all his fault, my lord, *she* was going to send me to a doctor—[*To* SHUI TA.] You were her worst enemy!
SHUI TA I was her only friend!
WONG Where is she then? Tell us where your good friend is!

[*The excitement of this exchange has run through the whole crowd.*]

ALL Yes, where is she? Where is Shen Te? [*Etc.*]
SHUI TA Shen Te . . . had to go.
WONG Where? Where to?
SHUI TA I cannot tell you! I cannot tell you!
ALL Why? Why did she have to go away? [*Etc.*]
WONG [*Into the din with the first words, but talking on beyond the others.*] Why not, why not? Why did she have to go away?
SHUI TA [*Shouting.*] Because you'd all have torn her to shreds, that's why! My lords, I have a request. Clear the court! When only the judges remain, I will make a confession.
ALL [*Except* WONG, *who is silent, struck by the new turn of events.*] So he's guilty? He's confessing! [*Etc.*]
FIRST GOD [*Using the gavel.*] Clear the court!
POLICEMAN Clear the court!
WONG Mr. Shui Ta has met his match this time.
MRS. SHIN [*With a gesture toward the judges.*] You're in for a little surprise.

[*The court is cleared. Silence.*]

SHUI TA Illustrious ones!

[*The* GODS *look at each other, not quite believing their ears.*]

SHUI TA Yes, I recognize you!
SECOND GOD [*Taking matters in hand, sternly.*] What have you done with our good woman of Setzuan?
SHUI TA I have a terrible confession to make: I am she! [*He takes off his mask, and tears away his clothes.* SHEN TE *stands there.*]
SECOND GOD Shen Te!

SHEN TE Shen Te, yes. Shui Ta *and* Shen Te. Both.

Your injunction
To be good and yet to live
Was a thunderbolt:
It has torn me in two
I can't tell how it was
But to be good to others
And myself at the same time
I could not do it
Your world is not an easy one, illustrious ones!
When we extend our hand to a beggar, he tears it off for us
When we help the lost, we are lost ourselves
And so
Since not to eat is to die
Who can long refuse to be bad?
As I lay prostrate beneath the weight of good intentions
Ruin stared me in the face
It was when I was unjust that I ate good meat
And hobnobbed with the mighty
Why?
Why are bad deeds rewarded?
Good ones punished?
I enjoyed giving
I truly wished to be the Angel of the Slums
But washed by a foster-mother in the water of the gutter
I developed a sharp eye
The time came when pity was a thorn in my side
And, later, when kind words turned to ashes in my mouth
And anger took over
I became a wolf
Find me guilty, then, illustrious ones,
But know:
All that I have done I did
To help my neighbor
To love my lover
And to keep my little one from want
For your great, godly deeds, I was too poor, too small.

[*Pause.*]

FIRST GOD [*Shocked.*] Don't go on making yourself miserable, Shen Te! We're overjoyed to have found you!

SHEN TE I'm telling you I'm the bad man who committed all those crimes!

FIRST GOD [*Using—or failing to use—his ear trumpet.*] The good woman who did all those good deeds?

SHEN TE Yes, but the bad man too!

FIRST GOD [*As if something had dawned.*] Unfortunate coincidences! Heartless neighbors!

THIRD GOD [*Shouting in his ear.*] But how is she to continue?

FIRST GOD Continue? Well, she's a strong, healthy girl . . .

SECOND GOD You didn't hear what she said!

FIRST GOD I heard every word! She is confused, that's all! [*He begins to bluster.*] And what about this book of rules—we can't renounce our rules, can we? [*More quietly.*] Should the world be changed? How? By whom? The world should *not* be changed! [*At a sign from him, the lights turn pink, and music plays.*]

And now the hour of parting is at hand.
Dost thou behold, Shen Te, yon fleecy cloud?
It is our chariot. At a sign from me
'Twill come and take us back from whence we came
Above the azure vault and silver stars. . . .

SHEN TE No! Don't go, illustrious ones!

FIRST GOD

Our cloud has landed now in yonder field
From which it will transport us back to heaven.
Farewell, Shen Te, let not thy courage fail thee. . . .

[*Exeunt* GODS.]

SHEN TE What about the old couple? They've lost their shop! What about the water seller and his hand? And I've got to defend myself against the barber, because I don't love him! And against Sun, because I do love him! How? How?

[SHEN TE*'s eyes follow the* GODS *as they are imagined to step into a cloud, which rises and moves forward over the orchestra and up beyond the balcony.*]

FIRST GOD [*From on high.*] We have faith in you, Shen Te!

SHEN TE There'll be a child. And he'll have to be fed. I can't stay here. Where shall I go?

FIRST GOD Continue to be good, good woman of Setzuan!

SHEN TE I need my bad cousin!

FIRST GOD But not very often!

SHEN TE Once a week at least!

FIRST GOD Once a month will be quite enough!

SHEN TE [*Shrieking.*] No, no! Help!

[*But the cloud continues to recede as the* GODS *sing.*]

VALEDICTORY HYMN

What rapture, oh, it is to know
  A good thing when you see it
And having seen a good thing, oh,
  What rapture 'tis to flee it

Be good, sweet maid of Setzuan
  Let Shui Ta be clever
Departing, we forget the man
  Remember your endeavor

Because through all the length of days
  Her goodness faileth never
Sing hallelujah! Make Shen Te's
  Good name live on forever!

SHEN TE Help!

1943

ZHANG AILING

1920–1995

In many ways the case of Zhang Ailing embodies the complexities and historical twists of a national literature finding its place in a global community—in this case, the literature of a nation with an immense, intellectually vibrant diaspora. Often acclaimed as the best Chinese writer of the mid-twentieth century, Zhang Ailing was recovered from a period of obscurity by a Chinese professor at Yale University. Zhang's fame then spread to Taiwan and Hong Kong, and at last to China itself. Although the literary work on which her fame rests was written in China and Hong Kong, Zhang Ailing herself lived more than half her life in the United States, and her best-known novel, *The Rice-Sprout Song*, from her second residence in Hong Kong, was written first in English and then rewritten in Chinese.

Zhang Ailing was born in Shanghai into an old family of imperial officialdom, with an irascible, opium-smoking father and a mother who left to study in France when Zhang Ailing was a child; thus the girl's family background combined the decadence and fierce independence of spirit of the Shanghai elite in the 1920s and 1930s. After her parents divorced, Zhang was mistreated by her father and fled his house to live with her mother. When the war in China broke out (1941), she left Shanghai to study at the University of Hong Kong; but after the fall of Hong Kong to the Japanese, Zhang returned to Shanghai, where, under Japanese occupation, she wrote her most famous shorter works. Her marriage, albeit brief, to the collaborator Hu Lancheng and her passive acceptance of Japanese rule made her suspect after the war, and her family background placed her in an even more uncomfortable position when the Communists took Shanghai and the People's Republic of china was established. In 1952 Zhang went again to Hong Kong, where she put her talent at the service of the anticommunist passions of the era. There she wrote two novels, both critical of the People's Republic: *The Rice-Sprout Song*, which enjoyed a modest success, and *Naked Earth*, which did not. In 1955 she left for the United States. After remarriage and the death of her second husband, Zhang went to Berkeley as a researcher and at last to Los Angeles, where she lived her last days in bleak austerity.

Far more than her novels, her stories from the 1940s, collected as *Tales* (sometimes translated as *Romances*), form the core of her work. One of the best known, a novella later turned into a novel, *The Golden Cangue*, describes a woman who must choose between love and financial advantage; her choice of the latter eventually destroys her and those around her, including her children. In addition to the stories and novels, Zhang Ailing wrote essays and memoirs that are much admired; she also did scholarly work on the *Story of the Stone* and an annotated translation of a late Qing novel, in Wu dialect, into Mandarin Chinese.

Zhang is sometimes called a postmodern writer, both for her experimental approach toward language and narrative structure and for her interest in unsettling and unmasking the discourses of modernity. Her fiction is infused with an atmosphere of desolation at odds with the optimism of the narratives of progress and revolutionary success. Her persistent focus on the trivial, the private feeling, the humble detail can be understood as a rejection of the nation-building myths that many of her contemporaries strove to develop.

The story selected here, "Sealed Off" (1943), opens in the city of Shanghai, the buzzing center of Chinese commercial life, technology, and urban activity. The images of geometric abstraction, with the parallel lines of the tramcar tracks extending seemingly into infinity, and even the air siren telegraphing a pattern of "cold little dots," suggest a rigid and rationalized world, a glowing plane along which the human tokens move in perfect, unending formation. But in shutting down the city, forcing buildings to seal their doors, the streets to clear of pedestrians, and even the tramcar to loiter on its tracks, the air siren imposes an unexpected calm on the metropolis. (The story takes place during the Second World War, when air sirens were a common feature of city life.) Sitting in enforced quietude, the citizens in the tramcar begin to ruminate, ponder, and dream: a groan of complaint, a meditation on food, a fantasy of romance. The narrative voice, too, enters a heavy, dreamlike mode. When the all-clear finally sounds and the hum of the metropolis resumes, a central character, who has been venturing a cautious flirtation with another passenger, is jolted into an awareness that the possibilities unfolding "while the city was sealed off" cannot belong to real life. Yet a form of life did surface: however fleetingly, the governing grid was locked in stasis, enabling a different kind of humanity to emerge.

The story's genre is psychological fiction, though not in the usual sense of entering directly into the thoughts of characters (although this does happen). Instead, the emphasis lies on the roiling, sensuous unconscious of the city, where the submerged desires and dreams of Shanghai's populace oppose the ruthlessness of the social order. Readers may detect the influence, through various postwar British writers, of Freud, with his stress on the unconscious and the irrational. Zhang's concern as a writer, she said, was not History with a capital H: "I cannot write what is commonly known as the memorials of the times, and I have no intention of attempting it, because there seems at present no such concentration of subject matter. I only write some little things between men and women; also there are no wars or revolution in my works, for I believe that a man is both simpler and freer when he is in love than when he is in war or revolution."

Sealed Off[1]

The tramcar driver drove his tram. The tramcar tracks, in the blazing sun, shimmered like two shiny eels crawling out of the water; they stretched and shrank, stretched and shrank, on their onward way—soft and slippery, long old eels, never ending, never ending . . . the driver fixed his eyes on the undulating tracks, and didn't go mad.

1. Translated by Karen Kingsbury.

If there hadn't been an air raid,[2] if the city hadn't been sealed, the tramcar would have gone on forever. The city was sealed. The alarm-bell rang. Ding-ding-ding-ding. Every "ding" was a cold little dot, the dots all adding up to a dotted line, cutting across time and space.

The tramcar ground to a halt, but the people on the street ran: those on the left side of the street ran over to the right, and those on the right ran over to the left. All the shops, in a single sweep, rattled down their metal gates. Matrons tugged madly at the railings. "Let us in for just a while," they cried. "We have children here, and old people!" But the gates stayed tightly shut. Those inside the metal gates and those outside the metal gates stood glaring at each other, fearing one another.

Inside the tram, people were fairly quiet. They had somewhere to sit, and though the place was rather plain, it still was better, for most of them, than what they had at home. Gradually, the street also grew quiet: not that it was a complete silence, but the sound of voices eased into a confused blur, like the soft rustle of a straw-stuffed pillow, heard in a dream. The huge, shambling city sat dozing in the sun, its head resting heavily on people's shoulders, its spittle slowly dripping down their shirts, an inconceivably enormous weight pressing down on everyone. Never before, it seemed, had Shanghai been this quiet—and in the middle of the day! A beggar, taking advantage of the breathless, birdless quiet, lifted up his voice and began to chant: "Good master, good lady, kind sir, kind ma'am, won't you give alms to this poor man? Good master, good lady . . ." But after a short while he stopped, scared silent by the eerie quiet.

Then there was a braver beggar, a man from Shandong,[3] who firmly broke the silence. His voice was round and resonant: "Sad, sad, sad! No money do I have!" An old, old song, sung from one century to the next. The tram driver, who also was from Shandong, succumbed to the sonorous tune. Heaving a long sigh, he folded his arms across his chest, leaned against the tram door, and joined in: "Sad, sad, sad! No money do I have!"

Some of the tram passengers got out. But there was still a little loose, scattered chatter; near the door, a group of office workers was discussing something. One of them, with a quick, ripping sound, shook his fan open and offered his conclusion: "Well, in the end, there's nothing wrong with him—it's just that he doesn't know how to act." From another nose came a short grunt, followed by a cold smile: "Doesn't know how to act? He sure knows how to toady up to the bosses!"

A middle-aged couple who looked very much like brother and sister stood together in the middle of the tram, holding onto the leather straps. "Careful!" the woman suddenly yelped. "Don't get your trousers dirty!" The man flinched, then slowly raised the hand from which a packet of smoked fish dangled. Very cautiously, very gingerly, he held the paper packet, which was brimming with oil, several inches away from his suit pants. His wife did not let up. "Do you know what dry-cleaning costs these days? Or what it costs to get a pair of trousers made?"

2. The Japanese frequently bombed Shanghai during the Second Sino-Japanese War (1937–45), which became part of the Second World War (1939–45).

3. A region in eastern China, located to the north of Shanghai.

Lu Zongzhen, accountant for Huamao Bank, was sitting in the corner. When he saw the smoked fish, he was reminded of the steamed dumplings stuffed with spinach that his wife had asked him to buy at a noodle stand near the bank. Women are always like that. Dumplings bought in the hardest-to-find, most twisty-windy little alleys had to be the best, no matter what. She didn't for a moment think of how it would be for him—neatly dressed in suit and tie, with tortoiseshell eyeglasses and a leather briefcase, then, tucked under his arm, these steaming hot dumplings wrapped in newspaper—how ludicrous! Still, if the city were sealed for a long time, so that his dinner was delayed, then he could at least make do with the dumplings.

He glanced at his watch; only four-thirty. Must be the power of suggestion. He felt hungry already. Carefully pulling back a corner of the paper, he took a look inside. Snowy white mounds, breathing soft little whiffs of sesame oil. A piece of newspaper had stuck to the dumplings, and he gravely peeled it off; the ink was printed on the dumplings, with all the writing in reverse, as though it were reflected in a mirror. He peered down and slowly picked the words out: "Obituaries . . . Positions Wanted . . . Stock Market Developments . . . Now Playing . . ." Normal, useful phrases, but they did look a bit odd on a dumpling. Maybe because eating is such serious business; compared to it, everything else is just a joke. Lu Zongzhen thought it looked funny, but he didn't laugh: he was a very straightforward kind of fellow. After reading the dumplings, he read the newspaper, but when he'd finished half a page of old news, he found that if he turned the page all the dumplings would fall out, and so he had to stop.

While Lu read the paper, others in the tram did likewise. People who had newspapers read them; those without newspapers read receipts, or lists of rules and regulations, or business cards. People who were stuck without a single scrap of printed matter read shop signs along the street. They simply had to fill this terrifying emptiness—otherwise, their brains might start to work. Thinking is a painful business.

Sitting across from Lu Zongzhen was an old man who, with a dull clacking sound, rolled two slippery, glossy walnuts in his palm: a rhythmic little gesture can substitute for thought. The old man had a clean-shaven pate, a reddish yellow complexion, and an oily sheen on his face. When his brows were furrowed, his head looked like a walnut. The thoughts inside were walnut-flavored: smooth and sweet, but in the end, empty-tasting.

To the old man's right sat Wu Cuiyuan, who looked like one of those young Christian wives, though she was still unmarried. Her Chinese gown of white cotton was trimmed with a narrow blue border—the navy blue around the white reminded one of the black borders around an obituary—and she carried a little blue-and-white checked parasol. Her hairstyle was utterly banal, so as not to attract attention. Actually, she hadn't much reason to fear. She wasn't bad-looking, but hers was an uncertain, unfocused beauty, an afraid-she-had-offended-someone kind of beauty. Her face was bland, slack, lacking definition. Even her own mother couldn't say for certain whether her face was long or round.

At home she was a good daughter, at school she was a good student. After graduating from college, Cuiyuan had become an English instructor at her alma mater. Now, stuck in the air raid, she decided to grade a few papers while she waited. The first one was written by a male student. It railed against the evils of the big city, full of righteous anger, the prose stiff, choppy, ungrammatical. "Painted prostitutes . . . cruising the Cosmo . . . low-class bars and dancing-halls." Cuiyuan paused for a moment, then pulled out her red pencil and gave the paper an "A." Ordinarily, she would have gone right on to the next one, but now, because she had too much time to think, she couldn't help wondering why she had given this student such a high mark. If she hadn't asked herself this question, she could have ignored the whole matter, but once she did ask, her face suffused with red. Suddenly, she understood: it was because this student was the only man who fearlessly and forthrightly said such things to her.

He treated her like an intelligent, sophisticated person; as if she were a man, someone who really understood. He respected her. Cuiyuan always felt that no one at school respected her—from the president on down to the professors, the students, even the janitors. The students' grumbling was especially hard to take: "This place is really falling apart. Getting worse every day. It's bad enough having to learn English from a Chinese, but then to learn it from a Chinese who's never gone abroad . . ." Cuiyuan took abuse at school, took abuse at home. The Wu household was a modern, model household, devout and serious. The family had pushed their daughter to study hard, to climb upwards step by step, right to the tip-top . . . A girl in her twenties teaching at a university! It set a record for women's professional achievement. But her parents' enthusiasm began to wear thin and now they wished she hadn't been quite so serious, wished she'd taken more time out from her studies, tried to find herself a rich husband.

She was a good daughter, a good student. All the people in her family were good people; they took baths every day and read the newspaper; when they listened to the wireless, they never tuned into local folk-opera, comic opera, that sort of thing, but listened only to the symphonies of Beethoven and Wagner; they didn't understand what they were listening to, but still they listened. In this world, there are more good people than real people . . . Cuiyuan wasn't very happy.

Life was like the Bible, translated from Hebrew into Greek, from Greek into Latin, from Latin into English, from English into Chinese. When Cuiyuan read it, she translated the standard Chinese into Shanghainese. Gaps were unavoidable.

She put the student's essay down and buried her chin in her hands. The sun burned down on her backbone.

Next to her sat a nanny with a small child lying on her lap. The sole of the child's foot pushed against Cuiyuan's leg. Little red shoes, decorated with tigers, on a soft but tough little foot . . . this at least was real.

A medical student who was also on the tram took out a sketchpad and carefully added the last touches to a diagram of the human skeleton. The other passengers thought he was sketching a portrait of the man who sat dozing across from him. Nothing else was going on, so they started sauntering over, crowding into little clumps of three or four, leaning on each other with their hands behind their backs, gathering around to watch the man sketch from life. The husband who dangled smoked fish from his fingers whispered to his wife:

"I can't get used to this cubism, this impressionism, which is so popular these days." "Your pants," she hissed.

The medical student meticulously wrote in the names of every bone, muscle, nerve, and tendon. An office worker hid half his face behind a fan and quietly informed his colleague: "The influence of Chinese painting. Nowadays, writing words in is all the rage in Western painting. Clearly a case of 'Eastern ways spreading Westward.'"

Lu Zongzhen didn't join the crowd, but stayed in his seat. He had decided he was hungry. With everyone gone, he could comfortably munch his spinach-stuffed dumplings. But then he looked up and caught a glimpse, in the third-class car, of a relative, his wife's cousin's son. He detested that Dong Peizhi was a man of humble origins who harbored a great ambition: he sought a fiancée of comfortable means, to serve as a foothold for his climb upwards. Lu Zongzhen's eldest daughter had just turned twelve, but already she had caught Peizhi's eye; having made, in his own mind, a pleasing calculation, Peizhi's manner grew ever softer, ever more cunning.

As soon as Lu Zongzhen caught sight of this young man, he was filled with quiet alarm, fearing that if he were seen, Peizhi would take advantage of the opportunity to press forward with his attack. The idea of being stuck in the same car with Dong Peizhi while the city was sealed off was too horrible to contemplate! Lu quickly closed his briefcase and wrapped up his dumplings, then fled, in a great rush, to a seat across the aisle. Now, thank God, he was screened by Wu Cuiyuan, who occupied the seat next to him, and his nephew could not possibly see him.

Cuiyuan turned and gave him a quick look. Oh no! The woman surely thought he was up to no good, changing seats for no reason like that. He recognized the look of a woman being flirted with—she held her face absolutely motionless, no hint of a smile anywhere in her eyes, her mouth, not even in the little hollows beside her nose; yet from some unknown place there was the trembling of a little smile that could break out at any moment. If you think you're simply too adorable, you can't keep from smiling.

Damn! Dong Peizhi had seen him after all, and was coming toward the first-class car, very humble, bowing even at a distance, with his long jowls, shiny red cheeks, and long, gray, monklike gown—a clean, cautious young man, hard-working no matter what the hardship, the very epitome of a good son-in-law. Thinking fast, Zongzhen decided to follow Peizhi's lead and try a bit of artful nonchalance. So he stretched one arm out across the window-sill that ran behind Cuiyuan, soundlessly announcing flirtatious intent. This would not, he knew, scare Peizhi into immediate retreat, because in Peizhi's eyes he already was a dirty old man. The way Peizhi saw it, anyone over thirty was old, and all the old were vile. Having seen his uncle's disgraceful behavior, the young man would feel compelled to tell his wife every little detail—well, angering his wife was just fine with him. Who told her to give him such a nephew, anyway? If she was angry, it served her right.

He didn't care much for this woman sitting next to him. Her arms were fair, all right, but were like squeezed-out toothpaste. Her whole body was like squeezed-out toothpaste, it had no shape.

"When will this air raid ever end?" he said in a low, smiling voice. "It's awful!"

Shocked, Cuiyuan turned her head, only to see that his arm was stretched out behind her. She froze. But come what may, Zongzhen could not let himself pull his arm back. His nephew stood just across the way, watching him with brilliant, glowing eyes, the hint of an understanding smile on his face. If, in the middle of everything, he turned and looked his nephew in the eye, maybe the little no-account would get scared, would lower his eyes, flustered and embarrassed like a sweet young thing; then again, maybe Peizhi would keep staring at him—who could tell?

He gritted his teeth and renewed the attack. "Aren't you bored? We could talk a bit, that can't hurt. Let's . . . let's talk." He couldn't control himself, his voice was plaintive.

Again Cuiyuan was shocked. She turned to look at him. Now he remembered, he had seen her get on the tram—a striking image, but an image concocted by chance, not by any intention of hers. "You know, I saw you get on the tram," he said softly. "Near the front of the car. There's a torn advertisement, and I saw your profile, just a bit of your chin, through the torn spot." It was an ad for Lacova powdered milk that showed a pudgy little child. Beneath the child's ear this woman's chin had suddenly appeared; it was a little spooky, when you thought about it. "Then you looked down to get some change out of your purse, and I saw your eyes, then your brows, then your hair." When you took her features separately, looked at them one by one, you had to admit she had a certain charm.

Cuiyuan smiled. You wouldn't guess that this man could talk so sweetly—you'd think he was the stereotypical respectable businessman. She looked at him again. Under the tip of his nose the cartilage was reddened by the sunlight. Stretching out from his sleeve, and resting on the newspaper, was a warm, tanned hand, one with feeling—a real person! Not too honest, not too bright, but a real person. Suddenly she felt flushed and happy; she turned away with a murmur. "Don't talk like that."

"What?" Zongzhen had already forgotten what he'd said. His eyes were fixed on his nephew's back—the diplomatic young man had decided that three's a crowd, and he didn't want to offend his uncle. They would meet again, anyway, since theirs was a close family, and no knife was sharp enough to sever the ties; and so he returned to the third-class car. Once Peizhi was gone, Zongzhen withdrew his arm; his manner turned respectable. Casting about for a way to make conversation, he glanced at the notebook spread out on her lap. "Shenguang University," he read aloud. "Are you a student there?"

Did he think she was that young? That she was still a student? She laughed, without answering.

"I graduated from Huaqi." He repeated the name. "Huaqi." On her neck was a tiny dark mole, like the imprint of a fingernail. Zongzhen absentmindedly rubbed the fingers of his right hand across the nails of his left. He coughed slightly, then continued: "What department are you in?"

Cuiyuan saw that he had moved his arm and thought that her stand-offish manner had wrought this change. She therefore felt she could not refuse to answer. "Literature. And you?"

"Business." Suddenly he felt that their conversation had grown stuffy. "In school I was busy with student activities. Now that I'm out, I'm busy earning a living. So I've never really studied much of anything."

"Is your office very busy?"

"Terribly. In the morning I go to work and in the evening I go home, but I don't know why I do either. I'm not the least bit interested in my job. Sure, it's a way to earn money, but I don't know who I'm earning it for."

"Everyone has family to think of."

"Oh, you don't know . . . my family . . ." A short cough. "We'd better not talk about it."

"Here it comes," thought Cuiyuan. "His wife doesn't understand him. Every married man in the world seems desperately in need of another woman's understanding."

Zongzhen hesitated, then swallowed hard and forced the words out: "My wife—she doesn't understand me at all."

Cuiyuan knitted her brow and looked at him, expressing complete sympathy.

"I really don't understand why I go home every evening. Where is there to go? I have no home, in fact." He removed his glasses, held them up to the light, and wiped the spots off with a handkerchief. Another little cough. "Just keep going, keep getting by, without thinking—above all, don't start thinking!" Cuiyuan always felt that when nearsighted people took their glasses off in front of other people it was a little obscene; improper, somehow, like taking your clothes off in public. Zongzhen continued: "You, you don't know what kind of woman she is."

"Then why did you . . . in the first place?"

"Even then I was against it. My mother arranged the marriage. Of course I wanted to choose for myself, but . . . she used to be very beautiful . . . I was very young . . . young people, you know . . ." Cuiyuan nodded her head.

"Then she changed into this kind of person—even my mother fights with her, and she blames me for having married her! She has such a temper—she hasn't even got a grade-school education."

Cuiyuan couldn't help saying, with a tiny smile, "You seem to take diplomas very seriously. Actually, even if a woman's educated it's all the same." She didn't know why she said this, wounding her own heart.

"Of course, you can laugh, because you're well-educated. You don't know what kind of—" He stopped, breathing hard, and took off the glasses he had just put back on.

"Getting a little carried away?" said Cuiyuan.

Zongzhen gripped his glasses tightly, made a painful gesture with his hands. "You don't know what kind of—"

"I know, I know," Cuiyuan said hurriedly. She knew that if he and his wife didn't get along, the fault could not lie entirely with her. He too was a person of simple intellect. He just wanted a woman who would comfort and forgive him.

The street erupted in noise, as two trucks full of soldiers rumbled by. Cuiyuan and Zongzhen stuck their heads out to see what was going on; to their surprise, their faces came very close together. At close range anyone's face is somehow different, is tension-charged like a close-up on the movie screen. Zongzhen and Cuiyuan suddenly felt they were seeing each other for the first time. To his eyes, her face was the spare, simple peony of a watercolor sketch, and the strands of hair fluttering at her temples were pistils ruffled by a breeze.

He looked at her, and she blushed. When she let him see her blush, he grew visibly happy. Then she blushed even more deeply.

Zongzhen had never thought he could make a woman blush, make her smile, make her hang her head shyly. In this he was a man. Ordinarily, he was an accountant, a father, the head of a household, a tram passenger, a store customer, an insignificant citizen of a big city. But to this woman, this woman who didn't know anything about his life, he was only and entirely a man.

They were in love. He told her all kinds of things: who was on his side at the bank and who secretly opposed him; how his family squabbled; his secret sorrows; his schoolboy dreams . . . unending talk, but she was not put off. Men in love have always liked to talk; women in love, on the other hand, don't want to talk, because they know, without even knowing that they know, that once a man really understands a woman he'll stop loving her.

Zongzhen was sure that Cuiyuan was a lovely woman—pale, wispy, warm, like the breath your mouth exhales in winter. You don't want her, and she quietly drifts away. Being part of you, she understands everything, forgives everything. You tell the truth, and her heart aches for you; you tell a lie, and she smiles as if to say, "Go on with you—what are you saying?"

Zongzhen was quiet for a moment, then said, "I'm thinking of marrying again."

Cuiyuan assumed an air of shocked surprise. "You want a divorce? Well . . . that isn't possible, is it?"

"I can't get a divorce. I have to think of the children's well-being. My oldest daughter is twelve, just passed the entrance exams for middle school, her grades are quite good."

"What," thought Cuiyuan, "what does this have to do with what you just said?" "Oh," she said aloud, her voice cold, "you plan to take a concubine."

"I plan to treat her like a wife," said Zongzhen. "I—I can make things nice for her. I wouldn't do anything to upset her."

"But," said Cuiyuan, "a girl from a good family won't agree to that, will she? So many legal difficulties . . ."

Zongzhen sighed. "Yes, you're right. I can't do it. Shouldn't have mentioned it . . . I'm too old. Thirty-four already."

"Actually," Cuiyuan spoke very slowly, "these days, that isn't considered very old."

Zongzhen was still. Finally he asked, "How old are you?"

Cuiyuan ducked her head. "Twenty-four."

Zongzhen waited awhile, then asked, "Are you a free woman?"

Cuiyuan didn't answer. "You aren't free," said Zongzhen. "But even if you agreed, your family wouldn't, right?"

Cuiyuan pursed her lips. Her family—her prim and proper family—how she hated them all. They had cheated her long enough. They wanted her to find them a wealthy son-in-law. Well, Zongzhen didn't have money, but he did have a wife—that would make them good and angry! It would serve them right!

Little by little, people started getting back on the tram. Perhaps it was rumored out there that "traffic will soon return to normal." The passengers got on and sat down, pressing against Zongzhen and Cuiyuan, forcing them a little closer, then a little closer again.

Zongzhen and Cuiyuan wondered how they could have been so foolish not to have thought of sitting closer before. Zongzhen struggled against his happiness. He turned to her and said, in a voice full of pain, "No, this won't do! I can't let you sacrifice your future! You're a fine person, with such a good education . . . I don't have much money, and don't want to ruin your life!"

Well, of course, it was money again. What he said was true. "It's over," thought Cuiyuan. In the end she'd probably marry, but her husband would never be as dear as this stranger met by chance—this man on the tram in the middle of a sealed-off city . . . it could never be this spontaneous again. Never again . . . oh, this man, he was so stupid! So very stupid! All she wanted was one small part of him, one little part that no one else could want. He was throwing away his own happiness. Such an idiotic waste! She wept, but it wasn't a gentle, maidenly weeping. She practically spit her tears into his face. He was a good person—the world had gained one more good person!

What use would it be to explain things to him? If a woman needs to turn to words to move a man's heart, she is a sad case.

Once Zongzhen got anxious, he couldn't get any words out, and just kept shaking the umbrella she was holding. She ignored him. Then he tugged at her hand. "Hey, there are people here, you know! Don't! Don't get so upset! Wait a bit, and we'll talk it over on the telephone. Give me your number."

Cuiyuan didn't answer. He pressed her. "You have to give me your phone number."

"Seven-five-three-six-nine." Cuiyuan spoke as fast as she could.

"Seven-five-three-six-nine?"

No response. "Seven-five-three-six-nine, seven-five . . ." Mumbling the number over and over, Zongzhen searched his pockets for a pen, but the more frantic he became, the harder it was to find one. Cuiyuan had a red pencil in her bag, but she purposely did not take it out. He ought to remember her telephone number; if he didn't, then he didn't love her, and there was no point in continuing the conversation.

The city started up again. "Ding-ding-ding-ding." Every "ding" a cold little dot, which added up to a line that cut across time and space.

A wave of cheers swept across the metropolis. The tram started clanking its way forward. Zongzhen stood up, pushed into the crowd, and disappeared. Cuiyuan turned her head away, as if she didn't care. He was gone. To her, it was as if he were dead.

The tram picked up speed. On the evening street, a tofu-seller had set his shoulder-pole down and was holding up a rattle; eyes shut, he shook it back and forth. A big-boned blonde woman, straw hat slung across her back, bantered with an Italian sailor. All her teeth showed when she grinned. When Cuiyuan looked at these people, they lived for that one moment. Then the tram clanked onward, and one by one they died away.

Cuiyuan shut her eyes fretfully. If he phoned her, she wouldn't be able to control her voice; it would be filled with emotion, for he was a man who had died, then returned to life.

The lights inside the tram went on; she opened her eyes and saw him sitting in his old seat, looking remote. She trembled with shock—he hadn't gotten off the tram, after all! Then she understood his meaning: everything that had happened while the city was sealed was a non-occurrence. The whole of Shanghai had dozed off, had dreamed an unreasonable dream.

The tramcar driver raised his voice in song: "Sad, sad, sad! No money do I have! Sad, sad, sad—" An old beggar, thoroughly dazed, limped across the street in front of the tram. The driver bellowed at her. "You swine!"

1943

MODERN POETRY

Modern poets often proclaimed their break with nineteenth-century precursors, notably the Romantics and the symbolists. Romanticism had aspired, according to the English poet **William Wordsworth**, to speak in the "real language of men," but a century later, Romantic reveries about natural beauty or the soul had become, in the eyes of the modernists, just another set of poetic clichés. Wordsworth had also claimed that "all good poetry is the spontaneous overflow of powerful feelings"; the modernists were more skeptical of emotion. They sought, instead, precision and clarity; in place of self-expression, they emphasized the construction of the literary work. Correspondingly, they turned away from ballads and narrative poetry and toward compressed lyrics that often used language in a shocking or an unfamiliar way, far from the everyday language that Wordsworth had praised.

Some modernists likewise saw the late nineteenth-century symbolism of the French poets **Charles Baudelaire** and **Stéphane Mallarmé** as merely an overwrought kind of Romanticism in which personal vision counted for more than precision and formal innovation. In fact, however, many modernists drew on the symbolist inheritance in their attempts to transform verse. One area of continuity was the role of images and symbols. **William Butler Yeats** and **Constantine Cavafy**, who were already writing poetry during the heyday of symbolism, stress the power of what Yeats called "masterful images"—striking visual creations hermetic or esoteric enough to require challenging acts of interpretation on the reader's part. Both poets found inspiration in the storehouse of images associated with myth and legend to create complex personal mythologies that enriched their poems, even for the reader who might be unaware of the poet's private associations.

Rainer Maria Rilke and **T. S. Eliot** likewise incorporated elements of ancient myth in their poetry, but they were less comfortable with symbolist subjectivity; their aim was to achieve impersonal objectivity. Rilke became known in particular for his "object poems," in which precise observation yields indirect commentary on human society. Eliot used complex metrical play and surprising rhymes to revitalize the resources of English verse. (A parallel movement in Russia, Acmeism, influenced the young **Anna Akhmatova**.) Eliot frequently alluded to or quoted other writers, creating layers of voices or registers that collide uneasily in the poems and keep the reader on edge. Yeats, who (like Cavafy in Greek and Rilke in German) generally relied on traditional stanza forms, used meter to achieve a high formality while evoking the rhythms of spoken English. Both English-language poets were substantially influenced by Ezra Pound, who, in arguing against adherence to the most widely used metrical pattern, iambic pentameter, asserted that poets should "compose in the sequence of the musical phrase, not the sequence of a metronome."

Photo of Rainer Maria Rilke taken by the Irish playwright George Bernard Shaw in 1906.

Although the modernists often undertook long poems, these works were seldom narrative epics but, rather, fragmentary collections of lyrics, like Eliot's ***The Waste Land*** (1922) and ***Four Quartets*** (1943) or Akhmatova's ***Requiem*** (1963). Eliot argued that "our civilization comprehends great variety and complexity, and this variety and complexity, playing upon a refined sensibility, must produce various and complex results. The poet must become more and more comprehensive, more allusive, more indirect, in order to force, to dislocate if necessary, language to his meaning." While many poets undertook the dislocation of language through play with traditional forms, rhymes, and meters, the literary avant-gardes—especially the advocates of surrealism—launched a fundamental attack on traditional poetry. Led by André Breton and inspired by Sigmund Freud and Karl Marx, the surrealists tapped into the unconscious and undermined the repressive tendencies of Western society. Many of them, moreover, hoped to transform society through a communist revolution. In different ways, **Aimé Césaire**, **Pablo Neruda**, and **Octavio Paz** were all influenced by surrealism's quest for political, erotic, and spiritual liberation. To varying degrees they embraced free verse, long and loose poetic lines, and the startling juxtaposition of images. That the three came from the developing or colonized world, and spent formative periods in Paris, helps to explain their openness to the surrealist revolution against traditional poetry.

The more politically oriented poets, notably Neruda, often found themselves balancing their interest in literary experiment with a desire to write in a direct, unadorned style that could attract a wide readership. Although **Federico García Lorca** befriended the early surrealists and shared their experimental attitude in his plays, his elegy "**Lament for the Death of Ignacio Sánchez Mejías**" (1935) is in many respects a more traditional poem than anything produced by the avant-gardes. His use of repetition and rhetorical techniques intended to move an audience shares something with the work of his friend Neruda, who would later memorialize Lorca himself in **"I'm Explaining a Few Things"** (1936).

Modernist poetry, particularly as exemplified by Eliot's *The Waste Land* and championed in his essays, has been rejected by some critics as elitist. It can certainly be challenging, inviting the reader to engage with untested literary forms and to respond to unexpected meaning. Whether cryptic like some of Yeats's symbols or direct like Neruda's odes, intricate like Rilke's poetry or explosive like Césaire's free verse, the poetry of the early twentieth century reinvents and reinvigorates language for an age in which words can all too easily lose their meanings and traditional forms their power to structure experience. The selection of modernist poetry that follows suggests the variety and complexity of this rich period in literary history, a period whose implications are still being worked out by poets and readers today.

CONSTANTINE CAVAFY

A private poet who circulated his work in folders to relatives and friends and never offered a book for sale, Constantine Cavafy became, almost in spite of himself, the most influential Greek poet of the twentieth century when a posthumous edition of 154 short poems was published in 1935. His precisely worded, obliquely evocative portraits of historical figures, displayed with their poignant desires and personal tragedies, subtly link the past and the present. The present-day world is present, too: glimpses of contemporary Alexandria spark the recall of erotic memories, and forgotten landscapes resurge with complex emotional and intellectual associations.

Cavafy was born in 1863 to Greek parents living in Alexandria, Egypt. The export-import firm of Cavafy Brothers had once been wealthy, but its fortunes declined and Constantine's father died in 1870. Two years later, Cavafy's mother took the family to England, where the boy's parents had lived in the 1850s and where she hoped they would prosper again. Unfortunately, the boy's two older brothers were inexperienced in business affairs; the rest of their funds vanished, obliging them to return to Alexandria, where they lived in straitened circumstances. During the poet's seven years in England, however, he became bilingual and read widely in English literature. In 1882, Cavafy's mother returned to her father's house outside Constantinople with Cavafy and his two brothers. They remained there for three years, during which time Cavafy discovered his homosexuality and had his first love affair. The young writer—who was now fluent in English, Greek, and French—began to write poems in the three languages. In 1885 the family returned to Alexandria where Cavafy settled for the rest of his life, living with his mother until 1899 and, after her death, sharing quarters with his unmarried brothers. Although he became the greatest of modern Greek poets, he did not visit Greece itself until he was almost fifty.

Cavafy continued to write poetry and essays while working for an Alexandrian newspaper and for the Egyptian Stock Exchange before receiving the position he would hold from then on: special clerk in the Irrigation Service of the Ministry of Public Works. Although Cavafy shared his poetry with friends and relatives, he seems to have had no interest in seeking a wider audience. He had several pamphlets printed privately—an initial booklet of fourteen poems in 1904, enlarged with seven more in 1910—but otherwise restricted himself to folders of poems given to a few readers. In his later years, his reputation spread internationally through the efforts of the British novelist E. M. Forster, who met Cavafy during the First World War in Alexandria and remained a friend for the next twenty years. Cavafy's poem "Ithaka" was published in **T. S. Eliot**'s journal *Criterion*; occasionally, European visitors to Alexandria came to meet its author. He was reportedly a sociable person and a fascinating conversationalist, but he kept to himself and his circle of friends. Forster described him as a Greek gentleman with a straw hat standing "at a slight angle to the universe," and he was virtually unknown in Greece when he died in 1933.

Cavafy's poetry draws his readers into an astonishingly real personal world, establishing a common bond between them and fictional characters in an immense variety of circumstances. The sense of participation comes not merely from the recognition of familiar emotional situations but also from Cavafy's ironic and philosophical perspective that makes subtle demands on the reader's imagination. Cavafy observed that his works could be divided into three broad categories—historical, philosophical, and erotic—and he arranged his folders of poetry in thematic as well as chronological order. It is easy to see how a primary division could be made: of the poems printed here, "Kaisarion" (1918) is historical; "The Next Table" (1919) is erotic; and "Ithaka" (1911) is philosophical. But isn't such compartmentalizing too simple? The young Kaisarion is "good-looking and sensitive," with a "dreamy, an appealing beauty"; "The Next Table" involves memory, self-deception, and a portrait of aging as much as the act of love; and "Ithaka" would not exist without its basis in historical legend. The primary categories are not only broad but (as Cavafy undoubtedly knew) they overlap and leave room for others, whether political allusion ("When the Watchman Saw the Light," 1900), psychological portrait ("The City," 1910, "A Sculptor from Tyana," 1911), devotion to art ("A Craftsman of Wine Bowls," 1921), or philosophical evocation of memory ("Evening," 1917).

In these poems history exists on several levels. It is not the better-known Homeric and Periclean ages of Greek history, but rather the Hellenistic period and the Byzantine Empire, whose tangled politics, sophisticated art, social decadence, and vulnerability to invasion have their analogue in twentieth-century Alexandria. Cavafy's Alexandria is a modern metropolis with a glorious past, and the poet searches history for dramatic anecdotes that reveal the texture of life in that turbulent earlier age. It is not merely the murdered Kaisarion—son of Caesar and Cleopatra—who interests him, but John Kantakuzinos, a minor, impoverished ruler forced to decorate his crown with glass jewels; King Dimitrios, who in 288 B.C.E. disguised himself in simple clothes to escape capture after being deserted by his soldiers; and the scheming Anna Komnina, furious at seeing the Byzantine throne slip out of her hands in 1137. Ancient Greece appears primarily as a reference point in the distant past: the home of heroes like Patroklos or the god Hermes, who are both subjects for the vain sculptor of Tyana; of gods who fleetingly appear in the streets of Alexandria or the landscape of Ionia; or of Odysseus, whose epic voyage becomes a lesson that you can't go home again. From whatever era, Cavafy's precisely rendered narratives invite readers to enter, for a moment, the world of his poetic imagination and to draw their own connections to contemporary life.

When the Watchman Saw the Light[1]

Winter and summer the watchman sat on the roof
of the palace of the sons of Atreus and looked out. Now he tells
the joyful news. He saw a fire flare in the distance.[2]
And he is glad, and his labor is over as well.
It is hard work night and day,
in heat or cold, to look far off
to Arachnaion[3] for a fire. Now the desired
omen has appeared. When happiness
arrives it brings a lesser joy
than expected.[4] Clearly,
we've gained this much: we are saved from hopes
and expectations. Many things will happen
to the Atreus dynasty. One doesn't have to be wise
to surmise this now that the watchman
has seen the light. So, no exaggeration.
The light is good, and those that will come are good.
Their words and deeds are also good.
And we hope all will go well. But
Argos can manage without the Atreus family.
Great houses are not eternal.
Of course, many will have much to say.
We'll listen. But we won't be fooled
by the Indispensable, the Only, the Great.
Some other indispensable, only, and great
is always instantly found.

1900

1. All poems in this selection are translated by Aliki Barnstone. This poem was written in 1900 and was not published during the poet's lifetime. The title, a reference to the prologue of Aeschylus's play *Agamemnon*, a speech given by the watchman who is waiting for the signal that announces the king's return to Argos, is a reminder of the hereditary curse on the family: King Atreus was Agamemnon's father, and Atreus himself was supposed to have revenged himself on his brother Thyestes by serving his children to him for dinner.

2. A chain of bonfires that stretched from Troy to Greece had been prepared as a way of announcing the long-awaited return of Agamemnon's ship from the Trojan War.

3. A mountain in the Epidauros (Argeia) region of Greece.

4. A general statement but also a reminder that Agamemnon is coming home to his death at the hands of his wife, Queen Clytemnestra. Just as in Aeschylus's play, the watchman knows that all is not well at home.

Waiting for the Barbarians[1]

—What are we waiting for, gathered in the agora?[2]

The barbarians are arriving today.

—Why is nothing happening in the Senate?
Why do the Senators sit making no laws?

Because the barbarians are arriving today.
What laws can the Senators make now?
When the barbarians come, they will make laws.
—Why did our emperor wake up so early,
and, in the city's grandest gate, sit in state
on his throne, wearing his crown?

Because the barbarians are arriving today,
and the emperor is waiting to receive
their leader. In fact, he prepared
a parchment to give them, where
he wrote down many titles and names.

—Why did our two consuls and the praetors[3]
come out today in their crimson embroidered togas;
why did they don bracelets with so many amethysts
and rings resplendent with glittering emeralds;
why do they hold precious staffs today,
beautifully wrought in silver and gold?

Because the barbarians are arriving today,
and such things dazzle barbarians.

—Why don't the worthy orators come as usual
to deliver their speeches and say their piece?

Because the barbarians are arriving today
and they are bored by eloquence and harangues.

—Why should this anxiety and confusion
suddenly begin. (How serious faces have become.)

1. Written in 1898; published in 1904. The setting appears to be ancient Rome during the decadence of the empire, when the city was sacked by the Visigoth leader Alaric in 410 C.E. Cavafy has specified that there is no precise reference, however, noting that the barbarians are only a symbol and that "the emperor, the senators and the orators are not necessarily Roman."
2. A large public area, containing temples, shops, and buildings; in Rome, the equivalent would be the forum, which also contained the Senate building.
3. Judicial officers in Rome who held preliminary hearings before cases were assigned to a judge. "Consuls": the two chief administrative officers of the state who presided over the Senate. They were elected by the people under the republic but named by the emperor during the empire.

Why have the streets and squares emptied so quickly,
and why has everyone returned home so pensive?

Because night's fallen and the barbarians have not arrived.
And some people came from the border
and they say the barbarians no longer exist.

Now what will become of us without barbarians?
Those people were some kind of solution.

1904

The City[1]

You said, "I'll go to another land, I'll go to another sea.
I'll find a city better than this one.
My every effort is a written indictment,
and my heart—like someone dead—is buried.
How long will my mind remain in this decaying state.
Wherever I cast my eyes, wherever I look,
I see my life in black ruins here,
where I spent so many years, and ruined and wasted them."

You will not find new lands, you will not find other seas.
The city will follow you. You will roam
the same streets. And you will grow old in the same neighborhood,
and your hair will turn white in the same houses.
You will always arrive in this city. Don't hope for elsewhere—
there is no ship for you, there is no road.
As you have wasted your life here,
in this small corner, so you have ruined it on the whole earth.

1910

A Sculptor from Tyana[1]

As you may have heard, I'm not a beginner.
Quite a lot of stone has taken shape in my hands.
In my homeland, Tyana, I am well known,
and here senators have commissioned
many statues from me.
Let me show you
a few right now. Observe this Rhea,[2]

1. Written in 1894 under the title "Once More in the Same City" and listed under "Prisons." It was published with the current title in 1910.

1. First written in June 1893, entitled "A Sculptor's Studio"; published in 1911. Tyana was a city in Cappadocia, a district in Asia Minor, but the scene—in Rome—is imaginary.

2. Daughter of heaven and earth, and mother of the gods on Olympus.

inspiring reverence, full of fortitude, wholly archaic.
Observe Pompey. Marius,
Paulus Aemilius, Scipio Africanus.[3]
Likenesses faithful as I could make them.
Patroklos (I'll retouch him a bit).
Near the yellowish marble—
those pieces over there—is Kaisarion.[4]

For some time now I've been working on
a Poseidon.[5] I'm particularly studying
his horses, how to form them.
They must be made so light
to show clearly that their bodies, their feet
don't tread on earth, only gallop on water.
But look, here is my work I love most,
made with feeling and greatest care.
With him, on a warm summer day,
when my mind was rising to the ideal,
he came to me in a dream, this young Hermes.[6]

1911

Ithaka[1]

As you set out on the journey to Ithaka,
wish that the way be long,
full of adventures, full of knowledge.
Don't be afraid of Laistrygonians, the Cyclops,
angry Poseidon,[2] you'll never find them on your way
if your thought stays exalted, if a rare
emotion touches your spirit and body.
You won't meet the Laistrygonians
and the Cyclops and wild Poseidon,

3. Scipio Africanus the Younger (185–129 B.C.E.) led the army that destroyed Carthage in 146 B.C.E. "Pompey": Gnaeus Pompeius Magnus (106–48 B.C.E.), Roman general and statesman who fled to Egypt after being defeated by Julius Caesar, was assassinated by King Ptolemy. Gaius Marius (157–86 B.C.E.), a popular general, was elected consul seven times. Lucius Aemilius Paulus (228–160 B.C.E.) was a Roman consul whose army was disastrously defeated by Hannibal at the Battle of Cannae (216 B.C.E.).
4. Kaisarion or Caesarion ("Little Caesar," 47–30 B.C.E.), the son of Cleopatra and Julius Caesar. Co-ruler of Egypt with his mother, he was killed by Octavian (the future emperor Augustus Caesar) for political reasons after her death. "Patroklos": Achilles' friend in Homer's *Iliad*, killed in battle.
5. Greek god of the sea.
6. Son of Zeus and messenger of the gods, often depicted as a nude youth bearing a herald's wand, or caduceus.
1. Ithaka is Odysseus's island kingdom and the destination of his homeward journey after the Trojan War. An early, different version of this poem was entitled "Second Odyssey."
2. Greek god of the sea. Odysseus encounters both the Laistrygonians (fierce, rock-throwing cannibal giants in *Odyssey* 10) and the Cyclops (one-eyed cannibal giant in *Odyssey* 9) on his voyage home.

if you don't bear them along in your soul,
if your soul doesn't raise them before you.

Wish that the way be long.
May there be many summer mornings
when with such pleasure, such joy
you enter ports seen for the first time;
may you stop in Phoenician emporia[3]
to buy fine merchandise,
mother-of-pearl and coral, amber and ebony,
and every kind of sensual perfume,
buy abundant sensual perfumes, as many as you can.
Travel to many Egyptian cities
to learn and learn from their scholars.
Always keep Ithaka in your mind.
Arriving there is your destination.
But don't hurry the journey at all.
Better if it lasts many years,
and you moor on the island when you are old,
rich with all you have gained along the way,
not expecting Ithaka to make you rich.

Ithaka gave you the beautiful journey.
Without her you would not have set out on your way.
She has no more to give you.

And if you find her poor, Ithaka did not betray you.
With all your wisdom, all your experience,
you understand by now what Ithakas mean.

1911

Evening[1]

Anyway, they would not have lasted long. So the experience
of the years shows me. But Fate came
somewhat hastily and stopped them.
The good life was short.
But how strong the perfumes were,
how divine the beds where we lay,
to what pleasure we gave our bodies.

An echo of the days of pleasure,
an echo of the days came close to me,

3. The Phoenicians (from Phoenicia, in modern Syria and Lebanon) were famous merchants and sailors who established trade routes throughout the Mediterranean.

1. Published in 1917; written in 1916 as "Alexandrian" (a reference to the city of Alexandria, Egypt).

something of our youth's fire, something of the two of us.
In my hands was a letter I picked up again,
and I read it again and again until the light was gone.

I went out on the balcony, melancholy—
I went out to change my thoughts, at least to see
a little of the beloved city,
a little of the activity in the streets and the stores.

1917

Kaisarion[1]

In part to verify an era,
in part to pass the time,
last night I chose a collection
of Ptolemaic epigraphs to read.
The extravagant praise and flattery
was the same for everybody. All are splendid,
glorious, powerful, and altruistic;
every undertaking very wise.
If you talk about the women of that generation, they, too,
all the Berenikis and Kleopatras,[2] were marvelous.

When I succeeded in verifying the era,
I would have put the book down if a small
and unimportant note about King Kaisarion
did not immediately attract my attention.

Ah, here you came with your ambiguous
charm. In history only a few
lines about you exist,
and so I created you more freely in my mind.
I created you handsome and sensitive.
My art gives your face
a dreamy, amiable beauty.

And I imagine you so fully
that late last night as my light
went out—I let it go out on purpose—
I imagined you came in my room,
it seemed to me you stood as before, as you would have
in the vanquished Alexandria,
pale and tired, ideal in your sorrow,

1. Kaisarion or Caesarion ("Little Caesar," 47–30 B.C.E.) was the son of Cleopatra and Julius Caesar.
2. Kleopatra or Cleopatra (69–30 B.C.E.) was queen of Egypt and mother of Kaisarion. Bereniki or Berenice (ca. 273–221 B.C.E.), the sister of Ptolemy III Euergetes (ca. 284–221 B.C.E.), married Antiochus II, king of Syria, and, after his death, would have married the emperor Titus if the Romans had not objected.

still hoping they might show you compassion,
the vicious ones—who whispered, "too many Caesars."[3]

1918

The Next Table

He[1] must be barely twenty-three years old.
And yet I am sure almost as many
years ago, I enjoyed this same body.

It isn't merely an erotic flush.
I've only been in the casino[2] a little while
and haven't even had time to drink a lot.
I enjoyed this same body.

And even if I don't recall where—one lapse of memory means nothing.

Ah, now, there, now that he sits at the next table,
I know each way he moves—and under his clothes,
naked, are the loved limbs I see again.

1919

A Craftsman of Wine Bowls[1]

On this wine bowl made of pure silver
that was made for the home of Irakleidis[2]
where good taste prevails supreme—
look, here are elegant flowers and streams and thyme,
and in the center I have placed a beautiful young man
naked, erotic; he still dangles one of his calves
in the water.— Oh, memory, I prayed
to find you my best helper, so I might make
the face of the young man I loved, as it was.
It turned out to be a vast difficulty
because almost fifteen years have passed since the day
he fell, a soldier in the defeat of Magnesia.[3]

1921

3. The teenage Kaisarion was killed because, as the son of Julius Caesar and Cleopatra, he represented a political threat to the future emperor Augustus (then Octavian). The reason for his execution was given in a sentence modeled on a line from Homer's *Iliad* (2.204): "It is not a good thing to have too many Caesars."

1. The language of the Greek original does not reveal the gender of the person seated at the next table, but this calculated ambiguity is not possible in English translation.

2. Casinos were respectable places of entertainment.

1. Printed in 1921; written in 1903 and twice revised.

2. Treasurer of Antiochus IV Epiphanus (ruled 175–163 B.C.E.).

3. In 190 B.C.E. at the battle of Magnesia, the Romans defeated Antiochus III the Great, the father of Antiochus IV.

WILLIAM BUTLER YEATS

The twentieth century's greatest English-language poet, William Butler Yeats (1865–1939) became a major voice of modern, independent Ireland. His captivating imagery and his fusion of history and vision continue to stir readers around the world, and many of his poetic phrases have entered the language. Yeats created a private mythology that helped him come to terms with personal and cultural pain and allowed him to explain—as symptoms of Western civilization's declining spiral—the plight of Irish society and the chaos in Europe in the period surrounding the First World War.

The eldest of four children born to John Butler and Susan Pollexfen Yeats, William came from a middle-class Protestant family. His father, a cosmopolitan Irishman who had turned from law to painting and whose inherited fortune had mostly evaporated, gave his son an unconventional education at home. J. B. Yeats was an argumentative religious skeptic who alternately terrorized his son and fostered the boy's interest in poetry and the visual arts, inspiring rebellion against scientific rationalism and belief in the superiority of art. His mother's ties to her home in County Sligo, where Yeats spent many summers and school holidays with his wealthy grandparents, introduced him to the beauties of the Irish countryside and to the folklore and supernatural legends that appear throughout his work. Living alternately in Ireland and England for much of his youth, Yeats became part of literary society in both countries and—though an Irish nationalist—rejected any narrowly patriotic point of view. Before he turned fully to literature in 1886, Yeats attended art school and had planned to become an artist. (His brother Jack became a well-known painter.) Yeats's early works show the influence of the Pre-Raphaelite school in art and in literature. Pre-Raphaelitism called for a return to the sensuous representation and concrete details found in Italian painting before Raphael (1483–1520); Pre-Raphaelite poetry evoked a realm of luminous supernatural beauty in allusive, erotic imagery. Yeats combined the Pre-Raphaelite fascination with the medieval with his exploration of Irish legend: in 1889 he published an archaically styled poem describing a traveler in fairyland ("The Wanderings of Oisin") that established his reputation and won the praise of the designer and writer William Morris. The musical style of Yeats's Pre-Raphaelite period is evident in one of his most popular poems, "The Lake Isle of Innisfree" (1890), with its hidden "bee-loud glade" where "peace comes dropping slow" and evening, after the "purple glow" of noon, is "full of the linnet's wings."

In 1887, Yeats's family moved to London, where the writer pursued his interest in mystical philosophy by studying theosophy under its Russian interpreter, Madame Blavatsky. She claimed mystical knowledge from Tibetan monks and preached the doctrine of the Universal Oversoul, individual spiritual evolution through cycles of reincarnation, and the world as a conflict of opposing forces. Yeats was taken with the grandeur of her cosmology, although he inconveniently wished to test it by experiment and analysis and, in 1890, was expelled from the Theosophical

Society. He found a more congenial literary model in the works of **William Blake**, which he coedited in 1893 with F. J. Ellis. The appeal that mysticism had for Yeats later waned but never disappeared; traces may be seen in the introduction he wrote in 1913 for *Gitanjali*, a collection of poems by the Indian author **Rabindranath Tagore**, the preeminent figure in modern Bengali literature.

Several anthologies of Irish folk and fairy tales and a book describing Irish traditions (*The Celtic Twilight*, 1893) demonstrated a corresponding interest in Irish national identity. In 1896 he had met Lady Augusta Gregory, a nationalist who invited him to spend summers at Coole Park, her country house in Galway, and who worked closely with him (and later J. M. Synge) in founding the Irish National Theater (later the Abbey Theater). Along with other participants in the Irish literary renaissance, Yeats aimed to create "a national literature that made Ireland beautiful in the memory . . . freed from provincialism by an exacting criticism." To this end, he wrote *Cathleen ni Houlihan* (1902), a play in which the title character personified Ireland; it became immensely popular with the nationalists. Yeats also established literary societies, promoted and reviewed Irish books, and lectured and wrote about the need for Irish community. Gradually Yeats became embittered by the barriers he believed nationalism was erecting around the free expression of Irish culture. He was outraged at the attacks on Synge's *Playboy of the Western World* (1907) for its supposed derogatory picture of Irish culture, and he commented scathingly in *Poems Written in Discouragement* (1913; reprinted in *Responsibilities*, 1914) on the inability of the middle class to appreciate art or literature.

Except for summers at Coole Park, Yeats in his middle age was spending more time in England than in Ireland. He began *Autobiographies* in 1914 and wrote symbolic plays intended for small audiences on the model of the Japanese Noh theater. His works of this period display a change in tone—a precision and epigrammatic quality that reflects partly his disappointment with Irish nationalism and partly the tastes in poetry promulgated by his friend Ezra Pound and by **T. S. Eliot**. Although Yeats had claimed in a poem just before the First World War that "Romantic Ireland's dead and gone," he found himself drawn again to politics as a subject for poetry and as an arena for action. Shocked by the aftermath of the Easter 1916 uprising against British rule, when sixteen leaders were shot for treason, Yeats wrote that, through their sacrifice, "a terrible beauty is born." The revolutionary figures whom Yeats had known in life took their place in a mythic framework within which he interpreted human history. In the subsequent Anglo-Irish War (1919–21) and Irish Civil War (1922–23), great violence, as Yeats had prophesied, attended the birth of the Irish nation-state. In the Irish Free State, Yeats became a senator from 1922 to 1928, Nobel Prize laureate in 1924, and a "sixty-year-old smiling public man," in the words of "Among School Children" (1926). Much of his best poetry was still to come.

Yeats's marriage in 1917 to Georgie Hyde-Lees provided him with much-needed stability. Intrigued by his wife's experiments with automatic writing (jotting down whatever comes to mind, without correction or rational intent), he viewed them as glimpses into a cosmic order; he gradually evolved his interpretation into a symbolic scheme. He explained the system in *A Vision* (1926): the wheel of history takes 26,000 years to turn; and inside the wheel, civilizations evolve in roughly 2,000-year gyres, spirals expanding outward until they collapse at the onset of a new gyre, which reverses the direction of the old. Within the system human personalities fall into various types, and both gyres and types relate to the phases of the moon. Yeats's later poems in *The Tower* (1928), *The Winding Stair* (1933), and *Last Poems* (1939) are set in the context of this system. His enthusiasms for mythical systems sometimes led him astray, notably when he flirted with the Irish Blue Shirts, a para-fascist movement in the 1930s. Throughout his life, he affected an aristocratic disdain for the rough-and-tumble of democratic politics; by the end of his life, he had abandoned practical politics and devoted himself to the reality of personal experience inside a mystic view of history. The final poem in his posthumous *Last Poems*, "Politics," suggests that events in Russia, Italy, and Spain (communism, fascism, and the impending Second World War) held less interest for the poet than a girl standing nearby: "maybe what they say is true / Of war and war's alarms / But O that I were young again / And held her in my arms."

For many readers Yeats's "masterful images" (in the words of another late poem, "The Circus Animals' Desertion," 1939) define his work. From his early use of symbols as metaphors for personal emotions, to the cosmology of his last work, Yeats created a poetry whose power derives from the interweaving of sharp-edged images. Symbols such as the Tower, Byzantium, Helen of Troy, the sun and the moon, birds of prey, the blind man, and the fool recur frequently and draw their meaning not from connections established inside the poem (as is true for the French symbolists) but from an underlying myth based on occult tradition, Irish folklore, history, and Yeats's private experience. Even readers unacquainted with his mythic system will respond to images that express a situation or state of mind—for example, golden Byzantium for intellect, art, wisdom—all that "body" cannot supply.

The nine poems included here cover the range of Yeats's career, which embraced several styles. A poem from his early, Pre-Raphaelite period, "When You Are Old" (1895), pleads his love for the beautiful actress and Irish nationalist Maud Gonne, whom he met in 1889 and who repeatedly refused to marry him. From the love poems of his youth to those of his old age, when in "The Circus Animals' Desertion" he describes Gonne as prey to fanaticism and hate, Yeats again and again examines his feelings for this woman, who for him personified love, beauty, and nationalism along with hope, frustration, and despair.

In middle age, when Yeats adopted a more political tone, he did so with an element of meditative distance. When he celebrates the abortive nationalist uprisings in "Easter 1916" (1916), it is from a universal, aesthetic point of view: "A terrible beauty is born" in the self-sacrifice that leads even a "drunken, vainglorious lout" (Major John MacBride, Maud Gonne's husband) to be "transformed utterly" by martyrdom. Yeats recognized that the Easter Rebellion, led by radicals whose politics and violence he disapproved, had altered not just the political situation in Ireland but its spiritual state as well.

His early poetry made substantial use of public, straightforward symbols, such as the rose for Ireland. Later on, Yeats employed symbols in a more indirect, allusive way. For example, in "The Second Coming" (1921), the "gyre," or spiral unfolding of history, is represented by the falcon's spiral flight. The sphinxlike beast slouching blank-eyed toward Bethlehem is an enigmatic but terrifying image. Yeats believed that contemporary society was witnessing a transformation similar to that of the fall of Troy or the birth of Christ: "twenty centuries of stony sleep" since Christ's birth are again to be "vexed to nightmare by a rocking cradle," the poem declares; he asks what sort of savior or Antichrist will announce the impending age. This poem demonstrates how Yeats, a master of English meter and rhyme, evolved a loose poetic line with only hints of rhyme. The fourteen lines of the second stanza can be read as an unconventional sonnet.

In form a more conventional sonnet, "Leda and the Swan" (1924) is an erotic retelling of a mythical rape. But it also foreshadows the Trojan War—brute force mirroring brute force. Yeats called the poem's subject "a violent annunciation": as the event that conceives Helen of Troy, Zeus's transformation into a swan and rape of Leda embodies a moment of world-historical change. Once again Yeats draws parallels between the upheavals of history and the catastrophic events of ancient narratives. The poem combines the Shakespearean sonnet in its first two quatrains (the eight lines rhyming *ababcdcd*) with the Petrarchan form in the sestet (the final six lines rhyming *defdef*).

In the two poems on the legendary city of Byzantium, "Sailing to Byzantium" (1926) and "Byzantium" (1930), Yeats admires an artistic civilization that "could answer all my questions" but that was, in fact, only a moment in history. Byzantine art, with its stylized perspectives and mosaics assembled from colored bits of stone, represents the opposite of the tendency of Western art to imitate nature, and it provides a kind of escape for the poet. The idea in "Sailing to Byzantium" of an inhuman, metallic, abstract beauty that art separates "out of nature" expresses a mystic, symbolist quest for an invulnerable world distinct from the ravages of time. This world is to be found in an idealized Byzantium, where the poet's body will be transmuted into artifice. By the time of the second of these poems, the possibility of achieving such a separation seems problematic: the speaker recognizes, on the one hand, that artistic images remain close to the living, suffering world—"the dolphin's mire and blood"—and, on the other hand, that such images have a life independent of the people who would merge with them—"Those images that yet / Fresh images beget."

At the close of "Among School Children," the sixty-year-old "public man" compensates for the passing of youth by dreaming of pure "Presences" that never fade. This poem, like "Sailing to Byzantium" and "The Circus Animals' Desertion," is written in a complex, courtly stanza form, ottava rima (eight lines rhyming *abababcc*), which Yeats often uses for philosophical reflection. He often adopts, as well, the persona of the old man for whom the perspectives of age, idealized beauty, and history are ways to keep human agony at a distance. In "Lapis Lazuli," the tragic figures of history transcend their roles by the calm "gaiety" with which they accept their fate: the ancient Chinamen carved in the blue stone climb toward a vantage point where they can gaze, without concern, upon the world's tragedies: "Their eyes mid many wrinkles, their eyes, / Their ancient, glittering eyes, are gay."

Yet the world is still there, tragedies still abound, and Yeats's poetry remains aware of the physical and emotional roots from which the words spring. Whatever the wished-for distance, his poems are full of passionate feelings, erotic desire and disappointment, delight in beauty, horror at civil war and anarchy, dismay at degradation and change. By the time of his death, on January 28, 1939, Yeats had rejected his Byzantine identity as the golden songbird and sought out "the brutality, the ill breeding, the barbarism of truth." In "The Circus Animals' Desertion," Yeats describes his former themes as so many performing creatures on display. Yeats's poetry, which draws its initial power from the formal mastery of images and verbal rhythm, resonates in the reader's mind for its attempt to come to terms with reality, to grasp and make sense of human experience in the language of art.

When You Are Old[1]

When you are old and grey and full of sleep,
And nodding by the fire, take down this book,
And slowly read, and dream of the soft look
Your eyes had once, and of their shadows deep;

How many loved your moments of glad grace,
And loved your beauty with love false or true,
But one man loved the pilgrim soul in you,
And loved the sorrows of your changing face;

And bending down beside the glowing bars,
Murmur, a little sadly, how Love fled
And paced upon the mountains overhead
And hid his face amid a crowd of stars.

1895

Easter 1916[1]

I have met them at close of day
Coming with vivid faces
From counter or desk among grey
Eighteenth-century houses.
I have passed with a nod of the head
Or polite meaningless words,
Or have lingered awhile and said
Polite meaningless words,
And thought before I had done
Of a mocking tale or a gibe
To please a companion
Around the fire at the club,
Being certain that they and I
But lived where motley is worn:
All changed, changed utterly:
A terrible beauty is born.

1. An adaptation of a love sonnet by the French Renaissance poet Pierre de Ronsard (1524–1585), which begins similarly ("Quand vous serez bien vieille") but ends by asking the beloved to "pluck the roses of life today."

1. On Easter Sunday 1916, Irish nationalists began an unsuccessful rebellion against British rule, which lasted throughout the week and ended in the surrender and execution of its leaders.

That woman's[2] days were spent
In ignorant good-will,
Her nights in argument
Until her voice grew shrill.
What voice more sweet than hers
When, young and beautiful,
She rode to harriers?
This man had kept a school
And rode our wingèd horse;
This other his helper and friend[3]
Was coming into his force;
He might have won fame in the end,
So sensitive his nature seemed,
So daring and sweet his thought.
This other man[4] I had dreamed
A drunken, vainglorious lout.
He had done most bitter wrong
To some who are near my heart,
Yet I number him in the song;
He, too, has resigned his part
In the casual comedy;
He, too, has been changed in his turn,
Transformed utterly:
A terrible beauty is born.

Hearts with one purpose alone
Through summer and winter seem
Enchanted to a stone
To trouble the living stream.
The horse that comes from the road,
The rider, the birds that range
From cloud to tumbling cloud,
Minute by minute they change;
A shadow of cloud on the stream
Changes minute by minute;
A horse-hoof slides on the brim,
And a horse plashes within it;
The long-legged moor-hens dive,
And hens to moor-cocks call;
Minute by minute they live:
The stone's in the midst of all.

Too long a sacrifice
Can make a stone of the heart.

2. Constance Gore-Booth (1868–1927), later Countess Markiewicz, an ardent nationalist.
3. Patrick Pearse (1879–1916) and his friend Thomas MacDonagh (1878–1916), both schoolmasters and leaders of the rebellion and both executed by the British. As a Gaelic poet, Pearse symbolically rode the winged horse of the Muses, Pegasus.
4. Major John MacBride (1865–1916), who had married and separated from Maud Gonne (1866–1953), Yeats's great love.

O when may it suffice?
That is Heaven's part, our part
To murmur name upon name,
As a mother names her child
When sleep at last has come
On limbs that had run wild.
What is it but nightfall?
No, no, not night but death;
Was it needless death after all?
For England may keep faith
For all that is done and said.
We know their dream; enough
To know they dreamed and are dead;
And what if excess of love
Bewildered them till they died?
I write it out in a verse—
MacDonagh and MacBride
And Connolly[5] and Pearse
Now and in time to be,
Wherever green is worn,
Are changed, changed utterly:
A terrible beauty is born.

1916

The Second Coming[1]

Turning and turning in the widening gyre[2]
The falcon cannot hear the falconer;
Things fall apart; the centre cannot hold;
Mere anarchy is loosed upon the world,
The blood-dimmed tide is loosed, and everywhere
The ceremony of innocence is drowned;
The best lack all conviction, while the worst
Are full of passionate intensity.

Surely some revelation is at hand;
Surely the Second Coming is at hand.
The Second Coming! Hardly are those words out
When a vast image out of *Spiritus Mundi*[3]

5. James Connolly (1870–1916), labor leader and nationalist executed by the British.

1. The Second Coming of Christ, believed by Christians to herald the end of the world, is transformed here into the prediction of a birth initiating an era and terminating the two-thousand-year cycle of Christianity.

2. The cone pattern of the falcon's flight and of historical cycles, in Yeats's vision.

3. World-soul (Latin) or, as *Anima Mundi* in Yeats's *Per Amica Silentia Lunae*, a "great memory" containing archetypal images; recalls C. G. Jung's collective unconscious.

Troubles my sight: somewhere in sands of the desert
A shape with lion body and the head of a man
A gaze blank and pitiless as the sun,
Is moving its slow thighs, while all about it
Reel shadows of the indignant desert birds.
The darkness drops again; but now I know
That twenty centuries of stony sleep
Were vexed to nightmare by a rocking cradle,
And what rough beast, its hour come round at last,
Slouches towards Bethlehem to be born?

1921

Leda and the Swan[1]

A sudden blow: the great wings beating still
Above the staggering girl, her thighs caressed
By the dark webs, her nape caught in his bill,
He holds her helpless breast upon his breast.

How can those terrified vague fingers push
The feathered glory from her loosening thighs?
And how can body, laid in that white rush,
But feel the strange heart beating where it lies?

A shudder in the loins engenders there
The broken wall, the burning roof and tower
And Agamemnon dead.[2]
Being so caught up,
So mastered by the brute blood of the air,
Did she put on his knowledge with his power
Before the indifferent beak could let her drop?

1924

1. Zeus, ruler of the Greek gods, took the form of a swan to rape the mortal Leda; she gave birth to Helen of Troy, whose beauty caused the Trojan War.
2. The ruins of Troy and the death of Agamemnon, the Greek leader, whose sacrifice of his daughter Iphigenia to win the gods' favor caused his wife, Clytemnestra (also a daughter of Leda), to assassinate him on his return.

Sailing to Byzantium[1]

1

That is no country for old men. The young
In one another's arms, birds in the trees
—Those dying generations—at their song,
The salmon-falls, the mackerel-crowded seas,
Fish, flesh, or fowl, commend all summer long
Whatever is begotten, born, and dies.
Caught in the sensual music all neglect
Monuments of unageing intellect.

2

An aged man is but a paltry thing,
A tattered coat upon a stick, unless
Soul clap its hands and sing, and louder sing
For every tatter in its mortal dress,
Nor is there singing school but studying
Monuments of its own magnificence;
And therefore I have sailed the seas and come
To the holy city of Byzantium.

3

O sages standing in God's holy fire
As in the gold mosaic of a wall,
Come from the holy fire, perne in a gyre,[2]
And be the singing-masters of my soul.
Consume my heart away; sick with desire
And fastened to a dying animal
It knows not what it is; and gather me
Into the artifice of eternity.

4

Once out of nature I shall never take
My bodily form from any natural thing,
But such a form as Grecian goldsmiths make
Of hammered gold and gold enamelling
To keep a drowsy Emperor awake;
Or set upon a golden bough to sing
To lords and ladies of Byzantium
Of what is past, or passing, or to come.

1926

1. The ancient name for modern Istanbul, the capital of the Eastern Roman Empire, which represented for Yeats (who had seen Byzantine mosaics in Italy) a highly stylized and perfectly integrated artistic world where "religious, aesthetic, and practical life were one."

2. I.e., come spinning down in a spiral. "Perne": a spool or bobbin. "Gyre": the cone pattern of the falcon's flight and of historical cycles, in Yeats's vision.

Among School Children

I

I walk through the long schoolroom questioning;
A kind old nun in a white hood replies;
The children learn to cipher and to sing,
To study reading-books and history,
To cut and sew, be neat in everything
In the best modern way—the children's eyes
In momentary wonder stare upon
A sixty-year-old smiling public man.[1]

2

I dream of a Ledaean[2] body, bent
Above a sinking fire, a tale that she
Told of a harsh reproof, or trivial event
That changed some childish day to tragedy—
Told, and it seemed that our two natures blent
Into a sphere from youthful sympathy,
Or else, to alter Plato's parable,
Into the yolk and white of the one shell.[3]

3

And thinking of that fit of grief or rage
I look upon one child or t'other there
And wonder if she stood so at that age—
For even daughters of the swan can share
Something of every paddler's heritage—
And had that color upon cheek or hair,
And thereupon my heart is driven wild:
She stands before me as a living child.

4

Her present image floats into the mind—
Did Quattrocento finger fashion it
Hollow of cheek[4] as though it drank the wind
And took a mess of shadows for its meat?
And I though never of Ledaean kind
Had pretty plumage once—enough of that,
Better to smile on all that smile, and show
There is a comfortable kind of old scarecrow.

1. Yeats was elected senator of the Irish Free State in 1922.
2. Beautiful as Leda or as her daughter, Helen of Troy.
3. In Plato's *Symposium*, Socrates explains love by telling how the gods split human beings into two halves—like halves of an egg—so that each half seeks its opposite throughout life. Yeats compares the two parts to the yolk and white of an egg.
4. Italian painters of the 15th century (the Quattrocento), such as Botticelli (1444–1510), were known for their delicate figures.

5

What youthful mother, a shape upon her lap
Honey of generation had betrayed,
And that must sleep, shriek, struggle to escape
As recollection or the drug decide,[5]
Would think her son, did she but see that shape
With sixty or more winters on its head,
A compensation for the pang of his birth,
Or the uncertainty of his setting forth?

6

Plato thought nature but a spume that plays
Upon a ghostly paradigm of things;
Solider Aristotle played the taws
Upon the bottom of a king of kings;
World-famous golden-thighed Pythagoras[6]
Fingered upon a fiddle-stick or strings
What a star sang and careless Muses heard:
Old clothes upon old sticks to scare a bird.

7

Both nuns and mothers worship images,
But those the candles light are not as those
That animate a mother's reveries,
But keep a marble or a bronze repose.
And yet they too break hearts—O Presences
That passion, piety, or affection knows,
And that all heavenly glory symbolize—
O self-born mockers of man's enterprise;

8

Labor is blossoming or dancing where
The body is not bruised to pleasure soul,
Nor beauty born out of its own despair,
Nor blear-eyed wisdom out of midnight oil.
O chestnut tree, great-rooted blossomer,
Are you the leaf, the blossom, or the bole?
O body swayed to music, O brightening glance,
How can we know the dancer from the dance?

1926

5. Yeats's note to this poem recalls the Greek scholar Porphyry (ca. 234–305), who associates "honey" with "the pleasure arising from copulation" that engenders children; the poet further describes honey as a drug that destroys the child's "'recollection' of pre-natal freedom."

6. Greek philosophers. Plato (427–337 B.C.E.) believed that nature was a series of illusionistic reflections or appearances cast by abstract "forms" that were the true realities. Aristotle (384–322 B.C.E.), more pragmatic, was Alexander the Great's tutor and spanked him with the "taws" (leather straps). Pythagoras (582–407 B.C.E.), a demigod to his disciples and thought to have a golden thigh bone, pondered the relationship between music, mathematics, and the stars.

Byzantium[1]

The unpurged images of day recede;
The Emperor's drunken soldiery are abed;
Night resonance recedes, night-walkers' song
After great cathedral gong;
A starlit or a moonlit dome[2] disdains
All that man is,
All mere complexities,
The fury and the mire of human veins.

Before me floats an image, man or shade,
Shade more than man, more image than a shade;
For Hades' bobbin bound in mummy-cloth
May unwind the winding path;[3]
A mouth that has no moisture and no breath
Breathless mouths may summon;
I hail the superhuman;
I call it death-in-life and life-in-death.

Miracle, bird or golden handiwork,
More miracle than bird or handiwork,
Planted on the starlit golden bough,
Can like the cocks of Hades crow,[4]
Or, by the moon embittered, scorn aloud
In glory of changeless metal
Common bird or petal
And all complexities of mire or blood.

At midnight on the Emperor's pavement flit
Flames that no faggot feeds, nor steel has lit,
Nor storm disturbs, flames begotten of flame,
Where blood-begotten spirits come
And all complexities of fury leave,
Dying into a dance,
An agony of trance,
An agony of flame that cannot singe a sleeve.

Astraddle on the dolphin's[5] mire and blood,
Spirit after spirit! The smithies break the flood,

1. The holy city of "Sailing to Byzantium" (p. 554), seen here as it resists and transforms the blood and mire of human life into its own transcendent world of art.

2. According to Yeats's system in *A Vision* (1925), the first "starlit" phase in which the moon does not shine and the fifteenth, opposing phase of the full moon represent complete objectivity (potential being) and complete subjectivity (the achievement of complete beauty). In between these absolute phases lie the evolving "mere complexities" of human life.

3. Unwinding the spool of fate that leads from mortal death to the superhuman. "Hades": the realm of the dead in Greek mythology.

4. To mark the transition from death to the dawn of new life.

5. A dolphin rescued the famous singer Arion by carrying him on his back over the sea. Dolphins were associated with Apollo, Greek god of music and prophecy, and in ancient art they are often shown escorting the souls of the dead to the Isles of the Blessed. Here, the dolphin is also flesh and blood, a part of life.

The golden smithies of the Emperor!
Marbles of the dancing floor
Break bitter furies of complexity,
Those images that yet
Fresh images beget,
That dolphin-torn, that gong-tormented sea.

1930

Lapis Lazuli[1]

For Harry Clifton

I have heard that hysterical women say
They are sick of the palette and fiddle-bow,
Of poets that are always gay,
For everybody knows or else should know
That if nothing drastic is done
Aeroplane and Zeppelin will come out,
Pitch like King Billy[2] bomb-balls in
Until the town lie beaten flat.
All perform their tragic play,
There struts Hamlet, there is Lear,
That's Ophelia, that Cordelia;[3]
Yet they, should the last scene be there,
The great stage curtain about to drop,
If worthy their prominent part in the play,
Do not break up their lines to weep.
They know that Hamlet and Lear are gay;
Gaiety transfiguring all that dread.
All men have aimed at, found and lost;
Black out; Heaven blazing into the head:[4]
Tragedy wrought to its uttermost.
Though Hamlet rambles and Lear rages,
And all the drop-scenes drop at once
Upon a hundred thousand stages,
It cannot grow by an inch or an ounce.

On their own feet they came, or on shipboard,
Camel-back, horse-back, ass-back, mule-back,

1. A deep blue semiprecious stone. One of Yeats's letters (to Dorothy Wellesley, July 6, 1935) describes a Chinese carving in lapis lazuli that depicts an ascetic and pupil about to climb a mountain: "Ascetic, pupil, hard stone, eternal theme of the sensual east . . . the east has its solutions always and therefore knows nothing of tragedy."
2. A linkage of past and present. According to an Irish ballad, King William III of England "threw his bomb-balls in" and set fire to the tents of the deposed James II at the Battle of the Boyne in 1690. Also a reference to Kaiser Wilhelm II (King William II) of Germany, who sent zeppelins to bomb London during World War I. "Zeppelin": a long, cylindrical airship, supported by internal gas chambers.
3. Tragic figures in Shakespeare's plays.
4. The loss of rational consciousness making way for the blaze of inner revelation or "mad" tragic vision. Also suggests the final curtain and an air raid curfew.

Old civilisations put to the sword.
Then they and their wisdom went to rack:
No handiwork of Callimachus[5]
Who handled marble as if it were bronze,
Made draperies that seemed to rise
When sea-wind swept the corner, stands;
His long lamp-chimney shaped like the stem
Of a slender palm, stood but a day;
All things fall and are built again,
And those that build them again are gay.
Two Chinamen, behind them a third,
Are carved in Lapis Lazuli,
Over them flies a long-legged bird,[6]
A symbol of longevity;
The third, doubtless a serving-man,
Carries a musical instrument.

Every discoloration of the stone,
Every accidental crack or dent,
Seems a water-course or an avalanche,
Or lofty slope where it still snows
Though doubtless plum or cherry-branch
Sweetens the little half-way house
Those Chinamen climb towards, and I
Delight to imagine them seated there;
There, on the mountain and the sky,
On all the tragic scene they stare.
One asks for mournful melodies;
Accomplished fingers begin to play.
Their eyes mid many wrinkles, their eyes,
Their ancient, glittering eyes, are gay.

1938

The Circus Animals' Desertion

I

I sought a theme and sought for it in vain,
I sought it daily for six weeks or so.
Maybe at last, being but a broken man,
I must be satisfied with my heart, although
Winter and summer till old age began
My circus animals were all on show,
Those stilted boys, that burnished chariot,
Lion and woman[1] and the Lord knows what.

5. Athenian sculptor (5th century B.C.E.), famous for a gold lamp in the Erechtheum (temple on the Acropolis) and for using drill lines in marble to give the effect of flowing drapery.

6. A crane.

1. Yeats enumerates images and themes from his earlier work; here, the sphinx of "The Double Vision of Michael Robartes."

2

What can I but enumerate old themes?
First that sea-rider Oisin led by the nose
Through three enchanted islands, allegorical dreams,[2]
Vain gaiety, vain battle, vain repose,
Themes of the embittered heart, or so it seems,
That might adorn old songs or courtly shows;
But what cared I that set him on to ride,
I, starved for the bosom of his faery bride?

And then a counter-truth filled out its play,
The Countess Cathleen[3] was the name I gave it;
She, pity-crazed, had given her soul away,
But masterful Heaven had intervened to save it.
I thought my dear must her own soul destroy,
So did fanaticism and hate enslave it,
And this brought forth a dream and soon enough
This dream itself had all my thought and love.

And when the Fool and Blind Man stole the bread
Cuchulain[4] fought the ungovernable sea;
Heart-mysteries there, and yet when all is said
It was the dream itself enchanted me:
Character isolated by a deed
To engross the present and dominate memory.
Players and painted stage took all my love,
And not those things that they were emblems of.

3

Those masterful images because complete
Grew in pure mind, but out of what began?
A mound of refuse or the sweepings of a street,
Old kettles, old bottles, and a broken can,
Old iron, old bones, old rags, that raving slut
Who keeps the till. Now that my ladder's gone,
I must lie down where all the ladders start,
In the foul rag-and-bone shop of the heart.

1939

2. In "The Wanderings of Oisin" (1889), an early poem in which Yeats describes a legendary Irish hero who wandered in fairyland for 150 years.

3. A play (1892), dedicated to Maud Gonne, in which the countess is saved by heaven after having sold her soul to the devil in exchange for food for the poor. The figure of Cathleen comes up frequently in Yeats's work and is often taken as a personification of nationalist Ireland.

4. A legendary Irish hero. Yeats is referring to the play *On Baile's Strand* (1904).

RAINER MARIA RILKE

In his intensely personal quest to understand the "great mysteries" of the universe, Rilke asks questions that we ordinarily think of as religious. Whether his gaze turns toward earth, which he describes with extraordinary clarity and affection, or toward a higher realm whose enigmas remain to be deciphered, he seeks a comprehensive vision of cosmic unity. Rilke's sharply focused yet visionary lyricism made him the best-known and most influential German poet of the twentieth century.

Born in Prague on December 4, 1875, to German-speaking parents who separated when he was nine, Rilke had an unhappy childhood. His mother dressed him as a girl to compensate for the earlier loss of a baby daughter; as a teenager he was sent to military academies, where he was lonely and miserable. After a year in business school, he worked in his uncle's law firm and studied at the University of Prague. His heart was already set on a literary career, however, and between his work and his studies, he stole enough time to publish two books of poetry and write plays, stories, and reviews. In 1897 he moved to Munich and fell in love with the married psychoanalyst Lou Andreas-Salomé, who would be an influence on him throughout his life. Accompanying Andreas-Salomé and her husband to Russia in 1899, Rilke met **Leo Tolstoy** and Boris Pasternak and—swayed by Russian mysticism and the Russian landscape—wrote some of his first successful poems.

Rilke met his future wife, the sculptor Clara Westhoff, when the two were living in the artists' colony Worpswede, in northern Germany; they soon separated, and Rilke moved to Paris to begin a book on the sculptor Auguste Rodin. In Rodin, who became his friend, the German poet found a dedication to the technical demands of his craft; an intense concentration on visible, tangible objects; and, above all, a belief in art as an essentially religious activity. In Paris Rilke was also struck by the poetry of **Charles Baudelaire**. Although he wrote in distress to Lou Andreas-Salomé, complaining of nightmares and a sense of failure, it is at this time (and with her encouragement) that Rilke launched his major work. The anguished, semiautobiographical spiritual confessions of *The Notebook of Malte Laurids Brigge* (1910) date from this period, as do *New Poems* (1907–8), in which the writer develops a symbolic vision focused on objects.

When a patron, Princess Marie von Thurn und Taxis-Hohenlohe, proposed that he stay by himself in her castle at Duino, near Trieste, during the winter of 1911–12, Rilke found the quiet and isolation that he needed as a writer. Walking on the rocks above the sea and puzzling over his answer to a bothersome business letter, Rilke seemed to hear in the roar of the wind the first lines of an elegy: "Who, if I cried out, would hear me among the angels' / hierarchies?" (An elegy is a mournful lyric poem, usually a lament for loss.) By February he had written two elegies, and when he left Duino Castle in May, he had conceived the cycle and written fragments of four other elegies, which would eventually be published in the sequence of ten poems called the *Duino Elegies* (1923).

Drafted into the German army during

the First World War, Rilke spent his days drawing precise vertical and horizontal lines on paper for the War Archives Office in Vienna. Released from military service in 1916, he produced few poems and feared that he would never be able to complete the Duino sequence. In 1922, however, a friend's purchase of the tiny Château de Muzot in Switzerland gave him a peaceful place to retire to and write. Not only did he complete the *Duino Elegies* in Muzot, he also wrote—as a memorial for the young daughter of a friend—a two-part sequence of fifty-five sonnets, *Sonnets to Orpheus* (1922). Affirming the essential unity of life and death, Rilke closed his two complementary sequences ("the little rust-colored sail of the Sonnets and the Elegies' gigantic white canvas") and wrote little—chiefly poems in French—over the next few years. Increasingly ill with leukemia, he died on December 29, 1926, as the result of an infection that developed after he pricked himself while cutting roses in his garden for a friend.

The five selections from *New Poems* (1907–8) printed here demonstrate Rilke's visual imagination of his "thing-poems" (*Dinggedichte*). *New Poems* emphasizes physical reality, the absolute otherness and "thing-like" nature of what is observed—be it fountain, panther, flower, human being, or the "Archaic Torso of Apollo," which is presented here in both English and German to give readers a sense of Rilke's original language. A letter to Andreas-Salomé describes the poet's sense that ancient art objects take on a peculiar luster once they are detached from history and are seen as "things" in and for themselves: "No subject matter is attached to them, no irrelevant voice interrupts the silence of their concentrated reality . . . no history casts a shadow over their naked clarity—: they *are*. That is all . . . one day one of them reveals itself to you, and shines like a first star." Such "things" are not dead or inanimate but supremely alive, filled with a strange vitality before the poet's glance: the charged sexuality of the marble torso, the caged panther padding around his prison, and the metamorphosis of the Spanish dancer. Faced with a physical presence that transcends words, the viewer is challenged on an existential level. The "archaic torso of Apollo" is not a living being but an ancient Greek sculpture on display in the Louvre Museum in Paris. This headless marble is truly a "thing": a lifeless, even defaced chunk of stone. Yet such is the perfection of its luminous sensuality—derived, the speaker suggests, from the brilliant gaze of its missing head and "ripening" eyes—that it seems alive, and an inner radiance bursts starlike from the marble. The torso puts to shame the observer's puny existence, demanding: "You must change your life."

In his poetry Rilke is haunted by the incompleteness of human experience and by the passage of time. His response is to turn to art to draw objects into a "human" world, infusing them with ideas, emotions, and value. The poet's role, according to Rilke, is to observe with renewed sensitivity "this fleeting world, which in some strange way / keeps calling to us," and to bear witness, by means of language, to the transfiguration of its materiality through human emotions.

From New Poems[1]

Archaic Torso of Apollo[2]

We did not know his legendary head[3]
in which the eyeballs ripened. But
his torso still glows like a candelabrum
in which his gaze only turned low,

holds and gleams. Else could not the curve
of the breast blind you, nor in the slight turn
of the loins could a smile be running
to that middle, which carried procreation.

Else would this stone be standing maimed and short
under the shoulders' translucent plunge
nor flimmering like the fell of beasts of prey

nor breaking out of all its contours
like a star: for there is no place
that does not see you. You must change your life.

Archaïscher Torso Apollos

Wir kannten nicht sein unerhörtes Haupt,
darin die Augenäpfel reiften. Aber
sein Torso glüht noch wie ein Kandelaber,
in dem sein Schauen, nur zurückgeschraubt,

sich hält und glänzt. Sonst könnte nicht der Bug
der Brust dich blenden, und im leisen Drehen
der Lenden könnte nicht ein Lächeln gehen
zu jener Mitte, die die Zeugung trug.

Sonst stünde dieser Stein entstellt und kurz
unter der Schultern durchsichtigem Sturz
und flimmerte nicht so wie Raubtierfelle

1. All Rilke selections are translated by M. D. Herter Norton.
2. The first poem in the second volume of Rilke's *New Poems* (1908), which were dedicated "to my good friend, Auguste Rodin" (the French sculptor [1840–1917] whose secretary Rilke was for a brief period and on whom he wrote two monographs, in 1903 and 1907). The poem itself was inspired by an ancient Greek statue discovered at Miletus (a Greek colony on the coast of Asia Minor) that was called simply the *Torso of a Youth from Miletus*; since the god Apollo was an ideal of youthful male beauty, his name was often associated with such statues.
3. In a torso, the head and limbs are missing.

und bräche nicht aus allen seinen Rändern
aus wie ein Stern: denn da ist keine Stelle,
die dich nicht sieht. Du musst dein Leben ändern.

The Panther

jardin des plantes,[1] *paris*

His vision from the passing of the bars
is grown so weary that it holds no more.
To him it seems there are a thousand bars
and behind a thousand bars no world.

The padding gait of flexibly strong strides,
that in the very smallest circle turns,
is like a dance of strength around a center
in which stupefied a great will stands.

Only sometimes the curtain of the pupil
soundlessly parts—. Then an image enters,
goes through the tensioned stillness of the limbs—
and in the heart ceases to be.

The Swan

This toiling to go through something yet
undone, heavily and as though in bonds,
is like the ungainly gait of the swan.

And dying, this no longer grasping
of that ground on which we daily stand,
like his anxious letting-himself-down—:

into the waters, which receive him smoothly
and which, as though happy and bygone,
draw back underneath him, flow on flow;
while he, infinitely still and sure,
ever more maturely and more royally
and more serenely deigns to draw along.

1. A zoo in Paris. Rilke also admired, at Rodin's studio, the plaster cast of an ancient statue of a panther.

Spanish Dancer[1]

As in one's hand a sulphur match, whitely,
before it comes aflame, to every side
darts twitching tongues—: within the circle
of close watchers hasty, bright and hot
her round dance begins twitching to spread itself.

And suddenly it is altogether flame.

With her glance she sets alight her hair
and all at once with daring art
whirls her whole dress within this conflagration,
out of which her naked arms upstretch
like startled snakes awake and rattling.[2]

And then: as though the fire were tightening round her,
she gathers it all in one and casts it off
very haughtily, with imperious gesture
and watches: it lies there raging on the ground
and still flames and will not give in—.
Yet conquering, sure and with a sweet
greeting smile she lifts her countenance
and stamps it out with little sturdy feet.

1907

1. The dance described in the poem is the flamenco (from *flamear*, "to flame").
2. The dancer accompanies herself with the rhythmic clicking of castanets (worn on the fingers).

T. S. ELIOT

Thomas Stearns Eliot (1888–1965) had a unique role in defining modernist taste and style. As a poet and as a literary critic, he rejected the narrative, moralizing, frequently "noble" style of late Victorian poetry, instead employing highly focused, startling images and an elliptical, ironic voice that has had enormous impact on modern poetry throughout the world. Readers in far-flung regions who know nothing of Eliot's other works are likely to be familiar with *The Waste Land* (1922), a literary-historical landmark representing the cultural crisis in Europe after the First World War. Although Eliot did not consider himself a generational icon, his challenging, quirky, memorable poetry is indissolubly linked with the spiritual and intellectual crises of modernism.

Two countries, England and the United States, claim Eliot as part of their national literature. Although Eliot was born in St. Louis, the Eliots were a distinguished New England family; Eliot's grandfather had gone west to found Washington University in St. Louis. Eliot attended Harvard (where his father's cousin was president of the university) for his undergraduate and graduate education. There he found literary models that would feed his work in future years: the poetry of Dante and John Donne, and the plays of Elizabethan and Jacobean dramatists. In 1908, Eliot read Arthur Symons's *The Symbolist Movement in Literature* and became acquainted with the French Symbolist poets, whose richly allusive images—and highly self-conscious, ironic, and craftsmanlike technique—he would adopt as his own. He began writing poetry while still in college and published his first major work, "The Love Song of J. Alfred Prufrock," in *Poetry* magazine in 1915.

At twenty-two he left for Europe to study at Oxford and the Sorbonne; the outbreak of the First World War prevented him from returning to Harvard, where he intended to continue graduate study in philosophy. Nonetheless, he completed a doctoral dissertation on the philosopher F. H. Bradley, whose examination of private consciousness became a theme of Eliot's later essays and poems. Settling in England, Eliot married, taught briefly, and worked for several years in the foreign department of Lloyd's Bank. Unhappy in his marriage and under pressure in his job at the bank, Eliot suffered from writer's block and then had a breakdown soon after the First World War. He wrote most of *The Waste Land* while recovering in a sanatorium in Lausanne, Switzerland. It was immediately hailed as one of the most important poems of the modernist movement and an expression of the postwar sense of social crisis. Already well known for his essays, collected in *The Sacred Wood* (1920), and his editorial work for the literary journals *The Egoist* and *The Criterion*, Eliot left Lloyd's for a position with the publishing firm Faber & Faber.

Raised an American Unitarian, Eliot joined the Church of England in 1927 and became a naturalized British subject the same year. He continued to write poetry and also turned to drama, composing a verse play on the death of the English St. Thomas à Becket (*Murder in the Cathedral*, 1935) as well as more conventional stage plays, *The Family Reunion* (1939), which recasts the Orestes story from Greek tragedy, and *The Cocktail Party* (1949), a drawing-room comedy that explores the search for salvation. During this time, Eliot became increasingly conservative in his political attitudes; the anti-Semitic remarks in his speeches and poems from this period have tarnished his reputation. By the time he received the Nobel Prize for Literature, in 1948, however, Eliot was recognized as a major contemporary writer in English. For such an influential poet, his output was relatively small; but in addition to writing some of the greatest verse of the twentieth century and essays that shaped literary opinion, he nurtured many younger writers as a director at Faber & Faber. Despite his social, political, and religious conservatism, Eliot ushered in the revolution in literary form known as modernism.

The selection here includes two of Eliot's major poems from different phases of his career. "The Love Song of J. Alfred Prufrock" displays the evocative yet confounding images, abrupt shifts in focus, and combination of human sympathy and ironic wit that would attract and puzzle readers of his later works. Clearly Prufrock's dramatic monologue aims to startle readers—by bidding them, in the opening lines, to imagine the evening spread out "like a patient etherised upon a table," and by shifting focus abruptly among metaphysical questions, drawing-room chatter, imaginary landscapes, and literary and biblical allusions. Tones of high seriousness jar against banal and even singsong speech: "I grow old . . . I grow old . . . / I shall wear the bottoms of my trousers rolled." The stanzas of "Prufrock" are individual scenes, each with a stylistic coherence (for example, the third stanza's yellow fog as a cat). Together, they create a symbolic landscape that unfolds in the narrator's mind as a combination of factual observation and subjective feelings. In its discontinuity, its precise yet evocative imagery, its mixture of romantic and everyday reference, and its formal and conversational speech, as well as in the complex and ironic self-consciousness of its very unheroic hero, "The Love Song of J. Alfred Prufrock" anticipates the modernist traits typical of Eliot's larger corpus. Also anticipating Eliot's later work are the theme of spiritual void and the disoriented protagonist helpless to cope with a crisis that is as much the face of modern Western culture as of his personal tragedy.

Eliot dedicated *The Waste Land*, the next selection, to his friend, fellow poet, and editor Ezra Pound, with a quotation from Dante that praises the "better craftsman." Quotations from, or allusions to, a vast range of sources—including Shakespeare, Dante, **Charles Baudelaire**, Richard Wagner, Ovid, St. Augustine, Buddhist sermons, folk songs, and the anthropologists Jessie Weston and James Frazer—punctuate this lengthy work, to which Eliot added explanatory notes when it appeared in book form. A poem that depicts society in a time of cultural and spiritual crisis, *The Waste Land* juxtaposes images of the fragmentation of modern experience, on the one hand, and references (some in foreign languages) to a more stable heritage, on the other. The classical prophet Tiresias is contrasted to the contemporary charlatan Madame Sosostris; the celebrated lovers Antony and Cleopatra, to a real estate agent's clerk who mechanically seduces a bored typist at the end of her workday; Buddhist sermons and the religious visions of St. Augustine, to a sterile world of rock and dust where "one can neither stand nor lie nor sit." Throughout the poem runs a series of oblique allusions to the legend of a knight passing trials in a Chapel Perilous and healing a Fisher King by asking the right questions about the Holy Grail and the Holy Lance. The implication is that the modern wasteland might be redeemed if its inhabitants learned to answer (or perhaps to ask) the appropriate questions. These and other references that Eliot integrates into the poem constitute, the speaker says, "fragments I have shored against my ruins"—pieces of a puzzle whose resolution might bring "shantih," or the peace that passeth understanding but that remains enigmatically out of reach, as the poem's final lines in a mosaic of foreign languages suggest.

The groundbreaking technical innovation in *The Waste Land* is the deliberate use of fragmentation and discontinuity. Eliot pointedly refused to provide transitional passages or narrative thread, relying on the reader to construct a pattern whose implications would make sense as a whole. The writer's approach represents a direct attack on the conventional experience of the written word; the poem undercuts readers' expectations of linearity by inserting unexplained literary references, sudden shifts in scene or perspective, interpolations of foreign language, and changes of verbal register from lofty diction to slang. Eliot's refusal to fulfill traditional expectations serves several functions: it contributes to the poem's picture of cultural disintegration; it allows Eliot to exploit the Symbolist or allusive powers of language, since the diction rather than the narrative content must carry the burden of meaning; and by drawing attention to itself as a technique, it exemplifies modernist self-reflexive, or self-conscious, style.

Eliot's early essays on literature and literary history helped to bring about a different understanding of poetry, which afterward was no longer seen as the expression of personal feeling but as a carefully made aesthetic object. Yet much of Eliot's impact was not merely formal but spiritual and philosophical. The search for meaning that pervades his work created a lasting picture of the barrenness of modern culture and of the search for alternatives. But while many later poets rejected Eliot's religious beliefs, they found inspiration in his expression of the dilemmas facing an anxious and infinitely vulnerable modern soul.

The Love Song of J. Alfred Prufrock

S'io credessi che mia risposta fosse
a persona che mai tornasse al mondo,
questa fiamma staria senza più scosse.
Ma per ciò che giammai di questo fondo
non tornò vivo alcun, s'i'odo il vero,
senza tema d'infamia ti rispondo.[1]

Let us go then, you and I,
When the evening is spread out against the sky
Like a patient etherised upon a table;
Let us go, through certain half-deserted streets,
The muttering retreats
Of restless nights in one-night cheap hotels
And sawdust restaurants with oyster-shells:
Streets that follow like a tedious argument
Of insidious intent
To lead you to an overwhelming question . . .
Oh, do not ask, "What is it?"
Let us go and make our visit.

In the room the women come and go
Talking of Michelangelo.[2]

The yellow fog that rubs its back upon the window-panes,
The yellow smoke that rubs its muzzle on the window-panes
Licked its tongue into the corners of the evening,
Lingered upon the pools that stand in drains,
Let fall upon its back the soot that falls from chimneys,
Slipped by the terrace, made a sudden leap,

1. From Dante's *Inferno* 27.61–66, in which the false counselor Guido da Montefeltro, enveloped in flame, explains that he would never reveal his past if he thought the traveler could report it: "If I thought my reply were meant for one / who ever could return into the world, / this flame would stir no more; and yet, since none— / if what I hear is true—ever returned / alive from this abyss, then without fear / of facing infamy, I answer you."

2. Michelangelo Buonarroti (1475–1564), famous Italian Renaissance sculptor, painter, architect, and poet; here, merely a topic of fashionable conversation.

And seeing that it was a soft October night,
Curled once about the house, and fell asleep.

And indeed there will be time[3]
For the yellow smoke that slides along the street,
Rubbing its back upon the window-panes;
There will be time, there will be time
To prepare a face to meet the faces that you meet;
There will be time to murder and create,
And time for all the works and days of hands[4]
That lift and drop a question on your plate;
Time for you and time for me,
And time yet for a hundred indecisions,
And for a hundred visions and revisions,
Before the taking of a toast and tea.

In the room the women come and go
Talking of Michelangelo.

And indeed there will be time
To wonder, "Do I dare?" and, "Do I dare?"
Time to turn back and descend the stair,
With a bald spot in the middle of my hair—
(They will say: "How his hair is growing thin!")
My morning coat, my collar mounting firmly to the chin,
My necktie rich and modest, but asserted by a simple pin—
(They will say: "But how his arms and legs are thin!")
Do I dare
Disturb the universe?
In a minute there is time
For decisions and revisions which a minute will reverse.

For I have known them all already, known them all—
Have known the evenings, mornings, afternoons,
I have measured out my life with coffee spoons;
I know the voices dying with a dying fall[5]
Beneath the music from a farther room.
So how should I presume?

And I have known the eyes already, known them all—
The eyes that fix you in a formulated phrase,
And when I am formulated, sprawling on a pin,
When I am pinned and wriggling on the wall,
Then how should I begin
To spit out all the butt-ends of my days and ways?
And how should I presume?

3. Echo of a love poem by Andrew Marvell (1621–1678), *To His Coy Mistress*: "Had we but world enough and time."
4. An implied contrast with the more productive agricultural labor of hands in the *Works and Days* of the Greek poet Hesiod (8th century B.C.E.).
5. Recalls Duke Orsino's description of a musical phrase in Shakespeare's *Twelfth Night* (1.1.4): "It has a dying fall."

And I have known the arms already, known them all—
Arms that are braceleted and white and bare
(But in the lamplight, downed with light brown hair!)
Is it perfume from a dress
That makes me so digress?
Arms that lie along a table, or wrap about a shawl.
And should I then presume?
And how should I begin?

• • •

Shall I say, I have gone at dusk through narrow streets
And watched the smoke that rises from the pipes
Of lonely men in shirt-sleeves, leaning out of windows? . . .

I should have been a pair of ragged claws
Scuttling across the floors of silent seas.

• • •

And the afternoon, the evening, sleeps so peacefully!
Smoothed by long fingers,
Asleep . . . tired . . . or it malingers,
Stretched on the floor, here beside you and me.
Should I, after tea and cakes and ices,
Have the strength to force the moment to its crisis?
But though I have wept and fasted, wept and prayed,
Though I have seen my head (grown slightly bald) brought in
upon a platter,
I am no prophet[6]—and here's no great matter;
I have seen the moment of my greatness flicker,
And I have seen the eternal Footman hold my coat, and snicker,
And in short, I was afraid.

And would it have been worth it, after all,
After the cups, the marmalade, the tea,
Among the porcelain, among some talk of you and me,
Would it have been worth while,
To have bitten off the matter with a smile,
To have squeezed the universe into a ball
To roll it toward some overwhelming question,[7]
To say: "I am Lazarus, come from the dead,[8]
Come back to tell you all, I shall tell you all"—
If one, settling a pillow by her head,
Should say: "That is not what I meant at all.
That is not it, at all."

6. Salome obtained the head of the prophet John the Baptist on a platter as a reward for dancing before the tetrarch Herod (Matthew 14.3–11).

7. Another echo of Marvell's "To His Coy Mistress," when the lover suggests rolling "all our strength and all / our sweetness up into one ball" to send against the "iron gates of life."

8. The story of Lazarus, raised from the dead, is told in John 11.1–44.

And would it have been worth it, after all,
Would it have been worth while,
After the sunsets and the dooryards and the sprinkled streets,
After the novels, after the teacups, after the skirts that trail along
the floor—
And this, and so much more?—
It is impossible to say just what I mean!
But as if a magic lantern[9] threw the nerves in patterns on a screen:
Would it have been worth while
If one, settling a pillow or throwing off a shawl,
And turning toward the window, should say:
"That is not it at all,
That is not what I meant, at all."

• • •

No! I am not Prince Hamlet, nor was meant to be;
Am an attendant lord, one that will do
To swell a progress,[1] start a scene or two,
Advise the prince; no doubt, an easy tool,
Deferential, glad to be of use,
Politic, cautious, and meticulous;
Full of high sentence, but a bit obtuse;
At times, indeed, almost ridiculous—
Almost, at times, the Fool.

I grow old . . . I grow old . . .
I shall wear the bottoms of my trousers rolled.

Shall I part my hair behind? Do I dare to eat a peach?
I shall wear white flannel trousers, and walk upon the beach.
I have heard the mermaids singing, each to each.

I do not think that they will sing to me.

I have seen them riding seaward on the waves
Combing the white hair of the waves blown back
When the wind blows the water white and black.

We have lingered in the chambers of the sea
By sea-girls wreathed with seaweed red and brown
Till human voices wake us, and we drown.

1915

9. A slide projector.
1. A procession of attendants accompanying a king or nobleman across the stage, as in Elizabethan drama.

The Waste Land[1]

"Nam Sibyllam quidem Cumis ego ipse oculis meis vidi in ampulla pendere, et cum illi pueri dicerent: Σίβυλλα τί θέλεισ; respondebat illa: αποθανεῖν θέλω."[2]

For Ezra Pound
il miglior fabbro.[3]

1. The Burial of the Dead[4]

April is the cruellest month, breeding
Lilacs out of the dead land, mixing
Memory and desire, stirring
Dull roots with spring rain.
Winter kept us warm, covering
Earth in forgetful snow, feeding
A little life with dried tubers.
Summer surprised us, coming over the Starnbergersee[5]
With a shower of rain; we stopped in the colonnade,
And went on in sunlight, into the Hofgarten,[6]
And drank coffee, and talked for an hour.
Bin gar keine Russin, stamm' aus Litauen, echt deutsch.[7]
And when we were children, staying at the arch-duke's,
My cousin's, he took me out on a sled,
And I was frightened. He said, Marie,
Marie, hold on tight. And down we went.[8]
In the mountains, there you feel free.
I read, much of the night, and go south in the winter.

What are the roots that clutch, what branches grow
Out of this stony rubbish? Son of man,[9]
You cannot say, or guess, for you know only

1. Eliot provided footnotes for *The Waste Land* when it was first published in book form; these notes are included here. A general note at the beginning referred readers to the religious symbolism described in Jessie L. Weston's study of the Grail legend, *From Ritual to Romance* (1920), and to fertility myths and vegetation ceremonies (especially those involving Adonis, Attis, and Osiris) as described in the *The Golden Bough* (1890–1918) by the anthropologist Sir James Frazer.
2. Lines from Petronius's *Satyricon* (ca. 60 C.E.) describing the Sibyl, a prophetess shriveled with age and suspended in a bottle. "For indeed I myself have seen with my own eyes the Sibyl at Cumae, hanging in a bottle, and when those boys would say to her: 'Sibyl, what do you want?' she would reply: 'I want to die.'"
3. The dedication to Pound, who suggested cuts and changes in the first manuscript of *The Waste Land*, borrows words used by Guido Guinizelli to describe his predecessor, the Provençal poet Arnaut Daniel, in Dante's *Purgatorio* (26.117): he is "the better craftsman."
4. From the burial service of the Anglican Church.
5. A lake near Munich.
6. A public park.
7. "I am certainly no Russian, I come from Lithuania and am pure German." German settlers in Lithuania considered themselves superior to the Baltic natives.
8. Lines 8–16 recall *My Past*, the memoirs of Countess Marie Larisch.
9. "Cf. Ezekiel II, i" [Eliot's note]. The passage reads "Son of man, stand upon thy feet, and I will speak unto thee."

A heap of broken images, where the sun beats,
And the dead tree gives no shelter, the cricket no relief,[1]
And the dry stone no sound of water. Only
There is shadow under this red rock,
(Come in under the shadow of this red rock),
And I will show you something different from either
Your shadow at morning striding behind you
Or your shadow at evening rising to meet you;
I will show you fear in a handful of dust.
Frisch weht der Wind
Der Heimat zu
Mein Irisch Kind,
Wo weilest du?[2]
"You gave me hyacinths first a year ago;
"They called me the hyacinth girl."
—Yet when we came back, late, from the hyacinth garden,
Your arms full, and your hair wet, I could not
Speak, and my eyes failed, I was neither
Living nor dead, and I knew nothing,
Looking into the heart of light, the silence.
Oed' und leer das Meer.[3]

Madame Sosostris,[4] famous clairvoyante,
Had a bad cold, nevertheless
Is known to be the wisest woman in Europe,
With a wicked pack of cards.[5] Here, said she,
Is your card, the drowned Phoenician Sailor,
(Those are pearls that were his eyes.[6] Look!)
Here is Belladonna, the Lady of the Rocks,

1. "Cf. Ecclesiastes XII, v" [Eliot's note]. "Also when they shall be afraid of that which is high, and fears shall be in the way, . . . the grasshopper shall be a burden, and desire shall fail."
2. "V. *Tristan und Isolde*, I, verses 5–8" [Eliot's note]. A sailor in Richard Wagner's opera sings, "The wind blows fresh / Towards the homeland / My Irish child / Where are you waiting?" (German)
3. "Id. III, verse 24" [Eliot's note]. "Barren and empty is the sea" (German) is the erroneous report the dying Tristan hears as he waits for Isolde's ship in the third act of Wagner's opera.
4. A fortune-teller with an assumed Egyptian name, possibly suggested by a similar figure in a novel by Aldous Huxley (*Crome Yellow*, 1921).
5. "I am not familiar with the exact constitution of the Tarot pack of cards, from which I have obviously departed to suit my own convenience. The Hanged Man, a member of the traditional pack, fits my purpose in two ways: because he is associated in my mind with the Hanged God of Frazer, and because I associate him with the hooded figure in the passage of the disciples to Emmaus in Part V. The Phoenician Sailor and the Merchant appear later; also the 'crowds of people,' and Death by Water is executed in Part IV. The Man with Three Staves (an authentic member of the Tarot pack) I associate, quite arbitrarily, with the Fisher King himself" [Eliot's note]. Tarot cards are used for telling fortunes; the four suits (cup, lance, sword, and coin) are life symbols related to the Grail legend; and, as Eliot suggests, various figures on the cards are associated with different characters and situations in *The Waste Land*. For example, the "drowned Phoenician Sailor" (line 47) recurs in the merchant from Smyrna (III) and Phlebas the Phoenician (IV). "Belladonna" (line 49)—a poison, hallucinogen, medicine, and cosmetic (in Italian, "beautiful lady"); also an echo of Leonardo da Vinci's painting of the Virgin, *Madonna of the Rocks*—heralds the neurotic society woman amid her jewels and perfumes (II). "The Wheel" (line 51) is the wheel of fortune. "The Hanged Man" (line 55) becomes the sacrificed fertility god whose death ensures resurrection and new life for his people.
6. A line from Ariel's song in Shakespeare's *The Tempest* (1.2.398), which describes the transformation of a drowned man.

The lady of situations.
Here is the man with three staves, and here the Wheel,
And here is the one-eyed merchant, and this card,
Which is blank, is something he carries on his back,
Which I am forbidden to see. I do not find
The Hanged Man. Fear death by water.
I see crowds of people, walking round in a ring.
Thank you. If you see dear Mrs. Equitone,
Tell her I bring the horoscope myself:
One must be so careful these days.

Unreal City,[7]
Under the brown fog of a winter dawn,
A crowd flowed over London Bridge, so many,
I had not thought death had undone so many.[8]
Sighs, short and infrequent, were exhaled,[9]
And each man fixed his eyes before his feet.
Flowed up the hill and down King William Street,
To where Saint Mary Woolnoth kept the hours
With a dead sound on the final stroke of nine.[1]
There I saw one I knew, and stopped him, crying: "Stetson!
"You who were with me in the ships at Mylae![2]
"That corpse you planted last year in your garden,
"Has it begun to sprout? Will it bloom this year?
"Or has the sudden frost disturbed its bed?
"Oh keep the Dog far hence, that's friend to men,[3]
"Or with his nails he'll dig it up again!
"You! hypocrite lecteur!—mon semblable,—mon frère!"[4]

7. "Cf. Baudelaire: 'Fourmillante cité, cité pleine de rêves, / Où le spectre en plein jour raccroche le passant'" [Eliot's note]. "Swarming city, city full of dreams, / Where the specter in broad daylight accosts the passerby"; a description of Paris from "The Seven Old Men" in *The Flowers of Evil* (1857).

8. "Cf. *Inferno* III, 55–57: 'si lunga tratta / di gente, ch'io non avrei mai creduto / che morte tanta n' avesse disfatta'" [Eliot's note]. "Behind that banner trailed so long a file / of people—I should never have believed / that death could have unmade so many souls"; not only is Dante amazed at the number of people who have died but he is also describing a crowd of people who were neither good nor bad—non-entities denied even the entrance to hell.

9. "Cf. *Inferno* IV, 25–27: 'Quivi, secondo che per ascoltare, / non avea pianto, ma' che di sospiri, / che l'aura eterna facevan tremare'" [Eliot's note]. "Here, so far as I could tell by listening, there was no weeping but so many sighs that they caused the everlasting air to tremble"; the first circle of hell, or limbo, contained the souls of virtuous people who lived before Christ or had not been baptized.

1. "A phenomenon which I have often noticed" [Eliot's note]. The church is in the financial district of London, where King William Street is also located.

2. An "average" modern name (with business associations) linked to the ancient battle of Mylae (260 B.C.E.), where Rome was victorious over its commercial rival, Carthage.

3. "Cf. the Dirge in Webster's *White Devil*" [Eliot's note]. The dirge, or song of lamentation, sung by Cornelia in John Webster's play (1625), asks to "keep the wolf far thence, that's foe to men," so that the wolf's nails may not dig up the bodies of her murdered relatives. Eliot's reversal of dog for wolf, and friend for foe, domesticates the grotesque scene; it may also foreshadow rebirth since (according to Weston's book) the rise of the Dog Star, Sirius, announced the flooding of the Nile and the consequent return of fertility to Egyptian soil.

4. "V. Baudelaire, Preface to *Fleurs du Mal*" [Eliot's note]. Baudelaire's poem preface, titled "To the Reader," ended "Hypocritical reader!—my likeness!—my brother!" The poet challenges the reader to recognize that both are caught up in the worst sin of all—the moral wasteland of *ennui* ("boredom") as lack of will, the refusal to care one way or the other.

II. A Game of Chess[5]

The Chair she sat in, like a burnished throne,[6]
Glowed on the marble, where the glass
Held up by standards wrought with fruited vines
From which a golden Cupidon peeped out
(Another hid his eyes behind his wing)
Doubled the flames of sevenbranched candelabra
Reflecting light upon the table as
The glitter of her jewels rose to meet it,
From satin cases poured in rich profusion.
In vials of ivory and coloured glass
Unstoppered, lurked her strange synthetic perfumes,
Unguent, powdered, or liquid—troubled, confused
And drowned the sense in odours; stirred by the air
That freshened from the window, these ascended
In fattening the prolonged candle-flames,
Flung their smoke into the laquearia,[7]
Stirring the pattern on the coffered ceiling.
Huge sea-wood fed with copper
Burned green and orange, framed by the coloured stone,
In which sad light a carvèd dolphin swam.
Above the antique mantel was displayed
As though a window gave upon the sylvan scene[8]
The change of Philomel,[9] by the barbarous king
So rudely forced; yet there the nightingale[1]
Filled all the desert with inviolable voice
And still she cried, and still the world pursues,
"Jug Jug"[2] to dirty ears.
And other withered stumps of time
Were told upon the walls; staring forms
Leaned out, leaning, hushing the room enclosed.
Footsteps shuffled on the stair.
Under the firelight, under the brush, her hair

5. Reference to a play, *A Game of Chess* (1627) by Thomas Middleton (1580–1627); see n. 5, p. 576. Part II juxtaposes two scenes of modern sterility: an initial setting of wealthy boredom, neurosis, and lack of communication, and a pub scene in which similar concerns of appearance, sexual attraction, and thwarted childbirth are brought out more visibly, and in more vulgar language.
6. "Cf. *Antony and Cleopatra*, II, ii, 1.190" [Eliot's note]. A paler version of Cleopatra's splendor as she met her future lover, Antony: "The barge she sat in, like a burnished throne, / Burned on the water."
7. "Laquearia. V. *Aeneid*, 1, 726: dependent lychni laquearibus aureis incensi, et noctem flammis funalia vincunt" [Eliot's note]. "Glowing lamps hang from the gold-paneled ceiling, and the torches conquer night with their flames"; the banquet setting of another classical love scene, in which Dido is inspired with a fatal passion for Aeneas.
8. "Sylvan scene. V. Milton, *Paradise Lost*, IV, 140" [Eliot's note]. Eden as first seen by Satan.
9. "V. Ovid, *Metamorphoses*, VI, Philomela" [Eliot's note]. Philomela was raped by her brother-in-law, King Tereus, who cut out her tongue so that she could not tell her sister, Procne. Later Procne is changed into a swallow and Philomela into a nightingale to save them from the king's rage after they have revenged themselves by killing his son.
1. "Cf. Part III, 1.204" [Eliot's note].
2. Represents the nightingale's song in Elizabethan poetry.

Spread out in fiery points
Glowed into words, then would be savagely still.

'My nerves are bad to-night. Yes, bad. Stay with me.
'Speak to me. Why do you never speak. Speak.
'What are you thinking of? What thinking? What?
'I never know what you are thinking. Think.'

I think we are in rats' alley[3]
Where the dead men lost their bones.

'What is that noise?'
The wind under the door.[4]
'What is that noise now? What is the wind doing?'
Nothing again nothing.
'Do
'You know nothing? Do you see nothing? Do you remember
'Nothing?'

I remember
Those are pearls that were his eyes.
'Are you alive, or not? Is there nothing in your head?'
But
O O O O that Shakespeherian Rag—
It's so elegant
So intelligent
'What shall I do now? What shall I do?'
'I shall rush out as I am, and walk the street
'With my hair down, so. What shall we do to-morrow?
'What shall we ever do?'
The hot water at ten.
And if it rains, a closed car at four.
And we shall play a game of chess,[5]
Pressing lidless eyes and waiting for a knock upon the door.

When Lil's husband got demobbed,[6] I said—
I didn't mince my words, I said to her myself,
HURRY UP PLEASE ITS TIME[7]
Now Albert's coming back, make yourself a bit smart.
He'll want to know what you done with that money he gave you
To get yourself some teeth. He did, I was there.
You have them all out, Lil, and get a nice set,
He said, I swear, I can't bear to look at you.
And no more can't I, I said, and think of poor Albert,

3. "Cf. Part III, 1.195" [Eliot's note].
4. "Cf. Webster: 'Is the wind in that door still?'" [Eliot's note]. From *The Devil's Law Case* (1623), 3.2.162, with the implied meaning "is there still breath in him?"
5. "Cf. the game of chess in Middleton's *Women Beware Women*" [Eliot's note]. In this scene, a woman is seduced in a series of strategic steps that parallel the moves of a chess game, which is occupying her mother-in-law at the same time.
6. Demobilized, discharged from the army.
7. The British bartender's warning that the pub is about to close.

He's been in the army four years, he wants a good time,
And if you don't give it him, there's others will, I said.
Oh is there, she said. Something o' that, I said.
Then I'll know who to thank, she said, and give me a straight look.
HURRY UP PLEASE ITS TIME
If you don't like it you can get on with it, I said.
Others can pick and choose if you can't.
But if Albert makes off, it won't be for lack of telling.
You ought to be ashamed, I said, to look so antique.
(And her only thirty-one.)
I can't help it, she said, pulling a long face,
It's them pills I took, to bring it off, she said.
(She's had five already, and nearly died of young George.)
The chemist[8] said it would be all right, but I've never been the same.
You are a proper fool, I said.
Well, if Albert won't leave you alone, there it is, I said,
What you get married for if you don't want children?
HURRY UP PLEASE ITS TIME
Well, that Sunday Albert was home, they had a hot gammon,[9]
And they asked me in to dinner, to get the beauty of it hot—
HURRY UP PLEASE ITS TIME
HURRY UP PLEASE ITS TIME
Goonight Bill. Goonight Lou. Goonight May. Goonight.
Ta ta. Goonight. Goonight.
Good night, ladies, good night, sweet ladies, good night, good night.[1]

III. The Fire Sermon[2]

The river's tent is broken: the last fingers of leaf
Clutch and sink into the wet bank. The wind
Crosses the brown land, unheard. The nymphs are departed.
Sweet Thames, run softly, till I end my song.[3]
The river bears no empty bottles, sandwich papers,
Silk handkerchiefs, cardboard boxes, cigarette ends
Or other testimony of summer nights. The nymphs are departed.
And their friends, the loitering heirs of city directors;
Departed, have left no addresses.
By the waters of Leman I sat down and wept[4] . . .
Sweet Thames, run softly till I end my song,

8. The druggist, who gave her pills to cause a miscarriage.

9. Ham.

1. The popular song for a party's end ("Good Night, Ladies") shifts into Ophelia's last words in *Hamlet* (4.5.72) as she goes off to drown herself.

2. Reference to the Buddha's Fire Sermon (see n. 2, p. 582), in which he denounced the fiery lusts and passions of earthly experience. "All things are on fire . . . with the fire of passion . . . of hatred . . . of infatuation." Part III describes the degeneration of even these passions in the sterile decadence of the modern Waste Land.

3. "V. Spenser, *Prothalamion*" [Eliot's note]. The line is the refrain of a marriage song by the Elizabethan poet Edmund Spenser (1552?–1599) and evokes a river of unpolluted pastoral beauty.

4. In Psalms 137.1, the exiled Hebrews sit by the rivers of Babylon and weep for their lost homeland. "Waters of Leman": Lake Geneva (where Eliot wrote much of *The Waste Land*). A "leman" is a mistress or lover.

Sweet Thames, run softly, for I speak not loud or long.
But at my back in a cold blast I hear[5]
The rattle of the bones, and chuckle spread from ear to ear.

A rat crept softly through the vegetation
Dragging its slimy belly on the bank
While I was fishing in the dull canal
On a winter evening round behind the gashouse
Musing upon the king my brother's wreck
And on the king my father's death before him.[6]
White bodies naked on the low damp ground
And bones cast in a little low dry garret,
Rattled by the rat's foot only, year to year.
But at my back from time to time I hear[7]
The sound of horns and motors, which shall bring[8]
Sweeney to Mrs. Porter in the spring.
O the moon shone bright on Mrs. Porter[9]
And on her daughter
They wash their feet in soda water
Et O ces voix d'enfants, chantant dans la coupole![1]

Twit twit twit
Jug jug jug jug jug jug
So rudely forc'd.
Tereu[2]

Unreal City
Under the brown fog of a winter noon
Mr. Eugenides, the Smyrna merchant
Unshaven, with a pocket full of currants
C.i.f. London: documents at sight,[3]

5. Distorted echo of Andrew Marvell's (1621–1678) poem "To His Coy Mistress." "But at my back I always hear / Time's wingèd chariot hurrying near."
6. "Cf. *The Tempest* I.ii" [Eliot's note]. Ferdinand, the king's son, believing his father drowned and mourning his death, hears in the air a song containing the line that Eliot quotes earlier at lines 48 and 125.
7. "Cf. Marvell, 'To His Coy Mistress'" [Eliot's note].
8. "Cf. Day, *Parliament of Bees*: 'When of the sudden, listening, you shall hear, / A noise of horns and hunting, which shall bring / Actaeon to Diana in the spring, / Where all shall see her naked skin'" [Eliot's note]. The young hunter Actaeon was changed into a stag, hunted down, and killed when he came upon the goddess Diana bathing. Sweeney is in no such danger from his visit to Mrs. Porter.
9. "I do not know the origin of the ballad from which these lines are taken: it was reported to me from Sydney, Australia" [Eliot's note]. A song popular among Allied troops during World War I. One version continues lines 199–201 as follows: "And so they oughter / To keep them clean."
1. "V. Verlaine, *Parsifal*" [Eliot's note]. "And O these children's voices, singing in the dome!" (French); the last lines of a sonnet by Paul Verlaine (1844–1896), which ambiguously celebrates the Grail hero's chaste restraint. In Richard Wagner's opera, Parsifal's feet are washed to purify him before entering the presence of the Grail.
2. Tereus, who raped Philomela (see line 99); also the nightingale's song.
3. "The currants were quoted at a price 'carriage and insurance free to London'; and the Bill of Lading etc. were to be handed to the buyer upon payment of the sight draft" [Eliot's note].

Asked me in demotic French
To luncheon at the Cannon Street Hotel
Followed by a weekend at the Metropole.[4]

At the violet hour, when the eyes and back
Turn upward from the desk, when the human engine waits
Like a taxi throbbing waiting,
I Tiresias,[5] though blind, throbbing between two lives,
Old man with wrinkled female breasts, can see
At the violet hour, the evening hour that strives
Homeward, and brings the sailor home from sea,[6]
The typist home at teatime, clears her breakfast, lights
Her stove, and lays out food in tins.
Out of the window perilously spread
Her drying combinations touched by the sun's last rays,
On the divan are piled (at night her bed)
Stockings, slippers, camisoles, and stays.
I Tiresias, old man with wrinkled dugs
Perceived the scene, and foretold the rest—
I too awaited the expected guest.
He, the young man carbuncular, arrives,
A small house agent's clerk, with one bold stare,
One of the low on whom assurance sits
As a silk hat on a Bradford[7] millionaire.
The time is now propitious, as he guesses,
The meal is ended, she is bored and tired,
Endeavours to engage her in caresses
Which still are unreproved, if undesired.
Flushed and decided, he assaults at once;
Exploring hands encounter no defence;
His vanity requires no response,
And makes a welcome of indifference.
(And I Tiresias have foresuffered all
Enacted on this same divan or bed;
I who have sat by Thebes below the wall

4. Smyrna is an ancient Phoenician seaport, and early Smyrna merchants spread the Eastern fertility cults. In contrast, their descendant Mr. Eugenides ("Well-born") invites the poet to lunch in a large commercial hotel and a weekend at a seaside resort in Brighton.

5. "Tiresias, although a mere spectator and not indeed a 'character,' is yet the most important personage in the poem, uniting all the rest. Just as the one-eyed merchant, seller of currants, melts into the Phoenician Sailor, and the latter is not wholly distinct from Ferdinand Prince of Naples, so all the women are one woman, and the two sexes meet in Tiresias. What Tiresias *sees*, in fact, is the substance of the poem. The whole passage from Ovid is one of great anthropological interest" [Eliot's note]. The passage then quoted from Ovid's *Metamorphoses* (3.320–38) describes how Tiresias spent seven years of his life as a woman and thus experienced love from the point of view of both sexes. Blinded by Juno, he was recompensed by Jove with the gift of prophecy.

6. "This may or may not appear as exact as Sappho's lines, but I had in mind the 'longshore' or 'dory' fisherman, who returns at nightfall" [Eliot's note]. The Greek poet Sappho's poem describes how the evening star brings home those whom dawn has sent abroad; there is also an echo of Robert Louis Stevenson's (1850–1894) *Requiem* 1.221: "Home is the sailor, home from the sea."

7. A manufacturing town in Yorkshire that prospered greatly during World War I.

And walked among the lowest of the dead.)[8]
Bestows one final patronising kiss,
And gropes his way, finding the stairs unlit . . .

She turns and looks a moment in the glass,
Hardly aware of her departed lover;
Her brain allows one half-formed thought to pass:
'Well now that's done: and I'm glad it's over.'
When lovely woman stoops to folly and[9]
Paces about her room again, alone,
She smoothes her hair with automatic hand,
And puts a record on the gramophone.

'This music crept by me upon the waters'[1]
And along the Strand, up Queen Victoria Street.
O City city,[2] I can sometimes hear
Beside a public bar in Lower Thames Street,
The pleasant whining of a mandoline
And a clatter and a chatter from within
Where fishmen lounge at noon: where the walls
Of Magnus Martyr[3] hold
Inexplicable splendour of Ionian white and gold.

The river sweats[4]
Oil and tar
The barges drift
With the turning tide
Red sails
Wide
To leeward, swing on the heavy spar.
The barges wash
Drifting logs
Down Greenwich reach
Past the Isle of Dogs.[5]

8. Tiresias prophesied in the marketplace at Thebes for many years before dying and continuing to prophesy in Hades.
9. "V. Goldsmith, the song in *The Vicar of Wakefield*" [Eliot's note]. "When lovely woman stoops to folly / And finds too late that men betray / What charm can soothe her melancholy, / What art can wash her guilt away?" Oliver Goldsmith (ca. 1730–1774), *The Vicar of Wakefield* (1766).
1. "V. *The Tempest*, as above" [Eliot's note, referring to line 191]. Spoken by Ferdinand as he hears Ariel sing of his father's transformation by the sea, his eyes turning to pearls, his bones to coral, and everything else he formerly was into "something rich and strange."
2. A double invocation: the city of London and the City as London's central financial district (see lines 60 and 207). See also lines 375–76, the great cities of Western civilization.
3. "The interior of St. Magnus Martyr is to my mind one of the finest among Wren's interiors. See *The Proposed Demolition of Nineteen City Churches*: (P. S. King & Son, Ltd)" [Eliot's note]. The architect was Christopher Wren (1632–1723), and the church is located just below London Bridge on Lower Thames Street.
4. "The Song of the (three) Thames-daughters begins here. From line 292 to 306 inclusive they speak in turn. V. *Götterdämmerung* III.i.: the Rhine-daughters" [Eliot's note]. In Wagner's opera *The Twilight of the Gods* (1876), the three Rhine-maidens mourn the loss of their gold, which gave the river its sparkling beauty; lines 277–78 here echo the Rhine-maidens' refrain.
5. A peninsula opposite Greenwich on the Thames.

Weialala leia
Wallala leialala

Elizabeth and Leicester[6]
Beating oars
The stern was formed
A gilded shell
Red and gold
The brisk swell
Rippled both shores
Southwest wind
Carried down stream
The peal of bells
White towers
Weialala leia
Wallala leialala

'Trams and dusty trees.
Highbury bore me. Richmond and Kew
Undid me.[7] By Richmond I raised my knees
Supine on the floor of a narrow canoe.'
'My feet are at Moorgate,[8] and my heart
Under my feet. After the event
He wept. He promised "a new start."
I made no comment. What should I resent?'

'On Margate Sands.[9]
I can connect
Nothing with nothing.
The broken fingernails of dirty hands.
My people humble people who expect
Nothing.'
la la

To Carthage then I came[1]

6. "V. Froude, *Elizabeth*, vol. I, ch. iv, letter of De Quadra to Philip of Spain: 'In the afternoon we were in a barge, watching the games on the river. (The queen) was alone with Lord Robert and myself on the poop, when they began to talk nonsense, and went so far that Lord Robert at last said, as I was on the spot there was no reason why they should not be married if the queen pleased" [Eliot's note]. Sir Robert Dudley (1532–1588), the earl of Leicester, was a favorite of Queen Elizabeth and at one point hoped to marry her.

7. "Cf. *Purgatorio*, V, 133: 'Ricorditi di me, che son la Pia; / Siena mi fe', disfecemi Maremma'" [Eliot's note]. La Pia, in Purgatory, recalls her seduction: "Remember me, who am La Pia. / Siena made me, Maremma undid me." Eliot's parody substitutes Highbury (a London suburb) and Richmond and Kew, popular excursion points on the Thames.

8. A London slum.

9. A seaside resort on the Thames.

1. "V. St. Augustine's *Confessions*: 'to Carthage then I came, where a cauldron of unholy loves sang all about mine ears'" [Eliot's note]. The youthful Augustine is described. Carthage is also the scene of Dido's faithful love for Aeneas, referred to in line 92.

Burning burning burning burning[2]
O Lord Thou pluckest me out[3]
O Lord Thou pluckest

burning

IV. Death by Water

Phlebas the Phoenician, a fortnight dead,
Forgot the cry of gulls, and the deep sea swell
And the profit and loss.
A current under sea
Picked his bones in whispers. As he rose and fell
He passed the stages of his age and youth
Entering the whirlpool.
Gentile or Jew
O you who turn the wheel and look to windward,
Consider Phlebas, who was once handsome and tall as you.

V. What the Thunder Said[4]

After the torchlight red on sweaty faces
After the frosty silence in the gardens
After the agony in stony places
The shouting and the crying
Prison and palace and reverberation
Of thunder of spring over distant mountains
He who was living is now dead[5]
We who were living are now dying
With a little patience

Here is no water but only rock
Rock and no water and the sandy road
The road winding above among the mountains
Which are mountains of rock without water
If there were water we should stop and drink

2. "The complete text of the Buddha's Fire Sermon (which corresponds in importance to the Sermon on the Mount) from which these words are taken, will be found translated in the late Henry Clarke Warren's *Buddhism in Translation* (Harvard Oriental Studies). Mr. Warren was one of the great pioneers of Buddhist studies in the Occident" [Eliot's note]. The Sermon on the Mount is in Matthew 5–7.
3. "From St. Augustine's *Confessions* again. The collocation of these two representatives of eastern and western asceticism, as the culmination of this part of the poem is not an accident" [Eliot's note]. See also Zechariah 3.2, where the high priest Joshua is described as a "brand plucked out of the fire."
4. "In the first part of Part V three themes are employed: the journey to Emmaus, the approach to the Chapel Perilous (see Miss Weston's book) and the present decay of eastern Europe" [Eliot's note]. On their journey to Emmaus (Luke 24.13–34), Jesus's disciples were joined by a stranger who later revealed himself to be the crucified and resurrected Christ. The *thunder* of the title is a divine voice in the Hindu *Upanishads* (see n. 3, p. 584).
5. Allusions to stages in Christ's Passion: the betrayal, prayer in the garden of Gethsemane, imprisonment, trial, crucifixion, and burial. Despair reigns, for this is death before the Resurrection.

Amongst the rock one cannot stop or think
Sweat is dry and feet are in the sand
If there were only water amongst the rock
Dead mountain mouth of carious teeth that cannot spit
Here one can neither stand nor lie nor sit
There is not even silence in the mountains
But dry sterile thunder without rain
There is not even solitude in the mountains
But red sullen faces sneer and snarl
From doors of mudcracked houses
If there were water
And no rock
If there were rock
And also water
And water
A spring
A pool among the rock
If there were the sound of water only
Not the cicada[6]
And dry grass singing
But sound of water over a rock
Where the hermit-thrush[7] sings in the pine trees
Drip drop drip drop drop drop drop
But there is no water

Who is the third who walks always beside you?
When I count, there are only you and I together[8]
But when I look ahead up the white road
There is always another one walking beside you
Gliding wrapt in a brown mantle, hooded
I do not know whether a man or a woman
—But who is that on the other side of you?

What is that sound high in the air[9]
Murmur of maternal lamentation
Who are those hooded hordes swarming
Over endless plains, stumbling in cracked earth
Ringed by the flat horizon only
What is the city over the mountains
Cracks and reforms and bursts in the violet air

6. Grasshopper or cricket; see line 23.
7. "The hermit-thrush which I have heard in Quebec Province. . . . Its 'water-dripping song' is justly celebrated" [Eliot's note].
8. "The following lines were stimulated by the account of one of the Antarctic expeditions (I forget which, but I think one of Shackleton's): it was related that the party of explorers, at the extremity of their strength, had the constant delusion that there was *one more member* than could actually be counted" [Eliot's note]. See also n. 4, p. 582.
9. Eliot's note to lines 367–77 refers to Hermann Hesse's *Blick ins Chaos* (Glimpse into Chaos) and a passage that reads, translated, "Already half of Europe, already at least half of Eastern Europe is on the way to Chaos, drives drunk in holy madness on the edge of the abyss and sings at the same time, sings drunk and hymn-like, as Dimitri Karamazov sang [in Dostoevsky's *The Brothers Karamazov*]. The offended bourgeois laughs at the songs; the saint and the seer hear them with tears."

Falling towers
Jerusalem Athens Alexandria
Vienna London
Unreal

A woman drew her long black hair out tight
And fiddled whisper music on those strings
And bats with baby faces in the violet light
Whistled, and beat their wings
And crawled head downward down a blackened wall
And upside down in air were towers
Tolling reminiscent bells, that kept the hours
And voices singing out of empty cisterns and exhausted wells.

In this decayed hole among the mountains
In the faint moonlight, the grass is singing
Over the tumbled graves, about the chapel
There is the empty chapel, only the wind's home.
It has no windows, and the door swings,
Dry bones can harm no one.
Only a cock stood on the rooftree
Co co rico co co rico[1]
In a flash of lightning. Then a damp gust
Bringing rain

Ganga was sunken, and the limp leaves
Waited for rain, while the black clouds
Gathered far distant, over Himavant.[2]
The jungle crouched, humped in silence.
Then spoke the thunder
DA
Datta: what have we given?[3]
My friend, blood shaking my heart
The awful daring of a moment's surrender
Which an age of prudence can never retract
By this, and this only, we have existed
Which is not to be found in our obituaries
Or in memories draped by the beneficent spider[4]
Or under seals broken by the lean solicitor
In our empty rooms
DA

1. European version of the cock's crow: *cock-a-doodle-doo*. The cock crowed in Matthew 26.34 and 74, after Peter had denied Jesus three times.
2. A mountain in the Himalayas. "Ganga": the river Ganges in India.
3. "'Datta, dayadhvam, damyata' (Give, sympathise, control). The fable of the meaning of the Thunder is found in the *Brihadaranyaka*—Upanishad 5,1" [Eliot's note]. In the fable, the word *DA*, spoken by the supreme being Prajapati, is interpreted as *Datta* ("to give alms"), *Dayadhvam* ("to sympathize or have compassion"), and *Damyata* ("to have self-control") by gods, human beings, and demons respectively. The conclusion is that when the thunder booms DA DA DA, Prajapati is commanding that all three virtues be practiced simultaneously.
4. "Cf. Webster, *The White Devil*, V, vi: '. . . they'll remarry / Ere the worm pierce your winding-sheet, ere the spider / Make a thin curtain for your epitaphs'" [Eliot's note].

Dayadhvam:[5] I have heard the key
Turn in the door once and turn once only
We think of the key, each in his prison
Thinking of the key, each confirms a prison
Only at nightfall, aethereal rumours
Revive for a moment a broken Coriolanus[6]
Da
Damyata: The boat responded
Gaily, to the hand expert with sail and oar
The sea was calm, your heart would have responded
Gaily, when invited, beating obedient
To controlling hands

I sat upon the shore
Fishing,[7] with the arid plain behind me
Shall I at least set my lands in order?
London Bridge is falling down falling down falling down

Poi s'ascose nel foco che gli affina[8]
Quando fiam uti chelidon[9]—O swallow swallow
Le Prince d'Aquitaine à la tour abolie[1]
These fragments I have shored against my ruins
Why then Ile fit you. Hieronymo's mad againe.[2]
Datta. Dayadhvam. Damyata.
Shantih shantih shantih[3]

1922

5. Eliot's note on the command "to sympathize" or reach outside the self cites two descriptions of helpless isolation. The first comes from Dante's *Inferno* 33.46: as Ugolino, imprisoned in a tower with his children to die of starvation, says, "And I heard below the door of the horrible tower being locked up." The second is a modern description by the English philosopher F. H. Bradley (1846–1924) of the inevitably self-enclosed or private nature of consciousness: "My external sensations are no less private to myself than are my thoughts or my feelings. In either case my experience falls within my own circle, a circle closed on the outside; and, with all its elements alike, every sphere is opaque to the others which surround it. . . . In brief, regarded as an existence which appears in a soul, the whole world for each is peculiar and private to that soul" (*Appearance and Reality*).
6. A proud Roman patrician who was exiled and led an army against his homeland. In Shakespeare's play, both his grandeur and his downfall come from a desire to be ruled only by himself.
7. "V. Weston: *From Ritual to Romance*; chapter on the Fisher King" [Eliot's note].
8. Eliot's note quotes a passage in the *Purgatorio* in which Arnaut Daniel (see n. 3, p. 572) asks Dante to remember his pain. The line cited here, "then he, too, hid himself in the fire that makes those spirits ready to go higher" (*Purgatorio* 26.148), shows Daniel departing in fire which—in Purgatory—exists as a purifying rather than a destructive element.
9. "V. *Pervigilium Veneris*. Cf. Philomela in Parts II and III" [Eliot's note]. "When shall I be as a swallow?" A line from the *Vigil of Venus*, an anonymous late Latin poem, that asks for the gift of song; here associated with Philomela as a swallow, not the nightingale of lines 99–103 and 203–06.
1. "V. Gerard de Nerval, Sonnet *El Desdichado*" [Eliot's note]. The Spanish title means "The Disinherited One," and the sonnet is a monologue describing the speaker as a melancholy, ill-starred dreamer: "the Prince of Aquitaine in his ruined tower."
2. "V. Kyd's *Spanish Tragedy*" [Eliot's note]. Thomas Kyd's revenge play (1594) is subtitled *Hieronymo's Mad Againe*. The protagonist "fits" his son's murderers into appropriate roles in a court entertainment so that they may all be killed.
3. "Shantih. Repeated as here, a formal ending to an Upanishad. 'The Peace which passeth understanding' is our equivalent to this word" [Eliot's note]. The *Upanishads* comment on the sacred Hindu scriptures, the *Vedas*.

ANNA AKHMATOVA

One of the great Russian poets of the twentieth century, Anna Akhmatova (1889–1966) expresses herself in an intensely personal, poetic voice, whether as lover, wife, and mother or as a national poet commemorating the mute agony of millions. From the subjective romantic lyrics of her earliest work to the communal mourning of *Requiem*, she conveys universal themes in terms of individual experience, and historical events through the filter of fear, love, hope, and pain. Yet what most distinguishes her work is the way these basic emotions arise from the historical traumas of Akhmatova's native land.

Born Anna Andreevna Gorenko, in a suburb of the Black Sea port of Odessa, she was the daughter of a maritime engineer and an independent woman of revolutionary sympathies. She took the pen name Akhmatova (accented on the second syllable) from her maternal great-grandmother, who was of Tatar descent. Anna attended the local school at Tsarskoe Selo, near St. Petersburg, but completed her degree in Kiev. In 1907 she briefly studied law at the Kiev College for Women before moving to St. Petersburg to study literature. In Tsarskoe Selo, Akhmatova met Nikolai Gumilyov, whom she married in 1910. Gumilyov helped organize the Poets Guild, which became the core of a small new literary movement. Acmeism rejected the romantic, quasi-religious aims of Russian symbolism and valued clarity, concreteness, and closeness to the things of this earth. The Symbolist–Acmeist debate went on inside a lively literary and social life, while the three main figures of the movement—Akhmatova, Gumilyov, and Osip Mandelstam—gained a reputation as important poets.

Although Akhmatova and Gumilyov divorced, his arrest and execution for counterrevolutionary activities in 1921 put her status into question. After 1922 she was no longer allowed to publish and was forced into the withdrawal from public activity that Russians call "internal emigration." Officially forgotten, she was not forgotten in fact; in the schools, students who would never hear her name mentioned in class copied out her poems by hand and circulated them secretly. Relying for her living on a meager, irregular pension, Akhmatova prepared essays on the life and works of the Russian author Aleksandr Pushkin (1799–1837) and wrote poems that would not appear until much later. Stalin's "Great Purge" of 1935–38 sent millions of people to prison camps and made the 1930s a time of terror and uncertainty for everyone.

Akhmatova's friend Osip Mandelstam was exiled to Voronezh in 1934 and then sent to a prison camp in 1938, where he died that year. In 1935 her partner, the art critic Nikolai Punin, was arrested briefly and her son Lev Gumilyov, then twenty-three, was imprisoned, an event that inspired the first poems of the cycle that would become *Requiem*. Lev was ultimately imprisoned for a total of fourteen years as the government sought a way to punish his mother for what it perceived as her disloyalty to the regime. Composing *Requiem* was a risky act carried out over several years, and Akhmatova and her friend Lidia Chukovskaya memorized the stanzas in order to preserve the poem in the absence of written copy.

During the Second World War, Akhmatova's interest in larger musical forms motivated her to develop cycles of poems instead of her accustomed individual lyrics. She also began work on *Poem Without a Hero*, a long, complex verse narrative in three parts that sums up many of her earlier themes: love, death, creativity, the unity of European culture, and the suffering of her people. The poet was allowed a partial return to public life, addressing women on the radio during the siege of Leningrad (St. Petersburg) in 1941 and writing patriotic lyrics such as the famous *Courage* (published in *Pravda* in 1942), which rallied the Russian people to defend their homeland (and their national language) from enslavement. Her son was briefly released to serve in the military before being imprisoned again after the war.

Despite her patriotic activities, Akhmatova was subject to vicious official attacks after the war. Because she was considered too independent and cosmopolitan to be tolerated by the authorities, Akhmatova's books were suppressed. Her works did not fit the government-approved model of literature: they were too "individualistic" and were not "socially useful." After the death of Joseph Stalin, in 1953, however, her collected poems—including poems of the war years and unknown texts written during the periods of enforced silence—brought the range of her work to public attention. *Requiem* was first published "without her consent" in Munich in 1963 (not until 1987 was the complete text published in the Soviet Union). Her death, in 1966, signaled the end of an era in modern Russian poetry, for she was the last of the famous "quartet" that also included Mandelstam, Marina Tsvetaeva, and Boris Pasternak.

Requiem (1940), presented here, is a lyrical cycle, a series of poems written on a theme, but it is also a short epic narrative. The story it tells is acutely personal, even autobiographical, but like an epic it transcends personal significance and describes (as in *The Song of Roland*) a moment in the history of a nation. Akhmatova, who had seen her husband and son arrested and her friends die in prison camps, was only one of millions who had suffered similar losses in the purges of the 1930s. "Instead of a Preface," "Dedication," "Prologue," and two epilogues to *Requiem* constitute a framework examining this image of a common fate, while the core group of numbered poems develops a subjective picture and stages an individual drama. The "Dedication" and "Prologue" establish the context for the poem as a whole: the mass arrests in the 1930s after the assassination on December 1, 1934, of Sergei Kirov, the top Communist Party official in Leningrad. In the inner poems, Akhmatova blends her individual personal losses—husband, son, and friends—to create a single focus: the figure of a mother grieving for her condemned son. The speaker identifies herself with the crowd of women with whom she waited for seventeen months outside the Kresty ("Crosses") prison in Leningrad; at dawn each day they would all arrive, hoping to be allowed to pass their loved ones a parcel or a letter, and fearing that the prisoners would be sentenced to death or exile to the prison camps of Siberia. Instead of experiencing a natural life—one in which "for someone the sunset luxuriates"—these women and the prisoners are forced into a suspended, uncertain existence where all values are inverted and the city itself has become merely the setting for its prisons.

The "I" of the speaker throughout remains anonymous, in spite of the fact that Akhmatova describes her personal emotions in the central poems; her identity is that of a sorrowing mother, and she is distinguished from her fellow sufferers only by the poetic gift that makes her the "exhausted mouth, / Through which a hundred million scream." *Requiem* is at once both public and private: a picture of individual grief linked to the country's disaster, and a vision of community suffering that extends beyond contemporary national tragedy into medieval Russian history and Greek mythology. The poem consistently figures the martyrdom of the Soviet people in religious terms, from the recurrent mention of crosses and Crucifixion to the culminating image of maternal suffering in Mary, the mother of Christ.

With the numbered poems, Akhmatova recounts the growing anguish of a mother as her son is arrested and sentenced to death. The speaker has described her partner's arrest at dawn, in the midst of the family. Her son is arrested later, and in the rest of the poem she relives her numb incomprehension as she struggles against the increasing likelihood that he will be condemned to death. After the sentence is passed, the mother can speak of his execution only in oblique terms, by shifting the image of death onto the plane of the Crucifixion and God's will. It is a tragedy that cannot be comprehended or beheld directly, just as, she suggests, at the Crucifixion "No one glanced and no one would have dared" to look at the grieving Mary.

In the two epilogues, the grieving speaker returns from religious transcendence to Earth and current history. Here she takes on a composite identity, seeing herself not as an isolated sufferer but as the women whose fate she has shared. It is their memory she perpetuates by writing *Requiem*, and it is in their memory that she herself lives on. No longer the victim of purely personal tragedy, she has become a bronze statue commemorating a community of suffering—a figure shaped by circumstances into a monument of public and private grief.

Requiem[1]

1935–1940

No, not under the vault of alien skies,[2]
And not under the shelter of alien wings—
I was with my people then,
There, where my people, unfortunately, were.

1961

Instead of a Preface

In the terrible years of the Yezhov terror,[3] I spent seventeen months in the prison lines of Leningrad. Once, someone "recognized" me. Then a woman with bluish lips standing behind me, who, of course, had never heard me called by name before, woke up from the stupor to which every one had succumbed and whispered in my ear (everyone spoke in whispers there):

"Can you describe this?"

And I answered: "Yes, I can."

1. Translated by Judith Hemschemeyer.
2. A phrase borrowed from *Message to Siberia* by the Russian poet Aleksandr Pushkin (1799–1837).
3. In 1937–38, mass arrests were carried out by the secret police, headed by Nikolai Yezhov.

Then something that looked like a smile passed over what had once been her face.

April 1, 1957
Leningrad[4]

Dedication

Mountains bow down to this grief,
Mighty rivers cease to flow,
But the prison gates hold firm,
And behind them are the "prisoners' burrows"
And mortal woe.
For someone a fresh breeze blows,
For someone the sunset luxuriates—
We[5] wouldn't know, we are those who everywhere
Hear only the rasp of the hateful key
And the soldiers' heavy tread.
We rose as if for an early service,
Trudged through the savaged capital
And met there, more lifeless than the dead;
The sun is lower and the Neva[6] mistier,
But hope keeps singing from afar.
The verdict . . . And her tears gush forth,
Already she is cut off from the rest,
As if they painfully wrenched life from her heart,
As if they brutally knocked her flat,
But she goes on . . . Staggering . . . Alone . . .
Where now are my chance friends
Of those two diabolical years?
What do they imagine is in Siberia's storms,[7]
What appears to them dimly in the circle of the moon?
I am sending my farewell greeting to them.

March 1940

Prologue

That was when the ones who smiled
Were the dead, glad to be at rest.
And like a useless appendage, Leningrad
Swung from its prisons.
And when, senseless from torment,
Regiments of convicts marched,

4. The prose preface was written after her son had been released from prison and it was possible to think of editing the poem for publication.
5. The women waiting in line before the prison gates.
6. The large river that flows through St. Petersburg.
7. Victims of the purges who were not executed were condemned to prison camps in Siberia. Their wives were allowed to accompany them into exile, although they had to live in towns at a distance from the camps.

And the short songs of farewell
Were sung by locomotive whistles.
The stars of death stood above us
And innocent Russia writhed
Under bloody boots
And under the tires of the Black Marias.[8]

I

They led you away at dawn,
I followed you, like a mourner,
In the dark front room the children were crying,[9]
By the icon shelf the candle was dying.
On your lips was the icon's chill.[1]
The deathly sweat on your brow . . . Unforgettable!—
I will be like the wives of the Streltsy,[2]
Howling under the Kremlin towers.

1935

II

Quietly flows the quiet Don,[3]
Yellow moon slips into a home.

He slips in with cap askew,
He sees a shadow, yellow moon.

This woman is ill,
This woman is alone,
Husband in the grave,[4] son in prison,
Say a prayer for me.

III

No, it is not I, it is somebody else who is suffering.
I would not have been able to bear what happened,
Let them shroud it in black,
And let them carry off the lanterns . . .
Night.

1940

8. Police cars for conveying those arrested.
9. Akhmatova's third husband, the art historian Nikolai Punin, was arrested at dawn while the children (his daughter and her cousin) cried.
1. The icon—a small religious painting—was set on a shelf before which a candle was kept lit. Punin had kissed the icon before being taken away.
2. Elite troops organized by Ivan the Terrible around 1550. They rebelled and were executed by Peter the Great in 1698. Pleading in vain, their wives and mothers saw the men killed under the towers of the Kremlin.
3. The great Russian river, often celebrated in folk songs. This poem is modeled on a simple, rhythmic, short folk song known as a *chastuska*.
4. Akhmatova's first husband, the poet Nikolai Gumilyov, was shot in 1921.

IV

You should have been shown, you mocker,
Minion of all your friends,
Gay little sinner of Tsarskoye Selo,[5]
What would happen in your life—
How three-hundredth in line, with a parcel,
You would stand by the Kresty prison,

Your tempestuous tears
Burning through the New Year's ice.
Over there the prison poplar bends,
And there's no sound—and over there how many
Innocent lives are ending now . . .

V

For seventeen months I've been crying out,
Calling you home.
I flung myself at the hangman's[6] feet,
You are my son and my horror.
Everything is confused forever,
And it's not clear to me
Who is a beast now, who is a man,
And how long before the execution.
And there are only dusty flowers,
And the chinking of the censer, and tracks
From somewhere to nowhere.
And staring me straight in the eyes,
And threatening impending death,
Is an enormous star.[7]

1939

VI

The light weeks will take flight,
I won't comprehend what happened.
Just as the white nights[8]
Stared at you, dear son, in prison

So they are staring again,
With the burning eyes of a hawk,
Talking about your lofty cross,
And about death.

1939

5. Akhmatova recalls her early, carefree, and privileged life in Tsarskoe Selo, outside St. Petersburg.
6. Stalin's. Akhmatova wrote a letter to him pleading for the release of her son.
7. The star, the censer, the foliage, and the confusion between beast and man recall apocalyptic passages in the Book of Revelation (8.5, 7, 10–11 and 9.7–10).
8. In St. Petersburg, because it is so far north, the nights around the summer solstice are never totally dark.

VII

THE SENTENCE

And the stone word fell
On my still-living breast.
Never mind, I was ready.
I will manage somehow.

Today I have so much to do:
I must kill memory once and for all,
I must turn my soul to stone,
I must learn to live again—

Unless . . . Summer's ardent rustling
Is like a festival outside my window.
For a long time I've foreseen this
Brilliant day, deserted house.

June 22, 1939[9]
Fountain House

VIII

TO DEATH

You will come in any case—so why not now?
I am waiting for you—I can't stand much more.
I've put out the light and opened the door
For you, so simple and miraculous.
So come in any form you please,
Burst in as a gas shell
Or, like a gangster, steal in with a length of pipe,
Or poison me with typhus fumes.
Or be that fairy tale you've dreamed up,[1]
So sickeningly familiar to everyone—
In which I glimpse the top of a pale blue cap[2]
And the house attendant white with fear.
Now it doesn't matter anymore. The Yenisey[3] swirls,
The North Star shines.
And the final horror dims
The blue luster of beloved eyes.

August 19, 1939
Fountain House

9. The date that her son was sentenced to labor camp.
1. A denunciation to the police for imaginary crimes, common during the purges as people hastened to protect themselves by accusing their neighbors.
2. The NKVD (secret police) wore blue caps.
3. A river in Siberia along which there were many prison camps.

IX

Now madness half shadows
My soul with its wing,
And makes it drunk with fiery wine
And beckons toward the black ravine.

And I've finally realized
That I must give in,
Overhearing myself
Raving as if it were somebody else.

And it does not allow me to take
Anything of mine with me
(No matter how I plead with it,
No matter how I supplicate):

Not the terrible eyes of my son—
Suffering turned to stone,
Not the day of the terror,
Not the hour I met with him in prison,

Not the sweet coolness of his hands,
Not the trembling shadow of the lindens,
Not the far-off, fragile sound—
Of the final words of consolation.

May 4, 1940
Fountain House

X

CRUCIFIXION

"Do not weep for Me, Mother,
I am in the grave."

1

A choir of angels sang the praises of that momentous hour,
And the heavens dissolved in fire.
To his Father He said: "Why hast Thou forsaken me!"[4]
And to his Mother: "Oh, do not weep for Me . . ."[5]

1940
Fountain House

4. Jesus' last words from the Cross (Matthew 27.46).
5. These words and the epigraph refer to a line from the Russian Orthodox prayer sung at services on Easter Saturday: "Weep not for Me, Mother, when you look upon the grave." Jesus is comforting Mary with the promise of his resurrection.

2

Mary Magdalene beat her breast and sobbed,
The beloved disciple[6] turned to stone,
But where the silent Mother stood, there
No one glanced and no one would have dared.

1943
Tashkent

Epilogue I

I learned how faces fall,
How terror darts from under eyelids,
How suffering traces lines
Of stiff cuneiform on cheeks,
How locks of ashen-blonde or black
Turn silver suddenly,
Smiles fade on submissive lips
And fear trembles in a dry laugh.
And I pray not for myself alone,
But for all those who stood there with me
In cruel cold, and in July's heat,
At that blind, red wall.

Epilogue II

Once more the day of remembrance[7] draws near.
I see, I hear, I feel you:

The one they almost had to drag at the end,
And the one who tramps her native land no more,

And the one who, tossing her beautiful head,
Said: "Coming here's like coming home."

I'd like to name them all by name,
But the list[8] has been confiscated and is nowhere to be found.

I have woven a wide mantle for them
From their meager, overheard words.

I will remember them always and everywhere,
I will never forget them no matter what comes.

And if they gag my exhausted mouth
Through which a hundred million scream,

6. The apostle John.
7. In the Russian Orthodox Church, a memorial service is held on the anniversary of a death.
8. Of prisoners.

Then may the people remember me
On the eve of my remembrance day.

And if ever in this country
They decide to erect a monument to me,

I consent to that honor
Under these conditions—that it stand

Neither by the sea, where I was born:
My last tie with the sea is broken,

Nor in the tsar's garden near the cherished pine stump,[9]
Where an inconsolable shade[1] looks for me,

But here, where I stood for three hundred hours,
And where they never unbolted the doors for me.

This, lest in blissful death
I forget the rumbling of the Black Marias,

Forget how that detested door slammed shut
And an old woman howled like a wounded animal.

And may the melting snow stream like tears
From my motionless lids of bronze,

And a prison dove coo in the distance,
And the ships of the Neva sail calmly on.

March 1940

1963

9. The gardens and park surrounding the summer palace in Tsarskoe Selo. Akhmatova writes elsewhere of the stump of a favorite tree in the gardens and of the poet Pushkin, whom she describes as walking in the park.

1. A ghost; probably the restless spirit of Akhmatova's executed husband, Gumilyov, who had courted her in Tsarskoe Selo.

FEDERICO GARCÍA LORCA

The poet and playwright Federico García Lorca, the best known writer of modern Spain and perhaps the greatest Spanish author since Cervantes, wrote poignantly about death and would himself suffer an early and infamous death. A member of the "Generation of 1927" who sought to revive the grandeur of Spanish poetry, Lorca is known for the striking imagery and lyric musicality of his work, which was both classical and modern, traditional and innovative, difficult and popular, regional and universal. The poetry and plays that began as personal statements took on larger significance, first as the expression of tragic conflicts in Spanish culture and then as poignant laments for humanity—especially the plight of those who are deprived, by society or simply by death, of the fulfillment that could have been theirs.

Lorca (despite the Spanish practice of using both paternal and maternal surnames—correctly, "García Lorca"—the author is generally called "Lorca") was born on June 5, 1898, in the small village of Fuentevaqueros, near the Andalusian city of Granada. He studied law at the University of Granada but left in 1919 for Madrid, where he entered the Residencia de Estudiantes, a college that provided a cosmopolitan education for Spanish youth. Madrid, the capital of Spain, was the center of intellectual and artistic ferment, and the Residencia attracted those who would become the most influential writers and artists of their generation (including the artist Salvador Dalí and the film director Luis Buñuel). Although Lorca lived at the Residencia almost continuously until 1928, he never seriously pursued a degree but spent his time reading, writing, improvising music and poetry with his friends, and producing his first plays.

Lorca's early poems celebrate his home province of Andalusia, a region known for its mixture of Arab and Spanish culture and for a tradition of wandering Gypsy singers who improvised, to guitar accompaniment, rhythmic laments of love and death, often with repetitive refrains such as that in the *Lament for the Death of Ignacio Sánchez Mejías*. Impelled by an emotional crisis, Lorca left Spain for New York in 1929 and there wrote a series of poems later published as *Poet in New York* (1940). Along with the familiar themes of doomed love and death is Lorca's tentative exploration of his homosexuality, which he could not reveal in conservative Spanish society and which, in this and later works, announced itself only with hesitation and anxiety. He traveled to Argentina, where he befriended the Chilean poet **Pablo Neruda**. From 1930 to his death, Lorca was active in the theater both as a writer and as a director of a traveling theatrical group (La Barraca) subsidized by the Spanish Republic. After a series of farces that mixed romantically tragic and comic themes, he presented the tragedies for which he is best known: *Blood Wedding* (1933) and *Yerma* (1934). All of Lorca's theater work rejects the conventionally realistic nineteenth-century drama, employing an openly poetic form that suggests musical patterns, with choruses, songs, and stylized movement.

Lorca published his *Lament for the Death of Ignacio Sánchez Mejías* in

1935. This long poem commemorates the death of a good friend, a famous toreador who was gored by a bull on August 11, 1934, and died two days later. Lorca's *Lament* celebrates both his friend and the value of human grace and courage in a world in which death is inevitable.

Lorca's *Lament*, cast as an elegy (a poem that mourns a death), recalls one of the most famous poems of Spanish literature: the *Verses on the Death of His Father*, by the late-medieval poet Jorge Manrique (1440–1479). Yet there is a fundamental difference between the two: while Manrique's elegy stresses religious themes and the prospect of eternal life, Lorca—in grim contrast—rejects such consolation and insists that his friend's death is permanent.

The four parts of the *Lament* incorporate diverse forms and perspectives, all working together to suggest a progression from the report of death in the first line—"At five in the afternoon"—to the close, where the dead man's nobility and elegance survive in "a sad breeze among the olive trees." The insistent refrain colors the first section, "Goring and Death," with its throbbing return to the moment of death. The scene in the arena wavers between objective reporting—the boy with the shroud, the coffin on wheels—and the shared agony of the bull's bellowing and wounds burning like suns. In the second section, the speaker refuses to accept his friend's death ("I don't want to see it!") and requests that images of whiteness cover up the spilled blood; he imagines Ignacio climbing steps in pursuit of a mystic meeting with his true self and instead, bewildered, encountering his own broken body. After paying his friend tribute, the speaker admits what he cannot force himself to envision: the finality of decay as moss and grass invade the bullfighter's buried skull.

At the end of section 3, the speaker accepts physical death ("The sea, too, dies") but signals in the rhythmic free verse of the final section that his poetry will preserve a vision of his noble countryman against complete obliteration. In life, Sánchez Mejías was known to his friends for the "ripe gleam of your wisdom. / Your appetite for death and the taste of its mouth." These qualities survive in memory. Echoing the pride with which the Latin poet Horace claimed to perpetuate his subjects in a "monument of lasting bronze," Lorca sings of his friend "for the future" and captures, in his poem, the death and life of Sánchez Mejías.

On August 16, 1936, shortly after the outbreak of the Spanish Civil War, when right-wing troops led by General Francisco Franco, with support from the Catholic Church, attacked the young Spanish Republic, and almost precisely two years after the death of Sánchez Mejías, Lorca was dragged from a friend's house by a squadron of Franco's fascist guards; three days later he was killed. Unlike that of his friend Ignacio, his body was never recovered. Lorca's murder, commemorated in Pablo Neruda's poem "**I'm Explaining a Few Things**," outraged the European and American literary and artistic community; it seemed to symbolize the mindless destruction of humane values that loomed with the approach of World War II.

Lament for the Death of Ignacio Sánchez Mejías[1]

1. Goring and Death

At five in the afternoon.
It was five sharp in the afternoon.
A boy brought the white sheet
at five in the afternoon.
A basket of lime[2] already set
at five in the afternoon.
The rest was death and only death
at five in the afternoon.

The wind swept away the cotton[3]
at five in the afternoon.
And rust planted crystal and nickel
at five in the afternoon.
Now the struggle of leopard and dove[4]
at five in the afternoon.
And a thigh with a desolate horn
at five in the afternoon.
And so began the bass notes
at five in the afternoon.
The arsenic bells[5] and the smoke
at five in the afternoon.

On the corners groups of silence
at five in the afternoon.
And the bull alone with heart on high
at five in the afternoon.
When the sweat of snow arrived
at five in the afternoon,
when the bullring filled with iodine[6]
at five in the afternoon,
death laid eggs in the wound
at five in the afternoon.
At five in the afternoon.
At five sharp in the afternoon.

The bed is a coffin on wheels
at five in the afternoon.
Bones and flutes blow in his ear[7]
at five in the afternoon.
The bull bellowed on his brow
at five in the afternoon.

1. Translated by Pablo Medina.
2. A disinfectant to be sprinkled on the body after death.
3. To stop the blood; the beginning of a series of medicinal, chemical, and inhuman images that emphasize the presence of death.
4. Traditional symbols for violence and peace; they struggle with one another as the bullfighter's thigh struggles with the bull's horn.
5. Bells are rung to announce a death. The bass notes of the guitar sound a lament.
6. A blood-colored disinfectant for wounds.
7. A suggestion of the medieval dance of death.

The room[8] iridescent with agony
at five in the afternoon.
Gangrene comes in the distance
at five in the afternoon.
Trumpet of lilies on green[9] groins
at five in the afternoon.
The wounds burned like suns
at five in the afternoon.
and the rabble broke the windows[1]
at five in the afternoon.
Oh, what a terrible five in the afternoon!
It was five on all the clocks.
It was five in shadow of the afternoon.

2. *Spilled Blood*

I don't want to see it!
Tell the moon to come.
I don't want to see
Ignacio's blood on the sand.

I don't want to see it!

The moon fully open,
a horse of quiet clouds
and the gray bullring of sleep
with willows over the barricades.[2]

I don't want to see it!
My memory burns.
Warn the jasmine[3]
to cover its whiteness!

I don't want to see it!

The cow of the old world
stroked a snout of blood
with its sorrowful tongue
and the bulls of Guisando[4]
almost death and almost stone
bellowed like two centuries
tired of walking the land.
No.

I don't want to see it.

8. The room adjoining the arena, where wounded bullfighters are taken for treatment.
9. Gangrene turns flesh a greenish color. "Lilies": the shape of the wound resembles this flower.
1. A Spanish idiom for the crowd's loud roar.
2. The barriers around the ring within which the fight takes place and over which a fighter may escape a charging bull. "Willows": symbols of mourning.
3. A more literal translation is "Notify the jasmines with their little whiteness." The speaker calls on the jasmine to cover the blood he does not want to see.
4. Carved stone bulls from the Celtic past, a tourist attraction in the province of Madrid.

Up the bleachers goes Ignacio[5]
with death on his shoulders.
He looks for dawn
and it isn't dawn.
He looks for his sensible profile
and sleep confuses him.
He looks for his beautiful body
and finds his open blood.
Don't ask me to see it!
I don't want to feel the spurt
growing weaker by the moment,
the spurt that illumines
the seats and spills
on the hide of the thirsty crowd.
Who orders me to look!
Don't make me see it!

His eyes didn't close
when he saw the horns approach,
but the terrible mothers
raised their heads[6]
and all through the cattle ranches[7]
there was an air of secret orders
thrown to celestial bulls
by the foremen of pale mists.
There wasn't a prince in Seville[8]
who could compare,
no sword like his sword
nor a heart so real.
His strength was a river of lions,
his prudence a torso of marble.
An air of Andalusian Rome
gilded his head[9]
where his smile was a rose
of salt and intelligence.
The great fighter of bulls!
The good mountaineer of the mountain![1]
How soft with the wheat stalk!
How hard with his spurs!
How tender with the dew!
How dazzling in the fair!
How grand with the last
banderillas[2] of dusk!

5. An imaginary scene in which the bullfighter mounts the stairs of the arena.
6. The three Fates traditionally raised their heads when the thread of life was cut.
7. Fighting bulls are raised on the ranches of Lorca's home province of Andalusia.
8. Leading city of Andalusia.
9. The image suggests a statue from Roman times, when Andalusia was part of the Roman Empire.
1. Sánchez Mejías is seen as a good *serrano* or "man of the hills."
2. The multicolored short spears that are thrust into the bull's shoulders to provoke him to attack.

But now he sleeps forever.
Now the grass and the moss
open with sure fingers
the flower of his skull.
And his blood comes singing:
singing through marshes and prairies,
sliding down shivering horns,
wandering soulless in fog,
stumbling on thousands of hoofs
like a long, dark, sorrowful tongue
to form a puddle of agony
by the Guadalquivir[3] of the stars.
Oh white wall of Spain!
Oh black bull of sorrow!
Oh hard blood of Ignacio!
Oh nightingale of his veins!
No.
I don't want to see it!
There is no chalice to hold it.
There are no swallows[4] that drink it,
no frost of light to cool it,
no song or deluge of lilies,
no crystal to bathe it in silver.
No.
I don't want to see it!

3. *The Laid-Out Body*[5]

The stone is a forehead where dreams moan
without the curve of water or the frozen cypress.
The stone is a shoulder weighed down by time
with trees of tears and ribbons and planets.[6]

I have seen gray rains race toward the waves
raising their tender bullet-ridden arms
not to be hunted by the horizontal stone
that tears out limbs without soaking up blood.

Because the stone gathers semen and clouds,
skeletons of larks and shadow wolves,

3. A river that passes through all the major cities of Andalusia. The "singing" stream of the bullfighter's blood suggests both the river and a nightingale.
4. According to a Spanish legend of the Crucifixion, swallows—a symbol of innocence—drank the blood of Christ on the Cross. The "chalice" refers to the legend of the Holy Grail, said to have held Christ's blood after the Crucifixion. The poet is seeking ways of concealing the dead man's blood.
5. Or "present body" (literal trans.), the Spanish expression for a funeral wake, when the body is laid out for public mourning. The title contrasts with that of the next section: *Absent Soul*.
6. Traditional funeral imagery carved on gravestones.

yet gives no sound or crystal or fire,
only bullrings and bullrings and other bullrings without walls.

Ignacio the well-born already lies on the stone.
It is over; what's the matter? Look at his figure:
death has covered him with a pale sulfur
and given him the head of a dark minotaur.[7]

It is over. Rain enters his mouth.
The mad wind leaves his sunken chest
and Love, soaked with tears of snow,
suns itself on the hills of the cattle ranches.

What is it they say? A stench-filled silence rests.
We stand before a laid-out body that vanishes,
with a clear form that held the nightingales,
and we see it fill with bottomless holes.

Who wrinkles the shroud? It is not true what they say![8]
No one is singing here, or weeps in the corner,
or uses his spurs or frightens the snake:
all I want here are wide open eyes
to see that body that can never rest.

Here I want to see men of powerful voices.
The breakers of stallions, masters of rivers,
the men whose skeletons rattle
and sing mouthfuls of sun and flint.

I want to see them here. Before the stone.
Before this body with the broken reins.
I want them to show me the way out
for this captain tied to death.

I want them to teach me to weep
like a river of sweet mists and deep shores,
to carry the body of Ignacio, to free him
from the double snorting of the bull.

To lose him in the round bullring of the moon
that feigns like a girl the sorrow of a quiet cow;
to lose him in the night where no fish sing
and in the white thicket of a frozen smoke.

I don't want them to cover his face with handkerchiefs.
Let him live with the death he bears.

7. A monster from Greek myth: half man, half bull.

8. The speaker criticizes the conventional pieties voiced by someone standing close to the shrouded body; he prefers a clear-eyed, realistic view of death.

Go, Ignacio, don't feel the hot bellowing.
Sleep, fly, rest. The sea, too, dies.

4. *Absent Soul*

Neither bull nor fig tree knows you,
not the horses or the ants of your house,
not your mute memory
because you have died forever.

The stone's loin doesn't know you
or the black satin where you shatter.
Your mute memory doesn't know you
because you have died forever.

Autumn will come with its seashells,[9]
its misty grapes, its gathering of hills,
but no one will want to look in your eyes
because you have died forever.

Because you have died forever
like all the dead of the earth,
like all the dead who are forgotten
under a mound of darkened dogs.[1]

No one knows you. No. But I sing to you.
I sing for the future your profile and your grace.
The ripe gleam of your wisdom.
Your appetite for death and the taste of its mouth.
The sadness borne in your valiant joy.

It will take a long time, if at all,
for an Andaluz to be born so clear,
so rich with adventure.
I sing his elegance with a whimper of words
and remember a sad breeze among the olive trees.

1935

9. Horns in the shape of conch shells; the shepherds' horns that sound in the hills each fall as the sheep are driven to new pastures.

1. Dogs as an image for undignified, inferior creatures.

PABLO NERUDA

The son of a railroad worker and a schoolteacher, with both Spanish and Indian ancestry, the Nobel Prize winner Pablo Neruda became Latin America's most important twentieth-century poet, as well as an advocate for social justice and a leading cultural figure on the communist left. He wrote in a variety of styles (lyrical, polemic, objective, and prophetic) on an array of subjects (love, daily life, the natural world, political oppression), evoking the most elemental levels of human emotion and experience. In the second half of his life, moved especially by the Spanish Civil War, Neruda adopted the role of public poet, putting his writing at the service of the people.

The writer was born Neftalí Ricardo Reyes y Basoalto, on July 12, 1904, in the small town of Parral, in southern Chile. His mother died a month after his birth. Two years later his father moved to Temuco, where he remarried and where Neruda had his early schooling. Temuco was a frontier town, and the boy's father, who disapproved of aesthetic pursuits, did not encourage his love of literature. Neruda was fortunate to find a mentor in the poet Gabriela Mistral, the principal of the girls' school at Temuco, who would herself win the Nobel Prize in Literature in 1945. To encourage the young writer, Mistral loaned him books. He began publishing his poetry at age thirteen. Seeking a pen name that would not be tied to the provinces, he chose the surname of a Czech writer, Jan Neruda, and the given name Pablo, which some critics have associated with Saint Paul the apostle.

After working and studying in poverty in Chile's capital, Santiago, from 1921 to 1927, Neruda was appointed the nation's consul to Rangoon, Burma (now Myanmar). He would serve in Ceylon (now Sri Lanka), Java (in Indonesia), and Singapore, and then, after 1933, in Buenos Aires, Barcelona, Madrid, Paris, and Mexico City. During his residence in Spain, Neruda, influenced by his friends the poets **Federico García Lorca**, Rafael Alberti, and Miguel Hernández, assumed a more activist political stance. In 1936, civil war broke out in Spain between the Republic and the forces of General Francisco Franco. Franco's fascist guards dragged Neruda's friend Lorca out of a friend's house; he was presumably shot, but his body was never recovered. (Neruda recalls the event in the poem "I'm Explaining a Few Things.") From that point on, Neruda would be a public poet, dedicating his voice to social issues rather than to private feelings and addressing a larger community.

Neruda returned to Chile in 1943, and, within two years, was elected to the Senate, as a representative of the Communist Party. When he criticized Chile's president in a speech on the Senate floor, Neruda's house was attacked, the government ordered his arrest, and he was forced to flee the country. Though he was celebrated internationally, with official honors from Latin America, the Soviet Union, Europe, India, and China, Neruda nonetheless could not return to Chile until 1952. He retained his close association with the Communist Party and even wrote a poem in praise of the Soviet dictator Joseph Stalin.

In 1970, Neruda ran for president of

Chile as the communist candidate, but he withdrew in favor of the socialist Salvador Allende, who won the election and appointed Neruda ambassador to Paris. In 1971, Neruda received the Nobel Prize for Literature; the following year he returned to his home in Isla Negra, gravely ill with cancer. The news at home was not good: political tensions were mounting, and Neruda watched television coverage of the rising unrest. On September 11, 1973, President Allende was assassinated in a military coup led by General Augusto Pinochet. Neruda died twelve days later. It was at Neruda's funeral that the first public demonstration against Pinochet's military government took place—a fitting tribute to Chile's national poet and representative of the people.

The selections presented here begin with Neruda's beautiful and popular early love poem "Tonight I Can Write . . ." (1924), which makes use of couplets, repetition, and chiasmus (rhetorical inversion) to explore the speaker's evolving consciousness of a love affair. While maintaining the lyrical and personal tone of his earlier poetry, "Walking Around" demonstrates Neruda's turn toward public subject matter—here expressed not in the political terms of his later work but as a description of urban life and the sufferings of the poor. In "I'm Explaining a Few Things" (1936), however, Neruda engages explicitly with politics, and his repeated exhortation, "Come and see the blood in the streets!" illustrates the speaker's intention to address his audience directly and to dedicate his voice to public issues rather than private feelings.

Canto General (1950) celebrates both Latin American identity and humanity at large. It also recreates the continent's history—anchored, for Neruda, especially after a spiritual experience he had in 1943, in the lost Inca city of Macchu Picchu, in Peru. (The usual spelling is "Machu Picchu," but Neruda uses "Macchu" throughout.) On climbing to the city's stone ruins in October of that year, the poet had an almost mystical vision showing the past linked with natural forces and the progress of humanity—a vision he described two years later in the crucial second canto of *Canto General: The Heights of Macchu Picchu*, published as a separate poem in 1946 and only later integrated into the larger work. Its twelve sections (also called cantos) are divided into two broad movements that express several philosophical attitudes and represent a turning point in the poet's thought. Throughout the first five cantos, the speaker struggles with a sense of loss and alienation; but, starting with Canto VI, as he depicts his ascent to Macchu Picchu, he comes to an understanding of a suffering human community that now gives meaning to his hitherto solitary existence. The portion printed here, the second half of *The Heights of Macchu Picchu*, begins with the speaker's invocation of the abandoned city, after climbing to its perch on a precipice in the Andes. He addresses the city as a "mother of stone"—the mother of the Latin American people—and bears witness to a lost civilization. Canto IX consists of a sequence of extraordinary metaphors that portray the city in fused images of nature and daily life—images of the passage of time and of intuited connections that transcend chronology. In Cantos X through XII, the speaker imagines the experience of the people who interest him most: the laborers who built Macchu Picchu and knew hunger and fatigue. Though they are long dead, he senses their voices and memories entering his flesh and blood, as both he and they are reborn in a unity of the people.

The final work here, "Ode to the Tomato" (1954), shows Neruda shifting his poetic style once again, employing an unadorned expression to focus on everyday subject matter. His *Elemental Odes*

(1954) examines such ordinary topics as fire, rain, bread, clothes, bees, and tomatoes. The new simplicity stemmed from Neruda's commitment to his role as public poet; he felt a responsibility to write for a broader audience, he said, including those who were just learning to read. "We must go back to what is simply human," he said; the joyous "Ode to the Tomato" responds to this need.

Tonight I Can Write . . .[1]

Tonight I can write the saddest lines.

Write, for example, 'The night is shattered
and the blue stars shiver in the distance.'

The night wind revolves in the sky and sings.

Tonight I can write the saddest lines.
I loved her, and sometimes she loved me too.

Through nights like this one I held her in my arms.
I kissed her again and again under the endless sky.

She loved me, sometimes I loved her too.
How could one not have loved her great still eyes.

Tonight I can write the saddest lines.
To think that I do not have her. To feel that I have lost her.

To hear the immense night, still more immense without her.
And the verse falls to the soul like dew to the pasture.

What does it matter that my love could not keep her.
The night is shattered and she is not with me.

This is all. In the distance someone is singing. In the distance.
My soul is not satisfied that it has lost her.

My sight searches for her as though to go to her.
My heart looks for her, and she is not with me.

The same night whitening the same trees.
We, of that time, are no longer the same.

I no longer love her, that's certain, but how I loved her.
My voice tried to find the wind to touch her hearing.

1. Translated by W. S. Merwin.

Another's. She will be another's. Like my kisses before.
Her voice. Her bright body. Her infinite eyes.

I no longer love her, that's certain, but maybe I love her.
Love is so short, forgetting is so long.

Because through nights like this one I held her in my arms
my soul is not satisfied that it has lost her.

Though this be the last pain that she makes me suffer
and these the last verses that I write for her.

1924

Walking Around[1]

It happens that I am tired of being a man.
It happens that I go into the tailors' shops and the movies
all shrivelled up, impenetrable, like a felt swan
navigating on a water of origin and ash.

The smell of barber shops makes me sob out loud.
I want nothing but the repose either of stones or of wool,
I want to see no more establishments, no more gardens,
nor merchandise, nor glasses, nor elevators.

It happens that I am tired of my feet and my nails
and my hair and my shadow.
It happens that I am tired of being a man.

Just the same it would be delicious
to scare a notary with a cut lily
or knock a nun stone dead with one blow of an ear.

It would be beautiful
to go through the streets with a green knife
shouting until I died of cold.

I do not want to go on being a root in the dark,
hesitating, stretched out, shivering with dreams,
downwards, in the wet tripe of the earth,
soaking it up and thinking, eating every day.

I do not want to be the inheritor of so many misfortunes.
I do not want to continue as a root and as a tomb,
as a solitary tunnel, as a cellar full of corpses,
stiff with cold, dying with pain.

1. Translated by W. S. Merwin.

For this reason Monday burns like oil
at the sight of me arriving with my jail-face,
and it howls in passing like a wounded wheel,
and its footsteps towards nightfall are filled with hot blood.

And it shoves me along to certain corners, to certain damp houses,
to hospitals where the bones come out of the windows,
to certain cobblers' shops smelling of vinegar,
to streets horrendous as crevices.

There are birds the colour of sulphur, and horrible intestines
hanging from the doors of the houses which I hate,
there are forgotten sets of teeth in a coffee-pot,
there are mirrors
which should have wept with shame and horror,
there are umbrellas all over the place, and poisons, and navels.

I stride along with calm, with eyes, with shoes,
with fury, with forgetfulness,
I pass, I cross offices and stores full of orthopaedic appliances,
and courtyards hung with clothes on wires,
underpants, towels and shirts which weep
slow dirty tears.

1933

I'm Explaining a Few Things[1]

You are going to ask: and where are the lilacs?
and the poppy-petalled metaphysics?
and the rain repeatedly spattering
its words and drilling them full
of apertures and birds?

I'll tell you all the news.

I lived in a suburb,
a suburb of Madrid,[2] with bells,
and clocks, and trees.

From there you could look out
over Castile's[3] dry face:
a leather ocean.
My house was called
the house of flowers, because in every cranny

1. Translated by Nathaniel Tarn.
2. The capital of Spain.
3. Spain.

geraniums burst: it was
a good-looking house
with its dogs and children.
                    Remember, Raúl?
Eh, Rafael?
          Federico,[4] do you remember
from under the ground
my balconies on which
the light of June drowned flowers in your mouth?
                              Brother, my brother!
Everything
loud with big voices, the salt of merchandises,
pile-ups of palpitating bread,
the stalls of my suburb of Argüelles with its statue
like a drained inkwell in a swirl of hake:[5]
oil flowed into spoons,
a deep baying
of feet and hands swelled in the streets,
metres, litres, the sharp
measure of life,
          stacked-up fish,
the texture of roofs with a cold sun in which
the weather vane falters,
the fine, frenzied ivory of potatoes,
wave on wave of tomatoes rolling down to the sea.

And one morning all that was burning,
one morning the bonfires
leapt out of the earth
devouring human beings—
and from then on fire,
gunpowder from then on,
and from then on blood.
Bandits with planes and Moors,
bandits with finger-rings and duchesses,
bandits with black friars[6] spattering blessings
came through the sky to kill children
and the blood of children ran through the streets
without fuss, like children's blood.

Jackals that the jackals would despise,
stones that the dry thistle would bite on and spit out,
vipers that the vipers would abominate!

4. I.e., the poet Federico García Lorca, who was murdered by the Fascists on August 19, 1936. "Rafael": his friend, the poet Rafael Alberti.

5. A fish similar to the cod. "Argüelles": a busy shopping area in Madrid, near the university.

6. "Finger-rings," "duchesses," "friars" imply a collusion of the wealthy, the aristocracy, and the church to suppress the people. "Bandits": Neruda lists categories of invaders. "Moors": probably an analogy between the early Muslim invaders of Spain and German and Italian pilots who bombed the village of Guernica in April 1937.

Face to face with you I have seen the blood
of Spain tower like a tide
to drown you in one wave
of pride and knives!

Treacherous
generals:
see my dead house,
look at broken Spain:
from every house burning metal flows
instead of flowers,
from every socket of Spain
Spain emerges
and from every dead child a rifle with eyes,
and from every crime bullets are born
which will one day find
the bull's eye of your hearts.

And you will ask: why doesn't his poetry
speak of dreams and leaves
and the great volcanoes of his native land?

Come and see the blood in the streets.
Come and see
the blood in the streets.
Come and see the blood
in the streets!

1936

General Song (Canto General)[1]

From *Canto II. The Heights of Macchu Picchu*[2]

VI

And so I scaled the ladder of the earth
amid the atrocious maze of lost jungles
up to you, Macchu Picchu.
High citadel of terraced stones,
at long last the dwelling of him whom the earth
did not conceal in its slumbering vestments.
In you, as in two parallel lines,
the cradle of lightning and man
was rocked in a wind of thorns.

1. Translated by Jack Schmitt.
2. Ancient city of the Incas, situated on a remote precipice in the Andes mountains of Peru; the city escaped the Spanish invaders and was rediscovered in 1911. The Inca empire flourished in the 14th century and was destroyed by Francisco Pizarro in 1532.

Mother of stone, sea spray of the condors.

Towering reef of the human dawn.

Spade lost in the primal sand.

This was the dwelling, this is the site:
here the full kernels of corn rose
and fell again like red hailstones.
Here the golden fiber emerged from the vicuña[3]
to clothe love, tombs, mothers,
the king, prayers, warriors.

Here man's feet rested at night
beside the eagle's feet, in the high gory
retreats, and at dawn
they trod the rarefied mist with feet of thunder
and touched lands and stones
until they recognized them in the night or in death.

I behold vestments and hands,
the vestige of water in the sonorous void,
the wall tempered by the touch of a face
that beheld with my eyes the earthen lamps,
that oiled with my hands the vanished
wood: because everything—clothing, skin, vessels,
words, wine, bread—
is gone, fallen to earth.

And the air flowed with orange-blossom
fingers over all the sleeping:
a thousand years of air, months, weeks of air,
of blue wind, of iron cordillera,[4]
like gentle hurricanes of footsteps
polishing the solitary precinct of stone.

VII

O remains of a single abyss, shadows of one gorge—
the deep one—the real, most searing death
attained the scale
of your magnitude,
and from the quarried stones,
from the spires,
from the terraced aqueducts
you tumbled as in autumn

3. A llama-like animal, found in the Andes, that has a fine soft fleece.

4. Mountain range.

to a single death.
Today the empty air no longer weeps,
no longer knows your feet of clay,
has now forgotten your pitchers that filtered the sky
when the lightning's knives emptied it,
and the powerful tree was eaten away
by the mist and felled by the wind.
It sustained a hand that fell suddenly
from the heights to the end of time.
You are no more, spider hands, fragile
filaments, spun web:
all that you were has fallen: customs, frayed
syllables, masks of dazzling light.
But a permanence of stone and word:
the citadel was raised like a chalice in the hands
of all, the living, the dead, the silent, sustained
by so much death, a wall, from so much life a stroke
of stone petals: the permanent rose, the dwelling:
this Andean reef of glacial colonies.

When the clay-colored hand
turned to clay, when the little eyelids closed,
filled with rough walls, brimming with castles,
and when the entire man was trapped in his hole,
exactitude remained hoisted aloft:
this high site of the human dawn:
the highest vessel that has contained silence:
a life of stone after so many lives.

VIII

Rise up with me, American[5] love.

Kiss the secret stones with me.
The torrential silver of the Urubamba[6]
makes the pollen fly to its yellow cup.
It spans the void of the grapevine,
the petrous plant, the hard wreath
upon the silence of the highland casket.
Come, minuscule life, between the wings
of the earth, while—crystal and cold, pounded air
extracting assailed emeralds—
O, wild water, you run down from the snow.

Love, love, even the abrupt night,
from the sonorous Andean flint

5. For Neruda (and for many Latin Americans), *America* refers to Latin America; North America is called "Saxon America."

6. The river flowing through the valley below Macchu Picchu, called Wilkamayu by the Indians.

Futurism, a modernist movement centered in Italy in the early twentieth century, focused on the technologies and dynamism of modern life. This photograph (*Dattilografa*, 1913) by Anton Giulio Bragaglia (1890–1960) captures the spirit of the futurist movement perfectly, portraying writing as an energetic and technology-enhanced activity.

The Reader (Woman in Grey), 1920, an oil painting by the twentieth-century's most

Soviet propaganda poster, 1921. The text reads, "From the gloom to the light; from battle to books; from grief to happiness."

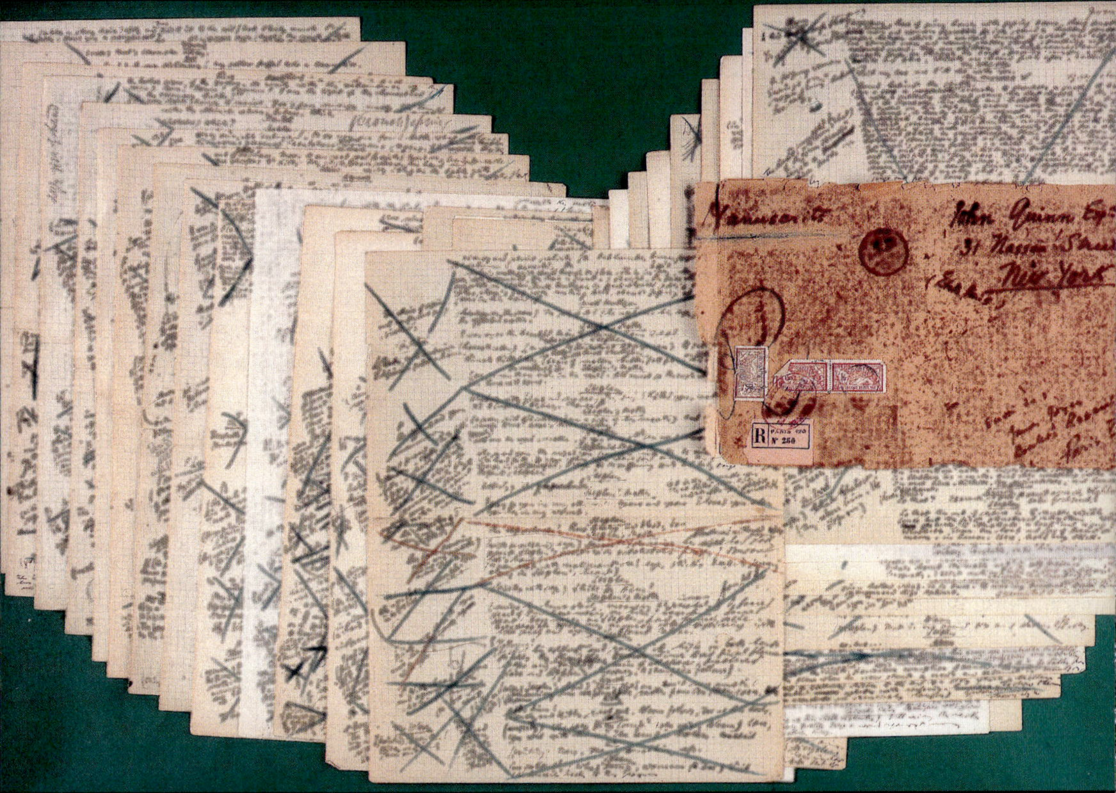

Manuscript pages—heavily marked with corrections and additions—from the "Circe" chapter of James Joyce's novel *Ulysses* (1922).

Portrait of Virginia Woolf (1882–1941) taken in 1902, and a page from Woolf's draft notebook for her novel *Mrs. Dalloway* (1925). Surveying the history of literature and finding so few women, Woolf had this to say in *A Room of One's Own* (1929): "I would venture to guess that Anon, who wrote so many poems without signing them, was often a woman."

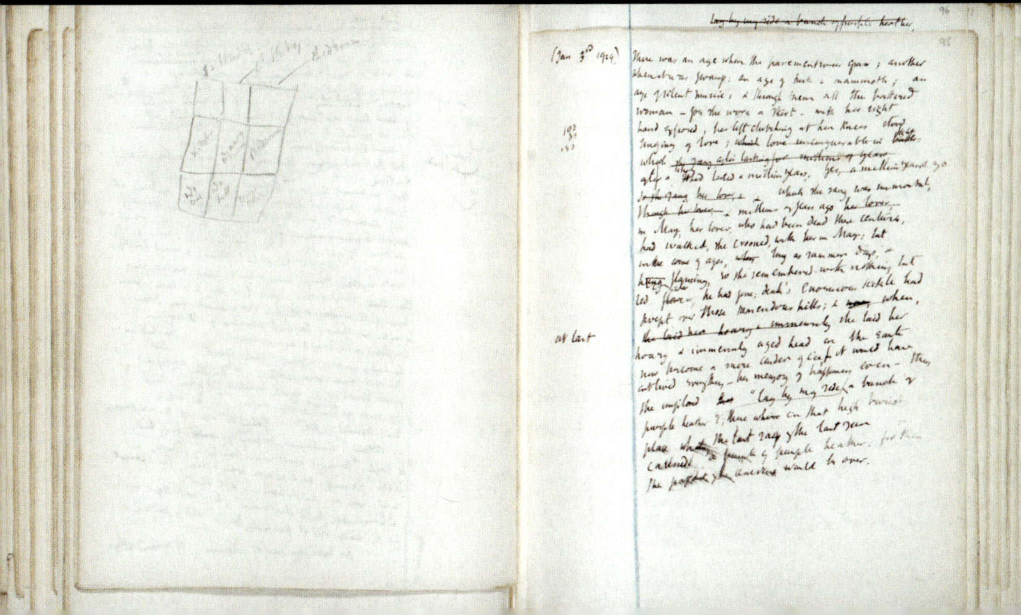

The Nigerian author Chinua Achebe (born 1930), photographed in 1960 holding two editions of his book *Things Fall Apart* (1958), which would become the most widely read and respected African novel in English.

Participants in a 2010 calligraphy contest in the city of Xian, Shanxi Province, China.

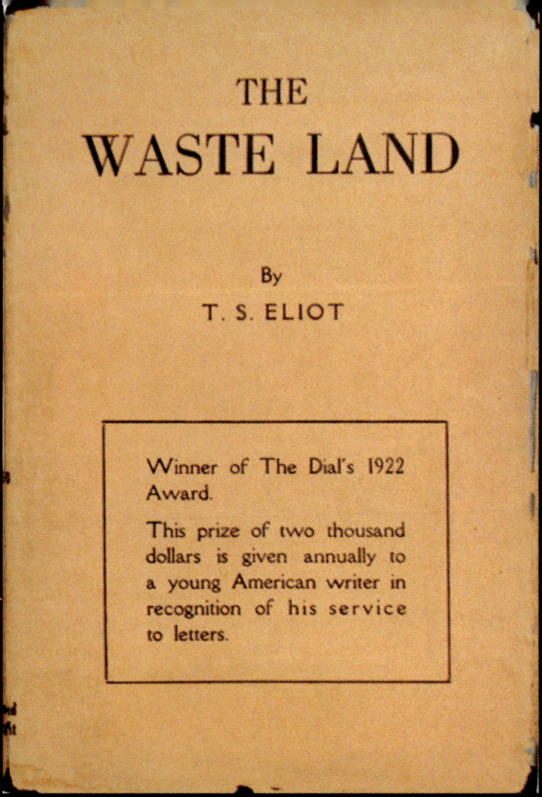

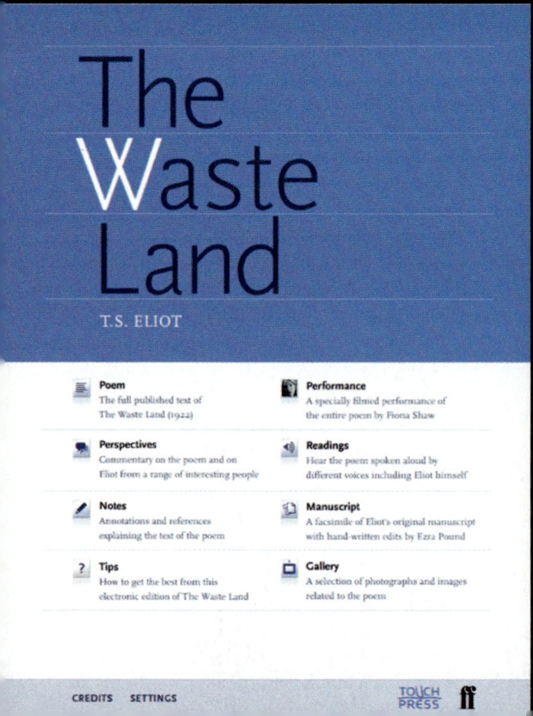

The cover of the first American edition of T. S. Eliot's modernist masterpiece, *The Waste Land*, published in 1922, and the opening menu of an ebook/app version of the poem, released in 2011. Clearly, the new media and technologies of the twenty-first century will change the way we read and experience poetry, drama, fiction, and other writing. But in what ways? How quickly?

to the dawn's red knees,
contemplates the snow's blind child.

O, sonorous threaded Wilkamayu,
when you beat your lineal thunder
to a white froth, like wounded snow,
when your precipitous storm
sings and batters, awakening the sky,
what language do you bring to the ear recently
wrenched from your Andean froth?

Who seized the cold's lightning
and left it shackled in the heights,
dispersed in its glacial tears,
smitten in its swift swords,
hammering its embattled stamens,
borne on its warrior's bed,
startled in its rocky end?

What are your tormented sparks saying?
Did your secret insurgent lightning
once journey charged with words?
Who keeps on shattering frozen syllables,
black languages, golden banners,
deep mouths, muffled cries,
in your slender arterial waters?

Who keeps on cutting floral eyelids
that come to gaze from the earth?
Who hurls down the dead clusters
that fell in your cascade hands
to strip the night stripped
in the coal of geology?

Who flings the branch down from its bonds?
Who once again entombs farewells?

Love, love, never touch the brink
or worship the sunken head:
let time attain its stature
in its salon of shattered headsprings,
and, between the swift water and the walls,
gather the air from the gorge,
the parallel sheets of the wind,
the cordilleras' blind canal,
the harsh greeting of the dew,
and, rise up, flower by flower, through the dense growth,
treading the hurtling serpent.

In the steep zone—forest and stone,
mist of green stars, radiant jungle—

Mantur explodes like a blinding lake
or a new layer of silence.

Come to my very heart, to my dawn,
up to the crowned solitudes.
The dead kingdom is still alive.

And over the Sundial the sanguinary shadow
of the condor[7] crosses like a black ship.

IX

Sidereal eagle, vineyard of mist.
Lost bastion, blind scimitar.
Spangled waistband, solemn bread.
Torrential stairway, immense eyelid.
Triangular tunic, stone pollen.
Granite lamp, stone bread.
Mineral serpent, stone rose.
Entombed ship, stone headspring.
Moonhorse, stone light.
Equinoctial square, stone vapor.
Ultimate geometry, stone book.
Tympanum fashioned amid the squalls.
Madrepore[8] of sunken time.
Rampart tempered by fingers.
Ceiling assailed by feathers.
Mirror bouquets, stormy foundations.
Thrones toppled by the vine.
Regime of the enraged claw.
Hurricane sustained on the slopes.
Immobile cataract of turquoise.
Patriarchal bell of the sleeping.
Hitching ring of the tamed snows.
Iron recumbent upon its statues.
Inaccessible dark tempest.
Puma hands, bloodstained rock.
Towering sombrero, snowy dispute.
Night raised on fingers and roots.
Window of the mists, hardened dove.
Nocturnal plant, statue of thunder.
Essential cordillera, searoof.
Architecture of lost eagles.
Skyrope, heavenly bee.

7. The heights of Macchu Picchu and the smaller Huayna Picchu were said to form the shape of a condor, a large vulturelike bird seen as the messenger of humanity. "Sundial": the *intihuatana*, or "hitching post of the sun," a large altar carved directly out of the granite; its shape and position served to predict the date of the winter solstice and other periods of importance to agriculture.

8. Coral.

Bloody level, man-made star.
Mineral bubble, quartz moon.
Andean serpent, brow of amaranth.[9]
Cupola of silence, pure land.
Seabride, tree of cathedrals.
Cluster of salt, black-winged cherry tree.
Snow-capped teeth, cold thunderbolt.
Scored moon, menacing stone.
Headdresses of the cold, action of the air.
Volcano of hands, obscure cataract.
Silver wave, pointer of time.

X

Stone upon stone, and man, where was he?
Air upon air, and man, where was he?
Time upon time, and man, where was he?
Were you too a broken shard
of inconclusive man, of empty raptor,
who on the streets today, on the trails,
on the dead autumn leaves, keeps
tearing away at the heart right up to the grave?
Poor hand, foot, poor life . . .
Did the days of light
unraveled in you, like raindrops
on the banners of a feast day,
give petal by petal of their dark food
to the empty mouth?
                                        Hunger, coral of mankind,
hunger, secret plant, woodcutters' stump,
hunger, did the edge of your reef rise up
to these high suspended towers?

I want to know, salt of the roads,
show me the spoon—architecture, let me
scratch at the stamens of stone with a little stick,
ascend the rungs of the air up to the void,
scrape the innards until I touch mankind.

Macchu Picchu, did you put
stone upon stone and, at the base, tatters?
Coal upon coal and, at the bottom, tears?
Fire in gold and, within it, the trembling
drop of red blood?
Bring me back the slave that you buried!
Shake from the earth the hard bread
of the poor wretch, show me

9. An annual plant with flowers and highly nutritious edible seeds.

the slave's clothing and his window.
Tell me how he slept when he lived.
Tell me if his sleep was
harsh, gaping, like a black chasm
worn by fatigue upon the wall.
The wall, the wall! If upon his sleep
each layer of stone weighed down, and if he fell beneath it
as beneath a moon, with his dream!
Ancient America, sunken bride,
your fingers too,
on leaving the jungle for the high void of the gods,
beneath the nuptial standards of light and decorum,
mingling with the thunder of drums and spears,
your fingers, your fingers too,
which the abstract rose, the cold line, and
the crimson breast of the new grain transferred
to the fabric of radiant substance, to the hard cavities—
did you, entombed America, did you too store in the depths
of your bitter intestine, like an eagle, hunger?

XI

Through the hazy splendor,
through the stone night, let me plunge my hand,
and let the aged heart of the forsaken beat in me
like a bird captive for a thousand years!
Let me forget, today, this joy, which is greater than the sea,
because man is greater than the sea and its islands,
and we must fall into him as into a well to emerge from the bottom
with a bouquet of secret water and sunken truths.
Let me forget, great stone, the powerful proportion,
the transcendent measure, the honeycombed stones,
and from the square let me today run
my hand over the hypotenuse of rough blood and sackcloth.
When, like a horseshoe of red elytra,[1] the frenzied condor
beats my temples in the order of its flight,
and the hurricane of cruel feathers sweeps the somber dust
from the diagonal steps, I do not see the swift brute,
I do not see the blind cycle of its claws,
I see the man of old, the servant, asleep in the fields,
I see a body, a thousand bodies, a man, a thousand women,
black with rain and night, beneath the black squall,
with the heavy stone of the statue:
Juan Stonecutter, son of Wiracocha[2]
Juan Coldeater, son of a green star,
Juan Barefoot, grandson of turquoise,
rise up to be born with me, my brother.

1. An insect's wing cases.
2. Inca rain god who taught the arts of civilization to humanity.

XII

Rise up to be born with me, my brother.

Give me your hand from the deep
zone of your disseminated sorrow.
You'll not return from the bottom of the rocks.
You'll not return from subterranean time.
Your stiff voice will not return.
Your drilled eyes will not return.
Behold me from the depths of the earth,
laborer, weaver, silent herdsman:
tamer of the tutelary guanacos:[3]
mason of the defied scaffold:
bearer of the Andean tears:
jeweler with your fingers crushed:
tiller trembling in the seed:
potter spilt in your clay:
bring to the cup of this new life, brothers,
all your timeless buried sorrows.
Show me your blood and your furrow,
tell me: I was punished here,
because the jewel did not shine or the earth
did not surrender the gemstone or kernel on time:
show me the stone on which you fell
and the wood on which you were crucified,
strike the old flintstones,
the old lamps, the whips sticking
throughout the centuries to your wounds
and the war clubs glistening red.
I've come to speak through your dead mouths.
Throughout the earth join all
the silent scattered lips
and from the depths speak to me all night long,
as if I were anchored with you,
tell me everything, chain by chain,
link by link, and step by step,
sharpen the knives that you've kept,
put them in my breast and in my hand,
like a river of yellow lightning,
like a river of buried jaguars,
and let me weep hours, days, years,
blind ages, stellar centuries.

Give me silence, water, hope.

Give me struggle, iron, volcanoes.

3. Reddish-brown grazing animals related to the llama.

Cling to my body like magnets.

Hasten to my veins and to my mouth.

Speak through my words and my blood.

1950

Ode to the Tomato[1]

The street
drowns in tomatoes:
noon,
summer,
light
breaks
in two
tomato
halves,
and the streets
run
with juice.
In December[2]
the tomato
cuts loose,
invades
kitchens,
takes over lunches,
settles
at rest
on sideboards,
with the glasses,
butter dishes,
blue salt-cellars.
It has
its own radiance,
a goodly majesty.
Too bad we must
assassinate:
a knife
plunges
into its living pulp,
red
viscera,
a fresh,

1. Translated by Nathaniel Tarn.

2. Summer in Chile.

deep,
inexhaustible
sun
floods the salads
of Chile,
beds cheerfully
with the blonde onion,
and to celebrate
oil
the filial essence
of the olive tree
lets itself fall
over its gaping hemispheres,
the pimento
adds
its fragrance,
salt its magnetism—
we have the day's
wedding:
parsley
flaunts
its little flags,
potatoes
thump to a boil,
the roasts
beat
down the door
with their aromas:
it's time!
let's go!
and upon
the table,
belted by summer,
tomatoes,
stars of the earth,
stars multiplied
and fertile
show off
their convolutions,
canals
and plenitudes
and the abundance
boneless,
without husk,
or scale or thorn,
grant us
the festival
of ardent colour
and all-embracing freshness.

1954

AIMÉ CÉSAIRE

Aimé Césaire has been called "Poet of the Black Diaspora." The title draws attention to the bitter historical experience of the black population of the New World, especially in the Caribbean—its uprooting, transplantation, and enslavement in America. This collective experience has profoundly influenced Césaire's subjects and themes: his poetry often works through the repercussions of slavery, both as a historical predicament and as a personal drama.

Césaire was born on June 26, 1913, at Basse-Pointe, in northern Martinique, the second child in a family of modest means. His father was a junior functionary of the French colonial administration; his mother, a dressmaker. The legacy of slavery weighed heavily on the black population in the highly stratified society of colonial Martinique, exerting a pressure that the young Césaire could not have escaped. Beyond this, Césaire's earliest impressions were shaped by the landscape of his birthplace, the moody ocean and abundant tropical vegetation near the volcano Mont Pelée. These surroundings would furnish significant elements of his imaginative universe.

Césaire received his primary schooling at Basse-Pointe, then went for his secondary education to the colony's capital, Fort-de-France, where he attended the Lycée Schoelcher (named after the prominent French abolitionist). After obtaining his *baccalauréat* (high school diploma) in 1931, he received a scholarship to continue his studies in France. Shortly after his arrival in Paris that year, and his enrollment in a preparatory class for the elite École Normale Supérieure, he met Léopold Sédar Senghor, with whom Césaire formed a lasting friendship. Through the close collaboration of the two men over the next few years, what came to be known as the Négritude ("blackness") movement developed. The term itself, which denotes a sense of common destiny and collective racial identity and culture among black peoples the world over, was coined by Césaire and first appeared in print in 1939 in his celebrated poem, *Notebook of a Return to the Native Land*, which remains his best-known work.

"When I met Senghor," Césaire later remarked, "I knew I was an African." By introducing Césaire to aspects of African civilization that formed Senghor's own background, Senghor helped to free his friend from the negative associations that Africa held for West Indians of his generation. The two men became intellectual companions, with a passion for Africa. Together they read and discussed the ethnographic literature that appeared during this period, which emphasized the coherence of African social systems and the value of the continent's indigenous cultures. In these works, Césaire encountered a positive image of Africa that enabled him to identify with his ancestors' homeland and to accept himself as a black person.

Césaire's relationship with Senghor was part of a black awakening that was already under way during the years between the world wars. In the United States the activities of W. E. B. Du Bois had given concrete form to the idea of

Pan-Africanism as a movement of solidarity concerned with the bleak situation of black people both in America and in Africa. By the time Césaire arrived in Paris, a strong anticolonial sentiment had developed among African and Caribbean students and intellectuals. The new militancy can be attributed to several factors. Foremost among them was a political, social, and cultural malaise, resulting from the First World War, that undermined the claim of Western civilization to moral superiority, a claim consistently used in justifying the colonial enterprise. Another factor was the rise of socialism, with its explicit challenge to imperialism. Finally, there was the Harlem Renaissance, at its height in the 1920s, which had introduced a decidedly affirmative note into black American literature.

The revolution of consciousness among French-speaking black intellectuals encouraged Césaire and Senghor to create works that questioned the premises on which colonial ideology was based. This they did through the journal *L'Étudiant noir* (*The Black Student*), founded in 1935 by a group of West Indian and African students. *L'Étudiant noir* had a pronounced Pan-African orientation, aiming to draw connections between peoples throughout Africa and the African diaspora, as well as to affirm what Césaire termed, in an article in the journal, "the primacy of self."

Césaire entered the École Normale Supérieure in 1935, and within two years earned the equivalent of a master's degree, writing a thesis on the South in black literature of the United States. He also began to write poetry and was especially drawn to the work of the surrealists, in particular **André Breton**, whose aesthetic of spontaneous expression held special appeal for Césaire. Surrealism offered not only a modern poetic idiom but also an instrument for sounding the depths of his consciousness and releasing the tension created by the conflict between his European training and what he considered to be his authentic, African self.

In the early stages of the Second World War, Césaire returned to Martinique. Within a short time, the German invasion of France was followed by the creation of the Vichy regime, which quickly established its control over the island colony and pursued authoritarian and racist policies. In response to this somber atmosphere, Césaire collaborated with his wife, Suzanne Roussi, and a few colleagues to found the journal *Tropiques* (*Tropics*), which examined the social and psychological problems of the island people. Césaire also taught in his old high school, where one of his students was the future theorist of colonialism Frantz Fanon. After the war, Césaire entered Martinican politics. He was elected mayor of Fort-de-France and deputy for Martinique in the French National Assembly, positions he held for almost half a century. (Unlike many colonies, Martinique remains politically part of France, an overseas department with representation in the National Assembly.) He originally ran for deputy as a representative of the French Communist Party, but left the party in 1956 to protest the Soviet suppression of the Hungarian revolt against communism. Subsequently, Césaire founded his own Martinique Progressive Party. When Césaire died in 2008, he received a state funeral in Fort-de-France, with the President of the French Republic in attendance.

While his activities as a leading political figure in his country kept him busy, Césaire, almost accidentally, became an internationally known poet. He began to compose *Notebook of a Return to the Native Land* in autumn 1936 and completed it in time for publication in the journal *Volontés* (*Wills*), in August 1939. Although the poem attracted little attention at the time, it was later to exert major influence in the French-speaking black world and beyond. The first issue of *Tropiques* had just appeared in Paris in April 1941 when Breton, passing through Martinique on his way to voluntary exile in the United States, found a copy in a local bookshop. Its tone and content made such an impression on him that he asked to meet Césaire and his colleagues and thus became acquainted with the first version of *Notebook*, released earlier in Paris. Later, Breton arranged the publication of a revised and expanded edition in volume form, along with an English translation. In the preface of this edition, issued in New York in 1947, he hailed Césaire's poem as "the greatest lyrical monument of the age."

With Breton's active promotion, Césaire's poems appeared in the mid-1940s in surrealist journals and were later collected in various volumes. Césaire's *Discourse on Colonialism* (1950), a vigorous denunciation of the brutal methods of colonial conquest, is often seen as a founding work of postcolonial theory.

Since the poem's republication in volume form, Césaire had been revising *Notebook*, and in 1956 the publishing house Présence Africaine brought out an enlarged, updated version. The poem quickly established itself as the centerpiece of the literature of Négritude. An impassioned statement of the radical sentiments of black peoples about their historical, social, and cultural relation to the Western world, it was also recognized as a masterpiece of modern French poetry, the only long poem in the surrealist tradition, which tends to emphasize compact lyrics. *Notebook* thus belongs to mainstream French literature and to the evolving canon of French-speaking literature in Africa and the Caribbean. Drawing on a long-standing European trope, Césaire relies on the imagery of darkness to indicate both his social status and his moral turmoil as a black man. Its dramatic use of slang and long free-verse paragraphs gives the work an almost biblical power.

The poem's long opening evocation of the physical and moral misery of the Antilles is a crucial step in attaining the self-knowledge the poem reaches toward. But this process also requires realization of a wider humanity, of other peoples also in need of spiritual renewal: "you know that it is not from hatred of other races / that I demand a digger for this unique race / that what I want / is for universal hunger / for universal thirst." Despite the force of its commitment to a collective social and political cause, the poem's enduring significance resides in its apprehension of a realm of transcendental values. The concluding stanzas affirm the interpenetration of the public, the private, and the absolute: the turbulent movement of a people through history mirrors the unfolding of the speaker's personal consciousness into a higher mode of being.

Notebook of a Return to the Native Land[1]

At the end of daybreak . . .

Beat it, I said to him, you cop, you lousy pig, beat it, I detest the flunkies of order and the cockchafers of hope. Beat it, evil grigri,[2] you bedbug of a petty monk. Then I turned toward paradises lost for him and his kin, calmer than the face of a woman telling lies, and there, rocked by the flux of a never exhausted thought I nourished the wind, I unlaced the monsters and heard rise, from the other side of disaster,[3] a river of turtledoves and savanna clover which I carry forever in my depths height-deep as the twentieth floor of the most arrogant houses and as a guard against the putrefying force of crepuscular surroundings, surveyed night and day by a cursed venereal sun.

At the end of daybreak burgeoning with frail coves, the hungry Antilles, the Antilles pitted with smallpox, the Antilles dynamited by alcohol, stranded in the mud of this bay, in the dust of this town sinisterly stranded.

At the end of daybreak, the extreme, deceptive desolate bedsore on the wound of the waters; the martyrs who do not bear witness; the flowers of blood that fade and scatter in the empty wind like the screeches of babbling parrots; an aged life mendaciously smiling, its lips opened by vacated agonies; an aged poverty rotting under the sun, silently; an aged silence bursting with tepid pustules, the awful futility of our raison d'être.[4]

At the end of daybreak, on this very fragile earth thickness exceeded in a humiliating way by its grandiose future—the volcanoes will explode,[5] the naked water will bear away the ripe sun stains and nothing will be left but a tepid bubbling pecked at by sea birds—the beach of dreams and the insane awakenings.

At the end of daybreak, this town sprawled-flat toppled from its common sense, inert, winded under its geometric weight of an eternally renewed cross, indocile to its fate, mute, vexed no matter what, incapable of growing with the juice of this earth, self-conscious, clipped, reduced, in breach of fauna and flora.

At the end of daybreak, this town sprawled flat . . .

And in this inert town, this squalling throng so astonishingly detoured from its cry as this town has been from its movement, from its meaning, not even worried, detoured from its true cry, the only cry you would have

1. Translated by Clayton Eshleman and Annette Smith.
2. Charms.
3. I.e., Africa before the historical disaster of slavery.
4. Reason for being (French, literal trans.).
5. A reference to Mont Pelée, which suddenly erupted in 1902 and destroyed Saint-Pierre, the former capital of Martinique.

wanted to hear because you feel it alone belongs to this town; because you feel it lives in it in some deep refuge and pride in this inert town, this throng detoured from its cry of hunger, of poverty, of revolt, of hatred, this throng so strangely chattering and mute.

In this inert town, this strange throng which does not pack, does not mix: clever at discovering the point of disencasement,[6] of flight, of dodging. This throng which does not know how to throng, this throng, clearly so perfectly alone under this sun, like a woman one thought completely occupied with her lyric cadence, who abruptly challenges a hypothetical rain and enjoins it not to fall; or like a rapid sign of the cross without perceptive motive; or like the sudden grave animality of a peasant, urinating standing, her legs parted, stiff.

In this inert town, this desolate throng under the sun, not connected with anything that is expressed, asserted, released in broad earth daylight, its own. Neither with Josephine, Empress of the French, dreaming way up there above the nigger scum. Nor with the liberator[7] fixed in his whitewashed stone liberation. Nor with the conquistador.[8] Nor with this contempt, with this freedom, with this audacity.

At the end of daybreak, this inert town and its beyond of lepers, of consumption, of famines, of fears squatting in the ravines, fears perched in the trees, fears dug in the ground, fears adrift in the sky, piles of fears and their fumaroles[9] of anguish.

At the end of daybreak, the morne[1] forgotten, forgetful of leaping.

At the end of daybreak, the morne in restless, docile hooves—its malarial blood routs the sun with its overheated pulse.

At the end of daybreak, the restrained conflagration of the morne like a sob gagged on the verge of a bloodthirsty burst, in quest of an ignition that slips away and ignores itself.

At the end of daybreak, the morne crouching before bulimia on the lookout for tuns[2] and mills, slowly vomiting out its human fatigue, the morne solitary and its blood shed, the morne bandaged in shades, the morne and its ditches of fear, the morne and its great hands of wind.

6. The point at which two pieces of machinery can be fitted into each other or disconnected.
7. Victor Schoelcher (1804–1893), French abolitionist, whose statue stands in a square in the capital, Fort-de-France. Josephine (1763–1814), the first wife of Napoléon Bonaparte, was born in Martinique into the white settler class: she became empress when Napoléon took the title "emperor of the French" in 1804.
8. Conqueror (Spanish), applied to Cortés, Pizarro, and other adventurers who conquered South America on behalf of Spain. Here, Bélain d'Estambue, who occupied Martinique in 1635 and claimed it for France.
9. In volcanic regions, ground holes that emit gases and vapors.
1. A little hill or hillock characteristic of Martinican landscape.
2. Casks, in which rum is stored. "Bulimia": here, excessive hunger. The references are to the economic life of the islands, dominated by the production of sugar and the distillation of rum.

At the end of daybreak, the famished morne and no one knows better than this bastard morne why the suicide choked with a little help from his hypoglossal jamming his tongue backward to swallow it;[3] why a woman seems to float belly up on the Capot River[4] (her chiaroscuro body submissively organized at the command of her navel) but she is only a bundle of sonorous water.

And neither the teacher in his classroom, nor the priest at catechism will be able to get a word out of this sleepy little nigger, no matter how energetically they drum on his shorn skull, for starvation has quicksanded his voice into the swamp of hunger (a word-one-single-word and we-will-forget-about-Queen-Blanche-of-Castille,[5] a-word-one-single-word, you-should-see-this-little savage-who-doesn't-know-any-of-The-Ten-Commandments)

for his voice gets lost in the swamp of hunger,
and there is nothing, really nothing to squeeze out of this little brat,
other than a hunger which can no longer climb to the rigging of his voice,
a sluggish flabby hunger,
a hunger buried in the depth of the Hunger of this famished morne.

At the end of daybreak, the disparate stranding,[6] the exacerbated stench of corruption, the monstrous sodomies of the host and the sacrificing priest, the impassable beakhead frames of prejudice and stupidity, the prostitutions, the hypocrisies, the lubricities, the treasons, the lies, the frauds, the concussions—the panting of a deficient cowardice, the heave-holess enthusiasm of supernumerary sahibs,[7] the greeds, the hysterias, the perversions, the clownings of poverty, the cripplings, the itchings, the hives, the tepid hammocks of degeneracy. Right here the parade of laughable and scrofulous buboes, the forced feedings of very strange microbes, the poisons without known alexins, the sanies[8] of really ancient sores, the unforeseeable fermentations of putrescible species.

At the end of daybreak, the great motionless night, the stars deader than a caved-in balafon,[9]

the teratical[1] bulb of night, sprouted from our vilenesses and our renunciations.

And our foolish and crazy stunts to revive the golden splashing of privileged moments, the umbilical cord restored to its ephemeral splendor,

3. Slaves committed suicide by choking on their own tongues. "Hypoglossal": the nerve under the tongue.
4. A stream in northern Martinique. The passage plays on an allusion to Ophelia, in Shakespeare's *Hamlet*, who floats downriver after her suicide by drowning.
5. A queen of France in the Middle Ages.
6. The heterogeneous character of the West Indian population.
7. Lord, commander (Hindi).
8. Fluid from a wound. "Scrofulous buboes": swellings caused by tuberculosis ("scrofula"). "Alexins": antidotes.
9. An African musical instrument similar to a xylophone.
1. Monstrous.

the bread, and the wine of complicity, the bread, the wine, the blood of honest weddings.

And this joy of former times making me aware of my present poverty, a bumpy road plunging into a hollow where it scatters a few shacks; an indefatigable road charging at full speed a morne at the top of which it brutally quicksands into a pool of clumsy houses, a road foolishly climbing, recklessly descending, and the carcass of wood, which I call "our house," comically perched on minute cement paws, its coiffure of corrugated iron in the sun like a skin laid out to dry, the main room, the rough floor where the nail heads gleam, the beams of pine and shadow across the ceiling, the spectral straw chairs, the grey lamp light, the glossy flash of cockroaches in a maddening buzz . . .

At the end of daybreak, this most essential land restored to my gourmandise,[2] not in diffuse tenderness, but the tormented sensual concentration of the fat tits of the mornes with an occasional palm tree as their hardened sprout, the jerky orgasm of torrents and from Trinité to Grand-Rivière,[3] the hysterical grandsuck of the sea.

And time passed quickly, very quickly.
After August and mango trees decked out in all their little moons, September begetter of cyclones, October igniter of sugar-cane, November who purrs in the distilleries, there came Christmas.
It had come in at first, Christmas did, with a tingling of desires, a thirst for new tenderness, a burgeoning of vague dreams, then with a purple rustle of its great joyous wings it had suddenly flown away, and then its abrupt fall out over the village that made the shack life burst like an overripe pomegranate.
Christmas was not like other holidays. It didn't like to gad about the streets,[4] to dance on public squares, to mount the wooden horses, to use the crowd to pinch women, to hurl fireworks in the faces of the tamarind trees. It had agoraphobia,[5] Christmas did. What it wanted was a whole day of bustling, preparing, a cooking and cleaning spree,
endless jitters
about-not-having-enough,
about-running-short,
about-getting-bored,

then at evening an unimposing little church, which would benevolently make room for the laughter, the whispers, the secrets, the love talk, the gossip and the guttural cacophony of a plucky singer and also boisterous pals and shameless hussies and shacks up to their guts in succulent goodies, and not stingy, and twenty people can crowd in, and the street is deserted, and the village turns into a bouquet of singing, and you are cozy in there, and you eat good, and you drink hearty and there are blood sausages, one kind only two fingers wide twined in coils, the other broad

2. Here, keen desire.
3. Towns in northern Martinique.
4. As during Carnival (just before Lent).
5. The fear of open spaces, the opposite of claustrophobia.

and stocky, the mild one tasting of wild thyme, the hot one spiced to an incandescence, and steaming coffee and sugared anise[6] and milk punch, and the liquid sun of rums, and all sorts of good things which drive your taste buds wild or distill them to the point of ecstasy or cocoon them with fragrances, and you laugh, and you sing, and the refrains flare on and on like coco-palms:

ALLELUIA
KYRIE ELEISON[7] . . . LEISON . . . LEISON
CHRISTE ELEISON . . . LEISON . . . LEISON.

And not only do the mouths sing, but the hands, the feet, the buttocks, the genitals, and your entire being liquefies into sounds, voices, and rhythm.

At the peak of its ascent, joy bursts like a cloud. The songs don't stop, but now anxious and heavy roll through the valleys of fear, the tunnels of anguish and the fires of hell.

And each one starts pulling the nearest devil by his tail, until fear imperceptibly fades in the fine sand lines of dream, and you really live as in a dream, and you drink and you shout and you sing as in a dream, and doze too as in a dream, with rose petal eyelids, and the day comes velvety as a sapodilla[8] tree, and the liquid manure smell of the cacao trees, and the turkeys which shell their red pustules[9] in the sun, and the obsessive bells, and the rain,
the bells . . . the rain . . .
that tinkle, tinkle, tinkle . . .

At the end of daybreak, this town sprawled-flat . . .

It crawls on its hands without the slightest desire to drill the sky with a stature of protest. The backs of the houses are afraid of the sky truffled with fire, their feet of the drownings of the soil, they chose to perch shallowly between surprises and treacheries. And yet it advances, the town does. It even grazes every day further out into its tide of tiled corridors, prudish shutters, gluey courtyards, dripping paintwork. And petty hushed-up scandals, petty unvoiced guilts, petty immense hatreds knead the narrow streets into bumps and potholes where the waste-water grins longitudinally through turds . . .

At the end of daybreak, life prostrate, you don't know how to dispose of your aborted dreams, the river of life desperately torpid in its bed, neither turgid nor low, hesitant to flow, pitifully empty, the impartial heaviness of boredom distributing shade equally on all things, the air stagnant, unbroken by the brightness of a single bird.

At the end of daybreak, another little house very bad-smelling in a very narrow street, a minuscule house which harbors in its guts of rotten wood dozens of rats and the turbulence of my six brothers and sisters, a

6. A liqueur made from aniseed.
7. Lord have mercy (Greek); a chant from the first part of the Catholic Mass.
8. A fleshy fruit found in the West Indies.
9. Pimples. The red skin hanging in a fold around the neck of turkeys seems to be covered with them.

cruel little house whose demands panic the ends of our months and my temperamental father gnawed by one persistent ache, I never knew which one, whom an unexpected sorcery could lull to melancholy tenderness or drive to towering flames of anger; and my mother whose legs pedal, pedal, night and day, for our tireless hunger, I was even awakened at night by these tireless legs which pedal the night and the bitter bite in the soft flesh of the night of a Singer[1] that my mother pedals, pedals for our hunger and day and night.

At the end of daybreak, beyond my father, my mother, the shack chapped with blisters, like a peach tree afflicted with curl,[2] and the thin roof patched with pieces of gasoline cans, which create swamps of rust in the stinking sordid grey straw pulp, and when the wind whistles, these odds and ends make a noise bizarre, first like the crackling of frying, then like a brand dropped into water the smoke of its twigs flying up. And the bed of boards from which my race arose, my whole entire race from this bed of boards, with its kerosene case paws, as if it had elephantiasis,[3] that bed, and its kidskin, and its dry banana leaves, and its rags, yearning for a mattress, my grandmother's bed. (Above the bed, in a jar full of oil a dim light whose flame dances like a fat cockroach . . . on the jar in gold letters: MERCI.[4])

And this rue Paille,[5] this disgrace,

an appendage repulsive as the private parts of the village which extends right and left, along the colonial highway, the grey surge of its shingled roofs. Here there are only straw roofs, spray browned and wind plucked.

Everybody despises rue Paille. It's there that the village youth go astray. It's there especially that the sea pours forth its garbage, its dead cats and its croaked dogs. For the street opens on to the beach, and the beach alone cannot satisfy the sea's foaming rage.

A blight this beach as well, with its piles of rotting muck, its furtive rumps relieving themselves, and the sand is black,[6] funereal, you've never seen a sand so black, and the scum glides over it yelping, and the sea pummels it like a boxer, or rather the sea is a huge dog licking and biting the shins of the beach, biting them so fiercely that it will end up devouring it, the beach and rue Paille along with it.

At the end of daybreak, the wind of long ago—of betrayed trusts, of uncertain evasive duty and that other dawn in Europe—arises . . .

To go away.
As there are hyena-men and panther-men, I would be a jew-man[7]

1. An old-model sewing machine that was powered by the movement of the legs.
2. An infection that attacks the leaves of the peach tree.
3. A disease that causes swelling of the legs.
4. Thank you (French); the inscription is presumably addressed to God.
5. Straw Road (French, literal trans.); a street whose houses are roofed with straw.
6. Because of its volcanic origin.
7. Césaire's identification with another persecuted people, extended in the lines below to other minorities.

a Kaffir-man
a Hindu-man-from-Calcutta
a Harlem-man-who-doesn't-vote[8]

the famine man, the insult-man, the torture man you can grab anytime, beat up, kill—no joke, kill—without having to account to anyone, without having to make excuses to anyone
a jew-man
a pogrom[9]-man
a puppy
a beggar
but *can* one kill Remorse, perfect as the stupefied face of an English lady discovering a Hottentot[1] skull in her soup-tureen?

I would rediscover the secret of great communications and great combustions. I would say storm. I would say river. I would say tornado. I would say leaf. I would say tree. I would be drenched by all rains, moistened by all dews. I would roll like frenetic blood on the slow current of the eye of words turned into mad horses into fresh children into clots into curfew into vestiges of temples into precious stones remote enough to discourage miners. Whoever would not understand me would not understand any better the roaring of a tiger.

And you ghosts rise blue from alchemy from a forest of hunted beasts of twisted machines of a jujube tree of rotten flesh of a basket of oysters of eyes of a network of straps in the beautiful sisal[2] of human skin I would have words vast enough to contain you earth taut earth drunk
earth great vulva raised to the sun
earth great delirium of God's mentula[3]
savage earth arisen from the storerooms of the sea a clump of Cecropia[4] in your mouth earth whose tumultuous face I can only compare to the virgin and mad forest which were it in my power I would show in guise of a face to the undeciphering eyes of men all I would need is a mouthful of jiculi milk[5] to discover in you always as distant as a mirage—a thousand times more native and made golden by a sun that no prism divides—the earth where everything is free and fraternal, my earth.

To go away. My heart was pounding with emphatic generosities. To go away . . . I would arrive sleek and young in this land of mine and I would say to this land whose loam is part of my flesh: "I have wandered for a long time and I am coming back to the deserted hideousness of your sores."

8. Harlem, the center of black life in New York City, is an appropriate reference for the denial of civil rights to blacks in the United States before corrective legislation in the 1960s. "Kaffir": a term of contempt formerly applied by whites to black South Africans. Calcutta, India, was noted for its extreme poverty.
9. Organized harassment of Jews, often leading to their massacre.
1. A people of southwest Africa, who were decimated by white invaders in the 19th century.
2. A fibrous plant. "Jujube tree": produces red fruit.
3. Penis, here ascribed to the sun.
4. A tree with a milky sap.
5. The juice of a tropical plant; it produces a hallucinatory effect.

I would go to this land of mine and I would say to it: "Embrace me without fear . . . And if all I can do is speak, it is for you I shall speak."
And again I would say:
"My mouth shall be the mouth of those calamities that have no mouth, my voice the freedom of those who break down in the solitary confinement of despair."
And on the way I would say to myself:
"And above all, my body as well as my soul, beware of assuming the sterile attitude of a spectator, for life is not a spectacle, a sea of miseries is not a proscenium,[6] a man screaming is not a dancing bear . . ."

And behold here I am!
Once again this life hobbling before me, what am I saying life, *this death*, this death without sense or piety, this death that so pathetically falls short of greatness, the dazzling pettiness of this death, this death hobbling from pettiness to pettiness; these shovelfuls of petty greeds over the conquistador; these shovelfuls of petty flunkies over the great-savage, these shovelfuls of petty souls over the three-souled Carib,[7]
and all these deaths futile
absurdities under the splashing of my open conscience
tragic futilities lit up by this single noctiluca[8]
and I alone, sudden stage of this daybreak when the apocalypse of
monsters cavorts then, capsized, hushes
warm election of cinders, of ruins and collapse
—One more thing! only one, but please make it only one: I have no right to measure life by my sooty finger span; to reduce myself to this little ellipsoidal nothing[9] trembling four fingers above the line,[1] I a man, to so overturn creation, that I include myself between latitude and longitude!

At the end of daybreak,
the male thirst and the desire stubborn,
here I am, severed from the cool oases of brotherhood
this so modest nothing bristles with hard splinters
this too safe horizon is startled like a jailer.

Your last triumph, tenacious crow of Treason.
What is mine, these few thousand deathbearers who mill in the calabash of an island and mine too, the archipelago arched[2] with an anguished desire to negate itself, as if from maternal anxiety to protect this impossibly delicate tenuity separating one America from another; and these loins which secrete for Europe the hearty liquor of a Gulf Stream,[3] and one of the two slopes of incandescence between which the

6. A platform that serves as a stage for a performance.
7. Indicating the indigenous as Carib Indians as well as the descendants of Africans and of Europeans.
8. Light from a glowworm.
9. That is, Martinique, which is oval-shaped.
1. A reference to Martinique's geographical position close to the equator.
2. Like a tense bow, an image suggested by the half circle formed by the islands across the Caribbean Sea.

Equator tightropewalks toward Africa. And my nonfence island, its brave audacity standing at the stern of this Polynesia, before it, Guadeloupe, split in two down its dorsal line and equal in poverty to us, Haiti where negritude rose for the first time[4] and stated that it believed in its humanity and the funny little tail of Florida where the strangulation of a nigger is being completed, and Africa gigantically caterpillaring up to the Hispanic foot of Europe, its nakedness where Death scythes widely.

And I say to myself Bordeaux and Nantes and Liverpool[5] and New York and San Francisco

not an inch of this world devoid of my fingerprint
and my calcaneum[6] on the spines of skyscrapers and my filth in the
glitter of gems!
Who can boast of being better off than I? Virginia.
Tennessee. Georgia. Alabama[7]
monstrous putrefactions of stymied
revolts
marshes of putrid blood
trumpets absurdly muted
land red, sanguineous, consanguineous[8] land.

What is also mine: a little
cell in the Jura,[9]
a little cell, the snow lines it with white bars
the snow is a jailer mounting
guard before a prison

What is mine
a lonely man imprisoned in
whiteness
a lonely man defying the white
screams of white death
(TOUSSAINT, TOUSSAINT L'OUVERTURE)

a man who mesmerizes
the white hawk of white death

3. An ocean current that flows from the West Indies to the north Atlantic; it has a tempering effect on the climate of western Europe. "Delicate tenuity": the thin strip of Central America, protected by the Caribbean from the full force of the Atlantic.

4. A reference to the slave revolt, led by Toussaint L'Ouverture (ca. 1743–1803), which led to the independence of Haiti in 1804. Guadeloupe, the other French West Indian colony, is now a French department. It lies north of Martinique and is made up of two islands (Basse-Terre and Grande-Terre). "Polynesia": in the sense of a group of islands.

5. Bordeaux and Nantes in France and Liverpool in England were the principal ports from which, in a triangular circuit, the slave ships sailed out to Africa and, after being loaded with their human cargo, crossed to America, returning with produce to Europe.

6. Heel, complementary to *fingerprint*.

7. Along with New York and San Francisco, symbols of the economic exploitation of the black people.

8. Linked by blood; here, that of the black slave.

9. L'Ouverture was captured by the French and taken to France, to be imprisoned in the fortress of Joue, in the Jura Mountains, where he eventually died.

a man alone in the sterile
sea of white sand
a coon grown old standing up to
the waters of the sky
Death traces a shining circle
above this man
death stars softly above his head
death breathes, crazed, in the ripened
cane field of his arms
death gallops in the prison like
a white horse[1]
death gleams in the dark like the
eyes of a cat
death hiccups like water under the Keys[2]
death is a struck bird
death wanes
death flickers
death is a very shy patyura[3]
death expires in a white pool
of silence.
Swellings of night in the four corners
of this dawn
convulsions of congealed death
tenacious fate
screams erect from mute earth
the splendor of this blood will it not burst open?

At the end of daybreak this land without a stele,[4] these paths without memory, these winds without a tablet.

So what?

We would tell. Would sing. Would howl.

Full voice, ample voice, you would be our wealth, our spear pointed.

Words?

Ah yes, words!

Reason, I crown you evening wind.[5]
Your name voice of order?
To me the whip's corolla.[6]
Beauty I call you the false claim of the stone.
But ah! my raucous laughter
smuggled in
Ah! my saltpetre[7] treasure!
Because we hate you

1. Refers both to Baron Samedi, the spirit of death in Haitian folk belief, and the horse of death in Western iconography.
2. Coral reefs in the Caribbean.
3. According to Césaire, a variation on "patira," the name for a peccary found in Paraguay [Translators' note].
4. Funeral monument to a military hero.
5. Boding death.
6. The strands of the whip commonly used on slaves.
7. Potassium nitrate, used in the manufacture of gunpowder.

and your reason, we claim kinship
with dementia praecox[8] with the flaming madness
of persistent cannibalism

Treasure, let's count:
the madness that remembers[9]
the madness that howls
the madness that sees
the madness that is unleashed
And you know the rest

That 2 and 2 are 5[1]
that the forest miaows
that the tree plucks the maroons from the fire[2]
that the sky strokes its beard
etc. etc. . . .

Who and what are we?
A most worthy question!

From staring too long at trees I have
become a tree and my long tree
feet have dug in the ground large
venom sacs high cities of bone
from brooding too long on the Congo[3]
I have become a Congo resounding with
forests and rivers
where the whip cracks like a great banner
the banner of a prophet
where the water goes
likouala-likouala
where the angerbolt hurls its greenish
axe[4] forcing the boars of
putrefaction to the lovely wild edge
of the nostrils.

At the end of daybreak the sun which
hacks and spits up its lungs
At the end of daybreak
a slow gait of sand
a slow gait of gauze
a slow gait of corn kernels

8. Schizophrenia.
9. The immediate reference is to the memory of slavery, but the phrase draws its full meaning from the surrealist belief in madness as a form of insight.
1. Deliberately irrational, again as part of the surrealist convention.
2. Runaway slaves (*maroons*) often made animal sounds as signals to each other. They also hid in the treetops to escape their pursuers; plays also on the French meaning of *marron* = chestnut.
3. A river that flows through dense tropical forests in central Africa.
4. "Angerbolt" refers to the uprising of the native population, an act that restores the people to harmony with their essential beings (*greenish axe*). The Likouala River is in the interior of the present-day Congo Republic.

At the end of daybreak
a full gallop of pollen
a full gallop of a slow gait of
little girls
a full gallop of hummingbirds[5]
a full gallop of daggers to stave in
the earth's breast

customs angels mounting guard over
prohibitions at the gates of foam

I declare my crimes[6] and that there is nothing
to say in my defense.
Dances. Idols. An apostate. I too
I have assassinated God with my laziness with
my words with my gestures
with my obscene songs

I have worn parrot plumes
musk cat skins
I have exhausted the missionaries' patience
insulted the benefactors of mankind.
Defied Tyre. Defied Sidon.
Worshipped the Zambezi.[7]
The extent of my perversity overwhelms me!

But why impenetrable jungle are you still hiding the raw zero of my
mendacity and from a self-conscious concern for nobility not celebrating
the horrible leap of my Pahouin[8] ugliness?

voum rooh oh[9]
voum rooh oh
to charm the snakes to conjure
the dead
voum rooh oh
to compel the rain to turn back
the tidal waves
voum rooh oh
to keep the shade from moving
voum rooh oh that my own skies
may open

—me on a road, a child chewing
sugar cane root
—a dragged man on a bloodspattered road
a rope around his neck

5. Symbols of Césaire's native land.
6. The stereotypes of Africans in colonial ideology are echoed in this ironic confession.
7. A river in southern Africa. The religious practices of Africans were often devalued as animism, of which river worship was a prominent feature. Tyre and Sidon were commercial ports in ancient Phoenicia, often mentioned in history books as early centers of civilization.
8. An ethnic group in present-day Gabon.
9. An incantation, by which Césaire assumes the powers enumerated in this stanza.

—standing in the center of a huge circus,
on my black forehead a crown of daturas[1]
voum rooh
to fly off
higher than quivering higher
than the sorceresses toward other stars
ferocious exultation of forests and
mountains uprooted at the hour
when no one expects it[2]
the islands linked for a thousand years!

voum rooh oh
that the promised times may return
and the bird who knew my name
and the woman[3] who had a thousand names
names of fountain sun and tears
and her hair of minnows[4]
and her steps my climates
and her eyes my seasons
and the days without injury
and the nights without offense
and the stars my confidence
and the wind my accomplice

But who misleads my voice? who grates
my voice? Stuffing my throat
with a thousand bamboo fangs. A thousand
sea urchin stakes. It is you dirty end
of the world. Dirty end of daybreak.
It is you dirty hatred. It is you weight
of the insult and a hundred years of whip
lashes. It is you one hundred years of my
patience, one hundred years of my effort
simply to stay alive
rooh oh
we sing of venomous flowers
flaring in fury-filled prairies;
the skies of love cut with bloodclots;
the epileptic mornings; the white blaze
of abyssal[5] sands, the sinking
of flotsam in nights electrified
with feline smells.

What can I do?

1. A mildly poisonous, hallucinatory plant, with which his brow is decked—as befits his combative role—instead of the laurels associated with classical tradition.
2. Another reference to the sudden eruption of Mont Pelée.
3. A guardian goddess, identified with Césaire's vision of Martinique's future. *The bird who knew my name*: the hummingbird (see n. 5, p. 634).
4. The woman is now presented as the sea goddess of folk mythology, with hair made of small fish.
5. Unfathomable.

One must begin somewhere.

Begin what?

The only thing in the world
worth beginning:
The End of the world of course.

Torte[6]
oh torte of the terrifying autumn
where the new steel and the perennial concrete
grow
torte oh torte
where the air rusts in great sheets
of evil glee
where the sanious[7] water sears the great
solar cheeks
I hate you

one still sees madras rags[8] around the loins
of women rings in their ears
smiles on their lips babies
at their nipples, these for starters:

ENOUGH OF THIS OUTRAGE!

So here is the great challenge and the satanic
compulsion and the insolent
nostalgic drift of April moons,[9]
of green fires, of yellow fevers!

Vainly in the tepidity of your throat
you ripen for the twentieth time the same indigent
solace that we are
mumblers of words

Words? while we handle
quarters of earth, while we wed
delirious continents, while
we force steaming gates,
words, ah yes, words! but
words of fresh blood, words that are
tidal waves and erysipelas[1]
malarias and lava and brush
fires, and blazes of flesh,
and blazes of cities . . .

Know this:
the only game I play is the millennium

6. A kind of crude peasant bread.
7. Pertaining to fluid from a wound.
8. The scarf of fine material worn around the waist by Martinican women.
9. Often reddish in hue and considered an ill omen.
1. An inflammation of the skin.

the only game I play is the Great
Fear[2]

Put up with me. I won't put up with you!

Sometimes you see me with a great display of brains
snap up a cloud too red
or a caress of rain, or a prelude
of wind,
don't fool yourself:

I am forcing the vitelline membrane[3] that separates
me from myself,
I am forcing the great waters which girdle me with blood

I and I alone choose
a seat on the last train of the last
surge of the last tidal wave

I and I alone
make contact with the latest
anguish

I and oh, only I
secure the first
drops of virginal milk through a straw!

And now a last boo:
to the sun (not strong enough to inebriate
my very tough head)
to the mealy night with its golden
hatchings of erratic fireflies
to the head of hair trembling at the very
top of the cliff
where the wind leaps in bursts of salty
cavalries
I clearly read in my pulse that for me
exoticism is no provender[4]

Leaving Europe utterly twisted with screams
the silent currents of despair
leaving timid Europe which
collects and proudly overrates itself
I summon this egotism beautiful
and bold
  and my ploughing reminds me of an implacable cutwater.[5]

2. The year 1000 C.E. was awaited in early Christendom with foreboding (*the Great Fear*) as the date that would mark the end of the world predicted in the Book of Revelation.

3. Protects the fetus in its mother's womb.

4. Animal feed.

5. The prow of a ship.

So much blood in my memory! In my memory are lagoons. They are covered with death's-heads.
They are not covered with water lilies.
In my memory are lagoons. No women's loincloths spread out on their shores.
My memory is encircled with blood. My memory has a belt of corpses!
and machine gun fire of rum barrels brilliantly sprinkling our ignominious revolts amorous glances swooning from having swigged too much ferocious freedom

(niggers-are-all-alike, I-tell-you vices-all-the-vices-believe-you-me
nigger-smell, that's-what-makes-cane-grow
remember-the-old-saying:
beat-a-nigger, and you feed him)
among "rocking chairs" contemplating the voluptuousness of quirts[6]
I circle about, an unappeased filly

Or else quite simply as they like to think of us!
Cheerfully obscene, completely nuts about jazz to cover their extreme boredom
I can boogie-woogie, do the Lindy-hop[7] and tap-dance.
And for a special treat the muting of our cries muffled with wah-wah.[8]
Wait . . . Everything is as it should be. My good angel grazes the neon.
I swallow batons. My dignity wallows in puke . . .
Sun, Angel Sun, curled Angel of the Sun
for a leap beyond the sweet and greenish
treading of the waters of abjection!

But I approached the wrong sorcerer, on this exorcised earth, cast adrift from its precious malignant purpose, this voice that cries, little by little hoarse, vainly, vainly hoarse,
and there remains only the accumulated droppings of our lies—and they do not respond.
What madness to dream up a marvelous caper above the baseness!
Oh Yes the Whites are great warriors hosannah to the master and to the nigger-gelder!
Victory! Victory, I tell you: the defeated are content!
Joyous stenches and songs of mud!
By a sudden and beneficent inner revolution, I now honour my repugnant ugliness.

On Midsummer Day, as soon as the first shadows fall on the village of Gros-Morne, hundreds of horse dealers gather on rue "De PROFUNDIS,"[9] a name at least honest enough to announce an onrush from the shoals of Death. And it truly is from Death, from its thousand petty local

6. Riding whips.
7. A dance named after Charles Lindbergh, who made aviation history in 1927 by being the first to fly solo across the Atlantic.
8. Sarcastic imitation of the muted trumpet.
9. Out of the depths (Latin), from a liturgy for the dead. Gros-Morne is north of Fort-de-France.

forms (cravings unsatisfied by Para grass[1] and tipsy bondage to the distilleries) that the astonishing cavalry of impetuous nags surges unfenced toward the great-life. What a galloping! what neighing! what sincere urinating! what prodigious droppings! "A fine horse difficult to mount!"—"A proud mare sensitive to the spur"—"A fearless foal superbly pasterned!"[2]

And the shrewd fellow whose waistcoat displays a proud watch chain, palms off instead of full udders, youthful mettle and genuine contours, either the systematic puffiness from obliging wasps, or the obscene stings from ginger, or the helpful distribution of several gallons of sugared water.[3]

I refuse to pass off my puffiness for authentic glory.

And I laugh at my former childish fantasies.

No, we've never been Amazons of the king of Dahomey, nor princes of Ghana with eight hundred camels, nor wise men in Timbuktu under Askia the Great, nor the architects of Djenne, nor Madhis,[4] nor warriors. We don't feel under our armpit the itch of those who in the old days carried a lance. And since I have sworn to leave nothing out of our history (I who love nothing better than a sheep grazing his own afternoon shadow), I may as well confess that we were at all times pretty mediocre dishwashers, shoeblacks without ambition, at best conscientious sorcerers and the only unquestionable record that we broke was that of endurance under the chicote[5] . . .

And this land screamed for centuries that we are bestial brutes; that the human pulse stops at the gates of the slave compound; that we are walking compost hideously promising tender cane and silky cotton and they would brand us with red-hot irons and we would sleep in our excrement and they would sell us on the town square and an ell[6] of English cloth and salted meat from Ireland cost less than we did, and this land was calm, tranquil, repeating that the spirit of the Lord was in its acts.

We the vomit of slave ships
We the venery of the Calabars[7]
what? Plug up our ears?
We, so drunk on jeers and inhaled fog that we rode the roll to death!
Forgive us fraternal whirlwind!

1. Coarse elephant grass on which the horses are fed.
2. Nobly built.
3. Ways in which the horses have been doctored to give them a false air of well-being.
4. In Islam, leaders in a holy war. "Amazons": female warriors in the ancient African kingdom of Dahomey. Ghana was the medieval West African empire after which the modern state is named. Timbuktu, on the river Niger, was an outstanding intellectual center in the Middle Ages. Askia the Great was ruler of the African empire of Songhai from the late 15th to the early years of the 16th century. Djenne, in present-day Mali, was a university town in the Middle Ages. This passage contains references to aspects of precolonial African history to which the West Indian has at best an ambiguous connection.
5. Whip.
6. A unit of measure that equals about 45 inches.
7. A coastal town in southeastern Nigeria; a major slave depot.

I hear coming up from the hold the enchained curses, the gasps of the dying, the noise of someone thrown into the sea . . . the baying of a woman in labor . . . the scrape of fingernails seeking throats . . . the flouts of the whip . . . the seethings of vermin amid the weariness . . .

Nothing could ever lift us toward a noble hopeless adventure.
So be it. So be it.
I am of no nationality recognized by the chancelleries.
I defy the craniometer. Homo sum etc.
Let them serve and betray and die
So be it. So be it. It was written in the shape of their pelvis.[8]

And I, and I,
I was singing the hard fist
You must know the extent of my cowardice. One evening on the streetcar facing me, a nigger.

A nigger big as a pongo[9] trying to make himself small on the streetcar bench. He was trying to leave behind, on this grimy bench, his gigantic legs and his trembling famished boxer hands. And everything had left him, was leaving him. His nose which looked like a drifting peninsula and even his negritude discolored as a result of untiring tawing.[1] And the tawer was Poverty. A big unexpected lop-eared bat whose claw marks in his face had scabbed over into crusty islands. Or rather, it was a tireless worker. Poverty was, working on some hideous cartouche.[2] One could easily see how that industrious and malevolent thumb had kneaded bumps into his brow, bored two bizarre parallel tunnels in his nose, overexaggerated his lips, and in a masterpiece of caricature, planed, polished and varnished the tiniest cutest little ear in all creation.

He was a gangly nigger without rhythm or measure.

A nigger whose eyes rolled a bloodshot weariness.

A shameless nigger and his toes sneered in a rather stinking way at the bottom of the yawning lair of his shoes.

Poverty, without any question, had knocked itself out to finish him off.

It had dug the socket, had painted it with a rouge of dust mixed with rheum.[3]

It had stretched an empty space between the solid hinge of the jaw and bone of an old tarnished cheek. Had planted over it the small shiny stakes of a two- or three-day beard. Had panicked his heart, bent his back.

And the whole thing added up perfectly to a hideous nigger, a grouchy nigger, a melancholy nigger, a slouched nigger, his hands joined in prayer

8. Ironic reference to physiological arguments employed to establish the inferiority of the black race, notably by the French writer Arthur Gobineau, whose actual words are quoted here. "Craniometer": an instrument for measuring the size of skulls, thought to be a factor in the evolution of the brain. "Homo sum": I am man (Latin); a quotation from *The Self-Tormentor* by the playwright Terence. The rest of the line reads, "and I consider nothing human foreign to me."

9. A genus of anthropoid apes.

1. Working of leather.

2. Portrait sketch.

3. Liquid from the eye.

on a knobby stick. A nigger shrouded in an old threadbare coat. A comical
and ugly nigger, with some women behind me sneering at him.
He was COMICAL AND UGLY,[4]
COMICAL AND UGLY for sure.
I displayed a big complicitous smile . . .
My cowardice rediscovered!
Hail to the three centuries which uphold my civil rights and my minimized blood!
My heroism, what a farce!
This town fits me to a t.
And my soul is lying down. Lying down like this town in its refuse and mud.
This town, my face of mud.
For my face I demand the vivid homage of spit! . . .
So, being what we are, ours the warrior thrust, the triumphant knee, the well-plowed plains of the future?
Look, I'd rather admit to uninhibited ravings, my heart in my brain like a drunken knee.
My star now, the funereal menfenil.[5]

And on this former dream my cannibalistic cruelties:

(The bullets in the mouth thick saliva
our heart from daily lowness bursts the continents break the fragile bond of isthmuses
lands leap in accordance with the fatal division of rivers
and the morne which for centuries kept its scream within itself, it is its turn to draw and quarter the silence and this people an ever-rebounding spirit
and our limbs vainly disjointed by the most refined tortures
and life even more impetuously jetting from this compost—unexpected as a soursop amidst the decomposition of jack tree[6] fruit!)

On this dream so old in me my cannibalistic cruelties

I was hiding behind a stupid vanity destiny called me I was hiding behind it and suddenly there was a man on the ground, his feeble defenses scattered.
his sacred maxims trampled underfoot, his pedantic rhetoric oozing air through each wound.
There is a man on the ground
and his soul is almost naked
and destiny triumphs in watching this soul which defied its metamorphosis in the ancestral slough.

4. An echo of Baudelaire's poem *The Albatross*. The individual is, of course, without the mystical significance Baudelaire attributes to the ungainly bird.
5. A Caribbean sparrow hawk with black plumage; hence "funereal."
6. Or breadfruit, which provided an important source of nourishment for the slaves. "Soursop": a tropical tree with a white fleshy fruit, which has a sharp taste.

I say that this is right
My back will victoriously exploit the chalaza[7] of fibers.
I will deck my natural obsequiousness with gratitude
And the silver-braided bullshit of the postillion of Havana,[8] lyrical baboon pimp for the glamour of slavery, will be more than a match for my enthusiasm.

I say that this is right
I live for the flattest part of my soul.
For the dullest part of my flesh!

Tepid dawn[9] of ancestral heat and fear
I now tremble with the collective trembling that our docile blood sings in the madrepore.[1]

And these tadpoles hatched in me by my prodigious ancestry!
Those who invented neither powder nor compass
those who could harness neither steam nor electricity
those who explored neither the seas nor the sky but who know
in its most minute corners the land of suffering
those who have known voyages only through uprootings
those who have been lulled to sleep by so much kneeling
those whom they domesticated and Christianized
those whom they inoculated with degeneracy
tom-toms of empty hands
inane tom-toms of resounding sores
burlesque tom-toms of tabetic treason[2]

Tepid dawn of ancestral heat and fears
overboard with alien riches
overboard with my genuine falsehoods
But what strange pride suddenly illuminates me!
let the hummingbird come
let the sparrow hawk come
the breach in the horizon
the cynocephalus
let the lotus[3] bearer of the world come
the pearly upheaval of dolphins
cracking the shell of the sea
let a plunge of islands come
let it come from the disappearing of days of dead

7. A whip made of hard fibers.
8. A port city in Cuba. "Postillion": a valet employed to welcome newly arrived slaves with a speech in praise of slavery.
9. Announces a new movement in the poem, leading to Césaire's celebration of his race.
1. Coral reef, symbolizing Martinique and, by extension, the Caribbean region.
2. Ineffectual revolt. "Tabetic": derives from the Latin *tabidus*, "wasting away."
3. A white flower, symbol of Isis, the ancient Egyptian goddess of the rising sun. "Cynocephalus": an African monkey, with a head resembling a dog's noted for its great strength.
4. An extremely compressed image that identifies Césaire's revolt with the action of *birds of prey* or *quicklime* (calcium oxide, which has a dissolving effect), both of which cleanse the land of dead bodies.

flesh in the quicklime of birds of prey[4]
let the ovaries of the water come where the future stirs its testicles
let the wolves come who feed in the untamed openings of the body at
the hour when my moon and your sun meet at the ecliptic inn[5]

under the reserve of my uvula[6] there is a wallow of boars
under the grey stone of the day there are your eyes which are a shim-
mering conglomerate of coccinella[7]
in the glance of disorder there is this swallow of mint and broom[8] which
melts always to be reborn in the tidal wave of your light
Calm and lull oh my voice the child who does not know that the map of
spring is always to be drawn again
the tall grass will sway gentle the ship of hope for the cattle
the long alcoholic sweep of the swell
the stars with the bezels[9] if their rings never in sight will cut the pipes
of the glass organ of evening zinnias
coryanthas[1]
will then pour into the rich extremity of my fatigue
and you star[2] please from your luminous foundation draw lemurian
being—of man's unfathomable
sperm the yet undared form

carried like an ore in woman's trembling belly!

oh friendly light
oh fresh source of light
those who have invented neither powder nor compass
those who could harness neither steam nor electricity
those who explored neither the seas nor the sky but those
without whom the earth would not be the earth
gibbosity[3] all the more beneficent as the bare earth even more earth
silo[4] where that which is earthiest about earth ferments and ripens
my negritude is not a stone, its deafness hurled against the clamor of
the day
my negritude is not a leukoma[5] of dead liquid over the earth's dead
eye
my negritude is neither tower nor cathedral
it takes root in the red flesh of the soil
it takes root in the ardent flesh of the sky
it breaks through the opaque prostration with its upright patience[6]

5. The partners fuse into one another as in an eclipse of the sun or moon.
6. The tissue at the back of the tongue, opening into the throat.
7. Beetles. The passage refers to Césaire's wife, Suzanne, whose bright eyes are compared to the shimmering of a swarm of beetles.
8. Medicinal plants. "Swallow": a harbinger of spring, associated with the health-restoring properties of medicinal plants.
9. The upper parts of rings in which the stones are set.
1. Tropical flowers.
2. Perhaps the sun.
3. An ugly swelling.
4. A granary. Here, the black race as the spiritual reservoir of humankind.
5. A film over the eye, caused by infection.
6. A reference to the Cross, symbol of Christ's Passion.

Eia for the royal Cailcedra[7]
Eia for those who have never invented anything
for those who never explored anything
for those who never conquered anything

but yield, captivated, to the essence of all things
ignorant of surfaces but captivated by the motion of all things
indifferent to conquering, but playing the game of the world
truly the eldest sons of the world
porous to all the breathing of the world
fraternal locus for all the breathing of the world
drainless channel for all the water of the world
spark of the sacred fire of the world
flesh of the world's flesh pulsating with the very motion of the world!
  Tepid dawn of ancestral virtues

Blood! Blood! all our blood aroused by the male heart of the sun
those who know about the femininity of the moon's oily body
the reconciled exultation of antelope and star
those whose survival travels in the germination of grass!
Eia perfect circle of the world, enclosed concordance!

Hear the white world
horribly weary from its immense efforts
its stiff joints crack under the hard stars
hear its blue steel rigidity pierce the mystic flesh
its deceptive victories tout its defeats
hear the grandiose alibis of its pitiful stumblings

Pity for our omniscient and naive conquerors!

Eia for grief and its udders of reincarnated tears
for those who have never explored anything
for those who have never conquered anything

Eia for joy
Eia for love
Eia for grief and its udders of reincarnated tears

and here at the end of this daybreak is my virile prayer that I hear neither
the laughter nor the screams, my eyes fixed on this town which I prophesy, beautiful,
grant me the savage faith of the sorcerer
grant my hands power to mold
grant my soul the sword's temper
I won't flinch. Make my head into a figurehead
and as for me, my heart, do not make me into a father nor a brother,
nor a son, but into the father, the brother, the son,
nor a husband, but the lover of this unique people.

7. A tree typical of the west African savannah, with royal significance. "Eia": a triumphant cry.

Make me resist any vanity, but espouse its genius as the fist the extended arm!

Make me a steward of its blood
make me trustee of its resentment
make me into a man for the ending
make me into a man for the beginning
make me into a man of meditation
but also make me into a man of germination

make me into the executor of these lofty works
the time has come to gird one's loins like a brave man[8]—

But in doing so, my heart, preserve me from all hatred
do not make me into that man of hatred for whom I feel only hatred
for entrenched as I am in this unique race
you still know my tyrannical love
you know that it is not from hatred of other races
that I demand a digger for this unique race
that what I want
is for universal hunger
for universal thirst

to summon it to generate,
free at last, from its intimate closeness
the succulence of fruit.

And be the tree of our hands!
it turns, for all, the wounds cut
in its trunk[9]
the soil works for all
and toward the branches a headiness of fragrant precipitation!

But before stepping on the shores of future orchards
grant that I deserve those on their belt of sea
grant me my heart while awaiting the earth
grant me on the ocean sterile
but somewhere caressed by the promise of the clew-line[1]
grant me on this diverse ocean
the obstinacy of the fierce pirogue[2]
and its marine vigor.
See it advance rising and falling on the pulverized wave
see it dance the sacred dance before the greyness of the village
see it trumpet from a vertiginous conch[3]

8. An echo of God's words to Job: "Gird up now thy loins like a man" (Job 38.3).
9. Like the rubber tree, which thrives on incisions made in its trunk to produce sap.
1. Rope by which a clew of an upper square sail is hauled up.
2. A dug-out canoe, in which local fishermen go out to sea.
3. A seashell that has a wound-up (*vertiginous*) shape. It can be made into a horn, which has a trumpeting sound like that of an elephant.

see the conch gallop up to the uncertainty of the morne

and see twenty times over the paddle
vigorously
plow the water
the pirogue rears under the attack of the swells
deviates for an instant
tries to escape, but the paddle's rough caress turns it,
then it charges, a shudder runs along the wave's spine,
the sea slobbers and rumbles
the pirogue like a sleigh glides onto the sand.

At the end of this daybreak, my virile prayer:

grant me pirogue muscles on this raging sea
and the irresistible gaiety of the conch of good tidings!
Look, now I am only a man, no degradation, no spit perturbs him, now
I am only a man who accepts emptied of anger
(nothing left in his heart but immense love, which burns)

I accept . . . I accept . . . totally, without reservation . . .
my race that no ablution of hyssop[4] mixed with lilies could purify
my race pitted with blemishes
my race a ripe grape for drunken feet
my queen of spittle and leprosy
my queen of whips and scrofula
my queen of squasma and chloasma[5] (oh those queens I once loved in
the remote gardens of spring against the illumination of all the candles
of the chestnut[6] trees!)
I accept. I accept.
and the flogged nigger saying: "Forgive me master"
and the twenty-nine legal blows[7] of the whip
and the four-feet-high cell
and the spiked iron-collar
and the hamstringing of my runaway audacity
and the fleur de lys[8] flowing from the red iron into the fat of my shoulder
and Monsieur VAULTIER MAYENCOURT'S dog house[9] where I
barked
six poodle months
and Monsieur BRAFIN
and Monsieur FOURNIOL
and Monsieur de la MAHAUDIERE[1]

4. An aromatic plant featured in a Latin chant said before High Mass in the Catholic Church.
5. Suggests sickness, possibly derived from the Greek word meaning "paleness." "Squasma": scales on the skin.
6. In the French, there is a play on the word *marron*, which means both chestnut and runaway slaves.
7. The limit prescribed by the *Code Noir* (Black Code), designed to regulate slaveowners' treatment of their slaves.
8. The lily flower (French); the emblem of the Bourbon Dynasty in France, with which recaptured slaves were branded.
9. Mayencourt, a slaveowner, caused the death of one of his slaves by caging him in a dog kennel for six months.
1. Slaveowners involved in an incident in which two slaves committed suicide.

and the yaws
the mastiff[2]
the suicide
the promiscuity
the bootkin[3]
the shackles
the rack
the cippus
the head screw[4]

Look, am I humble enough? Have I enough calluses on my knees?
Muscles on my loins?
Grovel in mud. Brace yourself in the thick of the mud. Carry.
Soil of mud. Horizon of mud. Sky of mud.
Dead of the mud, oh names to thaw in the palm of a feverish breathing!

Siméon Piquine, who never knew his father or mother; unheard of in any town hall[5] and who wandered his whole life—seeking a new name.

Grandvorka—of him I only know that he died, crushed one harvest evening, it was his job, apparently, to throw sand under the wheels of the running locomotive, to help it across bad spots.

Michel who used to write me signing a strange name. Lucky Michel address *Condemned District*[6] and you their living brothers Exélie Vêté Congolo Lemké Boussolongo what healer with his thick lips would suck from the depths of the gaping wound the tenacious secret of venom?

what cautious sorcerer would undo from your ankles the viscous tepidity of mortal rings?

Presences it is not on your back that I will make my peace with the world

Islands scars of the water
Islands evidence of wounds
Islands crumbs
Islands unformed

Islands cheap paper shredded upon the water
Islands stumps skewered side by side on the flaming sword of the Sun
Mulish reason you will not stop me from casting on the waters at the mercy of the currents of my thirst
your form, deformed islands,
your end, my defiance.

2. A bloodhound, used to hunt down runaway slaves. "Yaws": a tropical disease that attacks the skin and bones.
3. Stocks designed to lock in the victim's legs.
4. A form of punishment in which a cord was wound tightly around the slave's head. "Cippus": an elevated spot where slaves were whipped.
5. Where births and deaths are recorded.
6. Indicative of a mood of total despair.

Annulose[7] islands, single beautiful hull
And I caress you with my oceanic hands. And I turn you
around with the tradewinds of my speech. And I lick you with my seaweed tongues.
And I sail you unfreebootable!

O death your mushy marsh!
Shipwreck your hellish debris! I accept!

At the end of daybreak, lost puddles, wandering scents, beached hurricanes, demasted hulls, old sores, rotted bones, vapors, shackled volcanoes, shallow-rooted dead, bitter cry. I accept!

And my special geography too; the world map made for my own use,
not tinted with the arbitrary colors of scholars, but with the geometry
of my spilled blood, I accept both the determination of my biology, not
a prisoner to a facial angle, to a type of hair, to a well-flattened nose, to
a clearly Melanian coloring, and negritude, no longer a cephalic index,
or plasma, or soma, but measured by the compass of suffering[8]
and the Negro every day more base, more cowardly, more sterile, less profound, more spilled out of himself, more separated from himself, more wily with himself, less immediate to himself,

I accept, I accept it all

and far from the palatial sea that foams beneath the suppurating syzygy[9] of blisters, miraculously lying in the despair of my arms the body of my country, its bones shocked and, in its veins, the blood hesitating like a drop of vegetal milk at the injured point of the bulb . . .

Suddenly now strength and life assail me like a bull and the water of life overwhelms the papilla[1] of the morne, now all the veins and veinlets are bustling with new blood and the enormous breathing lung of cyclones and the fire hoarded in volcanoes and the gigantic seismic pulse which now beats the measure of a living body in my firm conflagration.

And we are standing now, my country and I, hair in the wind, my hand puny in its enormous fist and now the strength is not in us but above us, in a voice that drills the night and the hearing like the penetrance of an apocalyptic wasp.[2] And the voice proclaims that for centuries Europe has force-fed us with lies and bloated us with pestilence,

for it is not true that the work of man is done
that we have no business being on earth that we parasite the world
that it is enough for us to heel to the world
whereas the work has only begun

7. Strung out, as in a ceremonial procession.
8. Earlier in the 20th century physical anthropologists were interested in the worldwide distribution of various physical traits of humans (some of which are listed here). Others used such data to advance and justify racial theories. "Melanian": dark. "Cephalic": relating to the head. "Soma": body (Greek).
9. The alignment of the sun and the moon; also the movement of the tides.
1. Nipple.
2. An allusion to the plague that descended on the Egyptians before the liberation of the Israelites in Exodus 5–11.

and man still must overcome all the interdictions wedged in the recesses of his fervor and no race has a monopoly on beauty, on intelligence, on strength[3]

and there is room for everyone at the convocation of conquest and we know now that the sun turns around our earth lighting the parcel designated by our will alone and that every star falls from sky to earth at our omnipotent command.

I now see the meaning of this trial by the sword: my country is the "lance of night" of my Bambara[4] ancestors. It shrivels and its point desperately retreats toward the haft when it is sprinkled with chicken blood and it says that its nature requires the blood of man, his fat, his liver, his heart, not chicken blood.

And I seek for my country not date hearts, but men's hearts which, in order to enter the silver cities through the great trapezoidal[5] gate, beat with warrior blood, and as my eyes sweep my kilometers of paternal earth I number its sores almost joyfully and I pile one on top of the other like rare species, and my total is ever lengthened by unexpected mintings of baseness.

And there are those who will never get over not being made in the likeness of God but of the devil, those who believe that being a nigger is like being a second-class clerk; waiting for a better deal and upward mobility; those who beat the drum of compromise in front of themselves, those who live in their own dungeon pit; those who drape themselves in proud pseudomorphosis;[6] those who say to Europe: "You see, I *can* bow and scrape, like you I pay my respects, in short, I am no different from you; pay no attention to my black skin: the sun did it."[7]

And there is the nigger pimp, the nigger askari,[8] and all the zebras shaking themselves in various ways to get rid of their stripes in a dew of fresh milk.[9] And in the midst of all that I say right on! my grandfather dies, I say right on! the old negritude progressively cadavers itself.

No question about it: he was a good nigger. The Whites say he was a good nigger, a really good nigger, massa's good ole darky. I say right on!

He was a good nigger, indeed,
poverty had wounded his chest and back and they had stuffed into his poor brain that a fatality impossible to trap weighed on him; that he had no control over his own fate; that an evil Lord had for all eternity inscribed

3. A pointed reference to the writings of Gobineau, who argued the superiority of the white race in terms of the qualities stated here.
4. An ethnic group concentrated in present-day Mali. The passage refers to a ritual in which warriors sprinkled human blood on their spears to ensure their effectiveness.
5. A reference to a four-sided figure that has only two sides parallel; a frequent motif in the architecture of ancient civilizations.
6. A false personality.
7. Adapted from the Song of Solomon (1.6). The words have been attributed to the queen of Sheba.
8. African colonial soldiers in east Africa (Swahili).
9. Recalls the queen of Sheba's description of Solomon's eyes as "washed in milk" (Song of Solomon 5.12).

Thou Shall Not in his pelvic constitution; that he must be a good nigger; must sincerely believe in his worthlessness, without any perverse curiosity to check out the fatidic hieroglyphs.[1]

He was a very good nigger

and it never occurred to him that he could hoe, burrow, cut anything, anything else really than insipid cane

He was a very good nigger.

And they threw stones at him, bits of scrap iron, broken bottles, but neither these stones, nor this scrap iron, nor these bottles . . . O peaceful years of God on this terraqueous[2] clod!

and the whip argued with the bombilation[3] of the flies over the sugary dew of our sores.

I say right on! The old negritude
progressively cadavers itself
the horizon breaks, recoils and expands
and through the shredding of clouds the flashing of a sign[4]
the slave ship cracks everywhere . . . Its belly convulses and resounds
. . . The ghastly tapeworm[5] of its cargo gnaws the fetid guts of the strange suckling of the sea!

And neither the joy of sails filled like a pocket stuffed with doubloons,
nor the tricks played on the dangerous stupidity of the frigates of order[6]
prevent it from hearing the threat of its intestinal rumblings

In vain to ignore them the captain hangs the biggest loudmouth nigger from the main yard or throws him into the sea, or feeds him to his mastiffs

Reeking of fried onions the nigger scum rediscovers the bitter taste of freedom in its spilled blood

And the nigger scum is on its feet

the seated nigger scum
unexpectedly standing
standing in the hold
standing in the cabins
standing on deck
standing in the wind
standing under the sun
standing in the blood

1. Characters in ancient Egyptian writing. "Fatidic": pertaining to fate.
2. From the Latin *terra*, "of the earth."
3. Swarming.
4. Like the clap of thunder heard when Moses brought down the tablets from Mount Sinai (Genesis 19.1–3).
5. A tropical parasite that lives in the intestines of its victims.
6. Patrol ships sent out from England to enforce Britain's abolition of slavery. "Doubloons": old Spanish coins.

  standing
    and
      free
standing and no longer a poor madwoman in her maritime freedom and
destitution gyrating in perfect drift[7]
and there she is:
most unexpectedly standing
standing in the rigging
standing at the tiller
standing at the compass
standing at the map
standing under the stars
  standing
    and
      free
and the lustral[8] ship fearlessly advances on the crumbling water.

And now our ignominious plops are rotting away!
by the clanking noon sea
by the burgeoning midnight sun[9]
listen sparrow hawk who holds the keys to the orient
by the disarmed day
by the stony spurt of the rain
listen dogfish that watches over the occident

listen white dog of the north, black serpent of the south that cinches
the sky girdle
There still remains one sea to cross
oh still one sea to cross
that I may invent my lungs
that the prince may hold his tongue
that the queen may lay me
still one old man to murder
one madman to deliver
that my soul may shine bark shine
bark bark bark
and the owl[1] my beautiful inquisitive angel may hoot.
The master of laughter?
The master of ominous silence?
The master of hope and despair?
The master of laziness? Master of the dance?
  It is I!
and for this reason, Lord,
the frail-necked men
receive and perceive deadly triangular calm[2]

7. An allusion to the "Ship of Fools" in which the insane were packed off to sea and set adrift. The passage describes the momentary disarray on the ship after being taken over by the victorious slaves.
8. Purifying. The slaves have been cleansed by their act of revolt.
9. A phenomenon that can be observed at the height of summer in the Arctic and Antarctic.
1. Césaire's guardian angel. The owl was also associated with Minerva, the goddess of wisdom in Roman mythology.
2. The Holy Trinity of Christianity was represented as a triangle, a figure associated in Césaire's consciousness with the triangular circuit of the slave trade.

Rally to my side my dances
you bad nigger dances
the carcan-cracker[3] dance
the prison-break dance
the it-is-beautiful-good-and-legitimate-to-be-a-nigger-dance
Rally to my side my dances and let the sun bounce on the racket of my hands

but no the unequal sun is not enough for me
coil, wind, around my new growth
light on my cadenced fingers
to you I surrender my conscience and its fleshy rhythm
to you I surrender the fire in which my weakness smolders
to you I surrender the "chain-gang"
to you the swamps
to you the nontourist of the triangular circuit
devour wind
to you I surrender my abrupt words
devour and encoil yourself
and self-encoiling embrace me with a more ample shudder
embrace me unto furious us
embrace, embrace US
but after having drawn from us blood
drawn by our own blood!
embrace, my purity mingles only with yours
so then embrace
like a field of even filagos[4]
at dusk
our multicolored purities
and bind, bind me without remorse
bind me with your vast arms to the luminous clay
bind my black vibration to the very navel of the world
bind, bind me, bitter brotherhood
then, strangling me with your lasso of stars
rise,
Dove[5]
rise
rise
rise
I follow you who are imprinted on my ancestral white cornea.[6]
rise sky licker
and the great black hole where a moon ago I wanted to drown it is there
I will now fish the malevolent tongue of the night in its motionless veerition![7]

1939

3. A dance of freedom. "Carcan": an iron collar fixed around the necks of slaves.
4. The causuarina tree, which grows tall and straight.
5. The symbol of Pentecost in Christian iconology, from which it has acquired its conventional meaning of peace.
6. The transparent tissue that covers the front of the eye.
7. Coined on a Latin verb "verri," meaning "to sweep," "to scrape a surface," and ultimately "to scan" [Translators' note].

OCTAVIO PAZ

A leading Mexican writer of the twentieth century, the Nobel Prize winner Octavio Paz (1914–1998) drew on ancient myth to characterize urban life in his native land and around the world. A poet, cultural critic, diplomat, and public intellectual, Paz applied the experimental forms of Latin American and European modernism to the challenge of expressing contemporary Mexican identity.

Paz was born during the chaotic years of the Mexican Revolution. His father, a journalist and lawyer, supported the revolutionary Emiliano Zapata and was exiled from Mexico after Zapata's death in 1919. Although Paz lived briefly with his father in Los Angeles, he grew up mostly in the suburban Mexico City home of his paternal grandfather, a liberal intellectual whose library included great works of Spanish classical literature and Latin American modernism. Paz started writing poetry in his teens and soon became involved in the literary journal *Contemporáneos*, which published translations of many French- and English-language modernists. He particularly admired the poetry of **Stéphane Mallarmé** and **T. S. Eliot**'s ***The Waste Land.*** Paz studied law at college before dropping out to teach at a school for peasant children in the Yucatán peninsula.

Inspired by the ideals of social justice espoused by the revolution, Paz became active in international left-wing politics. In 1937, during the Spanish Civil War, he attended the second International Congress of Anti-Fascist Writers in Spain as the guest of the Chilean poet **Pablo Neruda,** whose work Paz admired. "For me," he wrote, "Neruda was the great destructor-creator of Hispanic poetry." Like Neruda, Paz entered his country's diplomatic service, first representing Mexico as a cultural attaché in Paris from 1946 to 1951. He had long been interested in surrealism and became friendly with the movement's founder, **André Breton.** Later he would represent Mexico in Geneva, New York, and India, where he developed an interest in Buddhism and Hinduism.

The writer's most famous work on Mexican history and culture, *The Labyrinth of Solitude* (1950), emphasized the condition of solitude and despair that affected Mexicans but was in some sense universal: "our situation of alienation is that of the majority of people." He saw the Mexican as by nature reserved, enclosed, and isolated. At this time, Paz still acknowledged the legacy of the Mexican Revolution in bringing individuals together as a community. He became disillusioned with Mexican politics and resigned his post as ambassador to India in 1968, however, in protest against the Mexican government massacre of student demonstrators. Paz returned to Mexico City and wrote a series of poems later collected as *Vuelta* (*Return*), which was also the title of a journal he edited from 1975 until his death. In 1990 he celebrated the end of communism in Eastern Europe by hosting a conference of leading writers and intellectuals from East and West in Mexico City. That same year the Nobel committee honored him for his "impassioned writing with wide horizons, characterized by sensuous intelligence and humanistic integrity."

The works selected here span the later stages of Paz's career, when he was at the height of his poetic powers. They combine intense lyricism with a surrealist-inspired fascination with the irrational and the unconscious. Surrealism, Buddhism, and Hinduism seemed to Paz to offer alternatives to the rationalism of traditional European culture. "Surrealism was not merely an esthetic, poetic and philosophical doctrine," he once said. "It was a vital attitude. A negation of the contemporary world and at the same time an attempt to substitute other values for those of democratic bourgeois society: eroticism, poetry, imagination, liberty, spiritual adventure, vision." Paz's long poem "I Speak of the City" (1976) evokes elements of the Mexican capital, New York City, London, and Rome and draws on the tradition of free verse from **Walt Whitman** and T. S. Eliot through the surrealists. Another late poem, specifically about New York, "Central Park" (1987) was inspired by a painting by the Belgian artist Pierre Alechinsky and contains the repeated warning (in English in the original) "Don't cross Central Park at night." "Small Variation" (1987), written when the poet was in his seventies, recollects the sorrow of Gilgamesh in the ancient epic and echoes other, later laments to create a moving meditation on human mortality. Throughout these lyrical and imaginative works, Paz uses rhythmic, loose poetic forms, in the tradition of free verse, to present a haunting vision of urban life that is in touch with the deeper, subterranean forces of the human spirit.

I Speak of the City[1]

for Eliot Weinberger

a novelty today, tomorrow a ruin from the past, buried and resurrected every day,
lived together in streets, plazas, buses, taxis, movie houses, theaters, bars, hotels, pigeon coops and catacombs,
the enormous city that fits in a room three yards square, and endless as a galaxy,
the city that dreams us all, that all of us build and unbuild and rebuild as we dream,
the city we all dream, that restlessly changes while we dream it,
the city that wakes every hundred years and looks at itself in the mirror of a word and doesn't recognize itself and goes back to sleep,
the city that sprouts from the eyelids of the woman who sleeps at my side, and is transformed,
with its monuments and statues, its histories and legends,
into a fountain made of countless eyes, and each eye reflects the same landscape, frozen in time,
before schools and prisons, alphabets and numbers, the altar and the law:
the river that is four rivers, the orchard, the tree, the Female and Male, dressed in wind—
to go back, go back, to be clay again, to bathe in that light, to sleep under those votive lights,

1. Translated by Eliot Weinberger, a frequent translator of Paz's work to whom the poem is dedicated.

to float on the waters of time like the flaming maple leaf the current drags along,
to go back—are we asleep or awake?—we are, we are nothing more, day breaks, it's early,
we are in the city, we cannot leave except to fall into another city, different yet identical,
I speak of the immense city, that daily reality composed of two words: *the others*,
and in every one of them there is an I clipped from a we, an I adrift,
I speak of the city built by the dead, inhabited by their stern ghosts, ruled by their despotic memory,
the city I talk to when I talk to nobody, the city that dictates these insomniac words,
I speak of towers, bridges, tunnels, hangars, wonders and disasters,
the abstract State and its concrete police, the schoolteachers, jailers, preachers,
the shops that have everything, where we spend everything, and it all turns to smoke,
the markets with their pyramids of fruit, the turn of the seasons, the sides of beef hanging from the hooks, the hills of spices and the towers of bottles and preserves,
all of the flavors and colors, all the smells and all the stuff, the tide of voices—water, metal, wood, clay—the bustle, the haggling and conniving as old as time,
I speak of the buildings of stone and marble, of cement, glass and steel, of the people in the lobbies and doorways, of the elevators that rise and fall like the mercury in thermometers,
of the banks and their boards of directors, of factories and their managers, of the workers and their incestuous machines,
I speak of the timeless parade of prostitution through streets long as desire and boredom,
of the coming and going of cars, mirrors of our anxieties, business, passions (why? toward what? for what?),
of the hospitals that are always full, and where we always die alone,
I speak of the half-light of certain churches and the flickering candles at the altars,
the timid voices with which the desolate talk to saints and virgins in a passionate, failing language,
I speak of dinner under a squinting light at a limping table with chipped plates,
of the innocent tribes that camp in the empty lots with their women and children, their animals and their ghosts,
of the rats in the sewers and the brave sparrows that nest in the wires, in the cornices and the martyred trees,
of the contemplative cats and their libertine novels in the light of the moon, cruel goddess of the rooftops,
of the stray dogs that are our Franciscans and *bhikkus*,[2] the dogs that scratch up the bones of the sun,
I speak of the anchorite and the libertarian brotherhood, of the secret plots of law enforcers and of bands of thieves,

2. Buddhist monks. "Franciscans": Catholic monks.

of the conspiracies of levelers and the Society of Friends of Crime, of the Suicide Club, and of Jack the Ripper,[3]
of the Friend of the People, sharpener of the guillotine, of Caesar, Delight of Humankind,[4]
I speak of the paralytic slum, the cracked wall, the dry fountain, the graffitied statue,
I speak of garbage heaps the size of mountains, and of melancholy sunlight filtered by the smog,
of broken glass and the desert of scrap iron, of last night's crime, and of the banquet of the immortal Trimalchio,[5]
of the moon in the television antennas, and a butterfly on a filthy jar,
I speak of dawns like a flight of herons on the lake, and the sun of transparent wings that lands on the rock foliage of the churches, and the twittering of light on the glass stalks of the palaces,
I speak of certain afternoons in early fall, waterfalls of immaterial gold, the transformation of this world, when everything loses its body, everything is held in suspense,
and the light thinks, and each one of us feels himself thought by that reflective light, and for one long moment time dissolves, we are air once more,
I speak of the summer, of the slow night that grows on the horizon like a mountain of smoke, and bit by bit it crumbles, falling over us like a wave,
the elements are reconciled, night has stretched out, and its body is a powerful river of sudden sleep, we rock in the waves of its breathing, the hour is tangible, we can touch it like a fruit,
they have lit the lights, and the avenues burn with the brilliancy of desire, in the parks electric light breaks through the branches and falls over us like a green and phosphorescent mist that illuminates but does not wet us, the trees murmur, they tell us something,
there are streets in the half-light that are a smiling insinuation, we don't know where they lead, perhaps to the ferry for the lost islands,
I speak of the stars over the high terraces and the indecipherable sentences they write on the stone of the sky,
I speak of the sudden downpour that lashes the windowpanes and bends the trees, that lasted twenty-five minutes and now, up above, there are blue slits and streams of light, steam rises from the asphalt, the cars glisten, there are puddles where ships of reflections sail,
I speak of nomadic clouds, and of a thin music that lights a room on the fifth floor, and a murmur of laughter in the middle of the night like water that flows far-off through roots and grasses,
I speak of the longed-for encounter with that unexpected form with which the unknown is made flesh, and revealed to each of us:

3. Famous serial killer in 19th-century London whose identity was never discovered. The Society of Friends of Crime is a fictional organization invented by the Marquis de Sade (1740–1814). The Suicide Club was a similar organization invented by the Scottish novelist Robert Louis Stevenson (1850–1894). All three references concern urban criminality.

4. An epithet of the Roman emperor Titus (39–81). Caesar was a title associated with several Roman emperors. The French revolutionary Jean-Paul Marat said that the king should be "a friend of the people." These references concern the power of a strong leader to control the mob.

5. Character in *The Satyricon* by Petronius (c. 27–66), famous for throwing ostentatious dinners of many courses.

eyes that are the night half-open and the day that wakes, the sea stretching out and the flame that speaks, powerful breasts: lunar tide,
lips that say *sesame*, and time opens, and the little room becomes a garden of change, air and fire entwine, earth and water mingle,
or the arrival of that moment there, on the other side that is really here, where the key locks and time ceases to flow:
the moment of *until now*, the last of the gasps, the moaning, the anguish, the soul loses its body and crashes through a hole in the floor, falling in itself, and time has run aground, and we walk through an endless corridor, panting in the sand,
is that music coming closer or receding, are those pale lights just lit or going out? space is singing, time has vanished: it is the gasp, it is the glance that slips through the blank wall, it is the wall that stays silent, the wall,
I speak of our public history, and of our secret history, yours and mine,
I speak of the forest of stone, the desert of the prophets, the ant-heap of souls, the congregation of tribes, the house of mirrors, the labyrinth of echoes,
I speak of the great murmur that comes from the depths of time, the incoherent whisper of nations uniting or splitting apart, the wheeling of multitudes and their weapons like boulders hurling down, the dull sound of bones falling into the pit of history,
I speak of the city, shepherd of the centuries, mother that gives birth to us and devours us, that creates us and forgets.

1976

Small Variation[1]

Like music come back to life—
who brings it from over there, from the other side,
who conducts it through the spirals
of the mind's ear?—
like the vanished
moment that returns
and is again the same
presence erasing itself,
the syllables unearthed
make sound without sound:
and at the hour of our death, amen.[2]

In the school chapel
I spoke them many times
without conviction. Now I hear them
spoken by a voice without lips,
a sound of sand sifting away,
while in my skull the hours toll
and time takes another turn around my night.

1. Translated by Mark Strand.
2. Final line of the Lord's Prayer.

I am not the first man on earth—
I tell myself in the manner of Epictetus[3]—
who is going to die.
And as I say this
the world breaks down in my blood.

The sorrow
of Gilgamesh[4] when he returned
from the land without twilight
is my sorrow. On our shadowy earth
each man is Adam:
with him the world begins,[5]
with him it ends.
Between after and before—
brackets of stone—
for an instant that will never return I shall be
the first man and I shall be the last.
And as I say it, the instant—
bodiless, weightless—
opens under my feet
and closes over me and is pure time.

1987

Central Park[1]

Green and black thickets, bare spots,
leafy river knotting into itself:
it runs motionless through the leaden buildings
and there, where light turns to doubt
and stone wants to be shadow, it vanishes.
Don't cross Central Park at night.[2]

Day falls, night flares up,
Alechinsky draws a magnetic rectangle,
a trap of lines, a corral of ink:
inside there is a fallen beast,
two eyes and a twisting rage.
Don't cross Central Park at night.

There are no exits or entrances,
enclosed in a ring of light
the grass beast sleeps with eyes open,
the moon exhumes razors,

3. Greek stoic philosopher who counseled acceptance of fate, including mortality.
4. Protagonist of the Mesopotamian *Epic of Gilgamesh*, who visits the underworld where the dead dwell.
5. Adam was punished with mortality for his disobedience (Genesis 2.17).

1. Translated by Eliot Weinberger. The poem was inspired by a painting by Belgian artist Pierre Alechinsky entitled *Central Park* (1965).
2. This line is in English in the Spanish version of the poem.

the water in the shadows has become green fire.
Don't cross Central Park at night.

There are no entrances but everyone,
in the middle of a phrase dangling from the telephone,
from the top of the fountain of silence or laughter,
from the glass cage of the eye that watches us,
everyone, all of us are falling in the mirror.
Don't cross Central Park at night.

The mirror is made of stone and the stone now is shadow,
there are two eyes the color of anger,
a ring of cold, a belt of blood,
there is a wind that scatters the reflections
of Alice, dismembered in the pond.
Don't cross Central Park at night.

Open your eyes: now you are inside yourself,
you sail in a boat of monosyllables
across the mirror-pond, you disembark
at the Cobra dock: it is a yellow taxi
that carries you to the land of flames
across Central Park at night.

1987

M. Slodki

Künstlerkneipe Voltaire

Allabendlich (mit Ausnahme von Freitag)

Musik-Vorträge und Rezitationen

Eröffnung Samstag den 5. Februar

im Saale der „Meierei“ Spiegelgasse 1

MANIFESTOS

The manifesto is one of the most distinctive genres of the twentieth century. Artists—painters, writers, composers, and other creative people—had always thought deeply about, and sometimes openly declared the principles of, their work, but in the twentieth century they devoted more time and attention to doing so than ever before. Individual artists and, more often, groups hammered out declarations with which they hoped to outdo their predecessors and rivals. Soon hundreds and even thousands of manifestos started to appear in newspapers, as leaflets, or as performance pieces declaimed loudly at gatherings large and small, announcing the birth of movements or "-isms." Some artists rejected these shrill pronouncements and recommended that their colleagues just get on with their work. But even detractors had to admit that they were living in an age of manifestos.

Manifestos came to dominate literature and the arts, but they originated in the world of politics. Inspired by political assertions such as the **Declaration of Independence** in the United States and the **Declaration of the Rights of Man and of the Citizen** in France, disenfranchised groups sought to articulate their demands and visions. In 1848, Karl Marx and Friedrich Engels penned the document that was, finally, to give specific meaning to the word: the *Manifesto of the Communist Party.* By the early twentieth century, the *Communist Manifesto*, as it came to be known, was a revolutionary bestseller, a text that had set out to change the world and had already partly succeeded.

This lithograph by Marcel Slodki advertised the opening of the Cabaret Voltaire in Zurich in 1916.

Both the notoriety and the success of Marx and Engels's text inspired artists to continue writing manifestos whose goal was to revolutionize literature and other forms of creative work. The Chinese communist **Chen Duxiu**, for example, praised the European experience of political revolution and sought to translate it into a literary revolution through his manifesto. The Italian **F. T. Marinetti**, who had been a socialist before he made common cause with the fascist Benito Mussolini, gained an unsavory reputation for the dozens of manifestos he wrote. He also changed their form. Whereas Marx and Engels had devoted a significant part of their manifesto to historical analysis, Marinetti condensed the genre to highlight a series of short, numbered declarations and demands. "Precision and clarity," he said, were the main features of the manifesto, but he forgot to include the third one: aggression. Yet not all writers of the genre employed an assertive style. **André Breton** wrote long, meandering manifestos, while Dadaists such as Tristan Tzara liked to poke fun at the form even as they used it to great effect.

World War II and the period of reconstruction that followed dampened the revolutionary ambitions of artists, but in the 1960s and 1970s a wave of both political and artistic proclamations emerged. The **Black Panther Party** harkened back to the Declaration of Independence in voicing its demands, while **Valerie Solanas** presented the more extreme fringe of feminism with her **SCUM Manifesto** (the acronym stood for Society for Cutting Up Men). Even though manifestos do not dominate contemporary literature, they continue to be written in large numbers, by groups and individuals alike.

F. T. MARINETTI

The Italian Filippo Tommaso Marinetti (1876–1944) began as a symbolist poet and socialist believer before he broke with socialism by agitating for Italy's entry into World War I. By this time, he had started a movement named futurism. Advertised through manifestos, futurism quickly became the paradigm for an avant-garde effort whose primary purpose was to attack what was inherited and to celebrate what was new. Museums, repositories of previous generations' achievements, were the chief target of futurist critique, together with Italy's beautiful old cities such as Venice. In fact, Marinetti carried numerous copies of one of his manifestos up the clock tower in Piazza San Marco, in Venice, and let them rain down on tourists and inhabitants alike. The writer did not set his eyes on modernizing just Italy, however. Dubbed "the caffeine of Europe," he traveled around, seeking to promote his cause. While Marinetti managed to turn futurism into a household word in art circles and beyond, he failed to turn the movement into an official fascist art. Mussolini tolerated Marinetti as a fellow fascist, but he nevertheless kept both him and his movement at arm's length.

The Foundation and Manifesto of Futurism[1]

My friends and I had stayed up all night, sitting beneath the lamps of a mosque, whose star-studded, filigreed brass domes resembled our souls, all aglow with the concentrated brilliance of an electric heart. For many hours, we'd been trailing our age-old indolence back and forth over richly adorned, oriental carpets, debating at the uttermost boundaries of logic and filling up masses of paper with our frenetic writings.

Immense pride filled our hearts, for we felt that at that hour we alone were vigilant and unbending, like magnificent beacons or guards in forward positions, facing an army of hostile stars, which watched us closely from their celestial encampments. Alone we were, with the stokers working feverishly at the infernal fires of great liners; alone with the black specters that rake through the red-hot bellies of locomotives, hurtling along at breakneck speed; alone with the floundering drunks, with the uncertain beating of our wings, along the city walls.

Suddenly we were startled by the terrifying clatter of huge, double-decker trams jolting by, all ablaze with different-colored lights, as if they were villages

1. Translated by Doug Thompson.

in festive celebration, which the River Po,[2] in full spate, suddenly shakes and uproots to sweep them away down to the sea, over the falls and through the whirlpools of a mighty flood.

Then the silence became more somber. Yet even while we were listening to the tedious, mumbled prayers of an ancient canal and the creaking bones of dilapidated palaces on their tiresome stretches of soggy lawn, we caught the sudden roar of ravening motorcars, right there beneath our windows.

"Come on! Let's go!" I said. "Come on, my lads, let's get out of here! At long last, all the myths and mystical ideals are behind us. We're about to witness the birth of a Centaur[3] and soon we shall witness the flight of the very first Angels! . . . We shall have to shake the gates of life itself to test their locks and hinges! . . . Let's be off! See there, the Earth's very first dawn! Nothing can equal the splendor of the sun's red sword slicing through our millennial darkness, for the very first time!"

We approached the three panting beasts to stroke their burning breasts, full of loving admiration. I stretched myself out on my car like a corpse on its bier, but immediately I was revived as the steering wheel, like a guillotine blade, menaced my belly.

A furious gust of madness tore us out of ourselves and hurled us along roads as deep and plunging as the beds of torrents. Every now and then a feeble light, flickering behind some windowpane, made us mistrust the calculations of our all-too-fallible eyes. I cried out: "The scent, nothing but the scent! That's all an animal needs!"

And we, like young lions, chased after Death, whose black pelt was dotted with pale crosses, as he sped away across the vast, violet-tinted sky, vital and throbbing.

And yet we had no idealized Lover whose sublime being rose up into the skies; no cruel Queen to whom we might offer up our corpses, contorted like Byzantine rings! Nothing at all worth dying for, other than the desire to divest ourselves finally of the courage that weighed us down!

But we sped on, squashing beneath our scorching tires the snarling guard dogs at the doorsteps of their houses, like crumpled collars under a hot iron. Death, tamed by this time, went past me at each bend, only to offer me his willing paw; and sometimes he would lie down, his teeth grinding, eyeing me with his soft, gentle look from every puddle in the road.

"Let's leave wisdom behind as if it were some hideous shell, and cast ourselves, like fruit, flushed with pride, into the immense, twisting jaws of the wind! . . . Let's become food for the Unknown, not out of desperation, but simply to fill up the deep wells of the Absurd to the very brim!"

I had hardly got these words out of my mouth when I swung the car right around sharply, with all the crazy irrationality of a dog trying to bite its own tail. Then suddenly a pair of cyclists came toward me, gesticulating that I was on the wrong side, dithering about in front of me like two different lines of thought, both persuasive but for all that, quite contradictory. Their stupid uncertainty was in my way . . . How ridiculous! What a nuisance! . . . I braked hard and to my disgust the wheels left the ground and I flew into a ditch . . .

O mother of a ditch, brimful with muddy water! Fine repair shop of a ditch! How I relished your strength-giving sludge that reminded me so much of the

2. Marinetti was living in Milan, not far from the Po River, to which the city is connected by the Navigilio Canal.

3. Half-horse, half-human (as the automobile with driver is half-machine, half-human).

saintly black breast of my Sudanese nurse . . . When I got myself up—soaked, filthy, foul-smelling rag that I was—from beneath my overturned car, I had a wonderful sense of my heart being pierced by the red-hot sword of joy!

A crowd of fishermen, with their lines, and some gouty old naturalists were already milling around this wondrous spectacle. Patiently, meticulously, they set up tall trestles and laid out huge iron-mesh nets to fish out my car, as if it were a great shark that had been washed up and stranded. Slowly the car's frame emerged, leaving its heavy, sober bodywork at the bottom of the ditch as well as its soft, comfortable upholstery, as though they were merely scales.

They thought it was dead, that gorgeous shark of mine, but a caress was all it needed to revive it, and there it was, back from the dead, darting along with its powerful fins!

So, with my face covered in repair-shop grime—a fine mixture of metallic flakes, profuse sweat, and pale-blue soot—with my arms all bruised and bandaged, yet quite undaunted, I dictated our foremost desires to all men on Earth who are truly alive:

THE FUTURIST MANIFESTO

1. We want to sing about the love of danger, about the use of energy and recklessness as common, daily practice.
2. Courage, boldness, and rebellion will be essential elements in our poetry.
3. Up to now, literature has extolled a contemplative stillness, rapture, and reverie. We intend to glorify aggressive action, a restive wakefulness, life at the double, the slap and the punching fist.
4. We believe that this wonderful world has been further enriched by a new beauty, the beauty of speed. A racing car, its bonnet decked out with exhaust pipes like serpents with galvanic breath . . . a roaring motorcar, which seems to race on like machine-gun fire, is more beautiful than the Winged Victory of Samothrace.[4]
5. We wish to sing the praises of the man behind the steering wheel, whose sleek shaft traverses the Earth, which itself is hurtling at breakneck speed along the racetrack of its orbit.
6. The poet will have to do all in his power, passionately, flamboyantly, and with generosity of spirit, to increase the delirious fervor of the primordial elements.
7. There is no longer any beauty except the struggle. Any work of art that lacks a sense of aggression can never be a masterpiece. Poetry must be thought of as a violent assault upon the forces of the unknown with the intention of making them prostrate themselves at the feet of mankind.
8. We stand upon the furthest promontory of the ages! . . . Why should we be looking back over our shoulders, if what we desire is to smash down the mysterious doors of the Impossible? Time and Space died yesterday. We are already living in the realms of the Absolute, for we have already created infinite, omnipresent speed.
9. We wish to glorify war—the sole cleanser of the world—militarism, patriotism, the destructive act of the libertarian, beautiful ideas worth dying for, and scorn for women.

4. A famous Hellenistic sculpture (2nd century B.C.E.) from the Greek island of Samothrace; now housed in the Louvre Museum, Paris.

10. We wish to destroy museums, libraries, academies of any sort, and fight against moralism, feminism, and every kind of materialistic, self-serving cowardice.
11. We shall sing of the great multitudes who are roused up by work, by pleasure, or by rebellion; of the many-hued, many-voiced tides of revolution in our modern capitals; of the pulsating, nightly ardor of arsenals and shipyards, ablaze with their violent electric moons; of railway stations, voraciously devouring smoke-belching serpents; of workshops hanging from the clouds by their twisted threads of smoke; of bridges which, like giant gymnasts, bestride the rivers, flashing in the sunlight like gleaming knives; of intrepid steamships that sniff out the horizon; of broad-breasted locomotives, champing on their wheels like enormous steel horses, bridled with pipes; and of the lissome flight of the airplane, whose propeller flutters like a flag in the wind, seeming to applaud, like a crowd excited.

It is from Italy that we hurl at the whole world this utterly violent, inflammatory manifesto of ours, with which today we are founding "Futurism," because we wish to free our country from the stinking canker of its professors, archaeologists, tour guides, and antiquarians.

For far too long has Italy been a marketplace for junk dealers. We want to free our country from the endless number of museums that everywhere cover her like countless graveyards. Museums, graveyards! . . . They're the same thing, really, because of their grim profusion of corpses that no one remembers. Museums. They're just public flophouses, where things sleep on forever, alongside other loathsome or nameless things! Museums: ridiculous abattoirs for painters and sculptors, who are furiously stabbing one another to death with colors and lines, all along the walls where they vie for space.

Sure, people may go there on pilgrimage about once a year, just as they do to the cemetery on All Souls Day—I'll grant you that! And yes, once a year a wreath of flowers is laid at the feet of the *Gioconda*[5]—I'll grant you that too! But what I won't allow is that all our miseries, our fragile courage, or our sickly anxieties get marched daily around these museums. Why should we want to poison ourselves? Why should we want to rot?

What on earth is there to be discovered in an old painting other than the labored contortions of the artist, trying to break down the insuperable barriers which prevent him from giving full expression to his artistic dream? . . . Admiring an old painting is just like pouring our purest feelings into a funerary urn, instead of projecting them far and wide, in violent outbursts of creation and of action.

Do you really want to waste all your best energies in this unending, futile veneration for the past, from which you emerge fatally exhausted, diminished, trampled down?

Make no mistake, I'm convinced that for an artist to go every day to museums and libraries and academies (the cemeteries of wasted effort, calvaries of crucified dreams, records of impulses cut short! . . .) is every bit as harmful as the prolonged overprotectiveness of parents for certain young people who get carried away by their talent and ambition. For those who are dying anyway, for

5. *La Gioconda* is the Italian name for the *Mona Lisa*, the famous painting by Leonardo da Vinci (1452–1519).

the invalids, for the prisoners—who cares? The admirable past may be a balm to their worries, since for them the future is a closed book . . . but we, the powerful young Futurists, don't want to have anything to do with it, the past!

So let them come, the happy-go-lucky fire raisers with their blackened fingers! Here they come! Here they are! . . . Come on then! Set fire to the library shelves! . . . Divert the canals so they can flood the museums! . . . Oh, what a pleasure it is to see those revered old canvases, washed out and tattered, drifting away in the water! . . . Grab your picks and your axes and your hammers and then demolish, pitilessly demolish, all venerated cities!

The oldest among us are thirty; so we have at least ten years in which to complete our task. When we reach forty, other, younger, and more courageous men will very likely toss us into the trash can, like useless manuscripts. And that's what we want!

Our successors will rise up against us, from far away, from every part of the world, dancing on the winged cadenzas[6] of their first songs, flexing their hooked, predatory claws, sniffing like dogs at the doors of our academies, at the delicious scent of our decaying minds, already destined for the catacombs of libraries.

But we won't be there . . . Eventually, they will find us, on a winter's night, in a humble shed, far away in the country, with an incessant rain drumming upon it, and they'll see us huddling anxiously together beside our airplanes, warming our hands around the flickering flames of our present-day books, which burn away beneath our images as they are taking flight.

They will rant and rave around us, gasping in outrage and fury, and then—frustrated by our proud, unwavering boldness—they will hurl themselves upon us to kill us, driven by a hatred made all the more implacable because their hearts overflow with love and admiration for us.

Strong, healthy Injustice will flash dazzlingly in their eyes. Art, indeed, can be nothing but violence, cruelty, and injustice.

The oldest among us are only thirty. And yet we have squandered fortunes, a thousand fortunes of strength, love, daring, cleverness, and of naked willpower. We have tossed them aside impatiently, in anger, without thinking of the cost, without a moment's hesitation, without ever resting, gasping for breath . . . Just look at us! We're not exhausted yet! Our hearts feel no weariness, for they feed on fire, on hatred and on speed! . . . Does that surprise you? . . . That's logical enough, I suppose, as you don't even remember having lived! Standing tall on the roof of the world, yet again we fling our challenge at the stars!

Do you have any objections? . . . All right! Sure, we know what they are . . . We have understood! . . . Our sharp, duplicitous intelligence tells us that we are the sum total and the extension of our forebears.—Well, maybe! . . . Be that as it may! . . . But what does it matter? We want nothing to do with it! . . . Woe betide anybody whom we catch repeating these infamous words of ours.

Look around you!

Standing tall on the roof of the world, yet once again, we hurl our defiance at the stars! . . .

1909

6. The close of a musical phrase.

CHEN DUXIU

Chen Duxiu (1879–1942) played an important role in modernizing China, in the realm of both politics and culture. A founding member of the Chinese Communist Party, he was later expelled and became associated with Leon Trotsky (1879–1940), the Russian communist leader who was himself discredited by officials of the party. To contribute to the renovation of Chinese culture, Chen Duxiu founded the journal *Jeunesse* (*New Youth*), which was allied with the May Fourth Movement advocating Chinese nationalism after the end of World War I. His manifesto "On Literary Revolution" (1917) celebrates Western revolutions and exhorts the journal's Chinese readers to embrace a similar attitude. In particular, Chen Duxiu sought to diminish his country's veneration of the Chinese classics as well as of other traditional forms of philosophy and literature, including Tang Dynasty writing. Demanding an end to the emulation of the classics, he advocated a free, unadorned form of literary expression that could be achieved only through literary revolution.

On Literary Revolution[1]

From whence arose the awesome and brilliant Europe of today? I say from the legacy of revolution. In European languages, "revolution" means the elimination of the old and the changeover to the new, not at all the same as the so-called dynastic cycles of our Middle Kingdom.[2] Since the literary renaissance, therefore, there have been a revolution in politics, a revolution in religion, and a revolution in morality and ethics. Literary art as well has not been without revolution: there is no literary art that does not renew itself and advance itself with revolution. The history of contemporary European modernization can simply be called the history of revolutions. So I say that the awesome and brilliant Europe of today is the legacy of revolution.

My oblivious and fainthearted countrymen are as fearful of revolution as they are of snakes and scorpions. So even after three political revolutions,[3] the darkness has yet to wane. The lesser reason is that all three revolutions started with a bang and ended with a whimper, unable to wash away old perspiration with fresh blood. The greater reason is the ethics, morality, and culture, layered in darkness and mired in shameful filth, that have occupied the very core of our people's spirit and have prevented the emergence of revolutions with either bangs or whimpers. That is the reason the political revolutions have not brought about any change, have not achieved any results, in our society. The

1. Translated by Timothy Wong.
2. Traditional name for China.
3. The Chinese Revolution of 1911 established a republic in 1912, but a power struggle followed, leading to the Second Revolution in 1913, a brief renewal of empire in 1915, and a reestablishment of the republic in 1916. Civil war was to continue almost uninterrupted for the next twenty years.

overall cause of all this is the ill-will our people bear toward revolution, not knowing that it is the cutting edge of modernization.

The problem of Confucianism[4] has been attracting much attention in the nation: this is the first indication of the revolution in ethics and morality. Literary revolution has been fermenting for quite some time. The immediate pioneer who first raised the flag is my friend Hu Shi.[5] I am willing to be the enemy of the nation's scholars and raise high the banner of the "Army of Literary Revolution," in vocal support of my friend. On the banner will be written large the three great ideological tenets of our revolutionary army: (1) Down with the ornate, sycophantic literature of the aristocracy; up with the plain, expressive literature of the people! (2) Down with stale, pompous classical literature; up with fresh, sincere realist literature! (3) Down with obscure, abstruse eremitic[6] literature; up with comprehensible popularized social literature!

The "Airs of the States" in the *Book of Songs* were full of the lowly speech of the streets, and the *Elegies of Chu*[7] employed rustic expressions in abundance, but both were unfailingly elegant and remarkable. In their wake, however, writers of *fu* poetry[8] in the Former and Later Han dynasties raised their eulogistic voices and produced ornate and sycophantic writings, dense with words but sparse in meaning. This was the beginning of the trend in classical aristocratic literature of making artifacts for the dead. The five-syllable poetry since the Wei and Jin[9] was expressive and descriptive, a change from the pedantic and allusive style of the preceding period. For its time, it could have been called a great literary revolution, and indeed, it was a great literary advance. Still, it relied on high antiquity and was artless in its diction and obscure in its meaning. It did not draw from social phenomena for its source material. So ultimately it remained the stuff of the upper class and cannot be called the popularized literature of the people. After the Qi and the Liang dynasties,[1] prosodic parallelism was still *de rigueur.*[2] In the Tang dynasty, it developed into regulated verse, while parallelism persisted in prose, as it has always done since the time of the *Book of History* and the *Book of Changes.*[3] (In prose compositions, the habit of the ancients was not only antithetical parallelism, but also the frequent employment of rhyme. For this reason, many experts in parallel prose favor the theory that parallelism is the most orthodox of Chinese prose forms. My late friend Wang Wusheng was one such person. They do not know that in ancient times it was not simple to write down compositions, and rhyme and parallelism helped to make them easier to recite and to transmit. How can later writers be so muddled about this?)

Since the Eastern Jin, parallel prose was used even for minor reports and notices; in the Tang, it became the antithetical form. That poetry should be "regulated" and prose "parallel" was an idea that originated in the Six Dynasties[4]

4. The philosophy associated with Confucius (551–479 B.C.E.).
5. Chinese philosopher and diplomat (1891–1962).
6. In this context, aimed at a small audience.
7. Classical Chinese poetry anthology, like *The Book of Songs* or *Classic of Poetry*, from the 1st millennium B.C.E.
8. Ancient Chinese prose poetry, popular in the Han Dynasty (206 B.C.E.–220 C.E.).
9. Chinese dynasties (220–420).
1. Chinese dynasties (479–557) preceding the Tang Dynasty (618–907).
2. Required by custom (French).
3. *I Ching*, an ancient book of Chinese philosophy. *The Book of History* is an anthology of classical Chinese documents.
4. A period from 220 to 589 when China was divided among six ruling dynasties.

and became well established in the Tang period. These genres developed further into linked verse and into "four-six" prose. At its best, this kind of ornate, sycophantic, pompous, and hollow classical literature of the aristocrats is no more than a clay doll applied with powder and rouge. Its value is hardly higher than that of "eight-legged" examination essays.[5] It can be considered a literary dead end.

The abrupt rise of Han Yu and Liu Zongyuan wiped away the effete and redundant style of their predecessors. The drift of the times was a transition between the aristocratic classical literature of the Six Dynasties and the popularized literature of the Song and Yuan. Han Yu, Liu Zongyuan, Yuan Zhen, and Bai Juyi[6] rose with the times and became the central figures of the new literary movement. It is commonly said that Han Yu's essays reversed the decline of the eight dynasties from the Eastern Han to the Sui. Even though this is not certain, he nevertheless is a giant for changing the literary practices of the eight dynasties and for opening the way to Song and Yuan literature. That we today are less than totally satisfied with Han Yu, however, can be traced to two points. The first is his idea that literature should follow ancient authority. Even though it is no longer classicist, his literature does not depart from the aristocratic mold. In terms of content, it is far less rich than that found in the various fictional works of the Tang. In the end, he succeeded only in creating a new kind of aristocratic literature. Second, his view of "literature to convey the Way" is erroneous. Literature was originally not designed to carry such burdens; the concept of "literature conveys the Way," which was established by Han Yu and ended with Zeng Guofan,[7] is no more than an extremely shallow and unsubstantial subterfuge co-opted from the tradition of Confucius and Mencius.[8] I have often said that the "literature to convey the Way" practiced by the great writers of the Tang and the Song dynasties is of a kind with the view of "speaking through the sages" in the "eight-legged" essay. From these two points, we can see that Han Yu's reversal of ancient traditions was brought about by his times. In terms of literary history, he himself was not extremely remarkable.

Brilliantly remarkable in the literature of more recent history are the plays of the Yuan and Ming dynasties and the fiction of the Ming and Qing dynasties.[9] Regrettably, the development of these genres was blocked by fiendish forces, and they were aborted before they could emerge naturally from the womb. The result is that China's literature today is lifeless and stale, unable to stand next to that of Europe. Now who were these fiends? They are none other than the Earlier and the Later Seven Masters of the Ming dynasty and those who followed Tang-Song literary thought, Gui Youguang, Fang Bao, Liu Dakui, and Yao Nai.[1] These eighteen fiends worshipped the past and despised the contemporary. They dominated

5. A style of essay required of candidates for the civil service examination under the Chinese Empire.

6. Han Yu (768–824), Liu Zongyuan (773–819), Yuan Zhen (779–831), and Bai Juyi (772–846) were much admired during the Song (960–1274) and Yuan (1271–1368) dynasties.

7. Zeng Guofan (1811–1872), a neo-Confucian scholar viewed as conservative by Chen Duxiu.

8. Major interpreter (ca. 372–289 B.C.E.) of Confucius.

9. The final Chinese imperial dynasties (1368–1644 and 1644–1912).

1. Founders of the Tongcheng school, who modernized the classicism of the fourteen masters in the Qing period. Chen Duxiu is criticizing all eighteen for their traditionalism.

the literary scene with their plodding, unspontaneous style, so that even the names of the era's real literary heroes—such as Ma Zhiyuan or Shi Nai'an or Cao Xueqin[2]—remained almost unknown to their countrymen. Poems like those of the Seven Masters are so intensely imitative of the ancients that we can consider them copies. The essays of Gui, Fang, Liu, and Yao are either elegies written for the sake of literary fame and glory, or wailings without woe, full of pedantic language. There are always back-and-forth discussions and circumlocutions—about what I don't know. These literary authors were not creative talents; there was nothing of substance in their hearts. Their only skills were in imitating the ancients and deceiving people, and they did not write a single word of lasting value. Even though they measured themselves by their writings, what they wrote had not a smidgen of relevance to the modernization or progress of contemporary society.

China's literature today has inherited the faults of previous eras. What is called the Tongcheng school is merely the amalgamation of Tang-Song style with that of the "eight-legged" essays. And the so-called "parallel prose" is merely the "four-six" prose of Zhang Zaogong and Yuan Mei,[3] just as the Xijiang School is the idolization of Huang Tingjian.[4] Look as one might, there are no representative literary giants who, naked and unadorned, expressed their inner feeling or described the world of their times. Not only are there none in our nation who can be considered literary giants representative of the times, the very idea of such a figure does not exist. So although our literary writings are not worth reading, our practical compositions are even more absurd. Inscriptional writings and epitaphs are so fulsome in their praise that readers definitely do not believe what they are reading even as writers must carry on pro forma. Everyday notices begin and end with all sorts of formulaic hyperbole. Someone in mourning for the dead may be living in luxury and eating well; but the funeral notice has to claim that he is "numb with grief on a mat of straw with an earthen pillow." A testimonial plaque presented to a physician will either say that "His skill surpasses that of the legendary healers Qi Bo and the Yellow Emperor"[5] or that "Cures come with every touch." Decorative couplets on the doorways of poor, rustic, and extremely tiny out-of-the-way bean curd shops will always say that "Business flourishes throughout the four seas, / Profits proliferate to reach the three rivers." This kind of unsightliness in the practical writings of the people can all be laid at the feet of the sycophantic, empty, and pompous classical literature of the upper class.

During this time of literary change and innovation, all literature classified as aristocratic, classical, and eremitic has been the subject of criticism. What is the reason for the criticism of these three? The answer is that aristocratic literature embellishes according to traditional practice and has lost its independence and self-confidence. Classical literature is pompous and pedantic and

2. Ma Zhiyuan (1260–1325), playwright; Shi Nai'an (1296–1327), novelist; and Cao Xueqin (ca. 1715–1763), author of the novel *The Dream of the Red Chamber*. All are praised by Chen Duxiu for their relative modernity.

3. Qing Dynasty writers.

4. An 11th-century poet admired by the 12th-century Jiangxi (here Xijiang) school.

5. Legendary emperor of the 3rd millennium B.C.E., said to have founded Chinese civilization and to have employed the mythical doctor Qi Bo.

has lost the principles of expressiveness and realistic description. Eremitic literature is highly obscure and abstruse and is self-satisfied writing that provides no benefit to the majority of its readers. In form, Chinese literature has followed old precedents; it has flesh without bones and body without soul. It is a decorative and not a practical product. In content, its vision does not go beyond kings, officials, spirits, ghosts, and the fortunes or misfortunes of individuals. As for the universe, or human life, or society—they are simply beyond its ken. Such are the common failings of these three kinds of literature.

Literature of this sort, I think, has a mutual cause-and-effect relationship with our sycophantic, self-aggrandizing, hypocritical, and impractical national character. Since we now want to reform our politics, we cannot by necessity ignore the reformation of the literature that has a hold on the spiritual world of those wielding political power. The present literature has prevented us from opening our eyes to the world, to society, to literary trends, and to the Zeitgeist.[6] We bury our heads day and night under a pile of old paper. What we train our eyes on and direct our hearts to are nothing other than kings and officials, ghosts and spirits, or the fortunes and misfortunes of single individuals. To seek reform of literature and reform of politics from this is to fight a formidable foe with hands and feet tied.

Much of European culture benefited from politics and science; it also benefited considerably from literature. If I love the France of Rousseau and Pasteur, I especially love the France of Hugo and Zola.[7] If I love the Germany of Kant and Hegel, I especially love the Germany of Goethe and Hauptmann.[8] And if I love the England of Bacon and Darwin, I especially love the England of Dickens and Wilde.[9] Among the outstanding literary figures of this nation, are there those who dare consider themselves China's Hugo, Zola, Goethe, Hauptmann, Dickens, or Wilde? Are there those who, without concern for the praise or blame of pedantic scholars, would with bright eyes and stout hearts declare war on the eighteen fiends? I wish to tow out the largest cannon in the world and lead the way.

1917

6. Spirit of the times (German).
7. Jean-Jacques Rousseau (1712–1778), philosopher; Louis Pasteur (1822–1895), scientist; Victor Hugo (1802–1885), poet and novelist; Emile Zola (1840–1902), novelist.
8. Immanuel Kant (1724–1804) and Georg Wilhelm Friedrich Hegel (1770–1831), philosophers; Johann Wolfgang von Goethe (1749–1832), poet, novelist, and playwright; Gerhard Hauptmann (1862–1946), playwright.
9. Francis Bacon (1561–1626), philosopher; Charles Darwin (1809–1882), scientist; Charles Dickens (1812–1870), novelist; Oscar Wilde (1854–1900), playwright.

TRISTAN TZARA

Born in Romania, Tristan Tzara (1896–1963) made his first contribution to the avant-garde in Zurich, Switzerland, during World War I, where a group of international pacifists had fled to escape the war. There they started the Cabaret Voltaire, a nightclub with a stage, presenting an array of outré artworks, performances, and concerts, as well as manifestos announcing a movement called Dadaism. Much less programmatic than futurism, Dadaism was only sure what it was *against*, not what it was *for*; the Dadaists could not even agree on the meaning of the word *Dada*. After the war Tzara moved to Paris, still the center of the art world, and founded the Paris branch of Dada. As was so often the case, one movement begot the next, and out of Dadaism emerged surrealism, whose chief advocate was **André Breton**. But Tzara could never accept the leadership of Breton and split off, continuing his pranks and activities as well as his involvement in various leftist causes throughout his life.

From Dada Manifesto 1918

DADAIST DISGUST[1]

Every product of disgust capable of becoming a negation of the family is *dada*; the whole being protesting in its destructive force with clenched fists: **DADA**; knowledge of all the means rejected up to this point by the timid sex of easy compromise and sociability: DADA; abolition of logic, dance of all those impotent to create: **DADA**; of all hierarchy and social equation installed for the preservation of values by our valets: DADA; each and every object, feelings and obscurities, apparitions and the precise shock of parallel lines, can be means for the combat: DADA; abolition of memory: **DADA**; abolition of archeology: *DADA*; abolition of the prophets: ***DADA***; abolition of the future: DADA; an absolute indisputable belief in each god immediate product of spontaneity: **DADA**; elegant and unprejudicial leap from one harmony to the other sphere; trajectory of a word tossed like a sonorous cry of phonograph record; respecting all individualities in their momentary madness: serious, fearful, timid, ardent, vigorous, determined, enthusiastic; stripping its chapel of every useless awkward accessory; spitting out like a luminous waterfall any unpleasant or amorous thought, or coddling it—with the lively satisfaction of knowing that it doesn't matter—with the same intensity in the bush of his soul, free of insects for the aristocrats, and gilded with archangels' bodies. Freedom: ***DADA DADA DADA***, shrieking of contracted pains, intertwining of contraries and of all contradictions, grotesqueries, nonsequiturs: LIFE.

1. Translated from the French by Mary Ann Caws. This is the last section of Tzara's "Dada Manifesto 1918."

ANDRÉ BRETON

André Breton (1896–1966) can be credited with turning surrealism into one of the most successful avant-garde movements, whose influence can still be felt today. Although he didn't invent the word *surrealism*, Breton developed the notion of incongruity and fantasy as the basis of creativity and turned it into a distinct cultural movement. Jealously guarding his leadership over the group, he would expel rivals when necessary. Briefly allied with the French Communist Party, surrealism remained a movement of the left even though its most lasting ambitions could not be reduced to party politics. Rather, its great task was to explore the world behind humdrum reality and human reason. To this purpose, Breton drew on Freud's theory of the unconscious as a resource for producing literature through "automatic writing," a technique of composition seeking to evade conscious planning. His most widely read work is his novel *Nadja* (1928), in which he sought to capture the effects of a chance encounter in the street. Breton laid down the principles of his art in his "First Manifesto of Surrealism" (1924), but this complex text is more than just a declaration of principles: a meandering and allusive composition, it is itself an example of surrealist art. Although Breton was a writer, surrealism's most lasting impact would be on photography, cinema, painting, and, later on, advertising.

Manifesto of Surrealism[1]

So strong is the belief in life, in what is most fragile in life—*real* life, I mean—that in the end this belief is lost. Man, that inveterate dreamer, daily more discontent with his destiny, has trouble assessing the objects he has been led to use, objects that his nonchalance has brought his way, or that he has earned through his own efforts, almost always through his own efforts, for he has agreed to work, at least he has not refused to try his luck (or what he calls his luck!). At this point he feels extremely modest: he knows what women he has had, what silly affairs he has been involved in; he is unimpressed by his wealth or poverty, in this respect he is still a newborn babe and, as for the approval of his conscience, I confess that he does very nicely without it. If he still retains a certain lucidity, all he can do is turn back toward his childhood which, however his guides and mentors may have botched it, still strikes him as somehow charming. There, the absence of any known restrictions allows him the perspective of several lives lived at once; this illusion becomes firmly rooted within him; now he is only interested in the fleeting, the extreme facility of everything. Children set off each day without a worry in the world. Everything is near at hand, the worst material conditions are fine. The woods are white or black, one will never sleep.

1. Translated by Richard Seaver and Helen Lane.

But it is true that we would not dare venture so far, it is not merely a question of distance. Threat is piled upon threat, one yields, abandons a portion of the terrain to be conquered. This imagination which knows no bounds is henceforth allowed to be exercised only in strict accordance with the laws of an arbitrary utility; it is incapable of assuming this inferior role for very long and, in the vicinity of the twentieth year, generally prefers to abandon man to his lusterless fate.

Though he may later try to pull himself together upon occasion, having felt that he is losing by slow degrees all reason for living, incapable as he has become of being able to rise to some exceptional situation such as love, he will hardly succeed. This is because he henceforth belongs body and soul to an imperative practical necessity which demands his constant attention. None of his gestures will be expansive, none of his ideas generous or far-reaching. In his mind's eye, events real or imagined will be seen only as they relate to a welter of similar events, events in which he has not participated, *abortive* events. What am I saying: he will judge them in relationship to one of these events whose consequences are more reassuring than the others. On no account will he view them as his salvation.

Beloved imagination, what I most like in you is your unsparing quality.

The mere word "freedom" is the only one that still excites me. I deem it capable of indefinitely sustaining the old human fanaticism. It doubtless satisfies my only legitimate aspiration. Among all the many misfortunes to which we are heir, it is only fair to admit that we are allowed the greatest degree of freedom of thought. It is up to us not to misuse it. To reduce the imagination to a state of slavery—even though it would mean the elimination of what is commonly called happiness—is to betray all sense of absolute justice within oneself. Imagination alone offers me some intimation of what *can be*, and this is enough to remove to some slight degree the terrible injunction; enough, too, to allow me to devote myself to it without fear of making a mistake (as though it were possible to make a bigger mistake). Where does it begin to turn bad, and where does the mind's stability cease? For the mind, is the possibility of erring not rather the contingency of good?

There remains madness, "the madness that one locks up," as it has aptly been described. That madness or another. . . . We all know, in fact, that the insane owe their incarceration to a tiny number of legally reprehensible acts and that, were it not for these acts their freedom (or what we see as their freedom) would not be threatened. I am willing to admit that they are, to some degree, victims of their imagination, in that it induces them not to pay attention to certain rules—outside of which the species feels itself threatened—which we are all supposed to know and respect. But their profound indifference to the way in which we judge them, and even to the various punishments meted out to them, allows us to suppose that they derive a great deal of comfort and consolation from their imagination, that they enjoy their madness sufficiently to endure the thought that its validity does not extend beyond themselves. And, indeed, hallucinations, illusions, etc., are not a source of trifling pleasure. The best controlled sensuality partakes of it, and I know that there are many evenings when I would gladly tame that pretty hand which, during the last pages of Taine's *L'Intelligence*,[2] indulges in some curious misdeeds. I could spend my whole life prying loose the secrets of the insane. These people are honest to a

2. An 1870 work by French historian and critic Hippolyte Taine (1828–1893).

fault, and their naiveté has no peer but my own. Christopher Columbus should have set out to discover America with a boatload of madmen. And note how this madness has taken shape, and endured.

* * *

We are still living under the reign of logic: this, of course, is what I have been driving at. But in this day and age logical methods are applicable only to solving problems of secondary interest. The absolute rationalism that is still in vogue allows us to consider only facts relating directly to our experience. Logical ends, on the contrary, escape us. It is pointless to add that experience itself has found itself increasingly circumscribed. It paces back and forth in a cage from which it is more and more difficult to make it emerge. It too leans for support on what is most immediately expedient, and it is protected by the sentinels of common sense. Under the pretense of civilization and progress, we have managed to banish from the mind everything that may rightly or wrongly be termed superstition, or fancy; forbidden is any kind of search for truth which is not in conformance with accepted practices. It was, apparently, by pure chance that a part of our mental world which we pretended not to be concerned with any longer—and, in my opinion by far the most important part—has been brought back to light. For this we must give thanks to the discoveries of Sigmund Freud.[3] On the basis of these discoveries a current of opinion is finally forming by means of which the human explorer will be able to carry his investigations much further, authorized as he will henceforth be not to confine himself solely to the most summary realities. The imagination is perhaps on the point of reasserting itself, of reclaiming its rights. If the depths of our mind contain within it strange forces capable of augmenting those on the surface, or of waging a victorious battle against them, there is every reason to seize them—first to seize them, then, if need be, to submit them to the control of our reason. The analysts themselves have everything to gain by it. But it is worth noting that no means has been designated a priori for carrying out this undertaking, that until further notice it can be construed to be the province of poets as well as scholars, and that its success is not dependent upon the more or less capricious paths that will be followed.

Freud very rightly brought his critical faculties to bear upon the dream. It is, in fact, inadmissible that this considerable portion of psychic activity (since, at least from man's birth until his death, thought offers no solution of continuity, the sum of the moments of dream, from the point of view of time, and taking into consideration only the time of pure dreaming, that is the dreams of sleep, is not inferior to the sum of the moments of reality, or, to be more precisely limiting, the moments of waking) has still today been so grossly neglected. I have always been amazed at the way an ordinary observer lends so much more credence and attaches so much more importance to waking events than to those occurring in dreams. It is because man, when he ceases to sleep, is above all the plaything of his memory, and in its normal state memory takes pleasure in weakly retracing for him the circumstances of the dream, in stripping it of any real importance, and in dismissing the only *determinant* from the point

3. Founder of psychoanalysis (1856–1939).

where he thinks he has left it a few hours before: this firm hope, this concern. He is under the impression of continuing something that is worthwhile. Thus the dream finds itself reduced to a mere parenthesis, as is the night. And, like the night, dreams generally contribute little to furthering our understanding. This curious state of affairs seems to me to call for certain reflections.

* * *

From the moment when it is subjected to a methodical examination, when, by means yet to be determined, we succeed in recording the contents of dreams in their entirety (and that presupposes a discipline of memory spanning generations; but let us nonetheless begin by noting the most salient facts), when its graph will expand with unparalleled volume and regularity, we may hope that the mysteries which really are not will give way to the great Mystery. I believe in the future resolution of these two states, dream and reality, which are seemingly so contradictory, into a kind of absolute reality, a *surreality*,[4] if one may so speak. It is in quest of this surreality that I am going, certain not to find it but too unmindful of my death not to calculate to some slight degree the joys of its possession.

A story is told according to which Saint-Pol-Roux,[5] in times gone by, used to have a notice posted on the door of his manor house in Camaret, every evening before he went to sleep, which read: THE POET IS WORKING.

A great deal more could be said, but in passing I merely wanted to touch upon a subject which in itself would require a very long and much more detailed discussion; I shall come back to it. At this juncture, my intention was merely to mark a point by noting the *hate of the marvelous* which rages in certain men, this absurdity beneath which they try to bury it. Let us not mince words: the marvelous is always beautiful, anything marvelous is beautiful, in fact only the marvelous is beautiful.

* * *

Completely occupied as I still was with Freud at that time, and familiar as I was with his methods of examination which I had had some slight occasion to use on some patients during the war, I resolved to obtain from myself what we were trying to obtain from them, namely, a monologue spoken as rapidly as possible without any intervention on the part of the critical faculties, a monologue consequently unencumbered by the slightest inhibition and which was, as closely as possible, akin to *spoken thought*. It had seemed to me, and still does—the way in which the phrase about the man cut in two had come to me[6] is an indication of it—that the speed of thought is no greater than the speed of speech, and that thought does not necessarily defy language, nor even the fast-moving pen. It was in this frame of mind that Philippe Soupault[7]—to whom I had confided these initial conclusions—and I decided to blacken some paper, with a praiseworthy disdain for what might result from a literary point of view. The ease of execution did the rest. By the end of the first day we were able to read to ourselves some fifty or so pages obtained in this manner, and begin to compare our results. All in all, Soupault's pages and mine proved to be remark-

4. I.e., something beyond or above reality.
5. French symbolist poet (1861–1940).
6. A phrase mentioned in an earlier section of the manifesto.
7. Dadaist and, later, surrealist poet (1897–1990).

ably similar: the same overconstruction, shortcomings of a similar nature, but also, on both our parts, the illusion of an extraordinary verve, a great deal of emotion, a considerable choice of images of a quality such that we would not have been capable of preparing a single one in longhand, a very special picturesque quality and, here and there, a strong comical effect. The only difference between our two texts seemed to me to derive essentially from our respective tempers, Soupault's being less static than mine, and, if he does not mind my offering this one slight criticism, from the fact that he had made the error of putting a few words by way of titles at the top of certain pages, I suppose in a spirit of mystification. On the other hand, I must give credit where credit is due and say that he constantly and vigorously opposed any effort to retouch or correct, however slightly, any passage of this kind which seemed to me unfortunate. In this he was, to be sure, absolutely right.[8] It is, in fact, difficult to appreciate fairly the various elements present; one may even go so far as to say that it is impossible to appreciate them at a first reading. To you who write, these elements are, on the surface, *as strange to you as they are to anyone else,* and naturally you are wary of them. Poetically speaking, what strikes you about them above all is their *extreme degree of immediate absurdity,* the quality of this absurdity, upon closer scrutiny, being to give way to everything admissible, everything legitimate in the world: the disclosure of a certain number of properties and of facts no less objective, in the final analysis, than the others.

In homage to Guillaume Apollinaire,[9] who had just died and who, on several occasions, seemed to us to have followed a discipline of this kind, without however having sacrificed to it any mediocre literary means, Soupault and I baptized the new mode of pure expression which we had at our disposal and which we wished to pass on to our friends, by the name of SURREALISM. I believe that there is no point today in dwelling any further on this word and that the meaning we gave it initially has generally prevailed over its Apollinarian sense. To be even fairer, we could probably have taken over the word SUPERNATURALISM employed by Gérard de Nerval in his dedication to the *Filles de feu.*[1] It appears, in fact, that Nerval possessed to a tee the spirit with which we claim a kinship, Apollinaire having possessed, on the contrary, naught but *the letter,* still imperfect, of Surrealism, having shown himself powerless to give a valid theoretical idea of it. Here are two passages by Nerval which seem to me to be extremely significant in this respect:

> I am going to explain to you, my dear Dumas,[2] the phenomenon of which you have spoken a short while ago. There are, as you know, certain storytellers who cannot invent without identifying with the characters their imagination has

8. "I believe more and more in the infallibility of my thought with respect to myself, and this is too fair. Nonetheless, with this *thought-writing,* where one is at the mercy of the first outside distraction, 'ebullutions' can occur. It would be inexcusable for us to pretend otherwise. By definition, thought is strong, and incapable of catching itself in error. The blame for these obvious weaknesses must be placed on suggestions that come to it from without." [Breton's note].

9. Poet and playwright (1880–1918) who coined the term *surrealism.*

1. "And also by Thomas Carlyle in *Sartor Resartus* ([Book III] Chapter VIII, 'Natural Supernaturalism'), 1833–34." [Breton's note]. *Filles de feu: Girls of Fire* by Gérard de Nerval, French Romantic poet (1808–1855). Carlyle (1795–1881) was a Scottish essayist.

2. Alexandre Dumas (1802–1870), French novelist, author of *The Three Musketeers.*

dreamt up. You may recall how convincingly our old friend Nodier[3] used to tell how it had been his misfortune during the Revolution to be guillotined; one became so completely convinced of what he was saying that one began to wonder how he had managed to have his head glued back on.

. . . And since you have been indiscreet enough to quote one of the sonnets composed in this SUPERNATURALISTIC dream-state, as the Germans would call it, you will have to hear them all. You will find them at the end of the volume. They are hardly any more obscure than Hegel's metaphysics or Swedenborg's MEMORABILIA, and would lose their charm if they were explained, if such were possible; at least admit the worth of the expression.[4] . . .

Those who might dispute our right to employ the term SURREALISM in the very special sense that we understand it are being extremely dishonest, for there can be no doubt that this word had no currency before we came along. Therefore, I am defining it once and for all:

SURREALISM, *n.* Psychic automatism in its pure state, by which one proposes to express—verbally, by means of the written word, or in any other manner—the actual functioning of thought. Dictated by thought, in the absence of any control exercised by reason, exempt from any aesthetic or moral concern.

ENCYCLOPEDIA. *Philosophy.* Surrealism is based on the belief in the superior reality of certain forms of previously neglected associations, in the omnipotence of dream, in the disinterested play of thought. It tends to ruin once and for all all other psychic mechanisms and to substitute itself for them in solving all the principal problems of life. The following have performed acts of ABSOLUTE SURREALISM: Messrs. Aragon, Baron, Boiffard, Breton, Carrive, Crevel, Delteil, Desnos, Eluard, Gérard, Limbour, Malkine, Morise, Naville, Noll, Péret, Picon, Soupault, Vitrac.[5]

They seem to be, up to the present time, the only ones, and there would be no ambiguity about it were it not for the case of Isidore Ducasse[6] about whom I lack information. And, of course, if one is to judge them only superficially by their results, a good number of poets could pass for Surrealists, beginning with Dante and, in his finer moments, Shakespeare.[7] *In the course of the various attempts I have made to reduce what is, by breach of trust, called genius, I have found nothing which in the final analysis can be attributed to any other method than that.*

3. Charles Nodier (1780–1844), French short-story writer.
4. "See also *L'idéoréalisme* by Saint-Pol-Roux" [Breton's note]. *L'idéoréalisme* translates into English as "ideorealism." Georg Wilhelm Friedrich Hegel (1770–1831) was a German idealist philosopher; Emanuel Swedenborg (1688–1772) was a mystical Swedish philosopher and religious leader.
5. Friends of Breton's who enlisted in the surrealist movement.
6. Also known as the Comte de Lautréamont (1846–1870); Uruguayan-born French poet, obscure during his lifetime, who was championed by the surrealists.
7. Breton here invokes two acknowledged geniuses as forerunners of surrealism.

Young's *Nights*[8] are Surrealist from one end to the other; unfortunately it is a priest who is speaking, a bad priest no doubt, but a priest nonetheless.

Swift is Surrealist in malice,
Sade is Surrealist in sadism.[9]
Chateaubriand is Surrealist in exoticism.[1]
Constant is Surrealist in politics.[2]
Hugo is Surrealist when he isn't stupid.[3]
Desbordes-Valmore is Surrealist in love.[4]
Bertrand is Surrealist in the past.[5]
Rabbe is Surrealist in death.[6]
Poe is Surrealist in adventure.[7]
Baudelaire is Surrealist in morality.[8]
Rimbaud is Surrealist in the way he lived, and elsewhere.[9]
Mallarmé is Surrealist when he is confiding.[1]
Jarry is Surrealist in absinthe.[2]
Nouveau is Surrealist in the kiss.[3]
Saint-Pol-Roux is Surrealist in his use of symbols.
Fargue is Surrealist in the atmosphere.[4]
Vaché is Surrealist in me.[5]
Reverdy is Surrealist at home.[6]
Saint-Jean-Perse is Surrealist at a distance.[7]
Roussel is Surrealist as a storyteller.[8]
Etc.

1924

8. *Night Thoughts*, a poem by Edward Young (1681–1765).
9. Jonathan Swift (1667–1745), Irish satirist and author of *Gulliver's Travels*; the Marquis de Sade (1740–1814), French aristocrat and author of libertine works.
1. François-Auguste-René de Chateaubriand (1768–1848), French Romantic writer with an interest in the East.
2. Benjamin Constant (1767–1830), liberal political theorist.
3. Victor Hugo (1802–1885), French Romantic poet and novelist.
4. Marceline Desbordes-Valmore (1786–1859), French poet and actress.
5. Aloysius Bertrand (1807–1841), French prose poet.
6. Alphonse Rabbe (1784–1829), author of *Album of a Pessimist*; he died from a drug overdose.
7. Edgar Allan Poe (1809–1849), American Romantic writer whose macabre tales were much admired by French modernists.
8. Charles Baudelaire (1821–1867), French Romantic poet who inspired modernism and who was charged with obscenity; he also translated Poe's works into French.
9. Arthur Rimbaud (1854–1891), French poet infamous for his decadent lifestyle.
1. Stéphane Mallarmé (1842–1898), French symbolist poet.
2. Alfred Jarry (1873–1907), avant-garde playwright who was addicted to absinthe, a strong alcoholic drink popular in 19th-century France.
3. Germain Nouveau (1851–1920), French symbolist poet, author of "The Kiss."
4. Léon-Paul Fargue (1876–1947), French symbolist poet.
5. Jacques Vaché (1895–1919), Breton's close friend, had died of an opium overdose.
6. Pierre Reverdy (1889–1960), surrealist poet.
7. St. John Perse (1887–1975), French poet who would win the Nobel Prize for Literature in 1960.
8. Raymond Roussel (1877–1933), experimental French writer.

BLACK PANTHER PARTY

Founded in the mid-1960s in Oakland, California, the Black Panther Party represents the radical wing of the civil rights movement. Disappointed with the ethos of nonviolent resistance advocated by civil rights activists such as Martin Luther King Jr., the Black Panthers vowed to defend themselves against police brutality, as well as political and social disenfranchisement. Demanding basic rights such as freedom to determine the fate of the black community and full employment, the Panthers espoused socialist doctrines to better the lot of African Americans. Their famous ten-point manifesto (1966) details the movement's demands in clear and hard-hitting phrases. Most remarkable, however, is the tenth point, which reprints, verbatim, the opening of the **Declaration of Independence**. The significance of the words is clear: the Black Panthers saw parallels between their insistence on human rights and that of the founders of the Republic, as stated in the document from the American Revolution.

Black Panther Platform

What we want

1. We want freedom. We want power to determine the destiny of our black community.
2. We want full employment for our people.
3. We want an end to the robbery by the white man of our black community.
4. We want decent housing, fit for shelter of human beings.
5. We want education for our people that exposes the true nature of this decadent American society. We want education that teaches us our true history and our role in the present day society.
6. We want all black men to be exempt from military service.
7. We want an immediate end to *police brutality* and *murder* of black people.
8. We want freedom for all black men held in federal, state, county, and city prisons and jails.
9. We want all black people when brought to trial to be tried in court by a jury of their peer group or people from their black communities as defined by the constitution of the United States.
10. We want land, bread, housing, education, clothing, justice and peace.

What we believe

1. We believe that black people will not be free until we are able to determine our destiny.
2. We believe that the federal government is responsible and obligated to give every man employment or a guaranteed income. We believe that if the white American businessmen will not give full employment, then the means of production should be taken from the businessmen and placed in the community so that the people of the community can organize and employ all of its people and give a high standard of living.

3. We believe that this racist government has robbed us and now we are demanding the overdue debt of forty acres and two mules.[1] Forty acres and two mules was promised 100 years ago as retribution for slave labor and mass murder of black people. We will accept the payment in currency which will be distributed to our many communities. The Germans murdered 6,000,000 Jews. The American racist has taken part in the slaughter of over 50,000,000 black people; therefore, we feel that this is a modest demand that we make.
4. We believe that if the white landlords will not give decent housing to our black community, then the housing and the land should be made into cooperatives so that our community, with government aid, can build and make decent housing for its people.
5. We believe in an educational system that will give to our people a knowledge of self. If a man does not have knowledge of himself and his position in society and the world, then he has little chance to relate to anything else.
6. We believe that black people should not be forced to fight in the military service to defend a racist government that does not protect us. We will not fight and kill other people of color in the world who, like black people, are being victimized by the white racist government of America. We will protect ourselves from the force and violence of the racist police and the racist military, by whatever means necessary.
7. We believe we can end police brutality in our black community by organizing black *self defense* groups that are dedicated to defending our black community from racist police oppression and brutality. The second amendment of the constitution of the United States gives us a right to bear arms. We therefore believe that all black people should arm themselves for *self defense.*
8. We believe that all black people should be released from the many jails and prisons because they have not received a fair and impartial trial.
9. We believe that the courts should follow the United States constitution so that black people will receive fair trials. The 14th Amendment of the U.S. Constitution gives a man a right to be tried by his peer group.[2] A peer is a person from a similar economic, social, religious, geographical, environmental, historical and racial background. To do this the court will be forced to select a jury from the black community from which the black defendant came. We have been, and are being tried by all white juries that have no understanding of the 'average reasoning man' of the black community.
10. When in the course of human events, it becomes necessary for one people to dissolve the political bonds which have connected them with another, and to assume among the powers of the earth the separate and equal station to which the laws of nature and nature's god entitle them, a decent respect to the opinions of mankind requires that they should declare the causes which impel them to separation. We hold these truths to be self-evident, that all men are created equal, that they are endowed by their creator with certain inalienable rights, that among these are life, liberty and the pursuit of happiness. That to secure these rights, governments are instituted among

1. Promised in 1865 to freed slaves who had served in the Union Army during the American Civil War.
2. Amendment to the U.S. Constitution, adopted in 1868, to confer citizenship rights on African Americans; it guarantees all citizens equal protection under the law and due process, including, by extension, the right to trial by jury, as established by the Sixth Amendment, adopted in 1791.

men, deriving their just power from the consent of the governed—that whenever any form of government becomes destructive of these ends, it is the right of people to alter or to abolish it, and to institute new government, laying its foundations on such principles and organizing its powers in such form as to them shall seem most likely to effect their safety and happiness. Prudence, indeed, will dictate that governments long established should not be changed for light and transient causes; and accordingly all experience hath shewn, that mankind are more disposed to suffer while evils are sufferable, than to right themselves by abolishing the forms to which they are accustomed. But when a long train of abuses and usurpations, pursuing invariably the same object, evinces a design to reduce them under absolute despotism, it is their right, it is their duty, to throw off such government, and to provide new guards for their future security.[3]

1966

3. The final paragraph is a verbatim transcription of the Preamble to the United States Declaration of Independence (1776).

VALERIE SOLANAS

Valerie Solanas (1936–1988) is known not so much for her writings as for the attempted assassination of Andy Warhol (1928–1987), a Pop Art icon. Solanas accused Warhol of losing her play, *Up Your Ass*, which she had given him for review. Warhol survived, and Solanas remained on the fringe of New York's bohemian Greenwich Village, whose appetite for radical causes she captured in her SCUM Manifesto (1968). The founding document of the Society for Cutting Up Men, of which she was the only member, this text is an outrageous provocation advocating the killing of all males and the creation of a female-only society. Littered with images of violence, it captures in an extreme form the spirit of 1960s radicalism.

SCUM Manifesto[1]

Life in this society being, at best, an utter bore and no aspect of society being at all relevant to women, there remains to civic-minded, responsible, thrill-seeking females only to overthrow the government, eliminate the money system, institute complete automation and destroy the male sex.

It is now technically possible to reproduce without the aid of males (or, for that matter, females) and to produce only females. We must begin immediately

1. *SCUM* stands for Society for Cutting Up Men.

to do so. The male is a biological accident: the y (male) gene is an incomplete x (female) gene, that is, has an incomplete set of chromosomes. In other words, the male is an incomplete female, a walking abortion, aborted at the gene stage. To be male is to be deficient, emotionally limited; maleness is a deficiency disease and males are emotional cripples.

The male is completely egocentric, trapped inside himself, incapable of empathizing or identifying with others, of love, friendship, affection or tenderness. He is a completely isolated unit, incapable of rapport with anyone. His responses are entirely visceral, not cerebral; his intelligence is a mere tool in the service of his drives and needs; he is incapable of mental passion, mental interaction; he can't relate to anything other than his own physical sensations. He is a half dead, unresponsive lump, incapable of giving or receiving pleasure or happiness; consequently, he is at best an utter bore, an inoffensive blob, since only those capable of absorption in others can be charming. He is trapped in a twilight zone halfway between humans and apes, and is far worse off than the apes because, unlike the apes, he is capable of a large array of negative feelings—hate, jealousy, contempt, disgust, guilt, shame, doubt—and, moreover he is *aware* of what he is and isn't.

* * *

Why produce even females? Why should there be future generations? What is their purpose? When aging and death are eliminated, why continue to reproduce? Even if they are not eliminated, why reproduce? Why should we care what happens when we're dead? Why should we care that there is no younger generation to succeed us?

Eventually the natural course of events, of social evolution, will lead to total female control of the world and, subsequently, to the cessation of the production of males and, ultimately, to the cessation of the production of females.

But SCUM is impatient; SCUM is not consoled by the thought that future generations will thrive; SCUM wants to grab some swinging living for itself. And, if a large majority of women were SCUM, they could acquire complete control of this country within a few weeks simply by withdrawing from the labor force, thereby paralyzing the entire nation. Additional measures, any one of which would be sufficient to completely disrupt the economy and everything else, would be for women to declare themselves off the money system, stop buying, just loot and simply refuse to obey all laws they don't care to obey. The police force, National Guard, Army, Navy and Marines combined couldn't squelch a rebellion of over half the population, particularly when it's made up of people they are utterly helpless without.

If all women simply left men, refused to have anything to do with any of them—ever, all men, the government, and the national economy would collapse completely. Even without leaving men, women who are aware of the extent of their superiority to and power over men, could acquire complete control over everything within a few weeks, could effect a total submission of males to females. In a sane society the male would trot along obediently after the female. The male is docile and easily led, easily subjected to the domination of any female who cares to dominate him. The male, in fact, wants desperately to be led by females, wants Mama in charge, wants to abandon himself to her care. But this is not a sane society, and most women are not even dimly aware of where they're at in relation to men.

The conflict, therefore, is not between females and males, but between SCUM—dominant, secure, self-confident, nasty, violent, selfish, independent, proud, thrill-seeking, free-wheeling, arrogant females, who consider themselves fit to rule the universe, who have free-wheeled to the limits of this "society" and are ready to wheel on to something far beyond what it has to offer—and nice, passive, accepting, "cultivated", polite, dignified, subdued, dependent, scared, mindless, insecure, approval-seeking Daddy's Girls, who can't cope with the unknown, who want to continue to wallow in the sewer that is, at least, familiar, who want to hang back with the apes, who feel secure only with Big Daddy standing by, with a big, strong man to lean on and with a fat, hairy face in the White House, who are too cowardly to face up to the hideous reality of what a man is, what Daddy is, who have cast their lot with the swine, who have adapted themselves to animalism, feel superficially comfortable with it and know no other way of "life", who have reduced their minds, thoughts and sights to the male level, who, lacking sense, imagination and wit can have value only in a male "society", who can have a place in the sun, or, rather, in the slime, only as soothers, ego boosters, relaxers and breeders, who are dismissed as inconsequents by other females, who project their deficiencies, their maleness, onto all females and see the female as a worm.

But SCUM is too impatient to hope and wait for the de-brainwashing of millions of assholes. Why should the swinging females continue to plod dismally along with the dull male ones? Why should the fates of the groovy and the creepy be intertwined? Why should the active and imaginative consult the passive and dull on social policy? Why should the independent be confined to the sewer along with the dependent who need Daddy to cling to?

A small handful of SCUM can take over the country within a year by systematically fucking up the system, selectively destroying property, and murder:

SCUM will become members of the unwork force, the fuck-up force; they will get jobs of various kinds and unwork. For example, SCUM salesgirls will not charge for merchandise; SCUM telephone operators will not charge for calls; SCUM office and factory workers, in addition to fucking up their work, will secretly destroy equipment. SCUM will unwork at a job until fired, then get a new job to unwork at.

SCUM will forcibly relieve bus drivers, cab drivers and subway token sellers of their jobs and run busses and cabs and dispense free tokens to the public.

SCUM will destroy all useless and harmful objects—cars, store windows, "Great Art", etc.

Eventually SCUM will take over the airwaves—radio and T.V. networks—by forcibly relieving of their jobs all radio and T.V. employees who would impede SCUM's entry into the broadcasting studios.

SCUM will couple-bust–barge into mixed (male-female) couples, wherever they are, and bust them up.

* * *

The sick, irrational men, those who attempt to defend themselves against their disgustingness, when they see SCUM barreling down on them, will cling in terror to Big Mama with her Big Bouncy Boobies, but Boobies won't protect them against SCUM; Big Mama will be clinging to Big Daddy, who will be in the corner shitting in his forceful, dynamic pants. Men who are rational, however, won't kick or struggle or raise a distressing fuss, but will just sit back, relax, enjoy the show and ride the waves to their demise.

1968

II
Postwar and Postcolonial Literature, 1945–1968

In the middle of the twentieth century, the two superpowers, the United States and the Soviet Union, having emerged from the bloody, or "hot," wars of the previous decades, found themselves locked in a Cold War: their most powerful weapons, though fired only in tests, would be capable of annihilating the planet. The two sides—the North Atlantic Treaty Organization, representing Western Europe and North America, and the Warsaw Pact, uniting the military forces of Soviet-dominated Eastern Europe—divided most of the globe into spheres of influence. By 1949, with the success of the Communist Revolution in China, led by Mao Zedong, almost half of the world's population lived under communism. The competing blocs, as they were called, understood that if either one launched a nuclear attack, the enemy would retaliate, an unstable balance known as "mutually assured destruction" (producing an ironic acronym).

To avoid planetary disaster, the two sides fought wars by proxy, notably in Korea (1950–53) and Vietnam (1955–75). Within the communist world, the purges and mass imprisonments initiated by the Soviet dictator Joseph Stalin were selectively

A photograph from October 1947 by Margaret Bourke-White (American, 1904–1971) of a refugee camp in Delhi. The picture was taken a month before British-ruled India was partitioned into two nations, India and Pakistan.

repudiated, after Stalin's death in 1953, by his successor, Nikita Khrushchev. It was during this period of de-Stalinization that the works of the dissident **Alexander Solzhenitsyn** were briefly allowed to be published. The bloody suppression of the Hungarian revolt against communism in 1956, however, showed the limits of de-Stalinization. Stalin's techniques spread, moreover, to Mao's China. The forced collectivization of the Great Leap Forward (1958–59) led to a famine that caused an estimated twenty million deaths, while the Cultural Revolution, which began in 1966 and lasted until Mao's death in 1976, attacked intellectuals and the middle classes, resulting in the destruction of most of the country's functioning institutions.

While the communist world was undergoing radical transformations, the colonial powers of Western Europe, facing pressure from nationalist movements among their subject peoples, began to relinquish direct political control of their colonies. The process of decolonization, often accompanied by conflicts over redrawn borders, became a major topic for a generation of writers who, though born in the formerly colonized nations, were likely to have been educated in Europe and who sought to give voice to the concerns of their recently independent nations. The initial stages of postcolonial development were frequently marked by internal conflicts, civil wars, and dictatorships, and by jockeying to align newly independent nations with either the United States or the Soviet Union (or to find an alternative, "nonaligned" path). It was also in these years, however, that the basis was laid for the prosperity of what was then known as the "third world" (in contrast to the liberal capitalist democracies of the developed first world and the rapidly industrializing second world of communist regimes). In particular, the Green Revolution of the 1960s and 1970s improved agricultural methods in the developing world and made it possible to feed a rapidly expanding population, while smallpox was eliminated and other serious illnesses, such as tuberculosis, malaria, and plague, were brought under control. Still, in the poorer countries of Africa and South Asia, it was common for as much as half the population to live in poverty.

In Western Europe, the postwar period saw rapid rebuilding and further industrialization, even as thinkers and writers struggled to comprehend the enormity of the Holocaust. The young Polish journalist **Tadeusz Borowski** shocked his compatriots with his account of life in the Nazi concentration camps, while the Romanian-born Jew **Paul Celan**, writing in German, turned his experiences in the camps into austere and beautiful poetry. In the wake of the Nazi occupation of France (1940–44), the theme of choice became critical to a generation of authors who had had to decide between allegiance to the collaborationist Vichy state or to the Resistance movement. The philosophy of existentialism, derived by Jean-Paul Sartre from the writings of the German philosophers Friedrich Nietzsche and Martin Heidegger, emphasized the role of free choice in human life. Glimpses of existentialism occur in the bleak humor of **Samuel Beckett**'s apocalyptic ***Endgame***. Like Beckett, **Albert Camus** had worked for the Resistance. He develops the theme of choice in his account of a schoolteacher's experiences in Algeria in "**The Guest**." In different ways, these writers turned to a stripped-down literary style—either direct and realistic, like Camus and Borowski, or elusive and minimalist, like Celan and Beckett—and thus away from the exuberant modernism of the earlier part of the century.

Partly because it had been incorporated into the French state (unlike British colonies, which tended to be governed locally), Algeria became one of the bloodiest colonial battlefields

The Algerian writer Albert Camus (1913–1960), on the balcony of his Paris publisher's office in 1955.

until its eventual independence in 1962. Elsewhere, decolonization occurred more rapidly. In the immediate aftermath of the war, faced with nationalist pressures in the colonies and with the moral bankruptcy of any claims to racial superiority, many colonial powers began granting independence. At midnight on August 14, 1947, Britain divided its territorial possessions in South Asia into two states, India and Pakistan. The partition took place along religious (or "communal") lines between Hindus and Muslims, but there remained many Muslims in India and Hindus in Pakistan. During the weeks before and after independence, large populations were transferred and an untold number were killed in communal violence—the subject of **Salman Rushdie**'s *Midnight's Children*. The following year, under a United Nations mandate, Britain left most of its former territories in Palestine in the hands of the new Jewish state, Israel. Its Arab neighbors attacked the new country and, during a series of short wars from 1948 to 1968, Israel expanded its national boundaries, at the same time occupying territories inhabited by Arab Palestinians. The continuing Arab-Israeli conflict and the Israeli Occupation are themes in the poetry of **Yehuda Amichai** in this volume.

Elsewhere in the Middle East and North Africa, a series of military coups created dictatorships, sometimes focused on the Pan-Arabist movement for Muslim unity, at other times oriented more toward socialism. It was in this context that Arabic writers such as **Naguib Mahfouz** combined traditional literary language with the European form of the novel to chronicle the transformations of their cultures. Sub-Saharan Africa also experienced a series of civil wars and dictatorships, as well as ongoing minority rule by the white settler communities in South Africa and Rhodesia, which **Doris Lessing** describes. Despite Africa's hardships, it developed a remarkable literature, typically in the languages of the former colonial powers, represented here by **Chinua Achebe**, **Ngugi Wa Thiong'o**, **Wole Soyinka**, **Bessie Head**, **Chimamanda Ngozi Adichie**, and **Ama Ata Aidoo**. Although they sometimes took inspiration from the

Egyptian premier Gamal Abdel Nasser Hussein (right) and the prime minister of the Sudan, Ismail Al Azhari, clasp hands among a crowd of supporters in Egypt in July 1954. Nasser, a central figure in the Egyptian revolution of 1952, which overthrew the monarchy of Egypt and Sudan, became Egypt's president in 1956.

celebration of African identity typical of the earlier French-speaking writers of the Négritude movement, these anglophone authors typically explore village life as it has been transformed by contact with Europeans and then by the process of establishing independence.

In the United States, too, racial segregation and the disenfranchisement of African Americans were challenged in the civil rights movement, whose landmarks included the Supreme Court decision *Brown v. Board of Education* of 1954, which ended public school segregation, and the Civil Rights Acts of 1964, which banned segregation in public accommodations and outlawed discriminatory voter registration. **James Baldwin** explores the challenges that African Americans faced in the North during and after the Second World War.

The postwar period also witnessed the increasing globalization of literature and the media, and writers frequently adapted certain genres, especially the short story and the novel but drama and lyric poetry as well, to local conditions. For example, authors might use the language of a traditional literature (Classical Chinese, Standard Arabic, and biblical Hebrew) to produce a colloquial, contemporary short story. In other cases, writers transformed a historically European genre by introducing elements of local customs and storytelling techniques (examples include magic realism in Latin America; the postcolonial African novel). More broadly, the encounters between indigenous societies and widely accepted literary forms caused writers to rethink the defining characteristics of their homeland; many authors valued hybrid qualities that tended to dismantle claims to cultural uniqueness or homogeneity.

Much of the writing of the postwar period engages in the movement toward "neorealism"—a return to political and social issues, in contrast to the interiority and linguistic inventiveness of the modernists. While sometimes drawing on modernist techniques such as the representation of individual consciousness and intense irony, the realists tended to use the chronological plot, omniscient narrator, and objective description typical of nineteenth-century European works. Such preferences apply equally to postcolonial writers eager to portray the history of their nations and to Western authors grappling with social issues such as civil rights, immigration, and gender relations. There are some notable exceptions, however, to the reinvigorated realism of postwar literature. Many politically oriented writers, such as Mahfouz and Solzhenitsyn, wove allegory into their seeming realism, sometimes conveying hidden political messages in apparently straightforward narratives, at other times using allegory openly as a way of commenting on current events. At the same time, writers of all nationalities continued to use language wittily, finding expressiveness in the sounds and unexpected meanings of words.

The most intense linguistic playfulness can be found in the works of **Vladimir Nabokov**, **Jorge Luis Borges**, **Julio Cortázar**, and (albeit in a minor key) Samuel Beckett. They are among the writers who introduced many of the characteristics associated with postmodernism, although the term itself became widespread only in the later decades of the twentieth century. Like the modernists before them, they called attention to their use of language and choice of literary form. They differ from the earlier group in their sense of the limits of literature's ability to find meaning in the world; an acute consciousness of the instability of language and of its potential to carry multiple meanings; and a particular concern with the boundary between fiction and reality—what is sometimes called "metafiction" or "metatheater." Although they did not think of themselves as postmodernists, these authors were conscious of succeeding the modernists **Proust**, **Joyce**, **Woolf**, and **Kafka**, and of seeking the possibilities for literary experiment even if they no longer believed that such efforts could reveal the ultimate meaningfulness of life.

JULIO CORTÁZAR

1914–1984

Known for his vivid sense of fantasy and his ability to portray alternative realities, Julio Cortázar was considered one of the leading figures of the Latin American "Boom" of the 1960s and 1970s—a period of great creativity and productivity—although by then he had left his native Argentina to live and work in Paris. His friend and mentor, **Jorge Luis Borges**, declared, "No one can retell the plot of a Cortázar story; each one consists of determined words in a determined order. If we try to summarize them, we realize that something precious has been lost." The compounded sense of perfect, shimmering order and underlying mystery pervades Cortázar's work.

Cortázar's parents, wealthy Argentines, were visiting Belgium on business in August 1914 when Germany invaded the country at the outbreak of the First World War. Three weeks later, Cortázar was born in Brussels. The

Cortázar family (like the Borges family) spent most of the war in neutral Switzerland. In 1918 the family returned to Argentina; but Cortázar's father soon abandoned the family, and the young boy was raised by his mother and a house full of female relatives in a suburb of Buenos Aires. A sickly child, Julio spent much of his youth reading science fiction and fantasy novels, with a particular interest in Jules Verne and other French writers. He expressed his writerly aspirations early, claiming to have completed his first novel at the age of nine. Cortázar trained as a teacher and taught high school in several small towns near Buenos Aires. He opposed the rise of the dictator Juan Perón, and in 1944 was even briefly imprisoned for political activities while teaching French at the University of Cuyo.

During his teaching years, Cortázar wrote in a variety of genres: poetry, short stories, plays, and essays. He published several essays and a collection of poems, *Presencia*, under the pseudonym Julio Denis. Later he would repudiate these early works, explaining that when he wrote them, he did not yet know what he really wanted to say. Only after 1945 did he begin publishing stories in his own name. The first of these, "House Taken Over," appeared in 1946 in a magazine under the editorship of Borges, who helped to launch Cortázar's career. The two writers share important affinities as inventors of imaginary worlds, but Borges is the more intellectual of the two, Cortázar the more playful, although his is a playfulness with a dark side. Cortázar's stories of the postwar period, which he often based on his nightmares, frequently concern themselves with imaginary beasts; he collected them in 1951 under the title *Bestiario* (*Bestiary*). That same year Cortázar emigrated to Paris, where he lived until his death. While there, he wrote his best-known novel, *Hopscotch* (1963), which can be read either sequentially (chapters 1–155) or by hopping through the chapters according to a series of patterns that the author provides. Sometimes called an "anti-novel," *Hopscotch* is an example of experimental fiction and is considered postmodernist because of the liberties it takes with narrative order. Cortázar also translated, into Spanish, Daniel Defoe's *Robinson Crusoe* and many short stories by Edgar Allan Poe, whose influence is evident throughout Cortázar's work. He remained politically engaged throughout his life, opposing human rights abuses by right-wing Latin American dictators, supporting the communist government of Fidel Castro in Cuba, and even giving royalties from his work to the Sandinistas in Nicaragua, a socialist organization.

The story selected here, "House Taken Over" (1946), was based on a dream. Cortázar later recalled the origin of the story, "which I dreamed with all the details which figure in the text and which I wrote upon jumping out of bed, still enveloped in the horrible nausea of its ending." The use Cortázar made of this dream owes something to surrealism and its rejection of rational thought in favor of responses arising from the unconscious. A tale that starts out representing everyday life in dreamlike simplicity soon takes on shivering distortions of a nightmare. The story begins with the peaceful lives of a middle-aged brother and sister who live in a large house in Buenos Aires; little information about them is provided, except that their family has lived in this house for generations. Although a suggestion of incest lingers in the idea of a "quiet, simple marriage of sister and brother," their existence seems straightforward until the strange events of the middle of the story. The siblings accept their sudden change of circumstance serenely, but it remains puzzling, even uncanny, for the reader: who are the "they" who have taken over the house?

Critics have analyzed the story as a commentary on life under the authoritarian regime of Perón, or as a critique of the backwardness and conservatism of postwar Argentine society. Written as it was near the end of the Second World War, "House Taken Over" may also refer to the occupation of Europe by the Nazis—an event that would have had special interest for Cortázar, who was born in German-occupied Belgium more than thirty years earlier. Yet while Cortázar's stories seem open to reading as allegories (coded statements about political events), they tend to remain evasive and ambiguous, to resist efforts at final interpretation. In this respect, the story resembles **Franz Kafka**'s ***The Metamorphosis***. Whatever its political or biographical implications, "House Taken Over" is haunting in its suggestion of forces beyond the grasp of rationality or even description. Cortázar complained that readers wanted his works to be less obscure and hermetic, more directly involved in political life; yet his genius lies precisely in creating those disturbing images and events that register historical conflicts so uneasily and obscurely.

House Taken Over[1]

We liked the house because, apart from its being old and spacious (in a day when old houses go down for a profitable auction of their construction materials), it kept the memories of great-grandparents, our paternal grandfather, our parents and the whole of childhood.

Irene and I got used to staying in the house by ourselves, which was crazy, eight people could have lived in that place and not have gotten in each other's way. We rose at seven in the morning and got the cleaning done, and about eleven I left Irene to finish off whatever rooms and went to the kitchen. We lunched at noon precisely; then there was nothing left to do but a few dirty plates. It was pleasant to take lunch and commune with the great hollow, silent house, and it was enough for us just to keep it clean. We ended up thinking, at times, that that was what had kept us from marrying. Irene turned down two suitors for no particular reason, and María Esther went and died on me before we could manage to get engaged. We were easing into our forties with the unvoiced concept that the quiet, simple marriage of sister and brother was the indispensable end to a line established in this house by our grandparents. We would die here someday, obscure and distant cousins would inherit the place, have it torn down, sell the bricks and get rich on the building plot; or more justly and better yet, we would topple it ourselves before it was too late.

Irene never bothered anyone. Once the morning housework was finished, she spent the rest of the day on the sofa in her bedroom, knitting. I couldn't tell you why she knitted so much; I think women knit when they discover that it's a fat excuse to do nothing at all. But Irene was not like that, she always knitted necessities, sweaters for winter, socks for me, handy morning robes and bedjackets for herself. Sometimes she would do a jacket, then unravel it the next moment because there was something that didn't please her; it was

1. Translated from Spanish by Paul Blackburn.

pleasant to see a pile of tangled wool in her knitting basket fighting a losing battle for a few hours to retain its shape. Saturdays I went downtown to buy wool; Irene had faith in my good taste, was pleased with the colors and never a skein had to be returned. I took advantage of these trips to make the rounds of the bookstores, uselessly asking if they had anything new in French literature. Nothing worthwhile had arrived in Argentina since 1939.[2]

But it's the house I want to talk about, the house and Irene, I'm not very important. I wonder what Irene would have done without her knitting. One can reread a book, but once a pullover is finished you can't do it over again, it's some kind of disgrace. One day I found that the drawer at the bottom of the chiffonier, replete with mothballs, was filled with shawls, white, green, lilac. Stacked amid a great smell of camphor—it was like a shop; I didn't have the nerve to ask her what she planned to do with them. We didn't have to earn our living, there was plenty coming in from the farms each month, even piling up. But Irene was only interested in the knitting and showed a wonderful dexterity, and for me the hours slipped away watching her, her hands like silver sea-urchins, needles flashing, and one or two knitting baskets on the floor, the balls of yarn jumping about. It was lovely.

How not to remember the layout of that house. The dining room, a living room with tapestries, the library and three large bedrooms in the section most recessed, the one that faced toward Rodríguez Peña.[3] Only a corridor with its massive oak door separated that part from the front wing, where there was a bath, the kitchen, our bedrooms and the hall. One entered the house through a vestibule with enameled tiles, and a wrought-iron grated door opened onto the living room. You had to come in through the vestibule and open the gate to go into the living room; the doors to our bedrooms were on either side of this, and opposite it was the corridor leading to the back section; going down the passage, one swung open the oak door beyond which was the other part of the house; or just before the door, one could turn to the left and go down a narrower passageway which led to the kitchen and the bath. When the door was open, you became aware of the size of the house; when it was closed, you had the impression of an apartment, like the ones they build today, with barely enough room to move around in. Irene and I always lived in this part of the house and hardly ever went beyond the oak door except to do the cleaning. Incredible how much dust collected on the furniture. It may be Buenos Aires is a clean city, but she owes it to her population and nothing else. There's too much dust in the air, the slightest breeze and it's back on the marble console tops and in the diamond patterns of the tooled-leather desk set. It's a lot of work to get it off with a feather duster; the motes rise and hang in the air, and settle again a minute later on the pianos and the furniture.

I'll always have a clear memory of it because it happened so simply and without fuss. Irene was knitting in her bedroom, it was eight at night, and I suddenly decided to put the water up for *mate*.[4] I went down the corridor as far as the

2. The outbreak of World War II, in 1939, prevented books from being exported from Europe.

3. Street in Buenos Aires.

4. A popular Argentine herbal tea made from the leaf *yerba mate*, a type of holly.

oak door, which was ajar, then turned into the hall toward the kitchen, when I heard something in the library or the dining room. The sound came through muted and indistinct, a chair being knocked over onto the carpet or the muffled buzzing of a conversation. At the same time or a second later, I heard it at the end of the passage which led from those two rooms toward the door. I hurled myself against the door before it was too late and shut it, leaned on it with the weight of my body; luckily, the key was on our side; moreover, I ran the great bolt into place, just to be safe.

I went down to the kitchen, heated the kettle, and when I got back with the tray of *mate*, I told Irene:

"I had to shut the door to the passage. They've taken over the back part."

She let her knitting fall and looked at me with her tired, serious eyes.

"You're sure?"

I nodded.

"In that case," she said, picking up her needles again, "we'll have to live on this side."

I sipped at the *mate* very carefully, but she took her time starting her work again. I remember it was a grey vest she was knitting. I liked that vest.

The first few days were painful, since we'd both left so many things in the part that had been taken over. My collection of French literature, for example, was still in the library. Irene had left several folios of stationery and a pair of slippers that she used a lot in the winter. I missed my briar pipe, and Irene, I think, regretted the loss of an ancient bottle of Hesperidin.[5] It happened repeatedly (but only in the first few days) that we would close some drawer or cabinet and look at one another sadly.

"It's not here."

One thing more among the many lost on the other side of the house.

But there were advantages, too. The cleaning was so much simplified that, even when we got up late, nine thirty for instance, by eleven we were sitting around with our arms folded. Irene got into the habit of coming to the kitchen with me to help get lunch. We thought about it and decided on this: while I prepared the lunch, Irene would cook up dishes that could be eaten cold in the evening. We were happy with the arrangement because it was always such a bother to have to leave our bedrooms in the evening and start to cook. Now we made do with the table in Irene's room and platters of cold supper.

Since it left her more time for knitting, Irene was content. I was a little lost without my books, but so as not to inflict myself on my sister, I set about reordering papa's stamp collection; that killed some time. We amused ourselves sufficiently, each with his own thing, almost always getting together in Irene's bedroom, which was the more comfortable. Every once in a while, Irene might say:

"Look at this pattern I just figured out, doesn't it look like clover?"

After a bit it was I, pushing a small square of paper in front of her so that she could see the excellence of some stamp or another from Eupen-et-Malmédy.[6]

5. A citrus-flavored Argentine aperitif. "Briar": a common wood used in making smoking pipes.

6. A region ceded by Germany to Belgium at the end of World War I, then reannexed to Germany during World War II; well-known among stamp collectors because a variety of stamps were issued there by the Belgian and German governments during the wars.

We were fine, and little by little we stopped thinking. You can live without thinking.

(Whenever Irene talked in her sleep, I woke up immediately and stayed awake. I never could get used to this voice from a statue or a parrot, a voice that came out of the dreams, not from a throat. Irene said that in my sleep I flailed about enormously and shook the blankets off. We had the living room between us, but at night you could hear everything in the house. We heard each other breathing, coughing, could even feel each other reaching for the light switch when, as happened frequently, neither of us could fall asleep.

Aside from our nocturnal rumblings, everything was quiet in the house. During the day there were the household sounds, the metallic click of knitting needles, the rustle of stamp-album pages turning. The oak door was massive, I think I said that. In the kitchen or the bath, which adjoined the part that was taken over, we managed to talk loudly, or Irene sang lullabies. In a kitchen there's always too much noise, the plates and glasses, for there to be interruptions from other sounds. We seldom allowed ourselves silence there, but when we went back to our rooms or to the living room, then the house grew quiet, half-lit, we ended by stepping around more slowly so as not to disturb one another. I think it was because of this that I woke up irremedially and at once when Irene began to talk in her sleep.)

Except for the consequences, it's nearly a matter of repeating the same scene over again. I was thirsty that night, and before we went to sleep, I told Irene that I was going to the kitchen for a glass of water. From the door of the bedroom (she was knitting) I heard the noise in the kitchen; if not the kitchen, then the bath, the passage off at that angle dulled the sound. Irene noticed how brusquely I had paused, and came up beside me without a word. We stood listening to the noises, growing more and more sure that they were on our side of the oak door, if not the kitchen then the bath, or in the hall itself at the turn, almost next to us.

We didn't wait to look at one another. I took Irene's arm and forced her to run with me to the wrought-iron door, not waiting to look back. You could hear the noises, still muffled but louder, just behind us. I slammed the grating and we stopped in the vestibule. Now there was nothing to be heard.

"They've taken over our section," Irene said. The knitting had reeled off from her hands and the yarn ran back toward the door and disappeared under it. When she saw that the balls of yarn were on the other side, she dropped the knitting without looking at it.

"Did you have time to bring anything?" I asked hopelessly.

"No, nothing."

We had what we had on. I remembered fifteen thousand pesos[7] in the wardrobe in my bedroom. Too late now.

I still had my wrist watch on and saw that it was 11 P.M. I took Irene around the waist (I think she was crying) and that was how we went into the street. Before we left, I felt terrible; I locked the front door up tight and tossed the key down the sewer. It wouldn't do to have some poor devil decide to go in and rob the house, at that hour and with the house taken over.

1946

7. About $3,500 at the time (worth about $40,000 today).

TADEUSZ BOROWSKI

1922–1951

Incarcerated in the extermination camps of Auschwitz-Birkenau, Dautmergen, and Dachau-Allach between the ages of twenty and twenty-two, a tormented suicide by gas at twenty-eight, Tadeusz Borowski wrote stories of life in the camps that have made him the foremost writer of what is called the "literature of atrocity." His fiction is still read for its powerful evocation of the death camps, for its analysis of human relationships under pressure, and for its agonizing portrayal of individuals forced to choose between physical or spiritual survival.

Tadeusz Borowski was born on November 12, 1922, to Polish Catholic parents in Żytomierz, a Soviet-controlled city with Polish, Ukrainian, Jewish, and Russian residents. When he was three years old, his father was sent to a labor camp in Siberia as a suspected dissident. Four years later, his mother was deported as well, and Tadeusz was separated from his twelve-year-old brother. Tadeusz was raised by an aunt and educated in a Soviet school until a prisoner exchange in 1932 brought his father home; his mother's release in 1934 reunited the family. Money was scarce, however, and the boy was sent away to a Franciscan boarding school where he could be educated inexpensively. Later he commented that he had never had a family life: "Either my father was sitting in Murmansk or my mother was in Siberia, or I was in a boarding school, on my own, or in a camp." The Second World War began when he was sixteen, and—since the Nazis did not permit higher education for Poles—Borowski continued his studies at Warsaw University via illegal underground classes. Unlike his fellow students, he refused to join political groups and did not become involved in the Resistance; he wanted merely to write poetry and continue his literary studies. Polish publications were illegal, however, and his first poetry collection, *Wherever the Earth* (1942)—run off in 165 copies on a clandestine mimeograph machine—was enough to condemn him. *Wherever the Earth* prefigures the bleak perspective of the concentration camp stories: prophesying the end of the human race, it sees the world as a gigantic labor camp and the sky as a "low, steel lid" or "a factory ceiling" (an oppressive image that he may have adapted from **Baudelaire**'s "**Spleen LXXXI**"). In late February 1943, Borowski and his fiancée, Maria Rundo, were arrested; they were sent to Auschwitz two months later. In the meantime, Borowski was able to see, from his cell window, both the Jewish uprising in the Warsaw ghetto and the ghetto's fiery destruction by Nazi soldiers.

On arriving in Auschwitz, Borowski was put to hard labor with the other prisoners. After a bout with pneumonia, he survived by taking a position as an orderly in the Auschwitz hospital—which was not just a clinic but a place where doctors used prisoners as experimental subjects. Rundo had been sent to the women's barracks at the same camp, and he wrote daily letters that were smuggled to her. He got to see her when he was sent to the women's camp to pick up the corpses of infants, and later when he was assigned to repair roofs in the women's camp. Borowski wrote about his camp experiences immediately after the war, when he was living in Munich with two other former Auschwitz prisoners, Janusz Nel Siedlecki and Krystyn Olszewski. The three men were transferred from Dachau-Allach to the Freimann repatriation camp, outside Munich, which they soon left when the Polish artist and publisher Anatol Girs located them and found them jobs. Sharing an apartment in Munich, they published their slightly fictionalized memoirs, including Borowski's "This Way for the Gas, Ladies and Gentlemen," in the 1946 collection *We Were in Auschwitz*. On his return to Poland, Borowski's searing talent was recognized and he became a prominent writer. He married Maria Rundo and was courted by Poland's Stalinist government. At the government's urging, he wrote journalism and weekly stories that followed communist political lines and employed a newly strident tone. The Cold War had begun, and Borowski was persuaded that he had joined a popular revolution that would prevent more horrors like Auschwitz. He went so far as to do intelligence work in Berlin for the Polish secret police in 1949. The revelation of Soviet prison camps, however, as well as the spectacle of political purges in Poland, gradually disillusioned him: once more, he was part of a concentration-camp system and complicit with the oppressors. Although he and his wife had a newborn daughter, he committed suicide by gas on July 1, 1951.

Narrated in an impersonal tone by one of the prisoners, "This Way for the Gas, Ladies and Gentlemen" describes the extermination camp of Birkenau, the largest of three concentration camps at Auschwitz (Polish: *Oświęcim*), an enclosed world of hierarchical authority and desperate struggles to survive. Food, shoes, shirts, underwear: this vital currency of the camp is obtained when prisoners are stripped of their belongings as they arrive in railway cattle cars. The story follows the narrator's first trip to the railroad station with the labor battalion "Canada." The trip will salvage goods from three trains bringing fifteen thousand Polish Jews, former inhabitants of the cities Sosnowiec and Będzin. By the end of the day, most of the travelers will be burning in the crematorium, and the camp will live for a few more days on the loot from "a good, rich transport."

Borowski suggests from the beginning the systematic dehumanization of the camps: prisoners are equated with lice, and they mill around by the naked thousands in blocked-off sections. The same gas is used in exterminating lice and humans—who will later be equated with sick horses (the converted stables retain their old signs), lumber and concrete trucked in from the railroad station, and insects whose jaws work away at moldy pieces of bread. Constantly supervised, subject to arbitrary rules and punishment, malnourished and pushed to exhaustion, their identities reduced to numerals tattooed on their arms, the prisoners live in the shadow of a hierarchical authority that is to be both feared and placated. Paradoxically, their common vulnerability leads to alienation and rage at their fellow victims rather than at the executioners. The Nazis have foreseen everything, explains the narrator's friend Henri, including the fact that weakness needs to vent itself on the weaker. The only way to cope is to distance oneself from what is happening, to become a cog in the machine so that one does not actually experience the events—to suspend, for the moment, one's humanity.

The story's brutal realism and matter-of-fact tone convey as no passionate oratory could the mind-numbing horror of a situation in which systematic slaughter was the background for everyday life. The narrator, Tadeusz, is modeled partly on Borowski, but he is also a composite figure; he has become another part of the concentration-camp system, a survivor. He has a job in the system; assists the Kapos, or senior prisoners who organize the camp; and carries a burden of guilt that his adopted impersonal attitude cannot quite suppress. Borowski's stories shocked their postwar audience with their uncompromising honesty: here were no saintly victims and demonic executioners, but rather human beings—human beings—going about the business of extermination or, reduced to near-animal level, cooperating in the destruction of themselves and others. It is a picture that sorely tests any belief in civilization, common humanity, or divine providence; Borowski's bleak outlook questions everything and does not pretend to offer encouragement.

The narrator's dispassionate tone, as he describes senseless cruelty and mass murder, individual scenes of desperation, or the eccentric emotions of people about to die, continues to shock many readers. Borowski is certainly describing a world of antiheroes, those who survive by accommodating themselves to things as they are and avoiding acts of heroism. Borowski wrote this story after the Nazi defeat, but for its duration the picture is one of a spiritual desolation that not only illustrates a shameful moment in modern history but raises questions about what it means to be civilized, or even human.

This Way for the Gas, Ladies and Gentlemen[1]

All of us[2] walk around naked. The delousing is finally over, and our striped suits are back from the tanks of Cyclone B[3] solution, an efficient killer of lice in clothing and of men in gas chambers. Only the inmates in the blocks cut off from ours by the 'Spanish goats'[4] still have nothing to wear. But all the same, all of us walk around naked: the heat is unbearable. The camp has been sealed off tight. Not a single prisoner, not one solitary louse, can sneak through the gate. The labour Kommandos have stopped working. All day, thousands of naked men shuffle up and down the roads, cluster around the squares, or lie against the walls and on top of the roofs. We have been sleeping on plain boards, since our mattresses and blankets are still being disinfected. From the rear blockhouses we have a view of the F.K.L.—*Frauen Konzentration Lager*;[5] there too the delousing is in full swing. Twenty-eight thousand women have been stripped naked and driven out of the barracks. Now they swarm around the large yard between the blockhouses.

The heat rises, the hours are endless. We are without even our usual diversion: the wide roads leading to the crematoria are empty. For several days now, no new transports have come in. Part of 'Canada'[6] has been liquidated and detailed to a labour Kommando—one of the very toughest—at Harmenz.[7] For there exists in the camp a special brand of justice based on envy: when the rich

1. Translated by Barbara Vedder.
2. Inmates in Auschwitz 11, or Birkenau, the largest of the Nazi extermination camps, established in October 1941 near the town of Birkenau, Poland. Its death toll is usually estimated between 1 million and 2.5 million people.
3. Gas used in extermination camps.
4. Crossed wooden beams wrapped in barbed wire.
5. Women's concentration camp (German).
6. The name given to the camp stores (as well as prisoners working there) where valuables and clothing taken from prisoners were sorted for dispatch to Germany. Like the nation of Canada, the store symbolized wealth and prosperity to the camp inmates.
7. One of the subcamps outside Birkenau itself.

and mighty fall, their friends see to it that they fall to the very bottom. And Canada, our Canada, which smells not of maple forests but of French perfume, has amassed great fortunes in diamonds and currency from all over Europe.

Several of us sit on the top bunk, our legs dangling over the edge. We slice the neat loaves of crisp, crunchy bread. It is a bit coarse to the taste, the kind that stays fresh for days. Sent all the way from Warsaw[8]—only a week ago my mother held this white loaf in her hands . . . dear Lord, dear Lord . . .

We unwrap the bacon, the onion, we open a can of evaporated milk. Henri, the fat Frenchman, dreams aloud of the French wine brought by the transports from Strasbourg, Paris, Marseille[9] . . . Sweat streams down his body.

'Listen, *mon ami*,[1] next time we go up on the loading ramp, I'll bring you real champagne. You haven't tried it before, eh?'

'No. But you'll never be able to smuggle it through the gate, so stop teasing. Why not try and "organize" some shoes for me instead—you know, the perforated kind, with a double sole,[2] and what about that shirt you promised me long ago?'

'*Patience, patience*. When the new transports come, I'll bring all you want. We'll be going on the ramp again!'

'And what if there aren't any more "cremo"[3] transports?' I say spitefully. 'Can't you see how much easier life is becoming around here: no limit on packages, no more beatings? You even write letters home . . . One hears all kind of talk, and, dammit, they'll run out of people!'

'Stop talking nonsense.' Henri's serious fat face moves rhythmically, his mouth is full of sardines. We have been friends for a long time, but I do not even know his last name. 'Stop talking nonsense,' he repeats, swallowing with effort. 'They can't run out of people, or we'll starve to death in this blasted camp. All of us live on what they bring.'

'All? We have our packages . . .'

'Sure, you and your friend, and ten other friends of yours. Some of you Poles get packages. But what about us, and the Jews, and the Russkis? And what if we had no food, no "organization" from the transports, do you think you'd be eating those packages of yours in peace? We wouldn't let you!'

'You would, you'd starve to death like the Greeks. Around here, whoever has grub, has power.'

'Anyway, you have enough, we have enough, so why argue?'

Right, why argue? They have enough, I have enough, we eat together and we sleep on the same bunks. Henri slices the bread, he makes a tomato salad. It tastes good with the commissary mustard.

Below us, naked, sweat-drenched men crowd the narrow barracks aisles or lie packed in eights and tens in the lower bunks. Their nude, withered bodies stink of sweat and excrement; their cheeks are hollow. Directly beneath me, in the bottom bunk, lies a rabbi. He has covered his head[4] with a piece of rag torn

8. Capital of Poland; most of its Jewish residents were executed by the Nazis.
9. A large French port on the Mediterranean Sea. Strasbourg is a city in northeast France.
1. My friend (French).
2. A Hungarian style.
3. The crematorium.
4. Jews are expected to keep their heads covered while at prayer.

off a blanket and reads from a Hebrew prayer book (there is no shortage of this type of literature at the camp), wailing loudly, monotonously.

'Can't somebody shut him up? He's been raving as if he'd caught God himself by the feet.'

'I don't feel like moving. Let him rave. They'll take him to the oven that much sooner.'

'Religion is the opium of the people,'[5] Henri, who is a Communist and a *rentier*,[6] says sententiously. 'If they didn't believe in God and eternal life, they'd have smashed the crematoria long ago.'

'Why haven't you done it then?'

The question is rhetorical; the Frenchman ignores it.

'Idiot,' he says simply, and stuffs a tomato in his mouth.

Just as we finish our snack, there is a sudden commotion at the door. The Muslims[7] scurry in fright to the safety of their bunks, a messenger runs into the Block Elder's shack. The Elder,[8] his face solemn, steps out at once.

'Canada! *Antreten!*[9] But fast! There's a transport coming!'

'Great God!' yells Henri, jumping off the bunk. He swallows the rest of his tomato, snatches his coat, screams '*Raus*'[1] at the men below, and in a flash is at the door. We can hear a scramble in the other bunks. Canada is leaving for the ramp.

'Henri, the shoes!' I call after him.

'*Keine Angst!*'[2] he shouts back, already outside.

I proceed to put away the food. I tie a piece of rope around the suitcase where the onions and the tomatoes from my father's garden in Warsaw mingle with Portuguese sardines, bacon from Lublin (that's from my brother), and authentic sweetmeats from Salonica.[3] I tie it all up, pull on my trousers, and slide off the bunk.

'*Platz!*'[4] I yell, pushing my way through the Greeks. They step aside. At the door I bump into Henri.

'*Was ist los?*'[5]

'Want to come with us on the ramp?'

'Sure, why not?'

'Come along then, grab your coat! We're short of a few men. I've already told the Kapo,' and he shoves me out of the barracks door.

We line up. Someone has marked down our numbers, someone up ahead yells, 'March, march,' and now we are running towards the gate, accompanied by the shouts of a multilingual throng that is already being pushed back to the barracks. Not everybody is lucky enough to be going on the ramp . . . We have almost reached the gate. *Links, zwei, drei, vier! Mützen ab!*[6] Erect, arms stretched stiffly along our hips, we march past the gate briskly, smartly, almost

5. A quotation from the German political philosopher Karl Marx (1818–1883).
6. Someone with unearned income, a stockholder (French).
7. Camp nickname for people who had given up, considered the camp pariahs.
8. A Kapo, or senior prisoner in charge of a group of prisoners.
9. Report (German).
1. Outside (German).
2. Don't panic (German).
3. Major port city in northeast Greece. Lublin is a city in eastern Poland.
4. Make room (German).
5. What's the matter? (German).
6. Left, two, three, four! Caps off! (German).

gracefully. A sleepy S.S.[7] man with a large pad in his hand checks us off, waving us ahead in groups of five.

'*Hundert!*'[8] he calls after we have all passed.

'*Stimmt!*'[9] comes a hoarse answer from out front.

We march fast, almost at a run. There are guards all around, young men with automatics. We pass camp II B, then some deserted barracks and a clump of unfamiliar green—apple and pear trees. We cross the circle of watchtowers and, running, burst on to the highway. We have arrived. Just a few more yards. There, surrounded by trees, is the ramp.

A cheerful little station, very much like any other provincial railway stop: a small square framed by tall chestnuts and paved with yellow gravel. Not far off, beside the road, squats a tiny wooden shed, uglier and more flimsy than the ugliest and flimsiest railway shack; farther along lie stacks of old rails, heaps of wooden beams, barracks parts, bricks, paving stones. This is where they load freight for Birkenau: supplies for the construction of the camp, and people for the gas chambers. Trucks drive around, load up lumber, cement, people—a regular daily routine.

And now the guards are being posted along the rails, across the beams, in the green shade of the Silesian chestnuts,[1] to form a tight circle around the ramp. They wipe the sweat from their faces and sip out of their canteens. It is unbearably hot; the sun stands motionless at its zenith.

'Fall out!'

We sit down in the narrow streaks of shade along the stacked rails. The hungry Greeks (several of them managed to come along, God only knows how) rummage underneath the rails. One of them finds some pieces of mildewed bread, another a few half-rotten sardines. They eat.

'*Schweinedreck*,'[2] spits a young, tall guard with corn-coloured hair and dreamy blue eyes. 'For God's sake, any minute you'll have so much food to stuff down your guts, you'll bust!' He adjusts his gun, wipes his face with a handkerchief.

'Hey you, fatso!' His boot lightly touches Henri's shoulder. '*Pass mal auf*,[3] want a drink?'

'Sure, but I haven't got any marks,' replies the Frenchman with a professional air.

'*Schade*, too bad.'

'Come, come, Herr[4] Posten, isn't my word good enough any more? Haven't we done business before? How much?'

'One hundred. *Gemacht?*'[5]

'*Gemacht*.'

7. Abbreviation for *Schutzstaffel* (Protective Echelon, German), the Nazi police system that began as Hitler's private guard and grew, by 1939, to a 250,000-member military and political organization that administered all state security functions. The SS was divided into numerous bureaucratic units, one of which, the Death's Head Battalions, managed the concentration camps. Selected for physical perfection and (Aryan) racial purity, SS members wore black or gray-green uniforms decorated with silver insignia.

8. A hundred! (German).

9. Right! (German).

1. Probably local chestnuts. Silesia, in central Europe, was partitioned among Poland, Czechoslovakia, and Germany after World War I; Germany occupied Polish Silesia in 1939.

2. Dirty pigs (German).

3. See here (German).

4. Mister (German).

5. Done? (German).

We drink the water, lukewarm and tasteless. It will be paid for by the people who have not yet arrived.

'Now you be careful,' says Henri, turning to me. He tosses away the empty bottle. It strikes the rails and bursts into tiny fragments. 'Don't take any money, they might be checking. Anyway, who the hell needs money? You've got enough to eat. Don't take suits, either, or they'll think you're planning to escape. Just get a shirt, silk only, with a collar. And a vest. And if you find something to drink, don't bother calling me. I know how to shift for myself, but you watch your step or they'll let you have it.'

'Do they beat you up here?'

'Naturally. You've got to have eyes in your ass. *Arschaugen*.'[6]

Around us sit the Greeks, their jaws working greedily, like huge human insects. They munch on stale lumps of bread. They are restless, wondering what will happen next. The sight of the large beams and the stacks of rails has them worried. They dislike carrying heavy loads.

'*Was wir arbeiten?*'[7] they ask.

'*Niks. Transport kommen, alles Krematorium, compris?*'[8]

'*Alles verstehen*,' they answer in crematorium Esperanto.[9] All is well—they will not have to move the heavy rails or carry the beams.

In the meantime, the ramp has become increasingly alive with activity, increasingly noisy. The crews are being divided into those who will open and unload the arriving cattle cars and those who will be posted by the wooden steps. They receive instructions on how to proceed most efficiently. Motor cycles drive up, delivering S.S. officers, bemedalled, glittering with brass, beefy men with highly polished boots and shiny, brutal faces. Some have brought their briefcases, others hold thin, flexible whips. This gives them an air of military readiness and agility. They walk in and out of the commissary—for the miserable little shack by the road serves as their commissary, where in the summertime they drink mineral water, Sudetenquelle,[1] and where in winter they can warm up with a glass of hot wine. They greet each other in the state-approved way, raising an arm Roman fashion, then shake hands cordially, exchange warm smiles, discuss mail from home, their children, their families. Some stroll majestically on the ramp. The silver squares on their collars glitter, the gravel crunches under their boots, their bamboo whips snap impatiently.

We lie against the rails in the narrow streaks of shade, breathe unevenly, occasionally exchange a few words in our various tongues, and gaze listlessly at the majestic men in green uniforms, at the green trees, and at the church steeple of a distant village.

'The transport is coming,' somebody says. We spring to our feet, all eyes turn in one direction. Around the bend, one after another, the cattle cars begin rolling in. The train backs into the station, a conductor leans out, waves his hand, blows a whistle. The locomotive whistles back with a shrieking noise, puffs, the

6. Eyes on your ass (German; literal trans.).
7. What are we working on? (German).
8. Nothing. Transport coming, everything crematorium, understood? (German; *compris* is French).
9. An artificial language, created in 1887 by L. L. Zamenhof, to simplify communication between nationalities. "*Alles verstehen*": Everything understood.
1. Water from the Sudetenland or Sudeten Mountains; a narrow strip of land on the northern and western borders of the Czech Republic. The Sudeten was annexed by Hitler in 1938.

train rolls slowly alongside the ramp. In the tiny barred windows appear pale, wilted, exhausted human faces, terror-stricken women with tangled hair, unshaven men. They gaze at the station in silence. And then, suddenly, there is a stir inside the cars and a pounding against the wooden boards.

'Water! Air!'—weary, desperate cries.

Heads push through the windows, mouths gasp frantically for air. They draw a few breaths, then disappear; others come in their place, then also disappear. The cries and moans grow louder.

A man in a green uniform covered with more glitter than any of the others jerks his head impatiently, his lips twist in annoyance. He inhales deeply, then with a rapid gesture throws his cigarette away and signals to the guard. The guard removes the automatic from his shoulder, aims, sends a series of shots along the train. All is quiet now. Meanwhile, the trucks have arrived, steps are being drawn up, and the Canada men stand ready at their posts by the train doors. The S.S. officer with the briefcase raises his hand.

'Whoever takes gold, or anything at all besides food, will be shot for stealing Reich property. Understand? *Verstanden?*'

'*Jawohl!*'[2] we answer eagerly.

'*Also los!*[3] Begin!'

The bolts crack, the doors fall open. A wave of fresh air rushes inside the train. People . . . inhumanly crammed, buried under incredible heaps of luggage, suitcases, trunks, packages, crates, bundles of every description (everything that had been their past and was to start their future). Monstrously squeezed together, they have fainted from heat, suffocated, crushed one another. Now they push towards the opened doors, breathing like fish cast out on the sand.

'Attention! Out, and take your luggage with you! Take out everything. Pile all your stuff near the exits. Yes, your coats too. It is summer. March to the left. Understand?'

'Sir, what's going to happen to us?' They jump from the train on to the gravel, anxious, worn-out.

'Where are you people from?'

'Sosnowiec-Będzin.[4] Sir, what's going to happen to us?' They repeat the question stubbornly, gazing into our tired eyes.

'I don't know. I don't understand Polish.'

It is the camp law: people going to their death must be deceived to the very end. This is the only permissible form of charity. The heat is tremendous. The sun hangs directly over our heads, the white, hot sky quivers, the air vibrates, an occasional breeze feels like a sizzling blast from a furnace. Our lips are parched, the mouth fills with the salty taste of blood, the body is weak and heavy from lying in the sun. Water!

A huge, multicoloured wave of people loaded down with luggage pours from the train like a blind, mad river trying to find a new bed. But before they have a chance to recover, before they can draw a breath of fresh air and look at the

2. Yes! (German). "*Verstanden*": understand? (German).
3. Then get going! (German).
4. Two cities in Katowice province (southern Poland). Będzin was also the site of a concentration camp, and more than ten thousand of its inhabitants were exterminated.

sky, bundles are snatched from their hands, coats ripped off their backs, their purses and umbrellas taken away.

'But please, sir, it's for the sun, I cannot . . .'

'*Verboten!*'[5] one of us barks through clenched teeth. There is an S.S. man standing behind your back, calm, efficient, watchful.

'*Meine Herrschaften*,[6] this way, ladies and gentlemen, try not to throw your things around, please. Show some goodwill,' he says courteously, his restless hands playing with the slender whip.

'Of course, of course,' they answer as they pass, and now they walk alongside the train somewhat more cheerfully. A woman reaches down quickly to pick up her handbag. The whip flies, the woman screams, stumbles, and falls under the feet of the surging crowd. Behind her, a child cries in a thin little voice 'Mamele!'—a very small girl with tangled black curls.

The heaps grow. Suitcases, bundles, blankets, coats, handbags that open as they fall, spilling coins, gold, watches; mountains of bread pile up at the exits, heaps of marmalade, jams, masses of meat, sausages; sugar spills on the gravel. Trucks, loaded with people, start up with a deafening roar and drive off amidst the wailing and screaming of the women separated from their children, and the stupefied silence of the men left behind. They are the ones who had been ordered to step to the right—the healthy and the young who will go to the camp. In the end, they too will not escape death, but first they must work.

Trucks leave and return, without interruption, as on a monstrous conveyor belt. A Red Cross van drives back and forth, back and forth, incessantly: it transports the gas that will kill these people. The enormous cross on the hood, red as blood, seems to dissolve in the sun.

The Canada men at the trucks cannot stop for a single moment, even to catch their breath. They shove the people up the steps, pack them in tightly, sixty per truck, more or less. Near by stands a young, cleanshaven 'gentleman', an S.S. officer with a notebook in his hand. For each departing truck he enters a mark; sixteen gone means one thousand people, more or less. The gentleman is calm, precise. No truck can leave without a signal from him, or a mark in his notebook: *Ordnung muss sein*.[7] The marks swell into thousands, the thousands into whole transports, which afterwards we shall simply call 'from Salonica', 'from Strasbourg', 'from Rotterdam'.[8] This one will be called 'Sosnowiec-Będzin'. The new prisoners from Sosnowiec-Będzin will receive serial numbers 131–2—thousand, of course, though afterwards we shall simply say 131–2, for short.

The transports swell into weeks, months, years. When the war is over, they will count up the marks in their notebooks—all four and a half million of them. The bloodiest battle of the war, the greatest victory of the strong, united Germany. *Ein Reich, ein Volk, ein Führer*[9]—and four crematoria.

The train has been emptied. A thin, pock-marked S.S. man peers inside, shakes his head in disgust and motions to our group, pointing his finger at the door.

'*Rein*.[1] Clean it up!'

5. Forbidden (German).
6. Gentlemen (German).
7. Order in everything (German).
8. Large port city in the Netherlands.
9. One State, One People, One Leader! (the slogan of Nazi Germany).
1. Clean (German).

We climb inside. In the corners amid human excrement and abandoned wrist-watches lie squashed, trampled infants, naked little monsters with enormous heads and bloated bellies. We carry them out like chickens, holding several in each hand.

'Don't take them to the trucks, pass them on to the women,' says the S.S. man, lighting a cigarette. His cigarette lighter is not working properly; he examines it carefully.

'Take them, for God's sake!' I explode as the women rush from me in horror, covering their eyes.

The name of God sounds strangely pointless, since the women and the infants will go on the trucks, every one of them without exception. We all know what this means, and we look at each other with hate and horror.

'What, you don't want to take them?' asks the pockmarked S.S. man with a note of surprise and reproach in his voice, and reaches for his revolver.

'You mustn't shoot, I'll carry them.' A tall, grey-haired woman takes the little corpses out of my hands and for an instant gazes straight into my eyes.

'My poor boy,' she whispers and smiles at me. Then she walks away, staggering along the path. I lean against the side of the train. I am terribly tired. Someone pulls at my sleeve.

'*En avant*,[2] to the rails, come on!'

I look up, but the face swims before my eyes, dissolves, huge and transparent, melts into the motionless trees and the sea of people . . . I blink rapidly: Henri.

'Listen, Henri, are we good people?'

'That's stupid. Why do you ask?'

'You see, my friend, you see, I don't know why, but I am furious, simply furious with these people—furious because I must be here because of them. I feel no pity. I am not sorry they're going to the gas chamber. Damn them all! I could throw myself at them, beat them with my fists. It must be pathological, I just can't understand . . .'

'Ah, on the contrary, it is natural, predictable, calculated. The ramp exhausts you, you rebel—and the easiest way to relieve your hate is to turn against someone weaker. Why, I'd even call it healthy. It's simple logic, *compris*?' He props himself up comfortably against the heap of rails. 'Look at the Greeks, they know how to make the best of it! They stuff their bellies with anything they find. One of them has just devoured a full jar of marmalade.'

'Pigs! Tomorrow half of them will die of the shits.'

'Pigs? You've been hungry.'

'Pigs!' I repeat furiously. I close my eyes. The air is filled with ghastly cries, the earth trembles beneath me, I can feel sticky moisture on my eyelids. My throat is completely dry.

The morbid procession streams on and on—trucks growl like mad dogs. I shut my eyes tight, but I can still see corpses dragged from the train, trampled infants, cripples piled on top of the dead, wave after wave . . . freight cars roll in, the heaps of clothing, suitcases and bundles grow, people climb out, look at the sun, take a few breaths, beg for water, get into the trucks, drive away. And again freight cars roll in, again people . . . The scenes become confused in my

2. Forward (French).

mind—I am not sure if all of this is actually happening, or if I am dreaming. There is a humming inside my head; I feel that I must vomit.

Henri tugs at my arm.

'Don't sleep, we're off to load up the loot.'

All the people are gone. In the distance, the last few trucks roll along the road in clouds of dust, the train has left, several S.S. officers promenade up and down the ramp. The silver glitters on their collars. Their boots shine, their red, beefy faces shine. Among them there is a woman—only now I realize she has been here all along—withered, flat-chested, bony, her thin, colourless hair pulled back and tied in a 'Nordic'[3] knot; her hands are in the pockets of her wide skirt. With a rat-like, resolute smile glued on her thin lips she sniffs around the corners of the ramp. She detests feminine beauty with the hatred of a woman who is herself repulsive, and knows it. Yes, I have seen her many times before and I know her well: she is the commandant of the F.K.L. She has come to look over the new crop of women, for some of them, instead of going on the trucks, will go on foot—to the concentration camp. There our boys, the barbers from Zauna,[4] will shave their heads and will have a good laugh at their 'outside world' modesty.

We proceed to load the loot. We lift huge trunks, heave them on to the trucks. There they are arranged in stacks, packed tightly. Occasionally somebody slashes one open with a knife, for pleasure or in search of vodka and perfume. One of the crates falls open; suits, shirts, books drop out on the ground . . . I pick up a small, heavy package. I unwrap it—gold, about two handfuls, bracelets, rings, brooches, diamonds . . .

'*Gib hier*,'[5] an S.S. man says calmly, holding up his briefcase already full of gold and colourful foreign currency. He locks the case, hands it to an officer, takes another, an empty one, and stands by the next truck, waiting. The gold will go to the Reich.[6]

It is hot, terribly hot. Our throats are dry, each word hurts. Anything for a sip of water! Faster, faster, so that it is over, so that we may rest. At last we are done, all the trucks have gone. Now we swiftly clean up the remaining dirt: there must be 'no trace left of the *Schweinerei*'. But just as the last truck disappears behind the trees and we walk, finally, to rest in the shade, a shrill whistle sounds around the bend. Slowly, terribly slowly, a train rolls in, the engine whistles back with a deafening shriek. Again weary, pale faces at the windows, flat as though cut out of paper, with huge, feverishly burning eyes. Already trucks are pulling up, already the composed gentleman with the notebook is at his post, and the S.S. men emerge from the commissary carrying briefcases for the gold and money. We unseal the train doors.

It is impossible to control oneself any longer. Brutally we tear suitcases from their hands, impatiently pull off their coats. Go on, go on, vanish! They go, they vanish. Men, women, children. Some of them know.

Here is a woman—she walks quickly, but tries to appear calm. A small child with a pink cherub's face runs after her and, unable to keep up, stretches out his little arms and cries: 'Mama! Mama!'

3. A northern (especially Scandinavian) style encouraged by the Nazis to establish an image of Teutonic racial purity.

4. The "sauna" barracks, in front of Canada, where prisoners were bathed, shaved, and deloused.

5. Give it to me (German).

6. The German state.

'Pick up your child, woman!'

'It's not mine, sir, not mine!' she shouts hysterically and runs on, covering her face with her hands. She wants to hide, she wants to reach those who will not ride the trucks, those who will go on foot, those who will stay alive. She is young, healthy, good-looking, she wants to live.

But the child runs after her, wailing loudly: 'Mama, mama, don't leave me!'

'It's not mine, not mine, no!'

Andrei, a sailor from Sevastopol,[7] grabs hold of her. His eyes are glassy from vodka and the heat. With one powerful blow he knocks her off her feet, then, as she falls, takes her by the hair and pulls her up again. His face twitches with rage.

'Ah, you bloody Jewess! So you're running from your own child! I'll show you, you whore!' His huge hand chokes her, he lifts her in the air and heaves her on to the truck like a heavy sack of grain.

'Here! And take this with you, bitch!' and he throws the child at her feet.

'*Gut gemacht*, good work. That's the way to deal with degenerate mothers,' says the S.S. man standing at the foot of the truck. '*Gut, gut, Russki*.'[8]

'Shut your mouth,' growls Andrei through clenched teeth, and walks away. From under a pile of rags he pulls out a canteen, unscrews the cork, takes a few deep swallows, passes it to me. The strong vodka burns the throat. My head swims, my legs are shaky, again I feel like throwing up.

And suddenly, above the teeming crowd pushing forward like a river driven by an unseen power, a girl appears. She descends lightly from the train, hops on to the gravel, looks around inquiringly, as if somewhat surprised. Her soft, blonde hair has fallen on her shoulders in a torrent, she throws it back impatiently. With a natural gesture she runs her hands down her blouse, casually straightens her skirt. She stands like this for an instant, gazing at the crowd, then turns and with a gliding look examines our faces, as though searching for someone. Unknowingly, I continue to stare at her, until our eyes meet.

'Listen, tell me, where are they taking us?'

I look at her without saying a word. Here, standing before me, is a girl, a girl with enchanting blonde hair, with beautiful breasts, wearing a little cotton blouse, a girl with a wise, mature look in her eyes. Here she stands, gazing straight into my face, waiting. And over there is the gas chamber: communal death, disgusting and ugly. And over in the other direction is the concentration camp: the shaved head, the heavy Soviet trousers in sweltering heat, the sickening, stale odour of dirty, damp female bodies, the animal hunger, the inhuman labour, and later the same gas chamber, only an even more hideous, more terrible death . . .

Why did she bring it? I think to myself, noticing a lovely gold watch on her delicate wrist. They'll take it away from her anyway.

'Listen, tell me,' she repeats.

I remain silent. Her lips tighten.

'I know,' she says with a shade of proud contempt in her voice, tossing her head. She walks off resolutely in the direction of the trucks. Someone tries to

7. A Soviet (now, Ukrainian) port on the Black Sea.

8. Good, good, Russky (German). "*Gut gemacht*": well done (German).

stop her; she boldly pushes him aside and runs up the steps. In the distance I can only catch a glimpse of her blonde hair flying in the breeze.

I go back inside the train; I carry out dead infants; I unload luggage. I touch corpses, but I cannot overcome the mounting, uncontrollable terror. I try to escape from the corpses, but they are everywhere: lined up on the gravel, on the cement edge of the ramp, inside the cattle cars. Babies, hideous naked women, men twisted by convulsions. I run off as far as I can go, but immediately a whip slashes across my back. Out of the corner of my eye I see an S.S. man, swearing profusely. I stagger forward and run, lose myself in the Canada group. Now, at last, I can once more rest against the stack of rails. The sun has leaned low over the horizon and illuminates the ramp with a reddish glow; the shadows of the trees have become elongated, ghostlike. In the silence that settles over nature at this time of day, the human cries seem to rise all the way to the sky.

Only from this distance does one have a full view of the inferno on the teeming ramp. I see a pair of human beings who have fallen to the ground locked in a last desperate embrace. The man has dug his fingers into the woman's flesh and has caught her clothing with his teeth. She screams hysterically, swears, cries, until at last a large boot comes down over her throat and she is silent. They are pulled apart and dragged like cattle to the truck. I see four Canada men lugging a corpse: a huge, swollen female corpse. Cursing, dripping wet from the strain, they kick out of their way some stray children who have been running all over the ramp, howling like dogs. The men pick them up by the collars, heads, arms, and toss them inside the trucks, on top of the heaps. The four men have trouble lifting the fat corpse on to the car, they call others for help, and all together they hoist up the mound of meat. Big, swollen, puffed-up corpses are being collected from all over the ramp; on top of them are piled the invalids, the smothered, the sick, the unconscious. The heap seethes, howls, groans. The driver starts the motor, the truck begins rolling.

'Halt! Halt!' an S.S. man yells after them. 'Stop, damn you.'

They are dragging to the truck an old man wearing tails and a band around his arm. His head knocks against the gravel and pavement; he moans and wails in an uninterrupted monotone: '*Ich will mit dem Herrn Kommandanten sprechen*[9]—I wish to speak with the commandant . . .' With senile stubbornness he keeps repeating these words all the way. Thrown on the truck, trampled by others, choked, he still wails: '*Ich will mit dem . . .*'

'Look here, old man!' a young S.S. man calls, laughing jovially. 'In half an hour you'll be talking with the top commandant! Only don't forget to greet him with a *Heil Hitler*!'

Several other men are carrying a small girl with only one leg. They hold her by the arms and the one leg. Tears are running down her face and she whispers faintly: 'Sir, it hurts, it hurts . . .' They throw her on the truck on top of the corpses. She will burn alive along with them.

The evening has come, cool and clear. The stars are out. We lie against the rails. It is incredibly quiet. Anaemic bulbs hang from the top of the high lampposts; beyond the circle of light stretches an impenetrable darkness. Just one

9. I want to speak with the commandant (German).

step, and a man could vanish for ever. But the guards are watching, their automatics ready.

'Did you get the shoes?' asks Henri.

'No.'

'Why?'

'My God, man, I am finished, absolutely finished!'

'So soon? After only two transports? Just look at me, I . . . since Christmas, at least a million people have passed through my hands. The worst of all are the transports from around Paris—one is always bumping into friends.'

'And what do you say to them?'

'That first they will have a bath, and later we'll meet at the camp. What would you say?'

I do not answer. We drink coffee with vodka; somebody opens a tin of cocoa and mixes it with sugar. We scoop it up by the handful, the cocoa sticks to the lips. Again coffee, again vodka.

'Henri, what are we waiting for?'

'There'll be another transport.'

'I'm not going to unload it! I can't take any more.'

'So, it's got you down? Canada is nice, eh?' Henri grins indulgently and disappears into the darkness. In a moment he is back again.

'All right. Just sit here quietly and don't let an S.S. man see you. I'll try to find you your shoes.'

'Just leave me alone. Never mind the shoes.' I want to sleep. It is very late.

Another whistle, another transport. Freight cars emerge out of the darkness, pass under the lamp-posts, and again vanish in the night. The ramp is small, but the circle of lights is smaller. The unloading will have to be done gradually. Somewhere the trucks are growling. They back up against the steps, black, ghostlike, their searchlights flash across the trees. *Wasser! Luft!*[1] The same all over again, like a late showing of the same film: a volley of shots, the train falls silent. Only this time a little girl pushes herself halfway through the small window and, losing her balance, falls out on to the gravel. Stunned, she lies still for a moment, then stands up and begins walking around in a circle, faster and faster, waving her rigid arms in the air, breathing loudly and spasmodically, whining in a faint voice. Her mind has given way in the inferno inside the train. The whining is hard on the nerves: an S.S. man approaches calmly, his heavy boot strikes between her shoulders. She falls. Holding her down with his foot, he draws his revolver, fires once, then again. She remains face down, kicking the gravel with her feet, until she stiffens. They proceed to unseal the train.

I am back on the ramp, standing by the doors. A warm, sickening smell gushes from inside. The mountain of people filling the car almost halfway up to the ceiling is motionless, horribly tangled, but still steaming.

'*Ausladen!*[2] comes the command. An S.S. man steps out from the darkness. Across his chest hangs a portable searchlight. He throws a stream of light inside.

'Why are you standing about like sheep? Start unloading!' His whip flies and falls across our backs. I seize a corpse by the hand; the fingers close tightly

1. Water! Air! (German).
2. Unload! (German).

around mine. I pull back with a shriek and stagger away. My heart pounds, jumps up to my throat. I can no longer control the nausea. Hunched under the train I begin to vomit. Then, like a drunk, I weave over to the stack of rails.

I lie against the cool, kind metal and dream about returning to the camp, about my bunk, on which there is no mattress, about sleep among comrades who are not going to the gas tonight. Suddenly I see the camp as a haven of peace. It is true, others may be dying, but one is somehow still alive, one has enough food, enough strength to work . . .

The lights on the ramp flicker with a spectral glow, the wave of people—feverish, agitated, stupefied people—flows on and on, endlessly. They think that now they will have to face a new life in the camp, and they prepare themselves emotionally for the hard struggle ahead. They do not know that in just a few moments they will die, that the gold, money, and diamonds which they have so prudently hidden in their clothing and on their bodies are now useless to them. Experienced professionals will probe into every recess of their flesh, will pull the gold from under the tongue and the diamonds from the uterus and the colon. They will rip out gold teeth. In tightly sealed crates they will ship them to Berlin.[3]

The S.S. men's black figures move about, dignified, businesslike. The gentleman with the notebook puts down his final marks, rounds out the figures: fifteen thousand.

Many, very many, trucks have been driven to the crematoria today.

It is almost over. The dead are being cleared off the ramp and piled into the last truck. The Canada men, weighed down under a load of bread, marmalade and sugar, and smelling of perfume and fresh linen, line up to go. For several days the entire camp will live off this transport. For several days the entire camp will talk about 'Sosnowiec-Będzin'. 'Sosnowiec-Będzin' was a good, rich transport.

The stars are already beginning to pale as we walk back to the camp. The sky grows translucent and opens high above our heads—it is getting light.

Great columns of smoke rise from the crematoria and merge up above into a huge black river which very slowly floats across the sky over Birkenau and disappears beyond the forests in the direction of Trzebinia.[4] The 'Sosnowiec-Będzin' transport is already burning.

We pass a heavily armed S.S. detachment on its way to change guard. The men march briskly, in step, shoulder to shoulder, one mass, one will.

'*Und morgen die ganze Welt* . . .'[5] they sing at the top of their lungs.

'*Rechts ran!*[6] To the right march!' snaps a command from up front. We move out of their way.

1946

3. The capital of Germany.
4. A town west of Auschwitz, near Krakow.
5. And tomorrow the whole world (German): the last line of the Nazi song "The Rotten Bones Are Shaking," written by Hans Baumann. The previous line reads "for today Germany belongs to us."
6. To the right, get going! (German).

PAUL CELAN
1920–1970

A survivor of the Holocaust, Paul Celan wrote spare, hauntingly beautiful lyric poems about suffering and loss. The critic Theodor Adorno famously noted that "to write a poem after Auschwitz is barbaric." Yet Celan, who lost both parents in Nazi prison camps and who himself spent much of the Second World War in a forced labor camp, managed to write poetry that spoke directly about the unspeakable.

Born Paul Antschel in Czernowitz, Romania, Celan came from a religious Jewish family. (Celan is an anagram of the Romanian spelling of his last name, Ancel.) He was raised speaking German, and his mother passed on to him her love of German literature, while his father transmitted his Zionism and concern with the Jewish tradition. Czernowitz was linguistically and ethnically diverse, and Celan quickly learned Yiddish and Romanian, as well as Hebrew; later in life, he learned French, Russian, Ukranian, and English as well.

In 1938, Celan enrolled in a premedical program in Paris, where he was exposed to avant-garde literary movements such as surrealism; he had recently begun writing poetry. Returning home in the summer of 1939, he was trapped in Czernowitz by the outbreak of the Second World War. Under the Hitler-Stalin pact, the Soviet Union occupied Czernowitz in 1940. Distressed by harsh Soviet rule, Celan abandoned his youthful support of communism. After the Nazi invasion of the Soviet Union in the summer of 1941, the Germans took control of Czernowitz, and the Jews of the city were attacked and confined to a ghetto by the Nazi SS (abbreviation for the German word *Schutzstaffel*, the elite security organization) and by Romanian soldiers. Celan was given the task of clearing trash and destroying Russian books. On June 27, 1942, while Celan was away from the house, the Germans seized his parents and deported them to Nazi prison camps in Ukraine. His father died of typhus later that year, and his mother was shot when she was no longer capable of working. Celan spent the next year and a half in labor camps in German-allied Romania, where, though conditions were severe, he was at less risk of being killed. He continued to write poetry. After the Soviet Red Army reoccupied eastern Romania and the full horror of the concentration camps came to be known, Celan, now released from his prison camp, wrote "Deathfugue," one of the first and most moving poems about the camps, published first in Romanian translation in 1947, then in German in 1952.

Near the end of the war, Celan left Czernowitz for Bucharest, where he worked translating literature, including some of **Franz Kafka**'s parables, into Romanian. For the remainder of his life, he was active as a translator of much modern French, Russian, and English poetry (and also Shakespeare) into German. Celan fled Bucharest in 1947, just before the Soviet takeover, and was smuggled with his poems over the border to Vienna. From there he went on to Paris and the prestigious École Normale Supérieure, where he received his degree and then taught German literature. He visited Germany occasionally, receiving the premier German literary award, the Büchner Prize, in 1960 and later meeting the existential philosopher Martin Heidegger, whose work had inspired Celan despite the German's support of the Nazi regime. In 1969, Celan visited Israel for the first time.

During the 1960s, however, Celan suffered periods of increasing paranoia, the result of his concerns about anti-Semitism and of false accusations of plagiarism that continually dogged him. He briefly entered a psychiatric clinic in 1965, and remained under psychiatric treatment for the following five years. On April 20, 1970, Celan committed suicide by jumping off a bridge into the Seine, in Paris.

The poems printed here represent a sampling of Celan's work. They show his use of a restrained and difficult language to bear witness to the horrors suffered by his parents and other victims of the Holocaust. "Deathfugue," his first published poem and eventually his most famous, originally appeared in Romanian translation as "Tangoul Mortii" (Tango of Death). That title refers to the dance music that an SS commander forced prisoners to play during marches and executions at the Janowska camp in L'vov, Ukraine. The poem contrasts the golden hair of the commander's beloved Margareta (a typically German name) with the dark hair of the Jewish Shulamith, a prisoner in the camp. Her hair is described as "ashen," recalling the crematoria where bodies of concentration camp victims were burned. Celan re-creates the musical quality of the tango or fugue—two very different musical forms both characterized by rhythmic repetition—in his repetition of short, rhythmic phrases. The fragmentation and absence of punctuation suggest a breakdown of the moral order. The translator, John Felstiner, has left some of the poem in German to give the sense of its original language. Of the German language and why he continued to write in it, Celan once said, "Only in the mother tongue can one speak one's own truth. In a foreign tongue the poet lies."

Later in life, Celan wrote poems that were less political and often more explicitly religious. "Zurich, at the Stork" (1963) recalls Celan's debate with an older poet, Nelly Sachs, about God's existence. Though deeply concerned with Jewish religious teaching, Celan never believed in God in a straightforward sense. And yet, in keeping with certain forms of Jewish mysticism, he believed in God as an absence.

Deathfugue[1]

Black milk of daybreak we drink it at evening
we drink it at midday and morning we drink it at night
we drink and we drink
we shovel a grave in the air where you won't lie too cramped
A man lives in the house he plays with his vipers he writes
he writes when it grows dark to Deutschland[2] your golden hair
  Margareta[3]
he writes it and steps out of doors and the stars are all sparkling he
  whistles his hounds to stay close

1. All selections translated from German by John Felstiner.

2. Germany (German).

3. A typically German name.

he whistles his Jews into rows has them shovel a grave in the ground
he commands us play up for the dance[4]

Black milk of daybreak we drink you at night
we drink you at morning and midday we drink you at evening
we drink and we drink
A man lives in the house he plays with his vipers he writes
he writes when it grows dark to Deutschland your golden hair
  Margareta
Your ashen hair Shulamith[5] we shovel a grave in the air
  where you won't lie too cramped

He shouts dig this earth deeper you lot there you others sing up and play
he grabs for the rod in his belt he swings it his eyes are so blue
stick your spades deeper you lot there you others play on for the dancing

Black milk of daybreak we drink you at night
we drink you at midday and morning we drink you at evening
we drink and we drink
a man lives in the house your goldenes Haar[6] Margareta
your aschenes Haar[7] Shulamith he plays with his vipers

He shouts play death more sweetly this Death is a master from
  Deutschland
he shouts scrape your strings darker you'll rise up as smoke to the sky[8]
you'll then have a grave in the clouds where you won't lie too cramped

Black milk of daybreak we drink you at night
we drink you at midday Death is a master aus Deutschland
we drink you at evening and morning we drink and we drink
this Death is ein Meister aus Deutschland his eye it is blue
he shoots you with shot made of lead shoots you level and true
a man lives in the house your goldenes Haar Margarete
he looses his hounds on us grants us a grave in the air
he plays with his vipers and daydreams der Tod ist ein Meister aus
  Deutschland[9]

dein goldenes Haar Margarete
dein aschenes Haar Shulamith

1947

4. Concentration camp commanders are reported to have forced prisoners to play dance tunes, sometimes while graves were being dug.
5. A typically Jewish name.
6. Golden hair (German). The translator has left some phrases in the original.
7. Ashen hair (German).
8. Murdered prisoners were burned in crematoria.
9. Death is a Master from Germany (German).

Zurich, at the Stork[1]

For Nelly Sachs

Our talk was of Too Much, of
Too Little. Of Thou
and Yet-Thou, of
clouding through brightness, of
Jewishness, of
your God.

Of
that.
On the day of an ascension, the
Minster stood over there, it came
with some gold across the water.

Our talk was of your God, I spoke
against him, I let the heart
I had
hope:
for
his highest, death-rattled, his
wrangling word—

Your eye looked at me, looked away,
your mouth
spoke toward the eye, I heard:

We
really don't know, you know,
we
really don't know
what
counts.

1963

1. A hotel where Celan had a theological conversation with his friend the poet Nelly Sachs (1891–1970).

DORIS LESSING

1919–2013

Conflicts between cultures, between values within a culture, and even between elements of a personality, are fundamental themes in Doris Lessing's work—as is the struggle to integrate these entities into a higher, unified order. The recipient of the 2007 Nobel Prize in Literature, Lessing has spent her life in the midst of such conflicts. A witness to harsh colonial policies toward native subjects in Rhodesia as well as to the sexual and feminist revolutions in Europe, she has used her writing to interrogate both the psychology of the self and the larger relations between the personal and the political.

Lessing was born Doris May Tayler in October 1919 in Persia (now Iran). Her parents were British: her mother was a nurse, and her father a clerk in the Imperial Bank of Persia who had been crippled in World War I; his horrific memories of combat would seep into his daughter's recollections of childhood. In 1925 the family moved to the British colony of Rhodesia (now Zimbabwe), where the colonial government was offering economic incentives to encourage the immigration of white settlers. For ten shillings an acre, the family bought three thousand acres of farmland in Mashonaland, a section of Southern Rhodesia that once had been the home of the Matabele tribe but from which the government had evicted most of the native population. The farm never prospered. Lessing attended a convent school until she was fourteen, but she considered herself largely self-educated, from her avid reading of the classics of European and American literature. Above all, she loved the nineteenth-century novel; realists such as Stendhal, **Tolstoy**, and **Dostoevsky** impressed her, she later said, with "the warmth, the compassion, the humanity, the love of people" that gave impetus and passion to their social criticism. Gradually Lessing became aware of the racial injustice in Southern Rhodesia, and of the fact that she was, as she later put it, "a member of the white minority pitted against a black majority that was abominably treated and still is."

Social awareness is a defining theme of her early work, especially her first novel, *The Grass Is Singing* (1949), and the collection *African Stories* (1964). Arguing that "literature should be committed" to political issues, Lessing was herself politically active in Rhodesia, as well as a member of the British Communist Party from 1952 until 1956, the year of the Soviet intervention in Hungary. Her activism and socially oriented writing made their mark, and in 1956 she was declared a prohibited alien in both Southern Rhodesia and South Africa.

While still in Rhodesia, Lessing worked in several office jobs in Salisbury and made two unsuccessful marriages. (Lessing is the name of her second husband.) In 1949 she moved to England with the son from her second marriage and took a gamble on a literary career: "I was working in a lawyer's office at the time, and I remember walking in and saying to my boss, 'I'm giving up my job and writing a novel.' He very properly laughed, and I indignantly walked home and wrote *The Grass Is Singing*." The novel was a surprising and immediate success, and she was able, from that point, to make a profession of writing. Her next project was the five-volume series, *Children of Violence* (1952–69): the portrait of an era, after the form of the nineteenth-century bildungsroman, or "education novel," *Children of Violence* follows the life of a symbolically named heroine, Martha Quest, while exploring social and moral issues including race relations, the conflict between autonomy and socialization, and the hopes and frustrations of political idealism.

Lessing's most famous novel, *The Golden Notebook* (1962), makes a sharp break with the linear narrative style that *Children of Violence* shares with the bildungsroman tradition. In this work, too, a female protagonist (Anna Wulf) struggles to build a unified identity from the multiple, fragmented elements that constitute her personality; yet the exploratory process by which she pursues this goal takes her story beyond the confines of chronological narrative. Although the book is framed by a conventional short novel called *Free Women*, the governing structure is a series of different-colored notebooks that Anna uses to record the distinct versions of her experience: black for Africa, red for politics, yellow for a fictionalized rendering of herself as a character named Ella, and blue for a factual diary. By analyzing her life from these varying perspectives, Anna learns to understand and reconcile her contradictions—to write, ultimately, the "Golden Notebook," which is "all of me in one book."

During the 1970s and early 1980s, Lessing embarked on a series of science-fiction novels, which she termed "inner-space fiction," extending her interest in psychology and consciousness into speculative and quasi-mystical regions of the imagination. She then shifted to realistic stories that carry a sharp satiric or symbolic twist, such as *The Good Terrorist* (1985), a satire in which a group of naïve British terrorists try to create a homey atmosphere in an empty house in London while carrying out bombing raids. She also published collections of essays and interviews that address politics, life, and art in a nonfiction voice. In presenting Lessing with the Nobel Prize in 2007, the committee praised her as an epic poet of "the female experience, who with scepticism, fire and visionary power has subjected a divided civilisation to scrutiny."

"The Old Chief Mshlanga" is one of Lessing's earliest African stories, written during the period, from 1950 to 1958, when she wrote most of her fiction set on that continent. The collection in which the story first appeared, *This Was the Old Chief's Country* (1951), together with *The Grass Is Singing* and *Five* (1953), a group of novellas set in Africa, established Lessing as an important interpreter of the colonial experience in contemporary Africa. The long act of dispossession that underlies "The Old Chief Mshlanga" began with the economic infiltration of the country by white settlers, under the leadership of the Chartered Company, a private firm that ruled the land under a British charter. Company policies soon formalized segregation by dividing land into tracts categorized as "alienated" (owned by white settlers) or "unalienated" (occupied by natives). The Land Apportionment Act of 1930 confirmed this arrangement by dividing the territory into areas called Native and European. In the story the figure of the Old Chief bridges the earlier dispensation, an era fifty years before, when his people owned the country, and the new, when they can be forcibly relocated to a Reserve after disagreeing with a white settler. Yet the Old Chief is not the protagonist here: significantly, his story comes into the foreground only some distance in, when it intrudes on the consciousness of a young white girl. The "vein of richness" that his tribe represents makes itself known only gradually. By the narrative's end, the tribe has disappeared altogether; the girl visits their village to find it disintegrating into the landscape.

Yet in spite of her remark that "there was nothing there," the girl's intimate description of the lush landscape shows that her encounter, however brief, with its former inhabitants has opened her eyes to an African presence that initially she had not been able to see. Nonetheless, the gain is one-sided: even her altered perceptions can bring her no closer to the members of the tribe, only throw light on the ground they occupied. For the Old Chief, there is no advantage: he and his people have disappeared into a symbolic essence, a "richness" that the settlers derive from the land they take over. Lessing's observant young girl has been changed by her encounter with the Old Chief, but the awakening is a bleak one that endows her with a sense of loss and responsibility. Perhaps, one day, she will write about it.

The Old Chief Mshlanga

They were good, the years of ranging the bush over her father's farm which, like every white farm, was largely unused, broken only occasionally by small patches of cultivation. In between, nothing but trees, the long sparse grass, thorn and cactus and gully, grass and outcrop and thorn. And a jutting piece of rock which had been thrust up from the warm soil of Africa unimaginable eras of time ago, washed into hollows and whorls by sun and wind that had travelled so many thousands of miles of space and bush, would hold the weight of a small girl whose eyes were sightless for anything but a pale willowed river, a pale gleaming castle—a small girl singing: "Out flew the web and floated wide, the mirror cracked from side to side . . ."[1]

Pushing her way through the green aisles of the mealie[2] stalks, the leaves arching like cathedrals veined with sunlight far overhead, with the packed red earth underfoot, a fine lace of red starred witchweed would summon up a black bent figure croaking premonitions: the Northern witch, bred of cold Northern forests, would stand before her among the mealie fields, and it was the mealie fields that faded and fled, leaving her among the gnarled roots of an oak, snow falling thick and soft and white, the woodcutter's fire glowing red welcome through crowding tree trunks.

A white child, opening its eyes curiously on a sun-suffused landscape, a gaunt and violent landscape, might be supposed to accept it as her own, to make the msasa trees and the thorn trees as familiars, to feel her blood running free and responsive to the swing of the seasons.

This child could not see a msasa tree,[3] or the thorn, for what they were. Her books held tales of alien fairies, her rivers ran slow and peaceful, and she knew the shape of the leaves of an ash or an oak, the names of the little creatures that lived in English streams, when the words "the veld"[4] meant strangeness, though she could remember nothing else.

1. The child is reciting lines 114–15 of Tennyson's "The Lady of Shalott."
2. Maize; corn.
3. A large tree of central Africa, notable for the vivid colorings (pink through copper) of its spring foliage and for the fragrance of its white flowers.
4. Unenclosed country, open grassland.

Because of this, for many years, it was the veld that seemed unreal; the sun was a foreign sun, and the wind spoke a strange language.

The black people on the farm were as remote as the trees and the rocks. They were an amorphous black mass, mingling and thinning and massing like tadpoles, faceless, who existed merely to serve, to say "Yes, Baas,"[5] take their money and go. They changed season by season, moving from one farm to the next, according to their outlandish needs, which one did not have to understand, coming from perhaps hundreds of miles north or east, passing on after a few months—where? Perhaps even as far away as the fabled gold mines of Johannesburg,[6] where the pay was so much better than the few shillings a month and the double handful of mealie meal twice a day which they earned in that part of Africa.

The child was taught to take them for granted: the servants in the house would come running a hundred yards to pick up a book if she dropped it. She was called "Nkosikaas"—Chieftainess, even by the black children her own age.

Later, when the farm grew too small to hold her curiosity, she carried a gun in the crook of her arm and wandered miles a day, from *vlei* to *vlei*, from *kopje*[7] to *kopje*, accompanied by two dogs: the dogs and the gun were an armour against fear. Because of them she never felt fear.

If a native came into sight along the kaffir[8] paths half a mile away, the dogs would flush him up a tree as if he were a bird. If he expostulated (in his uncouth language which was by itself ridiculous) that was cheek. If one was in a good mood, it could be a matter for laughter. Otherwise one passed on, hardly glancing at the angry man in the tree.

On the rare occasions when white children met together they could amuse themselves by hailing a passing native in order to make a buffoon of him; they could set the dogs on him and watch him run; they could tease a small black child as if he were a puppy—save that they would not throw stones and sticks at a dog without a sense of guilt.

Later still, certain questions presented themselves in the child's mind; and because the answers were not easy to accept, they were silenced by an even greater arrogance of manner.

It was even impossible to think of the black people who worked about the house as friends, for if she talked to one of them, her mother would come running anxiously: "Come away; you mustn't talk to natives."

It was this instilled consciousness of danger, of something unpleasant, that made it easy to laugh out loud, crudely, if a servant made a mistake in his English or if he failed to understand an order—there is a certain kind of laughter that is fear, afraid of itself.

5. Boss.
6. The largest city in the Union (now Republic) of South Africa.
7. A small hill (Afrikaans). "Vlei": a shallow pool or swamp (Afrikaans).
8. Black African; usually used disparagingly.

One evening, when I was about fourteen, I was walking down the side of a mealie field that had been newly ploughed, so that the great red clods showed fresh and tumbling to the vlei beyond, like a choppy red sea; it was that hushed and listening hour, when the birds send long sad calls from tree to tree, and all the colours of earth and sky and leaf are deep and golden. I had my rifle in the curve of my arm, and the dogs were at my heels.

In front of me, perhaps a couple of hundred yards away, a group of three Africans came into sight around the side of a big antheap. I whistled the dogs close in to my skirts and let the gun swing in my hand, and advanced, waiting for them to move aside, off the path, in respect for my passing. But they came on steadily, and the dogs looked up at me for the command to chase. I was angry. It was "cheek"[9] for a native not to stand off a path, the moment he caught sight of you.

In front walked an old man, stooping his weight on to a stick, his hair grizzled white, a dark red blanket slung over his shoulders like a cloak. Behind him came two young men, carrying bundles of pots, assegais,[1] hatchets.

The group was not a usual one. They were not natives seeking work. These had an air of dignity, of quietly following their own purpose. It was the dignity that checked my tongue. I walked quietly on, talking softly to the growling dogs, till I was ten paces away. Then the old man stopped, drawing his blanket close.

"Morning, Nkosikaas," he said, using the customary greeting for any time of the day.

"Good morning," I said. "Where are you going?" My voice was a little truculent.

The old man spoke in his own language, then one of the young men stepped forward politely and said in careful English: "My Chief travels to see his brothers beyond the river."

A Chief! I thought, understanding the pride that made the old man stand before me like an equal—more than an equal, for he showed courtesy, and I showed none.

The old man spoke again, wearing dignity like an inherited garment, still standing ten paces off, flanked by his entourage, not looking at me (that would have been rude) but directing his eyes somewhere over my head at the trees.

"You are the little Nkosikaas from the farm of Baas Jordan?"

"That's right," I said.

"Perhaps your father does not remember," said the interpreter for the old man, "but there was an affair with some goats. I remember seeing you when you were . . ." The young man held his hand at knee level and smiled.

We all smiled.

"What is your name?" I asked.

"This is Chief Mshlanga," said the young man.

"I will tell my father that I met you," I said.

The old man said: "My greetings to your father, little Nkosikaas."

"Good morning," I said politely, finding the politeness difficult, from lack of use.

"Morning, little Nkosikaas," said the old man, and stood aside to let me pass.

9. Impudence.
1. Spears.

I went by, my gun hanging awkwardly, the dogs sniffing and growling, cheated of their favourite game of chasing natives like animals.

Not long afterwards I read in an old explorer's book the phrase: "Chief Mshlanga's country." It went like this: "Our destination was Chief Mshlanga's country, to the north of the river; and it was our desire to ask his permission to prospect for gold in his territory."

The phrase "ask his permission" was so extraordinary to a white child, brought up to consider all natives as things to use, that it revived those questions, which could not be suppressed: they fermented slowly in my mind.

On another occasion one of those old prospectors who still move over Africa looking for neglected reefs, with their hammers and tents, and pans for sifting gold from crushed rock, came to the farm and, in talking of the old days, used that phrase again: "This was the Old Chief's country," he said. "It stretched from those mountains over there way back to the river, hundreds of miles of country." That was his name for our district: "The Old Chief's Country"; he did not use our name for it—a new phrase which held no implication of usurped ownership.

As I read more books about the time when this part of Africa was opened up, not much more than fifty years before, I found Old Chief Mshlanga had been a famous man, known to all the explorers and prospectors. But then he had been young; or maybe it was his father or uncle they spoke of—I never found out.

During that year I met him several times in the part of the farm that was traversed by natives moving over the country. I learned that the path up the side of the big red field where the birds sang was the recognized highway for migrants. Perhaps I even haunted it in the hope of meeting him: being greeted by him, the exchange of courtesies, seemed to answer the questions that troubled me.

Soon I carried a gun in a different spirit; I used it for shooting food and not to give me confidence. And now the dogs learned better manners. When I saw a native approaching, we offered and took greetings; and slowly that other landscape in my mind faded, and my feet struck directly on the African soil, and I saw the shapes of tree and hill clearly, and the black people moved back, as it were, out of my life: it was as if I stood aside to watch a slow intimate dance of landscape and men, a very old dance, whose steps I could not learn.

But I thought: this is my heritage, too; I was bred here; it is my country as well as the black man's country; and there is plenty of room for all of us, without elbowing each other off the pavements and roads.

It seemed it was only necessary to let free that respect I felt when I was talking with old Chief Mshlanga, to let both black and white people meet gently, with tolerance for each other's differences: it seemed quite easy.

Then, one day, something new happened. Working in our house as servants were always three natives: cook, houseboy, garden boy. They used to change as the farm natives changed: staying for a few months, then moving on to a new job, or back home to their kraals.[2] They were thought of as "good" or "bad" natives; which meant: how did they behave as servants? Were they lazy, efficient,

2. Native villages: collections of huts surrounding a central space.

obedient, or disrespectful? If the family felt good-humoured, the phrase was: "What can you expect from raw black savages?" If we were angry, we said: "These damned niggers, we would be much better off without them."

One day, a white policeman was on his rounds of the district, and he said laughingly: "Did you know you have an important man in your kitchen?"

"What!" exclaimed my mother sharply. "What do you mean?"

"A Chief's son." The policeman seemed amused. "He'll boss the tribe when the old man dies."

"He'd better not put on a Chief's son act with me," said my mother.

When the policeman left, we looked with different eyes at our cook: he was a good worker, but he drank too much at week-ends—that was how we knew him.

He was a tall youth, with very black skin, like black polished metal, his tightly growing black hair parted white man's fashion at one side, with a metal comb from the store stuck into it; very polite, very distant, very quick to obey an order. Now that it had been pointed out, we said: "Of course, you can see. Blood always tells."

My mother became strict with him now she knew about his birth and prospects. Sometimes, when she lost her temper, she would say: "You aren't the Chief yet, you know." And he would answer her very quietly, his eyes on the ground: "Yes, Nkosikaas."

One afternoon he asked for a whole day off, instead of the customary half-day, to go home next Sunday.

"How can you go home in one day?"

"It will take me half an hour on my bicycle," he explained.

I watched the direction he took; and the next day I went off to look for this kraal; I understood he must be Chief Mshlanga's successor: there was no other kraal near enough our farm.

Beyond our boundaries on that side the country was new to me. I followed unfamiliar paths past *kopjes* that till now had been part of the jagged horizon, hazed with distance. This was Government land, which had never been cultivated by white men; at first I could not understand why it was that it appeared, in merely crossing the boundary, I had entered a completely fresh type of landscape. It was a wide green valley, where a small river sparkled, and vivid water-birds darted over the rushes. The grass was thick and soft to my calves, the trees stood tall and shapely.

I was used to our farm, whose hundreds of acres of harsh eroded soil bore trees that had been cut for the mine furnaces and had grown thin and twisted, where the cattle had dragged the grass flat, leaving innumerable criss-crossing trails that deepened each season into gullies, under the force of the rains.

This country had been left untouched, save for prospectors whose picks had struck a few sparks from the surface of the rocks as they wandered by; and for migrant natives whose passing had left, perhaps, a charred patch on the trunk of a tree where their evening fire had nestled.

It was very silent: a hot morning with pigeons cooing throatily, the midday shadows lying dense and thick with clear yellow spaces of sunlight between and in all that wide green park-like valley, not a human soul but myself.

I was listening to the quick regular tapping of a woodpecker when slowly a chill feeling seemed to grow up from the small of my back to my shoulders, in a constricting spasm like a shudder, and at the roots of my hair a tingling sensation began and ran down over the surface of my flesh, leaving me goose-fleshed and cold, though I was damp with sweat. Fever? I thought; then uneasily, turned to look over my shoulder; and realized suddenly that this was fear. It was extraordinary, even humiliating. It was a new fear. For all the years I had walked by myself over this country I had never known a moment's uneasiness; in the beginning because I had been supported by a gun and the dogs, then because I had learnt an easy friendliness for the Africans I might encounter.

I had read of this feeling, how the bigness and silence of Africa, under the ancient sun, grows dense and takes shape in the mind, till even the birds seem to call menacingly, and a deadly spirit comes out of the trees and the rocks. You move warily, as if your very passing disturbs something old and evil, something dark and big and angry that might suddenly rear and strike from behind. You look at groves of entwined trees, and picture the animals that might be lurking there; you look at the river running slowly, dropping from level to level through the *vlei*, spreading into pools where at night the bucks come to drink, and the crocodiles rise and drag them by their soft noses into underwater caves. Fear possessed me. I found I was turning round and round, because of that shapeless menace behind me that might reach out and take me; I kept glancing at the files of *kopjes* which, seen from a different angle, seemed to change with every step so that even known landmarks, like a big mountain that had sentinelled my world since I first became conscious of it, showed an unfamiliar sunlit valley among its foothills. I did not know where I was. I was lost. Panic seized me. I found I was spinning round and round, staring anxiously at this tree and that, peering up at the sun which appeared to have moved into an eastern slant, shedding the sad yellow light of sunset. Hours must have passed! I looked at my watch and found that this state of meaningless terror had lasted perhaps ten minutes.

The point was that it was meaningless. I was not ten miles from home: I had only to take my way back along the valley to find myself at the fence; away among the foothills of the *kopjes* gleamed the roof of a neighbour's house, and a couple of hours' walking would reach it. This was the sort of fear that contracts the flesh of a dog at night and sets him howling at the full moon. It had nothing to do with what I thought or felt; and I was more disturbed by the fact that I could become its victim than of the physical sensation itself: I walked steadily on, quietened, in a divided mind, watching my own pricking nerves and apprehensive glances from side to side with a disgusted amusement. Deliberately I set myself to think of this village I was seeking, and what I should do when I entered it—if I could find it, which was doubtful, since I was walking aimlessly and it might be anywhere in the hundreds of thousands of acres of bush that stretched about me. With my mind on that village, I realized that a new sensation was added to the fear: loneliness. Now such a terror of isolation invaded me that I could hardly walk; and if it were not that I came over the crest of a small rise and saw a village below me, I should have turned and gone home. It was a cluster of thatched huts in a clearing among trees. There were neat patches of mealies and pumpkins and millet, and cattle grazed under some trees at a distance. Fowls scratched among the huts, dogs lay sleeping on the grass, and goats friezed a *kopje* that jutted up beyond a tributary of the river lying like an enclosing arm around the village.

As I came close I saw the huts were lovingly decorated with patterns of yellow and red and ochre mud on the walls; and the thatch was tied in place with plaits of straw.

This was not at all like our farm compound, a dirty and neglected place, a temporary home for migrants who had no roots in it.

And now I did not know what to do next. I called a small black boy, who was sitting on a lot playing a stringed gourd, quite naked except for the strings of blue beads round his neck, and said: "Tell the Chief I am here." The child stuck his thumb in his mouth and stared shyly back at me.

For minutes I shifted my feet on the edge of what seemed a deserted village, till at last the child scuttled off, and then some women came. They were draped in bright cloths, with brass glinting in their ears and on their arms. They also stared, silently; then turned to chatter among themselves.

I said again: "Can I see Chief Mshlanga?" I saw they caught the name; they did not understand what I wanted. I did not understand myself.

At last I walked through them and came past the huts and saw a clearing under a big shady tree, where a dozen old men sat crosslegged on the ground, talking. Chief Mshlanga was leaning back against the tree, holding a gourd in his hand, from which he had been drinking. When he saw me, not a muscle of his face moved, and I could see he was not pleased: perhaps he was afflicted with my own shyness, due to being unable to find the right forms of courtesy for the occasion. To meet me, on our own farm, was one thing; but I should not have come here. What had I expected? I could not join them socially: the thing was unheard of. Bad enough that I, a white girl, should be walking the veld alone as a white man might: and in this part of the bush where only Government officials had the right to move.

Again I stood, smiling foolishly, while behind me stood the groups of brightly clad, chattering women, their faces alert with curiosity and interest, and in front of me sat the old men, with old lined faces, their eyes guarded, aloof. It was a village of ancients and children and women. Even the two young men who kneeled beside the Chief were not those I had seen with him previously: the young men were all away working on the white men's farms and mines, and the Chief must depend on relatives who were temporarily on holiday for his attendants.

"The small white Nkosikaas is far from home," remarked the old man at last.

"Yes," I agreed, "it is far." I wanted to say: "I have come to pay you a friendly visit, Chief Mshlanga." I could not say it. I might now be feeling an urgent helpless desire to get to know these men and women as people, to be accepted by them as a friend, but the truth was I had set out in a spirit of curiosity: I had wanted to see the village that one day our cook, the reserved and obedient young man who got drunk on Sundays, would one day rule over.

"The child of Nkosi Jordan is welcome," said Chief Mshlanga.

"Thank you," I said, and could think of nothing more to say. There was a silence, while the flies rose and began to buzz around my head; and the wind shook a little in the thick green tree that spread its branches over the old men.

"Good morning," I said at last. "I have to return now to my home."

"Morning, little Nkosikaas," said Chief Mshlanga.

I walked away from the indifferent village, over the rise past the staring amber-eyed goats, down through the tall stately trees into the great rich green valley where the river meandered and the pigeons cooed tales of plenty and the woodpecker tapped softly.

The fear had gone; the loneliness had set into stiff-necked stoicism; there was now a queer hostility in the landscape, a cold, hard, sullen indomitability that walked with me, as strong as a wall, as intangible as smoke; it seemed to say to me: you walk here as a destroyer. I went slowly homewards, with an empty heart: I had learned that if one cannot call a country to heel like a dog, neither can one dismiss the past with a smile in an easy gush of feeling, saying: I could not help it, I am also a victim.

I only saw Chief Mshlanga once again.

One night my father's big red land was trampled down by small sharp hooves, and it was discovered that the culprits were goats from Chief Mshalanga's kraal. This had happened once before, years ago.

My father confiscated all the goats. Then he sent a message to the old Chief that if he wanted them he would have to pay for the damage.

He arrived at our house at the time of sunset one evening, looking very old and bent now, walking stiffly under his regally-draped blanket, leaning on a big stick. My father sat himself down in his big chair below the steps of the house; the old man squatted carefully on the ground before him, flanked by his two young men.

The palaver was long and painful, because of the bad English of the young man who interpreted, and because my father could not speak dialect, but only kitchen kaffir.

From my father's point of view, at least two hundred pounds' worth of damage had been done to the crop. He knew he could not get the money from the old man. He felt he was entitled to keep the goats. As for the old Chief, he kept repeating angrily: "Twenty goats! My people cannot lose twenty goats! We are not rich, like the Nkosi Jordan, to lose twenty goats at once."

My father did not think of himself as rich, but rather as very poor. He spoke quickly and angrily in return, saying that the damage done meant a great deal to him, and that he was entitled to the goats.

At last it grew so heated that the cook, the Chief's son, was called from the kitchen to be interpreter, and now my father spoke fluently in English, and our cook translated rapidly so that the old man could understand how very angry my father was. The young man spoke without emotion, in a mechanical way, his eyes lowered, but showing how he felt his position by a hostile uncomfortable set of the shoulders.

It was now in the late sunset, the sky a welter of colours, the birds singing their last songs, and the cattle, lowing peacefully, moving past us towards their sheds for the night. It was the hour when Africa is most beautiful; and here was this pathetic, ugly scene, doing no one any good.

At last my father stated finally: "I'm not going to argue about it. I am keeping the goats."

The old Chief flashed back in his own language: "That means that my people will go hungry when the dry season comes."

"Go to the police, then," said my father, and looked triumphant.

There was, of course, no more to be said.

The old man sat silent, his head bent, his hands dangling helplessly over his withered knees. Then he rose, the young men helping him, and he stood facing my father. He spoke once again, very stiffly; and turned away and went home to his village.

"What did he say?" asked my father of the young man, who laughed uncomfortably and would not meet his eyes.

"What did he say?" insisted my father.

Our cook stood straight and silent, his brows knotted together. Then he spoke. "My father says: All this land, this land you call yours, is his land, and belongs to our people."

Having made this statement, he walked off into the bush after his father, and we did not see him again.

Our next cook was a migrant from Nyasaland, with no expectations of greatness.

Next time the policeman came on his rounds he was told this story. He remarked: "That kraal has no right to be there; it should have been moved long ago. I don't know why no one has done anything about it. I'll have a chat with the Native Commissioner next week. I'm going over for tennis on Sunday, anyway."

Some time later we heard that Chief Mshlanga and his people had been moved two hundred miles east, to a proper Native Reserve; the Government land was going to be opened up for white settlement soon.

I went to see the village again, about a year afterwards. There was nothing there. Mounds of red mud, where the huts had been, had long swathes of rotting thatch over them, veined with the red galleries of the white ants. The pumpkin vines rioted everywhere, over the bushes, up the lower branches of trees so that the great golden balls rolled underfoot and dangled overhead: it was a festival of pumpkins. The bushes were crowding up, the new grass sprang vivid green.

The settler lucky enough to be allotted the lush warm valley (if he chose to cultivate this particular section) would find, suddenly, in the middle of a mealie field, the plants were growing fifteen feet tall, the weight of the cobs dragging at the stalks, and wonder what unsuspected vein of richness he had struck.

1951

JAMES BALDWIN

1924–1987

A leading African American novelist, James Baldwin was one of the great prose stylists of the twentieth century. He is best known for his remarkable essays that, in poetic rhetoric drawing on both the classics of English literature and the tones of biblical prophecy, combine personal reflection with a wider view of social justice. An icon of the civil rights movement, Baldwin nonetheless felt considerably alienated both from black culture and from white liberal society. He lived much of his life abroad but continually affirmed his American identity as a "native son."

Baldwin grew up in his "father's house"—that is, in the Harlem home of his stepfather, David Baldwin, a preacher whom his mother married when James was two. David Baldwin, a preacher in small black churches, reacted with suspicion when a white teacher, Orilla Miller, took James to plays, including Orson Welles's all-black production of Shakespeare's *Macbeth*. (The elder Baldwin did not approve of theater.) David Baldwin's mother, who had been born in slavery, lived with the family in Harlem. Although his acquaintance with secular literature strained his relationship to the church, James remained affiliated with various churches over the years and preached sermons as a young man.

As the United States mobilized for the Second World War, Baldwin found a job in a defense plant in New Jersey—and hated both the job and the place, where he had his first serious experiences of racial discrimination. When his stepfather died, in 1943, he was expected to move back home and take care of his mother and siblings. Instead, Baldwin moved to Greenwich Village, in lower Manhattan, to pursue his career as a writer. Here he met older writers, including Richard Wright. "Writing was an act of love," Baldwin would later say, "an attempt to be loved." While living in the Village, he became aware of his homosexuality.

After the war Baldwin left New York for Paris, following in the paths of a generation of famous American writers before him. Of this self-imposed expatriation, he later wrote, "In my own case, I think my exile saved my life." In the years that followed, Baldwin wrote and then suffered writer's block; he was arrested on a false charge of theft; he tried to commit suicide; and he succeeded in finishing *Go Tell It on the Mountain* (1953), his first published novel, an autobiographical story of a deeply religious young man who ultimately leaves the church. For the rest of his life, Baldwin divided his time between New York, Paris, Switzerland, and Turkey. Amid constant interpersonal turmoil (and additional suicide attempts), his literary career was now on the rise: in 1955, *Notes of a Native Son*, a collection of essays that cemented his public voice, was released; a year later, *Giovanni's Room*, a novel about a white American in Paris struggling with his homosexuality, appeared. Despite difficulties in finding a publisher, the work increased Baldwin's fame. Encouraged by the rise of the civil rights movement, he renewed his political engagement; with *The Fire Next Time* (1963), in which he commented on race and American history, he became an international figure.

Like other leading African Americans of the civil rights era, Baldwin was unhappy with the radicalization of movements with which he had been associated. Although he had known the Black Nationalist leader Malcolm X and met Elijah Muhammad of the Nation of Islam, their successors in such groups as the Black Panthers tended to think of Baldwin as a darling of white liberals who was more concerned with cosmopolitan life in Paris than with the plight of ordinary African Americans. Baldwin's generally optimistic, liberal views led him to exhort his readers to work together for change: "If we—and now I mean the relatively conscious whites and the relatively conscious blacks, who must, like lovers, insist on, or create, the consciousness of the others—do not falter in our duty now, we may be able, handful that we are, to end the racial nightmare, and achieve our country, and change the history of the world." In his later years, Baldwin's primary home was a farmhouse in Saint-Paul-de-Vence, a town in southern France, but he continued traveling in the United States, writing essays, and teaching in several colleges. He died in Saint-Paul in 1987.

Baldwin begins "Notes of a Native Son," the essay printed here, with the conjunction of two profound events in his personal life: the death of his father (actually his stepfather) and the birth of his father's youngest child. These personal rites of passage are, however, quickly placed in the context of broader social and political events—namely, the race riots that shook Detroit in June 1943. The protests, in which nearly three dozen people died, were a shocking episode in a series of conflicts between blacks and whites in the wake of the Great Migration between the two world wars. African Americans were leaving the segregated South in search of greater freedom, and work, in northern industrial cities, where they were not always welcomed. Baldwin's father had likewise moved to New York from New Orleans not long before the boy's birth, and Baldwin describes the racial tensions of wartime New York and New Jersey. The juxtaposition of experiences of great personal significance with momentous public events becomes a central issue in the essay.

While it offers a profound meditation on a relationship between a son and a father who was both physically and mentally ill, the essay explains how both men's encounters with racial discrimination contributed to the conflicts in their private lives. Baldwin represents the relationship, and his evolving consciousness of his place in the family and in American society, with subtlety and nuance. Baldwin's style—direct but meditative, confessional but aware of the broader context—gives this classic work its status as one of the most memorable personal meditations published in the twentieth century.

Notes of a Native Son[1]

On the 29th of July, in 1943, my father died. On the same day, a few hours later, his last child was born. Over a month before this, while all our energies were concentrated in waiting for these events, there had been, in Detroit, one of the bloodiest race riots of the century.[2] A few hours after my father's funeral, while he lay in state in the undertaker's chapel, a race riot broke out in Harlem. On the morning of the 3rd of August, we drove my father to the graveyard through a wilderness of smashed plate glass.

1. The title alludes to Richard Wright's novel *Native Son* (1940).
2. Three days of rioting in June 1943, in which 25 African Americans and 9 whites were killed.

The day of my father's funeral had also been my nineteenth birthday. As we drove him to the graveyard, the spoils of injustice, anarchy, discontent, and hatred were all around us. It seemed to me that God himself had devised, to mark my father's end, the most sustained and brutally dissonant of codas. And it seemed to me, too, that the violence which rose all about us as my father left the world had been devised as a corrective for the pride of his eldest son. I had declined to believe in that apocalypse which had been central to my father's vision; very well, life seemed to be saying, here is something that will certainly pass for an apocalypse until the real thing comes along. I had inclined to be contemptuous of my father for the conditions of his life, for the conditions of our lives. When his life had ended I began to wonder about that life and also, in a new way, to be apprehensive about my own.

I had not known my father very well. We had got on badly, partly because we shared, in our different fashions, the vice of stubborn pride. When he was dead I realized that I had hardly ever spoken to him. When he had been dead a long time I began to wish I had. It seems to be typical of life in America, where opportunities, real and fancied, are thicker than anywhere else on the globe, that the second generation has no time to talk to the first. No one, including my father, seems to have known exactly how old he was, but his mother had been born during slavery. He was of the first generation of free men. He, along with thousands of other Negroes, came North after 1919 and I was part of that generation which had never seen the landscape of what Negroes sometimes call the Old Country.[3]

He had been born in New Orleans and had been a quite young man there during the time that Louis Armstrong,[4] a boy, was running errands for the dives and honky-tonks of what was always presented to me as one of the most wicked of cities—to this day, whenever I think of New Orleans, I also helplessly think of Sodom and Gomorrah.[5] My father never mentioned Louis Armstrong, except to forbid us to play his records; but there was a picture of him on our wall for a long time. One of my father's strong-willed female relatives had placed it there and forbade my father to take it down. He never did, but he eventually maneuvered her out of the house and when, some years later, she was in trouble and near death, he refused to do anything to help her.

He was, I think, very handsome. I gather this from photographs and from my own memories of him, dressed in his Sunday best and on his way to preach a sermon somewhere, when I was little. Handsome, proud, and ingrown, "like a toe-nail," somebody said. But he looked to me, as I grew older, like pictures I had seen of African tribal chieftains: he really should have been naked, with war-paint on and barbaric mementos, standing among spears. He could be chilling in the pulpit and indescribably cruel in his personal life and he was certainly the most bitter man I have ever met; yet it must be said that there was something else in him, buried in him, which lent him his tremendous power and, even, a rather crushing charm. It had something to do with his blackness,

3. The South. Over a million African Americans left the South for the Midwest and the Northeast after the First World War (1914–18).

4. Armstrong (1901–1971), jazz trumpeter, cornetist, and singer.

5. Biblical cities destroyed by God for their wickedness. See Genesis 18–19.

I think—he was very black—with his blackness and his beauty, and with the fact that he knew that he was black but did not know that he was beautiful. He claimed to be proud of his blackness but it had also been the cause of much humiliation and it had fixed bleak boundaries to his life. He was not a young man when we were growing up and he had already suffered many kinds of ruin; in his outrageously demanding and protective way he loved his children, who were black like him and menaced, like him; and all these things sometimes showed in his face when he tried, never to my knowledge with any success, to establish contact with any of us. When he took one of his children on his knee to play, the child always became fretful and began to cry; when he tried to help one of us with our homework the absolutely unabating tension which emanated from him caused our minds and our tongues to become paralyzed, so that he, scarcely knowing why, flew into a rage and the child, not knowing why, was punished. If it ever entered his head to bring a surprise home for his children, it was, almost unfailingly, the wrong surprise and even the big watermelons he often brought home on his back in the summertime led to the most appalling scenes. I do not remember, in all those years, that one of his children was ever glad to see him come home. From what I was able to gather of his early life, it seemed that this inability to establish contact with other people had always marked him and had been one of the things which had driven him out of New Orleans. There was something in him, therefore, groping and tentative, which was never expressed and which was buried with him. One saw it most clearly when he was facing new people and hoping to impress them. But he never did, not for long. We went from church to smaller and more improbable church, he found himself in less and less demand as a minister, and by the time he died none of his friends had come to see him for a long time. He had lived and died in an intolerable bitterness of spirit and it frightened me, as we drove him to the graveyard through those unquiet, ruined streets, to see how powerful and overflowing this bitterness could be and to realize that this bitterness now was mine.

When he died I had been away from home for a little over a year. In that year I had had time to become aware of the meaning of all my father's bitter warnings, had discovered the secret of his proudly pursed lips and rigid carriage: I had discovered the weight of white people in the world. I saw that this had been for my ancestors and now would be for me an awful thing to live with and that the bitterness which had helped to kill my father could also kill me.

He had been ill a long time—in the mind, as we now realized, reliving instances of his fantastic intransigence in the new light of his affliction and endeavoring to feel a sorrow for him which never, quite, came true. We had not known that he was being eaten up by paranoia, and the discovery that his cruelty, to our bodies and our minds, had been one of the symptoms of his illness was not, then, enough to enable us to forgive him. The younger children felt, quite simply, relief that he would not be coming home anymore. My mother's observation that it was he, after all, who had kept them alive all these years meant nothing because the problems of keeping children alive are not real for children. The older children felt, with my father gone, that they could invite their friends to the house without fear that their friends would be insulted or, as had sometimes happened with me, being told that their friends were in league with the devil and intended to rob our family of everything we owned. (I didn't fail to wonder, and it made me hate him, what on earth we owned that anybody else would want.)

His illness was beyond all hope of healing before anyone realized that he was ill. He had always been so strange and had lived, like a prophet, in such unimaginably close communion with the Lord that his long silences which were punctuated by moans and hallelujahs and snatches of old songs while he sat at the living-room window never seemed odd to us. It was not until he refused to eat because, he said, his family was trying to poison him that my mother was forced to accept as a fact what had, until then, been only an unwilling suspicion. When he was committed, it was discovered that he had tuberculosis and, as it turned out, the disease of his mind allowed the disease of his body to destroy him. For the doctors could not force him to eat, either, and, though he was fed intravenously, it was clear from the beginning that there was no hope for him.

In my mind's eye I could see him, sitting at the window, locked up in his terrors; hating and fearing every living soul including his children who had betrayed him, too, by reaching towards the world which had despised him. There were nine of us. I began to wonder what it could have felt like for such a man to have had nine children whom he could barely feed. He used to make little jokes about our poverty, which never, of course, seemed very funny to us; they could not have seemed very funny to him, either, or else our all too feeble response to them would never have caused such rages. He spent great energy and achieved, to our chagrin, no small amount of success in keeping us away from the people who surrounded us, people who had all-night rent parties[6] to which we listened when we should have been sleeping, people who cursed and drank and flashed razor blades on Lenox Avenue.[7] He could not understand why, if they had so much energy to spare, they could not use it to make their lives better. He treated almost everybody on our block with a most uncharitable asperity and neither they, nor, of course, their children were slow to reciprocate.

The only white people who came to our house were welfare workers and bill collectors. It was almost always my mother who dealt with them, for my father's temper, which was at the mercy of his pride, was never to be trusted. It was clear that he felt their very presence in his home to be a violation: this was conveyed by his carriage, almost ludicrously stiff, and by his voice, harsh and vindictively polite. When I was around nine or ten I wrote a play which was directed by a young, white schoolteacher, a woman, who then took an interest in me, and gave me books to read and, in order to corroborate my theatrical bent, decided to take me to see what she somewhat tactlessly referred to as "real" plays. Theater-going was forbidden in our house, but, with the really cruel intuitiveness of a child, I suspected that the color of this woman's skin would carry the day for me. When, at school, she suggested taking me to the theater, I did not, as I might have done if she had been a Negro, find a way of discouraging her, but agreed that she should pick me up at my house one evening. I then, very cleverly, left all the rest to my mother, who suggested to my

6. Parties at which money was collected from the guests to help cover tenants' rent; normally, the parties included hired bands; during Prohibition (1920–33), bootlegged alcohol was served.

7. Major north–south thoroughfare in Harlem.

father, as I knew she would, that it would not be very nice to let such a kind woman make the trip for nothing. Also, since it was a schoolteacher, I imagine that my mother countered the idea of sin with the idea of "education," which word, even with my father, carried a kind of bitter weight.

Before the teacher came my father took me aside to ask *why* she was coming, what *interest* she could possibly have in our house, in a boy like me. I said I didn't know but I, too, suggested that it had something to do with education. And I understood that my father was waiting for me to say something—I didn't quite know what; perhaps that I wanted his protection against this teacher and her "education." I said none of these things and the teacher came and we went out. It was clear, during the brief interview in our living room, that my father was agreeing very much against his will and that he would have refused permission if he had dared. The fact that he did not dare caused me to despise him: I had no way of knowing that he was facing in that living room a wholly unprecedented and frightening situation.

Later, when my father had been laid off from his job, this woman became very important to us. She was really a very sweet and generous woman and went to a great deal of trouble to be of help to us, particularly during one awful winter. My mother called her by the highest name she knew: she said she was a "christian." My father could scarcely disagree but during the four or five years of our relatively close association he never trusted her and was always trying to surprise in her open, Midwestern face the genuine, cunningly hidden, and hideous motivation. In later years, particularly when it began to be clear that this "education" of mine was going to lead me to perdition, he became more explicit and warned me that my white friends in high school were not really my friends and that I would see, when I was older, how white people would do anything to keep a Negro down. Some of them could be nice, he admitted, but none of them were to be trusted and most of them were not even nice. The best thing was to have as little to do with them as possible. I did not feel this way and I was certain, in my innocence, that I never would.

But the year which preceded my father's death had made a great change in my life. I had been living in New Jersey, working in defense plants, working and living among southerners, white and black. I knew about the south, of course, and about how southerners treated Negroes and how they expected them to behave, but it had never entered my mind that anyone would look at me and expect *me* to behave that way. I learned in New Jersey that to be a Negro meant, precisely, that one was never looked at but was simply at the mercy of the reflexes the color of one's skin caused in other people. I acted in New Jersey as I had always acted, that is as though I thought a great deal of myself—I had to *act* that way—with results that were, simply, unbelievable. I had scarcely arrived before I had earned the enmity, which was extraordinarily ingenious, of all my superiors and nearly all my co-workers. In the beginning, to make matters worse, I simply did not know what was happening. I did not know what I had done, and I shortly began to wonder what *anyone* could possibly do, to bring about such unanimous, active, and unbearably vocal hostility. I knew about jim-crow[8] but I had never experienced it. I went to the same self-service restaurant three times and

8. System of laws and customs enforcing segregation of blacks and whites in southern states; some aspects of Jim Crow were also in force in northern states, including New Jersey.

stood with all the Princeton boys before the counter, waiting for a hamburger and coffee; it was always an extraordinarily long time before anything was set before me; but it was not until the fourth visit that I learned that, in fact, nothing had ever been set before me: I had simply picked something up. Negroes were not served there, I was told, and they had been waiting for me to realize that I was always the only Negro present. Once I was told this, I determined to go there all the time. But now they were ready for me and, though some dreadful scenes were subsequently enacted in that restaurant, I never ate there again.

It was the same story all over New Jersey, in bars, bowling alleys, diners, places to live. I was always being forced to leave, silently, or with mutual imprecations. I very shortly became notorious and children giggled behind me when I passed and their elders whispered or shouted—they really believed that I was mad. And it did begin to work on my mind, of course; I began to be afraid to go anywhere and to compensate for this I went places to which I really should not have gone and where, God knows, I had no desire to be. My reputation in town naturally enhanced my reputation at work and my working day became one long series of acrobatics designed to keep me out of trouble. I cannot say that these acrobatics succeeded. It began to seem that the machinery of the organization I worked for was turning over, day and night, with but one aim: to eject me. I was fired once, and contrived, with the aid of a friend from New York, to get back on the payroll; was fired again, and bounced back again. It took a while to fire me for the third time, but the third time took. There were no loopholes anywhere. There was not even any way of getting back inside the gates.

That year in New Jersey lives in my mind as though it were the year during which, having an unsuspected predilection for it, I first contracted some dread, chronic disease, the unfailing symptom of which is a kind of blind fever, a pounding in the skull and fire in the bowels. Once this disease is contracted, one can never be really carefree again, for the fever, without an instant's warning, can recur at any moment. It can wreck more important things than race relations. There is not a Negro alive who does not have this rage in his blood—one has the choice, merely, of living with it consciously or surrendering to it. As for me, this fever has recurred in me, and does, and will until the day I die.

My last night in New Jersey, a white friend from New York took me to the nearest big town, Trenton, to go to the movies and have a few drinks. As it turned out, he also saved me from, at the very least, a violent whipping. Almost every detail of that night stands out very clearly in my memory. I even remember the name of the movie we saw because its title impressed me as being so patly ironical. It was a movie about the German occupation of France, starring Maureen O'Hara and Charles Laughton and called *This Land Is Mine*. I remember the name of the diner we walked into when the movie ended: it was the "American Diner." When we walked in the counterman asked what we wanted and I remember answering with the casual sharpness which had become my habit: "We want a hamburger and a cup of coffee, what do you think we want?" I do not know why, after a year of such rebuffs, I so completely failed to anticipate his answer, which was, of course, "We don't serve Negroes here." This reply failed to discompose me, at least for the moment. I made some sardonic comment about the name of the diner and we walked out into the streets.

This was the time of what was called the "brown-out," when the lights in all American cities were very dim. When we re-entered the streets something happened to me which had the force of an optical illusion, or a nightmare. The streets were very crowded and I was facing north. People were moving in every direction but it seemed to me, in that instant, that all of the people I could see, and many more than that, were moving toward me, against me, and that everyone was white. I remember how their faces gleamed. And I felt, like a physical sensation, a *click* at the nape of my neck as though some interior string connecting my head to my body had been cut. I began to walk. I heard my friend call after me, but I ignored him. Heaven only knows what was going on in his mind, but he had the good sense not to touch me—I don't know what would have happened if he had—and to keep me in sight. I don't know what was going on in my mind, either; I certainly had no conscious plan. I wanted to do something to crush these white faces, which were crushing me. I walked for perhaps a block or two until I came to an enormous, glittering, and fashionable restaurant in which I knew not even the intercession of the Virgin would cause me to be served. I pushed through the doors and took the first vacant seat I saw, at a table for two, and waited.

I do not know how long I waited and I rather wonder, until today, what I could possibly have looked like. Whatever I looked like, I frightened the waitress who shortly appeared, and the moment she appeared all of my fury flowed towards her. I hated her for her white face, and for her great, astounded, frightened eyes. I felt that if she found a black man so frightening I would make her fright worth-while.

She did not ask me what I wanted, but repeated, as though she had learned it somewhere, "We don't serve Negroes here." She did not say it with the blunt, derisive hostility to which I had grown so accustomed, but, rather, with a note of apology in her voice, and fear. This made me colder and more murderous than ever. I felt I had to do something with my hands. I wanted her to come close enough for me to get her neck between my hands.

So I pretended not to have understood her, hoping to draw her closer. And she did step a very short step closer, with her pencil poised incongruously over her pad, and repeated the formula: ". . . don't serve Negroes here."

Somehow, with the repetition of that phrase, which was already ringing in my head like a thousand bells of a nightmare, I realized that she would never come any closer and that I would have to strike from a distance. There was nothing on the table but an ordinary watermug half full of water, and I picked this up and hurled it with all my strength at her. She ducked and it missed her and shattered against the mirror behind the bar. And, with that sound, my frozen blood abruptly thawed, I returned from wherever I had been, I *saw*, for the first time, the restaurant, the people with their mouths open, already, as it seemed to me, rising as one man, and I realized what I had done, and where I was, and I was frightened. I rose and began running for the door. A round, potbellied man grabbed me by the nape of the neck just as I reached the doors and began to beat me about the face. I kicked him and got loose and ran into the streets. My friend whispered, "*Run!*" and I ran.

My friend stayed outside the restaurant long enough to misdirect my pursuers and the police, who arrived, he told me, at once. I do not know what I said to him when he came to my room that night. I could not have said much. I felt, in the oddest, most awful way, that I had somehow betrayed him. I lived it over and over and over again, the way one relives an automobile accident after it has happened and one finds oneself alone and safe. I could not get over two facts, both equally difficult for the imagination to grasp, and one was that I could have been murdered. But the other was that I had been ready to commit murder. I saw nothing very clearly but I did see this: that my life, my *real* life, was in danger, and not from anything other people might do but from the hatred I carried in my own heart.

II

I had returned home around the second week in June—in great haste because it seemed that my father's death and my mother's confinement were both but a matter of hours. In the case of my mother, it soon became clear that she had simply made a miscalculation. This had always been her tendency and I don't believe that a single one of us arrived in the world, or has since arrived anywhere else, on time. But none of us dawdled so intolerably about the business of being born as did my baby sister. We sometimes amused ourselves, during those endless, stifling weeks, by picturing the baby sitting within in the safe, warm dark, bitterly regretting the necessity of becoming a part of our chaos and stubbornly putting it off as long as possible. I understood her perfectly and congratulated her on showing such good sense so soon. Death, however, sat as purposefully at my father's bedside as life stirred within my mother's womb and it was harder to understand why he so lingered in that long shadow. It seemed that he had bent, and for a long time, too, all of his energies towards dying. Now death was ready for him but my father held back.

All of Harlem, indeed, seemed to be infected by waiting. I had never before known it to be so violently still. Racial tensions throughout this country were exacerbated during the early years of the war,[9] partly because the labor market brought together hundreds of thousands of ill-prepared people and partly because Negro soldiers, regardless of where they were born, received their military training in the south. What happened in defense plants and army camps had repercussions, naturally, in every Negro ghetto. The situation in Harlem had grown bad enough for clergymen, policemen, educators, politicians, and social workers to assert in one breath that there was no "crime wave" and to offer, in the very next breath, suggestions as to how to combat it. These suggestions always seemed to involve playgrounds, despite the fact that racial skirmishes were occurring in the playgrounds, too. Playground or not, crime wave or not, the Harlem police force had been augmented in March, and the unrest grew—perhaps, in fact, partly as a result of the ghetto's instinctive hatred of policemen. Perhaps the most revealing news item, out of the steady parade of reports of muggings, stabbings, shootings, assaults, gang wars, and accusations of police brutality, is the item concerning six Negro girls who set upon a white girl in the subway because, as they all too accurately put it, she was stepping on their toes. Indeed she was, all over the nation.

I had never before been so aware of policemen, on foot, on horseback, on corners, everywhere, always two by two. Nor had I ever been so aware of small

9. The Second World War (1939–45), which the United States entered on December 8, 1941.

knots of people. They were on stoops and on corners and in doorways, and what was striking about them, I think, was that they did not seem to be talking. Never, when I passed these groups, did the usual sound of a curse or a laugh ring out and neither did there seem to be any hum of gossip. There was certainly, on the other hand, occurring between them communication extraordinarily intense. Another thing that was striking was the unexpected diversity of the people who made up these groups. Usually, for example, one would see a group of sharpies standing on the street corner, jiving the passing chicks;[1] or a group of older men, usually, for some reason, in the vicinity of a barber shop, discussing baseball scores, or the numbers,[2] or making rather chilling observations about women they had known. Women, in a general way, tended to be seen less often together—unless they were church women, or very young girls, or prostitutes met together for an unprofessional instant. But that summer I saw the strangest combinations: large, respectable, churchly matrons standing on the stoops or the corners with their hair tied up, together with a girl in sleazy satin whose face bore the marks of gin and the razor, or heavy-set, abrupt, no-nonsense older men, in company with the most disreputable and fanatical "race" men,[3] or these same "race" men with the sharpies, or these sharpies with the churchly women. Seventh Day Adventists and Methodists and Spiritualists seemed to be hobnobbing with Holyrollers[4] and they were all, alike, entangled with the most flagrant disbelievers; something heavy in their stance seemed to indicate that they had all, incredibly, seen a common vision, and on each face there seemed to be the same strange, bitter shadow.

The churchly women and the matter-of-fact, no-nonsense men had children in the Army. The sleazy girls they talked to had lovers there, the sharpies and the "race" men had friends and brothers there. It would have demanded an unquestioning patriotism, happily as uncommon in this country as it is undesirable, for these people not to have been disturbed by the bitter letters they received, by the newspaper stories they read, not to have been enraged by the posters, then to be found all over New York, which described the Japanese as "yellow-bellied Japs." It was only the "race" men, to be sure, who spoke ceaselessly of being revenged—how this vengeance was to be exacted was not clear—for the indignities and dangers suffered by Negro boys in uniform; but everybody felt a directionless, hopeless bitterness, as well as that panic which can scarcely be suppressed when one knows that a human being one loves is beyond one's reach, and in danger. This helplessness and this gnawing uneasiness does something, at length, to even the toughest mind. Perhaps the best way to sum all this up is to say that the people I knew felt, mainly, a peculiar kind of relief when they knew that their boys were being shipped out of the south, to do battle overseas. It was, perhaps, like feeling that the most dangerous part of a dangerous journey had been passed and that now, even if death should come, it would come with honor and without the complicity of their countrymen. Such a death would be, in short, a fact with which one could hope to live.

It was on the 28th of July, which I believe was a Wednesday, that I visited my father for the first time during his illness and for the last time in his life. The

1. Talking nonsense with the girls passing by. "Sharpies": tricksters or con men.
2. An illegal lottery.
3. Men who emphasized the importance of African American pride and mutual support.
4. Pentecostalists, who emphasized prophecy, healing, and speaking in tongues.

moment I saw him I knew why I had put off this visit so long. I had told my mother that I did not want to see him because I hated him. But this was not true. It was only that I *had* hated him and I wanted to hold on to this hatred. I did not want to look on him as a ruin: it was not a ruin I had hated. I imagine that one of the reasons people cling to their hates so stubbornly is because they sense, once hate is gone, that they will be forced to deal with pain.

We traveled out to him, his older sister and myself, to what seemed to be the very end of a very Long Island. It was hot and dusty and we wrangled, my aunt and I, all the way out, over the fact that I had recently begun to smoke and, as she said, to give myself airs. But I knew that she wrangled with me because she could not bear to face the fact of her brother's dying. Neither could I endure the reality of her despair, her unstated bafflement as to what had happened to her brother's life, and her own. So we wrangled and I smoked and from time to time she fell into a heavy reverie. Covertly, I watched her face, which was the face of an old woman; it had fallen in, the eyes were sunken and lightless; soon she would be dying, too.

In my childhood—it had not been so long ago—I had thought her beautiful. She had been quick-witted and quick-moving and very generous with all the children and each of her visits had been an event. At one time one of my brothers and myself had thought of running away to live with her. Now she could no longer produce out of her handbag some unexpected and yet familiar delight. She made me feel pity and revulsion and fear. It was awful to realize that she no longer caused me to feel affection. The closer we came to the hospital the more querulous she became and at the same time, naturally, grew more dependent on me. Between pity and guilt and fear I began to feel that there was another me trapped in my skull like a jack-in-the-box who might escape my control at any moment and fill the air with screaming.

She began to cry the moment we entered the room and she saw him lying there, all shriveled and still, like a little black monkey. The great, gleaming apparatus which fed him and would have compelled him to be still even if he had been able to move brought to mind, not beneficence, but torture; the tubes entering his arm made me think of pictures I had seen when a child, of Gulliver,[5] tied down by the pygmies on that island. My aunt wept and wept, there was a whistling sound in my father's throat; nothing was said; he could not speak. I wanted to take his hand, to say something. But I do not know what I could have said, even if he could have heard me. He was not really in that room with us, he had at last really embarked on his journey; and though my aunt told me that he said he was going to meet Jesus, I did not hear anything except that whistling in his throat. The doctor came back and we left, into that unbearable train again, and home. In the morning came the telegram saying that he was dead. Then the house was suddenly full of relatives, friends, hysteria, and confusion and I quickly left my mother and the children to the care of those impressive women, who, in Negro communities at least, automatically appear at times of bereavement armed with lotions, proverbs, and patience, and an ability to cook. I went downtown. By the time I returned, later the same day, my mother had been carried to the hospital and the baby had been born.

5. The hero of *Gulliver's Travels* (1726) by the English-Irish writer Jonathan Swift (1667–1745); Gulliver is washed ashore on Lilliput, an island inhabited by tiny people who tie him down with cords while he is sleeping.

III

For my father's funeral I had nothing black to wear and this posed a nagging problem all day long. It was one of those problems, simple, or impossible of solution, to which the mind insanely clings in order to avoid the mind's real trouble. I spent most of that day at the downtown apartment of a girl I knew, celebrating my birthday with whiskey and wondering what to wear that night. When planning a birthday celebration one naturally does not expect that it will be up against competition from a funeral and this girl had anticipated taking me out that night, for a big dinner and a night club afterwards. Sometime during the course of that long day we decided that we would go out anyway, when my father's funeral service was over. I imagine *I* decided it, since, as the funeral hour approached, it became clearer and clearer to me that I would not know what to do with myself when it was over. The girl, stifling her very lively concern as to the possible effects of the whiskey on one of my father's chief mourners, concentrated on being conciliatory and practically helpful. She found a black shirt for me somewhere and ironed it and, dressed in the darkest pants and jacket I owned, and slightly drunk, I made my way to my father's funeral.

The chapel was full, but not packed, and very quiet. There were, mainly, my father's relatives, and his children, and here and there I saw faces I had not seen since childhood, the faces of my father's one-time friends. They were very dark and solemn now, seeming somehow to suggest that they had known all along that something like this would happen. Chief among the mourners was my aunt, who had quarreled with my father all his life; by which I do not mean to suggest that her mourning was insincere or that she had not loved him. I suppose that she was one of the few people in the world who had, and their incessant quarreling proved precisely the strength of the tie that bound them. The only other person in the world, as far as I knew, whose relationship to my father rivaled my aunt's in depth was my mother, who was not there.

It seemed to me, of course, that it was a very long funeral. But it was, if anything, a rather shorter funeral than most, nor, since there were no overwhelming, uncontrollable expressions of grief, could it be called—if I dare to use the word—successful. The minister who preached my father's funeral sermon was one of the few my father had still been seeing as he neared his end. He presented to us in his sermon a man whom none of us had ever seen—a man thoughtful, patient, and forbearing, a Christian inspiration to all who knew him, and a model for his children. And no doubt the children, in their disturbed and guilty state, were almost ready to believe this; he had been remote enough to be anything and, anyway, the shock of the incontrovertible, that it was really our father lying up there in that casket, prepared the mind for anything. His sister moaned and this grief-stricken moaning was taken as corroboration. The other faces held a dark, non-committal thoughtfulness. This was not the man they had known, but they had scarcely expected to be confronted with *him*; this was, in a sense deeper than questions of fact, the man they had not known, and the man they had not known may have been the real one. The real man, whoever he had been, had suffered and now he was dead: this was all that was sure and all that mattered now. Every man in the chapel hoped that when his hour came he, too, would be eulogized, which is to say forgiven, and that all of his lapses, greeds, errors, and strayings from the truth would be invested with coherence and looked upon with charity. This was perhaps the last thing human beings could give each other and it was what they demanded, after all, of the Lord. Only the Lord saw the midnight tears, only He was present when one of His children, moaning and wringing hands, paced up and down the room. When one slapped one's child in anger the recoil in the heart reverberated through heaven and became part of the pain of the universe. And when the children were hungry and sullen and distrustful and one watched them, daily, growing wilder, and further away, and running headlong into danger, it was the Lord who knew what the charged heart endured as the strap was laid to the backside; the Lord alone who knew what one *would* have said if one had had, like the Lord, the gift of the living word. It was the Lord who knew of the impossibility every parent in that room faced: how to prepare the child for the day when the child would be despised and how to *create* in the child—by what means?—a stronger antidote to this poison than one had found for oneself. The avenues, side streets, bars, billiard halls, hospitals, police stations, and even the playgrounds of Harlem—not to mention the houses of correction, the jails, and the morgue—testified to the potency of the poison while remaining silent as to the efficacy of whatever antidote, irresistibly raising the question of whether or not such an antidote existed; raising, which was worse, the question of whether or not an antidote was desirable; perhaps poison should be fought with poison. With these several schisms in the mind and with more terrors in the heart than could be named, it was better not to judge the man who had gone down under an impossible burden. It was better to remember: *Thou knowest this man's fall; but thou knowest not his wrassling.*[6]

While the preacher talked and I watched the children—years of changing their diapers, scrubbing them, slapping them, taking them to school, and scolding them had had the perhaps inevitable result of making me love them, though I am not sure I knew this then—my mind was busily breaking out with a rash of disconnected impressions. Snatches of popular songs, indecent jokes, bits of books I had read, movie sequences, faces, voices, political issues—I thought I was going mad; all these impressions suspended, as it were, in the solution of the faint nausea produced in me by the heat and liquor. For a moment I had the impression that my alcoholic breath, inefficiently disguised with chewing gum, filled the entire chapel. Then someone began singing one of my father's favorite songs and, abruptly, I was with him, sitting on his knee, in the hot, enormous, crowded church which was the first church we attended. It was the Abyssinia Baptist Church on 138th Street.[7] We had not gone there long. With this image, a host of others came. I had forgotten, in the rage of my growing up, how proud my father had been of me when I was little. Apparently, I had had a voice and my father had liked to show me off before the members of the church. I had forgotten what he had looked like when he was pleased but now I remembered that he had always been grinning with pleasure when my solos ended. I even remembered certain expressions on his face when he teased my mother—had he loved her? I would never know. And when had it all

6. From the English author John Donne (1572–1631), *Biathanatos* (1608), a defense of suicide. "Wrassling": wrestling.

7. A famous African American church in Harlem.

begun to change? For now it seemed that he had not always been cruel. I remembered being taken for a haircut and scraping my knee on the footrest of the barber's chair and I remembered my father's face as he soothed my crying and applied the stinging iodine. Then I remembered our fights, fights which had been of the worst possible kind because my technique had been silence.

I remembered the one time in all our life together when we had really spoken to each other.

It was on a Sunday and it must have been shortly before I left home. We were walking, just the two of us, in our usual silence, to or from church. I was in high school and had been doing a lot of writing and I was, at about this time, the editor of the high school magazine. But I had also been a Young Minister and had been preaching from the pulpit. Lately, I had been taking fewer engagements and preached as rarely as possible. It was said in the church, quite truthfully, that I was "cooling off."

My father asked me abruptly, "You'd rather write than preach, wouldn't you?"

I was astonished at his question—because it was a real question. I answered, "Yes."

That was all we said. It was awful to remember that that was all we had *ever* said.

The casket now was opened and the mourners were being led up the aisle to look for the last time on the deceased. The assumption was that the family was too overcome with grief to be allowed to make this journey alone and I watched while my aunt was led to the casket and, muffled in black, and shaking, led back to her seat. I disapproved of forcing the children to look on their dead father, considering that the shock of his death, or, more truthfully, the shock of death as a reality, was already a little more than a child could bear, but my judgment in this matter had been overruled and there they were, bewildered and frightened and very small, being led, one by one, to the casket. But there is also something very gallant about children at such moments. It has something to do with their silence and gravity and with the fact that one cannot help them. Their legs, somehow, seem *exposed*, so that it is at once incredible and terribly clear that their legs are all they have to hold them up.

I had not wanted to go to the casket myself and I certainly had not wished to be led there, but there was no way of avoiding either of these forms. One of the deacons led me up and I looked on my father's face. I cannot say that it looked like him at all. His blackness had been equivocated by powder and there was no suggestion in that casket of what his power had or could have been. He was simply an old man dead, and it was hard to believe that he had ever given anyone either joy or pain. Yet, his life filled that room. Further up the avenue his wife was holding his newborn child. Life and death so close together, and love and hatred, and right and wrong, said something to me which I did not want to hear concerning man, concerning the life of man.

After the funeral, while I was downtown desperately celebrating my birthday, a Negro soldier, in the lobby of the Hotel Braddock,[8] got into a fight with a white policeman over a Negro girl. Negro girls, white policemen, in or out of uniform, and Negro males—in or out of uniform—were part of the furniture of

8. Hotel at Eighth Avenue and 126th Street in Harlem.

the lobby of the Hotel Braddock and this was certainly not the first time such an incident had occurred. It was destined, however, to receive an unprecedented publicity, for the fight between the policeman and the soldier ended with the shooting of the soldier. Rumor, flowing immediately to the streets outside, stated that the soldier had been shot in the back, an instantaneous and revealing invention, and that the soldier had died protecting a Negro woman. The facts were somewhat different—for example, the soldier had not been shot in the back, and was not dead, and the girl seems to have been as dubious a symbol of womanhood as her white counterpart in Georgia usually is,[9] but no one was interested in the facts. They preferred the invention because this invention expressed and corroborated their hates and fears so perfectly. It is just as well to remember that people are always doing this. Perhaps many of those legends, including Christianity, to which the world clings began their conquest of the world with just some such concerted surrender to distortion. The effect, in Harlem, of this particular legend was like the effect of a lit match in a tin of gasoline. The mob gathered before the doors of the Hotel Braddock simply began to swell and to spread in every direction, and Harlem exploded.

The mob did not cross the ghetto lines. It would have been easy, for example, to have gone over Morningside Park on the west side or to have crossed the Grand Central railroad tracks at 125th Street on the east side, to wreak havoc in white neighborhoods. The mob seems to have been mainly interested in something more potent and real than the white face, that is, in white power, and the principal damage done during the riot of the summer of 1943 was to white business establishments in Harlem. It might have been a far bloodier story, of course, if, at the hour the riot began, these establishments had still been open. From the Hotel Braddock the mob fanned out, east and west along 125th Street, and for the entire length of Lenox, Seventh, and Eighth avenues. Along each of these avenues, and along each major side street—116th, 125th, 135th, and so on—bars, stores, pawnshops, restaurants, even little luncheonettes had been smashed open and entered and looted—looted, it might be added, with more haste than efficiency. The shelves really looked as though a bomb had struck them. Cans of beans and soup and dog food, along with toilet paper, corn flakes, sardines and milk tumbled every which way, and abandoned cash registers and cases of beer leaned crazily out of the splintered windows and were strewn along the avenues. Sheets, blankets, and clothing of every description formed a kind of path, as though people had dropped them while running. I truly had not realized that Harlem *had* so many stores until I saw them all smashed open; the first time the word *wealth* ever entered my mind in relation to Harlem was when I saw it scattered in the streets. But one's first, incongruous impression of plenty was countered immediately by an impression of waste. None of this was doing anybody any good. It would have been better to have left the plate glass as it had been and the goods lying in the stores.

It would have been better, but it would also have been intolerable, for Harlem had needed something to smash. To smash something is the ghetto's chronic need. Most of the time it is the members of the ghetto who smash each other, and themselves. But as long as the ghetto walls are standing there will

9. Baldwin here refers to the origins of many lynchings in the South: allegations that black men had insulted white women.

always come a moment when these outlets do not work. That summer, for example, it was not enough to get into a fight on Lenox Avenue, or curse out one's cronies in the barber shops. If ever, indeed, the violence which fills Harlem's churches, pool halls, and bars erupts outward in a more direct fashion, Harlem and its citizens are likely to vanish in an apocalyptic flood. That this is not likely to happen is due to a great many reasons, most hidden and powerful among them the Negro's real relation to the white American. This relation prohibits, simply, anything as uncomplicated and satisfactory as pure hatred. In order really to hate white people, one has to blot so much out of the mind—and the heart—that this hatred itself becomes an exhausting and self-destructive pose. But this does not mean, on the other hand, that love comes easily: the white world is too powerful, too complacent, too ready with gratuitous humiliation, and, above all, too ignorant and too innocent for that. One is absolutely forced to make perpetual qualifications and one's own reactions are always canceling each other out. It is this, really, which has driven so many people mad, both white and black. One is always in the position of having to decide between amputation and gangrene. Amputation is swift but time may prove that the amputation was not necessary—or one may delay the amputation too long. Gangrene is slow, but it is impossible to be sure that one is reading one's symptoms right. The idea of going through life as a cripple is more than one can bear, and equally unbearable is the risk of swelling up slowly, in agony, with poison. And the trouble, finally, is that the risks are real even if the choices do not exist.

"But as for me and my house," my father had said, "we will serve the Lord." I wondered, as we drove him to his resting place, what this line had meant for him. I had heard him preach it many times. I had preached it once myself, proudly giving it an interpretation different from my father's. Now the whole thing came back to me, as though my father and I were on our way to Sunday school and I were memorizing the golden text: *And if it seem evil unto you to serve the Lord, choose you this day whom you will serve; whether the gods which your fathers served that were on the other side of the flood, or the gods of the Amorites, in whose land ye dwell: but as for me and my house, we will serve the Lord.*[1] I suspected in these familiar lines a meaning which had never been there for me before. All of my father's texts and songs, which I had decided were meaningless, were arranged before me at his death like empty bottles, waiting to hold the meaning which life would give them for me. This was his legacy: nothing is ever escaped. That bleakly memorable morning I hated the unbelievable streets and the Negroes and whites who had, equally, made them that way. But I knew that it was folly, as my father would have said, this bitterness was folly. It was necessary to hold on to the things that mattered. The dead man mattered, the new life mattered; blackness and whiteness did not matter; to believe that they did was to acquiesce in one's own destruction. Hatred, which could destroy so much, never failed to destroy the man who hated and this was an immutable law.

It began to seem that one would have to hold in the mind forever two ideas which seemed to be in opposition. The first idea was acceptance, the acceptance, totally without rancor, of life as it is, and men as they are: in the light of

1. Joshua 24.15.

this idea, it goes without saying that injustice is a commonplace. But this did not mean that one could be complacent, for the second idea was of equal power: that one must never, in one's own life, accept these injustices as commonplace but must fight them with all one's strength. This fight begins, however, in the heart and it now had been laid to my charge to keep my own heart free of hatred and despair. This intimation made my heart heavy and, now that my father was irrecoverable, I wished that he had been beside me so that I could have searched his face for the answers which only the future would give me now.

1955

ALBERT CAMUS

1913–1960

From his childhood among the most disadvantaged in Algiers to his later roles as journalist, Resistance fighter in World War II, iconic literary figure, and winner of the Nobel Prize in Literature, in 1957, Albert Camus was intensely aware of the basic levels of human existence and of the struggles of the poor and the oppressed. "I can understand only in human terms," he said. "I understand the things I touch, things that offer me resistance." He describes the raw experience of life that human beings share, the humble but ineradicable bond between them. Camus kept a sympathetic yet critical eye on the tensions of his day: observing the Soviet Union from afar, and the bloody battles for Algerian independence up-close, led him to examine the way people can respond to oppressive systems without themselves becoming oppressors.

Camus was born on November 7, 1913, into a "world of poverty and light" in Mondavi, Algeria, then a colony of France. He was the second son in a poor family of mixed Alsatian and Spanish descent, and his father died in an early battle of the First World War. Camus's mother was illiterate; an untreated childhood illness had left her deaf and with a speech impediment. The two boys lived together with their mother, uncle, and grandmother in a two-room apartment in the working-class section of the capital city, Algiers. Camus and his brother, Lucien, were raised by their strict grandmother while their mother worked as a cleaning woman to support the family. Images of the Mediterranean landscape, with the sensual appeal of sea and blazing sun, recur throughout his work, as does a profound compassion for those who—like his mother—labor unrecognized and in silence.

A passionate athlete as well as a scholarship recipient, Camus completed his secondary education and enrolled as a philosophy student at the University of Algiers before contracting, at seventeen, the tuberculosis that corroded his health and made him aware of the body's vulnerability to disease and death. Camus eventually finished his degree, but in the meantime his illness had provided a metaphor for the personal and natural events that oppose and limit human fulfillment and happiness: elements he was later to term the "plague," which infects bodies, minds, cities, and society. (*The Plague* is the title of his second novel.)

Camus lived and worked as a journalist and essayist. Then, as later, however, his work extended well beyond journalism. He founded a collective theater, Le Théâtre du Travail (The Labor Theater), for which he wrote and adapted a number of plays. The theater fascinated Camus, possibly because it involved groups of people and spontaneous interaction between actors and audience. Sponsored by the Communist Party, the Labor Theater was designed for the working people, with performances on the docks in Algiers. Like many intellectuals of his day, Camus joined the Communist Party, but he withdrew after a year to protest its opposition to Algerian nationalism. He eventually left the Labor Theater too and, with a group of young Algerians associated with the publishing house Charlot, organized the politically independent Team Theater (Théâtre de l'Équipe). In 1940 he moved to France after his political commentary, including a famous report on administrative mismanagement during a famine among the Berbers (tribal peoples in North Africa), so outraged the Algerian government that his newspaper was suspended and he himself refused a work permit.

Soon after leaving Algeria, Camus published his first and most famous novel, *The Stranger* (1942), the play *Caligula* (1944), and a lengthy essay defining his concept of the "absurd" hero, *The Myth of Sisyphus* (1942). During World War II, Camus worked in Paris as a reader for the publishing firm of Gallimard, a post that he kept until his death, in 1960. At the same time, he took part in the French Resistance and helped edit the underground journal *Combat*. His friendship with the existentialist philosopher Jean-Paul Sartre began in 1944; after the war he and Sartre were internationally known as uncompromising analysts of the modern conscience. Camus's second novel, *The Plague* (1947), portrays an epidemic in a quarantined city, Oran, Algeria, to symbolize the spread of evil during World War II ("the feeling of suffocation from which we all suffered, and the atmosphere of threat and exile") and to show the struggle against physical and spiritual death in its many forms. He continued, as well, to write plays (*Cross Purposes*, 1944; *The Just Assassins*, 1949). Not content to express his views symbolically in fiction, Camus also spoke out in philosophical essays and political statements. His independent mind and rejection of doctrinaire positions brought him attacks from both the left and the right.

Unlike many intellectuals of his day, Camus did not place a higher value on ideology than on its practical effects: when word emerged about Stalinist labor camps, for instance, he criticized the Soviets rather than defend the communist ideal, as many of his friends did. Camus's open anti-communism led to a spectacular break with Sartre, whose magazine, *Les Temps Modernes* (Modern Times), condemned Camus's book-length essay *The Rebel* (1951); the personal and public dispute between the old friends may have been unavoidable. In the bitter struggle over Algeria, Camus supported the claims of French colonists, including his own family, and therefore opposed Algerian independence, while at the same time attacking the violence of the French colonial regime. Camus did not live to witness the end of the Algerian conflict, which led to independence in 1962. After being awarded the Nobel Prize in 1957, he died in a car accident in 1960. His death at the height of his powers contributed to his posthumous fame as an analyst of the tragic elements of the human condition.

Camus is often linked with Sartre as an existentialist writer, and indeed—as novelist, playwright, and essayist—he is widely known for his analysis of two issues fundamental to existentialism: its distinctive assessment of the human condition and its search for authentic beliefs and values. Yet Camus rejected doctrinaire labels, and Sartre himself suggested that Camus was better placed in the tradition of French moralist writers, such as Michel de Montaigne and René Pascal, who observed human behavior within an implied ethical context that had its own standards of good and evil.

A consummate artist as well as a moralist, Camus was well aware of both the opportunities and the illusions of his craft. When he received the Nobel Prize, his acceptance speech emphasized the artificial but necessary "human" order that art imposes on the chaos of immediate experience. Artists are important as *creators*, because they shape a human perspective, allow understanding in human terms, and therefore provide a basis for action. By stressing the gap between art and reality, Camus provides a link between two poles of human understanding. His works juxtapose realistic detail and a philosophical, almost mythical dimension. The symbolism of his titles, from *The Stranger* to the last collection of stories, *Exile and the Kingdom* (1957), indicates the status of outsider, and the feeling of alienation in the world, while suggesting a search for the realm of human solidarity and agency.

The two terms around which Camus's thinking and writing revolve are the nouns *the absurd* and *revolt*. Camus's wartime output established his reputation as a philosopher of the absurd: the impossibility of "making sense" of a world that has no discernible sense. How to live in such an enviroment nevertheless becomes the main object of his philosophical and literary work. *Revolt*, for Camus, is more ethical than political, a rejection of the conventional and the inauthentic, but also an embrace of a shared humanity. Because the impulse to rebel is a basis for social tolerance and has no patience for master plans that prescribe patterns of thought or action, *revolt* actually opposes revolutionary nihilism.

In the story presented here, "The Guest" (1957), taken from *Exile and the Kingdom*, Camus returns to the landscape of his native Algeria. The colonial context is crucial in this story, not only to explain the real threat of guerrilla reprisal (Camus may be recalling the actual killing of rural schoolteachers in 1954) but to establish the dimensions of a political situation in which the government, police, educational system, and economic welfare of Algeria are all controlled by France. As in the works of **Doris Lessing**, **Naguib Mahfouz**, **Chinua Achebe**, and **Wole Soyinka**, the colonial (or newly postcolonial) setting generates a charged atmosphere. The beginning of the story illustrates how French colonial education emphasizes French rather than local concerns: the schoolteacher's geography lesson outlines the four main rivers of France. The Arab is led along like an animal behind the gendarme Balducci, who rides a horse (here too, Camus may be recalling a humiliation reported two decades before and used as a way to inspire Algerian nationalists). Within this specific context, however, Camus concentrates on wider issues: freedom, brotherhood, responsibility, and the ambiguity of actions along with the inevitability of choice.

The remote desert landscape establishes a complete physical and moral isolation for the story's events. "No one, in this desert, . . . mattered," and the schoolteacher and his guest must each decide, independently, what to do. When Balducci invades Daru's monastic solitude and tells him that he must deliver the Arab to prison, Daru is outraged to be given involvement in, and indeed responsibility for, another's fate. Cursing both the system that tries to force him into complicity and the Arab who has not had enough sense to get away, Daru tries, in every way possible, to avoid taking a stand. Yet he finds himself confronted with the essential human demand for hospitality, which creates burdens and links between guest and host. The choice that Daru must make leads to a further necessary choice by the Arab prisoner. As possible titles for this story, Camus considered "Cain" and "The Law" before settling on "The Guest": the title word, *l'hôte*, means both "guest" and "host" in French. Joined in their fundamental humanity, both guest and host are obliged to shoulder the ambiguous, and potentially fatal, burden of freedom.

The Guest[1]

The schoolmaster was watching the two men climb toward him. One was on horseback, the other on foot. They had not yet tackled the abrupt rise leading to the schoolhouse built on the hillside. They were toiling onward, making slow progress in the snow, among the stones, on the vast expanse of the high, deserted plateau. From time to time the horse stumbled. Without hearing anything yet, he could see the breath issuing from the horse's nostrils. One of the men, at least, knew the region. They were following the trail although it had disappeared days ago under a layer of dirty white snow. The schoolmaster calculated that it would take them half an hour to get onto the hill. It was cold; he went back into the school to get a sweater.

He crossed the empty, frigid classroom. On the blackboard the four rivers of France,[2] drawn with four different colored chalks, had been flowing toward their estuaries for the past three days. Snow had suddenly fallen in mid-October after eight months of drought without the transition of rain, and the twenty pupils, more or less, who lived in the villages scattered over the plateau had stopped coming. With fair weather they would return. Daru now heated only the single room that was his lodging, adjoining the classroom and giving also onto the plateau to the east. Like the class windows, his window looked to the south too. On that side the school was a few kilometers from the point where the plateau began to slope toward the south. In clear weather could be seen the purple mass of the mountain range where the gap opened onto the desert.

Somewhat warmed, Daru returned to the window from which he had first seen the two men. They were no longer visible. Hence they must have tackled the rise. The sky was not so dark, for the snow had stopped falling during the night. The morning had opened with a dirty light which had scarcely become brighter as the ceiling of clouds lifted. At two in the afternoon it seemed as if the day were merely beginning. But still this was better than those three days when the thick snow was falling amidst unbroken darkness with little gusts of wind that rattled the double door of the classroom. Then Daru had spent long hours in his room, leaving it only to go to the shed and feed the chickens or get some coal. Fortunately the delivery truck from Tadjid, the nearest village to the north, had brought his supplies two days before the blizzard. It would return in forty-eight hours.

1. Translated by Justin O'Brien.
2. The Seine, Loire, Rhone, and Gironde rivers. French geography was taught in the French colonies.

Besides, he had enough to resist a siege, for the little room was cluttered with bags of wheat that the administration left as a stock to distribute to those of his pupils whose families had suffered from the drought. Actually they had all been victims because they were all poor. Every day Daru would distribute a ration to the children. They had missed it, he knew, during these bad days. Possibly one of the fathers or big brothers would come this afternoon and he could supply them with grain. It was just a matter of carrying them over to the next harvest. Now shiploads of wheat were arriving from France and the worst was over. But it would be hard to forget that poverty, that army of ragged ghosts wandering in the sunlight, the plateaus burned to a cinder month after month, the earth shriveled up little by little, literally scorched, every stone bursting into dust under one's foot. The sheep had died then by thousands and even a few men, here and there, sometimes without anyone's knowing.

In contrast with such poverty, he who lived almost like a monk in his remote schoolhouse, nonetheless satisfied with the little he had and with the rough life, had felt like a lord with his whitewashed walls, his narrow couch, his unpainted shelves, his well, and his weekly provision of water and food. And suddenly this snow, without warning, without the foretaste of rain. This is the way the region was, cruel to live in, even without men—who didn't help matters either. But Daru had been born here. Everywhere else, he felt exiled.

He stepped out onto the terrace in front of the schoolhouse. The two men were now halfway up the slope. He recognized the horseman as Balducci, the old gendarme he had known for a long time. Balducci was holding on the end of a rope an Arab who was walking behind him with hands bound and head lowered. The gendarme waved a greeting to which Daru did not reply, lost as he was in contemplation of the Arab dressed in a faded blue jellaba, his feet in sandals but covered with socks of heavy raw wool, his head surmounted by a narrow, short *chèche*.[3] They were approaching. Balducci was holding back his horse in order not to hurt the Arab, and the group was advancing slowly.

Within earshot, Balducci shouted: "One hour to do the three kilometers from El Ameur!" Daru did not answer. Short and square in his thick sweater, he watched them climb. Not once had the Arab raised his head. "Hello," said Daru when they got up onto the terrace. "Come in and warm up." Balducci painfully got down from his horse without letting go the rope. From under his bristling mustache he smiled at the schoolmaster. His little dark eyes, deep-set under a tanned forehead, and his mouth surrounded with wrinkles made him look attentive and studious. Daru took the bridle, led the horse to the shed, and came back to the two men, who were now waiting for him in the school. He led them into his room. "I am going to heat up the classroom," he said. "We'll be more comfortable there." When he entered the room again, Balducci was on the couch. He had undone the rope tying him to the Arab, who had squatted near the stove. His hands still bound, the *chèche* pushed back on his head, he was looking toward the window. At first Daru noticed only his huge lips, fat, smooth, almost Negroid; yet his nose was straight, his eyes were dark and full of fever. The *chèche* revealed an obstinate forehead and, under the weathered skin now rather discolored by the cold, the whole face had a restless

3. Scarf; here, wound as a turban around the head. "Jellaba": a long hooded robe worn by Arabs in North Africa.

and rebellious look that struck Daru when the Arab, turning his face toward him, looked him straight in the eyes. "Go into the other room," said the schoolmaster, "and I'll make you some mint tea." "Thanks," Balducci said. "What a chore! How I long for retirement." And addressing his prisoner in Arabic: "Come on, you." The Arab got up and, slowly, holding his bound wrists in front of him, went into the classroom.

With the tea, Daru brought a chair. But Balducci was already enthroned on the nearest pupil's desk and the Arab had squatted against the teacher's platform facing the stove, which stood between the desk and the window. When he held out the glass of tea to the prisoner, Daru hesitated at the sight of his bound hands. "He might perhaps be untied." "Sure," said Balducci. "That was for the trip." He started to get to his feet. But Daru, setting the glass on the floor, had knelt beside the Arab. Without saying anything, the Arab watched him with his feverish eyes. Once his hands were free, he rubbed his swollen wrists against each other, took the glass of tea, and sucked up the burning liquid in swift little sips.

"Good," said Daru. "And where are you headed?"

Balducci withdrew his mustache from the tea. "Here, son."

"Odd pupils! And you're spending the night?"

"No. I'm going back to El Ameur. And you will deliver this fellow to Tinguit. He is expected at police headquarters."

Balducci was looking at Daru with a friendly little smile.

"What's this story?" asked the schoolmaster. "Are you pulling my leg?"

"No, son. Those are the orders."

"The orders? I'm not . . ." Daru hesitated, not wanting to hurt the old Corsican.[4] "I mean, that's not my job."

"What! What's the meaning of that? In wartime people do all kinds of jobs."

"Then I'll wait for the declaration of war!"

Balducci nodded.

"O.K. But the orders exist and they concern you too. Things are brewing, it appears. There is talk of a forthcoming revolt. We are mobilized, in a way."

Daru still had his obstinate look.

"Listen, son," Balducci said. "I like you and you must understand. There's only a dozen of us at El Ameur to patrol throughout the whole territory of a small department[5] and I must get back in a hurry. I was told to hand this guy over to you and return without delay. He couldn't be kept there. His village was beginning to stir; they wanted to take him back. You must take him to Tinguit tomorrow before the day is over. Twenty kilometers shouldn't faze a husky fellow like you. After that, all will be over. You'll come back to your pupils and your comfortable life."

Behind the wall the horse could be heard snorting and pawing the earth. Daru was looking out the window. Decidedly, the weather was clearing and the light was increasing over the snowy plateau. When all the snow was melted, the sun would take over again and once more would burn the fields of stone. For days, still, the unchanging sky would shed its dry light on the solitary expanse where nothing had any connection with man.

4. Balducci is a native of Corsica, a French island north of Sardinia.

5. French administrative and territorial division; like a county.

"After all," he said, turning around toward Balducci, "what did he do?" And, before the gendarme had opened his mouth, he asked: "Does he speak French?"

"No, not a word. We had been looking for him for a month, but they were hiding him. He killed his cousin."

"Is he against us?"[6]

"I don't think so. But you can never be sure."

"Why did he kill?"

"A family squabble, I think. One owed the other grain, it seems. It's not at all clear. In short, he killed his cousin with a billhook. You know, like a sheep, *kreezk*!"

Balducci made the gesture of drawing a blade across his throat and the Arab, his attention attracted, watched him with a sort of anxiety. Daru felt a sudden wrath against the man, against all men with their rotten spite, their tireless hates, their blood lust.

But the kettle was singing on the stove. He served Balducci more tea, hesitated, then served the Arab again, who, a second time, drank avidly. His raised arms made the jellaba fall open and the schoolmaster saw his thin, muscular chest.

"Thanks, kid," Balducci said. "And now, I'm off."

He got up and went toward the Arab, taking a small rope from his pocket.

"What are you doing?" Daru asked dryly.

Balducci, disconcerted, showed him the rope.

"Don't bother."

The old gendarme hesitated. "It's up to you. Of course, you are armed?"

"I have my shotgun."

"Where?"

"In the trunk."

"You ought to have it near your bed."

"Why? I have nothing to fear."

"You're crazy, son. If there's an uprising, no one is safe, we're all in the same boat."

"I'll defend myself. I'll have time to see them coming."

Balducci began to laugh, then suddenly the mustache covered the white teeth.

"You'll have time? O.K. That's just what I was saying. You have always been a little cracked. That's why I like you, my son was like that."

At the same time he took out his revolver and put it on the desk.

"Keep it; I don't need two weapons from here to El Ameur."

The revolver shone against the black paint of the table. When the gendarme turned toward him, the schoolmaster caught the smell of leather and horseflesh.

"Listen, Balducci," Daru said suddenly, "every bit of this disgusts me, and first of all your fellow here. But I won't hand him over. Fight, yes, if I have to. But not that."

The old gendarme stood in front of him and looked at him severely.

"You're being a fool," he said slowly. "I don't like it either. You don't get used to putting a rope on a man even after years of it, and you're even ashamed—yes, ashamed. But you can't let them have their way."

6. I.e., against the French colonial government.

"I won't hand him over," Daru said again.

"It's an order, son, and I repeat it."

"That's right. Repeat to them what I've said to you: I won't hand him over."

Balducci made a visible effort to reflect. He looked at the Arab and at Daru. At last he decided.

"No, I won't tell them anything. If you want to drop us, go ahead; I'll not denounce you. I have an order to deliver the prisoner and I'm doing so. And now you'll just sign this paper for me."

"There's no need. I'll not deny that you left him with me."

"Don't be mean with me. I know you'll tell the truth. You're from hereabouts and you are a man. But you must sign, that's the rule."

Daru opened his drawer, took out a little square bottle of purple ink, the red wooden penholder with the "sergeant-major" pen he used for making models of penmanship, and signed. The gendarme carefully folded the paper and put it into his wallet. Then he moved toward the door.

"I'll see you off," Daru said.

"No," said Balducci. "There's no use being polite. You insulted me."

He looked at the Arab, motionless in the same spot, sniffed peevishly, and turned away toward the door. "Good-by, son," he said. The door shut behind him. Balducci appeared suddenly outside the window and then disappeared. His footsteps were muffled by the snow. The horse stirred on the other side of the wall and several chickens fluttered in fright. A moment later Balducci reappeared outside the window leading the horse by the bridle. He walked toward the little rise without turning around and disappeared from sight with the horse following him. A big stone could be heard bouncing down. Daru walked back toward the prisoner, who, without stirring, never took his eyes off him. "Wait," the schoolmaster said in Arabic and went toward the bedroom. As he was going through the door, he had a second thought, went to the desk, took the revolver, and stuck it in his pocket. Then, without looking back, he went into his room.

For some time he lay on his couch watching the sky gradually close over, listening to the silence. It was this silence that had seemed painful to him during the first days here, after the war. He had requested a post in the little town at the base of the foothills separating the upper plateaus from the desert. There, rocky walls, green and black to the north, pink and lavender to the south, marked the frontier of eternal summer. He had been named to a post farther north, on the plateau itself. In the beginning, the solitude and the silence had been hard for him on these wastelands peopled only by stones. Occasionally, furrows suggested cultivation, but they had been dug to uncover a certain kind of stone good for building. The only plowing here was to harvest rocks. Elsewhere a thin layer of soil accumulated in the hollows would be scraped out to enrich paltry village gardens. This is the way it was: bare rock covered three quarters of the region. Towns sprang up, flourished, then disappeared; men came by, loved one another or fought bitterly, then died. No one in this desert, neither he nor his guest, mattered. And yet, outside this desert neither of them, Daru knew, could have really lived.

When he got up, no noise came from the classroom. He was amazed at the unmixed joy he derived from the mere thought that the Arab might have fled and that he would be alone with no decision to make. But the prisoner was there. He had merely stretched out between the stove and the desk. With eyes open, he was staring at the ceiling. In that position, his thick lips were particularly noticeable, giving him a pouting look. "Come," said Daru. The Arab got up and followed him. In the bedroom, the schoolmaster pointed to a chair near the table under the window. The Arab sat down without taking his eyes off Daru.

"Are you hungry?"

"Yes," the prisoner said.

Daru set the table for two. He took flour and oil, shaped a cake in a frying-pan, and lighted the little stove that functioned on bottled gas. While the cake was cooking, he went out to the shed to get cheese, eggs, dates, and condensed milk. When the cake was done he set it on the window sill to cool, heated some condensed milk diluted with water, and beat up the eggs into an omelette. In one of his motions he knocked against the revolver stuck in his right pocket. He set the bowl down, went into the classroom, and put the revolver in his desk drawer. When he came back to the room, night was falling. He put on the light and served the Arab. "Eat," he said. The Arab took a piece of the cake, lifted it eagerly to his mouth, and stopped short.

"And you?" he asked.

"After you. I'll eat too."

The thick lips opened slightly. The Arab hesitated, then bit into the cake determinedly.

The meal over, the Arab looked at the schoolmaster. "Are you the judge?"

"No, I'm simply keeping you until tomorrow."

"Why do you eat with me?"

"I'm hungry."

The Arab fell silent. Daru got up and went out. He brought back a folding bed from the shed, set it up between the table and the stove, perpendicular to his own bed. From a large suitcase which, upright in a corner, served as a shelf for papers, he took two blankets and arranged them on the camp bed. Then he stopped, felt useless, and sat down on his bed. There was nothing more to do or to get ready. He had to look at this man. He looked at him, therefore, trying to imagine his face bursting with rage. He couldn't do so. He could see nothing but the dark yet shining eyes and the animal mouth.

"Why did you kill him?" he asked in a voice whose hostile tone surprised him.

The Arab looked away.

"He ran away. I ran after him."

He raised his eyes to Daru again and they were full of a sort of woeful interrogation. "Now what will they do to me?"

"Are you afraid?"

He stiffened, turning his eyes away.

"Are you sorry?"

The Arab stared at him openmouthed. Obviously he did not understand. Daru's annoyance was growing. At the same time he felt awkward and self-conscious with his big body wedged between the two beds.

"Lie down there," he said impatiently. "That's your bed."

The Arab didn't move. He called to Daru:

"Tell me!"

The schoolmaster looked at him.

"Is the gendarme coming back tomorrow?"

"I don't know."

"Are you coming with us?"

"I don't know. Why?"

The prisoner got up and stretched out on top of the blankets, his feet toward the window. The light from the electric bulb shone straight into his eyes and he closed them at once.

"Why?" Daru repeated, standing beside the bed.

The Arab opened his eyes under the blinding light and looked at him, trying not to blink.

"Come with us," he said.

In the middle of the night, Daru was still not asleep. He had gone to bed after undressing completely; he generally slept naked. But when he suddenly realized that he had nothing on, he hesitated. He felt vulnerable and the temptation came to him to put his clothes back on. Then he shrugged his shoulders; after all, he wasn't a child and, if need be, he could break his adversary in two. From his bed he could observe him, lying on his back, still motionless with his eyes closed under the harsh light. When Daru turned out the light, the darkness seemed to coagulate all of a sudden. Little by little, the night came back to life in the window where the starless sky was stirring gently. The schoolmaster soon made out the body lying at his feet. The Arab still did not move, but his eyes seemed open. A faint wind was prowling around the schoolhouse. Perhaps it would drive away the clouds and the sun would reappear.

During the night the wind increased. The hens fluttered a little and then were silent. The Arab turned over on his side with his back to Daru, who thought he heard him moan. Then he listened for his guest's breathing, become heavier and more regular. He listened to that breath so close to him and mused without being able to go to sleep. In this room where he had been sleeping alone for a year, this presence bothered him. But it bothered him also by imposing on him a sort of brotherhood he knew well but refused to accept in the present circumstances. Men who share the same rooms, soldiers or prisoners, develop a strange alliance as if, having cast off their armor with their clothing, they fraternized every evening, over and above their differences, in the ancient community of dream and fatigue. But Daru shook himself; he didn't like such musings, and it was essential to sleep.

A little later, however, when the Arab stirred slightly, the schoolmaster was still not asleep. When the prisoner made a second move, he stiffened, on the alert. The Arab was lifting himself slowly on his arms with almost the motion of a sleepwalker. Seated upright in bed, he waited motionless without turning his head toward Daru, as if he were listening attentively. Daru did not stir; it had just occurred to him that the revolver was still in the drawer of his desk. It was better to act at once. Yet he continued to observe the prisoner, who, with the same slithery motion, put his feet on the ground, waited again, then began to stand up slowly. Daru was about to call out to him when the Arab began to walk, in a quite natural but extraordinarily silent way. He was heading toward the door at the end of the room that opened into the shed. He lifted the latch with precaution and went out, pushing the door behind him but without shutting it. Daru had not stirred. "He is running away," he merely thought. "Good riddance!" Yet he listened attentively. The hens were not fluttering; the guest must be on the plateau. A faint sound of water reached him, and he didn't know what it was until the Arab again stood framed in the doorway, closed the door carefully, and came back to bed without a sound. Then Daru turned his back on him and fell asleep. Still later he seemed, from the depths of his sleep, to hear furtive steps around the schoolhouse. "I'm dreaming! I'm dreaming!" he repeated to himself. And he went on sleeping.

When he awoke, the sky was clear; the loose window let in a cold, pure air. The Arab was asleep, hunched up under the blankets now, his mouth open, utterly relaxed. But when Daru shook him, he started dreadfully, staring at Daru with wild eyes as if he had never seen him and such a frightened expression that the schoolmaster stepped back. "Don't be afraid. It's me. You must eat." The Arab nodded his head and said yes. Calm had returned to his face, but his expression was vacant and listless.

The coffee was ready. They drank it seated together on the folding bed as they munched their pieces of the cake. Then Daru led the Arab under the shed and showed him the faucet where he washed. He went back into the room, folded the blankets and the bed, made his own bed and put the room in order. Then he went through the classroom and out onto the terrace. The sun was already rising in the blue sky; a soft, bright light was bathing the deserted plateau. On the ridge the snow was melting in spots. The stones were about to reappear. Crouched on the edge of the plateau, the schoolmaster looked at the deserted expanse. He thought of Balducci. He had hurt him, for he had sent him off in a way as if he didn't want to be associated with him. He could still hear the gendarme's farewell and, without knowing why, he felt strangely empty and vulnerable. At that moment, from the other side of the schoolhouse, the prisoner coughed. Daru listened to him almost despite himself and then, furious, threw a pebble that whistled through the air before sinking into the snow. That man's stupid crime revolted him, but to hand him over was contrary to honor. Merely thinking of it made him smart with humiliation. And he cursed at one and the same time his own people who had sent him this Arab and the Arab too who had dared to kill and not managed to get away. Daru got up, walked in a circle on the terrace, waited motionless, and then went back into the schoolhouse.

The Arab, leaning over the cement floor of the shed, was washing his teeth with two fingers. Daru looked at him and said: "Come." He went back into the room ahead of the prisoner. He slipped a hunting-jacket on over his sweater and put on walking-shoes. Standing, he waited until the Arab had put on his *chèche* and sandals. They went into the classroom and the schoolmaster pointed to the exit, saying: "Go ahead." The fellow didn't budge. "I'm coming," said Daru. The Arab went out. Daru went back into the room and made a package of pieces of rusk, dates, and sugar. In the classroom, before going out, he hesitated a second in front of his desk, then crossed the threshold and locked the door. "That's the way," he said. He started toward the east, followed by the prisoner. But, a short distance from the schoolhouse, he thought he heard a slight sound behind them. He retraced his steps and examined the surroundings of the house, there was no one there. The Arab watched him without seeming to understand. "Come on," said Daru.

They walked for an hour and rested beside a sharp peak of limestone. The snow was melting faster and faster and the sun was drinking up the puddles at once, rapidly cleaning the plateau, which gradually dried and vibrated like the air itself. When they resumed walking, the ground rang under their feet. From time to time a bird rent the space in front of them with a joyful cry. Daru breathed in deeply the fresh morning light. He felt a sort of rapture before the vast familiar expanse, now almost entirely yellow under its dome of blue sky. They walked an hour more, descending toward the south. They reached a level height made up of crumbly rocks. From there on, the plateau sloped down, eastward, toward a low plain where there were a few spindly trees and, to the south, toward outcroppings of rock that gave the landscape a chaotic look.

Daru surveyed the two directions. There was nothing but the sky on the horizon. Not a man could be seen. He turned toward the Arab, who was looking at him blankly. Daru held out the package to him. "Take it," he said. "There are dates, bread, and sugar. You can hold out for two days. Here are a thousand francs too." The Arab took the package and the money but kept his full hands at chest level as if he didn't know what to do with what was being given him. "Now look," the schoolmaster said as he pointed in the direction of the east, "there's the way to Tinguit. You have a two-hour walk. At Tinguit you'll find the administration and the police. They are expecting you." The Arab looked toward the east, still holding the package and the money against his chest. Daru took his elbow and turned him rather roughly toward the south. At the foot of the height on which they stood could be seen a faint path. "That's the trail across the plateau. In a day's walk from here you'll find pasturelands and the first nomads. They'll take you in and shelter you according to their law." The Arab had now turned toward Daru and a sort of panic was visible in his expression. "Listen," he said. Daru shook his head: "No, be quiet. Now I'm leaving you." He turned his back on him, took two long steps in the direction of the school, looked hesitantly at the motionless Arab, and started off again. For a few minutes he heard nothing but his own step resounding on the cold ground and did not turn his head. A moment later, however, he turned around. The Arab was still there on the edge of the hill, his arms hanging now, and he was looking at the schoolmaster. Daru felt something rise in his throat. But he swore with impatience, waved vaguely, and started off again. He had already gone some distance when he again stopped and looked. There was no longer anyone on the hill.

Daru hesitated. The sun was now rather high in the sky and was beginning to beat down on his head. The schoolmaster retraced his steps, at first somewhat uncertainly, then with decision. When he reached the little hill, he was bathed in sweat. He climbed it as fast as he could and stopped, out of breath, at the top. The rock-fields to the south stood out sharply against the blue sky, but on the plain to the east a steamy heat was already rising. And in that slight haze, Daru, with heavy heart, made out the Arab walking slowly on the road to prison.

A little later, standing before the window of the classroom, the schoolmaster was watching the clear light bathing the whole surface of the plateau, but he hardly saw it. Behind him on the blackboard, among the winding French rivers, sprawled the clumsily chalked-up words he had just read: "You handed over our brother. You will pay for this." Daru looked at the sky, the plateau, and, beyond, the invisible lands stretching all the way to the sea. In this vast landscape he had loved so much, he was alone.

1957

SAMUEL BECKETT
1906–1989

At once among the grimmest and funniest of modern writers, Samuel Beckett offers in his novels and plays a stark, spare representation of the human condition in its "absurd" emptiness. Beckett's world is haunted by an absence of meaning at the core, yet the absence of meaning becomes the occasion for puns, parodies, and clowning. Filling the void with desperate stagecraft and patter, Beckett's characters live out a hopeless attempt to find or to create meaning for themselves. Often they spend their lives waiting for an explanation that never comes; and yet Beckett makes this predicament a source of intense black humor.

Born near Dublin on April 13, 1906 (Good Friday), to a well-to-do Protestant family, Beckett was educated in Ireland and received a bachelor's degree from Trinity College in 1927. He then taught English for two years at the École Normale Supérieure in Paris, where he met **James Joyce** and was influenced by the older novelist's exuberant and punning use of language. Beckett wrote an essay on the early stages of Joyce's *Finnegans Wake* and later helped in the French translation of some portions of the book. In 1930, Beckett entered a competition for a poem on the subject of time and won first prize with a ninety-eight-line (and seventeen-footnote) dramatic monologue, *Whoroscope*; the poem's speaker is the seventeenth-century French philosopher René Descartes, whose ideas about the dualism between mind and body became an obsession of Beckett's literary work. Beckett returned to Trinity College, where he took a master's degree in 1931, published an essay on **Marcel Proust**, and briefly taught French. In 1937, after living in England, France, and Germany, Beckett made Paris his permanent home. During the Second World War, Beckett worked for the French Resistance, helping to collate intelligence reports from occupied France. Nearly discovered by the Nazis, he fled south to Roussillon, where he remained for the rest of the war. On a visit to his mother in Dublin after the war, Beckett experienced a revelation, seemingly connected with the concept of nothingness, that he recalled (in his characteristically elliptical way) in the later play *Krapp's Last Tape* (1958). In the scene the main character listens to a tape of his own voice recollecting an earlier vision:

> Spiritually a year of profound gloom and indigence until that memorable night in March, at the end of the jetty, in the howling wind, never to be forgotten, when suddenly I saw the whole thing. The vision, at last. . . . What I suddenly saw then was this, that the belief I had been going on all my life, namely—. . . that the dark I have always struggled to keep under is in reality my most . . .

Before this belief can be revealed, however, Krapp switches off the tape and winds it forward, so that the audience never learns the content of the revelation. Beckett later told his biographer that the missing words were "precious ally." Certainly, in the years after the war, Beckett made darkness his ally.

Although two highly amusing early novels, *Murphy* (1938) and *Watt* (published in 1953), were written in English, during the war Beckett turned to French as his preferred language for composition. In the years after the war, he wrote almost exclusively in French and only later translated the texts (often with substantial changes) into English. He explained his choice of language for creating his works: "in French it is easier to write without style"—without the native speaker's temptation to elegance and virtuoso display. Comparing the French and English versions of Beckett's works often suggests such a contrast, with the French text closer to basic grammatical forms and therefore possessing a harsher, starker focus. Indeed, Beckett claimed to care little about the formalities of language. "Grammar and Style," he wrote: "To me they seem to have become as irrelevant as a Victorian bathing suit or the imperturbability of a true gentleman. A mask. Let us hope the time will come . . . when language is most efficiently used where it is most efficiently misused." He sought a way to achieve a language of darkness, a language suitable to the postwar world in which old proprieties should be discarded in favor of a more austere, less artificial reality. Yet, as if against his will, he infused these dark and minimalist works with the wit and eloquence of his personal idiom. He later compared himself to his old friend Joyce: "The more Joyce knew the more he could. He's tending toward omniscience and omnipotence as an artist. I'm working with impotence, ignorance." The movement toward reductionism and minimalism helped to define postwar literature.

Beckett's first works in the spare style were a trilogy of novels, completed in 1949: *Molloy* (published in 1951), *Malone Dies* (1951), and *The Unnamable* (1953). The narrative perspective moves from a series of related monologues (in which a number of narrators, all of whose names begin with "M," come increasingly to resemble one another) to the ramblings, at the end, of an "unnamable" speaker who seems to represent them all. The reader can never be sure who is speaking, whether what the narrator is saying is true in the fictional world, or what the relationships among the various narrators might be. Beckett's early fiction received admiring attention from the philosopher Jean-Paul Sartre, among others, but Beckett's true fame came suddenly with the production of his first play, *Waiting for Godot* (published in 1952), first in French (1953), then in English (1955). The play's popularity showed that absurdist theater—with its empty, repetitive dialogue, its grotesquely bare yet evidently symbolic settings, and its refusal to build to a dramatic climax—could have meaning even for audiences accustomed to theatrical realism and logical plots. The audiences encountered two clownlike tramps, Vladimir and Estragon (Didi and Gogo), talking, quarreling, falling down, contemplating suicide, and generally filling up time with conversation that ranges from vaudeville patter to metaphysical speculation as they wait under a tree for "Godot," who never comes. Instead, the two are joined by another grotesque pair: the rich Pozzo and his brutally abused servant, Lucky, whom he leads around by a rope tied to the neck. As the first act comes to an end, Vladimir and Estragon agree to give up waiting, to leave; yet as the curtain falls, they stay where they are. A plot summary of the second act would be virtually identical with a summary of the first. As one critic put it, in *Waiting for Godot*, "nothing happens, twice." The popular interpretation of "Godot" as a diminutive for "God," and of the play as a statement of existential anguish at the inexplicable human condition, is scarcely defused by Beckett's caution that "If by Godot I had meant God, I would have said God." Yet identifying Godot is less important than identifying the wretched plight on stage as symbolically our own, and identifying *with* the characters as they express the anxious, often repugnant, but also comic picture of human relationships in an absurd universe. Both *Waiting for Godot* and *Endgame* draw on the full resources of modern theater while stripping the elements of traditional theater—plot, character, setting, dialogue—to a minimum.

After the popular success of *Waiting for Godot*, Beckett wrote *Endgame* (French version performed 1957; English, 1958) and a series of stage plays and brief pieces for the radio. The stage plays have the same bare yet striking settings: *Krapp's Last Tape* presents an old man sitting at a table with his tape recorder, recalling a love affair thirty years past; *Happy Days* (1961) portrays a married couple, with the wife chattering ceaselessly about her possessions, although she is buried in dirt up to her waist in the first act and up to her neck in the second. When he received the Nobel Prize for Literature in 1969, Beckett's wife declared the prize a "catastrophe" and another friend advised him to go into hiding—he was now a world-famous author, much sought after by admirers. In later years he wrote a number of shorter plays and novels, moving in the direction he had identified as distinguishing him from Joyce: toward minimalism, ignorance, and impotence. An unidentified voice in one of his final novellas, *Worstward Ho* (1983), says, "Fail again. Fail better." Beckett continued to produce successful works about failure for the rest of his long life. He died in a nursing home at the age of 83. The Nobel Prize conferred recognition on Beckett as the purest exponent of the twentieth century's chief philosophical dilemma: the notion of the "absurd," or the contradiction between human attempts to discover meaning in life and the simultaneous conviction that no "meaning" exists that we have not created ourselves.

Endgame, the play printed here, often called Beckett's major achievement, is a prime example of this dilemma. When the curtain rises on *Endgame*, the world seems to awaken from sleep. The sheets draping the furniture and central character are taken off, and Hamm sets himself in motion like an actor or a chess pawn: "Me . . . to play." Yet we are also near the story's end, for, as the title implies, nothing new will happen. An "endgame" is the final phase of a chess game, the stage at which the end is predictably in sight although the play must still be completed. Throughout, the theme of "end," "finish," "no more" resounds, even while Hamm notes the passage of time: "Something is taking its course." But time does not lead anywhere; it is either past or present and always barren. The past exists as Nagg's and Nell's memories, as Hamm's story, which may or may not describe Clov's entry into the home, and as a period when Clov once loved Hamm. The present shows four characters dwindling away, alone in a dead world, caught between bleak visions of hell and dreams of life reborn. In one of the biblical echoes that permeate the play, Hamm and Clov repeatedly evoke the final words of the crucified Jesus in the Gospel according to John: "It is finished." But this is not a biblical morality play, and *Endgame* describes a world not of divine creation but of self-creation. It is even possible that Hamm is composing and directing the entire performance: he is a storyteller and playwright with "asides" and "last soliloquy" whose "dialogue" keeps Clov onstage against his will, who (when looking out the window onto a clearly flourishing world) can see only dust and ashes, or a magician presiding over an imaginary kingdom who concludes a personal narrative and hopeless prayer with Prospero's line from Shakespeare's *The Tempest* (4.1.148): "Our revels now are ended." Or perhaps Hamm is simply the only character who is aware of his or her life *as* a performance, without other meaning. (As Shakespeare's passage continues later, "We are such stuff / As dreams are made on, and our little life / Is rounded with a sleep.") By the end of the play, the situation has changed little: it just becomes barer, as Hamm discards his stick, whistle, and dog, "reckoning closed and story ended." Yet as Hamm covers his face after this line, Clov is still waiting to depart rather than actually departing. It is not impossible that the play will resume in precisely the same terms tomorrow.

Like *Waiting for Godot*, *Endgame* has been given a number of interpretations. Some refer to Beckett's love of wordplay: Hamm as Hamm-actor, Hammlet, Hammer. The setting of a boxlike room with two windows is seen as a skull, the seat of consciousness, or (emphasizing the bloody handkerchief and the reference to fontanelles—the soft spot in the skull of a newborn) as a womb. The characters' isolation in a dead world after an unnamed catastrophe (which may be Hamm's fault) suggests the world after atomic holocaust. Or, for those who recall Beckett's fascination with the apathetic figure of Belacqua waiting, in the Purgatory of Dante's *Divine Comedy*, for his punishment to begin, *Endgame* evokes an image of pre-Purgatorial consciousness. The ash cans in which Hamm has "bottled" his parents, and the general cruelty between characters, may represent the dustbin of modern Western civilized values (while they also offer a sort of slapstick humor). Hamm and Clov represent the uneasy adjustment of soul and body, the class struggle of rich and poor, or the master-slave relationship in all senses (including the slave's acceptance of victimization). Clearly Beckett has created a structure that accommodates all these readings while authorizing none. He himself said to the director Alan Schneider that he was less interested in symbolism than in describing a "local situation," an interaction of four characters in a given set of circumstances, and that the audience's interpretation was its own responsibility.

Beckett both authorized and denied these interpretations. He pruned down an earlier, more anecdotal two-act play to achieve *Endgame*'s skeletal plot and almost anonymous characters, and in doing so, created a structure that immediately elicits the reader's instinct to "fill in the blanks." His puns and allusions point to a further meaning that *may* be contained in the implied reference but may also be part of an infinite regress of meaning—expressing the "absurd" itself. Working against too heavy an insistence on symbolic meanings is the fact that the play is funny—especially when performed on stage. The characters popping out of ash cans; the jerky, repetitive motions with which Clov carries out his master's commands; and the often obscene vaudeville patter accompanied by appropriate gestures—all provide a comic perspective that keeps *Endgame* from sinking into tragic despair. The intellectual distance offered by comedy is entirely in keeping with the more somber side of the play, which rejects pathos and constantly drags its characters' escapist fancies down to the minimal facts of survival: food, shelter, sleep, painkiller. Thus it is possible to say that *Endgame* describes—but only among many other things—what it is like to be alive, declining toward death in a world without meaning.

Endgame[1]

For Roger Blin

CHARACTERS

NAGG
NELL
HAMM
CLOV

Bare interior.
Gray light.
Left and right back, high up, two small windows, curtains drawn.
Front right, a door. Hanging near door, its face to wall, a picture.
Front left, touching each other, covered with an old sheet, two ashbins.
Center, in an armchair on castors, covered with an old sheet, HAMM.
Motionless by the door, his eyes fixed on HAMM, CLOV. *Very red face.*
Brief tableau.

[CLOV *goes and stands under window left. Stiff, staggering walk. He looks up at window left. He turns and looks at window right. He goes and stands under window right. He looks up at window right. He turns and looks at window left. He goes out, comes back immediately with a small step-ladder, carries it over and sets it down under window left, gets up on it, draws back curtain. He gets down, takes six steps (for example) towards window right, goes back for ladder, carries it over and sets it down under window right, gets up on it, draws back curtain. He gets down, takes three steps towards window right, goes back for ladder, carries it over and sets it down under window left, gets up on it, looks out of window. Brief laugh. He gets down, takes one step towards window right, goes back for ladder, carries it over and sets it down under window right, gets up on it, looks out of window. Brief laugh. He gets down, goes with ladder towards ashbins, halts, turns, carries back ladder and sets it down under window right, goes to ashbins, removes sheet covering them, folds it over his arm. He raises one lid, stoops and looks into bin. Brief laugh. He closes lid. Same with other bin. He goes to* HAMM, *removes sheet covering him, folds it over his arm. In a dressing-gown, a stiff toque*[2] *on his head, a large blood-stained handkerchief over his face, a whistle hanging from his neck, a rug over his knees, thick socks on his feet,* HAMM *seems to be asleep.* CLOV *looks him over. Brief laugh. He goes to door, halts, turns towards auditorium.*]

CLOV [*Fixed gaze, tonelessly.*] Finished, it's finished, nearly finished, it must be nearly finished. [*Pause.*] Grain upon grain, one by one, and one day, suddenly, there's a heap, a little heap, the impossible heap. [*Pause.*] I can't be punished any more. [*Pause.*] I'll go now to my kitchen, ten feet by ten feet by ten feet, and wait for him to whistle me. [*Pause.*] Nice dimensions, nice proportions, I'll lean on the table, and look at the wall, and wait for him to whistle me.

[*He remains a moment motionless, then goes out. He comes back immediately, goes to window right, takes up the ladder and carries it out. Pause.*

1. Translated by the author.
2. A fitted cloth hat with little or no brim, sometimes indicating official status, as with a judge's toque.

HAMM *stirs. He yawns under the handkerchief. He removes the handkerchief from his face. Very red face. Black glasses.*]

HAMM Me— [*He yawns.*] —to play[3] [*He holds the handkerchief spread out before him.*] Old Stancher![4] [*He takes off his glasses, wipes his eyes, his face, the glasses, puts them on again, folds the handkerchief and puts it back neatly in the breast-pocket of his dressing-gown. He clears his throat, joins the tips of his fingers.*] Can there be misery— [*He yawns.*] —loftier than mine? No doubt. Formerly. But now? [*Pause.*] My father? [*Pause.*] My mother? [*Pause.*] My . . . dog? [*Pause.*] Oh I am willing to believe they suffer as much as such creatures can suffer. But does that mean their sufferings equal mine? No doubt. [*Pause.*] No, all is a— [*He yawns.*] —bsolute, [*Proudly.*] the bigger a man is the fuller he is. [*Pause. Gloomily.*] And the emptier. [*He sniffs.*] Clov! [*Pause.*] No, alone. [*Pause.*] What dreams! Those forests! [*Pause.*] Enough, it's time it ended, in the shelter too. [*Pause.*] And yet I hesitate, I hesitate to . . . to end. Yes, there it is, it's time it ended and yet I hesitate to— [*He yawns.*] —to end. [*Yawns.*] God, I'm tired, I'd be better off in bed. [*He whistles. Enter* CLOV *immediately. He halts beside the chair.*] You pollute the air! [*Pause.*] Get me ready, I'm going to bed.

CLOV I've just got you up.

HAMM And what of it?

CLOV I can't be getting you up and putting you to bed every five minutes, I have things to do. [*Pause.*]

HAMM Did you ever see my eyes?

CLOV No.

HAMM Did you never have the curiosity, while I was sleeping, to take off my glasses and look at my eyes?

CLOV Pulling back the lids? [*Pause.*] No.

HAMM One of these days I'll show them to you. [*Pause.*] It seems they've gone all white. [*Pause.*] What time is it?

CLOV The same as usual.

HAMM [*Gesture towards window right.*] Have you looked?

CLOV Yes.

HAMM Well?

CLOV Zero.

HAMM It'd need to rain.

CLOV It won't rain. [*Pause.*]

HAMM Apart from that, how do you feel?

CLOV I don't complain.

HAMM You feel normal?

CLOV [*Irritably.*] I tell you I don't complain.

HAMM I feel a little queer. [*Pause.*] Clov!

CLOV Yes.

HAMM Have you not had enough?

CLOV Yes! [*Pause.*] Of what?

3. Hamm announces that it is his move at the beginning of *Endgame*: the comparison is with a game of chess, of which the "endgame" is the final stage.

4. The handkerchief that stanches his blood.

HAMM Of this . . . this . . . thing.

CLOV I always had. [*Pause.*] Not you?

HAMM [*Gloomily.*] Then there's no reason for it to change.

CLOV It may end. [*Pause.*] All life long the same questions, the same answers.

HAMM Get me ready. [CLOV *does not move.*] Go and get the sheet. [CLOV *does not move.*] Clov!

CLOV Yes.

HAMM I'll give you nothing more to eat.

CLOV Then we'll die.

HAMM I'll give you just enough to keep you from dying. You'll be hungry all the time.

CLOV Then we won't die. [*Pause.*] I'll go and get the sheet. [*He goes towards the door.*]

HAMM No! [CLOV *halts.*] I'll give you one biscuit per day. [*Pause.*] One and a half. [*Pause.*] Why do you stay with me?

CLOV Why do you keep me?

HAMM There's no one else.

CLOV There's nowhere else. [*Pause.*]

HAMM You're leaving me all the same.

CLOV I'm trying.

HAMM You don't love me.

CLOV No.

HAMM You loved me once.

CLOV Once!

HAMM I've made you suffer too much. [*Pause.*] Haven't I?

CLOV It's not that.

HAMM [*Shocked.*] I haven't made you suffer too much?

CLOV Yes!

HAMM [*Relieved.*] Ah you gave me a fright! [*Pause. Coldly.*] Forgive me. [*Pause. Louder.*] I said, Forgive me.

CLOV I heard you. [*Pause.*] Have you bled?

HAMM Less. [*Pause.*] Is it not time for my pain-killer?

CLOV No. [*Pause.*]

HAMM How are your eyes?

CLOV Bad.

HAMM How are your legs?

CLOV BAD.

HAMM But you can move.

CLOV Yes.

HAMM [*Violently.*] Then move! [CLOV *goes to back wall, leans against it with his forehead and hands.*] Where are you?

CLOV Here.

HAMM Come back! [CLOV *returns to his place beside the chair.*] Where are you?

CLOV Here.

HAMM Why don't you kill me?

CLOV I don't know the combination of the cupboard. [*Pause.*]

HAMM Go and get two bicycle-wheels.

CLOV There are no more bicycle-wheels.

HAMM What have you done with your bicycle?

CLOV I never had a bicycle.

HAMM The thing is impossible.

CLOV When there were still bicycles I wept to have one. I crawled at your feet. You told me to go to hell. Now there are none.

HAMM And your rounds? When you inspected my paupers. Always on foot?

CLOV Sometimes on horse. [*The lid of one of the bins lifts and the hands of* NAGG *appear, gripping the rim. Then his head emerges. Nightcap. Very white face.* NAGG *yawns, then listens.*] I'll leave you, I have things to do.

HAMM In your kitchen?

CLOV Yes.

HAMM Outside of here it's death. [*Pause.*] All right, be off. [*Exit* CLOV. *Pause.*] We're getting on.

NAGG Me pap![5]

HAMM Accursed progenitor!

NAGG Me pap!

HAMM The old folks at home! No decency left! Guzzle, guzzle, that's all they think of. [*He whistles. Enter* CLOV. *He halts beside the chair.*] Well! I thought you were leaving me.

CLOV Oh not just yet, not just yet.

NAGG Me pap!

HAMM Give him his pap.

CLOV There's no more pap.

HAMM [*To* NAGG.] Do you hear that? There's no more pap. You'll never get any more pap.

NAGG I want me pap!

HAMM Give him a biscuit. [*Exit* CLOV.] Accursed fornicator! How are your stumps?

NAGG Never mind me stumps.

[*Enter* CLOV *with biscuit.*]

CLOV I'm back again, with the biscuit. [*He gives biscuit to* NAGG *who fingers it, sniffs it.*]

NAGG [*Plaintively.*] What is it?

CLOV Spratt's medium.[6]

NAGG [*As before.*] It's hard! I can't!

HAMM Bottle him!

[CLOV *pushes* NAGG *back into the bin, closes the lid.*]

CLOV [*Returning to his place beside the chair.*] If age but knew!

HAMM Sit on him!

CLOV I can't sit.

HAMM True. And I can't stand.

CLOV So it is.

HAMM Every man his speciality. [*Pause.*] No phone calls? [*Pause.*] Don't we laugh?

5. Food, mush.
6. A common plain cookie.

CLOV [*After reflection.*] I don't feel like it.
HAMM [*After reflection.*] Nor I. [*Pause.*] Clov!
CLOV Yes.
HAMM Nature has forgotten us.
CLOV There's no more nature.
HAMM No more nature! You exaggerate.
CLOV In the vicinity.
HAMM But we breathe, we change! We lose our hair, our teeth! Our bloom! Our ideals!
CLOV Then she hasn't forgotten us.
HAMM But you say there is none.
CLOV [*Sadly.*] No one that ever lived ever thought so crooked as we.
HAMM We do what we can.
CLOV We shouldn't. [*Pause.*]
HAMM You're a bit of all right, aren't you?[7]
CLOV A smithereen.[8] [*Pause.*]
HAMM This is slow work. [*Pause.*] Is it not time for my pain-killer?
CLOV No. [*Pause.*] I'll leave you, I have things to do.
HAMM In your kitchen?
CLOV Yes.
HAMM What, I'd like to know.
CLOV I look at the wall.
HAMM The wall! And what do you see on your wall? Mene, mene?[9] Naked bodies?
CLOV I see my light dying.
HAMM Your light dying! Listen to that! Well, it can die just as well here, *your* light. Take a look at me and then come back and tell me what you think of *your* light. [*Pause.*]
CLOV You shouldn't speak to me like that. [*Pause.*]
HAMM [*Coldly.*] Forgive me. [*Pause. Louder.*] I said, Forgive me.
CLOV I heard you.

[*The lid of* NAGG*'s bin lifts. His hands appear, gripping the rim. Then his head emerges. In his mouth the biscuit. He listens.*]

HAMM Did your seeds come up?
CLOV No.
HAMM Did you scratch round them to see if they had sprouted?
CLOV They haven't sprouted.
HAMM Perhaps it's still too early.
CLOV If they were going to sprout they would have sprouted. [*Violently.*] They'll never sprout!

[*Pause.* NAGG *takes biscuit in his hand.*]

HAMM This is not much fun. [*Pause.*] But that's always the way at the end of the day, isn't it, Clov?
CLOV Always.

7. You're pretty good, aren't you? (British slang).
8. A tiny bit.
9. From Daniel 5.25: "Mene, mene, tekel, upharsin"; words written by a divine hand on the wall during the feast of Belshazzar, king of Babylon. They predict doom and tell the king "Thou art weighed in the balances, and art found wanting" (Daniel 5.27).

HAMM It's the end of the day like any other day, isn't it, Clov?

CLOV Looks like it. [*Pause.*]

HAMM [*Anguished.*] What's happening, what's happening?

CLOV Something is taking its course. [*Pause.*]

HAMM All right, be off. [*He leans back in his chair, remains motionless.* CLOV *does not move, heaves a great groaning sigh.* HAMM *sits up.*] I thought I told you to be off.

CLOV I'm trying. [*He goes to door, halts.*] Ever since I was whelped.
[*Exit* CLOV.]

HAMM We're getting on.
[*He leans back in his chair, remains motionless.* NAGG *knocks on the lid of the other bin. Pause. He knocks harder. The lid lifts and the hands of* NELL *appear, gripping the rim. Then her head emerges. Lace cap. Very white face.*]

NELL What is it, my pet? [*Pause.*] Time for love?

NAGG Were you asleep?

NELL Oh no!

NAGG Kiss me.

NELL We can't.

NAGG Try.
[*Their heads strain towards each other, fail to meet, fall apart again.*]

NELL Why this farce, day after day? [*Pause.*]

NAGG I've lost me tooth.

NELL When?

NAGG I had it yesterday.

NELL [*Elegiac.*] Ah yesterday!
[*They turn painfully towards each other.*]

NAGG Can you see me?

NELL Hardly. And you?

NAGG What?

NELL Can you see me?

NAGG Hardly.

NELL So much the better, so much the better.

NAGG Don't say that. [*Pause.*] Our sight has failed.

NELL Yes.
[*Pause. They turn away from each other.*]

NAGG Can you hear me?

NELL Yes. And you?

NAGG Yes. [*Pause.*] Our hearing hasn't failed.

NELL Our what?

NAGG Our hearing.

NELL No. [*Pause.*] Have you anything else to say to me?

NAGG Do you remember—

NELL No.

NAGG When we crashed on our tandem[1] and lost our shanks.
[*They laugh heartily.*]

NELL It was in the Ardennes.
[*They laugh less heartily.*]

1. A bicycle built for two.

NAGG On the road to Sedan.[2] [*They laugh still less heartily.*] Are you cold?

NELL Yes, perished. And you?

NAGG [*Pause.*] I'm freezing. [*Pause.*] Do you want to go in?

NELL Yes.

NAGG Then go in. [NELL *does not move.*] Why don't you go in?

NELL I don't know. [*Pause.*]

NAGG Has he changed your sawdust?

NELL It isn't sawdust. [*Pause. Wearily.*] Can you not be a little accurate, Nagg?

NAGG Your sand then. It's not important.

NELL It is important. [*Pause.*]

NAGG It was sawdust once.

NELL Once!

NAGG And now it's sand. [*Pause.*] From the shore. [*Pause. Impatiently.*] Now it's sand he fetches from the shore.

NELL Now it's sand.

NAGG Has he changed yours?

NELL No.

NAGG Nor mine. [*Pause.*] I won't have it! [*Pause. Holding up the biscuit.*] Do you want a bit?

NELL No. [*Pause.*] Of what?

NAGG Biscuit. I've kept you half. [*He looks at the biscuit. Proudly.*] Three quarters. For you. Here. [*He proffers the biscuit.*] No? [*Pause.*] Do you not feel well?

HAMM [*Wearily.*] Quiet, quiet, you're keeping me awake. [*Pause.*] Talk softer. [*Pause.*] If I could sleep I might make love. I'd go into the woods. My eyes would see . . . the sky, the earth. I'd run, they wouldn't catch me. [*Pause.*] Nature! [*Pause.*] There's something dripping in my head. [*Pause.*] A heart, a heart in my head. [*Pause.*]

NAGG [*Soft.*] Do you hear him? A heart in his head! [*He chuckles cautiously.*]

NELL One mustn't laugh at those things, Nagg. Why must you always laugh at them?

NAGG Not so loud!

NELL [*Without lowering her voice.*] Nothing is funnier than unhappiness, I grant you that. But—

NAGG [*Shocked.*] Oh!

NELL Yes, yes, it's the most comical thing in the world. And we laugh, we laugh, with a will, in the beginning. But it's always the same thing. Yes, it's like the funny story we have heard too often, we still find it funny, but we don't laugh any more. [*Pause.*] Have you anything else to say to me?

NAGG No.

NELL Are you quite sure? [*Pause.*] Then I'll leave you.

NAGG Do you not want your biscuit? [*Pause.*] I'll keep it for you. [*Pause.*] I thought you were going to leave me.

NELL I am going to leave you.

NAGG Could you give me a scratch before you go?

2. Town in northern France where the French were defeated in the Franco-Prussian War (1870). Ardennes is a forest in northern France, the scene of bitter fighting in both world wars.

NELL No. [*Pause.*] Where?
NAGG In the back.
NELL No. [*Pause.*] Rub yourself against the rim.
NAGG It's lower down. In the hollow.
NELL What hollow?
NAGG The hollow! [*Pause.*] Could you not? [*Pause.*] Yesterday you scratched me there.
NELL [*Elegiac.*] Ah yesterday!
NAGG Could you not? [*Pause.*] Would you like me to scratch you? [*Pause.*] Are you crying again?
NELL I was trying. [*Pause.*]
HAMM Perhaps it's a little vein. [*Pause.*]
NAGG What was that he said?
NELL Perhaps it's a little vein.
NAGG What does that mean? [*Pause.*] That means nothing. [*Pause.*] Will I tell you the story of the tailor?
NELL No. [*Pause.*] What for?
NAGG To cheer you up.
NELL It's not funny.
NAGG It always made you laugh. [*Pause.*] The first time I thought you'd die.
NELL It was on Lake Como.[3] [*Pause.*] One April afternoon. [*Pause.*] Can you believe it?
NAGG What?
NELL That we once went out rowing on Lake Como. [*Pause.*] One April afternoon.
NAGG We had got engaged the day before.
NELL Engaged!
NAGG You were in such fits that we capsized. By rights we should have been drowned.
NELL It was because I felt happy.
NAGG [*Indignant.*] It was not, it was not, it was my story and nothing else. Happy! Don't you laugh at it still? Every time I tell it. Happy!
NELL It was deep, deep. And you could see down to the bottom. So white. So clean.
NAGG Let me tell it again. [*Raconteur's voice.*] An Englishman, needing a pair of striped trousers in a hurry for the New Year festivities, goes to his tailor who takes his measurements. [*Tailor's voice.*] "That's the lot, come back in four days, I'll have it ready." Good. Four days later. [*Tailor's voice.*] "So sorry, come back in a week, I've made a mess of the seat." Good, that's all right, a neat seat can be very ticklish. A week later. [*Tailor's voice.*] "Frightfully sorry, come back in ten days. I've made a hash of the crotch." Good, can't be helped, a snug crotch is always a teaser. Ten days later. [*Tailor's voice.*] "Dreadfully sorry, come back in a fortnight, I've made a balls of the fly." Good, at a pinch, a smart fly is a stiff proposition. [*Pause. Normal voice.*] I never told it worse. [*Pause. Gloomy.*] I tell this story worse and worse. [*Pause. Raconteur's voice.*] Well, to make it short, the bluebells

3. A large lake and tourist resort in northern Italy, near the Swiss border.

are blowing and he ballockses[4] the buttonholes. [*Customer's voice.*] "God damn you to hell, Sir, no, it's indecent, there are limits! In six days, do you hear me, six days, God made the world. Yes Sir, no less Sir, the WORLD! And you are not bloody well capable of making me a pair of trousers in three months!" [*Tailor's voice, scandalized.*] "But my dear Sir, my dear Sir, look— [*Disdainful gesture, disgustedly.*] —at the world— [*Pause.*] and look— [*Loving gesture, proudly.*] —at my TROUSERS!"

[*Pause. He looks at* NELL *who has remained impassive, her eyes unseeing, breaks into a high forced laugh, cuts it short, pokes his head towards* NELL, *launches his laugh again.*]

HAMM Silence!

[NAGG *starts, cuts short his laugh.*]

NELL You could see down to the bottom.

HAMM [*Exasperated.*] Have you not finished? Will you never finish? [*With sudden fury.*] Will this never finish? [NAGG *disappears into his bin, closes the lid behind him.* NELL *does not move. Frenziedly.*] My kingdom for a nightman![5] [*He whistles. Enter* CLOV.] Clear away this muck! Chuck it in the sea!

[CLOV *goes to bins, halts.*]

NELL So white.

HAMM What? What's she blathering about?

[CLOV *stoops, takes* NELL*'s hand, feels her pulse.*]

NELL [*To* CLOV.] Desert!

[CLOV *lets go her hand, pushes her back in the bin, closes the lid.*]

CLOV [*Returning to his place beside the chair.*] She has no pulse.

HAMM What was she drivelling about?

CLOV She told me to go away, into the desert.

HAMM Damn busybody! Is that all?

CLOV No.

HAMM What else?

CLOV I didn't understand.

HAMM Have you bottled her?

CLOV Yes.

HAMM Are they both bottled?

CLOV Yes.

HAMM Screw down the lids. [CLOV *goes towards door.*] Time enough. [CLOV *halts.*] My anger subsides, I'd like to pee.

CLOV [*With alacrity.*] I'll go and get the catheter. [*He goes towards door.*]

HAMM Time enough. [CLOV *halts.*] Give me my pain-killer.

CLOV It's too soon. [*Pause.*] It's too soon on top of your tonic, it wouldn't act.

HAMM In the morning they brace you up and in the evening they calm you down. Unless it's the other way round. [*Pause.*] That old doctor, he's dead naturally?

CLOV He wasn't old.

HAMM But he's dead?

4. "Bollixes," botches.

5. Parody of Shakespeare's *Richard III*, where the defeated king seeks a horse to escape from the battlefield: "A horse! a horse! My kingdom for a horse!" (5.4.7). Nightman: a man who removes human waste at night.

CLOV Naturally. [*Pause.*] *You* ask *me* that? [*Pause.*]

HAMM Take me for a little turn. [CLOV *goes behind the chair and pushes it forward.*] Not too fast! [CLOV *pushes chair.*] Right round the world! [CLOV *pushes chair.*] Hug the walls, then back to the center again. [CLOV *pushes chair.*] I was right in the center, wasn't I?

CLOV [*Pushing.*] Yes.

HAMM We'd need a proper wheel-chair. With big wheels. Bicycle wheels! [*Pause.*] Are you hugging?

CLOV [*Pushing.*] Yes.

HAMM [*Groping for wall.*] It's a lie! Why do you lie to me?

CLOV [*Bearing closer to wall.*] There! There!

HAMM Stop! [CLOV *stops chair close to back wall.* HAMM *lays his hand against wall.*] Old wall! [*Pause.*] Beyond is the . . . other hell. [*Pause. Violently.*] Closer! Closer! Up against!

CLOV Take away your hand. [HAMM *withdraws his hand.* CLOV *rams chair against wall.*] There!

[HAMM *leans towards wall, applies his ear to it.*]

HAMM Do you hear? [*He strikes the wall with his knuckles.*] Do you hear? Hollow bricks! [*He strikes again.*] All that's hollow! [*Pause. He straightens up. Violently.*] That's enough. Back!

CLOV We haven't done the round.

HAMM Back to my place! [CLOV *pushes chair back to center.*] Is that my place?

CLOV Yes, that's your place.

HAMM Am I right in the center?

CLOV I'll measure it.

HAMM More or less! More or less!

CLOV [*Moving chair slightly.*] There!

HAMM I'm more or less in the center?

CLOV I'd say so.

HAMM You'd say so! Put me right in the center!

CLOV I'll go and get the tape.

HAMM Roughly! Roughly! [CLOV *moves chair slightly.*] Bang in the center!

CLOV There! [*Pause.*]

HAMM I feel a little too far to the left. [CLOV *moves chair slightly.*] Now I feel a little too far to the right. [CLOV *moves chair slightly.*] I feel a little too far forward. [CLOV *moves chair slightly.*] Now I feel a little too far back. [CLOV *moves chair slightly.*] Don't stay there, [*i.e., behind the chair*] you give me the shivers.

[CLOV *returns to his place beside the chair.*]

CLOV If I could kill him I'd die happy. [*Pause.*]

HAMM What's the weather like?

CLOV As usual.

HAMM Look at the earth.

CLOV I've looked.

HAMM With the glass?

CLOV No need of the glass.

HAMM Look at it with the glass.

CLOV I'll go and get the glass.

[*Exit* CLOV.]

HAMM No need of the glass!

[*Enter* CLOV *with telescope.*]

CLOV I'm back again, with the glass. [*He goes to window right, looks up at it.*] I need the steps.

HAMM Why? Have you shrunk? [*Exit* CLOV *with telescope.*] I don't like that, I don't like that.

[*Enter* CLOV *with ladder, but without telescope.*]

CLOV I'm back again, with the steps. [*He sets down ladder under window right, gets up on it, realizes he has not the telescope, gets down.*] I need the glass. [*He goes towards door.*]

HAMM [*Violently.*] But you have the glass!

CLOV [*Halting, violently.*] No, I haven't the glass!

[*Exit* CLOV.]

HAMM This is deadly.

[*Enter* CLOV *with telescope. He goes towards ladder.*]

CLOV Things are livening up. [*He gets up on ladder, raises the telescope, lets it fall.*] I did it on purpose. [*He gets down, picks up the telescope, turns it on auditorium.*] I see . . . a multitude . . . in transports . . . of joy.[6] [*Pause.*] That's what I call a magnifier. [*He lowers the telescope, turns towards* HAMM.] Well? Don't we laugh?

HAMM [*After reflection.*] I don't.

CLOV [*After reflection.*] Nor I. [*He gets up on ladder, turns the telescope on the without.*] Let's see. [*He looks, moving the telescope.*] Zero . . . [*he looks*] . . . zero . . . [*he looks*] . . . and zero.

HAMM Nothing stirs. All is—

CLOV Zer—

HAMM [*Violently.*] Wait till you're spoke to! [*Normal voice.*] All is . . . all is . . . all is what? [*Violently.*] All is what?

CLOV What all is? In a word? Is that what you want to know? Just a moment. [*He turns the telescope on the without, looks, lowers the telescope, turns towards* HAMM.] Corpsed. [*Pause.*] Well? Content?

HAMM Look at the sea.

CLOV It's the same.

HAMM Look at the ocean!

[CLOV *gets down, takes a few steps towards window left, goes back for ladder, carries it over and sets it down under window left, gets up on it, turns the telescope on the without, looks at length. He starts, lowers the telescope, examines it, turns it again on the without.*]

CLOV Never seen anything like that!

HAMM [*Anxious.*] What? A sail? A fin? Smoke?

CLOV [*Looking.*] The light is sunk.

HAMM [*Relieved.*] Pah! We all knew that.

CLOV [*Looking.*] There was a bit left.

HAMM The base.

CLOV [*Looking.*] Yes.

HAMM And now?

6. Echo of Revelation 7.9–10: "After this I beheld, and, lo, a great multitude, which . . . cried with a loud voice, saying, Salvation."

CLOV [*Looking.*] All gone.

HAMM No gulls?

CLOV [*Looking.*] Gulls!

HAMM And the horizon? Nothing on the horizon?

CLOV [*Lowering the telescope, turning towards* HAMM, *exasperated.*] What in God's name could there be on the horizon? [*Pause.*]

HAMM The waves, how are the waves?

CLOV The waves? [*He turns the telescope on the waves.*] Lead.

HAMM And the sun?

CLOV [*Looking.*] Zero.

HAMM But it should be sinking. Look again.

CLOV [*Looking.*] Damn the sun.

HAMM Is it night already then?

CLOV [*Looking.*] No.

HAMM Then what is it?

CLOV [*Looking.*] Gray. [*Lowering the telescope, turning towards* HAMM, *louder.*] Gray! [*Pause. Still louder.*] GRRAY! [*Pause. He gets down, approaches* HAMM *from behind, whispers in his ear.*]

HAMM [*Starting.*] Gray! Did I hear you say gray?

CLOV Light black. From pole to pole.

HAMM You exaggerate. [*Pause.*] Don't stay there, you give me the shivers.

[CLOV *returns to his place beside the chair.*]

CLOV Why this farce, day after day?

HAMM Routine. One never knows. [*Pause.*] Last night I saw inside my breast. There was a big sore.

CLOV Pah! You saw your heart.

HAMM No, it was living. [*Pause. Anguished.*] Clov!

CLOV Yes.

HAMM What's happening?

CLOV Something is taking its course. [*Pause.*]

HAMM Clov!

CLOV [*Impatiently.*] What is it?

HAMM We're not beginning to . . . to . . . mean something?

CLOV Mean something! You and I, mean something! [*Brief laugh.*] Ah that's a good one!

HAMM I wonder. [*Pause.*] Imagine if a rational being came back to earth, wouldn't he be liable to get ideas into his head if he observed us long enough. [*Voice of rational being.*] Ah, good, now I see what it is, yes, now I understand what they're at! [CLOV *starts, drops the telescope and begins to scratch his belly with both hands. Normal voice.*] And without going so far as that, we ourselves . . . [*With emotion.*] . . . we ourselves . . . at certain moments . . . [*Vehemently.*] To think perhaps it won't all have been for nothing!

CLOV [*Anguished, scratching himself.*] I have a flea!

HAMM A flea! Are there still fleas?

CLOV On me there's one. [*Scratching.*] Unless it's a crablouse.

HAMM [*Very perturbed.*] But humanity might start from there all over again! Catch him, for the love of God!

CLOV I'll go and get the powder.

[*Exit* CLOV.]

HAMM A flea! This is awful! What a day!

[*Enter* CLOV *with a sprinkling-tin.*]

CLOV I'm back again, with the insecticide.

HAMM Let him have it!

[CLOV *loosens the top of his trousers, pulls it forward and shakes powder into the aperture. He stoops, looks, waits, starts, frenziedly shakes more powder, stoops, looks, waits.*]

CLOV The bastard!

HAMM Did you get him?

CLOV Looks like it. [*He drops the tin and adjusts his trousers.*] Unless he's laying doggo.

HAMM Laying! Lying you mean. Unless he's *lying* doggo.

CLOV Ah? One says lying? One doesn't say laying?

HAMM Use your head, can't you. If he was laying we'd be bitched.

CLOV Ah. [*Pause.*] What about that pee?

HAMM I'm having it.

CLOV Ah that's the spirit, that's the spirit! [*Pause.*]

HAMM [*With ardour.*] Let's go from here, the two of us! South! You can make a raft and the currents will carry us away, far away, to other . . . mammals!

CLOV God forbid!

HAMM Alone, I'll embark alone! Get working on that raft immediately. Tomorrow I'll be gone for ever.

CLOV [*Hastening towards door.*] I'll start straight away.

HAMM Wait! [CLOV *halts.*] Will there be sharks, do you think?

CLOV Sharks? I don't know. If there are there will be. [*He goes towards door.*]

HAMM Wait! [CLOV *halts.*] Is it not yet time for my pain-killer?

CLOV [*Violently.*] No! [*He goes towards door.*]

HAMM Wait! [CLOV *halts.*] How are your eyes?

CLOV Bad.

HAMM But you can see.

CLOV All I want.

HAMM How are your legs?

CLOV Bad.

HAMM But you can walk.

CLOV I come . . . and go.

HAMM In my house. [*Pause. With prophetic relish.*] One day you'll be blind, like me. You'll be sitting there, a speck in the void, in the dark, for ever, like me. [*Pause.*] One day you'll say to yourself, I'm tired, I'll sit down, and you'll go and sit down. Then you'll say, I'm hungry, I'll get up and get something to eat. But you won't get up. You'll say, I shouldn't have sat down, but since I have I'll sit on a little longer, then I'll get up and get something to eat. But you won't get up and you won't get anything to eat. [*Pause.*] You'll look at the wall awhile, then you'll say, I'll close my eyes, perhaps have a little sleep, after that I'll feel better, and you'll close them. And when you open them again there'll be no wall any more. [*Pause.*] Infinite emptiness will be all around you, all the resurrected dead of all the ages wouldn't fill it, and there you'll be like a little bit of grit in the middle of the steppe. [*Pause.*] Yes, one day you'll know what it is, you'll be like me, except that you won't have anyone with you, because you won't have had pity on anyone and because there won't be anyone left to have pity on. [*Pause.*]

CLOV It's not certain. [*Pause.*] And there's one thing you forget.

HAMM Ah?

CLOV I can't sit down.

HAMM [*Impatiently.*] Well you'll lie down then, what the hell! Or you'll come to a standstill, simply stop and stand still, the way you are now. One day you'll say, I'm tired, I'll stop. What does the attitude matter? [*Pause.*]

CLOV So you all want me to leave you.

HAMM Naturally.

CLOV Then I'll leave you.

HAMM You can't leave us.

CLOV Then I won't leave you. [*Pause.*]

HAMM Why don't you finish us? [*Pause.*] I'll tell you the combination of the cupboard if you promise to finish me.

CLOV I couldn't finish you.

HAMM Then you won't finish me. [*Pause.*]

CLOV I'll leave you, I have things to do.

HAMM Do you remember when you came here?

CLOV No. Too small, you told me.

HAMM Do you remember your father?

CLOV [*Wearily.*] Same answer. [*Pause.*] You've asked me these questions millions of times.

HAMM I love the old questions. [*With fervor.*] Ah the old questions, the old answers, there's nothing like them! [*Pause.*] It was I was a father to you.

CLOV Yes. [*He looks at* HAMM *fixedly.*] You were that to me.

HAMM My house a home for you.

CLOV Yes. [*He looks about him.*] This was that for me.

HAMM [*Proudly.*] But for me, [*Gesture towards himself.*] no father. But for Hamm, [*Gesture towards surroundings.*] no home. [*Pause.*]

CLOV I'll leave you.

HAMM Did you ever think of one thing?

CLOV Never.

HAMM That here we're down in a hole. [*Pause.*] But beyond the hills? Eh? Perhaps it's still green. Eh? [*Pause.*] Flora! Pomona! [*Ecstatically.*] Ceres![7] [*Pause.*] Perhaps you won't need to go very far.

CLOV I can't go very far. [*Pause.*] I'll leave you.

HAMM Is my dog ready?

CLOV He lacks a leg.

HAMM Is he silky?

CLOV He's a kind of Pomeranian.

HAMM Go and get him.

CLOV He lacks a leg.

HAMM Go and get him! [*Exit* CLOV.] We're getting on.

[*Enter* CLOV *holding by one of its three legs a black toy dog.*]

CLOV Your dogs are here. [*He hands the dog to* HAMM *who feels it, fondles it.*]

HAMM He's white, isn't he?

7. In Roman mythology, the goddesses of flowers, fruits, and fertility.

CLOV Nearly.
HAMM What do you mean, nearly? Is he white or isn't he?
CLOV He isn't. [*Pause.*]
HAMM You've forgotten the sex.
CLOV [*Vexed.*] But he isn't finished. The sex goes on at the end. [*Pause.*]
HAMM You haven't put on his ribbon.
CLOV [*Angrily.*] But he isn't finished, I tell you! First you finish your dog and then you put on his ribbon! [*Pause.*]
HAMM Can he stand?
CLOV I don't know.
HAMM Try. [*He hands the dog to* CLOV *who places it on the ground.*] Well?
CLOV Wait! [*He squats down and tries to get the dog to stand on its three legs, fails, lets it go. The dog falls on its side.*]
HAMM [*Impatiently.*] Well?
CLOV He's standing.
HAMM [*Groping for the dog.*] Where? Where is he?
[CLOV *holds up the dog in a standing position.*]
CLOV There. [*He takes* HAMM*'s hand and guides it towards the dog's head.*]
HAMM [*His hand on the dog's head.*] Is he gazing at me?
CLOV Yes.
HAMM [*Proudly.*] As if he were asking me to take him for a walk?
CLOV If you like.
HAMM [*As before.*] Or as if he were begging me for a bone. [*He withdraws his hand.*] Leave him like that, standing there imploring me.
[CLOV *straightens up. The dog falls on its side.*]
CLOV I'll leave you.
HAMM Have you had your visions?
CLOV Less.
HAMM Is Mother Pegg's light on?
CLOV Light! How could anyone's light be on?
HAMM Extinguished!
CLOV Naturally it's extinguished. If it's not on it's extinguished.
HAMM No, I mean Mother Pegg.
CLOV But naturally she's extinguished! [*Pause.*] What's the matter with you today?
HAMM I'm taking my course. [*Pause.*] Is she buried?
CLOV Buried! Who would have buried her?
HAMM You.
CLOV Me! Haven't I enough to do without burying people?
HAMM But you'll bury me.
CLOV No I won't bury you. [*Pause.*]
HAMM She was bonny once, like a flower of the field. [*With reminiscent leer.*] And a great one for the men!
CLOV We too were bonny—once. It's a rare thing not to have been bonny—once. [*Pause.*]
HAMM Go and get the gaff.[8]
[CLOV *goes to door, halts.*]

8. A long stick with a hook, usually for catching fish.

CLOV Do this, do that, and I do it. I never refuse. Why?

HAMM You're not able to.

CLOV Soon I won't do it any more.

HAMM You won't be able to any more. [*Exit* CLOV.] Ah the creatures, the creatures, everything has to be explained to them.

[*Enter* CLOV *with gaff.*]

CLOV Here's your gaff. Stick it up. [*He gives the gaff to* HAMM *who, wielding it like a puntpole, tries to move his chair.*]

HAMM Did I move?

CLOV No.

[HAMM *throws down the gaff.*]

HAMM Go and get the oilcan.

CLOV What for?

HAMM To oil the castors.

CLOV I oiled them yesterday.

HAMM Yesterday! What does that mean? Yesterday!

CLOV [*Violently.*] That means that bloody awful day, long ago, before this bloody awful day. I use the words you taught me. If they don't mean anything any more, teach me others. Or let me be silent. [*Pause.*]

HAMM I once knew a madman who thought the end of the world had come. He was a painter—and engraver. I had a great fondness for him. I used to go and see him, in the asylum. I'd take him by the hand and drag him to the window. Look! There! All that rising corn! And there! Look! The sails of the herring fleet! All that loveliness! [*Pause.*] He'd snatch away his hand and go back into his corner. Appalled. All he had seen was ashes. [*Pause.*] He alone had been spared. [*Pause.*] Forgotten. [*Pause.*] It appears the case is . . . was not so . . . so unusual.

CLOV A madman! When was that?

HAMM Oh way back, way back, you weren't in the land of the living.

CLOV God be with the days!

[*Pause.* HAMM *raises his toque.*]

HAMM I had a great fondness for him. [*Pause. He puts on his toque again.*] He was a painter—and engraver.

CLOV There are so many terrible things.

HAMM No, no, there are not so many now. [*Pause.*] Clov!

CLOV Yes.

HAMM Do you not think this has gone on long enough?

CLOV Yes! [*Pause.*] What?

HAMM This . . . this . . . thing.

CLOV I've always thought so. [*Pause.*] You not?

HAMM [*Gloomily.*] Then it's a day like any other day.

CLOV As long as it lasts. [*Pause.*] All life long the same inanities.

HAMM I can't leave you.

CLOV I know. And you can't follow me. [*Pause.*]

HAMM If you leave me how shall I know?

CLOV [*Briskly.*] Well you simply whistle me and if I don't come running it means I've left you. [*Pause.*]

HAMM You won't come and kiss me goodbye?

CLOV Oh I shouldn't think so. [*Pause.*]

HAMM But you might be merely dead in your kitchen.

CLOV The result would be the same.

HAMM Yes, but how would I know, if you were merely dead in your kitchen?

CLOV Well . . . sooner or later I'd start to stink.

HAMM You stink already. The whole place stinks of corpses.

CLOV The whole universe.

HAMM [*Angrily.*] To hell with the universe. [*Pause.*] Think of something.

CLOV What?

HAMM An idea, have an idea. [*Angrily.*] A bright idea!

CLOV Ah good. [*He starts pacing to and fro, his eyes fixed on the ground, his hands behind his back. He halts.*] The pains in my legs! It's unbelievable! Soon I won't be able to think any more.

HAMM You won't be able to leave me. [CLOV *resumes his pacing.*] What are you doing?

CLOV Having an idea. [*He paces.*] Ah! [*He halts.*]

HAMM What a brain! [*Pause.*] Well?

CLOV Wait! [*He meditates. Not very convinced.*] Yes . . . [*Pause. More convinced.*] Yes! [*He raises his head.*] I have it! I set the alarm. [*Pause.*]

HAMM This is perhaps not one of my bright days, but frankly—

CLOV You whistle me. I don't come. The alarm rings. I'm gone. It doesn't ring. I'm dead. [*Pause.*]

HAMM Is it working? [*Pause. Impatiently.*] The alarm, is it working?

CLOV Why wouldn't it be working?

HAMM Because it's worked too much.

CLOV But it's hardly worked at all.

HAMM [*Angrily.*] Then because it's worked too little!

CLOV I'll go and see. [*Exit* CLOV. *Brief ring of alarm off. Enter* CLOV *with alarm-clock. He holds it against* HAMM*'s ear and releases alarm. They listen to it ringing to the end. Pause.*] Fit to wake the dead! Did you hear it?

HAMM Vaguely.

CLOV The end is terrific!

HAMM I prefer the middle. [*Pause.*] Is it not time for my pain-killer?

CLOV No! [*He goes to door, turns.*] I'll leave you.

HAMM It's time for my story. Do you want to listen to my story.

CLOV No.

HAMM Ask my father if he wants to listen to my story.

[CLOV *goes to bins, raises the lid of* NAGG*'s, stoops, looks into it. Pause. He straightens up.*]

CLOV He's asleep.

HAMM Wake him.

[CLOV *stoops, wakes* NAGG *with the alarm. Unintelligible words.* CLOV *straightens up.*]

CLOV He doesn't want to listen to your story.

HAMM I'll give him a bon-bon.

[CLOV *stoops. As before.*]

CLOV He wants a sugar-plum.

HAMM He'll get a sugar-plum.

[CLOV *stoops. As before.*]

CLOV It's a deal. [*He goes towards door.* NAGG*'s hands appear, gripping the rim. Then the head emerges.* CLOV *reaches door, turns.*] Do you believe in the life to come?

HAMM Mine was always that. [*Exit* CLOV.] Got him that time!

NAGG I'm listening.

HAMM Scoundrel! Why did you engender me?

NAGG I didn't know.

HAMM What? What didn't you know?

NAGG That it'd be you. [*Pause.*] You'll give me a sugar-plum?

HAMM After the audition.

NAGG You swear?

HAMM Yes.

NAGG On what?

HAMM My honor.

[*Pause. They laugh heartily.*]

NAGG Two.

HAMM One.

NAGG One for me and one for—

HAMM One! Silence! [*Pause.*] Where was I? [*Pause. Gloomily.*] It's finished, we're finished. [*Pause.*] Nearly finished. [*Pause.*] There'll be no more speech. [*Pause.*] Something dripping in my head, ever since the fontanelles. [*Stifled hilarity of* NAGG.] Splash, splash, always on the same spot. [*Pause.*] Perhaps it's a little vein. [*Pause.*] A little artery. [*Pause. More animated.*] Enough of that, it's story time, where was I? [*Pause. Narrative tone.*] The man came crawling towards me, on his belly. Pale, wonderfully pale and thin, he seemed on the point of— [*Pause. Normal tone.*] No, I've done that bit. [*Pause. Narrative tone.*] I calmly filled my pipe—the meerschaum, lit it with . . . let us say a vesta, drew a few puffs. Aah! [*Pause.*] Well, what is it *you* want? [*Pause.*] It was an extraordinarily bitter day, I remember, zero by the thermometer. But considering it was Christmas Eve there was nothing . . . extra-ordinary about that. Seasonable weather, for once in a way. [*Pause.*] Well, what ill wind blows you my way? He raised his face to me, black with mingled dirt and tears. [*Pause. Normal tone.*] That should do it. [*Narrative tone.*] No, no, don't look at me, don't look at me. He dropped his eyes and mumbled something, apologies I presume. [*Pause.*] I'm a busy man, you know, the final touches, before the festivities, you know what it is. [*Pause. Forcibly.*] Come on now, what is the object of this invasion? [*Pause.*] It was a glorious bright day, I remember, fifty by the heliometer,[9] but already the sun was sinking down into the . . . down among the dead. [*Normal tone.*] Nicely put, that. [*Narrative tone.*] Come on now, come on, present your petition and let me resume my labors. [*Pause. Normal tone.*] There's English for you. Ah well . . . [*Narrative tone.*] It was then he took the plunge. It's my little one, he said. Tsstss, a little one, that's bad. My little boy, he said, as if the sex mattered. Where did he come from? He named the hole. A good half-day, on horse. What are you insinuating? That the place is still inhabited? No no, not a soul, except himself and the child—assuming he existed. Good. I enquired about the situation at Kov, beyond the gulf. Not a sinner. Good. And you expect me to believe you have left your little one back there, all alone, and alive into the bargain? Come

9. Literally, a "sun meter." Ordinarily, a telescope used to measure distances between celestial bodies.

now! [*Pause.*] It was a howling wild day, I remember, a hundred by the anemometer.[1] The wind was tearing up the dead pines and sweeping them . . . away. [*Pause. Normal tone.*] A bit feeble, that. [*Narrative tone.*] Come on, man, speak up, what is you want from me, I have to put up my holly. [*Pause.*] Well to make it short it finally transpired that what he wanted from me was . . . bread for his brat? Bread? But I have no bread, it doesn't agree with me. Good. Then perhaps a little corn? [*Pause. Normal tone.*] That should do it. [*Narrative tone.*] Corn, yes, I have corn, it's true, in my granaries. But use your head. I give you some corn, a pound, a pound and a half, you bring it back to your child and you make him—if he's still alive—a nice pot of porridge, [NAGG *reacts.*] a nice pot and a half of porridge, full of nourishment. Good. The colors come back into his little cheeks—perhaps. And then? [*Pause.*] I lost patience. [*Violently.*] Use your head, can't you, use your head, you're on earth, there's no cure for that! [*Pause.*] It was an exceedingly dry day, I remember, zero by the hygrometer.[2] Ideal weather, for my lumbago. [*Pause. Violently.*] But what in God's name do you imagine? That the earth will awake in spring? That the rivers and seas will run with fish again? That there's manna in heaven still for imbeciles like you? [*Pause.*] Gradually I cooled down, sufficiently at least to ask him how long he had taken on the way. Three whole days. Good. In what condition he had left the child. Deep in sleep. [*Forcibly.*] But deep in what sleep, deep in what sleep already? [*Pause.*] Well to make it short I finally offered to take him into my service. He had touched a chord. And then I imagined already that I wasn't much longer for this world. [*He laughs. Pause.*] Well? [*Pause.*] Well? Here if you were careful you might die a nice natural death, in peace and comfort. [*Pause.*] Well? [*Pause.*] In the end he asked me would I consent to take in the child as well—if he were still alive. [*Pause.*] It was the moment I was waiting for. [*Pause.*] Would I consent to take in the child . . . [*Pause.*] I can see him still, down on his knees, his hands flat on the ground, glaring at me with his mad eyes, in defiance of my wishes. [*Pause. Normal tone.*] I'll soon have finished with this story. [*Pause.*] Unless I bring in other characters. [*Pause.*] But where would I find them? [*Pause.*] Where would I look for them? [*Pause. He whistles. Enter* CLOV.] Let us pray to God.

NAGG Me sugar-plum!

CLOV There's a rat in the kitchen!

HAMM A rat! Are there still rats?

CLOV In the kitchen there's one.

HAMM And you haven't exterminated him?

CLOV Half. You disturbed us.

HAMM He can't get away?

CLOV No.

HAMM You'll finish him later. Let us pray to God.

CLOV Again!

NAGG Me sugar-plum!

HAMM God first! [*Pause.*] Are you right?

CLOV [*Resigned.*] Off we go.

1. A wind meter.
2. A moisture meter.

HAMM [*To* NAGG.] And you?

NAGG [*Clasping his hands, closing his eyes, in a gabble.*] Our Father which art—

HAMM Silence! In silence! Where are your manners? [*Pause.*] Off we go. [*Attitudes of prayer. Silence. Abandoning his attitude, discouraged.*] Well?

CLOV [*Abandoning his attitude.*] What a hope! And you?

HAMM Sweet damn all! [*To* NAGG.] And you?

NAGG Wait! [*Pause. Abandoning his attitude.*] Nothing doing!

HAMM The bastard! He doesn't exist!

CLOV Not yet.

NAGG Me sugar-plum!

HAMM There are no more sugar-plums! [*Pause.*]

NAGG It's natural. After all I'm your father. It's true if it hadn't been me it would have been someone else. But that's no excuse. [*Pause.*] Turkish Delight,[3] for example, which no longer exists, we all know that, there is nothing in the world I love more. And one day I'll ask you for some, in return for a kindness, and you'll promise it to me. One must live with the times. [*Pause.*] Whom did you call when you were a tiny boy, and were frightened, in the dark? Your mother? No. Me. We let you cry. Then we moved you out of earshot, so that we might sleep in peace. [*Pause.*] I was asleep, as happy as a king, and you woke me up to have me listen to you. It wasn't indispensable, you didn't really need to have me listen to you. [*Pause.*] I hope the day will come when you'll really need to have me listen to you, and need to hear my voice, any voice. [*Pause.*] Yes, I hope I'll live till then, to hear you calling me like when you were a tiny boy, and were frightened, in the dark, and I was your only hope. [*Pause.* NAGG *knocks on lid of* NELL*'s bin. Pause.*] Nell! [*Pause. He knocks louder. Pause. Louder.*] Nell! [*Pause.* NAGG *sinks back into his bin, closes the lid behind him. Pause.*]

HAMM Our revels now are ended.[4] [*He gropes for the dog.*] The dog's gone.

CLOV He's not a real dog, he can't go.

HAMM [*Groping.*] He's not there.

CLOV He's lain down.

HAMM Give him up to me. [CLOV *picks up the dog and gives it to* HAMM. HAMM *holds it in his arms. Pause.* HAMM *throws away the dog.*] Dirty brute! [CLOV *begins to pick up the objects lying on the ground.*] What are you doing?

CLOV Putting things in order. [*He straightens up. Fervently.*] I'm going to clear everything away! [*He starts picking up again.*]

HAMM Order!

CLOV [*Straightening up.*] I love order. It's my dream. A world where all would be silent and still and each thing in its last place, under the last dust. [*He starts picking up again.*]

HAMM [*Exasperated.*] What in God's name do you think you are doing?

CLOV [*Straightening up.*] I'm doing my best to create a little order.

HAMM Drop it!

[CLOV *drops the objects he has picked up.*]

CLOV After all, there or elsewhere. [*He goes towards door.*]

3. A sticky sweet candy.
4. Lines spoken by Prospero in Shakespeare's *The Tempest* 4.1.148.

HAMM [*Irritably.*] What's wrong with your feet?
CLOV My feet?
HAMM Tramp! Tramp!
CLOV I must have put on my boots.
HAMM Your slippers were hurting you? [*Pause.*]
CLOV I'll leave you.
HAMM No!
CLOV What is there to keep me here?
HAMM The dialogue. [*Pause.*] I've got on with my story. [*Pause.*] I've got on with it well. [*Pause. Irritably.*] Ask me where I've got to.
CLOV Oh, by the way, your story?
HAMM [*Surprised.*] What story?
CLOV The one you've been telling yourself all your days.
HAMM Ah you mean my chronicle?
CLOV That's the one. [*Pause.*]
HAMM [*Angrily.*] Keep going, can't you, keep going!
CLOV You've got on with it, I hope.
HAMM [*Modestly.*] Oh not very far, not very far. [*He sighs.*] There are days like that, one isn't inspired. [*Pause.*] Nothing you can do about it, just wait for it to come. [*Pause.*] No forcing, no forcing, it's fatal. [*Pause.*] I've got on with it a little all the same. [*Pause.*] Technique, you know. [*Pause. Irritably.*] I say I've got on with it a little all the same.
CLOV [*Admiringly.*] Well I never! In spite of everything you were able to get on with it!
HAMM [*Modestly.*] Oh not very far, you know, not very far, but nevertheless, better than nothing.
CLOV Better than nothing! Is it possible?
HAMM I'll tell you how it goes. He comes crawling on his belly—
CLOV Who?
HAMM What?
CLOV Who do you mean, he?
HAMM Who do I mean! Yet another.
CLOV Ah him! I wasn't sure.
HAMM Crawling on his belly, whining for bread for his brat. He's offered a job as gardener. Before— [CLOV *bursts out laughing.*] What is there so funny about that?
CLOV A job as gardener!
HAMM Is that what tickles you?
CLOV It must be that.
HAMM It wouldn't be the bread?
CLOV Or the brat. [*Pause.*]
HAMM The whole thing is comical, I grant you that. What about having a good guffaw the two of us together?
CLOV [*After reflection.*] I couldn't guffaw again today.
HAMM [*After reflection.*] Nor I. [*Pause.*] I continue then. Before accepting with gratitude he asks if he may have his little boy with him.
CLOV What age?
HAMM Oh tiny.
CLOV He would have climbed the trees.

HAMM All the little odd jobs.
CLOV And then he would have grown up.
HAMM Very likely. [*Pause.*]
CLOV Keep going, can't you, keep going!
HAMM That's all. I stopped there. [*Pause.*]
CLOV Do you see how it goes on.
HAMM More or less.
CLOV Will it not soon be the end?
HAMM I'm afraid it will.
CLOV Pah! You'll make up another.
HAMM I don't know. [*Pause.*] I feel rather drained. [*Pause.*] The prolonged creative effort. [*Pause.*] If I could drag myself down to the sea! I'd make a pillow of sand for my head and the tide would come.
CLOV There's no more tide. [*Pause.*]
HAMM Go and see is she dead.

[CLOV *goes to bins, raises the lid of* NELL's, *stoops, looks into it. Pause.*]

CLOV Looks like it.

[*He closes the lid, straightens up.* HAMM *raises his toque. Pause. He puts it on again.*]

HAMM [*With his hand to his toque.*] And Nagg?

[CLOV *raises lid of* NAGG's *bin, stoops, looks into it. Pause.*]

CLOV Doesn't look like it. [*He closes the lid, straightens up.*]
HAMM [*Letting go his toque.*] What's he doing? [CLOV *raises lid of* NAGG's *bin, stoops, looks into it. Pause.*]
CLOV He's crying. [*He closes lid, straightens up.*]
HAMM Then he's living. [*Pause.*] Did you ever have an instant of happiness?
CLOV Not to my knowledge. [*Pause.*]
HAMM Bring me under the window. [CLOV *goes towards chair.*] I want to feel the light on my face. [CLOV *pushes chair.*] Do you remember, in the beginning, when you took me for a turn? You used to hold the chair too high. At every step you nearly tipped me out. [*With senile quaver.*] Ah great fun, we had, the two of us, great fun. [*Gloomily.*] And then we got into the way of it. [CLOV *stops the chair under window right.*] There already? [*Pause. He tilts back his head.*] Is it light?
CLOV It isn't dark.
HAMM [*Angrily.*] I'm asking you is it light.
CLOV Yes. [*Pause.*]
HAMM The curtain isn't closed?
CLOV No.
HAMM What window is it?
CLOV The earth.
HAMM I knew it! [*Angrily.*] But there's no light there! The other! [CLOV *stops the chair under window left.* HAMM *tilts back his head.*] That's what I call light! [*Pause.*] Feels like a ray of sunshine. [*Pause.*] No?
CLOV No.
HAMM It isn't a ray of sunshine I feel on my face?
CLOV No. [*Pause.*]
HAMM Am I very white? [*Pause. Angrily.*] I'm asking you am I very white!
CLOV Not more so than usual. [*Pause.*]

HAMM Open the window.

CLOV What for?

HAMM I want to hear the sea.

CLOV You wouldn't hear it.

HAMM Even if you opened the window?

CLOV No.

HAMM Then it's not worth while opening it?

CLOV No.

HAMM [*Violently.*] Then open it! [CLOV *gets up on the ladder, opens the window. Pause.*] Have you opened it?

CLOV Yes. [*Pause.*]

HAMM You swear you've opened it?

CLOV Yes. [*Pause.*]

HAMM Well . . . ! [*Pause.*] It must be very calm. [*Pause. Violently.*] I'm asking you is it very calm!

CLOV Yes.

HAMM It's because there are no more navigators. [*Pause.*] You haven't much conversation all of a sudden. Do you not feel well?

CLOV I'm cold.

HAMM What month are we? [*Pause.*] Close the window, we're going back. [CLOV *closes the window, gets down, pushes the chair back to its place, remains standing behind it, head bowed.*] Don't stay there, you give me the shivers! [CLOV *returns to his place beside the chair.*] Father! [*Pause. Louder.*] Father! [*Pause.*] Go and see did he hear me.

[CLOV *goes to* NAGG*'s bin, raises the lid, stoops. Unintelligible words.* CLOV *straightens up.*]

CLOV Yes.

HAMM Both times?

[CLOV *stoops. As before.*]

CLOV Once only.

HAMM The first time or the second?

[CLOV *stoops. As before.*]

CLOV He doesn't know.

HAMM It must have been the second.

CLOV We'll never know. [*He closes lid.*]

HAMM Is he still crying?

CLOV No.

HAMM The dead go fast. [*Pause.*] What's he doing?

CLOV Sucking his biscuit.

HAMM Life goes on. [CLOV *returns to his place beside the chair.*] Give me a rug. I'm freezing.

CLOV There are no more rugs. [*Pause.*]

HAMM Kiss me. [*Pause.*] Will you not kiss me?

CLOV No.

HAMM On the forehead.

CLOV I won't kiss you anywhere. [*Pause.*]

HAMM [*Holding out his hand.*] Give me your hand at least. [*Pause.*] Will you not give me your hand?

CLOV I won't touch you. [*Pause.*]

HAMM Give me the dog. [CLOV *looks round for the dog.*] No!

CLOV Do you not want your dog?

HAMM No.

CLOV Then I'll leave you.

HAMM [*Head bowed, absently.*] That's right.

[CLOV *goes to door, turns.*]

CLOV If I don't kill that rat he'll die.

HAMM [*As before.*] That's right. [*Exit* CLOV. *Pause.*] Me to play. [*He takes out his handkerchief, unfolds it, holds it spread out before him.*] We're getting on. [*Pause.*] You weep, and weep, for nothing, so as not to laugh, and little by little . . . you begin to grieve. [*He folds the handkerchief, puts it back in his pocket, raises his head.*] All those I might have helped. [*Pause.*] Helped! [*Pause.*] Saved. [*Pause.*] Saved! [*Pause.*] The place was crawling with them! [*Pause. Violently.*] Use your head, can't you, use your head, you're on earth, there's no cure for that! [*Pause.*] Get out of here and love one another! Lick your neighbor as yourself![5] [*Pause. Calmer.*] When it wasn't bread they wanted it was crumpets. [*Pause. Violently.*] Out of my sight and back to your petting parties! [*Pause.*] All that, all that! [*Pause.*] Not even a real dog! [*Calmer.*] The end is in the beginning and yet you go on. [*Pause.*] Perhaps I could go on with my story, end it and begin another. [*Pause.*] Perhaps I could throw myself out on the floor. [*He pushes himself painfully off his seat, falls back again.*] Dig my nails into the cracks and drag myself forward with my fingers. [*Pause.*] It will be the end and there I'll be, wondering what can have brought it on and wondering what can have . . . [*He hesitates.*] . . . why it was so long coming. [*Pause.*] There I'll be, in the old shelter, alone against the silence and . . . [*He hesitates.*] . . . the stillness. If I can hold my peace, and sit quiet, it will be all over with sound, and motion, all over and done with. [*Pause.*] I'll have called my father and I'll have called my . . . [*He hesitates.*] . . . my son. And even twice, or three times, in case they shouldn't have heard me, the first time, or the second. [*Pause.*] I'll say to myself, He'll come back. [*Pause.*] And then? [*Pause.*] And then? [*Pause.*] He couldn't, he has gone too far. [*Pause.*] And then? [*Pause. Very agitated.*] All kinds of fantasies! That I'm being watched! A rat! Steps! Breath held and then . . . [*He breathes out.*] Then babble, babble, words, like the solitary child who turns himself into children, two, three, so as to be together, and whisper together, in the dark. [*Pause.*] Moment upon moment, pattering down, like the millet grains of . . . [*He hesitates.*] . . . that old Greek,[6] and all life long you wait for that to mount up to a life. [*Pause. He opens his mouth to continue, renounces.*] Ah let's get it over! [*He whistles. Enter* CLOV *with alarm-clock. He halts beside the chair.*] What? Neither gone nor dead?

CLOV In spirit only.

HAMM Which?

5. Parody of Jesus's words in the Bible: "Thou shalt love thy neighbor as thyself" (Matthew 19.19).

6. Zeno of Elea, a Greek philosopher active around 450 B.C.E., known for logical paradoxes that reduce to absurdity various attempts to define *Being*. Aristotle reports that Zeno's paradox on sound questioned: If a grain of millet falling makes no sound, how can a bushel of grains make any sound? (Aristotle's *Physics* 5.250a.19).

CLOV Both.
HAMM Gone from me you'd be dead.
CLOV And vice versa.
HAMM Outside of here it's death! [*Pause.*] And the rat?
CLOV He's got away.
HAMM He can't go far. [*Pause. Anxious.*] Eh?
CLOV He doesn't need to go far. [*Pause.*]
HAMM Is it not time for my pain-killer?
CLOV Yes.
HAMM Ah! At last! Give it to me! Quick! [*Pause.*]
CLOV There's no more pain-killer. [*Pause.*]
HAMM [*Appalled.*] Good . . . ! [*Pause.*] No more pain-killer!
CLOV No more pain-killer. You'll never get any more pain-killer. [*Pause.*]
HAMM But the little round box. It was full!
CLOV Yes. But now it's empty.

[*Pause.* CLOV *starts to move about the room. He is looking for a place to put down the alarm-clock.*]

HAMM [*Soft.*] What'll I do? [*Pause. In a scream.*] What'll I do? [CLOV *sees the picture, takes it down, stands it on the floor with its face to the wall, hangs up the alarm-clock in its place.*] What are you doing?
CLOV Winding up.
HAMM Look at the earth.
CLOV Again!
HAMM Since it's calling to you.
CLOV Is your throat sore? [*Pause.*] Would you like a lozenge? [*Pause.*] No. [*Pause.*] Pity. [*He goes, humming, towards window right, halts before it, looks up at it.*]
HAMM Don't sing.
CLOV [*Turning towards* HAMM.] One hasn't the right to sing any more?
HAMM No.
CLOV Then how can it end?
HAMM You want it to end?
CLOV I want to sing.
HAMM I can't prevent you.

[*Pause.* CLOV *turns towards window right.*]

CLOV What did I do with that steps? [*He looks around for ladder.*] You didn't see that steps? [*He sees it.*] Ah, about time. [*He goes towards window left.*] Sometimes I wonder if I'm in my right mind. Then it passes over and I'm as lucid as before. [*He gets up on ladder, looks out of window.*] Christ, she's under water! [*He looks.*] How can that be? [*He pokes forward his head, his hand above his eyes.*] It hasn't rained. [*He wipes the pane, looks. Pause.*] Ah what a fool I am! I'm on the wrong side! [*He gets down, takes a few steps towards window right.*] Under water! [*He goes back for ladder.*] What a fool I am! [*He carries ladder towards window right.*] Sometimes I wonder if I'm in my right senses. Then it passes off and I'm as intelligent as ever. [*He sets down ladder under window right, gets up on it, looks out of window. He turns towards* HAMM.] Any particular sector you fancy? Or merely the whole thing?
HAMM Whole thing.

CLOV The general effect? Just a moment. [*He looks out of window. Pause.*]

HAMM Clov.

CLOV [*Absorbed.*] Mmm.

HAMM Do you know what it is?

CLOV [*As before.*] Mmm.

HAMM I was never there. [*Pause.*] Clov!

CLOV [*Turning towards* HAMM, *exasperated.*] What is it?

HAMM I was never there.

CLOV Lucky for you. [*He looks out of window.*]

HAMM Absent, always. It all happened without me. I don't know what's happened. [*Pause.*] Do you know what's happened? [*Pause.*] Clov!

CLOV [*Turning towards* HAMM, *exasperated.*] Do you want me to look at this muckheap, yes or no?

HAMM Answer me first.

CLOV What?

HAMM Do you know what's happened?

CLOV When? Where?

HAMM [*Violently.*] When! What's happened? Use your head, can't you! What has happened?

CLOV What for Christ's sake does it matter? [*He looks out of window.*]

HAMM I don't know.

[*Pause.* CLOV *turns towards* HAMM.]

CLOV [*Harshly.*] When old Mother Pegg asked you for oil for her lamp and you told her to get out to hell, you knew what was happening then, no? [*Pause.*] You know what she died of, Mother Pegg? Of darkness.

HAMM [*Feebly.*] I hadn't any.

CLOV [*As before.*] Yes, you had. [*Pause.*]

HAMM Have you the glass?

CLOV No, it's clear enough as it is.

HAMM Go and get it.

[*Pause.* CLOV *casts up his eyes, brandishes his fists. He loses balance, clutches on to the ladder. He starts to get down, halts.*]

CLOV There's one thing I'll never understand. [*He gets down.*] Why I always obey you. Can you explain that to me?

HAMM No. . . . Perhaps it's compassion. [*Pause.*] A kind of great compassion. [*Pause.*] Oh you won't find it easy, you won't find it easy.

[*Pause.* CLOV *begins to move about the room in search of the telescope.*]

CLOV I'm tired of our goings on, very tired. [*He searches.*] You're not sitting on it? [*He moves the chair, looks at the place where it stood, resumes his search.*]

HAMM [*Anguished.*] Don't leave me there! [*Angrily* CLOV *restores the chair to its place.*] Am I right in the center?

CLOV You'd need a microscope to find this— [*He sees the telescope.*] Ah, about time. [*He picks up the telescope, gets up on the ladder, turns the telescope on the without.*]

HAMM Give me the dog.

CLOV [*Looking.*] Quiet!

HAMM [*Angrily.*] Give me the dog!

[CLOV *drops the telescope, clasps his hands to his head. Pause. He gets down precipitately, looks for the dogs, sees it, picks it up, hastens towards* HAMM *and strikes him violently on the head with the dog.*]

CLOV There's your dog for you!

[*The dog falls to the ground. Pause.*]

HAMM He hit me!

CLOV You drive me mad, I'm mad!

HAMM If you must hit me, hit me with the axe. [*Pause.*] Or with the gaff, hit me with the gaff. Not with the dog. With the gaff. Or with the axe.

[CLOV *picks up the dog and gives it to* HAMM *who takes it in his arms.*]

CLOV [*Imploringly.*] Let's stop playing!

HAMM Never! [*Pause.*] Put me in my coffin.

CLOV There are no more coffins.

HAMM Then let it end! [CLOV *goes towards ladder.*] With a bang! [CLOV *gets up on ladder, gets down again, looks for telescope, sees it, picks it up, gets up ladder, raises telescope.*] Of darkness! And me? Did anyone ever have pity on me?

CLOV [*Lowering the telescope, turning towards* HAMM.] What? [*Pause.*] Is it me you're referring to?

HAMM [*Angrily.*] An aside, ape! Did you never hear an aside before? [*Pause.*] I'm warming up for my last soliloquy.

CLOV I warn you. I'm going to look at this filth since it's an order. But it's the last time. [*He turns the telescope on the without.*] Let's see. [*He moves the telescope.*] Nothing . . . nothing . . . good . . . good . . . nothing . . . goo— [*He starts, lowers the telescope, examines it, turns it again on the without. Pause.*] Bad luck to it!

HAMM More complications! [CLOV *gets down.*] Not an underplot, I trust.

[CLOV *moves ladder nearer window, gets up on it, turns telescope on the without.*]

CLOV [*Dismayed.*] Looks like a small boy!

HAMM [*Sarcastic.*] A small . . . boy!

CLOV I'll go and see. [*He gets down, drops the telescope, goes towards door, turns.*] I'll take the gaff. [*He looks for the gaff, sees it, picks it up, hastens towards door.*]

HAMM No! [CLOV *halts.*]

CLOV No? A potential procreator?

HAMM If he exists he'll die there or he'll come here. And if he doesn't . . . [*Pause.*]

CLOV You don't believe me? You think I'm inventing? [*Pause.*]

HAMM It's the end, Clov, we've come to the end. I don't need you any more. [*Pause.*]

CLOV Lucky for you. [*He goes towards door.*]

HAMM Leave me the gaff.

[CLOV *gives him the gaff, goes towards door, halts, looks at alarm-clock, takes it down, looks round for a better place to put it, goes to bins, puts it on lid of* NAGG*'s bin. Pause.*]

CLOV I'll leave you. [*He goes towards door.*]

HAMM Before you go . . . [CLOV *halts near door.*] . . . say something.

CLOV There is nothing to say.

HAMM A few words . . . to ponder . . . in my heart.

CLOV Your heart!

HAMM Yes. [*Pause. Forcibly.*] Yes! [*Pause.*] With the rest, in the end, the shadows, the murmurs, all the trouble, to end up with. [*Pause.*] Clov. . . . He never spoke to me. Then, in the end, before he went, without my having asked him, he spoke to me. He said . . .

CLOV [*Despairingly.*] Ah . . . !

HAMM Something . . . from your heart.

CLOV My heart!

HAMM A few words . . . from your heart. [*Pause.*]

CLOV [*Fixed gaze, tonelessly, towards auditorium.*] They said to me, That's love, yes, yes, not a doubt, now you see how—

HAMM Articulate!

CLOV [*As before.*] How easy it is. They said to me, That's friendship, yes, yes, no question, you've found it. They said to me, Here's the place, stop, raise your head and look at all that beauty. That order! They said to me. Come now, you're not a brute beast, think upon these things and you'll see how all becomes clear. And simple! They said to me, What skilled attention they get, all these dying of their wounds.

HAMM Enough!

CLOV [*As before.*] I say to myself—sometimes, Clov, you must learn to suffer better than that if you want them to weary of punishing you—one day. I say to myself—sometimes, Clov, you must be there better than that if you want them to let you go—one day. But I feel too old, and too far, to form new habits. Good, it'll never end, I'll never go. [*Pause.*] Then one day, suddenly, it ends, it changes, I don't understand, it dies, or it's me, I don't understand that either. I ask the words that remain—sleeping, waking, morning, evening. They have nothing to say. [*Pause.*] I open the door of the cell and go. I am so bowed I only see my feet, if I open my eyes, and between my legs a little trail of black dust. I say to myself that the earth is extinguished, though I never saw it lit. [*Pause.*] It's easy going. [*Pause.*] When I fall I'll weep for happiness. [*Pause. He goes towards door.*]

HAMM Clov! [CLOV *halts, without turning.*] Nothing. [CLOV *moves on.*] Clov!

[CLOV *halts, without turning.*]

CLOV This is what we call making an exit.

HAMM I'm obliged to you, Clov. For your services.

CLOV [*Turning, sharply.*] Ah pardon, it's I am obliged to you.

HAMM It's we are obliged to each other. [*Pause.* CLOV *goes towards door.*] One thing more. [CLOV *halts.*] A last favor. [*Exit* CLOV.] Cover me with the sheet. [*Long pause.*] No? Good. [*Pause.*] Me to play. [*Pause. Wearily.*] Old endgame lost of old, play and lose and have done with losing. [*Pause. More animated.*] Let me see. [*Pause.*] Ah yes! [*He tries to move the chair, using the gaff as before. Enter* CLOV, *dressed for the road. Panama hat, tweed coat, raincoat over his arm, umbrella, bag. He halts by the door and stands there, impassive and motionless, his eyes fixed on* HAMM, *till the end.* HAMM *gives up.*] Good. [*Pause.*] Discard. [*He throws away the gaff, makes to throw away the dog, thinks better of it.*] Take it easy. [*Pause.*] And now? [*Pause.*] Raise hat. [*He raises his toque.*] Peace to our . . . arses. [*Pause.*] And put on again. [*He puts on his toque.*] Deuce. [*Pause. He takes off his glasses.*] Wipe. [*He takes out his handkerchief and, without unfolding it, wipes his glasses.*] And put on again. [*He puts on his glasses, puts back the handkerchief in his pocket.*] We're coming. A few more squirms like that and I'll call. [*Pause.*] A little poetry. [*Pause.*] You prayed— [*Pause. He corrects himself.*] You CRIED for night; it comes— [*Pause. He corrects himself.*] It FALLS: now cry in darkness. [*He repeats, chanting.*] You cried for night; it falls: now cry in darkness.[7] [*Pause.*] Nicely put, that. [*Pause.*] And now? [*Pause.*] Moments for nothing, now as always, time was never and time is over, reckoning closed and story ended. [*Pause. Narrative tone.*] If he could have his child with him. . . . [*Pause.*] It was the moment I was waiting for. [*Pause.*] You don't want to abandon him? You want him to bloom while you are withering? Be there to solace your last million last moments? [*Pause.*] He doesn't realize, all he knows is hunger, and cold, and death to crown it all. But you! You ought to know what the earth is like, nowadays. Oh I put him before his responsibilities! [*Pause. Normal tone.*] Well, there we are, there I am, that's enough. [*He raises the whistle to his lips, hesitates, drops it. Pause.*] Yes, truly! [*He whistles. Pause. Louder. Pause.*] Good. [*Pause.*] Father! [*Pause. Louder.*] Father! [*Pause.*] Good. [*Pause.*] We're coming. [*Pause.*] And to end up with? [*Pause.*] Discard. [*He throws away the dog. He tears the whistle from his neck.*] With my compliments. [*He throws whistle towards auditorium. Pause. He sniffs. Soft.*] Clov! [*Long pause.*] No? Good. [*He takes out the handkerchief.*] Since that's the way we're playing it . . . [*He unfolds handkerchief.*] . . . let's play it that way . . . [*He unfolds.*] . . . and speak no more about it . . . [*He finishes unfolding.*] . . . speak no more. [*He holds handkerchief spread out before him.*] Old stancher! [*Pause.*] You . . . remain.

[*Pause. He covers his face with handkerchief, lowers his arms to armrests, remains motionless.*]

[*Brief tableau.*]

Curtain

1957

7. Parody of a line from the poem *Meditation*, by Baudelaire: "You were calling for evening; it falls; here it is."

VLADIMIR NABOKOV
1899–1977

Exiled first from revolutionary Russia and then from Nazi-dominated Western Europe, Vladimir Nabokov became one of the great literary explorers of the contemporary United States. An urbane European modernist, in middle age he traveled throughout his adoptive country, maintaining an ironic detachment from postwar American society even as he developed an intimate familiarity with American English. His extraordinary, playful use of the language to describe the culture from an outsider's point of view made him one of the most famous and controversial novelists of the twentieth century.

Born in St. Petersburg to a wealthy, aristocratic family, Nabokov grew up speaking Russian, English, and French; he later recalled with nostalgia the extraordinary family estate where he spent much of his childhood (he inherited the nearby estate of his uncle at age 17, only to lose it to the Russian Revolution the following year). His father, also named Vladimir, a prominent liberal politician, became a minister in the provisional government after the February 1917 Revolution. When the Communists came to power later that year in the October Revolution, the Nabokovs fled Moscow. They lived at first in noncommunist Russia, but once it was clear that the Communists would maintain power, the family moved to London, then to Berlin. In 1922, while attending a political conference, Nabokov's father was killed by right-wing assassins. A gunman had attacked another Russian exile speaking at the conference. While Nabokov's father tried to wrestle the gun away from him, he was shot by an accomplice of the first killer. The younger Nabokov remained haunted by his father's death, which would surface in disguised form in many of his novels.

After completing his studies at Cambridge University, Nabokov joined his family in Berlin and supported himself as a language teacher and tennis and boxing coach while beginning to publish his writing. He had written poetry and plays but gained most attention for his first nine novels, written in Russian, usually featuring Russian émigrés, as well as some of Nabokov's later obsessions, such as unreliable narrators, young girls, and chess problems. One of his major themes, like that of such modernists as **Marcel Proust**, was the mystery of consciousness and memory. Although widely recognized as a leading young novelist, Nabokov could reach only a small audience of Russian émigrés, since his works could not be published in his homeland.

Nabokov married Véra Slonim, a Russian-Jewish exile, and after the Nazis took power in Germany, the family, now impoverished, moved to Paris. Shortly before the Nazis conquered France, in 1940, the Nabokovs managed to escape yet again, this time to the United States, where Nabokov taught at Stanford University, Wellesley College, and later Cornell University. In addition to teaching Russian and comparative literature, Nabokov, an avid collector of butterflies, served for a time as curator of lepidoptery at Harvard University's Museum of Comparative Zoology. Having become an American citizen, Nabokov took lengthy summer road trips with his wife to collect butterflies and thus became familiar with the postwar highways and motels of the United States, while gaining glimpses of many small college towns.

Although Nabokov had previously translated some of his Russian novels into French and English, only in 1938 did he begin writing fiction in English. His first novel in his adopted language, *The Real Life of Sebastian Knight* (1941), takes the form of a highly subjective biography of a fictional Russian-born English novelist, written by his disturbed half brother, V. Like some of the works of his contemporary **Jorge Luis Borges**, the novel both draws on modernist themes and prefigures postmodernism by playing with the line between fiction and nonfiction, biography and novel. Nabokov has also often been compared with **Samuel Beckett**, another bilingual émigré novelist dedicated to wordplay and meditations on the status of fiction. This "metafictional" tendency is present, too, in *Lolita* (1955), which brought Nabokov his initial commercial success. Narrated in the first person by Humbert Humbert, who is, like Nabokov, a witty and urbane language professor but, unlike Nabokov, a child molester, the novel was controversial from the first. By creating an unreliable narrator, Nabokov challenges his readers to disentangle the pleasure they may take in Humbert's wit from the horror of Humbert's evil. Nabokov does not make it easy to separate one from the other.

Because of fear of censorship, the novel was originally published in Paris, but even in the less repressive French society, the work was banned for a brief period. In 1958, the novel was finally released in the United States, to great acclaim, huge sales, and frequent expressions of moral disapproval. The financial success of *Lolita* (and the 1962 film version, directed by Stanley Kubrick) allowed Nabokov to retire from academia and return to Europe. He took up residence in Switzerland, where he remained for the rest of his life, continuing to write in English. A major contributor to modern American literature, he had spent only two of his eight decades in the United States.

Nabokov considered "The Vane Sisters" (1959), presented here, his best story. It is a detective story of an unusual kind. What makes it unusual is the fact that the narrator himself does not quite understand the story he is telling; in this respect, he is an extreme form of the unreliable narrator. Though capable of witty observations about the Vane sisters and his friends, he is blinded by his arrogance. He believes himself to be supremely observant, "one big eyeball rolling in the world's socket," but in fact he misses the clues that the Vane sisters have left for him. One of the first hints that his visible world is in fact full of signs is the icicle shaped like an exclamation mark at the beginning of the story. In an explanatory letter to his editor at *The New Yorker* (who had rejected the story), Nabokov described the narrator, apparently so like the author, as "a somewhat obtuse scholar and a rather callous observer of the superficial planes of life." The reader's task, he suggested, was to see further than the narrator. Indeed, throughout his fiction, Nabokov encourages readers to seek signs and hints that the characters themselves may ignore. Although the surface of the story seems to depict the external world realistically—the narrator spots every visual detail of the scenes he observes—the story's plot suggests that this surface actually contains a complex set of indicators intended to lead, or mislead, the narrator and the reader. As Nabokov also explained to his editor, the reader is meant to discover the clues left by the author because "by means of various allusions to trick-reading I have arranged matters so that the reader almost automatically slips into this discovery, especially because of the abrupt change in *style*." Some readers dislike such trickiness, but the pleasure of discovery repays the reader who is attentive to Nabokov's clues.

The Vane Sisters

I

I might never have heard of Cynthia's death, had I not run, that night, into D., whom I had also lost track of for the last four years or so; and I might never have run into D. had I not got involved in a series of trivial investigations.

The day, a compunctious Sunday after a week of blizzards, had been part jewel, part mud. In the midst of my usual afternoon stroll through the small hilly town attached to the girls' college where I taught French literature, I had stopped to watch a family of brilliant icicles drip-dripping from the eaves of a frame house. So clear-cut were their pointed shadows on the white boards behind them that I was sure the shadows of the falling drops should be visible too. But they were not. The roof jutted too far out, perhaps, or the angle of vision was faulty, or, again, I did not chance to be watching the right icicle when the right drop fell. There was a rhythm, an alternation in the dripping that I found as teasing as a coin trick. It led me to inspect the corners of several house blocks, and this brought me to Kelly Road, and right to the house where D. used to live when he was instructor here. And as I looked up at the eaves of the adjacent garage with its full display of transparent stalactites backed by their blue silhouettes, I was rewarded at last, upon choosing one, by the sight of what might be described as the dot of an exclamation mark leaving its ordinary position to glide down very fast—a jot faster than the thaw-drop it raced. This twinned twinkle was delightful but not completely satisfying; or rather it only sharpened my appetite for other tidbits of light and shade, and I walked on in a state of raw awareness that seemed to transform the whole of my being into one big eyeball rolling in the world's socket.

Through peacocked lashes I saw the dazzling diamond reflection of the low sun on the round back of a parked automobile. To all kinds of things a vivid pictorial sense had been restored by the sponge of the thaw. Water in overlapping festoons flowed down one sloping street and turned gracefully into another. With ever so slight a note of meretricious appeal, narrow passages between buildings revealed treasures of brick and purple. I remarked for the first time the humble fluting—last echoes of grooves on the shafts of columns—ornamenting a garbage can, and I also saw the rippling upon its lid—circles diverging from a fantastically ancient center. Erect, dark-headed shapes of dead snow (left by the blades of a bulldozer last Friday) were lined up like rudimentary penguins along the curbs, above the brilliant vibration of live gutters.

I walked up, and I walked down, and I walked straight into a delicately dying sky, and finally the sequence of observed and observant things brought me, at my usual eating time, to a street so distant from my usual eating place that I decided to try a restaurant which stood on the fringe of the town. Night had fallen without sound or ceremony when I came out again. The lean ghost, the elongated umbra[1] cast by a parking meter upon some damp snow, had a strange ruddy tinge; this I made out to be due to the tawny red light of the restaurant sign above the sidewalk; and it was then—as I loitered there, wondering rather wearily if in the course of my return tramp I might be lucky enough to find the

1. Shadow.

same in neon blue—it was then that a car crunched to a standstill near me and D. got out of it with an exclamation of feigned pleasure.

He was passing, on his way from Albany to Boston, through the town he had dwelt in before, and more than once in my life have I felt that stab of vicarious emotion followed by a rush of personal irritation against travelers who seem to feel nothing at all upon revisiting spots that ought to harass them at every step with wailing and writhing memories. He ushered me back into the bar that I had just left, and after the usual exchange of buoyant platitudes came the inevitable vacuum which he filled with the random words: "Say, I never thought there was anything wrong with Cynthia Vane's heart. My lawyer tells me she died last week."

2

He was still young, still brash, still shifty, still married to the gentle, exquisitely pretty woman who had never learned or suspected anything about his disastrous affair with Cynthia's hysterical young sister, who in her turn had known nothing of the interview I had had with Cynthia when she suddenly summoned me to Boston to make me swear I would talk to D. and get him "kicked out" if he did not stop seeing Sybil at once—or did not divorce his wife (whom incidentally she visualized through the prism of Sybil's wild talk as a termagant and a fright). I had cornered him immediately. He had said there was nothing to worry about—had made up his mind, anyway, to give up his college job and move with his wife to Albany, where he would work in his father's firm; and the whole matter, which had threatened to become one of those hopelessly entangled situations that drag on for years, with peripheral sets of well-meaning friends endlessly discussing it in universal secrecy—and even founding, among themselves, new intimacies upon its alien woes—came to an abrupt end.

I remember sitting next day at my raised desk in the large classroom where a midyear examination in French Lit. was being held on the eve of Sybil's suicide. She came in on high heels, with a suitcase, dumped it in a corner where several other bags were stacked, with a single shrug slipped her fur coat off her thin shoulders, folded it on her bag, and with two or three other girls stopped before my desk to ask when I would mail them their grades. It would take me a week, beginning from tomorrow, I said, to read the stuff. I also remember wondering whether D. had already informed her of his decision—and I felt acutely unhappy about my dutiful little student as during 150 minutes my gaze kept reverting to her, so childishly slight in close-fitting gray, and kept observing that carefully waved dark hair, that small, small-flowered hat with a little hyaline veil as worn that season, and under it her small face broken into a cubist pattern by scars due to a skin disease, pathetically masked by a sunlamp tan that hardened her features, whose charm was further impaired by her having painted everything that could be painted, so that the pale gums of her teeth between cherry-red chapped lips and the diluted blue ink of her eyes under darkened lids were the only visible openings into her beauty.

Next day, having arranged the ugly copybooks alphabetically, I plunged into their chaos of scripts and came prematurely to Valevsky and Vane, whose books I had somehow misplaced. The first was dressed up for the occasion in a semblance of legibility, but Sybil's work displayed her usual combination of several demon hands. She had begun in very pale, very hard pencil which had conspicuously embossed the black verso,[2] but had produced little of permanent value on the upper side of the page. Happily the tip soon broke, and Sybil continued in another, darker lead, gradually lapsing into the blurred thickness of what looked almost like charcoal, to which, by sucking the blunt point, she had contributed some traces of lipstick. Her work, although even poorer than I had expected, bore all the signs of a kind of desperate conscientiousness, with underscores, transposes, unnecessary footnotes, as if she were intent upon rounding up things in the most respectable manner possible. Then she had borrowed Mary Valevsky's fountain pen and added: "*Cette examain est finie ainsi que ma vie. Adieu, jeunes filles!*[3] Please, *Monsieur le Professeur*, contact *ma soeur*[4] and tell her that Death was not better than D minus, but definitely better than Life minus D."

I lost no time in ringing up Cynthia, who told me it was all over—had been all over since eight in the morning—and asked me to bring her the note, and when I did, beamed through her tears with proud admiration for the whimsical use ("Just like her!") Sybil had made of an examination in French literature. In no time she "fixed" two highballs, while never parting with Sybil's notebook—by now splashed with soda water and tears—and went on studying the death message, whereupon I was impelled to point out to her the grammatical mistakes in it and to explain the way "girl" is translated in American colleges lest students innocently bandy around the French equivalent of "wench," or worse.[5] These rather tasteless trivialities pleased Cynthia hugely as she rose, with gasps, above the heaving surface of her grief. And then, holding that limp notebook as if it were a kind of passport to a casual Elysium (where pencil points do not snap and a dreamy young beauty with an impeccable complexion winds a lock of her hair on a dreamy forefinger, as she meditates over some celestial test), Cynthia led me upstairs to a chilly little bedroom, just to show me, as if I were the police or a sympathetic Irish neighbor, two empty pill bottles and the tumbled bed from which a tender, inessential body, that D. must have known down to its last velvet detail, had been already removed.

3

It was four or five months after her sister's death that I began seeing Cynthia fairly often. By the time I had come to New York for some vocational research in the Public Library she had also moved to that city, where for some odd reason (in vague connection, I presume, with artistic motives) she had taken what people, immune to gooseflesh, term a "cold water" flat,[6] down in the scale of the city's transverse streets. What attracted me was neither her ways, which I thought repulsively vivacious, nor her looks, which other men thought striking. She had wide-spaced eyes very much like her sister's, of a frank, frightened blue with dark points in a radial arrangement. The interval between her thick black eyebrows was always shiny, and shiny too were the fleshy volutes of her nostrils. The coarse texture of her epiderm looked almost masculine, and, in

2. Reverse side of a sheet of paper.
3. This exam is done, like my life. Goodbye, girls (misspelled French).
4. My sister (French). "Monsieur le Professeur": Professor (French).
5. *Jeune fille* (French for girl) could be used in American slang to refer to a prostitute.
6. An inexpensive, possibly illegal apartment.

the stark lamplight of her studio, you could see the pores of her thirty-two-year-old face fairly gaping at you like something in an aquarium. She used cosmetics with as much zest as her little sister had, but with an additional slovenliness that would result in her big front teeth getting some of the rouge. She was handsomely dark, wore a not too tasteless mixture of fairly smart heterogeneous things, and had a so-called good figure; but all of her was curiously frowzy, after a way I obscurely associated with left-wing enthusiasms in politics and "advanced" banalities in art, although, actually, she cared for neither. Her coily hairdo, on a part-and-bun basis, might have looked feral and bizarre had it not been thoroughly domesticated by its own soft unkemptness at the vulnerable nape. Her fingernails were gaudily painted, but badly bitten and not clean. Her lovers were a silent young photographer with a sudden laugh and two older men, brothers, who owned a small printing establishment across the street. I wondered at their tastes whenever I glimpsed, with a secret shudder, the higgledy-piggledy striation of black hairs that showed all along her pale shins through the nylon of her stockings with the scientific distinctness of a preparation flattened under glass; or when I felt, at her every movement, the dullish, stalish, not particularly conspicuous but all-pervading and depressing emanation that her seldom bathed flesh spread from under weary perfumes and creams.

Her father had gambled away the greater part of a comfortable fortune, and her mother's first husband had been of Slav origin, but otherwise Cynthia Vane belonged to a good, respectable family. For aught we know, it may have gone back to kings and soothsayers in the mists of ultimate islands. Transferred to a newer world, to a landscape of doomed, splendid deciduous trees, her ancestry presented, in one of its first phases, a white churchful of farmers against a black thunderhead, and then an imposing array of townsmen engaged in mercantile pursuits, as well as a number of learned men, such as Dr. Jonathan Vane, the gaunt bore (1780–1839), who perished in the conflagration of the steamer *Lexington* to become later an habitué of Cynthia's tilting table.[7] I have always wished to stand genealogy on its head, and here I have an opportunity to do so, for it is the last scion, Cynthia, and Cynthia alone, who will remain of any importance in the Vane dynasty. I am alluding of course to her artistic gift, to her delightful, gay, but not very popular paintings, which the friends of her friends bought at long intervals—and I dearly should like to know where they went after her death, those honest and poetical pictures that illumined her living room—the wonderfully detailed images of metallic things, and my favorite, *Seen Through a Windshield*—a windshield partly covered with rime,[8] with a brilliant trickle (from an imaginary car roof) across its transparent part and, through it all, the sapphire flame of the sky and a green-and-white fir tree.

4

Cynthia had a feeling that her dead sister was not altogether pleased with her—had discovered by now that she and I had conspired to break her romance; and so, in order to disarm her shade, Cynthia reverted to a rather primitive type

7. I.e., she attempted to contact his spirit through séances, where one proof of contact with the supernatural was an unexplained tilting or movement of a table.
8. Hard ice.

of sacrificial offering (tinged, however, with something of Sybil's humor), and began to send to D.'s business address, at deliberately unfixed dates, such trifles as snapshots of Sybil's tomb in a poor light; cuttings of her own hair which was indistinguishable from Sybil's; a New England sectional map with an inked-in cross, midway between two chaste towns, to mark the spot where D. and Sybil had stopped on October the twenty-third, in broad daylight, at a lenient motel, in a pink and brown forest; and, twice, a stuffed skunk.

Being as a conversationalist more voluble than explicit, she never could describe in full the theory of intervenient auras[9] that she had somehow evolved. Fundamentally there was nothing particularly new about her private creed since it presupposed a fairly conventional hereafter, a silent solarium of immortal souls (spliced with mortal antecedents) whose main recreation consisted of periodical hoverings over the dear quick.[1] The interesting point was a curious practical twist that Cynthia gave to her tame metaphysics. She was sure that her existence was influenced by all sorts of dead friends each of whom took turns in directing her fate much as if she were a stray kitten which a schoolgirl in passing gathers up, and presses to her cheek, and carefully puts down again, near some suburban hedge—to be stroked presently by another transient hand or carried off to a world of doors by some hospitable lady.

For a few hours, or for several days in a row, and sometimes recurrently, in an irregular series, for months or years, anything that happened to Cynthia, after a given person had died, would be, she said, in the manner and mood of that person. The event might be extraordinary, changing the course of one's life; or it might be a string of minute incidents just sufficiently clear to stand out in relief against one's usual day and then shading off into still vaguer trivia as the aura gradually faded. The influence might be good or bad; the main thing was that its source could be identified. It was like walking through a person's soul, she said. I tried to argue that she might not always be able to determine the exact source since not everybody has a recognizable soul; that there are anonymous letters and Christmas presents which anybody might send; that, in fact, what Cynthia called "a usual day" might be itself a weak solution of mixed auras or simply the routine shift of a humdrum guardian angel. And what about God? Did or did not people who would resent any omnipotent dictator on earth look forward to one in heaven? And wars? What a dreadful idea—dead soldiers still fighting with living ones, or phantom armies trying to get at each other through the lives of crippled old men.

But Cynthia was above generalities as she was beyond logic. "Ah, that's Paul," she would say when the soup spitefully boiled over, or: "I guess good Betty Brown is dead" when she won a beautiful and very welcome vacuum cleaner in a charity lottery. And, with Jamesian[2] meanderings that exasperated my French mind, she would go back to a time when Betty and Paul had not yet departed, and tell me of the showers of well-meant, but odd and quite unacceptable, bounties—beginning with an old purse that contained a check for three dollars which she picked up in the street and, of course, returned (to the aforesaid Betty Brown—this is where she first comes in—a decrepit colored

9. Spiritual energy fields that intervene in the material world.
1. Living.
2. I.e., in the style of the American novelist Henry James (1843–1916).

woman hardly able to walk), and ending with an insulting proposal from an old beau of hers (this is where Paul comes in) to paint "straight" pictures of his house and family for a reasonable remuneration—all of which followed upon the demise of a certain Mrs. Page, a kindly but petty old party who had pestered her with bits of matter-of-fact advice since Cynthia had been a child.

Sybil's personality, she said, had a rainbow edge as if a little out of focus. She said that had I known Sybil better I would have at once understood how Sybil-like was the aura of minor events which, in spells, had suffused her, Cynthia's, existence after Sybil's suicide. Ever since they had lost their mother they had intended to give up their Boston home and move to New York, where Cynthia's paintings, they thought, would have a chance to be more widely admired; but the old home had clung to them with all its plush tentacles. Dead Sybil, however, had proceeded to separate the house from its view—a thing that affects fatally the sense of home. Right across the narrow street a building project had come into loud, ugly, scaffolded life. A pair of familiar poplars died that spring, turning to blond skeletons. Workmen came and broke up the warm-colored lovely old sidewalk that had a special violet sheen on wet April days and had echoed so memorably to the morning footsteps of museum-bound Mr. Lever, who upon retiring from business at sixty had devoted a full quarter of a century exclusively to the study of snails.

Speaking of old men, one should add that sometimes these posthumous auspices and interventions were in the nature of parody. Cynthia had been on friendly terms with an eccentric librarian called Porlock[3] who in the last years of his dusty life had been engaged in examining old books for miraculous misprints such as the substitution of *l* for the second *h* in the word "hither." Contrary to Cynthia, he cared nothing for the thrill of obscure predictions; all he sought was the freak itself, the chance that mimics choice, the flaw that looks like a flower; and Cynthia, a much more perverse amateur of misshapen or illicitly connected words, puns, logogriphs,[4] and so on, had helped the poor crank to pursue a quest that in the light of the example she cited struck me as statistically insane. Anyway, she said, on the third day after his death she was reading a magazine and had just come across a quotation from an imperishable poem (that she, with other gullible readers, believed to have been really composed in a dream) when it dawned upon her that "Alph" was a prophetic sequence of the initial letters of Anna Livia Plurabelle[5] (another sacred river running through, or rather around, yet another fake dream), while the additional *h* modestly stood, as a private signpost, for the word that had so hypnotized Mr. Porlock. And I wish I could recollect that novel or short story (by some contemporary writer, I believe) in which, unknown to its author, the first letters of the words in its last paragraph formed, as deciphered by Cynthia, a message from his dead mother.

3. An allusion to Samuel Taylor Coleridge's poem "Kubla Khan" (1797). Coleridge claimed that the poem came to him in a dream that was interrupted by a visitor from the town of Porlock.

4. A word puzzle, such as an anagram.

5. An allusion to James Joyce's novel *Finnegans Wake* (1939). Anna Livia Plurabelle is a character based on the River Liffey in Dublin. Alph is the name of a river mentioned in Coleridge's "Kubla Khan." The name Alph contains the initials of Anna Livia Plurabelle plus the letter *h*, which the narrator interprets as standing for Hitler (the word that interested the librarian Porlock).

5

I am sorry to say that not content with these ingenious fancies Cynthia showed a ridiculous fondness for spiritualism. I refused to accompany her to sittings in which paid mediums took part: I knew too much about that from other sources. I did consent, however, to attend little farces rigged up by Cynthia and her two poker-faced gentlemen friends of the printing shop. They were podgy, polite, and rather eerie old fellows, but I satisfied myself that they possessed considerable wit and culture. We sat down at a light little table, and crackling tremors started almost as soon as we laid our fingertips upon it. I was treated to an assortment of ghosts that rapped out their reports most readily though refusing to elucidate anything that I did not quite catch. Oscar Wilde came in and in rapid garbled French, with the usual anglicisms, obscurely accused Cynthia's dead parents of what appeared in my jottings as "*plagiatisme.*"[6] A brisk spirit contributed the unsolicited information that he, John Moore, and his brother Bill had been coal miners in Colorado and had perished in an avalanche at "Crested Beauty" in January 1883. Frederic Myers,[7] an old hand at the game, hammered out a piece of verse (oddly resembling Cynthia's own fugitive productions) which in part reads in my notes:

What is this—a conjuror's rabbit,
Or a flawy but genuine gleam—
Which can check the perilous habit
And dispel the dolorous dream?

Finally, with a great crash and all kinds of shudderings and jiglike movements on the part of the table, Leo Tolstoy[8] visited our little group and, when asked to identify himself by specific traits of terrene habitation, launched upon a complex description of what seemed to be some Russian type of architectural woodwork ("figures on boards—man, horse, cock, man, horse, cock"), all of which was difficult to take down, hard to understand, and impossible to verify.

I attended two or three other sittings which were even sillier but I must confess that I preferred the childish entertainment they afforded and the cider we drank (Podgy and Pudgy were teetotalers) to Cynthia's awful house parties.

She gave them at the Wheelers' nice flat next door—the sort of arrangement dear to her centrifugal nature, but then, of course, her own living room always looked like a dirty old palette. Following a barbaric, unhygienic, and adulterous custom, the guests' coats, still warm on the inside, were carried by quiet, baldish Bob Wheeler into the sanctity of a tidy bedroom and heaped on the conjugal bed. It was also he who poured out the drinks, which were passed around by the young photographer while Cynthia and Mrs. Wheeler took care of the canapés.

A late arrival had the impression of lots of loud people unnecessarily grouped within a smoke-blue space between two mirrors gorged with reflections. Because,

6. Plagiarism (French). The narrator has accidentally written *t* for *r*. "Oscar Wilde": Irish writer (1854–1900).

7. Frederic Myers (1843–1901), British philosopher and noted researcher into spiritualism, the belief in supernatural powers and the possibility of communication with the dead. "Crested Butte": The Colorado site in mining country was subject to frequent avalanches, including a notably destructive one in March 1884.

8. Leo Tolstoy (1828–1910), Russian novelist and moralist, known for his mystical beliefs.

I suppose, Cynthia wished to be the youngest in the room, the women she used to invite, married or single, were, at the best, in their precarious forties; some of them would bring from their homes, in dark taxis, intact vestiges of good looks, which, however, they lost as the party progressed. It has always amazed me the ability sociable weekend revelers have of finding almost at once, by a purely empiric but very precise method, a common denominator of drunkenness, to which everybody loyally sticks before descending, all together, to the next level. The rich friendliness of the matrons was marked by tomboyish overtones, while the fixed inward look of amiably tight men was like a sacrilegious parody of pregnancy. Although some of the guests were connected in one way or another with the arts, there was no inspired talk, no wreathed, elbow-propped heads, and of course no flute girls.[9] From some vantage point where she had been sitting in a stranded mermaid pose on the pale carpet with one or two younger fellows, Cynthia, her face varnished with a film of beaming sweat, would creep up on her knees, a proffered plate of nuts in one hand, and crisply tap with the other the athletic leg of Cochran or Corcoran, an art dealer, ensconced, on a pearl-gray sofa, between two flushed, happily disintegrating ladies.

At a further stage there would come spurts of more riotous gaiety. Corcoran or Coransky would grab Cynthia or some other wandering woman by the shoulder and lead her into a corner to confront her with a grinning imbroglio of private jokes and rumors, whereupon, with a laugh and a toss of her head, she would break away. And still later there would be flurries of intersexual chumminess, jocular reconciliations, a bare fleshy arm flung around another woman's husband (he standing very upright in the midst of a swaying room), or a sudden rush of flirtatious anger, of clumsy pursuit—and the quiet half-smile of Bob Wheeler picking up glasses that grew like mushrooms in the shade of chairs.

After one last party of that sort, I wrote Cynthia a perfectly harmless and, on the whole, well-meant note, in which I poked a little Latin fun at some of her guests. I also apologized for not having touched her whiskey, saying that as a Frenchman I preferred the grape to the grain. A few days later I met her on the steps of the Public Library, in the broken sun, under a weak cloudburst, opening her amber umbrella, struggling with a couple of armpitted books (of which I relieved her for a moment), *Footfalls on the Boundary of Another World* by Robert Dale Owen,[1] and something on "Spiritualism and Christianity"; when, suddenly, with no provocation on my part, she blazed out at me with vulgar vehemence, using poisonous words, saying—through pear-shaped drops of sparse rain—that I was a prig and a snob; that I only saw the gestures and disguises of people; that Corcoran had rescued from drowning, in two different oceans, two men—by an irrelevant coincidence both called Corcoran; that romping and screeching Joan Winter had a little girl doomed to grow completely blind in a few months; and that the woman in green with the freckled chest whom I had snubbed in some way or other had written a national bestseller in 1932. Strange Cynthia! I had been told she could be thunderously rude to people whom she liked and respected; one had, however, to draw the

9. Missing are the trappings of the revels of Dionysus, Greek god of wine.
1. An 1860 book on the afterlife and communication with the dead by the Scottish-American social reformer Robert Dale Owen (1801–1877). "Spiritualism and Christianity": a 1900 lecture given by the Rev. H. R. Haweis (1838–1901), a leading spiritualist.

line somewhere and since I had by then sufficiently studied her interesting auras and other odds and ids,[2] I decided to stop seeing her altogether.

6

The night D. informed me of Cynthia's death I returned after eleven to the two-story house I shared, in horizontal section,[3] with an emeritus professor's widow. Upon reaching the porch I looked with the apprehension of solitude at the two kinds of darkness in the two rows of windows: the darkness of absence and the darkness of sleep.

I could do something about the first but could not duplicate the second. My bed gave me no sense of safety; its springs only made my nerves bounce. I plunged into Shakespeare's sonnets—and found myself idiotically checking the first letters of the lines to see what sacramental words they might form. I got FATE (LXX), ATOM (CXX), and, twice, TAFT (LXXXVIII, CXXXI).[4] Every now and then I would glance around to see how the objects in my room were behaving. It was strange to think that if bombs began to fall I would feel little more than a gambler's excitement (and a great deal of earthy relief) whereas my heart would burst if a certain suspiciously tense-looking little bottle on yonder shelf moved a fraction of an inch to one side. The silence, too, was suspiciously compact as if deliberately forming a black backdrop for the nerve flash caused by any small sound of unknown origin. All traffic was dead. In vain did I pray for the groan of a truck up Perkins Street. The woman above who used to drive me crazy by the booming thuds occasioned by what seemed monstrous feet of stone (actually, in diurnal life, she was a small dumpy creature resembling a mummified guinea pig) would have earned my blessings had she now trudged to her bathroom. I put out my light and cleared my throat several times so as to be responsible for at least *that* sound. I thumbed a mental ride with a very remote automobile but it dropped me before I had a chance to doze off. Presently a crackle (due, I hoped, to a discarded and crushed sheet of paper opening like a mean, stubborn night flower) started and stopped in the wastepaper basket, and my bed table responded with a little click. It would have been just like Cynthia to put on right then a cheap poltergeist show.

I decided to fight Cynthia. I reviewed in thought the modern era of raps and apparitions, beginning with the knockings of 1848, at the hamlet of Hydesville, New York, and ending with grotesque phenomena at Cambridge, Massachusetts; I evoked the ankle bones and other anatomical castanets of the Fox sisters (as described by the sages of the University of Buffalo);[5] the mysteri-

2. The founder of psychoanalysis, Sigmund Freud (1856–1939) theorized the existence of the *id* or "it" (Latin), a portion of the mind that sought to fulfill animal instincts regardless of social proprieties.

3. I.e., they each have one floor of the house.

4. The sonnets by Shakespeare indicated by the roman numerals in parentheses do in fact contain sequences of lines whose first letters spell out the words indicated. William Howard *Taft* (1857–1930) was the 27th president of the United States (1909–13).

5. In 1848 the three Fox sisters, Leah, Margaret, and Kate, claimed, as young girls in Hydesville, New York, to have made contact with the spirits of the dead; the claim began an international fad for spiritualism, which continued even after Margaret admitted in middle age that their spiritual contacts had been a hoax. Similar supernatural encounters were reported at *Tedworth* and *Epworth* in England, while spiritualism had a vogue in intellectual circles in *Peru*. Other famous mediums included Helen *Duncan*, Grace *Cooke* (who fooled the distinguished naturalist *Alfred Russel Wallace*), *Eusapia* Palladino, and *Margery* Crandon.

ously uniform type of delicate adolescent in bleak Epworth or Tedworth, radiating the same disturbances as in old Peru; solemn Victorian orgies with roses falling and accordions floating to the strains of sacred music; professional impostors regurgitating moist cheesecloth; Mr. Duncan, a lady medium's dignified husband, who, when asked if he would submit to a search, excused himself on the ground of soiled underwear; old Alfred Russel Wallace, the naive naturalist, refusing to believe that the white form with bare feet and unperforated earlobes before him, at a private pandemonium in Boston, could be prim Miss Cook whom he had just seen asleep, in her curtained corner, all dressed in black, wearing laced-up boots and earrings; two other investigators, small, puny, but reasonably intelligent and active men, closely clinging with arms and legs about Eusapia, a large, plump elderly female reeking of garlic, who still managed to fool them; and the skeptical and embarrassed magician, instructed by charming young Margery's "control" not to get lost in the bathrobe's lining but to follow up the left stocking until he reached the bare thigh—upon the warm skin of which he felt a "teleplastic" mass that appeared to the touch uncommonly like cold, uncooked liver.

7

I was appealing to flesh, and the corruption of flesh, to refute and defeat the possible persistence of discarnate[6] life. Alas, these conjurations only enhanced my fear of Cynthia's phantom. Atavistic peace came with dawn, and when I slipped into sleep the sun through the tawny window shades penetrated a dream that somehow was full of Cynthia.

This was disappointing. Secure in the fortress of daylight, I said to myself that I had expected more. She, a painter of glass-bright minutiae—and now so vague! I lay in bed, thinking my dream over and listening to the sparrows outside: Who knows, if recorded and then run backward, those bird sounds might not become human speech, voiced words, just as the latter become a twitter when reversed? I set myself to reread my dream—backward, diagonally, up, down—trying hard to unravel something Cynthia-like in it, something strange and suggestive that must be there.

I could isolate, consciously, little. Everything seemed blurred, yellow-clouded, yielding nothing tangible. Her inept acrostics, maudlin evasions, theopathies[7]—every recollection formed ripples of mysterious meaning. Everything seemed yellowly blurred, illusive, lost.

1959

6. Disembodied.
7. Spiritual emotions resulting from the contemplation of God. The first letter of each word in this paragraph spells out a message. Nabokov claimed that "by means of various allusions to trick-reading I have arranged matters so that the reader almost automatically slips into this discovery, especially because of the abrupt change in *style*."

CLARICE LISPECTOR

1920–1977

Reaching for an apple in the dark, claims Brazilian modernist Clarice Lispector, demonstrates the limits of our knowledge: we know that the object is an apple, but little more. Its color and ripeness remain shrouded in obscurity—tantalizingly *there* and *not there* at the same time. The characters in Lispector's novels and short stories live in the constant awareness of this kind of mystery; theirs is a plane of immediate experience and bodily sensations that has little to do with the orderly, daylight world of our shared rationality, where everything has been named and placed within a cognitive or social system. A pivotal figure in modern Brazilian literature, Lispector deploys a simple vocabulary but an unusual syntax; she makes extended use of interior monologues to evoke the immediacy of subjective consciousness.

Lispector was born in December 1920 in Tchetchelik, a small town in Ukraine, as her parents—Russian Jews who had been the victims of pogroms—made the long journey to a new home in Brazil. Upon their arrival, they changed their infant daughter's name from Chaya to Clarice. They settled in Recife, the capital of the northeastern state of Pernambuco, where Lispector received her early schooling, but later moved to Rio de Janeiro. There, Lispector entered law school and became the first woman reporter at the major newspaper *A Noite*. Her first novel, *Close to the Savage Heart*, published in 1943 (the title derives from a line in **James Joyce**'s *A Portrait of the Artist as a Young Man*), won her the Graça Aranha Prize and a reputation as an innovative young Brazilian writer.

Over the next fifteen years, she traveled widely with her husband, a diplomat she married when they were both in law school. They lived in Italy, Switzerland, England, and the United States. Lispector published some further fiction but spent much of her time in Washington, D.C., between 1952 and 1960, writing detailed notes that she would later incorporate into her fiction. Returning to Rio after separating from her husband, she made use of notes she had written during the previous eight years to compose her best-known short-story collection, *Family Ties* (1960), from which the selection here is taken. The collection won the prestigious Jabuti Prize, the foremost literary award in Brazil. Lispector published novels, short stories, chronicles (nonfiction pieces), and children's tales during the remaining years before her death from cancer in 1977.

Lispector is best known as a writer of intense, tightly structured short stories that portray the external world through a character's innermost thoughts and feelings and that emphasize sensuous perception to attain intuitive knowledge beyond words. She has often been compared, in this respect, with **Virginia Woolf**. Lispector's special contribution to literary modernism may lie in her ability to draw connections between bodily sensations, the limits of language, and the mysteries of existence—and to make these connections the unifying structure of her work. Her fluid, lyrical style has been called "feminine writing," because it explores the relationship of immediate bodily experience to language.

The work presented here, "The Daydreams of a Drunk Woman" (1960) is a disturbing tale. The title disposes of the protagonist in a few words: she is an alcoholic, and she imagines things. (The *rapariga* [young woman] of the original title suggests, in Brazilian Portuguese, that she may be promiscuous and possibly of poor immigrant stock.) The narrative's course confirms these descriptions: it begins with the protagonist in bed at home, possibly already drunk, and goes on to show her flying into alcoholic rages and bouts of self-pity. Yet the story reveals deeper possibilities in this woman. Oblique details and brilliant imagery suggest other dimensions to her life: the reasons for her misery and repressed rage, the choices that she has made while seeking security and protection, and the social conditions that foster such pitiable circumstances. From the beginning, when she stares at her reflection in a triple mirror and sees "the intersected breasts of several women," her identity appears fragmented, her self-image either in shards or swollen and unreachable. As she congratulates herself repeatedly on being "protected like everyone who had attained a position in life," and viciously criticizes a more stylish woman she sees in the restaurant, it gradually becomes clearer that she has arrived at her position, and escaped poverty, by exploiting her body to marry a man she neither loves nor respects. While filling in a devastatingly detailed picture of this abject modern figure in her day-to-day delusions, unhappiness, and destructive relationships, Lispector's prose evokes the existential dilemma that the young woman feels and half understands.

The Daydreams of a Drunk Woman[1]

It seemed to her that the trolley cars were about to cross through the room as they caused her reflected image to tremble. She was combing her hair at her leisure in front of the dressing table with its three mirrors, and her strong white arms shivered in the coolness of the evening. Her eyes did not look away as the mirrors trembled, sometimes dark, sometimes luminous. Outside, from a window above, something heavy and hollow fell to the ground. Had her husband and the little ones been at home, the idea would already have occurred to her that they were to blame. Her eyes did not take themselves off her image, her comb worked pensively, and her open dressing gown revealed in the mirrors the intersected breasts of several women.

"Evening News" shouted the newsboy to the mild breeze in Riachuelo Street,[2] and something trembled as if foretold. She threw her comb down on the dressing table and sang dreamily: "Who saw the little spar-row . . . it passed by the window . . . and flew beyond Minho!"[3]—but, suddenly becoming irritated, she shut up abruptly like a fan.

She lay down and fanned herself impatiently with a newspaper that rustled in the room. She clutched the bedsheet, inhaling its odor as she crushed its starched embroidery with her red-lacquered nails. Then, almost smiling, she started to fan herself once more. Oh my!—she sighed as she began to smile. She beheld the picture of her bright smile, the smile of a woman who was still

1. Translated by Giovanni Pontiero.
2. A street in Rio de Janeiro that intersects with Mem de Sá Street. Riachuelo is the name of a large department store; Mem de Sá was a 16th-century Portuguese governor-general of Brazil and the founder of Rio de Janeiro.
3. A river in northwest Portugal.

young, and she continued to smile to herself, closing her eyes and fanning herself still more vigorously. Oh my!—she would come fluttering in from the street like a butterfly.

"Hey there! Guess who came to see me today?" she mused as a feasible and interesting topic of conversation. "No idea, tell me," those eyes asked her with a gallant smile, those sad eyes set in one of those pale faces that make one feel so uncomfortable. "Maria Quiteria, my dear!" she replied coquettishly with her hand on her hip. "And who, might we ask, would she be?" they insisted gallantly, but now without any expression. "You!" she broke off, slightly annoyed. How boring!

Oh what a succulent room! Here she was, fanning herself in Brazil. The sun, trapped in the blinds, shimmered on the wall like the strings of a guitar. Riachuelo Street shook under the gasping weight of the trolley cars which came from Mem de Sá Street. Curious and impatient, she listened to the vibrations of the china cabinet in the drawing room. Impatiently she rolled over to lie face downward, and, sensuously stretching the toes of her dainty feet, she awaited her next thought with open eyes. "Whosoever found, searched," she said to herself in the form of a rhymed refrain, which always ended up by sounding like some maxim. Until eventually she fell asleep with her mouth wide open, her saliva staining the pillow.

She only woke up when her husband came into the room the moment he returned from work. She did not want to eat any dinner nor to abandon her dreams, and she went back to sleep: let him content himself with the leftovers from lunch.

And now that the kids were at the country house of their aunts in Jacarepaguá,[4] she took advantage of their absence in order to begin the day as she pleased: restless and frivolous in her bed . . . one of those whims perhaps. Her husband appeared before her, having already dressed, and she did not even know what he had prepared for his breakfast. She avoided examining his suit to see whether it needed brushing . . . little did she care if this was his day for attending to his business in the city. But when he bent over to kiss her, her capriciousness crackled like a dry leaf.

"Don't paw me!"

"What the devil's the matter with you?" the man asked her in amazement, as he immediately set about attempting some more effective caress.

Obstinate, she would not have known what to reply, and she felt so touchy and aloof that she did not even know where to find a suitable reply. She suddenly lost her temper. "Go to hell! . . . prowling round me like some old tomcat."

He seemed to think more clearly and said, firmly, "You're ill, my girl."

She accepted his remark, surprised, and vaguely flattered.

She remained in bed the whole day long listening to the silence of the house without the scurrying of the kids, without her husband who would have his meals in the city today. Her anger was tenuous and ardent. She only got up to go to the bathroom, from which she returned haughty and offended.

The morning turned into a long enormous afternoon, which then turned into a shallow night, which innocently dawned throughout the entire house.

She was still in bed, peaceful and casual. She was in love. . . . She was anticipating her love for the man whom she would love one day. Who knows, this

4. A quiet neighborhood in Rio de Janeiro with a beach where families would gather to picnic.

sometimes happened, and without any guilt or injury for either partner. Lying in bed thinking and thinking, and almost laughing as one does over some gossip. Thinking and thinking. About what? As if she knew. So she just stayed there.

The next minute she would get up, angry. But in the weakness of that first instant she felt dizzy and fragile in the room which swam round and round until she managed to grope her way back to bed, amazed that it might be true. "Hey, girl, don't you go getting sick on me!" she muttered suspiciously. She raised her hand to her forehead to see if there was any fever.

That night, until she fell asleep, her mind became more and more delirious—for how many minutes?—until she flopped over, fast asleep, to snore beside her husband.

She awoke late, the potatoes waiting to be peeled, the kids expected home that same evening from their visit to the country. "God, I've lost my self-respect, I have! My day for washing and darning socks. . . . What a lazy bitch you've turned out to be!" she scolded herself, inquisitive and pleased . . . shopping to be done, fish to remember, already so late on a hectic sunny morning.

But on Saturday night they went to the tavern in Tiradentes Square[5] at the invitation of a rich businessman, she with her new dress which didn't have any fancy trimmings but was made of good material, a dress that would last her a lifetime. On Saturday night, drunk in Tiradentes Square, inebriated but with her husband at her side to give her support, and being very polite in front of the other man who was so much more refined and rich—striving to make conversation, for she was no provincial ninny and she had already experienced life in the capital. But so drunk that she could no longer stand.

And if her husband was not drunk it was only because he did not want to show disrespect for the businessman, and, full of solicitude and humility, he left the swaggering to the other fellow. His manner suited such an elegant occasion, but it gave her such an urge to laugh! She despised him beyond words! She looked at her husband stuffed into his new suit and found him so ridiculous . . . so drunk that she could no longer stand, but without losing her self-respect as a woman. And the green wine[6] from her native Portugal slowly being drained from her glass.

When she got drunk, as if she had eaten a heavy Sunday lunch, all things which by their true nature are separate from each other—the smell of oil on the one hand, of a male on the other; the soup tureen on the one hand, the waiter on the other—became strangely linked by their true nature and the whole thing was nothing short of disgraceful . . . shocking!

And if her eyes appeared brilliant and cold, if her movements faltered clumsily until she succeeded in reaching the toothpick holder, beneath the surface she really felt so far quite at ease . . . there was that full cloud to transport her without effort. Her puffy lips, her teeth white, and her body swollen with wine. And the vanity of feeling drunk, making her show such disdain for everything, making her feel swollen and rotund like a large cow.

Naturally she talked, since she lacked neither the ability to converse nor topics to discuss. But the words that a woman uttered when drunk were like being

5. A square in Rio de Janeiro named after the Brazilian revolutionary patriot; he was executed by the Portuguese in 1792.

6. *Vinho Verde*, literally "green wine," is a soft wine produced in Portugal and often drunk cold before meals.

pregnant—mere words on her lips which had nothing to do with the secret core that seemed like a pregnancy. God, how queer she felt! Saturday night, her every-day soul lost, and how satisfying to lose it, and to remind her of former days, only her small, ill-kempt hands—and here she was now with her elbows resting on the white and red checked tablecloth like a gambling table, deeply launched upon a degrading and revolting existence. And what about her laughter? . . . this outburst of laughter which mysteriously emerged from her full white throat, in response to the polite manners of the businessman, an outburst of laughter coming from the depths of that sleep, and from the depths of that security of someone who has a body. Her white flesh was as sweet as lobster, the legs of a live lobster wriggling slowly in the air . . . that urge to be sick in order to plunge that sweetness into something really awful . . . and that perversity of someone who has a body.

She talked and listened with curiosity to what she herself was about to reply to the well-to-do businessman who had so kindly invited them out to dinner and paid for their meal. Intrigued and amazed, she heard what she was on the point of replying, and what she might say in her present state would serve as an augury for the future. She was no longer a lobster, but a harsher sign—that of the scorpion. After all, she had been born in November.

A beacon that sweeps through the dawn while one is asleep, such was her drunkenness which floated slowly through the air.

At the same time, she was conscious of such feelings! Such feelings! When she gazed upon that picture which was so beautifully painted in the restaurant, she was immediately overcome by an artistic sensibility. No one would get it out of her head that she had really been born for greater things. She had always been one for works of art.

But such sensibility! And not merely excited by the picture of grapes and pears and dead fish with shining scales. Her sensibility irritated her without causing her pain, like a broken fingernail. And if she wanted, she could allow herself the luxury of becoming even more sensitive, she could go still further, because she was protected by a situation, protected like everyone who had attained a position in life. Like someone saved from misfortune. I'm so miserable, dear God! If she wished, she could even pour more wine into her glass, and, protected by the position which she had attained in life, become even more drunk just so long as she did not lose her self-respect. And so, even more drunk, she peered round the room, and how she despised the barren people in that restaurant. Not a real man among them. How sad it really all seemed. How she despised the barren people in that restaurant, while she was plump and heavy and generous to the full. And everything in the restaurant seemed so remote, the one thing distant from the other, as if the one might never be able to converse with the other. Each existing for itself, and God existing there for everyone.

Her eyes once more settled on that female whom she had instantly detested the moment she had entered the room. Upon arriving, she had spotted her seated at a table accompanied by a man and all dolled up in a hat and jewelry, glittering like a false coin, all coy and refined. What a fine hat she was wearing! . . . Bet you anything she isn't even married for all that pious look on her face . . . and that fine hat stuck on her head. A fat lot of good her hypocrisy would do her, and she had better watch out in case her airs and graces proved her undoing! The more sanctimonious they were, the bigger frauds they turned out to be. And as for the waiter, he was a great nitwit, serving her, full of gestures and finesse, while the sallow man with her pretended not to notice. And that pious ninny so pleased with herself in that hat and so modest about her slim waistline, and I'll bet she couldn't even bear her man a child. All right, it was none of her business, but from the moment she arrived she felt the urge to give that blonde prude of a woman playing the grand lady in her hat a few good slaps on the face. She didn't even have any shape, and she was flat-chested. And no doubt, for all her fine hats, she was nothing more than a fishwife trying to pass herself off as a duchess.

Oh, how humiliated she felt at having come to the bar without a hat, and her head now felt bare. And that madam with her affectations, playing the refined lady! I know what you need, my beauty, you and your sallow boy friend! And if you think I envy you with your flat chest, let me assure you that I don't give a damn for you and your hats. Shameless sluts like you are only asking for a good hard slap on the face.

In her holy rage, she stretched out a shaky hand and reached for a toothpick.

But finally, the difficulty of arriving home disappeared; she now bestirred herself amidst the familiar reality of her room, now seated on the edge of the bed, a slipper dangling from one foot.

And, as she had half closed her blurred eyes, everything took on the appearance of flesh, the foot of the bed, the window, the suit her husband had thrown off, and everything became rather painful. Meanwhile, she was becoming larger, more unsteady, swollen and gigantic. If only she could get closer to herself, she would find she was even larger. Each of her arms could be explored by someone who didn't even recognize that they were dealing with an arm, and someone could plunge into each eye and swim around without knowing that it was an eye. And all around her everything was a bit painful. Things of the flesh stricken by nervous twinges. The chilly air had caught her as she had come out of the restaurant.

She was sitting up in bed, resigned and sceptical. And this was nothing yet, God only knew—she was perfectly aware that this was nothing yet. At this moment things were happening to her that would only hurt later and in earnest. When restored to her normal size, her anesthetized body would start to wake up, throbbing, and she would begin to pay for those big meals and drinks. Then, since this would really end up by happening, I might as well open my eyes right now (which she did) and then everything looked smaller and clearer, without her feeling any pain. Everything, deep down, was the same, only smaller and more familiar. She was sitting quite upright in bed, her stomach so full, absorbed and resigned, with the delicacy of one who sits waiting until her partner awakens. "You gorge yourself and I pay the piper," she said sadly, looking at the dainty white toes of her feet. She looked around her, patient and obedient. Ah, words, nothing but words, the objects in the room lined up in the order of words, to form those confused and irksome phrases that he who knows how will read. Boredom . . . such awful boredom. . . . How sickening! How very annoying! When all is said and done, heaven help me—God knows best. What was one to do? How can I describe this thing inside me? Anyhow, God knows best. And to think that she had enjoyed herself so much last night . . . and to think of how nice it all was—a restaurant to her liking—and how she had been seated elegantly at table. At table! The world would exclaim. But she made no reply, drawing herself erect with a bad-tempered click of her tongue . . . irritated . . . "Don't come to me with your endearments" . . . disenchanted, resigned, satiated, married, content, vaguely nauseated.

It was at this moment that she became deaf: one of her senses was missing. She clapped the palm of her hand over her ear, which only made things worse . . . suddenly filling her eardrum with the whirr of an elevator . . . life suddenly becoming loud and magnified in its smallest movements. One of two things: either she was deaf or hearing all too well. She reacted against this new suggestion with a sensation of spite and annoyance, with a sigh of resigned satiety. "Drop dead," she said gently . . . defeated.

"And when in the restaurant . . ." she suddenly recalled when she had been in the restaurant her husband's protector had pressed his foot against hers beneath the table, and above the table his face was watching her. By coincidence or intentionally? The rascal. A fellow, to be frank, who was not unattractive. She shrugged her shoulders.

And when above the roundness of her low-cut dress—right in the middle of Tiradentes Square! she thought, shaking her head incredulously—that fly had settled on her bare bosom. What cheek!

Certain things were good because they were almost nauseating . . . the noise like that of an elevator in her blood, while her husband lay snoring at her side . . . her chubby little children sleeping in the other room, the little villains. Ah, what's wrong with me! she wondered desperately. Have I eaten too much? Heavens above! What *is* wrong with me?

It was unhappiness.

Her toes playing with her slipper . . . the floor not too clean at that spot. "What a slovenly, lazy bitch you've become."

Not tomorrow, because her legs would not be too steady, but the day after tomorrow that house of hers would be a sight worth seeing: she would give it a scouring with soap and water which would get rid of all the dirt! "You mark my words," she threatened in her rage. Ah, she was feeling so well, so strong, as if she still had milk in those firm breasts. When her husband's friend saw her so pretty and plump he had immediately felt respect for her. And when she started to get embarrassed she did not know which way to look. Such misery! What was one to do? Seated on the edge of the bed, blinking in resignation. How well one could see the moon on these summer nights. She leaned over slightly, indifferent and resigned. The moon! How clearly one could see it. The moon high and yellow gliding through the sky, poor thing. Gliding, gliding . . . high up, high up. The moon! Then her vulgarity exploded in a sudden outburst of affection; "you slut," she cried out, laughing.

1960

CHINUA ACHEBE

1930–2013

The best-known African writer today is the Nigerian Chinua Achebe, whose first novel, *Things Fall Apart,* exploded the colonialist image of Africans as childlike people living in a primitive society. Achebe's novels, stories, poetry, and essays have made him a respected and prophetic figure in Africa and the West. In Western countries, where he has traveled, taught, and lectured widely, he is admired as a major writer who has given a new direction to the English-language novel. Achebe helped to create the African postcolonial novel with its themes and characters; he also developed a complex narrative voice that questions cultural assumptions with a subtle irony and compassion born from bicultural experience.

Achebe was born in Ogidi, an Igbo-speaking town of Eastern Nigeria, on November 16, 1930. He was the fifth of six children in the family of Isaiah Okafor Achebe, a teacher for the Church Missionary Society, and his wife, Janet. Achebe's parents christened him Albert after Prince Albert, husband of Queen Victoria. Two cultures coexisted in Ogidi: on the one hand, African social customs and traditional religion; on the other, British colonial authority and Christianity. Instead of being torn between the two, Achebe found himself curious about both ways of life and fascinated with the dual perspective that came from living "at the crossroads of cultures."

He attended church schools in Ogidi, where instruction was carried out in English. Achebe read the various books in his father's library, most of them primers or church related, but he also listened eagerly to his mother and sister when they told traditional Igbo stories. Entering a prestigious secondary school in Umuahia, he immediately took advantage of its well-stocked library. Achebe later recalled that when he read books about Africa, he tended to identify with the white narrators rather than the black inhabitants: "I did not see myself as an African in those books. I took sides with the white men against the savages." After graduating in 1948, Achebe entered University College, Ibadan, on a scholarship to study medicine. In the following year he changed to a program in liberal arts that combined English, history, and religious studies. Research in the last two fields deepened his knowledge of Nigerian history and culture; the assigned literary texts, however, brought into sharp focus the distorted image of African culture offered by British colonial literature. Reading Joyce Cary's *Mister Johnson* (1939), a novel recommended for its depiction of life in Nigeria, he was shocked to find Nigerians described as violent savages with passionate instincts and simple minds: "and so I thought if this was famous, then perhaps someone ought to try and look at this from the inside." While at the university, Achebe rejected his British name in favor of his indigenous name Chinua, which abbreviates *Chinualumogu*, or "My spirit come fight for me."

Achebe began writing while at the university, contributing articles and sketches to several campus papers and publishing four stories in the *University Herald*, a magazine whose editor he became in his third year. His first novel, *Things Fall Apart* (1958), was a conscious attempt to counteract the distortions of English literature about Africa by describing the richness and complexity of traditional African society before the colonial and missionary invasion. It was important, Achebe said, to "teach my readers that their past—with all its imperfections—was not one long night of savagery from which the first Europeans acting on God's behalf delivered them." The novel was recognized immediately as an extraordinary work of literature in English. It also became the first classic work of modern African fiction, translated into nine languages, and Achebe became, for many readers and writers, the teacher of a whole generation. His later novels continue to examine the individual and cultural dilemmas of Nigerian society, although their background varies from the traditional religious society of *Arrow of God* (1964) to thinly disguised accounts of contemporary political strife.

Achebe worked as a radio journalist for the Nigerian Broadcasting Service, ultimately rising to the position of director of external services in charge of the Voice of Nigeria. The radio position was more than a merely administrative post, for Achebe and his colleagues were creating a sense of shared national identity through the broadcasting of national news and information about Nigerian culture. Since the end of the Second World War, Nigeria had been torn by intellectual and political rivalries that overlaid the common struggle for independence (achieved in 1960). The three major ethnolinguistic groups—Yoruba, Hausa-Fulani, and Igbo—were increasingly locked in economic and political competition at the same time they were fighting to erase the vestiges of British colonial rule. These problems eventually boiled over in the Nigerian Civil War (1967–70).

It is hard to overestimate the influence of Nigerian politics on Achebe's life after 1966. In January a military coup d'état led by young Igbo officers overthrew the government; six months later a second coup led by non-Igbo officers took power. Ethnic strife intensified: thousands of Igbos were killed and driven out of the north. Soldiers were sent to find Achebe in Lagos; his wife and young children fled by boat to Eastern Nigeria, where after a dangerous and roundabout journey, Achebe joined them, taking up the post of senior research fellow at the University of Nigeria, Nsukka. In May 1967 the eastern region, mainly populated by Igbo-speakers, seceded as the new nation of Biafra. From then until the defeat of Biafra in January 1970, a bloody civil war was waged with high civilian casualties and widespread starvation. Achebe traveled in Europe, North America, and Africa to win support for Biafra, proclaiming that "no government, black or white, has the right to stigmatize and destroy groups of its own citizens without undermining the basis of its own existence." A group of his poems about the war won the Commonwealth Poetry Prize in 1972, the same year that he published a volume of short stories, *Girls at War*, and left Nigeria to take up a three-year position at the University of Massachusetts at Amherst. Returning to Nsukka as professor of literature in 1976, Achebe continued to participate in his country's political life. Badly hurt in a car accident in 1990, Achebe slowly recovered and returned to writing and teaching at Bard College in Annandale-on-Hudson, New York, where he stayed for most of the following two decades. Later, he taught at Brown University in Providence, Rhode Island. Among many other novels and memoirs, he published the essay collection *Education of a British Protected Child* (2009). Achebe died in Boston in 2013.

Chinua Achebe's writings emphasize an author's social responsibility. He draws frequent contrasts between the European "art for art's sake" tradition and the African belief in the indivisibility of art and society. His favorite example is the Owerri Igbo custom of *mbari*, a communal art project in which villagers selected by the priest of the earth goddess Ala live in a forest clearing for a year or more, working under the direction of master artists to prepare a temple of images in the goddess's honor. This creative communal enterprise and its culminating festival are diametrically opposed, the writer says, to the European custom of secluding art objects in museums or private collections. Instead, *mbari* celebrates art as a cultural process, affirming that "art belongs to all and is a 'function' of society." Achebe's own practice as novelist, poet, essayist, founder and editor of two journals, lecturer, and active representative of African letters exemplifies this commitment to the community.

"Chike's School Days" (1960), published in the year of Nigerian independence, tells the story of a child with a dual inheritance like Achebe's own. Like Achebe himself, the boy has three names: the Christian John, the familiar Chike, and the more formal African name Obiajulu, meaning "the mind at last is at rest." Yet if Chike is the answer to his parents' prayers for a son, he is also about to enter a transformative experience in a Christian school, where he will master the English language. Achebe's literary language is an English skillfully blended with Igbo vocabulary, proverbs, images, and speech patterns to create a voice embodying the linguistic pluralism of modern African experience. By including Standard English, Igbo, and pidgin in different contexts, Achebe demonstrates the existence of a diverse society that is otherwise concealed behind language barriers. He thereby acknowledges that his primary African audience is composed of younger, schooled readers who are relatively fluent in English, readers like Chike. Chike's story, however, focuses less on the school days of the title than on his background. Chike's education turns out to be the product of his paternal grandmother's conversion to Christianity, and of his father's marriage (following his own new Christian convictions) to an outcaste woman, an *Osu* (a member of the traditional Igbo slave caste). Thus a seemingly simple tale about a boy going to school turns out to be a story of historical change as it affects three generations. Chike's love of English, while it separates him from his neighbors, suggests the potential for a love of literature. Elsewhere, Achebe wrote that literature is important because it liberates the human imagination; it "begins as an adventure in self-discovery and ends in wisdom and human conscience."

Chike's School Days

Sarah's last child was a boy, and his birth brought great joy to the house of his father, Amos. The child received three names at his baptism—John, Chike, Obiajulu. The last name means "the mind at last is at rest."[1] Anyone hearing this name knew at once that its owner was either an only child or an only son. Chike was an only son. His parents had had five daughters before him.

Like his sisters Chike was brought up "in the ways of the white man," which meant the opposite of traditional. Amos had many years before bought a tiny bell with which he summoned his family to prayers and hymn-singing first

1. In the Igbo or Ibo language.

thing in the morning and last thing at night. This was one of the ways of the white man. Sarah taught her children not to eat in their neighbours' houses because "they offered their food to idols." And thus she set herself against the age-old custom which regarded children as the common responsibility of all so that, no matter what the relationship between parents, their children played together and shared their food.

One day a neighbour offered a piece of yam to Chike, who was only four years old. The boy shook his head haughtily and said, "We don't eat heathen food." The neighbour was full of rage, but she controlled herself and only muttered under her breath that even an *Osu*[2] was full of pride nowadays, thanks to the white man.

And she was right. In the past an *Osu* could not raise his shaggy head in the presence of the free-born. He was a slave to one of the many gods of the clan. He was a thing set apart, not to be venerated but to be despised and almost spat on. He could not marry a free-born, and he could not take any of the titles of his clan. When he died, he was buried by his kind in the Bad Bush.

Now all that had changed, or had begun to change. So that an *Osu* child could even look down his nose at a free-born, and talk about heathen food! The white man had indeed accomplished many things.

Chike's father was not originally an *Osu*, but had gone and married an *Osu* woman in the name of Christianity. It was unheard of for a man to make himself *Osu* in that way, with his eyes wide open. But then Amos was nothing if not mad. The new religion had gone to his head. It was like palm-wine. Some people drank it and remained sensible. Others lost every sense in their stomach.

The only person who supported Amos in his mad marriage venture was Mr. Brown, the white missionary, who lived in a thatch-roofed, red-earth-walled parsonage and was highly respected by the people, not because of his sermons, but because of a dispensary he ran in one of his rooms. Amos had emerged from Mr. Brown's parsonage greatly fortified. A few days later he told his widowed mother, who had recently been converted to Christianity and had taken the name of Elizabeth. The shock nearly killed her. When she recovered, she went down on her knees and begged Amos not to do this thing. But he would not hear; his ears had been nailed up. At last, in desperation, Elizabeth went to consult the diviner.

This diviner was a man of great power and wisdom. As he sat on the floor of his hut beating a tortoise shell, a coating of white chalk round his eyes, he saw not only the present, but also what had been and what was to be. He was called "the man of the four eyes." As soon as old Elizabeth appeared, he cast his stringed cowries[3] and told her what she had come to see him about. "Your son has joined the white man's religion. And you too in your old age when you should know better. And do you wonder that he is stricken with insanity? Those who gather ant-infested faggots must be prepared for the visit of lizards." He cast his cowries a number of times and wrote with a finger on a bowl of sand, and all the while his *nwifulu*,[4] a talking calabash, chatted to itself. "Shut up!" he roared, and it immediately held its peace. The diviner then mut-

2. An untouchable, the lowest caste in the Igbo class system.
3. Snail shells used as currency and, here, in fortune-telling.
4. A pipe made of a gourd.

tered a few incantations and rattled off a breathless reel of proverbs that followed one another like the cowries in his magic string.

At last he pronounced the cure. The ancestors were angry and must be appeased with a goat. Old Elizabeth performed the rites, but her son remained insane and married an *Osu* girl whose name was Sarah. Old Elizabeth renounced her new religion and returned to the faith of her people.

We have wandered from our main story. But it is important to know how Chike's father became an *Osu*, because even today when everything is upside down, such a story is very rare. But now to return to Chike who refused heathen food at the tender age of four years, or maybe five.

Two years later he went to the village school. His right hand could now reach across his head to his left ear, which proved that he was old enough to tackle the mysteries of the white man's learning. He was very happy about his new slate and pencil, and especially about his school uniform of white shirt and brown khaki shorts. But as the first day of the new term approached, his young mind dwelt on the many stories about teachers and their canes. And he remembered the song his elder sisters sang, a song that had a somewhat disquieting refrain:

Onye nkuzi ewelu itali piagbusie umuaka[5]

One of the ways an emphasis is laid in Ibo is by exaggeration, so that the teacher in the refrain might not actually have flogged the children to death. But there was no doubt he did flog them. And Chike thought very much about it.

Being so young, Chike was sent to what was called the "religious class" where they sang, and sometimes danced, the catechism. He loved the sound of words and he loved rhythm. During the catechism lesson the class formed a ring to dance the teacher's question. "Who was Caesar?"[6] he might ask, and the song would burst forth with much stamping of feet.

Siza bu eze Rome
Onye nachi enu uwa dum.[7]

It did not matter to their dancing that in the twentieth century Caesar was no longer ruler of the whole world.

And sometimes they even sang in English. Chike was very fond of "Ten Green Bottles." They had been taught the words but they only remembered the first and the last lines. The middle was hummed and hie-ed and mumbled:

Ten grin botr angin on dar war,
Ten grin botr angin on dar war,
Hm hm hm hm hm
Hm, hm hm hm hm hm,
An ten grin botr angin on dar war.[8]

5. "The teacher took a whip and flogged the pupils mercilessly" (Ibo).
6. Julius Caesar (100–44 B.C.E.), Roman general and political leader whose near-monopoly on power in the late days of the Roman Republic led to the creation of the Roman Empire.
7. "Caesar was the chief of Rome, / the ruler of the whole world" (Ibo).
8. A British children's song, "Ten green bottles hanging on the wall," as pronounced by African children who are learning English.

In this way the first year passed. Chike was promoted to the "Infant School," where work of a more serious nature was undertaken.

We need not follow him through the Infant School. It would make a full story in itself. But it was no different from the story of other children. In the Primary School, however, his individual character began to show. He developed a strong hatred for arithmetic. But he loved stories and songs. And he liked particularly the sound of English words, even when they conveyed no meaning at all. Some of them simply filled him with elation. "Periwinkle" was such a word. He had now forgotten how he learned it or exactly what it was. He had a vague private meaning for it and it was something to do with fairyland. "Constellation" was another.

Chike's teacher was fond of long words. He was said to be a very learned man. His favourite pastime was copying out jaw-breaking words from his *Chambers' Etymological Dictionary*. Only the other day he had raised applause from his class by demolishing a boy's excuse for lateness with unanswerable erudition. He had said: "Procrastination is a lazy man's apology." The teacher's erudition showed itself in every subject he taught. His nature study lessons were memorable. Chike would always remember the lesson on the methods of seed dispersal. According to teacher, there were five methods: by man, by animals, by water, by wind, and by explosive mechanism. Even those pupils who forgot all the other methods remembered "explosive mechanism."

Chike was naturally impressed by teacher's explosive vocabulary. But the fairyland quality which words had for him was of a different kind. The first sentences in his *New Method Reader* were simple enough and yet they filled him with a vague exultation: "Once there was a wizard. He lived in Africa. He went to China to get a lamp." Chike read it over and over again at home and then made a song of it. It was a meaningless song. "Periwinkles" got into it, and also "Damascus." But it was like a window through which he saw in the distance a strange, magical new world. And he was happy.

1960

CARLOS FUENTES

1928–2012

One of the first Mexican novelists to achieve international success, Carlos Fuentes helped to ignite the Latin American "Boom," or literary flowering, of the 1960s. Combining meditations on Mexican history with modern literary techniques, Fuentes became a leading novelist and public intellectual in his home country. His worldwide reputation rested on his experimental fiction, a precursor to postmodernism.

Born in Panama City, Fuentes was the son of a Mexican diplomat. With his parents, he lived in several Latin American capitals (Montevideo, Uruguay; Rio de Janeiro, Brazil; Santiago,

Chile; and Buenos Aires, Argentina)—and, from 1934 to 1940, in Washington, D.C., where he acquired an admiration for the liberal politics of Franklin Delano Roosevelt and the New Deal. In Washington, Fuentes learned about Mexico's relationship with its superpower neighbor. At the age of ten, he attended a film about the Texan Sam Houston. Fuentes wrote about the experience, "During the attack on the Alamo, I couldn't restrain my patriotism. I jumped on the seat, screaming, 'Viva Mexico—death to the gringo,'" using a generally unflattering term to refer to Mexico's neighbors to the north. His father hustled him out of the theater. As an adult, Fuentes often criticized U.S. policy in Latin America and was once prevented from entering the United States because of suspected Communist ties; but he remained relatively friendly toward the country where he had spent much of his childhood, and later in life he taught at American universities.

When he was a teenager, Fuentes and his family returned to Mexico City. Although he wanted to become a writer, he also worked in foreign affairs, for the United Nations and the International Labor Organization. Fuentes's first novel was the immensely successful *Where the Air Is Clear* (1958). Its hero is Mexico City itself, with its dramatic mixture of Spanish, indigenous, and mestizo cultures. Fuentes's novels draw on the techniques of modernism, such as stream-of-consciousness narration, to portray the inner lives of characters. After achieving fame as a novelist, he served briefly as Mexican ambassador to France.

In the novella presented here, *Aura* (1962), Fuentes makes use of second-person narration. By addressing the main character, Felipe Montero, as "you"—as if Montero were a reader—Fuentes draws his actual readers into the story, plunging them into the life of an unemployed Mexican intellectual. The unsettling quality is heightened by the advertisement Montero reads in the newspaper, on the first page of the story, which appears to have been written specifically for him. Montero seems closely identified with the author of the story, too. Like Fuentes, who wrote a panoramic overview of Latin American history, *The Buried Mirror* (1992), Montero is knowledgeable about history and fluent in French.

Montero journeys to the old center of Mexico City, which has fallen into disrepair, and mysteriously finds his way into a luxurious but faded apartment. There he is met by an old woman who seems to know all about him and who addresses him in French. As he learns what tasks the lady wants him to perform, the protagonist becomes fascinated by the role of her late, legendary husband in Mexican history and by the unreal beauty of her young niece, Aura. Like many uncanny stories (notably those of Henry James, whom Fuentes admired), *Aura* leaves us in suspense about which of the events may be real or imagined, natural or supernatural.

Fuentes recalled the origins of the story in his vision of a young woman in a certain light in a mirror-filled room in Paris:

> In this almost instantaneous succession, the girl I remembered when she was fourteen years old and who was now twenty suffered the same changes as the light coming through the windowpanes: that threshold between the parlour and the bedroom became the lintel between all the ages of this girl: the light that had been struggling against the clouds also fought against her flesh, took it, sketched it, granted her a shadow of years, sculpted a death in her eyes, tore the smile from her lips, waned through her hair with the floating melancholy of madness.

The next day, Fuentes sat down in a café to write *Aura*.

Aura[1]

Man hunts and struggles.
Woman intrigues and dreams;
she is the mother of fantasy,
the mother of the gods.
She has second sight,
the wings that enable her to fly
to the infinite of
desire and the imagination . . .
The gods are like men:
they are born and they die
on a woman's breast . . .

—JULES MICHELET[2]

I

You're reading the advertisement: an offer like this isn't made every day. You read it and reread it. It seems to be addressed to you and nobody else. You don't even notice when the ash from your cigarette falls into the cup of tea you ordered in this cheap, dirty café. You read it again. "Wanted, young historian, conscientious, neat. Perfect knowledge colloquial French." Youth . . . knowledge of French, preferably after living in France for a while . . . "Four thousand pesos a month, all meals, comfortable bedroom-study." All that's missing is your name. The advertisement should have two more words, in bigger, blacker type: Felipe Montero. Wanted, Felipe Montero, formerly on scholarship at the Sorbonne, historian full of useless facts, accustomed to digging among yellowed documents, part-time teacher in private schools, nine hundred pesos a month. But if you read that, you'd be suspicious, and take it as a joke. "Address, Donceles *815*."[3] No telephone. Come in person.

You leave a tip, reach for your brief case, get up. You wonder if another young historian, in the same situation you are, has seen the same advertisement, has got ahead of you and taken the job already. You walk down to the corner, trying to forget this idea. As you wait for the bus, you run over the dates you must have on the tip of your tongue so that your sleepy pupils will respect you. The bus is coming now, and you're staring at the tips of your black shoes. You've got to be prepared. You put your hand in your pocket, search among the coins, and finally take out thirty centavos. You've got to be prepared. You grab the handrail—the bus slows down but doesn't stop—and jump aboard. Then you shove your way forward, pay the driver the thirty centavos,[4] squeeze yourself in among the passengers already standing in the aisle, hang onto the over-head rail, press your brief case tighter under your left arm, and automatically put your left hand over the back pocket where you keep your billfold.

This day is just like any other day, and you don't remember the advertisement until the next morning, when you sit down in the same café and order

1. Translated from Spanish by Lysander Kemp.
2. French historian (1798–1874). The quotation is from *Satanism and Witchcraft* (1862).
3. In downtown Mexico City.
4. A few cents.

breakfast and open your newspaper. You come to the advertising section and there it is again: *young historian*. The job is still open. You reread the advertisement, lingering over the final words: four thousand pesos.

It's surprising to know that anyone lives on Donceles Street. You always thought that nobody lived in the old center of the city. You walk slowly, trying to pick out the number *815* in that conglomeration of old colonial mansions, all of them converted into repair shops, jewelry shops, shoe stores, drugstores. The numbers have been changed, painted over, confused. A *13* next to a *200*. An old plaque reading *47* over a scrawl in blurred charcoal: *Now 924*. You look up at the second stories. Up there, everything is the same as it was. The jukeboxes don't disturb them. The mercury streetlights don't shine in. The cheap merchandise on sale along the street doesn't have any effect on that upper level; on the baroque harmony of the carved stones; on the battered stone saints with pigeons clustering on their shoulders; on the latticed balconies, the copper gutters, the sandstone gargoyles; on the greenish curtains that darken the long windows; on that window from which someone draws back when you look at it. You gaze at the fanciful vines carved over the doorway, then lower your eyes to the peeling wall and discover *815, formerly 69*.

You rap vainly with the knocker, that copper head of a dog, so worn and smooth that it resembles the head of a canine foetus in a museum of natural science. It seems as if the dog is grinning at you and you let go of the cold metal. The door opens at the first light push of your fingers, but before going in you give a last look over your shoulder, frowning at the long line of stalled cars that growl, honk, and belch out the unhealthy fumes of their impatience. You try to retain some single image of that indifferent outside world.

You close the door behind you and peer into the darkness of a roofed alleyway. It must be a patio of some sort, because you can smell the mold, the dampness of the plants, the rotting roots, the thick drowsy aroma. There isn't any light to guide you, and you're searching in your coat pocket for the box of matches when a sharp, thin voice tells you, from a distance: "No, it isn't necessary. Please. Walk thirteen steps forward and you'll come to a stairway at your right. Come up, please. There are twenty-two steps. Count them."

Thirteen. To the right. Twenty-two.

The dank smell of the plants is all around you as you count out your steps, first on the paving-stones, then on the creaking wood, spongy from the dampness. You count to twenty-two in a low voice and then stop, with the matchbox in your hand, and the brief case under your arm. You knock on a door that smells of old pine. There isn't any knocker. Finally you push it open. Now you can feel a carpet under your feet, a thin carpet, badly laid. It makes you trip and almost fall. Then you notice the grayish filtered light that reveals some of the humps.

"Señora," you say, because you seem to remember a woman's voice. "Señora . . ."

"Now turn to the left. The first door. Please be so kind."

You push the door open: you don't expect any of them to be latched, you know they all open at a push. The scattered lights are braided in your eyelashes, as if you were seeing them through a silken net. All you can make out are the dozens of flickering lights. At last you can see that they're votive lights, all set on brackets or hung between unevenly-spaced panels. They cast a faint glow on the silver objects, the crystal flasks, the gilt-framed mirrors. Then you see the bed in the shadows beyond, and the feeble movement of a hand that seems to be beckoning to you.

But you can't see her face until you turn your back on that galaxy of religious lights. You stumble to the foot of the bed, and have to go around it in order to get to the head of it. A tiny figure is almost lost in its immensity. When you reach out your hand, you don't touch another hand, you touch the ears and thick fur of a creature that's chewing silently and steadily, looking up at you with its glowing red eyes. You smile and stroke the rabbit that's crouched beside her hand. Finally you shake hands, and her cold fingers remain for a long while in your sweating palm.

"I'm Felipe Montero. I read your advertisement."

"Yes, I know. I'm sorry, there aren't any chairs."

"That's all right. Don't worry about it."

"Good. Please let me see your profile. No, I can't see it well enough. Turn toward the light. That's right. Excellent."

"I read your advertisement . . ."

"Yes, of course. Do you think you're qualified? *Avez-vous fait des études?*"

"*A Paris, madame.*"

"*Ah, oui, ça me fait plaisir, toujours, toujours, d'entendre . . . oui . . . vous savez . . . on était tellement habitué . . . et après . . .*"[5]

You move aside so that the light from the candles and the reflections from the silver and crystal show you the silk coif that must cover a head of very white hair, and that frames a face so old it's almost childlike. Her whole body is covered by the sheets and the feather pillows and the high, tightly buttoned white collar, all except for her arms, which are wrapped in a shawl, and her pallid hands resting on her stomach. You can only stare at her face until a movement of the rabbit lets you glance furtively at the crusts and bits of bread scattered on the worn-out red silk of the pillows.

"I'll come directly to the point. I don't have many years ahead of me, Señor Montero, and therefore I decided to break a lifelong rule and place an advertisement in the newspaper."

"Yes, that's why I'm here."

"Of course. So you accept."

"Well, I'd like to know a little more."

"Yes. You're wondering."

She sees you glance at the night table, the different-colored bottles, the glasses, the aluminium spoons, the row of pillboxes, the other glasses—all stained with whitish liquids—on the floor within reach of her hand. Then you notice that the bed is hardly raised above the level of the floor. Suddenly the rabbit jumps down and disappears in the shadows.

"I can offer you four thousand pesos."

"Yes, that's what the advertisement said today."

"Ah, then it came out."

"Yes, it came out."

5. "Have you studied?"
"In Paris, Madame."
"Ah, yes, it always, always pleases me to hear . . . yes . . . you know . . . we were so accustomed to it . . . and afterwards . . ." (French).

"It has to do with the memoirs of my husband, General Llorente. They must be put in order before I die. I want them to be published. I decided that a short time ago."

"But the General himself? Wouldn't he be able to . . ."

"He died sixty years ago, Señor. They're his unfinished memoirs. They have to be completed before I die."

"But . . ."

"I can tell you everything. You'll learn to write in my husband's own style. You'll only have to arrange and read his manuscripts to become fascinated by his style . . . his clarity . . . his . . ."

"Yes, I understand."

"Saga, Saga. Where are you? *Ici*, Saga!"

"Who?"

"My companion."

"The rabbit?"

"Yes. She'll come back."

When you raise your eyes, which you've been keeping lowered, her lips are closed but you can hear her words again—"She'll come back"—as if the old lady were pronouncing them at that instant. Her lips remain still. You look in back of you and you're almost blinded by the gleam from the religious objects. When you look at her again you see that her eyes have opened very wide, and that they're clear, liquid, enormous, almost the same colour as the yellowish whites around them, so that only the black dots of the pupils mar that clarity. It's lost a moment later in the heavy folds of her lowered eyelids, as if she wanted to protect that glance which is now hiding at the back of its dry cave.

"Then you'll stay here. Your room is upstairs. It's sunny there."

"It might be better if I didn't trouble you, Señora. I can go on living where I am and work on the manuscripts there."

"My conditions are that you have to live here. There isn't much time left."

"I don't know if . . ."

"Aura . . ."

The old woman moves for the first time since you entered her room. As she reaches out her hand again, you sense that agitated breathing beside you, and another hand reaches out to touch the Señora's fingers. You look around and a girl is standing there, a girl whose whole body you can't see because she's standing so close to you and her arrival was so unexpected, without the slightest sound—not even those sounds that can't be heard but are real anyway because they're remembered immediately afterwards, because in spite of everything they're louder than the silence that accompanies them.

"I told you she'd come back."

"Who?"

"Aura. My companion. My niece."

"Good afternoon."

The girl nods and at the same instant the old lady imitates her gesture.

"This is Señor Montero. He's going to live with us."

You move a few steps so that the light from the candles won't blind you. The girl keeps her eyes closed, her hands at her sides. She doesn't look at you at first, then little by little she opens her eyes as if she were afraid of the light. Finally you can see that those eyes are sea green and that they surge, break to foam, grow calm again, then surge again like a wave. You look into them and tell yourself it isn't true, because they're beautiful green eyes just like all the beautiful green eyes you've ever known. But you can't deceive yourself: those eyes do surge, do change, as if offering you a landscape that only you can see and desire.

"Yes. I'm going to live with you."

2

The old woman laughs sharply and tells you that she is grateful for your kindness and that the girl will show you to your room. You're thinking about the salary of four thousand pesos, and how the work should be pleasant because you like these jobs of careful research that don't include physical effort or going from one place to another or meeting people you don't want to meet. You're thinking about this as you follow her out of the room, and you discover that you've got to follow her with your ears instead of your eyes: you follow the rustle of her skirt, the rustle of taffeta, and you're anxious now to look into her eyes again. You climb the stairs behind that sound in the darkness, and you're still unused to the obscurity. You remember it must be about six in the afternoon, and the flood of light surprises you when Aura opens the door to your bedroom—another door without a latch—and steps aside to tell you: "This is your room. We'll expect you for supper in an hour."

She moves away with the same faint rustle of taffeta, and you weren't able to see her face again.

You close the door and look up at the skylight that serves as a roof. You smile when you find that the evening light is blinding compared with the darkness in the rest of the house, and smile again when you try out the mattress on the gilded metal bed. Then you glance around the room: a red wool rug, olive and gold wallpaper, an easy chair covered in red velvet, an old walnut desk with a green leather top, an old Argand lamp with its soft glow for your nights of research, and a bookshelf over the desk in reach of your hand. You walk over to the other door, and on pushing it open you discover an outmoded bathroom: a four-legged bathtub with little flowers painted on the porcelain, a blue hand basin, an old-fashioned toilet. You look at yourself in the large oval mirror on the door of the wardrobe—it's also walnut—in the bathroom hallway. You move your heavy eyebrows and wide thick lips, and your breath fogs the mirror. You close your black eyes, and when you open them again the mirror has cleared. You stop holding your breath and run your hand through your dark, limp hair; you touch your fine profile, your lean cheeks; and when your breath hides your face again you're repeating her name: "Aura."

After smoking two cigarettes while lying on the bed, you get up, put on your jacket, and comb your hair. You push the door open and try to remember the route you followed coming up. You'd like to leave the door open so that the lamplight could guide you, but that's impossible because the springs close it behind you. You could enjoy playing with that door, swinging it back and forth. You don't do it. You could take the lamp down with you. You don't do it. This house will always be in darkness, and you've got to learn it and relearn it by touch. You grope your way like a blind man, with your arms stretched out wide, feeling your way along the wall, and by accident you turn on the light-switch.

You stop and blink in the bright middle of that long, empty hall. At the end of it you can see the bannister and the spiral staircase.

You count the stairs as you go down: another custom you've got to learn in Señora Llorente's house. You take a step backward when you see the reddish eyes of the rabbit, which turns its back on you and goes hopping away.

You don't have time to stop in the lower hallway because Aura is waiting for you at a half-open stained-glass door, with a candelabra in her hand. You walk toward her, smiling, but you stop when you hear the painful yowling of a number of cats—yes, you stop to listen, next to Aura, to be sure that they're cats—and then follow her to the parlor.

"It's the cats," Aura tells you. "There are lots of rats in this part of the city."

You go through the parlor: furniture upholstered in faded silk; glass-fronted cabinets containing porcelain figurines, musical clocks, medals, glass balls; carpets with Persian designs; pictures of rustic scenes; green velvet curtains. Aura is dressed in green.

"Is your room comfortable?"

"Yes. But I have to get my things from the place where . . ."

"It won't be necessary. The servant has already gone for them."

"You shouldn't have bothered."

You follow her into the dining room. She places the candelabra in the middle of the table. The room feels damp and cold. The four walls are paneled in dark wood carved in Gothic style, with fretwork arches and large rosettes. The cats have stopped yowling. When you sit down, you notice that four places have been set. There are two large, covered plates and an old, grimy bottle.

Aura lifts the cover from one of the plates. You breathe in the pungent odour of the liver and onions she serves you, then you pick up the old bottle and fill the cut-glass goblets with that thick red liquid. Out of curiosity you try to read the label on the wine bottle, but the grime has obscured it. Aura serves you some whole broiled tomatoes from the other plate.

"Excuse me," you say, looking at the two extra places, the two empty chairs, "but are you expecting someone else?"

Aura goes on serving the tomatoes. "No. Señora Consuelo feels a little ill tonight. She won't be joining us."

"Señora Consuelo? Your aunt?"

"Yes. She'd like you to go in and see her after supper."

You eat in silence. You drink that thick wine, occasionally shifting your glance so that Aura won't catch you in the hypnotized stare that you can't control. You'd like to fix the girl's features in your mind. Every time you look away you forget them again, and an irresistible urge forces you to look at her once more. As usual, she has her eyes lowered. While you're searching for the pack of cigarettes in your coat pocket, you run across that big key, and remember, and say to Aura: "Ah! I forgot that one of the drawers in my desk is locked. I've got my papers in it."

And she murmurs: "Then you want to go out?" She says it as a reproach.

You feel confused, and reach out your hand to her with the key dangling from one finger.

"It isn't important. The servant can go for them tomorrow."

But she avoids touching your hand, keeping her own hands on her lap. Finally she looks up, and once again you question your senses, blaming the wine for your bewilderment, for the dizziness brought on by those shining, clear green eyes, and you stand up after Aura does, running your hand over the wooden back of the Gothic chair, without daring to touch her bare shoulder or her motionless head.

You make an effort to control yourself, diverting your attention away from her by listening to the imperceptible movement of a door behind you—it must lead to the kitchen—or by separating the two different elements that make up the room: the compact circle of light around the candelabra, illuminating the table and one carved wall, and the larger circle of darkness surrounding it. Finally you have the courage to go up to her, take her hand, open it, and place your key-ring in her smooth palm as a token.

She closes her hand, looks up at you, and murmurs, "Thank you." Then she rises and walks quickly out of the room.

You sit down in Aura's chair, stretch your legs, and light a cigarette, feeling a pleasure you've never felt before, one that you knew was part of you but that only now you're experiencing fully, setting it free, bringing it out because this time you know it'll be answered and won't be lost . . . And Señora Consuelo is waiting for you, as Aura said. She's waiting for you after supper . . .

You leave the dining room, and with the candelabra in your hand you walk through the parlour and the hallway. The first door you come to is the old lady's. You rap on it with your knuckles, but there isn't any answer. You knock again. Then you push the door open because she's waiting for you. You enter cautiously, murmuring: "Señora . . . Señora . . ."

She doesn't hear you, for she's kneeling in front of that wall of religious objects, with her head resting on her clenched fists. You see her from a distance: she's kneeling there in her coarse woollen nightgown with her head sunk into her narrow shoulders; she's thin, even emaciated, like a medieval sculpture; her legs are like two sticks, and they're inflamed with erysipelas.[6] While you're thinking of the continual rubbing of that rough wool against her skin, she suddenly raises her fists and strikes feebly at the air, as if she were doing battle against the images you can make out as you tiptoe closer: Christ, the Virgin, St. Sebastian, St. Lucia, the Archangel Michael,[7] and the grinning demons in an old print, the only happy figures in that iconography of sorrow and wrath, happy because they're jabbing their pitchforks into the flesh of the damned, pouring cauldrons of boiling water on them, violating the women, getting drunk, enjoying all the liberties forbidden to the saints. You approach that central image, which is surrounded by the tears of Our Lady of Sorrows, the blood of Our Crucified Lord, the delight of Lucifer, the anger of the Archangel, the viscera preserved in bottles of alcohol, the silver heart: Señora Consuelo, kneeling, threatens them with her fists, stammering the words you can hear as you move even closer: "Come, City of God! Gabriel, sound your trumpet! Ah, how long the world takes to die!"[8]

She beats her breast until she collapses in front of the images and candles in a spasm of coughing. You raise her by the elbow, and as you gently help her to

6. Acute skin infection.
7. Catholic religious images.
8. The Archangel Gabriel will sound his trumpet to announce the return of the Messiah and the end of the world.

the bed you're surprised at her smallness: she's almost a little girl, bent over almost double. You realize that without your assistance she would have had to get back to bed on her hands and knees. You help her into that wide bed with its bread crumbs and old feather pillows, and cover her up, and wait until her breathing is back to normal, while the involuntary tears run down her parchment cheeks.

"Excuse me . . . excuse me, Señor Montero. Old ladies have nothing left but . . . the pleasure of devotion . . . Give me my handkerchief, please."

"Señorita Aura told me . . ."

"Yes, of course. I don't want to lose any time. We should . . . we should begin working as soon as possible. Thank you."

"You should try to rest."

"Thank you . . . Here . . ."

The old lady raises her hand to her collar, unbuttons it, and lowers her head to remove the frayed purple ribbon that she hands to you. It's heavy because there's a copper key hanging from it.

"Over in that corner . . . Open that trunk and bring me the papers at the right, on top of the others . . . They're tied with a yellow ribbon."

"I can't see very well . . ."

"Ah, yes . . . it's just that I'm so accustomed to the darkness. To my right . . . Keep going till you come to the trunk. They've walled us in, Señor Montero. They've built up all around us and blocked off the light. They've tried to force me to sell, but I'll die first. This house is full of memories for us. They won't take me out of here till I'm dead! Yes, that's it. Thank you. You can begin reading this part. I will give you the others later. Goodnight, Señor Montero. Thank you. Look, the candelabra has gone out. Light it outside the door, please. No, no, you can keep the key. I trust you."

"Señora, there's a rat's nest in the corner."

"Rats? I never go over there."

"You should bring the cats in here."

"The cats? What cats? Goodnight. I'm going to sleep. I'm very tired."

"Goodnight."

3

That same evening you read those yellow papers written in mustard-coloured ink, some of them with holes where a careless ash had fallen, others heavily fly-specked. General Llorente's French doesn't have the merits his wife attributed to it. You tell yourself you can make considerable improvements in the style, can tighten up his rambling account of past events: his childhood on a hacienda in Oaxaca, his military studies in France, his friendship with the duc de Morny and the intimates of Napoleon III, his return to Mexico on the staff of Maximilian, the imperial ceremonies and gatherings, the battles, the defeat in 1867, his exile in France.[9] Nothing that hasn't been described before. As you

9. Maximilian I (1832–1867) ruled Mexico from 1864 to 1867 with the support of French Emperor Napoleon III (1808–1873). Maximilian was executed by the Republican forces of Benito Juárez (1806–1872).

undress you think of the old lady's distorted notions, the value she attributes to these memoirs. You smile as you get into bed, thinking of the four thousand pesos.

You sleep soundly until a flood of light wakes you up at six in the morning: that glass roof doesn't have any curtain. You bury your head under the pillow and try to go back to sleep. Ten minutes later you give it up and walk into the bathroom, where you find all your things neatly arranged on a table and your few clothes hanging in the wardrobe. Just as you finish shaving the early morning silence is broken by that painful, desperate yowling.

You try to find out where it's coming from: you open the door to the hallway, but you can't hear anything from there: those cries are coming from up above, from the skylight. You jump up on the chair, from the chair onto the desk, and by supporting yourself on the bookshelf you can reach the skylight. You open one of the windows and pull yourself up to look out at that side garden, that square of yew trees and brambles where five, six, seven cats—you can't count them, can't hold yourself up there for more than a second—are all twined together, all writhing in flames and giving off a dense smoke that reeks of burnt fur. As you get down again you wonder if you really saw it: perhaps you only imagined it from those dreadful cries that continue, grow less, and finally stop.

You put on your shirt, brush off your shoes with a piece of paper, and listen to the sound of a bell that seems to run through the passageways of the house until it arrives at your door. You look out into the hallway. Aura is walking along it with a bell in her hand. She turns her head to look at you and tells you that breakfast is ready. You try to detain her but she goes down the spiral staircase, still ringing that black-painted bell as if she were trying to wake up a whole asylum, a whole boarding-school.

You follow her in your shirt-sleeves, but when you reach the downstairs hallway you can't find her. The door of the old lady's bedroom opens behind you and you see a hand that reaches out from behind the partly-opened door, sets a chamberpot in the hallway and disappears again, closing the door.

In the dining room your breakfast is already on the table, but this time only one place has been set. You eat quickly, return to the hallway, and knock at Señora Consuelo's door. Her sharp, weak voice tells you to come in. Nothing has changed: the perpetual shadows, the glow of the votive lights and the silver objects.

"Good morning, Señor Montero. Did you sleep well?"

"Yes. I read till quite late."

The old lady waves her hand as if in a gesture of dismissal. "No, no, no. Don't give me your opinion. Work on those pages and when you've finished I'll give you the others."

"Very well. Señora, would I be able to go into the garden?"

"What garden, Señor Montero?"

"The one that's outside my room."

"This house doesn't have any garden. We lost our garden when they built up all around us."

"I think I could work better outdoors."

"This house has only got that dark patio where you came in. My niece is growing some shade plants there. But that's all."

"It's all right, Señora."

"I'd like to rest during the day. But come to see me tonight."

"Very well, Señora."

You spend all morning working on the papers, copying out the passages you intend to keep, rewriting the ones you think are especially bad, smoking one cigarette after another and reflecting that you ought to space your work so that the job lasts as long as possible. If you can manage to save at least twelve thousand pesos, you can spend a year on nothing but your own work, which you've postponed and almost forgotten. Your great, inclusive work on the Spanish discoveries and conquests in the New World. A work that sums up all the scattered chronicles, makes them intelligible, and discovers the resemblances among all the undertakings and adventures of Spain's Golden Age, and all the human prototypes and major accomplishments of the Renaissance. You end up by putting aside the General's tedious pages and starting to compile the dates and summaries of your own work. Time passes and you don't look at your watch until you hear the bell again. Then you put on your coat and go down to the dining room.

Aura is already seated. This time Señora Llorente is at the head of the table, wrapped in her shawl and nightgown and coif, hunching over her plate. But the fourth place has also been set. You note it in passing. It doesn't bother you any more. If the price of your future creative liberty is to put up with all the manias of this old woman, you can pay it easily. As you watch her eating her soup you try to figure out her age. There's a time after which it's impossible to detect the passing of the years, and Señora Consuelo crossed that frontier a long time ago. The General hasn't mentioned her in what you've already read of the memoirs. But if the General was 42 at the time of the French invasion, and died in 1901, forty years later, he must have died at the age of 82. He must have married the Señora after the defeat at Querétaro[1] and his exile. But she would only have been a girl at that time . . .

The dates escape you because now the Señora is talking in that thin, sharp voice of hers, that bird-like chirping. She's talking to Aura and you listen to her as you eat, hearing her long list of complaints, pains, suspected illnesses, more complaints about the cost of medicines, the dampness of the house and so forth. You'd like to break in on this domestic conversation to ask about the servant who went for your things yesterday, the servant you've never even glimpsed and who never waits on table. You're going to ask about him but you're suddenly surprised to realize that up to this moment Aura hasn't said a word and is eating with a sort of mechanical fatality, as if she were waiting for some outside impulse before picking up her knife and fork, cutting a piece of liver—yes, it's liver again, apparently the favorite dish in this house—and carrying it to her mouth. You glance quickly from the aunt to the niece, but at that moment the Señora becomes motionless, and at the same moment Aura puts her knife on her plate and also becomes motionless, and you remember that the Señora put down her knife only a fraction of a second earlier.

There are several minutes of silence: you finish eating while they sit there rigid as statues, watching you. At last the Señora says, "I'm very tired. I ought not to eat at the table. Come, Aura, help me to my room."

1. One of Maximilian's final battles (1867).

The Señora tries to hold your attention: she looks directly at you so that you'll keep looking at her, although what she's saying is aimed at Aura. You have to make an effort in order to evade that look, which once again is wide, clear, and yellowish, free of the veils and wrinkles that usually obscure it. Then you look at Aura, who is staring fixedly at nothing and silently moving her lips. She gets up with a motion like those you associate with dreaming, takes the arm of the bent old lady, and slowly helps her from the dining room.

Alone now, you help yourself to the coffee that has been there since the beginning of the meal, the cold coffee you sip as you wrinkle your brow and ask yourself if the Señora doesn't have some secret power over her niece: if the girl, your beautiful Aura in her green dress, isn't kept in this dark old house against her will. But it would be so easy for her to escape while the Señora was asleep in her shadowy room. You tell yourself that her hold over the girl must be terrible. And you consider the way out that occurs to your imagination: perhaps Aura is waiting for you to release her from the chains in which the perverse, insane old lady, for some unknown reason, has bound her. You remember Aura as she was a few moments ago, spiritless, hypnotized by her terror, incapable of speaking in front of the tyrant, moving her lips in silence as if she were silently begging you to set her free; so enslaved that she imitated every gesture of the Señora, as if she were permitted to do only what the Señora did.

You rebel against this tyranny. You walk toward the other door, the one at the foot of the staircase, the one next to the old lady's room: that's where Aura must live, because there's no other room in the house. You push the door open and go in. This room is dark also, with whitewashed walls, and the only decoration is an enormous black Christ. At the left there's a door that must lead into the widow's bedroom. You go up to it on tiptoe, put your hands against it, then decide not to open it: you should talk with Aura alone.

And if Aura wants your help she'll come to your room. You go up there for a while, forgetting the yellowed manuscripts and your own notebooks, thinking only about the beauty of your Aura. And the more you think about her, the more you make her yours, not only because of her beauty and your desire, but also because you want to set her free: you've found a moral basis for your desire, and you feel innocent and self-satisfied. When you hear the bell again you don't go down to supper because you can't bear another scene like the one at the middle of the day. Perhaps Aura will realize it, and come up to look for you after supper.

You force yourself to go on working on the papers. When you're bored with them you undress slowly, get into bed, and fall asleep at once, and for the first time in years you dream, dream of only one thing, of a fleshless hand that comes toward you with a bell, screaming that you should go away, everyone should go away; and when that face with its empty eye-sockets comes close to yours, you wake up with a muffled cry, sweating, and feel those gentle hands caressing your face, those lips murmuring in a low voice, consoling you and asking you for affection. You reach out your hands to find that other body, that naked body with a key dangling from its neck, and when you recognize the key you recognize the woman who is lying over you, kissing you, kissing your whole body. You can't see her in the black of the starless night, but you can smell the fragrance of the patio plants in her hair, can feel her smooth, eager body in your arms; you kiss her again and don't ask her to speak.

When you free yourself, exhausted, from her embrace, you hear her first whisper: "You're my husband." You agree. She tells you it's daybreak, then leaves you, saying that she'll wait for you that night in her room. You agree again, and then fall asleep, relieved, unburdened, emptied of desire, still feeling the touch of Aura's body, her trembling, her surrender.

It's hard for you to wake up. There are several knocks on the door, and at last you get out of bed, groaning and still half asleep. Aura, on the other side of the door, tells you not to open it: she says that Señora Consuelo wants to talk with you, is waiting for you in her room.

Ten minutes later you enter the widow's sanctuary. She's propped up against the pillows, motionless, her eyes hidden by those drooping, wrinkled, dead-white lids; you notice the puffy wrinkles under her eyes, the utter weariness of her skin.

Without opening her eyes she asks you, "Did you bring the key to the trunk?"

"Yes, I think so . . . Yes, here it is."

"You can read the second part. It's in the same place. It's tied with a blue ribbon."

You go over to the trunk, this time with a certain disgust: the rats are swarming around it, peering at you with their glittering eyes from the cracks in the rotted floorboards, galloping toward the holes in the rotted walls. You open the trunk and take out the second batch of papers, then return to the foot of the bed. Señora Consuelo is petting her white rabbit. A sort of croaking laugh emerges from her buttoned-up throat, and she asks you, "Do you like animals?"

"No, not especially. Perhaps because I've never had any."

"They're good friends. Good companions. Above all when you're old and lonely."

"Yes, they must be."

"They're always themselves, Señor Montero. They don't have any pretensions."

"What did you say his name is?"

"The rabbit? She's Saga. She's very intelligent. She follows her instincts. She's natural and free."

"I thought it was a male rabbit."

"Oh? Then you still can't tell the difference."

"Well, the important thing is that you don't feel all alone."

"They want us to be alone, Señor Montero, because they tell us that solitude is the only way to achieve saintliness. They forget that in solitude the temptation is even greater."

"I don't understand, Señora."

"Ah, it's better that you don't. Get back to work now, please."

You turn your back on her, walk to the door, leave her room. In the hallway you clench your teeth. Why don't you have courage enough to tell her that you love the girl? Why don't you go back and tell her, once and for all, that you're planning to take Aura away with you when you finish the job? You approach the door again and start pushing it open, still uncertain, and through the crack you see Señora Consuelo standing up, erect, transformed, with a military tunic in her arms: a blue tunic with gold buttons, red epaulettes, bright medals with crowned eagles—a tunic the old lady bites ferociously, kisses tenderly, drapes over her shoulders as she performs a few teetering dance steps. You close the door.

"She was fifteen years old when I met her," you read in the second part of the memoirs. *"Elle avait quinze ans lorsque je l'ai connue et, si j'ose le dire, ce sont ses yeux verts qui ont fait ma perdition."*[2] Consuelo's green eyes, Consuelo who was only fifteen in 1867, when General Llorente married her and took her with him into exile in Paris. *"Ma jeune poupée,"* he wrote in a moment of inspiration, *"ma jeune poupée aux yeux verts; je t'ai comblée d'amour."*[3] He described the house they lived in, the outings, the dances, the carriages, the world of the Second Empire, but all in a dull enough way. *"J'ai même supporté ta haine des chats, moi qu'aimais tellement les jolies bêtes . . ."*[4] One day he found her torturing a cat: she had it clasped between her legs, with her crinoline skirt pulled up, and he didn't know how to attract her attention because it seemed to him that *"tu faisais ca d'une façon si innocent, par pur enfantillage,"*[5] and in fact it excited him so much that if you can believe what he wrote, he made love to her that night with extraordinary passion, *"parce que tu m'avais dit que torturer les chats était ta manière à toi de rendre notre amour favorable, par un sacrifice symbolique . . ."*[6] You've figured it up: Señora Consuelo must be 109. Her husband died fifty-nine years ago. *"Tu sais si bien t'habiller, ma douce Consuelo, toujours drappé dans de velours verts, verts comme tes yeux. Je pense que tu seras toujours belle, même dans cent ans . . ."*[7] Always dressed in green. Always beautiful, even after a hundred years. *"Tu es si fière de ta beauté; que ne ferais-tu pas pour rester toujours jeune?"*[8]

4

Now you know why Aura is living in this house: to perpetuate the illusion of youth and beauty in that poor, crazed old lady. Aura, kept here like a mirror, like one more icon on that votive wall with its clustered offerings, preserved hearts, imagined saints and demons.

You put the manuscript aside and go downstairs, suspecting there's only one place Aura could be in the morning—the place that greedy old woman has assigned to her.

Yes, you find her in the kitchen, at the moment she's beheading a kid; the vapour that rises from the open throat, the smell of spilt blood, the animal's glazed eyes, all give you nausea. Aura is wearing a ragged, blood-stained dress and her hair is dishevelled; she looks at you without recognition and goes on with her butchering.

2. "She was fifteen when I met her and, if I dare say so, her green eyes were my perdition" (French).
3. "My young doll . . . my young doll with green eyes; I filled you with love."
4. "I even endured your hatred of cats, I who so loved the pretty beasts."
5. "You did that in such an innocent way, from pure childishness."
6. "Because you told me that torturing the cats was your own way of making our love favorable, by a symbolic sacrifice . . ."
7. "You know how to dress so well, my sweet Consuelo, always draped in green velvet, green like your eyes. I think that you will always be beautiful, even in a hundred years . . ."
8. "You are so proud of your beauty; what would you not do to stay young forever?"

You leave the kitchen: this time you'll really speak to the old lady, really throw her greed and tyranny in her face. When you push open the door she's standing behind the veil of lights, performing a ritual with the empty air, one hand stretched out and clenched, as if holding something up, and the other clasped around an invisible object, striking again and again at the same place. Then she wipes her hands against her breast, sighs, and starts cutting the air again, as if—yes, you can see it clearly—as if she were skinning an animal . . .

You run through the hallway, the parlour, the dining room, to where Aura is slowly skinning the kid, absorbed in her work, heedless of your entrance or your words, looking at you as if you were made of air.

You climb up to your room, go in, and brace yourself against the door as if you were afraid someone would follow you: panting, sweating, victim of your horror, of your certainty. If something or someone should try to enter, you wouldn't be able to resist, you'd move away from the door, you'd let it happen. Frantically you drag the armchair over to that latchless door, push the bed up against it, then fall onto the bed, exhausted, drained of your willpower, with your eyes closed and your arms wrapped around your pillow—the pillow that isn't yours. Nothing is yours.

You fall into a stupor, into the depths of a dream that's your only escape, your only means of saying No to insanity. "She's crazy, she's crazy," you repeat again and again to make yourself sleepy, and you can see her again as she skins the imaginary kid with an imaginary knife. "She's crazy, she's crazy . . ."

in the depths of the dark abyss, in your silent dream with its mouths opening in silence, you see her coming toward you from the blackness of the abyss, you see her crawling toward you.

in silence,

moving her fleshless hand, coming toward you until her face touches yours and you see the old lady's bloody gums, her toothless gums, and you scream and she goes away again, moving her hand, sowing the abyss with the yellow teeth she carries in her blood-stained apron:

your scream is an echo of Aura's, she's standing in front of you in your dream, and she's screaming because someone's hands have ripped her green taffeta skirt in two, and then

she turns her head toward you

with the torn folds of the skirt in her hands, turns toward you and laughs silently, with the old lady's teeth superimposed on her own, while her legs, her naked legs, shatter into bits and fly toward the abyss . . .

There's a knock at the door, then the sound of the bell, the supper bell. Your head aches so much that you can't make out the hands on the clock, but you know it must be late: above your head you can see the night clouds beyond the skylight. You get up painfully, dazed and hungry. You hold the glass pitcher under the tap, wait for the water to run, fill the pitcher, then pour it into the basin. You wash your face, brush your teeth with your worn toothbrush that's clogged with greenish paste, dampen your hair—you don't notice you're doing all this in the wrong order—and comb it meticulously in front of the oval mirror on the walnut wardrobe. Then you tie your tie, put on your jacket and go down to the empty dining room, where only one place has been set—yours.

Beside your plate, under your napkin, there's an object you start caressing with your fingers: a clumsy little rag doll, filled with a powder that trickles from its badly-sewn shoulder; its face is drawn with India ink, and its body is naked, sketched with a few brush strokes. You eat the cold supper—liver, tomatoes, wine—with your right hand while holding the doll in your left.

You eat mechanically, without noticing at first your own hypnotized attitude, but later you glimpse a reason for your oppressive sleep, your nightmare, and finally identify your sleep-walking movements with those of Aura and the old lady. You're suddenly disgusted by that horrible little doll, in which you begin to suspect a secret illness, a contagion. You let it fall to the floor. You wipe your lips with the napkin, look at your watch, and remember that Aura is waiting for you in her room.

You go cautiously up to Señora Consuelo's door, but there isn't a sound from within. You look at your watch again: it's barely nine o'clock. You decide to feel your way down to that dark, roofed patio you haven't been in since you came through it, without seeing anything, on the day you arrived here.

You touch the damp, mossy walls, breathe the perfumed air, and try to isolate the different elements you're breathing, to recognize the heavy, sumptuous aromas that surround you. The flicker of your match lights up the narrow, empty patio, where various plants are growing on each side in the loose, reddish earth. You can make out the tall, leafy forms that cast their shadows on the walls in the light of the match. But it burns down, singeing your fingers, and you have to light another one to finish seeing the flowers, fruits and plants you remember reading about in old chronicles, the forgotten herbs that are growing here so fragrantly and drowsily: the long, broad, downy leaves of the henbane; the twining stems with flowers that are yellow outside, red inside; the pointed, heart-shaped leaves of the nightshade; the ash-colored down of the grape-mullein with its clustered flowers; the bushy gatheridge with its white blossoms; the bella-donna. They come to life in the flare of your match, swaying gently with their shadows, while you recall the uses of these herbs that dilate the pupils, alleviate pain, reduce the pangs of childbirth, bring consolation, weaken the will, induce a voluptuous calm.

You're all alone with the perfumes when the third match burns out. You go up to the hallway slowly, listen again at Señora Consuelo's door, then tiptoe on to Aura's. You push it open without knocking and go into the bare room, where a circle of light reveals the bed, the huge Mexican crucifix, and the woman who comes toward you when the door is closed. Aura is dressed in green, in a green taffeta robe from which, as she approaches, her moonpale thighs reveal themselves. The woman, you repeat as she comes close, the woman, not the girl of yesterday: the girl of yesterday—you touch Aura's fingers, her waist—couldn't have been more than twenty; the woman of today—you caress her loose black hair, her pallid cheeks—seems to be forty. Between yesterday and today, something about her green eyes has turned hard; the red of her lips has strayed beyond their former outlines, as if she wanted to fix them in a happy grimace, a troubled smile; as if, like that plant in the patio, her smile combined the taste of honey and the taste of gall. You don't have time to think of anything more.

"Sit down on the bed, Felipe."

"Yes."

"We're going to play. You don't have to do anything. Let me do everything myself."

Sitting on the bed, you try to make out the source of that diffuse, opaline light that hardly lets you distinguish the objects in the room, and the presence of Aura, from the golden atmosphere that surrounds them. She sees you looking up, trying to find where it comes from. You can tell from her voice that she's kneeling down in front of you.

"The sky is neither high nor low. It's over us and under us at the same time."

She takes off your shoes and socks and caresses your bare feet.

You feel the warm water that bathes the soles of your feet, while she washes them with a heavy cloth, now and then casting furtive glances at that Christ carved from black wood. Then she dries your feet, takes you by the hand, fastens a few violets in her loose hair, and begins to hum a melody, a waltz, to which you dance with her, held by the murmur of her voice, gliding around to the slow, solemn rhythm she's setting, very different from the light movements of her hands, which unbutton your shirt, caress your chest, reach around to your back and grasp it. You also murmur that wordless song, that melody rising naturally from your throat: you glide around together, each time closer to the bed, until you muffle the song with your hungry kisses on Aura's mouth, until you stop the dance with your crushing kisses on her shoulders and breasts.

You're holding the empty robe in your hands. Aura, squatting on the bed, places an object against her closed thighs, caressing it, summoning you with her hand. She caresses that thin wafer, breaks it against her thighs, oblivious of the crumbs that roll down her hips: she offers you half of the wafer and you take it, place it in your mouth at the same time she does, and swallow it with difficulty. Then you fall on Aura's naked body, you fall on her naked arms, which are stretched out from one side of the bed to the other like the arms of the crucifix hanging on the wall, the black Christ with that scarlet silk wrapped around his thighs, his spread knees, his wounded side, his crown of thorns set on a tangled black wig with silver spangles. Aura opens up like an altar.

You murmur her name in her ear. You feel the woman's full arms against your back. You hear her warm voice in your ear: "Will you love me forever?"

"Forever, Aura. I'll love you forever."

"Forever? Do you swear it?"

"I swear it."

"Even though I grow old? Even though I lose my beauty? Even though my hair turns white?"

"Forever, my love, forever."

"Even if I die, Felipe? Will you love me forever, even if I die?"

"Forever, forever. I swear it. Nothing can separate us."

"Come, Felipe, come . . ."

When you wake up, you reach out to touch Aura's shoulder, but you touch only the still-warm pillow and the white sheet that covers you.

You murmur her name.

You open your eyes and see her standing at the foot of the bed, smiling but not looking at you. She walks slowly toward the corner of the room, sits down on the floor, places her arms on the knees that emerge from the darkness you can't peer into, and strokes the wrinkled hand that comes forward from the lessening darkness: she's sitting at the feet of the old lady, of Señora Consuelo, who is seated in an armchair you hadn't noticed earlier: Señora Consuelo smiles at you, nodding her head, smiling at you along with Aura, who moves her head in rhythm with the old lady's: they both smile at you, thanking you. You lie back, without any will, thinking that the old lady has been in the room all the time;

you remember her movements, her voice, her dance,

though you keep telling yourself she wasn't there.

The two of them get up at the same moment, Consuelo from the chair, Aura from the floor. Turning their backs on you, they walk slowly toward the door that leads to the widow's bedroom, enter that room where the lights are forever trembling in front of the images, close the door behind them, and leave you to sleep in Aura's bed.

5

Your sleep is heavy and unsatisfying. In your dreams you had already felt the same vague melancholy, the weight on your diaphragm, the sadness that won't stop oppressing your imagination. Although you're sleeping in Aura's room, you're sleeping all alone, far from the body you believe you've possessed.

When you wake up, you look for another presence in the room, and realize it's not Aura who disturbs you but rather the double presence of something that was engendered during the night. You put your hands on your forehead, trying to calm your disordered senses: that dull melancholy is hinting to you in a low voice, the voice of memory and premonition, that you're seeking your other half, that the sterile conception last night engendered your own double.

And you stop thinking, because there are things even stronger than the imagination: the habits that force you to get up, look for a bathroom off this room without finding one, go out into the hallway rubbing your eyelids, climb the stairs tasting the thick bitterness of your tongue, enter your own room feeling the rough bristles on your chin, turn on the bath taps and then slide into the warm water, letting yourself relax into forgetfulness.

But while you're drying yourself, you remember the old lady and the girl as they smiled at you before leaving the room arm in arm; you recall that whenever they're together they always do the same things: they embrace, smile, eat, speak, enter, leave, at the same time, as if one were imitating the other, as if the will of one depended on the existence of the other . . . You cut yourself lightly on one cheek as you think of these things while you shave; you make an effort to get control of yourself. When you finish shaving you count the objects in your traveling case, the bottles and tubes which the servant you've never seen brought over from your boarding house: you murmur the names of these objects, touch them, read the contents and instructions, pronounce the names of the manufacturers, keeping to these objects in order to forget that other one, the one without a name, without a label, without any rational consistency. What is Aura expecting of you? you ask yourself, closing the traveling case. What does she want, what does she want?

In answer you hear the dull rhythm of her bell in the corridor telling you breakfast is ready. You walk to the door without your shirt on. When you open it you find Aura there: it must be Aura because you see the green taffeta she always wears, though her face is covered with a green veil. You take her by the wrist, that slender wrist which trembles at your touch . . .

"Breakfast is ready," she says, in the faintest voice you've ever heard.

"Aura, let's stop pretending."

"Pretending?"

"Tell me if Señora Consuelo keeps you from leaving, from living your own life. Why did she have to be there when you and I . . . Please tell me you'll go with me when . . ."

"Go away? Where?"

"Out of this house. Out into the world, to live together. You shouldn't feel bound to your aunt forever . . . Why all this devotion? Do you love her that much?"

"Love her?"

"Yes. Why do you have to sacrifice yourself this way?"

"Love her? She loves me. She sacrifices herself for me."

"But she's an old woman, almost a corpse. You can't . . ."

"She has more life than I do. Yes, she's old and repulsive . . . Felipe, I don't want to become . . . to be like her . . . another . . ."

"She's trying to bury you alive. You've got to be reborn, Aura."

"You have to die before you can be reborn . . . No, you don't understand. Forget about it, Felipe. Just have faith in me."

"If you'd only explain."

"Just have faith in me. She's going to be out today for the whole day."

"She?"

"Yes, the other."

"She's going out? But she never . . ."

"Yes, sometimes she does. She makes a great effort and goes out. She's going out today. For all day. You and I could . . ."

"Go away?"

"If you want to."

"Well . . . perhaps not yet. I'm under contract. But as soon as I can finish the work, then . . ."

"Ah, yes. But she's going to be out all day. We could do something."

"What?"

"I'll wait for you this evening in my aunt's bedroom. I'll wait for you as always."

She turns away, ringing her bell like the lepers who use a bell to announce their approach, telling the unwary: "Out of the way, out of the way." You put on your shirt and coat and follow the sound of the bell calling you to the dining room. In the parlour the widow Llorente comes toward you, bent over, leaning on a knobby cane; she's dressed in an old white gown with a stained and tattered gauze veil. She goes by without looking at you, blowing her nose into a handkerchief, blowing her nose and spitting. She murmurs, "I won't be at home today, Señor Montero. I have complete confidence in your work. Please keep at it. My husband's memoirs must be published."

She goes away, stepping across the carpets with her tiny feet, which are like those of an antique doll, and supporting herself with her cane, spitting and sneezing as if she wanted to clear something from her congested lungs. It's only by an effort of the will that you keep yourself from following her with your eyes, despite the curiosity you feel at seeing the yellowed bridal gown she's taken from the bottom of that old trunk in her bedroom.

You scarcely touch the cold coffee that's waiting for you in the dining room. You sit for an hour in the tall, arch-back chair, smoking, waiting for the sounds you never hear, until finally you're sure the old lady has left the house and can't catch you at what you're going to do. For the last hour you've had the key to the trunk clutched in your hand, and now you get up and silently walk through the parlor into the hallway, where you wait for another fifteen minutes—your watch tells you how long—with your ear against Señora Consuelo's door. Then you slowly push it open until you can make out, beyond the spider's web of candles, the empty bed on which her rabbit is gnawing at a carrot: the bed that's always littered with scraps of bread, and that you touch gingerly as if you thought the old lady might be hidden among the rumples of the sheets. You walk over to the corner where the trunk is, stepping on the tail of one of those rats; it squeals, escapes from your foot, and scampers off to warn the others. You fit the copper key into the rusted padlock, remove the padlock, and then raise the lid, hearing the creak of the old, stiff hinges. You take out the third portion of the memoirs—it's tied with a red ribbon—and under it you discover those photographs, those old, brittle dog-eared photographs. You pick them up without looking at them, clutch the whole treasure to your breast, and hurry up of the room without closing the trunk, forgetting the hunger of the rats. You close the door, lean against the wall in the hallway till you catch your breath, then climb the stairs to your room.

Up there you read the new pages, the continuation, the events of an agonized century. In his florid language General Llorente describes the personality of Eugenia de Montijo, pays his respects to Napoleon the Little, summons up his most martial rhetoric to proclaim the Franco-Prussian War, fills whole pages with his sorrow at the defeat, harangues all men of honor about the Republican monster, sees a ray of hope in General Boulanger, sighs for Mexico, believes that in the Dreyfus affairs the honor—always that word "honor"—of the army has asserted itself again.[9]

The brittle pages crumble at your touch: you don't respect them now, you're only looking for a reappearance of the woman with green eyes. "I know why you weep at times, Consuelo. I have not been able to give you children, although you are so radiant with life . . ." And later: "Consuelo, you should not tempt God. We must reconcile ourselves. Is not my affection enough? I know that you love me; I feel it. I am not asking you for resignation, because that would offend you. I am only asking you to see, in the great love which you say you have for me, something sufficient, something that can fill both of us, without the need of turning to sick imaginings . . ." On another page: "I told Consuelo that those medicines were utterly useless. She insists on growing her own herbs in the garden. She says she is not deceiving herself. The herbs are not to strengthen the body, but rather the soul." Later: "I found her in a delirium, embracing the pillow. She cried, 'Yes, yes, yes, I've done it, I've re-created

9. General Llorente reflects on the course of later 19th-century history. The Empress Eugenia de Montijo was the wife of Napoleon III (the "Little" because less great than Napoleon I). The Franco-Prussian War (1870–71) ended in the defeat of France and the fall of the empire. General Boulanger staged a failed coup against the new French Third Republic in 1888. Alfred Dreyfus, a French army captain, was falsely accused of treason, leading to a series of trials and social upheaval; General Llorente's views on all these matters are reactionary.

her! I can invoke her, I can give her life with my own life!' It was necessary to call the doctor. He told me he could not quiet her, because the truth was that she was under the effects of narcotics, not of stimulants." And finally: "Early this morning I found her walking barefooted through the hallways. I wanted to stop her. She went by without looking at me, but her words were directed to me. 'Don't stop me,' she said. 'I'm going toward my youth, and my youth is coming toward me. It's coming in, it's in the garden, it's come back . . .' Consuelo, my poor Consuelo! Even the devil was an angel once."

There isn't any more. The memoirs of General Llorente end with that sentence: *"Consuelo, le démon aussi était un ange, avant . . ."*[1]

And after the last page, the portraits. The portrait of an elderly gentleman in a military uniform, an old photograph with these words in one corner: *"Moulin, Photographe, 35 Boulevard Haussmann"* and the date *"1894."*[2] Then the photograph of Aura, of Aura with her green eyes, her black hair gathered in ringlets, leaning against a Doric column with a painted landscape in the background: the landscape of a Lorelei in the Rhine. Her dress is buttoned up to the collar, there's a handkerchief in her hand, she's wearing a bustle: Aura, and the date "*1876*" in white ink, and on the back of the daguerreotype, in spidery handwriting: *"Fait pour notre dixième anniversaire de mariage,"*[3] and a signature in the same hand, "*Consuelo Llorente*." In the third photograph you see both Aura and the old gentleman, but this time they're dressed in outdoor clothes, sitting on a bench in a garden. The photograph has become a little blurred: Aura doesn't look as young as she did in the other picture, but it's she, it's he, it's . . . it's you. You stare and stare at the photographs, then hold them up to the skylight. You cover General Llorente's beard with your finger, and imagine him with black hair, and you discover only yourself: blurred, lost, forgotten, but you, you, you.

Your head is spinning, overcome by the rhythms of that distant waltz, by the odor of damp, fragrant plants: you fall exhausted on the bed, touching your cheeks, your eyes, your nose, as if you were afraid that some invisible hand had ripped off the mask you've been wearing for twenty-seven years, the cardboard features that hid your true face, your real appearance, the appearance you once had but then forgot. You bury your face in the pillow, trying to keep the wind of the past from tearing away your own features, because you don't want to lose them. You lie there with your face in the pillow, waiting for what has to come, for what you can't prevent. You don't look at your watch again, that useless object tediously measuring time in accordance with human vanity, those little hands marking out the long hours that were invented to disguise the real passage of time, which races with a mortal and insolent swiftness no clock could ever measure. A life, a century, fifty years: you can't imagine those lying measurements any longer, you can't hold that bodiless dust within your hands.

When you look up from the pillow you find you're in darkness. Night has fallen.

Night has fallen. Beyond the skylight the swift black clouds are hiding the moon, which tries to free itself, to reveal its pale, round, smiling face. It escapes

1. "Consuelo, the demon was also an angel, before . . ." (French).
2. The picture was taken by the photographer Moulin in Paris.
3. "Taken on our tenth wedding anniversary."

for only a moment, then the clouds hide it again. You haven't got any hope left. You don't even look at your watch. You hurry down the stairs, out of that prison cell with its old papers and faded daguerreotypes, and stop at the door of Señora Consuelo's room, and listen to your own voice, muted and transformed after all those hours of silence: "Aura . . ."

Again: "Aura . . ."

You enter the room. The votive lights have gone out. You remember that the old lady has been away all day: without her faithful attention the candles have all burned up. You grope forward in the darkness to the bed.

And again: "Aura . . ."

You hear a faint rustle of taffeta, and the breathing that keeps time with your own. You reach out your hand to touch Aura's green robe.

"No. Don't touch me. Lie down at my side."

You find the edge of the bed, swing up your legs, and remain there stretched out and motionless. You can't help feeling a shiver of fear: "She might come back any minute."

"She won't come back."

"Ever?"

"I'm exhausted. She's already exhausted. I've never been able to keep her with me for more than three days."

"Aura . . ."

You want to put your hand on Aura's breasts. She turns her back: you can tell by the difference in her voice.

"No . . . Don't touch me . . ."

"Aura . . . I love you."

"Yes. You love me. You told me yesterday that you'd always love me."

"I'll always love you, always. I need your kisses, your body . . ."

"Kiss my face. Only my face."

You bring your lips close to the head that's lying next to yours. You stroke Aura's long black hair. You grasp that fragile woman by the shoulders, ignoring her sharp complaint. You tear off her taffeta robe, embrace her, feel her small and lost and naked in your arms, despite her moaning resistance, her feeble protests, kissing her face without thinking, without distinguishing, and you're touching her withered breasts when a ray of moonlight shines in and surprises you, shines in through a chink in the wall that the rats have chewed open, an eye that lets in a beam of silvery moonlight. It falls on Aura's eroded face, as brittle and yellowed as the memoirs, as creased with wrinkles as the photographs. You stop kissing those fleshless lips, those toothless gums: the ray of moonlight shows you the naked body of the old lady, of Señora Consuelo, limp, spent, tiny, ancient, trembling because you touch her. You love her, you too have come back . . .

You plunge your face, your open eyes, into Consuelo's silver-white hair, and you'll embrace her again when the clouds cover the moon, when you're both hidden again, when the memory of youth, of youth re-embodied, rules the darkness.

"She'll come back, Felipe. We'll bring her back together. Let me recover my strength and I'll bring her back . . ."

1962

ALEXANDER SOLZHENITSYN

1918–2008

Like his great predecessors **Tolstoy** and **Dostoevsky**, Alexander Solzhenitsyn was both a popular writer and a prophetic voice of moral conscience during the last decades of Soviet dictatorship. Solzhenitsyn used the techniques of nineteenth-century realism to explore a distinctively twentieth-century society. Imprisoned by the Stalinist regime, then later expelled from the Soviet Union and stripped of his citizenship, Solzhenitsyn criticized both the political oppression of the East and the materialism of the West, while proclaiming the virtues of an older, religious way of life.

He was born Alexander Isayevich Solzhenitsyn on December 11, 1918, a little more than a year after the Russian Revolution, in Kislovodsk, in the northern Caucasus. His father had died six months earlier, and his mother supported the family in Rostov-on-Don by working as a typist. They were extremely poor, and—although Solzhenitsyn would have preferred studying literature in Moscow—he was obliged, on graduation from high school, to enroll in the local Department of Mathematics at Rostov University. The choice, he later said, was a lucky one, for his double degree in mathematics and physics allowed him to spend four years of his prison-camp sentence in a relatively privileged *sharashka*, or research institute, instead of at hard manual labor. Unlike other writers (such as **Anna Akhmatova** and Boris Pasternak) who had known life before the revolution, Solzhenitsyn grew up a committed communist, supporting the regime even during the catastrophic famine of 1933, but during the Second World War he became disillusioned with the Soviet leadership.

Soon after graduating from the university, Solzhenitsyn was put in charge of an artillery reconnaissance battery at the front; he served for almost four years before his sudden arrest for treason in February 1945. The military censor had found passages in his letters to a friend that showed him to be—even under a pseudonym—disrespectful of the Soviet dictator Joseph Stalin, and Solzhenitsyn was sentenced to eight years in the prison camps. He worked at first as a mathematician in research institutes staffed by prisoners but in 1950 was taken to a new kind of camp for political prisoners, where he worked as a manual laborer. The hardships he endured there became the material for his most memorable writing, which combined autobiography, fiction, and historical events.

After his sentence was over, an administrative order sent him into permanent exile in southern Kazakhstan, a republic in Central Asia that was then a part of the Soviet Union. Solzhenitsyn spent the years of exile teaching physics and mathematics in a rural school and writing prose in secret. A cancerous tumor that had developed in his first labor camp grew worse, and in 1954 the author received treatment in a clinic in Tashkent (events recalled in the novel *Cancer Ward*, published in 1968). Solzhenitsyn remained in internal exile during the first phases of de-Stalinization, after the dictator's death in 1953, but was rehabilitated in 1957. He moved to Ryazan, in European Russia, where he continued to teach, while secretly writing fiction. The novella *Matryona's House* and the novel *One Day in the Life of Ivan Denisovich* were composed during this period.

At the age of forty-two, Solzhenitsyn had written a great deal but published nothing. In 1961, however, it looked as though the climate of political censorship might change. Soviet Premier Nikita Khrushchev publicly attacked the "cult of personality" and hero worship that had surrounded Stalin, and the poet and editor Alexander Tvardovsky called on writers to portray "truth," not the idealized picture of Soviet society that Stalin had preferred. Solzhenitsyn was encouraged to submit *One Day in the Life of Ivan Denisovich*, an account of a bricklayer in a Russian concentration camp, beset, from morning to night, by hunger, cold, and brutally demanding work. The novel appeared, with Khrushchev's approval, in the November 1962 issue of Tvardovsky's journal *Novy Mir* (*The New World*) and seemed to announce a more relaxed era in Soviet culture—never before had the prison camps been openly discussed. Solzhenitsyn's matter-of-fact narration of the prisoners' day-to-day struggle to survive and retain their humanity shocked readers in Russia and in the West. In January 1963, Tvardovsky issued *Matryona's House* and another novella, *An Incident at Krechetovka Station*, but—with the exception of two short stories and an article on style—Solzhenitsyn would not be allowed to publish anything more in his native land for more than twenty-five years. Even the highly praised *One Day in the Life of Ivan Denisovich* was removed from candidacy for the Lenin Prize in 1963.

Khrushchev himself was forced into retirement in October 1964, and the temporary loosening of censorship came to an end. The only means of publishing officially unacceptable works was to convey them to a Western publishing house or to circulate copies of typewritten manuscripts in *samizdat* ("self-publishing") form. Solzhenitsyn made arrangements to have his works, including the novels *Cancer Ward* and *The First Circle*, published in the West, in 1968. Within a year he was expelled from the official Writer's Union; in 1970 he was awarded the Nobel Prize in Literature, which he accepted in absentia because he was afraid that he would not be permitted to reenter the Soviet Union once he left. He continued work on his masterpiece, *The Gulag Archipelago* (1973–75), a three-volume, seven-section account of Stalin's widespread prison camp system, in which up to sixty million people suffered. Solzhenitsyn described the horror of these camps in quasi-anecdotal form, using personal experience, oral testimony, excerpts of documents, written eyewitness reports, and a massive collection of evidence accumulated inside *An Attempt at Artistic Investigation* (the subtitle). In the book there is a tension between the bare facts that Solzhenitsyn transmits and the spiritual interpretation of history into which they are made to fit. The author is overtly present, commenting, guessing intuitively from context when particular facts are missing, and stressing, in his own voice, the theme that has pervaded all his work: the purification of the soul through suffering. Solzhenitsyn tried to keep the work in progress a secret, but the KGB (the Soviet secret police) found a copy of the manuscript as a result of their interrogation of Solzhenitsyn's typist, who subsequently committed suicide. After the publication abroad of the first volume, Solzhenitsyn was arrested and expelled from the country. He went first to Zurich, then to the United States, where he lived in seclusion on a farm in Vermont.

The expulsion remained in effect until 1990, when the president of the Soviet Union, Mikhail S. Gorbachev, offered to restore Solzhenitsyn's citizenship as part of the rehabilitation of artists and writers disgraced during previous regimes. Solzhenitsyn did not accept the offer, though, and refused a prize awarded by the Russian Republic for *The Gulag Archipelago*—noting that the book was not widely available in the Soviet Union and that the "phenomenon of the Gulag" had not been overcome. In September 1991 the old charge of treason was officially dropped, and the writer returned to Russia in May 1994 to widespread public acclaim. The novelist expected, and was expected, to be a prominent voice in contemporary Russian society—for a while, he even had a television program. His moral strictures and nostalgia for a simpler past, however, proved alien to a post-Soviet society intent on prosperity. His massive series of historical novels about the Russian Revolution, *The Red Wheel*, on which he spent some thirty years, was poorly received. Disillusioned by post-Communist Russia, he increasingly supported authoritarian figures, including Russian president Vladimir Putin.

Since Solzhenitsyn was such a dedicated anti-Communist and anti-Marxist, many Westerners jumped to the conclusion—incorrectly, as it turned out—that he supported the capitalist, democratic system. Instead, he looked back to an earlier, more nationalist and spiritual authoritarianism represented for him by the image of Holy Russia: "For a thousand years Russia lived with an authoritarian order . . . that authoritarian order possessed a strong moral foundation . . . Christian Orthodoxy." In a speech given at Harvard in 1978, "A World Split Apart," he criticized Western democracy's "herd instinct" and "need to accommodate mass standards," its emphasis on "well-being" and "constant desire to have still more things," its "spiritual exhaustion" in which "mediocrity triumphs under the guise of democratic restraints." He returned to the theme of purification by suffering that permeates his fiction: "We have been through a spiritual training far in advance of Western experience. The complex and deadly crush of life has produced stronger, deeper, and more interesting personalities than those generated by standardized Western well-being."

One of those strong, deep personalities is surely Matryona in *Matryona's House*, the novella reprinted here. The story, which is probably modeled on the old Russian literary form of the saint's life, is a testimony to Matryona's absolute simplicity, her refusal to possess anything more than the necessities (she will not raise a pig to kill for food), her willingness to help others without promise of reward. The narrator, like Solzhenitsyn an ex-convict and mathematics teacher, has buried himself deep in the country to avoid signs of modern Soviet society and to find—if it still exists—an image of the Old Russia. The town of Tal'novo itself is tainted not just by the *kolkhoz* (collective farm) system, which ceases to consider Matryona part of the collective as soon as she becomes ill, but by the laziness, selfishness, and predatory greed of its inhabitants. Although Matryona's life has been filled with disappointment and deprivation, and she remains an outsider in a materialist society that despises her lack of acquisitive instinct, she seems to live in a dimension of spiritual contentment and love that is unknown to those around her. Only the narrator, who has learned to value essential qualities from his experience in the concentration camps, is able finally to recognize her as the "righteous" one (Genesis 18.23–33), one of those whose spiritual merit seems alien to modern society yet is needed to save society from divine retribution.

Matryona's House[1]

1

For at least six months after the incident took place every train used to slow down almost to a standstill at exactly a hundred and eighty-four kilometres from Moscow. The passengers would crowd to the windows and go out onto the open gangway at the end of the carriages to find out whether the track was under repair or if the train was ahead of schedule. But these were not the reasons for the delay. Once it had passed the level crossing, the train would pick up speed again and the passengers would go back to their seats. Only the drivers knew why they had to slow down.

And I knew too.

In the summer of 1953 I was returning from the hot, dusty wastelands, making my way aimlessly back to Russia. No one had sent for me and no one was waiting for me, because my return had been delayed by a little matter of ten years. I simply wanted to go somewhere in central Russia, somewhere where it was not too hot and where leaves rustled in the forest. I just wanted to creep away and vanish in the very heartland of Russia—if there were such a place.

A year earlier, the most that I could have got in the way of a job on the other side of the Urals[2] was labouring work. I would not even have been taken on as an electrician on a decent-sized construction site. And my ambition was to be a teacher. People in the teaching world told me that I was wasting money on a ticket, as the journey would be fruitless.

But the atmosphere in the country had already started to change.[3] As I climbed the stairs of the Regional Education Department and asked for the personnel branch, I was amazed to see that personnel was no longer situated behind a black leather door but simply on the other side of a glass partition as in a chemist's.

I approached the window timidly, bowed, and asked: "Excuse me, have you any vacancies for a mathematics teacher somewhere far away from civilisation? I want to settle there for good."

They scrutinised every detail of my documents, scuttled from room to room, and made telephone calls. I was a rare case for them; as a rule, everybody asked to be sent to a town and the bigger the better. Suddenly they presented me with a little place called High Field. The name of the place alone cheered me up.

It did not belie its name. Situated on a slope among hills, encircled by a wood, with a pond and a dyke, High Field was the very place where a man would be glad to live and die. I sat there on a tree stump in a copse for a long time, wishing that I could do without my daily meals and just stay here and listen to the branches rustling against the roofs at night, when there was no sound of a radio from any direction and everything in the world was at peace.

1. Translated by Michael Glenny.
2. Mountain chain separating European Russia from (Asiatic) Siberia.
3. Stalin's death, on March 5, 1953, brought a gradual relaxation of the Soviet state's repressive policies.

But it was no good. They did not bake their own bread there. They did not sell anything to eat. The whole village dragged its foodstuffs in sacks from the local town.

So back I went to the personnel branch and stood imploringly at their window. At first no one would see me. Then once again they scurried from room to room, made telephone calls, scratched their pens, and typed on my assignment form: "Peatproduce."

Peatproduce? If only Turgenev were alive today to see what violence is being done to the Russian language.[4]

On Peatproduce Station, consisting of a grey temporary wooden hut, hung a warning sign: "Trains may only be boarded from the platform." Someone had scratched on the notice with a nail: "Even if you haven't got a ticket," and beside the ticket office the following grimly humorous message was carved permanently in the woodwork: "No tickets." I realised the full meaning of these comments only much later. It was easy to get to Peatproduce but not to get out of it.

Before the Revolution and for some time after it, the place had been covered with silent, impenetrable forest. Then the forest had been cut down by the peat diggers and the nearby collective farm, whose chairman, Shashkov, had razed a considerable area of the forest to the ground and had sold it at a profit in the province of Odessa.

A straggling village was scattered among the peat diggings, consisting of some monotonous huts dating from the thirties and a few cottages put up in the fifties with fretwork trimmings and glassed-in verandahs. But in none of these cottages were there any partitions built right up to the ceiling, so that I could not find a room that had four proper walls.

A factory chimney poured smoke over the whole village. A narrow-gauge railway line wound its way through the place, and little engines, also puffing out thick clouds of smoke and emitting piercing whistles, pulled trainloads of raw peat, peat slabs, and briquettes. I was right when I guessed that a radiogram would be blaring out music all evening through the doors of the club, that drunks would be lurching about in the street, and that now and again they would knife each other.

This was the place to which my dream of a quiet corner of Russia had brought me. At least in the place I had come from I had lived in a mud hut that looked out over the desert, a fresh, clean wind had blown at night, and only the starry arc of heaven was stretched over my head.

I found it impossible to sleep on the station bench and it was hardly light when I set off to explore the village. Then I saw that it had a tiny market. Because it was so early, only one woman was there, selling milk. I bought a bottle and drank it on the spot.

The way she spoke surprised me. She did not so much talk as sing in an oddly touching way and her words made me feel nostalgic for Asia.

"Drink, drink, your heart's athirst. Are you a stranger here?"

"Where are you from?" I asked, delighted.

4. Ivan Sergeyevich Turgenev (1818–1883) was a master of Russian prose style, best known for the novel *Fathers and Sons* (1861) and for a series of sympathetic sketches of peasant life published as *A Sportsman's Sketches* (1882). "Peatproduce" (in the original Russian, *Torfoprodukt*): a word made by combining two words of Germanic origin: *torf* ("peat") and *produkt*.

I learned that the region was not all peat workings, that beyond the railway track there was a hill and over the hill a village called Tal'novo, which had been there from time immemorial, since the days when a "gypsy" lady had lived there and a haunted wood had stood all around. And beyond it a whole string of villages with names like Chaslitsy, Ovintsy, Spudni, Shevertni, Shestimirovo—each one more remote than the next as they stretched farther and farther away from the railway and nearer to the lakes.

The names wafted over me like a soothing breeze. They held a promise of the true, legendary Russia. So I asked my new-found friend to take me to Tal'novo when the market was over and help me look for a cottage where I could find lodgings.

As a lodger I was a good prospect: in addition to my rent, the school also provided a lorryload of peat for the winter. The woman's expression now betrayed a kind of concern that was less touching. She herself had no room to spare (she and her husband looked after her aged mother), so she took me around to some of her relatives; but their houses were noisy and crowded and none of them had a separate room to rent either.

By then we had walked as far as a little dammed-up stream crossed by a bridge. There was no prettier spot in the whole village—two or three willows, a crooked little shack, ducks swimming on the pond, and geese waddling up the bank to shake themselves.

"Well, I suppose we'd better try Matryona," said my guide, already growing tired of me. "Only her place isn't that well kept, she's let it go on account of her being so sick."

Matryona's house was nearby. It had a row of four windows along the side on which the sun never shone, a steep shingled roof with an elaborately ornamental dormer window. But the shingles were rotting away, the logs of the cottage walls and the once-mighty gateposts had turned grey with age, and much of the caulking between the logs had fallen out. Although the gate was shut, my guide did not bother to knock but thrust her hand underneath and undid the bolt—a simple precaution against stray cattle. There were no sheds in the yard, but instead the cottage had several outbuildings clustered under the one roof. Just inside the entrance, there were some steps leading up to a broad passage, open to the roof timbers. To the left, some more steps led up to the outhouse—a separate room but without a stove—and another flight of steps down to the storeroom. To the right were the living quarters with their attic and cellar.

It had been solidly built a long time ago, intended for a large family, but now a woman who was getting on towards sixty lived there alone.

The spacious room, and especially its brighter end by the windows, was set about with flower pots and tubs of fig plants on stools and benches. Silent yet alive, they filled the loneliness of Matryona's life, growing in wild profusion as they strained to catch the sparse northern light. As the light was fading and because she was hidden by the chimney, the owner's round face looked yellow and ill. Her bleary eyes showed how much her illness had exhausted her.

She talked to me lying prone on the stove,[5] without a pillow, her head facing the door, while I stood over her. She showed no sign of pleasure at the pros-

5. Russian stoves are large and built of masonry; they are used for both heating and cooking.

pect of acquiring a lodger but merely complained about the attack from which she was now recovering: the sickness did not come every month, but when it did strike, ". . . it stays for two or three days, so I wouldn't be able to get up or do anything for you. But the house isn't bad, you'd be all right here."

She listed other landladies whose cottages might be quieter and more comfortable and suggested that I should go and try them. But I could already tell that I was fated to settle in this dark cottage with its tarnished mirror, in which it was completely impossible to see yourself, and its two cheap, brightly coloured posters hung on the wall for decoration, one advertising the book trade and the other campaigning for the harvest.

Matryona made me try the village again, and when I arrived the second time she made countless excuses like "Don't expect any fancy cooking." But she was up and about and there was even a glint of something like pleasure in her eyes because I had come back.

We agreed about the rent and the peat that the school would supply.

I only found out later that Matryona Vasilievna had not earned a penny from anywhere for a long, long time, because she was not given a pension and her relatives hardly ever helped her out. She worked on the collective farm not for money but for ticks—the ticks entered in her well-thumbed workbook.

And so I settled in with Matryona Vasilievna. We did not divide up the room: her bed was in the corner by the door, near the stove; and I set up my camp bed by the window. I pushed Matryona's beloved fig plants aside to let in more light, and put a table by one of the windows. They had electricity in the village; it had been brought from Shatura as early as the twenties. In those days the newspapers used to publicise Lenin's electrification scheme with catchwords like "Ilyich lamps," while the peasants blinked and called it "magic fire."[6]

Perhaps to someone from a better-off village Matryona's cottage would not have seemed an ideal place to live, but we were very comfortable there that autumn and winter. Despite its age, it kept the rain out, and the embers in the stove warded off the icy winds pretty well—except towards morning, and hardly at all when the wind was blowing from the cold quarter.

Besides Matryona and myself, the other occupants of the house were a cat, some mice, and the cockroaches.

The cat was rather old and lame. Matryona had adopted it out of pity and it had settled down with her. Although it walked on four legs, it limped heavily in order to spare its one bad leg. When it jumped from the stove onto the floor, the sound it made when it landed was not a typical soft catlike sound but a thump of three legs hitting the floor simultaneously—crash!—a noise so loud that at first, before I got used to it, it startled me. It would land on three feet at once so as to spare the fourth.

It was not lameness that prevented the cat from dealing with the mice in the cottage; it would corner them and pounce like a flash of lightning and carry them off in its teeth. The reason why it caught so few was that once, when times were better, someone had papered Matryona's room with some greenish ribbed and checked wallpaper, and not just one layer but *five*. The coatings of wallpaper

6. The newspapers reflect the new order. "Ilyich": i.e., Vladimir Ilyich Lenin (1870–1924), leader of the 1917 Russian Revolution and first head of the new state. The peasants still think somewhat superstitiously.

were stuck firmly to each other but in many places all five layers had ceased to adhere to the wall, thus giving the house a sort of inner skin. The mice had made paths for themselves between the planks and the wallpaper where they pattered impudently back and forth, even running about under the ceiling. The cat would glare angrily at their rustling but could never get at them.

Sometimes the cat would even eat cockroaches, but they made it feel sick. The only thing that the cockroaches respected was the line of the partition dividing the stove and the kitchen from the clean part of the house. They never penetrated into the living room. But they made up for it by swarming all over the kitchen at night, and if I went into the kitchen late in the evening and switched on the light, the entire floor, the large bench, and even the walls were almost a solid, heaving mass of reddish-brown. Once when I brought home some borax from the chemistry lab at school, we mixed it with dough and slaughtered the cockroaches. Their numbers diminished, but Matryona was afraid of poisoning the cat as well, so we stopped putting down poison and the cockroaches flourished once more.

At night, when Matryona was asleep and I was working at my table, the occasional sound of the mice darting about behind the wallpaper was smothered by the ceaseless, monotonous rustle behind the partition, like the distant roar of the ocean. But I grew accustomed to it, for there was nothing false or deceptive about it. It was their nature; they couldn't help it.

I even got used to the crudely drawn girl on the poster, eternally offering me copies of Belinsky, Panfyorov,[7] and a pile of other books, but never speaking. I got used to everything in Matryona's house.

Matryona would get up at four or five o'clock in the morning. She had bought her old-fashioned kitchen clock at the village store twenty-seven years ago. It was always fast, but Matryona didn't mind; at least it wasn't slow, so she would not be late in the mornings.

She would switch on the light in the kitchen and quietly, considerately, trying not to make a noise, stoke up the stove. Then she would go and milk the goat (her entire livestock was one dirty white goat with a crooked horn), fetch water, put three saucepans on the stove to boil—one saucepan for me, one for herself, and one for the goat. From the store in the cellar she picked out the very smallest potatoes for the goat, small ones for herself, and a few for me the size of a hen's egg. Her kitchen garden was incapable of producing large potatoes; its sandy soil had not been manured since before the war and was never planted with anything but potatoes.

I hardly ever heard her doing her morning chores. I slept long, woke up late with the wintry sun and stretched, poking my head from underneath my blanket and sheepskin coat. With a quilted jacket from my prison-camp days which covered my feet, and a sack stuffed with straw as a mattress, I stayed warm all night, even when the north wind set our little windows rattling in their rotten frames. Hearing the muffled noises coming from behind the partition, I would solemnly say:

"Good morning, Matryona Vasilievna."

7. Fedor Ivanovich Panferov (1896–1960), socialist-realist writer popular in the 1920s, best known for his novel *The Iron Flood*. Vissarion Grigoryevich Belinsky (1811–1848), Russian literary critic who emphasized social and political ideas.

And always the same kindly response would be echoed from the other side. It began with a sort of low purring noise that grandmothers make in fairy tales: "Mm-m-m . . . and the same to you."

And a moment later: "Your breakfast's ready."

She never said what was for breakfast, but it was not hard to guess: an unpeeled potato, 'taty soup (as they called it in the village), or millet porridge. Any other kind of cereal was unobtainable in Peatproduce that year, and even millet was hard enough to get—as it was the cheapest sort, they bought it by the sackful for pig food. It was not always salted properly and it was often burnt; it left a film on your palate and gums, and it gave you heartburn. However, this was not Matryona's fault. There was no butter in Peatproduce either, margarine only now and then if you were lucky, and the only readily available fat was low-grade lard. What was more, the Russian stove, as I soon realised, was extremely awkward: the cook was unable to see the food cooking, and the heat reached the saucepans unevenly and sporadically. I suppose the reason why our forefathers have retained this kind of stove since the Stone Age is that once it is banked up before dawn, it keeps food and water for man and beast warm all day; and it's warm to sleep on.

I dutifully ate everything that was cooked for me, patiently removing any foreign bodies such as a hair, a lump of peat, or the leg of a cockroach. I did not have the heart to reproach Matryona. After all, she had warned me not to expect any fancy cooking.

"Thank you," I would say with absolute sincerity.

"What for? It's yours—you're paying for it." Having disarmed me with her dazzling smile, she would then look at me guilelessly with her pale blue eyes and ask: "Well, what shall I cook you for supper?"

I ate two meals a day, as we used to do on active service. What could I order for supper? It was always either potatoes or 'taty soup.

I reconciled myself to this, because experience had taught me not to regard eating as the main object of life. I set greater store by the smile on her round face, which, when I eventually took up photography, I tried in vain to capture on film. Whenever Matryona saw the cold eye of a lens staring at her, she would put on a look that was either strained or exaggeratedly stern. Only once did I manage to catch her smiling at something out of the window.

Matryona had a lot of trouble that autumn. Her neighbours had persuaded her to apply for a pension. She was all alone in the world, and since she had started being seriously ill, she had been dismissed from the collective farm. Altogether, Matryona was treated most unjustly: she was sick, but she was not certified as disabled; she had worked on the collective farm for a quarter of a century, yet because she had not been directly engaged on production she was not entitled to a personal pension but only to one on her husband's behalf—that is, on the grounds of loss of the breadwinner. But her husband had been dead for twelve years—since the beginning of the war, in fact—and it was not easy to get the necessary documents certifying how long he had worked and how much he had been paid. It had been trouble enough collecting all these certificates—getting someone to write down that he had earned three hundred roubles a month, then getting another to certify that she lived alone and was not supported by anyone, and for how long—then taking it all to the social-security office, then doing it all over again because something had been entered wrong. Even at the end she was still not sure whether she would get a pension at all.

All this effort was made still more difficult by the fact that the social-security office which dealt with Tal'novo was twenty kilometres to the east, the district soviet was ten kilometres to the west, and the village soviet was an hour's walk to the north. They chased her from office to office for two whole months—sometimes because of a missing period, sometimes because of a misplaced comma. Every journey meant a whole day. She would go to the district soviet, and the secretary would be out that day: he was just absent, for no particular reason, as happens in the country. Come again the day after tomorrow. And four days later she would have to go again; out of sheer carelessness (all Matryona's documents were pinned together in one sheaf), someone had signed the wrong piece of paper.

"They're wearing me out, Ignatich," she complained to me after several of these fruitless journeys. "I get so worried."

But her brow did not stay furrowed for long. I noticed that she had an infallible means of restoring her good spirits: work. She would immediately pick up her spade and dig potatoes, or go off with a sack under her arm to fetch some peat, or wander far into the woods with a wicker basket to pick berries. Instead of bowing to office desks, she would lean over the bushes in the forest. Then, her back bending under the weight of her burden, Matryona would come beaming back to her cottage, thoroughly delighted.

"Now, I really know where to get the good stuff, Ignatich," she would say about the peat she had dug. "You should see the place; it's a treat."

"Isn't my peat enough, Matryona Vasilievna? There's a whole lorryload of it, after all."

"Pooh, your peat! If you got twice as much, or more, it might just do. When the wind really starts blowing in the winter, you need all the peat you can get simply to keep warm. You should have seen how much we pinched last summer. I'd pinch three lorryloads if I could. But they catch you. They took one of our women to court."

She was right. The terrifying breath of winter was already starting to blow. We were surrounded by woods, but there was nowhere to gather fuel. Although excavators were digging peat out of the bogs all around us, none of it was sold to the local inhabitants; but if you were one of the bosses or ranked among the boss class—teachers, doctors, factory workers—then you got a lorryload. The local people in Tal'novo were not supposed to be given fuel, and it was no use asking for it. The chairman of the collective farm walked around the village looking at people earnestly or innocently and talking about everything under the sun except fuel. After all, he had his own supply. Winter didn't worry him.

Just as people had once stolen wood from the landlord, now they scrounged peat from the Trust. The peasant women banded together by fives and tens, because they felt bolder in a gang, and went in daytime. In summer the peat was stacked up all over the place to dry out. The great thing about peat is that when it is dug it cannot be removed right away: it has to dry out until the autumn, or until the snow if the roads are impassable from the autumn rains. It was then that the women stole it. You could get six slabs of peat into a sack if it was damp, or ten slabs if it was dry. A sackful, carried three or four kilometres (it weighed sixty pounds), was enough to fire the stove for one day. Winter lasts two hundred days, and you have to stoke two stoves every day—the Russian stove in the daytime, the tiled stove at night.

"There's no two ways about it," Matryona said, losing her temper with some invisible "them." "Since there's been no more horses, if you want stuff in the house you've got to fetch it yourself. My back never stops aching. If I'm not pulling a sledge in winter, I'm humping baskets in summer. It's true, you know."

The peasant women went more than once a day to scrounge peat. On a good day Matryona might bring home as many as half a dozen sackfuls. She made no secret about my peat, but hid her own under the passage, covering the hiding place every evening with a loose floorboard.

"Bet they can't guess where it is, the nosey-parkers." She grinned as she wiped the sweat from her forehead. "And if they can't, they'll never find it in a lifetime."

What could the Peat Trust do? They weren't allowed enough staff to post watchmen all over the bogs. They probably coped with the problem by exaggerating their production figures and then writing off a certain percentage to loss from the effects of rain and crumbling. Now and again, at random intervals, they would send out a patrol and catch the women as they returned to the village. The women would drop their sacks and scatter. Sometimes too, when an informer gave them a tip-off, they would make a house-to-house search, compile lists of people caught hoarding illegal peat, and threaten them with prosecution. The women would stop pilfering peat for a while, but winter was coming on and drove them to it again—at night this time, and with sledges.

Observing Matryona, I noticed that every day was taken up with some major task, in addition to cooking and housework. She somehow kept a record in her head of the proper routine of these jobs, and whenever she woke up in the morning, she always knew what she was going to be doing that day. Apart from collecting peat and scrounging old tree stumps rooted up by the tractors in the peat bogs, gathering bilberries, which she bottled for the winter ("Give yourself a treat, Ignatich," she would say as she offered me some), digging potatoes, and tramping the countryside seeing about her pension, she also had to find time to gather hay for her one and only nanny goat.

"Why don't you keep a cow, Matryona Vasilievna?"

"Well," Matryona explained as she stood in the kitchen doorway in her dirty apron and turned towards my table, "the goat gives enough milk for me. If I had a cow, she'd eat me out of house and home. No good cutting hay beside the railway track—that belongs to other people; the Forestry owns the hay in the woods, and they won't let me cut hay on the collective farm because I'm not a member any longer. The people on the farm won't give you the skin off their teeth. Ever tried looking for grass under the snow? There was a time when you could get all the hay you wanted on the verges, at hay harvest. Lovely hay, that was . . ."

Collecting hay for one milch goat was very hard work for Matryona. She would set off in the morning with a sack and a sickle and go to the places where she remembered that grass grew along the boundaries between fields, by the roadside, on tussocks among the peat bogs. Her sack stuffed with heavy, freshly cut grass, she would drag it home and spread it out to dry in her yard. A sackful of grass produced the equivalent of one pitchforkful of hay.

The first thing that the new town-bred chairman of the collective farm did was to reduce the size of the kitchen gardens allotted to disabled ex-members, so Matryona was left with fifteen square yards of sandy soil while the ten square yards docked from her old allotment simply lay fallow and went to waste on the other side of the fence. And when the farm was shorthanded and the women flatly refused to work overtime, the chairman's wife visited Matryona. She was a townswoman too, a determined creature in a short grey half-length coat, with a brisk, military air.

She went into the house and stared fiercely at Matryona without bothering to greet her. Matryona looked embarrassed.

"Right," the chairman's wife said crisply. "Comrade Grigorieva, you must come and lend a hand on the collective farm. We need some help to shift manure tomorrow."

Matryona's face creased into an apologetic smile, as though she was ashamed to tell the woman that the farm was not entitled to pay her for any work she did.

"Well," she said hesitantly, "I'm sick, you see, and I don't belong to the farm any longer." Then she hurriedly changed her mind. "What time shall I come?"

"Bring your own pitchfork," ordered the chairman's wife as she marched out with a swish of her stiff skirt.

"Huh!" Matryona fumed. "'Bring your own pitchfork!' The farm never has any pitchforks, or spades either. Here am I, without a man to stick up for me . . ."

She talked to me about it all that evening.

"What else can I do, Ignatich? Of course I'm bound to help them—what sort of a harvest will they have if the muck doesn't get spread? Only, the way that place is run, it's a wonder they ever get any work done; the women stand around leaning on their shovels just waiting till the factory whistle blows at twelve. And they waste time arguing about the hours they've worked, who's on and who's off. Now to *my* way of thinking, when you work, you work—no gossiping, but get on with the job, and before you know where you are, it's suppertime."

Next morning, off she went with her pitchfork.

Not only the collective farm but any distant relative or simply a neighbour might accost Matryona one evening and say: "Come and help me tomorrow, Matryona. I need the rest of my potatoes dug." And Matryona could never refuse. She would abandon her private affairs, go and help her neighbour, and then when she returned say without a trace of envy: "Oh, she's got such huge potatoes, Ignatich. It was a pleasure to dig them up. I didn't want to stop, honest."

Matryona was equally indispensable when it came to ploughing up the kitchen gardens. The Tal'novo women had very sensibly worked out that it was much slower and harder work for one person to dig her garden singlehanded than for them to borrow a plough, harness six of them to it, and plough up six kitchen gardens in one go. Here again, Matryona was always called in to help.

"Do they pay her for it?" I once asked.

"She won't take any money. You'd have to force it on her."

Another of Matryona's great problems came when it was her turn to feed the village goatherds. One was a big, strapping creature who was a deaf-mute, and the other a boy with a soggy cheroot permanently stuck between his teeth. The job only came round once every six weeks, but it cost Matryona a lot of money. She would go to the village store to buy tins of fish and even things which she herself never ate, such as sugar and butter. Apparently the housewives all competed with each other to see who could feed the goatherds best.

"You should beware of tailors and shepherds," she explained to me. "They go round every house in turn, and if things aren't just right for them, they'll say terrible things about you to all your neighbours."

As if she did not have cares enough in her busy life, Matryona was regularly laid low by her ferocious illness. She would collapse and lie prone for a day or two at a time. She never complained or groaned; in fact, she hardly moved at all. When this happened, Masha, her lifelong friend, would come and tend the goat and stoke the fire. Matryona herself never ate or drank when she was ill and never asked for anything. No one in Tal'novo ever thought of sending for the doctor from the village clinic to call on them at home; it was regarded as vaguely insulting to one's neighbours, who might think one was putting on airs. Once, when the doctor was sent for, it turned out to be a disagreeable woman who simply told Matryona to lie down until the pain went and then come to the clinic herself. Matryona went very unwillingly. They did some tests on her and sent her to the district hospital, where the illness just subsided. Matryona, of course, was blamed for wasting their time.

Her everyday chores were what summoned her back to life. Soon Matryona would start getting up, moving slowly at first, then more briskly.

"You never saw me in the old days, Ignatich," she explained. "I used to be the one who carried all the sacks—a hundred pounds was nothing. My father-in-law used to shout at me: 'You'll break your back, Matryona!' I never needed any help harnessing the horse into the shafts, either. Ours was an army horse, a tough brute called Wolfcub . . ."

"Why an army horse?"

"They took ours for the war and gave us a wounded army horse in exchange. He was a bit crazy. Once he shied at something and galloped off with the sledge, heading straight for the lake. The men all jumped out of his way, but I grabbed him by the bridle and stopped him—I did, you know! Liked his oats, did that horse. Our men always fed them on oats and then they could pull anything."

However, Matryona was by no means a fearless woman. She was afraid of fires and of lightning, and most of all she was terrified of trains.

"Once when I wanted to go to Cherusti[8] the train came from Nechayevka, flashing its great eyes, the rails humming; it brought me out in a sweat, I can tell you, and my knees started shaking." Matryona was amazed at herself and shrugged her shoulders.

"Perhaps you were nervous about not having a ticket, because they don't sell them at the local station."

"You mean at the ticket office? They do—but only 'soft' class. Anyway, when the train came in, it was one big scramble. We rushed up and down trying to find somewhere to get on. The men either hung on to the steps or climbed up on the roof. We found a door that wasn't locked and pushed straight in without tickets. And all the coaches were 'hard' class, best you could hope for was to lie down on a luggage rack. Don't know why they wouldn't give us any tickets, the brutes . . ."

That winter Matryona's life took a turn for the better. At long last she started to get her pension of eighty roubles a month, in addition to slightly over a hundred roubles paid by the school and by me for bed and board.

"Matryona doesn't need to die now!" Some of her neighbours were already starting to envy her. "The old woman's got more money than she knows what to do with."

8. About 100 miles east of Moscow and some 250 miles northwest of Nechayevka.

Matryona ordered a new pair of felt boots, bought a new quilted jacket, and had an overcoat made out of a second-hand railwayman's greatcoat which she had been given by an engine driver from Cherusti, the husband of her adopted daughter Kira. The hunchbacked village tailor lined the material with cotton-wool padding and made an overcoat more splendid than any she had made herself in all her sixty years.

In the middle of winter Matryona sewed two hundred roubles into the lining of that coat. The money was for her funeral and it gave her great satisfaction.

December and January passed, two whole months in which she was spared an attack of her illness. Matryona took to visiting her friend Masha more often in the evenings, when they would sit talking and cracking sunflower seeds. She never invited anyone to her home in the evening, out of consideration for my need to work. Only once when I came home from school did I find the cottage full of people dancing. It was a christening party and I was introduced to her three sisters. Since Matryona was considerably older than they were, they treated her more like an aunt or a nanny. Until then, we had seen or heard practically nothing of Matryona's sisters, probably because they were afraid Matryona needed help and would become a burden to them.

For Matryona this celebration was saddened by only one thing. She had walked three miles to church for the blessing of the water and had put her bowl among the others, but when the ceremony was over and the women jostled forward to collect their bowls, Matryona was at the back of the crowd; when she finally got there, her bowl was missing, gone as though the devil had spirited it away.

Matryona went around asking all the women in the congregation: "Did anybody take a bowl of someone else's holy water by mistake?"

As no one owned up, it was probably stolen by one of the little boys who had been brought to church. Matryona came sadly home.

However, this did not mean that Matryona was really a fervent believer. If anything, she was a pagan and, above all, superstitious: if you went into the garden on St. John's day, that meant there would be a bad harvest next year; if a storm was whirling the snowflakes round and round, it meant that someone had hanged himself; if you caught your foot in the door, it meant a visitor. For as long as I lodged with her, I never once saw her say her prayers or cross herself. Yet she always asked for God's blessing before doing anything and she invariably said "God bless you" to me whenever I set off for school in the morning. Perhaps she did say her prayers, but not ostentatiously, being embarrassed by my presence or afraid of disturbing me. There were ikons[9] in the cottage. On ordinary days they were unlit, but on the eve of feast days and on the feast days themselves Matryona would light the ikon lamp.

Yet she had even fewer sins to atone for than her lame cat. The cat, after all, did kill mice . . .

Having been slightly shaken out of the rut of her rather dull life, Matryona also started to listen more attentively to my radio (I had taken care to put up a good "area," as Matryona called it).

9. I.e., icons. Religious images or portraits, usually painted on wood. A small lamp was set in front of the icons to illuminate them.

When she heard on the radio that some new machine had been invented, she grumbled from the kitchen: "Nothing but newfangled things these days. People won't want to go on working with the old machines, so where'll they put them all?"

During a broadcast describing how rain was induced by "seeding" clouds from an aeroplane, Matryona shook her head as she bent over the stove. "If they tamper with things much more, we won't know whether it's winter or summer."

Once they played a record of Chaliapin[1] singing Russian folk songs. Matryona stood and listened for a long time, then said firmly: "He sings beautifully, but he doesn't sing our way."

"Oh, really, Matryona Vasilievna—just listen to him!"

She listened a bit longer, then pressed her lips together disapprovingly. "No. He hasn't got it right. That's not the way we sing. And he plays tricks with his voice."

Another time, Matryona made up for it. There was a recital of some of Glinka's[2] songs, and suddenly, after half a dozen of his concert arias, Matryona appeared excitedly from the kitchen, clutching her apron, with a film of tears misting her eyes.

"Now that's . . . our sort of singing," she whispered.

2

And so Matryona and I grew used to each other and got along excellently together. She never pestered me with questions. Either because she was devoid of the usual female curiosity or because she was so tactful, she never once asked me whether I were married or not. All the women in Tal'novo would badger her to find out everything about me, but all she would say to them was: "If you want to find out, ask him yourself. All I know is, he's from far away."

When after quite a while I told her that I had spent a long time in prison, she merely nodded in silence, as though she had already suspected it.

For my part, I only saw Matryona as she was then, a lonely old woman, and I too refrained from prying into her past; indeed, I never suspected that there was anything of interest in it. I knew that she had married before the Revolution and had immediately moved into the cottage in which we were now living and straight to this same stove. Neither her mother-in-law nor any elder sisters-in-law were still alive then, so from the very first day after her wedding Matryona had taken over all the housework. I knew that she had had six children and they had all died very young, one after the other, so that no two of them had been alive at one time. Then there was Kira, who was her adopted daughter.

Matryona's husband did not return from the last war, and not even a funeral service was held for him. Men from his village who had served in the same company said that he had either been taken prisoner or was missing without trace. By the time the war had been over for eight years, Matryona herself had come to the conclusion that he was dead. And it was just as well that she did. If he had

1. Feodor Ivanovich Shalyapin (or Chaliapin, 1873–1938), Russian operatic bass with an international reputation as a singer and actor; he included popular Russian music in his song recitals.

2. Mikhail Ivanovich Glinka (1804–1857), Russian composer who was instrumental in developing a "Russian" style of music, including the operas *A Life for the Czar* and *Ruslan and Ludmila.*

survived, he would probably be married and living somewhere in Brazil or Australia, and both the Russian language and the village of Tal'novo would have long since faded from his memory.

One day I came home from school to find a visitor in the cottage. A tall, dark, elderly man, his cap resting on his knee, was sitting on a chair which Matryona had put out for him in the middle of the room, near the Dutch stove. His whole face was framed in thick black hair that was scarcely touched with grey. His dense black beard merged with a thick black moustache that made his mouth almost invisible, while a pair of black side whiskers, almost hiding his ears, ran up in an unbroken line to join the black hair at his temples. To crown it all, his eyebrows met in an unbroken black line across the bridge of his nose, while his forehead rose like a gleaming dome towards the crown of his bald head. It seemed to me that the old man's whole appearance radiated wisdom and dignity. He was sitting there calmly with his arms folded on his walking stick, which was resting weightily on the floor, sitting in an attitude of patient expectation without making much attempt to talk to Matryona, who was busy behind the partition.

As I came in, he turned his magnificent head towards me in a dignified movement and suddenly spoke to me: "Good evening to you! I don't see very well, but you must be my son's teacher; his name's Antoshka Grigoriev . . ."

That was all he needed to say. For all my impulse to be helpful to this worthy old man, I knew exactly what he was going to say and I discounted it in advance as pointless. Antoshka Grigoriev was a chubby, red-cheeked lad in class 8-G who looked like a cat that has just eaten a bowl of cream. He treated school as a place to come for a good rest, where he could just sit at his desk, grinning idly. Needless to say, he never did his homework. But unfortunately, as part of our efforts to keep up the high success rate for which the schools of our region and the surrounding provinces were famous, he was regularly moved up by a class a year, and he had clearly grasped that, however much the teachers might threaten him, they would move him up at the end of the year just the same, and there was no need for him to do any work. He simply laughed at us. Although he was in class 8, he could not do fractions and he was unable to tell one sort of triangle from another. He had been a permanent candidate for bottom place in the class for my first two terms, and he would be in the same position next term too.

But how was I to tell this elderly, half-blind man, more of an age to be Antoshka's grandfather than his father, who had had the courtesy to call on me, that the school had been deceiving him regularly year after year? I could not keep up the deception, because if I too turned into a yes-man I would harm the children in my class, and that would be a betrayal of all my work and the ethics of my profession.

So I patiently explained to him that his son was a spoilt child, that he told lies both at school and at home, that we ought to check his attendance book more often, and that both parent and teacher should be much stricter with him.

"But I can't be much stricter with him," the visitor assured me. "I beat him at least once a week as it is. And I've got a heavy hand, believe me."

While we were talking, I remembered that Matryona herself had for some reason once put in a word on Antoshka Grigoriev's behalf, but I had not asked how he was related to her, and on that occasion too I had refused to intervene. Now Matryona appeared in the kitchen doorway, a wordless supplicant. After

Ilya Mironich, the boy's father, had gone out saying that he would come to the school and find out for himself, I asked her: "What has that boy Antoshka got to do with you, Matryona Vasilievna?"

"He's the son of my brother-in-law," Matryona replied curtly, and went out to milk the goat.

I finally worked out that this persistent old man was the brother of her husband, the one who had been posted missing without trace.

For the rest of the long evening Matryona did not refer to the subject again. Only much later that night, when I'd forgotten about the old man and was working in a silence disturbed only by the rustle of cockroaches and the tick of the kitchen clock, Matryona suddenly said from her dark corner: "I almost married him once, Ignatich."

I had forgotten about Matryona. She said it with as much emotion as if the old man were still courting her. It was obvious that she had been thinking about nothing else all evening.

She rose from her ragged bedclothes and slowly came over to me as though following her own words. I looked up in surprise, and for the first time I saw a new, unsuspected Matryona.

There was no overhead light in our big room, where the fig plants clustered like trees in a forest. The only illumination was from the table lamp shining downwards onto my exercise books, and if you looked up, the rest of the room seemed to be in half darkness tinged with pink. Matryona now emerged from this gloom and for a moment her cheeks did not look their usual yellow but were flushed.

"He courted me first, before Efim . . . He was the elder brother . . . I was nineteen; Ilya was twenty-three . . . They lived in this very house. Their father built it."

I gave an involuntary glance around. Suddenly, instead of this grey, decaying old house with mice running wild behind its pale green skin of wallpaper, I saw it just built, with its fresh, newly planed logs, and smelling deliciously of pitch.

"What happened?"

"That summer . . . he and I used to go and sit in the woods," she whispered. "Where the stables are now, there used to be a wood, but it was cut down . . . I all but married him, Ignatich. Then the German war started, and Ilya was taken off to fight."

As she said this, I had a momentary image of that blue, white, and golden July of 1914: the sky of a world still at peace, floating clouds, and the peasants busily gathering the ripe harvest. I imagined the pair of them side by side: the giant with his pitch-dark beard and a scythe over his shoulder; Matryona, rosy-cheeked, clasping a sheaf of wheat. And the singing in the open air, a singing such as we have forgotten in this machine age.

"He went to the war, and he was posted missing . . . I waited for three years—not a sound, not a word . . ."

Wrapped in her faded, old-woman's kerchief, Matryona's round face gazed at me, lit by the soft indirect light of the lamp, and I saw it as though all its wrinkles had been smoothed out and the shabby, workaday clothes were gone. I saw the face of a bewildered girl faced with a terrible choice. I could see it happening . . . the leaves withering and blowing away, the snow falling and melting again. Another season's ploughing, another sowing, another harvest.

Again autumn, again the snowfall; first one revolution, then another, and the whole world turned upside down.[3]

"Their mother died, and Efim began courting me. 'You wanted to come and live in our house,' he said, 'so you might as well come—as *my* wife.' Efim was a year younger than me. Well, marry in haste, repent at leisure, they say. On Trinity Sunday I married Efim, and at Michaelmas[4] . . . his brother Ilya came back from Hungary, where he'd been a prisoner of war."

Matryona closed her eyes.

I said nothing.

She turned towards the doorway as if someone were standing there.

"There he stood on the doorstep. I cried out and fell down on my knees to him. But it was no good. 'If he wasn't my own brother,' he said, 'I'd murder the pair of you.'"

I shuddered. Her anguish and fear had summoned up a vivid image of Ilya, black and angry, standing in the doorway and brandishing his axe at Matryona.

She calmed down, leaned on the chair back in front of her, and went on in her lilting voice: "Oh, the poor man! There were any number of nice girls in the village, but he wouldn't marry any of them. He said he'd only marry someone with the same name as mine. And he did, too. Brought a girl called Matryona from Lipki and built himself his own house. They still live there—you pass it every day on your way to school."

So that was it! I now realised that I had seen the other Matryona several times. I did not care for her: she was always coming to my Matryona to complain that her husband was beating her, that he was a skinflint and worked her to death. She would come and weep for hours and her voice always seemed to be on the edge of tears. Matryona, it seemed, had missed nothing by not marrying him; Ilya had beaten his Matryona throughout their married life and had terrorised the household right up to the present day.

"*He* never beat me once," Matryona said of her husband, Efim. "He'd punch another man in the street, but he never touched me . . . Well, there was one time—I'd quarrelled with his sister, and he hit me over the head with a ladle. I jumped up from the table and screamed at him: 'I hope you choke, you brute!' And I ran off into the woods. He never touched me after that."

Ilya apparently had no grounds for complaint either, because the other Matryona bore him six children (including my Antoshka, the youngest and the runt of the litter), and all of them survived, while none of the children of Matryona and Efim lived longer than three months, although they never actually fell ill.

"One of my daughters, Elena, died as soon as they'd washed her right after she was born. Just as I got married on St. Peter's day, so my sixth child, Alexander, was buried on St. Peter's day."

The village had decided that there was a curse on Matryona.

"Yes, there was a curse on me," Matryona said, obviously convinced of it herself. "They took me to a nun to be cured. She gave me something to make me cough, then waited for the curse to jump out of me like a frog. Well, it didn't . . ."

3. The February and October revolutions (1917).

4. "Michaelmas": October 12 (September 29, old style). "Trinity Sunday": June 23 (June 10, old style).

The years passed like running water . . . In '41 Ilya was not conscripted because of his poor eyesight, but Efim was called up, and just as the elder brother had vanished in the First World War, so the younger brother was lost without trace in the second—and he never returned. Empty, the cottage which had once been so lively and noisy grew decrepit and rotten, and Matryona aged too as she lived on in it all alone.

She begged the other Matryona to let her have one of her offspring, her youngest daughter, Kira—perhaps because it was a child of Ilya's. For ten years she brought her up in her home as if she were her own daughter, one of those she had lost. Not long before my arrival, she had married her off to a young engine driver in Cherusti. This was now her only source of help and comfort; occasionally they would send her some sugar, or some lard when they killed a pig.

Frequently ill and sensing that she had not long to live, Matryona expressed the wish that after her death the separate outhouse on the other side of the passage in her house was to be given to Kira.[5] She said nothing about the cottage itself; each of her three sisters was aiming to get it.

That evening Matryona told me everything about herself. And, as often happens, no sooner had I learned the secrets of her life than they began to appear in the flesh. Kira came over from Cherusti and old Ilya began to get very worried. Apparently, in order to validate their tenure of a plot of land in Cherusti they had to build on it, and Matryona's outhouse was ideal for the purpose: there was no hope of getting the timber anywhere else. The person who was keenest on getting the plot of land in Cherusti was neither Kira nor her husband but old Ilya on their behalf.

So he started calling on us; he came once and then again, talking persuasively to Matryona, urging her to give up the outhouse now, while she was still alive. During these visits he struck me as quite unlike the decrepit old man who had leaned on his stick and seemed liable to collapse at a push or a rough word. Although slightly hunched with lumbago, for a man over sixty he was still a handsome figure with his vigorous, youthful black hair, and he pressed his case with ardour.

Matryona could not sleep for two nights. It was a hard decision for her to make. She did not mind about the outhouse, which was empty anyway, just as she never grudged her own labour or property; it was, after all, already bequeathed to Kira. But she was upset by the thought of dismantling the roof which had sheltered her for forty years. Even I, a mere lodger, objected to them tearing down the planks and wrenching out the logs from her cottage. For Matryona, it meant the end of her life.

But her insistent relatives knew that they would succeed in breaking up her house while she was still alive.

Ilya and his sons and sons-in-law arrived one February morning, and soon there came the knocking sound of five axes, the squealing and creaking of planks being wrenched apart. There was a purposeful gleam in Ilya's eye. Although he could no longer properly straighten his back, he was nimble enough at clambering about under the rafters and shinning down to shout instructions to his assistants. Long ago, as a young boy, he had helped his own father build this cottage,

5. Lumber was scarce and valuable, and old houses were well built. Moving houses or sections of houses is still common in the Russian countryside.

and the extra room that they were now demolishing had been designed as the place where he, the eldest son, should bring home his bride. Now that the house belonged to someone else, he relished the idea of pulling it apart and carting it away.

Having numbered the joists and the planks of the ceiling, they dismantled the room and the cellar and made a temporary wooden wall for the rest of the cottage and its shortened passage. Carelessly they knocked holes in the wall; it was all too obvious that these wreckers were no builders and were acting on the assumption that Matryona was not going to live here much longer.

While the men hacked away, the women distilled moonshine vodka in preparation for the day when the timber would be loaded up; proper vodka would have been far too expensive. Kira brought thirty pounds of sugar from somewhere in the Moscow region, and under cover of night Matryona Vasilievna carried the sugar and the bottles to the still.

When all the timber had been dismantled and piled up in front of the gate, the engine driver son-in-law went off to Cherusti to fetch the tractor. But that day it began to snow. The blizzard swirled and howled for two days and obliterated the roads with vast snowdrifts. No sooner had the way been cleared, and one or two lorries had got through, than there was a sudden thaw in the space of a single day, a damp fog came down, the snow dissolved into gurgling rivulets and your boots sank up to the calves in mud.

It was two weeks before the tractor was able to come and fetch the dismantled outhouse, and throughout that time Matryona went around like a lost soul. She was particularly depressed by a visit from her three sisters, who cheerfully swore at her and called her a fool for having let the outhouse go. They departed, announcing that they were fed up with her. Soon afterwards her lame cat strayed out of the yard and was killed. These two incidents in quick succession greatly upset her.

At last a frost came and the thawing roads hardened again. The sun came out, which cheered everyone up, and Matryona had a pleasant dream before waking up. That morning she found out that I wanted to photograph someone working at an old hand loom (there were still two of them in working order in the village, used for weaving crude rugs). She smiled shyly.

"Wait a couple of days until we get rid of this timber, Ignatich, and I'll set up my loom—I've got one too, you know. Then you can take a picture of me."

She obviously liked the idea of being photographed working at the old craft. A faint pink light from the wintry sun filtered in through the frosted window of her truncated porch, and the glow lit up her face. People who are at ease with their consciences always look happy.

As I was returning from school before dusk, I noticed movement outside our house. A big new tractor-drawn sledge was already fully loaded with timber, but there was still plenty more. The whole of Ilya's family, and their friends who had been invited to help, were just completing a second, home-made sledge. They were all working like madmen, in the frenzied state that seizes people when there is big money or free drink in the offing, all shouting at each other and arguing.

The argument was about how to move the sledges—separately or together. One of Ilya's sons (the lame one) and his son-in-law (the engine driver) were saying that the tractor could not pull both sledges at once. The tractor driver, on the other hand, a burly, self-confident tough, insisted hoarsely that he knew what he was talking about, that *he* was in charge of the tractor and he was going to tow both sledges together. His motives were obvious: he was being paid a lump sum to transport a certain quantity of timber, rather than so much per trip. If he had to do it in two trips—it was thirty-five kilometres each way—he would never complete the job in one night, and at all costs he had to return the machine to its garage by the next morning, because he was "borrowing" it illegally.

Old Ilya was impatient to have the outhouse timber removed that same day, so he persuaded his family to agree to move the load in one trip. Hastily cobbled together, the second sledge was coupled behind the stronger one.

Matryona ran busily around among the menfolk, helping to pile the logs onto the sledge. It was then that I noticed that she was wearing my quilted jacket and had dirtied it when she rubbed against the frozen mud sticking to the timber. Annoyed, I pointed this out to her. I was fond of that jacket; it had seen me through some hard times.

For the first time I lost my temper with Matryona Vasilievna.

"Oh dear, oh dear, I am stupid," she said apologetically. "I just grabbed it without thinking, I forgot it was yours. Sorry, Ignatich." She took it off and hung it up to dry.

When the loading was finished, everyone who had helped, about ten men in all, clumped noisily through the living room past my table and ducked under the curtain that screened off the kitchen. There followed a muffled clinking of glasses, the occasional thump as a bottle was knocked over; the voices grew louder and the mutual congratulations more extravagant. The tractor driver was particularly boastful. The powerful reek of moonshine soon drifted through to me, but they did not drink for long because they had to hurry to start before darkness set in. Conceited and aggressive, the tractor driver came staggering out. Ilya's son-in-law, the lame son, and another nephew climbed on the sledge to go with it as far as Cherusti. The others went home. Waving his stick, Ilya ran after one of the men and hurriedly made some last-minute adjustment. The lame son stopped at my table to light a cigarette and quite unexpectedly began telling me how fond he was of Aunt Matryona, that he had recently got married and that a son had been born not long ago. Then someone shouted to him to hurry. Outside, the tractor's engine started with a roar.

The last person to emerge from the kitchen was Matryona. She shook her head anxiously as the men prepared to leave, then put on her quilted jacket and a headscarf. In the doorway she said to me: "Why didn't they get two tractors? If one broke down, the other could have pulled. As it is, God knows what'll happen if something goes wrong . . ." And she ran out after the others.

After the drinking bout, the arguments, and the tramping feet, the quiet in the empty cottage was particularly marked; the cottage had also been made extremely cold thanks to the constant opening of doors. Outside, it was now quite dark. I too put on my quilted jacket and sat down to correct exercise books. The sound of the tractor faded in the distance.

An hour passed, then another and a third. Matryona had not come back, but I was not surprised. Having seen the sledges on their way, she had probably gone to see her friend Masha.

Two more hours went by. The village was not only in darkness, but a profound silence seemed to have settled on it. At the time I couldn't understand it;

later I realised that not a single train had passed all evening along the railway line that ran a quarter of a mile away from us. My radio was silent and I noticed that the mice were unusually active, scurrying about behind the wallpaper, squeaking and scratching more noisily and impudently than ever.

I looked up, startled. It was one o'clock in the morning and Matryona had still not returned.

Suddenly I heard several loud voices out in the village street. They were still far away, but something told me they were coming to our cottage, and sure enough, before long there came a sharp knock on the gate. A brisk, unknown voice shouted to be let in. I went out into the dense blackness with a pocket torch. The whole village was asleep, none of the windows was lit, and the rapidly thawing snow gave off no reflection. I slid aside the lower bolt and let them in. Four men in service greatcoats marched into the house. It is extremely unpleasant to be visited at night by loud-voiced men in uniform.

In the light I noticed, however, that two of the men were in railway uniform. The senior, a stout man with the same sort of face as the tractor driver, asked me: "Where's the owner?"

"I don't know."

"Did some people drive a tractor away from here, pulling a sledge?"

"Yes, they did."

"Were they drinking before they left?"

All four men screwed up their eyes as they peered into the semi-darkness around the table lamp. It was obvious that they had made an arrest or were intending to arrest someone.

"What happened?"

"Answer when you're asked a question."

"But . . ."

"Were they drunk when they left?"

Had someone been killed? Had they run into trouble? They gave me quite a grilling, but I said nothing because I knew that Matryona could get a heavy sentence for dispensing illicitly distilled vodka. I placed myself across the doorway into the kitchen to keep them out.

"Not that I could see." (It was true: I hadn't seen them, only heard them.)

With an artless gesture I waved my hand around the room to emphasise the innocence of it all—the peaceful lamplight on my papers and books, the row of fig plants, Matryona's neat, spartan bed. There was not a trace of an orgy to be seen.

Agreeing reluctantly that no drinking bout could have taken place here, they turned to go. On the way out I heard them say that even if there had been no drinking here, they were still convinced that drink was involved somewhere. I saw them out and asked what had happened.

Only when they reached the gate did one of them bark at me: "The whole lot caught it. Hardly even any bits to pick up."

Another added: "That was nothing. The nine o'clock express was damn nearly derailed, that was the worst of it."

And they hurried away.

Appalled, I went indoors. What did he mean by "the whole lot"? How had they "caught it"? Where was Matryona?

I pushed the curtain aside and went into the kitchen. The reek of moonshine hit me like a punch in the face. It was a squalid sight—overturned stools and benches, empty bottles lying on their sides, an upright one with some moonshine still in it, glasses, half-chewed bits of salted herring, onion, a smear of dripping mixed with bread crumbs.

Everything was deathly still except for the cockroaches cheerfully swarming over the battlefield.

They had said something about the nine o'clock express. Why? What did that mean? I began to wonder whether I shouldn't have shown them the scene in the kitchen after all, but then I angrily remembered their highhanded manner and their refusal to give me any proper information.

Suddenly the gate creaked, and I hurried out into the passage. "Is that you, Matryona Vasilievna?"

The front door opened and Matryona's friend Masha tottered unsteadily in, wringing her hands. "Matryona . . . Our Matryona, Ignatich . . ."

I sat her down and she told me the story, between sobs.

There is a steep hill leading down to the level crossing, which is ungated. The tractor had almost managed to pull the first sledge across when the rope snapped. The second, makeshift sledge struck an obstacle on the tracks and began to fall apart, because the wood which Ilya had given them to make it with was mostly rotten. They pulled the first sledge clear, then the tractor driver, Ilya's lame son, and, for some reason, Matryona, came back to mend the rope and tow the second sledge away. What use could Matryona have been? She always had interfered in men's work; a horse had once bolted and nearly dragged her into the frozen lake. Why, oh why did she have to go back to that cursed level crossing? She'd given up her outhouse to them, done her duty by them and more . . . The tractor driver kept looking round to make sure there was no train coming from Cherusti, he would have been able to see its lights from miles away; but two engines coupled together, travelling backwards and without lights, came down the track from the other direction—from our station. Why they had no lights nobody knows, and when an engine travels in reverse, the driver is blinded by coal dust from the tender and can't see properly. The engines rammed the sledge at full tilt, and the three people standing between it and the tractor were smashed to mincemeat. The tractor was battered to pieces, the sledge reduced to splinters, the rails were ripped up, and both engines derailed and flung onto their sides.

"But why didn't they hear the engines coming?"

"Because of the noise from the tractor engine."

"What about the bodies?"

"They won't let anyone near them. It's been cordoned off."

"Didn't I hear something about the express? Was there an express?"

"The nine o'clock left our station on time and it was picking up speed towards the level crossing. But when the two engines crashed, the engine drivers managed to get out alive, and they ran down the track waving their arms and managed to stop the train . . . Ilya's nephew, too, was crippled by a falling log. Right now he's hiding with friends so the police won't find out he was at the crossing. They're pulling witnesses in as hard as they can—better keep your mouth shut if you want to stay out of trouble. And as for Kira's husband—not a scratch. He tried to hang himself and they had to pull his neck out of the noose. My brother and my aunt were killed because of me, he says. Then he went and gave himself up to the police, but he's being sent to the madhouse instead of prison. Oh, Matryona, Matryona . . ."

Matryona was no more. A beloved person was gone forever. And on her last day on earth I had scolded her for wearing my jacket.

The woman on the book poster, printed in bright yellows and reds, smiled joyfully.

Masha sat and wept a little longer. Then as she was getting up to go she suddenly asked: "Do you remember, Ignatich? Matryona had a grey shawl. She promised that after her death it should go to my little Tanya, didn't she?"

She looked hopefully at me in the semi-darkness, wondering whether I had forgetten.

But I remembered. "Yes, that's right, she promised it to her."

"Listen, then. Would you let me take it now? Tomorrow morning the whole clan will descend on this place and I might not get it."

She gave me a hopeful, imploring look. She had been Matryona's friend for fifty years and was the only person in the village who had been genuinely fond of her. It was surely right that she should have it.

"Of course, take it," I agreed.

She opened a chest, found the shawl, stuffed it under her skirts, and went.

The mice seemed to have been gripped by a kind of madness; they were racing furiously up and down the walls and the green wallpaper was heaving in almost visible waves.

Tomorrow I had to go and teach in school. It was three o'clock in the morning. The only refuge was to lock myself in and go to sleep. I could lock the door now, because Matryona would not be coming back.

I lay down, leaving the light on. The mice were squeaking so hard it was almost as if they were groaning. They raced tirelessly up and down. My exhausted, confused mind could not throw off an involuntary sense of horror. I had a feeling that Matryona was moving about, bidding farewell to her home. Suddenly, in the hallway by the front door I had a vision of Ilya, young, black-bearded, with axe raised: "If he wasn't my own brother, I'd murder you both."

Forty years that threat had laid in the corner, like an old abandoned blade—and it had finally struck.

3

At dawn the women brought home all that remained of Matryona, drawn on a sledge and covered with a dirty piece of sacking. They removed the sack to wash the corpse. It was hideously mangled—no legs, half the torso missing, and no left arm. One of the women said: "The Lord left her right arm so she can pray to Him in heaven."

All the fig plants were removed, the plants which Matryona had loved so much that once, when she had woken up with the cottage full of smoke, instead of trying to save the building she had thrown the fig plants to the floor so they would not suffocate. The floors were scrubbed clean. Matryona's dim mirror was draped with a large old towel of homespun cloth. The gay posters were taken down from the walls. My table was moved aside, and the roughly carpentered coffin was placed on stools near the window, under the ikon.

And there in the coffin lay Matryona. Her severed, disfigured body was covered with a clean sheet and her head was bound with a white cloth. Her face, calm and looking more alive than dead, had remained whole.

The villagers came to stand and look. Mothers brought young children to see the dead woman. And if anyone began to weep, all the women, even those who had come out of mere curiosity, inevitably started weeping in sympathy as they stood round the walls and in the doorway, like a choir accompanying a solo singer. The men stood stiffly to attention, silent and bareheaded.

It was the role of the female relatives to lead the mourning. I detected in their mourning an element of cold calculation, of an ancient, established procedure. The more distant relatives stepped up to the coffin for a short while and muttered as they bent over it. Those who regarded themselves as more closely related to the deceased began their keening at the very doorway and when they reached the coffin leaned over to say their piece right into the dead woman's face. Each mourner struck her own note and gave vent to her own particular thoughts and emotions.

I also observed that the keening was not merely an expression of grief but contained an element of "politics." Matryona's three sisters descended, took possession of the cottage, the goat, and the stove, locked her chest, ripped out of the lining of her coat the two hundred roubles she had put aside for her funeral, and explained to everyone present that they, her sisters, were Matryona's only close relatives. And this was what they said as they mourned over her coffin:

"Oh, our dearest, dearest only sister, you lived such a quiet, simple life, and we always loved you and cared for you. And your house was the death of you. The outhouse drove you to the grave. Why did you let them tear it down? Why didn't you listen to us?"

Thus the sisters' wailing was directed at her husband's clan—accusing them of having forced Matryona to surrender the timber from her house. And the further implication was: "You may have taken the outhouse but we won't let you have the rest of the cottage."

The husband's clan—Matryona's sisters-in-law, Efim's and Ilya's sisters, and various nieces—came and mourned in these terms:

"Oh, dearest Aunt Matryona, you never spared yourself or took care of yourself, and now *they* will say we were to blame. We loved you, but it was all your fault. The outhouse had nothing to do with it. Why did you go to the place where death was lying in wait for you? Nobody asked you to! Why didn't you stop and think?—then you mightn't have died! And why didn't you listen to us?"

These lamentations implied: "We weren't to blame for her death, and as for the cottage—we'll see about that!"

Then came the "other" Matryona, a coarse, ugly woman. But the substitute Matryona, who had once taken Ilya simply because her name was the same, broke the rules by wailing in unaffected sincerity over the coffin:

"Dearest, dearest sister of mine, promise me you weren't offended at me! Oh, what times we once had, you and I, and how we talked! Forgive me, poor Matryona! Oh, you've gone to join your mother now and you'll be telling tales about me! Oh, please don't, please . . ."

At this final "please" she seemed to sob out her very soul, and she beat her breast again and again against the side of the coffin. When her keening went too far beyond the ritual limits, the women, as though acknowledging that she had well and truly made her point, said kindly: "That's enough, dear. You'd better go now."

Matryona went, but she came back again and sobbed even more violently. Then a very old woman stepped forward from a corner, laid a hand on her shoulder, and said sternly: "There are two great riddles in this world: How was I born? I don't remember. How shall I die? I don't know."

At once Matryona was quiet, and everyone in the room fell completely silent.

But a little while later that same old woman, who was much older than all the others and who, I thought, had hardly even known Matryona during her lifetime, began to wail in her turn: "Poor, unhappy Matryona! Why was it you who died and I was spared?"

The one person whose mourning was completely unceremonious was Matryona's wretched adopted daughter, Kira from Cherusti, for whose sake the outhouse had been dismantled and removed. She could only weep the natural, commonplace tears of our time, an age that has been no stranger to suffering and bereavement. Her waved hair was pathetically disordered, her eyes bloodshot. Despite the cold, she was unaware that her headscarf had slipped off, and when she put on her overcoat, her arm could not find the sleeve. She walked numbly away from the coffin of her foster-mother in one cottage to her brother's coffin in another; they now feared for her reason, as her husband was certain to be sent for trial.

Her husband, it seemed, was doubly guilty: not only had he been responsible for moving the timber, but being an engine driver by profession and therefore thoroughly versed in the regulations for ungated level crossings, he should have first gone to Tal'novo Station to warn them about the tractor. That night the lives of a thousand people on board the Urals Express, sleeping peacefully in their berths by the light of shaded lamps, had been nearly destroyed. And all because of a few people's greed—the urge to grab a plot of land, the refusal to make two journeys by tractor; because of the outhouse, on which a curse had lain since Ilya had stretched out his covetous hands to seize it.

The tractor driver had already passed beyond the reach of earthly justice. But the railway management was also guilty for leaving a busy level crossing unguarded and for allowing two coupled engines to travel without lights. This was why they had at first made such strenuous efforts to prove that the party had been drinking, and were now doing their best to mislead the court.

The track and the rail bed were so badly damaged that no trains ran for the three days that the coffins lay in the village; traffic was diverted onto a loop line. Throughout Friday, Saturday, and Sunday—from the end of the police investigation until the funeral—the track was under repair day and night. To keep out the freezing cold and to provide light in the dark, the repair gangs lit bonfires with the free fuel provided by the planks and logs from the second sledge which were scattered all over the level crossing. The first sledge, still fully loaded, was left standing nearby on the roadside.

It was this—the tantalising fact that one sledge was there, ready to be towed away, and that the contents of the second sledge might have been saved from burning—that really tortured the black-bearded Ilya all Friday and Saturday. Yet his daughter was on the verge of insanity, his son-in-law was to be prosecuted, in his own house lay the body of his son, and across the street lay the woman he had once loved—both of whom he had killed. Ilya stood tugging at his beard and did not stay for long when he came to pay his last respects to the departed. To judge by his furrowed brow, he was obviously deep in thought; but what he was thinking about was how to save the rest of the timber from the bonfire and from the grasping claws of Matryona's sisters.

Later, when I came to know Tal'novo better, I realized that there were plenty of other people like him in the village. It is both revealing and bitterly ironic that our language itself equates "good" with "goods" and that to lose property is universally regarded as shameful and ridiculous.

Ilya set off on an unceasing round of visits, to the village soviet, to the station, from one department to another. His back bent, supported on his stick, he stood in each office in turn, begging the authorities to have pity on his old age and to give him permission to recover his timber.

Somewhere, someone gave him permission, and Ilya gathered his remaining sons, sons-in-law, and nephews, and borrowed some horses from the kolkhoz.[6] Then, by a roundabout route through three villages, he reached the far side of the damaged level crossing and carted the remains of the outhouse away to his own yard. He completed the work during the night between Saturday and Sunday.

On Sunday the funeral was held. The two coffins met in the middle of the village and the relatives quarrelled over which should go first. Then they placed them side by side on one sledge, aunt and nephew, and hauled them through the damp chill of an overcast February day to the cemetery that lay two villages distant. The weather was blustery and unpleasant; the priest and the deacon waited at the church, refusing to come out to meet the procession on the way.

Singing in chorus, the people slowly followed the procession as far as the village boundary. There they stopped and went home.

Even on Sunday morning the women were still busy at their rituals: one old woman sat mumbling psalms by the coffin: Matryona's sisters fussed around the stove, stoking up the heat with the slabs of peat that Matryona had brought in a sack from distant peat bogs. They baked some unappetising little pies out of cheap, nasty flour.

On Sunday evening, after the funeral, we assembled for the wake. Several tables, joined together to form a single long one, now occupied the space where the coffin had stood that morning. They began by all standing around the table while an old man, the husband of one of Ilya's sisters, recited the Lord's Prayer. Then a small quantity of melted honey was served to each person in a bowl, which we ate with spoons in memory of the departed. After that we ate something else, drank some vodka, and the talk grew more lively. Before eating the final dish of *kisel'*[7] we stood up and sang "In Eternal Memory."[8] They explained to me that traditionally this had to be sung before the *kisel'*. Then more vodka, after which the talk became louder still and no longer concerned with Matryona.

Ilya's brother-in-law said boastfully: "Did you notice at the church how they said *all* the prayers, without leaving any out? That's because Father Michael noticed I was there. He knows I know the service by heart. Otherwise he'd have just gabbled off half of it, tipped 'em in, and goodbye."

At last the meal was over. Once again we stood up, and sang "She is Worthy," then repeated "In Eternal Memory" three times. By now the voices were

6. Collective farm.
7. "*Kisel'*": a fruit jelly normally eaten with the *kutiia* at a Russian funeral. *Kutiia* is a wheat pudding with honey and almonds; the villagers are too poor to have the main ingredients and their honey and water are symbolic of the *kutiia*.
8. A dirge, or religious hymn sung to honor the dead. The village still follows religious rituals in times of crisis and does not use the civil ceremony proposed by the Soviet government.

hoarse and out of tune, the faces were drunken, and no one any longer put the slightest feeling into their "Eternal Memory."

Then most of the guests departed, leaving only the close relatives; cigarettes were produced and lit, there were jokes and laughter. The talk turned to Matryona's husband, Efim, who had been reported missing without trace. Thumping his chest, Ilya's brother-in-law explained about Efim to me and to a shoemaker who was married to one of Matryona's sisters: "Yes, he died all right, did Efim. Otherwise, why didn't he come back? Even if I knew I'd be hung if I came home, I'd still come back."

The shoemaker nodded in agreement. He had been a deserter and had spent the whole war at home, hiding in his mother's cellar.

The stern, silent old woman, the one who was much older than the others, had decided to stay in the cottage for the night and was already installed on top of the stove. She gazed down in silent disapproval on the indecently loud behaviour of all these youngsters of fifty and sixty.

Only the unhappy adopted daughter, who had grown up in this house, went behind the kitchen partition and wept.

Ilya did not come to Matryona's wake, because he was taking part in the memorial ceremony for his son, but during the next few days he came over to the cottage a couple of times for some ill-tempered discussions with Matryona's sisters and the shoemaker.

The argument was about who was to have the cottage—one of Matryona's sisters or the adopted daughter. It looked as if they might go to court over it, but they were fairly soon reconciled and reached a settlement, agreeing that the court would probably allot the house to neither party but would hand it over to the village soviet. So a deal was made. The goat went to one sister; the shoemaker and his wife got the cottage; and because he had "built the place with loving care," Ilya was allotted the outhouse timber plus the shed in which the goat had lived and the internal fence that divided the back yard from the kitchen garden.

Once more, overcoming his sickness and rheumatism, the insatiable old man began to perk up and look younger. Once more he summoned his remaining sons and sons-in-law. They demolished the shed and the fence and he personally removed the timber on a little sledge, helped by his young son Antoshka from class 8-G, who for once worked with a will.

Matryona's cottage was handed over before winter was out, so I moved over to one of her sisters-in-law who lived nearby. On various occasions she recalled things about Matryona and thus I learned to see the deceased in a new light.

"Efim didn't love her. He used to say that he liked to dress smartly, but she just wore any old thing, like a typical peasant woman. So once he realised he needn't spend any money on her, he blew all his spare cash on drink. And once, when he and I went to town to do a job and earn some money in the winter, he found himself a fancy woman and didn't want to go back to Matryona."

Everything she said about Matryona was disapproving: she was dirty, she was a bad housekeeper, she wasn't thrifty. She wouldn't even keep a pig, because she didn't like the idea of fattening up a beast to kill it. And she was stupid enough to work for other people without pay—though the very reason the sister-in-law had remembered Matryona was that she had been complaining that there was no longer anyone to help plough up the kitchen garden. Even though she acknowledged Matryona's kindness and simplicity, she did so in a tone of scornful pity.

Only then, listening to the disapproving comments of her sister-in-law, did I see an image of Matryona which I had never perceived before, even while living under her roof.

It was true: every other cottage had its pig, yet she had had none. What could be easier than to fatten up a greedy pig whose sole object in life was food? Boil it a bucketful of swill three times a day, make it the centre of one's existence, then slaughter it for lard and bacon. Yet Matryona never wanted one . . .

She was a poor housekeeper. In other words, she refused to strain herself to buy gadgets and possessions and then to guard them and care for them more than for her own life.

She never cared for smart clothes, the garments that embellish the ugly and disguise the wicked.

Misunderstood and rejected by her husband, a stranger to her own family despite her happy, amiable temperament, comical, so foolish that she worked for others for no reward, this woman, who had buried all her six children, had stored up no earthly goods. Nothing but a dirty white goat, a lame cat, and a row of fig plants.

None of us who lived close to her perceived that she was that one righteous person without whom, as the saying goes, no city can stand.

Neither can the whole world.[9]

1959

9. See Genesis 18.23–33, the story of Sodom.

NAGUIB MAHFOUZ

1911–2006

The first Arabic novelist to win the Nobel Prize, Naguib Mahfouz traced the roots of his work to the civilization of the ancient Egyptians, over five thousand years ago. Past and present combine in his novels and stories, as he explores the destiny of his people and their often traumatic adjustment to industrial society. To chronicle the rapidly changing culture, Mahfouz adapts the techniques of nineteenth-century European realism and combines them with a mystical outlook and a command of both the literary resources of classical Arabic and the idioms of contemporary speech.

Without Mahfouz, it is said, the turbulent history of twentieth-century Egypt would never be known. Indeed, he lived through almost a century of transition and documented the successive stages of social and political life from the time the country cast off foreign rule and became a postcolonial society. Mahfouz was born in Cairo on December 11, 1911, the youngest of seven children in the family of a civil servant. The family moved from its home in the old Jamaliya district to the suburbs of Cairo when Mahfouz was a young boy. He attended government schools and the University of Cairo, graduating in 1934 with a degree in philosophy. These were not quiet years: Egypt, officially under Ottoman rule, had been occupied by the British since 1883 and was declared a British protectorate at the start of the First World War, in 1914. Mahfouz grew up in the midst of the struggle for national independence that culminated in a violent uprising against the British in 1919 and the negotiation of a constitutional monarchy in 1923. The consistent focus on Egyptian cultural identity that permeates his work may well have its roots in this turbulent period.

While at the university, Mahfouz befriended the socialist and Darwinian thinker Salama Musa and began to write articles for Musa's journal *Al-Majalla al-Jadida* (*The Modern Magazine*). In 1938 he published his first collection of stories, *Whispers of Madness*, and in 1939 the first of three historical novels set in ancient Egypt. At that time he planned to write a set of forty books on the model of the historical romances written by the British novelist Sir Walter Scott (1771–1832). These first novels contained allegories of modern politics, and readers easily recognized the criticism of the reigning King Farouk in *Radubis* (1943) and the analogy in *The Struggle for Thebes* (1944) between the ancient Egyptian battle to expel Hyksos usurpers and twentieth-century rebellions against foreign rule. In 1945, Mahfouz shifted decisively to the realistic novel and a portrayal of modern society. He focused on the social and spiritual dilemmas of the middle class in Cairo, documenting in vivid detail the life of an urban society that represented Egypt.

The major work of this period, and Mahfouz's masterwork in many eyes, is *The Cairo Trilogy* (1956–57), three volumes depicting the experience of three generations of a Cairo family between 1918 and 1944. Into this story Mahfouz wove a social history of Egypt after the First World War. Mahfouz has been called the "Balzac of Egypt"—a comparison to the French novelist and panoramic chronicler of society Honoré de Balzac (1799–1850)—and he was well acquainted with the nineteenth-century realists. Traditional Arabic literature has many forms of narrative, but the novel is not one of them; Arabic writers like Mahfouz adapted the Western form to their own needs. He made use of familiar nineteenth-century strategies such as a chronological plot, unified characters, the inclusion of documentary information and realistic details, a panoramic view of society including a strong moral and humanistic perspective, and a picture of urban middle-class life. Mahfouz's achievement was recognized in the State Prize for literature in 1956, but he temporarily ceased to write after finishing the *Trilogy* in 1952.

In that year, an officers' coup headed by Gamal Abdel Nasser overthrew the monarchy and instituted a republic that promised democratic reforms, and Mahfouz described the changes in Egyptian society that resulted. Although the author was at first optimistic about the new order, he soon recognized that few improvements had occurred in the lives of the general population. When he started publishing again in 1959, Mahfouz's works included open criticism of the Nasser regime. Three years after *The Cairo Trilogy* brought him international praise, Mahfouz shocked many readers with a new book, *Children of Gebelawi*. An allegory of religious history, *Children of Gebelawi* scandalized orthodox believers by its personification of God and its depiction of the prophets chiefly as social reformers rather than as religious figures. The book was banned throughout the Arab world except in Lebanon, and the Jordan League of Writers attacked Mahfouz as a "delinquent man" whose novels were "plagued with sex and drugs." From this point on, Mahfouz tended to add an element of political or social allegory and subjective mysticism to his literary realism.

Although he had become the best-known writer in the Arab world, his works read by millions, Mahfouz was unable to make a living from his books. Copyright protection was minimal, and without such safeguards, even best-selling authors received only small sums for their books. Until he began writing for motion pictures in the 1960s, he supported himself and his family through various positions in governmental ministries and as a contributing editor for the leading newspaper, *Al-Ahram* (*The Pyramids*). Attached to the Ministry of Culture in 1954, he adapted novels for film and television and later became director-general of the governmental Cinema Organization, overseeing production and also, controversially, censorship. Eventually more than thirty of his stories and novels were made into films. After his retirement from the civil service in 1971, Mahfouz continued to publish articles and short stories in *Al-Ahram*, where most of his novels appeared in serialized form before being issued as paperbacks. When he received the Nobel Prize in Literature, in 1988, at the age of seventy-six, he was still contributing a weekly column, "Point of View," to *Al-Ahram*. Despite his fame, Mahfouz's books were censored and banned in many Arab nations; in his own country, he faced attacks from Islamic fundamentalists. Sheikh Omar Abdel-Rahman (later convicted in the first bombing of the World Trade Center, in New York, in 1993) condemned his work publicly and made death threats against Mahfouz in the early 1990s. In 1994, Mahfouz was stabbed in the neck by an assailant who fled the scene. Although the writer recovered from the attack, he lost most of his sight in old age and became reclusive. He died in Cairo at the age of ninety-four.

"Zaabalawi," the selection here, is a story from Mahfouz's second collection, *God's World* (1963). It contains many of the author's predominant themes and draws on an Islamic mystical tradition whose comprehensive tolerance is far from (and often opposed by) the rigid beliefs of contemporary Muslim fundamentalists. Written two years after *Children of Gebelawi*, it echoes the earlier work's religious symbolism in the mysterious character of Zaabalawi himself. It also demonstrates Mahfouz's shift from an "objective," realistic style toward one emphasizing subjective, mystical awareness. The perceptions of individual characters—here, the narrator—dominate many of his short stories. Mahfouz's later works would include adaptations of folk narratives like the *Arabian Nights*, and there is an element of the folktale in this story, as it draws on Arabic culture and comments, from a broader, often prophetic perspective, on the contemporary scene. Yet this story is also a social document: the narrator's quest for Zaabalawi brings him before various representatives of modern Egyptian society inside a realistically described Cairo. "Zaabalawi," therefore, takes on the character of a social and metaphysical allegory. Its terminally ill narrator seeks to be cured in a quest that implies not only physical healing but religious salvation as well. He has exhausted the resources of medical science and, in desperation, seeks out a holy man whose name he recalls from childhood tales.

Although he is never fully identified, Zaabalawi seems to stand for a spiritual principle of some sort. Zaabalawi's former acquaintances, whom the narrator interviews, form an allegorical portrait of

Egyptian society. The bureaucrats who depend on reason, technology, and businesslike efficiency seem least capable of encountering Zaabalawi, while the artists have a closer relationship with him, even if they cannot quickly find him. As the narrator's quest proceeds, he is continually surprised by the difficulty in locating this mystical figure. The story, which combines concreteness with mysticism, the spirit of nineteenth-century realism with that of the *Arabian Nights*, suggests that magic is still possible, even in twentieth-century industrial Cairo.

Zaabalawi[1]

Finally I became convinced that I had to find Sheikh[2] Zaabalawi.

The first time I had heard of his name had been in a song:

> Oh what's become of the world, Zaabalawi?
> They've turned it upside down and taken away its taste.

It had been a popular song in my childhood, and one day it had occurred to me to demand of my father, in the way children have of asking endless questions:

"Who is Zaabalawi?"

He had looked at me hesitantly as though doubting my ability to understand the answer. However, he had replied, "May his blessing descend upon you, he's a true saint of God, a remover of worries and troubles. Were it not for him I would have died miserably—"

In the years that followed, I heard my father many a time sing the praises of this good saint and speak of the miracles he performed. The days passed and brought with them many illnesses, for each one of which I was able, without too much trouble and at a cost I could afford, to find a cure, until I became afflicted with that illness for which no one possesses a remedy. When I had tried everything in vain and was overcome by despair, I remembered by chance what I had heard in my childhood: Why, I asked myself, should I not seek out Sheikh Zaabalawi? I recollected my father saying that he had made his acquaintance in Khan Gaafar[3] at the house of Sheikh Qamar, one of those sheikhs who practiced law in the religious courts, and so I took myself off to his house. Wishing to make sure that he was still living there, I made inquiries of a vendor of beans whom I found in the lower part of the house.

"Sheikh Qamar!" he said, looking at me in amazement. "He left the quarter ages ago. They say he's now living in Garden City and has his office in al-Azhar Square."[4]

I looked up the office address in the telephone book and immediately set off to the Chamber of Commerce Building, where it was located. On asking to see Sheikh Qamar, I was ushered into a room just as a beautiful woman with a most intoxicating perfume was leaving it. The man received me with a smile

1. Translated by Denys Johnson-Davies.
2. A title of respect (originally "old man"), often indicating rulership.
3. Gaafar Market, an area of shops.
4. An area of Cairo close to the famous mosque and university of al-Azhar.

and motioned me toward a fine leather-upholstered chair. Despite the thick soles of my shoes, my feet were conscious of the lushness of the costly carpet. The man wore a lounge suit and was smoking a cigar; his manner of sitting was that of someone well satisfied both with himself and with his worldly possessions. The look of warm welcome he gave me left no doubt in my mind that he thought me a prospective client, and I felt acutely embarrassed at encroaching upon his valuable time.

"Welcome!" he said, prompting me to speak.

"I am the son of your old friend Sheikh Ali al-Tatawi," I answered so as to put an end to my equivocal position.

A certain languor was apparent in the glance he cast at me; the languor was not total in that he had not as yet lost all hope in me.

"God rest his soul," he said. "He was a fine man."

The very pain that had driven me to go there now prevailed upon me to stay.

"He told me," I continued, "of a devout saint named Zaabalawi whom he met at Your Honor's. I am in need of him, sir, if he be still in the land of the living."

The languor became firmly entrenched in his eyes, and it would have come as no surprise if he had shown the door to both me and my father's memory.

"That," he said in the tone of one who has made up his mind to terminate the conversation, "was a very long time ago and I scarcely recall him now."

Rising to my feet so as to put his mind at rest regarding my intention of going, I asked, "Was he really a saint?"

"We used to regard him as a man of miracles."

"And where could I find him today?" I asked, making another move toward the door.

"To the best of my knowledge he was living in the Birgawi Residence in al-Azhar," and he applied himself to some papers on his desk with a resolute movement that indicated he would not open his mouth again. I bowed my head in thanks, apologized several times for disturbing him, and left the office, my head so buzzing with embarrassment that I was oblivious to all sounds around me.

I went to the Birgawi Residence, which was situated in a thickly populated quarter. I found that time had so eaten at the building that nothing was left of it save an antiquated façade and a courtyard that, despite being supposedly in the charge of a caretaker, was being used as a rubbish dump. A small, insignificant fellow, a mere prologue to a man, was using the covered entrance as a place for the sale of old books on theology and mysticism.

When I asked him about Zaabalawi, he peered at me through narrow, inflamed eyes and said in amazement, "Zaabalawi! Good heavens, what a time ago that was! Certainly he used to live in this house when it was habitable. Many were the times he would sit with me talking of bygone days, and I would be blessed by his holy presence. Where, though, is Zaabalawi today?"

He shrugged his shoulders sorrowfully and soon left me, to attend to an approaching customer. I proceeded to make inquiries of many shopkeepers in the district. While I found that a large number of them had never even heard of Zaabalawi, some, though recalling nostalgically the pleasant times they had spent with him, were ignorant of his present whereabouts, while others openly made fun of him, labeled him a charlatan, and advised me to put myself in the hands of a doctor—as though I had not already done so. I therefore had no alternative but to return disconsolately home.

With the passing of days like motes in the air, my pains grew so severe that I was sure I would not be able to hold out much longer. Once again I fell to wondering about Zaabalawi and clutching at the hope his venerable name stirred within me. Then it occurred to me to seek the help of the local sheikh of the district; in fact, I was surprised I had not thought of this to begin with. His office was in the nature of a small shop, except that it contained a desk and a telephone, and I found him sitting at his desk, wearing a jacket over his striped galabeya.[5] As he did not interrupt his conversation with a man sitting beside him, I stood waiting till the man had gone. The sheikh then looked up at me coldly. I told myself that I should win him over by the usual methods, and it was not long before I had him cheerfully inviting me to sit down.

"I'm in need of Sheikh Zaabalawi," I answered his inquiry as to the purpose of my visit.

He gazed at me with the same astonishment as that shown by those I had previously encountered.

"At least," he said, giving me a smile that revealed his gold teeth, "he is still alive. The devil of it is, though, he has no fixed abode. You might well bump into him as you go out of here, on the other hand you might spend days and months in fruitless searching."

"Even you can't find him!"

"Even I! He's a baffling man, but I thank the Lord that he's still alive!"

He gazed at me intently, and murmured, "It seems your condition is serious."

"Very."

"May God come to your aid! But why don't you go about it systematically?" He spread out a sheet of paper on the desk and drew on it with unexpected speed and skill until he had made a full plan of the district, showing all the various quarters, lanes, alleyways, and squares. He looked at it admiringly and said, "These are dwelling-houses, here is the Quarter of the Perfumers, here the Quarter of the Coppersmiths, the Mouski,[6] the police and fire stations. The drawing is your best guide. Look carefully in the cafés, the places where the dervishes perform their rites, the mosques and prayer-rooms, and the Green Gate,[7] for he may well be concealed among the beggars and be indistinguishable from them. Actually, I myself haven't seen him for years, having been somewhat preoccupied with the cares of the world, and was only brought back by your inquiry to those most exquisite times of my youth."

I gazed at the map in bewilderment. The telephone rang, and he took up the receiver.

"Take it," he told me, generously. "We're at your service."

Folding up the map, I left and wandered off through the quarter, from square to street to alleyway, making inquiries of everyone I felt was familiar with the place. At last the owner of a small establishment for ironing clothes told me, "Go to the calligrapher[8] Hassanein in Umm al-Ghulam—they were friends."

I went to Umm al-Ghulam,[9] where I found old Hassanein working in a deep, narrow shop full of signboards and jars of color. A strange smell, a mixture of

5. The traditional Arabic robe, over which this modernized district officer wears a European jacket.
6. The central bazaar.
7. A medieval gate in Cairo.
8. One who practices the art of decorative lettering (literally "beautiful writing"), which is respected as a fine art in Arabic and Asian cultures.
9. A street in Cairo.

glue and perfume, permeated its every corner. Old Hassanein was squatting on a sheepskin rug in front of a board propped against the wall; in the middle of it he had inscribed the word "Allah"[1] in silver lettering. He was engrossed in embellishing the letters with prodigious care. I stood behind him, fearful of disturbing him or breaking the inspiration that flowed to his masterly hand. When my concern at not interrupting him had lasted some time, he suddenly inquired with unaffected gentleness, "Yes?"

Realizing that he was aware of my presence, I introduced myself. "I've been told that Sheikh Zaabalawi is your friend; I'm looking for him," I said.

His hand came to a stop. He scrutinized me in astonishment. "Zaabalawi! God be praised!" he said with a sigh.

"He *is* a friend of yours, isn't he?" I asked eagerly.

"He was, once upon a time. A real man of mystery: he'd visit you so often that people would imagine he was your nearest and dearest, then would disappear as though he'd never existed. Yet saints are not to be blamed."

The spark of hope went out with the suddenness of a lamp snuffed by a power-cut.

"He was so constantly with me," said the man, "that I felt him to be a part of everything I drew. But where is he today?"

"Perhaps he is still alive?"

"He's alive, without a doubt. . . . He had impeccable taste, and it was due to him that I made my most beautiful drawings."

"God knows," I said, in a voice almost stifled by the dead ashes of hope, "how dire my need for him is, and no one knows better than you[2] of the ailments in respect of which he is sought."

"Yes, yes. May God restore you to health. He is, in truth, as is said of him, a man, and more. . . ."

Smiling broadly, he added, "And his face possesses an unforgettable beauty. But where is he?"

Reluctantly I rose to my feet, shook hands, and left. I continued wandering eastward and westward through the quarter, inquiring about Zaabalawi from everyone who, by reason of age or experience, I felt might be likely to help me. Eventually I was informed by a vendor of lupine[3] that he had met him a short while ago at the house of Sheikh Gad, the well-known composer. I went to the musician's house in Tabakshiyya,[4] where I found him in a room tastefully furnished in the old style, its walls redolent with history. He was seated on a divan, his famous lute beside him, concealing within itself the most beautiful melodies of our age, while somewhere from within the house came the sound of pestle and mortar and the clamor of children. I immediately greeted him and introduced myself, and was put at my ease by the unaffected way in which he received me. He did not ask, either in words or gesture, what had brought me, and I did not feel that he even harbored any such curiosity. Amazed at his understanding and kindness, which boded well, I said, "O Sheikh Gad, I am an admirer of yours, having long been enchanted by the renderings of your songs."

"Thank you," he said with a smile.

1. God (Arabic).
2. One of the calligrapher's major tasks is to write religious documents and prayers to Allah.
3. Beans.
4. A quarter named for the straw trays made and sold there.

"Please excuse my disturbing you," I continued timidly, "but I was told that Zaabalawi was your friend, and I am in urgent need of him."

"Zaabalawi!" he said, frowning in concentration. "You need him? God be with you, for who knows, O Zaabalawi, where you are."

"Doesn't he visit you?" I asked eagerly.

"He visited me some time ago. He might well come right now; on the other hand I mightn't see him till death!"

I gave an audible sigh and asked, "What made him like that?"

The musician took up his lute. "Such are saints or they would not be saints," he said, laughing.

"Do those who need him suffer as I do?"

"Such suffering is part of the cure!"

He took up the plectrum and began plucking soft strains from the strings. Lost in thought, I followed his movements. Then, as though addressing myself, I said, "So my visit has been in vain."

He smiled, laying his cheek against the side of the lute. "God forgive you," he said, "for saying such a thing of a visit that has caused me to know you and you me!"

I was much embarrassed and said apologetically, "Please forgive me; my feelings of defeat made me forget my manners."

"Do not give in to defeat. This extraordinary man brings fatigue to all who seek him. It was easy enough with him in the old days when his place of abode was known. Today, though, the world has changed, and after having enjoyed a position attained only by potentates, he is now pursued by the police on a charge of false pretenses. It is therefore no longer an easy matter to reach him, but have patience and be sure that you will do so."

He raised his head from the lute and skillfully fingered the opening bars of a melody. Then he sang:

I make lavish mention, even though I blame myself, of those I love,
For the stories of the beloved are my wine.[5]

With a heart that was weary and listless, I followed the beauty of the melody and the singing.

"I composed the music to this poem in a single night," he told me when he had finished. "I remember that it was the eve of the Lesser Bairam.[6] Zaabalawi was my guest for the whole of that night, and the poem was of his choosing. He would sit for a while just where you are, then would get up and play with my children as though he were one of them. Whenever I was overcome by weariness or my inspiration failed me, he would punch me playfully in the chest and joke with me, and I would bubble over with melodies, and thus I continued working till I finished the most beautiful piece I have ever composed."

"Does he know anything about music?"

5. From a poem by the medieval mystic poet Ibn al-Farid, who represents spiritual ecstasy as a kind of drunkenness.

6. A major Islamic holiday, celebrated for three days to end the month's fasting during Ramadan.

"He is the epitome of things musical. He has an extremely beautiful speaking voice, and you have only to hear him to want to burst into song and to be inspired to creativity. . . ."

"How was it that he cured those diseases before which men are powerless?"

"That is his secret. Maybe you will learn it when you meet him."

But when would that meeting occur? We relapsed into silence, and the hubbub of children once more filled the room.

Again the sheikh began to sing. He went on repeating the words "and I have a memory of her" in different and beautiful variations until the very walls danced in ecstasy. I expressed my wholehearted admiration, and he gave me a smile of thanks. I then got up and asked permission to leave, and he accompanied me to the front door. As I shook him by the hand, he said, "I hear that nowadays he frequents the house of Hagg Wanas al-Damanhouri. Do you know him?"

I shook my head, though a modicum of renewed hope crept into my heart.

"He is a man of private means," the sheikh told me, "who from time to time visits Cairo, putting up at some hotel or other. Every evening, though, he spends at the Negma Bar in Alfi Street."

I waited for nightfall and went to the Negma Bar. I asked a waiter about Hagg Wanas, and he pointed to a corner that was semisecluded because of its position behind a large pillar with mirrors on all four sides. There I saw a man seated alone at a table with two bottles in front of him, one empty, the other two-thirds empty. There were no snacks or food to be seen, and I was sure that I was in the presence of a hardened drinker. He was wearing a loosely flowing silk galabeya and a carefully wound turban; his legs were stretched out toward the base of the pillar, and as he gazed into the mirror in rapt contentment, the sides of his face, rounded and handsome despite the fact that he was approaching old age, were flushed with wine. I approached quietly till I stood but a few feet away from him. He did not turn toward me or give any indication that he was aware of my presence.

"Good evening, Mr. Wanas," I greeted him cordially.

He turned toward me abruptly, as though my voice had roused him from slumber, and glared at me in disapproval. I was about to explain what had brought me to him when he interrupted in an almost imperative tone of voice that was none the less not devoid of an extraordinary gentleness, "First, please sit down, and, second, please get drunk!"

I opened my mouth to make my excuses but, stopping up his ears with his fingers, he said, "Not a word till you do what I say."

I realized I was in the presence of a capricious drunkard and told myself that I should at least humor him a bit. "Would you permit me to ask one question?" I said with a smile, sitting down.

Without removing his hands from his ears he indicated the bottle. "When engaged in a drinking bout like this, I do not allow any conversation between myself and another unless, like me, he is drunk, otherwise all propriety is lost and mutual comprehension is rendered impossible."

I made a sign indicating that I did not drink.

"That's your lookout," he said offhandedly. "And that's my condition!"

He filled me a glass, which I meekly took and drank. No sooner had the wine settled in my stomach than it seemed to ignite. I waited patiently till I had grown used to its ferocity, and said, "It's very strong, and I think the time has come for me to ask you about—"

Once again, however, he put his fingers in his ears. "I shan't listen to you until you're drunk!"

He filled up my glass for the second time. I glanced at it in trepidation; then, overcoming my inherent objection, I drank it down at a gulp. No sooner had the wine come to rest inside me than I lost all willpower. With the third glass, I lost my memory, and with the fourth the future vanished. The world turned round about me and I forgot why I had gone there. The man leaned toward me attentively, but I saw him—saw everything—as a mere meaningless series of colored planes. I don't know how long it was before my head sank down onto the arm of the chair and I plunged into deep sleep. During it, I had a beautiful dream the like of which I had never experienced. I dreamed that I was in an immense garden surrounded on all sides by luxuriant trees, and the sky was nothing but stars seen between the entwined branches, all enfolded in an atmosphere like that of sunset or a sky overcast with cloud. I was lying on a small hummock of jasmine petals, more of which fell upon me like rain, while the lucent spray of a fountain unceasingly sprinkled the crown of my head and my temples. I was in a state of deep contentedness, of ecstatic serenity. An orchestra of warbling and cooing played in my ear. There was an extraordinary sense of harmony between me and my inner self, and between the two of us and the world, everything being in its rightful place, without discord or distortion. In the whole world there was no single reason for speech or movement, for the universe moved in a rapture of ecstasy. This lasted but a short while. When I opened my eyes, consciousness struck at me like a policeman's fist and I saw Wanas al-Damanhouri regarding me with concern. Only a few drowsy customers were left in the bar.

"You have slept deeply," said my companion. "You were obviously hungry for sleep."

I rested my heavy head in the palms of my hands. When I took them away in astonishment and looked down at them, I found that they glistened with drops of water.

"My head's wet," I protested.

"Yes, my friend tried to rouse you," he answered quietly.

"Somebody saw me in this state?"

"Don't worry, he is a good man. Have you not heard of Sheikh Zaabalawi?"

"Zaabalawi!" I exclaimed, jumping to my feet.

"Yes," he answered in surprise. "What's wrong?"

"Where is he?"

"I don't know where he is now. He was here and then he left."

I was about to run off in pursuit but found I was more exhausted than I had imagined. Collapsed over the table, I cried out in despair, "My sole reason for coming to you was to meet him! Help me to catch up with him or send someone after him."

The man called a vendor of prawns and asked him to seek out the sheikh and bring him back. Then he turned to me. "I didn't realize you were afflicted. I'm very sorry. . . ."

"You wouldn't let me speak," I said irritably.

"What a pity! He was sitting on this chair beside you the whole time. He was playing with a string of jasmine petals he had around his neck, a gift from one of his admirers, then, taking pity on you, he began to sprinkle some water on your head to bring you around."

"Does he meet you here every night?" I asked, my eyes not leaving the doorway through which the vendor of prawns had left.

"He was with me tonight, last night and the night before that, but before that I hadn't seen him for a month."

"Perhaps he will come tomorrow," I answered with a sigh.

"Perhaps."

"I am willing to give him any money he wants."

Wanas answered sympathetically, "The strange thing is that he is not open to such temptations, yet he will cure you if you meet him."

"Without charge?"

"Merely on sensing that you love him."

The vendor of prawns returned, having failed in his mission.

I recovered some of my energy and left the bar, albeit unsteadily. At every street corner I called out "Zaabalawi!" in the vague hope that I would be rewarded with an answering shout. The street boys turned contemptuous eyes on me till I sought refuge in the first available taxi.

The following evening I stayed up with Wanas al-Damanhouri till dawn, but the sheikh did not put in an appearance. Wanas informed me that he would be going away to the country and would not be returning to Cairo until he had sold the cotton crop.

I must wait, I told myself; I must train myself to be patient. Let me content myself with having made certain of the existence of Zaabalawi, and even of his affection for me, which encourages me to think that he will be prepared to cure me if a meeting takes place between us.

Sometimes, however, the long delay wearied me. I would become beset by despair and would try to persuade myself to dismiss him from my mind completely. How many weary people in this life know him not or regard him as a mere myth! Why, then, should I torture myself about him in this way?

No sooner, however, did my pains force themselves upon me than I would again begin to think about him, asking myself when I would be fortunate enough to meet him. The fact that I ceased to have any news of Wanas and was told he had gone to live abroad did not deflect me from my purpose; the truth of the matter was that I had become fully convinced that I had to find Zaabalawi.

Yes, I have to find Zaabalawi.

1963

榮興齋

III Contemporary World Literature

Certain years in world history stand out in the blaze of a revolution that transforms world politics: 1789 for the French Revolution, 1848 for a series of European revolutions, 1917 for the Russian Revolution. More recently, 1968, a year of student rebellion in Prague, Paris, Mexico City, and elsewhere, seemed at the time to be such a milestone. Challenges to traditional authority shook the 1960s. The subsequent changes to Western culture have shaped all that came after—especially in literature, where the intimate relations among men and women and the tensions between public responsibility and private desire play a central role. Meanwhile, the vision of a post-communist world that was glimpsed in Prague in the spring of 1968 found its realization in the dismantling of communist regimes in Eastern Europe in 1989 and the dissolution of the Soviet Union in 1991. The crushing of the Prague Spring led immediately to a period of pessimism and "normalization" (that is, a return to repressive practices) that restricted social movements. The only successful effort to thwart normalization was the Polish trade union Solidarity, which, however, was trampled by the imposition of martial law in 1981.

In the West, especially in the United States, the

A 1965 photograph by Marc Riboud of a street in Beijing as seen from inside an antique dealer's shop.

focus of protest was the Vietnam War—a conflict the Americans had taken over from the French—in which over half a million (mostly drafted) Americans had failed to defeat a guerrilla insurgency. Communist North Vietnam, backed by the Soviet Union (and for a time by China), eventually reached Saigon, the capital of South Vietnam, in 1975, and unified the country the following year. There were a number of other minor proxy wars between the superpowers during the 1970s and 1980s, but this was the period of détente, or relaxation of hostility, when the Soviet premier Leonid Brezhnev and American presidents including Richard Nixon and Jimmy Carter sought to defuse Cold War tensions and signed a number of treaties on arms control and human rights. Détente, eclipsed by the Soviet invasion of Afghanistan in 1979, was followed by a period of rearmament under President Ronald Reagan, which culminated, surprisingly, in the disarmament agreement with Russian premier Mikhail Gorbachev at Reykjavik, Iceland, in 1986. Seeking to transform the moribund economy and society he had inherited from his communist predecessors, Gorbachev introduced the principles of glasnost (or openness) and perestroika (or restructuring), intending to make the Soviet system more flexible and accountable. In the end, however, the restructuring went much further than Gorbachev had intended, resulting in the demise of the Communist Party and the dissolution of both the Warsaw Pact military alliance and the Soviet Union itself.

If 1968 marks the high point of the protest movements that would transform contemporary society, 1989 is an equally memorable year, during which the nations of Eastern Europe rebelled against—and finally overthrew—communist regimes, and the wall that had separated East and West Berlin fell. Also in 1989, the first steps were taken to dismantle the system of apartheid, or racial segregation and white minority rule in South Africa (white minority rule had ended in Zimbabwe, formerly Rhodesia, in 1980). That same year thousands of Chinese

Young men in Ho Chi Minh City (formerly Saigon, the capital of South Vietnam), in 1975, after "Liberation Day."

students mounted an unsuccessful rebellion against the communist government of the People's Republic of China; this brief uprising ended with a massacre in Tiananmen Square, in Beijing, the historic center of Chinese politics.

During the 1990s, as the Soviet Union disintegrated and as China moved closer to a capitalist economy, many hoped that humanity's bloodiest century would end with something like the accomplishment of world peace that had been such a bright dream at its beginning. The dictatorships of Latin America, supported by the United States as a bulwark against communism, gave way to democratically elected governments. Peace agreements in Northern Ireland and between Israel and Palestine seemed to confirm such promises. Another date, September 11, 2001, undermined such hopes: on that day, terrorists claiming to act in the name of Islam hijacked four airplanes and flew into the World Trade Center, in New York, and the Pentagon, near Washington, D.C. (one of the planes was forced, by the passengers, to crash in a remote field in Pennsylvania). The wars of the twenty-first century, which began in the aftermath of the terrorist attacks, have chilled the hope that ours would be a uniquely peaceful age. Likewise, the expectation that industrialization would lead inevitably to a more secular world has proved mistaken. Communal violence continues in India, and the Arab-Israeli conflict and Islamic fundamentalism have intensified during the first decades of the twenty-first century, while in much of the world outside Europe, religion is resurgent.

During the past half century or so, even if dreams of world peace have often appeared illusory, great improvement in the living standards of much of the world's still-expanding population has occurred. Four-fifths of the global population now benefits from the fruits of industrialization, even as one-fifth remains in poverty. The years since World War II have been an era of globalization in investment, knowledge, politics, and culture. The information revolution, made possible first by satellite television and then by ever-more-sophisticated computers and the Internet, has unified distant parts of the globe more rapidly than did the telegraph and telephone at the beginning of the twentieth century. Today, a world connected by telecommunications responds more quickly than ever before to news about politics, markets, and even sporting events. It is also a world of increased migration, in which the movements of people from poorer to richer nations have created immense cultural hybridity while sometimes producing tensions in the host countries. A diverse literature chronicles the

Supporters of antiapartheid activist Nelson Mandela gather outside the Victor Verster prison in Cape Town, South Africa, demanding his freedom. After twenty-seven years of confinement, Mandela was finally released in 1990. In 1994 he became South Africa's first black president.

ARCTIC OCEAN
Greenland (Den.)
Spitsbergen (Nor.)
Iceland
NORTH AMERICA
Canada
Chicago
New York
United States of America
Los Angeles
Mexico
Mexico City
Cuba
Haiti
Dominican Rep.
Jamaica
VIRGIN IS. (Br. & U.S.)
Antigua
Belize
Guatemala
Honduras
Martinique (Fr.)
St. Lucia
El Salvador
Nicaragua
Trinidad & Tobago
Costa Rica
Panama
Venezuela
Guyana
Surinam
French Guiana
Colombia
GALAPAGOS IS. (Ecuador)
Ecuador
Equator
Brazil
Peru
SOUTH AMERICA
Bolivia
Paraguay
Rio de Janeiro
Chile
Santiago
Buenos Aires
Uruguay
Argentina
FALKLAND IS. (Br.)
SOUTH PACIFIC OCEAN
NORTH ATLANTIC OCEAN
SOUTH ATLANTIC OCEAN
Norway
Sweden
Finland
Leningrad (St. Petersburg)
Union
Moscow
Northern Ireland
United Kingdom
Dublin
Ireland
Denmark
Netherlands
London
East Germany
Berlin
Poland
Warsaw
West Germany
Belgium
Paris
Prague
Czechoslovakia
France
Switz.
Austria
Vienna
Hungary
Venice
Yugoslavia
Romania
Italy
Albania
Bulgaria
Portugal
Madrid
Spain
Rome
Istanbul
Turkey
Greece
Tunisia
Mediterranean Sea
Syria
Lebanon
Beirut
Israel
Jerusalem
Iraq
Jordan
Kuwait
Morocco
Algeria
Libya
Alexandria
Cairo
Egypt
Bahrain
Qatar
Saudi Arabia
W. Sahara
AFRICA
Mauritania
Mali
Niger
Chad
Yemen
South Yemen
Eritrea
Senegal
Gambia
Guinea-Bissau
Guinea
Sierra Leone
Liberia
Burkina Faso
Ivory Coast
Ghana
Togo
Benin
Nigeria
Ibadan
Cameroon
Sudan
Central African Rep.
Ethiopia
Somalia
Equatorial Guinea
Gabon
Congo
Zaire
Uganda
Kenya
Rwanda
Burundi
Nairobi
Tanzania
Angola
Zambia
Malawi
Zimbabwe
Mozambique
Madagascar
Namibia
Botswana
Johannesburg
Swaziland
South Africa
Lesotho
MILES
0
1200
2400
3600
4800
AT THE EQUATOR
0
2400
4800
KILOMETERS

THE WORLD
1986
The Communist World
ARCTIC OCEAN
SIBERIA
ALASKA (U.S.)
Canada
oviet Socialist Republics
A S I A
Mongolia
disputed borders of Kashmir
Beijing
N. Korea
Seoul
S. Korea
China
Tokyo
Japan
Shanghai
Pakistan
New Delhi
Nepal
Bhutan
Bangladesh
India
Burma
Hanoi
Laos
Thailand
Vietnam
Kampuchea
Okinawa (Japan)
Taiwan
Philippines
Brunei
Sri Lanka
Malaysia
Indonesia
Papua
NORTH PACIFIC OCEAN
Los Angeles
HAWAIIAN IS. (U.S.)
Equator
SOUTH PACIFIC OCEAN
Australia
Sydney
New Zealand
INDIAN OCEAN
Kerguelen I.(Fr.)
ANTARCTICA

Speechless, 1996, by Shirin Neshat.

experiences of political refugees and immigrants, both documented and undocumented. The political upheavals of the twentieth century created millions of refugees and entrenched conflicts that remain unresolved. Within nations, many migrants left rural areas to move to expanding cities. In search of economic security, meanwhile, immigrants left poorer countries, often in the global south, for the developed world. The immigrant experience became a major theme of writers including **Junot Díaz** and **Jamaica Kincaid**.

Illness, too, travels faster than before; even as the general state of public health has improved, new epidemics, particularly AIDS, have ravaged populations in the West and much more broadly in Africa. In Europe and North America, AIDS at first affected mostly homosexuals. The decimation of gay communities by the disease led to more militant forms of activism, which built on antidiscrimination efforts dating back to the Stonewall uprising. A popular gay bar in the Greenwich Village neighborhood of New York City, Stonewall had been frequently targeted by the police. One evening in June 1969, patrons and their supporters resisted arrest, igniting the struggle for acceptance and equality. Yet another result of the gay rights movement was the introduction of same-sex marriages in much of the West, as well as in Brazil and South Africa. Tension over homosexuality remained, however: it is a theme in the writings of the Dominican American novelist Junot Díaz. At the same time, homosexuality remained illegal in much of Africa and the Muslim world.

The gay rights movement was one of several outgrowths of 1960s cultural conflicts. The most successful of these, feminism, achieved legal equality for women in the workplace and in the family throughout the industrialized world. Challenges remained, including violence against women and unequal pay, but by the end of the twentieth century, many successful young career women claimed to be "post-feminist." Another factor enabling these transformations was the availability of safe and reliable birth control, which allowed for family planning (the contraceptive pill was introduced in 1960). Works by writers as diverse as **Leslie Marmon Silko, Toni Morrison, Ama Ata Aidoo, Nawal El Saadawi**, and **Hanan Al Shaykh** touch on the changes in the status of women and in social norms governing sexuality. Abortion remained controversial in the United States and Ireland but was widely available elsewhere, except Latin America, Africa, and the Middle East, where homosexuality also remained illegal.

Even relatively conservative regions were not untouched by the youth culture born in the 1960s, broadcast by the mass media, and emphasizing the breaking of old taboos and the liberation of sexuality. Although the great writers were often skeptical of the appeal of mass culture, literature too participated in the breaking of taboos. Almost a century ago, **Virginia Woolf** spoke of a change in human character that the modernist generation registered: "All human relations have shifted—those between masters and servants, husbands and wives, parents and children." The literature of the last century has continually reimagined these perpetually shifting relations, and the theme of generational conflict or cultural transmission across the generations plays a prominent role in much contemporary literature.

The literature of the late twentieth century, presented here along with a few works from the twenty-first century, has responded in manifold ways to the period's unprecedented historical transformations. While the cultural hybridity that attends the movement of peoples and the sharing of information sometimes inspires literary innovations, it can also sharpen nostalgia for tradition and the past. Increasingly, writers are conscious of having an audience beyond their nation or region and even beyond their language. Writers with a global readership may feel both responsibility for representing their own people to the world and the need to accommodate their style of writing to the demands of the international marketplace. Indeed, Nobel Prize winners such as **Orhan Pamuk** have often been accused in their homelands of speaking primarily to an international audience. Writers thus find themselves striving to defend and honor the spirit and culture of historically marginalized groups while reaching out to a more elite international audience.

As in the immediate postwar period, many writers seeking to address the need for social change and the elimination of political inequality turn to traditional literary realism or to political allegory. A literary movement emerging in the 1960s, magic realism draws both on the realist tradition of the historical novel and on the inspiration of modernists such as **Franz Kafka**, who depicted his nightmarish worlds in lifelike detail. In various ways, Latin American novelists including **Gabriel García Marquéz**, **Carlos Fuentes**, and **Isabel Allende**, and the Indian-born **Salman Rushdie**, combine realistic historical narration with fanciful folktales in which individuals and societies seem to be transformed by distinctly nonrealistic events—a character who can fly, perhaps, or a mystical link among people born on the night of Indian independence. The juxtaposition emphasizes the coexistence of modern notions of causality and traditional, prescientific belief in the unexplainable and thus has had its greatest impact in zones of uneven economic development, where educated writers have incorporated the folk wisdom of their rural, sometimes illiterate communities. Toni Morrison has made effective use of such techniques in her writings on African American life. Like the magic realists, Morrison is sometimes described as a postmodernist. In common with an earlier generation inspired by the modernists (Borges, **Nabokov**, **Beckett**), postmodernists often question the boundary between fiction and history. While treating historical events, such writers as **Roberto Bolaño** and Orhan Pamuk may call attention to the fictionality of their reconstruction of those events—encouraging the reader to keep in mind that stories are the creations of writers who may, by the very act of narration, distort historical reality. These authors tend to present an oblique account of atrocities, whether involving colonization, genocide, or political repression. Both in magic realism and in postmodernism, stories may seem whimsical or fantastical even when they are playing for deadly serious stakes.

The twenty-first century began with reminders of the interconnectedness of a global society linked by industrial capitalism and communications technology but divided by religion and politics. While war, terrorism, and poverty are events that divide us, the greatest world literature suggests, as it always has, what unites us.

YEHUDA AMICHAI
1924–2000

Yehuda Amichai belongs to the first generation of Israeli poets to be fully naturalized into both the language and the landscape of modern Israel. Perhaps more than any other contemporary poet, Amichai established a language of poetry that was independent of the history of Hebrew as a sacred language. By juxtaposing the monumental and the ordinary, Amichai helped to appropriate the language of the epic, biblical struggles of the people of Israel for the mundane realities of the twentieth century.

Hebrew was a spoken language only up to the close of the biblical period in the sixth century B.C.E. For the next 2,500 years, beginning with the exile of the Jews to Babylonia and their long dispersion from the land of Israel and continuing to the present day—a period known as the Diaspora—Hebrew ceased to be a spoken language. During the Diaspora, Hebrew was principally a vehicle for the sacred and the liturgical writings, for biblical commentary, and for official communication, while local Jewish dialects like Yiddish and Ladino served the function of everyday communication. The movement to modernize medieval Hebrew began in the eighteenth century, and by the late nineteenth century, Hebrew had established itself as a vigorous literary language. But it was not revived as a modern spoken language and adapted to ordinary secular life until the early twentieth century, when European Jews started emigrating to Palestine. Along with other poets of his generation, Amichai sought to create a poetic idiom that was at home with the colloquial rhythms and idiomatic expressions of revived Hebrew.

Amichai was born Ludwig Pfeuffer in Würzburg, Germany, and came to Palestine with his family in 1936, when he was twelve. He had grown up in an Orthodox Jewish home and studied Hebrew since early childhood, however, and like so many other immigrants, he made the transition to modern Hebrew with relative ease. Despite the enforced move from Germany, in his poetry he speaks of his childhood as a time of happiness and peace. His adult life began during the turbulent struggle to establish the State of Israel. Amichai served with the Jewish Brigade in World War II and saw active duty as an infantryman with the elite Jewish army, the Palmach, during the Israeli War of Independence and with the Israeli army in 1956 and 1973.

After completing his studies at Hebrew University, Amichai became a secondary school teacher of Hebrew literature and the Bible, but his career as a teacher soon took second place to his work as a poet. He had begun writing poetry in 1949 and published his first collection, *Now and in Other Days*, in 1955. With his second collection, *Two Hopes Away* (1958), he established himself as a major poet. From the late 1950s until his death, in 2000, Amichai published more than nine volumes of poetry as well as novels—including the one translated as *Not of This Time, Not of This Place* (1968)—short stories, and plays.

At times there is a deceptive simplicity about Amichai's poems. They seem to address ordinary moments and casual encounters. And yet in their simplicity they capture the many, resonating layers of the language and the insistent and contradictory realities of contemporary

Israeli life. The writer's language is despairing, gently ironic, playful and passionate by turns, moving easily between a child's artlessness and the brusque directness of a war-hardened veteran. The scope of his poetry is enormous, but what he brings to each poem is a freshness of vision and metaphors that are rich in unexpected and illuminating juxtapositions—the city as mother, drying laundry and entrenched enmities, a lost child and a lost goat. These metaphors that thrust the deeply historical into the arms of the grittily immediate inspired critics to compare Amichai not with his contemporaries but with Donne and Shakespeare.

Amichai's form of choice was the short lyric, but he composed at least one memorable narrative poem, *The Travels of the Last Benjamin of Tudela,* and he often linked a number of shorter poems into cycles on a single theme. Many of his best poems are love poems, addressed to a woman or to Jerusalem—not as alternatives but as embedded in each other's essence. His poetry evokes with stunning immediacy that ancient city that other peoples and religions besides the Jews know as sacred and claim as home. Jerusalem is "an eternal heart . . . burning red," the place that must be remembered when all else is forgotten. Until 1967 it was a city divided only by a wall, across which intimate but hostile neighbors could watch each other's laundry drying.

In Israel, Amichai's poems are included in school anthologies and recited on public occasions. In the introduction to *The Selected Poetry of Yehuda Amichai,* Chana Bloch relates an anecdote that gives a more telling sense of the widespread popularity his works enjoy: "Some Israeli students were called up in the 1973 Yom Kippur War. As soon as they were notified, they went back to their rooms at the university, and each packed his gear, a rifle, and a book of Yehuda Amichai's poems." As she points out, despite the fact that his work "isn't patriotic in the ordinary sense of the word, it doesn't cry death to the enemy, and it offers no simple consolation for killing and dying." Amichai was originally brought to the attention of British and American readers by Ted Hughes, who published his work first in the journal *Modern Poetry in Translation* and then collaborated with Amichai in translating a volume of selections from his early poetry, *Amen* (1977). Eight volumes of his poetry have appeared in English translation, and there are numerous translations into other languages as well. It is for his renewal of the Hebrew language, however, that Amichai is best known; more than any other contemporary poet, he liberated Hebrew from the burden of its history.

If I Forget Thee, Jerusalem[1]

If I forget thee, Jerusalem,
Then let my right be forgotten.[2]
Let my right be forgotten, and my left remember.
Let my left remember, and your right close
And your mouth open near the gate.

1. Translated by Assia Gutmann. The title is from Psalm 137.5.

2. Compare Psalm 137.5: "If I forget thee, O Jerusalem, let my right hand forget its cunning."

I shall remember Jerusalem
And forget the forest—my love will remember,
Will open her hair, will close my window,
Will forget my right,
Will forget my left.

If the west wind does not come
I'll never forgive the walls,
Or the sea, or myself.
Should my right forget,
My left shall forgive,
I shall forget all water,
I shall forget my mother.

If I forget thee, Jerusalem,
Let my blood be forgotten.
I shall touch your forehead,
Forget my own,
My voice change
For the second and last time
To the most terrible of voices—
Or silence.

1968

Sleep in Jerusalem[1]

While a chosen people[2]
become a nation like all the nations,
building its houses, paving its highways,
breaking open its earth for pipes and water,
we lie inside, in the low house,
late offspring of this old landscape.
The ceiling is vaulted above us with love
and the breath of our mouth
is as it was given us
and as we shall give it back.

Sleep is where there are stones.
In Jerusalem there is sleep. The radio
brings day-tunes from a land
where there is day.
And words that here are bitter,
like last year's almond on a tree,
are sung in a far country, and sweet.

And like a fire
in the hollowed trunk of an olive tree

1. Translated by Harold Schimmel.
2. According to Hebrew Scriptures, God chose Abraham's descendants, the Jews, as the people through whom he would reveal himself.

an eternal heart is burning red
not far from the two sleepers.

1971

God Has Pity on Kindergarten Children[1]

God has pity on kindergarten children.
He has less pity on school children.
And on grownups he has no pity at all,
he leaves them alone,
and sometimes they must crawl on all fours
in the burning sand
to reach the first-aid station
covered with blood.

But perhaps he will watch over true lovers
and have mercy on them and shelter them
like a tree over the old man
sleeping on a public bench.

Perhaps we too will give them
the last rare coins of compassion
that Mother handed down to us,
so that their happiness will protect us
now and in other days.

1956

Jerusalem[1]

On a roof in the Old City[2]
laundry hanging in the late afternoon sunlight:
the white sheet of a woman who is my enemy,
the towel of a man who is my enemy,
to wipe off the sweat of his brow.

In the sky of the Old City
a kite.
At the other end of the string,
a child
I can't see
because of the wall.

We have put up many flags,
they have put up many flags.
To make us think that they're happy.
To make them think that we're happy.

1963

1. Translated by Stephen Mitchell.

1. Translated by Stephen Mitchell.

2. The oldest, walled portion of Jerusalem, around which the new city has been built.

An Arab Shepherd Is Searching for His Goat on Mount Zion[1]

An Arab shepherd is searching for his goat on Mount Zion
and on the opposite mountain I am searching
for my little boy.
An Arab shepherd and a Jewish father
both in their temporary failure.
Our voices meet above the Sultan's Pool[2]
in the valley between us. Neither of us wants
the child or the goat to get caught in the wheels
of the terrible *Had Gadya*[3] machine.

Afterward we found them among the bushes
and our voices came back inside us, laughing and crying.
Searching for a goat or a son
has always been the beginning
of a new religion in these mountains.

1980

1. Translated by Chana Bloch. The fortress of Jerusalem is built on Mount Zion.
2. Translation of the Hebrew name for a pool located in the valley just outside the walls of the Old City of Jerusalem.
3. One kid (Hebrew); alludes to a Passover song in which "the kid that Daddy bought is eaten by a cat that is bitten by a dog," and so on.

DEREK WALCOTT

1930–2017

A cosmopolitan poet from a small Caribbean island, a West Indian of mixed African and European ancestry, Derek Walcott depicted the hybridity of Caribbean culture while drawing on the traditions of English literature. In contemplating the violent uprising in Kenya against British colonialism, he wrote in an early poem, "A Far Cry from Africa" (1956), of his dual inheritance: "I who am poisoned with the blood of both / Where shall I turn, divided to the vein?" Yet if he treated his mixed blood as poison, he also made it a source of strength in his verse, which draws on the rhythms and idioms of Caribbean speech to enliven what he called, in the same poem, "the English tongue I love."

Derek Walcott was born, along with his twin brother, Roderick, on January 23, 1930, in Castries, the capital of the island of St. Lucia, then a British colony. (It had been occupied alternately by the French and the British since the seventeenth century and would not gain its independence from Britain until 1979.) Shortly after their first birthday, the boys' father, who was a government functionary and a talented artist, suddenly died, and the two boys were brought up by their mother, a schoolteacher who later became headmistress of the Methodist elementary school where they began their education. Both inherited their father's creative gift, Derek primarily in language, Roderick in the pictorial arts, and they remained intellectual and artistic companions until Roderick's death, in 1999. Their mother provided an environment in which their talents could be nurtured, an essential factor in Walcott's development as a poet.

Walcott acquired, early on, a sense of his singularity from the fact that he was of mixed ancestry in a predominantly black society (both his grandfathers were white, his grandmothers black). He was also a Protestant and member of the educated middle class in a peasant, Catholic community. Moreover, although he was brought up to speak Standard English as his first language, his exposure to the local French creole reinforced his sense of his ambiguous relation to the communal life around him. Far from unsettling Walcott, these factors of personal history became a source of strength and fascination. He began to write poetry in high school and published his first works as a teenager.

After high school education at St. Mary's College, Walcott studied at the University of West Indies in Jamaica, where he came to understand the Caribbean as a region unified by a common experience and a common historical legacy. His literary studies familiarized him with the great works of Western literature and particularly with the modern English poets **T. S. Eliot, W. B. Yeats**, and W. H. Auden. After his graduation, in 1953, Walcott taught school for a while in Kingston, while doing occasional work in journalism, before moving to Port of Spain, Trinidad, where he became a feature writer for a major local newspaper, the *Sunday Guardian*. In 1957, he was awarded a Rockefeller Fellowship to study theater at New York University. His encounter with the problems of race during his American sojourn gave further definition to his self-awareness as a West Indian; the experience confirmed for him the inescapable connection between race and history with which black people in the New World have to contend. On his return two years later to Port of Spain, he founded the Trinidad Theatre Workshop, to which he devoted his energies for nearly two decades. He was eager to bring the technical knowledge associated with the theater and stagecraft to the West Indies. He became well-known for his plays before he gained a following for his poetry, which won an international audience after the publication of his collection *In a Green Night* (1962) in England. Alienated by the Black Power revolts of the 1970s in Trinidad, Walcott resigned from the Trinidad Theatre Workshop and, after winning a MacArthur Fellowship ("genius" grant) in 1981, began teaching regularly at Boston University. He divided his time between the United States and St. Lucia until his death in 2017. He was awarded the Nobel Prize for Literature in 1992.

The poems selected here range from one Walcott wrote as a teenager to his mature masterpiece, *Omeros*. His early poems are marked by a striking eloquence of diction and a rich tapestry of imagery. "As John to Patmos" (1947), written when Walcott was only seventeen, already announces Walcott's poetic vocation: "To praise lovelong, the living and the brown dead." Here, as in later works, Walcott draws a parallel between St. Lucia and the Greek islands, specifically Patmos, where John the Divine was said to have written the Book of Revelation. In poems such as "Ruins of a Great House" (1956), Walcott assumes the weight of English literary tradition by translating its references and resources into a poetic register determined by his Caribbean experience and sensibility. Here, he recognizes the oppression of English colonizers, as he draws on the writings of Thomas Browne, William Blake, and John Donne to provide an alternative English heritage.

The next few poems, from *The Castaway* (1965), showing Walcott in his maturity as a poet, celebrate the role of the heroic or creative individual in the shaping of history. In poems such as "The Almond Trees," Walcott understands the poet as a type of castaway, the node of consciousness in the larger community but who will seldom be heeded by that community. "Crusoe's Journal" lends a poetic grandeur to such a figure, the lonely and bold adventurer who assumes the burden of pathfinder, creating a reality—and, indeed, a new world—out of the unpromising materials at hand. In "Verandah," he imagines himself in conversation with the English colonizers to whom he feels connected by his English grandfather.

All Walcott's poetry flows into his masterpiece *Omeros* (1990), which is best grasped as the imaginative summation of human history as seen from his Caribbean perspective. Its retrospective vision assumes an emotional value for the poet for whom, as he said, "Art is History's nostalgia." In an expansive recollection of his previous themes, *Omeros* sums up the West Indian experience through the adventures of Achille, a humble St. Lucian fisherman, whose travels take him to the compass points of the West Indian consciousness. Homer's great epics, the *Iliad* and the *Odyssey*, serve as explicit references for the work, and the figure of Homer himself, in his modern Greek rendering of "Omeros," is evoked in a key passage of the poem in which he is represented as the quintessential exile. Moreover, Walcott's use of the blind poet in the character of Seven Seas, modeled on Demodokos in Homer's *Odyssey*, reinforces the importance of this Greek frame of reference. The poem employs some of the standard tropes of the classical epic, such as descent into the underworld and conflict and contest.

Despite these connections, *Omeros* is not a mere rehash of Homer. Although the poem contains stretches of narration, they do not build up to a dramatic progression of events such as we find in a conventional epic. The rivalry between Achille and another local fisherman, Hector, over Helen (who is hardly idealized in the poem and remains, for all her beauty, an ordinary village woman) is presented as part of a strictly local history that features other characters such as the white settler couple, Major Plunkett and his wife, Maud, as well as minor characters who move in and out of the narrative. Thus the poem does not develop a linear plot, but represents, rather, a vast kaleidoscope, a series of episodes that are woven around its protagonist.

Walcott's epic explores the African element in Caribbean life and the theme of collective memory and its relation to identity. *Omeros* reconnects with Africa by emphasizing the continuing tie of the West Indians to the continent of their forbears yet helps its West Indian audience take cultural repossession of their island home. *Omeros* registers both the Afro-Caribbean quest for an established sense of place and of community and, at the same time, the compulsion to move toward the wider horizon of world literature.

As John to Patmos

As John to Patmos,[1] among the rocks and the blue, live air, hounded
His heart to peace, as here surrounded
By the strewn-silver on waves, the wood's crude hair, the rounded
Breasts of the milky bays,[2] palms, flocks, the green and dead

Leaves, the sun's brass coin on my cheek, where
Canoes brace the sun's strength, as John, in that bleak air,
So am I welcomed richer by these blue scapes, Greek there,[3]
So I shall voyage no more from home; may I speak here.

This island is heaven—away from the dustblown blood of cities;
See the curve of bay, watch the straggling flower, pretty is
The wing'd sound of trees, the sparse-powdered[4] sky, when lit is
The night. For beauty has surrounded
Its black children, and freed them of homeless ditties.[5]

As John to Patmos, in each love-leaping air,
O slave, soldier, worker under red trees sleeping,[6] hear
What I swear now, as John did:
To praise lovelong, the living and the brown dead.[7]

1947

Ruins of a Great House[1]

though our longest sun sets at right declensions and
makes but winter arches, it cannot be long before we
lie down in darkness, and have our light in ashes . . .

—BROWNE, *Urn Burial*[2]

Stones only, the disjecta membra[3] of this Great House,
Whose moth-like girls are mixed with candledust,
Remain to file the lizard's dragonish claws.[4]

1. The Evangelist John the Divine's name is associated with the Greek island of Patmos, where he was banished for several years and wrote the Book of Revelation.
2. Low hills (in French patois, *mornes*) rising on the gently sloping landscape against the background of the sea, a feature of many of the smaller Caribbean islands.
3. Walcott establishes a parallel between Patmos and the poet's own island home of St. Lucia.
4. Almost cloudless.
5. I.e., Negro spirituals, songs of exile.
6. The poet's self-dedication addressed to his fellow countrymen.
7. The total "organic" community.

1. The principal building around which life in the slave plantation revolved. As in the American South, many of the great houses in the Caribbean were constructed on a grand scale, modeled on classical Greek architectural style (cf. line 13).
2. Thomas Browne (1605–1682) was an English physician and essayist, best known for his book *Religio Medici*. The epigram here is taken from *Urn Burial* (1658), a work that dwells on the passing of time and on human mortality.
3. Disjointed limbs (Latin).
4. The dragon is often represented as a great lizard.

The mouths of those gate cherubs[5] shriek with stain;
Axle and coach wheel silted under the muck
Of cattle droppings
Three crows[6] flap for the trees
And settle, creaking the eucalyptus boughs.
A smell of dead limes quickens in the nose
The leprosy of empire[7]
"Farewell, green fields,
Farewell, ye happy groves!"[8]
Marble like Greece, like Faulkner's South in stone,[9]
Deciduous[1] beauty prospered and is gone,
But where the lawn breaks in a rash of trees
A spade below dead leaves will ring the bone
Of some dead animal or human thing
Fallen from evil days, from evil times.

It seems that the original crops were limes
Grown in the silt that clogs the river's skirt;
The imperious rakes[2] are gone, their bright girls gone,
The river flows, obliterating hurt.[3]
I climbed a wall with the grille ironwork
Of exiled craftsmen protecting that great house
From guilt,[4] perhaps, but not from the worm's rent[5]
Nor from the padded cavalry of the mouse.
And when a wind shook in the limes I heard
What Kipling[6] heard, the death of a great empire, the abuse
Of ignorance by Bible and by sword.[7]

A green lawn, broken by low walls of stone,
Dipped to the rivulet, and pacing, I thought next
Of men like Hawkins, Walter Raleigh, Drake,[8]
Ancestral murderers and poets, more perplexed
In memory now by every ulcerous crime.
The world's green age then was a rotting lime

5. Gates that display little angels with chubby cheeks and wings.
6. Birds of ill omen.
7. Slavery as moral blight.
8. The quotation is from Blake's poem "Night."
9. William Faulkner (1897–1962), considered by many to be the greatest writer of the American South.
1. Said of trees that shed their leaves in the winter. The idea here is that the splendor of the great house and the lifestyle associated with it are fleeting.
2. Young men in the slave-owning community who lived wild and riotous lives.
3. Symbolizing the impersonal flow of time.
4. Presumably of slavery.
5. I.e., inevitable decay and death, a tribute to time.
6. Rudyard Kipling (1865–1936), English writer born in India. He is often remembered for the slogan he coined, "the white man's burden," to justify European colonial domination of nonwhite races.
7. The two means by which native populations were conquered.
8. Significant figures of English imperial history. John Hawkins was a noted early slaver; Walter Raleigh was a favorite of Queen Elizabeth I of England, who knighted him for his exploration in America on behalf of the crown; Francis Drake was knighted for his daring acts of piracy against Spanish merchant ships.

Whose stench became the charnel galleon's text.
The rot remains with us, the men are gone.
But, as dead ash is lifted in a wind
That fans the blackening ember of the mind,
My eyes burned from the ashen prose of Donne.[9]

Ablaze with rage I thought,
Some slave is rotting in this manorial lake,
But still the coal of my compassion fought
That Albion[1] too was once
A colony like ours, "part of the continent, piece of the main,"
Nook-shotten, rook o'erblown, deranged
By foaming channels and the vain expense
Of bitter faction
                    All in compassion ends
So differently from what the heart arranged:
"as well as if a manor of thy friend's . . ."

1956

The Almond Trees[1]

There's nothing here
this early;
cold sand
cold churning ocean, the Atlantic,
no visible history,[2]

except this stand
of twisted, coppery, sea-almond trees[3]
their shining postures surely
bent as metal, and one
foam-haired, salt-grizzled fisherman,

9. John Donne (1572–1631) was dean of St. Paul's Cathedral in London and the leading figure among the Renaissance English poets known as "the Metaphysicals." The reference here is to Donne's sermons, specifically Meditation 17, which contains the sentence "Ask not for whom the bell tolls, it tolls for thee," a reminder of human mortality—hence, "ashen prose." The quotations in lines 45 and 51 are from the same sermon; they express the theme of our common humanity, summed up by the famous phrase "No Man is an island" that occurs elsewhere in the sermon.

1. Poetic name for England.

1. The tropical almond (also known as the Indian almond) is a tree that bears a fleshy fruit with a kernel that has some resemblance to the temperate variety. It denotes here a sense of place, the poet's rootedness in the resilience and enduring quality of his people.

2. I.e., one marked by monuments and a sense of achievement. This negative view of the Caribbean was first put forward by the English historian James Anthony Froude (1818–1894) and later echoed by the Caribbean novelist V. S. Naipaul (born 1932). The reprise of the phrase as a quotation eight lines further draws attention to these sources.

3. The trees have assimilated to the fauna and flora as elements of a common landscape of experience. The idea, restated in line 33, governs the poem's theme and imagery.

his mongrel growling, whirling on the stick
he pitches him; its spinning rays
'no visible history'
until their lengthened shapes amaze the sun.

By noon,
this further shore of Africa[4] is strewn
with the forked limbs of girls toasting their flesh
in scarves, sunglasses, Pompeian bikinis,[5]

brown daphnes,[6] laurels, they'll all have
like their originals, their sacred grove,
this frieze
of twisted, coppery, sea-almond trees.

The fierce acetylene[7] air
has singed
their writhing trunks with rust, the same
hues as a foundered, peeling barge.
It'll sear a pale skin copper with its flame.

The sand's white-hot ash underheel,
but their aged limbs have got their brazen sheen
from fire. Their bodies fiercely shine!
They're cured,
they endured their furnace.[8]

Aged trees and oiled limbs share a common colour!

Welded in one flame,
huddling naked, stripped of their name,
for Greek or Roman tags,[9] they were lashed
raw by wind, washed
out with salt and fire-dried,
bitterly nourished where their branches died,

their leaves' broad dialect[1] a coarse,
enduring sound
they shared together.
Not as some running hamadryad's[2] cries

4. The Caribbean as an extension of Africa in terms of climate, natural environment, ethnic composition, and, ultimately, forms of cultural expression.

5. The scantily clad girls evoke the liberal lifestyle for which the ancient Roman city of Pompeii was famous. Pompeii was destroyed in 79 C.E. by volcanic lava from the eruption of Mount Vesuvius.

6. The immediate reference is to the laurel tree. It also refers to the Greek myth of the nymph Daphne, who was turned into a laurel while fleeing from Apollo.

7. A gas-fired flame used to soften metal.

8. I.e., the furnace of history. The black people are represented as having gone through a trial by fire, becoming tempered like steel.

9. Slaves were often given classical names by their owners.

1. The language and expressive culture of a new, distinctive community that has emerged from a common history.

2. A nymph who lives in a tree.

rooted, broke slowly into leaf
her nipples peaking to smooth, wooden boles

Their grief[3]
howls seaward through charred, ravaged holes.

One sunburnt body now acknowledges
that past and its own metamorphosis
as, moving from the sun, she kneels to spread
her wrap within the beat arms of this grove
that grieves in silence,[4] like parental love.[5]

1965

Crusoe's Journal

I looked now upon the world as a thing remote, which I
had nothing to do with, no expectation from, and, indeed,
no desires about. In a word, I had nothing indeed
to do with it, nor was ever like to have; so I thought
it looked as we may perhaps look upon it hereafter,
viz., as a place I had lived in but was come out
of it; and well might I say, as Father Abraham
to Dives, "Between me and thee is a great gulf fixed."

—ROBINSON CRUSOE[1]

Once we have driven past Mundo Nuevo[2] trace
        safely to this beach house
perched between ocean and green, churning forest
        the intellect appraises
objects surely, even the bare necessities
        of style are turned to use,
like those plain iron tools he salvages
        from shipwreck,[3] hewing a prose
as odorous as raw wood to the adze;[4]
        out of such timbers
came our first book, our profane Genesis[5]
        whose Adam speaks that prose
which, blessing some sea-rock, startles itself
        with poetry's surprise,

3. The pathos of the slave experience.
4. I.e., that grieves not so much in resignation as in forgiveness.
5. A love marked by tolerance and understanding.
1. The epigraph from Daniel Defoe's (1660–1731) novel captures the Western frame of mind, a rational approach that establishes a rigorous separation between consciousness and the world of experience.
2. A route in Trinidad that leads to the house that Walcott is describing.
3. Apart from the reference to the Crusoe story, this is also a metaphor for the historical experience of slavery.
4. Sharp tool like a small ax used for carving wood.
5. The first book of the Judeo-Christian Bible containing the story of the world's creation and of Adam, the first man, who was entrusted by God to name the objects of the world.

in a green world, one without metaphors;
like Christofer[6] he bears
in speech mnemonic[7] as a missionary's
the Word to savages,
its shape an earthen, water-bearing vessel's
whose sprinkling alters us
into good Fridays[8] who recite His praise,
parroting our master's
style and voice, we make his language ours,
converted cannibals
we learn with him to eat the flesh of Christ[9]

All shapes, all objects multiplied from his,
our ocean's Proteus,[1]
in childhood, his derelict's old age
was like a god's. (Now pass
in memory, in serene parenthesis,
the cliff-deep leeward coast
of my own island filing past the noise
of stuttering canvas,[2]
some noon-struck village, Choiseul, Canaries,[3]
crouched crocodile canoes,
a savage settlement from Henty's novels,
Marryat or R.L.S.[4]
with one boy signalling at the sea's edge,
though what he cried is lost.)
So time, that makes us objects, multiplies
our natural loneliness.

For the hermetic skill,[5] that from earth's clays
shapes something without use,
and, separate from itself, lives somewhere else,[6]
sharing with every beach
a longing for those gulls that cloud the cays[7]
with raw, mimetic cries,

6. I.e., Christopher Columbus (1451–1506), acknowledged as the first European to encounter the New World.
7. Aiding memory.
8. Defoe's hero, Robinson Crusoe, gave the name Friday to the indigenous man he captured and made his manservant on the island. Note the punning allusion to the Christian observation of the Crucifixion of Christ.
9. In the Catholic doctrine of transubstantiation, the bread eaten at the Sacrament of Communion was deemed to be the body of Christ.
1. The Greek sea god who had the power of changing into various forms.
2. The Caribbean landscape envisioned as a work of art.
3. Villages in St. Lucia.
4. The works of Henty, Marryat, and R.L.S. were staples of colonial education throughout the former British Empire. George Alfred Henty (1832–1902) was a prolific writer of children's stories; Frederick Marryat (1792–1848) was an officer of the British navy who wrote a series of sea novels, of which the best known is *Mr. Midshipman Easy*; Robert Louis Stevenson (1850–1894) is renowned for his classic novel of adventure *Treasure Island*.
5. Poetry, which is sometimes regarded as a form of prophecy or divination. As an art form, it has no practical purpose ("without use") since its aesthetic significance is an end in itself.
6. In another dimension.
7. Inlets into the sea.

never surrenders wholly, for it knows
it needs another's praise
like hoar, half-cracked Ben Gunn,[8] until it cries
at last, "O happy desert!"
and learns again the self-creating peace
of islands. So from this house
that faces nothing but the sea, his journals
assume a household use;
we learn to shape from them, where nothing was
the language of a race,[9]
and since the intellect demands its mask
that sun-cracked, bearded face[1]
provides us with the wish to dramatize
ourselves at nature's cost,
to attempt a beard, to squint through the sea-haze,
posing as naturalists,
drunks, castaways, beachcombers, all of us
yearn for those fantasies
of innocence,[2] for our faith's arrested phase
when the clear voice
startled itself saying "water, heaven, Christ,"
hoarding such heresies[3] as
God's loneliness moves in His smallest creatures.

1965

Verandah

[for Ronald Bryden][1]

Grey apparitions[2] at verandah ends
like smoke,[3] divisible, but one
your age is ashes, its coherence gone,

Planters[4] whose tears were marketable gum,[5] whose voices
scratch the twilight like dried fronds
edged with reflection,

8. A character in Stevenson's *Treasure Island*. He had been marooned on the island and was found by the party of treasure seekers.
9. Like Crusoe, the inhabitants of the Caribbean have created a new culture out of the debris of their historical experience.
1. The physical outward aspect expressive of an inward attitude of stern resolution.
2. As of Eden, of new beginnings.
3. The pantheism given expression in the final line.

1. As literary editor of the Royal Shakespeare Company, he commissioned Walcott's *The Joker of Seville*.
2. Ghosts of the imperial past.
3. Insubstantial.
4. The term for white settlers in the West Indies who owned sugar plantations worked by slaves.
5. A pun on "medicinible gum" from Shakespeare's *Othello*, 5.2.360.

Colonels, hard as the commonwealth's greenheart,
middlemen, usurers whose art
kept an empire in the red,[6]

Upholders of Victoria's china seas[7]
lapping embossed around a drinking mug,
bully-boy roarers[8] of the empire club,

To the tarantara of the bugler, the sunset furled
round the last post,
the "flamingo colours"[9] of a fading world,

A ghost steps from you, my grandfather's ghost![1]
Uprooted from some rainy English shire,
you sought your Roman

End in suicide by fire.[2]
Your mixed son gathered your charred blackened bones
in a child's coffin.

And buried them himself on a strange coast.
Sire,
why do I raise you up? Because

Your house has voices, your burnt house
shrills with unguessed, lovely inheritors,[3]
your genealogical roof tree, fallen, survives,
like seasoned timber through green, little lives.

I ripen towards your twilight, sir, that dream
where I am singed in that sea-crossing, steam
towards that vaporous world, whose souls,

Like pressured trees, brought diamonds out of coals.[4]
The sparks pitched from your burning house are stars.
I am the man my father loved and was.

6. An allusion to the violent repression of colonized populations by the various imperial agents mentioned in the stanza.
7. Possibly an allusion to the attempt by the British to annex China and to the Opium Wars of 1839–1842 that resulted. "Victoria": queen of England from 1837 to 1901.
8. Pun on bullroarers, indigenous instruments that make a frightening sound.
9. The pageantry of empire exemplified by the ceremonial lowering of the flag at sunset to the sound of the bugle, a ritual that, ironically, anticipates the decline of empire ("fading world").
1. The poet is of English ancestry on his father's side.
2. In contrast to the Roman habit of falling on one's sword.
3. The black and mulatto children are the unlikely continuators of the white grandfather's ancestral line, which they rejuvenate ("green, little lives," line 28).
4. Of the same chemical composition and evolving into diamonds under intense pressure over time.

I climb the stair
and stretch a darkening hand to greet those friends[5]
who share with you the last inheritance
of earth, our shrine and pardoner,

grey, ghostly loungers at verandah ends.

1965

Sea Grapes[1]

That sail which leans on light,
tired of islands,
a schooner beating up the Caribbean

for home, could be Odysseus,[2]
home bound on the Aegean;[3]
that father and husband's

longing, under gnarled sour grapes, is
like the adulterer hearing Nausicaa's[4] name
in every gull's outcry.

This brings nobody peace. The ancient war
between obsession and responsibility
will never finish and has been the same

for the sea-wanderer or the one on shore
now wriggling on his sandals to walk home,
since Troy sighed its last flame,

and the blind giant's boulder heaved the trough[5]
from whose groundswell the great hexameters[6] come
to the conclusions of exhausted surf.

The classics can console. But not enough.

1976

5. Portraits of those who have passed away and now form part of the general life of the earth ("our shrine," line 38).
1. Type of bitter grape indigenous to the Caribbean.
2. Greek king of Ithaca, hero of Homer's epic poem the *Odyssey*.
3. Area in the Mediterranean Sea between Greece and Turkey.
4. The young princess of Phaeacia who moves Odysseus with her goodness and her beauty.
5. Polyphemus, a Cyclops (one-eyed giant), hurls a boulder that causes a great wave (trough) after Odysseus blinds him.
6. "Homer's meter," first used by early Greek poets of the oral tradition.

The Sea Is History

Where are your monuments, your battles, martyrs?
Where is your tribal memory? Sirs,
in that gray vault. The sea. The sea
has locked them up. The sea is History.

First, there was the heaving oil,
heavy as chaos;
then, like a light at the end of a tunnel,

the lantern of a caravel,
and that was Genesis.
Then there were the packed cries,
the shit, the moaning:

Exodus.[1]
Bone soldered by coral to bone,
mosaics
mantled by the benediction of the shark's shadow,
that was the Ark of the Covenant.[2]
Then came from the plucked wires
of sunlight on the sea floor

the plangent[3] harps of the Babylonian bondage,[4]
as the white cowries[5] clustered like manacles
on the drowned women,

and those were the ivory bracelets
of the Song of Solomon,[6]
but the ocean kept turning blank pages

looking for History.
Then came the men with eyes heavy as anchors
who sank without tombs,

brigands who barbecued cattle,
leaving their charred ribs like palm leaves on the shore,
then the foaming, rabid maw

of the tidal wave swallowing Port Royal,[7]
and that was Jonah,[8]
but where is your Renaissance?

1. Into exile in the New World, as opposed to the exodus of the Jews, under the leadership of Moses, out of bondage in Egypt.
2. A chest said to contain the tablets on which the Ten Commandments were recorded by God. Exodus 25:10–16.
3. Pouring out in waves of sound.
4. Which occurred between the fall of Jerusalem in 586 B.C.E. and the restoration of worship there by the decree of Cyrus the Great in 538 B.C.E.
5. Seashells that used to serve as currency in pre-colonial West Africa. They were also used in divination.
6. A book in the Hebrew Scriptures that is a collection of love poems; it is generally thought to be an allegory of God's love for Israel.
7. The former capital of Jamaica, destroyed in 1692 by an earthquake, during which most of the city sank into the sea.
8. In the Hebrew Scriptures, the man who lived in the belly of a whale for three days and nights before being disgorged alive.

Sir, it is locked in them sea sands
out there past the reef's moiling shelf,[9]
where the men-o'-war floated down;

strop[1] on these goggles, I'll guide you there myself.
It's all subtle and submarine,
through colonnades of coral,

past the gothic windows of sea fans
to where the crusty grouper,[2] onyx[3]-eyed,
blinks, weighted by its jewels, like a bald queen;

and these groined caves with barnacles
pitted like stone
are our cathedrals,

and the furnace before the hurricanes:
Gomorrah.[4] Bones ground by windmills
into marl[5] and cornmeal,

and that was Lamentations[6]—
that was just Lamentations,
it was not History;

then came, like scum on the river's drying lip,
the brown reeds of villages
mantling[7] and congealing into towns,

and at evening, the midges'[8] choirs,
and above them, the spires
lancing the side of God[9]

as His son set, and that was the New Testament.

Then came the white sisters clapping
to the waves' progress,
and that was Emancipation[1]—

jubilation, O jubilation—
vanishing swiftly
as the sea's lace dries in the sun,

9. "Shelf" here suggests the continental shelf, the relatively shallow stretch of coastal land ending in a sharp dip to the deep seabed. "Moiling": turbulent.
1. Strap (dialect).
2. A species of fish.
3. A highly valued gem, usually jet black.
4. A city often associated with Sodom, both synonymous with sin.
5. Finely ground sand.
6. Songs in the Hebrew Scriptures by the prophet Jeremiah, lamenting the fall of Jerusalem.
7. A reference to Shakespeare's *The Tempest,* where "mantling" apparently describes the scummy covering of the shore.
8. Small insects, chirping in chorus.
9. An allusion to the Roman soldier's piercing the side of the crucified Jesus to ascertain whether he was dead or not (see "His son set" in the following line).
1. Which, in the British West Indies, occurred in 1834.

but that was not History,
that was only faith,
and then each rock broke into its own nation;[2]

then came the synod of flies,
then came the secretarial heron,
then came the bullfrog bellowing for a vote,

fireflies with bright ideas
and bats like jetting ambassadors
and the mantis,[3] like khaki police,

and the furred caterpillars of judges[4]
examining each case closely,
and then in the dark ears of ferns

and in the salt chuckle of rocks
with their sea pools, there was the sound
like a rumor without any echo

of History, really beginning.

1979

Omeros

From Book One

From *Chapter I*

II

Achille looked up at the hole[1] the laurel had left.
He saw the hole silently healing with the foam
of a cloud like a breaker. Then he saw the swift[2]

crossing the cloud-surf, a small thing, far from its home,
confused by the waves of blue hills. A thorn vine gripped
his heel. He tugged it free. Around him, other ships

were shaping from the saw. With his cutlass he made
a swift sign of the cross, his thumb touching his lips
while the height rang with axes. He swayed back the blade,

2. A reference to the breakup of the West Indian Federation in 1962. The next two stanzas describe the ensuing confusion in the political life of the West Indies.
3. The characteristic posture of the praying mantis is generally interpreted as a demonstration of hypocrisy.
4. A reference to the dress of judges in formal sessions.

1. The opening stanza describes the ritual felling of a laurel tree from which a dugout canoe is to be made. This refers to the hole in the ground where the tree had stood. The section that follows describes the making of the canoe.
2. A small, plainly colored bird, related to the swallow, that serves as a guide to the wandering hero.

and hacked the limbs from the dead god,[3] knot after knot,
wrenching the severed veins from the trunk as he prayed:
"Tree! You can be a canoe! Or else you cannot!"

The bearded elders endured the decimation
of their tribe without uttering a syllable
of the language they had uttered as one nation,[4]

the speech taught their saplings: from the towering babble
of the cedar to green vowels of *bois-campêche*.
The *bois-flot* held its tongue with the *laurier-cannelle*,[5]

the red-skinned logwood endured the thorns in its flesh,
while the Aruacs' patois[6] crackled in the smell
of a resinous bonfire that turned the leaves brown

with curling tongues, then ash, and their language was lost.
Like barbarians striding columns they have brought down,
the fishermen shouted. The gods were down at last.

Like pygmies they hacked the trunks of wrinkled giants
for paddles and oars. They were working with the same
concentration as an army of fire-ants.[7]

But vexed by the smoke for defaming their forest,
blow-darts of mosquitoes kept needling Achille's trunk.
He frotted white rum on both forearms that, at least,

those that he flattened to asterisks would die drunk.
They went for his eyes. They circled them with attacks
that made him weep blindly. Then the host retreated

to high bamboo like the archers of Aruacs
running from the muskets of cracking logs,[8] routed
by the fire's banner and the remorseless axe

hacking the branches. The men bound the big logs first
with new hemp[9] and, like ants, trundled them to a cliff
to plunge through tall nettles.[1] The logs gathered that thirst

for the sea which their own vined bodies were born with.
Now the trunks in eagerness to become canoes
ploughed into breakers of bushes, making raw holes

3. The laurel tree, venerated as nature.
4. The flora as part of the total living environment.
5. *Bois-campêche, bois-flot, laurier-cannelle:* French for logwood, timber, and laurel, respectively.
6. Dialect. "Aruacs": the original inhabitants of the Caribbean; also Arawaks.
7. Omnivorous ants with powerful stingers in their tails.
8. Log houses from which white men shot at the Aruacs.
9. The vine is excellent for making ropes.
1. A plant that stings.

of boulders, feeling not death inside them, but use—
to roof the sea, to be hulls. Then, on the beach, coals[2]
were set in their hollows that were chipped with an adze.

A flat-bed truck had carried their rope-bound bodies.
The charcoals, smouldering, cored the dugouts for days
till heat widened the wood enough for ribbed gunwales.[3]

Under his tapping chisel Achille felt their hollows
exhaling to touch the sea, lunging towards the haze
of bird-printed islets, the beaks of their parted bows.

Then everything fit. The pirogues[4] crouched on the sand
like hounds with sprigs in their teeth. The priest
sprinkled them with a bell, then he made the swift's sign.[5]

When he smiled at Achille's canoe, *In God We Troust,*[6]
Achille said: "Leave it! Is God' spelling and mine."
After Mass one sunrise the canoes entered the troughs[7]

of the surpliced[8] shallows, and their nodding prows
agreed with the waves to forget their lives as trees;
one would serve Hector and another, Achilles.

From Book Seven

From *Chapter LXIV*

I

I sang[1] of quiet Achille, Afolabe's son,
who never ascended in an elevator,
who had no passport, since the horizon needs none,

never begged nor borrowed, was nobody's waiter,
whose end, when it comes, will be a death by water
(which is not for this book, which will remain unknown

and unread by him). I sang the only slaughter
that brought him delight, and that from necessity—
of fish, sang the channels of his back[2] in the sun.

2. They are used to fire the hollowed-out logs.
3. That is, the heat expanded the wood so that metal strips could be inserted to reinforce the sides of the boat.
4. French for dugout canoes.
5. The swift's wings are shaped like a cross.
6. The boat's name. The phrase "In God We Trust" is found on American money.
7. Sea channels.
8. The canoes make a lacelike pattern on the water, resembling the surplice worn by Catholic priests at Mass.
1. The invocation, usually placed at the beginning of an epic poem, is here put at the end and expressed in the past tense.
2. The ripples of muscles, denoting strength. The human frame represented as a furrowed landscape.

I sang our wide country, the Caribbean Sea.
Who hated shoes, whose soles were as cracked as a stone,
who was gentle with ropes, who had one suit alone,

whom no man dared insult and who insulted no one,
whose grin was a white breaker cresting, but whose frown
was a growing thunderhead, whose fist of iron

would do me a greater honour if it held on
to my casket's oarlocks[3] than mine lifting his own
when both anchors are lowered in the one island,

but now the idyll dies, the goblet is broken,
and rainwater trickles down the brown cheek of a jar
from the clay of Choiseul. So much left unspoken

by my chirping nib![4] And my earth-door lies ajar.
I lie wrapped in a flour-sack sail. The clods thud
on my rope-lowered canoe. Rasping shovels scrape

a dry rain of dirt on its hold, but turn your head
when the sea-almond rattles or the rust-leaved grape
from the shells of my unpharaonic pyramid[5]

towards paper shredded by the wind and scattered
like white gulls that separate their names from the foam
and nod to a fisherman[6] with his khaki dog

that skitters from the wave-crash, then frown at his form
for one swift second. In its earth-trough, my pirogue
with its brass-handled oarlocks is sailing. Not from

but with them, with Hector, with Maud[7] in the rhythm
of her beds[8] trowelled over, with a swirling log
lifting its mossed head from the swell; let the deep hymn

of the Caribbean continue my epilogue;
may waves remove their shawls as my mourners walk home
to their rusted villages, good shoes in one hand,

passing a boy who walked through the ignorant foam,
and saw a sail going out or else coming in,
and watched asterisks of rain[9] puckering the sand.

* * *

1990

3. At the poet's own funeral.
4. The point of a pen dipped in ink often makes a rasping noise on the paper.
5. Modest, without the monumental grandeur of Egypt's pyramids.
6. I.e., Philoctete.
7. The wife of an English colonial officer, Major Plunkett, whose adventures, intertwined with the life of the St. Lucians, are narrated in earlier passages of the poem. "Hector": rival of Achille who was killed in a car accident.
8. A reference to the flowerbeds tended by Maud. The image evokes her final resting place in the earth.
9. Which is life-giving.

SEAMUS HEANEY

1939–2013

Having reached his maturity as a poet during the sectarian violence known as the Troubles in his native Northern Ireland, Seamus Heaney developed a keen awareness of the poet's relationship to history and conflict. A student of the Irish language and of Anglo-Saxon (Old English), he has drawn on the resources of both in reinventing modern English poetry. His verse, alive to historical resonances, explores the ethical commitments of the poet in a world of enduring conflicts.

Born to a Catholic family on a farm in County Derry, Northern Ireland, Heaney was the eldest of nine children. He attended the nearby Anahorish School and then St. Columb's College, a Catholic boarding school in Derry, Northern Ireland's second city, before enrolling in Queen's University, Belfast, where he studied English language and literature. In addition to Anglo-Saxon, he learned Irish and Latin. After briefly teaching middle school, Heaney returned to Queen's in 1966 as an instructor in English literature. In the same year, his first major volume of poems, *Death of a Naturalist,* was released. During the following several years, as tensions heightened in Northern Ireland, Heaney addressed political concerns in his poetry, although often in an indirect fashion that was sometimes criticized for its lack of explicit commitment. In 1972, in a move that was seen at the time as indicating sympathies with the Nationalist cause (unification with the Republic of Ireland), Heaney moved to Dublin. He taught college there for several years, then, as his reputation as a poet grew, began an association with Harvard University, where he would teach part-time for a quarter of a century. He also taught at Oxford University, and in 1995, he received the Nobel Prize for Literature.

The late 1960s were a period of intense violence in Northern Ireland, a majority Protestant region that had remained part of the United Kingdom when the rest of Ireland gained its independence. Some members of the substantial Catholic population of Northern Ireland supported the illegal Irish Republican Army, which used violence to promote unification with the Irish Republic (the "Nationalist" position). Catholics often faced hostility and discrimination from Protestant groups, notably the paramilitary Ulster Volunteer Force, that favored continued union with Britain (the "Unionists"). British police and military forces were generally perceived as supporting the Unionists, particularly in the Bloody Sunday massacre of 1972, when thirteen unarmed Catholic protesters were killed by British army forces. The cycle of violence by the IRA, the UVF, and British forces continued until the Good Friday agreement of 1998, which ushered in a period of disarmament and power sharing by Nationalist and Unionist politicians.

The Northern Irish landscape of Heaney's youth plays a central role in his poetry. Regularly placed by Heaney at the beginning of collections of his poetry, "Digging" (1964) announces his poetic vocation by comparing the poet's pen to the shovels wielded by Heaney's father and grandfather, both farmers, and also to a gun. Heaney the poet will use a pen to make his mark. Although not following a strict form, the poem generally has four heavy accents per line and caesuras (pauses in the middle of a line); its rhythm and use of alliteration and assonance (repetition of vowel sounds) echo those of Old English poetry.

Heaney was interested in the sounds of words, and many of his poems draw on the significance and pronunciation of place-names. He frequently used words of Anglo-Saxon origin, which he associated with the land. His telling choice of diction can be observed in "The Tollund Man" (1972), one of the first of Heaney's poems about the bog people, an ancient folk, related to the Irish, whose bodies were preserved in the wetlands of Jutland, Denmark. In this poem and in "Punishment" (1975), the speaker contemplates the bodies of victims of sacrificial slaughter in the Iron Age society, hinting that such primitive violence is not all that different from the Troubles of Northern Ireland.

Heaney was attentive to the formal qualities of his verse, whether in loose blank verse (unrhymed iambic pentameter) or in his characteristic short quatrains (four-line stanzas). Although seldom making use of rhyme, these quatrains recall ballad forms associated with folk tradition, while in other poems (like "The Tollund Man" and "Punishment") they create a melancholy, meditative mood. Preferring relatively formal poetry rather than experimental verse, Heaney drew heavily on the literary tradition, including Dante, **T. S. Eliot**, and the medieval epic *Beowulf,* which he translated into modern English. His work is distinguished by its concreteness and descriptive precision.

Digging

Between my finger and my thumb
The squat pen rests; snug as a gun.

Under my window, a clean rasping sound
When the spade sinks into gravelly ground:
My father, digging. I look down

Till his straining rump among the flowerbeds
Bends low, comes up twenty years away
Stooping in rhythm through potato drills
Where he was digging.

The coarse boot nestled on the lug, the shaft
Against the inside knee was levered firmly.
He rooted out tall tops, buried the bright edge deep
To scatter new potatoes that we picked,
Loving their cool hardness in our hands.

By God, the old man could handle a spade.
Just like his old man.

My grandfather cut more turf in a day
Than any other man on Toner's bog.[1]

1. The boy belongs to a man named Toner. The speaker's father cuts turf for a fire.

Once I carried him milk in a bottle
Corked sloppily with paper. He straightened up
To drink it, then fell to right away
Nicking and slicing neatly, heaving sods
Over his shoulder, going down and down
For the good turf. Digging.

The cold smell of potato mould, the squelch and slap
Of soggy peat, the curt cuts of an edge
Through living roots awaken in my head.
But I've no spade to follow men like them.

Between my finger and my thumb
The squat pen rests.
I'll dig with it.

1964

The Tollund Man[1]

I

Some day I will go to Aarhus[2]
To see his peat-brown head,
The mild pods of his eyelids,
His pointed skin cap.

In the flat country nearby
Where they dug him out,
His last gruel of winter seeds
Caked in his stomach,

Naked except for
The cap, noose and girdle,
I will stand a long time.
Bridegroom to the goddess,

She tightened her torc[3] on him
And opened her fen,
Those dark juices working
Him to a saint's kept body,

Trove of the turf-cutters'
Honeycombed workings.
Now his stained face
Reposes at Aarhus.

1. The corpse of a man killed in the 4th century B.C.E, probably a sacrificial victim, preserved in a bog in Jutland, Denmark. Heaney had seen photographs of the Tollund Man and associated Denmark's bogs with those of Northern Ireland.
2. A town in Jutland (the Tollund Man is actually displayed in nearby Silkeborg).
3. An ancient style of metal necklace.

II

I could risk blasphemy,
Consecrate the cauldron bog
Our holy ground and pray
Him to make germinate

The scattered, ambushed
Flesh of labourers,
Stockinged corpses
Laid out in the farmyards,

Tell-tale skin and teeth
Flecking the sleepers
Of four young brothers,[4] trailed
For miles along the lines.

III

Something of his sad freedom
As he rode the tumbril
Should come to me, driving,
Saying the names

Tollund, Grauballe, Nebelgard,[5]
Watching the pointing hands
Of country people,
Not knowing their tongue.

Out there in Jutland
In the old man-killing parishes
I will feel lost,
Unhappy and at home.

1972

Punishment[1]

I can feel the tug
of the halter at the nape
of her neck, the wind
on her naked front.

It blows her nipples
to amber beads,
it shakes the frail rigging
of her ribs.

4. The speaker compares the Tollund Man to four Irish nationalist brothers killed by the Protestant Ulster Constabulary Force (forerunner of the Ulster Volunteer Force), in the early 1920s, in Northern Ireland.

5. Other places in Jutland where bog bodies had been found.

1. The speaker contemplates the body, preserved in a bog, of a young woman in ancient Scandinavia, drowned for adultery.

I can see her drowned
body in the bog,
the weighing stone,
the floating rods and boughs.

Under which at first
she was a barked sapling
that is dug up
oak-bone, brain-firkin:[2]

her shaved head
like a stubble of black corn,
her blindfold a soiled bandage,
her noose a ring

to store
the memories of love.

Little adulteress,
before they punished you

you were flaxen-haired,
undernourished, and your
tar-black face was beautiful.
My poor scapegoat,

I almost love you
but would have cast, I know,
the stones of silence.
I am the artful voyeur

of your brain's exposed
and darkened combs,
your muscles' webbing
and all your numbered bones:

I who have stood dumb
when your betraying sisters,
cauled in tar,
wept by the railings,

who would connive
in civilized outrage
yet understand the exact
and tribal, intimate revenge.

1975

2. Refers to a head covering on the dead body.

GABRIEL GARCÍA MÁRQUEZ

1928–2014

The best-known novelist of the Latin American "Boom" of the 1960s and 1970s, Gabriel García Márquez embodied, in his work, the mixture of fantasy and actuality known as "magic realism." Again and again García Márquez returned to certain themes: the contrast between dreamlike experiences and everyday reality; the enchanted or inexplicable aspect of fictional creation; and the solitude of individuals in societies that can never quite incorporate them. His fiction, which contains mythic dimensions that are often rooted in local folklore, reimagines regional tales to explore broader social and psychological conflicts. Even those works based in historical fact transform the characters and events into a fictional universe with its own set of laws.

García Márquez was born on March 6, 1928, in the small town of Aracataca, in the "banana zone" of Colombia. The first of twelve children, he was raised by his maternal grandparents until 1936, when his grandfather died. As an adult, he would attribute his love of fantasy to his grandmother, who told him fantastical tales whenever she wanted to shush his incessant questions. His grandfather, meanwhile, passed on a marked interest in politics, having fought on the Liberal side of a civil war early in the century. After receiving his undergraduate degree as a scholarship student at the National Colegio in Zipaquirá, García Márquez studied law at the University of Bogotá in 1947. It was there, he later claimed, that he read **Kafka's *The Metamorphosis,*** in a Spanish translation by **Jorge Luis Borges**. "Shit," he said to himself after reading the first sentence, "that's just the way my grandmother talked!" The next day he wrote "The Third Resignation," the Kafkaesque tale of a man in his coffin who continued to grow (and retain consciousness) for seventeen years after his death. It was the first of his works to be published. García Márquez found in Kafka the mobile balance of nonrealistic events and realistic detail that—combined with his grandmother's quixotic stories and his grandfather's political concerns—would become the genre known as magic realism. In this mode the narrator treats the subjective beliefs and experiences of the characters, often derived from folklore and supernatural beliefs, as if they were real, even when (to a scientifically minded observer) they seem impossible. Some of García Márquez's early novels also reflected the influence of **William Faulkner,** whom he later described as "my master"—in particular, Faulkner's representation of subjective experience through stream-of-consciousness technique and the southern writer's depiction of an underdeveloped geographical region beset by a long history of conflict.

In 1950, García Márquez abandoned his legal studies for journalism. As a correspondent for various Latin American newspapers, he traveled to Paris and later to Eastern Europe, Venezuela, Cuba, and New York. After writing several novels, short stories, and film scripts, he gained international fame for his novel *One Hundred Years of Solitude.* Published in 1967, it chronicles the rise and fall of the fortunes of the Buendía family in a mythical town called Macondo (based on the author's hometown of Aracataca). A global best seller, it was soon translated into multiple languages and received prizes in Italy and France. When it was published in English, in 1970, American critics praised it as one of the best books of the year, and it has since become a monument of world literature.

The author's later work was preoccupied with contemporary events, especially the prevalence of dictatorship in Latin American societies. As García Márquez continued to publish successful novels, he also became an advocate for social justice, speaking out for revolutionary governments in Latin America and organizing assistance for political prisoners. There were even rumors of a plot, backed by the Colombian government, to assassinate García Márquez because of his antigovernment activities; in 1981 he sought asylum in Mexico. In his later years, he lived primarily in Mexico City, although he spent time in Colombia and Europe as well.

The story printed here, "Death Constant Beyond Love" (1970), dates from the author's later, more politically active period. It has a political background, although its protagonist, Senator Onésimo Sánchez, appears chiefly through the lens of his struggles with the existential problem of death. García Márquez presents an essentially satirical portrait of Sánchez, a corrupt politician who accepts bribes and stays in power by helping the local property owners avoid reform. His electoral train is a traveling circus with carnival wagons, fireworks, a ready-made audience of hired Indians, and a cardboard village with imitation brick houses and a painted ocean liner to represent the (shallow) promise of prosperity. Among the citizenry, Sánchez uses carefully placed gifts to encourage support and a feeling of dependence.

Yet the spectacle of the senator's campaign for office, and even the sordid background of poverty and corruption that enables it, fade into insignificance before the broader themes of life and death. Forty-two, happily married, and in full control, as a powerful politician in mid-career, of the lives of himself and others, he is made suddenly to feel—when told that he will be dead "forever" by next Christmas—helpless, vulnerable, and alone. Theoretically he knows that death is inevitable and that the course of nature cannot be defeated. He has read Marcus Aurelius (121–180 C.E.) and refers to the Stoic philosopher's *Meditations*, which criticizes the delusions of those "who have tenaciously stuck to life" and recommends the cheerful acceptance of natural order, including death.

In this crisis the senator is reduced to basic, instinctual existence, drawing him deeper into García Márquez's recurrent themes of solitude, love, and death. The beautiful Laura provides an opportunity for him to submerge his fear of death in erotic passion. This choice means scandal and the destruction of his political career, but by now Onésimo Sánchez has felt the emptiness of his earlier activities—and has given them up for the hopeless struggle to cheat death. "Death Constant Beyond Love" reverses the ambitious claim of a famous sonnet by the Spanish Golden Age writer Quevedo (1580–1645), according to which there is "Love Constant Beyond Death." Such love is an illusion, for it is death, beyond everything else, that awaits us.

Gabriel García Márquez received the Nobel Prize in Literature in 1982. In his acceptance speech he drew connections between his novels and the sufferings of the peoples of Latin America through dictatorship and civil war. Voicing hope for an end to the nuclear arms race, the writer spoke of a "new and sweeping utopia of life, where no one will be able to decide for others how they die, where love will prove true and happiness be possible, and where the races condemned to one hundred years of solitude will have, at last and forever, a second opportunity on earth."

Death Constant beyond Love[1]

Senator Onésimo Sánchez had six months and eleven days to go before his death when he found the woman of his life. He met her in Rosal del Virrey,[2] an illusory village which by night was the furtive wharf for smugglers' ships, and on the other hand, in broad daylight looked like the most useless inlet on the desert, facing a sea that was arid and without direction and so far from everything no one would have suspected that someone capable of changing the destiny of anyone lived there. Even its name was a kind of joke, because the only rose in that village was being worn by Senator Onésimo Sánchez himself on the same afternoon when he met Laura Farina.

It was an unavoidable stop in the electoral campaign he made every four years. The carnival wagons had arrived in the morning. Then came the trucks with the rented Indians[3] who were carried into the towns in order to enlarge the crowds at public ceremonies. A short time before eleven o'clock, along with the music and rockets and jeeps of the retinue, the ministerial automobile, the color of strawberry soda, arrived. Senator Onésimo Sánchez was placid and weatherless inside the air-conditioned car, but as soon as he opened the door he was shaken by a gust of fire and his shirt of pure silk was soaked in a kind of light-colored soup and he felt many years older and more alone than ever. In real life he had just turned forty-two, had been graduated from Göttingen[4] with honors as a metallurgical engineer, and was an avid reader, although without much reward, of badly translated Latin classics. He was married to a radiant German woman who had given him five children and they were all happy in their home, he the happiest of all until they told him, three months before, that he would be dead forever by next Christmas.

While the preparations for the public rally were being completed, the senator managed to have an hour alone in the house they had set aside for him to rest in. Before he lay down he put in a glass of drinking water the rose he had kept alive all across the desert, lunched on the diet cereals that he took with him so as to avoid the repeated portions of fried goat that were waiting for him during the rest of the day, and he took several analgesic pills before the time prescribed so that he would have the remedy ahead of the pain. Then he put the electric fan close to the hammock and stretched out naked for fifteen minutes in the shadow of the rose, making a great effort at mental distraction so as not to think about death while he dozed. Except for the doctors, no one knew that he had been sentenced to a fixed term, for he had decided to endure his secret all alone, with no change in his life, not because of pride but out of shame.[5]

He felt in full control of his will when he appeared in public again at three in the afternoon, rested and clean, wearing a pair of coarse linen slacks and a floral shirt, and with his soul sustained by the anti-pain pills. Nevertheless, the erosion of death was much more pernicious than he had supposed, for as he

1. Translated by Gregory Rabassa.
2. The Rosebush of the Viceroy (governor).
3. People descended from the original inhabitants of the continent; generally poorer and less privileged than those descended from Spanish or Portuguese colonists.
4. A well-known German university.
5. "Death is such as generation is, a mystery of nature . . . altogether not a thing of which any man should be ashamed" (Marcus Aurelius, *Meditations* 4.5).

went up onto the platform he felt a strange disdain for those who were fighting for the good luck to shake his hand, and he didn't feel sorry as he had at other times for the groups of barefoot Indians who could scarcely bear the hot saltpeter coals of the sterile little square. He silenced the applause with a wave of his hand, almost with rage, and he began to speak without gestures, his eyes fixed on the sea, which was sighing with heat. His measured, deep voice had the quality of calm water, but the speech that had been memorized and ground out so many times had not occurred to him in the nature of telling the truth, but, rather, as the opposite of a fatalistic pronouncement by Marcus Aurelius in the fourth book of his *Meditations*.

"We are here for the purpose of defeating nature," he began, against all his convictions. "We will no longer be foundlings in our own country, orphans of God in a realm of thirst and bad climate, exiles in our own land. We will be different people, ladies and gentlemen, we will be a great and happy people."

There was a pattern to his circus. As he spoke his aides threw clusters of paper birds into the air and the artificial creatures took on life, flew about the platform of planks, and went out to sea. At the same time, other men took some prop trees with felt leaves out of the wagons and planted them in the saltpeter soil behind the crowd. They finished by setting up a cardboard façade with make-believe houses of red brick that had glass windows, and with it they covered the miserable real-life shacks.

The senator prolonged his speech with two quotations in Latin in order to give the farce more time. He promised rainmaking machines, portable breeders for table animals, the oils of happiness which would make vegetables grow in the saltpeter and clumps of pansies in the window boxes. When he saw that his fictional world was all set up, he pointed to it. "That's the way it will be for us, ladies and gentlemen," he shouted. "Look! That's the way it will be for us."

The audience turned around. An ocean liner made of painted paper was passing behind the houses and it was taller than the tallest houses in the artificial city. Only the senator himself noticed that since it had been set up and taken down and carried from one place to another the superimposed cardboard town had been eaten away by the terrible climate and that it was almost as poor and dusty as Rosal del Virrey.

For the first time in twelve years, Nelson Farina didn't go to greet the senator. He listened to the speech from his hammock amidst the remains of his siesta, under the cool bower of a house of unplaned boards which he had built with the same pharmacist's hands with which he had drawn and quartered his first wife. He had escaped from Devil's Island[6] and appeared in Rosal del Virrey on a ship loaded with innocent macaws, with a beautiful and blasphemous black woman he had found in Paramaribo[7] and by whom he had a daughter. The woman died of natural causes a short while later and she didn't suffer the fate of the other, whose pieces had fertilized her own cauliflower patch, but was buried whole and with her Dutch name in the local cemetery. The daughter had inherited her color and her figure along with her father's yellow and astonished eyes, and he had good reason to imagine that he was rearing the most beautiful woman in the world.

6. A former French penal colony off the coast of French Guiana in northern South America.

7. Capital of Suriname (formerly Dutch Guiana) and a large port.

Ever since he had met Senator Onésimo Sánchez during his first electoral campaign, Nelson Farina had begged for his help in getting a false identity card which would place him beyond the reach of the law. The senator, in a friendly but firm way, had refused. Nelson Farina never gave up, and for several years, every time he found the chance, he would repeat his request with a different recourse. But this time he stayed in his hammock, condemned to rot alive in that burning den of buccaneers. When he heard the final applause, he lifted his head, and looking over the boards of the fence, he saw the back side of the farce: the props for the buildings, the framework of the trees, the hidden illusionists who were pushing the ocean liner along. He spat without rancor.

"*Merde,*" he said. "*C'est le Blacamán de la politique.*"[8]

After the speech, as was customary, the senator took a walk through the streets of the town in the midst of the music and the rockets and was besieged by the townspeople, who told him their troubles. The senator listened to them good-naturedly and he always found some way to console everybody without having to do them any difficult favors. A woman up on the roof of a house with her six youngest children managed to make herself heard over the uproar and the fireworks.

"I'm not asking for much, Senator," she said. "Just a donkey to haul water from Hanged Man's Well."

The senator noticed the six thin children. "What became of your husband?" he asked.

"He went to find his fortune on the island of Aruba,"[9] the woman answered good-humoredly, "and what he found was a foreign woman, the kind that put diamonds on their teeth."

The answer brought on a roar of laughter.

"All right," the senator decided, "you'll get your donkey."

A short while later an aide of his brought a good pack donkey to the woman's house and on the rump it had a campaign slogan written in indelible paint so that no one would ever forget that it was a gift from the senator.

Along the short stretch of street he made other, smaller gestures, and he even gave a spoonful of medicine to a sick man who had had his bed brought to the door of his house so he could see him pass. At the last corner, through the boards of the fence, he saw Nelson Farina in his hammock, looking ashen and gloomy, but nonetheless the senator greeted him, with no show of affection.

"Hello, how are you?"

Nelson Farina turned in his hammock and soaked him in the sad amber of his look.

"*Moi, vous savez,*"[1] he said.

His daughter came out into the yard when she heard the greeting. She was wearing a cheap, faded Guajiro Indian[2] robe, her head was decorated with

8. Shit. He's the Blacamán of politics (French). Blacamán is a charlatan and huckster who appears in several of García Márquez's stories, including *Blacamán the Good, Vendor of Miracles.*

9. Off the coast of Venezuela, famous as a tourist resort.

1. "Oh well, as for me, you know" (French).

2. Inhabitant of the rural Guajira Peninsula of northern Colombia. The figure of Laura Farina is thus connected with the rustic poor, with earthy reality (*farina* means "flour"), and with erotic inspiration. (*Laura* was the beloved celebrated by the Italian Renaissance poet Francis Petrarch, 1304–1374.)

colored bows, and her face was painted as protection against the sun, but even in that state of disrepair it was possible to imagine that there had never been another so beautiful in the whole world. The senator was left breathless. "I'll be damned!" he breathed in surprise. "The Lord does the craziest things!"

That night Nelson Farina dressed his daughter up in her best clothes and sent her to the senator. Two guards armed with rifles who were nodding from the heat in the borrowed house ordered her to wait on the only chair in the vestibule.

The senator was in the next room meeting with the important people of Rosal del Virrey, whom he had gathered together in order to sing for them the truths he had left out of his speeches. They looked so much like all the ones he always met in all the towns in the desert that even the senator himself was sick and tired of that perpetual nightly session. His shirt was soaked with sweat and he was trying to dry it on his body with the hot breeze from an electric fan that was buzzing like a horse fly in the heavy heat of the room.

"We, of course, can't eat paper birds," he said. "You and I know that the day there are trees and flowers in this heap of goat dung, the day there are shad[3] instead of worms in the water holes, that day neither you nor I will have anything to do here, do I make myself clear?"

No one answered. While he was speaking, the senator had torn a sheet off the calendar and fashioned a paper butterfly out of it with his hands. He tossed it with no particular aim into the air current coming from the fan and the butterfly flew about the room and then went out through the half-open door. The senator went on speaking with a control aided by the complicity of death.

"Therefore," he said, "I don't have to repeat to you what you already know too well: that my reelection is a better piece of business for you than it is for me, because I'm fed up with stagnant water and Indian sweat, while you people, on the other hand, make your living from it."

Laura Farina saw the paper butterfly come out. Only she saw it because the guards in the vestibule had fallen asleep on the steps, hugging their rifles. After a few turns, the large lithographed butterfly unfolded completely, flattened against the wall, and remained stuck there. Laura Farina tried to pull it off with her nails. One of the guards, who woke up with the applause from the next room, noticed her vain attempt.

"It won't come off," he said sleepily. "It's painted on the wall."

Laura Farina sat down again when the men began to come out of the meeting. The senator stood in the doorway of the room with his hand on the latch, and he only noticed Laura Farina when the vestibule was empty.

"What are you doing here?"

"*C'est de la part de mon père,*"[4] she said.

The senator understood. He scrutinized the sleeping guards, then he scrutinized Laura Farina, whose unusual beauty was even more demanding than his pain, and he resolved then that death had made his decision for him.

"Come in," he told her.

Laura Farina was struck dumb standing in the doorway to the room: thousands of bank notes were floating in the air, flapping like the butterfly. But the

3. A kind of fish.

4. "My father sent me" (French).

senator turned off the fan and the bills were left without air and alighted on the objects in the room.

"You see," he said, smiling, "even shit can fly."

Laura Farina sat down on a schoolboy's stool. Her skin was smooth and firm, with the same color and the same solar density as crude oil, her hair was the mane of a young mare, and her huge eyes were brighter than the light. The senator followed the thread of her look and finally found the rose, which had been tarnished by the saltpeter.

"It's a rose," he said.

"Yes," she said with a trace of perplexity. "I learned what they were in Riohacha."[5]

The senator sat down on an army cot, talking about roses as he unbuttoned his shirt. On the side where he imagined his heart to be inside his chest he had a corsair's tattoo of a heart pierced by an arrow. He threw the soaked shirt to the floor and asked Laura Farina to help him off with his boots.

She knelt down facing the cot. The senator continued to scrutinize her, thoughtfully, and while he was untying the laces he wondered which one of them would end up with the bad luck of that encounter.

"You're just a child," he said.

"Don't you believe it," she said. "I'll be nineteen in April."

The senator became interested.

"What day?"

"The eleventh," she said.

The senator felt better. "We're both Aries,"[6] he said. And smiling, he added: "It's the sign of solitude."

Laura Farina wasn't paying attention because she didn't know what to do with the boots. The senator, for his part, didn't know what to do with Laura Farina, because he wasn't used to sudden love affairs and, besides, he knew that the one at hand had its origins in indignity. Just to have some time to think, he held Laura Farina tightly between his knees, embraced her about the waist, and lay down on his back on the cot. Then he realized that she was naked under her dress, for her body gave off the dark fragrance of an animal of the woods, but her heart was frightened and her skin disturbed by a glacial sweat.

"No one loves us," he sighed.

Laura Farina tried to say something, but there was only enough air for her to breathe. He laid her down beside him to help her, he put out the light and the room was in the shadow of the rose. She abandoned herself to the mercies of her fate. The senator caressed her slowly, seeking her with his hand, barely touching her, but where he expected to find her, he came across something iron that was in the way.

"What have you got there?"

"A padlock,"[7] she said.

"What in hell!" the senator said furiously and asked what he knew only too well. "Where's the key?"

5. A port on the Guajira Peninsula.
6. Sign in the zodiac; people born between March 21 and April 19 are said to be under the sign of Aries.
7. She is wearing a chastity belt, a medieval device worn by women to prevent sexual intercourse.

Laura Farina gave a breath of relief.

"My papa has it," she answered. "He told me to tell you to send one of your people to get it and to send along with him a written promise that you'll straighten out his situation."

The senator grew tense. "Frog[8] bastard," he murmured indignantly. Then he closed his eyes in order to relax and he met himself in the darkness. *Remember,* he remembered, *that whether it's you or someone else, it won't be long before you'll be dead and it won't be long before your name won't even be left.*[9]

He waited for the shudder to pass.

"Tell me one thing," he asked then. "What have you heard about me?"

"Do you want the honest-to-God truth?"

"The honest-to-God truth."

"Well," Laura Farina ventured, "they say you're worse than the rest because you're different."

The senator didn't get upset. He remained silent for a long time with his eyes closed, and when he opened them again he seemed to have returned from his most hidden instincts.

"Oh, what the hell," he decided. "Tell your son of a bitch of a father that I'll straighten out his situation."

"If you want, I can go get the key myself," Laura Farina said.

The senator held her back.

"Forget about the key," he said, "and sleep awhile with me. It's good to be with someone when you're so alone."

Then she laid his head on her shoulder with her eyes fixed on the rose. The senator held her about the waist, sank his face into woods-animal armpit, and gave in to terror. Six months and eleven days later he would die in that same position, debased and repudiated because of the public scandal with Laura Farina and weeping with rage at dying without her.

1970

8. Epithet for "French."
9. A direct translation of a sentence from Marcus Aurelius's *Meditations* (4.6).

AMA ATA AIDOO

born 1942

Poet, playwright, and novelist, Ama Ata Aidoo documents the rapidly changing role of women in Africa. Like older African writers such as **Chinua Achebe** and **Bessie Head,** Aidoo depicts a society in transition. Her particular emphasis on the urban life of young women demonstrates the specific conditions of the sexual revolution and feminism in African culture. She combines realistic exploration of women's plight in Africa with fine experimental passages that give her stories a universal appeal.

Born a chief's daughter in Abeadzi Kyakor, Ghana, Christina Ama Ata Aidoo graduated from Wesley Girls' High School in Cape Coast and the University of Ghana, Legon. Her first play, *The Dilemma of a Ghost* (1964), was produced by the Students' Theatre in Legon. In assessing the plight of African women, Aidoo has written, "For African women, the struggle begins with the right to be born as a girl child . . . to have a whole body . . . to go to school; the right to be heard." Given her relatively privileged upbringing, she recalls that writing always seemed a natural occupation to her. "As a young woman growing up in Ghana," she has said, "I didn't know that as a woman I wasn't supposed to write. Those of us who started to write so early were at an advantage because we didn't know what was good for us, in terms of one's self as a writer."

Aidoo went to the United States for graduate study at the Harvard International Seminar and the Stanford University Creative Writing Program. She then returned to teach at the University of Cape Coast, where she published a highly successful first collection of short stories, *No Sweetness Here* (1970). Her first, semiautobiographical novel, *Our Sister Killjoy* (1977), follows the protagonist, Sissie, as she travels through Europe, inciting black students to rebel against "soul-destroying white capitalism" and to return to Africa. While sharing an earlier generation's concerns with national liberation, Aidoo sought a form of African society that would be more respectful of women's roles. She herself became active in politics, briefly holding the position of minister of education in Ghana under Jerry Rawlings, who had taken power in a 1981 coup but was later democratically elected. Finding her role opposed by conservative forces, Aidoo resigned and went into self-imposed exile in Zimbabwe, where she lived for many years. Later she helped found the Women's World Organization for Rights, Literature, and Development, an organization that campaigns against censorship and for the rights of women. She taught at Brown University in Providence, Rhode Island, from 2003 to 2010.

The story presented here, "Two Sisters" (1970), uses the two main characters to portray the central tensions that interest Aidoo: the conflicts between traditional sexual mores and sexual liberation; between private life and political conflict; between past and present. The two sisters, Connie and Mercy, take very different attitudes to sexual matters and to the political transformations they witness in Ghana. Connie (presumably short for Constance) stands for traditional values, including marriage and self-reliance. Her younger sister, Mercy, wants to enjoy her sexual prime but also intends to profit from her relationships with powerful men.

Aidoo uses a number of realistic literary techniques, while sometimes startling the reader with brief experimental passages. The story starts out in the third person but closely follows Mercy's perspective until, in the middle of the sisters' conversation, it suddenly leaps into Connie's stream of consciousness. The formal opposition between the third-person narrator and Connie's first-person reflections calls attention to the moral conflict underlying the story. When Mercy visits the seashore with her boyfriend, the narrator personifies the Gulf of Guinea as a god who looks with compassion on Mercy's folly. Aidoo thus adjusts realistic techniques to her subject matter. The story explores the limits and risks of sexual experimentation as they intersect with the turbulent political history of Ghana. Aidoo's sympathetic rendering of the two sisters' competing viewpoints demonstrates her subtlety as a chronicler of African life and shows why she is a major voice in African fiction.

Two Sisters

As she shakes out the typewriter cloak and covers the machine with it, the thought of the bus she has to hurry to catch goes through her like a pain. It is her luck, she thinks. Everything is just her luck. Why, if she had one of those graduates for a boy-friend, wouldn't he come and take her home every evening? And she knows that a girl does not herself have to be a graduate to get one of those boys. Certainly, Joe is dying to do exactly that—with his taxi. And he is as handsome as anything, and a good man, but you know . . . Besides there are cars and there are cars. As for the possibility of the other actually coming to fetch her—oh well. She has to admit it will take some time before she can bring herself to make demands of that sort on *him*. She has also to admit that the temptation is extremely strong. Would it really be so dangerously indiscreet? Doesn't one government car look like another? The hugeness of it? Its shaded glass? The uniformed chauffeur? She can already see herself stepping out to greet the dead-with-envy glances of the other girls. To begin with, she will insist on a little discretion. The driver can drop her under the neem trees in the morning and pick her up from there in the evening . . . anyway, she will have to wait a little while for that and it is all her luck.

There are other ways, surely. One of these, for some reason, she has sworn to have nothing of. Her boss has a car and does not look bad. In fact the man is alright. But she keeps telling herself that she does not fancy having some old and dried-out housewife walking into the office one afternoon to tear her hair out and make a row. . . . Mm, so for the meantime, it is going to continue to be the municipal bus with its grimy seats, its common passengers and impudent conductors. . . . Jesus! She doesn't wish herself dead or anything so stupidly final like that. Oh no. She just wishes she could sleep deep and only wake up on the morning of her glory.

The new pair of black shoes are more realistic than their owner, though. As she walks down the corridor, they sing:

Count, Mercy, count your blessings
Count, Mercy, count your blessings
Count, count, count your blessings.[1]

They sing along the corridor, into the avenue, across the road and into the bus. And they resume their song along the gravel path, as she opens the front gate and crosses the cemented courtyard to the door.

'Sissie!' she called.

'Hei Mercy,' and the door opened to show the face of Connie, big sister, six years or more older and now heavy with her second child. Mercy collapsed into the nearest chair.

'Welcome home. How was the office today?'

'Sister, don't ask. Look at my hands. My fingers are dead with typing. Oh God, I don't know what to do.'

'Why, what is wrong?'

1. An 1897 hymn by John Oatman; Aidoo may also be referring to a 1954 popular song by Irving Berlin.

'You tell me what is right. Why should I be a typist?'

'What else would you be?'

'What a strange question. Is typing the only thing one can do in this world? You are a teacher, are you not?'

'But . . . but . . .'

'But what? Or you want me to know that if I had done better in the exams, I could have trained to be a teacher too, eh, sister? Or even a proper secretary?'

'Mercy, what is the matter? What have I done? What have I done? Why have you come home so angry?'

Mercy broke into tears.

'Oh I am sorry. I am sorry, Sissie. It's just that I am sick of everything. The office, living with you and your husband. I want a husband of my own, children. I want . . . I want . . .'

'But you are so beautiful.'

'Thank you. But so are you.'

'You are young and beautiful. As for marriage, it's you who are postponing it. Look at all these people who are running after you.'

'Sissie, I don't like what you are doing. So stop it.'

'Okay, okay, okay.'

And there was a silence.

'Which of them could I marry? Joe is—mm, fine—but, but I just don't like him.'

'You mean . . .'

'Oh, Sissie!'

'Little sister, you and I can be truthful with one another.'

'Oh yes.'

'What I would like to say is that I am not that old or wise. But still I could advise you a little. Joe drives someone's car now. Well, you never know. Lots of taxi drivers come to own their taxis, sometimes fleets of cars.'

'Of course. But it's a pity you are married already. Or I could be a go-between for you and Joe!'

And the two of them burst out laughing. It was when she rose up to go to the bedroom that Connie noticed the new shoes.

'Ei, those are beautiful shoes. Are they new?'

From the other room, Mercy's voice came interrupted by the motions of her body as she undressed and then dressed again. However, the uncertainty in it was due to something entirely different.

'Oh, I forgot to tell you about them. In fact, I was going to show them to you. I think it was on Tuesday I bought them. Or was it Wednesday? When I came home from the office, you and James had taken Akosua out. And later, I forgot all about them.'

'I see. But they are very pretty. Were they expensive?'

'No, not really.' This reply was too hurriedly said.

And she said only last week that she didn't have a penny on her. And I believed her because I know what they pay her is just not enough to last anyone through any month, even minus rent. . . . I have been thinking she manages very well. But these shoes. And she is not the type who would borrow money just to buy a pair of shoes, when she could have gone on wearing her old pairs until things get better. Oh I wish I knew what to do. I mean I am not her mother. And I wonder how James will see these problems.

'Sissie, you look worried.'

'Hmm, when don't I? With the baby due in a couple of months and the government's new ruling on salaries and all. On top of everything, I have reliable information that James is running after a new girl.'

Mercy laughed.

'Oh Sissie. You always get reliable information on these things.'

'But yes. And I don't know why.'

'Sissie, men are like that.'

'They are selfish.'

'No, it's just that women allow them to behave the way they do instead of seizing some freedom themselves.'

'But I am sure that even if we were free to carry on in the same way, I wouldn't make use of it.'

'But why not?'

'Because I love James. I love James and I am not interested in any other man.' Her voice was full of tears. But Mercy was amused.

'O God. Now listen to that. It's women like you who keep all of us down.'

'Well, I am sorry but it's how the good God created me.'

'Mm. I am sure that I can love several men at the same time.'

'Mercy!'

They burst out laughing again. And yet they are sad. But laughter is always best.

Mercy complained of hunger and so they went to the kitchen to heat up some food and eat. The two sisters alone. It is no use waiting for James. And this evening, a friend of Connie's has come to take the baby girl, Akosua, for the day, and had threatened to keep her until her bedtime.

'Sissie, I am going to see a film.' This from Mercy.

'Where?'

'The Globe.'

'Are you going with Joe?'

'No.'

'Are you going alone?'

'No.'

Careful Connie.

'Whom are you going with?'

Careful Connie, please. Little sister's nostrils are widening dangerously. Look at the sudden creasing-up of her mouth and between her brows. Connie, a sister is a good thing. Even a younger sister. Especially when you have no mother or father.

'Mercy, whom are you going out with?'

'Well, I had food in my mouth! And I had to swallow it down before I could answer you, no?'

'I am sorry.' How softly said.

'And anyway, do I have to tell you everything?'

'Oh no. It's just that I didn't think it was a question I should not have asked.'

There was more silence. Then Mercy sucked her teeth with irritation and Connie cleared her throat with fear.

'I am going out with Mensar-Arthur.'

As Connie asked the next question, she wondered if the words were leaving her lips.

'Mensar-Arthur?'

'Yes.'

'Which one?'

'How many do you know?'

Her fingers were too numb to pick up the food. She put the plate down. Something jumped in her chest and she wondered what it was. Perhaps it was the baby.

'Do you mean that member of Parliament?'

'Yes.'

'But Mercy . . .'

Little sister only sits and chews her food.

'But Mercy . . .'

Chew, chew, chew.

'But Mercy.'

'What?'

She startled Connie.

'He is so old.'

Chew, chew, chew.

'Perhaps, I mean, perhaps that really doesn't matter, does it? Not very much anyway. But they say he has so many wives and girl-friends.'

Please little sister. I am not trying to interfere in your private life. You said yourself a little while ago that you wanted a man of your own. That man belongs to so many women already. . . .

That silence again. Then there was only her footsteps as she went to put her plate in the kitchen sink, running water as she washed her plate and her hand. She drank some water and coughed. Then as tears streamed down her sister's averted face, there was the sound of her footsteps as she left the kitchen. At the end of it all, she banged a door. Connie only said something like, 'O Lord, O Lord,' and continued sitting in the kitchen. She had hardly eaten anything at all. Very soon Mercy went to have a bath. Then Connie heard her getting ready to leave the house. The shoes. Then she was gone. She needn't have carried on like that, eh? Because Connie had not meant to probe or bring on a quarrel. What use is there in this old world for a sister, if you can't have a chat with her? What more, things like this never happen to people like Mercy. Their parents were good Presbyterians. They feared God. Mama had not managed to give them all the rules of life before she died. But Connie knows that running around with an old and depraved public man would have been considered an abomination by the parents.

The sound of a big car with a super-smooth engine purred into the drive. It actually purrs: this huge machine from the white man's land. Indeed, its well-mannered protest as the tyres slid on to the gravel seemed like a lullaby compared to the loud thumping of the girl's stiletto shoes. When Mensar-Arthur saw Mercy, he stretched his arm and opened the door to the passenger seat. She sat down and the door closed with a civilised thud. The engine hummed into motion and the car sailed away.

After a distance of a mile or so from the house, the man started conversation.

'And how is my darling today?'

'I am well,' and only the words did not imply tragedy.

'You look solemn today, why?'

She remained silent and still.

'My dear, what is the matter?'

'Nothing.'

'Oh . . .' he cleared his throat again. 'Eh, and how were the shoes?'

'Very nice. In fact, I am wearing them now. They pinch a little but then all new shoes are like that.'

'And the handbag?'

'I like it very much too. . . . My sister noticed them. I mean the shoes.' The tragedy was announced.

'Did she ask you where you got them from?'

'No.'

He cleared his throat again.

'Where did we agree to go tonight?'

'The Globe, but I don't want to see a film.'

'Is that so? Mm, I am glad because people always notice things.'

'But they won't be too surprised.'

'What are you saying, my dear?'

'Nothing.'

'Okay, so what shall we do?'

'I don't know.'

'Shall I drive to the Seaway?'

'Oh yes.'

He drove to the Seaway. To a section of the beach they knew very well. She loves it here. This wide expanse of sand and the old sea. She has often wished she could do what she fancied: one thing she fancies. Which is to drive very near to the end of the sands until the tyres of the car touched the water. Of course it is a very foolish idea as he pointed out sharply to her the first time she thought aloud about it. It was in his occasional I-am-more-than-old-enough-to-be-your-father tone. There are always disadvantages. Things could be different. Like if one had a younger lover. Handsome, maybe not rich like this man here, but well-off, sufficiently well-off to be able to afford a sports car. A little something very much like those in the films driven by the white racing drivers. With tyres that can do everything . . . and they would drive exactly where the sea and the sand meet.

'We are here.'

'Don't let's get out. Let's just sit inside and talk.'

'Talk?'

'Yes.'

'Okay. But what is it, my darling?'

'I have told my sister about you.'

'Good God. Why?'

'But I had to. I couldn't keep it to myself any longer.'

'Childish. It was not necessary at all. She is not your mother.'

'No. But she is all I have. And she has been very good to me.'

'Well, it was her duty.'

'Then it is my duty to tell her about something like this. I may get into trouble.'

'Don't be silly,' he said, 'I normally take good care of my girl-friends.'

'I see,' she said and for the first time in the one month since she agreed to be this man's lover, the tears which suddenly rose into her eyes were not forced.

'And you promised you wouldn't tell her.' It was father's voice now.

'Don't be angry. After all, people talk so much, as you said a little while ago. She was bound to hear it one day.'

'My darling, you are too wise. What did she say?'

'She was pained.'

'Don't worry. Find out something she wants very much but cannot get in this country because of the import restrictions.'

'I know for sure she wants an electric motor for her sewing machine.'

'Is that all?'

'That's what I know of.'

'Mm. I am going to London next week on some delegation, so if you bring me the details on the make of the machine, I shall get her the motor.'

'Thank you.'

'What else is worrying my Black Beauty?'

'Nothing.'

'And by the way, let me know as soon as you want to leave your sister's place. I have got you one of the government estate houses.'

'Oh . . . oh,' she said, pleased, contented for the first time since this typically ghastly day had begun, at half-past six in the morning.

Dear little child came back from the playground with her toe bruised. Shall we just blow cold air from our mouth on it or put on a salve? Nothing matters really. Just see that she does not feel unattended. And the old sea roared on. This is a calm sea, generally. Too calm in fact, this Gulf of Guinea. The natives sacrifice to him on Tuesdays and once a year celebrate him.[2] They might save their chickens, their eggs and their yams. And as for the feast once a year, he doesn't pay much attention to it either. They are always celebrating one thing or another and they surely don't need him for an excuse to celebrate one day more. He has seen things happen along these beaches. Different things. Contradictory things. Or just repetitions of old patterns. He never interferes in their affairs. Why should he? Except in places like Keta where he eats houses away because they leave him no choice. Otherwise he never allows them to see his passions. People are worms, and even the God who created them is immensely bored with their antics. Here is a fifty-year-old 'big man' who thinks he is somebody. And a twenty-three-year-old child who chooses a silly way to conquer unconquerable problems. Well, what did one expect of human beings? And so as those two settled on the back seat of the car to play with each other's bodies, he, the Gulf of Guinea, shut his eyes with boredom. It is right. He could sleep, no? He spread himself and moved further ashore. But the car was parked at a very safe distance and the rising tides could not wet its tyres.

James has come home late. But then he has been coming back late for the past few weeks. Connie is crying and he knows it as soon as he enters the bedroom. He hates tears, for like so many men, he knows it is one of the most potent weapons in women's bitchy and inexhaustible arsenal. She speaks first.

'James.'

2. The Gulf of Guinea, personified as a god.

'Oh, you are still awake?' He always tries to deal with these nightly funeral parlour doings by pretending not to know what they are about.

'I couldn't sleep.'

'What is wrong?'

'Nothing.'

So he moves quickly and sits beside her.

'Connie, what is the matter? You have been crying again.'

'You are very late again.'

'Is that why you are crying? Or is there something else?'

'Yes.'

'Yes to what?'

'James, where were you?'

'Connie, I have warned you about what I shall do if you don't stop examining me, as though I were your prisoner, every time I am a little late.'

She sat up.

'A little late! It is nearly two o'clock.'

'Anyway, you won't believe me if I told you the truth, so why do you want me to waste my breath?'

'Oh well.' She lies down again and turns her face to the wall. He stands up but does not walk away. He looks down at her. So she remembers every night: they have agreed, after many arguments, that she should sleep like this. During her first pregnancy, he kept saying after the third month or so that the sight of her tummy the last thing before he slept always gave him nightmares. Now he regrets all this. The bed creaks as he throws himself down by her.

'James.'

'Yes.'

'There is something much more serious.'

'You have heard about my newest affair?'

'Yes, but that is not what I am referring to.'

'Jesus, is it possible that there is anything more important than that?'

And as they laugh they know that something has happened. One of those things which, with luck, will keep them together for some time to come.

'He teases me on top of everything.'

'What else can one do to you but tease when you are in this state?'

'James! How profane!'

'It is your dirty mind which gave my statement its shocking meaning.'

'Okay! But what shall I do?'

'About what?'

'Mercy. Listen, she is having an affair with Mensar-Arthur.'

'Wonderful.'

She sits up and he sits up.

'James, we must do something about it. It is very serious.'

'Is that why you were crying?'

'Of course.'

'Why shouldn't she?'

'But it is wrong. And she is ruining herself.'

'Since every other girl she knows has ruined herself prosperously, why shouldn't she? Just forget for once that you are a teacher. Or at least, remember she is not your pupil.'

'I don't like your answers.'

'What would you like me to say? Every morning her friends who don't earn any more than she does wear new dresses, shoes, wigs and what-have-you to work. What would you have her do?'

'The fact that other girls do it does not mean that Mercy should do it too.'

'You are being very silly. If I were Mercy, I am not sure that's exactly what I would do. And you know I mean it too.'

James is cruel. He is terrible and mean. Connie breaks into fresh tears and James comforts her. There is one point he must drive home though.

'In fact, encourage her. He may be able to intercede with the Ministry for you so that after the baby is born they will not transfer you from here for some time.'

'James, you want me to use my sister!'

'She is using herself, remember.'

'James, you are wicked.'

'And maybe he would even agree to get us a new car from abroad. I shall pay for everything. That would be better than paying a fortune for that old thing I was thinking of buying. Think of that.'

'You will ride in it alone.'

'Well . . .'

That was a few months before the *coup*.[3] Mensar-Arthur did go to London for a conference and bought something for all his wives and girl-friends, including Mercy. He even remembered the motor for Connie's machine. When Mercy took it to her she was quite confused. She had wanted this thing for a long time, and it would make everything so much easier, like the clothes for the new baby. And yet one side of her said that accepting it was a betrayal. Of what, she wasn't even sure. She and Mercy could never bring the whole business into the open and discuss it. And there was always James supporting Mercy, to Connie's bewilderment. She took the motor with thanks and sold even her right to dissent. In a short while, Mercy left the house to go and live in the estate house Mensar-Arthur had procured for her. Then, a couple of weeks later, the *coup*. Mercy left her new place before anyone could evict her. James never got his car. Connie's new baby was born. Of the three, the one who greeted the new order with undisguised relief was Connie. She is not really a demonstrative person but it was obvious from her eyes that she was happy. As far as she was concerned, the old order as symbolised by Mensar-Arthur was a threat to her sister and therefore to her own peace of mind. With it gone, things could return to normal. Mercy would move back to the house, perhaps start to date someone more—ordinary, let's say. Eventually, she would get married and then the nightmare of those past weeks would be forgotten. God being so good, he brought the *coup* early before the news of the affair could spread and brand her sister. . . .

The arrival of the new baby has magically waved away the difficulties between James and Connie. He is that kind of man, and she that kind of woman. Mercy has not been seen for many days. Connie is beginning to get worried. . . .

3. A coup d'état, or violent overthrow of the government (French).

James heard the baby yelling—a familiar noise, by now—the moment he opened the front gate. He ran in, clutching to his chest the few things he had bought on his way home.

'We are in here.'

'I certainly could hear you. If there is anything people of this country have, it is a big mouth.'

'Don't I agree? But on the whole, we are well. He is eating normally and everything. You?'

'Nothing new. Same routine. More stories about the overthrown politicians.'

'What do you mean, nothing new? Look at the excellent job the soldiers have done, cleaning up the country of all that dirt. I feel free already and I am dying to get out and enjoy it.'

James laughed mirthlessly.

'All I know is that Mensar-Arthur is in jail. No use. And I am not getting my car. Rough deal.'

'I never took you seriously on that car business.'

'Honestly, if this were in the ancient day, I could brand you a witch. You don't want me, your husband, to prosper?'

'Not out of my sister's ruin.'

'Ruin, ruin, ruin! Christ! See Connie, the funny thing is that I am sure you are the only person who thought it was a disaster to have a sister who was the girl-friend of a big man.'

'Okay; now all is over, and don't let's quarrel.'

'I bet the *coup* could have succeeded on your prayers alone.'

And Connie wondered why he said that with so much bitterness. She wondered if . . .

'Has Mercy been here?'

'Not yet, later, maybe. Mm. I had hoped she would move back here and start all over again.'

'I am not surprised she hasn't. In fact, if I were her, I won't come back here either. Not to your nagging, no thank you, big sister.'

And as the argument progressed, as always, each was forced in to a more aggressive defensive stand.

'Well, just say what pleases you, I am very glad about the soldiers. Mercy is my only sister, brother; everything. I can't sit and see her life going wrong without feeling it. I am grateful to whatever forces there are which put a stop to that. What pains me now is that she should be so vague about where she is living at the moment. She makes mention of a girl-friend but I am not sure that I know her.'

'If I were you, I would stop worrying because it seems Mercy can look after herself quite well.'

'Hmm,' was all she tried to say.

Who heard something like the sound of a car pulling into the drive? Ah, but the footsteps are unmistakably Mercy's. Are those shoes the old pair which were new a couple of months ago? Or are they the newest pair? And here she is herself, the pretty one. A gay Mercy.

'Hello, hello, my clan!' and she makes a lot of her nephew.

'Dow-dah-dee-day! And how is my dear young man today? My lord, grow up fast and come to take care of Auntie Mercy.'

Both Connie and James cannot take their eyes off her. Connie says, 'He says to Auntie Mercy he is fine.'

Still they watch her, horrified, fascinated and wondering what it's all about. Because they both know it is about something.

'Listen people, I brought a friend to meet you. A man.'

'Where is he?' from James.

'Bring him in,' from Connie.

'You know, Sissie, you are a new mother. I thought I'd come and ask you if it's all right.'

'Of course,' say James and Connie, and for some reason they are both very nervous.

'He is Captain Ashey.'

'Which one?'

'How many do you know?'

James still thinks it is impossible. 'Eh . . . do you mean the officer who has been appointed the . . . the . . .'

'Yes.'

'Wasn't there a picture in *The Crystal* over the weekend about his daughter's wedding? And another one of him with his wife and children and grandchildren?'

'Yes.'

'And he is heading a commission to investigate something or other?'

'Yes.'

Connie just sits there with her mouth open that wide. . . .

1970

LESLIE MARMON SILKO

born 1948

Novelist, poet, memoirist, and writer of short fiction, Leslie Marmon Silko can comfortably alternate between prose and poetry within the confines of a single work, in a manner reminiscent of traditional Native American storytellers. For all its seriousness and lyricism, Silko's work is marked by a touch of irreverence. Well acquainted with the proverbial trickster Coyote, Silko has demonstrated her own wit and versatility as a narrator of Coyote tales. But storytelling is a game with serious ends. "I will tell you something about stories," warns an unnamed voice in one of her novels: "They aren't just entertainment. Don't be fooled."

Silko was born in Albuquerque but grew up in Laguna Pueblo, New Mexico. "I am of mixed-breed ancestry," she has written, "but what I know is Laguna. This place I am from is everything I am as a writer and human being." A Keresan-speaking district,

Laguna Pueblo is an old Native community that whites first joined in the mid-nineteenth century when two government employees from Ohio, Walter and Robert Marmon, arrived as surveyors and set down roots. The brothers wrote a constitution for Laguna modeled after the U.S. Constitution; each served a term as governor of the pueblo, an office that no non-Native had held before. They also married Laguna women: Robert Marmon is the great-grandfather of Leslie Marmon Silko. Silko attended Laguna Day School until fifth grade, when she was transferred to Manzano Day School, a small private academy in Albuquerque. Between 1964 and 1969, she studied English at the University of New Mexico, married while still in college, and gave birth to the older of her two sons, Cazimir Silko. During these years she published her first story, "Tony's Story," a provocative tale of witchery.

Following graduation, Silko stayed on at the university and taught courses in creative writing and oral literature. She studied for a time in the university's American Indian Law Program, with the intention of working in the legal area of Native land claims. In 1971, however, a National Endowment for the Arts Discovery Grant changed Silko's mind about law school, and she quit to devote herself to writing. Seven of her stories, including "Yellow Woman," were published in 1974 in a collection edited by Kenneth Rosen—*The Man to Send Rain Clouds: Contemporary Stories by American Indians.* The novel *Ceremony,* her first large-scale work, appeared in 1977. An enormously complex novel that appeared just after the Vietnam War, *Ceremony* follows a Second World War veteran of mixed ancestry through his struggle for healing. Widely hailed, the novel propelled its author to the front of the growing ranks of indigenous writers in the United States. On the strength of *Ceremony,* Silko was awarded a MacArthur Fellowship (known as the "genius grant") in 1981.

Although much of Silko's work emphasizes the healing of conflicts—between white and Native Americans, between the human and natural worlds, between warring aspects of the self—some of her novels also reveal a more aggressive and despairing tone. Such a novel is *Almanac of the Dead* (1991), which turns a merciless eye on an America that drugs, prostitution, torture, organized crime, and forms of sexual violence have corrupted and deformed. On the map that opens the book read the stern lines: "The Indian Wars have never ended in the Americas. Native Americans acknowledge no borders; they seek nothing less than the return of all tribal lands." Formerly a professor at the University of Arizona, Silko continues to live and write in Tucson.

The story presented here, "Yellow Woman," is one of Silko's shortest and earliest pieces, that has, all the same, come to occupy a still-growing place in the canon of short fiction. Often reprinted, it became the subject of a volume of critical essays published in 1993. In traditional Laguna lore, Yellow Woman is either the heroine or a minor character in a wide range of tales. In her earliest incarnations, she might possibly have been a corn spirit—occasionally, Yellow Woman is named together with her three sisters, Blue Woman, Red Woman, and White Woman, thus completing the four colors of corn—but in Laguna lore she eventually became a kind of Everywoman. A traditional Laguna prayer song, recited at the naming ceremony for a newborn daughter, begins, "Yellow Woman is born, Yellow Woman is born." In narrative lore Yellow Woman most frequently appears in tales of abduction, where she is said to have been captured by a strange man at a stream while she is fetching water. Her captor, who carries her off to another world, is sometimes a kachina, or ancestral spirit; and when at last she returns to her home, she is imbued with power that proves of value for her people. In Silko's version of the tale, traditional elements remain constantly in the foreground. Yet whether the central figures in the story are human or supernatural remains unclear; the story's ambiguity is the source of its fascination. Thus Silko draws on Native tradition to make a major contribution to contemporary American fiction.

Yellow Woman

My thigh clung to his with dampness, and I watched the sun rising up through the tamaracks and willows. The small brown water birds came to the river and hopped across the mud, leaving brown scratches in the alkali-white crust. They bathed in the river silently. I could hear the water, almost at our feet where the narrow fast channel bubbled and washed green ragged moss and fern leaves. I looked at him beside me, rolled in the red blanket on the white river sand. I cleaned the sand out of the cracks between my toes, squinting because the sun was above the willow trees. I looked at him for the last time, sleeping on the white river sand.

I felt hungry and followed the river south the way we had come the afternoon before, following our footprints that were already blurred by lizard tracks and bug trails. The horses were still lying down, and the black one whinnied when he saw me but he did not get up—maybe it was because the corral was made out of thick cedar branches and the horses had not yet felt the sun like I had. I tried to look beyond the pale red mesas to the pueblo. I knew it was there, even if I could not see it, on the sandrock hill above the river, the same river that moved past me now and had reflected the moon last night.

The horse felt warm underneath me. He shook his head and pawed the sand. The bay whinnied and leaned against the gate trying to follow, and I remembered him asleep in the red blanket beside the river. I slid off the horse and tied him close to the other horse, I walked north with the river again, and the white sand broke loose in footprints over footprints.

"Wake up."

He moved in the blanket and turned his face to me with his eyes still closed. I knelt down to touch him.

"I'm leaving."

He smiled now, eyes still closed. "You are coming with me, remember?" He sat up now with his bare dark chest and belly in the sun.

"Where?"

"To my place."

"And will I come back?"

He pulled his pants on. I walked away from him, feeling him behind me and smelling the willows.

"Yellow Woman," he said.

I turned to face him. "Who are you?" I asked.

He laughed and knelt on the low, sandy bank, washing his face in the river. "Last night you guessed my name, and you knew why I had come."

I stared past him at the shallow moving water and tried to remember the night, but I could only see the moon in the water and remember his warmth around me.

"But I only said that you were him and that I was Yellow Woman—I'm not really her—I have my own name and I come from the pueblo on the other side of the mesa. Your name is Silva and you are a stranger I met by the river yesterday afternoon."

He laughed softly. "What happened yesterday has nothing to do with what you will do today, Yellow Woman."

"I know—that's what I'm saying—the old stories about the ka'tsina[1] spirit and Yellow Woman can't mean us."

My old grandpa liked to tell those stories best. There is one about Badger and Coyote who went hunting and were gone all day, and when the sun was going down they found a house. There was a girl living there alone, and she had light hair and eyes and she told them that they could sleep with her. Coyote wanted to be with her all night so he sent Badger into a prairie-dog hole, telling him he thought he saw something in it. As soon as Badger crawled in, Coyote blocked up the entrance with rocks and hurried back to Yellow Woman.

"Come here," he said gently.

He touched my neck and I moved close to him to feel his breathing and to hear his heart. I was wondering if Yellow Woman had known who she was—if she knew that she would become part of the stories. Maybe she'd had another name that her husband and relatives called her so that only the ka'tsina from the north and the storytellers would know her as Yellow Woman. But I didn't go on; I felt him all around me, pushing me down into the white river sand.

Yellow Woman went away with the spirit from the north and lived with him and his relatives. She was gone for a long time, but then one day she came back and she brought twin boys.

"Do you know the story?"

"What story?" He smiled and pulled me close to him as he said this. I was afraid lying there on the red blanket. All I could know was the way he felt, warm, damp, his body beside me. This is the way it happens in the stories, I was thinking, with no thought beyond the moment she meets the ka'tsina spirit and they go.

"I don't have to go. What they tell in stories was real only then, back in time immemorial, like they say."

He stood up and pointed at my clothes tangled in the blanket. "Let's go," he said.

I walked beside him, breathing hard because he walked fast, his hand around my wrist. I had stopped trying to pull away from him, because his hand felt cool and the sun was high, drying the river bed into alkali. I will see someone, eventually I will see someone, and then I will be certain that he is only a man—some man from nearby—and I will be sure that I am not Yellow Woman. Because she is from out of time past and I live now and I've been to school and there are highways and pickup trucks that Yellow Woman never saw.

1. Kachina, an ancestral spirit.

It was an easy ride north on horseback. I watched the change from the cottonwood trees along the river to the junipers that brushed past us in the foothills, and finally there were only piñons, and when I looked up at the rim of the mountain plateau I could see pine trees growing on the edge. Once I stopped to look down, but the pale sandstone had disappeared and the river was gone and the dark lava hills were all around. He touched my hand, not speaking, but always singing softly a mountain song and looking into my eyes.

I felt hungry and wondered what they were doing at home now—my mother, my grandmother, my husband, and the baby. Cooking breakfast, saying, "Where did she go?—maybe kidnapped." And Al going to the tribal police with the details: "She went walking along the river."

The house was made with black lava rock and red mud. It was high above the spreading miles of arroyos and long mesas. I smelled a mountain smell of pitch and buck brush. I stood there beside the black horse, looking down on the small, dim country we had passed, and I shivered.

"Yellow Woman, come inside where it's warm."

He lit a fire in the stove. It was an old stove with a round belly and an enamel coffeepot on top. There was only the stove, some faded Navajo blankets, and a bedroll and cardboard box. The floor was made of smooth adobe plaster, and there was one small window facing east. He pointed at the box.

"There's some potatoes and the frying pan." He sat on the floor with his arms around his knees pulling them close to his chest and he watched me fry the potatoes. I didn't mind him watching me because he was always watching me—he had been watching me since I came upon him sitting on the river bank trimming leaves from a willow twig with his knife. We ate from the pan and he wiped the grease from his fingers on his Levi's.

"Have you brought women here before?" He smiled and kept chewing, so I said, "Do you always use the same tricks?"

"What tricks?" He looked at me like he didn't understand.

"The story about being a ka'tsina from the mountains. The story about Yellow Woman."

Silva was silent; his face was calm.

"I don't believe it. Those stories couldn't happen now," I said.

He shook his head and said softly, "But someday they will talk about us, and they will say, 'Those two lived long ago when things like that happened.' "

He stood up and went out. I ate the rest of the potatoes and thought about things—about the noise the stove was making and the sound of the mountain wind outside. I remembered yesterday and the day before, and then I went outside.

I walked past the corral to the edge where the narrow trail cut through the black rim rock. I was standing in the sky with nothing around me but the wind that came down from the blue mountain peak behind me. I could see faint mountain images in the distance miles across the vast spread of mesas and valleys and plains. I wondered who was over there to feel the mountain wind on those sheer blue edges—who walks on the pine needles in those blue mountains.

"Can you see the pueblo?" Silva was standing behind me.

I shook my head. "We're too far away."

"From here I can see the world." He stepped out on the edge. "The Navajo reservation begins over there." He pointed to the east. "The Pueblo boundaries are over here." He looked below us to the south, where the narrow trail seemed to come from. "The Texans have their ranches over there, starting with that valley, the Concho Valley. The Mexicans run some cattle over there too."

"Do you ever work for them?"

"I steal from them," Silva answered. The sun was dropping behind us and the shadows were filling the land below. I turned away from the edge that dropped forever into the valleys below.

"I'm cold," I said, "I'm going inside." I started wondering about this man who could speak the Pueblo language so well but who lived on a mountain and rustled cattle. I decided that this man Silva must be Navajo, because Pueblo men didn't do things like that.

"You must be a Navajo."

Silva shook his head gently. "Little Yellow Woman," he said, "you never give up, do you? I have told you who I am. The Navajo people know me, too." He knelt down and unrolled the bedroll and spread the extra blankets out on a piece of canvas. The sun was down, and the only light in the house came from outside—the dim orange light from sundown.

I stood there and waited for him to crawl under the blankets.

"What are you waiting for?" he said, and I lay down beside him. He undressed me slowly like the night before beside the river—kissing my face gently and running his hands up and down my belly and legs. He took off my pants and then he laughed.

"Why are you laughing?"

"You are breathing so hard."

I pulled away from him and turned my back to him.

He pulled me around and pinned me down with his arms and chest. "You don't understand, do you, little Yellow Woman? You will do what I want."

And again he was all around me with his skin slippery against mine, and I was afraid because I understood that his strength could hurt me. I lay underneath him and I knew that he could destroy me. But later, while he slept beside me, I touched his face and I had a feeling—the kind of feeling for him that overcame me that morning along the river. I kissed him on the forehead and he reached out for me.

When I woke up in the morning he was gone. It gave me a strange feeling because for a long time I sat there on the blankets and looked around the little house for some object of his—some proof that he had been there or maybe that he was coming back. Only the blankets and the cardboard box remained. The .30-30 that had been leaning in the corner was gone, and so was the knife I had used the night before. He was gone, and I had my chance to go now. But first I had to eat, because I knew it would be a long walk home.

I found some dried apricots in the cardboard box, and I sat down on a rock at the edge of the plateau rim. There was no wind and the sun warmed me. I was surrounded by silence. I drowsed with apricots in my mouth, and I didn't believe that there were highways or railroads or cattle to steal.

When I woke up, I stared down at my feet in the black mountain dirt. Little black ants were swarming over the pine needles around my foot. They must have smelled the apricots. I thought about my family far below me. They would be wondering about me, because this had never happened to me before. The tribal police would file a report. But if old Grandpa weren't dead he would tell them what happened—he would laugh and say, "Stolen by a ka'tsina, a mountain spirit. She'll come home—they usually do." There are enough of them to handle things. My mother and grandmother will raise the baby like they raised me. Al will find someone else, and they will go on like before, except that there will be a story about the day I disappeared while I was walking along the river. Silva had come for me; he said he had. I did not decide to go. I just went. Moonflowers blossom in the sand hills before dawn, just as I followed him. That's what I was thinking as I wandered along the trail through the pine trees.

It was noon when I got back. When I saw the stone house I remembered that I had meant to go home. But that didn't seem important any more, maybe because there were little blue flowers growing in the meadow behind the stone house and the gray squirrels were playing in the pines next to the house. The horses were standing in the corral, and there was a beef carcass hanging on the shady side of a big pine in front of the house. Flies buzzed around the clotted blood that hung from the carcass. Silva was washing his hands in a bucket full of water. He must have heard me coming because he spoke to me without turning to face me.

"I've been waiting for you."

"I went walking in the big pine trees."

I looked into the bucket full of bloody water with brown-and-white animal hairs floating in it. Silva stood there letting his hand drip, examining me intently.

"Are you coming with me?"

"Where?" I asked him.

"To sell the meat in Marquez."

"If you're sure it's O.K."

"I wouldn't ask you if it wasn't," he answered.

He sloshed the water around in the bucket before he dumped it out and set the bucket upside down near the door. I followed him to the corral and watched him saddle the horses. Even beside the horses he looked tall, and I asked him again if he wasn't Navajo. He didn't say anything; he just shook his head and kept cinching up the saddle.

"But Navajos are tall."

"Get on the horse," he said, "and let's go."

The last thing he did before we started down the steep trail was to grab the .30-30 from the corner. He slid the rifle into the scabbard that hung from his saddle.

"Do they ever try to catch you?" I asked.

"They don't know who I am."

"Then why did you bring the rifle?"

"Because we are going to Marquez where the Mexicans live."

The trail leveled out on a narrow ridge that was steep on both sides like an animal spine. On one side I could see where the trail went around the rocky gray hills and disappeared into the southeast where the pale sandrock mesas stood in the distance near my home. On the other side was a trail that went west, and as I looked far into the distance I thought I saw the little town. But Silva said no, that I was looking in the wrong place, that I just thought I saw houses. After that I quit looking off into the distance; it was hot and the wildflowers were closing up their deep-yellow petals. Only the waxy cactus flowers bloomed in the bright sun, and I saw every color that a cactus blossom can be; the white ones and the red ones were still buds, but the purple and the yellow were blossoms, open full and the most beautiful of all.

Silva saw him before I did. The white man was riding a big gray horse, coming up the trail towards us. He was traveling fast and the gray horse's feet sent rocks rolling off the trail into the dry tumbleweeds. Silva motioned for me to stop and we watched the white man. He didn't see us right away, but finally his horse whinnied at our horses and he stopped. He looked at us briefly before he lapped the gray horse across the three hundred yards that separated us. He stopped his horse in front of Silva, and his young fat face was shadowed by the brim of his hat. He didn't look mad, but his small, pale eyes moved from the blood-soaked gunny sacks hanging from my saddle to Silva's face and then back to my face.

"Where did you get the fresh meat?" the white man asked.

"I've been hunting," Silva said, and when he shifted his weight in the saddle the leather creaked.

"The hell you have, Indian. You've been rustling cattle. We've been looking for the thief for a long time."

The rancher was fat, and sweat began to soak through his white cowboy shirt and the wet cloth stuck to the thick rolls of belly fat. He almost seemed to be panting from the exertion of talking, and he smelled rancid, maybe because Silva scared him.

Silva turned to me and smiled. "Go back up the mountain, Yellow Woman."

The white man got angry when he heard Silva speak in a language he couldn't understand. "Don't try anything, Indian. Just keep riding to Marquez. We'll call the state police from there."

The rancher must have been unarmed because he was very frightened and if he had a gun he would have pulled it out then. I turned my horse around and the rancher yelled, "Stop!" I looked at Silva for an instant and there was something ancient and dark—something I could feel in my stomach—in his eyes, and when I glanced at his hand I saw his finger on the trigger of the .30-30 that was still in the saddle scabbard. I slapped my horse across the flank and the sacks of raw meat swung against my knees as the horse leaped up the trail. It was hard to keep my balance, and once I thought I felt the saddle slipping backward; it was because of this that I could not look back.

I didn't stop until I reached the ridge where the trail forked. The horse was breathing deep gasps and there was a dark film of sweat on its neck. I looked down in the direction I had come from, but I couldn't see the place. I waited. The wind came up and pushed warm air past me. I looked up at the sky, pale blue and full of thin clouds and fading vapor trails left by jets.

I think four shots were fired—I remember hearing four hollow explosions that reminded me of deer hunting. There could have been more shots after that, but I couldn't have heard them because my horse was running again and the loose rocks were making too much noise as they scattered around his feet.

Horses have a hard time running downhill, but I went that way instead of uphill to the mountain because I thought it was safer. I felt better with the horse running southeast past the round gray hills that were covered with cedar trees and black lava rock. When I got to the plain in the distance I could see the dark green patches of tamaracks that grew along the river; and beyond the river I could see the beginning of the pale sandrock mesas. I stopped the horse and looked back to see if anyone was coming; then I got off the horse and turned the horse around, wondering if it would go back to its corral under the pines on the mountain. It looked back at me for a moment and then plucked a mouthful of green tumbleweeds before it trotted back up the trail with its ears pointed forward, carrying its head daintily to one side to avoid stepping on the dragging reins. When the horse disappeared over the last hill, the gunny sacks full of meat were still swinging and bouncing.

I walked toward the river on a wood-hauler's road that I knew would eventually lead to the paved road. I was thinking about waiting beside the road for someone to drive by, but by the time I got to the pavement I had decided it wasn't very far to walk if I followed the river back the way Silva and I had come.

The river water tasted good, and I sat in the shade under a cluster of silvery willows. I thought about Silva, and I felt sad at leaving him; still, there was something strange about him, and I tried to figure it out all the way back home.

I came back to the place on the river bank where he had been sitting the first time I saw him. The green willow leaves that he had trimmed from the branch were still lying there, wilted in the sand. I saw the leaves and I wanted to go back to him—to kiss him and to touch him—but the mountains were too far away now. And I told myself, because I believe it, he will come back sometime and be waiting again by the river.

I followed the path up from the river into the village. The sun was getting low, and I could smell supper cooking when I got to the screen door of my house. I could hear their voices inside—my mother was telling my grandmother how to fix the Jell-O and my husband, Al, was playing with the baby. I decided to tell them that some Navajo had kidnaped me, but I was sorry that old Grandpa wasn't alive to hear my story because it was the Yellow Woman stories he liked to tell best.

1974

NGUGI WA THIONG'O

born 1938

As the first successful English-language novelist from East Africa, Ngugi Wa Thiong'o made the surprising decision in middle age to stop writing in English. Believing that Africans should use their native tongues, he began writing in Kikuyu, a language spoken by about six million Kenyans (a quarter of the country's population). At the same time, Ngugi's politics became more radical and he turned from the experimental style of his early fiction to a form of socialist realism and satire in his Kikuyu works. Imprisoned for his criticisms of the Kenyan regime in the late 1970s, Ngugi soon became a symbol of the resistance of African writers to the abuse of state power.

Born James Ngugi in 1938 in British-ruled Kenya, the author lived as a youth through the Mau Mau uprising, in which the Mau Mau (a primarily Kikuyu group) rebelled against British laws that gave land to white settlers and forced Africans to work the land for little compensation. His stepbrother was killed in the rebellion; his mother was tortured. The uprising lasted for a decade, until 1963, when Kenya gained its independence. By this time, Ngugi had graduated from Makerere University College in Kampala, the capital of Uganda, and had his first play, *The Black Hermit* (1962), produced by the Uganda National Theatre. Like many African authors of his generation, Ngugi found early inspiration in the modern classics of Western literature, including the works of **Joseph Conrad.** For a brief period he became a Christian.

Shortly after Kenyan independence, Ngugi enrolled at the University of Leeds in England, where he completed three novels. While in England, he became interested in the radical theorists Karl Marx and Frantz Fanon; he would later visit the Soviet Union. In 1967 he was appointed the first African faculty member in the English Department of University College, Nairobi, rising to head of the department within a few years. In the 1970s the author decided to leave behind the name James Ngugi and the English language as his primary vehicle for creative expression. His first experiments with writing in Kikuyu began at this time, although he continued to publish some English-language fiction.

A turning point came in 1977, as he released his first novel in a decade, *Petals of Blood*. His last in English and his most explicitly political novel to date, it focused on Marxist analysis of relations among social classes rather than on the nationalist questions that had concerned the author earlier. In the same year, a play in Kikuyu, *I Will Marry When I Want*, had great success with its criticism of capitalism and Christianity. Its indirect attacks on government policies drew the attention of Daniel arap Moi, then vice president, who ordered Ngugi detained. He was imprisoned for almost a year; during this time Moi became president of Kenya, and when Ngugi was released, he was refused employment as a professor and eventually reimprisoned. His time in confinement led to his being declared a Prisoner of Conscience by Amnesty International; in 1978 an open letter calling for his release was published, signed by many Western authors. While in prison, Ngugi composed the first full-length novel written in Kikuyu, *Devil on the Cross* (1980), using prison toilet paper as stationery.

Shortly after his release, he left Kenya to live in London, and did not return until 2004, after Moi's departure from office.

Ngugi has continued his career as a novelist and a playwright, a journalist and a teacher, and an essayist and a postcolonial theorist. He has argued for the importance of writing in native languages rather than in English and has maintained his socialist ideological commitments, although he currently lives in the United States, where he is a professor of English and Comparative Literature at the University of California, Irvine.

Like **Chinua Achebe**, Ngugi explores the disastrous consequences for Africans of contact with the British. In the English-language work from the earliest years of his career, Ngugi wrote historical fiction about colonial rule in Kenya. By the middle years of his career, he turned his eye to independent Kenya and his writings became increasingly satirical and critical of Kenyan society and government. In the story included here, "Wedding at the Cross" (1975), Ngugi shows the effects of the previous decades of Kenyan history on a particular married couple and thus chronicles the compromises made by the Westernized middle classes in the pursuit of prosperity. He said of the collection in which it appears, *Secret Lives* (1975), his only collection of stories in English, that it contained his "creative autobiography over the last twelve years," that is, the years since independence.

Christianity plays an ambiguous role in Ngugi's works. On the one hand, it is an antimaterialist religion that exalts the poor; on the other hand, it is the religion of the colonizers and thus potentially a vehicle for social advancement. The story begins with the rebellious and charismatic Wariuki seeking to marry Miriamu, the daughter of a wealthy grocer in the years of colonial rule. Miriamu's father, a Christian who gets along well with the British authorities, opposes the match because of Wariuki's poverty. The young couple elopes, and the initial tone of the story is positive, even romantic. As the narrator relates the history of their marriage, however, it becomes clear that Wariuki's sense of manhood and self-worth has suffered from his rejection by Miriamu's father. He fights for the British during the Second World War, becomes a Christian, and takes an English name, but even as he gains in prosperity, his resentment of Miriamu's father remains. As independence comes and Wariuki benefits from the discriminatory policies of the Kenyan government against his employers (South Asian Kenyans who were expelled from the country in the late 1960s), Miriamu discovers a more authentic, but unofficial, Christianity, the Religion of Sorrows. The conflict between their values leads to the crisis of "Wedding at the Cross." Ngugi's subtle rendering of the tensions between official Christianity and popular religion adds depth to his memorable portrayal of postcolonial African society.

Wedding at the Cross

Everyone said of them: what a nice family; he, the successful timber merchant; and she, the obedient wife who did her duty to God, husband and family. Wariuki and his wife Miriamu were a shining example of what cooperation between man and wife united in love and devotion could achieve: he tall, correct, even a little stiff, but wealthy; she, small, quiet, unobtrusive, a diminishing shadow beside her giant of a husband.

He had married her when he was without a cent buried anywhere, not even for the rainiest day, for he was then only a milk clerk in a settler farm earning thirty shillings a month—a fortune in those days, true, but drinking most of it by the first of the next month. He was young; he did not care; dreams of material possessions and power little troubled him. Of course he joined the other workers in collective protests and demands, he would even compose letters for them; from one or two farms he had been dismissed as a dangerous and subversive character. But his heart was really elsewhere, in his favourite sports and acts. He would proudly ride his Raleigh Bicycle[1] around, whistling certain lines from old records remembered, yodelling in imitation of Jim Rogers,[2] and occasionally demonstrating his skill on the machine to an enthusiastic audience in Molo township. He would stand on the bicycle balancing with the left leg, arms stretched about to fly, or he would simply pedal backwards to the delight of many children. It was an old machine, but decorated in loud colours of red, green and blue with several Wariuki home-manufactured headlamps and reflectors and with a warning scrawled on a signboard mounted at the back seat: Overtake Me, Graveyard Ahead. From a conjurer on a bicycle, he would move to other roles. See the actor now mimicking his white bosses, satirizing their way of talking and walking and also their mannerisms and attitudes to black workers. Even those Africans who sought favours from the whites were not spared. He would vary his acts with dancing, good dancer too, and his mwomboko steps, with the left trouser leg deliberately split along the seam to an inch above the knee, always attracted approving eyes and sighs from maids in the crowd.

That's how he first captured Miriamu's heart.

On every Sunday afternoon she would seize any opportunity to go to the shopping square where she would eagerly join the host of worshippers. Her heart would then rise and fall with his triumphs and narrow escapes, or simply pound in rhythm with his dancing hips. Miriamu's family was miles better off than most squatters in the Rift Valley. Her father, Douglas Jones, owned several groceries and tea-rooms around the town. A God-fearing couple he and his wife were: they went to church on Sundays, they said their prayers first thing in the morning, last thing in the evening and of course before every meal. They were looked on with favour by the white farmers around; the District Officer would often stop by for a casual greeting. Theirs then was a good Christian home and hence they objected to their daughter marrying into sin, misery and poverty: what could she possibly see in that Murebi, Murebi bii-u?[3] They told her not to attend those heathen Sunday scenes of idleness and idol worship. But Miriamu had an independent spirit, though it had since childhood been schooled into inactivity by Sunday sermons—thou shalt obey thy father and mother and those that rule over us—and a proper upbringing with rules straight out of the Rt. Reverend Clive Schomberg's classic: *British Manners for Africans*.[4] Now Wariuki with his Raleigh bicycle, his milkman's tunes, his baggy trousers and dance which gave freedom to the body, was the light that beckoned her from the sterile world of Douglas Jones to a neon-lit city in a far

1. A British make of bicycle.
2. American country singer Jimmie Rodgers (1897–1933), known for his yodeling.
3. Drunkard, complete drunkard (Kikuyu).
4. A work encouraging Africans to imitate a British lifestyle.

horizon. Part of her was suspicious of the heavy glow, she was even slightly revolted by his dirt and patched-up trousers, but she followed him, and was surprised at her firmness. Douglas Jones relented a little: he loved his daughter and only desired the best for her. He did not want her to marry one of those useless half-educated upstarts, who disturbed the ordered life, peace and prosperity on European farms. Such men, as the Bwana District Officer[5] often told him, would only end in jails: they were motivated by greed and wanted to cheat the simple-hearted and illiterate workers about the evils of white settlers and missionaries. Wariuki looked the dangerous type in every way.

He summoned Wariuki, 'Our would-be-son-in-law', to his presence. He wanted to find the young man's true weight in silver and gold. And Wariuki, with knees weakened a little, for he, like most workers, was a little awed by men of that Christian and propertied class, carefully mended his left trouser leg, combed and brushed his hair and went there. They made him stand at the door, without offering him a chair, and surveyed him up and down. Wariuki, bewildered, looked alternately to Miriamu and to the wall for possible deliverance. And then when he finally got a chair, he would not look at the parents and the dignitaries invited to sit in judgement but fixed his eyes to the wall. But he was aware of their naked gaze and condemnation. Douglas Jones, though, was a model of Christian graciousness: tea for our—well—our son—well—this young man here. What work? Milk clerk? Ahh, well, well—no man was born with wealth—wealth was in the limbs you know and you, you are so young—salary? Thirty shillings a month?[6] Well, well, others had climbed up from worse and deeper pits: true wealth came from the Lord on high, you know. And Wariuki was truly grateful for these words and even dared a glance and a smile at old Douglas Jones. What he saw in those eyes made him quickly turn to the wall and wait for the execution. The manner of the execution was not rough: but the cold steel cut deep and clean. Why did Wariuki want to marry when he was so young? Well, well, as you like—the youth today—so different from our time. And who 'are we' to tell what youth ought to do? We do not object to the wedding: but we as Christians have a responsibility. I say it again: we do not object to this union. But it must take place at the cross. A church wedding, Wariuki, costs money. Maintaining a wife also costs money. Is that not so? You nod your head? Good. It is nice to see a young man with sense these days. All that I now want, and that is why I have called in my counsellor friends, is to see your savings account. Young man, can you show these elders your post office book?

Wariuki was crushed. He now looked at the bemused eyes of the elders present. He then fixed them on Miriamu's mother, as if in appeal. Only he was not seeing her. Away from the teats and rich udder of the cows, away from his bicycle and the crowd of rich admirers, away from the anonymous security of bars and tea-shops, he did not know how to act. He was a hunted animal, now cornered: and the hunters, panting with anticipation, were enjoying every moment of that kill. A buzz in his head, a blurring vision, and he heard the still gracious voice of Douglas Jones trailing into something about not signing his daughter to a life of misery and drudgery. Desperately Wariuki looked to the door and to the open space.

5. Highest-ranking British officer in a locality.
6. About $5 in the period of the story, or around $60 today.

Escape at last: and he breathed with relief. Although he was trembling a little, he was glad to be in a familiar world, his own world. But he looked at it slightly differently, almost as if he had been wounded and could not any more enjoy what he saw. Miriamu followed him there: for a moment he felt a temporary victory over Douglas Jones. They ran away and he got a job with Ciana Timber Merchants in Ilmorog forest. The two lived in a shack of a room to which he escaped from the daily curses of his Indian[7] employers. Wariuki learnt how to endure the insults. He sang with the movement of the saw: kneeling down under the log, the other man standing on it, he would make up words and stories about the log and the forest, sometimes ending on a tragic note when he came to the fatal marriage between the saw and the forest. This somehow would lighten his heart so that he did not mind the falling saw-dust. Came his turn to stand on top of the log and he would experience a malicious power as he sawed through it, gingerly walking backwards step by step and now singing of Demi na Mathathi[8] who, long ago, cleared woods and forests more dense than Ilmorog.

And Miriamu the erstwhile daughter of Douglas Jones would hear his voice rising above the whispering or uproarious wind and her heart rose and fell with it. This, this, dear Lord, was so different from the mournful church hymns of her father's compound, so, so, different and she felt good inside. On Saturdays and Sundays he took her to dances in the wood. On their way home from the dances and the songs, they would look for a suitable spot on the grass and make love. For Miriamu these were nights of happiness and wonder as the thorny pine leaves painfully but pleasantly pricked her buttocks even as she moaned under him, calling out to her mother and imaginary sisters for help when he plunged into her.

And Wariuki too was happy. It always seemed to him a miracle that he, a boy from the streets and without a father (he had died while carrying guns and food for the British in their expeditions against the Germans in Tanganyika[9] in the first European World War), had secured the affections of a girl from that class. But he was never the old Wariuki. Often he would go over his life beginning with his work picking pyrethrum[1] flowers for others under a scorching sun or icy cold winds in Limuru, to his recent job as a milk clerk in Molo:[2] his reminiscences would abruptly end with that interview with Douglas Jones and his counsellors. He would never forget that interview: he was never to forget the cackling throaty laughter as Douglas Jones and his friends tried to diminish his manhood and selfworth in front of Miriamu and her mother.

Never. He would show them. He would yet laugh in their faces.

But soon a restless note crept into his singing: bitterness of an unfulfilled hope and promise. His voice became rugged like the voice-teeth of the saw and he tore through the air with the same greedy malice. He gave up his job with the Ciana Merchants and took Miriamu all the way to Limuru. He dumped Miriamu with his aged mother and he disappeared from their lives. They heard of him in Nairobi, Mombasa, Nakuru, Kisumu and even Kampala.[3] Rumours

7. Indians often worked in Africa as merchants.
8. Mythical Kikuyu (Kenyan) giants.
9. Modern Tanzania, south of Kenya.
1. A relative of the chrysanthemum.
2. A town in western Kenya; Limuru is a town in central Kenya.
3. The capital of Uganda; the other towns listed are in various regions of Kenya.

reached them: that he was in prison, that he had even married a Muganda girl.[4] Miriamu waited: she remembered her moments of pained pleasure under Ilmorog woods, ferns and grass and endured the empty bed and the bite of Limuru cold in June and July. Her parents had disowned her and anyway she would not want to go back. The seedling he had planted in her warmed her. Eventually the child arrived and this together with the simple friendship of her mother-in-law consoled her. Came more rumours: white men were gathering arms for a war amongst themselves, and black men, sons of the soil, were being drafted to aid in the slaughter. Could this be true? Then Wariuki returned from his travels and she noticed the change in her man. He was now of few words: where was the singing and the whistling of old tunes remembered? He stayed a week. Then he said: I am going to war. Miriamu could not understand: why this change? Why this wanderlust? But she waited and worked on the land.

Wariuki had the one obsession: to erase the memory of that interview, to lay for ever the ghost of those contemptuous eyes. He fought in Egypt, Palestine, Burma and in Madagascar.[5] He did not think much about the war, he did not question what it meant for black people, he just wanted it to end quickly so that he might resume his quest. Why, he might even go home with a little loot from the war. This would give him the start in life he had looked for, without success, in towns all over Colonial Kenya. A lucrative job even: the British had promised them jobs and money-rewards once the wicked Germans were routed. After the war he was back in Limuru, a little emaciated in body but hardened in resolve.

For a few weeks after his return, Miriamu detected a little flicker of the old fires and held him close to herself. He made a few jokes about the war, and sang a few soldiers' songs to his son. He made love to her and another seed was planted. He again tried to get a job. He heard of a workers' strike in a Limuru shoe factory. All the workers were summarily dismissed. Wariuki and others flooded the gates to offer their sweat for silver. The striking workers tried to picket the new hands, whom they branded traitors to the cause, but helmeted police were called to the scene, baton charged the old workers away from the fenced compound and escorted the new ones into the factory. But Wariuki was not among them. Was he born into bad luck? He was back in the streets of Nairobi joining the crowd of the unemployed recently returned from the War. No jobs no money-rewards: the 'good' British and the 'wicked' Germans were shaking hands with smiles. But questions as to why black people were not employed did not trouble him: when young men gathered in Pumwani, Kariokor, Shauri Moyo[6] and other places to ask questions he did not join them: they reminded him of his old association and flirtation with farm workers before the war: those efforts had come to nought: even these ones would come to nought: he was in any case ashamed of that past: he thought that if he had been less of a loafer and more enterprising he would never have been so humiliated in front of Miriamu and her mother. The young men's talk of processions, petitions and pistols, their talk of gunning the whites out of the country, seemed too

4. From a Ugandan ethnic group.

5. Theaters of action in the Second World War (1939–45).

6. Neighborhoods of Nairobi, Kenya.

remote from his ambition and quest. He had to strike out on his own for moneyland. On arrival, he would turn round and confront old Douglas Jones and contemptuously flaunt success before his face. With the years the memory of that humiliation in the hands of the rich became so sharp and fresh that it often hurt him into sleepless nights. He did not think of the whites and the Indians as the real owners of property, commerce and land. He only saw the picture of Douglas Jones in his grey woollen suit, his waistcoat, his hat and his walking stick of a folded umbrella. What was the secret of that man's success? What? What? He attempted odd jobs here and there: he even tried his hand at trading in the hawk market at Bahati.[7] He would buy pencils and handkerchiefs from the Indian Bazaar and sell them at a retail price that ensured him a bit of profit. Was this his true vocation?

But before he could find an answer to his question, the Mau Mau war of national liberation broke out. A lot of workers, employed and unemployed, were swept off the streets of Nairobi into concentration camps. Somehow he escaped the net and was once again back in Limuru. He was angry. Not with the whites, not with the Indians, all of whom he saw as permanent features of the land like the mountains and the valleys, but with his own people. Why should they upset the peace? Why should they upset the stability just when he had started gathering a few cents from his trade? He now believed, albeit without much conviction, the lies told by the British about imminent prosperity and widening opportunities for blacks. For about a year he remained aloof from the turmoil around: he was only committed to his one consuming passion. Then he drifted into the hands of the colonial regime and cooperated. This way he avoided concentration camps and the forest. Soon his choice of sides started bearing fruit: he was excited about the prospects for its ripening. While other people's strips of land were being taken by the colonialists, his piece, although small, was left intact. In fact, during land consolidation forced on women and old men while their husbands and sons were decaying in detention or resisting in the forest, he, along with other active collaborators, secured additional land. Wariuki was not a cruel man: he just wanted this nightmare over so that he might resume his trade. For even in the midst of battle the image of D. Jones never really left him: the humiliation ached: he nursed it like one nurses a toothache with one's tongue, and felt that a day would come when he would stand up to that image.

Jomo Kenyatta[8] returned home from Maralal. Wariuki was a little frightened, his spirits were dampened: what would happen to his kind at the gathering of the braves to celebrate victory? Alas, where were the Whites he had thought of as permanent features of the landscape? But with independence approaching, Wariuki had his first real reward: the retreating colonialists gave him a loan: he bought a motor-propelled saw and set up as a Timber Merchant.

For a time after Independence, Wariuki feared for his life and business as the sons of the soil streamed back from detention camps and from the forests: he expected a retribution, but people were tired. They had no room in their hearts for vengeance at the victorious end of a just struggle. So Wariuki

7. A neighborhood in Nairobi.
8. Leader of the independence movement and later prime minister and president of Kenya (ca. 1894–1978).

prospered undisturbed: he had, after all, a fair start over those who had really fought for Uhuru.[9]

He joined the Church in gratitude. The Lord had spared him: he dragged Miriamu into it, and together they became exemplary Church-goers.

But Miriamu prayed a different prayer, she wanted her man back. Her two sons were struggling their way through Siriana Secondary School. For this she thanked the Lord. But she still wanted her real Wariuki back. During the Emergency[1] she had often cautioned him against excessive cruelty. It pained her that his singing, his dancing and his easy laughter had ended. His eyes were hard and set and this frightened her.

Now in Church he started singing again. Not the tunes that had once captured her soul, but the mournful hymns she knew so well; how sweet the name of Jesus sounds in a believer's ears. He became a pillar of the Church Choir. He often beat the drum which, after Independence, had been introduced into the church as a concession to African culture. He attended classes in baptism and great was the day he cast away Wariuki and became Dodge W. Livingstone, Jr. Thereafter he sat in the front bench. As his business improved, he gradually worked his way to the holy aisle. A new Church elder.

Other things brightened. His parents-in-law still lived in Molo, though their fortunes had declined. They had not yet forgiven him. But with his eminence, they sent out feelers: would their daughter pay them a visit? Miriamu would not hear of it. But Dodge W. Livingstone was furious: where was her Christian forgiveness? He was insistent. She gave in. He was glad. But that gesture, by itself, could not erase the memory of his humiliation. His vengeance would still come.

Though his base was at Limuru, he travelled to various parts of the country. So he got to know news concerning his line of business. It was the year of the Asian exodus.[2] Ciana Merchants were not Kenya Citizens. Their licence would be withdrawn. They quickly offered Livingstone partnership on a fifty-fifty share basis. Praise the Lord and raise high his name. Truly God never ate Ugali.[3] Within a year he had accumulated enough to qualify for a loan to buy one of the huge farms in Limuru previously owned by whites. He was now a big timber merchant: they made him a senior elder of the church.

Miriamu still waited for her Wariuki in vain. But she was a model wife. People praised her Christian and wifely meekness. She was devout in her own way and prayed to the Lord to rescue her from the dreams of the past. She never put on airs. She even refused to wear shoes. Every morning, she would wake early, take her Kiondo,[4] and go to the farm where she would work in the tea estate alongside the workers. And she never forgot her old strip of land in the Old Reserve. Sometimes she made lunch and tea for the workers. This infuriated her husband: why, oh why did she choose to humiliate him before these people? Why would she not conduct herself like a Christian lady? After all, had she not come from a Christian home? Need she dirty her hands now, he asked her, and with labourers too? On clothes, she gave in: she put on shoes

9. Independence (Swahili).
1. State of emergency during the anticolonial Mau Mau uprising of the 1950s.
2. In 1968–69, under pressure from a nationalist Kenyan government, South Asian residents of Kenya fled the country.
3. A type of porridge.
4. Woven basket (Kikuyu).

and a white hat especially when going to Church. But work was in her bones and this she would not surrender. She enjoyed the touch of the soil: she enjoyed the free and open conversation with the workers.

They liked her. But they resented her husband. Livingstone thought them a lazy lot: why would they not work as hard as he himself had done? Which employer's wife had ever brought him food in a shamba[5]? Miriamu was spoiling them and he told her so. Occasionally he would look at their sullen faces: he would then remember the days of the Emergency or earlier when he received insults from Ciana employers. But gradually he learnt to silence these unsettling moments in prayer and devotion. He was aware of their silent hatred but thought this a natural envy of the idle and the poor for the rich.

Their faces brightened only in Miriamu's presence. They would abandon their guarded selves and joke and laugh and sing. They gradually let her into their inner lives. They were members of a secret sect that believed that Christ suffered and died for the poor. They called theirs *The Religion of Sorrows*.[6] When her husband was on his business tours, she would attend some of their services. A strange band of men and women: they sang songs they themselves had created and used drums, guitars, jingles and tambourines, producing a throbbing powerful rhythm that made her want to dance with happiness. Indeed they themselves danced around, waving hands in the air, their faces radiating warmth and assurance, until they reached a state of possession and heightened awareness. Then they would speak in tongues strange and beautiful. They seemed united in a common labour and faith: this was what most impressed Miriamu. Something would stir in her, some dormant wings would beat with power inside her, and she would go home trembling in expectation. She would wait for her husband and she felt sure that together they could rescue something from a shattered past. But when he came back from his tours, he was still Dodge W. Livingstone, Jr., senior church elder, and a prosperous farmer and timber merchant. She once more became the model wife listening to her husband as he talked business and arithmetic for the day: what contracts he had won, what money he had won and lost, and tomorrow's prospects. On Sunday man and wife would go to church as usual: same joyless hymns, same prayers from set books; same regular visits to brothers and sisters in Christ; the inevitable tea-parties and charity auctions to which Livingstone was a conspicuous contributor. What a nice family everyone said in admiration and respect: he, the successful farmer and timber merchant; and she, the obedient wife who did her duty to God and husband.

One day he came home early. His face was bright—not wrinkled with the usual cares and worries. His eyes beamed with pleasure. Miriamu's heart gave a gentle leap, could this be true? Was the warrior back? She could see him trying to suppress his excitement. But the next moment her heart fell again. He had said it. His father-in-law, Douglas Jones, had invited him, had begged him to visit them at Molo. He whipped out the letter and started reading it aloud. Then he knelt down and praised the Lord, for his mercy and tender under-

5. Vegetable garden (Kikuyu).
6. Christianity has frequently been called a "religion of sorrow" because of its emphasis on sin and suffering (although it also emphasizes redemption).

standing. Miriamu could hardly join in the Amen. Lord, Lord, what has hardened my heart so, she prayed and sincerely desired to see the light.

The day of reunion drew near. His knees were becoming weak. He could not hide his triumph. He reviewed his life and saw in it the guiding finger of God. He the boy from the gutter, a mere milk clerk . . . but he did not want to recall the ridiculous young man who wore patched-up trousers and clowned on a bicycle. Could that have been he, making himself the laughing stock of the whole town? He went to Benbros and secured a new Mercedes Benz 220S. This would make people look at him differently. On the day in question, he himself wore a worsted woollen suit, a waistcoat, and carried a folded umbrella. He talked Miriamu into going in an appropriate dress bought from Nairobi Drapers in Government Road.[7] His own mother had been surprised into a frock and shoe-wearing lady. His two sons in their school uniform spoke nothing but English. (They affected to find it difficult speaking Kikuyu,[8] they made so many mistakes.) A nice family, and they drove to Molo. The old man met them. He had aged, with silver hair covering his head, but he was still strong in body. Jones fell on his knees; Livingstone fell on his knees. They prayed and then embraced in tears. Our son, our son. And my grandchildren too. The past was drowned in tears and prayers. But for Miriamu, the past was vivid in the mind.

Livingstone, after the initial jubilations, found that the memories of that interview rankled a little. Not that he was angry with Jones: the old man had been right, of course. He could not imagine himself giving his own daughter to such a ragamuffin of an upstart clerk. Still he wanted that interview erased from memory forever. And suddenly, and again he saw in that revelation the hand of God, he knew the answer. He trembled a little. Why had he not thought of it earlier? He had a long intimate conversation with his father-in-law and then made the proposal. Wedding at the cross. A renewal of the old. Douglas Jones immediately consented. His son had become a true believer. But Miriamu could not see any sense in the scheme. She was ageing. And the Lord had blessed her with two sons. Where was the sin in that? Again they all fell on her. A proper wedding at the cross of Jesus would make their lives complete. Her resistance was broken. They all praised the Lord. God worked in mysterious ways, his wonders to perform.[9]

The few weeks before the eventful day were the happiest in the life of Livingstone. He savoured every second. Even anxieties and difficulties gave him pleasure. That this day would come: a wedding at the cross. A wedding at the cross, at the cross where he had found the Lord. He was young again. He bounced in health and a sense of well-being. The day he would exchange rings at the cross would erase unsettling memories of yesterday. Cards were printed and immediately despatched. Cars and buses were lined up. He dragged Miriamu to Nairobi. They went from shop to shop all over the city: Kenyatta Avenue, Muindi Bingu Streets, Bazaar, Government Road, Kimathi Street, and back again to Kenyatta Avenue. Eventually he bought her a snow-white long-sleeved satin

7. An expensive commercial area in Nairobi.
8. The language of the Kikuyu ethnic group, to which Ngugi belongs.
9. Paraphrase of a hymn by William Cowper (1731–1800), "Light Shining Out of Darkness."

dress, a veil, white gloves, white shoes and stockings and of course plastic roses. He consulted Rev. Clive Schomberg's still modern classic on good manners for Africans and he hardly departed from the rules and instructions in the matrimonial section. Dodge W. Livingstone, Jr. did not want to make a mistake.

Miriamu did not send or give invitation cards to anybody. She daily prayed that God would give her the strength to go through the whole affair. She wished that the day would come and vanish as in a dream. A week before the day, she was driven all the way back to her parents. She was a mother of two; she was no longer the young girl who once eloped; she simply felt ridiculous pretending that she was a virgin maid at her father's house. But she submitted almost as if she were driven by a power stronger than man. Maybe she was wrong, she thought. Maybe everybody else was right. Why then should she ruin the happiness of many? For even the church was very happy. He, a successful timber merchant, would set a good example to others. And many women had come to congratulate her on her present luck in such a husband. They wanted to share in her happiness. Some wept.

The day itself was bright. She could see some of the rolling fields in Molo: the view brought painful memories of her childhood. She tried to be cheerful. But attempts at smiling only brought out tears: What of the years of waiting? What of the years of hope? Her face-wrinkled father was a sight to see: a dark suit with tails, a waist jacket, top hat and all. She inclined her head to one side, in shame. She prayed for yet more strength: she hardly recognized anybody as she was led towards the holy aisle. Not even her fellow workers, members of the *Religion of Sorrows*, who waited in a group among the crowd outside.

But for Livingstone this was the supreme moment. Sweeter than vengeance. All his life he had slaved for this hour. Now it had come. He had specially dressed for the occasion: a dark suit, tails, top hat and a beaming smile at any dignitary he happened to recognize, mostly MPs,[1] priests and businessmen. The church, Livingstone had time to note, was packed with very important people. Workers and not so important people sat outside. Members of the *Religion of Sorrows* wore red wine-coloured dresses and had with them their guitars, drums and tambourines. The bridegroom as he passed gave them a rather sharp glance. But only for a second. He was really happy.

Miriamu now stood before the cross: her head was hidden in the white veil. Her heart pounded. She saw in her mind's eye a grandmother pretending to be a bride with a retinue of aged bridesmaids. The Charade. The Charade. And she thought: there were ten virgins when the bridegroom came. And five of them were wise—and five of them were foolish—Lord, Lord that this cup would soon be over—over me, and before I be a slave . . .[2] and the priest was saying: 'Dodge W. Livingstone, Jr., do you accept this woman for a wife in sickness and health until death do you part?' Livingstone's answer was a clear and loud yes. It was now her turn; . . . Lord that this cup . . . this cup . . . over meeeee. . . . 'Do you Miriamu accept this man for a husband . . .' She tried to answer. Saliva blocked

1. Members of Parliament.
2. Miriamu is thinking of the parable of the wise and foolish virgins in Matthew 25; the foolish virgins seek oil to light their lamps and thus miss the opportunity to meet the bridegroom.

her throat . . . five virgins . . . five virgins . . . came bridegroom . . . groom . . . and the Church was now silent in fearful expectation.

Suddenly, from outside the Church, the silence was broken. People turned their eyes to the door. But the adherents of the *Religion of Sorrows* seemed unaware of the consternation on people's faces. Maybe they thought the ceremony was over. Maybe they were seized by the spirit. They beat their drums, they beat their tambourines, they plucked their guitars all in a jazzy bouncing unison. Church stewards rushed out to stop them, ssh, ssh, the wedding ceremony was not yet over—but they were way beyond hearing. Their voices and faces were raised to the sky, their feet were rocking the earth.

For the first time Miriamu raised her head. She remembered vaguely that she had not even invited her friends. How had they come to Molo? A spasm of guilt. But only for a time. It did not matter. Not now. The vision had come back . . . At the cross, at the cross where I found the Lord . . . she saw Wariuki standing before her even as he used to be in Molo. He rode a bicycle: he was playing his tricks before a huge crowd of respectful worshippers . . . At the cross, at the cross where I found the Lord . . . he was doing it for her . . . he had singled only her out of the thrilling throng . . . of this she was certain . . . came the dancing and she was even more certain of his love . . . He was doing it for her. Lord, I have been loved once . . . once . . . I have been loved, Lord . . . And those moments in Ilmorog forest and woods were part of her: what a moaning, oh, Lord what a moaning . . . and the drums and the tambourines were now moaning in her dancing heart. She was truly Miriamu. She felt so powerful and strong and raised her head even more proudly; . . . and the priest was almost shouting: 'Do you Miriamu . . .' The crowd waited. She looked at Livingstone, she looked at her father, and she could not see any difference between them. Her voice came in a loud whisper: 'No.'

A current went right through the church. Had they heard the correct answer? And the priest was almost hysterical: 'Do you Miriamu . . .' Again the silence made even more silent by the singing outside. She lifted the veil and held the audience with her eyes. 'No, I cannot . . . I cannot marry Livingstone . . . because . . . because . . . I have been married before. I am married to . . . to . . . Wariuki . . . and he is dead.'

Livingstone became truly a stone. Her father wept. Her mother wept. They all thought her a little crazed. And they blamed the whole thing on these breakaway churches that really worshipped the devil. No properly trained priest, etc. . . . etc. . . . And the men and women outside went on singing and dancing to the beat of drums and tambourines, their faces and voices raised to the sky.

1975

WOLE SOYINKA

born 1934

A political activist as well as a playwright, Wole Soyinka portrays modern Africa in transition, capturing the transformations in life, sensibility, and thought that have taken place as Western modernity impinges on indigenous customs. But Soyinka shows, as well, the tensions within the Yoruba world, its own struggle for modernity. To move beyond a simple division between Western and Yoruba traditions, Soyinka draws on both Yoruba and Greek myths, weaving them into a poetic system. It is perhaps his reliance on this frame of reference that has allowed Soyinka to turn the violence of British colonialism into the material for compelling novels and plays, which combine satire and myth with a meditation on the most fundamental human and historical conflicts of the twentieth century.

Soyinka's sense of Africa as a divided culture owes much to his personal background. He was born on July 13, 1934, in Abeokuta, western Nigeria, the second child in a family that had ties to the traditional Yoruba ruling class as well as to the educated elite that arose from Christian missionary activity; his father was a Christian clergyman. Soyinka has written extensively about his childhood and the growth of the Yoruba intelligentsia, whose nationalist aspirations and modernizing zeal have been largely responsible for the making of present-day Nigeria.

Soyinka began his education at the parsonage school at Aké, where his father was headmaster. He later attended Government College, an elite English-style boarding school at Ibadan, some sixty miles north of his native city. After two years at the newly founded University College, Ibadan, Soyinka entered the University of Leeds, in England, to study English literature; he had a particular interest in Shakespeare. After graduating, Soyinka evaluated new plays for the Royal Court Theatre in London, an influential institution that produced innovative works by **Samuel Beckett**, John Osborne, and Arnold Wesker. Soyinka was also influenced by the verse drama of **T. S. Eliot** and the "theatre of ideas" of George Bernard Shaw and **Bertolt Brecht**. From these sources and his knowledge of Yoruba culture, the writer developed a type of performance that combines dialogue in verse and prose with mime and song, a version of the "total theater" that has intrigued modernist and postmodernist playwrights elsewhere in the West. Soyinka's first plays were performed at the University Arts Theatre at Ibadan, where he returned in 1960 (the year of Nigerian independence) with the intention of researching traditional West African drama. He later taught at the universities of Ife and Lagos.

In writing plays for his recently independent nation, Soyinka was motivated by his conception of the creative artist as one who must serve as a public agent of moral insight and renewal. He thus incorporated Yoruba folktales, performance styles, and even religious practices into his English-language dramas. Soyinka founded the Orisun Theatre, a semiprofessional company that he trained and directed in a wide range of plays. His own works were already appearing in print, helping to establish his reputation beyond Nigeria. His first novel, *The Interpreters* (1965), portrayed a group of young Nigerian intellectuals seeking to give purpose to their lives and to chart a moral course for their society.

During these turbulent postindependence years, Soyinka became involved in Nigerian politics. Arrested in 1965 for broadcasting a message critical of rigged elections and accused of storming a government radio station, Soyinka was acquitted at his trial for lack of evidence. Civil war broke out in Nigeria in 1967, and Soyinka was arrested again for his efforts at reconciliation with the rebel regime of Biafra; he was held without trial until October 1969. His prison experience gave urgency to his moral concerns. As he writes in *The Man Died* (1972), a moving account of his detention and a searing indictment of the military regime, "The man dies in all who keep silent in the face of tyranny." These years of crisis and war account for the somber mood that runs through Soyinka's subsequent plays. In 1971, the author went into exile, living mostly in England until it was safe to return home to Nigeria, where he continued his teaching and writing. Awarded the Nobel Prize for Literature in 1986, he devoted his acceptance speech to condemning apartheid, the system of racial segregation and minority rule in South Africa. During the 1990s he was sentenced to death in absentia under the government of dictator Sani Abacha; again he went into exile. Soyinka has remained a prominent critic of dictatorships in Nigeria and elsewhere in Africa; in the years following the terrorist attacks of September 11, 2001, he has spoken against both Islamic fundamentalism and racial profiling. Since his homeland's return to democracy, in 1999, Soyinka has divided his time between Nigeria and the United States, where he has held a number of professorships.

Death and the King's Horseman (1975) is based on an actual event: a British colonial officer's intervention to prevent the ritual suicide, following the death of the king of Oyo, of his "horseman," a minor chief whose privileges were conditional on his accompanying the king to the afterworld. The officer does not realize the dire consequences his intervention will have for the village and, most important, for the King's Horseman's son, who is also the officer's protégé. In depicting historical figures, Soyinka shifts the focus from the story's symbolic and ethnographic interest to the concrete response of human beings to death.

The opening scene offers a view of Yoruba society. The market setting, with its fusion of economic, social, and religious life, projects the people's belief system in festive tones. Elesin, the King's Horseman destined to die, prepares to accept his burden joyously. Although the opening scene seems to display the original coherence of the Yoruba world, it hints at its latent tensions. Essential for this effect is the presence of the oral tradition, for much of the language the characters exchange, especially that between Elesin and his praise singer, derives from familiar forms of oral poetry, proverbs, and lineage praise names (*oriki orile*) that situate the individual within a network of social relations and obligations.

The intensity of this scene contrasts with the deliberate flatness of the second, when the ignorance of the British colonial officers becomes the object of satire and, in fact, the British colonial system is depicted as offensive and violent. Pilkings, the colonial official, for example, wears traditional Yoruba dress, which is reserved for specific ritual uses, as costume for a masked ball. When he learns of the impending suicide of the King's Horseman and seeks to prevent it, the colonial and indigenous worlds collide. Yet Soyinka insists that the play should not be reduced to a simple conflict between two cultures. And indeed, the play spends considerable energy bridging this gulf: for instance, Soyinka shows that both cultures have a tradition of honorable suicide and that both have rituals involving masked dancing. Mediating figures such as Mrs. Pilkings and Olunde, the son of the King's Horseman, offer more nuanced perspectives on the central conflict, which nevertheless cannot yield to an easy solution. This impasse reflects the challenges of Soyinka's attempt to negotiate, in his work, the competing claims of Yoruba tradition and Western theater, as he seeks to help shape a Nigerian culture that would draw on native traditions without barricading them from the wider world.

The different forms of ceremony, ritual, and dance that make up this complex play are mirrored and reinforced by its unusual language and poetry. Certain Yoruba songs are rendered in poetic English. The idiom of the non-British characters is informed by the syntax, expressions, proverbs, and metaphors of Yoruba. The result is a multilayered English that draws on the Yoruba world, its flora, fauna, social structure, and cosmology, for comparison and insight. The play contrasts and intermingles languages, cultures, characters, and forms of theater and performance.

Such juxtaposing is perhaps the most important innovation of *Death and the King's Horseman*. The play certainly shows the violence that occurs at a moment of contact between British and Yoruba ways of life. By revealing the tensions within each society, however, Soyinka avoids blaming the conflicts arising under colonialism on each side's ignorance, and often intolerance, of the other. Yoruba culture, for Soyinka, is never simple, authentic, or monolithic. Rather, for Soyinka, it has itself undergone a process of modernization; it therefore is compatible with the international, cosmopolitan world represented by the son of the King's Horseman. At the same time, Soyinka points to the traditionalist, even ritualistic, aspects of British life. This way, both the Yoruba people and the British are divided between tradition and modernization—even if Soyinka never lets us forget that it was the British who sought to interrupt and dismiss Yoruba traditions, not the other way around.

Death and the King's Horseman is Soyinka's masterpiece. In it the verbal resourcefulness and mastery of theatrical effects evident in his earlier plays unite to produce a work whose evocative power ensures its appeal as both a model of connection to an indigenous tradition and an exploration of a universal human dilemma.

Death and the King's Horseman

Cast

PRAISE-SINGER
ELESIN, *Horseman of the King*
IYALOJA, *"Mother" of the market*
SIMON PILKINGS, *District Officer*
JANE PILKINGS, *his wife*
SERJEANT AMUSA
JOSEPH, *houseboy to the Pilkingses*
BRIDE
H. R. H. THE PRINCE
THE RESIDENT
AIDE-DE-CAMP
OLUNDE, *eldest son of Elesin*
DRUMMERS, WOMEN, YOUNG GIRLS, DANCERS *at the Ball*

Scene One

A passage through a market in its closing stages. The stalls are being emptied, mats folded. A few WOMEN *pass through on their way home, loaded with baskets. On a cloth-stand, bolts of cloth are taken down, display pieces folded and piled on a tray.*

ELESIN OBA *enters along a passage before the market, pursued by his* DRUMMERS *and* PRAISE-SINGERS. *He is a man of enormous vitality, speaks, dances and sings with that infectious enjoyment of life which accompanies all his actions.*

PRAISE-SINGER: Elesin o! Elesin Oba! Howu![1] What tryst is this the cockerel goes to keep with such haste that he must leave his tail behind?

ELESIN: [*Slows down a bit, laughing.*] A tryst where the cockerel needs no adornment.

PRAISE-SINGER: O-oh, you hear that my companions? That's the way the world goes. Because the man approaches a brand new bride he forgets the long faithful mother of his children.

ELESIN: When the horse sniffs the stable does he not strain at the bridle? The market is the long-suffering home of my spirit and the women are packing up to go. That Esu[2]-harrassed day slipped into the stewpot while we feasted. We ate it up with the rest of the meat. I have neglected my women.

PRAISE-SINGER: We know all that. Still it's no reason for shedding your tail on this day of all days. I know the women will cover you in damask and *alari*[3] but when the wind blows cold from behind, that's when the fowl knows his true friends.

ELESIN: Olohun-iyo![4]

PRAISE-SINGER: Are you sure there will be one like me on the other side?

ELESIN: Olohun-iyo!

PRAISE-SINGER: Far be it for me to belittle the dwellers of that place but, a man is either born to his art or he isn't. And I don't know for certain that you'll meet my father, so who is going to sing these deeds in accents that will pierce the deafness of the ancient ones. I have prepared my going—just tell me: Olohun-iyo, I need you on this journey and I shall be behind you.

ELESIN: You're like a jealous wife. Stay close to me, but only on this side. My fame, my honour are legacies to the living; stay behind and let the world sip its honey from your lips.

PRAISE-SINGER: Your name will be like the sweet berry a child places under his tongue to sweeten the passage of food. The world will never spit it out.

ELESIN: Come then. This market is my roost. When I come among the women I am a chicken with a hundred mothers. I become a monarch whose palace is built with tenderness and beauty.

PRAISE-SINGER: They love to spoil you but beware. The hands of women also weaken the unwary.

ELESIN: This night I'll lay my head upon their lap and go to sleep. This night I'll touch feet with their feet in a dance that is no longer of this earth. But the smell of their flesh, their sweat, the smell of indigo[5] on their cloth, this is the last air I wish to breathe as I go to meet my great forebears.

PRAISE-SINGER: In their time the world was never tilted from its groove, it shall not be in yours.

ELESIN: The gods have said No.

1. An exclamation of surprise.
2. The god of fate in the Yoruba pantheon: also a trickster figure.
3. A rich woven cloth, brightly coloured [Author's note].
4. "Sweet voice": affectionate nickname for the praise-singer.
5. A deep blue dye.

PRAISE-SINGER: In their time the great wars came and went, the little wars came and went; the white slavers came and went, they took away the heart of our race, they bore away the mind and muscle of our race. The city fell and was rebuilt; the city fell and our people trudged through mountain and forest to find a new home but—Elesin Oba do you hear me?

ELESIN: I hear your voice Olohun-iyo.

PRAISE-SINGER: Our world was never wrenched from its true course.

ELESIN: The gods have said No.

PRAISE-SINGER: There is only one home to the life of a river-mussel; there is only one home to the life of a tortoise; there is only one shell to the soul of man; there is only one world to the spirit of our race. If that world leaves its course and smashes on boulders of the great void, whose world will give us shelter?

ELESIN: It did not in the time of my forebears, it shall not in mine.

PRAISE-SINGER: The cockerel must not be seen without his feathers.

ELESIN: Nor will the Not-I bird be much longer without his nest.

PRAISE-SINGER: [*Stopped in his lyric stride.*] The Not-I bird, Elesin?

ELESIN: I said, the Not-I bird.

PRAISE-SINGER: All respect to our elders but, is there really such a bird?

ELESIN: What! Could it be that he failed to knock on your door?

PRAISE-SINGER: [*Smiling.*] Elesin's riddles are not merely the nut in the kernel that breaks human teeth; he also buries the kernel in hot embers and dares a man's fingers to draw it out.

ELESIN: I am sure he called on you, Olohun-iyo. Did you hide in the loft and push out the servant to tell him you were out?

[ELESIN *executes a brief, half-taunting dance. The* DRUMMER *moves in and draws a rhythm out of his steps.* ELESIN *dances towards the market-place as he chants the story of the Not-I bird, his voice changing dexterously to mimic his characters. He performs like a born raconteur,*[6] *infecting his retinue with his humour and energy. More* WOMEN *arrive during his recital, including* IYALOJA.]

Death came calling
Who does not know his rasp of reeds?
A twilight whisper in the leaves before
The great araba[7] falls? Did you hear it?
Not I! swears the farmer. He snaps
His fingers round his head,[8] abandons
A hard-worn harvest and begins
A rapid dialogue with his legs.

"Not I," shouts the fearless hunter, "but—
It's getting dark, and this night-lamp
Has leaked out all its oil. I think
It's best to go home and resume my hunt
Another day." But now he pauses, suddenly
Lets out a wail: "Oh foolish mouth, calling
Down a curse on your own head! Your lamp

6. A storyteller.
7. A tall and majestic tropical tree.
8. The gesture for warding off evil.

Has leaked out all its oil, has it?"
Forwards or backwards now he dare not move.
To search for leaves and make etutu[9]
On that spot? Or race home to the safety
Of his hearth? Ten market-days have passed
My friends, and still he's rooted there
Rigid as the plinth of Orayan[1]

The mouth of the courtesan barely
Opened wide enough to take a ha'penny *robo*[2]
When she wailed: "Not I." All dressed she was
To call upon my friend the Chief Tax Officer.
But now she sends her go between instead:
"Tell him I'm ill: my period[3] has come suddenly
But not—I hope—my time."

Why is the pupil crying?
His hapless head was made to taste
The knuckles of my friend the Mallam:[4]
"If you were then reciting the Koran
Would you have ears for idle noises
Darkening the trees, you child of ill omen?"
He shuts down school before its time
Runs home and rings himself with amulets.
And take my good kinsman Ifawomi.[5]
His hands were like a carver's, strong
And true. I saw them
Tremble like wet wings of a fowl.
One day he cast his time-smoothed opele[6]
Across the divination board. And all because
The suppliant looked him in the eye and asked,
"Did you hear that whisper in the leaves?"
"Not I," was his reply; "perhaps I'm growing deaf—
Good-day." And Ifa spoke no more that day
The priest locked fast his doors,
Sealed up his leaking roof—but wait!
This sudden care was not for Fawomi
But for Osenyin,[7] a courier-bird of Ifa's
Heart of wisdom. I did not know a kite
Was hovering in the sky
And Ifa now a twittering chicken in
The brood of Fawomi the Mother Hen.[8]

9. Rites of propitiation, often involving a sacrifice.
1. The mythical founder of Ife, the sacred city of the Yoruba people. "Plinth": a tall stone column planted into the earth at Ife, reputed to have been the staff of Orayan.
2. A delicacy made from crushed melon seeds, fried in tiny balls [author's note].
3. That is, she is menstruating.
4. A teacher in a koranic school.
5. A name (later shortened to Fawomi) that designates a devotee of Ifa, the god of divination, referred to further in the passage.
6. A string of beads used in Ifa divination [Author's note].
7. The tutelary deity of Yoruba traditional healers.
8. That is, reduced in status, humiliated. Even a god as powerful as Ifa can be cowed by death.

Ah, but I must not forget my evening
Courier from the abundant palm, whose groan
Became Not I, as he constipated down
A wayside bush. He wonders if Elegbara[9]
Has tricked his buttocks to discharge
Against a sacred grove. Hear him
Mutter spells to ward off penalties
For an abomination he did not intend.
If any here
Stumbles on a gourd of wine, fermenting
Near the road, and nearby hears a stream
Of spells issuing from a crouching form.
Brother to a *sigidi*,[1] bring home my wine,
Tell my tapper I have ejected
Fear from home and farm. Assure him,
All is well.

PRAISE-SINGER: In your time we do not doubt the peace of farmstead and home, the peace of road and hearth, we do not doubt the peace of the forest.

ELESIN: There was fear in the forest too.
Not-I was lately heard even in the lair
Of beasts. The hyena cackled loud. Not I,
The civet twitched his fiery tail and glared:
Not I. Not-I became the answering name
Of the restless bird,[2] that little one
Whom Death found nesting in the leaves
When whisper of his coming ran
Before him on the wind. Not-I
Has long abandoned home. This same dawn
I heard him twitter in the gods' abode.
Ah, companions of this living world
What a thing this is, that even those
We call immortal
Should fear to die.

IYALOJA: But you, husband of multitudes?

ELESIN: I, when that Not-I bird perched
Upon my roof, bade him seek his nest again.
Safe, without care or fear. I unrolled
My welcome mat for him to see. Not-I
Flew happily away, you'll hear his voice
No more in this lifetime—You all know
What I am.

PRAISE-SINGER: That rock which turns its open lodes
Into the path of lightning. A gay
Thoroughbred whose stride disdains
To falter though an adder[3] reared
Suddenly in his path.

9. Another name for Esu.
1. A malevolent spirit.
2. Most likely the canary, which, when caged, is constantly making short, rapid movements.
3. Or puff-adder, an extremely poisonous snake.

ELESIN: My rein is loosened.
I am master of my Fate. When the hour comes
Watch me dance along the narrowing path
Glazed by the soles of my great precursors.
My soul is eager. I shall not turn aside.
WOMEN: You will not delay?
ELESIN: Where the storm pleases, and when, it directs
The giants of the forest. When friendship summons
Is when the true comrade goes.
WOMEN: Nothing will hold you back?
ELESIN: Nothing. What! Has no one told you yet
I go to keep my friend and master company.
Who says the mouth does not believe in
"No, I have chewed all that before?" I say I have.
The world is not a constant honey-pot.
Where I found little I made do with little.
Where there was plenty I gorged myself.
My master's hands and mine have always
Dipped together and, home or sacred feast,
The bowl was beaten bronze, the meats
So succulent our teeth accused us of neglect.
We shared the choicest of the season's
Harvest of yams. How my friend would read
Desire in my eyes before I knew the cause—
However rare, however precious, it was mine.
WOMEN: The town, the very land was yours.
ELESIN: The world was mine. Our joint hands
Raised housepots[4] of trust that withstood
The siege of envy and the termites of time.
But the twilight hour brings bats and rodents—
Shall I yield them cause to foul the rafters?
PRAISE-SINGER: Elesin Oba! Are you not that man who
Looked out of doors that stormy day
The god of luck[5] limped by, drenched
To the very lice that held
His rags together? You took pity upon
His sores and wished him fortune.
Fortune was footloose this dawn, he replied,
Till you trapped him in a heartfelt wish
That now returns to you. Elesin Oba!
I say you are that man who
Chanced upon the calabash of honour
You thought it was palm wine[6] and
Drained its contents to the final drop.

4. Used for storing the household's water.
5. Esu, who is represented as lame.
6. The sweet sap of the palm oil tree, which ferments naturally to become a potent drink. "Calabash": container made from the fruit of a vine.

ELESIN: Life has an end. A life that will outlive
Fame and friendship begs another name.
What elder takes his tongue to his plate,
Licks it clean of every crumb?[7] He will encounter
Silence when he calls on children to fulfill
The smallest errand! Life is honour.
It ends when honour ends.

WOMEN: We know you for a man of honour.

ELESIN: Stop! Enough of that!

WOMEN: [*Puzzled, they whisper among themselves, turning mostly to* IYALOJA.] What is it? Did we say something to give offence? Have we slighted him in some way?

ELESIN: Enough of that sound I say. Let me hear no more in that vein. I've heard enough.

IYALOJA: We must have said something wrong. [*Comes forward a little.*] Elesin Oba, we ask forgiveness before you speak.

ELESIN: I am bitterly offended.

IYALOJA: Our unworthiness has betrayed us. All we can do is ask your forgiveness. Correct us like a kind father.

ELESIN: This day of all days . . .

IYALOJA: It does not bear thinking. If we offend you now we have mortified the gods. We offend heaven itself. Father of us all, tell us where we went astray. [*She kneels, the other* WOMEN *follow.*]

ELESIN: Are you not ashamed? Even a tear-veiled
Eye preserves its function of sight.
Because my mind was raised to horizons
Even the boldest man lowers his gaze
In thinking of, must my body here
Be taken for a vagrant's?

IYALOJA: Horseman of the King, I am more baffled than ever.

PRAISE-SINGER: The strictest father unbends his brow when the child is penitent, Elesin. When time is short, we do not spend it prolonging the riddle. Their shoulders are bowed with the weight of fear lest they have marred your day beyond repair. Speak now in plain words and let us pursue the ailment to the home of remedies.

ELESIN: Words are cheap. "We know you for
A man of honour." Well tell me, is this how
A man of honour should be seen?
Are these not the same clothes in which
I came among you a full half-hour ago?

[*He roars with laughter and the* WOMEN, *relieved, rise and rush into stalls to fetch rich clothes.*]

WOMEN: The gods are kind. A fault soon remedied is soon forgiven. Elesin Oba, even as we match our words with deed, let your heart forgive us completely.

ELESIN: You who are breath and giver of my being
How shall I dare refuse you forgiveness
Even if the offence was real.

7. Elders are expected to deny themselves for the young.

IYALOJA: [*Dancing round him. Sings.*]
He forgives us. He forgives us.
What a fearful thing it is when
The voyager sets forth
But a curse remains behind.

WOMEN: For a while we truly feared
Our hands had wrenched the world adrift
In emptiness.

IYALOJA: Richly, richly, robe him richly
The cloth of honour is alari
Sanyan[8] is the band of friendship
Boa-skin makes slippers of esteem.

WOMEN: For a while we truly feared
Our hands had wrenched the world adrift
In emptiness.

PRAISE-SINGER: He who must, must voyage forth
The world will not roll backwards
It is he who must, with one
Great gesture overtake the world.

WOMEN: For a while we truly feared
Our hands had wrenched the world
In emptiness.

PRAISE-SINGER: The gourd[9] you bear is not for shirking.
The gourd is not for setting down
At the first crossroad or wayside grove.
Only one river may know its contents.

WOMEN: We shall all meet at the great market
We shall all meet at the great market
He who goes early takes the best bargains
But we shall meet, and resume our banter.

[ELESIN *stands resplendent in rich clothes, cap, shawl, etc. His sash is of a bright red alari cloth. The* WOMEN *dance round him. Suddenly, his attention is caught by an object off-stage.*]

ELESIN: The world I know is good.

WOMEN: We know you'll leave it so.

ELESIN: The world I know is the bounty
Of hives after bees have swarmed.
No goodness teems with such open hands
Even in the dreams of deities.

WOMEN: And we know you'll leave it so.

ELESIN: I was born to keep it so. A hive
Is never known to wander. An anthill
Does not desert its roots. We cannot see
The still great womb of the world—
No man beholds his mother's womb—
Yet who denies it's there? Coiled

8. Richly decorated woven cloth.

9. Used for carrying water.

To the navel of the world is that
Endless cord that links us all
To the great origin. If I lose my way
The trailing cord will bring me to the roots.

WOMEN: The world is in your hands.

[*The earlier distraction, a beautiful young girl, comes along the passage through which* ELESIN *first made his entry.*]

ELESIN: I embrace it. And let me tell you, women—
I like this farewell that the world designed,
Unless my eyes deceive me, unless
We are already parted, the world and I,
And all that breeds desire is lodged
Among our tireless ancestors. Tell me friends,
Am I still earthed in that beloved market
Of my youth? Or could it be my will
Has outleapt the conscious act and I have come
Among the great departed?

PRAISE-SINGER: Elesin Oba why do your eyes roll like a bush-rat who sees his fate like his father's spirit, mirrored in the eye of a snake? And all those questions! You're standing on the same earth you've always stood upon. This voice you hear is mine, Oluhun-iyo, not that of an acolyte in heaven.

ELESIN: How can that be? In all my life
As Horseman of the King, the juiciest
Fruit on every tree was mine. I saw,
I touched, I wooed, rarely was the answer No.
The honour of my place, the veneration I
Received in the eye of man or woman
Prospered my suit and
Played havoc with my sleeping hours.
And they tell me my eyes were a hawk
In perpetual hunger. Split an iroko tree[1]
In two, hide a woman's beauty in its heartwood
And seal it up again—Elesin, journeying by,
Would make his camp beside that tree
Of all the shades in the forest.

PRAISE-SINGER: Who would deny your reputation, snake-on-the-loose in dark passages of the market! Bed-bug who wages war on the mat and receives the thanks of the vanquished! When caught with his bride's own sister he protested—but I was only prostrating myself to her as becomes a grateful in-law. Hunter who carries his powder-horn on the hips and fires crouching or standing! Warrior who never makes that excuse of the whining coward—but how can I go to battle without my trousers?—trouserless or shirtless it's all one to him. Oka[2]-rearing-from-a-camouflage-of-leaves, before he strikes the victim is already prone! Once they told me, Howu, a stallion does not feed on the grass beneath him; he replied, true, but surely he can roll on it!

1. A tropical hardwood tree: it is a large tree with abundant foliage.

2. The python, a huge snake that swallows its victims whole.

WOMEN: Ba-a-a-ba O![3]

PRAISE-SINGER: Ah, but listen yet. You know there is the leaf-nibbling grub and there is the cola-chewing beetle; the leaf-nibbling grub lives on the leaf, the cola-chewing beetle lives in the colanut. Don't we know what our man feeds on when we find him cocooned in a woman's wrapper?

ELESIN: Enough, enough, you all have cause
To know me well. But, if you say this earth
Is still the same as gave birth to those songs,
Tell me who was that goddess through whose lips
I saw the ivory pebbles of Oya's[4] river-bed.
Iyaloja, who is she? I saw her enter
Your stall; all your daughters I know well.
No, not even Ogun[5]-of-the-farm toiling
Dawn till dusk on his tuber patch
Not even Ogun with the finest hoe he ever
Forged at the anvil could have shaped
That rise of buttocks, not though he had
The richest earth between his fingers.
Her wrapper was no disguise
For thighs whose ripples shamed the river's
Coils around the hills of Ilesi.[6] Her eyes
Were new-laid eggs glowing in the dark.
Her skin . . .

IYALOJA: Elesin Oba . . .

ELESIN: What! Where do you all say I am?

IYALOJA: Still among the living.

ELESIN: And that radiance which so suddenly
Lit up this market I could boast
I knew so well?

IYALOJA: Has one step already in her husband's home. She is betrothed.

ELESIN: [*Irritated.*] Why do you tell me that?

[IYALOJA *falls silent. The* WOMEN *shuffle uneasily.*]

IYALOJA: Not because we dare give you offence Elesin. Today is your day and the whole world is yours. Still, even those who leave town to make a new dwelling elsewhere like to be remembered by what they leave behind.

ELESIN: Who does not seek to be remembered?
Memory is Master of Death, the chink
In his armour of conceit. I shall leave
That which makes my going the sheerest
Dream of an afternoon. Should voyagers
Not travel light? Let the considerate traveller
Shed, of his excessive load, all
That may benefit the living.

WOMEN: [*Relieved.*] Ah Elesin Oba, we knew you for a man of honour.

ELESIN: Then honour me. I deserve a bed of honour to lie upon.

3. A form of salute to an elder male.
4. A Yoruba goddess said to live in the River Niger.
5. The Yoruba god of iron and of war (equivalent in some ways to Mars).
6. A town.

IYALOJA: The best is yours. We know you for a man of honour. You are not one who eats and leaves nothing on his plate for children. Did you not say it yourself? Not one who blights the happiness of others for a moment's pleasure.

ELESIN: Who speaks of pleasure? O women, listen!
Pleasure palls. Our acts should have meaning.
The sap of the plantain[7] never dries.
You have seen the young shoot swelling
Even as the parent stalk begins to wither.
Women, let my going be likened to
The twilight hour of the plantain.

WOMEN: What does he mean Iyaloja? This language is the language of our elders, we do not fully grasp it.

IYALOJA: I dare not understand you yet Elesin.

ELESIN: All you who stand before the spirit that dares
The opening of the last door of passage,
Dare to rid my going of regrets! My wish
Transcends the blotting out of thought
In one mere moment's tremor of the senses.
Do me credit. And do me honour.
I am girded for the route beyond
Burdens of waste and longing.
Then let me travel light. Let
Seed that will not serve the stomach
On the way remain behind. Let it take root
In the earth of my choice, in this earth
I leave behind.

IYALOJA: [*Turns to* WOMEN.] The voice I hear is already touched by the waiting fingers of our departed. I dare not refuse.

WOMAN: But Iyaloja . . .

IYALOJA: The matter is no longer in our hands.

WOMAN: But she is betrothed to your own son. Tell him.

IYALOJA: My son's wish is mine. I did the asking for him, the loss can be remedied. But who will remedy the blight of closed hands on the day when all should be openness and light? Tell him, you say! You wish that I burden him with knowledge that will sour his wish and lay regrets on the last moments of his mind. You pray to him who is your intercessor to the world—don't set this world adrift in your own time; would you rather it was my hand whose sacrilege wrenched it loose?

WOMAN: Not many men will brave the curse of a dispossessed husband.

IYALOJA: Only the curses of the departed are to be feared. The claims of one whose foot is on the threshold of their abode surpasses even the claims of blood. It is impiety even to place hindrances in their ways.

ELESIN: What do my mothers[8] say? Shall I step
Burdened into the unknown?

7. A plant related to the banana. It constantly regenerates itself from its young shoots ("suckers").

8. Here, a term of affection.

IYALOJA: Not we, but the very earth says No. The sap in the plantain does not dry. Let grain that will not feed the voyager at his passage drop here and take root as he steps beyond this earth and us. Oh you who fill the home from hearth to threshold with the voices of children, you who now bestride the hidden gulf and pause to draw the right foot across and into the resting-home of the great forebears, it is good that your loins be drained into the earth we know, that your last strength be ploughed back into the womb that gave you being.

PRAISE-SINGER: Iyaloja, mother of multitudes in the teeming market of the world, how your wisdom transfigures you!

IYALOJA: [*Smiling broadly, completely reconciled.*] Elesin, even at the narrow end of the passage I know you will look back and sigh a last regret for the flesh that flashed past your spirit in flight. You always had a restless eye. Your choice has my blessing. [*To the* WOMEN.] Take the good news to our daughter and make her ready. [*Some* WOMEN *go off.*]

ELESIN: Your eyes were clouded at first.

IYALOJA: Not for long. It is those who stand at the gateway of the great change to whose cry we must pay heed. And then, think of this—it makes the mind tremble. The fruit of such a union is rare. It will be neither of this world nor of the next. Nor of the one behind us. As if the timelessness of the ancestor world and the unborn have joined spirits to wring an issue of the elusive being of passage . . . Elesin!

ELESIN: I am here. What is it?

IYALOJA: Did you hear all I said just now?

ELESIN: Yes.

IYALOJA: The living must eat and drink. When the moment comes, don't turn the food to rodents' droppings in their mouth. Don't let them taste the ashes of the world when they step out at dawn to breathe the morning dew.

ELESIN: This doubt is unworthy of you Iyaloja.

IYALOJA: Eating the awusa nut is not so difficult as drinking water afterwards.[9]

ELESIN: The waters of the bitter stream are honey to a man
Whose tongue has savoured all.

IYALOJA: No one knows when the ants desert their home; they leave the mound intact. The swallow is never seen to peck holes in its nest when it is time to move with the season. There are always throngs of humanity behind the leave-taker. The rain should not come through the roof for them, the wind must not blow through the walls at night.

ELESIN: I refuse to take offence.

IYALOJA: You wish to travel light. Well, the earth is yours. But be sure the seed you leave in it attracts no curse.

ELESIN: You really mistake my person Iyaloja.

IYALOJA: I said nothing. Now we must go prepare your bridal chamber. Then these same hands will lay your shrouds.

ELESIN: [*Exasperated.*] Must you be so blunt? [*Recovers.*] Well, weave your shrouds, but let the fingers of my bride seal my eyelids with earth and wash my body.

9. The awasa nut eaten alone has a pleasant taste, but it turns bitter in the mouth if water is drunk just after.

IYALOJA: Prepare yourself Elesin.

[*She gets up to leave. At that moment the* WOMEN *return, leading the* BRIDE. ELESIN'*s face glows with pleasure. He flicks the sleeves of his agbada*[1] *with renewed confidence and steps forward to meet the group. As the girl kneels before* IYALOJA, *lights fade out on the scene.*]

Scene Two

The verandah of the District Officer's bungalow. A tango is playing from an old hand-cranked gramophone and, glimpsed through the wide windows and doors which open onto the forestage verandah, are the shapes of SIMON PILKINGS *and his wife,* JANE, *tangoing in and out of shadows in the living room. They are wearing what is immediately apparent as some form of fancy-dress. The dance goes on for some moments and then the figure of a "Native Administration"* POLICEMAN *emerges and climbs up the steps onto the verandah. He peeps through and observes the dancing couple, reacting with what is obviously a long-standing bewilderment. He stiffens suddenly, his expression changes to one of disbelief and horror. In his excitement he upsets a flower-pot and attracts the attention of the couple. They stop dancing.*

PILKINGS: Is there anyone out there?

JANE: I'll turn off the gramophone.

PILKINGS: [*Approaching the verandah.*] I'm sure I heard something fall over. [*The* CONSTABLE *retreats slowly, open-mouthed as* PILKINGS *approaches the verandah.*] Oh it's you Amusa. Why didn't you just knock instead of knocking things over?

AMUSA: [*Stammers badly and points a shaky finger at his dress.*] Mista Pirinkin . . . Mista Pirinkin . . .

PILKINGS: What is the matter with you?

JANE: [*Emerging.*] Who is it dear? Oh, Amusa . . .

PILKINGS: Yes it's Amusa, and acting most strangely.

AMUSA: [*His attention now transferred to* MRS. PILKINGS.] Mammadam[2] . . . you too!

PILKINGS: What the hell is the matter with you man!

JANE: Your costume darling. Our fancy dress.

PILKINGS: Oh hell, I'd forgotten all about that. [*Lifts the face mask over his head showing his face. His wife follows suit.*]

JANE: I think you've shocked his big pagan heart bless him.

PILKINGS: Nonsense, he's a Moslem. Come on Amusa, you don't believe in all that nonsense do you? I thought you were a good Moslem.

AMUSA: Mista Pirinkin, I beg you sir, what you think you do with that dress? It belong to dead cult, not for human being.

PILKINGS: Oh Amusa, what a let down you are. I swear by you at the club you know—thank God for Amusa, he doesn't believe in any mumbo-jumbo. And now look at you!

AMUSA: Mista Pirinkin, I beg you, take it off. Is not good for man like you to touch that cloth.

1. A long flowing robe.

2. A confused stammer of the word "madam."

PILKINGS: Well, I've got it on. And what's more Jane and I have bet on it we're taking first prize at the ball. Now, if you can just pull yourself together and tell me what you wanted to see me about . . .

AMUSA: Sir, I cannot talk this matter to you in that dress. I no fit.

PILKINGS: What's that rubbish again?

JANE: He is dead earnest too Simon. I think you'll have to handle this delicately.

PILKINGS: Delicately my . . . ! Look here Amusa, I think this little joke has gone far enough hm? Let's have some sense. You seem to forget that you are a police officer in the service of His Majesty's Government. I order you to report your business at once or face disciplinary action.

AMUSA: Sir, it is a matter of death. How can man talk against death to person in uniform of death? Is like talking against government to person in uniform of police. Please sir, I go and come back.

PILKINGS: [*Roars.*] Now! [AMUSA *switches his gaze to the ceiling suddenly, remains mute.*]

JANE: Oh Amusa, what is there to be scared of in the costume? You saw it confiscated last month from those *egungun*[3] men who were creating trouble in town. You helped arrest the cult leaders yourself—if the juju[4] didn't harm you at the time how could it possibly harm you now? And merely by looking at it?

AMUSA: [*Without looking down.*] Madam, I arrest the ringleaders who make trouble but me I no touch *egungun*. That *egungun* inself,[5] I no touch. And I no abuse 'am. I arrest ringleader but I treat *egungun* with respect.

PILKINGS: It's hopeless. We'll merely end up missing the best part of the ball. When they get this way there is nothing you can do. It's simply hammering against a brick wall. Write your report or whatever it is on that pad Amusa and take yourself out of here. Come on Jane. We only upset his delicate sensibilities by remaining here.

[AMUSA *waits for them to leave, then writes in the notebook, somewhat laboriously. Drumming from the direction of the town wells up.* AMUSA *listens, makes a movement as if he wants to recall* PILKINGS *but changes his mind. Completes his note and goes. A few moments later* PILKINGS *emerges, picks up the pad and reads.*]

Jane!

JANE: [*From the bedroom.*] Coming darling. Nearly ready.

PILKINGS: Never mind being ready, just listen to this.

JANE: What is it?

PILKINGS: Amusa's report. Listen. "I have to report that it come to my information that one prominent chief, namely, the Elesin Oba, is to commit death tonight as a result of native custom. Because this is criminal offence I await further instruction at charge office. Sergeant Amusa."

[JANE *comes out onto the verandah while he is reading.*]

JANE: Did I hear you say commit death?

PILKINGS: Obviously he means murder.

JANE: You mean a ritual murder?

3. Ancestral masks.
4. Charms and the occult power they possess.
5. Itself (pidgin English).

PILKINGS: Must be. You think you've stamped it all out but it's always lurking under the surface somewhere.

JANE: Oh. Does it mean we are not getting to the ball at all?

PILKINGS: No-o. I'll have the man arrested. Everyone remotely involved. In any case there may be nothing to it. Just rumours.

JANE: Really? I thought you found Amusa's rumours generally reliable.

PILKINGS: That's true enough. But who knows what may have been giving him the scare lately. Look at his conduct tonight.

JANE: [*Laughing.*] You have to admit he had his own peculiar logic. [*Deepens her voice.*] How can man talk against death to person in uniform of death? [*Laughs.*] Anyway, you can't go into the police station dressed like that.

PILKINGS: I'll send Joseph with instructions. Damn it, what a confounded nuisance!

JANE: But don't you think you should talk first to the man, Simon?

PILKINGS: Do you want to go to the ball or not?

JANE: Darling, why are you getting rattled? I was only trying to be intelligent. It seems hardly fair just to lock up a man—and a chief at that—simply on the er . . . what is the legal word again? uncorroborated word of a sergeant.

PILKINGS: Well, that's easily decided. Joseph!

JOSEPH: [*From within.*] Yes master.

PILKINGS: You're quite right of course, I am getting rattled. Probably the effect of those bloody drums. Do you hear how they go on and on?

JANE: I wondered when you'd notice. Do you suppose it has something to do with this affair?

PILKINGS: Who knows? They always find an excuse for making a noise . . . [*Thoughtfully.*] Even so . . .

JANE: Yes Simon?

PILKINGS: It's different Jane. I don't think I've heard this particular—sound—before. Something unsettling about it.

JANE: I thought all bush drumming sounded the same.

PILKINGS: Don't tease me now Jane. This may be serious.

JANE: I'm sorry. [*Gets up and throws her arms around his neck. Kisses him. The houseboy enters, retreats and knocks.*]

PILKINGS: [*Wearily.*] Oh, come in Joseph! I don't know where you pick up all these elephantine notions of tact. Come over here.

JOSEPH: Sir?

PILKINGS: Joseph, are you a Christian or not?

JOSEPH: Yessir.

PILKINGS: Does seeing me in this outfit bother you?

JOSEPH: No sir, it has no power.

PILKINGS: Thank God for some sanity at last. Now Joseph, answer me on the honour of a Christian—what is supposed to be going on in town tonight?

JOSEPH: Tonight sir? You mean the chief who is going to kill himself?

PILKINGS: What?

JANE: What do you mean, kill himself?

PILKINGS: You do mean he is going to kill somebody don't you?

JOSEPH: No master. He will not kill anybody and no one will kill him. He will simply die.

JANE: But why Joseph?

JOSEPH: It is native law and custom. The King die last month. Tonight is his burial. But before they can bury him, the Elesin must die so as to accompany him to heaven.

PILKINGS: I seem to be fated to clash more often with that man than with any of the other chiefs.

JOSEPH: He is the King's Chief Horseman.

PILKINGS: [*In a resigned way.*] I know.

JANE: Simon, what's the matter?

PILKINGS: It would have to be him!

JANE: Who is he?

PILKINGS: Don't you remember? He's that chief with whom I had a scrap some three or four years ago. I helped his son get to a medical school in England, remember? He fought tooth and nail to prevent it.

JANE: Oh now I remember. He was that very sensitive young man. What was his name again?

PILKINGS: Olunde.[6] Haven't replied to his last letter come to think of it. The old pagan wanted him to stay and carry on some family tradition or the other. Honestly I couldn't understand the fuss he made. I literally had to help the boy escape from close confinement and load him onto the next boat. A most intelligent boy, really bright.

JANE: I rather thought he was much too sensitive you know. The kind of person you feel should be a poet munching rose petals in Bloomsbury.[7]

PILKINGS: Well, he's going to make a first-class doctor. His mind is set on that. And as long as he wants my help he is welcome to it.

JANE: [*After a pause.*] Simon.

PILKINGS: Yes?

JANE: This boy, he was the eldest son wasn't he?

PILKINGS: I'm not sure. Who could tell with that old ram?

JANE: Do you know, Joseph?

JOSEPH: Oh yes madam. He was the eldest son. That's why Elesin cursed master good and proper. The eldest son is not supposed to travel away from the land.

JANE: [*Giggling.*] Is that true Simon? Did he really curse you good and proper?

PILKINGS: By all accounts I should be dead by now.

JOSEPH: Oh no, master is white man. And good Christian. Black man juju can't touch master.

JANE: If he was his eldest, it means that he would be the Elesin to the next king. It's a family thing isn't it Joseph?

JOSEPH: Yes madam. And if this Elesin had died before the King, his eldest son must take his place.

JANE: That would explain why the old chief was so mad you took the boy away.

PILKINGS: Well it makes me all the more happy I did.

6. "My lord or deliverer has come"; a contraction of Olumide.

7. An area in central London associated with a brilliant group of writers in the years between the world wars; Virginia Woolf was the principal figure among them.

JANE: I wonder if he knew.

PILKINGS: Who? Oh, you mean Olunde?

JANE: Yes. Was that why he was so determined to get away? I wouldn't stay if I knew I was trapped in such a horrible custom.

PILKINGS: [*Thoughtfully.*] No, I don't think he knew. At least he gave no indication. But you couldn't really tell with him. He was rather close you know, quite unlike most of them. Didn't give much away, not even to me.

JANE: Aren't they all rather close, Simon?

PILKINGS: These natives here? Good gracious. They'll open their mouths and yap with you about their family secrets before you can stop them. Only the other day . . .

JANE: But Simon, do they really give anything away? I mean, anything that really counts. This affair for instance, we didn't know they still practised that custom did we?

PILKINGS: Ye-e-es, I suppose you're right there. Sly, devious bastards.

JOSEPH: [*Stiffly.*] Can I go now master? I have to clean the kitchen.

PILKINGS: What? Oh, you can go. Forgot you were still here.

[JOSEPH goes.]

JANE: Simon, you really must watch your language. Bastard isn't just a simple swear-word in these parts, you know.

PILKINGS: Look, just when did you become a social anthropologist, that's what I'd like to know.

JANE: I'm not claiming to know anything. I just happen to have overheard quarrels among the servants. That's how I know they consider it a smear.

PILKINGS: I thought the extended family system took care of all that. Elastic family, no bastards.

JANE: [*Shrugs.*] Have it your own way.

[*Awkward silence. The drumming increases in volume.* JANE *gets up suddenly, restless.*]

That drumming Simon, do you think it might really be connected with this ritual? It's been going on all evening.

PILKINGS: Let's ask our native guide. Joseph! Just a minute Joseph. [JOSEPH *re-enters.*] What's the drumming about?

JOSEPH: I don't know master.

PILKINGS: What do you mean you don't know? It's only two years since your conversion. Don't tell me all that holy water nonsense also wiped out your tribal memory.

JOSEPH: [*Visibly shocked.*] Master!

JANE: Now you've done it.

PILKINGS: What have I done now?

JANE: Never mind. Listen Joseph, just tell me this. Is that drumming connected with dying or anything of that nature?

JOSEPH: Madam, this is what I am trying to say: I am not sure. It sounds like the death of a great chief and then, it sounds like the wedding of a great chief. It really mix me up.

PILKINGS: Oh get back to the kitchen. A fat lot of help you are.

JOSEPH: Yes master. [*Goes.*]

JANE: Simon . . .

PILKINGS: All right, all right. I'm in no mood for preaching.

JANE: It isn't my preaching you have to worry about, it's the preaching of the missionaries who preceded you here. When they make converts they really convert them. Calling holy water nonsense to our Joseph is really like insulting the Virgin Mary before a Roman Catholic. He's going to hand in his notice tomorrow you mark my word.

PILKINGS: Now you're being ridiculous.

JANE: Am I? What are you willing to bet that tomorrow we are going to be without a steward-boy? Did you see his face?

PILKINGS: I am more concerned about whether or not we will be one native chief short by tomorrow. Christ! Just listen to those drums. [*He strides up and down, undecided.*]

JANE: [*Getting up.*] I'll change and make up some supper.

PILKINGS: What's that?

JANE: Simon, it's obvious we have to miss this ball.

PILKINGS: Nonsense. It's the first bit of real fun the European club has managed to organise for over a year, I'm damned if I'm going to miss it. And it is a rather special occasion. Doesn't happen every day.

JANE: You know this business has to be stopped Simon. And you are the only man who can do it.

PILKINGS: I don't have to stop anything. If they want to throw themselves off the top of a cliff or poison themselves for the sake of some barbaric custom what is that to me? If it were ritual murder or something like that I'd be duty-bound to do something. I can't keep an eye on all the potential suicides in this province. And as for that man—believe me it's good riddance.

JANE: [*Laughs.*] I know you better than that Simon. You are going to have to do something to stop it—after you've finished blustering.

PILKINGS: [*Shouts after her.*] And suppose after all it's only a wedding? I'd look a proper fool if I interrupted a chief on his honeymoon, wouldn't I? [*Resumes his angry stride, slows down.*] Ah well, who can tell what those chiefs actually do on their honeymoon anyway? [*He takes up the pad and scribbles rapidly on it.*] Joseph! Joseph! Joseph! [*Some moments later* JOSEPH *puts in a sulky appearance.*] Did you hear me call you? Why the hell didn't you answer?

JOSEPH: I didn't hear master.

PILKINGS: You didn't hear me! How come you are here then?

JOSEPH: [*Stubbornly.*] I didn't hear master.

PILKINGS: [*Controls himself with an effort.*] We'll talk about it in the morning. I want you to take this note directly to Sergeant Amusa. You'll find him at the charge office. Get on your bicycle and race there with it. I expect you back in twenty minutes exactly. Twenty minutes, is that clear?

JOSEPH: Yes master [*Going.*]

PILKINGS: Oh er . . . Joseph.

JOSEPH: Yes master?

PILKINGS: [*Between gritted teeth.*] Er . . . forget what I said just now. The holy water is not nonsense. *I* was talking nonsense.

JOSEPH: Yes master [*Goes.*]

JANE: [*Pokes her head round the door.*] Have you found him?

PILKINGS: Found who?

JANE: Joseph. Weren't you shouting for him?

PILKINGS: Oh yes, he turned up finally.

JANE: You sounded desperate. What was it all about?

PILKINGS: Oh nothing. I just wanted to apologise to him. Assure him that the holy water isn't really nonsense.

JANE: Oh? And how did he take it?

PILKINGS: Who the hell gives a damn! I had a sudden vision of our Very Reverend Macfarlane[8] drafting another letter of complaint to the Resident about my unchristian language towards his parishioners.

JANE: Oh I think he's given up on you by now.

PILKINGS: Don't be too sure. And anyway, I wanted to make sure Joseph didn't "lose" my note on the way. He looked sufficiently full of the holy crusade to do some such thing.

JANE: If you've finished exaggerating, come and have something to eat.

PILKINGS: No, put it all away. We can still get to the ball.

JANE: Simon . . .

PILKINGS: Get your costume back on. Nothing to worry about. I've instructed Amusa to arrest the man and lock him up.

JANE: But that station is hardly secure Simon. He'll soon get his friends to help him escape.

PILKINGS: A-ah, that's where I have out-thought you. I'm not having him put in the station cell. Amusa will bring him right here and lock him up in my study. And he'll stay with him till we get back. No one will dare come here to incite him to anything.

JANE: How clever of you darling. I'll get ready.

PILKINGS: Hey.

JANE: Yes darling.

PILKINGS: I have a surprise for you. I was going to keep it until we actually got to the ball.

JANE: What is it?

PILKINGS: You know the Prince is on a tour of the colonies don't you? Well, he docked in the capital only this morning but he is already at the Residency. He is going to grace the ball with his presence later tonight.

JANE: Simon! Not really.

PILKINGS: Yes he is. He's been invited to give away the prizes and he has agreed. You must admit old Engleton is the best Club Secretary we ever had. Quick off the mark that lad.

JANE: But how thrilling.

PILKINGS: The other provincials are going to be damned envious.

JANE: I wonder what he'll come as.

PILKINGS: Oh I don't know. As a coat-of-arms perhaps. Anyway it won't be anything to touch this.

JANE: Well that's lucky. If we are to be presented I won't have to start looking for a pair of gloves. It's all sewn on.[9]

8. Irish priests were predominant in Catholic missionary activity in Nigeria.

9. The masquerade costume is designed to cover the entire body of the wearer, to conceal his or her identity.

PILKINGS: [*Laughing.*] Quite right. Trust a woman to think of that. Come on, let's get going.

JANE: [*Rushing off.*] Won't be a second. [*Stops.*] Now I see why you've been so edgy all evening. I thought you weren't handling this affair with your usual brilliance—to begin with, that is.

PILKINGS: [*His mood is much improved.*] Shut up woman and get your things on.

JANE: All right boss, coming.

[PILKINGS *suddenly begins to hum the tango to which they were dancing before. Starts to execute a few practice steps. Lights fade.*]

Scene Three

A swelling, agitated hum of women's voices rises immediately in the background. The lights come on and we see the frontage of a converted cloth stall in the market. The floor leading up to the entrance is covered in rich velvets and woven cloth. The WOMEN *come on stage, borne backwards by the determined progress of Sergeant* AMUSA *and his two* CONSTABLES *who already have their batons out and use them as a pressure against the* WOMEN. *At the edge of the cloth-covered floor however the* WOMEN *take a determined stand and block all further progress of the* MEN. *They begin to tease them mercilessly.*

AMUSA: I am tell you women for last time to commot my road.[1] I am here on official business.

WOMAN: Official business you white man's eunuch? Official business is taking place where you want to go and it's a business you wouldn't understand.

WOMAN: [*Makes a quick tug at the* CONSTABLE'*s baton.*] That doesn't fool anyone you know. It's the one you carry under your government knickers that counts. [*She bends low as if to peep under the baggy shorts. The embarrassed* CONSTABLE *quickly puts his knees together. The* WOMEN *roar.*]

WOMAN: You mean there is nothing there at all?

WOMAN: Oh there was something. You know that handbell which the whiteman uses to summon his servants . . . ?

AMUSA: [*He manages to preserve some dignity throughout.*] I hope you women know that interfering with officer in execution of his duty is criminal offence.

WOMAN: Interfere? He says we're interfering with him. You foolish man we're telling you there's nothing to interfere with.

AMUSA: I am order you now to clear the road.

WOMAN: What road? The one your father built?

WOMAN: You are a policeman not so? Then you know what they call trespassing in court. Or—[*pointing to the cloth-lined steps*]—do you think that kind of road is built for every kind of feet.

WOMAN: Go back and tell the white man who sent you to come himself.

AMUSA: If I go I will come back with reinforcement. And we will all return carrying weapons.

1. Get out of my way.

WOMAN: Oh, now I understand. Before they can put on those knickers the white man first cuts off their weapons.

WOMAN: What a cheek! You mean you come here to show power to women and you don't even have a weapon.

AMUSA: [*Shouting above the laughter.*] For the last time I warn you women to clear the road.

WOMAN: To where?

AMUSA: To that hut. I know he dey dere.

WOMAN: Who?

AMUSA: The chief who call himself Elesin Oba.

WOMAN: You ignorant man. It is not he who calls himself Elesin Oba, it is his blood that says it. As it called out to his father before him and will to his son after him. And that is in spite of everything your white man can do.

WOMAN: Is it not the same ocean that washes this land and the white man's land? Tell your white man he can hide our son away as long as he likes. When the time comes for him, the same ocean will bring him back.

AMUSA: The government say dat kin' ting[2] must stop.

WOMAN: Who will stop it? You? Tonight our husband and father will prove himself greater than the laws of strangers.

AMUSA: I tell you nobody go prove anything tonight or anytime. Is ignorant and criminal to prove dat kin' prove.

IYALOJA: [*Entering from the hut. She is accompanied by a group of young girls who have been attending the* BRIDE.] What is it Amusa? Why do you come here to disturb the happiness of others.

AMUSA: Madame Iyaloja, I glad you come. You know me, I no like trouble but duty is duty. I am here to arrest Elesin for criminal intent. Tell these women to stop obstructing me in the performance of my duty.

IYALOJA: And you? What gives you the right to obstruct our leader of men in the performance of his duty.

AMUSA: What kin' duty be dat one Iyaloja.

IYALOJA: What kin' duty? What kin' duty does a man have to his new bride?

AMUSA: [*Bewildered, looks at the women and at the entrance to the hut.*] Iyaloja, is it wedding you call dis kin' ting?

IYALOJA: You have wives haven't you? Whatever the white man has done to you he hasn't stopped you having wives. And if he has, at least he is married. If you don't know what a marriage is, go and ask him to tell you.

AMUSA: This no to wedding.[3]

IYALOJA: And ask him at the same time what he would have done if anyone had come to disturb him on his wedding night.

AMUSA: Iyaloja, I say dis no to wedding.

IYALOJA: You want to look inside the bridal chamber? You want to see for yourself how a man cuts the virgin knot?

AMUSA: Madam . . .

WOMAN: Perhaps his wives are still waiting for him to learn.

AMUSA: Iyaloja, make you tell dese women make den no insult me again. If I hear dat kin' insult once more . . .

2. That kind of thing.

3. This is not a wedding.

GIRL: [*Pushing her way through.*] You will do what?

GIRL: He's out of his mind. It's our mothers you're talking to, do you know that? Not to any illiterate villager you can bully and terrorise. How dare you intrude here anyway?

GIRL: What a cheek, what impertinence!

GIRL: You've treated them too gently. Now let them see what it is to tamper with the mothers of this market.

GIRL: Your betters dare not enter the market when the women say no!

GIRL: Haven't you learnt that yet, you jester in khaki and starch?

IYALOJA: Daughters . . .

GIRL: No no Iyaloja, leave us to deal with him. He no longer knows his mother, we'll teach him.

[*With a sudden movement they snatch the batons of the two* CONSTABLES. *They begin to hem them in.*]

GIRL: What next? We have your batons? What next? What are you going to do?

[*With equally swift movements they knock off their hats.*]

GIRL: Move if you dare. We have your hats, what will you do about it? Didn't the white man teach you to take off your hats before women?

IYALOJA: It's a wedding night. It's a night of joy for us. Peace . . .

GIRL: Not for him. Who asked him here?

GIRL: Does he dare go to the Residency without an invitation?

GIRL: Not even where the servants eat the left-overs.

GIRLS: [*In turn. In an "English" accent.*] Well well it's Mister Amusa. Were you invited? [*Play acting to one another. The older* WOMEN *encourage them with their titters.*]

—Your invitation card please?
—Who are you? Have we been introduced?
—And who did you say you were?
—Sorry, I didn't quite catch your name.
—May I take your hat?
—If you insist. May I take yours? [*Exchanging the* POLICEMEN's *hats.*]
—How very kind of you.
—Not at all. Won't you sit down?
—After you.
—Oh no.
—I insist.
—You're most gracious.
—And how do you find the place?
—The natives are all right.
—Friendly?
—Tractable.
—Not a teeny-weeny bit restless?
—Well, a teeny-weeny bit restless.
—One might, even say, difficult?
—Indeed one might be tempted to say, difficult.
—But you do manage to cope?
—Yes indeed I do. I have a rather faithful ox called Amusa.
—He's loyal?

—Absolutely.
—Lay down his life for you what?
—Without a moment's thought.
—Had one like that once. Trust him with my life.
—Mostly of course they are liars.
—Never known a native to tell the truth.
—Does it get rather close around here?
—It's mild for this time of the year.
—But the rains may still come.
—They are late this year aren't they?
—They are keeping African time.[4]
—Ha ha ha ha
—Ha ha ha ha
—The humidity is what gets me.
—It used to be whisky
—Ha ha ha ha
—Ha ha ha ha
—What's your handicap old chap?
—Is there racing by golly?
—Splendid golf course, you'll like it.
—I'm beginning to like it already.
—And a European club, exclusive.
—You've kept the flag flying.
—We do our best for the old country.
—It's a pleasure to serve.
—Another whisky old chap?
—You are indeed too too kind.
—Not at all sir. Where is that boy? [*With a sudden bellow.*] Sergeant!

AMUSA: [*Snaps to attention.*] Yessir!

[*The* WOMEN *collapse with laughter.*]

GIRL: Take your men out of here.

AMUSA: [*Realising the trick, he rages from loss of face.*] I'm give you warning . . .

GIRL: All right then. Off with his knickers! [*They surge slowly forward.*]

IYALOJA: Daughters, please.

AMUSA: [*Squaring himself for defence.*] The first woman wey touch me . . .

IYALOJA: My children, I beg of you . . .

GIRL: Then tell him to leave this market. This is the home of our mothers. We don't want the eater of white left-overs at the feast their hands have prepared.

IYALOJA: You heard them Amusa. You had better go.

GIRL: Now!

AMUSA: [*Commencing his retreat.*] We dey go now, but make you no say we no warn you.[5]

GIRLS: Now!

4. A standard colonial prejudice was that Africans lack a sense of time.

5. Don't say that we didn't warn you.

GIRL: Before we read the riot act—you should know all about that.

AMUSA: Make we go. [*They depart, more precipitately.*]

[*The* WOMEN *strike their palms across in the gesture of wonder.*]

WOMEN: Do they teach you all that at school?

WOMAN: And to think I nearly kept Apinke[6] away from the place.

WOMAN: Did you hear them? Did you see how they mimicked the white man?

WOMAN: The voices exactly. Hey, there are wonders in this world!

IYALOJA: Well, our elders have said it: Dada[7] may be weak, but he has a younger sibling who is truly fearless.

WOMAN: The next time the white man shows his face in this market I will set Wuraola[8] on his tail.

[*A* WOMAN *bursts into song and dance of euphoria—"Tani l'awa o l'ogbeja? Kayi! A l'ogbeja. Omo Kekere l'ogbeja."*[9] *The rest of the* WOMEN *join in, some placing the* GIRLS *on their back like infants, others dancing round them. The dance becomes general, mounting in excitement.* ELESIN *appears, in wrapper only. In his hands a white velvet cloth folded loosely as if it held some delicate object. He cries out.*]

ELESIN: Oh you mothers of beautiful brides! [*The dancing stops. They turn and see him, and the object in his hands.* IYALOJA *approaches and gently takes the cloth from him.*] Take it. It is no mere virgin stain, but the union of life and the seeds of passage. My vital flow, the last from this flesh is intermingled with the promise of future life. All is prepared. Listen! [*A steady drum beat from the distance.*] Yes. It is nearly time. The King's dog has been killed. The King's favourite horse is about to follow his master. My brother chiefs know their task and perform it well. [*He listens again.*]

[*The* BRIDE *emerges, stands shyly by the door. He turns to her.*]

Our marriage is not yet wholly fulfilled. When earth and passage wed, the consummation is complete only when there are grains of earth on the eyelids of passage. Stay by me till then. My faithful drummers, do me your last service. This is where I have chosen to do my leave-taking, in this heart of life, this hive which contains the swarm of the world in its small compass. This is where I have known love and laughter away from the palace. Even the richest food cloys when eaten days on end; in the market, nothing ever cloys. Listen. [*They listen to the drums.*] They have begun to seek out the heart of the King's favourite horse. Soon it will ride in its bolt of raffia[1] with the dog at its feet. Together they will ride on the shoulders of the King's grooms through the pulse centres of the town. They know it is here I shall await them. I have told them. [*His eyes appear to cloud. He passes his hand over them as if to clear his sight. He gives a faint smile.*] It promises well; just then I felt my spirit's eagerness. The kite makes for wide spaces and the wind creeps up behind its tail; can the kite say less than—thank you, the quicker the better? But wait a while my spirit. Wait. Wait for the coming of

6. "One Who Is Equally Cherished by All"; the name of one of the girls.
7. A child born with tangled hair.
8. "Dear as Gold"; a woman's name.
9. Who says we haven't a defender? Silence! We have our defenders. Little children are our champions [Author's translation].
1. The stem of this shrub is used for the decorative skirt worn in many African dances.

the courier of the King. Do you know friends, the horse is born to this one destiny, to bear the burden that is man upon its back. Except for this night, this night alone when the spotless stallion will ride in triumph on the back of man. In the time of my father I witnessed the strange sight. Perhaps tonight also I shall see it for the last time. If they arrive before the drums beat for me, I shall tell him to let the Alafin[2] know I follow swiftly. If they come after the drums have sounded, why then, all is well for I have gone ahead. Our spirits shall fall in step along the great passage. [*He listens to the drums. He seems again to be falling into a state of semi-hypnosis; his eyes scan the sky but it is in a kind of daze. His voice is a little breathless.*] The moon has fed, a glow from its full stomach fills the sky and air, but I cannot tell where is that gateway through which I must pass. My faithful friends, let our feet touch together this last time, lead me into the other market with sounds that cover my skin with down yet make my limbs strike earth like a thoroughbred. Dear mothers, let me dance into the passage even as I have lived beneath your roofs. [*He comes down progressively among them. They make way for him, the drummers playing. His dance is one of solemn, regal motions, each gesture of the body is made with a solemn finality. The* WOMEN *join him, their steps a somewhat more fluid version of his. Beneath the* PRAISE-SINGER*'s exhortations the* WOMEN *dirge "Ale le le, awo mi lo."*]

PRAISE-SINGER: Elesin Alafin, can you hear my voice?
ELESIN: Faintly, my friend, faintly.
PRAISE-SINGER: Elesin Alafin, can you hear my call?
ELESIN: Faintly my king, faintly.
PRAISE-SINGER: Is your memory sound Elesin?
Shall my voice be a blade of grass and
Tickle the armpit of the past?
ELESIN: My memory needs no prodding but
What do you wish to say to me?
PRAISE-SINGER: Only what has been spoken. Only what concerns
The dying wish of the father of all.
ELESIN: It is buried like seed-yam in my mind
This is the season of quick rains, the harvest
Is this moment due for gathering.
PRAISE-SINGER: If you cannot come, I said, swear
You'll tell my favourite horse. I shall
Ride on through the gates alone.
ELESIN: Elesin's message will be read
Only when his loyal heart no longer beats.
PRAISE-SINGER: If you cannot come Elesin, tell my dog.
I cannot stay the keeper too long
At the gate.
ELESIN: A dog does not outrun the hand
That feeds it meat. A horse that throws its rider
Slows down to a stop. Elesin Alafin
Trusts no beasts with messages between
A king and his companion.

2. "Owner of the Palace" (literal trans.); the title of the king of Oyo.

PRAISE-SINGER: If you get lost my dog will track
The hidden path to me.
ELESIN: The seven-way crossroads confuses
Only the stranger. The Horseman of the King
Was born in the recesses of the house.
PRAISE-SINGER: I know the wickedness of men. If there is
Weight on the loose end of your sash, such weight
As no mere man can shift; if your sash is earthed
By evil minds who mean to part us at the last . . .
ELESIN: My sash is of the deep purple *alari*;
It is no tethering-rope. The elephant
Trails no tethering-rope; that king
Is not yet crowned who will peg an elephant—
Not even you my friend and King.
PRAISE-SINGER: And yet this fear will not depart from me
The darkness of this new abode is deep—
Will your human eyes suffice?
ELESIN: In a night which falls before our eyes
However deep, we do not miss our way.
PRAISE-SINGER: Shall I now not acknowledge I have stood
Where wonders met their end? The elephant deserves
Better than that we say "I have caught
A glimpse of something."[3] If we see the tamer
Of the forest let us say plainly, we have seen
An elephant.
ELESIN: [*His voice is drowsy.*]
I have freed myself of earth and now
It's getting dark. Strange voices guide my feet.
PRAISE-SINGER: The river is never so high that the eyes
Of a fish are covered. The night is not so dark
That the albino fails to find his way.[4] A child
Returning homewards craves no leading by the hand.
Gracefully does the mask[5] regain his grove at the end of the day . . .
Gracefully. Gracefully does the mask dance
Homeward at the end of the day, gracefully . . .
[ELESIN'*s trance appears to be deepening, his steps heavier.*]
IYALOJA: It is the death of war that kills the valiant,
Death of water is how the swimmer goes
It is the death of markets that kills the trader
And death of indecision takes the idle away
The trade of the cutlass blunts its edge
And the beautiful die the death of beauty.
It takes an Elesin to die the death of death . . .
Only Elesin . . . dies the unknowable death of death . . .

3. A Yoruba saying, meaning that an outstanding person or deed must be granted proper recognition.
4. Many albinos have poor eyesight.
5. Of the *egungun* masquerade.

Gracefully, gracefully does the horseman regain
The stables at the end of day, gracefully . . .

PRAISE-SINGER: How shall I tell what my eyes have seen? The Horseman gallops on before the courier, how shall I tell what my eyes have seen? He says a dog may be confused by new scents of beings he never dreamt of, so he must precede the dog to heaven. He says a horse may stumble on strange boulders and be lamed, so he races on before the horse to heaven. It is best, he says, to trust no messenger who may falter at the outer gate, oh how shall I tell what my ears have heard? But do you hear me still Elesin, do you hear your faithful one?

[ELESIN *in his motions appears to feel for a direction of sound, subtly, but he only sinks deeper into his trance dance.*]

Elesin Alafin, I no longer sense your flesh. The drums are changing now but you have gone far ahead of the world. It is not yet noon in heaven; let those who claim it is begin their own journey home. So why must you rush like an impatient bride: why do you race to desert your Olohun-iyo?

[ELESIN *is now sunk fully deep in his trance, there is no longer sign of any awareness of his surroundings.*]

Does the deep voice of *gbedu*[6] cover you then, like the passage of royal elephants? Those drums that brook no rivals, have they blocked the passage to your ears that my voice passes into wind, a mere leaf floating in the night? Is your flesh lightened Elesin, is that lump of earth I slid between your slippers to keep you longer slowly sifting from your feet? Are the drums on the other side now tuning skin to skin with ours in *osugbo*?[7] Are there sounds there I cannot hear, do footsteps surround you which pound the earth like *gbedu*, roll like thunder round the dome of the world? Is the darkness gathering in your head Elesin? Is there now a streak of light at the end of the passage, a light I dare not look upon? Does it reveal whose voices we often heard, whose touches we often felt, whose wisdoms come suddenly into the mind when the wisest have shaken their heads and murmured: It cannot be done? Elesin Alafin, don't think I do not know why your lips are heavy, why your limbs are drowsy as palm oil in the cold of harmattan.[8] I would call you back but when the elephant heads for the jungle, the tail is too small a handhold for the hunter that would pull him back. The sun that heads for the sea no longer heeds the prayers of the farmer. When the river begins to taste the salt of the ocean, we no longer know what deity to call on, the river-god or Olokun.[9] No arrow flies back to the string, the child does not return through the same passage that gave it birth. Elesin Oba, can you hear me at all? Your eyelids are glazed like a courtesan's, is it that you see the dark groom and master of life? And will you see my father? Will you tell him that I stayed with you to the last? Will my voice ring in your ears awhile, will you remember Olohun-iyo even if the music on the other side surpasses his mortal craft? But will they know you over there? Have they eyes to gauge

6. Drums. Their deep resonance is caused by the hardwood from which they are made.
7. The secret executive cult of the Yoruba; its meeting place [Author's note].
8. A sharp, dry wind from the Sahara that blows over western Africa in December. The wind brings dust and noticeably cools the air. Palm oil congeals in cold weather and is thus said to sleep. Compare the American "slow as molasses in January."
9. Goddess of the sea.

your worth, have they the heart to love you, will they know what thoroughbred prances towards them in caparisons[1] of honour? If they do not Elesin, if any there cuts your yam with a small knife, or pours you wine in a small calabash, turn back and return to welcoming hands. If the world were not greater than the wishes of Olohun-iyo, I would not let you go . . .

[He appears to break down. ELESIN *dances on, completely in a trance. The dirge wells up louder and stronger.* ELESIN*'s dance does not lose its elasticity but his gestures become, if possible, even more weighty. Lights fade slowly on the scene.]*

Scene Four

A Masque. The front side of the stage is part of a wide corridor around the great hall of the Residency extending beyond vision into the rear and wings. It is redolent of the tawdry decadence of a far-flung but key imperial frontier. The COUPLES *in a variety of fancy-dress are ranged around the walls, gazing in the same direction. The guest-of-honour is about to make an appearance. A portion of the local police brass band with its white* CONDUCTOR *is just visible. At last, the entrance of* ROYALTY. *The band plays "Rule Britannia," badly, beginning long before he is visible. The couples bow and curtsey as he passes by them. Both he and his companions are dressed in seventeenth century European costume. Following behind are the* RESIDENT *and his* PARTNER *similarly attired. As they gain the end of the hall where the orchestra dais begins the music comes to an end. The* PRINCE *bows to the guests. The* BAND *strikes up a Viennese waltz and the* PRINCE *formally opens the floor. Several bars later the* RESIDENT *and his companion follow suit. Others follow in appropriate pecking order. The orchestra's waltz rendition is not of the highest musical standard.*

Some time later the PRINCE *dances again into view and is settled into a corner by the* RESIDENT *who then proceeds to select* COUPLES *as they dance past for introduction, sometimes threading his way through the dancers to tap the lucky* COUPLE *on the shoulder. Desperate efforts from many to ensure that they are recognised in spite of perhaps, their costume. The ritual of introductions soon takes in* PILKINGS *and his* WIFE. *The* PRINCE *is quite fascinated by their costume and they demonstrate the adaptations they have made to it, pulling down the mask to demonstrate how the* egungun *normally appears, then showing the various press-button controls they have innovated for the face flaps, the sleeves, etc. They demonstrate the dance steps and the guttural sounds made by the* egungun, *harass other dancers in the hall,* MRS. PILKINGS *playing the "restrainer"[2] to* PILKINGS' *manic darts. Everyone is highly entertained, the Royal Party especially who lead the applause.*

At this point a liveried FOOTMAN *comes in with a note on a salver and is intercepted almost absent-mindedly by the* RESIDENT *who takes the note and reads it. After polite coughs he succeeds in excusing the* PILKINGS *from the* PRINCE *and takes them aside. The* PRINCE *considerately offers the* RESIDENT'S WIFE *his hand and dancing is resumed.*

On their way out the RESIDENT *gives an order to his* AIDE-DE-CAMP. *They come into the side corridor where the* RESIDENT *hands the note to* PILKINGS.

1. Rich ceremonial cloth draped over the saddle of a horse.
2. Masqueraders sometimes become possessed and go berserk; ropes are, therefore, tied to their waists and held by "restrainers."

RESIDENT: As you see it says "emergency" on the outside. I took the liberty of opening it because His Highness was obviously enjoying the entertainment. I didn't want to interrupt unless really necessary.

PILKINGS: Yes, yes of course, sir.

RESIDENT: Is it really as bad as it says? What's it all about?

PILKINGS: Some strange custom they have, sir. It seems because the King is dead some important chief has to commit suicide.

RESIDENT: The King? Isn't it the same one who died nearly a month ago?

PILKINGS: Yes, sir.

RESIDENT: Haven't they buried him yet?

PILKINGS: They take their time about these things, sir. The pre-burial ceremonies last nearly thirty days. It seems tonight is the final night.

RESIDENT: But what has it got to do with the market women? Why are they rioting? We've waived that troublesome tax haven't we?

PILKINGS: We don't quite know that they are exactly rioting yet, sir. Sergeant Amusa is sometimes prone to exaggerations.

RESIDENT: He sounds desperate enough. That comes out even in his rather quaint grammar. Where is the man anyway? I asked my aide-de-camp to bring him here.

PILKINGS: They are probably looking in the wrong verandah. I'll fetch him myself.

RESIDENT: No no you stay here. Let your wife go and look for them. Do you mind my dear . . . ?

JANE: Certainly not, your Excellency. [*Goes.*]

RESIDENT: You should have kept me informed, Pilkings. You realise how disastrous it would have been if things had erupted while His Highness was here.

PILKINGS: I wasn't aware of the whole business until tonight, sir.

RESIDENT: Nose to the ground Pilkings, nose to the ground. If we all let these little things slip past us where would the empire be eh? Tell me that. Where would we all be?

PILKINGS: [*Low voice.*] Sleeping peacefully at home I bet.

RESIDENT: What did you say, Pilkings?

PILKINGS: It won't happen again, sir.

RESIDENT: It mustn't, Pilkings. It mustn't. Where is that damned sergeant? I ought to get back to His Highness as quickly as possible and offer him some plausible explanation for my rather abrupt conduct. Can you think of one, Pilkings?

PILKINGS: You could tell him the truth, sir.

RESIDENT: I could? No no no no Pilkings, that would never do. What! Go and tell him there is a riot just two miles away from him? This is supposed to be a secure colony of His Majesty, Pilkings.

PILKINGS: Yes, sir.

RESIDENT: Ah, there they are. No, these are not our native police. Are these the ring-leaders of the riot?

PILKINGS: Sir, these are my police officers.

RESIDENT: Oh, I beg your pardon officers. You do look a little . . . I say, isn't there something missing in their uniform? I think they used to have some rather colourful sashes. If I remember rightly I recommended them myself in my young days in the service. A bit of colour always appeals to the natives, yes, I remember putting that in my report. Well well well, where are we? Make your report man.

PILKINGS: [*Moves close to* AMUSA, *between his teeth.*] And let's have no more superstitious nonsense from you Amusa or I'll throw you in the guardroom for a month and feed you pork![3]

RESIDENT: What's that? What has pork to do with it?

PILKINGS: Sir, I was just warning him to be brief. I'm sure you are most anxious to hear his report.

RESIDENT: Yes yes yes of course. Come on man, speak up. Hey, didn't we give them some colourful fez[4] hats with all those wavy things, yes, pink tassells . . .

PILKINGS: Sir, I think if he was permitted to make his report we might find that he lost his hat in the riot.

RESIDENT: Ah yes indeed. I'd better tell His Highness that. Lost his hat in the riot, ha ha. He'll probably say well, as long as he didn't lose his head. [*Chuckles to himself.*] Don't forget to send me a report first thing in the morning young Pilkings.

PILKINGS: No, sir.

RESIDENT: And whatever you do, don't let things get out of hand. Keep a cool head and—nose to the ground Pilkings. [*Wanders off in the general direction of the hall.*]

PILKINGS: Yes, sir.

AIDE-DE-CAMP: Would you be needing me, sir?

PILKINGS: No thanks, Bob. I think His Excellency's need of you is greater than ours.

AIDE-DE-CAMP: We have a detachment of soldiers from the capital, sir. They accompanied His Highness up here.

PILKINGS: I doubt if it will come to that but, thanks, I'll bear it in mind. Oh, could you send an orderly with my cloak.

AIDE-DE-CAMP: Very good, sir. [*Goes.*]

PILKINGS: Now, sergeant.

AMUSA: Sir . . . [*Makes an effort, stops dead. Eyes to the ceiling.*]

PILKINGS: Oh, not again.

AMUSA: I cannot against death to dead cult. This dress get power of dead.

PILKINGS: All right, let's go. You are relieved of all further duty Amusa. Report to me first thing in the morning.

JANE: Shall I come, Simon?

PILKINGS: No, there's no need for that. If I can get back later I will. Otherwise get Bob to bring you home.

JANE: Be careful Simon . . . I mean, be clever.

PILKINGS: Sure I will. You two, come with me. [*As he turns to go, the clock in the Residency begins to chime.* PILKINGS *looks at his watch then turns, horror-stricken, to stare at his wife. The same thought clearly occurs to her. He swallows hard. An* ORDERLY *brings his cloak.*] It's midnight. I had no idea it was that late.

3. Muslims are prohibited from eating pork.
4. Red caps worn by African officials in the colonial service.

JANE: But surely . . . they don't count the hours the way we do. The moon, or something . . .

PILKINGS: I am . . . not so sure.

[*He turns and breaks into a sudden run. The two* CONSTABLES *follow, also at a run.* AMUSA, *who has kept his eyes on the ceiling throughout waits until the last of the footsteps has faded out of hearing. He salutes suddenly, but without once looking in the direction of the* WOMAN.]

AMUSA: Goodnight, madam.

JANE: Oh. [*She hesitates.*] Amusa . . . [*He goes off without seeming to have heard.*] Poor Simon . . . [*A figure emerges from the shadows, a young black* MAN *dressed in a sober western suit. He peeps into the hall, trying to make out the figures of the dancers.*]
Who is that?

OLUNDE: [*Emerges into the light.*] I didn't mean to startle you madam. I am looking for the District Officer.

JANE: Wait a minute . . . don't I know you? Yes, you are Olunde, the young man who . . .

OLUNDE: Mrs. Pilkings! How fortunate. I came here to look for your husband.

JANE: Olunde! Let's look at you. What a fine young man you've become. Grand but solemn. Good God, when did you return? Simon never said a word. But you do look well Olunde. Really!

OLUNDE: You are . . . well, you look quite well yourself Mrs. Pilkings. From what little I can see of you.

JANE: Oh, this. It's caused quite a stir I assure you, and not all of it very pleasant. You are not shocked I hope?

OLUNDE: Why should I be? But don't you find it rather hot in there? Your skin must find it difficult to breathe.

JANE: Well, it is a little hot I must confess, but it's all in a good cause.

OLUNDE: What cause Mrs. Pilkings?

JANE: All this. The ball. And His Highness being here in person and all that.

OLUNDE: [*Mildly.*] And that is the good cause for which you desecrate an ancestral mask?

JANE: Oh, so you are shocked after all. How disappointing.

OLUNDE: No I am not shocked, Mrs. Pilkings. You forget that I have now spent four years among your people. I discovered that you have no respect for what you do not understand.

JANE: Oh. So you've returned with a chip on your shoulder. That's a pity Olunde. I am sorry.

[*An uncomfortable silence follows.*]

I take it then that you did not find your stay in England altogether edifying.

OLUNDE: I don't say that. I found your people quite admirable in many ways, their conduct and courage in this war[5] for instance.

JANE: Ah yes, the war. Here of course it is all rather remote. From time to time we have a black-out drill just to remind us that there is a war on. And the rare convoy passes through on its way somewhere or on manoeuvres.

5. That is, World War II.

Mind you there is the occasional bit of excitement like that ship that was blown up in the harbour.[6]

OLUNDE: Here? Do you mean through enemy action?

JANE: Oh no, the war hasn't come that close. The captain did it himself. I don't quite understand it really. Simon tried to explain. The ship had to be blown up because it had become dangerous to the other ships, even to the city itself. Hundreds of the coastal population would have died.

OLUNDE: Maybe it was loaded with ammunition and had caught fire. Or some of those lethal gases they've been experimenting on.

JANE: Something like that. The captain blew himself up with it. Deliberately. Simon said someone had to remain on board to light the fuse.

OLUNDE: It must have been a very short fuse.

JANE: [*Shrugs.*] I don't know much about it. Only that there was no other way to save lives. No time to devise anything else. The captain took the decision and carried it out.

OLUNDE: Yes . . . I quite believe it. I met men like that in England.

JANE: Oh just look at me! Fancy welcoming you back with such morbid news. Stale too. It was at least six months ago.

OLUNDE: I don't find it morbid at all. I find it rather inspiring. It is an affirmative commentary on life.

JANE: What is?

OLUNDE: That captain's self-sacrifice.

JANE: Nonsense. Life should never be thrown deliberately away.

OLUNDE: And the innocent people around the harbour?

JANE: Oh, how does one know? The whole thing was probably exaggerated anyway.

OLUNDE: That was a risk the captain couldn't take. But please Mrs. Pilkings, do you think you could find your husband for me? I have to talk to him.

JANE: Simon? [*As she recollects for the first time the full significance of* OLUNDE*'s presence.*] Simon is . . . there is a little problem in town. He was sent for. But . . . when did you arrive? Does Simon know you're here?

OLUNDE: [*Suddenly earnest.*] I need your help Mrs. Pilkings. I've always found you somewhat more understanding than your husband. Please find him for me and when you do, you must help me talk to him.

JANE: I'm afraid I don't quite . . . follow you. Have you seen my husband already?

OLUNDE: I went to your house. Your houseboy told me you were here. [*He smiles.*] He even told me how I would recognise you and Mr. Pilkings.

JANE: Then you must know what my husband is trying to do for you.

OLUNDE: For me?

JANE: For you. For your people. And to think he didn't even know you were coming back! But how do you happen to be here? Only this evening we were talking about you. We thought you were still four thousand miles away.

OLUNDE: I was sent a cable.

6. A reference to an incident that occurred in Lagos, the capital of Nigeria, in 1944.

JANE: A cable? Who did? Simon? The business of your father didn't begin till tonight.

OLUNDE: A relation sent it weeks ago, and it said nothing about my father. All it said was, Our King is dead. But I knew I had to return home at once so as to bury my father. I understood that.

JANE: Well, thank God you don't have to go through that agony. Simon is going to stop it.

OLUNDE: That's why I want to see him. He's wasting his time. And since he has been so helpful to me I don't want him to incur the enmity of our people. Especially over nothing.

JANE: [*Sits down open mouthed.*] You . . . you Olunde!

OLUNDE: Mrs. Pilkings, I came home to bury my father. As soon as I heard the news I booked my passage home. In fact we were fortunate. We travelled in the same convoy as your Prince, so we had excellent protection.

JANE: But you don't think your father is also entitled to whatever protection is available to him?

OLUNDE: How can I make you understand? He *has* protection. No one can undertake what he does tonight without the deepest protection the mind can conceive. What can you offer him in place of his peace of mind, in place of the honour and veneration of his own people? What would you think of your Prince if he refused to accept the risk of losing his life on this voyage? This . . . showing the flag tour of colonial possessions.

JANE: I see. So it isn't just medicine you studied in England.

OLUNDE: Yet another error into which your people fall. You believe that everything which appears to make sense was learnt from you.

JANE: Not so fast Olunde. You have learnt to argue I can tell that, but I never said you made sense. However clearly you try to put it, it is still a barbaric custom. It is even worse—it's feudal! The king dies and a chieftan must be buried with him. How feudalistic can you get!

OLUNDE: [*Waves his hand towards the background. The* PRINCE *is dancing past again—to a different step—and all the guests are bowing and curtseying as he passes.*] And this? Even in the midst of a devastating war, look at that. What name would you give to that?

JANE: Therapy, British style. The preservation of sanity in the midst of chaos.

OLUNDE: Others would call it decadence. However, it doesn't really interest me. You white races know how to survive; I've seen proof of that. By all logical and natural laws this war should end with all the white races wiping out one another, wiping out their so-called civilisation for all time and reverting to a state of primitivism the like of which has so far only existed in your imagination when you thought of us. I thought all that at the beginning. Then I slowly realised that your greatest art is the art of survival. But at least have the humility to let others survive in their own way.

JANE: Through ritual suicide?

OLUNDE: Is that worse than mass suicide? Mrs. Pilkings, what do you call what those young men are sent to do by their generals in this war? Of course you have also mastered the art of calling things by names which don't remotely describe them.

JANE: You talk! You people with your long-winded, roundabout way of making conversation.

OLUNDE: Mrs. Pilkings, whatever we do, we never suggest that a thing is the opposite of what it really is. In your newsreels I heard defeats, thorough, murderous defeats described as strategic victories. No wait, it wasn't just on your newsreels. Don't forget I was attached to hospitals all the time. Hordes of your wounded passed through those wards. I spoke to them. I spent long evenings by their bedsides while they spoke terrible truths of the realities of that war. I know now how history is made.

JANE: But surely, in a war of this nature, for the morale of the nation you must expect . . .

OLUNDE: That a disaster beyond human reckoning be spoken of as a triumph? No, I mean, is there no mourning in the home of the bereaved that such blasphemy is permitted?

JANE: [*After a moment's pause.*] Perhaps I can understand you now. The time we picked for you was not really one for seeing us at our best.

OLUNDE: Don't think it was just the war. Before that even started I had plenty of time to study your people. I saw nothing, finally, that gave you the right to pass judgement on other peoples and their ways. Nothing at all.

JANE: [*Hesitantly.*] Was it the . . . colour thing? I know there is some discrimination.

OLUNDE: Don't make it so simple, Mrs. Pilkings. You make it sound as if when I left, I took nothing at all with me.

JANE: Yes . . . and to tell the truth, only this evening, Simon and I agreed that we never really knew what you left with.

OLUNDE: Neither did I. But I found out over there. I am grateful to your country for that. And I will never give it up.

JANE: Olunde, please . . . promise me something. Whatever you do, don't throw away what you have started to do. You want to be a doctor. My husband and I believe you will make an excellent one, sympathetic and competent. Don't let anything make you throw away your training.

OLUNDE: [*Genuinely surprised.*] Of course not. What a strange idea. I intend to return and complete my training. Once the burial of my father is over.

JANE: Oh, please . . . !

OLUNDE: Listen! Come outside. You can't hear anything against that music.

JANE: What is it?

OLUNDE: The drums. Can you hear the drums? Listen.

[*The drums come over, still distant but more distinct. There is a change of rhythm, it rises to a crescendo and then, suddenly, it is cut off. After a silence, a new beat begins, slow and resonant.*]

There it's all over.

JANE: You mean he's . . .

OLUNDE: Yes, Mrs. Pilkings, my father is dead. His will power has always been enormous; I know he is dead.

JANE: [*Screams.*] How can you be so callous! So unfeeling! You announce your father's own death like a surgeon looking down on some strange . . . stranger's body! You're just a savage like all the rest.

AIDE-DE-CAMP: [*Rushing out.*] Mrs. Pilkings. Mrs. Pilkings. [*She breaks down, sobbing.*] Are you all right, Mrs. Pilkings?

OLUNDE: She'll be all right. [*Turns to go.*]

AIDE-DE-CAMP: Who are you? And who the hell asked your opinion?

OLUNDE: You're quite right, nobody. [*Going.*]

AIDE-DE-CAMP: What the hell! Did you hear me ask you who you were?

OLUNDE: I have business to attend to.

AIDE-DE-CAMP: I'll give you business in a moment you impudent nigger. Answer my question!

OLUNDE: I have a funeral to arrange. Excuse me. [*Going.*]

AIDE-DE-CAMP: I said stop! Orderly!

JANE: No, no, don't do that. I'm all right. And for heaven's sake don't act so foolishly. He's a family friend.

AIDE-DE-CAMP: Well he'd better learn to answer civil questions when he's asked them. These natives put a suit on and they get high opinions of themselves.

OLUNDE: Can I go now?

JANE: No no don't go. I must talk to you. I'm sorry about what I said.

OLUNDE: It's nothing, Mrs. Pilkings. And I'm really anxious to go. I couldn't see my father before, it's forbidden for me, his heir and successor to set eyes on him from the moment of the king's death. But now . . . I would like to touch his body while it is still warm.

JANE: You will. I promise I shan't keep you long. Only, I couldn't possibly let you go like that. Bob, please excuse us.

AIDE-DE-CAMP: If you're sure . . .

JANE: Of course I'm sure. Something happened to upset me just then, but I'm all right now. Really.

[*The* AIDE DE CAMP *goes, somewhat reluctantly.*]

OLUNDE: I mustn't stay long.

JANE: Please, I promise not to keep you. It's just that . . . oh you saw yourself what happens to one in this place. The Resident's man thought he was being helpful, that's the way we all react. But I can't go in among that crowd just now and if I stay by myself somebody will come looking for me. Please, just say something for a few moments and then you can go. Just so I can recover myself.

OLUNDE: What do you want me to say?

JANE: Your calm acceptance for instance, can you explain that? It was so unnatural. I don't understand that at all. I feel a need to understand all I can.

OLUNDE: But you explained it yourself. My medical training perhaps. I have seen death too often. And the soldiers who returned from the front, they died on our hands all the time.

JANE: No. It has to be more than that. I feel it has to do with the many things we don't really grasp about your people. At least you can explain.

OLUNDE: All these things are part of it. And anyway, my father has been dead in my mind for nearly a month. Ever since I learnt of the King's death. I've lived with my bereavement so long now that I cannot think of him alive. On that journey on the boat, I kept my mind on my duties as the one who must perform the rites over his body. I went through it all again and again in my mind as he himself had taught me. I didn't want to do anything wrong, something which might jeopardise the welfare of my people.

JANE: But he had disowned you. When you left he swore publicly you were no longer his son.

OLUNDE: I told you, he was a man of tremendous will. Sometimes that's another way of saying stubborn. But among our people, you don't disown a child just like that. Even if I had died before him I would still be buried like his eldest son. But it's time for me to go.

JANE: Thank you. I feel calmer. Don't let me keep you from your duties.

OLUNDE: Goodnight, Mrs. Pilkings.

JANE: Welcome home.

[*She holds out her hand. As he takes it footsteps are heard approaching the drive. A short while later a woman's sobbing is also heard.*]

PILKINGS: [*Off.*] Keep them here till I get back. [*He strides into view, reacts at the sight of* OLUNDE *but turns to his wife.*] Thank goodness you're still here.

JANE: Simon, what happened?

PILKINGS: Later Jane, please. Is Bob still here?

JANE: Yes, I think so. I'm sure he must be.

PILKINGS: Try and get him out here as quickly as you can. Tell him it's urgent.

JANE: Of course. Oh Simon, you remember . . .

PILKINGS: Yes yes. I can see who it is. Get Bob out here. [*She runs off.*] At first I thought I was seeing a ghost.

OLUNDE: Mr. Pilkings, I appreciate what you tried to do. I want you to believe that. I can tell you it would have been a terrible calamity if you'd succeeded.

PILKINGS: [*Opens his mouth several times, shuts it.*] You . . . said what?

OLUNDE: A calamity for us, the entire people.

PILKINGS: [*Sighs.*] I see. Hm.

OLUNDE: And now I must go. I must see him before he turns cold.

PILKINGS: Oh ah . . . em . . . but this is a shock to see you. I mean er thinking all this while you were in England and thanking God for that.

OLUNDE: I came on the mail boat. We travelled in the Prince's convoy.

PILKINGS: Ah yes, a ah, hm . . . er well . . .

OLUNDE: Goodnight. I can see you are shocked by the whole business. But you must know by now there are things you cannot understand—or help.

PILKINGS: Yes. Just a minute. There are armed policemen that way and they have instructions to let no one pass. I suggest you wait a little. I'll er . . . give you an escort.

OLUNDE: That's very kind of you. But do you think it could be quickly arranged.

PILKINGS: Of course. In fact, yes, what I'll do is send Bob over with some men to the er . . . place. You can go with them. Here he comes now. Excuse me a minute.

AIDE-DE-CAMP: Anything wrong sir?

PILKINGS: [*Takes him to one side.*] Listen Bob, that cellar in the disused annex of the Residency, you know, where the slaves were stored before being taken down to the coast . . .

AIDE-DE-CAMP: Oh yes, we use it as a storeroom for broken furniture.

PILKINGS: But it's still got the bars on it?

AIDE-DE-CAMP: Oh yes, they are quite intact.

PILKINGS: Get the keys please. I'll explain later. And I want a strong guard over the Residency tonight.

AIDE-DE-CAMP: We have that already. The detachment from the coast . . .

PILKINGS: No, I don't want them at the gates of the Residency. I want you to deploy them at the bottom of the hill, a long way from the main hall so they can deal with any situation long before the sound carries to the house.

AIDE-DE-CAMP: Yes of course.

PILKINGS: I don't want His Highness alarmed.

AIDE-DE-CAMP: You think the riot will spread here?

PILKINGS: It's unlikely but I don't want to take a chance. I made them believe I was going to lock the man up in my house, which was what I had planned to do in the first place. They are probably assailing it by now. I took a roundabout route here so I don't think there is any danger at all. At least not before dawn. Nobody is to leave the premises of course—the native employees I mean. They'll soon smell something is up and they can't keep their mouths shut.

AIDE-DE-CAMP: I'll give instructions at once.

PILKINGS: I'll take the prisoner down myself. Two policemen will stay with him throughout the night. Inside the cell.

AIDE-DE-CAMP: Right sir. [*Salutes and goes off at the double.*]

PILKINGS: Jane. Bob is coming back in a moment with a detachment. Until he gets back please stay with Olunde. [*He makes an extra warning gesture with his eyes.*]

OLUNDE: Please, Mr. Pilkings . . .

PILKINGS: I hate to be stuffy old son, but we have a crisis on our hands. It has to do with your father's affair if you must know. And it happens also at a time when we have His Highness here. I am responsible for security so you'll simply have to do as I say. I hope that's understood.

[*Marches off quickly, in the direction from which he made his first appearance.*]

OLUNDE: What's going on? All this can't be just because he failed to stop my father killing himself.

JANE: I honestly don't know. Could it have sparked off a riot?

OLUNDE: No. If he'd succeeded that would be more likely to start the riot. Perhaps there were other factors involved. Was there a chieftancy dispute?

JANE: None that I know of.

ELESIN: [*An animal bellow from off.*] Leave me alone! Is it not enough that you have covered me in shame! White man, take your hand from my body!

[OLUNDE *stands frozen to the spot.* JANE *understanding at last, tries to move him.*]

JANE: Let's go in. It's getting chilly out here.

PILKINGS: [*Off.*] Carry him.

ELESIN: Give me back the name you have taken away from me you ghost from the land of the nameless!

PILKINGS: Carry him! I can't have a disturbance here. Quickly! stuff up his mouth.

JANE: Oh God! Let's go in. Please Olunde.

[OLUNDE *does not move.*]

ELESIN: Take your albino's hand from me you . . .

[*Sounds of a struggle. His voice chokes as he is gagged.*]

OLUNDE: [*Quietly.*] That was my father's voice.

JANE: Oh you poor orphan, what have you come home to?

[*There is a sudden explosion of rage from off-stage and powerful steps come running up the drive.*]

PILKINGS: You bloody fools, after him!

[*Immediately* ELESIN, *in handcuffs, comes pounding in the direction of* JANE *and* OLUNDE, *followed some moments afterwards by* PILKINGS *and the* CONSTABLES. ELESIN, *confronted by the seeming statue of his son, stops dead.* OLUNDE *stares above his head into the distance. The* CONSTABLES *try to grab him.* JANE *screams at them.*]

JANE: Leave him alone! Simon, tell them to leave him alone.

PILKINGS: All right, stand aside you. [*Shrugs.*] Maybe just as well. It might help to calm him down.

[*For several moments they hold the same position.* ELESIN *moves a step forward, almost as if he's still in doubt.*]

ELESIN: Olunde? [*He moves his head, inspecting him from side to side.*] Olunde! [*He collapses slowly at* OLUNDE'S *feet.*] Oh son, don't let the sight of your father turn you blind!

OLUNDE: [*He moves for the first time since he heard his voice, brings his head slowly down to look on him.*] I have no father, eater of left-overs.

[*He walks slowly down the way his father had run. Light fades out on* ELESIN, *sobbing into the ground.*]

Scene Five

A wide iron barred gate stretches almost the whole width of the cell in which ELESIN *is imprisoned. His wrists are encased in thick iron bracelets, chained together; he stands against the bars, looking out. Seated on the ground to one side on the outside is his recent* BRIDE, *her eyes bent perpetually to the ground. Figures of the two* GUARDS *can be seen deeper inside the cell, alert to every movement* ELESIN *makes.* PILKINGS *now in a police officer's uniform enters noiselessly, observes him a while. Then he coughs ostentatiously and approaches. Leans against the bars near a corner, his back to* ELESIN. *He is obviously trying to fall in mood with him. Some moments' silence.*

PILKINGS: You seem fascinated by the moon.

ELESIN: [*After a pause.*] Yes, ghostly one. Your twin-brother up there engages my thoughts.

PILKINGS: It is a beautiful night.

ELESIN: Is that so?

PILKINGS: The light on the leaves, the peace of the night . . .

ELESIN: The night is not at peace, District Officer.

PILKINGS: No? I would have said it was. You know, quiet . . .

ELESIN: And does quiet mean peace for you?

PILKINGS: Well, nearly the same thing. Naturally there is a subtle difference . . .

ELESIN: The night is not at peace, ghostly one. The world is not at peace. You have shattered the peace of the world for ever. There is no sleep in the world tonight.

PILKINGS: It is still a good bargain if the world should lose one night's sleep as the price of saving a man's life.

ELESIN: You did not save my life, District Officer. You destroyed it.

PILKINGS: Now come on . . .

ELESIN: And not merely my life but the lives of many. The end of the night's work is not over. Neither this year nor the next will see it. If I wished you well, I would pray that you do not stay long enough on our land to see the disaster you have brought upon us.

PILKINGS: Well, I did my duty as I saw it. I have no regrets.

ELESIN: No. The Regrets of life always come later.

[*Some moments' pause.*]

You are waiting for dawn, white man. I hear you saying to yourself: only so many hours until dawn and then the danger is over. All I must do is to keep him alive tonight. You don't quite understand it all but you know that tonight is when what ought to be must be brought about. I shall ease your mind even more, ghostly one. It is not an entire night but a moment of the night, and that moment is past. The moon was my messenger and guide. When it reached a certain gateway in the sky, it touched that moment for which my whole life has been spent in blessings. Even I do not know the gateway. I have stood here and scanned the sky for a glimpse of that door but, I cannot see it. Human eyes are useless for a search of this nature. But in the house of *osugbo*, those who keep watch through the spirit recognised the moment, they sent word to me through the voice of our sacred drums to prepare myself. I heard them and I shed all thoughts of earth. I began to follow the moon to the abode of the gods . . . servant of the white king, that was when you entered my chosen place of departure on feet of desecration.

PILKINGS: I'm sorry, but we all see our duty differently.

ELESIN: I no longer blame you. You stole from me my first-born, sent him to your country so you could turn him into something in your own image. Did you plan it all beforehand? There are moments when it seems part of a larger plan. He who must follow my footsteps is taken from me, sent across the ocean. Then, in my turn, I am stopped from fulfilling my destiny. Did you think it all out before, this plan to push our world from its course and sever the cord that links us to the great origin?

PILKINGS: You don't really believe that. Anyway, if that was my intention with your son, I appear to have failed.

ELESIN: You did not fail in the main, ghostly one. We know the roof covers the rafters, the cloth covers blemishes; who would have known that the white skin covered our future, preventing us from seeing the death our enemies had prepared for us. The world is set adrift and its inhabitants are lost. Around them, there is nothing but emptiness.

PILKINGS: Your son does not take so gloomy a view.

ELESIN: Are you dreaming now, white man? Were you not present at my reunion of shame? Did you not see when the world reversed itself and the father fell before his son, asking forgiveness?

PILKINGS: That was in the heat of the moment. I spoke to him and . . . if you want to know, he wishes he could cut out his tongue for uttering the words he did.

ELESIN: No. What he said must never be unsaid. The contempt of my own son rescued something of my shame at your hands. You have stopped me in my duty but I know now that I did give birth to a son. Once I mistrusted him for seeking the companionship of those my spirit knew as enemies of our race. Now I understand. One should seek to obtain the secrets of his enemies. He will avenge my shame, white one. His spirit will destroy you and yours.

PILKINGS: That kind of talk is hardly called for. If you don't want my consolation . . .

ELESIN: No white man, I do not want your consolation.

PILKINGS: As you wish. Your son anyway, sends his consolation. He asks your forgiveness. When I asked him not to despise you his reply was: I cannot judge him, and if I cannot judge him, I cannot despise him. He wants to come to you and say goodbye and to receive your blessing.

ELESIN: Goodbye? Is he returning to your land?

PILKINGS: Don't you think that's the most sensible thing for him to do? I advised him to leave at once, before dawn, and he agrees that is the right course of action.

ELESIN: Yes, it is best. And even if I did not think so, I have lost the father's place of honour. My voice is broken.

PILKINGS: Your son honours you. If he didn't he would not ask your blessing.

ELESIN: No. Even a thoroughbred is not without pity for the turf he strikes with his hoof. When is he coming?

PILKINGS: As soon as the town is a little quieter. I advised it.

ELESIN: Yes, white man, I am sure you advised it. You advise all our lives although on the authority of what gods, I do not know.

PILKINGS: [*Opens his mouth to reply, then appears to change his mind. Turns to go. Hesitates and stops again.*] Before I leave you, may I ask just one thing of you?

ELESIN: I am listening.

PILKINGS: I wish to ask you to search the quiet of your heart and tell me—do you not find great contradictions in the wisdom of your own race?

ELESIN: Make yourself clear, white one.

PILKINGS: I have lived among you long enough to learn a saying or two. One came to my mind tonight when I stepped into the market and saw what was going on. You were surrounded by those who egged you on with song and praises. I thought, are these not the same people who say: the elder grimly approaches heaven and you ask him to bear your greetings yonder; do you really think he makes the journey willingly? After that, I did not hesitate.

[*A pause.* ELESIN *sighs. Before he can speak a sound of running feet is heard.*]

JANE: [*Off.*] Simon! Simon!

PILKINGS: What on earth . . . ! [*Runs off.*]

[ELESIN *turns to his new wife, gazes on her for some moments.*]

ELESIN: My young bride, did you hear the ghostly one? You sit and sob in your silent heart but say nothing to all this. First I blamed the white man, then I blamed my gods for deserting me. Now I feel I want to blame you for the mystery of the sapping of my will. But blame is a strange peace offering for a man to bring a world he has deeply wronged, and to its innocent dwellers. Oh little mother, I have taken countless women in my life but you were more than a desire of the flesh. I needed you as the abyss across which my body must be drawn, I filled it with earth and dropped my seed in it at the moment of preparedness for my crossing. You were the final gift of the living to their emissary to the land of the ancestors, and perhaps your warmth and youth brought new insights of this world to me and turned my feet leaden on this side of the abyss. For I confess to you, daughter, my weakness came not merely from the abomination of the white man who came violently into my fading presence, there was also a weight of longing on my earth-held limbs. I would have shaken it off, already my foot had begun to lift but then, the white ghost entered and all was defiled.

[*Approaching voices of* PILKINGS *and his wife.*]

JANE: Oh Simon, you will let her in won't you?

PILKINGS: I really wish you'd stop interfering.

[*They come into view.* JANE *is in a dressing gown.* PILKINGS *is holding a note to which he refers from time to time.*]

JANE: Good gracious, I didn't initiate this. I was sleeping quietly, or trying to anyway, when the servant brought it. It's not my fault if one can't sleep undisturbed even in the Residency.

PILKINGS: He'd have done the same thing if we were sleeping at home so don't sidetrack the issue. He knows he can get round you or he wouldn't send you the petition in the first place.

JANE: Be fair Simon. After all he was thinking of your own interests. He is grateful you know, you seem to forget that. He feels he owes you something.

PILKINGS: I just wish they'd leave this man alone tonight, that's all.

JANE: Trust him Simon. He's pledged his word it will all go peacefully.

PILKINGS: Yes, and that's the other thing. I don't like being threatened.

JANE: Threatened? [*Takes the note.*] I didn't spot any threat.

PILKINGS: It's there. Veiled, but it's there. The only way to prevent serious rioting tomorrow—what a cheek!

JANE: I don't think he's threatening you Simon.

PILKINGS: He's picked up the idiom all right. Wouldn't surprise me if he's been mixing with commies or anarchists over there. The phrasing sounds too good to be true. Damn! If only the Prince hadn't picked this time for his visit.

JANE: Well, even so Simon, what have you got to lose? You don't want a riot on your hands, not with the Prince here.

PILKINGS: [*Going up to* ELESIN.] Let's see what he has to say. Chief Elesin, there is yet another person who wants to see you. As she is not a next-of-kin I don't really feel obliged to let her in. But your son sent a note with her, so it's up to you.

ELESIN: I know who that must be. So she found out your hiding place. Well, it was not difficult. My stench of shame is so strong, it requires no hunter's dog to follow it.

PILKINGS: If you don't want to see her, just say so and I'll send her packing.

ELESIN: Why should I not want to see her? Let her come. I have no more holes in my rag of shame. All is laid bare.

PILKINGS: I'll bring her in. [*Goes off.*]

JANE: [*Hesitates, then goes to* ELESIN.] Please, try and understand. Everything my husband did was for the best.

ELESIN: [*He gives her a long strange stare, as if he is trying to understand who she is.*] You are the wife of the District Officer?

JANE: Yes. My name, is Jane.

ELESIN: That is my wife sitting down there. You notice how still and silent she sits? My business is with your husband.

[PILKINGS *returns with* IYALOJA.]

PILKINGS: Here she is. Now first I want your word of honour that you will try nothing foolish.

ELESIN: Honour? White one, did you say you wanted my word of honour?

PILKINGS: I know you to be an honourable man. Give me your word of honour you will receive nothing from her.

ELESIN: But I am sure you have searched her clothing as you would never dare touch your own mother. And there are these two lizards[7] of yours who roll their eyes even when I scratch.

PILKINGS: And I shall be sitting on that tree trunk watching even how you blink. Just the same I want your word that you will not let her pass anything to you.

ELESIN: You have my honour already. It is locked up in that desk in which you will put away your report of this night's events. Even the honour of my people you have taken already; it is tied together with those papers of treachery[8] which make you masters in this land.

PILKINGS: All right. I am trying to make things easy but if you must bring in politics we'll have to do it the hard way. Madam, I want you to remain along this line and move no nearer to the cell door. Guards! [*They spring to attention.*] If she moves beyond this point, blow your whistle. Come on Jane. [*They go off.*]

IYALOJA: How boldly the lizard struts before the pigeon when it was the eagle itself he promised us he would confront.

ELESIN: I don't ask you to take pity on me Iyaloja. You have a message for me or you would not have come. Even if it is the curses of the world, I shall listen.

IYALOJA: You made so bold with the servant of the white king who took your side against death. I must tell your brother chiefs when I return how bravely you waged war against him. Especially with words.

ELESIN: I more than deserve your scorn.

IYALOJA: [*With sudden anger.*] I warned you, if you must leave a seed behind, be sure it is not tainted with the curses of the world. Who are you to open a new life when you dared not open the door to a new existence? I say who are you to make so bold? [*The* BRIDE *sobs and* IYALOJA *notices her. Her contempt noticeably increases as she turns back to* ELESIN.] Oh you self-vaunted stem of the plantain, how hollow it all proves. The pith is gone in the parent stem, so how will it prove with the new shoot? How will it go with that earth that bears it? Who are you to bring this abomination on us!

ELESIN: My powers deserted me. My charms, my spells, even my voice lacked strength when I made to summon the powers that would lead me over the last measure of earth into the land of the fleshless. You saw it, Iyaloja. You

7. That is, the guards.
8. The treaties of annexation forced by the British on African traditional rulers, who often did not understand their implications.

saw me struggle to retrieve my will from the power of the stranger whose shadow fell across the doorway and left me floundering and blundering in a maze I had never before encountered. My senses were numbed when the touch of cold iron came upon my wrists. I could do nothing to save myself.

IYALOJA: You have betrayed us. We fed you sweetmeats such as we hoped awaited you on the other side. But you said No, I must eat the world's left-overs. We said you were the hunter who brought the quarry down; to you belonged the vital portions of the game. No, you said, I am the hunter's dog and I shall eat the entrails of the game and the faeces of the hunter. We said you were the hunter returning home in triumph, a slain buffalo pressing down on his neck; you said wait, I first must turn up this cricket hole with my toes. We said yours was the doorway at which we first spy the tapper when he comes down from the tree, yours was the blessing of the twilight wine, the purl[9] that brings night spirits out of doors to steal their portion before the light of day. We said yours was the body of wine whose burden shakes the tapper like a sudden gust on his perch. You said, No, I am content to lick the dregs from each calabash when the drinkers are done. We said, the dew on earth's surface was for you to wash your feet along the slopes of honour. You said No, I shall step in the vomit of cats and the droppings of mice; I shall fight them for the left-overs of the world.

ELESIN: Enough Iyaloja, enough.

IYALOJA: We called you leader and oh, how you led us on. What we have no intention of eating should not be held to the nose.[1]

ELESIN: Enough, enough. My shame is heavy enough.

IYALOJA: Wait. I came with a burden.

ELESIN: You have more than discharged it.

IYALOJA: I wish I could pity you.

ELESIN: I need neither pity nor the pity of the world. I need understanding. Even I need to understand. You were present at my defeat. You were part of the beginnings. You brought about the renewal of my tie to earth, you helped in the binding of the cord.

IYALOJA: I gave you warning. The river which fills up before our eyes does not sweep us away in its flood.

ELESIN: What were warnings beside the moist contact of living earth between my fingers? What were warnings beside the renewal of famished embers lodged eternally in the heart of man. But even that, even if it overwhelmed one with a thousandfold temptations to linger a little while, a man could overcome it. It is when the alien hand pollutes the source of will, when a stranger's force of violence shatters the mind's calm resolution, this is when a man is made to commit the awful treachery of relief, commit in his thought the unspeakable blasphemy of seeing the hand of the gods in this alien rupture of his world. I know it was this thought that killed me, sapped my powers and turned me into an infant in the hands of unnamable strangers. I made to utter my spells anew but my tongue merely rattled in my mouth. I fingered hidden charms and the contact was damp; there was

9. The frothy head of the palm wine. "Tapper": one who climbs to the very top of the palm tree for its wine. The profession is a highly specialized one. "Cricket hole": hunting crickets is a favorite game of Yoruba boys.

1. Considered uncouth by Yorubas.

no spark left to sever the life-strings that should stretch from every fingertip. My will was squelched in the spittle of an alien race, and all because I had committed this blasphemy of thought—that there might be the hand of the gods in a stranger's intervention.

IYALOJA: Explain it how you will, I hope it brings you peace of mind. The bush rat fled his rightful cause, reached the market and set up a lamentation. "Please save me!"—are these fitting words to hear from an ancestral mask? "There's a wild beast at my heels" is not becoming language from a hunter.

ELESIN: May the world forgive me.

IYALOJA: I came with a burden I said. It approaches the gates which are so well guarded by those jackals whose spittle will from this day be on your food and drink. But first, tell me, you who were once Elesin Oba, tell me, you who know so well the cycle of the plantain: is it the parent shoot which withers to give sap to the younger or, does your wisdom see it running the other way?

ELESIN: I don't see your meaning Iyaloja?

IYALOJA: Did I ask you for a meaning? I asked a question. Whose trunk withers to give sap to the other? The parent shoot or the younger?

ELESIN: The parent.

IYALOJA: Ah. So you do know that. There are sights in this world which say different Elesin. There are some who choose to reverse the cycle of our being. Oh you emptied bark that the world once saluted for a pith-laden being, shall I tell you what the gods have claimed of you?

[*In her agitation she steps beyond the line indicated by* PILKINGS *and the air is rent by piercing whistles. The two* GUARDS *also leap forward and place safe-guarding hands on* ELESIN. IYALOJA *stops, astonished.* PILKINGS *comes racing in, followed by* JANE.]

PILKINGS: What is it? Did they try something?

GUARD: She stepped beyond the line.

ELESIN: [*In a broken voice.*] Let her alone. She meant no harm.

IYALOJA: Oh Elesin, see what you've become. Once you had no need to open your mouth in explanation because evil-smelling goats, itchy of hand and foot had lost their senses. And it was a brave man indeed who dared lay hands on you because Iyaloja stepped from one side of the earth onto another. Now look at the spectacle of your life. I grieve for you.

PILKINGS: I think you'd better leave. I doubt you have done him much good by coming here. I shall make sure you are not allowed to see him again. In any case we are moving him to a different place before dawn, so don't bother to come back.

IYALOJA: We foresaw that. Hence the burden I trudged here to lay beside your gates.

PILKINGS: What was that you said?

IYALOJA: Didn't our son explain? Ask that one. He knows what it is. At least we hope the man we once knew as Elesin remembers the lesser oaths he need not break.

PILKINGS: Do you know what she is talking about?

ELESIN: Go to the gates, ghostly one. Whatever you find there, bring it to me.

IYALOJA: Not yet. It drags behind me on the slow, weary feet of women. Slow as it is Elesin, it has long overtaken you. It rides ahead of your laggard will.

PILKINGS: What is she saying now? Christ! Must your people forever speak in riddles?

ELESIN: It will come white man, it will come. Tell your men at the gates to let it through.

PILKINGS: [*Dubiously.*] I'll have to see what it is.

IYALOJA: You will. [*Passionately.*] But this is one oath he cannot shirk. White one, you have a king here, a visitor from your land. We know of his presence here. Tell me, were he to die would you leave his spirit roaming restlessly on the surface of earth? Would you bury him here among those you consider less than human? In your land have you no ceremonies of the dead?

PILKINGS: Yes. But we don't make our chiefs commit suicide to keep him company.

IYALOJA: Child, I have not come to help your understanding. [*Points to* ELESIN.] This is the man whose weakened understanding holds us in bondage to you. But ask him if you wish. He knows the meaning of a king's passage; he was not born yesterday. He knows the peril to the race when our dead father, who goes as intermediary, waits and waits and knows he is betrayed. He knows when the narrow gate was opened and he knows it will not stay for laggards who drag their feet in dung and vomit, whose lips are reeking of the left-overs of lesser men. He knows he has condemned our king to wander in the void of evil with beings who are enemies of life.

PILKINGS: Yes er . . . but look here . . .

IYALOJA: What we ask is little enough. Let him release our King so he can ride on homewards alone. The messenger is on his way on the backs of women. Let him send word through the heart that is folded up within the bolt. It is the least of all his oaths, it is the easiest fulfilled.

[*The* AIDE-DE-CAMP *runs in.*]

PILKINGS: Bob?

AIDE-DE-CAMP: Sir, there's a group of women chanting up the hill.

PILKINGS: [*Rounding on* IYALOJA.] If you people want trouble . . .

JANE: Simon, I think that's what Olunde referred to in his letter.

PILKINGS: He knows damned well I can't have a crowd here! Damn it, I explained the delicacy of my position to him. I think it's about time I got him out of town. Bob, send a car and two or three soldiers to bring him in. I think the sooner he takes his leave of his father and gets out the better.

IYALOJA: Save your labour white one. If it is the father of your prisoner you want, Olunde, he who until this night we knew as Elesin's son, he comes soon himself to take his leave. He has sent the women ahead, so let them in.

[PILKINGS *remains undecided.*]

AIDE-DE-CAMP: What do we do about the invasion? We can still stop them far from here.

PILKINGS: What do they look like?

AIDE-DE-CAMP: They're not many. And they seem quite peaceful.

PILKINGS: No men?

AIDE-DE-CAMP: Mm, two or three at the most.

JANE: Honestly, Simon, I'd trust Olunde. I don't think he'll deceive you about their intentions.

PILKINGS: He'd better not. All right then, let them in Bob. Warn them to control themselves. Then hurry Olunde here. Make sure he brings his baggage because I'm not returning him into town.

AIDE-DE-CAMP: Very good, sir. [*Goes.*]

PILKINGS: [*To* IYALOJA.] I hope you understand that if anything goes wrong it will be on your head. My men have orders to shoot at the first sign of trouble.

IYALOJA: To prevent one death you will actually make other deaths? Ah, great is the wisdom of the white race. But have no fear. Your Prince will sleep peacefully. So at long last will ours. We will disturb you no further, servant of the white king. Just let Elesin fulfil his oath and we will retire home and pay homage to our King.

JANE: I believe her Simon, don't you?

PILKINGS: Maybe.

ELESIN: Have no fear ghostly one. I have a message to send my King and then you have nothing more to fear.

IYALOJA: Olunde would have done it. The chiefs asked him to speak the words but he said no, not while you lived.

ELESIN: Even from the depths to which my spirit has sunk, I find some joy that this little has been left to me.

[*The* WOMEN *enter, intoning the dirge "Ale le le" and swaying from side to side. On their shoulders is borne a longish object roughly like a cylindrical bolt, covered in cloth. They set it down on the spot where* IYALOJA *had stood earlier, and form a semi-circle round it. The* PRAISE-SINGER *and* DRUMMER *stand on the inside of the semi-circle but the drum is not used at all. The* DRUMMER *intones under the* PRAISE-SINGER'S *invocations.*]

PILKINGS: [*As they enter.*] What is *that*?

IYALOJA: The burden you have made white one, but we bring it in peace.

PILKINGS: I said *what* is it?

ELESIN: White man, you must let me out. I have a duty to perform.

PILKINGS: I most certainly will not.

ELESIN: There lies the courier of my King. Let me out so I can perform what is demanded of me.

PILKINGS: You'll do what you need to do from inside there or not at all. I've gone as far as I intend to with this business.

ELESIN: The worshipper who lights a candle in your church to bear a message to his god bows his head and speaks in a whisper to the flame. Have I not seen it ghostly one? His voice does not ring out to the world. Mine are no words for anyone's ears. They are not words even for the bearers of this load. They are words I must speak secretly, even as my father whispered them in my ears and I in the ears of my first-born. I cannot shout them to the wind and the open night sky.

JANE: Simon . . .

PILKINGS: Don't interfere. Please!

IYALOJA: They have slain the favourite horse of the king and slain his dog. They have borne them from pulse to pulse centre of the land receiving prayers for their king. But the rider has chosen to stay behind. Is it too much to ask that he speak his heart to heart of the waiting courier? [PILKINGS *turns his back on her.*] So be it. Elesin Oba, you see how even the mere leavings are denied you. [*She gestures to the* PRAISE SINGER.]

PRAISE-SINGER: Elesin Oba! I call you by that name only this last time. Remember when I said, if you cannot come, tell my horse. [*Pause.*] What? I cannot hear you? I said, if you cannot come, whisper in the ears of my horse. Is your tongue severed from the roots? Elesin? I can hear no response. I said, if there are boulders you cannot climb, mount my horse's back, this spotless black stallion, he'll bring you over them. [*Pauses.*] Elesin Oba, once you had a tongue that darted like a drummer's stick. I said, if you get lost my dog will track a path to me. My memory fails me but I think you replied: My feet have found the path, Alafin.

[*The dirge rises and falls.*]

I said at the last, if evil hands hold you back, just tell my horse there is weight on the hem of your smock. I dare not wait too long.

[*The dirge rises and falls.*]

There lies the swiftest ever messenger of a king, so set me free with the errand of your heart. There lie the head and heart of the favourite of the gods, whisper in his ears. Oh my companion, if you had followed when you should, we would not say that the horse preceded its rider. If you had followed when it was time, we would not say the dog has raced beyond and left his master behind. If you had raised your will to cut the thread of life at the summons of the drums, we would not say your mere shadow fell across the gateway and took its owner's place at the banquet. But the hunter, laden with slain buffalo, stayed to root in the cricket's hole with his toes. What now is left? If there is a dearth of bats, the pigeon must serve us for the offering.[2] Speak the words over your shadow which must now serve in your place.

ELESIN: I cannot approach. Take off the cloth. I shall speak my message from heart to heart of silence.

IYALOJA: [*Moves forward and removes the covering.*] Your courier Elesin, cast your eyes on the favoured companion of the King.

[*Rolled up in the mat, his head and feet showing at either end, is the body of* OLUNDE.]

There lies the honour of your household and of our race. Because he could not bear to let honour fly out of doors, he stopped it with his life. The son has proved the father Elesin, and there is nothing left in your mouth to gnash but infant gums.

PRAISE-SINGER: Elesin, we placed the reins of the world in your hands yet you watched it plunge over the edge of the bitter precipice. You sat with folded arms while evil strangers tilted the world from its course and crashed it beyond the edge of emptiness—you muttered, there is little that one man can do, you left us floundering in a blind future. Your heir has taken the burden on himself. What the end will be, we are not gods to tell. But this young shoot has poured its sap into the parent stalk, and we know this is not the way of life. Our world is tumbling in the void of strangers, Elesin.

[ELESIN *has stood rock-still, his knuckles taut on the bars, his eyes glued to the body of his son. The stillness seizes and paralyses everyone, including* PILKINGS *who has turned to look. Suddenly* ELESIN *flings one arm round his neck, once, and with the loop of the chain, strangles himself in a swift,*

2. Sacrifice.

decisive pull. The GUARDS *rush forward to stop him but they are only in time to let his body down.* PILKINGS *has leapt to the door at the same time and struggles with the lock. He rushes within, fumbles with the handcuffs and unlocks them, raises the body to a sitting position while he tries to give resuscitation. The* WOMEN *continue their dirge, unmoved by the sudden event.*]

IYALOJA: Why do you strain yourself? Why do you labour at tasks for which no one, not even the man lying there would give you thanks? He is gone at last into the passage but oh, how late it all is. His son will feast on the meat and throw him bones. The passage is clogged with droppings from the King's stallion; he will arrive all stained in dung.

PILKINGS: [*In a tired voice.*] Was this what you wanted?

IYALOJA: No child, it is what you brought to be, you who play with strangers' lives, who even usurp the vestments of our dead, yet believe that the stain of death will not cling to you. The gods demanded only the old expired plantain but you cut down the sap-laden shoot to feed your pride. There is your board, filled to overflowing. Feast on it. [*She screams at him suddenly, seeing that* PILKINGS *is about to close* ELESIN*'s staring eyes.*] Let him alone! However sunk he was in debt he is no pauper's carrion abandoned on the road. Since when have strangers donned clothes of indigo[3] before the bereaved cries out his loss?

[*She turns to the* BRIDE *who has remained motionless throughout.*]

Child.

[*The girl takes up a little earth, walks calmly into the cell and closes* ELESIN*'s eyes. She then pours some earth over each eyelid and comes out again.*]

Now forget the dead, forget even the living. Turn your mind only to the unborn.

[*She goes off, accompanied by the* BRIDE. *The dirge rises in volume and the* WOMEN *continue their sway. Lights fade to a black-out.*]

1975

3. Worn for mourning.

BESSIE HEAD

1937–1986

Bessie Head's works combine myth, legend, and oral tradition with realistic detail to portray the struggles of newly liberated southern Africa. Drawing on folktales, she relates them to modern African life to create a picture of contemporary society that is at once convincing and dreamlike. While suffering from mental illness and the effects of political oppression, Head managed to give voice in her writings to the people of Africa.

Born to a single mother in a South African mental asylum, Bessie Amelia Emery was adopted at birth by Nellie and George Heathcote. She grew up thinking of the Heathcotes as her parents and learned only as a teenager that she had a black father and a white mother; her mother had a history of mental illness and had been committed to the asylum when she became pregnant with a servant's child. The apartheid system of racial classification was formalized during her youth, and her adoptive parents were considered "colored" (that is, mixed race). Educated at St. Monica's Home, an Anglican mission school for colored girls, Head later taught at Clairwood Colored School. There, inspired by the teachings and writings of Mahatma Gandhi, Head developed an interest in Hinduism. "Never have I read anything that aroused my feelings like Gandhi's political statements," she later wrote. "There was a simple and astonishing clarity in the way he summarized political truths, there was an appalling tenderness and firmness in the man. I paused every now and then over his paper, almost swooning with worship because I recognized that this could only be God as man." She later worked as a court reporter in Cape Town, where she became interested in the Négritude and Pan-Africanist movements and began writing stories about social injustice. In 1960 she started a newspaper, *The Citizen*, focused on the injustices of apartheid. After marrying a fellow journalist, Harold Head, she moved to Serowe, Botswana, taking her infant son with her but leaving her husband behind in South Africa.

In Botswana, which had recently gained its independence from Britain, Head taught high school and continued writing fiction, receiving favorable reviews internationally for her first novel, *When the Rain Clouds Gather* (1969), which concerns a South African political prisoner who flees to Botswana. Around this time, Head began to suffer symptoms of bipolar disorder and schizophrenia. After denouncing the president of Botswana, Seretse Khama, as an assassin, Head was arrested by the police and confined in Lobatse Mental Hospital. As she recovered, she continued to write and in 1977 attended the University of Iowa's International Writing Program. In the next several years, she published a collection of short stories, two novels, an oral history of the village of Serowe, and *A Question of Power* (1974), a combination of fiction, autobiography, and political statement. These works often take up themes of cultural conflict similar to those in the works of her contemporary **Chinua Achebe.** Head traveled frequently to writers' conferences around the world, but after her estranged husband filed for divorce, she began to drink heavily, slipped into a coma, and died at age forty-eight. In one of her last published essays, "Why Do I Write?" she explained: "I am building a stairway to the stars. I have the authority to take the whole of mankind up there with me. That is why I write."

Head's works, many of which are set in Botswana, depict in realistic detail the lives of the downtrodden. They also have a mythic element. In "The Deep River: A Story of Ancient Tribal Migration," presented here, a traditional tale about the origins of a Botswanan ethnic group inspires a meditation on the conflicts between an imagined communal past and the pull of modern individuality, between a mythic origin in the "deep river" of the people, when individuals had no identity apart from the group, and a present defined by the sense of self and by notions of romantic love. Although Head narrates the story in a manner sympathetic to the claims of the individual, she laments the passing of what she sees as the unified traditional society. Similarly, while she quotes the opinions of old men about the events in the story, she attends to the concerns of the youngest wife, Rankwana. It is in the balance of these sympathies that Head manages to retell the old tale for a contemporary audience, both celebrating traditional culture and acknowledging its limitations.

The Deep River: A Story of Ancient Tribal Migration

Long ago, when the land was only cattle tracks and footpaths, the people lived together like a deep river. In this deep river which was unruffled by conflict or a movement forward, the people lived without faces, except for their chief, whose face was the face of all the people; that is, if their chief's name was Monemapee, then they were all the people of Monemapee. The Talaote tribe have forgotten their origins and their original language during their journey southwards—they have merged and remerged again with many other tribes—and the name, Talaote,[1] is all they have retained in memory of their history. Before a conflict ruffled their deep river, they were all the people of Monemapee, whose kingdom was somewhere in the central part of Africa.

They remembered that Monemapee ruled the tribe for many years as the hairs on his head were already saying white! by the time he died. On either side of the deep river there might be hostile tribes or great dangers, so all the people lived in one great town. The lands where they ploughed their crops were always near the town. That was done by all the tribes for their own protection, and their day-to-day lives granted them no individual faces either for they ploughed their crops, reared their children, and held their festivities according to the laws of the land.

Although the people were given their own ploughing lands, they had no authority to plough them without the chief's order. When the people left home to go to plough, the chief sent out the proclamation for the beginning of the ploughing season. When harvest time came, the chief perceived that the corn was ripe. He gathered the people together and said:

'Reap now, and come home.'

When the people brought home their crops, the chief called the thanksgiving for the harvest. Then the women of the whole town carried their corn in flat baskets, to the chief's place. Some of that corn was accepted on its arrival, but the rest was returned so that the women might soak it in their own yards. After a few days, the chief sent his special messenger to proclaim that the harvest thanksgiving corn was to be pounded. The special messenger went around the whole town and in each place where there was a little hill or mound, he climbed it and shouted:

'Listen, the corn is to be pounded!'

So the people took their sprouting corn and pounded it. After some days the special messenger came back and called out:

'The corn is to be fermented now!'

1. An ethnic group in central Botswana, originally from Zimbabwe.

A few days passed and then he called out:

'The corn is to be cooked now!'

So throughout the whole town the beer was boiled and when it had been strained, the special messenger called out for the last time:

'The beer is to be brought now!'

On the day on which thanksgiving was to be held, the women all followed one another in single file to the chief's place. Large vessels had been prepared at the chief's place, so that when the women came they poured the beer into them. Then there was a gathering of all the people to celebrate thanksgiving for the harvest time. All the people lived this way, like one face, under their chief. They accepted this regimental levelling down of their individual souls, but on the day of dispute or when strife and conflict and greed blew stormy winds over their deep river, the people awoke and showed their individual faces.

Now, during his lifetime Monemapee had had three wives. Of these marriages he had four sons: Sebembele by the senior wife; Ntema and Mosemme by the second junior wife; and Kgagodi by the third junior wife. There was a fifth son, Makobi, a small baby who was still suckling at his mother's breast by the time the old chief, Monemapee, died. This mother was the third junior wife, Rankwana. It was about the fifth son, Makobi, that the dispute arose. There was a secret there. Monemapee had married the third junior wife, Rankwana, late in his years. She was young and beautiful and Sebembele, the senior son, fell in love with her—but in secret. On the death of Monemapee, Sebembele, as senior son, was installed chief of the tribe and immediately made a blunder. He claimed Rankwana as his wife and exposed the secret that the fifth son, Makobi, was his own child and not that of his father.

This news was received with alarm by the people as the first ripples of trouble stirred over the even surface of the river of their lives. If both the young man and the old man were visiting the same hut, they reasoned, perhaps the old man had not died a normal death. They questioned the councillors who knew all secrets.

'Monemapee died just walking on his own feet,' they said reassuringly.

That matter settled, the next challenge came from the two junior brothers, Ntema and Mosemme. If Sebembele were claiming the child, Makobi, as his son, they said, it meant that the young child displaced them in seniority. That they could not allow. The subtle pressure exerted on Sebembele by his junior brothers and the councillors was that he should renounce Rankwana and the child and all would be well. A chief lacked nothing and there were many other women more suitable as wives. Then Sebembele made the second blunder. In a world where women were of no account, he said truthfully:

'The love between Rankwana and I is great.'

This was received with cold disapproval by the councillors.

'If we were you,' they said, 'we would look for a wife somewhere else. A ruler must not be carried away by his emotions. This matter is going to cause disputes among the people.'

They noted that on being given this advice, Sebembele became very quiet, and they left him to his own thoughts, thinking that sooner or later he would come to a decision that agreed with theirs.

In the meanwhile the people quietly split into two camps. The one camp said: 'If he loves her, let him keep her. We all know Rankwana. She is a lovely person, deserving to be the wife of a chief.'

The other camp said:

'He must be mad. A man who is influenced by a woman is no ruler. He is like one who listens to the advice of a child. This story is really bad.'

There was at first no direct challenge to the chieftaincy which Sebembele occupied. But the nature of the surprising dispute, that of his love for a woman and a child, caused it to drag on longer than time would allow. Many evils began to rear their heads like impatient hissing snakes, while Sebembele argued with his own heart or engaged in tender dialogues with his love, Rankwana.

'I don't know what I can do,' Sebembele said, torn between the demands of his position and the strain of a love affair which had been conducted in deep secrecy for many, many months. The very secrecy of the affair seemed to make it shout all the louder for public recognition. At one moment his heart would urge him to renounce the woman and child, but each time he saw Rankwana it abruptly said the opposite. He could come to no decision.

It seemed little enough that he wanted for himself—the companionship of a beautiful woman to whom life had given many other attractive gifts; she was gentle and kind and loving. As soon as Sebembele communicated to her the advice of the councillors, she bowed her head and cried a little.

'If that is what they say, my love,' she said in despair, 'I have no hope left for myself and the child. It were better if we were both dead.'

'Another husband could be chosen for you,' he suggested.

'You doubt my love for you, Sebembele,' she said. 'I would kill myself if I lose you. If you leave me, I would kill myself.'

Her words had meaning for him because he was trapped in the same kind of anguish. It was a terrible pain which seemed to paralyse his movements and thoughts. It filled his mind so completely that he could think of nothing else, day and night. It was like a sickness, this paralysis, and like all ailments it could not be concealed from sight; Sebembele carried it all around with him.

'Our hearts are saying many things about this man,' the councillors said among themselves. They were saying that he was unmanly; that he was unfit to be a ruler; that things were slipping from his hands. Those still sympathetic approached him and said:

'Why are you worrying yourself like this over a woman, Sebembele? There are no limits to the amount of wives a chief may have, but you cannot have that woman and that child.'

And he only replied with a distracted mind: 'I don't know what I can do.'

But things had been set in motion. All the people were astir over events; if a man couldn't make up his mind, other men could make it up for him.

Everything was arranged in secret and on an appointed day Rankwana and the child were forcibly removed back to her father's home. Ever since the controversy had started, her father had been harassed day and night by the councillors as an influence that could help to end it. He had been reduced to a state of agitated muttering to himself by the time she was brought before him. The plan was to set her up with a husband immediately and settle the matter. She was not yet formally married to Sebembele.

'You have put me in great difficulties, my child,' her father said, looking away from her distressed face. 'Women never know their own minds and once this has passed away and you have many children you will wonder what all the fuss was about.'

'Other women may not know their minds . . .' she began, but he stopped her with a raised hand, indicating the husband who had been chosen for her. In all the faces surrounding her there was no sympathy or help, and she quietly allowed herself to be led away to her new home.

When Sebembele arrived in his own yard after a morning of attending to the affairs of the land, he found his brothers, Ntema and Mosemme there.

'Why have you come to visit me?' he asked, with foreboding. 'You never come to visit me. It would seem that we are bitter enemies rather than brothers.'

'You have shaken the whole town with your madness over a woman,' they replied mockingly. 'She is no longer here so you don't have to say any longer "I-don't-know-what-I-can-do". But we still request that you renounce the child, Makobi, in a gathering before all the people, in order that our position is clear. You must say: "That child Makobi is the younger brother of my brothers, Ntema and Mosemme, and not the son of Sebembele who rules".'

Sebembele looked at them for a long moment. It was not hatred he felt but peace at last. His brothers were forcing him to leave the tribe.

'Tell the people that they should all gather together,' he said. 'But what I say to them is my own affair.'

The next morning the people of the whole town saw an amazing sight which stirred their hearts. They saw their ruler walk slowly and unaccompanied through the town. They saw him pause at the yard of Rankwana's father. They saw Sebembele and Rankwana's father walk to the home of her new husband where she had been secreted. They saw Rankwana and Sebembele walk together through the town. Sebembele held the child Makobi in his arms. They saw that they had a ruler who talked with deeds rather than words. They saw that the time had come for them to offer up their individual faces to the face of this ruler. But the people were still in two camps. There was a whole section of the people who did not like this face; it was too out-of-the-way and shocking; it made them very uneasy. Theirs was not a tender, compassionate, and romantic world. And yet in a way it was. The arguments in the other camp which supported Sebembele had flown thick and fast all this time, and they said:

'Ntema and Mosemme are at the bottom of all this trouble. What are they after for they have set a difficult problem before us all? We don't trust them. But why not? They have not yet had time to take anything from us. Perhaps we ought to wait until they do something really bad; at present they are only filled with indignation at the behaviour of Sebembele. But no, we don't trust them. We don't like them. It is Sebembele we love, even though he has shown himself to be a man with a weakness . . .'

That morning, Sebembele completely won over his camp with his extravagant, romantic gesture, but he lost everything else and the rulership of the kingdom of Monemapee.

When all the people had gathered at the meeting place of the town, there were not many arguments left. One by one the councillors stood up and condemned the behaviour of Sebembele. So the two brothers, Ntema and Mosemme won the day. Still working together as one voice, they stood up and asked if their senior brother had any words to say before he left with his people.

'Makobi is my child,' he said.

'Talaote,' they replied, meaning in the language then spoken by the tribe—'all right, you can go'.

And the name Talaote was all they were to retain of their identity as the people of the kingdom of Monemapee. That day, Sebembele and his people packed their belongings on the backs of their cattle and slowly began the journey southwards. They were to leave many ruins behind them and it is said that they lived, on the journey southwards, with many other tribes like the Baphaleng, Bakaa, and Batswapong until they finally settled in the land of the Bamangwato.[2] To this day there is a separate Botalaote ward in the capital village of the Bamangwato, and the people refer to themselves still as the people of Talaote. The old men there keep on giving confused and contradictory accounts of their origins, but they say they lost their place of birth over a woman. They shake their heads and say that women have always caused a lot of trouble in the world. They say that the child of their chief was named, Talaote, to commemorate their expulsion from the kingdom of Monemapee.

FOOTNOTE:
The story is an entirely romanticized and fictionalized version of the history of the Botalaote tribe. Some historical data was given to me by the old men of the tribe, but it was unreliable as their memories had tended to fail them. A reconstruction was made therefore in my own imagination; I am also partly indebted to the London Missionary Society's *'Livingstone Tswana Readers', Padiso III*, school textbook, for those graphic paragraphs on the harvest thanksgiving ceremony which appear in the story.

B. HEAD.

1977

2. Ethnic groups in Botswana.

NAWAL EL SAADAWI

born 1931

In her autobiography *A Daughter of Isis* (1999), the Egyptian novelist Nawal El Saadawi writes that she realized early in her life how gender discrimination limits the opportunities of women in the Arab-Islamic world: "I had been born a female in a world that wanted only males." Her acute awareness of the damaging impact of this burden and her sense of solidarity with women around the world have sustained her abundant output—novels, short stories, autobiography, essays, and addresses as well as scientific treatises and sociological studies—in an active career that has spanned some sixty years.

Nawal El Saadawi was born in 1931 in Kafir Tahla, a small village on the banks of the Nile, into a well-to-do middle-class family with strong connections to the ruling elite of the country. Her mother descended from the traditional aristocracy; her father, a government functionary, had been active in the Egyptian Revolution of 1919. Both parents saw to it that their nine children all received a university education. Nawal El Saadawi herself studied medicine at the University of Cairo and participated in student protests against the British occupation. She also began writing short articles about her childhood for Egyptian newspapers. After her graduation in 1955, she practiced as a psychiatrist before being appointed to the Ministry of Health, where she rose to become director of public health. She was dismissed from her post in 1972, however, after the publication of her book *Woman and Sex*, which aroused the displeasure of the Egyptian authorities for its frank treatment of a subject that was considered taboo. Among other things, the book criticized the practice of female circumcision, or genital mutilation. This was the beginning of her long struggle for the right of expression and of her crusade for female emancipation in Egypt and the Arab world.

After losing her government position, El Saadawi devoted herself to research on women; she also worked for a year with the United Nations as an advisor on women's development in the Middle East and Africa. In 1981 she was imprisoned for three months during the campaign of repression against intellectuals by the Sadat regime, an experience that inspired El Saadawi's novel *The Fall of the Imam* (1987). On her release, in 1982, she founded the Arab Women's Solidarity Association (AWSA), a nongovernmental organization dedicated to informed discussion of women's issues. The association was dissolved by the government in 1991 and its assets confiscated. El Saadawi sued the government, but, despite support from a distinguished panel of lawyers, she could not prevail against the forces ranged against her. Because she had also incurred the wrath of Islamic fundamentalists and ran a real risk of being assassinated, she went into exile in the United States in 1992, returning to Egypt in 1999. She joined the opposition to the government in 2011 and became a symbol for the young people who crowded Tahrir Square, the hub of the uprising that unseated Egypt's president Hosni Mubarak. She remains well-known in Egypt for her political activism as well as her writing.

Internationally, El Saadawi is probably best known for her novel *Woman at Point Zero* (1979), an account of a female prisoner condemned to death for killing a pimp. The main character had come to the city and become a prostitute in order to escape a forced marriage and the constricted existence it promised. The psychological and moral dilemmas highlighted by El Saadawi's works and the simplicity of her narrative style allow her to explore customs and religious beliefs as they affect women in her society, especially women whose freedom has been taken from them by government institutions. In their bleak depiction of the female predicament, her novels seek to document, albeit in fictional form, the vicissitudes in the lives of Egyptian women, denied fulfillment by forces beyond their control.

The short story "In Camera," taken from the collection entitled *Death of an Ex-Minister* (1980), is a representative sample of her work. The story criticizes the social system and state machinery in a fictional kingdom, which might be any dictatorial regime. Its political theme is developed through the narrative of the trial and the irreverent portrayal of the king and the agents of the state. The story's emphasis, however, is firmly on the ordeal of the female protagonist, on trial for an act of defiance against the system. Her physical violation and mental agony are reconstructed through the series of flashbacks that shape the story's atmosphere. As El Saadawi explores both the protagonist's perspective and that of her parents during the trial, the writer shows both the private and the public dimensions of the unfolding tragedy.

For El Saadawi, writing about the inner workings of female consciousness is an effort to break the silence that surrounds the culture of abuse and repression of which women are often victims. Her work is politically engaged; she calls on her readers not just to sympathize with her characters but to undertake political action in order to meet the moral challenges of a repressive society.

In Camera[1]

The first thing she felt was a blinding light. She saw nothing. The light was painful, even though her eyes were still shut. The cold air hit her face and bare neck, crept down to her chest and stomach and then fell lower to the weeping wound, where it turned into a sharp blow. She put one hand over her eyes to protect them from the light, whilst with the other she covered her neck, clenching her thighs against the sudden pain. Her lips too were clenched tight against a pain the like of which her body had never known, like the sting of a needle in her eyes and breasts and armpits and lower abdomen. From sleeping so long while standing and standing so long while sleeping, she no longer knew what position her body was in, whether vertical or horizontal, dangling in the air by her feet or standing on her head in water.

The moment they sat her down and she felt the seat on which she was sitting with the palms of her hands, the muscles of her face relaxed and resumed their human form. A shudder of sudden and intense pleasure shook her from inside when her body took up a sitting position on the wooden seat and her lips curled into a feeble smile as she said to herself: Now I know what pleasure it is to sit!

The light was still strong and her eyes still could not see, but her eyes were beginning to catch the sound of voices and murmurings. She lifted her hand off her eyes and gradually began to open them. Blurred human silhouettes moved before her on some elevated construction. She suddenly felt frightened, for human forms frightened her more than any others. Those long, rapid and agile bodies, legs inside trousers and feet inside shoes. Everything had been done in the dark with the utmost speed and agility. She could not cry or scream. Her tongue, her eyes, her mouth, her nose, all the parts of her body, were constrained. Her body was no longer hers but was like that of a small calf struck by the heels of boots. A rough stick entered between her thighs to tear at her insides. Then she was kicked into a dark corner where she remained curled up until the following day. By the third day, she still had not returned to normal but remained like a small animal incapable of uttering the simple words: My God! She said to herself: Do animals, like humans, know of the existence of something called God?

1. Translated by Shirley Eber. "In camera": the judicial term for "closed session." The oppressive atmosphere of the trial scene is immediately conveyed by the title.

Her eyes began to make out bodies sitting on that elevated place, above each head a body, smooth heads without hair, in the light as red as monkeys' rumps. They must all be males, for however old a woman grew, her head could never look like a monkey's rump. She strained to see more clearly. In the centre was a fat man wearing something like a black robe, his mouth open; in his hand something like a hammer. It reminded her of the village magician, when her eyes and those of all the other children had been mesmerized by the hand which turned a stick into a snake or into fire. The hammer squirmed in his hand like a viper and in her ears a sharp voice resounded: The Court! To herself she said: He must be the judge. It was the first time in her life she'd seen a judge or been inside a court. She'd heard the word 'court' for the first time as a child. She'd heard her aunt tell her mother: The judge did not believe me and told me to strip so he could see where I'd been beaten. I told him that I would not strip in front of a strange man, so he rejected my claim and ordered me to return to my husband. Her aunt had cried and at that time she had not understood why the judge had told her aunt to strip. I wonder if the judge will ask me to strip and what he will say when he sees that wound, she said to herself.

Gradually, her eyes were growing used to the light. She began to see the judge's face more clearly. His face was as red as his head, his eyes as round and bulging as a frog's, moving slowly here and there, his nose as curved as a hawk's beak, beneath it a yellow moustache as thick as a bundle of dry grass, which quivered above the opening of a mouth as taut as wire and permanently gaping like a mousetrap.

She did not understand why his mouth stayed open. Was he talking all the time or breathing through it? His shiny bald head moved continually with a nodding movement. It moved upwards a little and then backwards, entering into something pointed; then it moved downwards and forwards, so that his chin entered his neck opening. She could not yet see what was behind him, but when he raised his head and moved it backwards, she saw it enter something pointed which looked like the cap of a shoe. She focused her vision and saw that it really was a shoe, drawn on the wall above the judge's head. Above the shoe she saw taut legs inside a pair of trousers of expensive leather or leopard skin or snakeskin and a jacket, also taut, over a pair of shoulders. Above the shoulders appeared the face she'd seen thousands of times in the papers, eyes staring into space filled with more stupidity than simplicity, the nose as straight as though evened out by a hammer, the mouth pursed to betray that artificial sincerity which all rulers and kings master when they sit before a camera. Although his mouth was pinched in arrogance and sincerity, his cheeks were slack, beneath them a cynical and comical smile containing chronic corruption and childish petulance.

She had been a child in primary school the first time she saw a picture of the king. The face was fleshy, the eyes narrow, the lips thin and clenched in impudent arrogance. She recalled her father's voice saying: he was decadent and adulterous. But they were all the same. When they stood in front of a camera, they thought they were god.

Although she could still feel her body sitting on the wooden seat, she began to have doubts. How could they allow her to sit all this time? Sitting like this was so very relaxing. She could sit, leaving her body in a sitting position, and enjoy that astounding ability which humans have. For the first time she understood that the human body differed from that of an animal in one important way—sitting. No animal could sit the way she could. If it did, what would it do with its four legs? She remembered a scene that had made her laugh as a child, of a calf which had tried to sit on its backside and had ended up on its back. Her lips curled in a futile attempt to open her mouth and say something or smile. But her mouth remained stuck, like a horizontal line splitting the lower part of her face into two. Could she open her mouth a little to spit? But her throat, her mouth, her neck, her chest, everything, was dry, all except for that gaping wound between her thighs.

She pressed her legs together tighter to close off the wound and the pain and to enjoy the pleasure of sitting on a seat. She could have stayed in that position for ever, or until she died, had she not suddenly heard a voice calling her name: Leila Al-Fargani.

Her numbed senses awoke and her ears pricked up to the sound of that strange name: Leila Al-Fargani. As though it wasn't her name. She hadn't heard it for ages. It was the name of a young woman named Leila, a young woman who had worn young woman's clothes, had seen the sun and walked on two feet like other human beings. She had been that woman a very long time ago, but since then she hadn't worn a young woman's clothes nor seen the sun nor walked on two feet. For a long time she'd been a small animal inside a dark and remote cave and when they addressed her, they only used animal names.

Her eyes were still trying to see clearly. The judge's head had grown clearer and moved more, but it was still either inside the cap of the shoe whenever he raised it or was inside his collar whenever he lowered it. The picture hanging behind him had also become clearer. The shiny pointed shoes, the suit as tight as a horseman's, the face held taut on the outside by artificial muscles full of composure and stupidity, on the inside depraved and contentious.

The power of her sight was no longer as it had been, but she could still see ugliness clearly. She saw the deformed face and remembered her father's words: They only reach the seat of power, my girl, when they are morally deformed and internally corrupt.

And what inner corruption! She had seen their real corruption for herself. She wished at that moment they would give her pen and paper so that she could draw that corruption. But would her fingers still be capable of holding a pen or of moving it across a piece of paper? Would she still have at least two fingers which could hold a pen? What could she do if they cut off one of those two fingers? Could she hold a pen with one finger? Could a person walk on one leg? It was one of those questions her father used to repeat. But she hated the questions of the impotent and said to herself: I will split the finger and press the pen into it, just as Isis split the leg of Osiris.[2] She remembered that old story, still saw the split leg pouring with blood. What a long nightmare she was living! How she wanted her mother's hand to shake her so she could open her

2. Isis and Osiris were a royal couple in Egyptian mythology. In the celebrated story of the couple, Isis wandered the land in search of the body of her murdered husband (who was also her brother), whose body had been thrown into the Nile in a golden casket. She recovered the body, into which she was able to breathe life and from which she conceived a son. However, the body was discovered by his murderer, who tore it into pieces, leaving Isis to collect the limbs and other parts, into which she again breathed life. Osiris soon died again and descended into the underworld, where he reigned over the dead.

eyes and wake up. She used to be so happy when, as a child, she opened her eyes and realized that the monster which had tried to rip her body to pieces was nothing but a dream, or a nightmare as her mother used to call it. Each time she had opened her eyes, she was very happy to discover that the monster had vanished, that it was only a dream. But now she opened her eyes and the monster did not go away. She opened her eyes and the monster stayed on her body. Her terror was so great that she closed her eyes again to sleep, to make believe that it was a nightmare. But she opened her eyes and knew it was no dream. And she remembered everything.

The first thing she remembered was her mother's scream in the silence of the night. She was sleeping in her mother's arms, like a child of six even though she was an adult and in her twenties. But her mother had said: You'll sleep in my arms so that even if they come in the middle of the night, I will know it and I'll hold on to you with all my might and if they take you they'll have to take me as well.

Nothing was as painful to her as seeing her mother's face move further and further away until it disappeared. Her face, her eyes, her hair, were so pale. She would rather have died than see her mother's face so haggard. To herself she said: Can you forgive me, Mother, for causing you so much pain? Her mother always used to say to her: What's politics got to do with you? You're not a man. Girls of your age think only about marriage. She hadn't replied when her mother had said: Politics is a dirty game which only ineffectual men play.

The voices had now become clearer. The picture also looked clearer, even though the fog was still thick. Was it winter and the hall roofless, or was it summer and they were smoking in a windowless room? She could see another man sitting not far from the judge. His head, like the judge's, was smooth and red but, unlike the judge's, it was not completely under the shoe. He was sitting to one side and above his head hung another picture in which there was something like a flag or a small multicoloured banner. And for the first time, her ears made out some intelligible sentences:

Imagine, ladies and gentlemen. This student, who is not yet twenty years old, refers to Him, whom God protect to lead this noble nation all his life, as 'stupid'.

The word 'stupid' fell like a stone in a sea of awesome silence, making a sound like the crash of a rock in water or the blow of a hand against something solid, like a slap or the clap of one hand against another.

Was someone clapping? She pricked up her ears to catch the sound. Was it applause? Or a burst of laughter, like a cackle? Then that terrifying silence pervaded the courtroom once again, a long silence in which she could hear the beating of her heart. The sound of laughter or of applause echoed in her ears. She asked herself who could be applauding at so serious a moment as when the mighty one was being described as stupid, and aloud too.

Her body was still stuck to the wooden seat, clinging on to it, frightened it would suddenly be taken away. The wound in her lower abdomen was still weeping. But she was able to move her head and half opened her eyes to search for the source of that applause. Suddenly she discovered that the hall was full of heads crammed together in rows, all of them undoubtedly human. Some of the heads appeared to have a lot of hair, as if they were those of women or girls. Some of them were small, as if those of children. One head seemed to be like that of her younger sister. Her body trembled for a moment on the seat as her eyes searched around. Had she come alone or with her father and mother? Were they looking at her now? How did she look? Could they recognize her face or her body?

She turned her head to look. Although her vision had grown weak, she could just make out her mother. She could pick out her mother's face from among thousands of faces even with her eyes closed. Could her mother really be here in the hall? Her heartbeats grew audible and anxiety grew inside her. Anxiety often gripped her and she felt that something terrible had happened to her mother. One night, fear had overcome her when she was curled up like a small animal and she'd told herself: She must have died and I will not see her when I get out. But the following day, she had seen her mother when she came to visit. She'd come, safe and sound. She was happy and said: Don't die, Mother, before I get out and can make up for all the pain I've caused you.

The sound was now clear in her ears. It wasn't just one clap but a whole series of them. The heads in the hall were moving here and there. The judge was still sitting, his smooth head beneath the shoe. The hammer in his hand was moving impatiently, banging rapidly on the wooden table. But the clapping did not stop. The judge rose to his feet so that his head was in the centre of the stomach in the picture. His lower lip trembled as he shouted out words of rebuke which she couldn't hear in all the uproar.

Then silence descended for a period. She was still trying to see, her hands by her side holding on to the seat, clinging on to it, pressing it as if she wanted to confirm that it was really beneath her or that she was really sitting on it. She knew she was awake and not asleep with her eyes closed. Before, when she opened her eyes, the monster would disappear and she'd be happy that it was only a dream. But now she was no longer capable of being happy and had become frightened of opening her eyes.

The noise in the hall had died down and the heads moved as they had done before. All except one head. It was neither smooth nor red. It was covered in a thick mop of white hair and was fixed and immobile. The eyes also did not move and were open, dry and fixed on that small body piled on top of the wooden seat. Her hands were clasped over her chest, her heart under her hand beating fast, her breath panting as if she were running to the end of the track and could no longer breathe. Her voice broke as she said to herself: My God! Her eyes turn in my direction but she doesn't see me. What have they done to her eyes? Or is she fighting sleep? God of Heaven and Earth, how could you let them do all that? How, my daughter, did you stand so much pain? How did I stand it together with you? I always felt that you, my daughter, were capable of anything, of moving mountains or of crumbling rocks, even though your body is small and weak like mine. But when your tiny feet used to kick the walls of my stomach, I'd say to myself: God, what strength and power there is inside my body? Your movements were strong while you were still a foetus and shook me from inside, like a volcano shakes the earth. And yet I knew that you were as small as I was, your bones as delicate as your father's, as tall and slim as your grandmother, your feet as large as the feet of prophets.[3] When I gave birth to you, your grandmother

3. The passage conjures up an image of devoted pupils sitting at the feet of the prophets.

pursed her lips in sorrow and said: A girl and ugly too! A double catastrophe! I tensed my stomach muscles to close off my womb to the pain and the blood and, breathing with difficulty, for your birth had been hard and I suffered as though I'd given birth to a mountain, I said to her: She's more precious to me than the whole world! I held you to my breast and slept deeply. Can I, my daughter, again enjoy another moment of deep sleep whilst you are inside me or at least near to me so that I can reach out to touch you? Or whilst you are in your room next to mine so that I can tiptoe in to see you whilst you sleep? The blanket always used to fall off you as you slept, so I'd lift it and cover you. Anxiety would waken me every night and make me creep into your room. What was that anxiety and at what moment did it happen? Was it the moment the cover fell off your body? I could always feel you, even if you had gone away and were out of my sight. Even if they were to bury you under the earth or build a solid wall of mud or iron around you, I would still feel a draught of air on your body as though it were on mine. I sometimes wonder whether I ever really gave birth to you or if you are still inside me. How else could I feel the air when it touches you and hunger when it grips you. Your pain is mine, like fire burning in my breast and stomach. God of Heaven and Earth, how did your body and mine stand it? But I couldn't have stood it were it not for the joy of you being my daughter, of having given birth to you. And you can raise your head high above the mountains of filth. For three thousand and twenty-five hours (I've counted them one by one), they left you with the vomit and pus and the weeping wound in your stomach. I remember the look in your eyes when you told me, the bars between us: If only the weeping were red blood. But it's not red. It's white and has the smell of death. What was it I said to you that day? I don't know, but I said something. I said that the smell becomes normal when we get used to it and live with it every day. I could not look into your emaciated face, but I heard you say: It's not a smell, mother, like other smells which enter through the nose or mouth. It's more like liquid air or steam turned to viscid[4] water or molten lead flowing into every opening of the body. I don't know, mother, if it is burning hot or icy cold. I clasped my hands to my breast, then grasped your slender hand through the bars, saying: When heat became like cold, my daughter, then everything is bearable. But as soon as I left you, I felt my heart swell and swell until it filled my chest and pressed on my lungs so I could no longer breathe. I felt I was choking and tilted my head skywards to force air into my lungs. But the sky that day was void of air and the sun over my head was molten lead like the fire of hell. The eyes of the guards stung me and their uncouth voices piled up inside me. If the earth had transformed into the face of one of them, I'd have spat and spat and spat on it until my throat and chest dried up. Yes, my daughter, brace the muscles of your back and raise your head and turn it in my direction, for I'm sitting near you. You may have heard them when they applauded you. Did you hear them? I saw you move your head towards us. Did you see us? Me and your father and little sister? We all applauded with them. Did you see us?

Her eyes were still trying to penetrate the thick fog. The judge was still standing, his head smooth and red, his lower lip trembling with rapid words. To his right and to his left, she saw smooth red heads begin to move away from that

4. Sticky.

elevated table. The judge's head and the others vanished, although the picture on the wall remained where it was. The face and the eyes were the same as they had been, but now one eye appeared to her to be smaller, as though half-closed or winking at her, that common gesture that a man makes to a woman when he wants to flirt with her. Her body trembled in surprise. Was it possible that he was winking at her? Was it possible for his eyes in the picture to move? Could objects move? Or was she sick and hallucinating? She felt the seat under her palm and raised her hand to touch her body. A fierce heat emanated from it, like a searing flame, a fire within her chest. She wanted to open her mouth and say: Please, a glass of water. But her lips were stuck together, a horizontal line as taut as wire. Her eyes too were stuck on the picture, while the eye in the picture continued to wink at her. Why was it winking at her? Was it flirting with her? She had only discovered that winking was a form of greeting when, two years previously, she'd seen a file of foreign tourists walking in the street. She'd been on her way to the university. Whenever she looked at the faces of one of the men or women, an eye would suddenly wink at her strangely. She had been shocked and hadn't understood how a woman could flirt with her in such a way. Only later had she understood that it was an American form of greeting.

The podium was still empty, without the judge and the smooth heads around him. Silence prevailed. The heads in the hall were still close together in rows and her eyes still roamed in search of a mop of white hair, a pair of black eyes which she could see with eyes closed. But there were so many heads close together she could only see a mound of black and white, circles or squares or oblongs. Her nose began to move as if she were sniffing, for she knew her mother's smell and could distinguish it from thousands of others. It was the smell of milk when she was a child at the breast or the smell of the morning when it rises or the night when it sleeps or the rain on wet earth or the sun above the bed or hot soup in a bowl. She said to herself: Is it possible that you're not here, Mother? And Father, have you come?

The fog before her eyes was still thick. Her head continued to move in the direction of the rows of crammed heads. The black and white circles were interlocked in tireless movement. Only one circle of black hair was immobile above a wide brown forehead, two firm eyes in a pale slender face and a small body piled on to a chair behind bars. His large gaunt hands gripped his knees, pressing on them from the pain. But the moment he heard the applause, he took his hands off his knees and brought them together to clap. His hands did not return to his knees, the pain in his legs no longer tangible. His heart beat loudly in time to his clapping which shook his slender body on the seat. His eyes began to scour the faces and eyes, and his lips parted a little as though he were about to shout: I'm her father, I'm Al-Fargani who fathered her and whose name she bears. My God, how all the pain in my body vanished in one go with the burst of applause. What if I were to stand up now and reveal my identity to them? This moment is unique and I must not lose it. Men like us live and die for one moment such as this, for others to recognize us, to applaud us, for us to become heroes with eyes looking at us and fingers pointing at us. I have suffered the pain and torture with her, day after day, hour after hour, and now I have the right to enjoy some of the reward and share in her heroism.

He shifted his body slightly on his seat as if he were about to stand up. But he remained seated, though his head still moved. His eyes glanced from face to face, as if he wanted someone to recognize him. The angry voice of the judge and the sharp rapid blows of his hammer on the table broke into the applause. Presently the judge and those with him withdrew to the conference chambers. Silence again descended on the hall, a long and awesome silence, during which some faint whispers reached his ears: They'll cook up the case in the conference chamber . . . That's common practice . . . Justice and law don't exist here . . . In a while they'll declare the public hearing closed . . . She must be a heroine to have stayed alive until now . . . Imagine that young girl who is sitting in the dock causing the government so much alarm . . . Do you know how they tortured her? Ten men raped her, one after the other. They trampled on her honour and on her father's honour. Her poor father! Do you know him! They say he's ill in bed. Maybe he can't face people after his honour was violated!

At that moment he raised his hands to cover his ears so as not to hear, to press on his head so that it sunk into his chest, pushing it more and more to merge his body into the seat or underneath it or under the ground. He wanted to vanish so that no one would see or know him. His name was not Al-Fargani, not Assharqawi, not Azziftawi, not anything. He had neither name nor existence. What is left of a man whose honour is violated? He had told her bitterly: Politics, my girl, is not for women and girls. But she had not listened to him. If she had been a man, he would not be suffering now the way he was. None of those dogs would have been able to violate his honour and dignity. Death was preferable for him and for her now.[5]

Silence still reigned over the hall. The judge and his entourage had not yet reappeared. Her eyes kept trying to see, searching out one face amongst the faces, for eyes she recognized, for a mop of white hair the colour of children's milk. But all she could see were black and white circles and squares intermingled and constantly moving. Is it possible you're not here, Mother? Is Father still ill? Her nose too continued to move here and there, searching for a familiar smell, the smell of a warm breast full of milk, the smell of the sun and of drizzle on grass. But her nose was unable to pick up the smell. All it could pick up was the smell of her body crumpled on the seat and the weeping wound between her thighs. It was a smell of pus and blood and the putrid stench of the breath and sweat of ten men, the marks of whose nails were still on her body, with their uncouth voices, their saliva and the sound of their snorting. One of them, lying on top of her, had said: This is the way we torture you women—by depriving you of the most valuable thing you possess. Her body under him was as cold as a corpse but she had managed to open her mouth and say to him: You fool! The most valuable thing I possess is not between my legs. You're all stupid. And the most stupid among you is the one who leads you.

She craned her neck to raise her head and penetrate the fog with her weak eyes. The many heads were still crammed together and her eyes still strained. If only she could have seen her mother for a moment, or her father or little sister, she would have told them something strange. She would have told them

5. According to the Arab-Islamic code of honor, decreed and upheld by men.

that they had stopped using that method of torture when they discovered that it didn't torture her. They began to search for other methods.

In the conference chamber next to the hall, the judge and his aides were meeting, deliberating the case. What should they do now that the public had applauded the accused? The judge began to face accusations in his turn:

—We're not accusing you, Your Honour, but you did embarrass us all. As the saying goes: 'The road to hell is paved with good intentions'! You did what you thought was right, but you only managed to make things worse. How could you say, Your Honour, about Him, whom God protect to lead this noble nation all his life, that he is stupid?

—God forbid, sir! I didn't say that, I said that *she* said he was stupid.

—Don't you know the saying, 'What the ear doesn't hear, the heart doesn't grieve over'? You declared in public that he's stupid.

—I didn't say it, sir. I merely repeated what the accused said to make the accusation stick. That's precisely what my job is.

—Yes, that's your job, Your Honour. We know that. But you should have been smarter and wiser than that.

—I don't understand.

—Didn't you hear how the people applauded her?

—Is that my fault?

—Don't you know why they applauded?

—No, I don't.

—Because you said in public what is said in private and it was more like confirming a fact than proving an accusation.

—What else could I have done, sir?

—You could have said that she cursed the mighty one without saying exactly *what* she said.

—And if I'd been asked what kind of curse it was?

—Nobody would have asked you. And besides, you volunteered the answer before anyone asked, as though you'd seized the opportunity to say aloud and in her words, what you yourself wanted to say or perhaps what you do say to yourself in secret.

—Me? How can you accuse me in this way? I was simply performing my duty as I should. Nobody can accuse me of anything. Perhaps I was foolish, but you cannot accuse me of bad faith.

—But foolishness can sometimes be worse than bad faith. You must know that foolishness is the worst label you can stick on a man. And as far as he's concerned, better that he be a swindler, a liar, a miser, a trickster, even a thief or a traitor, rather than foolish. Foolishness means that he doesn't think, that he's mindless, that he's an animal. That's the worst thing you can call an ordinary man. And all the more so if he's a ruler. You don't know rulers, Your Honour, but I know them well. Each of them fancies his brain to be better than any other man's. And it's not just a matter of fantasy, but of blind belief, like the belief in God. For the sake of this illusion, he can kill thousands.[6]

—I didn't know that, sir. How can I get out of this predicament?

6. An overt critique of the murderous inclinations fostered by religious fanaticism.

—I don't know why you began with the description 'stupid', Your Honour. If you'd read everything she said, you'd have found that she used other less ugly terms to describe him.

—Such as what, sir? Please, use your experience to help me choose some of them. I don't want to leave here accused, after coming in this morning to raise an accusation.

—Such descriptions cannot be voiced in public. The session must be closed. Even a less ugly description will find an echo in the heart of the people if openly declared. That's what closed sessions are for, Your Honour. Many matters escape you and it seems you have little experience in law.

A few minutes later, utter silence descended on the hall. The courtroom was completely emptied. As for her, they took her back to where she'd been before.

1980

ŌE KENZABURŌ

born 1935

Ōe Kenzaburō ranks among the most important Japanese writers in the latter decades of the twentieth century. The second Japanese writer to receive the Nobel Prize, in 1994, he remains active in Japanese letters as a prolific author, a public intellectual, and a provocative moral voice. His fiction, often described as "grotesque realism," combines political and psychological themes to explore moral dilemmas in the Cold War, and now post–Cold War, eras.

Ōe was born in a rural area on Shikoku, the smallest of the four main Japanese islands. He vividly remembers that, as a student in primary school during Japan's wars in Asia and the Pacific, he had to pledge daily to die for the emperor if called to do so. Equally vivid is his account of the emperor's radio broadcast in August 1945 announcing the end of hostilities with the Allied countries: the first time his voice was carried on radio, the emperor's stilted speech was unintelligible to the villagers, and to many of the children sounded comical. Ōe's formative years passed during the American Occupation and its aftermath; Japan's dependent relationship with the United States during these years, when a "demilitarized" Japan supported the US position in the Cold War by hosting extensive US military bases, would later become a recurring theme in his work.

In 1954, Ōe entered the University of Tokyo, where he majored in French literature and wrote a senior thesis on the French existentialist philosopher Jean-Paul Sartre. He began publishing stories while still a university student. Two events shook his life in 1963: he visited Hiroshima to attend a world conference against the atomic and hydrogen bombs; and his wife gave birth to a son with severe brain damage.

Within a few years the major themes and motifs of his work emerged: the threat of nuclear weapons to human survival, the compromised innocence of the young, and the role of individual choice and responsibility in response to overwhelming issues.

The Japan in which Ōe grew up was a place both of optimism and of disappointment. Initially the American Occupation espoused principles drawn from the New Deal of US President Franklin D. Roosevelt, favoring labor unions and giving women the right to vote. At the same time, the postwar constitution reduced the emperor to a figurehead and foreswore armed conflict, policies meant to encourage the growth of peaceful democracy in Japan. Yet as the United States began confronting the Soviet Union in the late 1940s, the Occupation became more concerned with securing Japan as a reliable ally in the Cold War. It turned against labor unions because of their many communist members and, instead, supported anticommunist politicians. In the early 1950s, a rising conservative government expanded these reactionary policies and restricted the activities of the left. Ōe has described himself as an heir to the writers who opposed Japanese participation in the US alliance and the conservative turn in postwar politics. Although many critics and ordinary citizens sought to ignore or downplay military events in the years immediately after 1945, these writers called for all, not just the country's leaders, to acknowledge their responsibility for the war.

The story presented here, "The Clever Rain Tree" (1980), draws on the tradition of autobiographical fiction in Japan. This genre, which has precedents in classical literature, emerged in its modern form around the turn of the century and reached its peak of popularity during the 1920s. Its influence can be found in the meditative narrative voice of "The Clever Rain Tree," whose references are specific enough that we can assume the events to have a basis in the author's experiences. The author subjects the material to ghoulish transformation, however, creating a story that is at once otherworldly, parodic, and self-critical.

The setting of "The Clever Rain Tree" is a seminar on East-West understanding that takes place during the mid-1970s. As a public intellectual, Ōe would be familiar with such well-intentioned but perhaps naive efforts to ease international tensions through dialogue, as well as with the types likely to take part. There is the domineering American "beatnik," apparently modeled on the poet Allen Ginsberg, who subjects the others to clichéd opinions on the "Far East" and inept stabs at composing haiku. (The poem he produces does not follow the rules of the form, which requires phrases of five, seven, and five syllables.) South Asians attempt to communicate using "many distinct forms of English"; bombastic Americans try to dominate the proceedings; participants from South Korea and Iran, both pro-US dictatorships at the time, fear punishment for the free exchange of ideas. Meanwhile, middle-aged female "sponsors" throw receptions that the attendees find awkward. As in so many of the author's works, human psychology and political behavior slide back and forth along a continuum.

Against this social and political satire, the story depicts the mystery and sadness of the insane. (This theme has surfaced often in Ōe's writing since the birth of his son with mental disabilities.) The quest for human understanding that the seminar pursues, and the reader's glimpses behind it of minds in isolation, might be said to represent opposing poles of the narrative. As the awkward situation at the party becomes surreal, these poles converge—until, in a moment emblematic of Ōe's grotesque realism, the participants find themselves experiencing disillusionment, and the niceties that held the reception together quickly unravel.

In his acceptance speech for the Nobel Prize, Ōe described Japan as a place of profound ambiguities: an Asian nation, long industrialized; "modern," yet still not "Western"; the target of European imperialism in the nineteenth century and an imperial aggressor in Asia in the twentieth. The task of the novelist is to address such ambiguities, he said, at least to help diagnose the pains and sorrows they entail: "I wish my task as a novelist to enable both those who express themselves with words and their readers to recover from their own sufferings and the sufferings of their time, and to cure their souls of the wounds."

The Clever Rain Tree[1]

"You'd rather see the tree than these people, wouldn't you?" inquired the American woman of German descent as she ushered me from the room jammed with partygoers, along a wide corridor, and onto the porch where we faced a broad expanse of darkness. Enveloped in the laughter and hubbub behind me, I gazed into the damp-smelling dark. That the greater part of this darkness was filled with a single huge tree was evident from the fact that at the rim of the darkness the faintly reflecting shapes of innumerable layers of radiating, board-like roots spread out in our direction. I gradually realized that these shapes like black board fences were glowing softly with a luster of grayish blue. The tree—how many hundred tree-years old was it, with its well-developed board-roots?—in this darkness eclipsed the sky and the sea far below the slope. From where we stood beneath the eaves of the porch of this large New England-style building, even at broad noon one could probably see no further than its shins, to speak of the tree anthropomorphically. It befitted the old style of the building, or rather its actual age, that around this house whose sole illumination was so quietly restrained the tree in the garden formed a wall of total darkness.

"The local name for this tree, which you said you wanted to know, is 'rain tree,' but this one of ours is a particularly clever rain tree." So said the American woman, a middle-aged woman whom I called Agatha, since we didn't know each other's surnames . . . Writing like this smacks of a romance set abroad, like those we see from time to time in contemporary Japanese novels, whose hero is a compatriot proficient in foreign languages. In my case, however, it was with no such leisure that I passed these ten days. I was attending a seminar sponsored by the University of Hawaii's East-West Center on the issue of "Reappraisal of Cultural Exchange and Traditions." As for my English ability, it was such that I mistook three delegates from India for delegates from Canada, and didn't realize until halfway through the conference that they were actually from the Kannada region of India. In fact, since the conference was dedicated to the memory of the Indian humanist Coomaraswamy,[2] there were participants from various regions in India, fluent in many distinct forms of English. Listening to the presentation of a Jewish Indian poet from Bombay, for example—his manner of speaking was

1. Translated by Brett de Bary and Carolyn Haynes.

2. Ananda Kentish Coomaraswamy (1877–1947), South Asian philosopher and art critic.

extremely Indian, yet there was something unmistakably Jewish about it—I was able to enjoy his sense of humor, but if I didn't question him about each point after his lecture, it was difficult to give my response in the following sessions.

The participant from the American mainland, the poet who defined an era as spokesman for the beatnik generation,[3] would arrive at the meeting every morning with a youth who looked physically exhausted and psychologically scarred (at least to me he appeared in this pitiful state) and would cast tender glances toward the youth, who napped on the floor behind the round table where the seminar participants were seated, saying "He is my wife." Although the speech of this New Yorker so combined discipline and unpredictability in its unique way of unfolding that I could hardly follow his English, he elicited my comments on the so-called haiku[4] of his I've inserted below. He even sketched on a napkin from the cafeteria the scene depicted: a snowy mountain glimpsed through the wings of a fly mashed on a window. In brief, he was determined to get an authentic critique from a writer from the land of haiku. Having thus become his friend, I could hardly sit through his presentation daydreaming of other things.

Snow mountain fields
seen thru transparent wings
of a fly on windowpane.

At the end of the schedule of meetings that day I returned to the student dormitory which served as our lodging—a girls' dormitory, at that—intending to rest before the nightly party, when I was accosted by an American, a man of small stature with damaged facial muscles, who seemed to be in great torment. He had apparently worked until five years ago assisting deserters from the Vietnam War in a provincial city on the Japan Sea coast. At that time he became aware that rumors were spreading among his co-workers that he was a spy for the CIA, so he quietly slipped off to Tokyo and returned to America from there. "I imagine the leaders of the movement still think of me as a spy. Even if I wanted to renew contact with them now, I can't remember their names myself. I've always been hard of hearing, which makes it difficult for me to understand the English spoken by the Japanese, to say nothing of Japanese itself. Actually, even when I was with the movement, this led to a lot of misunderstandings and I was often confused."

This garrulous young American had become so distraught over the insubstantial rumors that he was a spy that he was now in a private institution for the psychologically disturbed. There are many classes of such institutions here in Hawaii, from the very expensive on down. This fellow lived in the kind that charged little more than the actual cost of living, yet he still went out to work during the day to earn his expenses. But how was I to comfort this poor, tormented young American, this character whose small frame was completely covered with grime (apparently related to his work)? This thoroughly depressed man who kept cocking his head toward me like a bird as if to press his ear to

3. US literary movement of the 1950s and early 1960s; a principal figure was the poet Allen Ginsberg (1926–1997), on whom the poet here is modeled.

4. Verse form that in Japanese consists of three phrases of five, seven, and five syllables.

my mouth, yet who still couldn't grasp with his bad ear what my English—a Japanese English—meant.

Engulfing the foreground of the darkness, only the expanse of the margin of the tree's well-developed roots was faintly discernible . . . It seemed that the middle-aged woman who showed me the tree also ran a private psychiatric clinic like those the tormented American had described, this one plainly of the higher class, in this spacious, old New England-style building.

There are often groups of so-called sponsors affiliated with public seminars at universities and research institutes throughout America. Usually late middle-aged or elderly women who have contributed no significant sum of money, they come as auditors to surround the seminar participants. Sometimes they put things in the form of questions, but they are also ready to express their own opinions. Then at night the sponsors take turns inviting the seminar members to their homes for a party. For those participants whose native tongue is not English, especially for those with my degree of language ability, these parties are a mortification no less severe than the days' seminars proper. Moreover the sponsors, having attended the day's seminar, beleaguer one with questions of which they never seem to tire.

The German-American woman whom people called Agatha was one of these sponsors, and her leading me out of the large adjoining rooms where the party was going on to view from the porch the tree in the dark garden was also related to something I had said that day at the seminar. Among the items in a collection of Coomaraswamy memorabilia on exhibit in conjunction with the seminar was a piece of Indian folk art, *Krishna in a Tree*, rendered in a minute sketch on a bound banana leaf. Naked women were calling to Krishna[5] from the river below. "The bodies of these women are typically Indian in every manifestation," the beatnik poet who was also a specialist in Hindu culture stated at the outset. "This has been captured in such a way that the form of an Indian woman's body, especially the breasts and belly, is distinctive from that of women from any other country. And, in fact, when one travels through India one sees women of precisely this physical type." Comments from other areas of the Far East were solicited to reply to this, whereupon a group of Indian women who were auditing reacted against the American poet, and I articulated my thoughts by turning the discussion to trees.

"Regarding what Allen has said, I obviously agree with his point that the style of representing the human form in Indian folk art contains idiosyncracies that are typically Indian. I would even partially support the view that, conversely, the form of the body has itself been influenced. It is probably fair to assume that this means that the physiology of the Indian people determines the style of their folk art, which is a manner of speaking typical of Allen. However, since I myself am not qualified to speak from experience about the bodies of Indian women, I would like to see the same theories applied to trees.

"This black tree Krishna has climbed is undoubtedly what would be called an Indian bo tree[6] in my country. It has certainly been depicted through the sensibility and techniques of the Indian folk art style. That is, its distinctive

5. Hindu god, one of the incarnations of the principal deity, Vishnu.
6. Also known as pipal; the Buddha is said to have reached enlightenment while sitting under a bo tree.

features are exaggerated, and yet the substantial feel of its trunk and curve of its branches, or again the way the tips of its leaves are elongated like a tail—these are all grounded in realistic observation. Nevertheless, the tree as a whole still strikes me as distinctively Indian. With this concrete example, I would like to propose a hypothesis paralleling Allen's idea. I feel there are close resemblances between a region's trees and the people who live and die there. Don't the trees of Cranach[7] give every appearance of being the bodies of Upper Franconian people standing there?"

I also mentioned the particular fondness I have for trees and the names that identify them in various lands. "When I travel to a foreign country I take delight in seeing within that landscape the trees particular to that region. Moreover, it is only by learning the region's unique designation and thus for the first time really knowing the trees that I feel I have truly encountered them. As I said before, the Japanese call this tree of Krishna's a bo tree. For us, this is a form of expression completely different from its classification as *Ficus religiosa Linn.* As for its scientific name, I interpret it as an explanation of the tree, which is different from the tree's name . . ."

It was with such a set of prior circumstances that Agatha uprooted me from the party to lead me before the huge tree that occupied the garden in front of the building. Nevertheless, since dusk had already fallen when I had been brought to the house, even when I got off the minibus I had been unable to see the entire tree; as a matter of fact even now I was only peering into the darkness where the tree purportedly stood. In any event, Agatha had tried to teach me the local name for the tree.

"It's called a 'rain tree' because, when there's a shower at night, drops of water fall from its foliage until past noon the next day, as if the tree were raining. Other trees dry off quickly, but this one stores water in its closely packed leaves, no larger than fingertips. Isn't it a clever tree?"

At dusk of that day which had threatened to rain, there had also been a shower. The moisture I smelled coming from the darkness, therefore, was the rain that the dense fingertip leaves were causing to fall anew on the ground. By concentrating my attention in front of me and ignoring the din of the party behind, I could, it seemed, hear the sound made by the fine rain as it fell from the tree over a fairly broad area. As I listened, I began to feel that, in the wall of black before my eyes, there were two different shades of darkness. One darkness was something like a giant baobab tree,[8] bulb-shaped; around its rim was a second vortex of darkness which fell away into bottomless depths, a darkness so profound that even if the rays of the waning moon had penetrated it no oceans or mountain ranges, nothing in our human universe, would have been visible. The immigrants who came to Hawaii from the American mainland a century—perhaps a century and a half—ago to build this house must have seen the same darkness on their first night, I mused. But was this darkness that yawned beyond the garden, ready to suck in body and soul of whoever looked at it, an appropriate setting for a home for the mentally ill?

7. Lucas Cranach the Elder (1472–1553), painter and engraver, originally from the Franconia region of southern Germany.

8. Indian and African tree of wide girth but low height.

Thanks to my habit of censoring my statements before I articulate them in a foreign tongue, I stopped short of putting this question to Agatha. It was probably just as well, since Agatha, as someone who lived in the building and was responsible for its residents, would no doubt have taken my words as a direct criticism of herself. Nevertheless, I realized that my perception of the two darknesses—the rim of the darkness shaped like the tree I had created in my imagination, and the darkness that engulfed it—was shared by the German-born American woman who stood just behind me. For I could clearly hear the long sigh, like an arrow of darkness released into the universe, that escaped from the sharp-chinned, oval face supported by her erect spine. We turned away from the tree that emanated the smell of water into the night and retraced our steps over the wide, wooden planks of the porch.

Agatha, like all the American women associated with this conference, was a realist, pragmatist, and activist in every sphere, and she could not restrain herself from infusing even the simple, quiet process of withdrawing from the dark garden with a sense of purpose. She came to a halt before one of the many first-floor rooms that lined the long porch and, bending slightly from the hips, peered in at something on the opposite wall with a truly affectionate gaze. Intrigued, I, too, peeked through the door and saw inside a wall covered with bookshelves, dimly illuminated by a lamp that hung from the high, plastered ceiling. (Soft lights, as opposed to the psychedelic lights I had often seen used in Hawaii, had also been used in the rooms where the party was being held, convincing me that this was, indeed, a facility for the mentally ill.) For someone of my height, it wasn't even necessary to bend as much as Agatha did.

As my eyes adjusted to the dim light after staring into darkness, I could see that an oil painting about six feet square was suspended in a most unusual manner, in midair, about halfway down the wall covered with bookshelves, hiding from sight all the books behind it. The painting almost seemed to have been hung at precisely the angle that would make it visible to someone peering in from the porch, as we were, or from the roots of the tree of darkness in the garden. Come to think of it, hadn't I noticed a steel chair, painted in a somber color, among the prolific board-like roots of the tree?

"*A Girl on Horseback*," Agatha intoned, apparently reading the title on the painting; I realized I was looking at a painting of a young girl seated on a saddle that sank deep into the flanks of a sturdy, chestnut farm horse. The girl was surrounded by gloomy, forbidding walls which could have been those of a prison or concentration camp, and were strangely out of keeping with the sporty atmosphere of horseback riding. It dawned on me that this *Girl on Horseback* was a portrait of Agatha herself as a child. I mentioned this and noticed in the dimness that blood seethed up beneath the thin skin of Agatha's face as she answered, "Yes, this is me when I was still in Germany, a girl on horseback, in the days before the truly frightful, unhappy things began to occur." Something intense and powerful in Agatha's burning blue eyes and in her cheeks, so flushed that heat seemed to radiate from the gold tips of her facial hair, prohibited me from asking what those "frightful, unhappy things" were. I knew only that Agatha had left her motherland, Germany (whether East or West, I was uncertain), and emigrated to Hawaii. Yet if I forced myself to make a connection between the two things, I could understand the meaning of the boycott of tonight's party by the European and American Jews at the seminar. (The Jewish Indian poet from Bombay, who deplored taking a single crab from the beach, viewed the lives and deaths of humans in the political context with the detachment of a Bodhisattva.)[9] But some kind of wisdom which makes it possible for seminars and parties like this to proceed peacefully must come into play just one step before a person attempts to scrutinize and pass judgment on such an issue.

When we returned to the adjoining rooms where the party was taking place we discovered that, during our absence, a new central character had appeared and had taken over the role that was previously Agatha's. In fact, the bearing of this new figure contrasted sharply with Agatha's demeanor as hostess; he seemed to constitute a dominating center of the gathering, like a tyrant reigning over the party. He was a dwarfish man of about fifty, ensconced in a wheelchair, who at first glance might have been taken for a child dressed up like a witch for a play. His long, ivory-colored hair had been trimmed and shaped so that it turned under along the collar of his red satin jacket. His mouth, like a dog's, was the largest feature in his face, while his aquiline nose and double-lidded gray eyes had a proud beauty to them. The impression created when his powerfully vibrating voice issued forth from his large mouth was one of arrogance, yet he directed unflagging attention to the young people who sat at his knees and stood around his wheelchair. It was to the beatnik poet, standing directly in front of his wheelchair as if to block its path, that he addressed a steady stream of words. Yet it was clear that the exchange between the two was a sort of game or theatrical performance, and that the man in the wheelchair, if not the poet, was more conscious of his audience than of his opponent.

"The architect Komarovich—our brilliant architect! What high spirits he's in tonight!" Agatha explained brightly, as if displaying her proudest possession. Her voice had instantly adapted to the gay tone of the party before us; the note of exaltation, underlain by pent-up gloom, that suffused her words when she spoke to me about *A Girl on Horseback* had vanished. She left me behind and walked with long, brisk strides to join the young men beside the wheelchair, deftly skirting the legs and knees of those who were seated on the floor.

I stayed at my post beside the entrance to the room and observed the debate between the architect and the beatnik poet, which was beginning to seem like entertainment provided as the party's main event. In fact, if I were to give a perfectly balanced description of all that transpired that night, I would have to present the debate between poet and architect as a one-act play, consisting purely of dialogue without any action. This is because the hour-long debate, after which our soirée in the mental institution came to an abrupt end, consumed the major portion of the evening. However, as I mentioned at the outset, with my level of comprehension it was impossible to grasp precisely the multiple levels of meaning of this dialogue between the architect, with his strangely high-pitched, florid speech, and the poet, who barely opened his lips when he spoke, and whose words combined Manhattan-style sophistication with an unconventionality befitting an idol of the beatnik movement. The only way I could interpret the play of logic and illogic in their words was to follow one step behind, reconstructing whatever I could from bits and pieces of the

9. In Buddhism, someone who has attained enlightenment and thus is free from worldly ties, but remains in the world to help others.

conversation. Thus, in my own way, I managed to fend off boredom during the hour-long session.

What I have written here, then, is merely a recasting of a reconstruction I performed that evening, no doubt distorted both by memory and the passage of time. To keep myself from degenerating into tedious summarizing, I have interspersed my own perceptions of the atmosphere surrounding the talks. This is also because of the extremely "colorful" nature (to borrow a word used frequently during the seminar), not only of the debaters' performance itself, but of the responses of the guests at the party—who listened intently, and even seemed to participate without actually intruding—and of the waiters and waitresses who were serving them food and drink.

At the feet of the poet, who remained standing throughout the debate, sat three boys of fifteen or sixteen similar enough to be brothers, in the sense that the face and body of each one conformed to the poet's tastes. These boys, unlike the athletic youths of Hawaii, looked as if they had never been to the beach in their lives, and they sat with pale faces cast down, lost in thought. One was a boy who had followed the poet to the seminar that morning, looking as stunned as a virgin who had just been deflowered, and whom everyone tried not to look at. Surrounding these three boys and covering the floor were other young people who were admirers of the poet, among them a girl attired in a Judo outfit (though she showed no traces of physical exertion) who seemed to be trying to attract the poet's attention by acting like a boy. She was, of course, already quite drunk, and no sooner had she nodded vigorously in agreement with something Allen had said than her head would slump and she would doze off, only to struggle awake again, shaking her head as if she had been listening attentively all along.

Encircling the architect in his wheelchair on three sides, like stalwart supporters of his genius, Agatha and the other middle-aged and elderly ladies sat primly on sofas and chairs and cast stealthy, pitying glances at the drunken young woman of the opposing camp in her Judo suit. It was at the poet that they directed their unvoiced disapproval, and they let the architect act as their advocate, expressing the full burden of their moral sentiment. Needless to say, these matrons, whose silence formed a shield for the architect championing their cause, consumed more alcohol than the young people on the floor. Of the three types of drinks—beer, gin and tonic, and whiskey—being served by the bartenders, waiters, and waitresses (apparently students working part-time) in attendance at this midnight party, it was not beer but the more potent stuff that filled the glasses of the matrons, who looked for all the world like spinsters or widows in uniform as they sat in matching girlish frocks with lacy collars. With deft gestures, calculated to escape the notice of the other guests, they drained their glasses and then signaled immediately for refills. Agatha was no exception. In fact, the only people drinking beer at the party were the seminar participants, who formed the outermost flank of those surrounding the debate.

Although I assumed the young people catering at the party were students hired for the occasion, they were a mysterious bunch who seemed to have developed a unique style in their dress and deportment by training together as a group. The men all wore old-fashioned vests and silk shirts with puffy sleeves; the girls wore the same frocks as those of the matrons, covered with frilly aprons. All were pale, terribly thin, and showed signs of what, to a superficial observer like myself, appeared to be autism. For example, they weaved in and out of the partygoers without ever looking anyone in the eye, even when they handed you a canapé or a drink. And despite their graceful bearing, or perhaps even because of the excessive agility of their movements, I detected the sound of violent breathing, as if from sheer exhaustion, whenever one of them brushed past me. A strangely antique, musty body odor, which in no way contradicted their cleanliness, clung to each one. This seemed to mystify those seminar participants whose interest had not been aroused by the debate, and they whispered about it among themselves.

It was against such a backdrop that the debate between architect and poet took place . . . that is to say, the verbal offensive of the architect and the defensive maneuvers of the poet, who managed to deflect the attack without ever appearing underhanded. The following is a summary of what I was able to pick up of the attacker's argument:

"You are a passionate lover of boys and young men and this is a beautiful thing, in and of itself. It is a standpoint we hold in common. Yet it is clear that even here, at our very point of departure, there are insurmountable differences between us. Your passion develops in a direction that debases and corrupts the young. Mine uplifts and enlightens them. Perhaps you will say that you are introducing young people to dark, mystical knowledge and depths of feeling. Just now you insisted that carnal love was as central to human experience as spiritual love since both were dark and mystical in their essence." (It was by taking the terse, acerbic rejoinders uttered jestingly by the poet and turning them upside down, in this manner, within the context of his own flowery and effusive speech that the architect was able to furnish his alcoholic supporters with a taste of victory. The poet, for his part, actually seemed to be enjoying his successive routs on the surface level of the debate and made no effort to probe the deep-seated weaknesses of his opponent. Where he could easily have exposed the architect's argument for its imprecision or its fatuousness, he simply shrugged his shoulders and chortled like a Santa Claus.) "But carnal love and spiritual love must be like a spiral stairway, constantly ascending toward their bright, sacred essence. Especially that physical and spiritual love which sees itself as educating the young . . ."

The architect went on to deliver a lecture—he had by now assumed the air of someone speaking from a podium—about the special features of this facility of the mentally ill as he, the designer of the building, had envisioned them, and about how the management of the facility was structured around his vision. "Those who seek refuge in this old house after fleeing the American mainland are the possessors of keen, delicate, ailing spirits. I felt I should provide each one with a place of retreat tailored to his or her own body. If there could be one hill, one valley, for every patient in this facility, what a wonderful thing that would be! Like the castles and estates that insane monarchs in Europe, suffering their various fates, made into hermitages in those wonderful eras of the past! The naked, wounded soul in America today is not even guaranteed a private dwelling place. Accordingly, I've devoted my energies to ensuring that, in this building at least, every person who seeks shelter will have a 'position' of his or her own. For my own 'position' I chose the lowest place in the building: my workshop is in the basement garage. And now, I'd like to ask you to take your cues from me, pretend you're going down to my workshop, right below the floor you're standing on, and from my 'position' try to imagine the 'positions' of the people who live in every partition of every room in this house. My structure incorporates each one of these 'positions' in such a way as to give a sense of constant movement upward. This should strike you immediately. I planned and carried out the renovations of the interior with the aim of providing any individual (particularly a young individual) inside the assemblage of 'positions' with an awareness of existing on a stairway where the self was being elevated on a spiral course into the heavens. Those residents of the facility who are not young people have been assigned to 'positions' that make them a foundation for the constant movement upward of the young. They are primarily ladies in the later years of life who watch with admiring hearts as the children—our youth—ascend toward the sacred heights." (At this point the poet raised several objections. Although he found the conception inspiring, he wondered whether those in the lower "positions" would be happy. Furthermore, as one can see by looking at a pyramid, the number of people who can occupy "positions" at the top is extremely limited. Wouldn't this create antagonism toward the idea in society at large, so that the young people who participated might be subjected to abuse, rather than benefiting from their participation? This could even happen in the closed society of the institution itself. In response, the architect drew himself up with a mighty effort and assumed a godlike posture.) "You are a passionate lover of boys and young men. Yet you are afraid to ask society to sanction the path that leads them to the heights. This is why your love brings them to decadence and degradation. To hide in dark, low places where you pollute and befoul each other—it is this, and this alone, that arouses your passion for the young! The passion of a necrophiliac is no different! But between us there is a fundamental difference. What I have accomplished in this building I wish to propagate outside our 'closed society,' across the American mainland, throughout the world! I am launching an architectural movement to place young people everywhere in 'positions' on stairways of ascent. We must begin with schools, libraries, and theaters for children. The reason I have compressed and reduced my own body, once that of a normal adult, into the child's body you see in this wheelchair is in order to ready myself by seeing and sensing the world from a child's height, from a child's 'position,' from the eyes of a child's body and soul. My goal is to create a model of the entire world on the scale of the child's body and soul and I am trying to live in the world as a physical and spiritual child speculating day and night about the types of space and structure most suitable to architecture for children. My compressed and shrunken body itself will be a model for architects of the future!"

As the architect made his proclamation I scrutinized his body more closely: it did indeed seem possible that he had transformed himself into a dwarf by sitting in the wheelchair and compressing the area between his chest and his hips into two or three accordion-like pleats. The wheelchair was merely a device he needed to manipulate his external appearance. Now, raising his arms in their red satin sleeves over his head with a flourish, he became a rose-colored king with the mouth of a small adorable dog, and the matrons behind him (made even more genteel by drink) let out a discreet burst of applause. Even his debating opponent, the beatnik poet with the face of a bearded Bodhidharma,[1] shouted, "This man is fantastic! He's out of his mind!" Eyes twinkling behind thick glasses, he urged on his disciples, who joined without hesitation in the applause.

It was probably inevitable at this point that the guests at the party decided to tour the inside of the building to see how the architect's master plan had been implemented. With the wheelchair that carried the architect as our masthead, we filed out to inspect the part of the building that was the heart of the architect's vision: the rooms designed to impart a sense of upward motion. Since, aside from the area where the party was being held, the first floor consisted only of conference rooms and a library, we flocked to the stairway and began climbing toward the second floor. The young people who just minutes earlier had flaunted their silent antagonism toward the architect now bore his wheelchair aloft, supporting it on three sides. A mood of exaltation united us as we threaded our way through the vast structure, peering into one empty room after another and discovering, every time we turned a corner, a short flight of stairs. Empty rooms? More accurately, I would describe each room as an assemblage of boxes with bases at differing levels of height. Each of the large rooms of the original structure had been divided into four or five partitions of parallelepiped[2] shape, arranged so that the unit as a whole gave one a sense of moving from a lower to a higher level. This was because, as one went from one of the large rooms to another, one repeatedly had the impression, created through an illusory use of color, of ascending beyond the level of the highest box in the room before (which would have been impossible in actuality). On the stairways, moreover, this illusion of ascent was reinforced by tangible reality, so that while climbing them I had the sense of being suspended in a lofty tower. As we went higher, I even began to wonder if we had been transformed into a herd of rats, racing up the stairs of this tower in the grip of some kind of group insanity. There were, in fact, some members of our band who found the emotion that united us disagreeable and dropped out of the procession.

As those of us who continued in the file reached the top floor of the building (the design created the illusion there was still one more room above) I could sense, outside the darkened windows of the square rooms of ever decreasing size, the dense leaves of the "clever rain tree" whose existence I had merely been able to assent to earlier in the evening. Or perhaps I should say that the rooms themselves seemed like birdhouses enveloped in a vast growth of leaves. We circled around the empty cubicles until we discovered that, in just one of the four partitions into which the corner room of the top floor had been divided, there was someone living.

As I mentioned before, there were a number of people in our group who had gradually become disenchanted with the atmosphere of the procession; still others were by nature apprehensive about the fragility of the wooden corridors and staircases, or had become bored with the unusual but repetitious formula according to which all the rooms had been renovated. Therefore, those who were left to approach the innermost chamber included only Agatha, myself, the Jewish Indian poet from Bombay, the beatnik poet, and the architect in his

1. Legendary Indian monk of the 6th century C.E., credited with establishing Zen Buddhism in China, from where it traveled to Korea and Japan.

2. A solid geometrical figure whose faces are parallelograms.

wheelchair, carried by two young men. I realize now that it was probably better that way. There, in that least accessible of all the rooms—a cubicle that appeared to jut right out from the wall of the house—we saw a woman about forty years old, crouching in a metal washtub which occupied almost the entire area of the floor. To judge from her facial expression alone, she might have been a close relative of those self-contained matrons who had gathered around the architect's wheelchair earlier in the evening, savoring his eloquence with their sips of alcohol. But from the neck down this woman, crouching there completely naked and with one knee drawn up, had daubed herself with a blackish red liquid. Now, turning the small, black holes of her eyes toward us, she smeared a single line of the dark, sticky substance across her narrow forehead.

The beatnik poet was silent, and even seemed impressed by the scene, while the always candid Jewish Indian poet made it known that he found the stench unbearable. This remark shattered the architect's mood of exaltation, and he explained glumly that the room the woman was now in was not her "position"; she had simply been moved here temporarily because of that night's party, and the change in surroundings had disoriented her. Agatha gave vent to the antagonism aroused by the poet's complaint even more bluntly. She told him that it was necessary for the woman to put her stale blood to some use, that no one could reproach her for this, and that she was perfectly capable of doing the same thing with fresh, living blood, but only at very special moments in her life.

Then, as if triggered by Agatha's words, a number of things occurred simultaneously. First the Indian poet, and a few seconds later I myself, came to a similar realization. In that instant of recognition, when we were also communicating to each other with our eyes that the beatnik poet had surely known everything all along . . . at that very moment when we understood that the midnight party had been organized entirely by patients in this mental institution (with the exception of the woman in front of us smeared with blood from her sexual organs) and that these patients were none other than the waiters and waitresses who had served us cocktails and canapés, not to mention the placid ladies sipping their liquor . . . an Iranian journalist who had been a member of the seminar came dashing up the stairs. He informed us that all of the members had decided to withdraw from the premises immediately.

My next clear memory is of the architect, so boyish-looking when he sat in his wheelchair, pulling himself to his feet in a single effort that made his body appear to double in size; I watched from behind as he hurried down the stairs, his surprisingly large body bent forward and supported by Agatha's shoulder. The beatnik poet, mindful not to disturb the woman covered with blood, waited until he had reached the floor below before bursting into peals of merry laughter. The Iranian then told all of us his story. It seemed that when everyone else had started climbing to the upper stories, he and an English teacher from the Republic of Korea,[3] who had already sensed something strange in the air, had descended to the architect's workshop in the basement. There they discovered a scene straight out of an American gangster film: two enormous men in uniform were bound and lying on the floor. In the neighboring compartment, a

3. South Korea, under the authoritarian rule of Park Chung Hee at the time the story takes place.

bathroom, they found three nurses who were also bound. They worked out an agreement with the nurses and night watchmen whereby the seminar participants would return to their dormitories immediately by minibus, on the condition that they would not be implicated in any of the events of the evening. In addition, they requested that any reprisals carried out against the patients who had staged the rebellion would in no way involve the seminar participants. Since the facility was itself subsidized by the high fees paid by the families of the patients, however, it was unlikely that any significant punishment would be meted out to them. Finally, the Iranian warned us that if word that he and the Korean representative were involved in the scandal leaked out to the press, they might find themselves in trouble once they returned home. (This was several years before the Khomeini revolution.)[4]

At that point, without further ado, we began to head toward the front garden, where the engine of the minibus was already humming. Far from bidding farewell to the inebriated women, moving unsteadily down the stairways and corridors in search of their "position," or to the young people, who still walked with their eyes cast down, we simply elbowed our way through them and boarded the bus. I saw no sign of the night watchmen who were supposedly presiding over our departure, and merely glimpsed the heads and shoulders of two nurses who towered over the throng of bent figures. But in my last moments in the building I heard, from the direction of the "clever rain tree" which had never materialized before my eyes out of the darkness, a woman cry out two or three times with sobs so loud it seemed her body was being ripped apart by grief.

Our bus, preceded and followed by young guests escaping on their motorcycles, sped over the steep, winding mountain road as if in desperate flight. But in the darkness inside the bus, reverberations of that sobbing voice seemed to echo all around us, and even the face of the beatnik poet (who had been laughing uproariously until then) took on an expression of pensive melancholy little different from the gloomy expressions of the Iranian and Korean representatives, who were brooding over the possible repercussions of the scandal in their native dictatorships. Yet for all that, I now find it strange that I never once looked back through the windows of the bus to the giant rain tree, which should have loomed up in its black entirety, no matter how dark the night, if I had only gazed into that part of the sky where the day was dawning. Strange, because I frequently picture to myself Agatha, who chose her "position" by setting her chair at the place where tree and earth came together, in among the board-roots that jutted out like great pleats in the ground; Agatha, who stared at the painting of *A Girl on Horseback* in the library across the porch, and looked up at the building designed to spiral endlessly toward heaven like an enormous twin of the tree . . . Agatha, whom I can still see in my mind's eye, although what kind of tree it was that she called her "clever rain tree" I shall never know.

1980

4. Iran's 1979 Islamic revolution, led by Ayatollah Ruhollah Khomeini (1900–1989).

SALMAN RUSHDIE
born 1947

Salman Rushdie, whose extended family lives in India as well as Pakistan, published his fourth novel, *The Satanic Verses*, in England in September 1988. On Valentine's Day 1989, Ayatollah Ruholla Khomeini, then the leader of Shi'a Muslims in Iran, issued a *fatwa*, or religious decree, urging Muslims around the world to murder Rushdie for his acts of blasphemy against Islam in writing the novel. With typical irony, Rushdie called the *fatwa* an unusually harsh "book review." The incident sparked off a global controversy about freedom of expression, modernity, and "Islam versus the West," and Rushdie had to live underground for a decade, with maximum security provided by the British secret service. For many readers ever since, the international fallout from *The Satanic Verses* has been a public measure of its literary value, and a confirmation of Rushdie's status as the world's most important living writer.

Rushdie was born into a wealthy Muslim business family in Bombay in 1947, a few weeks before the end of British colonial rule and the partition of the subcontinent into the two new nations of India and Pakistan. After early education in the city, Rushdie attended boarding school in England and received his undergraduate and master's degrees from the University of Cambridge, where he studied Islamic history. He worked in advertising in London for several years, and wrote his first book—a science-fiction novel—on the side. With the publication of *Midnight's Children* (1980) and its immense literary and commercial success, however, Rushdie was able to turn to writing full time, contributing to periodicals throughout the anglophone world in the 1980s while producing his next two novels, *Shame* (1983) and *The Satanic Verses*.

During his retreat from public view for a dozen years after the Ayatollah Khomeini's *fatwa*, Rushdie's "normal" life was seriously interrupted—two of his first three marriages ended—but seemingly the experience did not affect his creativity. In fact, the voluminous, multifarious criticism of his work and the continued threat to his life strengthened his resolve to imagine, write, and speak his mind as freely as possible. Among his important works published during this period were *The Moor's Last Sigh* (1995), the surreal saga of an Indian family of Jewish Portuguese descent, with connections to the last Muslim ruler of Moorish Spain in the fifteenth century, and *The Ground Beneath Her Feet* (1999), a novel about a love triangle interwoven with the Greek myth of Orpheus and Eurydice. Around the end of the millennium, Rushdie eased back into public life by moving to the United States, teaching at various universities as a writer-in-residence, and reading from his work and speaking to large audiences. His more recent novels—such as *Shalimar the Clown* (2005) and *The Enchantress of Florence* (2008)—and a book for children, *Luka and the Fire of Life* (2010), have not won as much acclaim as his early work. Rushdie's preeminence among his contemporaries was affirmed when the Booker Prize was awarded to *Midnight's Children* in 1981; the novel's enduring achievement was confirmed by special Booker awards, in 1993 and 2008. As a naturalized British citizen, Rushdie was knighted in 2007; toward the end of the decade, he began to spend time in London again, helping his third (former) wife to raise their son.

Rushdie has frequently described himself as a "historian of ideas," and many of his novels are "novels of ideas" rather than narratives centered on plot or character. He is not a realistic writer; he is the foremost practitioner in English of magic realism. Invented before the middle of the twentieth century by Latin American fiction writers, who popularized the genre in the 1950s and 1960s, magic realism is a mode or style in which "reality" is permeated by supernatural forces, miraculous events, larger-than-life presences, and extraordinary characters who may possess magical powers. In his works of magic realism, Rushdie creates characters, objects, and occurrences that break the rules of everyday logic and causality: a person may be present in two places at once, for example, or a human being may travel in time, or live for centuries. Rushdie's goal is to bring the reader closer to reality, which has its rational or rationally explicable features (as described by science) but is also irrational, unpredictable, and bizarre. If magic realism gives Rushdie's work its dimension of fantasy, his fascination with ideas gives it the quality of abstraction. Many of his characters are allegorical, or personifications of ideas: Saleem Sinai, the protagonist of *Midnight's Children*, for instance, is an embodiment of "the idea of India," with his large nose shaped like the country's peninsula on a map, and his physique threatening to break up into 580 million pieces, as many as India's population at the time of writing. In *The Satanic Verses*, a voice asks one of the novel's characters: "What kind of idea are you?" Unlike realistically represented characters, Rushdie's have inner conflicts not of emotions or passions but of ideas.

Rushdie builds his narratives around conflicting ideas and fantastic characters and events with wit and playfulness, and with precise attention to the sensuous details of everyday life. A significant element of his disorienting realism comes from the use of newspaper reports of current events and historical accounts. *Midnight's Children* and *Shame*, for example, draw extensively on the journalistic record on contemporary India and Pakistan, respectively; much of *The Satanic Verses*, *The Moor's Last Sigh*, and *The Enchantress of Florence* relies on readers' historical knowledge of diverse regions of the world, from Arabia in the seventh century, and Spain and Portugal between the eighth and fifteenth centuries, to Italy in the high Renaissance. These shifts in place and time stem from Rushdie's interest in large-scale flux and transformation in human societies: he is the foremost writer of our times on migration, immigrant communities, diasporas, and cultural mixing, or hybridity.

"The Perforated Sheet," the selection below, reads like a self-contained short story but is actually an excerpt, prepared by Rushdie himself, from the first two chapters of *Midnight's Children*, with a few connecting lines not found in the novel. It introduces us to Saleem Sinai, the protagonist and narrator, and to the story of his life and origins, which constitutes the novel's Protean narrative. Saleem is born at midnight, between August 14 and 15, 1947, the moment at which India and Pakistan became separate nations; as a "child" of that historic hour, he finds that his destiny is entwined with India's fate as a nation, so that his life unfolds as a precise parallel to the country's collective history thereafter. In "The Perforated Sheet" we encounter the beginning of that story as Saleem sees it: the time, almost half a century before his birth, when his grandfather returns from Europe with a medical degree; sets up a practice in his hometown of Srinagar, Kashmir; and meets the woman who is destined to become his wife, thereby launching the cascade of events that will culminate, two generations later, in Saleem's momentous arrival.

In the novel itself, every important event in the history of the Sinai family, from Saleem's grandparents onward, is a funny, farcical echo of every major event in the history of the Indian subcontinent. Thus Saleem's birth coincides with the birth of the nation of India. And, since the twin nations of India and Pakistan (which represent the religions of Hinduism and Islam, respectively) are born at the same moment, the birth of Saleem (a Muslim boy) coincides, as well, with the birth of his hateful "nemesis," Shiva (a Hindu boy). Saleem and Shiva's lives, from infancy to adulthood, then replicate the simultaneous histories of India/Hinduism and Pakistan/Islam. This comical story is complicated by the fact that a poor Christian nurse at the hospital where Saleem and Shiva are born (to different mothers) switches the babies, as an act of impersonal class revenge on their well-to-do parents. Saleem, who grows up in the Sinai family believing that he is a Muslim, is actually the biological son of a Hindu mother, and the reverse is true of Shiva.

A further fictional complication then ensues. During the first hour after the fateful midnight of August 14–15, 1947, exactly 1,001 children are born in India and Pakistan, and all of them—including Saleem and Shiva—possess magical powers. They are, as it were, the Chosen Ones; they are all "Midnight's Children" (hence the novel's title), they can telepathically connect with one another, and their individual destinies are intertwined with their nations' and each other's destinies, down to the last detail. Saleem grows up with an inexplicable "buzzing" in his head, and discovers that it is the buzz of the voices of hundreds of other Midnight's Children, with whom he can communicate directly. The culmination of the narrative is that everything that happens on the Indian subcontinent after 1947 has only one objective: to destroy these gifted children. "The Perforated Sheet" is thus the beginning of a story that is at once comic and tragic, on an epic scale.

The Perforated Sheet[1]

I was born in the city of Bombay . . . once upon a time. No, that won't do, there's no getting away from the date: I was born in Doctor Narlikar's Nursing Home on August 15th, 1947.[2] And the time? The time matters, too. Well then: at night. No, it's important to be more . . . On the stroke of midnight, as a matter of fact. Clock-hands joined palms in respectful greeting as I came. Oh, spell it out, spell it out: at the precise instant of India's arrival at independence, I tumbled forth into the world. There were gasps. And, outside the window, fireworks and crowds. A few seconds later, my father broke his big toe; but his accident was a mere trifle when set beside what had befallen me in that benighted moment, because thanks to the occult tyrannies of those blandly saluting clocks I had been mysteriously handcuffed to history, my destinies

1. Excerpted by the author from the first two chapters of *Midnight's Children*, with connecting material not in the original novel.

2. The date is that of India's official independence from British colonial rule.

indissolubly chained to those of my country. For the next three decades, there was to be no escape. Soothsayers had prophesied me, newspapers celebrated my arrival, politicos ratified my authenticity. I was left entirely without a say in the matter. I, Saleem Sinai, later variously called Snotnose, Stainface, Baldy, Sniffer, Buddha and even Piece-of-the-Moon, had become heavily embroiled in Fate—at the best of times a dangerous sort of involvement. And I couldn't even wipe my own nose at the time.

Now, however, time (having no further use for me) is running out. I will soon be thirty-one years old. Perhaps. If my crumbling, over-used body permits. But I have no hope of saving my life, nor can I count on having even a thousand nights and a night. I must work fast, faster than Scheherazade,[3] if I am to end up meaning—yes, meaning—something. I admit it: above all things, I fear absurdity.

And there are so many stories to tell, too many, such an excess of intertwined lives events miracles places rumours, so dense a commingling of the improbable and the mundane! I have been a swallower of lives; and to know me, just the one of me, you'll have to swallow the lot as well. Consumed multitudes are jostling and shoving inside me; and guided only by the memory of a large white bedsheet with a roughly circular hole some seven inches in diameter cut into the centre, clutching at the dream of that holey, mutilated square of linen, which is my talisman, my open-sesame, I must commence the business of remaking my life from the point at which it really began, some thirty-two years before anything as obvious, as *present*, as my clock-ridden crime-stained birth.

(The sheet, incidentally, is stained too, with three drops of old, faded redness. As the Quran tells us: *Recite, in the name of the Lord thy Creator, who created Man from clots of blood.*)

One Kashmiri morning in the early spring of 1915, my grandfather Aadam Aziz[4] hit his nose against a frost-hardened tussock of earth while attempting to pray. Three drops of blood plopped out of his left nostril, hardened instantly in the brittle air and lay before his eyes on the prayer-mat, transformed into rubies. Lurching back until he knelt with his head once more upright, he found that the tears which had sprung to his eyes had solidified, too; and at that moment, as he brushed diamonds contemptuously from his lashes, he resolved never again to kiss earth for any god or man. This decision, however, made a hole in him, a vacancy in a vital inner chamber, leaving him vulnerable to women and history. Unaware of this at first, despite his recently completed medical training, he stood up, rolled the prayer-mat into a thick cheroot, and holding it under his right arm surveyed the valley through clear, diamond-free eyes.

The world was new again. After a winter's gestation in its eggshell of ice, the valley had beaked its way out into the open, moist and yellow. The new grass bided its time underground: the mountains were retreating to their hill-stations for the warm season. (In the winter, when the valley shrank under the ice, the mountains closed in and snarled like angry jaws around the city on the lake.)

3. Shahrazad, the narrator in the *Arabian Nights*, who, night after night, tells stories to Prince Shahrayar, the kingdom's ruler, in order to defer, perhaps indefinitely, her execution.

4. A Muslim name; "Aadam" is the Arabic equivalent of Adam.

In those days the radio mast had not been built and the temple of Sankara Acharya, a little black blister on a khaki hill, still dominated the streets and lake of Srinagar.[5] In those days there was no army camp at the lakeside, no endless snakes of camouflaged trucks and jeeps clogged the narrow mountain roads, no soldiers hid behind the crests of the mountains past Baramulla and Gulmarg.[6] In those days travellers were not shot as spies if they took photographs of bridges, and apart from the Englishmen's houseboats on the lake, the valley had hardly changed since the Mughal Empire,[7] for all its springtime renewals; but my grandfather's eyes—which were, like the rest of him, twenty-five years old—saw things differently . . . and his nose had started to itch.

To reveal the secret of my grandfather's altered vision: he had spent five years, five springs, away from home. (The tussock of earth, crucial though its presence was as it crouched under a chance wrinkle of the prayer-mat, was at bottom no more than a catalyst.) Now, returning, he saw through travelled eyes. Instead of the beauty of the tiny valley circled by giant teeth, he noticed the narrowness, the proximity of the horizon; and felt sad, to be at home and feel so utterly enclosed. He also felt—inexplicably—as though the old place resented his educated, stethoscoped return. Beneath the winter ice, it had been coldly neutral, but now there was no doubt; the years in Germany had returned him to a hostile environment. Many years later, when the hole inside him had been clogged up with hate, and he came to sacrifice himself at the shrine of the black stone god in the temple on the hill, he would try and recall his childhood springs in Paradise,[8] the way it was before travel and tussocks and army tanks messed everything up.

On the morning when the valley, gloved in a prayer-mat,[9] punched him on the nose, he had been trying, absurdly, to pretend that nothing had changed. So he had risen in the bitter cold of four-fifteen, washed himself in the prescribed fashion, dressed and put on his father's astrakhan cap; after which he had carried the rolled cheroot of the prayer-mat into the small lakeside garden in front of their old dark house and unrolled it over the waiting tussock. The ground felt deceptively soft under his feet and made him simultaneously uncertain and unwary. 'In the Name of God, the Compassionate, the Merciful . . .'—the exordium, spoken with hands joined before him like a book, comforted a part of him, made another, larger part feel uneasy—'. . . Praise be to Allah, Lord of the Creation . . .'[1]—but now Heidelberg invaded his head; here was Ingrid, briefly his Ingrid, her face scorning him for this

5. The main city in the Valley of Kashmir, now in the northernmost state of India, Srinagar is set on Lake Dal. In the late classical period (ca. 8th to 11th centuries), Kashmir was a Hindu kingdom famous for its patronage of learning and the arts; Shankara Acharya (ca. 8th century) was the period's most influential Hindu philosopher and theologian.

6. Situated close to the western edge of Kashmir, Baramulla is the second-largest city in the region, after Srinagar. Gulmarg is a famous ski resort near Baramulla.

7. The subcontinent's largest and wealthiest empire, the Mughal Empire lasted from 1526 to 1858. "Mughal" is a variation on "Mongol"; the Mughals were descended matrilineally from the Mongolian conqueror Genghis Khan (late 12th–early 13th centuries).

8. The Mughal emperor Jahangir (ruled 1600–25) called Kashmir "Paradise," and the epithet has been popular ever since.

9. As prescribed for Muslims, Aadam Aziz prays five times a day, kneeling on his prayer mat; his injury occurs during one of his prayers.

1. Aadam Aziz's words of prayer are from the Qur'an, and invoke Allah, the one and only true God in Islam.

Mecca-turned parroting; here, their friends Oskar and Ilse Lubin the anarchists, mocking his prayer with their anti-ideologies—'. . . The Compassionate, the Merciful. King of the Last Judgment! . . .'—Heidelberg, in which, along with medicine and politics, he learned that India—like radium—had been 'discovered' by the Europeans; even Oskar was filled with admiration for Vasco da Gama,[2] and this was what finally separated Aadam Aziz from his friends, this belief of theirs that he was somehow the invention of their ancestors—'. . . You alone we worship, and to You alone we pray for help . . .'—so here he was, despite their presence in his head, attempting to re-unite himself with an earlier self which ignored their influence but knew everything it ought to have known, about submission for example, about what he was doing now, as his hands, guided by old memories, fluttered upwards, thumbs pressed to ears, fingers spread, as he sank to his knees—'. . . Guide us to the straight path. The path of those whom You have favoured . . .' But it was no good, he was caught in a strange middle ground, trapped between belief and disbelief, and this was only a charade after all—'. . . Not of those who have incurred Your wrath. Nor of those who have gone astray.' My grandfather bent his forehead towards the earth. Forward he bent, and the earth, prayer-mat-covered, curved up towards him. And now it was the tussock's time. At one and the same time a rebuke from Ilse-Oskar-Ingrid-Heidelberg as well as valley-and-God, it smote him upon the point of the nose. Three drops fell. There were rubies and diamonds. And my grandfather, lurching upright, made a resolve. Stood. Rolled cheroot. Stared across the lake. And was knocked forever into that middle place, unable to worship a God in whose existence he could not wholly disbelieve. Permanent alteration: a hole.

The lake was no longer frozen over. The thaw had come rapidly, as usual; many of the small boats, the shikaras,[3] had been caught napping, which was also normal. But while these sluggards slept on, on dry land, snoring peacefully beside their owners, the oldest boat was up at the crack as old folk often are, and was therefore the first craft to move across the unfrozen lake. Tai's shikara . . . this, too, was customary.

Watch how the old boatman,[4] Tai, makes good time through the misty water, standing stooped over at the back of his craft! How his oar, a wooden heart on a yellow stick, drives jerkily through the weeds! In these parts he's considered very odd because he rows standing up . . . among other reasons. Tai, bringing an urgent summons to Doctor Aziz, is about to set history in motion . . . while Aadam, looking down into the water, recalls what Tai taught him years ago: 'The ice is always waiting, Aadam baba,[5] just under the water's skin.' Aadam's eyes are a clear blue, the astonishing blue of mountain sky, which has a habit of dripping into the pupils of Kashmiri men; they have not forgotten how to look. They see—there! like the skeleton of a ghost, just beneath the surface of

2. Vasco da Gama (ca. 1460–1524), Portuguese explorer and first European to navigate the sea route from Europe, around Africa, to India, in 1498.

3. A "shikara" is a distinctive, long rowboat used on Lake Dal, similar to a British double skiff used on the Thames. It transports people and goods around Srinagar.

4. Tai operates a ferry boat on Lake Dal in Srinagar.

5. In Hindu and Urdu, "baba" is a term of respect (for a social superior) as well as of affection (for a child, an adult, or an old person); here Tai, an old man, uses it in both senses at once.

Lake Dal!—the delicate tracery, the intricate crisscross of colourless lines, the cold waiting veins of the future. His German years, which have blurred so much else, haven't deprived him of the gift of seeing. Tai's gift. He looks up, sees the approaching V of Tai's boat, waves a greeting. Tai's arm rises—but this is a command. 'Wait!' My grandfather waits; and during this hiatus, as he experiences the last peace of his life, a muddy, ominous sort of peace, I had better get round to describing him.

Keeping out of my voice the natural envy of the ugly man for the strikingly impressive, I record that Doctor Aziz was a tall man. Pressed flat against a wall of his family home, he measured twenty-five bricks (a brick for each year of his life), or just over six foot two. A strong man also. His beard was thick and red—and annoyed his mother, who said only Hajis, men who had made the pilgrimage to Mecca, should grow red beards. His hair, however, was rather darker. His sky-eyes you know about. Ingrid had said, 'They went mad with the colours when they made your face.' But the central feature of my grandfather's anatomy was neither colour nor height, neither strength of arm nor straightness of back. There it was, reflected in the water, undulating like a mad plantain in the centre of his face . . . Aadam Aziz, waiting for Tai, watches his rippling nose. It would have dominated less dramatic faces than his easily; even on him, it is what one sees first and remembers longest. 'A cyranose,' Ilse Lubin said, and Oskar added, 'A proboscissimus.' Ingrid announced, 'You could cross a river on that nose.' (Its bridge was wide.)

My grandfather's nose: nostrils flaring, curvaceous as dancers. Between them swells the nose's triumphal arch, first up and out, then down and under, sweeping in to his upper lip with a superb and at present red-tipped flick. An easy nose to hit a tussock with. I wish to place on record my gratitude to this mighty organ—if not for it, who would ever have believed me to be truly my mother's son, my grandfather's grandson?—this colossal apparatus which was to be my birthright, too. Doctor Aziz's nose—comparable only to the trunk of the elephant-headed god Ganesh—established incontrovertibly his right to be a patriarch. It was Tai who taught him that, too. When young Aadam was barely past puberty the dilapidated boatman said, 'That's a nose to start a family on, my princeling. There'd be no mistaking whose brood they were. Mughal Emperors would have given their right hands for noses like that one. There are dynasties waiting inside it,'—and here Tai lapsed into coarseness—'like snot.'

Nobody could remember when Tai had been young. He had been plying this same boat, standing in the same hunched position, across the Dal and Nageen Lakes . . . forever. As far as anyone knew. He lived somewhere in the insanitary bowels of the old wooden-house quarter and his wife grew lotus roots and other curious vegetables on one of the many 'floating gardens' lilting on the surface of the spring and summer water. Tai himself cheerily admitted he had no idea of his age. Neither did his wife—he was, she said, already leathery when they married. His face was a sculpture of wind on water: ripples made of hide. He had two golden teeth and no others. In the town, he had few friends. Few boatmen or traders invited him to share a hookah when he floated past the shikara moorings or one of the lakes' many ramshackle, waterside provision-stores and tea-shops.

The general opinion of Tai had been voiced long ago by Aadam Aziz's father the gemstone merchant: 'His brain fell out with his teeth.' It was an impression the boatman fostered by his chatter, which was fantastic, grandiloquent and ceaseless, and as often as not addressed only to himself. Sound carries over water, and the lake people giggled at his monologues; but with undertones of awe, and even fear. Awe, because the old halfwit knew the lakes and hills better than any of his detractors; fear, because of his claim to an antiquity so immense it defied numbering, and moreover hung so lightly round his chicken's neck that it hadn't prevented him from winning a highly desirable wife and fathering four sons upon her . . . and a few more, the story went, on other lakeside wives. The young bucks at the shikara moorings were convinced he had a pile of money hidden away somewhere—a hoard, perhaps, of priceless golden teeth, rattling in a sack like walnuts. And, as a child, Aadam Aziz had loved him.

He made his living as a simple ferryman, despite all the rumours of wealth, taking hay and goats and vegetables and wood across the lakes for cash; people, too. When he was running his taxi-service he erected a pavilion in the centre of the shikara, a gay affair of flowered-patterned curtains and canopy, with cushions to match; and deodorised his boat with incense. The sight of Tai's shikara approaching, curtains flying, had always been for Doctor Aziz one of the defining images of the coming of spring. Soon the English sahibs would arrive and Tai would ferry them to the Shalimar Gardens and the King's Spring, chattering and pointy and stooped, a quirky, enduring familiar spirit of the valley.[6] A watery Caliban, rather too fond of cheap Kashmiri brandy.

The Boy Aadam, my grandfather-to-be, fell in love with the boatman Tai precisely because of the endless verbiage which made others think him cracked. It was magical talk, words pouring from him like fools' money, past his two gold teeth, laced with hiccups and brandy, soaring up to the most remote Himalayas[7] of the past, then swooping shrewdly on some present detail, Aadam's nose for instance, to vivisect its meaning like a mouse. This friendship had plunged Aadam into hot water with great regularity. (Boiling water. Literally. While his mother said. 'We'll kill that boatman's bugs if it kills you.') But still the old soliloquist would dawdle in his boat at the garden's lakeside toes and Aziz would sit at his feet until voices summoned him indoors to be lectured on Tai's filthiness and warned about the pillaging armies of germs his mother envisaged leaping from that hospitably ancient body on to her son's starched white loose-pajamas. But always Aadam returned to the water's edge to scan the mists for the ragged reprobate's hunched-up frame steering its magical boat through the enchanted waters of the morning.

'But how old are you really, Taiji?'[8] (Doctor Aziz, adult, red-bearded, slanting towards the future, remembers the day he asked the unaskable question.) For an instant, silence, noisier than a waterfall. The monologue, interrupted. Slap of oar in water. He was riding in the shikara with Tai, squatting amongst goats, on a pile of straw, in full knowledge of the stick and bathtub waiting for him at

6. The Shalimar Gardens are the modern form of the Mughal-style rose garden first laid near Srinagar for Emperor Jahangir in 1619.
7. The western end of the Himalayas, the world's highest mountain range, wraps around the north of Kashmir.
8. In Hindi and Urdu, the main languages of northern India, the suffix "-ji" is an honorific added to names and epithets, to address elders and superiors. Aadam Aziz addresses the "lowly" boatman as "Taiji" out of respect for the latter's age.

home. He had come for stories—and with one question had silenced the storyteller.

'No, tell, Taiji, how old, *truly*?' And now a brandy bottle, materialising from nowhere: cheap liquor from the folds of the great warm chugha-coat.[9] Then a shudder, a belch, a glare. Glint of gold. And—at last!—speech. 'How old? You ask how old, you little wet-head, you nosey . . .' Tai pointed at the mountains. 'So old, nakkoo!' Aadam, the nakkoo, the nosey one, followed his pointing finger. 'I have watched the mountains being born; I have seen Emperors die. Listen. Listen, nakkoo[1] . . .'—the brandy bottle again, followed by brandy-voice, and words more intoxicating than booze—'. . . I saw that Isa, that Christ, when he came to Kashmir.[2] Smile, smile, it is your history I am keeping in my head. Once it was set down in old lost books. Once I knew where there was a grave with pierced feet carved on the tombstone, which bled once a year. Even my memory is going now; but I know, although I can't read.' Illiteracy, dismissed with a flourish; literature crumbled beneath the rage of his sweeping hand. Which sweeps again to chugha-pocket, to brandy bottle, to lips chapped with cold. Tai always had woman's lips. 'Nakkoo, listen, listen. I have seen plenty. Yara,[3] you should've seen that Isa when he came, beard down to his balls, bald as an egg on his head. He was old and fagged-out but he knew his manners. "You first, Taiji," he'd say, and "Please to sit"; always a respectful tongue, he never called me crackpot, never called me *tu* either. Always *aap*.[4] Polite, see? And what an appetite! Such a hunger, I would catch my ears in fright. Saint or devil, I swear he could eat a whole kid in one go. And so what? I told him, eat, fill your hole, a man comes to Kashmir to enjoy life, or to end it, or both. His work was finished. He just came up here to live it up a little.' Mesmerised by this brandied portrait of a bald, gluttonous Christ, Aziz listened, later repeating every word to the consternation of his parents, who dealt in stones and had no time for 'gas'.

'Oh, you don't believe?'—licking his sore lips with a grin, knowing it to be the reverse of the truth; 'Your attention is wandering?'—again, he knew how furiously Aziz was hanging on his words. 'Maybe the straw is pricking your behind, hey? Oh, I'm so sorry, babaji, not to provide for you silk cushions with gold brocade-work—cushions such as the Emperor Jehangir[5] sat upon! You think the Emperor Jehangir as a gardener only, no doubt,' Tai accused my grandfather, 'because he built Shalimar. Stupid! What do you know? His name meant Encompasser of the Earth. Is that a gardener's name? God knows what they teach you boys these days. Whereas I'. . . puffing up a little here . . .'I knew his precise weight, to the tola! Ask me how many maunds, how many seers! When he was happy he got heavier and in Kashmir he was heaviest of all. I used to

9. "Chuga" or "choga," the Persian word for a loose, cassocklike garment for Muslim men.
1. "Nakkoo," literally "nosy" in Hindi and Urdu, is Tai's playful epithet for the large-nosed Aadam Aziz.
2. An apocryphal legend in the Muslim and Hindu worlds is that at the end of his life, as recorded in the Bible, Jesus Christ left Jerusalem, living out his last days in Kashmir.
3. "Yara" is the common Urdu term of endearment for friend, buddy, loved one, or close companion.
4. In Hindi and Urdu, *tu* is the intimate or familiar form of "you," whereas *aap* is the formal, respectful form of the pronoun.
5. The fourth ruler in the Mughal dynasty, on the throne from 1600 to 1625.

carry his litter . . . no, no, look, you don't believe again, that big cucumber in your face is waggling like the little one in your pajamas! So, come on, come on, ask me questions! Give examination! Ask how many times the leather thongs wound round the handles of the litter—the answer is thirty-one. Ask me what was the Emperor's dying word—I tell you it was "Kashmir". He had bad breath and a good heart. Who do you think I am? Some common ignorant lying pie-dog? Go, get out of the boat now, your nose makes it too heavy to row; also your father is waiting to beat my gas out of you, and your mother to boil off your skin.'

Despite beating and boiling, Aadam Aziz floated with Tai in his shikara, again and again, amid goats hay flowers furniture lotus-roots, though never with the English sahibs,[6] and heard again and again the miraculous answers to that single terrifying question: 'But Taiji, how old are you, *honestly?*'

From Tai, Aadam learned the secrets of the lake—where you could swim without being pulled down by weeds; the eleven varieties of water-snake; where the frogs spawned; how to cook a lotus-root; and where the three English women had drowned a few years back. 'There is a tribe of feringhee women who come to this water to drown,' Tai said. 'Sometimes they know it, sometimes they don't, but I know the minute I smell them. They hide under the water from God knows what or who—but they can't hide from me, baba!' Tai's laugh, emerging to infect Aadam—a huge, booming laugh that seemed macabre when it crashed out of that old, withered body, but which was so natural in my giant grandfather that nobody knew, in later times, that it wasn't really his. And, also from Tai, my grandfather heard about noses.

Tai tapped his left nostril. 'You know what this is, nakkoo? It's the place where the outside world meets the world inside you. If they don't get on, you feel it here. Then you rub your nose with embarrassment to make the itch go away. A nose like that, little idiot, is a great gift. I say: trust it. When it warns you, look out or you'll be finished. Follow your nose and you'll go far.' He cleared his throat; his eyes rolled away into the mountains of the past. Aziz settled back on the straw. 'I knew one officer once—in the army of that Iskandar the Great. Never mind his name. He had a vegetable just like yours hanging between his eyes. When the army halted near Gandhara,[7] he fell in love with some local floozy. At once his nose itched like crazy. He scratched it, but that was useless. He inhaled vapours from crushed boiled eucalyptus leaves. Still no good, baba! The itching sent him wild; but the damn fool dug in his heels and stayed with his little witch when the army went home. He became—what?—a stupid thing, neither this nor that, a half-and-halfer with a nagging wife and an itch in the nose, and in the end he pushed his sword into his stomach. What do you think of that?'

6. "Sahib" is the Anglicized form of the Persian *saheb*, a respectful term of address for a rich or powerful man, a ruler or administrator, or a superior; it became the common epithet for British colonial administrators in India.

7. "Iskandar" or "Sikandar" is the Indian equivalent of "Alexander" the Great, whose army reached the subcontinent in 327 B.C.E. The farthest north Alexander went was to Gandhara, the region now around Peshawar and the Swat Valley in northwest Pakistan. When he turned back, Alexander left behind a Greek colony in Gandhara, which flourished there for several centuries as the eastern outpost of his empire.

Doctor Aziz in 1915, whom rubies and diamonds have turned into a half-and-halfer, remembers this story as Tai enters hailing distance. His nose is itching still. He scratches, shrugs, tosses his head; and then Tai shouts.

'Ohé! Doctor Sahib! Ghani the landowner's daughter is sick.'

. . . The young Doctor has entered the throes of a most unhippocratic excitement at the boatman's cry, and shouts, 'I'm coming just now! Just let me bring my things!' The shikara's prow touches the garden's hem. Aadam is rushing indoors, prayer-mat rolled like a cheroot under one arm, blue eyes blinking in the sudden interior gloom; he has placed the cheroot on a high shelf on top of stacked copies of *Vorwärts* and Lenin's *What Is To Be Done?*[8] and other pamphlets, dusty echoes of his half-faded German life; he is pulling out, from under his bed, a second-hand leather case which his mother called his 'doctori-attaché',[9] and as he swings it and himself upwards and runs from the room, the word HEIDELBERG is briefly visible, burned into the leather on the bottom of the bag. A landowner's daughter is good news indeed to a doctor with a career to make, even if she is ill. No: *because* she is ill.

. . . Slap of oar in water. Plop of spittle in lake. Tai clears his throat and mutters angrily, 'A fine business. A wet-head nakkoo child goes away before he's learned one damn thing and he comes back a big doctor sahib with a big bag full of foreign machines, and he's still as silly as an owl. I swear: a too bad business.'

. . .'Big shot,' Tai is spitting into the lake, 'big bag, big shot. Pah! We haven't got enough bags at home that you must bring back that thing made of a pig's skin that makes one unclean just by looking at it? And inside, God knows what all.' Doctor Aziz, seated amongst flowery curtains and the smell of incense, has his thoughts wrenched away from the patient waiting across the lake. Tai's bitter monologue breaks into his consciousness, creating a sense of dull shock, a smell like a casualty ward overpowering the incense . . . the old man is clearly furious about something, possessed by an incomprehensible rage that appears to be directed at his erstwhile acolyte, or, more precisely and oddly, at his bag. Doctor Aziz attempts to make small talk . . .'Your wife is well? Do they still talk about your bag of golden teeth?'. . . tries to remake an old friendship; but Tai is in full flight now, a stream of invective pouring out of him. The Heidelberg bag quakes under the torrent of abuse. 'Sistersleeping pigskin bag[1] from Abroad full of foreigners' tricks. Big-shot bag. Now if a man breaks an arm that bag will not let the bone-setter bind it in leaves. Now a man must let his wife lie beside that bag and watch knives come and cut her open. A fine business, what these foreigners put in our young men's heads. I swear: it is a too-bad thing. That bag should fry in Hell with the testicles of the ungodly.'

. . .'Do you still pickle water-snakes in brandy to give you virility, Taiji? Do you still like to eat lotus-root without any spices?' Hesitant questions, brushed aside by the torrent of Tai's fury. Doctor Aziz begins to diagnose. To the ferryman, the

8. Vladimir Lenin's small book, first published in 1902, quickly became a classic of socialist and communist theory and polemics, outlining a program that culminated in the Bolshevik Revolution of 1917 in Russia.

9. "Doctori-attaché" is an Indianized term for a doctor's satchel or attache case.

1. Muslims and Semitic people consider the pig a polluting animal; a pigskin bag is therefore a proscribed object in this context. "Sistersleeping" is the narrator's playful variation on the most common curse word in Hindi and Urdu.

bag represents Abroad; it is the alien thing, the invader, progress. And yes, it has indeed taken possession of the young Doctor's mind: and yes, it contains knives, and cures for cholera and malaria and smallpox; and yes, it sits between doctor and boatman, and has made them antagonists. Doctor Aziz begins to fight, against sadness, and against Tai's anger, which is beginning to infect him, to become his own, which erupts only rarely, but comes, when it does come, unheralded in a roar from his deepest places, laying waste everything in sight; and then vanishes, leaving him wondering why everyone is so upset . . . They are approaching Ghani's house. A bearer[2] awaits the shikara, standing with clasped hands on a little wooden jetty. Aziz fixes his mind on the job in hand.

The bearer holds the shikara steady as Aadam Aziz climbs out, bag in hand. And now, at last, Tai speaks directly to my grandfather. Scorn in his face, Tai asks, 'Tell me this, Doctor Sahib: have you got in that bag made of dead pigs one of those machines that foreign doctors use to smell with?' Aadam shakes his head, not understanding. Tai's voice gathers new layers of disgust. 'You know, sir, a thing like an elephant's trunk.' Aziz, seeing what he means, replies: 'A stethoscope? Naturally.' Tai pushes the shikara off from the jetty. Spits. Begins to row away. 'I knew it,' he says. 'You will use such a machine now, instead of your own big nose.'

My grandfather does not trouble to explain that a stethoscope is more like a pair of ears than a nose. He is stifling his own irritation, the resentful anger of a cast-off child; and besides, there is a patient waiting.

The house was opulent but badly lit. Ghani was a widower and the servants clearly took advantage. There were cobwebs in corners and layers of dust on ledges. They walked down a long corridor; one of the doors was ajar and through it Aziz saw a room in a state of violent disorder. This glimpse, connected with a glint of light in Ghani's dark glasses, suddenly informed Aziz that the landowner was blind. This aggravated his sense of unease . . . They halted outside a thick teak door. Ghani said, 'Wait here two moments,' and went into the room behind the door.

In later years, Doctor Aadam Aziz swore that during those two moments of solitude in the gloomy spidery corridors of the landowner's mansion he was gripped by an almost uncontrollable desire to turn and run away as fast as his legs would carry him. Unnerved by the enigma of the blind art-lover, his insides filled with tiny scrabbling insects as a result of the insidious venom of Tai's mutterings, his nostrils itching to the point of convincing him that he had somehow contracted venereal disease, he felt his feet begin slowly, as though encased in boots of lead, to turn; felt blood pounding in his temples; and was seized by so powerful a sensation of standing upon a point of no return that he very nearly wet his German woollen trousers. He began, without knowing it, to blush furiously; and at this point a woman with the biceps of a wrestler appeared, beckoning him to follow her into the room. The state of her sari[3] told him that she was a servant; but she was not servile. 'You look green as a fish,' she said. 'You young doctors. You come into a strange house and your liver

2. Common British-Indian colonial-era term for a servant, helper, or waiter.

3. The sari, a full-body wrap, is the most common attire for adult Hindu women.

turns to jelly. Come, Doctor Sahib, they are waiting for you.' Clutching his bag a fraction too tightly, he followed her through the dark teak door.

. . . Into a spacious bedchamber that was as ill-lit as the rest of the house; although here there were shafts of dusty sunlight seeping in through a fanlight high on one wall. These fusty rays illuminated a scene as remarkable as anything the Doctor had ever witnessed: a tableau of such surpassing strangeness that his feet began to twitch towards the door once again. Two more women, also built like professional wrestlers, stood stiffly in the light, each holding one corner of an enormous white bedsheet, their arms raised high above their heads so that the sheet hung between them like a curtain.[4] Mr Ghani welled up out of the murk surrounding the sunlit sheet and permitted the nonplussed Aadam to stare stupidly at the peculiar tableau for perhaps half a minute, at the end of which, and before a word had been spoken, the Doctor made a discovery:

In the very centre of the sheet, a hole had been cut, a crude circle about seven inches in diameter.

'Close the door, ayah.' Ghani instructed the first of the lady wrestlers, and then, turning to Aziz, became confidential. 'This town contains many good-for-nothings who have on occasion tried to climb into my daughter's room. She needs,' he nodded at the three musclebound women, 'protectors.'

Aziz was still looking at the perforated sheet. Ghani said, 'All right, come on, you will examine my Naseem right now. *Pronto*.'

My grandfather peered around the room. 'But where is she, Ghani Sahib?' he blurted out finally. The lady wrestlers adopted supercilious expressions and, it seemed to him, tightened their musculatures, just in case he intended to try something fancy.

'Ah, I see your confusion,' Ghani said, his poisonous smile broadening. 'You Europe-returned chappies forget certain things. Doctor Sahib, my daughter is a decent girl, it goes without saying. She does not flaunt her body under the noses of strange men. You will understand that you cannot be permitted to see her, no, not in any circumstances; accordingly I have required her to be positioned behind that sheet. She stands there, like a good girl.'

A frantic note had crept into Doctor Aziz's voice. 'Ghani Sahib, tell me how I am to examine her without looking at her?' Ghani smiled on.

'You will kindly specify which portion of my daughter it is necessary to inspect. I will then issue her with my instructions to place the required segment against that hole which you see there. And so, in this fashion the thing may be achieved.'

'But what, in any event, does the lady complain of?'—my grandfather, despairingly. To which Mr Ghani, his eyes rising upwards in their sockets, his smile twisting into a grimace of grief, replied: 'The poor child! She has a terrible, a too dreadful stomach-ache.'

'In that case,' Doctor Aziz said with some restraint, 'will she show me her stomach, please.'

4. Muslim women are required to be fully veiled in the presence of men not belonging to their families or intimate social circles. In this part of the novel, the bedsheet serving as a "curtain" between patient and doctor becomes an elaborate, comical proxy for the traditional Muslim veil.

My grandfather's premonitions in the corridor were not without foundation. In the succeeding months and years, he fell under what I can only describe as the sorcerer's spell of that enormous—and as yet unstained—perforated cloth.

In those years, you see, the landowner's daughter Naseem Ghani contracted a quite extraordinary number of minor illnesses, and each time a shikara-wallah was dispatched to summon the tall young Doctor Sahib with the big nose who was making such a reputation for himself in the valley. Aadam Aziz's visits to the bedroom with the shaft of sunlight and the three lady wrestlers became weekly events; and on each occasion he was vouchsafed a glimpse, through the mutilated sheet, of a different seven-inch circle of the young woman's body. Her initial stomach-ache was succeeded by a very slightly twisted right ankle, an ingrowing toenail on the big toe of the left foot, a tiny cut on the lower left calf. 'Tetanus is a killer, Doctor Sahib,' the landowner said. 'My Naseem must not die for a scratch.' There was the matter of her stiff right knee, which the Doctor was obliged to manipulate through the hole in the sheet . . . and after a time the illnesses leapt upwards, avoiding certain unmentionable zones, and began to proliferate around her upper half. She suffered from something mysterious which her father called Finger Rot, which made the skin flake off her hands; from weakness of the wrist-bones, for which Aadam prescribed calcium tablets; and from attacks of constipation, for which he gave her a course of laxatives, since there was no question of being permitted to administer an enema. She had fevers and she also had subnormal temperatures. At these times his thermometer would be placed under her armpit and he would hum and haw about the relative inefficiency of the method. In the opposite armpit she once developed a slight case of tineachloris and he dusted her with yellow powder; after this treatment—which required him to rub the powder in, gently but firmly, although the soft secret body began to shake and quiver and he heard helpless laughter coming through the sheet, because Naseem Ghani was very ticklish—the itching went away, but Naseem soon found a new set of complaints. She waxed anaemic in the summer and bronchial in the winter. ('Her tubes are most delicate,' Ghani explained, 'like little flutes.') Far away the Great War moved from crisis to crisis, while in the cobwebbed house Doctor Aziz was also engaged in a total war against his sectioned patient's inexhaustible complaints. And, in all those war years, Naseem never repeated an illness. 'Which only shows,' Ghani told him, 'that you are a good doctor. When you cure, she is cured for good. But alas!'—he struck his forehead—'She pines for her late mother, poor baby, and her body suffers. She is a too loving child.'

So gradually Doctor Aziz came to have a picture of Naseem in his mind, a badly-fitting collage of her severally-inspected parts. This phantasm of a partitioned woman began to haunt him, and not only in his dreams. Glued together by his imagination, she accompanied him on all his rounds, she moved into the front room of his mind, so that waking and sleeping he could feel in his fingertips the softness of her ticklish skin or the perfect tiny wrists or the beauty of the ankles; he could smell her scent of lavender and chambeli; he could hear her voice and her helpless laughter of a little girl; but she was headless, because he had never seen her face.

By 1918, Aadam Aziz had come to live for his regular trips across the lake. And now his eagerness became even more intense, because it became clear that, after three years, the landowner and his daughter had become willing to lower certain barriers. Now, for the first time, Ghani said, 'A lump in the right chest. Is it worrying, Doctor? Look. Look well.' And there, framed in the hole, was a perfectly-formed and lyrically lovely . . .'I must touch it,' Aziz said, fighting with his voice. Ghani slapped him on the back. 'Touch, touch!' he cried. 'The hands of the healer! The curing touch, eh, Doctor?' And Aziz reached out a hand . . .'Forgive me for asking; but is it the lady's time of the month?' . . . Little secret smiles appearing on the faces of the lady wrestlers. Ghani, nodding affably: 'Yes. Don't be so embarrassed, old chap. We are family and doctor now.' And Aziz, 'Then don't worry. The lumps will go when the time ends.' . . . And the next time, 'A pulled muscle in the back of her thigh, Doctor Sahib. Such pain!' And there, in the sheet, weakening the eyes of Aadam Aziz, hung a superbly rounded and impossible buttock . . . And now Aziz: 'Is it permitted that . . .' Whereupon a word from Ghani; an obedient reply from behind the sheet; a drawstring pulled; and pajamas fall from the celestial rump, which swells wondrously through the hole. Aadam Aziz forces himself into a medical frame of mind . . . reaches out . . . feels. And swears to himself, in amazement, that he sees the bottom reddening in a shy, but compliant blush.

That evening, Aadam contemplated the blush. Did the magic of the sheet work on both sides of the hole? Excitedly, he envisaged his headless Naseem tingling beneath the scrutiny of his eyes, his thermometer, his stethoscope, his fingers, and trying to build a picture in her mind of *him*. She was at a disadvantage, of course, having seen nothing but his hands . . . Aadam began to hope with an illicit desperation for Naseem Ghani to develop a migraine or graze her unseen chin, so they could look each other in the face. He knew how unprofessional his feelings were; but did nothing to stifle them. There was not much he could do. They had acquired a life of their own. In short: my grandfather had fallen in love, and had come to think of the perforated sheet as something sacred and magical, because through it he had seen the things which had filled up the hole inside him which had been created when he had been hit on the nose by a tussock and insulted by the boatman Tai.

On the day the World War ended, Naseem developed the longed-for headache. Such historical coincidences have littered, and perhaps befouled, my family's existence in the world.

He hardly dared to look at what was framed in the hole in the sheet. Maybe she was hideous; perhaps that explained all this performance . . . he looked. And saw a soft face that was not at all ugly, a cushioned setting for her glittering, gemstone eyes, which were brown with flecks of gold: tiger's-eyes. Doctor Aziz's fall was complete. And Naseem burst out, 'But Doctor, my God, what a *nose!*' Ghani, angrily, 'Daughter, mind your . . .' But patient and doctor were laughing together, and Aziz was saying, 'Yes, yes, it is a remarkable specimen. They tell me there are dynasties waiting in it . . .' And he bit his tongue because he had been about to add, '. . . like snot.'

And Ghani, who had stood blindly beside the sheet for three long years, smiling and smiling and smiling, began once again to smile his secret smile, which was mirrored in the lips of the wrestlers.

1980

JAMAICA KINCAID

born 1949

Born and raised among an extended family of "poor, ordinary people," "banana and citrus-fruit farmers, fishermen, carpenters and obeah women," Jamaica Kincaid rose from humble beginnings to become a successful contemporary writer, well known for her books and magazine articles about the immigrant experience. These works often convey a sense of immediacy through Kincaid's use of first-person narration or imagined dialogue.

Born Elaine Cynthia Potter Richardson in Antigua, a small island in the Caribbean, Kincaid grew up in the island's capital city of St. Johns. Part of the British Leeward Island chain, Antigua was a colony of Britain throughout the writer's childhood and adolescence; it gained political independence in 1981 and now belongs to the British Commonwealth. Kincaid's mother was a homemaker, and her stepfather worked as a carpenter (her biological father, a taxi driver, showed no interest in his children). Though Kincaid and her brothers were raised as Methodists, her mother and grandmother also practiced obeah, West Indian voodoo. Kincaid learned from them how to protect herself against the evil eye, how to appease local spirits, how to use herbs to conjure and heal—a familiarity with the supernatural that she later incorporated into her fiction.

At school, Kincaid was a quick student, taking a special interest in history and botany. Although her family had high aspirations for her three brothers and intended them to enter the professions, because Kincaid was a girl, they placed no value on her gifts: "No one expected anything from me at all," she later said. Her teachers often treated her eagerness in the classroom as a disciplinary problem. At thirteen, when Kincaid was about to take university qualifying examinations, her stepfather fell ill, forcing her to leave school and help raise her siblings. Angry and dispirited, she withdrew into books. Later she said that her passion for reading "saved her life." The island's colonial status meant that the local libraries and bookstores carried almost exclusively British literature, mainly of the nineteenth century. The lack of access to more recent works, or to the West Indian literary canon to which Kincaid would contribute so prominent a voice, prevented her at first from seeing art as more than an escape: "I thought writing was something that people just didn't do anymore, that went out of fashion, like the bustle."

Still, she chafed against her colonial upbringing and looked for ways to enter a wider world. At the age of seventeen she accepted a job as a nanny in the United States, and for four years lived with families in the New York City borough of Manhattan and in suburban Scarsdale. She earned a general equivalency diploma and briefly attended a college in New Hampshire before deciding she was too old. Back in Manhattan, and now determined to write, she started freelancing for magazines and weekly newspapers, including the *Village Voice*. It was during this period that she changed her name. Jamaica refers to the West Indies; Kincaid, to an unfinished novel by the playwright George Bernard Shaw. She explained that the alteration allowed her to evade her family, who opposed her writing, as well as her broader colonial inheritance: the new name was "a way for me to do things without being the same person who couldn't do them—the same person who had all these weights."

Kincaid's first collection of short stories, *At the Bottom of the River*, appeared in 1983. An autobiographical novel, *Annie John*, followed in 1985; her second and third novels also draw on her own and her family's experiences in Antigua. She has continued to publish books and magazine articles and has won many prestigious awards, including the 2000 French Prix Femina Etranger. In recent years the author has turned her attention to nature writing and to botanical studies of the landscape. Throughout her career, though, Kincaid has retained a strong commitment to issues of identity, colonialism, and the color line. In *A Small Place*, written following Kincaid's first visit to Antigua since her youth, she criticizes what she sees as the island's complicity in its exploitation, carried over from the colonial past.

The story selected here, "Girl" (1978), was the first piece of fiction that Kincaid published. It consists of a single, winding sentence; the speaker is a mother giving instructions to her daughter on the rules and rites of womanhood. (The daughter's replies break into the narration in two passages, both printed in italics.) The setting is Antigua, although this point is never explicitly stated and can only be inferred from the story's details. Some of the instructions refer to folk medicine and obeah; for example, the warning against throwing stones at blackbirds, which might be malicious spirits in disguise. As the speaker discusses with equal matter-of-factness such topics as keeping house, enduring a cruel husband, and aborting unwanted pregnancies, a picture emerges of the harshness of countless women's lives, not just in this setting but throughout history and across the globe. During the lecture, the mother stresses how important it is for a young woman to maintain a sense of sexual propriety: the woman warns her daughter repeatedly that she will look like a "slut" if she does not behave properly. The edict against squatting to play marbles suggests that the listener has not left childhood entirely, but the early reference to washing "your little cloths" indicates that she has reached puberty and that the time when these instructions will come into use is not far off.

Girl

Wash the white clothes on Monday and put them on the stone heap; wash the color clothes on Tuesday and put them on the clothesline to dry; don't walk barehead in the hot sun; cook pumpkin fritters in very hot sweet oil; soak your little cloths[1] right after you take them off; when buying cotton to make yourself a nice blouse, be sure that it doesn't have gum on it, because that way it won't hold up well after a wash; soak salt fish overnight before you cook it; is it true that you sing benna[2] in Sunday school?; always eat your food in such a way that it won't turn someone else's stomach; on Sundays try to walk like a lady and not like the slut you are so bent on becoming; don't sing benna in Sunday

1. Pads for menstruation.
2. Improvised Antiguan folk song with African roots.

school; you mustn't speak to wharf-rat boys, not even to give directions; don't eat fruits on the street—flies will follow you; *but I don't sing benna on Sundays at all and never in Sunday school*; this is how to sew on a button; this is how to make a buttonhole for the button you have just sewed on; this is how to hem a dress when you see the hem coming down and so to prevent yourself from looking like the slut I know you are so bent on becoming; this is how you iron your father's khaki shirt so that it doesn't have a crease; this is how you iron your father's khaki pants so that they don't have a crease; this is how you grow okra—far from the house, because okra tree harbors red ants; when you are growing dasheen,[3] make sure it gets plenty of water or else it makes your throat itch when you are eating it; this is how you sweep a corner; this is how you sweep a whole house; this is how you sweep a yard; this is how you smile to someone you don't like too much; this is how you smile to someone you don't like at all; this is how you smile to someone you like completely; this is how you set a table for tea; this is how you set a table for dinner; this is how you set a table for dinner with an important guest; this is how you set a table for lunch; this is how you set a table for breakfast; this is how to behave in the presence of men who don't know you very well, and this way they won't recognize immediately the slut I have warned you against becoming; be sure to wash every day, even if it is with your own spit; don't squat down to play marbles—you are not a boy, you know; don't pick people's flowers—you might catch something; don't throw stones at blackbirds, because it might not be a blackbird at all; this is how to make a bread pudding; this is how to make doukona;[4] this is how to make pepper pot;[5] this is how to make a good medicine for a cold; this is how to make a good medicine to throw away a child before it even becomes a child; this is how to catch a fish; this is how to throw back a fish you don't like, and that way something bad won't fall on you; this is how to bully a man; this is how a man bullies you; this is how to love a man, and if this doesn't work there are other ways, and if they don't work don't feel too bad about giving up; this is how to spit up in the air if you feel like it, and this is how to move quick so that it doesn't fall on you; this is how to make ends meet; always squeeze bread to make sure it's fresh; *but what if the baker won't let me feel the bread?*; you mean to say that after all you are really going to be the kind of woman who the baker won't let near the bread?

1978

3. A type of taro, a root vegetable.
4. A pudding made of plantains.
5. A spicy stew.

PARK WANSUH

1931–2011

The recent history of the Korean peninsula has been one of extremes. Within a century, it has gone from colonial rule under the Japanese Empire to liberation, national division, and in the South, democratization; from abject poverty to the economic "Miracle on the Han River" (of Seoul, the capital city) that has made South Korea into one of the world's richest nations and a powerhouse of high-tech innovation; from a downtrodden nation lacerated by foreign interests to an indisputable trendsetter of global popular culture. All these dramatic events brought along sweeping changes that included the dismantling of the aristocratic, patriarchic Confucian society of premodern Korea; the trauma of mass destruction, invasion, and occupation; the unresolved aftermath of Japanese colonization; and the deep rifts between communist and anticommunist forces that divided Korea into North and South, ripping apart fates and families. In addition, in the twentieth century Korea experienced the sudden public visibility of women in the workforce and of the "new woman" who dressed Western-style, asserted her right to self-determination, and fulfilled new roles as "modern" wife, mother, and, simply, woman, refusing to be subservient to her husband and in-laws as Confucian custom had required for centuries. All of these changes are at the heart of the work of Park Wansuh, one of the most perceptive and witty voices in modern Korean literature. She lets us feel the relentless individual pain of the aftermath of war atrocities, reveals the contradictions of the "new woman" ideal, and initiates us to the intimacies of family dramas that embody the complexities of Korea's path from a Japanese colony to South Korea's capitalist democracy.

Born in a small village in 1931 at the height of Japanese colonization, Park Wansuh was schooled exclusively in Japanese until the age of 14. She once confessed that the first word she ever learned in school was "Hōanden," the name of a small shrine typically set up in elementary schools to display portraits of the Japanese imperial family and the edict outlining the educational principles of the Japanese empire. After the liberation (in 1945) she was admitted to the Korean literature department of Seoul National University, one of Korea's top schools, but dropped out almost immediately after the outbreak of the Korean War (1950–53) and the death of her elder brother, which affected her deeply. Her hometown, Pakchŏk Village near Kaesŏng, became part of North Korea after 1953. The war and its aftermath was to haunt her for all her life. She went on to raise five children and, in her forties, embarked upon a prolific writing career, eventually producing about two dozen novels and numerous short stories.

In a literary establishment dominated by men, Park Wansuh was one of the first women to achieve critical success. She won all major South Korean literary awards during the four decades of her career and came to be regarded as the "Grande Dame of Korean Letters."

Korea has often fallen under the sway of colonial conquest and foreign dominance. As the Korean peninsula is wedged between the Japanese archipelago and the Chinese mainland, it has repeatedly suffered from its neighbors' aggressions, invasions, and even occupation. China's Han Dynasty (206 B.C.E.–220 C.E.) established several small "commanderies," and subsequent Chinese dynasties continued to influence Korea's royal court. Twice during the last decade of the late sixteenth century the Japanese warlord Toyotomi Hideyoshi invaded Korea and laid waste to the peninsula, decimating the population and looting or destroying vast amounts of cultural treasures. Japan's victories in the First Sino-Japanese War (1894–95) and the Russo-Japanese War (1904–5) paved the way to the annexation of Korea in 1910.

The Japanese government ruled its colony with a harsh hand, especially during the Pacific War (1937–45): Korean-language newspapers were suppressed; instruction in the new educational system was switched to Japanese and a Japanese curriculum; Koreans were forced to adopt Japanese names and to observe Japan's Shinto religion, including worship of the emperor. As in other Japanese colonies, Korean males were herded into labor camps to support the war effort. Innumerable Korean women were forced into sexual slavery in army brothels serving the Japanese imperial army. To this day, the Japanese government's reluctance to officially recognize the fate of these "comfort women" is still one of the most contentious and tragic issues hampering Japanese–Korean relations. While unquestionably one of the darkest periods in Korean history, Japanese rule also brought along many of the "blessings" of Western civilization, such as a general education system, judicial reform, modern medicine, and social reform. The fact that the formative phase of Korean modernization was ushered in by Japanese colonization makes any judgment of the colonial period and its depiction in literary works highly sensitive and paradoxical.

At the time of its liberation from Japanese colonial rule in 1945, the Korean peninsula was divided along the 38th parallel into the Soviet-backed North and the US-backed South. With tensions between former allies Soviet Russia and the United States hardening into the Cold War, in 1950 North Korean forces launched an attack on the South in an attempt to reunite the peninsula. Unprepared and taken by surprise, South Korean forces were driven to the southeastern corner of the peninsula, but a landing of US-led United Nations troops at Incheon, close to Seoul, managed to trap much of the North Korean army and inflict crushing losses. This triggered China's entry into the war to support its communist ally, resulting in a number of major battles and heavy casualties on both sides. Technically the war is still ongoing, as only an armistice but no formal peace treaty has been signed, and the occasional clashes on the 38th parallel can be considered a continuation of the Korean War.

Park Wansuh committed herself to confronting the most painful and controversial moments of recent Korean history, but she does so in subtle tones, giving us an intimate picture of how history works its way through people's everyday lives. By capturing the unbearable pain of colonization, war, and trauma in semi-autobiographical family dramas in a deeply personal, self-consciously tragicomic, and often wry voice, Park became the spokeswoman for an entire generation. Her work has served a cathartic function, helping her compatriots come to terms with the big challenges of the Korean peninsula's transformation through wars from a Japanese colony to a capitalist democracy, in the South.

Mother's Hitching Post (1980, 1981, 1991) is a trilogy of short stories, whose second part, included here, was honored with the coveted Yi Sang Literature

Prize. As the title suggests, the plot revolves around a mother's resolute attempts to put a "stake" in the ground and create a new home and life for her children and grandchildren. The trilogy traces the tumultuous and often bittersweet relationship between a mother from the traditional provincial nobility and her daughter, as they live through the 1930s to the 1990s. The first part of the trilogy is set in the colonial period of the 1930s and shows the young mother leaving the countryside for the big city of Seoul in search for a better life and education for her children. The second part deals with memories of the Korean War drawn into the narrative present of the 1980s, with the mother now a grandmother and her daughter the mother of her own children. The third part is set around the time of its publication, in 1991, when the economy was booming and national division had become an accepted reality.

The trilogy is narrated by the daughter, who portrays her mother as a headstrong woman with bold dreams, fearless in the pursuit of her dreams. After the early death of her husband she takes a chance on a new life, abandoning the safety of her status as a respected daughter belonging to a local *yangban* (ruling elite) family in the countryside. Traditionally, the so-called *yangban* (comprising the "two orders" of civil bureaucrats and military officers) was recruited through the civil service examination system based on the Chinese Confucian Classics. Successful candidates staffed the offices of the central government and served in local administration. When the mother decides to leave the security of her patriarchal home and move to the big city of Seoul, she does not shy away from the humiliation of taking on manual labor as a seamstress serving *kisaeng* (female entertainers considered low-class), to enable her daughter's transformation into a modern "new woman." Yet, even in the midst of her new life, the mother retains the aristocratic pride of her traditional *yangban* origins, and she disdains both low-class people and more-affluent hypocritical urbanites.

In the second part of the trilogy, the mother has grown into a matriarch of a large family comprising her daughter's family and the wife and offspring of her late son.

This part continues the family story with little plot, but all the more drama. The mother's boldness is undiminished as she refuses to succumb to the many political and economical changes rattling Korean society. The daughter, on the other hand, does cherish her more traditional role as the indispensable head of the household, but despite her maternal zeal she indulges in occasional adventures away from home that jolt her out of her everyday routine. The daughter thus embodies the two sides of a new Korea: she is a responsible mother in control of her life and duties, but at the same time she is a woman hungry for change, liberation, and oblivious pleasures. Mysteriously, the daughter's brief absences often coincide with minor domestic catastrophes—burns and broken bones, bad falls, car accidents, drug poisoning.

It is one such escapade that leads to a family crisis, which unleashes atrocious wartime memories and challenges deeply held beliefs about both tradition and modernity. Because Park Wansuh evokes such grand themes through the particular struggles, contradictions, and sufferings of individual people rather than through the abstractions of national discourse and ideology, her writing is profoundly human and emotionally "realistic," resounding far beyond the particular circumstances of the tortuous modern history of the Korean peninsula.

Mother's Hitching Post[1]

PART 2

Every disaster that has ever befallen my family, no matter how large or small, happened while I was away from home. I know by experience that if I leave home, body and soul, and thoroughly indulge in the delights of the outside world, oblivious to my family, I can expect an accident to be waiting for me when I return.

It was so when I had just weaned my first child. Dizzy with the relief that comes from having made it through the most difficult part of child rearing, I had stayed on after a get-together with friends to play *hwat'u* as if I had all the time in the world. My experience with the card game was limited to occasionally watching friends play before I would hurriedly take my leave, giving the lame excuse of living with parents-in-law and having to take care of my baby. But this time, winning with the proverbial beginner's luck, I had become caught up in the freshly learned merriment and was unaware the afternoon was waning.

"Look at her. I wonder if it's all right for a girl with a mother-in-law at home to stay out late," I heard someone murmur behind me and sobered up at once. Although even in those days I wasn't so naive as to let fear of my mother-in-law keep me from staying out late with friends, whom I met only occasionally, a very strange sensation came over me as I realized I'd never once thought about my home the whole day. I was also flustered to realize that I had let the charms of *hwat'u* thoroughly distract me from the mother's role I'd been so anxiously performing for my firstborn. A chill ran up my spine as it suddenly dawned on me that my fascination with the card game was due to a malevolent trick of fate, not of gambling; I had played right into the hands of destiny.

I knew immediately it was a preposterous thought but the uncanny sensation remained as vivid as a living creature. To shake off the nasty feeling I fussed over my winnings. I tried to cheer myself up with a cunning accounting of them. I told myself that besides having fun enough to lose all track of time, I had earned a small bundle.

I was soon to realize that the uncanny sensation was a premonition. While I was away from home, my toddler turned a kettle of boiling water over on her leg and had to be treated for severe burns in the emergency room. As soon as she saw me, my mother-in-law, who had been crying by the side of my groaning child, jumped up, not to scold me for being away from home all day, but to apologize.

"It happened in the blink of an eye. I got a bit hungry toward evening, so I boiled us some eggs, one for her and one for me. I brought the kettle into the room and was just turning around to get the salt—" She couldn't finish her explanation because her lips puckered like a child's and she burst into tears.

"It's my fault," was all I could stammer.

"Babysitting sure is a thankless job. . . ."

"It's all my fault, I tell you."

"The doctor says the burn won't scar as long as it doesn't get infected. And it won't get infected because she's got my skin. I was just like her when I was little. I spilled a piping hot bowl of soup on my left foot. It was so bad that when they pulled my sock off, my skin came off with it. That was a long, long time ago when

1. Translated by Kim Miza and Suzanne Crowder Han. This is the second part of the *Mother's Hitching Post* trilogy.

soy sauce was the only thing we had to treat burns with. All they did was brush the burn with soy sauce several times but I healed like new. My skin sure deserves taking after. And they have so many good medicines these days. Oh, by the way, they also gave her some shots."

She was trying to make me feel better but I could hardly stand her endless babbling. What good was such talk when my child was suffering? It made me crazy that I couldn't share with my little girl even a feather's worth of the horrible pain she was going through. For the first time in her life, my little girl, a mere child who had come into this world because of me, was experiencing pain. She was too small and too young to know that people are strangers to each other; we're all on our own. Perhaps that's why I kept trying to attach significance to the eeriness I felt after neglecting her the whole day. I thought that uncanny sensation must have been a warning message sent through a mysterious cord invisible but surely existing between my child and me. If only I'd realized it was a warning, she wouldn't have had to suffer. I hated myself for being so dense I hadn't recognized the warning and vowed I'd never be guilty of such stupidity again.

Whether it was because her skin took after my mother-in-law's or because she was given good medicine, my daughter's burn healed without scarring. I had four more children at intervals of two years. Raising five children, I had gone through not just burns but broken bones, bad falls, car accidents, drug poisoning, and countless other accidents that made my heart sink and the sky pale. And just like the first accident, they all happened when I was away from home. The strange feeling that always seemed to accompany my thorough neglect of my family was always the same as it was the first time but, as is true with everything, I became used to it and began to doubt its potency. If it was truly a premonition or a warning, the sensation should come before an accident, but I realized in retrospect that I felt it almost always *after* an accident happened. Although my children's accidents all occurred when I was away, what about the accidents that had nothing to do with my flesh and blood? Why did my mother-in-law's fall, a boiler explosion, a burglary, and the like have to happen when I was away? The answer was simple: it was the nature of an accident to occur in the absence of the person who was responsible for the safety of the family.

The eerie feeling was probably due more to my total negligence than to any mysterious ties of blood. The temporary neglect of my family and home was due only to my immersion in work or play. It was comforting to think that the eerie feeling was brought on by nothing more than the guilt and embarrassment any housewife who normally holds her family sacred would experience upon realizing she has been neglecting them. Once I had provided a rather sensible, if not reasonable, explanation for a work of supernatural energy assumed to exist between one's inner state of mind and the physical world, the magic of the eerie sensation dulled gradually.

In fact, the sensation was a false alarm more often than not. It was quite understandable, too. Now that all my children were grown up, my mother-in-law long dead, and we had moved into an apartment that seemed to have been built to be unlived in, it became quite natural for me to leave it locked up at every opportunity. There wasn't anyone or anything left at home to be involved in an accident. If an accident were to befall my family, it would occur outside our home rather than inside.

Strangely enough, I sometimes missed that unsettling sensation, and its uncanniness. It was not an ordinary feeling that would come over me every time I left home. I had to leave home in mind and body. After all, isn't it a housewife's lot to worry and wonder about her home even when she's away from it? My own superstition that the thorough neglect of family and home was the cause of accidents made me vigilant when I was away from home, and sometimes I would actually put the superstitious belief into play by telephoning home. Nevertheless, every now and then I would get carried away with the delights of the outside world and completely forget about my home, and each time I would be sobered up by that uncanny sensation. I came to love that feeling. For it cast a lightning flash on the dump of meaningless sediments of the routine that was my life and illuminated the ancient dust of my household vividly and beautifully. Thanks to the magic of such moments, I was able to return to my routine anew, fresh and breathless like an actress on her first stage. How could it not be exhilarating to have boredom shine like happiness and dust sparkle like gold even if it was only the illusion of an evanescent moment? It was an unexpected blessing of life.

How I loved that uncanny, ominous feeling. When I was young, it was hardly ever wrong. I guess that's why I feel the way I do about my family and home, that I'm their mainstay, their foundation.

What's going to happen to the household without me? I would grumble as I flailed a duster after returning from a trip of only a couple of days. Perhaps I grumbled out of a vain memory of the glory of those days. At such times, it was a big disappointment to find that the only bad things that had happened during my absence were that the shelves had become covered with dust and a couple of dirty socks had been thrown in the corner. That would only make me reiterate my routine threats of what dire things would happen without me. My children would giggle and roll their eyes in mock despair. Of course I also grumbled I couldn't wait until the day I would be free from the worries and boring chores that come with being a housewife. Perhaps I said that a bit more often than the what-will-become-of-the-household line. However, it was only a halfhearted exaggeration, my secret intention being a lifelong reign as mistress of the household.

On that day, I had more fun than I had had in a long time. The snow that began to fall lightly on my way to my friend's farm turned heavy in the afternoon. The big trees at the entrance to the village were a soft blur like in a painting, their limbs misty in minimal lines of nobleness. Every now and then a tree branch would break with a wail under the weight of the snow. The fresh-smelling pine branches burning in the fireplace warmed the room and our hearts as well. In the garden just outside the window a Nanking cherry bloomed with snow flowers. It was heavenly. I never imagined there was such a place so near Seoul, near enough that my friend's husband could easily drive to his office at the center of the city every day with no difficulty. I had been invited here last spring when the cherry trees were in full bloom. I had come with my friends. Our cars packed the lanes in the garden and the orchard and our children's laughter rang through the clouds of blossoms, making the place look like a suburban tourist farm. In my mind that farm and the one I was now visiting were two different places, each of which I liked for a different reason. Because they were different, the sense of distance was also different for me. I felt peaceful and sweetly weary like the faithful followers of the mystical Chonggamnok faith once they had found refuge at their promised haven on hallowed Kyeryong Mountain.[2]

As I listened to the crackling of the unseasoned wood in the fireplace, I imagined the trees singing. It was still snowing outside and the window looked like a lace curtain swaying in the wind. It made the room seem like it was floating to some faraway place. If the room was moving, it was moving in time, not in space, and I was willing to move with it. The thickly falling snow was erasing not just the footprints of humans but their achievements and was returning the world to primordial times.

My friend poured a red liquid from a moonlike glass jar into a crystal glass. "Try it. It's Nanking cherry wine."

The wine was as beautiful and clear as a ruby.

"I've come to learn there's nothing better than farming. Take the cherries in the garden. I thought they were plain old garden plants, but I was grossly mistaken. They bore so much fruit we got three bushels from as many trees, and that was after our helper's children gorged themselves on them and I gave heaps of them to relatives, friends, and every visitor to show them off. The jar I used to use to make grape wine wouldn't hold them all, so I put them in a huge earthen pot and buried it. You can drink as much as you like."

"So, you think I'm a lush," I quipped.

I kept sipping the lovely, sweet wine without giving it a second thought. I could not stop marveling at the cherry trees, the days between spring and winter, between cherry blossoms and snow blossoms, when they were weighed down by three bushels, no, five bushels of fruit clustered on their short little limbs.

"This farming business, you see—" My friend was about to boast some more about farming.

Recalling the housewarming party she had had during the cherry blossom season, I couldn't help becoming sarcastic. "How can you talk as though you've been farming for years? You're making me green with envy. Wait until you've gone through some bad times. This city slicker who's been stuck in a concrete chicken coop her whole life wouldn't mind hearing some regrets coming from you."

"I've been farming less than a year, but why should the future be any different?"

She was right. Although she and her husband owned the orchard and surrounding farmland, they had other people do the farming, but not as tenant farmers because they did not expect any income from them. All they wanted from the farm was to be able to pick fruit to their heart's content and know that it was all theirs. They had more than enough income from their business in the city. They had bought the farm in the belief that a change of air would be good for my friend, who had been unexplainably sick for a number of years. So what she meant by farming was gathering the fruit from the few cherry trees in the garden.

I found the whole idea ridiculous. The farm was too extravagant for a simple change of air for a nervous condition or some other minor illness. But I didn't let

2. The *Record of Chŏng Kam*, a coded text that prophesied the founding of a new ideal dynasty on Mount Kyeryong, was banned in pre-20th-century Korea.

the thought bother me for long. Drinking always made me different—elated, talkative, and much too ready to laugh. Thoughts stowed away tightly inside me, absurd anxieties, and heartaches would pour out like water from a crystal-clear spring. I didn't care if my audience found them crystal clear or murky, enraptured as I was with the verbal release of the things that had long been pent up inside me. It meant liberation from them. Perhaps that was the way I could experience freedom, which for me was a star hung at the tip of a tree branch. I would climb the tree in vain to pick it. The higher I climbed, the farther away the star became and the farther away became the ground to which I had to return, so that in the end I was left with only a sense of crisis.

Maybe that was why I tried to indulge myself in freedom in such a tasteless manner, like a drunkard. My friend's farming truly deserved endless boasting. The cherry wine was so sweet, clear, and beautiful and its fragrance so pure that it made me giddy and lighthearted the whole day.

My friend's husband came home. The snow had stopped, but his trip through the snow-covered fields, guided only by the headlights of his trusty car, was like the homing of a wild animal. My tipsiness made me shower him with praise. Fortunately, whenever I drank, I could never get beyond being tipsy.

Flustered at my flattery, he offered to drive me home because the road to Seoul was hazardous. My friend hugged him and jumped up and down saying happily, "Would you? I've been wondering how I could dare entrust my precious guest to that rattly old country bus and expect to have a good night's sleep."

"Rattly or not, there's no bus. The drivers all got scared and disappeared some time ago. If your friend isn't going to stay the night, my car is her only way home. So if . . ."

So if they were to get rid of me, their only choice was to drive me was what he wanted to say, I fathomed even in my drunken state, and I promptly stood up to leave.

"I don't want you to fall asleep driving," said my friend, and so she came along. She sat in the front seat beside her husband, and I gladly went to sleep in back.

I had no idea how long the drive took. I struggled awake as they helped me into the elevator. When I opened my purse for my compact, I found a pack of gum on top. "Here, chew this so you won't smell," I seemed to remember my friend saying as she shoved it into my purse. I couldn't remember at what point during our journey she did so, but it showed she was concerned about me returning to my husband and children smelling of alcohol. Then I realized that I'd not even thought about my family until my friend mentioned them. No, not even then. I had forgotten them completely. A familiar feeling crept down my back. It was the most uncanny I had ever experienced. It felt like some reptile was creeping down my spine. The pleasure the day had given me disappeared like a dream. I staggered. Not out of drunkenness. I had already sobered up completely. I counted my years. I thought I couldn't go through another disaster or misfortune. In the order of things, it was my turn to become the disaster for my family. Although in recent years these uncanny feelings had proven to be false alarms more times than not, I didn't have a moment's doubt that one of my family had had an accident; the uncanny feeling that came over me that day was so powerful and vivid. The elevator stopped and the door opened. All of my family were there, each one hale and hearty, but rigid like a statue.

Yes, they were like people immortalized in stone, motionless but looking at me. Their stiff expressions not changing. They seemed not to know me. How could it be like this. It was a disaster. A disaster of my own making. I can't go through with it, I thought.

How lovely the tedious life from which I had run away could suddenly become when I was to be denied re-entry to it. Oozing flattery from every pore, I tried to give them a big smile. But one would have thought I was trying to smile for the first time in my life because my whole face tensed up, making it impossible for me to smile naturally.

"Sorry I'm so late. What a snowstorm. It was really terrible. The buses stopped running. They wanted me to stay overnight but I begged and begged so they drove me home. Them, not their driver. I was so uncomfortable, making my friend's husband drive me. They risked their lives to bring me home. Oh, it's really a horrendous snowfall," I babbled, looking over their shoulders and down the hall of our apartment, which was a far cry from the snowy scene.

"Mom, don't be alarmed."

"Dear, don't be alarmed."

"Something happened while you were away."

"Don't be alarmed, Mom."

Is there anything more alarming than being warned not to be alarmed? But then, that was the only thing I could say to myself to calm my pounding heart. Don't be alarmed. All your family are right in front of you, all in one piece. As long as they were healthy and intact, nothing could scare me. No, never. Even if they were conspiring to deny my very existence, I was not going to be scared.

"Grandma got hurt, Mom."

"She fell in the snow."

"It looks serious."

"She hasn't regained consciousness."

"We've been waiting for you."

"We couldn't wait any longer so we were just leaving for the hospital. Will you come with us?"

Everyone had something to say. There was not even the faintest trace of disapproval, but I felt so ashamed I wanted to hide from them.

"Oh, no. Please go ahead. I'll be along soon. My heart is pounding. And my legs are wobbly," I whimpered, covering my burning face with both hands.

"See, I told you she'd be shocked. We shouldn't have dumped the news on her that way."

"Why not? We had to tell her."

"Okay, okay. I've heard of people hiding bad things that happened to a child from its parents but I've never heard of hiding a parent's accident from a child."

The children argued among themselves. Quietly my husband hustled them out of the apartment, leaving one behind to keep an eye on his traumatized wife. Declining her company, I locked myself in my room and collapsed in a heap on the floor. Not because of trauma but because of my shame and sleepiness. How relieved I was when I realized it wasn't one of my immediate family but my mother on whom the disaster had befallen in my absence. I was embarrassed and ashamed, but my sense of guilt was not enough to keep sleep away. Feigning sorrow to my child who was so eager to offer me moral support, I slipped into sleep, a sleep as sweet as a clandestine affair.

The first thing that surged into my mind like an icy stream after the short but deep sleep was that my mother was as much a family member as my children, that she was as much my flesh and blood as them. Still I was relieved to have shoved a disaster that could have happened to one of my children onto my mother as if she were a total stranger.

Moreover, I was the only first-of-kin my mother had left. I had five children but she only had me now. People say that though you have ten fingers, there is none that wouldn't hurt if you were to bite it, meaning that one's love for one's children cannot be halved and quartered into smaller pieces like a watermelon. Still, wouldn't a person cherish a finger all the more if it were that person's last one? This thought made me come to my senses.

I thought about my brother, who died during the Korean War. He was well known far and wide among our relatives and neighbors for being a model filial son. A vivid image of him as a young boy popped into my mind. When he, Mother, and I were in the pit of abject poverty, I used to pester Mother for candy money, although she only earned a pittance as a seamstress, and I finally caused her great financial difficulty by breaking the window of the candy shop. My brother took me to the old stone wall on Mount Inwang and beat me, crying all the time he was doing it. As if he were beating me awake now, my sleepiness disappeared completely and for the first time in a truly long time I felt him near me. His tears of that time made me cry even now. The nearer I felt him, the greater became my longing for him.

I could no longer avoid the reality that I was responsible for my mother. I pulled myself together and headed to the hospital.

To my surprise, Mother had regained consciousness; she even smiled faintly when she saw me. The two sons my brother had left in this world were now older than he ever was and had children of their own. With my big family and theirs, my mother's cubicle in the emergency room was impressively crowded. Because I had been thinking of my brother, I was saddened at the simple truth that the dead could not age.

As was appropriate for the first-of-kin, I hurriedly shoved them aside and grabbed Mother's hand. It was the proverbial arrival of the first-of-kin that is said to move even a corpse to tears. Tears welled up in Mother's eyes and streamed down her cheeks. The sorrow that I was the only child left to her crystallized into streams of tears for the two of us.

"How did this happen, Mom?"

"I was looking out the window at Sŏgi's dad clearing the snow and I thought I could help him, I'm not *that* old, but my first step out in the yard, I just . . ."

Sŏgi's dad was my brother's eldest son, my mother's grandson, and my nephew. Mother lived with him.

"Help him, my foot. You just wanted to meddle," muttered Sŏgi's mom.

"You mean all of you were there and let this happen?" I said, blaming my nephew and his wife automatically.

"You know how Grandma has to supervise everything. What could we do?" My nephew promptly sided with his wife.

My mother was long past eighty, and my nephew and his wife were both barely over thirty. It would be an understatement to say it wasn't easy for young people to live with a grandparent, when some people downright refused to live with their parents-in-law. Even so, never was my mother's unwanted presence so dramatically revealed.

I could hear the moaning and groaning of sick people and the agitation of their families coming from every corner of the emergency room.

"So where did you get hurt?"

My nephew's wife lifted the sheet and pointed. Mother's left leg was twisted to the outside and was so swollen it looked like someone else's leg was stitched to her body.

"They should be fixing it soon," Mother murmured as if to comfort us.

"Does it hurt?"

"It hurts so bad I wish I could faint again."

"Oh, Mother!"

A nurse called at that moment, and we all rushed over to the doctor who was with her. The resident in charge of the emergency room, he looked too young and too exhausted. The red hand on the clock on the wall was already past the twelve, and on the X-ray screen the bare bones of my mother's hip and thigh awaited judgment.

"We'll have to admit her and, depending on her progress, we'll operate."

"Excuse me?"

"What I mean is we have to determine if she can endure surgery. There's no possibility of natural healing."

"But she's eighty-six years old. Surgery would be too . . . Oh, my mother wants a cast. It doesn't matter how long it will take. Please put her leg in a cast."

"I'm mentioning surgery because she's too old for the fracture to mend in a cast. To put her leg in a cast at her age is to put her in a coffin. She would develop all kinds of complications and definitely end up dead," the young doctor said coldly.

"She believes she's getting a cast. Er, are you sure a cast won't do?" I implored.

"It's not a patient's job to diagnose or treat."

"So you're saying we don't have any choice."

"That's right. Surgery is the only way."

"Will she be able to walk?"

"If she makes good progress . . ."

"So you can't even guarantee the result of the surgery. This is pure nonsense!" I lifted my voice, hackles raised, but the young doctor was singularly unperturbed. His calm seemed to stem not so much from his medical knowledge as from fatigue.

"You can talk in detail with the doctor in charge tomorrow. In the meantime, you need to take care of her hospital admission."

"If you're not the doctor in charge, how can you be so positive she needs surgery?"

"Because that's practically the only thing today's medicine can do for her."

"Ha! You can't even guarantee the result!"

"I told you it was the only way. I didn't say it was the safe way. Sometimes the only way is risky," said the doctor, his temper finally roused.

"Come on, Auntie. This is a hospital. We've got to do as the doctor says." My two nephews, who had been watching in silence, stepped in.

"But you don't know anything. You don't know!" I shrieked in a blind outburst of emotion that was boiling up in me.

"What don't we know?"

"Your grandma is eighty-six. Do you think she can survive a big operation?"

"What else can we do? Let's get her admitted first. Then we can discuss it with the doctor tomorrow. This is an emergency room, Auntie."

My nephews manhandled me out to the hall as if I were a mobster. Little did we know that those few words we exchanged with the young doctor were to be the most comprehensive discussion we would ever have with Mother's doctors.

As is true of doctors' rounds at any big university hospital, the doctor in charge entered Mom's room with an entourage of residents, interns, and nurses the next morning and acted very dependable and authoritative. Perhaps it's their authoritative manner that makes people refrain from voicing what they want to say. I stood aside deferentially and waited for him to speak. He said several things to the residents that sounded like a foreign language and the next thing I knew he was gone. I hurried after him but all I could do was buttonhole the resident who'd been in the emergency room the previous night. Before I could utter a word, he told me the surgery would take place about three days later and disappeared into another room.

In the next three days, the only information I was able to glean from the doctor by chasing him here and there was that the prognosis was not very good for a person with a fracture in the place where Mom's was, that the broken bones would have to be hooked together with metal pins because the bones of someone her age would not fuse together on their own, and that the operation was not a simple procedure. The doctor hadn't told me this in so many words at one time, but that's what it added up to when I patched together the few words he reluctantly and sparingly dropped from time to time.

I don't know if it was because I was overwhelmed by his authoritativeness or whether reticence was contagious, but whenever I came face-to-face with the doctor, I could not properly voice what I had been determined to say. As much as the doctor frustrated our family, we were frustrating my mother.

"You know, we could have done better with the old bonesetter. A bonesetter can work wonders with broken bones. And here I am, lying up in this fancy hospital doing nothing but making you spend a fortune. Instead of getting busy fixing what's broken, these people just keep drawing blood out of this old bag of bones to do this test and that test. I can't understand it for the life of me. It hurts awfully. And it isn't as if they're doing it for free, is it? I guess they think there's not much money in fixing bones so they're just trying to bleed a fortune out of us. Go tell them we don't have any money. Aw, my leg. Is this my leg or a mortal enemy? If it's going to hurt this much after they fix it then I want to die. Let me die. It's shameful enough to have lived this long when my own son had to go before me. What other sin have I committed to have to go through this kind of pain?"

Despite saying such things, my mother was looking forward to having her leg in a cast, and never imagined anything else. All the family balked at the idea of informing her otherwise. Of course, the task naturally came to me as I was her daughter.

When a "Nothing By Mouth" sign was hung on her bed the night before the surgery, I had no choice but to tell her of the impending operation.

"Operation? Who wants an operation? No. Never. I'd go to the devil before I'd let them take a knife to me. Don't think it's from any fear of dying that I haven't ended my life of unjust burdens before now. I was afraid of what would happen if I took the life I was given. Let me be, even if they tell you I'll die if I don't get an operation. I'm soon going to be ninety. No one would blame you if you just let me be."

Mother was adamantly opposed. But her eldest grandson had already signed the surgery consent form and tomorrow morning she was scheduled to be hauled off to the operating room regardless of her wishes. But I did not want to heap insults on the shell of a body that was my mother. Except for the hideously swollen leg, Mother's body was so fragile it wouldn't be more than a handful if wadded up. As long as there was any pride left in it, I believed she had the right to know what was going to happen to it. My belief stemmed from the love and hate I harbored for my mother as her only remaining offspring.

Without mincing words, I explained in detail all I knew about the operation she was to undergo. I even had the presence of mind to compare the fracture of her thighbone to a broken stick.

"Just think about it. If you had a broken stick and wanted to fix it because you really needed it, would you glue the pieces together or would you join them together with nuts and bolts? Which would be stronger? And then, what if you didn't have any glue or not enough of it? There's nothing to worry about, Mom. The doctors are going to fix your bones good and strong with nuts and bolts. No matter how many more days you're going to live, you want to be able to use all your limbs, don't you? That's living, isn't it, Mom?"

A bright smile came over Mother's face. Her eyes, which had been dim a long time, suddenly shone like a dreamy girl's.

"You mean the mountain marrow[3] is still the best remedy for broken bones?"

"Huh?"

I had no idea what she was talking about. Her sudden change of attitude was so weird I almost screamed.

"So, there's still nothing better than mountain marrow. Yes, indeed. Mountain marrow is the best. It sure is a godsend," Mother chanted sweetly in a dreamy voice as if remembering a long-forgotten nursery rhyme.

"Mother, what are you talking about? Straighten up, Mom." I shook her emaciated shoulders.

"If only it were a small bone, I could just swallow a little mountain marrow. But since it's a big bone that's broken, they'll have to open me up and put the mountain marrow in. Children, I'm not a bit afraid of surgery. Don't you worry. I know bones fixed with mountain marrow are stronger than ever. Just look at this wrist of mine."

Wielding her right arm proudly, Mother beamed a knowing smile. But anybody could see her wrist was deformed. It had a crook in it and looked larger than her left one.

I knew why it was like that. And then I realized what she meant by mountain marrow.

3. Pyrite, used in traditional Korean medicine.

The next morning found Mother still smiling. She looked like a baby because her dentures had been removed in preparation for surgery. The secret that made her smile so broadly in the face of a serious trial at an age nearer to ninety than to eighty made me unbearably sad.

Our first winter in the house with the purse-sized yard at the top of Hyŏnjŏdong, which we managed to buy our first time in Seoul, was harsh. It was brutally cold and once snow began to fall, it kept falling for days like rain during the monsoon. Even our waterman, Mr. Kim, dared not trudge through the deep snow to deliver to us. No water was no big deal for us, however. All we had to do was shovel some of the snow that had accumulated in the yard, on the soy-crock terrace, on the roof, everywhere, and heat it in an iron pot. Water wasn't a serious problem, but fire was.

Every day we had to buy two bundles of thin pieces of firewood. Mother never bought firewood at the neighborhood store but went all the way down to the firewood market near the streetcar terminal, saying that even though they looked alike, the bundles from the market were heavier. The vendor would deliver them if she bought ten bundles at a time, but we must have been unable to afford even that, for every day my mother would bring one or two bundles herself. When the steep alleys of our neighborhood became dangerously slippery with the snow that fell night and day, my brother said he would fetch the wood, but my mother was not one to let her son do such a chore.

"I don't need such trivial shows of filial piety as fetching firewood. You're an only son so you should do far greater deeds. You must study hard so you can be successful and make lots of money. Then we'll be able to buy logs by the cartload at the Ch'ŏngnyangni[4] market to cut and chop into enough firewood to fill the shed. Then we'll be warm all winter."

"That's then. We have to think about now. People will make fun of us if you keep doing it when you have a big, strapping son. It's not the way for a son, either."

"And sending him on good-for-nothing errands is no way for a mother to treat a son who's going to be a great person some day."

Because my mother was so stubborn, there was little my brother could do, even as deeply devoted as he was.

Then one viciously cold day, Mother returned home with cuts and bruises all over because she had slipped and fallen while carrying firewood bundles on her head. The injuries were not serious, although they looked frightful for some time. Her wrist, however, swelled up very large and caused her great pain.

My brother and I lay awake through the night listening to her stifled moans. We felt as if our very pillar of strength had been shaken. The next morning, my mother did the household chores as usual and was as bright and spirited as ever with no sign of pretending. But try though she might, she could not do her needlework. She asked the old woman who used to bring orders from *kisaeng*[5] to come retrieve the unfinished dresses, apologizing over and over. On seeing my mother's swollen wrist, the woman immediately cited a string of excellent acu-

4. Neighborhood in Seoul.
5. Women trained to work for upperclass clients as artists, entertainers, and courtesans.

puncturists, each and every one known to be the best in the city, but it was obvious that my mother had no thought of listening to her.

"I'll be all right soon. It's already much easier to move today than it was yesterday."

The old woman came back later with a few pods of gardenia seeds and said, "Try a gardenia paste. It does wonders for swelling."

Then she muttered to herself, "But what good will it do if the swelling goes away. She's got to have her bones joined. Mountain marrow is wonderful for joining broken bones, but that woman won't listen to anything that costs money. She's just too stubborn for her own good. When will she realize she has to take care of herself first if she's to take care of those children."

Brother also heard her. He got me out of Mother's earshot and asked me if I knew where the old woman lived. Without telling Mother, we went to that woman's house and Brother asked her what mountain marrow was and where we could find some.

"Your mom didn't send you, did she? I should think not. You certainly are nice kids. You're acting the way good young'uns should. That's why people have children. What's the use of bundles of money if you don't have any kids. Money's just useless," the woman fussed. Then she told us stories about mountain marrow that were outlandish, to say the least, but as fascinating as ancient legends. We had already taken our first step into the world of myth. To us in the throes of despair, without even a needle's eye of hope, myth had swung open its door, beckoning us to become its heroes.

The woman told us that there was only one cave in the whole country that produced mountain marrow and that it was on the ridge of Muak Hill not far from our place in Hyŏnjŏ-dong.[6] She said the grains of marrow were shaped like tiny dice, just a bit bigger than millet and shiny like metal, and that each side of one had to be perfectly square for it to have a medicinal effect. She warned us that even though the vendor always did his best to select good ones, we should double-check them. Mountain marrow was very powerful, she said. One time they were moving the grave of a man who had taken mountain marrow for a broken bone and found the bone rejoined with a cluster of sparkling metal pieces so hard they could not break them free from the body.

It was more than enough to convince us that once swallowed, the mountain marrow would go directly to Mom's broken bone and put it back together.

"Is it expensive?" asked my brother, blushing.

"No, not at all. There's no reason for it to be expensive. It's formed naturally, like earth or sand. The man who's in charge of the cave charges something in the way of a premium, but it's not much. The people who go there are mostly people who can't afford a single prick of acupuncture—though there are plenty who go there after doctors and acupuncturists have failed to cure them."

"Let's go."

My brother and I climbed up Muak Hill. The climb was quite difficult, as the day was extremely cold and deep crusted snow lay everywhere. Still, it was not far from our house and it wasn't as though we had to climb up and down twelve steep hills as in a legendary journey after a miracle drug. So it was a good thing that the road was rough; that way, we felt the catharsis of myth.

6. Neighborhood in Seoul.

The mountain marrow cave that we finally found after asking people again and again for directions was a grotto closed with a door. Although it was daytime, there were candles burning. We could tell at once that the cave was different from others. The walls and the ceiling, covered with tiny metal granules, sparkled, undulating to the dance of the candle flames, creating a mysterious, dreamy world. The master of the cave was a young man clad in a long white cotton coat. If he had been an old man with a white beard, we might have thrown ourselves at his feet and begged him to give us the divine medicine for our mother.

Nonetheless, we deified him. Emaciated and otherworldly, he had a spiritual air about him. My brother was a strapping figure compared with him. Looking up at him, I clung to my brother.

My brother bowed politely and told the man the purpose of our visit. The man went to a small table lit by a pair of candles and began to select some mountain marrow. Confirming what the old woman had said, he told us that not all of the marrow in the cave was medicinal, only the perfectly square cubes that had no blemishes. However, he didn't go so far as to say they would cluster around broken bones to rejoin them.

He selected the marrow in a most peculiar way. He knelt down in front of a table on which marrow was piled and nodding his head slightly as if dozing picked up a few grains at a time and wrapped them in white paper. Being so entranced in his work made his pale, emaciated face look even more spiritual. He seemed to be doing the selecting with his mind's eye rather than his eye.

Seeing that my brother was stooped in a reverential bow with his hands clasped together, I quickly did the same.

"I'll give you enough for ten days to begin with," said the man, bundling up the white paper packs. His voice was dry and hollow. "Come over here. It will work better if you pray to the Mountain Spirit."

Beyond the table in a deep corner of the cave, two candles illuminated a painting of the Mountain Spirit enshrined on an altar of mountain marrow. A bowl of water was on the altar and ten-*chŏn* and twenty-*chŏn* coins[7] were scattered around it.

"Here, bow to the spirit and offer payment if you brought any. Pray to him for healing, like this."

Brother did as he was told. He prostrated himself again and again. Although I loved him dearly, I couldn't help being somewhat reserved and well behaved in my manner toward him, not only because there was a ten-year age gap between us, but also because he had a certain air about him that others found sobering. Clear intelligence and dignity that would never be tainted by stupidity or blinded by cunning superstition were his most prominent characteristics. Those marks of character that set him apart from the lowly brood of our impoverished neighborhood were the mantle I wore with pride.

And that brother of mine was kowtowing again and again to a cheap painting of the Mountain Spirit that even I could tell was the work of an amateur. Oddly enough, that superstitious ritual seemed to make him more dignified rather than degrade him. Maybe when you do something with so much care and heart, con-

7. 100 *chŏn* amount to I Korean *wŏn*. After World War II the official exchange rate was 15 *wŏn* to 1 US dollar.

tradictory ways do not contradict but harmonize of their own accord. Unbid, I stooped reverentially and watched my brother absorbed in his ritual.

I have no idea if the amount of money my brother dedicated to the Mountain Spirit was enough for the mountain marrow, but his devotion was obviously more than enough to please the marrow man.

"I told you to try ten days to begin with but I can see that she will be hale and hearty in no more than ten. I'm never mistaken. You wait and see. Mountain marrow is a mysterious thing that works spiritually more than physically, and what spirit on earth could remain unmoved by your devotion? Besides, the Mountain Spirit is truly a miracle worker."

Needless to say, my brother's mountain marrow moved Mother deeply. She was much happier than before she got injured and, after reporting the decrease in swelling and pain every day with hourglass precision, on exactly the tenth day she announced she was completely healed.

Still, her wrist didn't look normal. She said the bulging was due to the mountain marrow that had clustered there to join the bones. To prove she was healed, she resumed her needlework on the tenth day and her quality was as good as ever. She would lift heavy objects just to demonstrate how strong the mountain marrow had made her bone. And of course she resumed her routine of buying one or two bundles of firewood at the Yŏngch'ŏn market and adamantly refused my brother's offer to fetch the wood until the arrival of spring.

"Don't worry, son. If I slip again, I have this hand to break the fall. It's strong as iron," she boasted, flaunting her ugly, misshapen arm.

The meeting between a surgeon and the patient's family immediately before the patient goes into surgery is a heartwarming event in a TV show, a drama, or a movie. For a brief moment, the doctor sheds his armor of authority and shows warmth and compassion for the anxious family. The family is comforted by the feeling that, possibilities of failure notwithstanding, they have made the right choice to entrust their loved one to a fellow human being rather than a robot that doesn't make mistakes. That comfortable feeling makes them play the baby with the doctor and shamelessly beg and plead, and the doctor becomes generous enough to indulge their all-too-human weaknesses, though it is questionable if it is genuine generosity rather than condescension or sentimentalism.

I too hoped to have such a warm, if only brief, encounter with Dr. Hong outside the operating room. I couldn't bear the thought of entrusting him with my mother's ancient, frail, female body, made lifeless by anesthesia. I needed to be comforted by him.

But the operating room of the large medical center was more like an arena than a room. A multitude were operated on every day. Like products on an assembly line, patients were put through one process after another until they entered the operating room for a final processing and, after some time, were sent out. Many people did things to Mother before she entered the operating room, but I didn't feel that a single one of them was the type of person to whom I could pour out my heart.

The operating room was off limits to family, and we could not see anyone who was in charge, much less what was going on inside. Either the surgeons had a permanent residence in the operating room or they had their own private entrance somewhere, for I could not catch a glimpse of any doctor, including Dr. Hong, no matter how long I hung around outside.

I sorely missed the pre-operational ritual and rapport that was only natural to have when entrusting a human life to another person. I believed it was more important than signing the surgical consent form. In the midst of everything, my mother's cheerful innocence as she entered the operating room was a great comfort for me. It was a wonder she could be so relaxed and free of anxiety when her more than eighty-year-old body was going to undergo a major operation. She was comfortable because she identified the operation with the mountain marrow treatment. For my mother, my brother was still her religion.

The surgery was a large L-shaped area with an entrance at one end and an exit at the other. The exit was no better than the entrance for peeping inside. A great many people, relatives of people undergoing surgery, hovered around the exit. A young mother who had sent her child all alone into the operating room was crying on her husband's shoulder, and an olderly woman was chanting with prayer beads for her grown-up son. A nurse came out every now and then to write some numerals next to names on a roster of patients. The numerals indicated the time the surgery was over and the patient was moved to the recovery room. It took another hour for the patient to be wheeled out. Every time a patient was brought out, people flocked around the gurney to see if it was their loved one.

There were TV scenes in which the door of the operating room swishes open and a doctor emerges and, still swathed in his surgical gown, calmly removes a mask that covers all but his twinkling eyes to reveal a fatigued but content smile peculiar to a person who has successfully accomplished a difficult task, and finally announces "It's all right. The operation was a success," whereupon the patient's family all look up at him adoringly or kowtow, spilling tears of gratitude. Such scenes never took place this side of the exit. There was only the entrance swallowing up the patients and the exit spitting them out, the families looking on helplessly.

The list on the wall had the name, gender, and age of all the patients scheduled for surgery. At eighty-six, my mother was the oldest. The next oldest was fifty-seven, which made having an operation at eighty-six seem all the more risky. Although it was nine in the morning when Mother went into surgery, it was not until after one in the afternoon that her name was listed as having been moved to the recovery room. We heard nothing more for the longest time. Every time the door opened and a patient was carted out, I would rush to the gurney to see if it was her. My eyes dimmed because of all my misgivings, fatigue, and hunger, and I took longer and longer checking each patient.

"God, Auntie. Do you think Grandma had her wrinkles removed?"

I hated my nephews' ability to joke at such a time, but I found their presence comforting nonetheless.

At last my mother was brought out. She muttered something when she recognized us, but we couldn't make it out because she was so feeble and she didn't have her dentures in. The cotton sheet printed with the hospital's logo was not over her bare shoulders. Indignant about such mistreatment, I pulled up the sheet and tried to cover them, but the IV and drainage tubes made it difficult to cover her properly. Her naked body was shivering under the sheet.

"Cold?"

"No, I just can't keep from shivering."

Excited to hear her speaking lucidly, all the family flocked around and one after another tried to test her.

"Grandma, do you know who I am?"

"You're Sŏgi's dad, who else?"

"Grandma, Grandma, what about me?"

"Sŏgi's mom."

"And who am I?"

"Kyŏnga's dad."

Passing the tests with flying colors, Mother smiled at me proudly. The eerie sensation with which I was so familiar shot through me.

Two robust orderlies wheeled the gurney rapidly down the long corridor and stopped at the elevator. Believing them to be proof the operation was a success, we continued our ridiculous questions as we hurried alongside, but once inside the elevator we began to ignore her.

"God, am I worn out. Tonight I'm going to have a real good sleep for a change."

"My stomach's hurting because I didn't have lunch. How was the beef soup in the hospital restaurant, Brother?"

"Whose turn is it to stay tonight?"

"Don't worry. I'll stay with her. She seems all right now but I expect she'll have a rough time tonight when the anesthesia wears off. All of you go home and get some rest."

"Yeah, that's a good idea. You stay tonight, Auntie, and I'll send Sŏgi's mom first thing in the morning to relieve you."

"Grandma's really something, so wiry and tough. Can you imagine someone being so clearheaded after such a big operation, and almost ninety at that!"

"You naughty boys. Would you have been happier if she hadn't come around? She took forever in the recovery room. I was scared something bad had happened. After all, one can't cheat one's age. It took her more than three hours to regain consciousness when it took others less than an hour to come around."

"No, it didn't. I woke up soon enough," Mother butted in, having heard our whispered words. "I woke up and hollered for someone to take me back to my children, but nobody ever paid me any attention. And I was shivering all over. I told them I was dying of cold but it was no use. Although I was in my right mind, my voice just wouldn't come out. It was like something was pulling it back inside. Those folks in there were just heartless."

We winked at each other, our eyes conveying both our amazement and our disdain at the unbecoming toughness of the woman pushing ninety.

Back in her room, everyone became even more garrulous and Mother had to put in a word regardless of what we talked about. Even I became fed up with her toughness and began to ignore her now and then. It was tiresome to try to understand her speech, which was garbled because of the absence of her dentures, and worse still, it was embarrassing in front of my nephews and their wives. I wished she would pretend to be critically ill as was expected of someone who had gone through major surgery. Finally, I hustled them out even though visiting hours hadn't ended.

"Why don't you all go home. You look more worn out than your grandma does. Have a good meal and go to bed early. Besides, Grandma won't go to sleep with all of you around. She thinks she's all right, but who knows what will happen, her being so old. We should be extra careful so she can pull through without a hitch."

Even after they left, Mother kept babbling. She looked like a cow chewing its cud. I became increasingly irked at her inexhaustible strength.

In the evening, Dr. Hong appeared with residents and interns in tow. As it was not time for doctors to make their regular rounds, I assumed he was probably checking on the people on whom he had operated that day. However, it was no better than his regular visits, for he and his encourage left as soon as they arrived. The doctors I saw in the halls were no less hurried. They made rounds like a whirlwind. They swept by cold and fast like a wind that will not stay in one place.

I had prepared the highest words of appreciation to say to Dr. Hong but I couldn't. Such words should be said courteously, with a little hesitant stammer, but there was too little time for me to catch the right moment to do so. I hurried out into the hall after him and, after mumbling my thanks in the tritest, most desultory fashion, asked Mother's prognosis.

"The operation was a success. There's not much to worry about. But because of her age, she needs to be watched very carefully."

I dared not ask another question, overwhelmed as I was with his words, the most I had ever heard him utter, but I was far from satisfied.

Mother kept mumbling. Residents and nurses came and went frequently to check her and the many hoses and tubes that came out of her. They also instructed me how to care for her and to keep a log on her condition throughout the night. I was to encourage her to cough and spit out mucus every now and then, inform the nurses when the IV was running short and when the drainage bag for the incision was full, and keep a record of her urine output.

I tried to ask them all the things I had failed to ask Dr. Hong, but all I could get out of them was that Mother was progressing normally. And not a one of them failed to add that she was extremely old. Old age understandably was not a malady or health problem but an annotation.

Mother refused to cough, pleading a lack of energy, and gave me a fright every time she began to choke on mucus. It was useless to warn her that she would get pneumonia if she didn't cough up the mucus. She just kept mumbling, sounding like dry autumn leaves rustling in a breeze.

"Close your eyes and try to sleep, for god's sake," I blurted out when I could no longer put up with it.

Mother stared at me wide-eyed, her eyes pools of chilling resentment.

"Shall I turn off the light?" I asked shakily.

"No," Mother said, shaking her head.

"I'll cover your eyes. Relax and try to sleep."

I held her hand and, with my other hand, gently covered her eyes. She soon became impatient and brushed my hand away.

"The place that was cut hurts, doesn't it? It will tonight. But it'll be much better tomorrow. Tell me if it hurts too much and I'll ask them to give you something for the pain."

"No, it doesn't hurt a bit. I just can't sleep."

"Then I'll ask them to give you a sleeping pill."

I went to the nurses' station, asked them to give her something, and was told to wait in the room. Soon an intern brought a tiny pill and suggested I keep the room dark. After helping my mother take the pill, I turned off all the lights except for a dim lamp on the wall next to the guest cot. Mother didn't protest this time. Relieved by the knowledge that the pill would soon take effect, I became unbearably sleepy. After making sure there was more than half a bottle of IV to go and the urine bag and drainage bag were less than half full, I lay down on the cot with the intention of dozing for a few minutes.

I had no idea how long I'd been sleeping when I was awakened by a strange stirring. The room was astir with silent restlessness. My mother was beating the air with her hands. But not recklessly beating. She seemed to be working hard at something, beating the air regularly and purposefully. I jumped up and turned on the lights. Mother squinted for a moment but her hands never stopped.

"What are you doing, Mommy?" I asked, unconsciously speaking in the way I used to when I was a little girl.

"Can't you see? When you do laundry, you've got to put the blouses with the blouses, the panties with the panties, and the socks with the socks. It won't do to bundle everything up together," she said in a strong voice.

"Laundry? You should be sleeping. . . ."

"How can I go to sleep with these things scattered all over the place? You naughty kids."

Screeching in a metallic voice, Mother stared at me. The look in her eyes was so cold it gave me the shivers. I wanted to run for help. She kept her hands busy sorting and folding laundry only she could see. Where did she find such energy after all the fasting and enemas of the previous day and the anesthesia and surgery of today? I was more frightened than amazed. A nurse walked in at that moment.

"My mother is acting strangely. She keeps beating the air. It seems like she's hallucinating."

"Some patients become like that because of the anesthesia. She'll get over it," the nurse said perfunctorily and, after checking Mom's temperature and pulse, left. I followed her out into the hall and begged her to do something to make Mother sleep.

"But she was given a pill already. You asked us to."

"It didn't work. Come to think of it, she's become worse after taking that pill. That must be it. Before she took it, she wasn't hallucinating even though she couldn't sleep. What should we do?"

"I don't think it's because of the pill. But even if it is, it's nothing serious. She was given a tranquilizer clinically proven to have the least side-effects."

"What could be more serious than this? She's out of her mind."

"She'll get better."

"Why don't you forget the tranquilizer and give her a sleeping pill or a shot."

"I can't."

"Why not? It doesn't make sense that a patient can't be helped to sleep in this big medical center where all kinds of operations are done."

"We know much better than you how to take care of patients. Families should cooperate instead of making such unreasonable demands," the nurse said, turning away in a huff. Angry and humiliated, I returned to Mother's room, vowing never to plead with the likes of her again.

It seemed Mother had not finished her laundry. Her hands continued the folding action until she suddenly thrust them out in front of her, palms outward, as if to defend herself. Her eyes, which had been like icy pits, now popped out with fear.

"What's wrong, Mom?"

I ran over to her. She threw her arms around my neck and hung on so tightly I could hardly breathe. Her strength was unbelievable. As I tried to catch my breath, she whispered in my ear in a terror-stricken voice coming from hell, "He's back. My god, he's come again."

Mother stared at the door, a hand still held defensively. I turned around to see who had followed me but there was nobody. My hair stood on end.

"Mom!"

Fear gave me the strength to shake her off. Her face contorted and she stared at the door, her body shaking uncontrollably. She was confronting whomever she saw there with all her body and soul. It suddenly dawned on me that she might be seeing the messenger from the other world come to fetch her. Terror-stricken, I dared not take a step toward the door to go for help. It was only natural the messenger from the other world would lurk at the doorway of this eighty-six-year-old woman. In all likelihood she was probably not only the oldest person to undergo surgery that day but also the oldest patient in the whole medical center. It was useless to whine and fuss if the messenger was that discerning. I had already made up my mind to let him take her. No one would complain that she had not lived out her allotted time. Still it was certainly abominable of Death to drag her away when the blood from her wound had not yet dried. But then Death would not be Death if he did not cause the survivors pain.

We're ready but for god's sake don't you show your ghastly self to her, I begged the messenger. It is us mortals' nature not to welcome death even after we have lived a hundred years. The greatest act of mercy you could do is not revealing yourself until the very last minute. Go away, I beg you. Go away, I implored silently, unable to bear the terror that was gripping Mother. I was also afraid that he might decide to reveal himself to me as well. Instead of going away, he was obviously coming nearer. I could see it in Mother's blazing eyes. My god, I was facing her death alone.

"It's him again. What're you doing? We've got to hide your brother. Hurry!"

"Please, Mom. Don't do this. Where's there a brother for us to hide?"

"Have they already taken him away, then?"

"Please, Mom."

Mother groped all around with her hands and, coming upon her bandaged leg, whispered anxiously, "Ah, here you are, my poor boy. Sit tight. I'll protect you."

Mother tried to hug her leg with her shaky hands. From that moment on, her leg was her son. Shielding her leg with her body, Mother glared at her enemy. It wasn't the messenger from the other world after all.

"Comrade Officer, Comrade, sir. There are just us women here in the house."

The chill in her eyes wavered pitifully, and a groveling smile appeared on her face. I realized what she was seeing in her hallucination. Poor Mother. It would have been much better for her had it been the messenger from the other world.

Mother was trying desperately to hide her leg but of course she couldn't.

"Comrade Officer, there's no one but us women, I tell you. You don't need to search, Comrade Officer."

I watched helplessly as she became even more frantic. As she clung to a strand of hope, beads of sweat popped out on her face, which was distorted with fear and servility. Her hands and emaciated shoulders trembled like tree limbs in the wind.

Poor Mother. God can be so heartless. It would have been better to let her die than make her undergo this horror again.

"Mother, Mother. Don't do this. Please calm down," I cried, shaking her shoulders. With a strength I could not fathom, she thrashed violently and shook me off as easily as one would a dead leaf.

"No. No. You wretched creature. You brute! You brute!"

Backed up against the wall and shaking helplessly, I could only watch her becoming increasingly agitated by the minute. Except for her wounded leg, all of her body was heaving up like raging waves. That made the leg look even more bizarre and alien, anything but part of her body. The leg frightened me. Identifying her leg with her son was contagious.

In her violent writhing, which was punctuated with harsh cries of "No, you brute!" and sly flattery of "Mister Officer," "Comrade Officer," and "Officer, sir," the IV needle was dislodged and blood ran out onto her hospital gown and bed sheet. The sight of the blood upset her even more.

"Stop right there, you brute. You'll have to kill me before I'll let you go in there."

With tears streaming down her face, Mother ground her gums together. There can be nothing more gruesome than to see a toothless person trying to grind her teeth. If only I were dreaming. Mother emitted ghastly shrieks and pulled at her hair. She pulled out her catheter. I felt faint from the smell of blood. I tried to pull myself together and was just turning to go for help when a nurse ran into the room, obviously reacting to Mother's shrieks. The duty nurse followed her.

It took a lot of people to get all the things reattached to Mother. She was as strong as a wrestler. It took me and two nurses to pin her down so the duty nurse could replace all the tubes and gadgets she had pulled out. This time the nurse put the IV needle in her foot.

"How can things like this happen?" I addressed the head nurse bitterly.

"Don't be upset. This type of reaction is extraordinary but it is certainly not uncommon. She'll be better in no time," the nurse told me soothingly.

They thought my mother's nightmare was the result of her peculiar physical disposition. But then, who could really understand another person's nightmare?

My mother's writhing was desperate and hell-bent. The head nurse had Mother's arms and legs tied and the side rails of the bed put up on both sides.

"I know it's not easy to see one's mother like this, but you have to put up with it. This is the only way to deal with this kind of situation. Try to get some sleep. Otherwise, you'll end up sick, too. Don't worry about your mother, she'll soon be all right."

The nurses left me after making sure the restraints were tied securely. I was so tired I flopped down on the cot without even bothering to remove my shoes. But lo and behold, Mother, who had been growling like a rabid animal, let out a yell and the restraints broke with a crack. She was driven by an inhuman power. She was not uttering incoherent words but chilling shrieks and venomous curses. With a gut-ripping pain, the same inhuman power surged up inside me. I gritted my teeth and dashed to her. This time I wasn't about to ask for help. I would confront her head on. This was nobody's business but our own and we were the only ones who could deal with it.

I threw myself on Mother, practically straddling her. My body convulsed with hers. I knew I could not relent lest she should ride me instead. Still, I could not match her strength, and I had to slap her when she almost overpowered me.

"Calm down, Mom. Calm down."

I slapped her. Startled by the unprecedented immoral action committed by my hand, I slapped her even harder, and at the sight of the swelling hand mark on her face, I slapped her again. I was losing touch with reality. We were in either a nightmare or hell. Mother's strength was terrifying, but her face was even more terrifying. It was not my mother's face. Now I was not fighting with my mother but with the terror inside myself.

I loved my mother and I loved her face. My mother was one of those rare people who became more beautiful with age. Perhaps it had something to do with Buddhism, in which she had become steeped in her old age. Her trust in Buddha had helped her overcome the terrible rancor she harbored about her son's wretched death. As she aged, her face took on the gentle, complacent look of a Buddha. Although she lost her son, she still had his children and their wives and children to love. Loving them but never to the extent of obsession, she was aging happily. Watching my mother age more peacefully and beautifully than anybody I knew, so enchantingly beautifully, I thought she was a Boddhisatva.[8]

The human heart is fathomless, but never did I imagine such violent emotion was hidden in my mother's heart. I was shattered to find that it was not goodness, peace, and love but resentment, curses, and hatred that were hidden deep inside her. Even if all other humans were hopeless bundles of sins, my mother could not be so.

She finally began to lose the violent and ruthless battle between two evils. Only then did I cry aloud, rubbing my cheek on the swollen finger marks on her cheek.

I don't know why at that time Mother thought that hilly slope in Hyŏnjŏ-dong[9] would be a good hiding place. By then we had long risen above the poverty of that slummy neighborhood and had no reason to envy others, but we were in a predicament truly undeserved and unmanageable. We were helpless. I think it was this sense of helplessness that made my mother turn to the neighborhood that she had made her hitching post the first time she came to Seoul. It was also caused by the peculiar nature of our situation. Although it was only a tiny part in the great tragedy that gripped the nation during the Korean War, our predicament at that time was directly related to the hypocrisy and treacherous nature of that respectable middle-class neighborhood.

It had to do with my brother joining the North Korean Volunteer Army. He had participated in the leftist movement for a brief time soon after Korea was liberated from Japanese colonial rule. When we were unable to evacuate to the south and were trapped in Seoul under the Red army, he was extremely nervous lest his conversion from communism be revealed. He anxiously tried to learn what other converters in similar situations had done. The dubious information he managed to glean was that they had fled to the south at all costs and those who failed to do so had converted again. Unfortunately, that knowledge only increased his anxiety.

He cursed himself for gullibly trusting in the government that had proclaimed it would defend Seoul to the last, instead of heeding the ominous roaring of can-

8. In Buddhism, a Sanskrit term for someone motivated by compassion to help all sentient beings attain Buddhahood and transcend suffering.

9. Village near Seoul. During the Korean War, Seoul was overrun and captured by the Red Army of North Korea several times before the communists were finally driven back north of the 38th parallel in 1951.

nons, thus missing the chance to seek refuge elsewhere. He cursed the government leaders for irresponsibly misleading people and then fleeing themselves. Nevertheless, he was not clever enough even to think about converting to the left again. Even though he had courageously converted from the left when he realized his mistake, my brother was the type of person for whom the word *convert* caused moral indignation. If he had thought his choice of communism was a lesser mistake, he would have stuck to his original choice just to be consistent and faithful to himself rather than rectify the wrong by converting.

My brother was like the literati of old, who valued integrity as the highest ideal. His conflict was inevitable, as the literati spirit could not tolerate the true nature of communism, which justified means for its ends. The only reason I was unaffected by the leftist movement that attracted so many young people on the eve of the Korean War was my belief that there had to be something wrong with it to cause a man like my brother to convert from it.

As one who loathed even the thought of converting as a means to survive, he greatly resented the bureaucrats who sweet-talked people into staying in the city, only to sneak out themselves, abandoning those people to the Red army. Day by day his mind was increasingly wracked by resentment, suspicion, anxiety, and loneliness. He was already ill when, betrayed by a neighbor, he was hauled away. There was nothing we could do but watch helplessly. We expected to hear that he was executed on the spot at a people's court, tortured, or even worse, so we were shocked when word came that he had joined the army, the first to volunteer at a large people's rally, and had even encouraged a great many young people to join. We had no way to check if it was true or what kind of trick fate was dealing him.

But then fate was playing tricks on all of us. The neighbor who had harassed us and reported my brother to the authorities now wielded great power under the Red regime. He changed his attitude completely and became a self-appointed patron for us. Although the conscription of young people had not been so severe at the beginning of the Red army occupation, it was now being undertaken at such a pace that there was virtually no family who had not lost a son to the Volunteer Army. Thus my brother's joining the Volunteer Army was no reason for us to deserve special treatment, but we received special benefits in food rations and other things, all because of that neighbor's influence on the People's Committee of our district. We didn't have the presence of mind or the nerve to question whether we should take the benefits. Just trying to make it through a day made us stuporous, and food was unquestionably necessary.

We would stop with a start while greedily gobbling down boiled barley, not because we were eating when others did not even have thin porridge, but because we were eating at the cost of selling a member of our family.

"A sharp stomach makes short devotion, they say, but how can I eat this well and this easily when I got this in exchange for my son, my precious son's life," my mother would lament, dropping her spoon abruptly. But she had no forebodings.

Three months later, when the world changed back to what it had been, we were persecuted by our neighbors. We were reported as being Reds, and members of the young men's association came with clubs and guns and ransacked our house. They broke our furniture and pots and pans and with their clubs they poked my sister-in-law's stomach that was huge with a baby, while our neighbors looked on with the same enjoyment with which they would watch a shaman entertaining spirits. The target of their revenge for the ordeal they had gone through in the three months Seoul was in the hands of North Korea, we could do very little to defend ourselves against their wrath.

"Listen. Who was it that abandoned people in the pit of fire and took to his heels? I will gladly die if you want to kill me for the crime of surviving that fiery pit but just let me die after I look that person in the face and ask of his crime." Sometimes Mother would wail and rail like this, but all she got in return were scornful comments that she was a cold-blooded cheat and that Reds sure were glib talkers.

That was nothing compared with the charge that we were hiding the high-ranking Red who had used and protected us. My mother, my sister-in-law, and I were summoned and interrogated for days, each separately and at different times. The ill treatment my young nephew received at our relative's home during those days left an indelible scar on every member of the family. At that time, the whole world would shudder with revulsion at the mere mention of the word "red."

Then the war reversed again and the army began to retreat. The first thing Mother did was send my brother's wife and son to her parents because her baby was almost due. Needless to say, Mother wanted to remain in Seoul to the last minute in the hope that my brother might come back. It was a reasonable hope, because quite a number of young men ran away from the Volunteer Army and returned home. Mother trusted her son would return, even if it was with the Red army, were he unable to run away from it. She didn't care if he was a Red or not, her only worry being if he was dead or alive.

My brother did return. But his return was more like an omen than a miracle. Even my mother, who had been waiting for his return with so much trust and hope, dared not welcome him on the spot. His hideous appearance was understandable after a long period of starvation and ragged existence, but he was reduced to a complete wreck from deep inside. His eyes were glazed uneasily, never focusing on anything, and his body was emaciated due to acute insomnia. He became paranoiac and would suffer anxiety attacks countless times a day. He showed no affection for his family, nor did he miss or want to know the whereabouts of his wife and child. There was no way to know what harrowing experiences had wrecked him so completely. Like a timid child left alone at home, he locked himself inside his shell and denied the outside world.

To make matters worse, the war was turning from bad to worse and everyone was leaving Seoul, fleeing southward. This time the government didn't make the mistake it had made in the summer; it warned the people of Seoul of the impending crisis well in advance and helped them to evacuate. En masse the city's residents joined the ranks of refugees, preferring to risk freezing to death than go through another Red occupation.

His mind wracked as it was, my brother was more than eager to leave when it came to the matter of evacuation. He was desperate to leave. The only lucid thought left in his disheveled mind was that he should flee from the Reds. In his wretched condition, it would not have been possible in the first place without that obsession of his to break through the fierce battle ground.

My brother did not have an identification card so he could not prove he was a resident of Seoul. Because of the possibility of spies or enemy soldiers hiding among the refugees, ID checks were getting stricter by the day. A young man would not dare step outside his home without proper identification, to say nothing of leaving the city. A person needed guarantees from two people in one's neighborhood to apply for an identification card, otherwise the person would have to go through a police screening. My mother begged and begged our neighbors to help, but no one would vouch for my brother. They would ask why someone should be afraid of being screened if he were not a Red, which was actually a quite reasonable question. When, before the return of my brother, the three grown-ups in our family applied for cards, we had to report to the police numerous times for investigation because none of the neighbors would vouch for us. We were the last in our neighborhood to get cards.

My brother's case was far more complicated, however, for he became petrified and trembled abjectly at the mere mention of the police. He begged us not to take him to the police even if it meant he would not be able to seek refuge or to go out of the house for the rest of his life. But then he would rave, "Let's go. We can't sit here and get stuck again. Let's seek refuge." He was so nervous he drove us nuts. When we proposed that we just set out, card or no card, our situation being risky whichever course we chose, he glared at its with those glazed eyes of his and accused us of wanting to get him shot.

We were driven up the wall. My brother wanted us to get him a card by whatever means necessary as long as we did not involve him.

"Mother, sell everything. Sell the house and the furniture and buy me that damned card. What do you want to keep these things for?" He nagged Mother like a child until she burst into heart-wrenching tears. He clamored after me with unspeakable demands. "How come you don't get out there and hook up with someone powerful to save your poor brother, huh? What's the good of having a sister?"

These fits of shameful petulance were in truth the last convulsions of his wrecked spirit. The day the government announced its last evacuation order, warning that it was abandoning Seoul and that those still remaining should evacuate in an orderly fashion, the three of us left our house carrying bundles on our heads and backs. We had to show the few neighbors who had wavered to the last minute with false hopes that we too were fleeing lest they accuse us later of being Reds. Besides, we were deathly afraid of being in that house when the Reds returned. Running away from the Reds' Volunteer Army was obviously a far more serious crime than converting and deserved the supreme punishment. In those days, all of our thoughts and deeds were controlled entirely by the question of whether someone was a Red.

We mingled in the throng of refugees surging toward the south like a tidal wave, but we did little more than circle the downtown area several times to keep away from the checkpoints. Having no mind or will of his own, my brother was good for nothing except sensing the whereabouts of the check-points and dodging them, which he did with an animal-like instinct. I was so sick of the burden he had become that I was looking for a chance to run away by myself, when Mother suddenly said, "Children, let's go to Hyŏnjŏ-dong."

The moment I heard those words, I became as humble and meek as a prodigal who decided to return home after prolonged straying. Something like joy flickered through my brother's glazed eyes.

"Those shabby, ragged folds of Hyŏnjŏ-dong will be the best place to hide," Mother said calmly, obviously relieved at the thought. Her description of the village as shabby, ragged folds was more nostalgic than derogatory.

"That village must be deserted too. We can hide in any of the empty houses there and go back home when the National Army returns. I've never been so scared of people. Either I'm evil or the world is. But I wouldn't mind coming across one or two people there, they're all so good-natured."

The remembrance of the classic poverty and good-natured neighborliness of the shabby village where we had weathered our first hard years in Seoul glimmered like a key to salvation for us after we had been sneered at and hurt by our pompous neighbors. We hoped that even my brother's wrecked spirit could be healed there. We climbed up the mountain slope to Hyŏnjŏ-dong, brimming with quiet happiness as if we were returning home, as if we were returning to the arms of the Buddha. Every little alley, familiar and friendly, seemed to welcome us. Being the evening of the last night of the evacuation, the village was completely deserted with no trace of any living thing. At our foot the city lay unlit and deserted in the dusk like an empty expanse of marsh.

Mother sighed softly and murmured, "The Reds are a hopeless lot. How can they say they will rule the Red way when they can't win even the support of the poverty-stricken people here?"

We went around to the houses of several people with whom Mother had kept in touch but of course they were all empty. We chose a house with a well and let ourselves in. Being a humbly built shack, it was easy to unlock. We could have chosen a better house, the whole neighborhood being empty and ready for us to break in, but Mother wanted to take one owned by people she knew so that later she could apologize and thank them.

For the next several days, we never came across anybody and had no way of knowing if the world had changed or not. We had brought staples that would last about a month and there were various grains, pots of kimchi,[1] firewood, and water in the house. We were content. I wondered if it was a life like this that my brother had dreamed of as he ran away all that long distance. I became hopeful that not having the pressure of having to pretend in speech and behavior to impress others might help my brother. Already I could see tiny signs of healing. He indicated, though vaguely, worries about his wife and son, who had gone down south. He wondered if she had given birth at her parents' house. It was the first time he had shown any concern for them since his return, so we became excited at the possibility that he was beginning to open up to the people closest to him.

Overjoyed at finding a perfect shelter, we were blissfully unaware of its vulnerability. We were found one day by a party of soldiers of the People's Army who were wearing white bed sheets for overcoats. Stationed at the Sŏdaemun Penitentiary in the foothills, they had noticed smoke rising morning and evening from a few houses on the upper slopes. They had checked every house from which they had seen smoke rising, only to find invalids and old people who were half dead. But now their luck had changed, they said, greedily eyeing me as I opened the gate for them.

"Sure. Sure. There are just the two of us women here. You don't even need to check." Mother rushed out after me and rambled about things that would have been better left unsaid. They pushed her aside and went inside the house.

"You, too, are a woman, Comrade?" the officer at the head of the troop asked my brother with an icy sneer.

My brother became speechless at the sight of the soldiers and could utter only tortured moans and no coherent words.

1. Pickled cabbage, a Korean staple.

"That's not a woman, but an idiot. He's worse than a woman 'cause he's a useless idiot. He's my curse, my deathly curse." Terror, humility, and flattery crossed each other on Mother's face. It was needless for her to emphasize this; my brother was not a whole person in anybody's eyes. He looked even more wretched because of the contrast with the rough, coarse soldiers. He was pale and emaciated, with vacant pits for eyes, and could utter only monosyllabic sounds no one could understand. If only Mother had not emphasized he was an idiot.

After that day, the soldiers took turns coming to our house. One of them was an intelligence officer who seemed to have a hunch about my brother. He would be talking to us good-naturedly about his home and family when out of the blue he would glare at my brother and in a piercing voice say things like "Did you run away from the People's Army, Comrade?" or "Didn't you straggle out of the National Army?" My liver would shrivel up to the size of a pea every time. My brother's pitiful trembling did not get worse or better no matter how often they showed up and the aphasic symptom he acquired the moment he first saw the soldiers did not go away. His idiot act was so flawless that we no longer thought it was an act. Sad and bitter as it was, we had to admit there seemed no chance of his returning to normal.

Nonetheless, the intelligence officer was exceptionally tenacious. He threatened, cajoled, and sometimes begged to learn the truth.

"I can't help being sorry for you, Mother. What happened to cause your only son to become such a mess? He wasn't born like that, was he? If he wasn't born an idiot, he can be cured. The medical advancements in North Korea are world famous. And the poor are given priority. I can send him to any number of good doctors. Just tell me the truth. Tell me when he became like that."

The man called Mom "Mother" and often talked to her like a pampered child, which made her more frightened than when he was icy and ruthless so that she would cringe and ramble helplessly. Her rambling made me nervous. When the man left, she would wink at me and say she was playacting. It was amazing.

There's nothing a person won't do to survive. Every day was a blood-curdling, life-splitting acrobatic act like dancing with a viper.

The sound of cannons loomed near again and the soldiers' eyes became bloodshot. Mother prayed day in and day out that they would leave without causing any harm. "Please, let them not harm my boy. Please let them not harm my poor boy."

At last the intelligence officer came to say goodbye to us. But his way of saying goodbye was special.

"Comrades, did you think I could be deceived by such sly lots as you? It's not too late to tell the truth. Let's see if you really can't talk," he said, drawing his pistol and taking aim at my brother.

"No, you can't do this to us. No, you bastard!" Mother screamed and threw herself onto his arm. My brother only groaned like a stricken animal. The officer shook Mother off.

"Talk. Or I'll make you talk."

The gun went off. The bullet hit my brother's leg. Still, he merely groaned like an animal.

"All right. You asked for it."

The gun went off again. The same speech and the same sound were repeated over and over again. The officer aimed at the lower part of my brother so he wouldn't die on the spot.

My brother collapsed in a pool of blood and my mother, who had fallen down when the soldier shook her off his arm, let out a blood-curdling scream and fainted.

"I'm not going to kill you right away. I'm going to give you a chance to tell the truth before you die."

But the officer never returned, for in a few days the world changed again.

None of my brother's wounds was fatal, but he died in a few days from loss of blood and lack of proper medical treatment. He remained aphasic till the end. We could never forget all that blood and the unrequited grief of those few days that reached to Heaven. We could not forget those things, but we could hide them. I by meeting a man, falling in love with him, having children, and loving them, and my mother through raising and caring for her grandchildren and trusting in Buddha.

Mother was so exhausted from her exertions that she lay utterly spent for a long time. She was like a sheet of paper, thin, weightless, and breathless, ready to blow away at a whisper of wind. Relatives and friends who visited looked grim and shook their heads at the chance of her recovering. Some of them, thinking she was in a coma, would talk openly about funeral procedures, and some, as if they were already at her funeral, would say not to grieve because she had lived out her allotted life. We did not try to tell them otherwise nor did we resent their insensitivity. Mother showed only slight signs of consciousness, grimacing when the nurses gave her injections or when we fed her one or two spoons of liquid.

A friend came to visit me at the hospital. She took one look at Mother and said straight out, "Have you prepared her shroud?"

"No, why should I prepare such an awful thing in advance?"

"My, my! Then, how about her grave?"

"Grave? Do we have to get it in advance?"

"You haven't done that either, huh? You're really hopeless."

"What do you mean?"

"You're hopeless as a daughter, you dummy. What a pitiful thing to have no son, only a dummy for a daughter."

I didn't mind her calling me hopeless or a dummy, but it made my mother look rather bad and I thought I should do some explaining.

"We have our ancestral burial ground."

"Where is it?"

"You know. Kaep'ung County, near Kaesōng."

"What's the use of having a burial ground in North Korea?"

"Still."

"Still? That's the most miserable excuse I've ever heard. Next, you'll be trying to get a loan on your land and home in North Korea," chided my sarcastic friend.

"I mean it's a kind of unspoken promise between us. Mother would want to be buried in her ancestral land even if she could never return there in her life. How could I get a burial plot elsewhere when I know only too well that she really pines to return even though she doesn't say it in so many words? Of course, it won't matter after she's dead. It won't be too late to buy some land for her grave when that happens. After all, a grave is just a house one needs only after death."

Mother opened her eyes. They were so clear and bright in her paper-pale face that my friend shrieked and grabbed hold of me.

"Come here," Mother called to me in a clear voice.

"Yes, Mother." I approached her nervously. She grabbed my hand. The warmth and strength of her hand surprised and saddened me.

"Don't bury me in a grave when I die," she said, her voice as calm and irrefutable as usual.

"Ah, you heard us."

"Yes, and I'm glad I did. I've been meaning to tell you. You think of this as my will and you do as I tell you. When I die, do for me as I did for your brother. Don't mind what others say, just do as I tell you. I'm asking you because only you can override what others say."

"Like you did for Brother?"

"Yes, exactly like that. You haven't forgotten, have you?"

"Forgotten? How could I ever forget?"

My mother's hand was as strong and commanding as when she was healthy, as when she pulled me over Nongbawi Hill when I was a little girl and we were moving from her hometown to Seoul the first time.

We buried my brother in a temporary grave at a corner of someone's field on the other side of Muak Hill. The burial was a shabby affair without formality, no better than a burial for a vagrant, but anything better was beyond the ability of us two women stranded in the deserted city.

As soon as Seoul was recovered and the crematorium resumed operations, Mother broached the idea of cremation. My sister-in-law, who had rejoined us by then, maintained that we should move his remains to the public cemetery because the least we could do for her fatherless children was to give them their father's grave. Mother had been meek with her daughter-in-law as if her young widowhood was her fault, but she would not give an inch in that matter. Although my sister-in-law was understandably hurt and disgusted by Mother's hardheartedness in emptying her husband's grave when she was still grieving for him, she eventually obeyed, overwhelmed by Mother's undefiable dignity and grief-stricken determination to carry on.

My brother's flesh became smoke and his bones a fistful of dust. Without a word, we followed Mother to the terminal for buses to Kanghwa Island.[2] On the island, asking directions again and again, Mother found the seashore that overlooked Kaep'ung County in the north across the sea. There, toward the land that lay so near yet was so forbidding, she threw the dust to the wind. Granted, Kaep'ung County was the site of our family's ancestral burial ground, but I didn't think she was doing all this to appease my brother's spirit for not being buried there. There was no trace of a frail, pliant woman who meekly obeyed her destiny with sorrowful acceptance. She looked spirited and daring like a warrior heading into battle. With her fistful of dust cast on the wind, Mother was challenging something far too tremendous for her. The dust and wind were her only weapons to defy the monster called national division that trampled her life and destroyed everything she held precious.

Mother wanted me to repeat what she had done. This time she was going to become the dust on the wind and I had to do what she had done. Thirty years have passed. Is there no other way we can nullify that monster?

2. Island off the west coast of South Korea near Kaep'ung County of North Korea.

"I'm sorry. Please do as I ask. I beg you with all my heart."

Mother looked pathetic. She appeared truly apologetic that she had no other legacy to give me.

Ah, it seems I have to go through it again.

Mother is still fighting.

1981

HANAN AL-SHAYKH

born 1945

Lebanese writer Hanan Al-Shaykh explores the conflicts between tradition and modernity as they affect women in the Arab world. Her feminist critique of Arab culture shares much with that of **Nawal El-Saadawi**, but Al-Shaykh's fiction is more intimate, focused less on government oppression and more on the daily choices women must make to assert their freedom in a social system that often constrains them. By examining life through the innocent perspectives of girls and young women, the author provides social commentary while concentrating on the human dimensions of the issues raised.

Born in southern Lebanon, Hanan Al-Shaykh was raised in Beirut by her strict Shiite family. Later, Al-Shaykh would recall that her family's traditional religious practices seemed out of place in the cosmopolitan capital: "we lived in a street full of Beirutis. We were from the south, we always felt like outsiders. The whole street thought my father was mad: he wore a shawl on his head and would wash the stairs of the whole building." Her father, a conservative merchant, and her mother, an illiterate homemaker, divorced when she was young, and Al-Shaykh began to write short stories in part as an act of rebellion against the restrictive influences of her father and brothers.

Al-Shaykh attended a traditional Muslim girls' primary school and, later, the more cosmopolitan Ahliyyah School and the American College for Girls in Cairo. After graduating, she worked as a journalist for the magazine *al-Hasna (Beautiful Woman)* and for the journal *al-Nahar (The Day)*, which published her earliest short stories. Her first novel, *Suicide of a Dead Man* (1970), relates a teenage girl's affair with a middle-aged man but, surprisingly, from the man's point of view. It brought comparisons to the work of **Naguib Mahfouz**, particularly for its faithful representation of the spoken language. As Al-Shaykh later explained, "My generation of Arab writers adopted a language between the classical and the spoken dialect. The dialogue is, at times, even colloquial and thus much closer to the way people really speak."

During the Lebanese Civil War (1975–90), Al-Shaykh left the country to live in London and in Saudi Arabia, where she wrote *The Story of Zahra* (1980). She released the novel at her own expense, as no publisher in Lebanon would accept the manuscript, but it became her first international success. The protagonist of the story, Zahra, is a young woman mired in the oppressive and misogynistic milieu of war-torn Lebanon. Trapped in a loveless marriage, she falls in love with a sniper, who at some point turns on her as one of his political targets. Al-Shaykh's later novels likewise focus on the life experiences of Arab women, especially during the civil war. *Only in London* (2000) was her first novel set in Europe, although the main figures in it are Middle Eastern immigrants. She has written two experimental plays, performed by the Hampstead Theatre in London. Her frank treatment of such topics as abortion, adultery, homosexuality, prostitution, rape, and transvestism has made her work controversial in the Arab world. She has lived in London since 1983.

The story presented here, "The Women's Swimming Pool" (1982), although it addresses none of these controversial subjects, nonetheless concerns the breaking of taboos. The narrator, accustomed to having to cover her head and wear long-sleeve clothes in the fierce heat of southern Lebanese tobacco fields, wants to visit the sea and to bathe in a swimming pool that her friend has seen in Beirut. With great sensitivity Al-Shaykh portrays the innocent perspective of the narrator, an orphan who simply wants to go swimming but who, because of social customs barring women from displaying their bodies, has never had access to a swimming pool. Her grandmother, hoping to fulfill the little girl's wishes, takes her on a long bus ride from their home village, but she is as bewildered as her granddaughter by the metropolis of Beirut. The girl and the old woman have a close, loving relationship, but, as the story progresses, the narrator sees her grandmother, and indeed the customs of her village, in a new light. Although the narrator says little about her adult life, this recollection of childhood seems to mark a turning point, setting the girl on the path to become the woman who writes stories of liberation and separating her from the grandmother she loves but does not want to emulate.

The Women's Swimming Pool[1]

I am in the tent for threading the tobacco, amidst the mounds of tobacco plants and the skewers. Cross-legged, I breathe in the green odor, threading one leaf after another. I find myself dreaming and growing thirsty and dreaming. I open the magazine: I devour the words and surreptitiously gaze at the pictures. I am exasperated at being in the tent, then my exasperation turns to sadness.

Thirsty, I rise to my feet. I hear Abu Ghalib say, "Where are you off to, little lady?" I make my way to my grandmother, saying, "I'm thirsty." I go out. I make my way to the cistern, stumbling in the sandy ground. I see the greenish-blue water. I stretch out my hand to its still surface, hot from the harsh sun. I stretch out my hand and wipe it across my brow and face and neck, across my chest. Before being able to savor its relative coldness, I hear my name and see my grandmother standing in her black dress at the doorway of the tent. Aloud I express the wish that someone else had called to me. We have become like an

1. Translated from the Arabic by Denys Johnson-Davies.

orange and its navel: my grandmother has welded me so close to her that the village girls no longer dare to make friends with me, perhaps for fear of rupturing this close union.

I returned to the tent, growing thirsty and dreaming, with the sea ever in my mind. What were its waters like? What color would they be now? If only this week would pass in a flash, for I had at last persuaded my grandmother to go down to Beirut and the sea, after my friend Sumayya had sworn that the swimming pool she'd been at had been for women only.

My grandmother sat on the edge of a jagged slab of stone, leaning on my arm. Her hand was hot and rough. She sighed as she chased away a fly.

What is my grandmother gazing at? There was nothing in front of us but the asphalt road, which, despite the sun's rays, gave off no light, and the white marble tombs that stretched along the high mountainside, while the houses of upper Nabatieh[2] looked like deserted Crusader castles, their alleyways empty, their windows of iron. Our house likewise seemed to be groaning in its solitude, shaded by the fig tree. The washing line stirs with the wind above the tomb of my grandfather, the celebrated religious scholar, in the courtyard of the house. What is my grandmother staring at? Or does someone who is waiting not stare?

Turning her face toward me, she said, "Child, what will we do if the bus doesn't come?" Her face, engraved in my mind, seemed overcast, also her half-closed eyes and the blue tattoo mark on her chin.[3] I didn't answer her for fear I'd cry if I talked. This time I averted my gaze from the white tombs; moving my foot away from my grandmother's leg clothed in thick black stockings, I began to walk about, my gaze directed to the other side where lay the extensive fields of green tobacco, towering and gently swaying, their leaves glinting under the sun, leaves that were imprinted on my brain, their marks still showing on my hands.

My gaze reached out behind the thousands of plants, then beyond them, moving away till it arrived at the tent where the tobacco was threaded. I came up close to my grandmother, who was still sitting in her place, still gazing in front of her. As I drew close to her, I heard her give a sigh. A sprinkling of sweat lay on the pouches under her eyes. "Child, what do you want with the sea? Don't you know that the sea puts a spell on people?" I didn't answer her: I was worried that the morning would pass, that noonday would pass, and that I wouldn't see the green bus come to a stop by the stone my grandmother sat on, to take us to the sea, to Beirut. Again I heard my grandmother mumbling. "That devil Sumayya . . ." I pleaded with her to stop, and my thoughts rose up and left the stone upon which my grandmother sat, the rough road, left everything. I went back to my dreams, to the sea.

The sea had always been my obsession, ever since I had seen it for the first time inside a colored ball; with its blue color it was like a magic lantern, wide open, the surface of its water unrippled unless you tilted the piece of glass, with its small shells and white specks like snow. When I first became aware of things, this ball, which I had found in the parlor, was the sole thing that animated and amused me. The more I gazed at it, the cooler I felt its waters to be,

2. A town in southern Lebanon.

3. Shia Islam allows tattooing, a cultural practice that preceded the introduction of Islam and that is prohibited by Sunni Islam. Blue tattoos on the face and hands are a marker for a generation of aging women.

and the more they invited me to bathe in them; they knew that I had been born amidst dust and mud and the stench of tobacco.

If only the green bus would come along—and I shifted my bag from one hand to the other. I heard my grandmother wail, "Child, bring up a stone and sit down. Put down the bag and don't worry." My distress increased, and I was no longer able to stop it turning into tears that flowed freely down my face, veiling it from the road. I stretched up to wipe them with my sleeve; in this heat I still had to wear that dress with long sleeves, that head covering over my braids,[4] despite the hot wind that set the tobacco plants and the sparse poplars swaying. Thank God I had resisted her and refused to wear my stockings. I gave a deep sigh as I heard the bus's horn from afar. Fearful and anxious, I shouted at my grandmother as I helped her to her feet, turning round to make sure that my bag was still in my hand and my grandmother's hand in the other. The bus came to a stop and the conductor helped my grandmother on. When I saw myself alongside her and the stone on its own, I tightened my grip on my bag in which lay Sumayya's bathing costume, a sleeveless dress, and my money.

I noticed as the bus slowly made its way along the road that my anxiety was still there, that it was in fact increasing: Why didn't the bus pass by all these trees and fallow land like lightning? Why was it crawling along? My anxiety was still there and increased till it predominated over my other sensations, my nausea and curiosity.

How would we find our way to the sea? Would we see it as soon as we arrived in Beirut? Was it at the other end of it? Would the bus stop in the district of Zeytouna,[5] at the door of the women's swimming pool? Why, I wondered, was it called Zeytouna?—were there olive trees there? I leaned toward my grandmother and her silent face and long nose that almost met up with her mouth. Thinking that I wanted a piece of cane sugar, she put her hand to her bosom to take out a small twist of cloth. Impatiently I asked her if she was sure that Maryam at-Taweela knew Zeytouna, to which she answered, her mouth sucking at the cane sugar and making a noise with her tongue, "God will look after everything." Then she broke the silence by saying. "All this trouble is that devil Sumayya's fault—it was she who told you she'd seen with her own eyes the swimming pool just for women and not for men." "Yes, Grandma," I answered her. She said, "Swear by your mother's grave." I thought to myself absently: "Why only my mother's grave? What about my father? Or did she only acknowledge her daughter's death . . .?" "By my mother's grave, it's for women." She inclined her head and still munching the cane sugar and making a noise with her tongue, she said, "If any man were to see you, you'd be done for, and so would your mother and father and your grandfather, the religious scholar—and I'd be done for more than anyone because it's I who agreed to this and helped you."

I would have liked to say to her, "They've all gone, they've all died, so what do we have to be afraid of?" But I knew what she meant: that she was frightened they wouldn't go to heaven.

4. Islamic custom requires girls and women to keep their hair, arms, and legs covered.

5. A cosmopolitan district of Lebanon; the name means "olive."

I began to sweat, and my heart again contracted as Beirut came into view with its lofty buildings, car horns, the bared arms of the women, the girls' hair, the tight trousers they were wearing. People were sitting on chairs in the middle of the pavement, eating and drinking; the trams; the roasting chickens revolving on spits. Ah, these dresses for sale in the windows, would anyone be found actually to wear them? I see a Japanese man, the first-ever member of the yellow races outside of books; the Martyrs' monument; Riad Solh Square.[6] I was wringing wet with sweat and my heart pounded—it was as though I regretted having come to Beirut, perhaps because I was accompanied by my grandmother. It was soon all too evident that we were outsiders to the capital. We began walking after my grandmother had asked the bus driver the whereabouts of the district of Khandaq al-Ghamiq[7] where Maryam at-Taweela lived. Once again my body absorbed all the sweat and allowed my heart to flee its cage. I find myself treading on a pavement on which for long years I have dreamed of walking; I hear sounds that have been engraved on my imagination; and everything I see I have seen in daydreams at school or in the tobacco-threading tent. Perhaps I shouldn't say that I was regretting it, for after this I would never forget Beirut. We begin walking and losing our way in a Beirut that never ends, that leads nowhere. We begin asking and walking and losing our way, and my going to the sea seems an impossibility; the sea is fleeing from me. My grandmother comes to a stop and leans against a lamppost, or against the litter bin attached to it, and against my shoulders, and puffs and blows. I have the feeling that we shall never find Maryam at-Taweela's house. A man we had stopped to ask the way walks with us. When we knock at the door and no one opens to us, I become convinced that my bathing in the sea is no longer possible. The sweat pours off me, my throat contracts. A woman's voice brings me back to my senses as I drown in a lake of anxiety, sadness, and fear; then it drowns me once again. It was not Maryam at-Taweela but her neighbor who is asking us to wait at her place. We go down the steps to the neighbor's outdoor stone bench, and my grandmother sits down by the door but gets to her feet again when the woman entreats her to sit in the cane chair. Then she asks to be excused while she finishes washing down the steps. While she is cursing the heat of Beirut in the summer, I notice the tin containers lined up side by side containing red and green peppers. We have a long wait, and I begin to weep inwardly as I stare at the containers.

I wouldn't be seeing the sea today, perhaps not for years, but the thought of its waters would not leave me, would not be erased from my dreams. I must persuade my grandmother to come to Beirut with Sumayya. Perhaps I should not have mentioned the swimming pool in front of her. I wouldn't be seeing the sea today—and once again I sank back into a lake of doubt and fear and sadness. A woman's voice again brought me back to my senses: it was Maryam at-Taweela, who had stretched out her long neck and had kissed me, while she asked my grandmother: 'She's the child of your late daughter, isn't she?'—and she swore by the Imam[8] that we must have lunch with her,

6. One of the main squares in Beirut's commercial district; the Martyrs' monument commemorates Lebanese nationalists who opposed Ottoman rule in the early 20th century.

7. A well-to-do neighborhood in West Beirut.

8. The Imam Ali (ca. 600–661), cousin and son-in-law of the prophet Muhammad and founder of the Shia branch of Islam.

doing so before we had protested, feeling perhaps that I would do so. When she stood up and took the primus stove from under her bed and brought out potatoes and tomatoes and bits of meat, I had feelings of nausea, then of frustration. I nudged my grandmother, who leant over and whispered "What is it, dear?" at which Maryam at-Taweela turned and asked "What does your granddaughter want—to go to the bathroom?" My mouth went quite dry and my tears were all stored up waiting for a signal from my heartbeats to fall. My grandmother said with embarrassment, "She wants to go to the sea, to the women's swimming pool—that devil Sumayya put it into her head." To my amazement Maryam at-Taweela said loudly, "And why not? Right now Ali Mousa, our neighbor, will be coming and he'll take you, he's got a car"—and Maryam at-Taweela began peeling the potatoes at a low table in the middle of the room and my grandmother asked, "Where's Ali Mousa from? Where does he live?"

I can't wait, I shan't eat, I shan't drink. I want to go now, now. I remained seated, crying inwardly because I was born in the South, because there's no escape for me from the South, and I go on rubbing my fingers and gnawing at my nails. Again I begin to sweat: I shan't eat, I shan't drink, I shan't reply to Maryam at-Taweela. It was as though I was taking vengeance on my grandmother for some wrong she did not know about. My patience vanished. I stood up and said to my grandmother before I should burst out sobbing, "Come along, Grandma, get up, and let's go." I helped her to her feet, and Maryam at-Taweela asked in bewilderment what had suddenly come over me. I went on dragging my grandmother out to the street so that I might stop the first taxi.

Only moments passed before the driver shut off his engine and said, "Zeytouna." I looked about me but saw no sea. As I gave him a lira I asked him, "Where's the women's swimming pool?" He shrugged his shoulders. We got out of the car with difficulty, as was always the case with my grandmother. To my astonishment the driver returned, stretching out his head in concern at us. "Jump in," he said, and we got in. He took us round and round, stopping once at a petrol station and then by a newspaper seller, asking about the women's swimming pool and nobody knowing where it was. Once again he dropped us in the middle of Zeytouna Street.

Then, behind the hotels and the beautiful buildings and the date palms, I saw the sea. It was like a blue line of quicksilver: it was as though pieces of silver paper were resting on it. The sea that was in front of me was more beautiful than it had been in the glass ball. I didn't know how to get close to it, how to touch it. Cement lay between us. We began inquiring about the whereabouts of the swimming pool, but no one knew. The sea remains without waves, a blue line. I feel frustrated. Perhaps this swimming pool is some secret known only to the girls of the South. I began asking every person I saw. I tried to choke back my tears; I let go of my grandmother's hand as though wishing to reproach her, to punish her for having insisted on accompanying me instead of Sumayya. Poor me. Poor Grandma. Poor Beirut. Had my dreams come to an end in the middle of the street? I clasp my bag and my grandmother's hand, with the sea in front of me, separating her from me. My stubbornness and vexation impel me to ask and go on asking. I approached a man leaning against a bus, and to my surprise he pointed to an opening between two shops. I hurried back to my grandmother, who was supporting herself against a lamppost, to tell her I'd found it. When I saw with what difficulty she attempted to walk, I asked her to wait for me while I made sure. I went through the opening but didn't see the sea. All I saw was a fat woman with bare shoulders sitting behind a table. Hesitating, I stood and looked at her, not daring to step forward. My enthusiasm had vanished, taking with it my courage. "Yes," said the woman. I came forward and asked her, "Is the women's swimming pool here?" She nodded her head and said, "The entrance fee is a lira." I asked her if it was possible for my grandmother to wait for me here and she stared at me and said, "Of course." There was contempt in the way she looked at me: Was it my southern accent or my long-sleeved dress? I had disregarded my grandmother and had taken off my head shawl and hidden it in my bag. I handed her a lira and could hear the sounds of women and children—and still I did not see the sea. At the end of the portico were steps; which I was certain led to the roofed-in sea. The important thing was that I'd arrived, that I would be tasting the salty spray of its waters. I wouldn't be seeing the waves; never mind, I'd be bathing in its waters.

I found myself saying to the woman, or rather to myself because no sound issued from my throat, "I'll bring my grandmother." Going out through the opening and still clasping my bag to my chest, I saw my grandmother standing and looking up at the sky. I called to her, but she was reciting to herself under her breath as she continued to look upward: she was praying, right there in the street, praying on the pavement at the door of the swimming pool. She had spread out a paper bag and had stretched out her hands to the sky. I walked off in another direction and stopped looking at her. I would have liked to persuade myself that she had nothing to do with me, that I didn't know her. How, though? She's my grandmother whom I've dragged with my entreaties from the tobacco-threading tent, from the jagged slab of stone, from the winds of the South; I have crammed her into the bus and been lost with her in the streets as we searched for Maryam at-Taweela's house. And now here were the two of us standing at the door of the swimming pool, and she, having heard the call to prayers,[9] had prostrated herself in prayer. She was destroying what lay in my bag, blocking the road between me and the sea. I felt sorry for her, for her knees that knelt on the cruelly hard pavement, for her tattooed hands that lay on the dirt. I looked at her again and saw the passers-by staring at her. For the first time her black dress looked shabby to me. I felt how far removed we were from these passers-by, from this street, this city, this sea. I approached her, and she again put her weight on my hand.

1982

9. The Islamic call to prayer, heard five times a day in Muslim countries but ignored by secular residents of some large cities like Beirut.

TONI MORRISON
born 1931

Nobel laureate Toni Morrison combines realistic depictions of African American experience with a strong sense of the past's hold on the present. She often conveys this sensitivity to the power of history by invoking magic or supernatural occurrences. The combination of techniques resembles at times the magic realism of the Latin American Boom; at other times, Morrison's concern with the border between fiction and history seems postmodernist. Her writing also addresses the role of racial and gender discrimination in contemporary society. In all her work, while drawing on the experimental fictional techniques of the early twentieth century, she maintains a close connection to African American oral and literary traditions and to everyday life in the United States.

Born Chloe Ardelia Wofford in Lorain, Ohio, Morrison took the saint's name Anthony (later shortened to Toni) as her middle name when she converted to Catholicism, at the age of twelve. Her family had participated in the Great Migration of African Americans from the South in the early decades of the century. Her father was born in Georgia and worked at miscellaneous jobs in construction and shipbuilding, while her maternal grandparents had been sharecroppers in Alabama who came to Ohio to seek a better life for their daughters. Morrison studied English at Howard University, where she was active in student theater. Her master's thesis, at Cornell University, examined the role of suicide in the fiction of **Virginia Woolf** and **William Faulkner**; her later fictional practice made use both of the subject of violent death and of the stream-of-consciousness techniques of Woolf and Faulkner. After returning to Howard to teach, the author met and married the Jamaican architect Harold Morrison, also a faculty member; the couple would later divorce. She also began work on her first novel, *The Bluest Eye* (1970). Leaving behind her academic career, she was employed, for twenty years, as an editor at Random House, where she encouraged other African American women writers. She continued to produce novels and journalism; the works received critical praise, literary awards, and a growing audience. For her fifth novel, *Beloved* (1987), arguably her masterpiece, Morrison received the Pulitzer Prize. She has continued to write novels, essays, musical lyrics, and the libretto for an opera, and taught at Princeton University from 1989 until her retirement in 2006. In 1993, she was awarded the Nobel Prize for Literature.

Morrison's early novels focus on contemporary African American life and the impact of racism on the prospects and self-image of the young. In *The Bluest Eye,* Pecola Breedlove, a young African American girl in Morrison's hometown of Lorain, longs for blue eyes and what she imagines is the exclusively white preserve of beauty. Her family and others in the community share this false idea of attractiveness as associated with light skin, and their self-hatred leads to destructive consequences, including child molestation, incest, and insanity. With *Song of Solomon* (1977), Morrison chose a broader historical canvas, encompassing the roots of African American folk customs in the South. Here, Morrison explores the supernatural, drawing from oral tradition such as the ghost stories her family told her as a child, to create characters who can fly or talk to the dead. The novel, which also incorporates biblical archetypes, marks an experimental turn in Morrison's writing, as she makes use of multiple perspectives. *Beloved* treats a still earlier period of African American history, the time of slavery, and does so with extensive evocation of the supernatural. Based on the true story of a runaway slave who killed her child in order to prevent the child's reenslavement, it is Morrison's most moving novel as well as one of her most experimental. Throughout her works, characters find themselves caught in patterns of violence and prejudice that threaten to destroy them, but a few manage to transcend this history and achieve a measure of freedom and self-worth.

"Recitatif" (1983), Morrison's only published short story, examines a friendship between two girls of different races. The title refers to passages of narrative or dialogue in an opera that are sung in the rhythm of ordinary speech, as opposed to the formal arias or songs. The story focuses on the dialogue between the two main characters at several junctures of life that may independently seem insignificant but that, when combined in a narrative, reveal the nature of their relationship. The narrator, Twyla, meets Roberta at "St. Bonny's," the fictional St. Bonaventure Orphanage just outside New York City. They are the only two girls there whose mothers are still alive, but neither mother is up to the task of caring for her daughter. In the course of the short story, Morrison effectively presents Twyla's childlike perspective on events at St. Bonny's and the maturation of her point of view as she grows up, has children, and looks back on half-forgotten events.

Although Twyla and Roberta have much in common, they are divided by race. Morrison later explained that she intended the story as "an experiment in the removal of all racial codes from a narrative about two characters of different races for whom racial identity is crucial." Twyla never specifies her own race or that of Roberta. Maggie, who works in the kitchen, is also of ambiguous race. "Until very recently," Morrison has written, "and regardless of the race of the author, the readers of virtually all of American fiction have been positioned as white." In other words, writers have tended to assume a white audience; conversely, readers, unless specifically told otherwise, have assumed that the characters in fiction are white. "Recitatif" represents Morrison's effort to challenge such assumptions. Although racial conflict in society affects the girls' relationship later in life, "Recitatif" envisions the possibility of transcending racial divisions and embracing a common humanity.

This experiment in narrative ambiguity reflects Morrison's interest in the transformation of traditional narrative techniques. Inspired in part by the modernists, but equally by jazz music and African American oral tradition, Morrison has expanded the possibilities of contemporary American fiction.

Recitatif[1]

My mother danced all night and Roberta's was sick. That's why we were taken to St. Bonny's.[2] People want to put their arms around you when you tell them you were in a shelter, but it really wasn't bad. No big long room with one hundred beds like Bellevue.[3] There were four to a room, and when Roberta and me came, there was a shortage of state kids,[4] so we were the only ones assigned to 406 and could go from bed to bed if we wanted to. And we wanted to, too. We changed beds every night and for the whole four months we were there we never picked one out as our own permanent bed.

It didn't start out that way. The minute I walked in and the Big Bozo introduced us, I got sick to my stomach. It was one thing to be taken out of your own bed early in the morning—it was something else to be stuck in a strange place with a girl from a whole other race. And Mary, that's my mother, she was right. Every now and then she would stop dancing long enough to tell me something important and one of the things she said was that they never washed their hair and they smelled funny. Roberta sure did. Smell funny, I mean. So when the Big Bozo (nobody ever called her Mrs. Itkin, just like nobody ever said St. Bonaventure)—when she said, "Twyla, this is Roberta. Roberta, this is Twyla. Make each other welcome," I said, "My mother won't like you putting me in here."

"Good," said Bozo. "Maybe then she'll come and take you home."

How's that for mean? If Roberta had laughed I would have killed her, but she didn't. She just walked over to the window and stood with her back to us.

"Turn around," said the Bozo. "Don't be rude. Now Twyla. Roberta. When you hear a loud buzzer, that's the call for dinner. Come down to the first floor. Any fights and no movie." And then, just to make sure we knew what we would be missing, "*The Wizard of Oz*."

Roberta must have thought I meant that my mother would be mad about my being put in the shelter. Not about rooming with her, because as soon as Bozo left she came over to me and said, "Is your mother sick too?"

"No," I said. "She just likes to dance all night."

"Oh," she nodded her head and I liked the way she understood things so fast. So for the moment it didn't matter that we looked like salt and pepper standing there and that's what the other kids called us sometimes. We were eight years old and got F's all the time. Me because I couldn't remember what I read or what the teacher said. And Roberta because she couldn't read at all and didn't even listen to the teacher. She wasn't good at anything except jacks,[5] at which she was a killer: pow scoop pow scoop pow scoop.

We didn't like each other all that much at first, but nobody else wanted to play with us because we weren't real orphans with beautiful dead parents in the sky. We were dumped. Even the New York City Puerto Ricans and the upstate Indians ignored us. All kinds of kids were in there, black ones, white ones, even two Koreans. The food was good, though. At least I thought so.

1. A passage of narrative or dialogue in an opera sung in the rhythm of ordinary speech (French).
2. St. Bonaventure's, a fictional orphanage outside New York City.
3. A major hospital in New York City, famous for its psychiatric ward.
4. Children placed in the Catholic orphanage by the state of New York.
5. A traditional game in which children take turns picking up five- or six-pronged metal or plastic pieces between bounces of a ball.

Roberta hated it and left whole pieces of things on her plate: Spam, Salisbury steak—even jello with fruit cocktail in it, and she didn't care if I ate what she wouldn't. Mary's idea of supper was popcorn and a can of Yoo-Hoo. Hot mashed potatoes and two weenies was like Thanksgiving for me.

It really wasn't bad, St. Bonny's. The big girls on the second floor pushed us around now and then. But that was all. They wore lipstick and eyebrow pencil and wobbled their knees while they watched TV. Fifteen, sixteen, even, some of them were. They were put-out girls, scared runaways most of them. Poor little girls who fought their uncles off but looked tough to us, and mean. God did they look mean. The staff tried to keep them separate from the younger children, but sometimes they caught us watching them in the orchard where they played radios and danced with each other. They'd light out after us and pull our hair or twist our arms. We were scared of them, Roberta and me, but neither of us wanted the other one to know it. So we got a good list of dirty names we could shout back when we ran from them through the orchard. I used to dream a lot and almost always the orchard was there. Two acres, four maybe, of these little apple trees. Hundreds of them. Empty and crooked like beggar women when I first came to St. Bonny's but fat with flowers when I left. I don't know why I dreamt about that orchard so much. Nothing really happened there. Nothing all that important, I mean. Just the big girls dancing and playing the radio. Roberta and me watching. Maggie fell down there once. The kitchen woman with legs like parentheses. And the big girls laughed at her. We should have helped her up, I know, but we were scared of those girls with lipstick and eyebrow pencil. Maggie couldn't talk. The kids said she had her tongue cut out, but I think she was just born that way: mute. She was old and sandy-colored and she worked in the kitchen. I don't know if she was nice or not. I just remember her legs like parentheses and how she rocked when she walked. She worked from early in the morning till two o'clock, and if she was late, if she had too much cleaning and didn't get out till two-fifteen or so, she'd cut through the orchard so she wouldn't miss her bus and have to wait another hour. She wore this really stupid little hat—a kid's hat with ear flaps—and she wasn't much taller than we were. A really awful little hat. Even for a mute, it was dumb—dressing like a kid and never saying anything at all.

"But what about if somebody tries to kill her?" I used to wonder about that. "Or what if she wants to cry? Can she cry?"

"Sure," Roberta said. "But just tears. No sounds come out."

"She can't scream?"

"Nope. Nothing."

"Can she hear?"

"I guess."

"Let's call her," I said. And we did.

"Dummy! Dummy!" She never turned her head.

"Bow legs! Bow legs!" Nothing. She just rocked on, the chin straps of her baby-boy hat swaying from side to side. I think we were wrong. I think she could hear and didn't let on. And it shames me even now to think there was somebody in there after all who heard us call her those names and couldn't tell on us.

We got along all right, Roberta and me. Changed beds every night, got F's in civics and communication skills and gym. The Bozo was disappointed in us, she said. Out of 130 of us state cases, 90 were under twelve. Almost all were real orphans with beautiful dead parents in the sky. We were the only ones dumped and the only ones with F's in three classes including gym. So we got along—what with her leaving whole pieces of things on her plate and being nice about not asking questions.

I think it was the day before Maggie fell down that we found out our mothers were coming to visit us on the same Sunday. We had been at the shelter twenty-eight days (Roberta twenty-eight and a half) and this was their first visit with us. Our mothers would come at ten o'clock in time for chapel, then lunch with us in the teachers' lounge. I thought if my dancing mother met her sick mother it might be good for her. And Roberta thought her sick mother would get a big bang out of a dancing one. We got excited about it and curled each other's hair. After breakfast we sat on the bed watching the road from the window. Roberta's socks were still wet. She washed them the night before and put them on the radiator to dry. They hadn't, but she put them on anyway because their tops were so pretty—scalloped in pink. Each of us had a purple construction-paper basket that we had made in craft class. Mine had a yellow crayon rabbit on it. Roberta's had eggs with wiggly lines of color. Inside were cellophane grass and just the jelly beans because I'd eaten the two marshmallow eggs they gave us. The Big Bozo came herself to get us. Smiling she told us we looked very nice and to come downstairs. We were so surprised by the smile we'd never seen before, neither of us moved.

"Don't you want to see your mommies?"

I stood up first and spilled the jelly beans all over the floor. Bozo's smile disappeared while we scrambled to get the candy up off the floor and put it back in the grass.

She escorted us downstairs to the first floor, where the other girls were lining up to file into the chapel. A bunch of grown-ups stood to one side. Viewers mostly. The old biddies who wanted servants and the fags who wanted company looking for children they might want to adopt. Once in a while a grandmother. Almost never anybody young or anybody whose face wouldn't scare you in the night. Because if any of the real orphans had young relatives they wouldn't be real orphans. I saw Mary right away. She had on those green slacks I hated and hated even more now because didn't she know we were going to chapel? And that fur jacket with the pocket linings so ripped she had to pull to get her hands out of them. But her face was pretty—like always, and she smiled and waved like she was the little girl looking for her mother—not me.

I walked slowly, trying not to drop the jelly beans and hoping the paper handle would hold. I had to use my last Chiclet[6] because by the time I finished cutting everything out, all the Elmer's[7] was gone. I am left-handed and the scissors never worked for me. It didn't matter, though; I might just as well have chewed the gum. Mary dropped to her knees and grabbed me, mashing the basket, the jelly beans, and the grass into her ratty fur jacket.

"Twyla, baby. Twyla, baby!"

I could have killed her. Already I heard the big girls in the orchard the next time saying, "Twyyyyyla, baby!" But I couldn't stay mad at Mary while she was smiling and hugging me and smelling of Lady Esther[8] dusting powder. I wanted to stay buried in her fur all day.

6. A brand of chewing gum.
7. A brand of glue.
8. A brand of cosmetics.

To tell the truth I forgot about Roberta. Mary and I got in line for the traipse into chapel and I was feeling proud because she looked so beautiful even in those ugly green slacks that made her behind stick out. A pretty mother on earth is better than a beautiful dead one in the sky even if she did leave you all alone to go dancing.

I felt a tap on my shoulder, turned, and saw Roberta smiling. I smiled back, but not too much lest somebody think this visit was the biggest thing that ever happened in my life. Then Roberta said, "Mother, I want you to meet my roommate, Twyla. And that's Twyla's mother."

I looked up it seemed for miles. She was big. Bigger than any man and on her chest was the biggest cross I'd ever seen. I swear it was six inches long each way. And in the crook of her arm was the biggest Bible ever made.

Mary, simple-minded as ever, grinned and tried to yank her hand out of the pocket with the raggedy lining—to shake hands, I guess. Roberta's mother looked down at me and then looked down at Mary too. She didn't say anything, just grabbed Roberta with her Bible-free hand and stepped out of line, walking quickly to the rear of it. Mary was still grinning because she's not too swift when it comes to what's really going on. Then this light bulb goes off in her head and she says "That bitch!" really loud and us almost in the chapel now. Organ music whining; the Bonny Angels singing sweetly. Everybody in the world turned around to look. And Mary would have kept it up—kept calling names if I hadn't squeezed her hand as hard as I could. That helped a little, but she still twitched and crossed and uncrossed her legs all through service. Even groaned a couple of times. Why did I think she would come there and act right? Slacks. No hat like the grandmothers and viewers, and groaning all the while. When we stood for hymns she kept her mouth shut. Wouldn't even look at the words on the page. She actually reached in her purse for a mirror to check her lipstick. All I could think of was that she really needed to be killed. The sermon lasted a year, and I knew the real orphans were looking smug again.

We were supposed to have lunch in the teachers' lounge, but Mary didn't bring anything, so we picked fur and cellophane grass off the mashed jelly beans and ate them. I could have killed her. I sneaked a look at Roberta. Her mother had brought chicken legs and ham sandwiches and oranges and a whole box of chocolate-covered grahams. Roberta drank milk from a thermos while her mother read the Bible to her.

Things are not right. The wrong food is always with the wrong people. Maybe that's why I got into waitress work later—to match up the right people with the right food. Roberta just let those chicken legs sit there, but she did bring a stack of grahams up to me later when the visit was over. I think she was sorry that her mother would not shake my mother's hand. And I liked that and I liked the fact that she didn't say a word about Mary groaning all the way through the service and not bringing any lunch.

Roberta left in May when the apple trees were heavy and white. On her last day we went to the orchard to watch the big girls smoke and dance by the radio. It didn't matter that they said, "Twyyyyyla, baby." We sat on the ground and breathed. Lady Esther. Apple blossoms. I still go soft when I smell one or the other. Roberta was going home. The big cross and the big Bible was coming to get her and she seemed sort of glad and sort of not. I thought I would die in that room of four beds without her and I knew Bozo had plans to move some other dumped kid in there with me. Roberta promised to write every day, which was really sweet of her because she couldn't read a lick so how could she write anybody. I would have drawn pictures and sent them to her but she never gave me her address. Little by little she faded. Her wet socks with the pink scalloped tops and her big serious-looking eyes—that's all I could catch when I tried to bring her to mind.

I was working behind the counter at the Howard Johnson's[9] on the Thruway just before the Kingston exit. Not a bad job. Kind of a long ride from Newburgh, but okay once I got there. Mine was the second night shift—eleven to seven. Very light until a Greyhound checked in for breakfast around six-thirty. At that hour the sun was all the way clear of the hills behind the restaurant. The place looked better at night—more like shelter—but I loved it when the sun broke in, even if it did show all the cracks in the vinyl and the speckled floor looked dirty no matter what the mop boy did.

It was August and a bus crowd was just unloading. They would stand around a long while: going to the john, and looking at gifts and junk-for-sale machines, reluctant to sit down so soon. Even to eat. I was trying to fill the coffee pots and get them all situated on the electric burners when I saw her. She was sitting in a booth smoking a cigarette with two guys smothered in head and facial hair. Her own hair was so big and wild I could hardly see her face. But the eyes. I would know them anywhere. She had on a powder-blue halter and shorts outfit and earrings the size of bracelets. Talk about lipstick and eyebrow pencil. She made the big girls look like nuns. I couldn't get off the counter until seven o'clock, but I kept watching the booth in case they got up to leave before that. My replacement was on time for a change, so I counted and stacked my receipts as fast as I could and signed off. I walked over to the booth, smiling and wondering if she would remember me. Or even if she wanted to remember me. Maybe she didn't want to be reminded of St. Bonny's or to have anybody know she was ever there. I know I never talked about it to anybody.

I put my hands in my apron pockets and leaned against the back of the booth facing them.

"Roberta? Roberta Fisk?"

She looked up. "Yeah?"

"Twyla."

She squinted for a second and then said, "Wow."

"Remember me?"

"Sure. Hey. Wow."

"It's been a while," I said, and gave a smile to the two hairy guys.

"Yeah. Wow. You work here?"

"Yeah," I said. "I live in Newburgh."

"Newburgh? No kidding?" She laughed then a private laugh that included the guys but only the guys, and they laughed with her. What could I do but laugh too and wonder why I was standing there with my knees showing out from under that uniform. Without looking I could see the blue and white tri-

9. A modestly priced restaurant and hotel chain; this branch is off the New York State Thruway near Kingston, north of New York City.

angle on my head, my hair shapeless in a net, my ankles thick in white oxfords. Nothing could have been less sheer than my stockings. There was this silence that came down right after I laughed. A silence it was her turn to fill up. With introductions, maybe, to her boyfriends or an invitation to sit down and have a Coke. Instead she lit a cigarette off the one she'd just finished and said, "We're on our way to the Coast. He's got an appointment with Hendrix." She gestured casually toward the boy next to her.

"Hendrix? Fantastic," I said. "Really fantastic. What's she doing now?"

Roberta coughed on her cigarette and the two guys rolled their eyes up at the ceiling.

"Hendrix. Jimi Hendrix,[1] asshole. He's only the biggest—Oh, wow. Forget it."

I was dismissed without anyone saying goodbye, so I thought I would do it for her.

"How's your mother?" I asked. Her grin cracked her whole face. She swallowed. "Fine," she said. "How's yours?"

"Pretty as a picture," I said and turned away. The backs of my knees were damp. Howard Johnson's really was a dump in the sunlight.

James is as comfortable as a house slipper. He liked my cooking and I liked his big loud family. They have lived in Newburgh all of their lives and talk about it the way people do who have always known a home. His grandmother has a porch swing[2] older than his father and when they talk about streets and avenues and buildings they call them names they no longer have. They still call the A & P[3] Rico's because it stands on property once a mom and pop store owned by Mr. Rico. And they call the new community college Town Hall because it once was. My mother-in-law puts up jelly and cucumbers and buys butter wrapped in cloth from a dairy. James and his father talk about fishing and baseball and I can see them all together on the Hudson in a raggedy skiff. Half the population of Newburgh is on welfare now, but to my husband's family it was still some upstate paradise of a time long past. A time of ice houses and vegetable wagons, coal furnaces and children weeding gardens. When our son was born my mother-in-law gave me the crib blanket that had been hers.

But the town they remembered had changed. Something quick was in the air. Magnificent old houses, so ruined they had become shelter for squatters and rent risks, were bought and renovated. Smart IBM[4] people moved out of their suburbs back into the city and put shutters up and herb gardens in their backyards. A brochure came in the mail announcing the opening of a Food Emporium. Gourmet food it said—and listed items the rich IBM crowd would want. It was located in a new mall at the edge of town and I drove out to shop there one day—just to see. It was late in June. After the tulips were gone and the Queen Elizabeth roses were open everywhere. I trailed my cart along the aisle tossing in smoked oysters and Robert's sauce and things I knew would sit

1. African American rock guitarist (1942–1970).
2. I.e., even older; porch swings are proverbially old.
3. An inexpensive grocery store, originally the Great Atlantic & Pacific Tea Company.
4. International Business Machines, the leading computer company of the time, with headquarters in Armonk, New York.

in my cupboard for years. Only when I found some Klondike ice cream bars did I feel less guilty about spending James's fireman's salary so foolishly. My father-in-law ate them with the same gusto little Joseph did.

Waiting in the check-out line I heard a voice say, "Twyla!"

The classical music piped over the aisles had affected me and the woman leaning toward me was dressed to kill. Diamonds on her hand, a smart white summer dress. "I'm Mrs. Benson," I said.

"Ho. Ho. The Big Bozo," she sang.

For a split second I didn't know what she was talking about. She had a bunch of asparagus and two cartons of fancy water.

"Roberta!"

"Right."

"For heaven's sake. Roberta."

"You look great," she said.

"So do you. Where are you? Here? In Newburgh?"

"Yes. Over in Annandale."[5]

I was opening my mouth to say more when the cashier called my attention to her empty counter.

"Meet you outside." Roberta pointed her finger and went into the express line.

I placed the groceries and kept myself from glancing around to check Roberta's progress. I remembered Howard Johnson's and looking for a chance to speak only to be greeted with a stingy "wow." But she was waiting for me and her huge hair was sleek now, smooth around a small, nicely shaped head. Shoes, dress, everything lovely and summery and rich. I was dying to know what happened to her, how she got from Jimi Hendrix to Annandale, a neighborhood full of doctors and IBM executives. Easy, I thought. Everything is so easy for them. They think they own the world.

"How long," I asked her. "How long have you been here?"

"A year. I got married to a man who lives here. And you, you're married too, right? Benson, you said."

"Yeah. James Benson."

"And is he nice?"

"Oh, is he nice?"

"Well, is he?" Roberta's eyes were steady as though she really meant the question and wanted an answer.

"He's wonderful, Roberta. Wonderful."

"So you're happy."

"Very."

"That's good," she said and nodded her head. "I always hoped you'd be happy. Any kids? I know you have kids."

"One. A boy. How about you?"

"Four."

"Four?"

She laughed. "Step kids. He's a widower."

5. Annandale-on-Hudson, a prosperous small town north of New York City. Newburgh, across the Hudson River and slightly south, is less prosperous.

"Oh."

"Got a minute? Let's have a coffee."

I thought about the Klondikes melting and the inconvenience of going all the way to my car and putting the bags in the trunk. Served me right for buying all that stuff I didn't need. Roberta was ahead of me.

"Put them in my car. It's right here."

And then I saw the dark blue limousine.

"You married a Chinaman?"

"No," she laughed. "He's the driver."

"Oh, my. If the Big Bozo could see you now."

We both giggled. Really giggled. Suddenly, in just a pulse beat, twenty years disappeared and all of it came rushing back. The big girls (whom we called gar girls—Roberta's misheard word for the evil stone faces[6] described in a civics class) there dancing in the orchard, the ploppy mashed potatoes, the double weenies, the Spam with pineapple. We went into the coffee shop holding on to one another and I tried to think why we were glad to see each other this time and not before. Once, twelve years ago, we passed like strangers. A black girl and a white girl meeting in a Howard Johnson's on the road and having nothing to say. One in a blue and white triangle waitress hat—the other on her way to see Hendrix. Now we were behaving like sisters separated for much too long. Those four short months were nothing in time. Maybe it was the thing itself. Just being there, together. Two little girls who knew what nobody else in the world knew—how not to ask questions. How to believe what had to be believed. There was politeness in that reluctance and generosity as well. Is your mother sick too? No, she dances all night. Oh—and an understanding nod.

We sat in a booth by the window and fell into recollection like veterans.

"Did you ever learn to read?"

"Watch." She picked up the menu. "Special of the day. Cream of corn soup. Entrées. Two dots and a wriggly line. Quiche. Chef salad, scallops . . ."

I was laughing and applauding when the waitress came up.

"Remember the Easter baskets?"

"And how we tried to *introduce* them?"

"Your mother with that cross like two telephone poles."

"And yours with those tight slacks."

We laughed so loudly heads turned and made the laughter hard to suppress.

"What happened to the Jimi Hendrix date?"

Roberta made a blow-out sound with her lips.

"When he died I thought about you."

"Oh, you heard about him finally?"

"Finally. Come on, I was a small-town country waitress."

"And I was a small-town country dropout. God, were we wild. I still don't know how I got out of there alive."

"But you did."

"I did. I really did. Now I'm Mrs. Kenneth Norton."

"Sounds like a mouthful."

6. I.e., gargoyles.

"It is."

"Servants and all?"

Roberta held up two fingers.

"Ow! What does he do?"

"Computers and stuff. What do I know?"

"I don't remember a hell of a lot from those days, but Lord, St. Bonny's is as clear as daylight. Remember Maggie? The day she fell down and those gar girls laughed at her?"

Roberta looked up from her salad and stared at me. "Maggie didn't fall," she said.

"Yes, she did. You remember."

"No, Twyla. They knocked her down. Those girls pushed her down and tore her clothes. In the orchard."

"I don't—that's not what happened."

"Sure it is. In the orchard. Remember how scared we were?"

"Wait a minute. I don't remember any of that."

"And Bozo was fired."

"You're crazy. She was there when I left. You left before me."

"I went back. You weren't there when they fired Bozo."

"What?"

"Twice. Once for a year when I was about ten, another for two months when I was fourteen. That's when I ran away."

"You ran away from St. Bonny's?"

"I had to. What do you want? Me dancing in that orchard?"

"Are you sure about Maggie?"

"Of course I'm sure. You've blocked it, Twyla. It happened. Those girls had behavior problems, you know."

"Didn't they, though. But why can't I remember the Maggie thing?"

"Believe me. It happened. And we were there."

"Who did you room with when you went back?" I asked her as if I would know her. The Maggie thing was troubling me.

"Creeps. They tickled themselves in the night."

My ears were itching and I wanted to go home suddenly. This was all very well but she couldn't just comb her hair, wash her face and pretend everything was hunky-dory. After the Howard Johnson's snub. And no apology. Nothing.

"Were you on dope or what that time at Howard Johnson's?" I tried to make my voice sound friendlier than I felt.

"Maybe, a little. I never did drugs much. Why?"

"I don't know, you acted sort of like you didn't want to know me then."

"Oh, Twyla, you know how it was in those days: black—white. You know how everything was."

But I didn't know. I thought it was just the opposite. Busloads of blacks and whites came into Howard Johnson's together. They roamed together then: students, musicians, lovers, protesters. You got to see everything at Howard Johnson's and blacks were very friendly with whites in those days. But sitting there with nothing on my plate but two hard tomato wedges wondering about the melting Klondikes it seemed childish remembering the slight. We went to her car, and with the help of the driver, got my stuff into my station wagon.

"We'll keep in touch this time," she said.

"Sure," I said. "Sure. Give me a call."

"I will," she said, and then just as I was sliding behind the wheel, she leaned into the window. "By the way. Your mother. Did she ever stop dancing?"

I shook my head. "No. Never."

Roberta nodded.

"And yours? Did she ever get well?"

She smiled a tiny sad smile. "No. She never did. Look, call me, okay?"

"Okay," I said, but I knew I wouldn't. Roberta had messed up my past somehow with that business about Maggie. I wouldn't forget a thing like that. Would I?

Strife came to us that fall. At least that's what the paper called it. Strife. Racial strife. The word made me think of a bird—a big shrieking bird out of 1,000,000,000 B.C. Flapping its wings and cawing. Its eye with no lid always bearing down on you. All day it screeched and at night it slept on the rooftops. It woke you in the morning and from the *Today* show to the eleven o'clock news it kept you an awful company. I couldn't figure it out from one day to the next. I knew I was supposed to feel something strong, but I didn't know what, and James wasn't any help. Joseph was on the list of kids to be transferred from the junior high school to another one at some far-out-of-the-way place and I thought it was a good thing until I heard it was a bad thing. I mean I didn't know.[7] All the schools seemed dumps to me, and the fact that one was nicer looking didn't hold much weight. But the papers were full of it and then the kids began to get jumpy. In August, mind you. Schools weren't even open yet. I thought Joseph might be frightened to go over there, but he didn't seem scared so I forgot about it, until I found myself driving along Hudson Street out there by the school they were trying to integrate and saw a line of women marching. And who do you suppose was in line, big as life, holding a sign in front of her bigger than her mother's cross? MOTHERS HAVE RIGHTS TOO! it said.

I drove on, and then changed my mind. I circled the block, slowed down, and honked my horn.

Roberta looked over and when she saw me she waved. I didn't wave back, but I didn't move either. She handed her sign to another woman and came over to where I was parked.

"Hi."

"What are you doing?"

"Picketing. What's it look like?"

"What for?"

"What do you mean, 'What for?' They want to take my kids and send them out of the neighborhood. They don't want to go."

"So what if they go to another school? My boy's being bussed too, and I don't mind. Why should you?"

"It's not about us, Twyla. Me and you. It's about our kids."

7. In the 1970s and 1980s, many municipalities, often under court order, transported students to schools distant from their neighborhoods in order to desegregate racially segregated public schools; the practice, called busing, was controversial.

"What's more *us* than that?"

"Well, it is a free country."

"Not yet, but it will be."

"What the hell does that mean? I'm not doing anything to you."

"You really think that?"

"I know it."

"I wonder what made me think you were different."

"I wonder what made me think you were different."

"Look at them," I said. "Just look. Who do they think they are? Swarming all over the place like they own it. And now they think they can decide where my child goes to school. Look at them, Roberta. They're Bozos."

Roberta turned around and looked at the women. Almost all of them were standing still now, waiting. Some were even edging toward us. Roberta looked at me out of some refrigerator behind her eyes. "No, they're not. They're just mothers."

"And what am I? Swiss cheese?"

"I used to curl your hair."

"I hated your hands in my hair."

The women were moving. Our faces looked mean to them of course and they looked as though they could not wait to throw themselves in front of a police car, or better yet, into my car and drag me away by my ankles. Now they surrounded my car and gently, gently began to rock it. I swayed back and forth like a sideways yo-yo. Automatically I reached for Roberta, like the old days in the orchard when they saw us watching them and we had to get out of there, and if one of us fell the other pulled her up and if one of us was caught the other stayed to kick and scratch, and neither would leave the other behind. My arm shot out of the car window but no receiving hand was there. Roberta was looking at me sway from side to side in the car and her face was still. My purse slid from the car seat down under the dashboard. The four policemen who had been drinking Tab in their car finally got the message and strolled over, forcing their way through the women. Quietly, firmly they spoke. "Okay, ladies. Back in line or off the streets."

Some of them went away willingly; others had to be urged away from the car doors and the hood. Roberta didn't move. She was looking steadily at me. I was fumbling to turn on the ignition, which wouldn't catch because the gear shift was still in drive. The seats of the car were a mess because the swaying had thrown my grocery coupons all over it and my purse was sprawled on the floor.

"Maybe I am different now, Twyla. But you're not. You're the same little state kid who kicked a poor old black lady when she was down on the ground. You kicked a black lady and you have the nerve to call me a bigot."

The coupons were everywhere and the guts of my purse were bunched under the dashboard. What was she saying? Black? Maggie wasn't black.

"She wasn't black," I said.

"Like hell she wasn't, and you kicked her. We both did. You kicked a black lady who couldn't even scream."

"Liar!"

"You're the liar! Why don't you just go on home and leave us alone, huh?"

She turned away and I skidded away from the curb.

The next morning I went into the garage and cut the side out of the carton our portable TV had come in. It wasn't nearly big enough, but after a while I had a decent sign: red spray-painted letters on a white background—AND SO DO CHILDREN* * * *. I meant just to go down to the school and tack it up somewhere so those cows on the picket line across the street could see it, but when I got there, some ten or so others had already assembled—protesting the cows across the street. Police permits and everything. I got in line and we strutted in time on our side while Roberta's group strutted on theirs. That first day we were all dignified, pretending the other side didn't exist. The second day there was name calling and finger gestures. But that was about all. People changed signs from time to time, but Roberta never did and neither did I. Actually my sign didn't make sense without Roberta's. "And so do children what?" one of the women on my side asked me. Have rights, I said, as though it was obvious.

Roberta didn't acknowledge my presence in any way and I got to thinking maybe she didn't know I was there. I began to pace myself in the line, jostling people one minute and lagging behind the next, so Roberta and I could reach the end of our respective lines at the same time and there would be a moment in our turn when we would face each other. Still, I couldn't tell whether she saw me and knew my sign was for her. The next day I went early before we were scheduled to assemble. I waited until she got there before I exposed my new creation. As soon as she hoisted her MOTHERS HAVE RIGHTS TOO I began to wave my new one, which said, HOW WOULD YOU KNOW? I know she saw that one, but I had gotten addicted now. My signs got crazier each day, and the women on my side decided that I was a kook. They couldn't make heads or tails out of my brilliant screaming posters.

I brought a painted sign in queenly red with huge black letters that said, IS YOUR MOTHER WELL? Roberta took her lunch break and didn't come back for the rest of the day or any day after. Two days later I stopped going too and couldn't have been missed because nobody understood my signs anyway.

It was a nasty six weeks. Classes were suspended and Joseph didn't go to anybody's school until October. The children—everybody's children—soon got bored with that extended vacation they thought was going to be so great. They looked at TV until their eyes flattened. I spent a couple of mornings tutoring my son, as the other mothers said we should. Twice I opened a text from last year that he had never turned in. Twice he yawned in my face. Other mothers organized living room sessions so the kids would keep up. None of the kids could concentrate so they drifted back to *The Price Is Right* and *The Brady Bunch*. When the school finally opened there were fights once or twice and some sirens roared through the streets every once in a while. There were a lot of photographers from Albany. And just when ABC was about to send up a news crew, the kids settled down like nothing in the world had happened. Joseph hung my HOW WOULD YOU KNOW? sign in his bedroom. I don't know what became of AND SO DO CHILDREN* * * *. I think my father-in-law cleaned some fish on it. He was always puttering around in our garage. Each of his five children lived in Newburgh and he acted as though he had five extra homes.

I couldn't help looking for Roberta when Joseph graduated from high school, but I didn't see her. It didn't trouble me much what she had said to me in the car. I mean the kicking part. I know I didn't do that, I couldn't do that. But I was puzzled by her telling me Maggie was black. When I thought about it I actually couldn't be certain. She wasn't pitch-black, I knew, or I would have remembered that. What I remember was the kiddie hat, and the semicircle legs. I tried to reassure myself about the race thing for a long time until it dawned on me that the truth was already there, and Roberta knew it. I didn't kick her; I didn't join in with the gar girls and kick that lady, but I sure did want to. We watched and never tried to help her and never called for help. Maggie was my dancing mother. Deaf, I thought, and dumb. Nobody inside. Nobody who would hear you if you cried in the night. Nobody who could tell you anything important that you could use. Rocking, dancing, swaying as she walked. And when the gar girls pushed her down, and started roughhousing, I knew she wouldn't scream, couldn't—just like me—and I was glad about that.

We decided not to have a tree, because Christmas would be at my mother-in-law's house, so why have a tree at both places? Joseph was at SUNY New Paltz[8] and we had to economize, we said. But at the last minute, I changed my mind. Nothing could be that bad. So I rushed around town looking for a tree, something small but wide. By the time I found a place, it was snowing and very late. I dawdled like it was the most important purchase in the world and the tree man was fed up with me. Finally I chose one and had it tied onto the trunk of the car. I drove away slowly because the sand trucks were not out yet and the streets could be murder at the beginning of a snowfall. Downtown the streets were wide and rather empty except for a cluster of people coming out of the Newburgh Hotel. The one hotel in town that wasn't built out of cardboard and Plexiglas. A party, probably. The men huddled in the snow were dressed in tails and the women had on furs. Shiny things glittered from underneath their coats. It made me tired to look at them. Tired, tired, tired. On the next corner was a small diner with loops and loops of paper bells in the window. I stopped the car and went in. Just for a cup of coffee and twenty minutes of peace before I went home and tried to finish everything before Christmas Eve.

"Twyla?"

There she was. In a silvery evening gown and dark fur coat. A man and another woman were with her, the man fumbling for change to put in the cigarette machine. The woman was humming and tapping on the counter with her fingernails. They all looked a little bit drunk.

"Well. It's you."

"How are you?"

I shrugged. "Pretty good. Frazzled. Christmas and all."

"Regular?" called the woman from the counter.

"Fine," Roberta called back and then, "Wait for me in the car."

8. The State University of New York at New Paltz, north of New York City.

She slipped into the booth beside me. "I have to tell you something, Twyla. I made up my mind if I ever saw you again, I'd tell you."

"I'd just as soon not hear anything, Roberta. It doesn't matter now, anyway."

"No," she said. "Not about that."

"Don't be long," said the woman. She carried two regulars to go and the man peeled his cigarette pack as they left.

"It's about St. Bonny's and Maggie."

"Oh, please."

"Listen to me. I really did think she was black. I didn't make that up. I really thought so. But now I can't be sure. I just remember her as old, so old. And because she couldn't talk—well, you know, I thought she was crazy. She'd been brought up in an institution like my mother was and like I thought I would be too. And you were right. We didn't kick her. It was the gar girls. Only them. But, well, I wanted to. I really wanted them to hurt her. I said we did it, too. You and me, but that's not true. And I don't want you to carry that around. It was just that I wanted to do it so bad that day—wanting to is doing it."

Her eyes were watery from the drinks she'd had, I guess. I know it's that way with me. One glass of wine and I start bawling over the littlest thing.

"We were kids, Roberta."

"Yeah. Yeah. I know, just kids."

"Eight."

"Eight."

"And lonely."

"Scared, too."

She wiped her cheeks with the heel of her hand and smiled. "Well, that's all I wanted to say."

I nodded and couldn't think of any way to fill the silence that went from the diner past the paper bells on out into the snow. It was heavy now. I thought I'd better wait for the sand trucks before starting home.

"Thanks, Roberta."

"Sure."

"Did I tell you? My mother, she never did stop dancing."

"Yes. You told me. And mine, she never got well." Roberta lifted her hands from the tabletop and covered her face with her palms. When she took them away she really was crying. "Oh shit, Twyla. Shit, shit, shit. What the hell happened to Maggie?"

1983

MO YAN
born 1955

Mo Yan burst onto China's literary scene in 1986 with the publication of his novel *Red Sorghum*, which won high critical praise and was subsequently made into a film directed by Zhang Yimou. Since then he has published a host of novels and short stories, many of which have been translated into English by Howard Goldblatt, his longtime collaborator (the selection here was translated by Janice Wickeri). Much of Mo Yan's fiction is set in his native Gaomi County, in Shandong province—a real place, albeit one that Mo Yan's fictions enhance and transform almost into myth. Rich language and creative description are hallmarks of his style, which serves to create a mythic and surreal world that at once romanticizes and mourns the past. In 2012, Mo Yan was awarded the Nobel Prize for Literature.

Many critics describe Mo Yan's work as exemplary of the literary movement called "Roots Seeking." This movement arose in the 1980s, one of many waves of response in China to the collective experience of swift modernization in the preceding decades. The optimistic narratives of revolutionary progress that had buoyed the nation through the middle part of the century had declined by this period, giving way to fresh anxieties over China's eroding cultural identity as well as its continuing technological and economic lag behind the West. The writers of the Roots movement, most of them young men, sought to turn from grand models of the future and instead to look for Chinese selfhood in the intimate, local, and rooted places around them: in the rural past, in family lines, in small-h history. These sources, they argued, are the strongest materials for building a cultural identity on which a modern China can rise.

The Roots school tends to favor a decidedly masculine aesthetic, celebrating raw potency, toughness, and bravado, a tone that some feminist critics have challenged. The novelist Can Xue has criticized Mo Yan for what she regards as his excessive celebration of virility and masculinity, presenting a biting parody of his school's worst excesses: "His hometown is in the country where his ancestors were bandits. The village raises so many dogs to bite strangers that no outsiders can go in. It is a special village situated on top of a mountain which is covered by clouds and fog all year round. The village consists of eight hundred strong men and bewitching women with bound feet."

The story selected here, "The Old Gun" (written in 1985), is in many respects a typical Roots text, since it portrays a younger generation trying to reconnect with its ancestors. Narrated in the third person, the story revolves around a boy and his relation to his dead father through the trope of the "old gun." The story is typical of the movement, too, in its masculine emphases, narrating a young male's relationship with the spirit of a lost, primitive, masculine past. The boy has been in a sense emasculated, a condition that (as critics have noted) offers a metaphor for the general unmanning of the Chinese people by their Confucian and Maoist pasts. His desire to perform a difficult and symbolically charged act, namely firing a gun, represents compensation for wrongs done to him in the past, but it also represents the larger desire for control, vitality, and power. In the end, after the narration of the events surrounding his low estate, he manages to fire the gun in a violent explosion. Like much of Mo Yan's fiction, the story expresses a desire for a world lost, a world that possessed a vitality that the present lacks. That the protagonist's victory is a pyrrhic one, leading to ultimate failure, reflects the mood of pessimism and despondency that pervades so much of the work of this school. There is a sense of fatality to the quest these writers portray, as though it were a final test of resolve, or as though from a suspicion that the search for paradise entails the search for something lost.

The story narrates the boy's attempt to kill wild ducks in some local sorghum fields, which have transformed, almost magically, into primitive swampland. As is typical for Mo Yan, the most important aspect of the work is the richness and suggestiveness of the descriptive language. The language creates an almost mythical world of wild ducks, flooding waters, waving sorghum stalks, kaleidoscopic colors as the sun slants across the landscape—an untamed natural world, for feeding, hunting, and killing. As the boy prepares to fire his gun, we learn that part of his index finger is missing. The boy's observations and reflections are presented in free indirect discourse, a realist technique in which the narrator reports the thoughts of the character in the third person.

Through flashbacks, the story shows how the boy lost his finger, and how his father and grandfather died. The narrative returns periodically to the present, where the boy ruminates as he prowls through the sorghum fields, having defied his mother and taken down the gun to go hunting. Part of his motivation is simple hunger—he reflects that he hasn't eaten meat for what feels like ages—but more than that, he is overcome by the desire to kill, to attain explosive power, to connect with his paternal lineage, to recover a missing part of himself that he feels the gun represents. The narrative carefully builds a picture of the boy's mind and thoughts as he approaches a crisis in his existence.

The Old Gun[1]

As he swung the gun down from his right shoulder with his index-finger-less right hand, he was caught in a ray of golden sunlight. The sun was sinking rapidly in a smooth shallow arc; fragmentary sounds like those of a receding tide rippled from the fields, along with an air of desolation by turns pronounced and faint. Gingerly he placed the gun on the ground among the patches of coin-shaped moss, feeling a sense of distress as he saw how damp the earth was. The long-barrelled, home-made musket, its butt mahogany, lay unevenly on the soggy ground; beside it the evening sun picked out a fallen sorghum ear on which a great cluster of delicate, tender golden shoots had sprouted, casting discolouring shadows onto the black gun-barrel and deep-red butt. He took the powder-horn from around his waist, at the same time slipping off his black jacket to reveal a raw-boned torso. He wrapped the gun and the powder-horn in the jacket and lay them on the ground, then took three paces forward. Bending down, he stretched out his sun-drenched arms and dragged out one sheaf from among the great clump of sorghum stalks.

The autumn floods had been heavy and the land, water-logged for thousands of hectares, looked like an ocean. In the water the sorghum held high its

1. Translated from Chinese by Duncan Hewitt.

crimson heads; whole platoons of rats scurried across them as nimbly as birds in flight. By harvest time the water was at chest height, and the people waded in and took the ears of sorghum away on rafts. Red-finned carp and black-backed grass carp appeared from nowhere to dart about among the green aerial roots of the sorghum stalks. Now and again an emerald green kingfisher shot into the water, then shot back out with a tiny glistening fish in its beak. In August the flood waters gradually subsided, revealing roads covered in mud. On the low-lying land the water remained, forming pools of all shapes and sizes. The cut sorghum stalks could not be hauled away; they were dragged out of the water and stacked on the road or on the higher ground around the edges of the pools. A glorious sunlight shone on the low-lying plains. For miles around there was hardly a village; the pools sparkled; the clumps of sorghum stood like clusters of blockhouses.

Silhouetted against the bright warm sun and a big expanse of water, he dragged aside sheaf after sheaf of sorghum, piling them up at the edge of the pool until he had made a square hide half a man's height. Then he picked up the gun, jumped into the hide and sat down. His head came just level with the top of the hide. From outside he was invisible, but through the holes he had left he could clearly see the pool and the sand-bar which rose in its middle like a solitary island; he could see the rosy sky and the brown earth, too. The sky seemed very low; the sun's rays daubed the surface of the water a deep red. The pool stretched away into the hazy dusk, sparkling brilliantly, darts of radiance dancing around its edge like a ring of warm eyelashes. On the sand-bar in the pool, by now a pale shade of blue, clumps of yellow reeds stood solemnly upright. The sand-bar itself, surrounded by flickering light, seemed gently adrift. The hazier the surroundings grew, the brighter the water gleamed, and the more pronounced the impression that the sand-bar was drifting—he felt that it was floating towards him, floating nearer, until it was only a few steps away and he could have jumped onto it. They still hadn't arrived on the sand-bar; he gazed uneasily at the sky once more, thinking, it's about time, they ought to be here by now.

He had no idea where they came from. That day the workers had spent the whole afternoon shifting sorghum stalks. When the team leader said time to down tools, the men headed for home by the dozen, their long shadows swaying as they went. He had rushed over here to relieve himself when suddenly he caught sight of them. It was as though he had been punched in the chest—his heart faltered for a moment before it resumed beating. His eyes were dazzled by the great flock of wild ducks landing on the sand-bar. Every night for two weeks he hid among the sorghum sheafs watching them; he observed that they always arrived, cawing loudly, at around this time of the evening, as if they had come flying from beyond the sky. Before landing they would circle elegantly above the pool, like a great grey-green cloud now unfurling, now rolling back . . . When they descended onto the sand-bar, their wings beating the air, he was beside himself with excitement. Never before had he come across so many wild ducks on such a small piece of land, never . . .

They still weren't here—by now they really should have been. They weren't here *yet* . . . or they weren't coming? He was feeling anxious, even began to suspect that what he had seen before had been just an illusion—all along he had never quite believed there could really be such a large flock of wild ducks in this place. He had often heard the old people in the village telling tales of heavenly ducks, but the ducks in the stories were always pure white, and this flock of wild ducks was not. The ones with pretty green feathers on their heads and necks, a white ring round their throats and wings like blue mirrors—weren't they drakes? Those with golden-brown bodies, dappled with dark brown markings—weren't they females? They certainly weren't heavenly ducks, for they left little green and brown feathers all over the sand-bar. He felt greatly reassured at the sight of these feathers. He sat down, picked up his jacket and shook it open, revealing the gun and the shiny powder-horn. The gun lay peacefully on top of the sorghum stalks, its body gleaming dark-red, almost the colour of rust. In the past red rust had covered it several times and had eaten away at the metal, leaving it pocked and pitted. Now, though, there was no rust—he had sandpapered it all away. The gun lay there twisted like a hibernating snake; at any moment, he felt, it might wake up, fly into the air and start thrashing the sorghum stalks with its steel tail. When he stretched out his hand to touch the gun, his first sensation was an iciness in his fingertips, and the chill spread to his chest and made him shiver for a long while. The sun was sinking faster now, its shape altering all the while, flattening out and distorting, like a semi-fluid sphere hitting a smooth steel surface. Its underside was a flat line, its curved surfaces under extreme tension; at last they burst and the bubbling icy red liquid meandered away in every direction. A trance-like calm descended on the pool as the crimson liquid seeped down, turning its depths into a thick red broth, while the surface remained crystal clear and blindingly bright. Suddenly, he caught sight of a gold-hooped dragonfly suspended from a tall, withered blade of grass, its bulging eyes like purple gems, turning now to the left, now to the right, refracting light as they did so.

He reached for the gun and laid it across his legs, its body stretching out behind him along the right-angle of his thighs and belly; the barrel peeped out from beneath his chin at the pale grey southern sky. He opened the lid of the powder-horn, then pulled from his pocket a long, thin measuring cylinder which he filled with gunpowder. He poured this measure into the gun barrel, the smooth sound it made as it fell echoed from the muzzle. He then took a pinch of iron shot from a small iron box and tipped it into the muzzle of the gun; from inside the barrel there came a clatter. Now he pulled out a long rod from below the barrel and tamped down the mixture of gunpowder and shot with its uneven head. He moved as gingerly as if he were scratching a drowsy tiger's itch, nerve-ends tingling, heart pounding. As soon as he had put the third measure of gunpowder and the third handful of shot into the barrel, an icy cold clutched him; beads of cold sweat broke out on his forehead. His hands were trembling as he took out the cotton-wool stopper he had prepared for the purpose and plugged the mouth of the gun. He felt starving, his whole body limp. He snapped a piece of grass from the ground, rubbed the mud from it, put it into his mouth and began to chew on it, but this only made his hunger worse . . .

Just then, though, he heard the whistle of wings beating the air above the water-flats. He had to hurry and complete his final task of preparation: attaching the percussion cap. He pulled back the protruding head of the hammer, revealing a nipple-shaped protuberance connected to the gun barrel. There was a round groove in the top of the protuberance with a tiny hole in its centre. With great care he tore away several layers of paper from around the golden percussion cap, then fitted it into this groove. The percussion cap contained yellow gunpowder; as soon as the hammer struck it, this would explode, igniting the powder in the barrel and sending a fiery snake leaping from the muzzle, slender at first, then bigger until finally the gun looked like an iron broom. This gun had hung on the pitch-black gable in their house for so long that he had learned the mystery of its workings as if by revelation. Two days before, when he took it down and rubbed it clean of the rust which pocked its surface, he was actually completely at ease with it.

The wild ducks were here. At first they circled a hundred metres up in the air, wings beating. They dived and climbed, merged, then scattered again, hurtling down from all directions to skim across the sparkling surface of the reddened water. He got to his knees, holding his breath, eyes glued to the circle upon circle of purple radiance. Gently he edged the barrel of the gun through the gap in the sorghum stalks, heart pounding crazily. The wild ducks were still whirling around in circles of ever-changing size; it was almost as if the water-flats were spinning with them. Several times, some of the green-feathered drakes almost flew straight into the muzzle of his gun; he caught a glimpse of their pale green beaks and the gleam of cunning in their black eyes. The sun had grown wider and flatter still, turning black around the edges, its centre still like molten iron, crackling and spitting sparks.

The ducks suddenly started calling, the "quack quack quack" of the drakes merging with the "quack quack quack" of the females in a great cacophony. He knew they were about to land—after observing them minutely for a dozen days now he knew they always cried out just before they landed. It was only a few moments since their silhouettes had first appeared in the sky, but already he felt as if an extremely long time had passed; the violent cramps in his stomach reminded him again of his hunger. At last the ducks descended, only extending their purple legs and stretching their wings out flat when they were almost on the ground. Their snowy tails fluffed out like feathery fans, they hit the ground at such speed that the momentum made them stagger a couple of paces. Suddenly the mud was no longer brown: countless suns shimmered in the ducks' brilliant plumage as the entire flock waddled to and fro, carrying the sunlight with it.

Stealthily he raised the gun, rested the butt on his shoulder, and trained the muzzle on the increasingly dense pack of ducks. Another piece had vanished from the sun, which looked distorted, bizarre. Some of the wild ducks had settled on the ground, some were standing, some flew a little way then landed again. It's time, he thought, I should open fire, but he didn't do it. As he ran his hand over the trigger he suddenly realized his great disadvantage, recalling with a sense of pain his index finger: two of the joints were missing, the last one alone remained, a gnarled tree stump squatting between his thumb and his middle finger.

He was only six years old when his mother came back from his father's funeral, dressed in mourning—a long white cotton gown with a hempen cord tied around the waist, her hair flowing loose. Her eyelids were so swollen they were transparent, her eyes merely narrow slits from which her tear-stained, darkling gaze flashed out. She called out his name: "Dasuo, come here." He approached her with trepidation. She grabbed hold of his hand and gulped twice, craning her neck as though trying to swallow something hard. "Dasuo, your dad's died, do you realize that?" she said. He nodded, and heard her carry on, "Your dad's died. When you die you can never come back to life, do you realize that?" He gazed perplexedly at her, nodding energetically all the while. "You know how your dad died?" she asked. "He was shot with this gun; this gun was handed down from your grandmother. You're never to touch it: I'm going to hang it on the wall; you're going to look at it every day. And when you look at it you should think of your father, and study hard so you can live a decent life and bring a bit of credit to your ancestors." He wasn't sure how well he understood his mum's words, but he carried on nodding energetically.

And so the gun hung in their house on the gable, which was stained black and shiny by the smoke of decades. Every day he saw it. Later, when he went up from first to second grade, his mum hung a paraffin lamp on the gable every evening to give him enough light to study by. Whenever he saw the black characters in the books his head started spinning, and he couldn't help thinking of the gun and the story behind it. The wind off the desolate plain seeped through the lattice window, buffeting the flames in the oil lamp; the flames looked like the head of a writing brush, with wisps of black smoke shimmering at its tip. Though he appeared intent on his books, he was always aware of the spirit of the gun; he even seemed to hear it clicking. He felt like you do when you see a snake—wanting to look but scared at the same time. The gun hung there, barrel pointing down, butt upwards, a gloomy black glow emanating from its body. The powder-horn hung alongside, tangled up with it, its slender waist resting against the hammer. It was red-gold in colour, its big end facing downwards, its small end upwards. How high the gun and the powder-horn hung, how beautiful they looked hanging there—an ancient gun and an ancient powder-horn hanging on an ancient gable, tormenting his soul.

One evening he climbed up on a high stool and took the gun and the powder-horn down. Holding them up to the lamp-light, he inspected them carefully; the leaden weight of the gun in his hands brought him an acute sense of grief. Just at this moment, his mum walked in from the other room. She was not yet forty, but her hair was already grey, and she said: "Dasuo, what are you doing?" He just stood there blankly, the gun in one hand and the powder-horn in the other. "Where did you come in your class exams?" she asked him. "Second from bottom," he replied. "You good-for-nothing! Hang that gun back up!" He replied stubbornly, "No, I want to go and kill . . ." His mum slapped him round the face and said, "Hang it up. The only thing you're going to do is get on with your studies, and don't you forget it." He hung the gun on the wall. His mum went over to the stove, picked up a chopper and told him calmly, "Hold out your index finger." He stretched it out obediently. She pressed the finger onto the edge of the *kang*;[2] he began to squirm with fear. "Don't move," she told him. "Now remember this, you're never to touch that gun again." She raised the chopper . . . it fell in a flash of cold steel, a violent jolt surged from his fingertips up to his shoulders, his vertebrae arched with the strain. Blood oozed slowly from the severed finger. His mother was weeping as she staunched the wound with a handful of lime . . .

As he looked at the stub of his finger with its single joint, his nose began to twitch. How many days had he gone without meat now? Couldn't remember

2. A type of bed found in northern China that is heated with fire from below.

exactly; but he could distinctly remember all the meat he had eaten in the past. He seemed never to have eaten his fill of meat. The first time he caught sight of those plump wild ducks, meat was the first thing he thought of. The next thing he thought of was the gun—he had come out in goose-pimples all over as he recalled how his mum had chopped off his finger at the joint because of it. But in the end, yesterday afternoon, he had taken the gun down. Its body was covered in dust, as thick as a coin, and it was enmeshed from top to bottom in a tangle of spider's webs. The leather strap, chewed through by insects, snapped as soon as he touched it. There was still a lot of gunpowder in the horn—when he poured it out to dry he discovered a golden percussion cap. He picked up this single percussion cap, hands trembling with excitement. The first thing that came into his mind was his father: he felt how lucky he was, for where would you get one of these percussion caps nowadays? . . . I haven't got any money, even if I had some I still wouldn't be able to get a meat coupon;[3] I'm thick, even if I wasn't I still wouldn't get a chance to go to school, and anyway what use would it be? Looking at the stump of his finger, he tried to console himself. His mum had only chopped off the tip, but afterwards the wound had turned septic and he had lost another section—hence its present state. As he thought of all these things, he became filled with hatred for this flock of wild ducks with all their fine feathers. I'm going to kill you, kill the lot of you if it's the last thing I do! Then I'll eat you, chew your bones to a pulp and swallow them down. He imagined how crispy and aromatic their bones must be. He stretched his middle finger into the trigger guard.

Still he didn't pull the trigger. This was because another gaggle of wild ducks was swirling down from the sky in another spinning cloud of colour. There was a great commotion among the ducks on the sand-bar. Some stamped their feet, some took off; it was hard to tell whether they were expressing welcome or anger towards their fellows. He gazed irritably at the flurry of birds and gently withdrew the gun. The sun had grown pointed like a sweet potato, its rays now dark green and brilliant purple. The ducks' activity startled the gold-hooped dragonfly into flight. It skimmed low across the surface of the water and came to rest on his hide, its six legs clamped fast to a sorghum leaf, its long golden-hooped tail dangling down. He saw the two bright beads of light in its eyes. The flock of wild ducks was gradually regrouping and growing calmer. On the water's surface, shattered by their claws, concentric ripples spread out, creating new ripples where they collided.

The two flocks of ducks had merged into one. If I had a big net, he thought, and suddenly flung it over them . . . but he knew he had no net, just a gun. Gingerly he removed the percussion cap, pulled out the cotton wool stopper, and poured three more measures of gunpowder and three more measures of shot into the muzzle . . . Once more he took aim at the ducks, his heart filled with a primitive blood-lust . . . Such a huge flock of ducks, such a slender gun barrel . . . He edged stealthily back once more and poured another two cylinders of gunpowder into the muzzle, then plugged it again. The barrel was almost full now, and when he lifted the gun up he felt how heavy it was. His trembling middle finger pressed on the trigger—at the split second of firing he closed his eyes.

3. A ration coupon required for purchasing basic items in Communist China under Mao Zedong (ruled 1949–76).

The head of the hammer struck the golden percussion cap with a click, but no shot rang out. The rings on the water's surface seemed to be slowly contracting; the purple vapour which hung between heaven and earth was denser than ever, the red glow fading fast, the brightness of the water's surface undiminished but gradually assuming a deeper hue. Clustered together, the ducks looked so solid, beautiful, warm, their soft, clean plumage dazzling. Their cunning eyes seemed to be staring disdainfully at the muzzle of his gun, as if in mockery of his impotence. He took out the percussion cap, glancing at the mark left on the firing plate by the hammer. A warm breath of putrid air wafted over from the flock of ducks; their bodies gave off a soft, smooth sound as they rubbed against each other. He replaced the percussion cap, not believing that this could really have happened. Dad, Granny, hadn't it fired for them at the first attempt? It was ten or more years since his dad died, but his story was still common currency in the village. He could dimly recall a very tall man with a pitted face and yellow whiskers.

His dad's story had been so widely repeated that it had already taken on the status of a legend among the villagers: he had only to close his eyes for it to unfold in all its detail. It began on the grey dirt road to the fields, with his dad setting out with a throng of hard-headed peasants to sow the sorghum, a heavy wooden seed-drill across his shoulders. The road was lined with mulberry trees, their out-stretched leaves as big as copper coins. Birds were chattering; the grass along the roadside was very green. The water in the ditches lay deep, patches of frogspawn shimmered on the pale yellow reeds. Dad was panting noisily under the weight of the seed-drill, when a bicycle suddenly shot out of nowhere and crashed sidelong into him. He staggered a few paces but didn't fall over, unlike the bicycle which did. Dad flung down his seed-drill, picked up the bicycle, then picked up its rider. The latter was a short-arsed individual; as soon as he tried to walk his knee-joints began cracking. Dad greeted him respectfully, Officer Liu.

Officer Liu said: Have you gone blind, you dog?

Dad said: Yes, the dog is blind, don't be angry sir.

Liu: You dare to insult me? You sonofabitch bastard!

Dad: Officer, it was you who bumped into me.

Liu: Up yours!

Dad: Don't swear, sir, it was you who bumped into me.

Liu: x x x x.

Dad: You're being unreasonable, sir. Even in the old society there were honest officials who listened to reason.

Liu: What, are you saying the New Society[4] is worse than the old society?

Dad: I never said that.

Liu: Counter-revolutionary! Renegade! I'll blow you away! Officer Liu pulled a Mauser[5] from his waistband and pointed the gaping black muzzle at dad's chest.

Dad: I haven't done anything to deserve the death penalty.

Liu: Near as damn it you have.

Dad: Go on then, shoot me.

Liu: I didn't bring any bullets.

Dad: Fuck off then!

4. Communist society, officially egalitarian.

5. A German-made pistol.

Liu: Maybe I can't shoot you, but there's nothing to stop me beating you up.

Officer Liu leapt at Dad like an arrow, knees cracking, and stabbed straight at the bridge of his nose with the long barrel of the pistol. Black blood began to trickle slowly from Dad's nostrils. The peasants pulled him away, and some of the older ones tried to placate Officer Liu. Officer Liu said angrily: I'll let you off this once. Dad was standing to one side, wiping away the blood with his fingers; he lifted them up and inspected them carefully. Liu said: That'll teach you some respect.

Dad: My friends, you all saw it, you'll be my witnesses—He wiped his face vigorously a couple of times, it was covered in blood—Old Liu, fuck your ancestors to the eighth generation.

As Dad stomped towards him, Old Liu raised his gun, and shouted: Come any nearer and I'll shoot. Dad said: You won't get a peep out of that gun. Dad seized Old Liu's wrist, wrested the gun away from him and flung it viciously into the ditch, sending spray flying high into the air. Clasping Old Liu by the scruff of the neck, he shook him backwards and forwards for a moment, then took aim at his buttocks and gave them a gentle kick. Officer Liu plunged head-first into the ditch, buttocks skywards; his head lodged in the sludge and his legs splashed noisily in the water. The crowd of onlookers turned pale; some edged away, others rushed down into the ditch to drag the officer out. One old man said to Dad: Quick, nephew, run for it! Dad said: Fourth uncle, we'll meet again on the road to the yellow springs.[6] And he strode off towards home.

Officer Liu was extracted by the locals, weeping and wailing like a baby. He begged the crowd to find his gun for him, and at least a dozen of them went down into the ditch. Their searching hands stirred up plenty of mud, but they couldn't find the gun.

Dad felt among the dust on the beam and pulled down a long oil-paper sack, from which he withdrew a long, twisted gun. His eyes were glistening with tears. You mean we've still got a gun in the house? Mum asked him in astonishment. Dad said: Haven't you heard how my mum shot my dad? This was the gun she used. Mum was wide-eyed with fear. Get rid of it quick, she said. Dad said: No. Mum said: What are you going to do? Dad said: Kill someone. He now took down a powder-horn with a narrow waist, and a tin box, and deftly filled the gun with powder and shot. Dad said: Make sure that Dasuo studies hard. Make sure that he looks at this gun every day, just looks, mind, you're not to let him touch it. Have you got that? Mum said: Are you crazy? Dad pointed the gun at her: Get back!

Dad walked into the pear-orchard. The blossom on the trees was like a layer of snow. He hung the gun from a tree, muzzle downwards, and tied a thin piece of string to the hammer. Then he lay on his back on the ground and put the muzzle into his mouth. Eyes wide, he gazed at the golden bees and gave a sharp tug on the string. Pear blossom swirled down like snowflakes. A few bees fell to the ground, dead.[7]

He pulled the trigger again, but still there was no report. He sat down, disheartened. The sun lay across the horizon like a doughnut, its colour the same deep-

6. The underworld, where souls go after the body dies.

7. There is a long tradition in China of suicide as a form of political protest.

fried golden brown. The pool had shrunk even smaller, the fringes of the plain grew even hazier, the white half-moon was already visible. In the distance, on a clump of reeds, insects sparkled with a green light. The ducks tucked their beaks under their wings and gazed mockingly at him. They were so close to him, getting even closer now as the sky grew darker. His stomach protested bitterly; countless roast ducks, dripping with oil, flashed before his eyes. He pulled the trigger again and again, until the percussion cap was knocked out of shape by the hammer and embedded itself inextricably in the groove. He slumped disconsolately against the hide, like an animal which had just been filleted; the sorghum stalks cracked beneath him. The wild ducks paid not the slightest heed to the noise; they were silent, motionless, a heap of dappled cobble-stones. The sun disappeared, taking with it all the reds and greens, all shades of colour, leaving a world returned to its original state of grey and white. The crickets and cicadas beat their wings, their chirring merging into a constant drone. On the verge of tears, he stared up at the alfalfa-coloured vault of the sky, casting a sidelong glance, filled with hatred, at the gun. Was this decrepit old gun really the same one? Could such a foul-looking old wreck really have such an extraordinary history?

But when Wang Laoka started telling his tales of the old days, it really was as if they were unfolding before the villagers' eyes, and so everyone young and old loved to listen to him talking. Wang Laoka told them:

In the days of the Republic[8] none of the three counties controlled these parts—there were more bandits round here than hairs on a cow's back; men, women, they'd all turn violent at the drop of a hat, they'd kill a man as calmly as slicing a melon. Have you heard the story of Dasuo here's granny? Well, Dasuo's grandad was a compulsive gambler who lived off Dasuo's granny—that little woman was tough, she built up a home from nothing, all by herself, and that ain't easy for a woman. She sweated her guts out for three years and managed to buy a few dozen hectares of land, even a couple of horses. And what a beauty she was, Dasuo's granny, people called her "the queen of the eight villages". Lovely pointed bound feet she had, a fringe like a curtain of black silk.[9] To protect her house and home she swapped a stone and two pecks of grain for a gun. Now this gun had a long, long barrel and a mahogany butt, and they say that in the dead of night the hammer used to start clicking. She used to sling that gun across her back and ride off into the fields on her big horse to hunt foxes. A dead-shot she was—always shot 'em right up the arse. But then she got sick, a terrible thing, she was in a fever for seven whole weeks of seven whole days. Dasuo's grandad saw his chance—off he went roistering with whores and gambling to his heart's content: he lost all their land, even lost those two fine steeds. When the winner came to collect the horses, Dasuo's granny was lying on the *kang*, gasping for breath. Dasuo's dad was just a lad of five or six then, and when he saw that some people were trying to lead their horses away, he yelled: Mum, someone's taking the horses! The second she heard this, Dasuo's granny rolled straight off the *kang*, grabbed the gun from the wall, and dragged herself painfully into the courtyard. And what right have you to take out the horses, pray? she shouted. The two fellers leading the horses knew that this woman took no prisoners, so they said: Your man lost

8. The Republic of China (1912–49), before the Communist revolution.
9. Until the early 20th century, the Chinese bound the feet of young girls so that they would not grow to full size; the practice caused severe deformity.

these horses to our boss, lady. She said: Since that's the case, might I trouble you two brothers to bring my man to see me, there's something I'd like to say to him. Dasuo's grandad—his name was Santao—was so afraid of his wife he was skulking outside the door, too scared to come in. But when he heard her shouting he knew it was too late to chicken out. He plucked up courage, did his best to look tough, marched into the courtyard, thrust out his chest and said: Hot today, isn't it. Dasuo's granny smiled and said: You lost the horses, didn't you? Santao said: Sure did. She said: So, you lost the horses, what are you going to lose next? Santao said: I'm going to lose you. She said: Good old Santao. Fate must bring enemies together, it was really my luck to marry you. You've lost my horses, lost my land, forty-nine days I've been lying here sick and you haven't so much as brought me a bowl of water. And now you think you can lose me—I reckon I'd rather lose you first. On this day next year, Santao, I'll bring the child to your grave and burn paper money for you . . . The words were hardly out of her mouth when there was a great boom; the courtyard filled with a red flash . . . and his grandad was dead . . .

When he heard this story his dad was still alive. He asked his dad where the gun was, but his dad screamed furiously at him: You get the hell out of here.

The half-moon was becoming brighter, fireflies flitted unhurriedly, tracing a series of green-tinted arcs across his face. The pool had assumed a sombre, dim, steely-grey hue, but the sky was not yet completely black—he could still make out the pale green eyes of the gold-hooped dragonflies. The chirring of the insects came in bursts, each close on the heels of the last. The damp air congealed and wafted heavenwards. He wasn't watching the flock of ducks any more, he was thinking only about eating duck, again feeling the sharp contractions in his stomach. The image of the hunter with dead ducks slung all around his body became superimposed on the image of the woman warrior on horseback, her gun slung over her shoulder; at last they merged with that of the decent man under a covering of pear blossoms.

The sun had finally gone out. All that remained was a strip of fading golden warmth on the western horizon. The tip of the half-moon was rising in the south-west, scattering a tender feeling as soft as water. Mist rose from the pool like so many clumps of vegetation, the wild ducks shimmered in and out of sight through the gaps in the mist, and the splashing of big fish echoed from the water. He stood up, as if drunk or in a trance, and flexed his stiff, numb joints. He strapped on the powder-horn, slung the gun over his shoulder and strode out of the hide. Why doesn't anything happen when I pull the trigger? He swung the gun down, cradled it in his arms and stared at it. It shimmered with a blue glow in the moonlight. Why don't you fire? he thought. He cocked the hammer and casually pulled the trigger.

The low, rumbling explosion rolled in waves across the autumn fields and a ball of red light lit up the water-flats and the wild ducks. Shreds of iron and shards of wood hurtled through the air; the ducks took off in startled flight. He toppled slowly to the ground, trying with all his strength to open his eyes. He seemed to see the ducks floating down around him like rocks, falling onto his body, piling up into a great mound, pressing down on him so that it became difficult to breathe.

1985

YU HUA
born 1960

Since I grew up in a time and a place where there were no books, it's hard to say just how I began to read. . . . Since the bulk of the library's holdings had perished in all the Red Guard book burning, there was very little left to read. The fiction shelf featured only twenty-odd titles, all so-called socialist revolutionary literature of the home-grown variety. . . . This kind of reading has left no traces on my life, for in these books I encountered neither emotions nor characters nor even stories. All I found was grindingly dull accounts of class struggle. This did not stop me from reading each book through to the end, because my life at the time was even more grindingly dull.

Even though Yu Hua's early reading and writing experiences were limited to socialist propaganda literature and campaign posters, he has become a star of China's contemporary literary scene, combining the roles of star author and whimsical critic of China's current politics and society. His graphic descriptions of violence are notorious; his critical views of China's recent history under the rule of the Communist Party, well known; and his taste for the work of fate in people's lives—rise and fall, weakness and suffering, aging, death and misery—has produced memorable works about the vagaries of the human condition.

Yu Hua was born in the southeastern city of Hangzhou, now a bustling city with a thriving art and literary scene. He was six years old when the Cultural Revolution broke out; the memories of the denunciations and persecutions of political enemies, the sheer violence of those years, have haunted his life's work. They also sparked his interest in foreign novels, back then considered "poisonous weeds," as he puts it. In one memorable all-night marathon session, he feverishly copied out a translation of Alexandre Dumas' romantic *The Lady of the Camellias* with a classmate, just to discover the next day that during the late night hour their careless handwriting had become illegible. But the experience taught him what it meant to become "hooked" by a literary work, completely absorbed by its characters, their emotions, their worlds.

While developing his voice as a writer and sending pieces to literary magazines, Yu Hua supported himself for a number of years as a dentist. After many rejections, a literary magazine in Beijing accepted a few of his stories for publication and invited him for a tour of the grand city. This launched him on a career as one of today's most popular Mainland Chinese writers. His breakthrough to world fame came with his novel *To Live* (1993), a parable of China's tragic history in the twentieth century that traces the life of one man from the civil war of the mid twentieth century through communist rule. When the well-known film director Zhang Yimou made the novel into a film that was banned in China, Yu Hua became famous overnight.

Yu Hua is not an explicit dissident like the conceptual artist Ai Weiwei, who draws the world's attention with his ingenious multimedia art projects, or the writer Liao Yiwu, who recently went into exile in Germany. But he speaks out on issues of political concern, as in *China in Ten Words* (2011), an essay collection that allows us to eavesdrop on Yu Hua's thoughts about such concepts as "the people," "leader," "reading," "writing," "revolution," "grassroots," or "bamboozle." Yu Hua decided to publish it abroad, which might imply a critique of the regime in ways that are not immediately visible in his domestic bestsellers. In recent years Yu Hua has also appeared as a contributing op-ed writer in the *New York Times*, writing critically on issues of pollution, abuses during the Cultural Revolution, China's nouveau riche, and the need for democratic elections. On this last topic, he writes, "I am fifty-four, but have never in my life seen an election ballot. 'Have you seen one?' I ask people, out of curiosity. Like me, most of them have no idea what a ballot looks like and have only seen pictures on television of people completely unknown to them clutching a ballot and voting on their behalf." Yu Hua is also an open critic of the mainland's literary scene. He laments the lack of literary journals where writers can receive honest feedback, and the absence of a blind peer-review system that would hone writers' skills and eventually allow for brilliant work to emerge. He scorns the practice of buying favorable reviews and churning out repetitive work.

Graphic description of violence and cruelty is a recurrent feature of Yu Hua's novels and stories, beginning in the 1980s. He tells us that at the time he was plagued by nightmares and the memory of witnessing an execution at close range during the Cultural Revolution, when he saw a victim's head blown open by a bullet. In *To Live* he depicts the violence of China's tragic recent history, the brutality of political change, human greed, and willful cruelty, but also human helplessness gnawing bite by bite at the lives of one man and his family.

In the story selected here, "On the Road at Eighteen," first published in 1986, we see flashes of this kind of brutality as well: we have to watch as our young, idealistic protagonist is severely beaten and humiliated—but the real cruelty lies in the outrageous behavior of the bystanders. The story puts us in the shoes of an eighteen-year-old whose father sends him off into the wide world on the birthday marking the beginning of his adult life. The fresh gaze of our enthusiastic protagonist on a world full of excitement and irresistible novelty is contagious. We are venturing out with him into his very real "dream world," where everything—humans, mountains, trucks—is full of life. The bliss of hungering for new experiences tinges every perception; only an increasing worry over finding a new place to stay, "a home," distracts the young man from his happiness. He does finally find a place to stay the night, but not where and how the reader would expect it.

The story moves us through an archetypal landscape with vaguely surreal characters. Although this is the story of a road trip, nobody seems to know or care about where they are going. Why would the truck driver, who gives the young man a ride, not care that his apples are stolen by peasants who loot his fruit baskets and dismember the truck for parts? And why would he steal the—symbolically red—backpack of the young man, which his father had given him and which contains his entire livelihood? The strange, unexplained actions of these characters suggest an allegorical reading of the story as a parable of Chinese society in the unruly 1980s, when Deng Xiaoping, China's new political leader, introduced economic reforms that launched China on the path towards its current status as a global economic powerhouse. Despite the spirit of Deng Xiaoping's newly implemented "Four Modernizations" (in agriculture, industry, national defense, and science and technology), the old rhetoric of the socialist revolution remained, while a new economically privileged class emerged that robbed the peasants and simple folk of the fruits of their labor. Discontentment with the new political and social conditions eventually erupted in the pro-democracy movement in June 1989, three years after the publication of this story. The red back pack of socialist idealism, a truck driver who doesn't care about the theft of his fruit and is actually a thief himself, an endless road with, in the end, a wrecked and bleeding truck as a new "home"—Yu Hua's suggestive narrative does not deliver any of this as an explicit allegory. And yet, the enthusiastic reception of this story by the Chinese reading public at the time suggests that it struck a chord and encouraged a political reading. Who was it that stole the idealism of the Chinese people?

On the Road at Eighteen[1]

The asphalt road rolls up and down like it's pasted on top of ocean waves. Walking down this little highway in the mountains, I'm like a boat. This year, I turned eighteen. The few brownish whiskers that have sprouted on my chin flutter in the breeze. They've only just taken up residence on my chin, so I really treasure them. I've spent the whole day walking down the road, and I've already seen lots of mountains and lots of clouds. Every one of the mountains and every one of the clouds made me think of people I know. I shouted out each of their nicknames as I walked by. So even though I've walked all day, I'm not tired, not at all. I walked through the morning, now it's the tail end of the afternoon, and it won't be long until I see the tip of dusk. But I haven't found an inn.

I've encountered quite a few people along the road, but none of them has known where the road goes or whether there's an inn there. They all tell me: "Keep walking. You'll see when you get there." I think what everyone said was just terrific. I really am just seeing when I get there. But I haven't found an inn. I feel like I should be worried about that.

I think it's weird that I've walked all day and only seen one car. That was around noon, when I'd just begun to think about hitchhiking. But all I was doing was thinking about hitchhiking. I hadn't started to worry about finding an inn—I was only thinking about how amazing it would be to get a lift from someone. I stood by the side of the road waving at the car, trying my best to look casual. But the driver hardly even looked at me. The car or the driver. They hardly even looked at me. All they fucking did was drive right by. So I ran, chasing the car as fast as I could, just for fun, because I still hadn't started to worry about finding an inn. I ran until the car had disappeared, and then I laughed at myself, but I discovered that laughing too hard made it difficult to breathe, so I stopped. After that I kept walking, happy and excited, except that I started to regret that I hadn't picked up a rock before I started waving at the car.

Now I really want a lift, because dusk is about to fall and I can't get that inn out of my goddamned head. But there haven't been any cars all afternoon. If a car came now, I think I could make it stop. I'd lie down in the middle of the road,

1. Translated by Andrew F. Jones.

and I'm willing to bet that any car would come to a screeching halt before it got to my head. But I don't even hear the rumble of an engine, let alone see a car. Now I'm just going to have to keep walking and see when I get there. Not bad at all: keep walking and see when you get there.

The road rolls up and down from hill to valley, and the hills tempt me every time, because before I charge up to the top, I think I'll see an inn on the other side. But each time I charge up the slope, all I see is another hill in the distance, with a depressing trough in between. And still I charge up each hill as if my life depended on it. And now I'm charging up another one, but this time I see it. Not an inn, but a truck. The truck is pointed toward me, stalled in the middle of the highway in a gully between two hills. I can see the driver's ass pointing skyward and, behind it, all the colors of the approaching sunset. I can't see the driver's head because it's stuffed under the hood. The truck's hood slants up into the air like an upside-down lip. The back of the truck is piled full of big wicker baskets. I'm thinking that they definitely must be packed with some kind of fruit. Of course, bananas would be best of all. There are probably some in the cab too, so when I hop in, I can eat a few. And I don't really care if the truck's going in the opposite direction as me. I need to find an inn, and if there's no inn, I need a truck. And the truck's right here in front of me.

Elated, I run down to the truck and say, "Hi!"

The driver doesn't seem to have heard me. He's still fiddling with something under the hood.

"Want a smoke?"

Only now does he pull his head out from under the hood, stretch out a black, grimy hand, and take the cigarette between his fingers. I rush to give him a light, and he sucks several mouthfuls of smoke into his mouth before stuffing his head back under the hood.

I'm satisfied. Since he accepted the smoke, that means he has to give me a lift. So I wander around to the back of the truck to investigate what's in the wicker baskets. But they're covered, and I can't see, so I sniff. I smell the fragrance of apples. And I think: Apples aren't too bad either.

In just a little bit, he's done repairing the truck, and he jumps down from the hood. I rush over and say, "Hey, I need a ride." What I don't expect is that he gives me a hard shove with those grimy hands and barks, "Go away!"

I'm so angry I'm speechless, but he just swings on over to the driver's side, opens the door, slides into the cab, and starts the engine. I know that if I blow this opportunity, I'll never get another one. I know I should not just give up. So I run over to the other side, open the door and hop in. I'm ready to fight if necessary. I turn to him and yell: "Then give me back my cigarette!" The truck's already started to move by now.

He turns to look at me with a big, friendly smile and asks, "Where you headed?"

I'm bewildered by this turnaround. I say, "Doesn't matter. Wherever."

He asks me very nicely, "Want an apple?" He's still glancing over at me.

"That goes without saying."

"Go get one from the back."

How am I supposed to climb out of the cab to the back of the truck when he's driving so fast? So I say, "Forget it."

He says, "Go get one." He's still looking at me.

I say, "Stop staring at me. There's no road on my face."

With this, he twists his eyes back onto the highway.

The truck's driving back in the direction I just came from; I'm sitting comfortably in the cab, looking out the window and chatting with the driver. By now we're already the best of friends. I've found out that he's a private entrepreneur. It's his own truck. The apples are his too. I hear change jingling in his pockets. I ask him, "Where are you going?"

He says, "I just keep driving and see when I get there."

It sounds just like what everyone else said. That's so nice. I feel closer to him. I want everything I see outside the window to be just as close, just as familiar, and soon all those hills and clouds start to bring more friends to mind, so I shout out their nicknames as we drive by.

Now I'm not crying out for an inn anymore. What with the truck, the driver, the seat in the cab, I'm completely at peace. I don't know where the truck's going, and neither does he. Anyway, it doesn't matter, because all we have to do is keep driving, and we'll see when we get there.

But the truck broke down. By that time, we were as close as friends can be. My arm was draped over his shoulder and his over mine. He was telling me about his love life, and right when he'd got to the part about how it felt the first time he held a woman's body in his arms, the truck broke down. The truck was climbing up a hill when it broke down. All of a sudden the squeal of the engine went quiet like a pig right after it's been slaughtered. So he jumped out of the truck, climbed onto the hood, opened up that upside-down lip, and stuffed his head back under it. I couldn't see his ass. But I could hear the sound of him fiddling with the engine.

After a while, he pulled his head out from under the hood and slammed it shut. His hands were even blacker than before. He wiped them on his pants, wiped again, jumped down, and walked back to the cab.

"Is it fixed?" I asked.

"It's shot. There's no way to fix it."

I thought that over and finally asked, "Now what do we do?"

"Wait and see," he said, nonchalantly.

I was sitting in the cab wondering what to do. Then I started to think about finding an inn again. The sun was just falling behind the mountains, and the hazy dusk clouds looked like billows of steam. The notion of an inn stole back into my head and began to swell until my mind was stuffed full of it. By then, I didn't even have a mind. An inn was growing where my mind used to be.

At that point, the driver started doing the official morning calisthenics that they always play on the radio, right there in the middle of the highway. He went from the first exercise to the last without missing a beat. When he was finished, he started to jog circles around the truck. Maybe he had been sitting too long in the driver's seat and needed some exercise. Watching him moving from my vantage point inside the truck, I couldn't sit still either, so I opened the door and jumped out. But I didn't do calisthenics or jog in place. I was thinking about an inn and an inn and an inn.

Just then, I noticed five people rolling down the hill on bicycles. Each bike had a carrying pole fastened to the back with two big baskets on either end. I thought they were probably local peasants on their way back from selling vegetables at market. I was delighted to see people riding by, so I welcomed them with a big, "Hi!" They rode up beside me and dismounted. Excited, I greeted them and asked, "Is there an inn around here?"

Instead of responding they asked me, "What's in the truck?"

I said, "Apples."

All five of them pushed their bikes over to the side of the truck. Two of them climbed onto the back, picked up about ten baskets full of apples, and passed them upside down to the ones below, who proceeded to tear open the plastic covering the top of the wicker and pour the apples into their own baskets. I was dumbstruck. When I finally realized exactly what was going on, I made for them and asked, "Just what do you think you're doing?"

None of them paid the slightest bit of attention to me. They continued to pour the apples. I tried to grab hold of someone's arm and screamed, "They're stealing all the apples!" A fist came crashing into my nose, and I landed several feet away. I staggered up, rubbed my nose. It felt soft and sticky, like it wasn't stuck to my face anymore but only dangling from it. Blood was flowing like tears from a broken heart. When I looked up to see which of them had hit me, they were already astride their bikes, riding away.

The driver was taking a walk, lips curling out as he sucked in deep draughts of air. He had probably lost his breath running. He didn't seem to be at all aware of what had just happened. I yelled toward him, "They stole your apples!" But he kept on walking without paying any attention to what I had yelled. I really wanted to run over and punch him so hard that his nose would be left dangling too. I ran over and screamed into his ear, "They stole your apples." Only then did he turn to look at me, and I realized that his face was getting happier and happier the longer he looked at my nose.

At that point, yet another group of bicycles descended down the slope. Each bike had two big baskets fastened to the back. There were even a few children among the riders. They swarmed by me and surrounded the truck. A lot of people climbed onto the back, and the wicker baskets flew faster than I could count them. Apples poured out of broken baskets like blood out of my nose. They stuffed apples into their own baskets as if they were possessed. In just a few seconds, all the apples in the truck had been lowered to the ground. Then a few motorized tractor carts chugged down the hill and stopped next to the truck. A few big men dismounted and started to stuff apples into the carts. One by one, the empty wicker baskets were tossed to the side. The ground was covered with rolling apples, and the peasants scrabbled on their hands and knees like ants to pick them all up.

It was at that point that I rushed into their midst, risking life and limb, and cursed them: "Thieves!" I started swinging. My attack was met with countless fists and feet. It seemed like every part of my body got hit at the same time. I climbed back up off the ground. A few children began to hurl apples at me. The apples broke apart on my head, but my head didn't break. Just as I was about to rush the kids, a foot came crashing into my waist. I wanted to cry, but when I opened my mouth, nothing came out. There was nothing to do but fall to the ground and watch them steal the apples. I started to look around for the driver. He was standing a good distance away, looking right at me, and laughing as hard as he could. Just so I knew that I looked even better now than I had with a bloody nose.

I didn't even have the strength for anger. All I could do was gaze out at everything that was making me so angry. And what made me the angriest of all was the driver.

Another wave of bicycles and tractors rolled down the hill and threw themselves into the disaster area. There were fewer and fewer apples rolling on the ground. A few people left. A few more arrived. The ones who had arrived too late for apples began to busy themselves with the truck. I saw them remove the window glass, strip the tires, pry away the planks that covered the truck bed. Without its tires, the truck obviously felt really low, because it sank to the ground. A few children began to gather the wicker baskets that had been tossed to the side a moment before. As the road got cleaner and cleaner, there were fewer and fewer people. But all I could do was watch, because I didn't even have the strength for anger. I sat on the ground without moving, letting my eyes wander back and forth between the driver and the thieves.

Now there's nothing left but a single tractor parked beside the sunken truck. Someone's looking around to see if there's anything left to take. He looks for a while and then hops on his tractor and starts the engine.

The truck driver hops onto the back of the tractor and looks back toward me, laughing. He's holding my red backpack in his hand. He's stealing my backpack. My clothes and my money are in the backpack. And food and books. But he's stealing my backpack.

I'm watching the tractor climb back up the slope. It disappears over the crest. I can still hear the rumble of its engine, but soon I can't even hear that. All of a sudden, everything's quiet, and the sky starts to get really dark. I'm still sitting on the ground. I'm hungry, and I'm cold, but there's nothing left.

I sit there for a long time before I slowly stand up. It isn't easy because my whole body aches like crazy every time I move, but still I stand up and limp over to the truck. The truck looks miserable, battered. I know I've been battered too.

The sky's black now. There's nothing here. Just a battered truck and battered me. I'm looking at the truck, immeasurably sad, and the truck's looking at me, immeasurably sad. I reach out to stroke it. It's cold all over. The wind starts to blow, a strong wind, and the sound of the wind rustling the trees in the mountains is like ocean waves. The sound terrifies me so much that my body gets as cold as the truck's.

I open the door and hop in. I'm comforted by the fact that they didn't pry away the seat. I lie down in the cab. I smell leaking gas and think of the smell of the blood that leaked out of me. The wind's getting stronger and stronger, but I feel a little warmer lying on the seat. I think that even though the truck's been battered, its heart is still intact, still warm. I know that my heart's warm too. I was looking for an inn, and I never thought I'd find you here.

I lie inside the heart of the truck, remembering that clear warm afternoon. The sunlight was so pretty. I remember that I was outside enjoying myself in the sunshine for a long time, and when I got home I saw my dad through the window packing things into a red backpack. I leaned against the window frame and asked, "Dad, are you going on a trip?"

He turned and very gently said, "No, I'm letting you go on a trip."

"Letting me go on a trip?"

"That's right. You're eighteen now, and it's time you saw a little of the outside world."

Later I slipped that pretty red backpack onto my back. Dad patted my head from behind, just like you would pat a horse's rump. Then I gladly made for the door and excitedly galloped out of the house, as happy as a horse.

1986

NGUYEN HUY THIEP

born 1950

Nguyen Huy Thiep introduced a fresh style into modern Vietnamese literature, which had languished for decades under government censorship. Thiep's stories are distinguished by a complex, flexible image of human character: he considers the Vietnamese of today to be mutable, complex, and self-contradictory. Writing in short, cold, clear sentences, Thiep presents a view of a society in transition that, while realistic in its details, has the simplicity and clarity of parable.

Thiep was born in Hanoi in 1950, when Vietnam was still a colony of France. His mother was a peddler who made a living by selling goods from a street cart; she spent periods of time working as an agricultural laborer. Trading was a job that required constant travel, and the boy spent his childhood and adolescence moving from place to place in the rural provinces in the north. Theirs was a hard peasant existence, with money only for bare necessities.

These were especially difficult years for the laboring classes. In 1954 the Ho Chi Minh government instituted a Maoist "land reform" program that redistributed property to loyal party supporters, while conducting purges of people suspected of counterrevolutionary sympathies. The program escalated fear and distrust among the rural poor, who were already struggling under economic crisis. It was also a time of warfare: the Ho Chi Minh government had been fighting to repel the French army since 1946. Only in 1954 did the two sides reach a cease-fire, leading to the country's division between a communist north and a French-occupied, non-communist south. Soon enough, however, the North and South were at war again.

Despite this repressive background, Thiep developed a taste for books and classical learning, enhanced perhaps by a desire, fostered by extensive travels, to understand the even wider world. He enrolled in the National Vietnamese Teachers' College in Hanoi, where he studied history and pursued a personal interest in classical Chinese literature. He also read the nineteenth-century Russian novelists in translation.

In 1970, at the peak of United States involvement in the Vietnam War, Thiep earned his diploma and took a job as a history teacher in Son La Province, in northwest Vietnam. There he was employed for ten years, writing and painting in his spare time. In 1980 he returned to Hanoi with his wife and children, working as an illustrator and in other small jobs. When he was thirty-six, he published his first story, in a major publication: "The Breezes of Hua Tat" (1987), which appeared in *Literature and Art*, the journal of the National Writers Association.

The 1980s were a period of liberalization in Vietnam. The Communist Party had announced that it would give writers and publishers slightly more room for free expression; previously, its official policy had been watchful oversight and censorship. Although Vietnamese writers and publishers hardly greeted the announcement as the start of true freedom of speech, they at least took up subjects and themes they might not have before. The result was a reinvigoration, now called the renovation movement, of Vietnamese literature.

Thiep's renown grew quickly as a powerful voice of social critique. In 1988, two publishers brought out collected editions of his works; the following year a Vietnamese film company produced a cinematic version of "The General Retires." The spirit of free expression was not to last, however. In 1988 the National Writers Association fired the editor of *Literature and Art*, an event that many critics connected with the journal's publication of Thiep's story "Chastity," which portrays one of Vietnam's legendary heroes as a thuggish philanderer. Two years later, as world events were giving communist regimes new reasons to feel threatened, the Vietnamese government declared an end to the looser restrictions that writers and publishers had enjoyed for the past decade. The renovation movement largely dried up.

The renovation movement was in part a reaction against the socialist realism that had pervaded Vietnamese literature since the 1940s. That genre often created characters to represent heroic ideals rather than human psychological truths—to represent "the people" rather than ordinary men and women. Renovation literature sought to correct the balance, replacing the oversized hero with individuals, and replacing sweeping historical narratives with studies of history in the light of its effects on private lives. Thiep belongs to this transition: his stories present a complex vision of humanity in which characters struggle primarily not against vast social forces but against each other and even between conflicting aspects of themselves.

Thiep is widely recognized as the foremost of the renovation writers. Although his stories share the antiheroic commitment of the movement, they are not subordinated to it. He often writes in a hard, coolly literal realism, but many of his stories incorporate surreal and dreamlike elements.

The story selected here, "The General Retires," is Thiep's most famous work. It concerns an old military general who comes home after a lifetime away in service. Yet the society he returns to is quite different from the one he left. The narrator, the general's son, relates the old man's struggle to adjust to a strange world during the period of liberalization, when the communist government was embracing free-market economics. The head of the household is now the son's wife, who earns the main income (through various entrepreneurial schemes) and sees to the family's management. The planning and execution of a funeral, that most traditional of social rites, highlights the way society is fragmenting, with some burial customs retained but many more discarded. Meanwhile, Thiep's portrayal of the household's financial situation represents a potentially dangerous critique of the socialist system: the characters feel the need to supplement their income—presumably because, under socialist policies, they cannot legally earn adequate wages to sustain a family—but the pursuit of the extra money leads the wife to horrific actions, which most of her family accepts.

The narrator describes himself as odd and "old-fashioned"; and while this sense of reserve might position him as judge of the excesses of the other characters, its greater significance, in the real world, is that he has detached himself from contemporary life, abdicating his proper role governing the household. The true measure for the characters' failings, including the son's, is the implied perspective of the old general—who, though rarely in the foreground of the action, nevertheless remains in the reader's sight, a focal point for the story. As a whole, the story presents a harsh double portrait that shows both the unsustainability of the old society and the abominable compromises of the new. Contrasting his writing style with that of a previous generation of writers dominated by socialist realism, Thiep has said: "I try to rely on the ancient Vietnamese literary traditions: idioms, folk-poetry, fairy-tales, narratives written in demotic characters, anonymous Vietnamese verse. I feel that a writer must first and foremost be a storyteller." His lasting influence has been to restore the ancient art of Vietnamese storytelling to modern Vietnamese literature.

The General Retires[1]

I

In writing the following lines, I've reawakened in some of my acquaintances feelings that time had diluted, and I've also violated the sanctity of my own father's grave. I had to force myself to do this, and I beg the reader, out of respect for the strong emotion that compelled me, to judge lightly my weak pen. This emotion, I will state from the beginning, is the need for me to protect my father's name.

My father, Thuan, was the oldest son of the Nguyen family. In our village, the Nguyens are a very large family, with more male descendants than just about anyone except for maybe the Vus. My grandfather was a Confucian scholar who, later in life, taught school. He had two wives. His first wife died a few days after giving birth to my father, forcing my grandfather to take another step. His second wife was a cloth dyer. Although I never saw her face, I was told that she was extremely bad-tempered. Living with a stepmother, my father went through many bitter experiences during his youth. At twelve, he ran away from home. He joined the army and rarely came back.

Around the year 19__, my father went back to his village to marry. Love was certainly not involved in this arrangement. He had a ten-day leave, with much to do. Love has its prerequisites, and one of them is time.

Growing up, I knew nothing about my father. I'm sure my mother also knew very little about him. His whole life was linked to bullets, guns, and war.

When I grew up, I went to work, married, had children. My mother aged. My father was far away. Although occasionally he would return, each visit was short. Even his letters were short. Within those few lines, however, I recognized a great deal of love and concern.

I'm the only child, and am indebted to my father for everything I have. Because of him, I was able to study and travel abroad. He even provided for the assets of my own family. My house, on the outskirts of Hanoi, was built eight years before my father retired. It is a beautiful villa but rather uncomfortable. I had it built according to the plan of a famous architect, a friend of my father's, a colonel only adept at building barracks. At seventy, my father retired with the rank of major-general.

Although I knew about it beforehand, I still felt startled when my father returned. My mother had already grown senile (she was six years older than my father), so I was really the only one in the household who felt special emotions on this occasion. My children were small. My wife knew little about my father

1. Translated from the Vietnamese by Linh Dinh.

because we had gotten married during the war,[2] when we had no news of him. In our household, however, we always thought of my father with feelings of glory and pride. Even in our extended family, in our village, his name was held in tremendous esteem.

My father came home carrying simple luggage. He was healthy. He said, "I've already completed the big task in my life!"

I said, "Yes."

My father smiled. Strong feelings spread throughout the house. For half a month we celebrated, with routines disrupted and nights when dinner wasn't served until twelve. Visitors arrived in throngs. My wife said, "It can't go on like this." I had a pig killed and invited relatives and neighbors to come take part in the festivities. Although my village was near the city, we still kept to rural ways.

Not until exactly a month later did I have a chance to sit down and talk with my father about family matters.

II

Before I continue, I want to talk about my family.

I was thirty-seven years old, an engineer. I worked at the Institute of Physics. Thuy, my wife, was a doctor working in a maternity ward. We had two daughters, who were twelve and fourteen years old. My mother was senile. All day long she sat in one place.

Aside from the people I mentioned above, our household also included Co and his slow-witted daughter, Lai.

Co was sixty years old, from Thanh Hoa.[3] My wife met him and his daughter when their house burnt down, a disaster that wiped out all their possessions. Seeing that they were decent people, deserving of pity, my wife arranged for them to live with us. They lived separately, in a house in the back, but my wife took care of all their needs. Without a residency permit, they couldn't buy subsidized food like the other residents of the city.[4]

Co was kind and hard-working. He was responsible for the garden, the pigs, the chickens, and the dogs. We raised German Shepherds.[5] I never suspected that it would be such a profitable business. It accounted for our greatest income. Although Lai was slow-witted, she was exceptionally strong and good at housework. My wife taught her how to cook pork rinds, mushrooms, and chicken stew. Lai said, "I never eat like that." And she really didn't.

My wife, my daughters, and I did not have to worry about housework. From the meals to laundry, everything was relegated to the help. My wife kept a tight grip on our expenses. As for me, I was preoccupied with many things. At that point, my head was buried in the application of electrolysis.

There is one other point that needs to be stated: The relationship between myself and my wife was warm. Thuy was educated and lived a modern life. We thought independently and held rather simple views on social issues. Thuy was

2. The Vietnam War, sometimes known in Vietnamese as the American War (1955–75).
3. A rural region in North Vietnam.
4. Under the system of household registration in communist Vietnam, unregistered individuals would have difficulty receiving food, employment, or medical and social services.
5. Presumably as guard dogs for the newly wealthy during Vietnam's transition to a free-market economy in the 1980s, during which the story is set.

in charge of our finances as well as the children's education. As for me, I'm perhaps a little old-fashioned, clumsy, and loaded with anxieties.

III

Now I'll return to the discussion I had with my father about family matters. My father said, "Now that I'm retired, what should I do?"

I said, "Write a memoir."

My father said, "No!"

My wife said, "Father should raise parrots." Nowadays, a lot of people in the city raise nightingales and parrots.

My father said, "To make money?"

My wife didn't answer him. My father said, "I'll think about it."

My father gave each person in the household four meters of military cloth. He gave Co and Lai the same. I laughed. "You're very egalitarian, Father!"

My father said, "It's a way of life."

My wife said, "With everyone in a uniform this house will turn into a barracks." Everyone burst out laughing.

My father wanted to live in a room in the back of my house, like my mother did. My wife wouldn't allow it. My father was sad. The fact that my mother ate separately and lived separately made him uneasy. My wife said, "It's because she's senile." My father brooded.

I couldn't understand why my two daughters were not closer to their grandfather. I had them study foreign languages and music. They were always busy. My father said to them, "You girls give Grandfather some books to read."

Mi smiled. Vi said, "What do you like to read, Grandfather?"

My father said, "Whatever's easy."

The two of them said, "We don't have anything like that."

I subscribed to the daily newspaper for him. My father didn't like literature. These days, it's hard to digest the new writing.

When I came home from work one day, I found my father standing near where my wife kept the dogs and chickens. He didn't look happy. I said, "What's going on?"

He said, "Co and Lai work too hard. They can't finish all their tasks. Can I help them?"

I said, "Let me ask Thuy."

When I asked her, my wife said, "Father is a general. He may be retired, but he's still a general. He's the commander. If he acts like a common soldier, there'll be chaos."

My father said nothing.

Although retired, my father still had many visitors. This fact surprised me, and I was pleased. My wife said, "Don't be so happy about it. They only want favors. Father, don't exert yourself."

My father smiled. "It's nothing major. I'm only writing letters. For example, I write, 'Dear N., commander of Military District X. I'm writing this letter to you, and so on. In over fifty years, this is the first time I've celebrated the Floating Cake Festival[6] under my own roof. In the war zone, we used to dream, and

6. A festival at which sacrifices are offered to the gods and ancestors.

so on. Do you remember the little village on the side of the road, where Miss Hue made floating cakes with moldy flour? She had flour all over her back, and so on. By the way, M. is an acquaintance of mine, and wants to work under you, and so on.' Is it all right for me to write like that?"

I said, "It's all right."

My wife said, "It's not all right."

My father scratched his chin. "They've asked me."

Normally, my father inserted his letters into official hardpaper envelopes, measuring 20 × 30 centimeters,[7] with the words "Department of Defense" printed on them. Then he would give them to the person who had asked him for the favor. After three months, all these envelopes were gone. For a while, he made his own with students' construction paper, also measuring 20 × 30 centimeters. A year later, he put his letters into ordinary envelopes, the kind they sell at the post office at five dong[8] for ten.

That July, three months after my father retired, one of my uncles, Bong, had a wedding for his son.

IV

Bong and my father had the same father but different mothers. Tuan, Bong's son, drove an ox cart. Both father and son were grotesque characters, as big as giants and extremely foul-mouthed. It was the second marriage for Tuan. He hit the first one too hard and she left him. At court, he testified that she had a lover, so the judge had to let him go. The wife this time was named Kim Chi. She worked as a babysitter and came from an educated family. Tuan and Kim Chi messed around and he got her pregnant, or so we were told. Kim Chi was a beautiful girl, and as Tuan's wife, it was truly a case of "planting a sprig of jasmine on a pile of buffalo shit." Honestly speaking, we were fond of neither Bong nor his son, but, since "a drop of blood is worth more than a pond of water," we unfortunately still had to see them on holidays. We often heard Bong say of us, "Damn those intellectuals! They look down on working people. If I didn't respect his father, I'd never knock on their door." Having said that, he'd still come by to borrow money. My wife would be tough, and always made him sign a promissory note. Bong was bitter. He said, "I'm their uncle, and I only borrow from them as a last resort, but they act as if they were my landlords." Most of his debts to us he never paid back.

For his son's wedding, Bong said to my father, "You have to be the master of ceremonies. Kim Chi's father is a deputy.[9] You are a general. You two are compatible in status. My son and his wife will need your blessings. As a cart driver, I'm trash!" My father agreed to do it.

The wedding in our suburb was a ridiculous and quite obscene affair. Three cars. The filtered cigarettes ran out near the end, and we had to switch to rolled cigarettes. There were fifty trays of food, but twelve of them went untouched. The groom wore a black suit with a red tie. I had to lend him the best tie in my closet. The word is "lend," but I doubt I'll ever see it again. The groomsmen were six youths, all dressed alike, in jeans, with wild facial hair. At

7. 8 × 12 inches.
8. A tiny sum.
9. Deputy head of a government department, i.e., of high status.

the start of the party, a live band played "Ave Maria."[1] A guy from the same ox cart collective as Tuan jumped up and did a monstrous number:

"Ooh . . . eh . . . the roasted chicken
I wade through lakes and streams
Trying to find my fortune
Oh, money, fall quickly into my pocket
Ooh . . . eh . . . the sick chicken . . ."

After that, it was my father's turn. He was uncomfortable and awkward. His carefully prepared speech became irrelevant. A clarinet provided sloppy accompaniments after each pause. Loud fireworks. Inane discussions between children. My father skipped entire sections. While holding the paper, his whole body trembled. The unruliness of the event—quite ordinary, natural, rustic, and a little unclean—pained and disgusted him. The bride's father, the deputy, was also bewildered and awkward, and he even spilled wine on the bride's dress. No one could hear a thing. The live band drowned out everything with the upbeat and familiar songs of Abba and the Beatles.[2]

After that, the first trouble came to my father because only ten days after the wedding Kim Chi gave birth to a child. Bong's family was irresponsible. Drunk, Bong threw his daughter-in-law out of the house. Tuan tried to stab his father, but missed, fortunately.

With no other possible solution, my father had to take Kim Chi into our house. That meant two more mouths to feed in our household. My wife said nothing. Lai had one more responsibility. Luckily, Lai was scatterbrained. Moreover, she was fond of children.

V

One night, as I was reading *Sputnik*,[3] my father quietly walked in. He said, "I want to talk to you." I made coffee. He didn't drink it. He said, "Have you been paying attention to Thuy's business? It's very creepy."

My wife worked in the maternity ward, doing abortions.[4] Every day she carried home an ice-chest with fetuses in it. Co cooked them for the dogs and the pigs. To be honest, I already knew about it, but I chose to ignore it since it wasn't all that important. My father led me to the kitchen and pointed to the slop bucket, which had little bits of fetus in it. I didn't know what to say. My father picked up the ice-chest and threw it at the German Shepherds. "Damn it!" he began to cry. "I don't need this kind of wealth!" The dogs barked. My father went into the other room.

A moment later, my wife came in and said to Co, "Why didn't you put this through the grinder? Why did you let Father find out?"

Co said, "I forgot. I'm very sorry."

1. A musical setting of the Catholic prayer "Hail Mary" (Latin), fashionable as a Western import during the period of free-market reforms in the 1980s.
2. Western popular music is a sign of a modern lifestyle in Vietnam.
3. A Soviet newsmagazine named after the first human-made satellite to orbit the earth.
4. Abortion became widespread in Vietnam during the 1980s. Fears of overpopulation led to government sponsorship of birth control, abortion, and disincentives for childbearing.

In December, my wife sold all of our German Shepherds. She told me, "You'd better stop smoking those 'Gallant' cigarettes. This year our income is down by twenty-seven thousand, and our expenses are up by eighteen thousand, which adds up to forty-five thousand."[5]

Kim Chi finished her maternity leave and had to go back to work. She said, "Thank you, Brother and Sister. I'll take my baby home now."

I said, "What home?" Tuan had been locked up for disturbing the peace. Kim Chi took her baby home to her parents. My father escorted her right to the door in a hired taxi. He stayed at the deputy's house for a day. This man had just returned from an assignment in India. As presents, he gave my father a piece of silk with a flower design and fifty grams of ointment. My father gave the silk to Lai and the ointment to Co.

VI

Before New Year's, Co said to my wife and me, "I need a favor from you."

My wife said, "What favor?"

Co talked in a roundabout way and made very little sense. Basically, he wanted to go back to his village for a visit. Having lived with us for six years, he had saved a little money, and now he wanted to rebury his wife's remains.[6] After so long, the coffin must have caved in, for sure, but, as they say, "Loyalty to the dead is the ultimate loyalty." Co talked about living in the city and wanting to go back to the old village to see relatives and friends. Of course, he'd been away for so long, but, as they say, "Even the fox, dead for three years, still looks back toward the mountain."

My wife cut him off, "When do you want to go?"

Co scratched his head. "I'll be gone for ten days, and will be back in Hanoi before the ceremonies marking the 23rd of the final month."

My wife calculated. "All right. Thuan (Thuan is my name), can you take time off from work?"

"Yes."

Co said, "We want to invite Grandfather to visit our village."

My wife said, "I don't like that idea. What did he say?"

"He wants to come. Without him, I wouldn't have remembered this business about transferring my wife's grave."

My wife said, "How much money do you and your daughter have?"

Co said, "I had three thousand, but Grandfather gave me another two thousand."

My wife said, "Good. Don't take the two thousand from Grandfather. I'll make it up to you, plus another five thousand. That's ten thousand for you and your daughter. It's enough for a trip."

The day before the trip, my wife cooked. Everyone sat down to eat, including Co and Lai. Wearing her new clothes made from the military fabric my father had given her when he came home, Lai was very happy. Mi and Vi teased, "Lai is the most beautiful."

Lai giggled. "That's not true. Your mother is the most beautiful."

5. The story was written during a period of high inflation in Vietnam.

6. The Vietnamese rebury the remains of the dead three years after the original burial.

My wife said, "Lai, remember to look after Grandfather on buses."

My father said, "Do you think I shouldn't go?"

Co protested. "No! Please come. I already sent the telegram. It would give me a bad reputation!"

My father sighed. "What reputation do I have?"

VII

My father went to Thanh Hoa with Co and Lai on a Sunday morning. On Monday night, as I was watching TV, I heard a "whoosh." I rushed outside and saw my mother collapsed in a corner of the garden. My mother had been senile for four years, could eat and drink when fed, and had to be led to the toilet. Normally, with Lai taking care of her, we had no problems. That day, I had fed her but forgot to take her to the toilet. When I helped her back inside, her head slumped on her chest. I didn't see any injuries, but when I woke up in the middle of the night I noticed that my mother's body was very cold and her eyes were wild. I was scared and called my wife. Thuy said, "Mother is very old." The next day mother didn't eat. And the day after that she didn't eat and couldn't control her bowels. I washed everything, changed the mat. Some days twelve times. Knowing that Thuy and the children liked cleanliness, I did mother's laundry all the time, and not in the house but down at the canal. Whatever medicine we poured down her throat she threw up.

On Saturday she was suddenly able to sit up. She trudged alone to the garden. She was able to eat. I said, "She's fine now."

My wife said nothing, but came back that evening with ten meters of white cloth, and even called the carpenter. I said, "You're preparing for her death?"

My wife said, "No."

Two days later, my mother was bedridden, and, like before, could neither eat nor control her bowels. She declined rapidly and excreted a sort of brown, pasty, very strong-smelling liquid. I gave her ginseng. My wife said, "Don't give her ginseng. It's bad for her." I burst into loud sobs. It had been a long time since I'd sobbed like that. My wife stayed silent, then said, "It's up to you."

Bong came to visit. He said, "The way she's tossing and turning on that bed is very bad." Then he turned to my mother and asked, "Sister, do you recognize me?"

My mother said, "Yes."

"Then who am I?"

My mother said, "A human being."

Bong burst into loud sobs. "Then you must love me the most, Sister," he said. "The whole village calls me a dog. My wife calls me a fraud. Tuan calls me a bastard. Only you, Sister, call me a human being."

For the first time, my ox-cart-driving uncle, who's hot-tempered, vulgar, and immoral, turned into a child before my very eyes.

VIII

My father had been home for six hours when my mother died. Co and Lai said, "It's all our fault. If we had been home, Grandmother wouldn't have died."

My wife said, "Nonsense."

Lai cried, "Grandmother, why did you play a trick on me like this? Why didn't you allow me to come with you so I could serve you?"

Bong laughed. "If you want to go with Grandmother, go ahead. I'll tell them to make another coffin."

During the enshroudment of my mother's corpse, my father cried and asked Bong, "Why did her body decline so quickly? Does every old person die in such pain?"

Bong said, "You're being silly. Every single day, thousands of people in our country die a painful and humiliating death. The only exceptions are soldiers like you. One sweet 'Bang!' and that's it."

I had a shelter built and hired a carpenter to make the coffin. Co was always hovering around the pile of wood my wife had brought home. The carpenter barked, "Are you afraid I'm going to steal the wood?"

Bong asked, "How thick is that wood?"

"Four centimeters," I told him.

Bong said, "There goes a damn sofa. Who else would have made a coffin with such good wood? When you rebury her, make sure you give this wood to me."

My father sat in silence, and appeared to be in deep agony.

Bong said, "Thuy, boil a chicken and prepare a pot of sticky rice for me."

My wife said, "How many kilograms of rice, Uncle?"

Bong said, "Your damned mother! Why are you so sweet today? Three kilograms."

My wife said to me, "Your relatives are disgusting."

Bong asked me, "Who's in charge of the finances in this household?"

I said, "My wife."

Mr. Bong said, "That's normal. What I mean is, who's in charge of the finances for this funeral?"

"My wife."

Bong said, "That won't do, my boy! Different blood stinks up the intestines. I'll talk to your father, all right?"

"No, I'll take care of it."

Bong said, "Give me four thousand. How many trays of food were you thinking of preparing?"

"Ten trays."

"That won't even be enough to flush out the coffin bearers' bellies. You talk to your wife. I'd say you need forty trays."

I gave him four thousand dong, then went inside. My wife said, "I heard the whole conversation. I was thinking thirty trays, at eight hundred dong per tray. Three times eight is twenty-four. Twenty-four thousand. For miscellaneous costs, add six thousand. I'll take care of the shopping. Lai will cook. Don't listen to Bong. He's a shifty old man."

"I already gave him four thousand."

My wife said, "I'm really disappointed in you."

"I'll ask for it back."

"Forget about it. We'll consider it a payment for his service. He's nice, but poor."

We hired four traditional musicians for the funeral. My father went out to greet them. My mother's body was placed in the coffin at four in the afternoon. Bong pried open her mouth to place nine Khai Dinh and aluminum coins inside. He said, "For the ferry."[7] He also placed inside the coffin an incomplete set of to tom cards mixed together with some tam cuc cards.[8] "It's all right," he said. "She always used to play tam cuc."

That night, I stayed up to watch over my mother's coffin, and aimlessly pondered many things. Death will come to all of us, sparing none.

In the courtyard, Bong and the coffin bearers were playing tam cuc for money. Whenever he had a good hand, Bong ran to the coffin, bowed down and said, "Dearest Sister, please help me so I can clean out their pockets."

Mi and Vi stayed up with me. Mi asked, "Why do you still have to pay for the ferry after you've died? Why were coins put in Grandmother's mouth?"

Vi said, "Father, does it have to do with the saying, 'Shut your mouth, keep the money'?"

I was crying. "You kids won't understand," I said. "I don't understand myself. It's all superstition."

Vi said, "I understand. You need a lot of money in this life. Even when you're dead."

I felt very lonely. My children also seemed lonely. And so did the gamblers. And so did my father.

IX

My house was only five hundred meters from the cemetery, but if you took the main road through the village gate it would be two kilometers. On the small road it wasn't possible to push a hearse so the coffin had to be carried on the pallbearers' shoulders. There were thirty of them taking turns, with many men my wife and I didn't recognize. They carried the coffin casually, as if it were a most natural thing to do, as if they were carrying a house-pillar. They chewed betel nuts, smoked, and chattered as they walked. When they rested, they stood and sat carelessly next to the coffin. One man, who was all sprawled out, said, "It's so cool here. If I weren't busy, I'd sleep here until nightfall."

Bong said, "I beg you guys. Hurry up so we can all go home and eat."

We continued on. I walked backward with a cane in front of the coffin, according to the custom: 'Escort your father; Greet your mother.'

Bong said, "When I die, all of my pallbearers will be hard-core gamblers, and instead of pork at the banquet, there'll be dog meat."

My father said, "Please, Brother, how can you joke at a time like this?"

Bong shut up; then he cried, "Sister, why did you trick me and leave like this . . . You've abandoned me . . ."

I wondered why he said "trick." Had all the dead people tricked the ones who were still alive? Were there only tricksters in this cemetery?

After the burial, everyone went back to the house. Twenty-eight trays of food were laid out simultaneously. Looking at the banquet, I felt nothing but respect for Lai. At each table, people were yelling: "Where's Lai?" And she accommodated them all, fluttering about with whiskey and meat. Not until after dark, after she had washed up and changed into new clothes, did Lai go in front of the

7. At a traditional Vietnamese funeral (as in ancient Greece), coins are placed in the mouth of the deceased to pay for the passage to the afterlife. Here, some of the coins were minted during the reign of the emperor Khai Dinh (1916–25).

8. Traditional Vietnamese playing cards.

altar and cry, "Grandmother, I apologize. I didn't take you out to the field . . . And on that day you craved crab soup and I didn't feel like making it, you didn't get any . . . Now when I go to the market, who will I buy a present for?"

I felt very remorseful when I heard that. I realized that I hadn't bought my mother a cake or a bag of candy in ten years. Lai continued to cry, "If I had been here, then would you have died, Grandmother?"

My wife said, "Don't cry."

I got cranky. "Let her cry," I said. "It's very sad if there are no sounds of crying at a funeral. In this house, who else could grieve for Mother like that?"

My wife said, "Thirty-two trays. Aren't you in awe of how close my estimate was?"

I said, "It was pretty close."

Bong said, "I checked her burying hour on the horoscope. Your mother has 'one grave invasion, two overlapping deaths, and a migration.'[9] Should we invoke a talisman?"

My father said, "Talisman, my ass. In my life, I've buried three thousand men and it's never been like this."

Bong said, "That's happiness. 'Bang!' and it's over." He stuck out an index finger and pretended to pull a trigger.

X

That New Year we neither bought peach blossoms nor wrapped square rice cakes. On the evening of January 2nd, my father's old unit sent people over to pay homage to my mother. They gave five hundred dong.[1] Chuong, my father's old deputy who was now a general, went to the gravesite to light incense sticks. Thanh, a captain who accompanied him, pulled out his pistol and fired three shots into the air. Later, the children in the village would say that soldiers fired twenty-one cannon shots in honor of Mrs. Thuan. General Chuong asked my father, "Would you like to pay a last visit to the old unit? There'll be maneuvers in May. We can send a car down to get you."

My father said, "Fine."

General Chuong took a tour of our house, with Co as his guide. General Chuong said to my father, "Damn nice place you've got here. A garden, a fish pond, a pig sty, a chicken coop, a villa. No worries at all."

My father said, "My son built all this."

I said, "It was my wife."

My wife said, "Actually, it was Lai."

Lai giggled. Lately, her head would bob nonstop, as if she were having a seizure. "That's not true," she said.

My father joked, "It's the product of the Garden-Fish Pond-Pen Campaign."

January 3rd. Kim Chi and her baby rode a cyclo[2] by for a visit. My wife gave the baby one thousand dong for good luck. My father asked, "Does Tuan write?"

Kim Chi said, "No."

My father said, "It's my fault. I didn't know you were pregnant."

9. Horoscopes were consulted to determine an auspicious time for a funeral.

1. Worth about one dollar at the time the story was published, but considerably more a few years earlier.

2. Pedicab or bicycle rickshaw.

My wife said, "These things are common. There are no virgins these days. I work in a maternity ward, so I know."

Kim Chi looked embarrassed. I said, "Don't talk like that. Although, admittedly, it is tough to be a virgin."

Kim Chi cried, "Brother, it's humiliating to be a woman. Giving birth to a daughter tore my whole insides out."

My wife said, "And, I even have two daughters."

I said, "So you people don't think it's humiliating to be a man?"

My father said, "For men, the ones who have hearts are humiliated. The bigger the heart, the bigger the humiliation."

My wife said, "We all talk like crazy people in this household. Let's eat. Today, with Miss Kim Chi, I'll serve each person a chicken stewed with lotus hearts. Now that's 'heart' for you. Eating comes before everything else."

XI

Near my house lived a young man, Khong, whom the children called Confucius.[3] Khong worked at the fish sauce factory but liked poetry, which he wrote and sent to the magazine *Literature and Art*.[4] Khong came by often. Khong said, "Poetry is most superior." He read me Lorca, Whitman,[5] etc. I didn't like Khong, and half-suspected he came by for something even more adventurous than poetry. Once, I noticed a handwritten poetry manuscript on my wife's bed. My wife said, "These are Khong's poems. Would you like to read them?" I shook my head. My wife said, "You're already old." I shuddered.

One day I was busy at work and had to come home late. My father greeted me at the gate. He said, "Khong came over at dusk. He and your wife have been tittering away, and he hasn't left yet. It's very annoying."

I said, "You should go to bed, Father. Why pay attention to this?" My father shook his head and went upstairs. I walked the motorbike to the street, and rode aimlessly around town until I ran out of gas. I walked the motorbike to a corner of a park and sat down like some vagabond. A woman with a powdered face walked by and asked, "Brother, do you want some fun?" I shook my head.

Khong was trying to avoid me. Co hated him. One day, Co said, "Will you let me beat him up?"

I almost nodded. Then I thought, "Don't."

I went to the library to borrow some books as an experiment. I read Lorca, Whitman, etc. I vaguely felt that exceptional artists are frighteningly lonely. Suddenly, I saw that Khong was right. I was only pissed off that he was so ill-bred. Why didn't he show his poems to somebody else besides my wife?

My father said, "You're meek. And that's because you can't stand to live alone."

I said, "That's not true. There are many jokes in life."

My father said, "You think this is a joke?"

I said, "It's neither a joke nor something serious."

My father said, "Why do I feel like I belong to a different species?"

3. Chinese philosopher (ca. 551–479 B.C.E.), known in Vietnamese as Khong tu.
4. The journal of the Vietnamese National Writers Association, in which "The General Retires" was originally published.
5. Walt Whitman (1819–1892), American poet; Federico García Lorca (1898–1936), Spanish poet.

The institute wanted to send me on assignment to the south. I said to my wife, "I'll go, all right?"

My wife said, "Don't go. Tomorrow, you can fix the bathroom door. It's broken. The other day, when Mi was taking a shower, Khong walked by and tried something obscene. He scared her out of her wits. I've forbidden that bastard from ever walking through the door of this house again." Then she burst into tears, saying, "I really owe you and the children an apology."

I was uncomfortable and turned away. If Vi had been around, she would have asked me, "Father, are those crocodile tears?"[6]

XII

In May, my father's old unit sent a car down to pick him up. Thanh, the captain, carried a letter from General Chuong. My father trembled while holding the letter, which said, ". . . We need you and are waiting for you . . . If you can come, then come. There's no pressure." I didn't think my father should go, but it would have been awkward to say so. Although my father had aged noticeably since his retirement, holding the letter that day, he appeared vivacious and considerably younger. I felt happy for him. My wife wanted to pack his travel things in a tourist bag. He wouldn't hear of it. He said, "Stuff them in my rucksack."

My father made the rounds to say goodbye to the entire village. He even went to my mother's grave and told Thanh to fire three shots into the air again. That night, my father called for Co and gave him two thousand dong. He instructed him to have a stone marker made to be sent to Thanh Hoa and placed over his wife's grave. My father called Lai over and said, "You should find yourself a husband, my child."

Lai burst out crying. "I'm so ugly, no one will marry me," she said. "I'm also very naive."

My father became choked up. "My dear child," he told her. "Don't you understand that naiveté is the strength that allows one to live?"

I didn't recognize all of these preparations as signs that my father would not come back from his trip.

Before he stepped into the car, my father pulled a student's notebook from his rucksack. He gave it to me. He said, "I've jotted down a few things in this book. Read it and see what you think."

Mi and Vi said goodbye to their grandfather. Mi said, "Are you going to the battlefield, Grandfather?"

My father said, "Yes."

Vi quoted from a song: "'The road to the battlefield is beautiful at this time of year.'[7] Right, Grandfather?"

My father cursed. "Your mother! Know-it-all!"

XIII

A hilarious incident occurred a few days after my father left. It so happened that, as Co and Bong were dredging mud from the pond (my wife paid Bong two hundred dong a day plus meals), they suddenly saw the bottom of an

6. Insincere tears.
7. A line from a popular, patriotic North Vietnamese song of the Vietnam War period.

earthen jar appear above the surface. Both of them dug on enthusiastically and discovered the bottom of a second jar. Bong was sure that people in the old days had used these jars to hide their valuables. The two men reported the news to my wife. Thuy went for a look and proceeded to wade into the pond to join them, digging. Then Lai went in, then Mi, then Vi and I. We were all smeared with mud. My wife ordered that the pond be blocked off, and even rented a Kohler pump to siphon the water. The atmosphere grew deadly serious. Bong loved it. "I saw it first," he said. "I'll get to keep one of those jars for myself." After a day of digging, and finding two cracked jars with nothing inside, Bong said, "There's got to be more." More digging. One more jar was discovered. It was also cracked. Everyone was exhausted and starving. My wife sent for some bread so we could regain our strength to continue digging. At the depth of nearly ten meters we found a porcelain jar. Everyone was ecstatic and assumed there had to be gold inside. We opened it up only to find a string of rusty, bronze Bao Dai coins[8] and the shreds of a fabric medal. Bong said, "Damn it! I remember now. A long time ago, after I robbed Han Tin's[9] house with that hoodlum Nhan, we were being chased and Nhan threw this jar into the pond." Everyone had a good round of laughs. This hoodlum was a very famous thief on the outskirts of town. Han Tin was a soldier in the Colonial army. He had participated in a movement called "Coin-Spitting Southern Dragon to Expel the German Bandits"[1] during World War I. Both Han Tin and Nhan had been rotting in their graves for years already. Bong said, "It doesn't matter. Should this entire village die, I'll have enough ferry money to stuff into everyone's mouth."

The next morning, I woke up and heard someone calling at the gate. I went outside and saw Khong. I thought, "What a pain. This son of a bitch is the biggest curse in my entire life."

Khong said, "Brother Thuan, you have a telegram. Your father died."

XIV

The telegram from General Chuong said, "Major-General Nguyen Thuan sacrificed his life in the line of duty at __ on __. Services at the military cemetery will be at __ on __." I was stunned. My wife quickly made all the arrangements. I went out to hire a car and when I came back everything was ready. My wife said, "Lock the main house. Co will stay behind."

The car went to Cao Bang on Highway One. When we got there, the funeral had already been over for two hours.

General Chuong said, "We owe your family an apology."

I said, "That's not necessary. Each life has its destiny."

General Chuong said, "Your father was someone deserving of respect."

"Was the ceremony conducted according to military rites?" I asked.

"Yes."

8. Coins minted during the reign of the last Vietnamese emperor, Bao Dai (1926–45).

9. The character shares the Vietnamese name of Han Xin (d. 196 B.C.E.), the Chinese military hero who helped establish the Han Dynasty.

1. A slogan of the French administration of Vietnam (1887–55) encouraging people to buy government bonds to support the defeat of Germany in World War I (1914–18).

"Thank you," I told him.

General Chuong said, "He went to the battlefield and insisted on staying near the front."

I said, "I understand, Sir. You don't have to explain."

I cried. I had never cried like that before. Now I understood what it means to grieve the death of one's father. Perhaps it is the biggest grief in a person's lifetime.

My father's grave lay in the military cemetery. My wife took a camera along and had pictures taken in different poses. The next day, we declined General Chuong's invitation to stay and took our leave.

On the way home, my wife suggested we go slowly. It was Bong's first long trip, and he loved it. He said, "Our country is as beautiful as a painting. Now I understand why one must love one's country. Back home, even though Hanoi is so modern, I see nothing at all to love."

My wife said, "That's because you're used to it. Elsewhere, people are the same. They're the ones who love Hanoi."

Bong said, "Then one place loves the other place, and people here love people there. It's still one country, one people. Long live our country! Long live our people! Hurrah for the spinning lantern!"

XV

Perhaps my story ends here. After that, our lives reverted to what they were before my father retired. My wife continued her work as usual. I finished my electrolysis research. Co turned quiet, partly because Lai's condition had worsened. When I had time, I read over what my father had written. Now I understand him better.

I've recorded here the confusing events that occurred during the year or so of my father's retirement. I consider these lines as sticks of incense lit in his remembrance. If you have had the patience to read what I've written, I beg you to forgive my indulgences. Thank you.

1987

ISABEL ALLENDE

born 1942

One of the best known contemporary Latin American writers, the Chilean novelist Isabel Allende brought the tradition of magic realism to bear on women's experience. Drawing on the earlier experiments by **Gabriel García Márquez** and other writers of the Latin American Boom, Allende has portrayed women's spiritual lives in the context of the political world of her childhood and youth, adding a dimension to magic realism while bringing her a wide international audience.

Born in Peru, where her father was a diplomat representing Chile, Allende returned to Chile with her mother at the age of three when her parents divorced. She lived for much of her childhood with her grandparents. Her mother's second husband, also a diplomat, later took the family to Bolivia and Beirut. As a young woman, Allende became involved in international affairs herself, working for the Food and Agriculture Organization of the United Nations, before beginning a career in journalism. In 1973 her father's cousin, Salvador Allende, the first elected socialist president of Chile, was deposed in a coup led by General Augusto Pinochet. Historians still debate whether he killed himself or was assassinated by Pinochet's forces. In the coup's aftermath, Isabel Allende and her family left Chile for Venezuela, where she continued to work as a journalist. She has said that the departure from Chile made her a serious writer: "I don't think I would be a writer if I had stayed in Chile. I would be trapped in the chores, in the family, in the person that people expected me to be. I was not supposed to be in any way a liberated person. I was a female born in the '40s in a patriarchal family; I was supposed to marry and make everyone around me happy." Instead, she chose a liberated, cosmopolitan lifestyle, although she would marry and have two children.

When she received news, in 1981, that her ninety-nine-year-old grandfather was dying, Allende began writing him a long letter—which developed, transformed, and expanded to become her first novel, *The House of the Spirits* (1982). This novel chronicles the experiences of a South American family haunted by spirits and torn by political events over several decades of the twentieth century. The subjects and style drew comparisons to the magic realism of García Márquez, whom Allende described as "the great writer of the century." The novel was an international success, and Allende moved to California, where she continues to live, teaching at universities throughout the United States. Her daughter died of a rare illness, porphyria, in 1992, and Allende wrote a moving personal memoir with her in mind, *Paula* (1994).

The story presented here, "And of Clay Are We Created" (1989), belongs to a stage of her career in which Allende chose a more direct, less magic, realism. The title refers to the proverb "we are all made of the same clay," which in turn refers to biblical passages (Psalms 103.14, Job 33.6, and Genesis 2–3), in which humans are said to be created of clay or earth. As God reminds Adam on his expulsion from the Garden of Eden, "dust thou art, and unto dust shalt thou return" (Gen. 3.19). In the context of the soil smothering the victims of a volcanic eruption, this passage reminds us not only of our shared humanity but of our mortality as well. The narrator is the heroine of Allende's novel *Eva Luna* (1985). The plot offers a generally straightforward account of the aftermath of a volcanic eruption, based closely on a real event, the eruption of Nevado del Ruiz, in Colombia in 1985. The one element that might represent a form of magic is the role of television and media. Technology (flight, telecommunications, labor-saving devices) has often seemed to fulfill magicians' ancient dreams of dominating the world. In this story, though, even the awe-inspiring presence of television journalism fails to reverse the effects of natural forces. The story begins with an implicit critique of the way people may experience natural disasters through the mass media: Eva Luna's longtime companion, a television reporter named Rolf Carlé, takes a helicopter to the site of an avalanche caused by volcanic activity. While he and crowds of other journalists bring broadcasting equipment to the visually exciting disaster zone, no one in the mob can locate a simple pump that would help rescue a girl trapped under fallen earth. (This character is based on a real thirteen-year-old, Omaira Sánchez.) The child is only one of thousands of victims, but because her plight is caught on television, she becomes famous. The camera brings the public face-to-face, in a sense, with the victims, while emphasizing the distance between its operator and the victims; over the course of the story, however, the distance starts to collapse. What began as a criticism of the media becomes personal as the story focuses on the effects of the girl's fate on Rolf Carlé, who recollects his childhood in wartime Eastern Europe. Meanwhile, as the narrator watches the events unfold on television, she is powerless to help either the girl or Rolf.

The story demonstrates a keen awareness, typical of Allende, of the plight of the poor and disenfranchised; it reveals, as well, her attention to the ethical questions posed by a media-saturated society. Magic realism, for Allende, is not so much a return to an older mode of storytelling as a way of addressing the problems of the contemporary world. Allende's works provide a feminist perspective on the complex history of twentieth-century Latin America.

And of Clay Are We Created[1]

They discovered the girl's head protruding from the mudpit, eyes wide open, calling soundlessly. She had a First Communion name, Azucena.[2] Lily. In that vast cemetery where the odor of death was already attracting vultures from far away, and where the weeping of orphans and wails of the injured filled the air, the little girl obstinately clinging to life became the symbol of the tragedy. The television cameras transmitted so often the unbearable image of the head budding like a black squash from the clay that there was no one who did not recognize her and know her name. And every time we saw her on the screen, right behind her was Rolf Carlé, who had gone there on assignment, never suspecting that he would find a fragment of his past, lost thirty years before.

First a subterranean sob rocked the cotton fields, curling them like waves of foam. Geologists had set up their seismographs weeks before and knew that the mountain had awakened again. For some time they had predicted that the heat of the eruption could detach the eternal ice from the slopes of the volcano, but no one heeded their warnings; they sounded like the tales of frightened old women. The towns in the valley went about their daily life, deaf to the moaning of the earth, until that fateful Wednesday night in November when a prolonged roar announced the end of the world, and walls of snow broke loose, rolling in an avalanche of clay, stones, and water that descended on the villages and buried them beneath unfathomable meters of telluric[3] vomit. As soon as the survivors emerged from the paralysis of that first awful terror, they could see that houses, plazas, churches, white cotton plantations, dark coffee forests, cattle pastures—all had disappeared. Much later, after soldiers and volunteers had arrived to rescue the living and try to assess the magnitude of the

1. Translated by Margaret Sayers Peden.
2. Azucena is a type of lily, known in English as the Madonna lily or white lily. "First communion name": a name, often of a saint, bestowed at the time of First Communion or confirmation in the Catholic Church.
3. Earthy.

cataclysm, it was calculated that beneath the mud lay more than twenty thousand human beings and an indefinite number of animals putrefying in a viscous soup. Forests and rivers had also been swept away, and there was nothing to be seen but an immense desert of mire.

When the station called before dawn, Rolf Carlé and I were together. I crawled out of bed, dazed with sleep, and went to prepare coffee while he hurriedly dressed. He stuffed his gear in the green canvas backpack he always carried, and we said goodbye, as we had so many times before. I had no presentiments. I sat in the kitchen, sipping my coffee and planning the long hours without him, sure that he would be back the next day.

He was one of the first to reach the scene, because while other reporters were fighting their way to the edges of that morass in jeeps, bicycles, or on foot, each getting there however he could, Rolf Carlé had the advantage of the television helicopter, which flew him over the avalanche. We watched on our screens the footage captured by his assistant's camera, in which he was up to his knees in muck, a microphone in his hand, in the midst of a bedlam of lost children, wounded survivors, corpses, and devastation. The story came to us in his calm voice. For years he had been a familiar figure in newscasts, reporting live at the scene of battles and catastrophes with awesome tenacity. Nothing could stop him, and I was always amazed at his equanimity in the face of danger and suffering; it seemed as if nothing could shake his fortitude or deter his curiosity. Fear seemed never to touch him, although he had confessed to me that he was not a courageous man, far from it. I believe that the lens of the camera had a strange effect on him; it was as if it transported him to a different time from which he could watch events without actually participating in them. When I knew him better, I came to realize that this fictive distance seemed to protect him from his own emotions.

Rolf Carlé was in on the story of Azucena from the beginning. He filmed the volunteers who discovered her, and the first persons who tried to reach her; his camera zoomed in on the girl, her dark face, her large desolate eyes, the plastered-down tangle of her hair. The mud was like quicksand around her, and anyone attempting to reach her was in danger of sinking. They threw a rope to her that she made no effort to grasp until they shouted to her to catch it; then she pulled a hand from the mire and tried to move, but immediately sank a little deeper. Rolf threw down his knapsack and the rest of his equipment and waded into the quagmire, commenting for his assistant's microphone that it was cold and that one could begin to smell the stench of corpses.

"What's your name?" he asked the girl, and she told him her flower name. "Don't move, Azucena," Rolf Carlé directed, and kept talking to her, without a thought for what he was saying, just to distract her, while slowly he worked his way forward in mud up to his waist. The air around him seemed as murky as the mud.

It was impossible to reach her from the approach he was attempting, so he retreated and circled around where there seemed to be firmer footing. When finally he was close enough, he took the rope and tied it beneath her arms, so they could pull her out. He smiled at her with that smile that crinkles his eyes and makes him look like a little boy; he told her that everything was fine, that he was here with her now, that soon they would have her out. He signaled the others to pull, but as soon as the cord tensed, the girl screamed. They tried again, and her shoulders and arms appeared, but they could move her no farther; she was trapped. Someone suggested that her legs might be caught in the collapsed walls of her house, but she said it was not just rubble, that she was also held by the bodies of her brothers and sisters clinging to her legs.

"Don't worry, we'll get you out of here," Rolf promised. Despite the quality of the transmission, I could hear his voice break, and I loved him more than ever. Azucena looked at him, but said nothing.

During those first hours Rolf Carlé exhausted all the resources of his ingenuity to rescue her. He struggled with poles and ropes, but every tug was an intolerable torture for the imprisoned girl. It occurred to him to use one of the poles as a lever but got no result and had to abandon the idea. He talked a couple of soldiers into working with him for a while, but they had to leave because so many other victims were calling for help. The girl could not move, she barely could breathe, but she did not seem desperate, as if an ancestral resignation allowed her to accept her fate. The reporter, on the other hand, was determined to snatch her from death. Someone brought him a tire, which he placed beneath her arms like a life buoy, and then laid a plank near the hole to hold his weight and allow him to stay closer to her. As it was impossible to remove the rubble blindly, he tried once or twice to dive toward her feet, but emerged frustrated, covered with mud, and spitting gravel. He concluded that he would have to have a pump to drain the water, and radioed a request for one, but received in return a message that there was no available transport and it could not be sent until the next morning.

"We can't wait that long!" Rolf Carlé shouted, but in the pandemonium no one stopped to commiserate. Many more hours would go by before he accepted that time had stagnated and reality had been irreparably distorted.

A military doctor came to examine the girl, and observed that her heart was functioning well and that if she did not get too cold she could survive the night.

"Hang on, Azucena, we'll have the pump tomorrow," Rolf Carlé tried to console her.

"Don't leave me alone," she begged.

"No, of course I won't leave you."

Someone brought him coffee, and he helped the girl drink it, sip by sip. The warm liquid revived her and she began telling him about her small life, about her family and her school, about how things were in that little bit of world before the volcano had erupted. She was thirteen, and she had never been outside her village. Rolf Carlé, buoyed by a premature optimism, was convinced that everything would end well: the pump would arrive, they would drain the water, move the rubble, and Azucena would be transported by helicopter to a hospital where she would recover rapidly and where he could visit her and bring her gifts. He thought, She's already too old for dolls, and I don't know what would please her; maybe a dress. I don't know much about women, he concluded, amused, reflecting that although he had known many women in his lifetime, none had taught him these details. To pass the hours he began to tell Azucena about his travels and adventures as a newshound, and when he exhausted his memory, he called upon imagination, inventing things he thought might entertain her. From time to time she dozed, but he kept talking in the darkness, to assure her that he was still there and to overcome the menace of uncertainty.

That was a long night.

Many miles away, I watched Rolf Carlé and the girl on a television screen. I could not bear the wait at home, so I went to National Television, where I often spent entire nights with Rolf editing programs. There, I was near his world, and I could at least get a feeling of what he lived through during those three decisive days. I called all the important people in the city, senators, commanders of the armed forces, the North American[4] ambassador, and the president of National Petroleum, begging them for a pump to remove the silt, but obtained only vague promises. I began to ask for urgent help on radio and television, to see if there wasn't *someone* who could help us. Between calls I would run to the newsroom to monitor the satellite transmissions that periodically brought new details of the catastrophe. While reporters selected scenes with most impact for the news report, I searched for footage that featured Azucena's mudpit. The screen reduced the disaster to a single plane and accentuated the tremendous distance that separated me from Rolf Carlé; nonetheless, I was there with him. The child's every suffering hurt me as it did him; I felt his frustration, his impotence. Faced with the impossibility of communicating with him, the fantastic idea came to me that if I tried, I could reach him by force of mind and in that way give him encouragement. I concentrated until I was dizzy—a frenzied and futile activity. At times I would be overcome with compassion and burst out crying; at other times, I was so drained I felt as if I were staring through a telescope at the light of a star dead for a million years.

I watched that hell on the first morning broadcast, cadavers of people and animals awash in the current of new rivers formed overnight from the melted snow. Above the mud rose the tops of trees and the bell towers of a church where several people had taken refuge and were patiently awaiting rescue teams. Hundreds of soldiers and volunteers from the Civil Defense[5] were clawing through rubble searching for survivors, while long rows of ragged specters awaited their turn for a cup of hot broth. Radio networks announced that their phones were jammed with calls from families offering shelter to orphaned children. Drinking water was in scarce supply, along with gasoline and food. Doctors, resigned to amputating arms and legs without anesthesia, pled that at least they be sent serum and painkillers and antibiotics; most of the roads, however, were impassable, and worse were the bureaucratic obstacles that stood in the way. To top it all, the clay contaminated by decomposing bodies threatened the living with an outbreak of epidemics.

Azucena was shivering inside the tire that held her above the surface. Immobility and tension had greatly weakened her, but she was conscious and could still be heard when a microphone was held out to her. Her tone was humble, as if apologizing for all the fuss. Rolf Carlé had a growth of beard, and dark circles beneath his eyes; he looked near exhaustion. Even from that enormous distance I could sense the quality of his weariness, so different from the fatigue of other adventures. He had completely forgotten the camera; he could not look

4. I.e., United States.
5. A group of trained workers prepared to respond to disasters.

at the girl through a lens any longer. The pictures we were receiving were not his assistant's but those of other reporters who had appropriated Azucena, bestowing on her the pathetic responsibility of embodying the horror of what had happened in that place. With the first light Rolf tried again to dislodge the obstacles that held the girl in her tomb, but he had only his hands to work with; he did not dare use a tool for fear of injuring her. He fed Azucena a cup of the cornmeal mush and bananas the Army was distributing, but she immediately vomited it up. A doctor stated that she had a fever, but added that there was little he could do: antibiotics were being reserved for cases of gangrene. A priest also passed by and blessed her, hanging a medal of the Virgin around her neck. By evening a gentle, persistent drizzle began to fall.

"The sky is weeping," Azucena murmured, and she, too, began to cry.

"Don't be afraid," Rolf begged. "You have to keep your strength up and be calm. Everything will be fine. I'm with you, and I'll get you out somehow."

Reporters returned to photograph Azucena and ask her the same questions, which she no longer tried to answer. In the meanwhile, more television and movie teams arrived with spools of cable, tapes, film, videos, precision lenses, recorders, sound consoles, lights, reflecting screens, auxiliary motors, cartons of supplies, electricians, sound technicians, and cameramen: Azucena's face was beamed to millions of screens around the world. And all the while Rolf Carlé kept pleading for a pump. The improved technical facilities bore results, and National Television began receiving sharper pictures and clearer sound; the distance seemed suddenly compressed, and I had the horrible sensation that Azucena and Rolf were by my side, separated from me by impenetrable glass. I was able to follow events hour by hour; I knew everything my love did to wrest the girl from her prison and help her endure her suffering; I overheard fragments of what they said to one another and could guess the rest; I was present when she taught Rolf to pray, and when he distracted her with the stories I had told him in a thousand and one nights[6] beneath the white mosquito netting of our bed.

When darkness came on the second day, Rolf tried to sing Azucena to sleep with old Austrian folk songs he had learned from his mother, but she was far beyond sleep. They spent most of the night talking, each in a stupor of exhaustion and hunger, and shaking with cold. That night, imperceptibly, the unyielding floodgates that had contained Rolf Carlé's past for so many years began to open, and the torrent of all that had lain hidden in the deepest and most secret layers of memory poured out, leveling before it the obstacles that had blocked his consciousness for so long. He could not tell it all to Azucena; she perhaps did not know there was a world beyond the sea or time previous to her own; she was not capable of imagining Europe in the years of the war.[7] So he could not tell her of defeat, nor of the afternoon the Russians had led them to the concentration camp to bury prisoners dead from starvation. Why should he describe to her how the naked bodies piled like a mountain of firewood resembled fragile china? How could he tell this dying child about ovens[8] and gallows? Nor did he mention the

6. A reference to the collection of medieval Arabic tales, *The Thousand and One Nights*. In the collection, King Shahryar has killed a series of wives after spending a single night with each. Queen Scheherezade tells the king suspenseful stories each night, leaving the endings for the following night; her husband does not kill her because he wants to hear the endings of the stories.

7. The Second World War (1939–45).

8. Crematoria in which the Nazis incinerated their victims during the Second World War.

night that he had seen his mother naked, shod in stiletto-heeled red boots, sobbing with humiliation. There was much he did not tell, but in those hours he relived for the first time all the things his mind had tried to erase. Azucena had surrendered her fear to him and so, without wishing it, had obliged Rolf to confront his own. There, beside that hellhole of mud, it was impossible for Rolf to flee from himself any longer, and the visceral terror he had lived as a boy suddenly invaded him. He reverted to the years when he was the age of Azucena, and younger, and, like her, found himself trapped in a pit without escape, buried in life, his head barely above ground; he saw before his eyes the boots and legs of his father, who had removed his belt and was whipping it in the air with the never-forgotten hiss of a viper coiled to strike. Sorrow flooded through him, intact and precise, as if it had lain always in his mind, waiting. He was once again in the armoire where his father locked him to punish him for imagined misbehavior, there where for eternal hours he had crouched with his eyes closed, not to see the darkness, with his hands over his ears, to shut out the beating of his heart, trembling, huddled like a cornered animal. Wandering in the mist of his memories he found his sister Katharina, a sweet, retarded child who spent her life hiding, with the hope that her father would forget the disgrace of her having been born. With Katharina, Rolf crawled beneath the dining room table, and with her hid there under the long white tablecloth, two children forever embraced, alert to footsteps and voices. Katharina's scent melded with his own sweat, with aromas of cooking, garlic, soup, freshly baked bread, and the unexpected odor of putrescent clay. His sister's hand in his, her frightened breathing, her silk hair against his cheek, the candid gaze of her eyes. Katharina . . . Katharina materialized before him, floating on the air like a flag, clothed in the white tablecloth, now a winding sheet, and at last he could weep for her death and for the guilt of having abandoned her. He understood then that all his exploits as a reporter, the feats that had won him such recognition and fame, were merely an attempt to keep his most ancient fears at bay, a stratagem for taking refuge behind a lens to test whether reality was more tolerable from that perspective. He took excessive risks as an exercise of courage, training by day to conquer the monsters that tormented him by night! But he had come face to face with the moment of truth; he could not continue to escape his past. He *was* Azucena; he was buried in the clayey mud; his terror was not the distant emotion of an almost forgotten childhood, it was a claw sunk in his throat. In the flush of his tears he saw his mother, dressed in black and clutching her imitation-crocodile pocketbook to her bosom, just as he had last seen her on the dock when she had come to put him on the boat to South America.[9] She had not come to dry his tears, but to tell him to pick up a shovel: the war was over and now they must bury the dead.

"Don't cry. I don't hurt anymore. I'm fine," Azucena said when dawn came.

"I'm not crying for you," Rolf Carlé smiled. "I'm crying for myself. I hurt all over."

The third day in the valley of the cataclysm began with a pale light filtering through storm clouds. The President of the Republic visited the area in his tailored safari jacket to confirm that this was the worst catastrophe of the century; the country was in mourning; sister nations had offered aid; he had ordered a state of siege; the Armed Forces would be merciless, anyone caught stealing or committing other offenses would be shot on sight. He added that it was impossible to remove all the

9. Many refugees fled to South America during and immediately after the Second World War.

corpses or count the thousands who had disappeared; the entire valley would be declared holy ground, and bishops would come to celebrate a solemn mass for the souls of the victims. He went to the Army field tents to offer relief in the form of vague promises to crowds of the rescued, then to the improvised hospital to offer a word of encouragement to doctors and nurses worn down from so many hours of tribulations. Then he asked to be taken to see Azucena, the little girl the whole world had seen. He waved to her with a limp statesman's hand, and microphones recorded his emotional voice and paternal tone as he told her that her courage had served as an example to the nation. Rolf Carlé interrupted to ask for a pump, and the President assured him that he personally would attend to the matter. I caught a glimpse of Rolf for a few seconds kneeling beside the mudpit. On the evening news broadcast, he was still in the same position, and I, glued to the screen like a fortuneteller to her crystal ball, could tell that something fundamental had changed in him. I knew somehow that during the night his defenses had crumbled and he had given in to grief; finally he was vulnerable. The girl had touched a part of him that he himself had no access to, a part he had never shared with me. Rolf had wanted to console her, but it was Azucena who had given him consolation.

I recognized the precise moment at which Rolf gave up the fight and surrendered to the torture of watching the girl die. I was with them, three days and two nights, spying on them from the other side of life. I was there when she told him that in all her thirteen years no boy had ever loved her and that it was a pity to leave this world without knowing love. Rolf assured her that he loved her more than he could ever love anyone, more than he loved his mother, more than his sister, more than all the women who had slept in his arms, more than he loved me, his life companion, who would have given anything to be trapped in that well in her place, who would have exchanged her life for Azucena's, and I watched as he leaned down to kiss her poor forehead, consumed by a sweet, sad emotion he could not name. I felt how in that instant both were saved from despair, how they were freed from the clay, how they rose above the vultures and helicopters, how together they flew above the vast swamp of corruption and laments. How, finally, they were able to accept death. Rolf Carlé prayed in silence that she would die quickly, because such pain cannot be borne.

By then I had obtained a pump and was in touch with a general who had agreed to ship it the next morning on a military cargo plane. But on the night of that third day, beneath the unblinking focus of quartz lamps and the lens of a hundred cameras, Azucena gave up, her eyes locked with those of the friend who had sustained her to the end. Rolf Carlé removed the life buoy, closed her eyelids, held her to his chest for a few moments, and then let her go. She sank slowly, a flower in the mud.

You are back with me, but you are not the same man. I often accompany you to the station and we watch the videos of Azucena again; you study them intently, looking for something you could have done to save her, something you did not think of in time. Or maybe you study them to see yourself as if in a mirror, naked. Your cameras lie forgotten in a closet; you do not write or sing; you sit long hours before the window, staring at the mountains. Beside you, I wait for you to complete the voyage into yourself, for the old wounds to heal. I know that when you return from your nightmares, we shall again walk hand in hand, as before.

1989

CHU T'IEN-HSIN
born 1958

Chu T'ien-hsin (whose name can also be transliterated Zhu Tianxin) and her sister, Chu T'ien-wen, are among the best-known authors in contemporary Taiwan. Both began their careers in the 1970s, writing fiction that explores the importance of place and allegiance. The two grew up in a literary family: their mother worked as a translator of Japanese literature, concentrating on the works of modern authors such as **Kawabata Yasunari**; their father, also a celebrated writer, fled with his family from mainland China in the late 1940s. Much of Chu's mature writing deals with the relationship between China and Taiwan, gradually moving from an emphasis on Chinese identity, expressing nostalgic longing for a lost homeland, toward a direct engagement with Taiwan.

While studying at Taiwan National University, Chu and her sister started a literary magazine, *Three Three Quarterly*. During those years, Chu later said,

> we really began to develop a highly self-conscious sense of "mission." We didn't want to simply hone the technical skills and techniques of writing, we were aiming toward something more like the concept of *shi*, or traditional Chinese scholar. . . . Back when we were running the *Three Three Quarterly*, we very consciously decided that we didn't want to settle for being mere writers. After all, what's the big deal about being a novelist? All it's based on is technique. Like the traditional Chinese *shi*, we wanted to develop our understanding of politics, economics, and a whole array of other fields. Living in this world, we wanted to feel involved with what was happening in our country and our society.

Chu's more recent fiction, particularly the stories in the collection *Ancient Capital* (1997), is more stylistically experimental, exploring narrative structures that depart from traditional linear plots in order to explore complex questions of personal and cultural memory. The stories in *Ancient Capital* focus primarily on the history, memory, and cultural traditions of Taipei, a city that has been occupied at various times by the Dutch, the Manchus, the Japanese, and finally the Chinese nationalists, who fled there after their defeat in the civil war with the communists. A recipient of many literary honors, including the prestigious *China Times* prize for fiction, Chu is also a prolific screenwriter for the New Taiwan cinema movement, where she often collaborates with the writer-director Hou Hsiao-Hsien.

The story selected here, "Man of La Mancha" (1994), examines memory and identity in ways that are at once penetrating and oblique. Although the narration is in the first person, the speaker is a blurred and mysterious figure; we can guess at a profession (writer), but we cannot determine much else about the speaker. The plot revolves around the preparation for death. Unable to sleep one night, the speaker goes to a coffee shop, where the radio is broadcasting a bulletin about the death of "a second-generation descendant of the *ancien régime*" (the old order that precedes a revolution). Feeling faint, either because of the news, the stress, or the coffee, the narrator leaves the shop and heads to a Japanese-style medical clinic, and is diagnosed with arrhythmia. After leaving the clinic—and briefly passing out—the narrator imagines what would happen if the fainting spell had lasted longer and a passerby had to search the body for identification. Nothing the narrator is presently carrying would provide a useful clue.

This observation leads to a series of reflections on the life stories that we carry on our persons, in the form of trinkets and small documents. Gradually the speaker's list of preparations for an unexpected death becomes more intricate and even obsessive. The story ends with a quotation alluding to Don Quixote, the fictional country gentleman created by Miguel de Cervantes who sets out—absurdly, since even in the don's own time and place, the adventures of chivalric legend are not literally true—to win lasting honor and fame as a knight-errant.

The central topic that the speaker addresses—the question of how people are remembered after death—has deep roots in Chinese literature—most famously in the works of Sima Qian, a second-century historian who provided important models for the writers who followed. How one is remembered is critical to one's sense of identity, perhaps more critical than many of us would imagine. The story's subtle references to the fading lineage of the ancien régime, to the spread of Japanese institutions through Taiwan, to international travel and culturally specific forms of self-definition link these meditations to issues of cultural memory and Taiwanese identity. How much of the old Taiwan remains available to each generation's memory? And what are we to make of the distance between the generations? In short, what does it mean to be Taiwanese?

Man of La Mancha[1]

Strictly speaking, that was the day I began thinking about making preparations for my own death.

I should probably start from the night before.

Because a short essay of absolutely no importance was due the following noon, my brain, as usual, defied orders and turned itself on, ignoring the lure of the dream world and causing me to stay awake till dawn.

A few hours later, barely making it there before breakfast hours ended, I set to work in a Japanese-style chain coffee shop, effortlessly finishing that short, unimportant essay. It was then that I had the leisure to notice that, in order to fortify myself against the cold blasts from the air conditioner, I'd already downed five or six scalding refills of coffee, which had turned my fingers and toes numb, as if I'd been poisoned. I quietly stretched in my cramped seat, only to discover that my lips were so numb I couldn't open them to yawn. Even more strange was that my internal organs, whose existence had pretty much gone unnoticed over the three decades or so they'd been with me, were now frozen and shrunken, like little clenched fists, hanging tightly in their places inside me. I looked up at the girl who, in her clean, crisply pressed, nurselike uniform and apron, diligently refilled my cup over and over, and just about called out to her for help.

1. Translated by Howard Goldblatt.

I was anxiously pondering the language to use in seeking help from a stranger— even though this stranger was all smiles and would never refuse requests such as "Please give me another pat of butter," "Let me have another look at the menu," "Where can I make a phone call?" etc. But, "Help me?" "Please call me an ambulance?" "Please help me stand up?". . .

Yet for someone else, obviously, it was too late. The noontime headline news over the coffee shop radio announced that a certain second-generation descendant of the *ancien régime*[2] had been discovered early that morning dead in a hospital examination room, still in the prime of his youth, cause of death unknown, a peaceful look on his face. Which meant he hadn't even had time to struggle or call out for help.

That was all I needed: picking up my essay and bag, I paid and left.

I refused to pass out during the few minutes I spent waiting for a bus or a taxi (whichever came first), but if I'd wanted to, I could have slumped to the pavement and plunged into a deep slumber. Then a series of screams would have erupted around me, mixed with whisperings, and many heads, framed in the light behind them, would have bent down and appeared on the retina of my enlarged iris, as in the camera shot used in all movies for such scenes.

No matter how you looked at it, it would have been a pretty loutish way to go, so I refused to fall or even to rest, though by then the chill from my internal organs was spreading out to my flesh and skin. I forced myself to head toward an old and small nearby clinic. My mind was a blank; I have no idea how long it took me to get there. "I'm going to faint, please help me," I said to the work-study student nurse, who was about the same age as the coffee shop girl who'd served me.

When I came to, I was lying on a narrow examination bed; the gray-haired old doctor, mixing Mandarin and Taiwanese, answered the puzzled look and questions brimming in my eyes with a voice that seemed very loud, very far away, and very slow: "Not enough oxygen to your heart. We're giving you an IV.[3] Lie here a while before you leave. The nurse can help you phone your family, if you want. Don't stay up too late or eat anything that might upset you. Arrhythmia is a serious matter."

With that warning, he went off to see the next patient.

So concise, so precise, he'd pinpointed my problems: insomnia, too much coffee, and arrhythmia. Strange, why was a very, very cold tear hanging in the corner of each of my eyes?

I still felt cold, but it was only the chill of the old Japanese-style clinic, no longer the deadly silent, numbing cold from the gradual loss of vital signs I'd experienced a few minutes earlier. But I hesitated, like a spirit floating in the air, as if I could choose not to return to my body. I missed the body that had nearly slumped to the pavement a few minutes before. The site of the near fall was the bus stop in front of McDonald's, so there would have been young mothers with their children and old men with grandchildren waiting for the bus. The sharp-eyed youngsters would be the first to spot it, then the mothers

2. The old regime (French) of Chinese nationalist politicians who ruled Taiwan from 1949 until the end of the 20th century; a reference to the monarchy before the French Revolution of 1789. The descendant mentioned here is Jiang Xiaowu (1945–1991), grandson of nationalist leader Chiang Kai-shek (1887–1975).

3. Intravenous drip.

would vigilantly pull them away or draw them under their wings for protection, instinctively believing that it must be a beggar, a vagrant, or a mental patient, or maybe someone suffering from the effects of the plague, cholera, or epilepsy. But some of the grandpas who'd seen more of the world would come up to check and then, judging from my more or less respectable attire, take me off the list of the aforementioned suspects and decide to save me.

Looking into my wide-open but enlarged irises, they'd shout, "Who are you? Who should we call? What's the number?" They'd also order one of the gawking young women, "Go call an ambulance."

Who am I? Who should I call? What number?

I'd think back to how, on busy mornings, my significant other would lay out his schedule for the day, and I'd promptly forget; it would go something like this: "At ten-thirty I'm going to X's office; at noon I have to be at XX Bank as a guarantor. Do we have bills to pay? In the afternoon I'll go. . . . Want me to get you. . . . Or page me when you decide. . . ."

So I'd give up searching for and trying to recall his whereabouts.

Grandpa would say, "We have no choice, we have to go through his bag."

And, under watchful eyes, so as to avoid suspicion, he'd open my bag. Let's see, plenty of money—coins and bills—some ATM receipts, one or two unused lengths of dental floss, a claim ticket for film developing and a coupon for a free enlargement from the same photo studio; here, here's a business card . . . given to me yesterday by a friend, for a super-cheap London B&B[4] (16 pounds a night), at 45 Lupton Street, phone and fax (071) 4854075. Even though it would have an address and a phone number, it would of course provide no clue to my identity. So Grandpa would have to check my pockets; in one he'd find a small packet of facial tissues, in the other, after ordering the onlookers to help turn me over, a small stack of napkins with the name of the Japanese coffee shop I'd just visited printed in the corner. Different from the plain, unprinted McDonald's napkins in their pockets.

Then someone would take out that short, insignificant essay and start to read, but be unable to retrieve, from my insignificant pen name, any information to decipher my identity.

Finally a tender-hearted, timid young mother would cover her sobbing face and cry out, "Please, someone hurry, send him to the hospital."

That's what scared me most. Just like that, I could become a nameless vegetable lying in a hospital for who knows how long; of course, even more likely, I'd become an anonymous corpse picked up on a sidewalk and lie for years in cold storage at the city morgue.

Could all this really result from an absence of identifiable items?

From that moment on, from that very moment on, I began to think about making preparations for my own death—or should I say, it occurred to me that I ought to prepare for unpredictable, unpreventable circumstances surrounding my death?

Maybe you'll say nothing could be easier; all I had to do was start carrying a picture ID or a business card, like someone with a heart condition who's never without a note that says: whoever finds this please send the bearer to a certain hospital, phone the following family members, in the order their numbers

4. Bed and breakfast (a small, informal hotel).

appear here, and, most important, take a glycerin pill out of the little bottle in my pocket and place it under my tongue. But no, that's not what I meant. Maybe I should say that was the genesis of my worries but, as my thoughts unfolded, they went far beyond that.

Let me cite a couple of examples by way of explanation.

Not long ago I found a wallet in a phone booth. It was a poor-quality knock-off of a name-brand item. So I opened it without much curiosity, with the simple intention of finding the owner's address in order to, as my good deed for the day, mail it back to him or her—before opening it, I couldn't get a sense of the owner's gender, given its unisex look.

The wallet was quite thick, even though the money inside amounted to a meager 400 NT. In addition to a color photo of Amy Lau, it was all puffed up with over a dozen cards: a phone card, a KTV[5] member discount card, a student card from a chain hair salon, a point-collecting card from a bakery, a raffle ticket stub, a membership exchange card for a TV video game club, an iced tea shop manager's business card, an honor card for nonsmokers, etc.

I probably didn't look beyond the third card before I was confident I could describe the wallet's owner: a sixteen- or seventeen-year-old insipid (in my view) female student. That, in fact, turned out to be the case; my assumption was corroborated by a swimming pool membership card, which included her school and grade, so I could return the wallet to her when I found the time.

Here's another example. I don't know if you've read the autobiography of the Spanish director, Luis Buñuel,[6] but I recall that he said he stopped going on long trips after turning sixty because he was afraid of dying in a foreign land, afraid of the movielike scene of opened suitcases and documents strewn all over the ground, ambulance sirens and flashing police lights, hotel owners, local policemen, small-town reporters, gawkers, total chaos, awkward and embarrassing. Most important, he was probably afraid that, lacking the ability to defend himself, he'd be identified and labeled, whether or not he'd led a life that was serious, complex, worthy.

Here's another related example, although it doesn't concern death, taken from a certain short story that nicely describes the extramarital affair of a graceful and refined lady. When, by chance, she encounters her lover, and sex is on the agenda, she changes her mind. What stops her is surely not morality, nor her loving husband, who treats her just fine, nor the enjoyment-killing idea that there's no time for birth control measures. Rather, it's that she left home that day on the spur of the moment to take a stroll and do some shopping during a time when everything was scarce, and she was wearing ordinary cotton undergarments that were tattered from too many washings.

What would you have done?

Let me put it this way: these examples quickly convinced me that, if death came suddenly and without warning, who could manage to follow the intention of "a dying tiger leaves its skin intact"?

And that's why I envy chronically ill patients and old folks nearing the end of their lives, like Buñuel, for they have adequate time to make their preparations, since death is anticipated. I don't mean just writing a will or making their

5. Karaoke TV, a private karaoke studio.
6. Spanish surrealist filmmaker (1900–1983), author of the memoir *My Last Sigh* (1982).

own funeral arrangements, stuff like that. What I'm saying is: they have enough time to decide what to burn and destroy and what to leave behind—the diaries, correspondence, photographs, and curious objects from idiosyncratic collecting habits they've treasured and kept throughout their lives.

For example, I was once asked by the heartbroken wife of a teacher who had died unexpectedly to go through the effects in his office. Among the mountains of research material on the Zhou[7] dynasty city-state, I found a notebook recording the dates of conjugal bliss with his wife over the thirty years of their marriage. The dates were accompanied by complicated notations that were clearly secret codes, perhaps to describe the degree of satisfaction he'd achieved. I couldn't decide whether to burn it to protect the old man or treat it as a rare treasure and turn it over to his wife.

Actually, in addition to destroying things, I should also fabricate or arrange things in such a way that people would think what I wanted them to think about me. A minor ruse might be to obtain some receipts for charitable donations or copy down some occasional, personal notes that are more or less readable and might even be self-published by the surviving family. Even more delicate was a case I once read about in the health and medical section of the newspaper: a gramps in his seventies who had a penile implant wrote to ask if he should have it removed before emigrating to mainland China, for he was afraid that, after he died and was cremated, his children and grandchildren would discover his secret from the curious object that neither burned nor melted.

So you need to understand that the advance preparations I'm talking about go far beyond passive procedures to prevent becoming a nameless vegetable or an anonymous corpse; in fact, they have developed into an exquisite, highly proactive state.

I decided to begin by attending to my wallet.

The first thing I threw away was the sloppy-looking dental floss; then I tossed some business cards I'd taken out of politeness from people whose names I could no longer remember, a few baffling but colorful paper clips, a soft drink pull-tab to exchange for a free can, a book coupon, etc. In sum, a bunch of junk whose only significance was to show how shabby I was.

What then are the things that are both meaningful and fully explanatory, and are reasonably found in a wallet?

First of all, my career does not require business cards, and I had no employee ID card or work permit. I didn't have a driver's license and hadn't joined any serious organization or recreational club, so I had no membership cards. I didn't even have a credit card!

—Speaking of credit cards, they create a mystery that causes considerable consternation. I'm sure you've experienced this: you're in a department store or a large shop or a restaurant, and the cashier asks, "Cash or charge?"

Based on my observations, even though the cashier's tone is usually neutral and quite proper, those who pay cash stammer their response, while those who pay with a credit card answer loud and clear. Isn't that weird? Aren't the credit card users, simply put, debtors? The implication, at least, is: I have the money to pay you, but for now, or for the next few weeks, the credit guarantee system of my bank lets me owe you without having to settle up.

7. Dynasty of Chinese rulers (1046–221 B.C.E.).

But what about those who pay cash? They are able to hand over the money with one hand and take possession of the goods with the other, with neither party owing the other a thing. Why then should they be so diffident? And what makes those paying with a credit card so self-assured?

Could it be that the latter, after a credit check to prove that they are now and in the future will continue to be productive, can enter the system and be completely trusted? And the former, those who owe nothing to anyone, why are they so irretrievably timid? Is it possible they cannot be incorporated into the control system of an industrial, commercial society because their mode of production or their productivity is regarded as somehow uncivilized, unscientific, and unpredictable, the equivalent of an agricultural-age barter system? Simply put, when you are not a cog with a clearly defined purpose and prerequisite in the system, their trust in you is based on what they can see, and that must be a one-time exchange of money and goods, since there is no guarantee of exchange credit for the next time, or the time after that. You are neither trusted nor accepted by a gigantic, intimidating system, and that is why you are diffident, timid, even though you could well be able and diligent, and are not necessarily poor, at least not a beggar or a homeless person who pays no taxes.

By contrast, those whose wallets are choked with cards of every kind are trusted by organizations, big and small, which vie to admit them and consider them indispensable. They are so complacent, so confident, and all because: "I have credit, therefore I am."

Can a person living in this world be without a name, or a dwelling place?

My wallet was empty, with nothing to fill it up and no way to disguise that, but I didn't want the person who opened it to see at first glance that it belonged to one of life's losers. So I put in a few thousand-NT bills, which I wouldn't use for so long they'd begin to look as if they were part of the wallet itself.

The wallet may have been empty, but since it wouldn't hold a passport, I debated whether to include my ID card to establish my identity—when 20 million ID cards are attached to 20 million people, you see, the meaning is nullified—and I could not follow your suggestion to, in a feigned casual manner, insert a small note with my name and phone number on it. Which meant that putting aside the issue of becoming a nameless vegetable or an anonymous corpse on the sidewalk, this anonymous wallet would, sooner or later, become nonreturnable, even if found by a Samaritan.

Ah! A savorless, flavorless, colorless, odorless wallet. Sometimes I pretended to be a stranger, examining and fondling it, speculating how the Samaritan who found it would sigh emotionally: "What an uninteresting and unimportant person your owner must be!"

After I lost interest in the disguise and the construction of my wallet, for a while I turned my attention to my clothes. Especially my underwear. To be ready for an unexpected sexual encounter—no, I mean for the unannounced visit of death.

Underwear is very important, and it's not enough just to keep it from becoming tattered or turning yellow. On psychological, social, even political levels, it describes its owner more vividly than many other things. Didn't Bill Clinton respond shyly that his underpants weren't those trendy plaid boxers, but were skin-hugging briefs?[8]

8. In April 1994, a student asked US president Bill Clinton what kind of underwear he wore, boxer shorts or briefs; he replied, "usually briefs."

And just look at his foreign policy!

Still, I gave serious consideration to changing and washing my underwear religiously, and to the purchase of new sets. For starters, I tossed my black and purple sets, along with my Clinton-style briefs, all of which might have caused undue speculation. After mulling over the replacements, I decided to go to the open-rack garment section of Watson's,[9] where no salesperson would bother me, and picked out several pairs of white Calvin Klein 100 percent cotton underpants, though their yuppie style didn't quite match my antisocial tendencies. My significant other was all but convinced I had a new love interest, and we had a big fight over that. But I didn't reveal the truth. If one day I happened to depart this world before him, then my clear, white underwear would remind that grief-stricken man of what I looked like after my shower on so many nights. Those sweet memories might comfort him, at least a little.

But my preparatory work didn't end there.

On some days, when I had to go to work, I passed the site where I'd nearly fallen, knowing full well that the strength that had sustained me and would not let me fall came from the thought: "I'll not be randomly discovered and identified like this."

Randomly discovered. In addition to the state I was in, the wallet, my clothes, there was also location.

That's right, location. I thought back carefully to the routes I took when I went out and realized that, even though I was in the habit of roaming a bit, there was a definite sense of order and, in the end, it would be easy for a secret agent, even a neophyte P.I., to follow me. Even so, I strove to simplify my routes, avoiding places that would be hard to explain, even if I was just passing by.

Let me put it this way. An upright, simple, extremely religious, and highly disciplined college classmate of mine died in a fire at a well-known sex sauna last year. The firefighters found him, neatly dressed, dead of asphyxiation, in the hallway. We went to give our condolences to his wife, also a college classmate, and as we warmly recalled all the good deeds he'd performed when alive and said he'd definitely be ushered into heaven, we couldn't completely shake the subtle sense of embarrassment—what exactly was the good fellow, our classmate, doing there?

We could not ask, and she could not answer.

So I was determined to avoid vulgar, tasteless little local temples, shrouded in incense smoke; I didn't want to die in front of a spirit altar, giving my significant other the impression I'd changed religions.

And I didn't want to go to the Ximen-ding[1] area, which I'd pretty much avoided since graduating from college, afraid I'd end up dead in an area honeycombed with dilapidated sex-trade alleys, fall under suspicion, like that good classmate of mine, and be unable to defend myself.

From then on, I quickened my steps whenever I walked by some of my favorite deep-green alleys, with their Japanese-style houses, where time seemed to stand still. I no longer stopped or strolled there, afraid that my significant other would suspect I'd hidden away an illegitimate child or was having a secret rendezvous with an old flame.

9. A Chinese drugstore chain.
1. A shopping district in Taipei, the capital of Taiwan.

I even stopped roaming wherever my feet took me, as I'd done when I was younger, just so I wouldn't be found dead on a beach where people came to watch the sunset. Otherwise, my credit card–carrying significant other would be embroiled in a lifelong puzzle and be mired in deep grief.

After all, death only visits us once in our lifetime, so we should make advance preparations for its arrival.

Hundreds of years ago, the Man of La Mancha[2]
  howled at the sky—
A windblown quest
Seeking love in steel and rocks
Using manners with savages

And me, afraid that the handwriting would be eaten away by mites and no longer legible, I wrote this down.

1994

2. The nickname for Cervantes' Don Quixote, who hailed from the La Mancha region of Spain and tried to model his life on the knights in chivalric romances; *Man of La Mancha* was a play by Dale Wasserman, produced for television in 1959, transformed into a Broadway musical in 1965, and made into a successful feature film in 1972.

JUNOT DÍAZ
born 1968

Pulitzer Prize–winning novelist Junot Díaz is one of the most distinctive literary voices of any Latino writing today. Díaz has a remarkable ability to create a convincing narrative by drawing on New Jersey and Hispanic slang and to combine the street talk with a high degree of linguistic inventiveness. He thus mixes high style and low, even vulgar, language to impressive effect.

An immigrant of African descent from the Dominican Republic, Díaz, at the age of six, moved with his family to Parlin, New Jersey. Of his first days in an American school, he recalls: "I showed up at school not knowing a word of English and dressed like something out of a wetback comedy. We stood out so much in this community it was remarkable." He later worked his way through college, graduating with a bachelor's degree from Rutgers University and a master of fine arts from Cornell University; he now teaches at the Massachusetts Institute of Technology.

His first novel, *The Brief Wondrous Life of Oscar Wao* (2007), describes the lives of an immigrant family as they experience poverty and persecution in the Dominican Republic under the dictatorship of Rafael Leonidas Trujillo. In this novel, and in his short stories, Díaz interweaves techniques of the magic realism of **Gabriel García Márquez** with references to North American popular culture. He also mixes Spanish and English, in a combination often called "Spanglish." While some readers may object to the presence of Spanglish, Díaz has argued, "I've almost never read an adult book where I didn't have to pick up a dictionary. . . . I want there to be an element of incomprehension. What's language without incomprehension? What's art?"

"Drown," first published in the *New Yorker* magazine in 1996, lent its title to Díaz's first book, a collection of interlocking short stories. This memorable, one-word title refers only indirectly to any events in the story; it may represent the threat of drowning in the municipal swimming pool that the characters visit at night, but more broadly it suggests that the main character is drowning in the poverty of his surroundings and in the culture to which his parents have brought him. Díaz creates a first-person narrator whose biography is similar to his own. Many of the stories in *Drown* are narrated by Yunior de las Casas, a Dominican immigrant who arrived in the United States at the age of nine. Like **James Joyce** in *Ulysses,* Díaz has based the collection partly on Homer's *Odyssey*. Yunior, like Odysseus's son Telemachus, lives alone with his unhappy mother. In Díaz's work, the mother is waiting for the boy's father to return to her from Florida, where he is living with another woman. Díaz thus places his immigrant characters in the context of the epic tradition.

In this story, the narrator (elsewhere identified as Yunior), a drug dealer, has not gone to college. His mother tells him that his old friend Beto, who is attending college (probably Rutgers), is back in the neighborhood. She wants to know why her son no longer spends time with his old friend. Yunior reveals a key fact about Beto in the third sentence of the story: "He's a pato now." Only those with a knowledge of Latino slang will understand the meaning of *pato*, and not until much later in the story does the importance of the information become apparent, when Díaz makes the meaning of the term clear. Thus Díaz develops a level of suspense and vividly evokes the minority subculture to which the narrator belongs. Later he makes extensive use of New Jersey place-names, both to ground the story in reality and to suggest the relatively limited geographic scope of the narrator's experience—while indicating, as well, the young man's command over a territory that he can call his own. Compared by a teacher to a space shuttle crashing before it goes into orbit, Yunior senses that he is going nowhere—living at home with his mother, selling drugs, occasionally shoplifting, on the verge of drowning in poverty—while his friend Beto, by going to college, may just have saved himself.

Drown

My mother tells me Beto's home, waits for me to say something, but I keep watching the TV. Only when she's in bed do I put on my jacket and swing through the neighborhood to see. He's a pato[1] now but two years ago we were friends and he would walk into the apartment without knocking, his heavy voice rousing my mother from the Spanish of her room and drawing me up from the basement, a voice that crackled and made you think of uncles or grandfathers.

1. Homosexual (Caribbean Spanish slang); literally, duck.

We were raging then, crazy the way we stole, broke windows, the way we pissed on people's steps and then challenged them to come out and stop us. Beto was leaving for college at the end of the summer and was delirious from the thought of it—he hated everything about the neighborhood, the break-apart buildings, the little strips of grass, the piles of garbage around the cans, and the dump, especially the dump.

I don't know how you can do it, he said to me. I would just find me a job anywhere and go.

Yeah, I said. I wasn't like him. I had another year to go in high school, no promises elsewhere.

Days we spent in the mall or out in the parking lot playing stickball, but nights were what we waited for. The heat in the apartments was like something heavy that had come inside to die. Families arranged on their porches, the glow from their TVs washing blue against the brick. From my family apartment you could smell the pear trees that had been planted years ago, four to a court, probably to save us all from asphyxiation. Nothing moved fast, even the daylight was slow to fade, but as soon as night settled Beto and I headed down to the community center and sprang the fence into the pool. We were never alone, every kid with legs was there. We lunged from the boards and swam out of the deep end, wrestling and farting around. At around midnight abuelas, with their night hair swirled around spiky rollers, shouted at us from their apartment windows. ¡Sinvergüenzas![2] Go home!

I pass his apartment but the windows are dark; I put my ear to the busted-up door and hear only the familiar hum of the air conditioner. I haven't decided yet if I'll talk to him. I can go back to my dinner and two years will become three.

Even from four blocks off I can hear the racket from the pool—radios too—and wonder if we were ever that loud. Little has changed, not the stink of chlorine, not the bottles exploding against the lifeguard station. I hook my fingers through the plastic-coated hurricane fence. Something tells me that he will be here; I hop the fence, feeling stupid when I sprawl on the dandelions and the grass.

Nice one, somebody calls out.

Fuck me, I say. I'm not the oldest motherfucker in the place, but it's close. I take off my shirt and my shoes and then knife in. Many of the kids here are younger brothers of the people I used to go to school with. Two of them swim past, black and Latino, and they pause when they see me, recognizing the guy who sells them their shitty dope. The crackheads have their own man, Lucero, and some other guy who drives in from Paterson,[3] the only full-time commuter in the area.

The water feels good. Starting at the deep end I glide over the slick-tiled bottom without kicking up a spume or making a splash. Sometimes another swimmer churns past me, more a disturbance of water than a body. I can still go far without coming up. While everything above is loud and bright, everything below is whispers. And always the risk of coming up to find the cops stabbing their

2. Shameless people. "Abuelas": grandmothers.
3. A town in northern New Jersey; the name Lucero, like Lucifer in English, means "morningstar."

searchlights out across the water. And then everyone running, wet feet slapping against the concrete, yelling, Fuck you, officers, you puto sucios,[4] fuck you.

When I'm tired I wade through to the shallow end, past some kid who's kissing his girlfriend, watching me as though I'm going to try to cut in, and I sit near the sign that runs the pool during the day. *No Horseplay, No Running, No Defecating, No Urinating, No Expectorating*. At the bottom someone has scrawled in *No Whites, No Fat Chiks* and someone else has provided the missing *c*. I laugh. Beto hadn't known what expectorating meant though he was the one leaving for college. I told him, spitting a greener by the side of the pool.

Shit, he said. Where did you learn that?

I shrugged.

Tell me. He hated when I knew something he didn't. He put his hands on my shoulders and pushed me under. He was wearing a cross and cutoff jeans. He was stronger than me and held me down until water flooded my nose and throat. Even then I didn't tell him; he thought I didn't read, not even dictionaries.

We live alone. My mother has enough for the rent and groceries and I cover the phone bill, sometimes the cable. She's so quiet that most of the time I'm startled to find her in the apartment. I'll enter a room and she'll stir, detaching herself from the cracking plaster walls, from the stained cabinets, and fright will pass through me like a wire. She has discovered the secret to silence: pouring café[5] without a splash, walking between rooms as if gliding on a cushion of felt, crying without a sound. You have traveled to the East and learned many secret things, I've told her. You're like a shadow warrior.

And you're like a crazy, she says. Like a big crazy.

When I come in she's still awake, her hands picking clots of lint from her skirt. I put a towel down on the sofa and we watch television together. We settle on the Spanish-language news: drama for her, violence for me. Today a child has survived a seven-story fall, busting nothing but his diaper. The hysterical babysitter, about three hundred pounds of her, is head-butting the microphone.

It's a goddamn miraclevilla,[6] she cries.

My mother asks me if I found Beto. I tell her that I didn't look.

That's too bad. He was telling me that he might be starting at a school for business.

So what?

She's never understood why we don't speak anymore. I've tried to explain, all wise-like, that everything changes, but she thinks that sort of saying is only around so you can prove it wrong.

He asked me what you were doing.

What did you say?

I told him you were fine.

You should have told him I moved.

And what if he ran into you?

I'm not allowed to visit my mother?

She notices the tightening of my arms. You should be more like me and your father.

4. Dirty faggots (Spanish slang).
5. Coffee.
6. Mixes English "miracle" and Spanish "maravilla" (marvel).

Can't you see I'm watching television?

I was angry at him, wasn't I? But now we can talk to each other.

Am I watching television here or what?

Saturdays she asks me to take her to the mall. As a son I feel I owe her that much, even though neither of us has a car and we have to walk two miles through redneck territory to catch the M15.[7]

Before we head out she drags us through the apartment to make sure the windows are locked. She can't reach the latches so she has me test them. With the air conditioner on we never open windows but I go through the routine anyway. Putting my hand on the latch is not enough—she wants to hear it rattle. This place just isn't safe, she tells me. Lorena got lazy and look what they did to her. They punched her and kept her locked up in her place. Those morenos[8] ate all her food and even made phone calls. Phone calls!

That's why we don't have long-distance, I tell her but she shakes her head. That's not funny, she says.

She doesn't go out much, so when she does it's a big deal. She dresses up, even puts on makeup. Which is why I don't give her lip about taking her to the mall even though I usually make a fortune on Saturdays, selling to those kids going down to Belmar or out to Spruce Run.[9]

I recognize like half the kids on the bus. I keep my head buried in my cap, praying that nobody tries to score.[1] She watches the traffic, her hands somewhere inside her purse, doesn't say a word.

When we arrive at the mall I give her fifty dollars. Buy something, I say, hating the image I have of her, picking through the sale bins, wrinkling everything. Back in the day, my father would give her a hundred dollars at the end of each summer for my new clothes and she would take nearly a week to spend it, even though it never amounted to more than a couple of t-shirts and two pairs of jeans. She folds the bills into a square. I'll see you at three, she says.

I wander through the stores, staying in sight of the cashiers so they won't have reason to follow me. The circuit I make has not changed since my looting days. Bookstore, record store, comic-book shop, Macy's. Me and Beto used to steal like mad from these places, two, three hundred dollars of shit in an outing. Our system was simple—we walked into a store with a shopping bag and came out loaded. Back then security wasn't tight. The only trick was in the exit. We stopped right at the entrance of the store and checked out some worthless piece of junk to stop people from getting suspicious. What do you think? we asked each other. Would she like it? Both of us had seen bad shoplifters at work. All grab and run, nothing smooth about them. Not us. We idled out of the stores slow, like a fat seventies car. At this, Beto was the best. He even talked to mall security, asked them for directions, his bag all loaded up, and me, standing ten feet away, shitting my pants. When he finished he smiled, swinging his shopping bag up to hit me.

You got to stop that messing around, I told him. I'm not going to jail for bullshit like that.

7. A public bus.
8. Black men (Spanish).
9. A state park in central New Jersey; "Belmar": a beach resort on the New Jersey shore.
1. Purchase drugs.

You don't go to jail for shoplifting. They just turn you over to your old man.

I don't know about you, but my pops hits like a motherfucker.

He laughed. You know my dad. He flexed his hands. The nigger's got arthritis.

My mother never suspected, even when my clothes couldn't all fit in my closet, but my father wasn't that easy. He knew what things cost and knew that I didn't have a regular job.

You're going to get caught, he told me one day. Just you wait. When you do I'll show them everything you've taken and then they'll throw your stupid ass away like a bad piece of meat.

He was a charmer, my pop, a real asshole, but he was right. Nobody can stay smooth forever, especially kids like us. One day at the bookstore, we didn't even hide the drops. Four issues of the same *Playboy* for kicks, enough audio books to start our own library. No last minute juke either. The lady who stepped in front of us didn't look old, even with her white hair. Her silk shirt was half unbuttoned and a silver horn necklace sat on the freckled top of her chest. I'm sorry fellows, but I have to check your bag, she said. I kept moving, and looked back all annoyed, like she was asking us for a quarter or something. Beto got polite and stopped. No problem, he said, slamming the heavy bag into her face. She hit the cold tile with a squawk, her palms slapping the ground. There you go, Beto said.

Security found us across from the bus stop, under a Jeep Cherokee. A bus had come and gone, both of us too scared to take it, imagining a plainclothes waiting to clap the cuffs on. I remember that when the rent-a-cop tapped his nightstick against the fender and said, You little shits better come out here real slow, I started to cry. Beto didn't say a word, his face stretched out and gray, his hand squeezing mine, the bones in our fingers pressing together.

Nights I drink with Alex and Danny. The Malibou Bar is no good, just washouts and the sucias[2] we can con into joining us. We drink too much, roar at each other and make the skinny bartender move closer to the phone. On the wall hangs a cork dartboard and a Brunswick Gold Crown blocks the bathroom, its bumpers squashed, the felt pulled like old skin.

When the bar begins to shake back and forth like a rumba, I call it a night and go home, through the fields that surround the apartments. In the distance you can see the Raritan,[3] as shiny as an earthworm, the same river my homeboy goes to school on. The dump has long since shut down, and grass has spread over it like a sickly fuzz, and from where I stand, my right hand directing a colorless stream of piss downward, the landfill might be the top of a blond head, square and old.

In the mornings I run. My mother is already up, dressing for her housecleaning job. She says nothing to me, would rather point to the mangu[4] she has prepared than speak.

I run three miles easily, could have pushed a fourth if I were in the mood. I keep an eye out for the recruiter who prowls around our neighborhood in his dark K-car. We've spoken before. He was out of uniform and called me over,

2. Sluts (Spanish slang).
3. A major river in central New Jersey.
4. Plantain-based dish originating in the Dominican Republic.

jovial, and I thought I was helping some white dude with directions. Would you mind if I asked you a question?

No.

Do you have a job?

Not right now.

Would you like one? A real career, more than you'll get around here?

I remember stepping back. Depends on what it is, I said.

Son, I know somebody who's hiring. It's the United States government.

Well. Sorry, but I ain't Army material.

That's exactly what I used to think, he said, his ten piggy fingers buried in his carpeted steering wheel. But now I have a house, a car, a gun and a wife. Discipline. Loyalty. Can you say that you have those things? Even one?

He's a southerner, red-haired, his drawl so out of place that the people around here laugh just hearing him. I take to the bushes when I see his car on the road. These days my guts feel loose and cold and I want to be away from here. He won't have to show me his Desert Eagle or flash the photos of the skinny Filipino girls sucking dick. He'll only have to smile and name the places and I'll listen.

When I reach the apartment, I lean against my door, waiting for my heart to slow, for the pain to lose its edge. I hear my mother's voice, a whisper from the kitchen. She sounds hurt or nervous, maybe both. At first I'm terrified that Beto's inside with her but then I look and see the phone cord, swinging lazily. She's talking to my father, something she knows I disapprove of. He's in Florida now, a sad guy who calls her and begs for money. He swears that if she moves down there he'll leave the woman he's living with. These are lies, I've told her, but she still calls him. His words coil inside of her, wrecking her sleep for days. She opens the refrigerator door slightly so that the whir of the compressor masks their conversation. I walk in on her and hang up the phone. That's enough, I say.

She's startled, her hand squeezing the loose folds of her neck. That was him, she says quietly.

On school days Beto and I chilled at the stop together but as soon as that bus came over the Parkwood hill I got to thinking about how I was failing gym and screwing up math and how I hated every single living teacher on the planet.

I'll see *you* in the p.m., I said.

He was already standing on line. I just stood back and grinned, my hands in my pockets. With our bus drivers you didn't have to hide. Two of them didn't give a rat fuck and the third one, the Brazilian preacher, was too busy talking Bible to notice anything but the traffic in front of him.

Being truant without a car was no easy job but I managed. I watched a lot of TV and when it got boring I trooped down to the mall or the Sayreville library, where you could watch old documentaries for free. I always came back to the neighborhood late, so the bus wouldn't pass me on Ernston[5] and nobody could yell Asshole! out the windows. Beto would usually be home or down by the swings, but other times he wouldn't be around at all. Out visiting other neighborhoods. He knew a lot of folks I didn't—a messed-up black kid from Madi-

5. Ernston and Sayreville are towns in central New Jersey.

son Park, two brothers who were into that N.Y. club scene, who spent money on platform shoes and leather backpacks. I'd leave a message with his parents and then watch some more TV. The next day he'd be out at the bus stop, too busy smoking a cigarette to say much about the day before.

You need to learn how to walk the world, he told me. There's a lot out there.

Some nights me and the boys drive to New Brunswick.[6] A nice city, the Raritan so low and silty that you don't have to be Jesus to walk over it. We hit the Melody and the Roxy, stare at the college girls. We drink a lot and then spin out onto the dance floor. None of the chicas[7] ever dance with us, but a glance or a touch can keep us talking shit for hours.

Once the clubs close we go to the Franklin Diner, gorge ourselves on pancakes, and then, after we've smoked our pack, head home. Danny passes out in the back seat and Alex cranks the window down to keep the wind in his eyes. He's fallen asleep in the past, wrecked two cars before this one. The streets have been picked clean of students and townies and we blow through every light, red or green. At the Old Bridge Turnpike[8] we pass the fag bar, which never seems to close. Patos are all over the parking lot, drinking and talking.

Sometimes Alex will stop by the side of the road and say, Excuse me. When somebody comes over from the bar he'll point his plastic pistol at them, just to see if they'll run or shit their pants. Tonight he just puts his head out the window. Fuck you! he shouts and then settles back in his seat, laughing.

That's original, I say.

He puts his head out the window again. Eat me, then!

Yeah, Danny mumbles from the back. Eat me.

Twice. That's it.

The first time was at the end of that summer. We had just come back from the pool and were watching a porn video at his parents' apartment. His father was a nut for these tapes, ordering them from wholesalers in California and Grand Rapids. Beto used to tell me how his pop would watch them in the middle of the day, not caring a lick about his moms, who spent the time in the kitchen, taking hours to cook a pot of rice and gandules.[9] Beto would sit down with his pop and neither of them would say a word, except to laugh when somebody caught it in the eye or the face.

We were an hour into the new movie, some vaina[1] that looked like it had been filmed in the apartment next door, when he reached into my shorts. What the fuck are you doing? I asked, but he didn't stop. His hand was dry. I kept my eyes on the television, too scared to watch. I came right away, smearing the plastic sofa covers. My legs started shaking and suddenly I wanted out. He didn't say anything to me as I left, just sat there watching the screen.

The next day he called and when I heard his voice I was cool but I wouldn't go to the mall or anywhere else. My mother sensed that something was wrong and pestered me about it, but I told her to leave me the fuck alone, and my

6. Town in north-central New Jersey where Rutgers University is located; the Melody and the Roxy were dance clubs on French Street in New Brunswick in the 1980s and 1990s.

7. Girls.

8. A road in north-central New Jersey.

9. Pigeon peas (Spanish).

1. Worthless item (Spanish).

pops, who was home on a visit, stirred himself from the couch to slap me down. Mostly I stayed in the basement, terrified that I would end up abnormal, a fucking pato, but he was my best friend and back then that mattered to me more than anything. This alone got me out of the apartment and over to the pool that night. He was already there, his body pale and flabby under the water. Hey, he said. I was beginning to worry about you.

Nothing to worry about, I said.

We swam and didn't talk much and later we watched a Skytop crew pull a bikini top from a girl stupid enough to hang out alone. Give it, she said, covering herself, but these kids howled, holding it up over her head, the shiny laces flopping just out of reach. When they began to pluck at her arms, she walked away, leaving them to try the top on over their flat pecs.

He put his hand on my shoulder, my pulse a code under his palm. Let's go, he said. Unless of course you're not feeling good.

I'm feeling fine, I said.

Since his parents worked nights we pretty much owned the place until six the next morning. We sat in front of his television, in our towels, his hands bracing against my abdomen and thighs. I'll stop if you want, he said and I didn't respond. After I was done, he laid his head in my lap. I wasn't asleep or awake, but caught somewhere in between, rocked slowly back and forth the way surf holds junk against the shore, rolling it over and over. In three weeks he was leaving. Nobody can touch me, he kept saying. We'd visited the school and I'd seen how beautiful the campus was, with all the students drifting from dorm to class. I thought of how in high school our teachers loved to crowd us into their lounge every time a space shuttle took off from Florida. One teacher, whose family had two grammar schools named after it, compared us to the shuttles. A few of you are going to make it. Those are the orbiters. But the majority of you are just going to burn out. Going nowhere. He dropped his hand onto his desk. I could already see myself losing altitude, fading, the earth spread out beneath me, hard and bright.

I had my eyes closed and the television was on and when the hallway door crashed open, he jumped up and I nearly cut my dick off struggling with my shorts. It's just the neighbor, he said, laughing. He was laughing, but I was saying, Fuck this, and getting my clothes on.

I believe I see him in his father's bottomed-out Cadillac, heading towards the turnpike, but I can't be sure. He's probably back in school already. I deal close to home, trooping up and down the same dead-end street where the kids drink and smoke. These punks joke with me, pat me down for taps, sometimes too hard. Now that strip malls line Route 9,[2] a lot of folks have part-time jobs; the kids stand around smoking in their aprons, name tags dangling heavily from pockets.

When I get home, my sneakers are filthy so I take an old toothbrush to their soles, scraping the crap into the tub. My mother has thrown open the windows and propped open the door. It's cool enough, she explains. She has prepared dinner—rice and beans, fried cheese, tostones. Look what I bought, she says, showing me two blue t-shirts. They were two for one so I bought you one. Try it on.

2. A north-south federal highway that runs through New Jersey.

It fits tight but I don't mind. She cranks up the television. A movie dubbed into Spanish, a classic, one that everyone knows. The actors throw themselves around, passionate, but their words are plain and deliberate. It's hard to imagine anybody going through life this way. I pull out the plug of bills from my pockets. She takes it from me, her fingers soothing the creases. A man who treats his plata[3] like this doesn't deserve to spend it, she says.

We watch the movie and the two hours together makes us friendly. She puts her hand on mine. Near the end of the film, just as our heroes are about to fall apart under a hail of bullets, she takes off her glasses and kneads her temples, the light of the television flickering across her face. She watches another minute and then her chin lists to her chest. Almost immediately her eyelashes begin to tremble, a quiet semaphore. She is dreaming, dreaming of Boca Raton, of strolling under the jacarandas[4] with my father. You can't be anywhere forever, was what Beto used to say, what he said to me the day I went to see him off. He handed me a gift, a book, and after he was gone I threw it away, didn't even bother to open it and read what he'd written.

I let her sleep until the end of the movie and when I wake her she shakes her head, grimacing. You better check those windows, she says. I promise her I will.

1996

3. Money (Spanish slang).

4. Tropical flowering plant.

ROBERTO BOLAÑO

1953–2003

Celebrated after his premature death as one of the first great novelists of the twenty-first century, Roberto Bolaño extends the Latin American tradition of combining fantasy and reality to comment on the region's tragic history. Bolaño wrote that violence appears in his works "in an accidental way, which is how violence functions everywhere." While following the lives of writers and other middle-class figures apparently unaffected by the turbulent history of their region, Bolaño reveals, almost casually, how deeply shaped their lives have in fact been by its political upheavals.

Mystery also pervades much of Bolaño's biography. Born in Chile to a truck driver and a teacher, he moved to Mexico City with his family as a teenager. After dropping out of school, Bolaño joined several friends to form a poetic movement called infrarealism, influenced by the Dadaists and vehemently opposing the hero of Mexican culture, **Octavio Paz**, for his alleged conservatism. The infrarealist manifesto declared that "the poem is a journey, and the poet is a hero who reveals heroes." True to this vision, Bolaño's later fiction would trace the journeys of many real and fictional poets.

Bolaño soon became involved in left-wing politics; he claimed to have been imprisoned while fighting against the dictatorship of Augusto Pinochet in Chile in the 1970s, although his friends later disputed his assertion. (He also claimed, in later years, to have been a longtime heroin addict, a story that his wife strenuously denied, but his death from a liver ailment that may have been hepatitis seemed to confirm it.) After further travels in Central America and Europe, Bolaño settled near Barcelona, Spain, around 1980, working for a time as a night watchman and writing poetry in his spare hours. After the birth of his son, in 1990, he switched to writing fiction, in the hope that it would provide a better living. (He was indeed able to supplement his meager income by entering minor literary contests.) Suffering from the liver disease that eventually killed him, he wrote a series of brilliant novels that drew on the tradition of Latin American fiction that intertwines fantastical phenomena with the political events of the late twentieth century. In their style, his fictions suggest the invented worlds of **Jorge Luis Borges**. "I could live under a table reading Borges," he once said, although he was not above defying the master with a boastful challenge: "My life has been infinitely more savage than Borges's." Most of his novels were published in the 1990s, but his last work, *2666*, was published posthumously in 2004. Its English translation won the National Book Critics Circle award for fiction in 2008.

Bolaño's fascination with the effects of large-scale history on everyday life, as well as his frequent allusions to other writers, seem to mark him as a postmodernist, but in many respects his stories are more straightforward and less experimental than typical postmodernism. Like earlier writers of the Latin American "Boom," such as **Julio Cortázar** and **Gabriel García Márquez**, Bolaño concerns himself with politics; but rather than take sides, he tends to show his protagonists (almost all of whom are writers) making compromises with political violence in order to get by. As the novelist and critic Francisco Goldman once remarked, "the inseparable dangers of life and literature, and the relationship of life to literature, were the constant themes of Bolaño's writings and also of his life." Although the extent to which Bolaño participated in political struggle remains a mystery, there is no doubt that social and economic turmoil of the late twentieth century helped shape his fiction into a richly imagined world, very similar to—but at times a crazed glass reflecting—our own.

The story presented here, "Sensini" (1997), starts out as the chronicle of a young writer's life and his interest in the literary prizes sponsored by various Spanish towns. Drawing on Bolaño's experience, the work is set in the early 1980s, when the author was in his late twenties; like the author himself, the narrator is Chilean. The narrator, who lives near Barcelona, befriends an older, Argentine writer named Sensini, who lives with his wife and daughter in poverty in Madrid. (Sensini's character seems to be based in part on the writer Antonio di Benedetto, 1922–1986.) What begins as a simple tale of the narrator's apprenticeship and youthful literary ambitions becomes more troubling when he realizes that Sensini is looking for a substitute for his son, Gregorio, who has recently disappeared in the Argentine Dirty War (1976–83)—an extrajudicial campaign of murder and terror that the dictator Jorge Rafael Videla conducted against students, intellectuals, and opponents of his regime. Still, despite the narrator's frequent discussion of real-life Argentine authors, this is no straightforward historical account. The narrator develops a fascination with Sensini's daughter, Miranda, named after the character in Shakespeare's *The Tempest* whom the slave Caliban desires (and almost rapes). And Sensini's son,

Gregorio, is named after Gregor Samsa of **Franz Kafka**'s ***The Metamorphosis***, another story about complicated family relationships. Wondering whether to become an adoptive son to the writer he admires, the narrator finds himself increasingly entangled in the older man's family life, in a maze of literary allusions, and in the tragedies of Latin American political life in the 1980s.

Sensini[1]

The way in which my friendship with Sensini developed was somewhat unusual. At the time I was twenty-something and poorer than a church mouse. I was living on the outskirts of Girona,[2] in a dilapidated house that my sister and brother-in-law had left me when they moved to Mexico, and I had just lost my job as a night watchman in a Barcelona campground, a job that had exacerbated my tendency not to sleep at night. I had practically no friends and all I did was write and go for long walks, starting at seven in the evening, just after getting up, with a feeling like jet lag—an odd sensation of fragility, of being there and not there, somehow distant from my surroundings. I was living on what I had saved during the summer, and although I spent very little my savings dwindled as autumn drew on. Perhaps that was what prompted me to enter the Alcoy National Literature Competition, open to writers in Spanish, whatever their nationality or place of residence. There were three categories: for poems, stories, and essays. First I thought about trying for the poetry prize, but I felt it would be demeaning to send what I did best into the arena with the lions (or hyenas). Then I thought about the essay, but when they sent me the conditions, I discovered that it had to be about Alcoy,[3] its environs, its history, its eminent sons, its future prospects, and I couldn't face it. So I decided to go for the story prize and sent off three copies of the best one I had (not that I had many) and sat down to wait.

When the winners were announced I was working as a vendor in a handcrafts market where absolutely no one was selling anything handcrafted. I won fourth prize and ten thousand pesetas,[4] which the Alcoy Council paid with scrupulous promptitude. Shortly afterward I received the anthology, with the winning story and those of the six finalists, liberally peppered with typos. Naturally my story was better than the winner's, so I cursed the judges and told myself, Well, what can you expect? But the real surprise was coming across the name Luis Antonio Sensini,[5] the Argentinean writer, who had won third prize with a story in which the narrator went to the countryside and when he got there his son died, or went away to the country because his son had died in the city—it was hard to tell—in any case, out there in the countryside, on the bare plains, the narrator's son went on dying, that much was clear. It was a claustrophobic story, very much in Sensini's manner, set in a world where vast geographical spaces could suddenly shrink to the dimensions of a coffin, and it was better than the winning story and the one that came in second, as well as those that came in fourth, fifth, and sixth.

1. Translated by Chris Andrews.
2. City in northeastern Catalonia, Spain.
3. A city in Alicante province, south of Barcelona, on the Mediterranean coast of Spain.
4. Approximately $125 in the early 1980s, when the story is set (about $275 today).
5. Based on the real-life Argentine writer Antonio di Benedetto (1922–1986).

I don't know what moved me to ask the Alcoy Council for Sensini's address. I had read one of his novels and some of his stories in Latin American magazines. The novel was the kind of book that finds its own readers by word of mouth. Entitled *Ugarte*, it was about a series of moments in the life of Juan de Ugarte, a bureaucrat in the Viceroyalty of the Río de la Plata[6] at the end of the eighteenth century. Some (mainly Spanish) critics had dismissed it as Kafka[7] in the colonies, but gradually the novel had made its way, and by the time I came across Sensini's name in the Alcoy anthology, *Ugarte* had recruited a small group of devoted readers, scattered around Latin America and Spain, most of whom knew each other, either as friends or as gratuitously bitter enemies. He had published other books, of course, in Argentina, and with Spanish publishers who had since gone broke, and he belonged to that intermediate generation of Argentinean writers, born in the twenties, after Cortázar, Bioy Casares, Sábato, and Mújica Laínez, a generation whose best-known representative (to me, back then, at any rate) was Haroldo Conti,[8] who disappeared in one of the special camps set up by Videla[9] and his henchmen during the dictatorship. It was a generation (although perhaps I am using the word too loosely) that hadn't come to much, but not for want of brilliance or talent: followers of Roberto Arlt,[1] journalists, teachers, and translators; in a sense they foreshadowed what was to come, in their own sad and skeptical way, which led them one by one to the abyss.

I had a soft spot for those writers. In years gone by, I had read Abelardo Castillo's plays and the stories of Daniel Moyano and Rodolfo Walsh[2] (who was killed under the dictatorship, like Conti). I read their work piecemeal, whatever I could find in Argentinean, Mexican, or Cuban magazines, or the secondhand bookshops of Mexico City: pirated anthologies of Buenos Aires writing, probably the twentieth century's best writing in Spanish. They were part of that tradition, and although, of course, they didn't have the stature of Borges or Cortázar, and were soon overtaken by Manuel Puig and Osvaldo Soriano,[3] their concise, intelligent texts were a constant source of complicit delight. Needless to say, my favorite was Sensini, and having been his fellow runner-up in a provincial literary competition—an association that I found at once flattering and profoundly depressing—encouraged me to make contact with him, to pay my respects and tell him how much his work meant to me.

The Alcoy Council sent me his address without delay—he lived in Madrid—and one night, after dinner or a light meal or just a snack, I wrote him a long letter, which rambled from *Ugarte* and the stories of his that I had read in magazines to myself, my house on the outskirts of Girona, the competition (I

6. The last Spanish-controlled government of South America before the independence of Argentina (1776–1810). Juan de Ugarte (1662–1730): actually the name of a Jesuit missionary in Mexico about a century before the Viceroyalty of the Río de la Plata.

7. Franz Kafka (1883–1924), German-Jewish-Czech author of *The Metamorphosis* (1915), in which Gregor Samsa is transformed into a giant insect.

8. Julio Cortázar (1914–1984); Adolfo Bioy Casares (1914–1999); Ernesto Sábato (1911–2011); Manuel Mújica Laínez (1910–1984); Haroldo Conti (1925–1976): Argentine writers and critics.

9. Jorje Rafael Videla (b. 1925), dictator of Argentina from 1976 to 1981, responsible for human rights abuses including kidnapping, extrajudicial murder of political opponents, and use of concentration camps.

1. Roberto Arlt (1900–1942), Argentine writer.

2. Abelardo Castillo (b. 1935); Daniel Mayano (1930–1992); Rodolfo Walsh (1927–1977); Argentine writers.

3. Jorge Luis Borges (1899–1986); Manuel Puig (1932–1990); Osvaldo Soriano (1943–1997): Argentine writers.

made fun of the winner), the political situation in Chile and in Argentina (both dictatorships were still firmly in place),[4] Walsh's stories (along with Sensini, Walsh was my other favorite in that generation), life in Spain, and life in general. To my surprise, I received a reply barely a week later. He began by thanking me for my letter; he said that the Alcoy Council had sent him the anthology, too, but that, unlike me, he hadn't found time to look at the winning story or those of the other finalists (later on, in a passing reference, he admitted that it wasn't so much a lack of time as a lack of "fortitude"), although he had just read mine and thought it well done, "a first-rate story," he said (I kept the letter), and he urged me to persevere, not, as I thought at first, to persevere with my writing, but to persevere with the competitions, as he intended to do himself, he assured me. He went on to ask me which competitions were "looming on the horizon," imploring me to notify him as soon as I heard of one. In exchange he sent me the submission guidelines for two short-story competitions, one in Plasencia and the other in Écija,[5] with prizes of 25,000 and 30,000 pesetas respectively. He had tracked these down, as I later discovered, in Madrid newspapers or magazines whose mere existence was a crime or a miracle, depending on your point of view. There was still time for me to enter both competitions, and Sensini finished his letter on a curiously enthusiastic note, as if the pair of us were on our marks for a race that, as well as being hard and meaningless, would never end. "Pen to paper now, no shirking!" he wrote.

I remember thinking, What a strange letter. I remember reading a few chapters of *Ugarte*. Around that time the traveling booksellers came to Girona to set up their stalls in the square where the movie theaters are, laying out their mostly unsaleable stock: remaindered books published by recently bankrupt companies, books printed during World War II, romance novels and wild west sagas, and collections of postcards. At one of the stalls I found a book of stories by Sensini and bought it. It was as good as new—in fact it *was* new, one of those titles that publishers sell off to the traveling salesmen when no one else can move it, when there's not a bookshop or a distributor left who's willing to take it on—and for the following week I lived and breathed Sensini. I read his letter over and over, leafed through *Ugarte*, and when I wanted a little action, something new, I turned to the stories. Although the themes and situations varied, the settings were generally rural, and the protagonists were the fabled gauchos of the pampa,[6] that is to say armed and unfortunate individuals, either loners or endowed with peculiar notions of sociability. Whereas *Ugarte* was a cold book, written with neurosurgical precision, the collection of stories was all warmth: brave and aimless characters adrift in landscapes that seemed to be gradually drawing away from the reader (and sometimes taking the reader with them).

I didn't manage to send in an entry for the Plasencia competition, but I did for the Écija one. As soon as I had mailed off the copies of my story (under the pseudonym Aloysius Acker),[7] I realized that sitting around waiting for the results could only make things worse. So I decided to look for more competitions; that way at least I'd be able to comply with Sensini's request. Over the

4. Reference to Jorge Rafael Videla's dictatorship in Argentina (1976–81) and to Augusto Pinochet's dictatorship in Chile (1973–90).
5. City in the province of Seville near the Mediterranean coast of Spain; "Plasencia": city in the Extremadura region in western Spain.
6. Cowboys of the South American plains.
7. "Aloysius Acker" is the title of a poem by Martín Adán, the pseudonym of the Peruvian writer Rafael de la Fuente Benavides (1908–1985).

next few days, when I went down to Girona, I spent hours looking through back copies of newspapers in search of announcements. Some papers put them in a column next to the society news; in others, they came after the crime reports and before the sports section; the most serious paper had them wedged between the weather and the obituaries. They were never with the book reviews, of course. In my search I discovered a magazine put out by the Catalonian government, which, along with advertisements for scholarships, exchanges, jobs, and postgraduate courses, published announcements of literary competitions, mostly for Catalans writing in Catalan, but there were some exceptions. I soon found three for which Sensini and I were eligible, and they were still open, so I wrote him a letter.

Like the first time, I received a reply by return mail. Sensini's letter was short. He answered some of my questions, mainly about the book of stories I had recently bought, but also included photocopies of the details for three more short-story competitions, one of which was sponsored by the National Railway Company, with a tidy sum for the winner and "50,000 pesetas per head" (as he put it) for the ten finalists: no prize for dreaming, you have to be in it to win it. I wrote back saying I didn't have enough stories for all six competitions, but most of my letter was about other things (in fact I got rather carried away): travel, lost love, Walsh, Conti, Francisco Urondo . . . I asked him about Gelman,[8] whom he was bound to have known, gave him a summary of my life story, and somehow ended up going on about the tango and labyrinths, as I always do with Argentineans (it's something Chileans are prone to).

Sensini's reply was prompt and voluble, at least as far as writing and competitions were concerned. On one sheet, recto and verso,[9] single-spaced, he set out a kind of general strategy for the pursuit of provincial literary prizes. I speak from experience, he wrote. The letter began with a blessing on prizes (whether in earnest or in jest, I have never been able to tell), those precious supplements to the writer's modest income. He referred to the sponsors—town councils and credit unions—as "those good people with their touching faith in literature" and "those disinterested and dutiful readers." He entertained no illusions, however, about the erudition of the "good people" in question, who presumably exercised their touching faith on these ephemeral anthologies (or not). He told me I must compete for as many prizes as possible, although he suggested I take the precaution of changing a story's title if I was entering it for, say, three competitions that were due to be judged around the same time. He cited the example of his story "At Dawn," a story I didn't know, which he had used to test his method, as a guinea pig is used to test the effects of a new vaccine. For the first competition, with the biggest prize, "At Dawn" was entered as "At Dawn"; for the second, he changed the title to "The Gauchos"; for the third, it was called "The Other Pampa"; and for the last, "No Regrets." Of these four competitions, it won the second and the fourth, and with the money from the prizes he was able to pay a month-and-half's rent (in Madrid the rents had gone through the roof). Of course no one realized that "The Gauchos" and "No Regrets" were the same story with different titles, although there was always the risk that one of the judges might have read the story in another contest (in Spain the peculiar occupation of judging literary prizes was obstinately monopolized by a clique of

8. Francisco Urondo (1910–1976); Juan Gelman (1930–2014): Argentine writers.

9. Front and back.

minor poets and novelists, plus former laureates). The little world of letters is terrible as well as ridiculous, he wrote. And he added that even if one's story did come before the same judge twice, the danger was minimal, since they generally didn't read the entries or only skimmed them. Furthermore, who was to say that "The Gauchos" and "No Regrets" were not two different stories whose singularity resided precisely in their respective titles? Similar, very similar even, but different. Toward the end of the letter he said that, of course, in a perfect world, he would be otherwise occupied, living and writing in Buenos Aires, for example, but the way things were, he had to earn a crust somehow (I'm not sure they say that in Argentina; we do in Chile) and, for now, the competitions were helping him get by. It's like a lesson in Spanish geography, he wrote. At the end, or maybe in a postscript, he declared: I'm going on sixty, but I feel as if I were twenty-five. At first this struck me as very sad, but when I read it for the second or third time I realized it was his way of asking me: How old are you, kid? I remember I replied immediately. I told him I was twenty-eight, three years older than him. That morning I felt not exactly happy again but more alive, as if an infusion of energy were reanimating my sense of humor and my memory.

Although I didn't follow Sensini's advice and become a full-time prize hunter, I did enter the competitions he and I had recently discovered, without any success. Sensini pulled off another double in Don Benito[1] and Écija, with a story originally called "The Sabre," renamed "Two Swords" for Écija and "The Deepest Cut" for Don Benito. And in the competition sponsored by the railways he was one of the finalists. As well as a cash sum, he won a pass that entitled him to travel free on Spanish trains for a year.

Little by little I learned more about him. He lived in a flat in Madrid with his wife and his daughter, Miranda,[2] who was seventeen years old. He had a son, from his first marriage, who had gone to ground somewhere in Latin America, or that was what he wanted to believe. The son's name was Gregorio; he was thirty-five and had worked as a journalist. Sometimes Sensini would tell me about the inquiries he was making through human rights organizations and the European Union in an attempt to determine Gregorio's whereabouts. When he got on to this subject, his prose became heavy and monotonous, as if he were trying to exorcise his ghosts by describing the bureaucratic labyrinth. I haven't lived with Gregorio, he once told me, since he was five years old, just a kid. He didn't elaborate, but I imagined a five-year-old boy and Sensini typing in a newspaper office: even then it was already too late. I also wondered about the boy's name and somehow came to the conclusion that it must have been an unconscious homage to Gregor Samsa.[3] Of course I never mentioned this to Sensini. When he got on to the subject of Miranda he cheered up. Miranda was young and ready to take on the world, insatiably curious, pretty too, and kind. She looks like Gregorio, he wrote, except that (obviously) she's a girl and she has been spared what my son had to go through.

Gradually, Sensini's letters grew longer. The district where he lived in Madrid was run-down; his apartment had two bedrooms, a dining-room-cum-living-room, a kitchen, and a bathroom. At first I was surprised to discover that his place was smaller than mine; then I felt ashamed. It seemed unfair. Sensini

1. City in the Extremadura region.
2. The name of Prospero's daughter in Shakespeare's *The Tempest*. The slave Caliban loves her and attempts to rape her.
3. Protagonist of *The Metamorphosis* (1915), by Franz Kafka.

wrote in the dining room, at night, "when the wife and the girl are asleep," and he was a heavy smoker. He earned his living doing some kind of work for a publisher (I think he edited translations) and by sending his stories out to do battle in the provinces. Every now and then he received a royalty check for one of his many books, but most of the publishers were chronically forgetful or had gone broke. The only book that went on selling well was *Ugarte*, which had been published by a company in Barcelona. It didn't take me long to realize that he was living in poverty: not destitution, but the genteel poverty of a middle-class family fallen on hard times. His wife (her name was Carmela Zadjman, a story in itself) did freelance work for publishers and gave English, French, and Hebrew lessons, although she'd been obliged to take on cleaning jobs occasionally. The daughter was busy with her studies and would soon be going on to university. In one of my letters I asked Sensini whether Miranda wanted to be a writer too. He wrote back: No, thank God, she's going to study medicine.

One night I wrote and asked for a photo of his family. Only after putting the letter in the mail did I realize that what I really wanted was to see what Miranda looked like. A week later I received a photo, no doubt taken in the Retiro, which showed an old man and a middle-aged woman next to a tall, slim adolescent girl with straight hair and very large breasts. The old man was smiling happily, the middle-aged woman was looking at her daughter, as if saying something to her, and Miranda was facing the photographer with a serious look that I found both moving and disturbing. Sensini also sent me a photocopy of another photo, showing a young man more or less my age, with sharp features, very thin lips, prominent cheekbones and a broad forehead. He was strongly built and probably tall, and he was gazing at the camera (it was a studio photo) with a confident and perhaps slightly impatient expression. It was Gregorio Sensini, at the age of twenty-two, before he disappeared, quite a bit younger than me, in fact, but he had an air of experience that made him seem older.

The photo and the photocopy lived on my desk for a long time. I would sit there staring at them or take them to the bedroom and look at them until I fell asleep. Sensini had asked me to send a photograph of myself. I didn't have a recent one, so I decided to go to the photo booth in the station, which at the time was the only photo booth in the whole of Girona. But I didn't like the way the photos came out. I thought I looked ugly and skinny and scruffy haired. So I kept putting off sending any of them and going back to spend more money at the photo booth. Finally I chose one at random, put it in an envelope with a postcard, and sent it to him. It was a while before I received a reply. In the meantime I remember I wrote a very long, very bad poem, full of voices and faces that seemed different at first, but all belonging to Miranda Sensini, and when, in the poem, I finally realized this and could put it into words, when I could say to her, Miranda it's me, your father's friend and correspondent, she turned around and ran off in search of her brother, Gregorio Samsa, in search of Gregorio Samsa's eyes, shining at the end of a dim corridor in which the shadowy masses of Latin America's terror were shifting imperceptibly.

The reply, when it came, was long and friendly. Sensini and Carmela's verdict on my photo was positive: they thought I looked nice, like they imagined me, a bit on the skinny side maybe, but fit and well, and they liked the postcard of the Girona cathedral, which they hoped to see for themselves in the near future, as soon as they had sorted out a few financial and household problems. It was clear that they were hoping to stay at my place when they came. In return they offered to put me up whenever I wanted to go to Madrid. It's a modest apartment, and it isn't clean either, wrote Sensini, quoting a comic-strip gaucho who was famous in South America at the beginning of the seventies.[4] He didn't say anything about his literary projects. Nor did he mention any contests.

At first I thought of sending Miranda my poem, but after much hesitation and soul-searching I decided not to. I must be going mad, I thought: if I sent her that poem, there'd be no more letters from Sensini, and who could blame him? So I didn't send it. For a while I applied myself to the search for new literary prizes. In one of his letters Sensini said he was worried that he might have run his race. I misunderstood; I thought he meant he was running out of competitions to enter.

I wrote back to say they must come to Girona; he and Carmela were most welcome to stay at my house. I even spent several days cleaning, sweeping, mopping, and dusting, having convinced myself (quite unreasonably) that they might turn up at any moment, with Miranda. Since they had one free pass they'd only have to buy two tickets, and Catalonia, I stressed, was full of wonderful things to see and do. I mentioned Barcelona, Olot, the Costa Brava,[5] and talked about the happy days we could spend together. In a long reply, thanking me for my invitation, Sensini said that for the moment they couldn't leave Madrid. Unlike any of the preceding letters, this one was rather confused, although in the middle he returned to the theme of prizes (I think he had won another one) and encouraged me not to give up, to keep on trying. He also said something about the writer's trade or profession, and I had the impression that his words were meant partly for me and partly for himself, as a kind of reminder. The rest, as I said, was a muddle. When I got to the end I had the feeling that someone in his family wasn't well.

Two or three months later Sensini wrote to tell me that one of the bodies in a recently discovered mass grave was probably Gregorio's.[6] His letter was restrained. There was no outpouring of grief; all he said was that on a certain day, at a certain time, a group of forensic pathologists and officials from human rights organizations had opened a mass grave containing the bodies of more than fifty young people, etc. For the first time, I didn't want to reply in writing. I would have liked to call him, but I don't think he had a telephone, and if he did I didn't know his number. My letter was brief. I said I was sorry, and ventured to point out that they still didn't know for sure that the body was Gregorio's.

Summer came and I took a job in a hotel on the coast. In Madrid that summer there were numerous lectures, courses, and all sorts of cultural activities, but Sensini didn't participate in any of them, or if he did, it wasn't mentioned in the newspaper I was reading.

At the end of August I sent him a card. I said that maybe when the season was over I would visit him. That was all. When I got back to Girona in the middle of September, in the small pile of letters slipped under the door, I found one from Sensini dated August seventh. He had written to say good-bye. He was going back to Argentina; with the return of democracy[7] he would be

4. An allusion to Roberto Fontanarrosa, *Inodoro Pereyra (el renegáu)* (*Stinky Pereyra, the Renegade*), a famous comic strip about the life of a gaucho.

5. A coastal region of Catalonia, Spain. Barcelona and Olot are cities in Catalonia.

6. Political enemies of Videla's regime were buried in mass graves.

7. The return to democracy in Argentina took place in late 1983.

safe now, so there was no point staying away any longer. And it was the only way he would be able to find out for sure what had happened to Gregorio. Carmela, of course, is returning with me, he said, but Miranda will stay. I wrote to him immediately, at the only address I had, but received no reply.

Gradually I came to accept that Sensini had gone back to Argentina for good and that, unless he wrote to me again, our correspondence had come to an end. I waited a long time for a letter from him, or so it seems to me now, looking back. The letter, of course, never came. I tried to tell myself that life in Buenos Aires must be hectic, an explosion of activity, hardly time to breathe or blink. I wrote to him again at the Madrid address, hoping that the letter would be sent on to Miranda, but a month later it was returned to me stamped "Addressee Unknown." So I gave up and let the days go by and gradually forgot about Sensini, although on my rare visits to Barcelona I would sometimes spend whole afternoons in secondhand bookshops looking for his other books, the ones I knew by their titles but was destined never to read. All I could find in the shops were old copies of *Ugarte* and the collection of stories published in Barcelona by a company that had recently gone into receivership, as if to send a message to Sensini (and to me).

A year or two later I found out that he had died. I think I read it in a newspaper, I don't know which one. Or maybe I didn't read it; maybe someone told me, but I can't remember talking around that time with anyone who knew him, so I probably did read the death notice somewhere. It was brief, as I remember it: the Argentinean writer Luis Antonio Sensini, who lived for several years in exile in Spain, had died in Buenos Aires. I think there was also a mention of *Ugarte* at the end. I don't know why, but it didn't come as a surprise. I don't know why, but it seemed logical that Sensini would go back to Buenos Aires to die.

Some time later, when the photo of Sensini, Carmela, and Miranda and the photocopied image of Gregorio were packed away with my other memories in a cardboard box that I still haven't committed to the flames for reasons I prefer not to expand upon here, there was a knock on my door. It must have been about midnight, but I was awake. It gave me a shock all the same. I knew only a few people in Girona and none of them would have turned up like that unless something out of the ordinary had happened. When I opened the door there was a woman with long hair, wearing a big black overcoat. It was Miranda Sensini, although she had changed a good deal in the years since her father had sent me the photo. Next to her was a tall young man with long blond hair and an aquiline nose. I'm Miranda Sensini, she said to me with a smile. I know, I said, and invited them in. They were on their way to Italy; after that they planned to cross the Adriatic to Greece. Since they didn't have much money they were hitchhiking. They slept in my house that night. I made them something to eat. The young man was called Sebastian Cohen, and he had been born in Argentina too, although he had lived in Madrid since he was a child. He helped me prepare the meal while Miranda looked around the house. Have you known her for long? he asked. Until a moment ago, I'd only seen her in a photo, I replied.

After dinner, I set them up in one of the rooms and said they could go to bed whenever they wanted. I thought about going to bed myself, but realized it would be hard, if not impossible, to sleep, so I gave them a while to get settled, then went downstairs and put on the television with the volume down low and sat there thinking about Sensini.

Soon I heard someone on the stairs. It was Miranda. She couldn't get to sleep either. She sat down beside me and asked for a cigarette. At first we talked about their trip, Girona (they had been in the city all day, but I didn't ask why they had come to my house so late), and the cities they were planning to visit in Italy. Then we talked about her father and her brother. According to Miranda, Sensini never got over Gregorio's death. He went back to look for him, although we all knew he was dead. Carmela too? I asked. He was the only one who hadn't accepted it, she said. I asked her how things had gone in Argentina. Same as here, same as in Madrid, said Miranda, same as everywhere. But he was well-known and loved in Argentina, I said. Same as here, she said. I got a bottle of cognac from the kitchen and offered her a drink. You're crying, she said. When I looked at her she turned away. Were you writing? she asked. No, I was watching TV. No, I mean when we arrived. Yes, I said. Stories? No, poems. Ah, said Miranda. For a long time we sat there drinking in silence, watching the black and white images on the television screen. Tell me something, I said, Why did your father choose the name Gregorio? Because of Kafka, of course, said Miranda. Gregor Samsa? Of course, she said. I thought so, I said. Then Miranda told me the story of Sensini's last months in Buenos Aires.

He was already sick when he left Madrid, against the advice of various Argentinean doctors, who never billed him and had even arranged a couple of hospital stays, paid for by the national health insurance. Returning to Buenos Aires was a painful and happy experience. In the first week he started taking steps to locate Gregorio. He wanted to go back to his job at the university, but what with bureaucracy and the inevitable jealousies and bitterness, it wasn't going to happen, so he had to make do with translating for a couple of publishing houses. Carmela, however, got a teaching position and toward the end they lived exclusively on her earnings. Each week, Sensini wrote to Miranda. He knew he didn't have long to live, she said, and sometimes it was like he was impatient, like he wanted to use up the last of his strength and get it over with. As for Gregorio, there was nothing conclusive. Some of the pathologists thought his bones might have been in the pile exhumed from the mass grave, but to be sure they would have to perform a DNA test, and the government didn't have the money or didn't really want the tests done, so they kept being postponed. Sensini also went searching for a girl who had probably been Greg's girlfriend when he was in hiding, but he couldn't find her either. Then his health deteriorated and he had to go to the hospital. He didn't even write after that, said Miranda. It had always been very important to him, writing every day, whatever else was happening. Yes, I said, that's the way he was. I asked her if he'd found any literary contests to enter in Buenos Aires. Miranda looked at me and smiled. Of course! You were the one he used to enter the competitions with; he met you through a competition. Then it struck me: the reason she had my address was simply that she had all her father's addresses, and she had only just that moment realized who I was. That's me, I said. Miranda poured me out some more cognac and said there was a year when her father used to talk about me quite a lot. I noticed she was looking at me differently. I must have annoyed him so much, I said. Annoyed him? You've got to be joking; he loved your letters. He always read them to Mom and me. I hope they were funny, I said, without much conviction. They were really funny, said Miranda, my mother even gave you guys a name. A name? Which guys? Dad and you. She called you the gunslingers or the bounty hunters, I can't remember now, something like that, or the buccaneers. I see, I said, but the real bounty hunter was your father. I just passed on some information. Yes, he was a professional, said Miranda, suddenly serious. How many prizes did he win altogether? I asked her. About fifteen, she said with an absent look. And you? So far just the one, I said. A place in the Alcoy competition, that's how I got to know your father. Did you know that Borges wrote to him once in Madrid, to say how much he liked one of his stories? No, I didn't know, I said. And Cortázar wrote about him, and Mújica Laínez too. Well, he was a very good writer, I said. Jesus! said Miranda, then she got up and went out onto the terrace as if I had said something to offend her. I let a few seconds go by, picked up the bottle of cognac, and followed her. Miranda was leaning on the balustrade, looking at the lights of Girona. You have a good view, she said. I filled her glass, then my own, and we stood there for a while looking at the moonlit city. Suddenly I realized that we were at peace, that for some mysterious reason the two of us had reached a state of peace, and that from now on, imperceptibly, things would begin to change. As if the world really was shifting. I asked her how old she was. Twenty-two, she said. I must be over thirty then, I said, and even my voice sounded different.

1997

ORHAN PAMUK

born 1952

Orhan Pamuk's life and work are closely bound up with Istanbul, a historic city at the border between East and West. Pamuk described looking out his window and seeing both the Asian and the European portions of the city, separated by the Bosphorus strait. Of his attachment to Istanbul, Pamuk has written: "Conrad, Nabokov, and Naipaul—these are writers known for having managed to migrate between languages, cultures, countries, continents, even civilizations. Their imaginations were fed by exile, a nourishment drawn not through roots but through rootlessness. My imagination, however, requires that I stay in the same city, on the same street, in the same house, gazing at the same view. Istanbul's fate is my fate." Combining Turkish and European influences, Pamuk's work re-creates the city of his childhood in realistic detail colored by the transformative power of memory and imagination.

Born in Istanbul to a wealthy, secularized Muslim family whose fortune had recently declined, Pamuk grew up in Westernized surroundings. Educated at the elite Robert College, he considered becoming a painter or an architect, but after three years at the Istanbul Technical University, he decided instead to become a writer and studied journalism at Istanbul University. His first novel, *Cevdet Bey ve Ogullari* (*Cevet Bey and His Sons*, 1982), offered a partly autobiographical panorama spanning three generations of a Turkish family. The more realistic tone of his early works gave way to greater experimentation in a series of novels set in Istanbul, often involving multiple narrators, doppelgängers, and mysterious coincidences and containing commentary on Turkish history. Some of these works have been described as postmodernist for their play with the relationship between history and fiction, reality and imagination. After winning a number of Turkish literary prizes, Pamuk's work began to be translated into foreign languages, and he received international acclaim, culminating in the Nobel Prize in 2006. His views on Turkish history have sometimes been controversial, especially in his criticisms of the Armenian genocide, conducted by the Turkish government during the First World War, and the later killings of Turkish Kurds. Many in Turkey deny both events, and right-wing nationalists charged Pamuk in court with "insulting Turkish-ness." Pamuk's books were burned by angry crowds, but the charges were later dropped. While continuing to live mostly in Istanbul, Pamuk has also taught abroad, notably at Columbia University in New York.

Pamuk has often considered his work to be at the crossroads of the West and Islam, Europe and the Middle East. In his Nobel lecture, he spoke of a suitcase bequeathed to him that was full of his father's youthful attempts at writing (composed mainly in Paris):

> As for my place in the world—in life, as in literature, my basic feeling was that I was "not in the centre." In the centre of the world, there was a life richer and more exciting than our own, and with all of Istanbul, all of Turkey, I was outside it. . . . My father's library was evidence of this. At one end, there were Istanbul's books—our literature, our local world, in all its beloved detail—and at the other end were the books from this other, Western, world, to which our own bore no resemblance, to which our lack of resemblance gave us both pain and hope. To write, to read, was like leaving one world to find consolation in the other world's otherness, the strange and the wondrous.

"To Look Out the Window" (1999) returns to the theme of East and West, as the narrator recalls his boyhood in Istanbul and his father's departure for Paris. Pamuk has written that the story "is so autobiographical that the hero's name might well have been Orhan." (Pamuk's brother, however, was not as cruel as the brother in the story.) The story also involves a return to the realistic, autobiographical writing of Pamuk's early work, although the way that the experience is filtered through memory and longing, and the emphasis on the naive viewpoint of the child, evoke the modernism of **Marcel Proust**. Like Proust, Pamuk is able to call up the emotions of childhood, including the child's incomprehension in the face of adult conflicts and the child's not always innocent response to this bewilderment.

Pamuk writes in the tradition of the great modernists, attentive to the finer points of the individual consciousness faced with a hostile or incomprehensible world. Yet what is perhaps most distinctive about Pamuk is his awareness of the way such consciousness is shaped by the movements of history. The author's re-creations of Turkish and Ottoman history, sometimes playful and sometimes terrifying, have occasionally caused him to be described as a postmodernist. Such labels ultimately tell us little about Pamuk's main contribution to world literature: his rich and vivid imagination.

To Look Out the Window[1]

I

If there's nothing to watch and no stories to listen to, life can get tedious. When I was a child, boredom was something we fought off by listening to the radio or looking out the window into neighboring apartments or at people passing in the street below. In those days, in 1958, there was still no television in Turkey. But we didn't like to admit it: We talked about television optimistically, just as we did the Hollywood adventure films that took four or five years to reach Istanbul's film theaters, saying it "had yet to arrive."

Looking out the window was such an important pastime that when television did finally come to Turkey, people acted the same way in front of their sets as they had in front of their windows. When my father, my uncles, and my grandmother watched television, they would argue without looking at one another, pausing now and again to report on what they'd just seen, just as they did while gazing out the window.

"If if keeps snowing like this, it's going to stick," my aunt would say, looking at the snowflakes swirling past.

"That man who sells *helva* is back on the Nişantaşi[2] corner!" I would say, peering from the other window, which looked out over the avenue with the streetcar lines.

On Sundays, we'd go upstairs with my uncles and aunts and everyone else who lived in the downstairs apartments to have lunch with my grandmother. As I stood at the window, waiting for the food to arrive, I'd be so happy to be there with my mother, my father, my aunts, and my uncles that everything before me seemed to glow with the pale light of the crystal chandelier hanging over the long dining table. My grandmother's sitting room was dark, as were the downstairs sitting rooms, but to me it always seemed darker. Maybe this was because of the tulle curtains and the heavy drapes that hung at either side of the never-opened balcony doors, casting fearsome shadows. Or maybe it was the screens inlaid with mother-of-pearl, the massive tables, the chests, and the baby grand piano, with all those framed photographs on top, or the general clutter of this airless room that always smelled of dust.

The meal was over, and my uncle was smoking in one of the dark adjoining rooms. "I have a ticket to a football match, but I'm not going," he'd say. "Your father is going to take you instead."

"Daddy, take us to the football match!" my older brother would cry from the other room.

"The children could use some fresh air," my mother would call from the sitting room.

"Then you take them out," my father said to my mother.

"I'm going to my mother's," my mother replied.

"We don't want to go to Granny's," said my brother.

"You can have the car," said my uncle.

"Please, Daddy!" said my brother.

There was a long, strange silence. It was as if everyone in the room was

1. Translated by Maureen Freely.
2. An elegant neighborhood in central Istanbul. "Helva": a sweet made of sesame seeds (or similar nuts), popular throughout the Middle East, Eastern Europe, and South Asia.

thinking certain thoughts about my mother, and as if my father could tell what those thoughts were.

"So you're giving me your car, are you?" my father asked my uncle.

Later, when we had gone downstairs, while my mother was helping us put on our pullovers and our thick checked woolen socks, my father paced up and down the corridor, smoking a cigarette. My uncle had parked his "elegant, cream colored" '52 Dodge in front of the Teşvikiye Mosque. My father allowed both of us to sit in the front seat and managed to get the motor started with one turn of the key.

There was no line at the stadium. "This ticket for the two of them," said my father to the man at the turnstile. "One is eight, and the other is ten." As we went through, we were afraid to look into the man's eyes. There were lots of empty seats in the stands, and we sat down at once.

The two teams had already come out to the muddy field, and I enjoyed watching the players run up and down in their dazzling white shorts to warm up. "Look, that's Little Mehmet," said my brother, pointing to one of them. "He's just come from the junior team."

"We know."

The match began, and for a long time we didn't speak. A while later my thoughts wandered from the match to other things. Why did footballers all wear the same strip when their names were all different? I imagined that there were no longer players running up and down the field, just names. Their shorts were getting dirtier and dirtier. A while later, I watched a ship with an interesting smokestack passing slowly down the Bosphorus,[3] just behind the bleachers. No one had scored by halftime, and my father bought us each a cone of chickpeas and a cheese pita.

"Daddy, I can't finish this," I said, showing him what was left in my hand.

"Put it over there," he said. "No one will see you."

We got up and moved around to warm up, just like everyone else. Like our father, we had shoved our hands into the pockets of our woolen trousers and turned away from the field to look at the people sitting behind us, when someone in the crowd called out to my father. My father brought his hand to his ear, to indicate that he couldn't hear a thing with all the noise.

"I can't come," he said, as he pointed in our direction. "I have my children with me."

The man in the crowd was wearing a purple scarf. He fought his way to our row, pushing the seatbacks and shoving quite a few people to reach us.

"Are these your boys?" he asked, after he had embraced my father. "They're so big. I can hardly believe it."

My father said nothing.

"So when did these children appear?" said the man, looking at us admiringly. "Did you get married as soon as you finished school?"

"Yes," said my father, without looking him in his face. They spoke for a while longer. The man with the purple scarf turned to my brother and me and put an unshelled American peanut into each of our palms. When he left, my father sat down in his seat and for a long time said nothing.

Not long after the two teams had returned to the field in fresh shorts, my father said, "Come on, let's go home. You're getting cold."

3. The strait that bisects Istanbul, traditionally the border between Asia and Europe. The story takes place on the European side of the city.

"I'm not getting cold," said my brother.

"Yes, you are," said my father. "And Ali's cold. Come on, let's get going."

As we were making our way past the others in our row, jostling against knees and sometimes stepping on feet, we stepped on the cheese pita I'd left on the ground. As we walked down the stairs, we heard the referee blowing his whistle to signal the start of the second half.

"Were you getting cold?" my brother asked. "Why didn't you say you weren't cold?" I stayed quiet. "Idiot," said my brother.

"You can listen to the second half on the radio at home," said my father.

"This match is not on the radio," my brother said.

"Quiet, now," said my father. "I'm taking you through Taksim on our way back."

We stayed quiet. Driving across the square, my father stopped the car just before we got to the off-track betting shop—just as we'd guessed. "Don't open the door for anyone," he said. "I'll be back in a moment."

He got out of the car. Before he had a chance to lock the car from the outside, we'd pressed down on the buttons and locked it from the inside. But my father didn't go into the betting shop; he ran over to the other side of the cobblestone street. There was a shop over there that was decorated with posters of ships, big plastic airplanes, and sunny landscapes, and it was even open on Sundays, and that's where he went.

"Where did Daddy go?"

"Are we going to play upstairs or downstairs when we get home?" my brother asked.

When my father got back, my brother was playing with the accelerator. We drove back to Nişantaşi and parked again in front of the mosque. "Why don't I buy you something!" said my father. "But please, don't ask for that Famous People series again."

"Oh, please, Daddy!" we pleaded.

When we got to Alaaddin's shop, my father bought us each ten packs of chewing gum from the Famous People series. We went into our building; I was so excited by the time we got into the lift that I thought I might wet my pants. It was warm inside and my mother wasn't back yet. We ripped open the chewing gum, throwing the wrappers on the floor. The result:

I got two Field Marshal Fevzi Çakmaks; one each of Charlie Chaplin, the wrestler Hamit Kaplan, Gandhi, Mozart, and De Gaulle; two Atatürks, and one Greta Garbo—number 21—which my brother didn't have yet. With these I now had 173 pictures of Famous People, but I still needed another 27 to complete the series. My brother got four Field Marshal Fevzi Çakmaks, five Atatürks, and one Edison.[4] We tossed the chewing gum into our mouths and began to read the writing on the backs of the cards.

4. Thomas Alva Edison (1847–1931), American inventor. The cards include internationally famous figures from history and popular culture as well as many Turks whose fame was more local. Fevzi Çakmak (1876–1950), Turkish general in the War of Independence (1919–23), fought against the occupying Allied forces after the First World War (1914–18). Charlie Chaplin, British-American movie star (1889–1977). Hamit Kaplan, Turkish world champion Olympic wrestler (1934–1976). Mahondas K. (Mahatma) Gandhi (1869–1948), leader of the movement for Indian independence and philosopher of nonviolence. Wolfgang Amadeus Mozart (1756–1791), Austrian classical composer. Charles de Gaulle (1890–1970), wartime leader of Free French forces and later president of France. Mustafa Kemal Atatürk (1881–1938), leader of the movement for Turkish independence and first president of Turkey. Greta Garbo (1905–1990), Swedish movie star.

Field Marshal Fevzi Çakmak
General in the War of Independence
(1876–1950)

MAMBO SWEETS CHEWING GUM, INC
A leather soccer ball will be awarded to the lucky person who collects all 100 famous people.

My brother was holding his stack of 165 cards. "Do you want to play Tops or Bottoms?"

"No."

"Would you give me your Greta Garbo for my twelve Fevzi Çakmaks?" he asked. "Then you'll have one hundred and eighty-four cards."

"No."

"But now you have two Greta Garbos."

I said nothing.

"When they do our inoculations at school tomorrow, it's really going to hurt," he said. "Don't expect me to take care of you, okay?"

"I wouldn't anyway."

We ate supper in silence. When *World of Sports* came on the radio, we found out that the match had been a draw, 2–2, and then our mother came into our room to put us to bed. My brother started getting his bag ready for school, and I ran into the sitting room. My father was at the window, staring down at the street.

"Daddy, I don't want to go to school tomorrow."

"Now how can you say that?"

"They're giving us those inoculations tomorrow. I come down with a fever, and then I can hardly breathe. Ask Mummy."

He looked at me, saying nothing. I raced over to the drawer and got out a pen and a piece of paper.

"Does your mother know about this?" he asked, putting the paper down on the volume of Kierkegaard[5] that he was always reading but never managed to finish. "You're going to school, but you won't have that injection," he said. "That's what I'll write."

He signed his name. I blew on the ink and then folded up the paper and put it in my pocket. Running back to the bedroom, I slipped it into my bag, and then I climbed up onto my bed and began to bounce on it.

"Calm down," said my mother. "It's time to go to sleep."

2

I was at school, and it was just after lunch. The whole class was lined up two by two, and we were going back to that stinking cafeteria to have our inoculations. Some children were crying; others were waiting in nervous anticipation. When a whiff of iodine floated up the stairs, my heart began to race. I stepped out of line and went over to the teacher standing at the head of the stairs. The whole class passed us noisily.

5. Søren Kierkegaard, Danish philosopher (1813–1855), forerunner of existentialism.

"Yes?" said the teacher. "What is it?"

I took out the piece of paper my father had signed and gave it to the teacher. She read it with a frown. "Your father's not a doctor, you know," she said. She paused to think. "Go upstairs. Wait in Room Two-A."

There were six or seven children in 2-A who like me had been excused. One was staring in terror out the window. Cries of panic came floating down the corridor; a fat boy with glasses was munching on pumpkin seeds and reading a Kinova comic book. The door opened and in came thin, gaunt Deputy Headmaster Seyfi Bey.

"Probably some of you are genuinely ill, and if you are, we won't take you downstairs," he said. "But I have this to say to those of you who've lied to get excused. One day you will grow up, serve our country, and maybe even die for it. Today it's just an injection you're running away from—but if you try something like this when you grow up, and if you don't have a genuine excuse, you'll be guilty of treason. Shame on you!"

There was a long silence. I looked at Atatürk's picture, and tears came to my eyes.

Later, we slipped unnoticed back to our classrooms. The children who'd had their inoculations started coming back: Some had their sleeves rolled up, some had tears in their eyes, some scuffled in with very long faces.

"Children living close by can go home," said the teacher. "Children with no one to pick them up must wait until the last bell. Don't punch one another on the arm! Tomorrow there's no school."

Everyone started shouting. Some were holding their arms as they left the building; others stopped to show the janitor, Hilmi Efendi, the iodine tracks on their arms.

When I got out to the street, I slung my bag over my shoulder and began to run. A horse cart had blocked traffic in front of Karabet's butcher shop, so I weaved between the cars to get to our building on the other side. I ran past Hayri's fabric shop and Salih's florist shop. Our janitor, Hazim Efendi, let me in.

"What are you doing here all alone at this hour?" he asked.

"They gave us our inoculations today. They let us out early."

"Where's your brother? Did you come back alone?"

"I crossed the streetcar lines by myself. Tomorrow we have the day off."

"Your mother's out," he said. "Go up to your grandmother's."

"I'm ill," I said. "I want to go to our house. Open the door for me."

He took a key off the wall and we got into the lift. By the time we had reached our floor, his cigarette had filled the whole cage with smoke that burned my eyes. He opened our door. "Don't play with the electrical sockets," he said, as he pulled the door closed.

There was no one at home, but I still shouted out, "Is anyone here, anyone home? Isn't there anyone home?" I threw down my bag, opened up my brother's drawer, and began to look at the film ticket collection he'd never shown me. Then I had a good long look at the pictures of football matches that he'd cut out of newspapers and glued into a book. I could tell from the footsteps that it wasn't my mother coming in now, it was my father. I put my brother's tickets and his scrapbook back where they belonged, carefully, so he wouldn't know I'd been looking at them.

My father was in his bedroom; he'd opened up his wardrobe and was looking inside.

"You're home already, are you?"

"No, I'm in Paris," I said, the way they did at school.

"Didn't you go to school today?"

"Today they gave us our inoculations."

"Isn't your brother here?" he asked. "All right then, go to your room and show me how quiet you can be."

I did as he asked. I pressed my forehead against the window and looked outside. From the sounds coming from the hallway I could tell that my father had taken one of the suitcases out of the cupboard there. He went back into his room and began to take his jackets and his trousers out of the wardrobe; I could tell from the rattling of the hangers. He began to open and close the drawers where he kept his shirts, his socks, and his underpants. I listened to him put them all into the suitcase. He went into the bathroom and came out again. He snapped the suitcase latches shut and turned the lock. He came to join me in my room.

"So what have you been up to in here?"

"I've been looking out the window."

"Come here, let's look out the window together."

He took me on his lap, and for a long time we looked out the window together. The tips of the tall cypress tree that stood between us and the apartment building opposite began to sway in the wind. I liked the way my father smelled.

"I'm going far away," he said. He kissed me. "Don't tell your mother. I'll tell her myself later."

"Are you going by plane?"

"Yes," he said, "to Paris. Don't tell this to anyone either." He took a huge two-and-a-half-lira coin from his pocket and gave it to me, and then he kissed me again. "And don't say you saw me here."

I put the money right into my pocket. When my father had lifted me from his lap and picked up his suitcase, I said, "Don't go, Daddy." He kissed me one more time, and then he left.

I watched him from the window. He walked straight to Alaaddin's store, and then he stopped a passing taxi. Before he got in, he looked up at our apartment one more time and waved. I waved back, and he took off.

I looked at the empty avenue for a long, long time. A streetcar passed, and then the water seller's horse cart. I rang the bell and called Hazim Efendi.

"Did you ring the bell?" he said, when he got to the door. "Don't play with the bell."

"Take this two-and-a-half-lira coin," I said, "go to Alaaddin's shop, and buy me ten chewing gums from the Famous People series. Don't forget to bring back the fifty kuruş change."

"Did your father give you this money?" he asked. "Let's hope your mother doesn't get angry."

I said nothing, and he left. I stood at the window and watched him go into Alaaddin's shop. He came out a little later. On his way back, he ran into the janitor from the Marmara Apartments across the way, and they stopped to chat.

When he came back, he gave me the change. I immediately ripped open the chewing gum: three more Fevzi Çakmaks, one Atatürk, and one each of Leonardo da Vinci and Süleyman the Magnificent, Churchill, General Franco,[6] and one more number 21, the Greta Garbo that my brother still didn't have. So now I had 183 pictures in all. But to complete the full set of 100, I still needed 26 more.

I was admiring my first 91, which showed the plane in which Lindbergh had crossed the Atlantic,[7] when I heard a key in the door. My mother! I quickly gathered up the gum wrappers that I had thrown on the floor and put them in the bin.

"We had our inoculations today, so I came home early," I said. "Typhoid, typhus, tetanus."

"Where's your brother?"

"His class hadn't had their inoculations yet," I said. "They sent us home. I crossed the avenue all by myself."

"Does your arm hurt?"

I said nothing. A little later, my brother came home. His arm was hurting. He lay down on his bed, resting on his other arm, and looked miserable as he fell asleep. It was very dark out by the time he woke up. "Mummy, it hurts a lot," he said.

"You might have a fever later on," my mother said, as she was ironing in the other room. "Ali, is your arm hurting too? Lie down, keep still."

We went to bed and kept still. After sleeping for a little my brother woke up and began to read the sports page, and then he told me it was because of me that we'd left the match early yesterday, and because we'd left early our team had missed four goals.

"Even if we hadn't left, we might not have made those goals," I said.

"What?"

After dozing a little longer, my brother offered me six Fevzi Çakmaks, four Atatürks, and three other cards I already had in exchange for one Greta Garbo, and I turned him down.

"Shall we play Tops or Bottoms?" he asked me.

"Okay, let's play."

You press the whole stack between the palms of your hands. You ask, "Tops or Bottoms?" If he says Bottoms, you look at the bottom picture, let's say number 68, Rita Hayworth.[8] Now let's say it's number 18, Dante the Poet, on top. If it is, then Bottoms wins and you give him the picture you like the least, the one you already have the most of. Field Marshal Fevzi Çakmak pictures passed back and forth between us until it was evening and time for supper.

"One of you go upstairs and take a look," said my mother. "Maybe your father's come back."

6. Francisco Franco (1892–1975), Spanish general and fascist dictator. Leonardo da Vinci, Renaissance artist and inventor (1452–1519). Süleyman the Magnificent, sultan of the Ottoman Empire (1494–1566). Winston Churchill (1874–1965), British wartime prime minister.

7. Charles Lindbergh (1902–1974), American pilot, first to fly nonstop across the Atlantic Ocean.

8. American movie star and sex symbol (1918–1987).

We both went upstairs. My uncle was sitting, smoking, with my grandmother; my father wasn't there. We listened to the news on the radio, we read the sports page. When my grandmother sat down to eat, we went downstairs.

"What kept you?" said my mother. "You didn't eat anything up there, did you? Why don't I give you your lentil soup now. You can eat it very slowly until your father gets home."

"Isn't there any toasted bread?" my brother asked.

While we were silently eating our soup, our mother watched us. From the way she held her head and the way her eyes darted away from us, I knew she was listening for the lift. When we finished our soup, she asked, "Would you like some more?" She glanced into the pot. "Why don't I have mine before it gets cold," she said. But instead she went to the window and looked down at Nişantaşi Square; she stood there looking for some time. Then she turned around, came back to the table, and began to eat her soup. My brother and I were discussing yesterday's match.

"Be quiet! Isn't that the lift?"

We fell quiet and listened carefully. It wasn't the lift. A streetcar broke the silence, shaking the table, the glasses, the pitcher, and the water inside it. When we were eating our oranges, we all definitely heard the lift. It came closer and closer, but it didn't stop at our floor; it went right up to my grandmother's. "It went all the way up," said my mother.

After we had finished eating, my mother said, "Take your plates to the kitchen. Leave your father's plate where it is." We cleared the table. My father's clean plate sat alone on the empty table for a long time.

My mother went over to the window that looked down at the police station; she stood there looking for a long time. Then suddenly she made up her mind. Gathering up my father's knife and fork and empty plate, she took them into the kitchen. "I'm going upstairs to your grandmother's," she said. "Please don't get into a fight while I'm gone."

My brother and I went back to our game of Tops or Bottoms.

"Tops," I said, for the first time.

He revealed the top card: number 34, Koca Yusuf, the world-famous wrestler. He pulled out the card from the bottom of the stack: number 50, Atatürk. "You lose. Give me a card."

We played for a long time and he kept on winning. Soon he had taken nineteen of my twenty Fevzi Çakmaks and two of my Atatürks.

"I'm not playing anymore," I said, getting angry. "I'm going upstairs. To Mummy."

"Mummy will get angry."

"Coward! Are you afraid of being home all alone?"

My grandmother's door was open as usual. Supper was over. Bekir, the cook, was washing the dishes; my uncle and my grandmother were sitting across from each other. My mother was at the window looking down on Nişantaşi Square.

"Come," she said, still looking out the window. I moved straight into the empty space that seemed to be reserved just for me. Leaning against her, I too looked down at Nişantaşi Square. My mother put her hand on my head and gently stroked my hair.

"Your father came home early this afternoon, I hear. You saw him."

"Yes."

"He took his suitcase and left. Hazim Efendi saw him."

"Yes."

"Did he tell you where he was going, darling?"

"No," I said. "He gave me two and a half lira."

Down in the street, everything—the dark stores along the avenue, the car lights, the little empty space in the middle where the traffic policemen stood, the wet cobblestones, the letters on the advertising boards that hung from the trees—everything was lonely and sad. It began to rain, and my mother passed her fingers slowly through my hair.

That was when I noticed that the radio that sat between my grandmother's chair and my uncle's—the radio that was always on—was silent. A chill passed through me.

"Don't stand there like that, my girl," my grandmother said then.

My brother had come upstairs.

"Go to the kitchen, you two," said my uncle. "Bekir!" he called. "Make these boys a ball; they can play football in the hallway."

In the kitchen, Bekir had finished the dishes. "Sit down over there," he said. He went out to the glass-enclosed balcony that my grandmother had turned into a greenhouse and brought back a pile of newspapers that he began to crumple into a ball. When it was as big as a fist, he asked, "Is this good enough?"

"Wrap a few more sheets around it," said my brother.

While Bekir was wrapping a few more sheets of newsprint around the ball, I looked through the doorway to watch my mother, my grandmother, and my uncle on the other side. With a rope he took from a drawer, Bekir bound the paper ball until it was as round as it could be. To soften its sharp edges, he wiped it lightly with a damp rag and then he compressed it again. My brother couldn't resist touching it.

"Wow. It's hard as a rock."

"Put your finger down there for me." My brother carefully placed his finger on the spot where the last knot was to be tied. Bekir tied the knot and the ball was done. He tossed it into the air and we began to kick it around.

"Play in the hallway," said Bekir. "If you play in here, you'll break something."

For a long time we gave our game everything we had. I was pretending to be Lefter from Fenerbahçe, and I twisted and turned like he did. Whenever I did a wall pass, I ran into my brother's bad arm. He hit me, too, but it didn't hurt. We were both perspiring, the ball was falling to pieces, and I was winning five to three when I hit his bad arm very hard. He threw himself down on the floor and began to cry.

"When my arm gets better I'm going to kill you!" he said, as he lay there.

He was angry because he'd lost. I left the hallway for the sitting room; my grandmother, my mother, and my uncle had all gone into the study. My grandmother was dialing the phone.

"Hello, my girl," she said then, in the same voice she used when she called my mother the same thing. "Is that Yeşilköy Airport? Listen, my girl, we want to make an inquiry about a passenger who flew out to Europe earlier today." She gave my father's name and twisted the phone cord around her finger while she waited. "Bring me my cigarettes," she said then to my uncle. When my uncle had left the room, she took the receiver away from her ear.

"Please, my girl, tell us," my grandmother said to my mother. "You would know. Is there another woman?"

I couldn't hear my mother's answer. My grandmother was looking at her as if she hadn't said a thing. Then the person at the other end of the line said something and she got angry. "They're not going to tell us," she said, when my uncle returned with a cigarette and an ashtray.

My mother saw my uncle looking at me, and that was when she noticed I was there. Taking me by the arm, she pulled me back into the hallway. When she'd felt my back and the nape of my neck, she saw how much I'd perspired, but she didn't get angry at me.

"Mummy, my arm hurts," said my brother.

"You two go downstairs now, I'll put you both to bed."

Downstairs on our floor, the three of us were silent for a long time. Before I went to bed I padded into the kitchen in my pajamas for a glass of water, and then I went into the sitting room. My mother was smoking in front of the window, and at first she didn't hear me.

"You'll catch cold in those bare feet," she said. "Is your brother in bed?"

"He's asleep. Mummy, I'm going to tell you something." I waited for my mother to make room for me at the window. When she had opened up that sweet space for me, I sidled into it. "Daddy went to Paris," I said. "And you know what suitcase he took?"

She said nothing. In the silence of the night, we watched the rainy street for a very long time.

3

My other grandmother's house was next to Şişli Mosque[9] and the end of the streetcar line. Now the square is full of minibus and municipal bus stops, and high ugly buildings and department stores plastered with signs, and offices whose workers spill out onto the pavements at lunchtime and look like ants, but in those days it was at the edge of the European city. It took us fifteen minutes to walk from our house to the wide cobblestone square, and as we walked hand in hand with my mother under the linden and mulberry trees, we felt as if we had come to the countryside.

My other grandmother lived in a four-story stone and concrete house that looked like a matchbox turned on its side; it faced Istanbul to the west and in the back the mulberry groves in the hills. After her husband died and her three daughters were married, my grandmother had taken to living in a single room of this house, which was crammed with wardrobes, tables, trays, pianos, and other furniture. My aunt would cook her food and bring it over or pack it in a metal container and have her driver deliver it for her. It wasn't just that my grandmother would not leave her room to go two flights down to the kitchen to cook; she didn't even go into the other rooms of the house, which were covered with a thick blanket of dust and silky cobwebs. Like her own mother, who had spent her last years alone in a great wooden mansion, my grandmother had succumbed to a mysterious solitary disease and would not even permit a caretaker or a daily cleaner.

9. A mosque in the European part of Istanbul.

When we went to visit her, my mother would press down on the bell for a very long time and pound on the iron door, until my grandmother would at last open the rusty iron shutters on the second-floor window overlooking the mosque and peer down on us, and because she didn't trust her eyes—she could no longer see very far—she would ask us to wave at her.

"Come out of the doorway so your grandmother can see you, children," said my mother. Coming out into the middle of the pavement with us, she waved and cried, "Mother dear, it's me and the children; it's us, can you hear us?"

We understood from her sweet smile that she had recognized us. At once she drew back from the window, went into her room, took out the large key she kept under her pillow, and, after wrapping it in newsprint, threw it down. My brother and I pushed and shoved each other, struggling to catch it.

My brother's arm was still hurting, and that slowed him down, so I got to the key first, and I gave it to my mother. With some effort, my mother managed to unlock the great iron door. The door slowly yielded as the three of us pushed against it, and out from the darkness came that smell I would never come across again: decay, mold, dust, age, and stagnant air. On the coat rack right next to the door—to make the frequent robbers think there was a man in the house—my grandmother had left my grandfather's felt hat and his fur-collared coat, and in the corner were the boots that always scared me so.

A little later, at the end of two straight flights of wooden stairs, far, far away, standing in a white light, we saw our grandmother. She looked like a ghost, standing perfectly still in the shadows with her cane, lit only by the light filtering through the frosted Art Deco[1] doors.

As she walked up the creaking stairs, my mother said nothing to my grandmother. (Sometimes she would say, "How are you, darling Mother?" or "Mother dear, I've missed you; it's very cold out, dear Mother!") When I reached the top of the stairs, I kissed my grandmother's hand, trying not to look at her face, or the huge mole on her wrist. But still we were frightened by the lone tooth in her mouth, her long chin, and the whiskers on her face, so once we were in the room we huddled next to our mother. My grandmother went back to the bed, where she spent most of the day in her long nightgown and her woolen vest, and she smiled at us, giving us a look that said, All right, now entertain me.

"Your stove isn't working so well, Mother," said my mother. She took the poker and stirred the coals.

My grandmother waited for a while, and then she said, "Leave the stove alone now. Give me some news. What's going on in the world?"

"Nothing at all," said my mother, sitting at our side.

"You have nothing to tell me at all?"

"Nothing at all, Mother dear."

After a short silence, my grandmother asked, "Haven't you seen anyone?"

"You know that already, Mother dear."

"For God's sake, have you no news?"

There was a silence.

"Grandmother, we had our inoculations at school," I said.

"Is that so?" said my grandmother, opening up her large blue eyes as if she were surprised. "Did it hurt?"

"My arm still hurts," said my brother.

1. Decorative style, originating in Western Europe in the early 20th century.

"Oh, dear," said my grandmother with a smile.

There was another long silence. My brother and I got up and looked out the window at the hills in the distance, the mulberry trees, and the empty old chicken coop in the back garden.

"Don't you have any stories for me at all?" pleaded my grandmother. "You go up to see the mother-in-law. Doesn't anyone else?"

"Dilruba Hanim came yesterday afternoon," said my mother. "They played bezique with the children's grandmother."

In a rejoicing voice, our grandmother then said what we'd expected: "That's the palace lady!"

We knew she was talking not about one of the cream-colored palaces we read so much about in fairy tales and newspapers in those years but about Dolmabahçe Palace;[2] it was only much later I realized that my grandmother looked down on Dilruba Hanim—who had come from the last sultan's harem—because she had been a concubine before marrying a businessman, and that she also looked down on my grandmother for having befriended this woman.[3] Then they moved to another subject that they discussed every time my mother visited: Once a week, my grandmother would go to Beyoğlu to lunch alone at a famous and expensive restaurant called Aptullah Efendi, and afterward she would complain at great length about everything she'd eaten. She opened the third ready-made topic by asking us this question: "Children, does your other grandmother make you eat parsley?"

We answered with one voice, saying what our mother told us to say. "No, Grandmother, she doesn't."

As always, our grandmother told us how she'd seen a cat peeing on parsley in a garden, and how it was highly likely that the same parsley had ended up barely washed in some idiot's food, and how she was still arguing about this with the greengrocers of Şişli and Nişantaşi.

"Mother dear," said my mother, "the children are getting bored; they want to take a look at the other rooms. I'm going to open up the room next door."

My grandmother locked all the rooms in the house from the outside, to keep any thief who might enter through a window from reaching any other room in the house. My mother opened up the large cold room that looked out on the avenue with the streetcar line, and for a moment she stood there with us, looking at the armchairs and the divans under their dust covers, the rusty, dusty lamps, trays, and chairs, the bundles of old newspaper; at the worn saddle and the drooping handlebars of the creaky girl's bicycle listing in the corner. But she did not take anything out of the trunk to show us, as she had done on happier days. ("Your mother used to wear these sandals when she was little, children; look at your aunt's school uniform, children; would you like to see your mother's childhood piggy bank, children?")

"If you get cold, come and tell me," she said, and then she left.

My brother and I ran to the window to look at the mosque and the streetcar in the square. Then we read about old football matches in the newspapers. "I'm bored," I said. "Do you want to play Tops or Bottoms?"

2. 19th-century palace where the sultans kept their harems.

3. The children's maternal grandmother looks down at Dilruba Hanim for being a former concubine; she also looks down on the children's paternal grandmother for befriending Dilruba Hanim.

"The defeated wrestler still wants to fight," said my brother, without looking up from his newspaper. "I'm reading the paper."

We'd played again that morning, and my brother had won again.

"Please."

"I have one condition: If I win, you have to give me two pictures, and if you win, I only give you one."

"No, one."

"Then I'm not playing," said my brother. "As you can see, I'm reading the paper."

He held the paper just like the English detective in a black-and-white film we'd seen recently at the Angel Theater. After looking out the window a little longer, I agreed to my brother's conditions. We took our Famous People cards from our pockets and began to play. First I won, but then I lost seventeen more cards.

"When we play this way, I always lose," I said. "I'm not playing anymore unless we go back to the old rules."

"Okay," said my brother, still imitating that detective. "I wanted to read those newspapers anyway."

For a while I looked out the window. I carefully counted my pictures: I had 121 left. When my father left the day before, I'd had 183! But I didn't want to think about it. I had agreed to my brother's conditions.

In the beginning, I'd been winning, but then he started winning again. Hiding his joy, he didn't smile when he took my cards and added them to his pack.

"If you want, we can play by some other rules," he said, a while later. "Whoever wins takes one card. If I win, I can choose which card I take from you. Because I don't have any of some of them, and you never give me those."

Thinking I would win, I agreed. I don't know how it happened. Three times in a row I lost my high card to his, and before I knew it I had lost both my Greta Garbos (21) and my only King Faruk (78). I wanted to take them all back at once, so the game got bigger: This was how a great many other cards I had and he didn't—Einstein (63), Rumi (3), Sarkis Nazaryan, the founder of Mambo Chewing Gum–Candied Fruit Company (100), and Cleopatra (51)[4]—passed over to him in only two rounds.

I couldn't even swallow. Because I was afraid I might cry, I ran to the window and looked outside: How beautiful everything had seemed only five minutes earlier—the streetcar approaching the terminus, the apartment buildings visible in the distance through the branches that were losing their leaves, the dog lying on the cobblestones, scratching himself so lazily! If only time had stopped. If only we could go back five squares as we did when we played Horse Race Dice. I was never playing Tops or Bottoms with my brother again.

"Shall we play again?" I said, without taking my forehead off the windowpane.

"I'm not playing," said my brother. "You'll only cry."

"Cevat, I promise. I won't cry," I insisted, as I went to his side. "But we have to play the way we did at the beginning, by the old rules."

"I'm going to read my paper."

4. Egyptian queen (69–30 B.C.E.). Faruk (1920–1965), king of Egypt. Albert Einstein (1879–1955), German-Swiss-American founder of modern physics. Rumi (1207–1273), Persian poet.

"Okay," I said. I shuffled my thinner-than-ever stack. "With the old rules. Tops or Bottoms?"

"No crying," he said. "Okay, high."

I won and he gave me one of his Field Marshal Fevzi Çakmaks. I wouldn't take it. "Can you please give me seventy-eight, King Faruk?"

"No," he said. "That isn't what we agreed."

We played two more rounds, and I lost. If only I hadn't played that third round: When I gave him my 49, Napoleon,[5] my hand was shaking.

"I'm not playing anymore," said my brother.

I pleaded. We played two more rounds, and instead of giving him the pictures he asked for, I threw all the cards I had left at his head and into the air: the cards I had been collecting for two and a half months, thinking about each and every one of them every single day, hiding them and nervously accumulating them with care—number 28, Mae West, and 82, Jules Verne; 7, Mehmet the Conqueror, and 70, Queen Elizabeth; 41, Celal Salik the columnist, and 42, Voltaire[6]—they went flying through the air to scatter all over the floor.

If only I was in a completely different place, in a completely different life. Before I went back into my grandmother's room, I crept quietly down the creaky stairs, thinking about a distant relative who had worked in insurance and committed suicide. My father's mother had told me that suicides stayed in a dark place underground and never went to Heaven. When I'd gone a long way down the stairs, I stopped to stand in the darkness. I turned around and went upstairs and sat on the last step, next to my grandmother's room.

"I'm not well off like your mother-in-law," I heard my grandmother say. "You are going to look after your children and wait."

"But please, Mother dear, I beg you. I want to come back here with the children," my mother said.

"You can't live here with two children, not with all this dust and ghosts and thieves," said my grandmother.

"Mother dear," said my mother, "don't you remember how happily we lived here, just the two of us, after my sisters got married and my father passed away?"

"My lovely Mebrure, all you did all day was to leaf through old issues of your father's *Illustrations*."

"If I lit the big stove downstairs, this house would be cosy and warm in the space of two days."

"I told you not to marry him, didn't I?" said my grandmother.

"If I bring in a maid, it will only take us two days to get rid of all this dust," said my mother.

"I'm not letting any of those thieving maids into this house," said my grandmother. "Anyway, it would take six months to sweep out all this dust and cobwebs. By then your errant husband will be back home again."

5. French emperor Napoleon Bonaparte (1769–1821).

6. Pen name of François-Marie Arouet (1694–1778), French Enlightenment philosopher. Mae West, American actress and sex symbol (1893–1980). Jules Verne, French novelist (1828–1905), author of *Twenty Thousand Leagues Under the Sea*. Mehmet the Conqueror, sultan (1432–1481) who conquered Constantinople (modern Istanbul) in 1453, establishing the Ottoman Empire. Elizabeth I, queen of England (1533–1603), long-reigning monarch celebrated in Renaissance literature. Celal Salik, Turkish journalist much admired by Orhan Pamuk.

"Is that your last word, Mother dear?" my mother asked.

"Mebrure, my lovely girl, if you came here with your two children what would we live on, the four of us?"

"Mother dear, how many times have I asked you—pleaded with you—to sell the lots in Bebek before they're expropriated?"

"I'm not going to the deeds office to give those dirty men my signature and my picture."

"Mother dear, please don't say this: My older sister and I brought a notary right to your door," said my mother, raising her voice.

"I've never trusted that notary," said my grandmother. "You can see from his face that he's a swindler. Maybe he isn't even a notary. And don't shout at me like that."

"All right, then, Mother dear, I won't!" said my mother. She called into the room for us. "Children, children, come on now, gather up your things; we're leaving."

"Slow down!" said my grandmother. "We haven't even said two words."

"You don't want us, Mother dear," my mother whispered

"Take this, let the children have some Turkish delight."[7]

"They shouldn't eat it before lunch," said my mother, and as she left the room she passed behind me to enter the room opposite. "Who threw these pictures all over the floor? Pick them up at once. And you help him," she said to my brother.

As we silently gathered the pictures, my mother lifted the lids of the old trunks and looked at the dresses from her childhood, her ballet costumes, the boxes. The dust underneath the black skeleton of the pedal sewing machine filled my nostrils, making my eyes water, filling my nose.

As we washed our hands in the little lavatory, my grandmother pleaded in a soft voice. "Mebrure dear, you take this teapot; you love it so much, you have a right to," she said. "My grandfather brought it for my dear mother when he was the governor of Damascus.[8] It came all the way from China. Please take it."

"Mother dear, from now on I don't want anything from you," my mother said. "And put that into your cupboard or you'll break it. Come, children, kiss your grandmother's hand."

"My little Mebrure, my lovely daughter, please don't be angry at your poor mother," said my grandmother, as she let us kiss her hand. "Please don't leave me here without any visitors, without anyone."

We raced down the stairs, and when the three of us had pushed open the heavy metal door, we were greeted by brilliant sunlight as we breathed in the clean air.

"Shut the door firmly behind you!" cried my grandmother. "Mebrure, you'll come to see me again this week, won't you?"

As we walked hand in hand with my mother, no one spoke. We listened in silence as the other passengers coughed and waited for the streetcar to leave. When finally we began to move, my brother and I moved to the next row, saying we wanted to watch the conductor, and began to play Tops or Bottoms. First I lost some cards, then I won a few back. When I upped the ante, he happily agreed, and I quickly began to lose again. When we had reached the

7. A nut-based sweet.
8. Capital of Syria, ruled by the Ottoman Empire until 1918.

Osmanbey[9] stop, my brother said, "In exchange for all the pictures you have left, here is this Fifteen you want so much."

I played and lost. Without letting him see, I removed two cards from the stack before handing it to my brother. I went to the back row to sit with my mother. I wasn't crying. I looked sadly out the window as the streetcar moaned and slowly gathered speed, and I watched them pass us by, all those people and places that are gone forever: the little sewing shops, the bakeries, the pudding shops with their awnings, the Tan cinema where we saw those films about ancient Rome, the children standing along the wall next to the front selling used comics, the barber with the sharp scissors who scared me so, and the half-naked neighborhood madman, always standing in the barbershop door.

We got off at Harbiye. As we walked toward home, my brother's satisfied silence was driving me mad. I took out the Lindbergh, which I'd hidden in my pocket.

This was his first sight of it. "Ninety-one: Lindbergh!" he read in admiration. "With the plane he flew across the Atlantic! Where did you find this?"

"I didn't have my injection yesterday," I said. "I went home early, and I saw Daddy before he left. Daddy bought it for me."

"Then half is mine," he said. "In fact, when we played that last game, the deal was you'd give me all the pictures you had left." He tried to grab the picture from my hand, but he couldn't manage it. He caught my wrist, and he twisted it so badly that I kicked his leg. We laid into each other.

"Stop!" said my mother. "Stop! We're in the middle of the street!"

We stopped. A man in a suit and a woman wearing a hat passed us. I felt ashamed for having fought in the street. My brother took two steps and fell to the ground. "It hurts so much," he said, holding his leg.

"Stand up," whispered my mother. "Come on now, stand up. Everyone's watching."

My brother stood up and began to hop down the road like a wounded soldier in a film. I was afraid he was really hurt, but I was still glad to see him that way. After we had walked for some time in silence, he said, "Just you see what happens when we get home. Mummy, Ali didn't have his injection yesterday."

"I did too, Mummy!"

"Be quiet!" my mother shouted.

We were now just across from our house. We waited for the streetcar coming up from Maçka[1] to pass before we crossed the street. After it came a truck, a clattering Beşiktaş[2] bus spewing great clouds of exhaust, and, in the opposite direction, a light violet De Soto.[3] That was when I saw my uncle looking down at the street from the window. He didn't see me; he was staring at the passing cars. For a long time, I watched him.

The road had long since cleared. I turned to my mother, wondering why she had not yet taken our hands and crossed us over to the other side, and saw that she was silently crying.

1999

9. District in the European part of Istanbul.
1. District in central Istanbul.
2. District in the European part of Istanbul.
3. A model produced by the Chrysler Motor Company (1928–61).

CHIMAMANDA NGOZI ADICHIE

born 1977

A leading contemporary novelist, Chimamanda Ngozi Adichie ranges over the historical and modern experiences of Nigerians, especially Nigerian women, from before colonization through the Biafran War of the 1960s to contemporary immigrant communities in Britain and the United States. Her acute observations of contemporary life and deep sense of history have made her work timeless, even as she has become a famous spokesperson for feminism. Her novels have been adapted as films, and her lectures on race and gender are widely admired; one of them was sampled by the artist Beyoncé in her song "Flawless."

A member of the Igbo people of southern Nigeria, Adichie was born in 1977, after the defeat of the Igbo independence movement in the Biafran War, also known as the Nigerian Civil War (1967–70). She was strongly influenced by the historical legacy of the war, in which several of her family members died, and it seems to have shaped her understanding of the ways that private life can be transformed by political events. Born in Enugu, in southern Nigeria, the fifth of six children, Adichie grew up mostly in Nsukka, where her parents worked at the University of Nigeria. Her father was a professor of statistics while her mother served as the university's first female registrar. Adichie began her studies in medicine there but later studied at a number of universities in the United States. She graduated from Eastern Connecticut State University and received master's degrees in writing from Johns Hopkins University and in African Studies from Yale. She was awarded the MacArthur Fellowship (informally known as the "genius grant") in 2008 and currently spends time in both Nigeria and the United States. She has one daughter.

As a young girl, Adichie discovered the writings of **Chinua Achebe**, who had previously taught at the university where her parents worked and who had by that time achieved worldwide fame for his portrayals of the colonization of Nigeria. (Her family even lived in a house once inhabited by the renowned writer.) Adichie has credited the influence of Achebe's work in helping her to imagine what it would be like to be an African writer. As a child, Adichie read British and American books voraciously. When she began writing her own stories, her characters had blue eyes and white skin, ate apples, played in the snow, and talked about the weather. Adichie notes that she herself was black, ate mangoes, had never seen snow, and never heard talk of the weather, as on the equator it stays more or less the same. Reading Achebe's work convinced her that Africans could be the subject of fiction, although her approach to African history was distinctively shaped by her perspective as a woman and a feminist.

Her first novel, *Purple Hibiscus* (2003), opens with a reference to Achebe's novel *Things Fall Apart* (1958) and goes on to describe the effects of Nigeria's postcolonial history on a well-to-do Igbo family. The novel juxtaposes the power of the abusive father in the family with that of African dictators. Adichie uses the relatively small canvas of private family life to portray the sweeping historical changes affecting Nigeria in the late twentieth century, especially the dictatorship of General Sani Abacha from 1993 to 1998. More broadly, she chronicles the move from the traditional mores of the countryside to the more impersonal interactions of life in Africa's growing cities.

Adichie's work is distinguished by her strong sense of historical empathy. In her second novel, *Half of a Yellow Sun* (2006), for example, while recounting the horrors of the Biafran War, she describes the suffering of a rape victim but also explores the life story of one of her attackers. In 1967, massacres in northern Nigeria of the southeastern Igbo resulted in the people of southeastern Nigeria seceding to form Biafra, their own nation. Nigeria invaded Biafra, and more than 1 million people lost their lives in the conflict. Adichie's novel describes the effects of the war on two middle-class female twins, their male partners, and one of their servants (the houseboy Ugwu). They endure violent air raids, invading Nigerian soldiers, and economic deprivation: their worlds turn upside down, and they must change as a result. Adichie's poignant and nuanced portrayal of human relationships during the ravages of war makes this a particularly powerful novel.

Her third novel, *Americanah* (2013), the most autobiographical of her works to date, shifts focus to describe the experiences of a young Nigerian woman who has come to the United States to study. Her life is contrasted with that of her boyfriend who moves to England and eventually becomes an undocumented immigrant. Adichie's vivid characterizations and shifting geographical focus create a moving portrait of both the Nigerian diaspora and American society in the age of President Barack Obama. It is also the funniest of Adichie's novels. Although she writes frequently on political issues, she seldom takes simple or straightforward political positions; rather, she tends to see the complexity of social issues as they intersect with questions of personal identity.

Adichie has also written incisive essays on such subjects as Nigerian and American politics. Her prose style is clear, direct, and can be deceptively simple, as under the surface she often explores deep and troubling tensions and conflicts, whether social or familial. Her works have won a number of honors, including the O. Henry Prize, the Commonwealth Writers' Prize for Best First Book, and the National Book Critics Circle Award.

The story presented here, "The Headstrong Historian," comes from her collection of short stories, *The Thing Around Your Neck* (2009). This work returns to her earlier inspiration by the novels of Chinua Achebe. The story begins in nineteenth-century western Africa during the "scramble for Africa," in which colonial powers sought influence on the continent. Written from a woman's perspective and thus showing a different side of the events chronicled by Achebe in *Things Fall Apart* and his other writings, "The Headstrong Historian" describes how an Igbo woman of the late nineteenth century negotiates native marriage practices, the competing demands of missionaries from the Catholic and Anglican churches, and the education of her son. (Several of the characters have the same names as characters in Achebe's *Things Fall Apart*, and the study *The Pacification of the Primitive Tribes of Southern Nigeria*, mentioned in the story, was invented by Achebe in his fiction.) The story displays Adichie's characteristic empathy as she imagines how Nwamgba, a woman raised in a traditional culture, tries to understand and succeed in a world that is being transformed by European colonialism. She sends her son to a missionary school in hopes that acquiring English will allow him to reclaim land that once belonged to his father. But her son eventually becomes almost a foreigner to her, no longer following traditional customs and moving far away. Ultimately, though, she develops a close relationship with her granddaughter Afamefuna, or Grace. The character Grace, who is introduced in the last pages of the story, shares the given name of Adichie's mother, Grace Ifeoma.

Although it is difficult to tell how much of the story is closely based on family history and how much is literary invention, Adichie has found an effective way to link Africa's pre-colonial and colonial history to its contemporary reality. At least in an imaginative sense, Nwamgba is the author's great-grandmother, and the writing of the story becomes a link to a living but distant past. This ability to use the everyday details of modern life to telescope two centuries of African history marks out Adichie's work as great historical writing that also has tremendous contemporary relevance.

The Headstrong Historian

Many years after her husband died, Nwamgba still closed her eyes from time to time to relive his nightly visits to her hut and the mornings after, when she would walk to the stream humming a song, thinking of the smoky scent of him, the firmness of his weight, those secrets she shared with herself, and feeling as if she were surrounded by light. Other memories of Obierika remained clear—his stubby fingers curled around his flute when he played in the evenings, his delight when she set down his bowls of food, his sweaty back when he returned with baskets filled with fresh clay for her pottery. From the moment she first saw him at a wrestling match, both of them staring and staring at each other, both of them too young, her waist not yet wearing the menstruation cloth, she had believed with a quiet stubbornness that her chi[1] and his chi had destined their marriage, and so when he came to her father a few years later bringing pots of palm wine and accompanied by his relatives, she told her mother that this was the man she would marry. Her mother was aghast. Did Nwambga not know that Obierika was an only child, that his late father had been an only child whose wives had lost pregnancies and buried babies? Perhaps somebody in their family had committed the taboo of selling a girl into slavery and the earth god Ani was visiting misfortune on them. Nwamgba ignored her mother. She went into her father's *obi*[2] and told him she would run away from any other man's house if she was not allowed to marry Obierika. Her father found her exhausting, this sharp-tongued, headstrong daughter who had once wrestled her brother to the ground. (After which her father had warned everybody not to let the news leave the compound that the girl had thrown a boy.) He, too, was concerned about the infertility in Obierika's family, but it was not a bad family: Obierika's late father had taken the *ozo*[3] title; Obierika was already giving out his seed yams to share-

1. In Igbo cultural practice, individuals have *chi*, or spiritual beings, which are parallel to their physical beings.

2. Central building in an Igbo family compound.

3. Title of highest distinction in Igbo society.

croppers. Nwamgba would not do badly if she married him. Besides, it was better that he let her go with the man she chose, to save himself years of trouble when she would keep returning home after confrontations with in-laws. And so he gave his blessing and she smiled and called him by his praise name.

To pay her bride price, Obierika came with two maternal cousins, Okafo and Okoye, who were like brothers to him. Nwamgba loathed them at first sight. She saw a grasping envy in their eyes that afternoon as they drank palm wine in her father's obi, and in the following years, years in which Obierika took titles and widened his compound and sold his yams to strangers from afar, she saw their envy blacken. But she tolerated them, because they mattered to Obierika, because he pretended not to notice that they didn't work but came to him for yams and chickens, because he wanted to imagine that he had brothers. It was they who urged him, after her third miscarriage, to marry another wife. Obierika told them he would give it some thought but when he and Nwamgba were alone in her hut at night, he told her that he was sure they would have a home full of children, and that he would not marry another wife until they were old, so that they would have somebody to care for them. She thought this strange of him, a prosperous man with only one wife, and she worried more than he did about their childlessness, about the songs that people sang, melodious mean-spirited words: *She has sold her womb. She has eaten his penis. He plays his flute and hands over his wealth to her.*

Once, at a moonlight gathering, the square full of women telling stories and learning new dances, a group of girls saw Nwamgba and began to sing, their aggressive breasts pointing at her. She stopped and asked whether they would mind singing a little louder so that she could hear the words and then show them who was the greater of two tortoises.[4] They stopped singing. She enjoyed their fear, the way they backed away from her, but it was then that she decided to find a wife for Obierika herself.

Nwamgba liked going to the Oyi stream, untying her wrapper from her waist and walking down the slope to the silvery rush of water that burst out from a rock. The waters of Oyi were fresher than those of the other stream, Ogalanya, or perhaps it was simply that she felt comforted by the shrine of the Oyi goddess, tucked away in a corner; as a child she had learned that Oyi was the protector of women, the reason women were not to be sold into slavery. Her closest friend, Ayaju, was already at the stream, and as Nwamgba helped her raise her pot to her head, she asked Ayaju who might be a good second wife for Obierika.

She and Ayaju had grown up together and married men from the same clan. The difference between them, though, was that Ayaju was of slave descent; her father had been brought as a slave after a war. Ayaju did not care for her husband, Okenwa, who she said resembled and smelled like a rat, but her marriage prospects had been limited; no man from a freeborn family would have come for her hand. Ayaju's long-limbed, quick-moving body spoke of her many trading journeys; she had traveled even beyond Onicha.[5] It was she who had first brought tales of the strange customs of the Igala and Edo traders, she who first told of the

4. The tortoise is a symbol of wisdom in folktales told by the Igbo people.

5. Major port city on the Niger River.

white-skinned men who arrived in Onicha with mirrors and fabrics and the biggest guns the people of those parts had ever seen. This cosmopolitanism earned her respect, and she was the only person of slave descent who talked loudly at the Women's Council, the only person who had answers for everything.

And so she promptly suggested, for Obierika's second wife, the young girl from the Okonkwo family; the girl had beautiful wide hips and was respectful, nothing like the young girls of today with their heads full of nonsense. As they walked home from the stream, Ayaju said that perhaps Nwamgba should do what other women in her situation did—take a lover and get pregnant in order to continue Obierika's lineage. Nwamgba's retort was sharp, because she did not like Ayaju's tone, which suggested that Obierika was impotent, and as if in response to her thoughts she felt a furious stab in her back and knew that she was pregnant again, but she said nothing, because she knew, too, that she would lose the baby again.

Her miscarriage happened a few weeks later, lumpy blood running down her legs. Obierika comforted her and suggested they go to the famous oracle, Kisa, as soon as she was well enough for the half day's journey. After the *dibia*[6] had consulted the oracle, Nwamgba cringed at the thought of sacrificing a whole cow; Obierika certainly had greedy ancestors. But they did the ritual cleansings and the sacrifices, and when she suggested he go and see the Okonkwo family about their daughter, he delayed and delayed until another sharp pain spliced her back; and months later, she was lying on a pile of freshly washed banana leaves behind her hut, straining and pushing until the baby slipped out.

They named him Anikwenwa: the earth god Ani had finally granted a child. He was dark and solidly built and had Obierika's happy curiosity. Obierika took him to pick medicinal herbs, to collect clay for Nwamgba's pottery, to twist yam vines at the farm. Obierika's cousins Okafo and Okoye visited too often. They marveled at how well Anikwenwa played the flute, how quickly he was learning poetry and wrestling moves from his father, but Nwamgba saw the glowing malevolence that their smiles could not hide. She feared for her child and her husband, and when Obierika died—a man who had been hearty and laughing and drinking palm wine moments before he slumped—she knew that they had killed him with medicine. She clung to his corpse until a neighbor slapped her to make her let go; she lay in the cold ash for days; she tore at the patterns shaved into her hair.[7] Obierika's death left her with an unending despair. She thought often of the woman who, after her tenth successive child died, had gone to her backyard and hanged herself on a kola tree. But she would not do it, because of Anikwenwa.

Later, she wished she had insisted that his cousins drink Obierika's *mmili ozu*[8] before the oracle. She had witnessed this once, when a wealthy man died and his family insisted his rival drink his *mmili ozu*. Nwamgba had watched the unmarried woman take a cupped leaf full of water, touch it to the dead man's body, all the time speaking solemnly, and give the leaf-cup to the accused man. He drank. Everyone watched to make sure he swallowed, a grave silence in the air because they knew that if he was guilty he would die. He died days later, and his family

6. Doctor and priest (Igbo).
7. Igbo mourning customs.
8. Literally "corpse water"; an Igbo cultural practice for determining responsibility for a person's death.

lowered their heads in shame and Nwamgba felt strangely shaken by it all. She should have insisted on this with Obierika's cousins, but she had been blinded by grief and now Obierika was buried and it was too late.

His cousins, during the funeral, took his ivory tusk, claiming that the trappings of titles went to brothers and not to sons. It was when they emptied his barn of yams and led away the adult goats in his pen that she confronted them, shouting, and when they brushed her aside, she waited until evening and then walked around the clan singing about their wickedness, the abominations they were heaping on the land by cheating a widow, until the elders asked them to leave her alone. She complained to the Women's Council, and twenty women went at night to Okafo and Okoye's home, brandishing pestles, warning them to leave Nwamgba alone. Members of Obierika's age grade, too, told them to leave her alone. But Nwamgba knew those grasping cousins would never really stop. She dreamed of killing them. She certainly could—those weaklings who had spent their lives scrounging off Obierika instead of working—but of course she would be banished and there would be nobody to care for her son. So she took Anikwenwa on long walks, telling him that the land from that palm tree to that plantain tree was theirs, that his grandfather had passed it on to his father. She told him the same things over and over, even though he looked bored and bewildered, and she did not let him go and play at moonlight unless she was watching.

Ayaju came back from a trading journey with another story: the women in Onicha were complaining about the white men. They had welcomed the white men's trading station, but now the white men wanted to tell them how to trade, and when the elders of Agueke, a clan of Onicha, refused to place their thumbs on a paper, the white men came at night with their normal-men helpers and razed the village. There was nothing left. Nwamgba did not understand. What sort of guns did these white men have? Ayaju laughed and said their guns were nothing like the rusty thing her own husband owned. Some white men were visiting different clans, asking parents to send their children to school, and she had decided to send Azuka, the son who was laziest on the farm, because although she was respected and wealthy, she was still of slave descent, her sons still barred from taking titles. She wanted Azuka to learn the ways of these foreigners, since people ruled over others not because they were better people but because they had better guns; after all, her own father would not have been brought as a slave if his clan had been as well armed as Nwamgba's clan. As Nwamgba listened to her friend, she dreamed of killing Obierika's cousins with the white men's guns.

The day that the white men visited her clan, Nwamgba left the pot she was about to put in her oven, took Anikwenwa and her girl apprentices, and hurried to the square. She was at first disappointed by the ordinariness of the two white men; they were harmless-looking, the color of albinos, with frail and slender limbs. Their companions were normal men, but there was something foreign about them, too, and only one spoke a strangely accented Igbo. He said that he was from Elele;[9] the other normal men were from Sierra Leone, and the white men from France, far across the sea. They were all of the Holy Ghost Congregation;[1] they had arrived in Onicha in 1885 and were building their school and

9. Town in Rivers State, Nigeria.

1. Roman Catholic missionary organization.

church there. Nwamgba was first to ask a question: Had they brought their guns by any chance, the ones used to destroy the people of Agueke, and could she see one? The man said unhappily that it was the soldiers of the British government and merchants of the Royal Niger Company[2] who destroyed villages; they, instead, brought good news. He spoke about their god, who had come to the world to die, and who had a son but no wife, and who was three but also one. Many of the people around Nwamgba laughed loudly. Some walked away, because they had imagined that the white man was full of wisdom. Others stayed and offered cool bowls of water.

Weeks later, Ayaju brought another story: the white men had set up a courthouse in Onicha where they judged disputes. They had indeed come to stay. For the first time, Nwamgba doubted her friend. Surely the people of Onicha had their own courts. The clan next to Nwamgba's, for example, held its courts only during the new yam festival, so that people's rancor grew while they awaited justice. A stupid system, Nwamgba thought, but surely everyone had one. Ayaju laughed and told Nwamgba again that people ruled others when they had better guns. Her son was already learning about these foreign ways, and perhaps Anikwenwa should, too. Nwamgba refused. It was unthinkable that her only son, her single eye, should be given to the white men, never mind how superior their guns might be.

Three events, in the following years, caused Nwamgba to change her mind. The first was that Obierika's cousins took over a large piece of land and told the elders that they were farming it for her, a woman who had emasculated their dead brother and now refused to remarry even though suitors were coming and her breasts were still round. The elders sided with them. The second was that Ayaju told a story of two people who took a land case to the white men's court; the first man was lying but could speak the white men's language, while the second man, the rightful owner of the land, could not, and so he lost his case, was beaten and locked up and ordered to give up his land. The third was the story of the boy Iroegbunam, who had gone missing many years ago and then suddenly reappeared, a grown man, his widowed mother mute with shock at his story: a neighbor, whom his father often shouted down at age-grade meetings, had abducted him when his mother was at the market and taken him to the Aro slave dealers, who looked him over and complained that the wound on his leg would reduce his price. Then he and some others were tied together by the hands, forming a long human column, and he was hit with a stick and asked to walk faster. There was only one woman among them. She shouted herself hoarse, telling the abductors that they were heartless, that her spirit would torment them and their children, that she knew she was to be sold to the white man, and did they not know that the white man's slavery was very different, that people were treated like goats, taken on large ships a long way and eventually eaten? Iroegbunam walked and walked and walked, his feet bloodied, his body numb, with a little water poured into his mouth from time to time, until all he could remember later was the smell of dust. Finally they stopped at a coastal clan, where a man spoke a nearly incomprehensible Igbo, but Iroegbunam made out enough to understand that another man, who was to sell the abductees to the white people on

2. 19th-century British mercantile company.

the ship, had gone up to bargain with the white people but had himself been kidnapped. There were loud arguments, scuffling; some of the abductees yanked at the ropes and Iroegbunam passed out. He awoke to find a white man rubbing his feet with oil, and at first he was terrified, certain that he was being prepared for the white man's meal. But this was a different kind of white man, a missionary who bought slaves only to free them, and he took Iroegbunam to live with him and trained him to be a Christian missionary.

Iroegbunam's story haunted Nwamgba, because this, she was sure, was the way Obierika's cousins were likely to get rid of her son. Killing him was too dangerous, the risk of misfortunes from the oracle too high, but they would be able to sell him as long as they had strong medicine to protect themselves. She was struck, too, by how Iroegbunam lapsed into the white man's language from time to time. It sounded nasal and disgusting. Nwamgba had no desire to speak such a thing herself, but she was suddenly determined that Anikwenwa would speak it well enough to go to the white men's court with Obierika's cousins and defeat them and take control of what was his. And so, shortly after Iroegbunam's return, she told Ayaju that she wanted to take her son to school.

They went first to the Anglican mission. The classroom had more girls than boys—a few curious boys wandered in with their catapaults[3] and then wandered out. The students sat with slates on their laps while the teacher stood in front of them, holding a big cane, telling them a story about a man who transformed a bowl of water into wine. Nwamgba was impressed by the teacher's spectacles, and she thought that the man in the story must have had fairly powerful medicine to be able to transform water into wine. But when the girls were separated and a woman teacher came to teach them how to sew, Nwamgba found this silly; in her clan girls learned to make pottery and a man sewed cloth. What dissuaded her completely about the school, however, was that the instruction was done in Igbo. Nwamgba asked the first teacher why. He said that of course the students were taught English—he held up the English primer—but children learned best in their own language, and the children in the white men's land were taught in their own language, too. Nwamgba turned to leave. The teacher stood in her way and told her that the Catholic missionaries were harsh and did not have the best interests of the natives at heart. Nwamgba was amused by these foreigners, who did not seem to know that one must, in front of strangers, pretend to have unity. But she had come in search of English, and so she walked past him and went to the Catholic mission.

Father Shanahan told her that Anikwenwa would have to take an English name, because it was not possible to be baptized with a heathen name. She agreed easily. His name was Anikwenwa as far as she was concerned; if they wanted to name him something she could not pronounce before teaching him their language, she did not mind at all. All that mattered was that he learn enough of the language to fight his father's cousins. Father Shanahan looked at Anikwenwa, a dark-skinned, well-muscled child, and guessed that he was about twelve, although he found it difficult to estimate the ages of these people; sometimes a mere boy would look like a man, nothing like in Eastern Africa, where he had previously worked and where the natives tended to be slender, less confusingly muscular. As he poured

3. I.e., slingshots.

some water on the boy's head, he said, "Michael, I baptize you in the name of the Father and of the Son and of the Holy Spirit."

He gave the boy a singlet and a pair of shorts, because the people of the living God did not walk around naked, and he tried to preach to the boy's mother, but she looked at him as if he were a child who did not know any better. There was something troublingly assertive about her, something he had seen in many women here; there was much potential to be harnessed if their wildness could be tamed. This Nwamgba would make a marvelous missionary among the women. He watched her leave. There was a grace in her straight back, and she, unlike others, had not spent too much time going round and round in her speech. It infuriated him, their overlong talk and circuitous proverbs, their never getting to the point, but he was determined to excel here; it was the reason he had joined the Holy Ghost Congregation, whose special vocation was the redemption of black heathens.

Nwamgba was alarmed by how indiscriminately the missionaries flogged students—for being late, for being lazy, for being slow, for being idle. And once, as Anikwenwa told her, Father Lutz had put metal cuffs around a girl's wrists to teach her a lesson about lying, all the time saying in Igbo—for Father Lutz spoke a broken brand of Igbo—that native parents pampered their children too much, that teaching the Gospel also meant teaching proper discipline. The first weekend Anikwenwa came home, Nwamgba saw angry welts on his back. She tightened her wrapper on her waist and went to the school. She told the teacher that she would gouge out the eyes of everyone at the mission if they ever did that to him again. She knew that Anikwenwa did not want to go to school, and she told him that it was only for a year or two, so that he would learn English, and although the mission people told her not to come so often, she insistently came every weekend to take him home. Anikwenwa always took off his clothes even before they left the mission compound. He disliked the shorts and shirt that made him sweat, the fabric that was itchy around his armpits. He disliked, too, being in the same class as old men and missing out on wrestling contests.

Perhaps it was because he began to notice the admiring glances his clothes brought in the clan but Anikwenwa's attitude to school slowly changed. Nwamgba first noticed this when some of the other boys with whom he swept the village square complained that he no longer did his share because he was at school, and Anikwenwa said something in English, something sharp-sounding, which shut them up and filled Nwamgba with an indulgent pride. Her pride turned to a vague worry when she noticed that the curiosity in his eyes had diminished. There was a new ponderousness in him, as if he had suddenly found himself bearing the weight of a too-heavy world. He stared at things for too long. He stopped eating her food, because, he said, it was sacrificed to idols. He told her to tie her wrapper around her chest instead of her waist, because her nakedness was sinful. She looked at him, amused by his earnestness, but worried nonetheless, and asked why he had only just begun to notice her nakedness.

When it was time for his *ima mmuo* ceremony,[4] he said he would not participate, because it was a heathen custom for boys to be initiated into the world of

4. Rite of passage through which Igbo boys become men by joining with ancestral spirits.

spirits, a custom that Father Shanahan had said would have to stop. Nwamgba roughly yanked his ear and told him that a foreign albino could not determine when their customs would change, so until the clan itself decided that the initiation would stop, he would participate or else he would tell her whether he was her son or the white man's son. Anikwenwa reluctantly agreed, but as he was taken away with a group of boys, she noticed that he lacked their excitement. His sadness saddened her. She felt her son slipping away from her, and yet she was proud that he was learning so much, that he could become a court interpreter or a letter writer, and that with Father Lutz's help he had brought home some papers that showed that their lands belonged to him and his mother. Her proudest moment was when he went to his father's cousins Okafo and Okoye and asked for his father's ivory tusk back. And they gave it to him.

Nwamgba knew that her son now inhabited a mental space that was foreign to her. He told her that he was going to Lagos to learn how to be a teacher, and even as she screamed—How can you leave me? Who will bury me when I die?—she knew he would go. She did not see him for many years, years during which his father's cousin Okafo died. She often consulted the oracle to ask whether Anikwenwa was still alive; the *dibia* admonished her and sent her away, because of course he was alive. At last Anikwenwa returned, in the year that the clan banned all dogs after a dog killed a member of the Mmangala age grade, the age grade to which Anikwenwa would have belonged if he had not said that such things were devilish.

Nwamgba said nothing when he announced that he had been appointed catechist at the new mission. She was sharpening her *aguba*[5] on the palm of her hand, about to shave patterns in the hair of a little girl, and she continued to do so—*flick-flick-flick*—while Anikwenwa talked about winning souls in their clan. The plate of breadfruit seeds she had offered him was untouched—he no longer ate anything at all of hers—and she looked at him, this man wearing trousers, and a rosary around his neck, and wondered whether she had meddled with his destiny. Was this what his chi had ordained for him, this life in which he was like a person diligently acting a bizarre pantomime?

The day that he told her about the woman he would marry, she was not surprised. He did not do it as it was done, did not consult people to ask about the bride's family, but simply said that somebody at the mission had seen a suitable young woman from Ifite Ukpo[6] and the suitable young woman would be taken to the Sisters of the Holy Rosary[7] in Onicha to learn how to be a good Christian wife. Nwamgba was sick with malaria on that day, lying on her mud bed, rubbing her aching joints, and she asked Anikwenwa the young woman's name. Anikwenwa said it was Agnes. Nwamgba asked for the young woman's real name. Anikwenwa cleared his throat and said she had been called Mgbeke before she became a Christian, and Nwamgba asked whether Mgbeke would at least do the confession ceremony even if Anikwenwa would not follow the other marriage rites of their clan. He shook his head furiously and told her that the confession made by a woman before marriage, in which she, surrounded by female relatives, swore that no man had touched her since her husband had declared his interest, was sinful, because Christian wives should not have been touched *at all*.

5. Razor (Igbo).
6. Town in Nigeria about 10 miles northeast of Onicha.
7. Roman Catholic order of missionary nuns.

The marriage ceremony in church was laughably strange, but Nwamgba bore it silently and told herself that she would die soon and join Obierika and be free of a world that increasingly made no sense. She was determined to dislike her son's wife, but Mgbeke was difficult to dislike; she was small-waisted and gentle, eager to please the man to whom she was married, eager to please everyone, quick to cry, apologetic about things over which she had no control. And so, instead, Nwamgba pitied her. Mgbeke often visited Nwamgba in tears, saying that Anikwenwa had refused to eat dinner because he was upset with her or that Anikwenwa had banned her from going to a friend's Anglican wedding because Anglicans did not preach the truth, and Nwamgba would silently carve designs on her pottery while Mgbeke cried, uncertain of how to handle a woman crying about things that did not deserve tears.

Mgbeke was called "missus" by everyone, even the non-Christians, all of whom respected the catechist's wife, but on the day she went to the Oyi stream and refused to remove her clothes because she was a Christian, the women of the clan, outraged that she dared to disrespect the goddess, beat her and dumped her at the grove. The news spread quickly. Missus had been harassed. Anikwenwa threatened to lock up all the elders if his wife was treated that way again, but Father O'Donnell, on his next trek from his station in Onicha, visited the elders and apologized on Mgbeke's behalf and asked whether perhaps Christian women could be allowed to fetch water fully clothed. The elders refused—if one wanted Oyi's waters, then one had to follow Oyi's rules—but they were courteous to Father O'Donnell, who listened to them and did not behave like their own son Anikwenwa.

Nwamgba was ashamed of her son, irritated with his wife, upset by their rarefied life in which they treated non-Christians as if they had smallpox, but she held out her hope for a grandchild; she prayed and sacrificed for Mgbeke to have a boy, because it would be Obierika come back and would bring a semblance of sense back into her world. She did not know of Mgbeke's first or second miscarriage, it was only after the third that Mgbeke, sniffling and blowing her nose, told her. They had to consult the oracle, as this was a family misfortune, Nwamgba said, but Mgbeke's eyes widened with fear. Michael would be very angry if he ever heard of this oracle suggestion. Nwamgba, who still found it difficult to remember that Michael was Anikwenwa, went to the oracle herself, and afterwards thought it ludicrous how even the gods had changed and no longer asked for palm wine but for gin. Had they converted, too?

A few months later, Mgbeke visited, smiling, bringing a covered bowl of one of those concoctions that Nwamgba found inedible, and Nwamgba knew that her chi was still wide awake and that her daughter-in-law was pregnant. Anikwenwa had decreed that Mgbeke would have the baby at the mission in Onicha, but the gods had different plans and she went into early labor on a rainy afternoon; somebody ran in the drenching rain to Nwamgba's hut to call her. It was a boy. Father O'Donnell baptized him Peter, but Nwamgba called him Nnamdi, because she believed he was Obierika come back. She sang to him, and when he cried she pushed her dried-up nipple into his mouth, but try as she might, she did not feel the spirit of her magnificent husband Obierika. Mgbeke had three more miscarriages and Nwamgba went to the oracle many times until a pregnancy stayed and the second baby was born, this time at the mission in Onicha.

A girl. From the moment Nwamgba held her, the baby's bright eyes delightfully focused on her, she knew that it was the spirit of Obierika that had returned; odd, to have come in a girl, but who could predict the ways of the ancestors? Father O'Donnell baptized her Grace, but Nwamgba called her Afamefuna, "My Name Will Not Be Lost," and was thrilled by the child's solemn interest in her poetry and her stories, the teenager's keen watchfulness as Nwamgba struggled to make pottery with newly shaky hands. But Nwamgba was not thrilled that Afamefuna was to go away to secondary school (Peter was already living with the priest in Onicha), because she feared that, at boarding school, the new ways would dissolve her granddaughter's fighting spirit and replace it either with an incurious rigidity, like Anikwenwa's, or a limp helplessness, like Mgbeke's.

The year that Afamefuna left for secondary school in Onicha, Nwamgba felt as if a lamp had been blown out on a moonless night. It was a strange year, the year that darkness suddenly descended on the land in the middle of the afternoon, and when Nwamgba felt the deep-seated ache in her joints, she knew her end was near. She lay on her bed gasping for breath, while Anikwenwa pleaded with her to be baptized and anointed so that he could hold a Christian funeral for her, as he could not participate in a heathen ceremony. Nwamgba told him that if he dared to bring anybody to rub some filthy oil on her, she would slap that person with her last strength. All she wanted was to see Afamefuna before she joined the ancestors, but Anikwenwa said that Grace was taking exams in school and could not come home. But she came. Nwamgba heard the squeaky swing of her door and there was Afamefuna, her granddaughter who had come on her own from Onicha because she had been unable to sleep for days, her restless spirit urging her home. Grace put down her schoolbag, inside of which was her textbook with a chapter called "The Pacification of the Primitive Tribes of Southern Nigeria," by an administrator from Worcestershire[8] who had lived among them for seven years.

It was Grace who would read about these savages, titillated by their curious and meaningless customs, not connecting them to herself until her teacher, Sister Maureen, told her she could not refer to the call-and-response her grandmother had taught her as poetry because primitive tribes did not have poetry. It was Grace who would laugh loudly until Sister Maureen took her to detention and then summoned her father, who slapped Grace in front of the teachers to show them how well he disciplined his children. It was Grace who would nurse a deep scorn for her father for years, spending holidays working as a maid in Onicha so as to avoid the sanctimonies, the dour certainties, of her parents and brother. It was Grace who, after graduating from secondary school, would teach elementary school in Agueke, where people told stories of the destruction of their village years before by the white men's guns, stories she was not sure she believed, because they also told stories of mermaids appearing from the River Niger holding wads of crisp cash. It was Grace who, as one of the few women at the University College in Ibadan[9] in 1950, would change her degree from chemistry to history after she heard, while drinking tea at the home of a friend, the story of Mr. Gboyega. The eminent Mr. Gboyega, a chocolate-skinned Nigerian,

8. County in England.
9. Oldest and most prestigious Nigerian university.

educated in London, distinguished expert on the history of the British Empire, had resigned in disgust when the West African Examinations Council began talking of adding African history to the curriculum, because he was appalled that African history would even be considered a subject. Grace would ponder this story for a long time, with great sadness, and it would cause her to make a clear link between education and dignity, between the hard, obvious things that are printed in books and the soft, subtle things that lodge themselves into the soul. It was Grace who would begin to rethink her own schooling—how lustily she had sung, on Empire Day, "God bless our Gracious King. Send him victorious, happy and glorious. Long to reign over us," how she had puzzled over words like "wallpaper" and "dandelions" in her textbooks, unable to picture those things; how she had struggled with arithmetic problems that had to do with mixtures, because what was coffee and what was chicory[1] and why did they have to be mixed? It was Grace who would begin to rethink her father's schooling and then hurry home to see him, his eyes watery with age, telling him she had not received all the letters she had ignored, saying amen when he prayed, pressing her lips against his forehead. It was Grace who, driving past Agueke on her way back, would become haunted by the image of a destroyed village and would go to London and to Paris and to Onicha, sifting through moldy files in archives, reimagining the lives and smells of her grandmother's world, for the book she would write called *Pacifying with Bullets: A Reclaimed History of Southern Nigeria*. It was Grace who, in a conversation about the early manuscript with her fiancé, George Chikadibia—stylish graduate of Kings College, Lagos;[2] engineer-to-be; wearer of three-piece suits; expert ballroom dancer who often said that a grammar school without Latin was like a cup of tea without sugar—knew that the marriage would not last when George told her she was misguided to write about primitive culture instead of a worthwhile topic like African Alliances in the American-Soviet Tension. They would divorce in 1972, not because of the four miscarriages Grace had suffered but because she woke up sweating one night and realized that she would strangle him to death if she had to listen to one more rapturous monologue about his Cambridge days. It was Grace who, as she received faculty prizes, as she spoke to solemn-faced people at conferences about the Ijaw and Ibibio and Igbo and Efik peoples of Southern Nigeria, as she wrote reports for international organizations about commonsense things for which she nevertheless received generous pay, would imagine her grandmother looking on and chuckling with great amusement. It was Grace who, feeling an odd rootlessness in the later years of her life, surrounded by her awards, her friends, her garden of peerless roses, would go to the courthouse in Lagos and officially change her first name from Grace to Afamefuna.

But on that day as she sat at her grandmother's bedside in the fading evening light, Grace was not contemplating her future. She simply held her grandmother's hand, the palm thickened from years of making pottery.

2008

1. Herbaceous root substituted for coffee during wartime in England.

2. Elite Nigerian secondary school for boys.

Selected Bibliographies

I. Modernity and Modernism, 1900–1945

Pericles Lewis, *The Cambridge Introduction to Modernism* (2007), offers an overview of developments in England and Europe. Ástráður Eysteinsson and Vivian Lisca, eds., *Modernism*, 2 vols. (2007) provides detailed studies of particular national contexts. Harry Levin, "What Was Modernism?" (1962, repr. in *Refractions*, 1966) is a survey of modernist writers as humanists and inheritors of the Enlightenment. Many of the original critical writings on modern literature and art are collected in Vassiliki Kolocotroni, Jane Goldman, and Olga Taxidoe, eds., *Modernism: An Anthology of Sources and Documents* (1998). Richard Gilman, *The Making of Modern Drama* (1974) treats developments in drama, while Martin Puchner, *Stage Fright: Modernism, Anti-Theatricality, and Drama* (2002) explores the modernists' ambivalence toward theater. H. H. Arnason and Elizabeth Mansfield, *History of Modern Art: Painting, Sculpture, Architecture* (6th ed., 2009, illus.) follows the evolution of the arts in the West, from the nineteenth century to the 1960s. Matei Calinescu, *Five Faces of Modernity* (1987) is an informative collection of essays on the aesthetics of modernism, avant-garde, decadence, and kitsch. Peter Gay, *Modernism: The Lure of Heresy* (2007) places the movement in historical context.

Anna Akhmatova
Eileen Feinstein, *Anna of All the Russias: A Life of Anna Akhmatova* (2007) is a good recent biography. Roberta Reeder, *Anna Akhmatova: Poet and Prophet* (1994) is thorough. David Wells, *Anna Akhmatova: Her Poetry* (1996) is a readable, well-documented study that discusses works in chronological order. Amanda Haight, *Anna Akhmatova: A Poetic Pilgrimage* (1976) and Susan Amert, *In a Shattered Mirror: The Later Poetry of Anna Akhmatova* (1992) are perceptive book-length studies. Ronald Hingley, *Nightingale Fever: Russian Poets in Revolution* (1981) discusses Akhmatova, Pasternak, Tsvetaeva, and Mandelstam in the context of Russian literary history and Soviet politics up to the early years of World War II. Anna Akhmatova, *My Half Century: Selected Prose*, ed. Ronald Meyer (1992), includes autobiographical material, correspondence, short pieces on other writers, and an essay on Akhmatova's prose.

Akutagawa Ryūnosuke
Akutagawa's masterpieces are all works of short fiction. *Rashōmon and Seventeen Other Stories* (2006) collects many, including "Rashōmon," "Hell Screen," "The Nose," "The Spider Thread," "Spinning Gears," and "The Life of a Stupid Man." *Kappa* (1970) is his most treasured longer piece. On the writer's career as a whole, see Yu Beongcheon, *Akutagawa* (1972) and the chapter on the author in Donald Keene, *Dawn to the West* (1984). Seiji M. Lippit devotes a chapter to Akutagawa's late works in *Topographies of Japanese Modernism* (2002).

Jorge Luis Borges
Useful biographies include James Woodall, *The Man in the Mirror of the Book: A Life of Jorge Luis Borges* (1996); James Woodall, *Borges: A Life* (1996); and Jason Wilson, *Jorge Luis Borges* (2006). George R. McMurray, *Jorge Luis Borges* (1980) and Martin S. Stabb,

Borges Revisited (1991) are general introductions to the man and his work. Jaime Alazraki, ed., *Critical Essays on Jorge Luis Borges* (1987) assembles articles and reviews (including the 1970 *Autobiographical Essay*), four comparative essays, and a general introduction that offer valuable perspectives on Borges's writing as well as his impact on writers and critics in the United States. Edna Aizenberg, ed., *Borges and His Successors: The Borgesian Impact on Literature and the Arts* (1990) is a wide-ranging collection of essays describing Borges as the precursor of postmodern fiction and criticism. Anna Maria Barrenechea, *Borges the Labyrinth Maker* (1965) discusses the writer's intricate style, while Daniel Balderston, *Out of Context: Historical Reference and the Representation of Reality in Borges* (1993) focuses on the texts' manipulation of fictional and historical reality. Fernando Sorrentino, *Seven Conversations with Jorge Luis Borges* (1981) is a series of informal, widely ranging interviews from 1972, with a list of the topics of each conversation. Recent translations into English include *Collected Fictions*, trans. Andrew Hurley (1998) and *Selected Non-Fictions*, ed. Eliot Weinberger (2000).

Bertolt Brecht

Martin Esslin, *Brecht, the Man and His Work* (1974), John Fuegi, *Brecht and Company: Sex, Politics, and the Making of Modern Drama* (1994), and John Willett, *The Theatre of Bertolt Brecht: A Study from Eight Aspects* (1959) offer biographical and critical perspectives on the author and his work. John Willett, ed. and trans., *Brecht on Theatre: The Development of an Aesthetic* (1964) contains Brecht's essays and lectures on his theater. Ronald Hayman, *Brecht: A Biography* (1983) offers a detailed view of the playwright's life. Eric Bentley, *The Brecht Commentaries 1943–1986* (1987) presents lively essays by a friend and sometime colleague on the major plays, on Brecht's stagecraft, and on his place in modern culture. The essays in Walter Benjamin, *Understanding Brecht* (1983) provide insights, by a friend and major intellectual figure, into Brecht's work and modern thought. *The Cambridge Companion to Brecht*, ed. Peter Thompson and Glendry Sacks (1994), contains an essay on *The Good Person of Szechwan*. Fredric Jameson, *Brecht and Method* (1998) is the best book on Brecht's theory. Interesting comparative studies include Anthony Tatlow, *The Mask of Evil: Brecht's Response to the Poetry, Theatre and Thought of China and Japan* (1977).

Constantine Cavafy

Biographical information is available in Peter Bien, *Constantine Cavafy* (1964) and Robert Liddell, *Cavafy: A Critical Biography* (1974, repr. 2000), which contains a bibliography. The best full-length study in English is Edmund Keeley, *Cavafy's Alexandria* (1996). A wide-ranging collection of essays is Denise Harvey, ed., *The Mind and Art of C. P. Cavafy* (1983).

Aimé Césaire

The fullest critical account of Césaire's work is to be found in A. James Arnold, *Négritude and Modernism: The Poetry and Poetics of Aimé Césaire* (1981); Arnold has developed his views in his introduction to Clayton Eshleman and Annette Smith, trans., *Aimé Césaire: Lyrical and Dramatic Poetry* (1992). In *Négritude and Literary Criticism* (1996), Belinda E. Jack offers a comprehensive general introduction to the major works of the Négritude movement. Gregson Davis, *Aimé Césaire* (1997) is an insightful examination of the evolution of the writer's work; it contains chapters on *Notebook* and the poet's surrealist period as well as a chronology and a bibliography. The translation of *Notebook* printed here is taken from Clayton Eshleman and Annette Smith, trans., *Aimé Césaire: The Collected Poetry* (1983), which contains, in addition to translations of Césaire's poetry up to the late 1970s, a valuable introduction.

Joseph Conrad

Among the many sources of biographical information are Conrad's *The Mirror of the Sea* (1906) and *A Personal Record* (1912) and Jocelyn Baines, *Joseph Conrad: A Critical Biography* (1960). The best general biography is Zdzislaw Najder, *Joseph Conrad: A Life* (2007). Albert J. Guérard's critical study, *Conrad the Novelist* (1958), is also recommended. The best general critical study, Ian Watt's *Conrad in the Nineteenth Century* (1979), discusses Conrad's impressionist and symbolist techniques. Chinua Achebe's essay "An Image of Africa: Racism in Conrad's *Heart of Darkness*" is published in his *Hopes and Impediments* (1988). J. H. Stape, ed., *The Cambridge Companion to Joseph Conrad* (1996) offers a wide variety of perspectives on Conrad's work, including *Heart of Darkness*; Allan Simmons, *Heart of Darkness: A Reader's*

Guide (2007) provides an introduction to the critical themes of the novella. Adam Hochschild, *King Leopold's Ghost: A Story of Greed, Terror, and Heroism in Colonial Africa* (1998) is a detailed and informative study of the Congo setting of Conrad's novella.

T. S. Eliot

Peter Ackroyd, *T. S. Eliot* (1984) and Tony Sharpe, *T. S. Eliot: A Literary Life* (1991) are brief, readable introductions to Eliot's life and works. Lyndall Gordon, *T. S. Eliot: An Imperfect Life* (1998) is a fuller biography. Several volumes of Eliot's correspondence are being published in Valerie Eliot and Hugh Haughton, ed., *The Letters of T. S. Eliot* (2009–). The influence of Eliot's life on his poems is the subject of Ronald Schuchard, *Eliot's Dark Angel: Intersections of Life and Art* (1999). Martin Scofield, *T. S. Eliot: The Poems* (1988) offers a concise, balanced discussion of the evolution of Eliot's poetry. A fine study is Denis Donogue, *Words Alone: The Poet T. S. Eliot* (2000). Useful general collections are Linda Wagner, ed., *T. S. Eliot: A Collection of Criticism* (1974); Ronald Bush, ed., *T. S. Eliot: The Modernist in History* (1991); A. David Moody, ed., *The Cambridge Companion to T. S. Eliot* (1995); and Harold Bloom, ed., *T. S. Eliot* (1999).

William Faulkner

Stephen B. Oates, *William Faulkner, The Man and the Artist: A Biography* (1987) is vividly written. Joseph Blotner, *Faulkner: A Biography*, 2 vols. (1974; repr. in 1 vol., 2005) is the authorized, immensely detailed account of the writer's life. Other studies include Cleanth Brooks, *William Faulkner: The Yoknapatawpha Country* (1963), a basic literary analysis and exploration of Faulkner's mythical South, with a list of his fictional characters; James B. Carothers, *William Faulkner's Short Stories* (1985), an examination of the short stories in the context of the novels; and Richard C. Moreland, ed., *A Companion to William Faulkner* (2007), a collection of recent essays.

James Joyce

Harry Levin, *James Joyce: A Critical Introduction* (1941) is an excellent, readable general introduction. The standard, detailed biography, with illustrations, is Richard Ellmann, *James Joyce* (1982). Morris Beja, *James Joyce: A Literary Life* (1992) includes recent scholarship. Derek Attridge, ed., *The Cambridge Companion to James Joyce* (1990) and Mary T. Reynolds, ed., *James Joyce: A Collection of Critical Essays* (1993) treat various aspects of the work. Daniel R. Schwarz, ed., *The Dead* (1994) is a useful short book that contains the text and contextual material, an account of *Dubliners*' history and criticism from the 1950s, and analyses by several authors using five critical perspectives. John Wyse Jackson and Bernard McGinley, eds., *Joyce's* Dubliners: *An Illustrated Edition with Annotations* (1995) is a fascinating, copiously illustrated and documented edition that includes allusions to other works and a capsule essay after each story. A valuable recent introduction is David Pierce, *Reading Joyce* (2008). Pierce's earlier *James Joyce's Ireland* (1992) provides contemporary photographs by Dan Harper and uses documents, photographs, and quotations to reconstruct Joyce's biography in historical context.

Franz Kafka

Kafka's life has been the subject of many studies, starting with Max Brod, *Franz Kafka: A Biography* (English trans., 1960). One of the best recent works is Nicholas Murray, *Kafka: A Biography* (2004). Readable introductions to the author's life and work include Klaus Wagenbach, *Kafka* (2003) and Louis Begley, *The Tremendous World I Have Inside My Head: Franz Kafka: A Biographical Essay* (2008). Heinz Politzer, *Franz Kafka: Parable and Paradox* (1962) is an interesting early study concerned with Kafka's symbolism. *Kafka: A Collection of Critical Essays*, ed. Ronald Gray (1962), introduces the main themes of Kafka criticism, while more recent essays, specifically on the selection here, are collected in Harold Bloom, ed., *Franz Kafka's The Metamorphosis* (1988) and Stanley Corngold, ed., *The Metamorphosis* (1996). Kafka's religious background is the subject of Sander Gilman, *Franz Kafka: The Jewish Patient* (1995), while the Czech context is discussed by Scott Spector, *Prague Territories* (2000).

Kawabata Yasunari

Even in translation, the eloquent reticence of Kawabata's style shines through, and it is reasonable to assume that Edward Seidensticker's English versions were influential in bringing Kawabata the Nobel Prize. Especially recommended are *Snow Country* (1947), *Thousand Cranes* (1959), *The Sound of the Mountain* (1970), *The Master of Go* (1972), *The Izu Dancer and Other Stories* (1974), and *House of the Sleeping Beauties and Other Stories* (1969).

A collection of Kawabata's short pieces has been translated by Lane Dunlop and J. Martin Holman, *Palm-of-the-Hand Stories* (1988). For background on Kawabata, see Seidensticker, "On Kawabata Yasunari," in *This Country, Japan* (1979). There are chapter-length studies of the author in Masao Miyoshi, *Accomplices of Silence: The Modern Japanese Novel* (1974); Dennis Washburn, *The Dilemma of the Modern in Japanese Fiction* (1995); and Roy Starrs, *Soundings in Time: The Fictive Art of Yasunari Kawabata* (1998).

Kushi Fusako

Although "Memoirs of a Declining Ryukyuan Woman" was Kushi's only published work, a selection of other short stories and poetry from Okinawa can be found in *Southern Exposure: Modern Japanese Literature from Okinawa* (2000). A pair of important longer works has been translated in *Okinawa: Two Postwar Novellas* (1989). Davinder Bhowmik discusses the work of Kushi and her generation in *Writing Okinawa: Narrative Acts of Identity and Resistance* (2008). Michael Molasky, *The American Occupation of Japan and Okinawa: Literature and Memory* (1999) focuses on the period after 1945.

Lao She

Lao She's political context is the subject of Ranbir Vohra, *Lao She and the Chinese Revolution* (1974). David Der-Wei Wang, *Fictional Realism in Twentieth-Century China: Mao Dun, Lao She, Shen Congwen* (1992) examines the broader literary movement in which Lao She participated.

Federico García Lorca

Leslie Stainton, *Lorca: A Dream of Life* (1998) is an extensive biography. Carl W. Cobb, *Federico García Lorca* (1967) is a good general biography, while Gwynne Edwards, *Lorca: Living in the Theatre* (2003) focuses on his dramatic work. Candelas Newton, *Understanding Federico García Lorca* (1995) is a brief discussion of the work; E. Honig, *García Lorca* (1980) provides a critical introduction in literary historical context; and C. B. Morris, *Son of Andalusia: The Lyrical Landscapes of Federico García Lorca* (1997) offers a more specialized view, with illustrations. Federico Bonaddio, ed., *Companion to Federico García Lorca* (2007) is a valuable collection of essays on the poet and his work.

Lu Xun

A valuable and readable biography is David Pollard, *The True Story of Lu Xun* (2002). Leo Ou-fan Lee, *Voices from the Iron House: A Study of Lu Xun* (1987) is an excellent introduction to Lu Xun's work, placing it in the context of his life and Chinese cultural history; and Lee, *Lu Xun and His Legacy* (1985) is a collection of scholarly articles treating Lu's literary work, his politics, and his influence. William A. Lyell, *Lu Hsün's Vision of Reality* (1976) is also useful.

Thomas Mann

Hermann Kurzke, *Thomas Mann: A Biography* (2002) provides a thorough account of Mann's life. Harold Bloom, ed., *Thomas Mann* (1986) and Ritchie Robertson, ed., *The Cambridge Companion to Thomas Mann* (2001) present essays on different works and brief biographical information. Terence J. Reed, *Thomas Mann: The Uses of Tradition* (2nd ed., 1996), is an excellent, well-written general study incorporating recent material. Richard Winston, *Thomas Mann: The Making of an Artist 1875–1911* (1981), the first volume of an unfinished study, is a detailed and authoritative presentation by the translator of Mann's diaries and letters. Ellis Shookman reviews almost a century's worth of criticism in *Thomas Mann's* Death in Venice: *A Novella and Its Critics* (2003).

Ch'ae Man-sik

Representative colonial Korean short stories are collected in Kim Chung-un and Bruce Fulton, trans., *A Ready-Made Life: Early Masters of Korean Fiction* (1998); the title is from Ch'ae Man-sik's famous short story of that name. His most important novel, *Peace Under Heaven*, has been masterfully translated by Chun Kyung-Ja (1992). For an excellent selection of post-1945 short stories, see Marshall R. Phil, Bruce Fulton, and Ju-Chan Fulton, eds., *Land of Exile: Contemporary Korean Fiction* (2007).

Modern Poetry

C. K. Stead, *The New Poetic* (1964) and David Perkins, *A History of Modern Poetry: From the 1890s to the High Modernist Mode* (1976) trace the development of modernism in English poetry. Frank Lentricchia, *Modernist Quartet* (1994) explores American modernism, with a chapter devoted to T. S. Eliot. More recent poetry is well represented in Jeffery Paine, ed., *The Poetry of Our World: An International Anthology of Contemporary Poetry* (2001).

Pablo Neruda
Pablo Neruda, *Memoirs*, trans. Hardie St. Martin (1977) contains much biographical information. A good recent biography in English is Adam Feinstein, *Pablo Neruda: A Passion for Life* (2004). Manuel Duran and Margery Safir, *Earth Tones: The Poetry of Pablo Neruda* (1981) is an excellent thematic study that includes a short biography. *Pablo Neruda*, ed. Harold Bloom (1989), contains nineteen valuable essays and reminiscences by scholars, translators, and those who knew Neruda. John Felstiner, *Translating Neruda: The Way to Macchu Picchu* (1980) describes in detail the process of translating *The Heights of Macchu Picchu* in terms of Neruda's life and perspectives. Louis Poirot, *Pablo Neruda: Absence and Presence* (1990) matches photographs of Neruda, his friends, and his homes with related passages from the poet, his wife, and friends. A recent work is *The Poetry of Pablo Neruda*, trans. Ilan Stavans (2005).

Octavio Paz
Paz discusses the development of his ideas in *Itinerary: An Intellectual Journey*, trans. Jason Wilson (1999). Wilson analyzes the Mexican writer's surrealist poetry in *Octavio Paz: A Study of His Poetics* (1979), while the essays in Harold Bloom, ed., *Octavio Paz* (2002) explore a range of perspectives on his work. Nick Caistor, *Octavio Paz* (2007) provides an overview of the poet's life and works.

Luigi Pirandello
Gaspare Guidice's *Pirandello: A Biography* (1975), trans. Alastair Hamilton provides a good overview of the artist's life. The best essay on Pirandello and metatheater is by Maurizio Grande, "Pirandello and the Theatre-within-the-Theatre: Thresholds and Frames in *Cascuno a suo modo*" (in *Luigi Pirandello: Contemporary Perspectives* [1999]). Roger W. Oliver's *Dreams of Passion: The Theater of Luigi Pirandello* (1979) focuses on Pirandello's theory of humor and applies it to his best-known plays, including *Six Characters*. Ann Hallamore Caesar's *Characters and Authors in Luigi Pirandello* (1998) offers a wide-ranging discussion of Pirandello through the diversity of genres in which he worked, from novels and poetry to drama and film. Pirandello's work in the theater is captured in *Luigi Pirandello in the Theatre: A Documentary Record* (1993), ed. Susan Bassnett and Jennifer Lorch, and in A. Richard Sogliuzzo's *Luigi Pirandello, Director: The Playwright in the Theatre* (1982).

Marcel Proust
Roger Shattuck, *Proust's Way* (2001) is a general study including advice on how to read Proust. Malcolm Bowie, *Proust Among the Stars* (2000) offers a slightly more advanced starting point. George D. Painter, in *Marcel Proust: A Biography* (rev. 1996), presents a comprehensive biography. Excellent recent biographies include William C. Carter, *Marcel Proust* (2000) and Jean-Yves Tadié, *Marcel Proust* (2000). Terence Kilmartin, *A Reader's Guide to* Remembrance of Things Past (1984) is a handbook to Proust's characters, persons referred to in the text, places, and themes, all keyed to the revised translation. René Girard, *Proust: A Collection of Critical Essays* (1962); Harold Bloom, ed., *Marcel Proust's Remembrance of Things Past* (1987); and Barbara J. Bucknall, ed., *Critical Essays on Marcel Proust* (1987) are also recommended.

Rainer Maria Rilke
J. F. Hendry, *The Sacred Threshold: A Life of Rainer Maria Rilke* (1983) and Patricia Pollock Brodsky, *Rainer Maria Rilke* (1988) are brief, readable biographies with numerous citations from Rilke's letters and work. A more recent, comprehensive biography is Ralph Freedman's *Life of a Poet: Rainer Maria Rilke* (1998). Heinz F. Peters, *Rainer Maria Rilke: Masks and the Man* (1977) is a biographical and thematic study of the poet's work and influence. William H. Gass, *Reading Rilke: Reflections on the Problems of Translation* (1999) combines biography, philosophy, and commentary on specific translation problems in the *Duino Elegies*. Judith Ryan, *Rilke, Modernism and Poetic Tradition* (1999) places his work in its literary-historical context.

Virginia Woolf
Hermione Lee's biography, *Virginia Woolf* (1996) is now, and surely for a while to come, the definitive work on Woolf's life. Julia Briggs has also produced a detailed recent biography that pays close attention to the author's works and their creation, *Virginia Woolf: An Inner Life* (2005). Alison Light's study, *Mrs. Woolf and the Servants* (2007), examines Woolf's place amid the shifting social and economic issues of the era through the lens of her relationships with the domestic help. Two valuable collections of essays on Woolf's writing and her position in the modernist tradition are Patricia Clements and Isobel Grundy, eds., *Virginia Woolf: New Critical Essays* (1983)

and Margaret Homans, ed., *Virginia Woolf: A Collection of Critical Essays* (1993). S. P. Rosenbaum, ed., *Virginia Woolf: Women and Fiction* (1992) transcribes and edits two draft manuscripts that are the basis for *A Room of One's Own.* Gillian Beer, *Virginia Woolf: The Common Ground* (1996) offers four useful general essays and four discussions of specific novels.

William Butler Yeats

Edward Malins presents a brief introduction with biography, illustrations, and maps in *A Preface to Yeats* (1994). Richard Ellmann, *The Identity of Yeats* (1964) is an excellent discussion of the poet's work as a whole. Norman A. Jeffares has revised his major study, *A New Commentary on the Collected Poems of W. B. Yeats* (1983); a useful reference work is Lester I. Conner, *A Yeats Dictionary: Persons and Places in the Poetry of William Butler Yeats* (1998). The most thorough and balanced biographical study is R. F. Foster, *W. B. Yeats: A Life*, 2 vols. (1997–2003). A major account of Yeats's use of poetic form is Helen Vendler, *Our Secret Discipline: Yeats and Lyric Form* (2007). Essay collections include Harold Bloom, ed., *William Butler Yeats* (1986); Richard J. Finneran, ed., *Critical Essays on W. B. Yeats* (1986); and Marjorie Howes and John Kelly, eds., *Cambridge Companion to W. B. Yeats* (2006).

Zhang Ailing

C. T. Hsia's *A History of Modern Chinese Fiction* (1961) contains the first study of Zhang Ailing's work. *The Rice-Sprout Song* (repr. 1988) has an excellent introduction by David Der-Wei Wang.

II. Postwar and Colonial Literature, 1945–1968

Ihab and Sally Hassan, eds., *Essays in Innovation/Renovation: New Perspectives on the Humanities* (1983) explores change in Western culture in the second half of the twentieth century. Tony Judt, *Postwar: A History of Europe Since 1945* (2005) explores the historical context in Europe, while Michael Howard and William Roger Louis, eds., *The Oxford History of the Twentieth Century* (1998) includes informative essays on other parts of the world. Janheinz Jahn, *Muntu: African Culture and the Western World*, trans. Marjorie Grene (1990, orig. 1961) is an influential discussion of the interface of two cultures. Anthony Appiah, *In My Father's House: Africa in the Philosophy of Culture* (1992) explores similar issues in a postcolonial context. Marjorie Perloff, ed., *Postmodern Genres* (1989) collects essays on postmodernism in art and literature. Linda Hutcheon, *A Poetics of Postmodernism* (1988) analyzes the movement's literary forms.

Chinua Achebe

A good reference is Ezenwa Ohaeto, *Chinua Achebe: A Biography* (1997). Achebe has written a series of memoirs of his early life, collected as *The Education of a British-Protected Child* (2009). C. L. Innes, *Chinua Achebe* (1990) is a comprehensive study of the writer's work through 1988 that emphasizes his literary techniques and Africanization of the novel. Simon Gikandi, *Reading Chinua Achebe: Language and Ideology in Fiction* (1991) is also recommended. Also of interest is *Conversations with Chinua Achebe* (1997), ed. Bernth Lindfors. Jago Morrison, *The Fiction of Chinua Achebe* (2007) is a guide to criticism that includes discussions of his short fiction.

James Baldwin

David Leeming, who served as Baldwin's personal secretary, later recollected his friend and employer in *James Baldwin: A Biography* (1995). Also recommended is James Campbell, *Talking at the Gates: A Life of James Baldwin* (1991). A collection of essays published near the end of Baldwin's life, Harold Bloom, ed., *James Baldwin: Modern Critical Views* (1986) represents a range of views by Baldwin's contemporaries. A more recent collection, Dwight A. McBride, ed., *James Baldwin Now* (1999) includes a number of essays on race and sexuality.

Samuel Beckett

Beckett's works have been collected in four volumes in the Grove Centenary Edition

(2006), ed. Paul Auster. *The Letters of Samuel Beckett* (first vol., 2009) are being published in an edition by Martha Dow Fehsenfeld and Lois More Overbeck. Samuel Beckett, *Endgame: with a Revised Text* (1992), ed. S. E. Gontarski is based on productions directed or supervised by Beckett; the attached theatrical notebooks often clarify situations and settings. Arthur N. Athanason, *Endgame: The Ashbin Play* (1993) is a brief introduction; and Alexander Astro, *Understanding Samuel Beckett* (1990) discusses the complete work with interpretations emphasizing cultural and linguistic aspects. Mark S. Byron, ed., *Samuel Beckett's Endgame* (2007) collects essays on this play. Andrew Kennedy, *Samuel Beckett* (1989) provides a compact, comprehensive overview of Beckett's work, with chapters on the major plays and novels. Richard Begam, *Samuel Beckett and the End of Modernity* (1996) discusses Beckett in the context of postmodernism. Cathleen Culotta Andonian organizes *The Critical Response to Samuel Beckett* (1998) in ten sections that represent the various stages in the reception of his work. Useful biographies are Deirdre Bair, *Samuel Beckett: A Biography* (1993); Anthony Cronin, *Samuel Beckett: The Last Modernist* (1996); Lois G. Gordon, *The World of Samuel Beckett, 1906–1946* (1996); and James Knowlson, *Damned to Fame: The Life of Samuel Beckett* (1996). Hugh Kenner, *Samuel Beckett: A Critical Study* (1974) is an earlier but still valuable discussion of the writer's work. Useful essay collections are Jennifer Birkett and Kate Ince, eds., *Samuel Beckett* (2000) and Steven Connor, ed., *Waiting for Godot and Endgame—Samuel Beckett* (1992), which includes eleven essays, of which seven are wholly or partially on *Endgame*.

Tadeusz Borowski

Brief discussions of Borowski are found in Czeslaw Milosz, *The History of Polish Literature* (1969); and from a different perspective, Sidra DeKoven Ezrahi, *By Words Alone: The Holocaust in Literature* (1980) and James Hatley, *Suffering Witness: The Quandary of Responsibility after the Irreparable* (2000). Jan Kott, "Introduction," *This Way for the Gas, Ladies and Gentlemen* (1976), and Jan Walc, "When the Earth Is No Longer a Dream and Cannot Be Dreamed through to the End," *Polish Review* (1987), combine biography and literary analysis, while Czeslaw Milosz, *The Captive Mind* (1953) analyzes Borowski's later communism in relation to his generation. Selections from the poetry are available in *Selected Poems* (1990), trans. Tadeusz Pióro with Larry Rafferty. Tadeusz Drewnowski, ed., *Postal Indiscretions: The Correspondence of Tadeusz Borowski* (2007), trans. Alicia Nitecki, includes letters written to his family from Auschwitz.

Albert Camus

Germaine Brée, *Albert Camus* (1964) is an excellent general study. Catherine Savage Brosman, *Albert Camus* (2001) is a short introduction and biography. Herbert Lottman, *Albert Camus: A Biography* (1979) and Oliver Todd, *Albert Camus: A Life* (1997) are detailed accounts. English Showalter, *Exiles and Strangers: A Reading of Camus's* Exile and the Kingdom (1984) offers essays on the six stories in Camus's collection and separate comments on translations. For a collection of recent essays on Camus, see Edward J. Hughes, ed., *The Cambridge Companion to Camus* (2007), which contains a bibliography.

Paul Celan

A translator of Celan discusses the poet's life and the challenges that his works pose for translation in John Felstiner, *Paul Celan: Poet, Survivor, Jew* (2001). A friend of the poet and distinguished critic interprets three of his major poems in Peter Szondi, *Celan Studies* (2003). Celan has attracted much commentary from philosophers, notably Hans-Georg Gadamer, *Gadamer on Celan*, ed. and trans. Richard Heinemann and Bruce Krajewski (1997), and Philippe Lacoue-Labarthe, *Poetry as Experience*, trans. by Andrea Tarnowski (1999). Aris Fioretos, ed., *Word Traces: Readings of Paul Celan* (1994) is a valuable collection of essays.

Julio Cortázar

A useful overview is Peter Standish, *Understanding Julio Cortázar* (2001). Essays on the writer are collected in three helpful volumes in English: Harold Bloom, ed., *Julio Cortázar* (2005); Jaime Alazraki, ed., *Critical Essays on Julio Cortázar* (1999); and Carlos J. Alonso, ed., *Julio Cortázar: New Readings* (1998). His stories are discussed at greater length in Ilan Stavans, *Julio Cortázar: A Study of the Short Fiction* (1996). For further bibliography, see Sara de Mundo Lo, *Julio Cortázar: His Works and His Critics* (1985).

Carlos Fuentes

Daniel de Guzman, *Carlos Fuentes* (1972) is a brief biography. Maarten van Delden, *Carlos Fuentes, Mexico, and Modernity* (1998) explores the tension between nationalism and cosmopolitanism in Fuentes's fiction and nonfiction. Robert Brody and Charles Rossman, eds., *Carlos Fuentes, A Critical View* (1982), a collection of essays, features several notable critics of Latin American literature, writing on such topics as Fuentes's use of myth and his formal experimentation. It includes an essay on the second-person narration of *Aura*.

Doris Lessing

The most comprehensive biography is Carol Klein, *Doris Lessing* (2000). Ruth Whittaker, *Doris Lessing* (1988) is a concise, informative discussion of the writer's fiction to 1985; it includes biographical contexts and selective bibliography. Two volumes of Lessing's autobiography are published as *Under My Skin* (1995) and *Walking in the Shade* (1997). A good critical study of the novels is Roberta Rubenstein, *The Novelistic Vision of Doris Lessing* (1979). Perspectives on women and literature are the focus of Gayle Greene, *Doris Lessing: The Poetics of Change* (1994).

Clarice Lispector

The best biography is Benjamin Moser, *Why This World: A Biography of Clarice Lispector* (2008). Earl E. Fitz, *Clarice Lispector* (1985), a valuable introduction to her life and work, contains an annotated bibliography. Hélène Cixous, *Reading with Clarice Lispector*, ed., trans., and intro. Verena Andermatt Conley (1990), discusses Lispector's style with reference to three stories and three novels.

Naguib Mahfouz

Roger M. A. Allen, *The Arabic Novel: An Historical and Critical Introduction* (1982) is an authoritative introduction that situates Mahfouz in the context of modern Arabic literature and includes a bibliography of works in Arabic and Western languages. The author's own perspective is given in Najib Mahfuz, *Echoes of an Autobiography*, trans. Denys Johnson-Davies (1997). Sasson Somekh, *"Za 'balawi"*—Author, Theme and Technique," in *Journal of Arabic Literature* (1970), examines the story as a "double-layered" structure governed by references to Sufi mysticism. Michael Beard and Adnan Haydar, eds., *Naguib Mahfouz: From Regional Fame to Global Recognition* (1993) assembles eleven original essays on themes, individual works, and cultural contexts in Mahfouz's work. Trevor le Gassick, ed., *Critical Perspectives on Naguib Mahfouz* (1991) reprints articles on the writer's work up to the 1970s. Rasheed El-Enany, ed., *Naguib Mahfouz: The Pursuit of Meaning* (1993) is an excellent study that offers biography; analyses of novels, short stories, and plays; and a guide for further reading. Comparative studies include Mona Mikhail, *Studies in the Short Fiction of Mahfouz and Idris* (1992), an introductory work juxtaposing themes in Hemingway, Yusuf Idris, Mahfouz, and Camus, and Samia Mehrez, *Egyptian Writers Between History and Fiction: Essays on Naguib Mahfouz, Sonallah Ibrahim, and Gamal al-Ghitani* (1994). Rasheed El-Enany discusses the place of religion in Mahfouz's work in "The Dichotomy of Islam and Modernity in the Fiction of Naguib Mahfouz," in John C. Hawley, ed., *The Postcolonial Crescent: Islam's Impact on Contemporary Literature* (1998).

Manifestos

The best collection is Mary Ann Caws's *Manifestos: A Century of Isms* (2001). Critical studies of the genre include Janet Lyon's *Manifestoes: Provocations of the Modern* (1999), which emphasizes declarations written by women, and Martin Puchner's *Poetry of the Revolution: Marx, Manifestos, and the Avant-Gardes* (2006), which focuses on the relation between artistic manifestos and political ones.

Vladimir Nabokov

A thorough scholarly biography in two volumes is Brian Boyd, *Vladimir Nabokov* (1990–1991). A shorter biography that also introduces Nabokov's works is Neil Cornwell, *Vladimir Nabokov* (1999). For more on his life, see Dmitri Nabokov and Matthew J. Bruccoli, eds., *Vladimir Nabokov: Selected Letters, 1940–1977* (1989). Nabokov's memoir, *Speak, Memory* (1966) is unforgettable, while his idiosyncratic observations on literature are collected in *Strong Opinions* (1973) and *Lectures on Literature*, ed. Fredson Bowers (1980). Valuable critical essays are collected in Julian Connolly, ed., *The Cambridge Companion to Nabokov* (2005).

Alexander Solzhenitsyn

Andrej Kodjak, *Alexander Solzhenitsyn* (1978) provides a biographical and critical introduction up to the writer's deportation from the Soviet Union in 1974; it includes a discussion of Russian terms. Michael Scammell's detailed *Solzhenitsyn: A Biography* (1984) is complemented by Joseph Pearce, *Solzhenitsyn: A Soul in Exile* (1999). Kathryn B. Feuer, ed., *Solzhenitsyn: A Collection of Critical Essays* (1976) and Harold Bloom, ed., *Alexander Solzhenitsyn* (2000) contain a range of essays on aspects and particular works, including *Matryona's House*. John B. Dunlop, Richard S. Haugh, and Michael Nicholson, eds., *Solzhenitsyn in Exile: Critical Essays and Documentary Material* (1985) offers critical essays and discussions of Solzhenitsyn's reception in several countries. A collection of shorter works is available in Edward E. Ericson Jr., and Daniel J. Mahoney, eds., *The Solzhenitsyn Reader: New and Essential Writings 1946–2005* (2006).

III. Contemporary World Literature

Lois Parkinson Zamora and Wendy B. Faris, eds., *Magical Realism: Theory, History, Community* (1997) examines the theoretical and cultural implications of the style in Latin America and elsewhere. Nancy K. Miller, ed., *The Poetics of Gender* (1986) presents essays on various aspects of feminist criticism. Sarah Lawall, ed., *Reading World Literature: Theory, History, Practice* (1994) includes a theoretical introduction to the subject of world literature and twelve essays on specific topics. David Damrosch, *What Is World Literature?* (2003) explores a range of issues in the study of world literature, while Pascale Casanova, *The World Republic of Letters* (2004) offers a sociological view of the development of literary reputations. Accounts of crucial moments in contemporary history include Jeremi Suri, ed., *The Global Revolutions of 1968* (2007); Timothy Garton Ash, *The Magic Lantern: The Revolution of '89 Witnessed in Warsaw, Budapest, Berlin, and Prague* (1993); and Thomas L. Friedman, *The World Is Flat 3.0: A Brief History of the Twenty-First Century* (2007).

Chimamanda Ngozi Adichie

Adichie gives expression to some of her political and social views in *We Should All be Feminists* (2017). She outlines her views on literary representation in her Commonwealth Lecture, "To Instruct and Delight: A Case for Realist Literature" (2012). Ernest N. Emenyonu, ed., *A Companion to Chimamanda Ngozi Adichie*, includes essays on various facets of Adichie's work. Her earlier works are studied in Allwell Abalogu Onukaogu, *Chimamanda Ngozi Adichie: The Aesthetics of Commitment and Narrative* (2010).

Ama Ata Aidoo

Ada Uzoamaka Azodo and Gay Wilentz, eds., *Emerging Perspectives on Ama Ata Aidoo* (1999) contains essays on a range of Aidoo's works. She is well-known for her plays as well as her fiction; Biodun Jeyifo, ed., *Modern African Drama* (2002) includes Aidoo's play *The Dilemma of a Ghost* and works by other African playwrights, as well as relevant essays. The political context of Aidoo's work is the subject of Vincent O. Odamtten, *The Art of Ama Ata Aidoo* (1994).

Isabel Allende

Interviews are collected in Celia Correas Zapata, *Isabel Allende: Life and Spirits* (2002) and in John Rodden, ed., *Conversations with Isabel Allende* (2004). Harold Bloom offers a critical assessment of Allende's work but collects the best early essays on her in *Isabel Allende* (2003). General introductions are available in Linda Gould Levine, *Isabel Allende* (2002) and Karen Castellucci Cox, *Isabel Allende: A Critical Companion* (2003), which contains a bibliography.

Hanan al-Shaykh

Several of al-Shaykh's novels, and her memoir, *The Locust and the Bird: My Mother's Story* (2010), have been translated into English. A lengthy interview by Paula W. Sunderman was published in *Literary Review* in 1997 as "Between

Two Worlds: An Interview with Hanan al-Shaykh."

Yehuda Amichai
Glenda Abramson, *The Writing of Yehuda Amichai: A Thematic Approach* (1989) provides a comprehensive overview of the poet's work. Nili Scharf Gold, *Yehuda Amichai: The Making of Israel's National Poet* (2008) treats his work in relation to his biography. Joseph Cohen, *Voices of Israel* (1990) includes a long essay on Amichai as well as an extended interview. Articles by Glenda Abramson, Naomi B. Sokoloff, and Nili Scharf Gold appear in "Amichai at Sixty" (1984), a special issue of *Prooftexts*.

Roberto Bolaño
Selected short stories, including "Sensini," appear in *Last Evenings on Earth*, trans. Chris Andrews (2006). The best overview of Bolaño's career in English is Francisco Goldman, "The Great Bolaño," *The New York Review of Books*, July 19, 2007. Bolaño discusses his life and work in his characteristically indirect way in Mónica Maristain, *Roberto Bolaño: The Last Interview & Other Conversations* (2009). Tod Thilleman and Richard Blevins, *Breathing Bolaño* (2009) contains the poet Richard Blevins's amusing meditations on Bolaño's novels and stories about poets.

Chu T'ien-Hsin
Essays on Chu T'ien-Hsin and other contemporary Taiwanese writers are collected in David Der-Wei Wang and Carlos Rojas, eds., *Writing Taiwan: A New Literary History*. "Man of La Mancha" is one of five loosely connected chapters in Chu T'ien-Hsin, *The Old Capital: A Novel of Taipei*, trans. Howard Goldblatt (2007).

Junot Díaz
Díaz is interviewed in Ilan Stavans, *Conversations with Ilan Stavans* (2005). Díaz's work is discussed in Harold Augenbraum and Margarite Fernández Olmos, eds., *U.S. Latino Literature: A Critical Guide for Students and Teachers* (2000) and in Lyn Di Iorio Sandin and Richard Perez, eds., *Contemporary U.S. Latino/a Literary Criticism* (2007), which includes a bibliography.

Nawal El Saadawi
Several articles in journals and collective volumes offer views and assessments of Nawal El Saadawi's work, but Fedwa Malti-Douglas, *Men, Women and God(s): Nawal El Saadawi and Arab Feminist Poetics* (1995) is the only study so far devoted to a systematic account and critical interpretation of the corpus in the light of its social and cultural background. El Saadawi has published two volumes of autobiography, translated by Sherif Hetata as *Daughter of Isis* (1999) and *Walking Through Fire* (2002). A recent collection of essays is Ernest N. Emenyonu and Maureen N. Eke, eds., *Emerging Perspectives on Nawal El Saadawi* (2010).

Gabriel García Márquez
The best biography is Gerald Martin, *Gabriel García Márquez* (2008). A shorter overview is Rubén Pelayo, *Gabriel García Márquez: A Biography* (2009). García Márquez has himself published a remarkable autobiography, *Living to Tell the Tale* (2003). Regina Janes, *Gabriel García Márquez, Revolutions in Wonderland* (1981) is an excellent early study on the author in a Latin American context. Other useful introductions to the writer and his work are George P. McMurray, *Gabriel García Márquez* (1977); Robin W. Fiddian, *García Márquez* (1995); and Joan Mellen, *Gabriel García Márquez* (2000). See also Julio Ortega, ed., *Gabriel García Márquez and the Powers of Fiction* (1988) and Isabel Rodriguez-Vergara, *Haunting Demons: Critical Essays on the Works of Gabriel García Márquez* (1998). Harley D. Oberhelman, ed., *Gabriel García Márquez: A Study of the Short Fiction* (1991) includes a bibliography.

Bessie Head
Gillian Stead Eilerson presents the author's biography in *Bessie Head: Thunder Behind Her Ears, Her Life and Writing* (1995). Some of her letters are collected, with a memoir by a close friend, in Patrick Cullinan, ed., *Imaginative Trespasser: Letters Between Bessie Head and Patrick and Wendy Cullinan, 1963–1977* (2005). Craig MacKenzie provides a helpful overview of her work in *Bessie Head* (1999).

Seamus Heaney
Michael Parker, *Seamus Heaney: The Making of a Poet* (1993) combines biography with literary criticism, while the best overall critical study is Helen Vendler, *Seamus Heaney* (1998), which focuses on Heaney's intellectual and aesthetic experiments. Bernard O'Donoghue, ed., *The Cambridge Companion to Seamus Heaney* (2009) includes several essays on Heaney's relationship to other poets. A number of the poet's interviews are collected in Dennis

O'Driscoll, ed., *Stepping Stones: Interviews with Seamus Heaney* (2008).

Jamaica Kincaid
Diane Simmons provides an overview of Kincaid's work, with biographical information, in *Jamaica Kincaid* (1994). Elizabeth Paravisini-Gebert, *Jamaica Kincaid: A Critical Companion* (1999) focuses on the early short stories and the first three novels. A more recent overview is Justin Edwards, *Understanding Jamaica Kincaid* (2007).

Mo Yan
The Roots literary movement, to which Mo Yan belongs, is discussed in Xueping Zhong, *Masculinity Besieged: Issues of Modernity and Male Subjectivity in Chinese Literature of the Late Twentieth Century* (2000). David Der-Wei Wang's essay, "The Literary World of Mo Yan," in *World Literature Today* (2000), offers a general introduction to the work of Mo Yan, with a focus on his novels and their complex narration.

Toni Morrison
John Duvall's critical study *The Identifying Fictions of Toni Morrison: Modernist Authenticity and Postmodern Blackness* (2000) interprets the writer's novels as deeply autobiographical and presents an account of her early life. Another valuable critical study is Linden Peach, *Toni Morrison* (2000). Mark C. Connor, ed., *The Aesthetics of Toni Morrison: Speaking the Unspeakable* (2000) includes a number of excellent essays on Morrison's fiction and nonfiction. A more comprehensive overview is Justine Tally, ed., a *Cambridge Companion to Toni Morrison* (2007). Several of the author's interviews are collected in Danille K. Taylor-Guthrie, ed., *Conversations with Toni Morrison* (1994).

Ngugi wa Thiong'o
A good overview of Ngugi's works is David Cook and Michael Okenimkpe, *Ngugi wa Thiong'o: An Exploration of His Writings* (2nd ed., 1997). Thorough critical accounts include Simon Gikandi, *Ngugi wa Thiong'o* (2000) and Patrick Williams, *Ngugi wa Thiong'o* (1999). Oliver Lovesey provides a biography with relevant historical context in *Ngugi wa Thiong'o* (2000). The historical background is comprehensively treated in Carol Sicherman, ed., *Ngugi wa Thiong'o: The Making of a Rebel. A Source Book in Kenyan Literature and Resistance* (1990).

Ōe Kenzaburō
Ōe's early works are frequently considered "pastoral," although they depict the rural area of his childhood in critical terms. Examples are *Nip the Buds, Shoot the Kids* (1995) and the story "Prize Stock," collected in *Teach Us to Outgrow Our Madness* (1977). The political themes in Ōe's fiction appeared in the early 1960s, in stories such as "Seventeen," collected in *Two Novels: Seventeen, J* (1996). *A Personal Matter* (1969) and *Hiroshima Notes* (1981) reflect the twin events that changed Ōe's life, the birth of his son and a conference he attended on nuclear arms. *The Silent Cry* (1974) is often seen as Ōe's finest long work. Yasuko Claremont traces the author's career in *The Novels of Ōe Kenzaburō* (2008). Michiko N. Wilson, *The Marginal World of Ōe Kenzaburō* (1986) examines Ōe's techniques and compares him to English and American writers. Mary N. Layoun devotes a chapter of *Travels of a Genre: The Modern Novel and Ideology* (1990) to Ōe's work and its relationship to the European novel.

Orhan Pamuk
Pamuk's melancholic memoir, *Istanbul: Memories and the City*, trans. Maureen Freely (2004), intersperses autobiographical reflections with historical analysis of Turkey and descriptions of literary figures associated with the country. Michael D. McGaha, *Autobiographies of Orhan Pamuk: The Writer in His Novels* (2008) explores the relationship between Pamuk's life and his work. Nilgun Anadolu-Okur, ed., *Essays Interpreting the Writings of Novelist Orhan Pamuk: The Turkish Winner of the Nobel Prize* (2009) explores Pamuk's stature as a global writer.

Park Wansuh
For a bilingual translation of the first part of Park Wansuh's trilogy, see *Mother's Stake I*, translated by Yu Young-nan (2012). For a perceptive study, see Kyeong-Hee Choi, "Neither Colonial nor National: The Making of the 'New Woman' in Pak Wansŏ's 'Mother's Stake 1,'" in *Colonial Modernity in Korea*, ed. Gi-Wook Shin and Michael Edson Robinson (1999).

Salman Rushdie
Midnight's Children (1980) has been in print since its first publication. Among the many books about Rushdie and his work, particularly helpful and informative are Damian Grant, *Salman Rushdie* (1999), for an overview of

much of his career; Jaina C. Sanga, *Salman Rushdie's Postcolonial Metaphors* (2001) and Sabrina Hassumani, *Salman Rushdie* (2002), for analyses of his style and major themes. Discussions of the writer's work in wider literary contexts appear in Timothy Brennan, *Salman Rushdie and the Third World* (1989) and Fawzia Afzal-Khan, *Cultural Imperialism and the Indo-English Novel* (1993). Important documentary sources include Lisa Appignanesi and Sara Maitland, *The Rushdie File* (1990); Michael R. Reder, *Conversations with Salman Rushdie* (2000); and Pradyumna S. Chauhan, *Salman Rushdie Interviews* (2001).

Leslie Marmon Silko

Gregory Salyer, *Leslie Marmon Silko* (1997) is a brief introduction to the author and her work; Brewster E. Fitz offers an updated view of the author's career in *Silko: Writing Storyteller and Medicine Woman* (2004). Helen Jaskoski, *Leslie Marmon Silko: A Study of the Short Fiction* (1998) focuses on the stories. Leslie Marmon Silko, *Sacred Water: Narratives and Pictures* (1994) is an autobiographical narrative. Melody Graulich, ed., *"Yellow Woman": Leslie Marmon Silko* (1993) collects pertinent critical essays. "Yellow Woman" and other works are treated in Louise K. Barnett and James L. Thorson, eds., *Leslie Marmon Silko: A Collection of Critical Essays* (1999). For traditional texts on Yellow Woman and other figures in Laguna mythology, the best source is Franz Boas, *Keresan Texts* (1928); the stories in Boas's volume were obtained in 1919–1921 from several Laguna informants, including Leslie Silko's great-grandfather, Robert Marmon.

Wole Soyinka

For an authoritative text and extensive background readings on *Death and the King's Horseman*, consult the Norton Critical Edition of that play (2003). Derek Wright, *Wole Soyinka Revisited* (1993) provides a nuanced analysis of the dramatic oeuvre, focusing on theatrical categories, such as ritual, tragedy, and satire, that are central to an understanding of Soyinka's work. Ketu H. Katrak, *Wole Soyinka and Modern Tragedy* (1986) focuses on the author's attempt to create a Yoruba tragedy. By far the best of the critical literature on the playwright is Biodun Jeyifo, *Wole Soyinka: Politics, Poetics and Postcoloniality* (2004), which analyzes the complex relations among colonial culture, independence, and literature that mark this playwright's oeuvre. See also a collection of interviews, *Conversations with Wole Soyinka*, ed. Biodun Jeyifo (2001). The philosopher K. Anthony Appiah has devoted attention to Soyinka in his work *In My Father's House: Africa in the Philosophy of Culture* (1992). There are several useful collections of essays on Soyinka, including James Gibbs, ed., *Critical Perspectives on Wole Soyinka* (1980) and Biodun Jeyifo, ed., *Perspectives on Wole Syoinka*.

Nguyen Huy Thiep

Nguyen Huy Thiep, *The General Retires and Other Stories* (1992), ed. Greg Lockhart, is the best general anthology of Thiep's short fiction in English translation. Lockhart's introductory essay gives an overview of Thiep's life, context, and the style and themes of his fiction. Nguyen Huy Thiep, *Crossing the River: Short Fiction* (2003), ed. Nguyen Nguyet Hep and Dana Sachs, is another strong anthology of the author's short fiction, with an illuminating introductory essay. Lin Dinh, ed., *Night Again: Contemporary Fiction from Vietnam* (1996), an anthology of contemporary Vietnamese fiction, helps contextualize Thiep's works within a national literary tradition. Mark W. McLeod and Nguyen Thi Dieu, *Culture and Customs of Vietnam* (2001) offers an overview of contemporary Vietnamese literature and culture that includes discussion of Thiep's works and their reception.

Derek Walcott

Derek Walcott, *Another Life* (1973), an autobiography in verse, traces the poet's artistic development. A full biography is Bruce King, *Derek Walcott: A Caribbean Life* (2000). Walcott's collection of essays, *What the Twilight Says* (1998), is an indispensable compendium of his social and aesthetic ideas. Robert Hamner, *Derek Walcott* (1978, rev. 1993), is a comprehensive and accessible full-length study of the writer's work; John Thieme, *Derek Walcott* (1999) is more up-to-date and provides commentaries on the key poems in Walcott's various collections and on the dramatic works. Robert Hamner, *Epic of the Dispossessed* (1997) offers a detailed discussion of *Omeros* that considers its adaptation of epic idiom to the experience and life dilemmas of the common folk. *The Art of Derek Walcott*, ed. Stewart Brown (1991), and *Crit-*

ical Perspectives on Derek Walcott, ed. Robert Hamner (1993), are collective volumes that cover Walcott's work up to the dates of their publication.

Yu Hua

To explore more of Yu Hua's work, begin with his most famous novel, *To Live*, translated by Michael Berry (1993) (and the film based on the novel, directed by Zhang Yimou in 1994); *Chronicle of a Blood Merchant*, translated by Andrew F. Jones (2003); *Brothers*, translated by Eileen Cheng-yin Chow and Carlos Rojas (2009); or his essay collection *China in Ten Words*, translated by Allan H. Barr (2011). For a study of Yu Hua's coming-of-age fiction in particular, see Hua Li, *Contemporary Chinese Fiction by Su Tong and Yu Hua* (2011).

Timeline

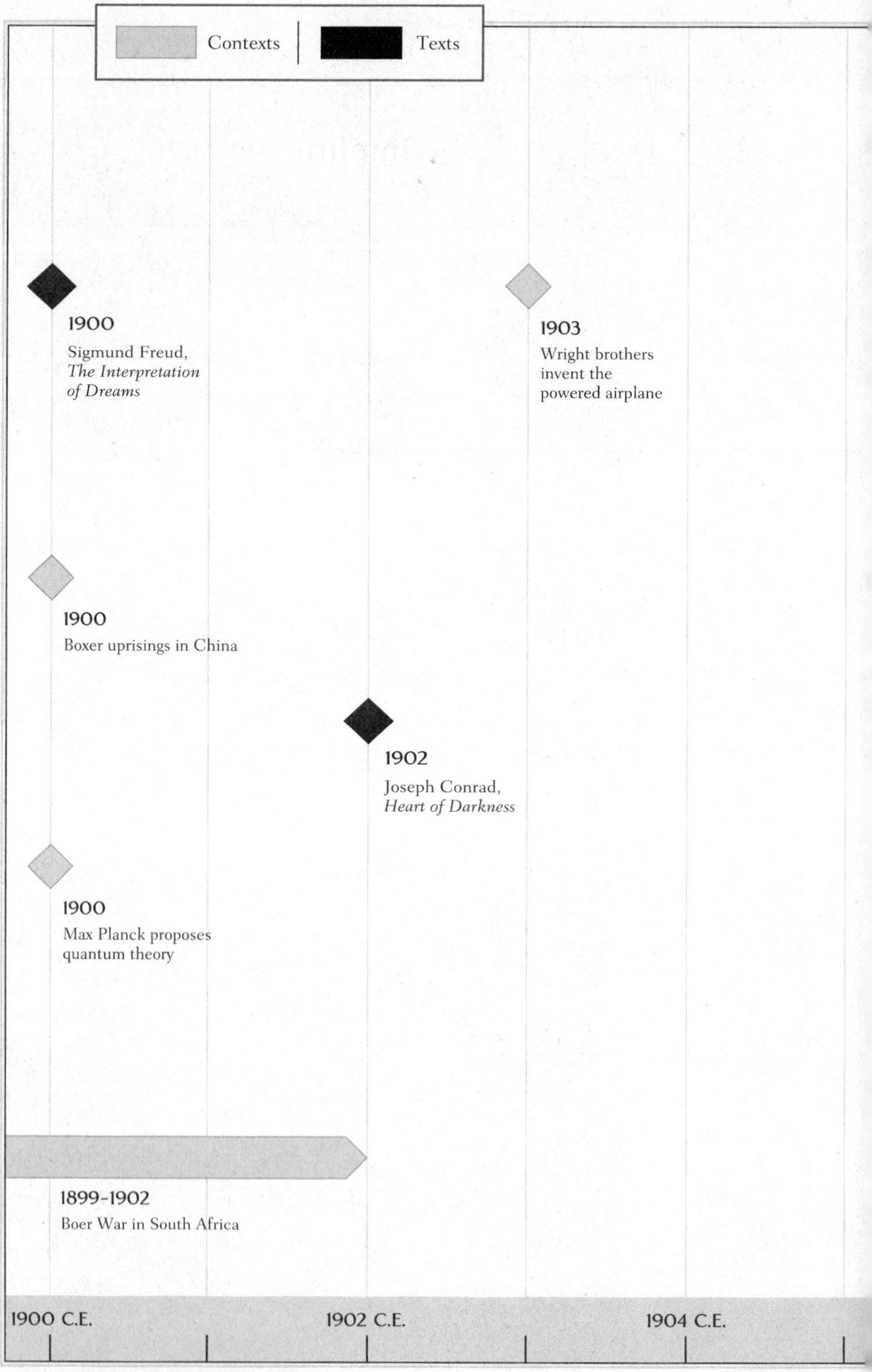
Contexts
Texts
1900
Sigmund Freud, *The Interpretation of Dreams*
1903
Wright brothers invent the powered airplane
1900
Boxer uprisings in China
1902
Joseph Conrad, *Heart of Darkness*
1900
Max Planck proposes quantum theory
1899–1902
Boer War in South Africa
1900 C.E.
1902 C.E.
1904 C.E.

1905
Partition of Bengal based on Hindu and Muslim populations

1909
F. T. Marinetti, *Futurist Manifesto*

1907
August Strindberg, *The Ghost Sonata*

1909
Commercial manufacture of plastic begins

1905
Foundation of International Workers of the World (IWW)

1908
Gertrude Stein, *Three Lives*

1907
Japanese immigration to the United States prohibited

1908
Rainer Maria Rilke, *New Poems*

1906 C.E. | 1908 C.E. | 1910 C.E.

Contexts | Texts

1910
China abolishes slavery

1913
Marcel Proust,
Swann's Way

1910
NAACP founded in
United States

1910
Tanizaki Jun'ichirō,
The Tattooer

1912–1913
Balkan wars

1910
Rabindranath Tagore,
Gitanjali

1914–1918
World War I

1911
Revolution establishes
Chinese Republic

1914
James Joyce,
Dubliners

1910
Post-Impressionist
exhibition in London

1913
D. H. Lawrence,
Sons and Lovers

1912
Thomas Mann,
Death in Venice

1910–1911
Mexican Revolution

1910 C.E. | 1912 C.E. | 1914 C.E.

1917
Chen Duxiu,
On Literary Revolution

1915
First transcontinental
phone call, in America

1918–1920
Global influenza
epidemic kills millions

1917
Russian Revolution
overthrows Romanov Dynasty

1919
Treaty of Versailles

1915
Albert Einstein
formulates general
theory of relativity

1918
Women over 30 given
vote in Great Britain

1917
T. S. Eliot,
*Prufrock and
Other Observations*

1915
Franz Kafka,
The Metamorphosis

1919
League of Nations
formed

1916
James Joyce,
*A Portrait of the Artist
as a Young Man*

1918
Lu Xun,
Diary of a Madman

1916 C.E. 1918 C.E. 1920 C.E.

Contexts | Texts

1920
Mahatma Gandhi leads India's struggle for independence from Britain

1921
Marianne Moore, *Poems*

1921
Luigi Pirandello, *Six Characters in Search of an Author*

1921–1929
Harlem Renaissance

1922
USSR formed

1922
Irish Free State established

1922
James Joyce, *Ulysses*

1922
Turkey becomes a republic

1922
Discovery of Egyptian pharaoh Tutankhamen's tomb

1922
T. S. Eliot, *The Waste Land*

1922
Rainer Maria Rilke, *Sonnets to Orpheus*

1923
Earthquakes destroy centers of Tokyo and Yokohama

1923
Rainer Maria Rilke, *Duino Elegies*

1923
Wallace Stevens, *Harmonium*

1924
Premchand, *The Road to Salvation*

1924
Thomas Mann, *The Magic Mountain*

1924
André Breton, *First Surrealist Manifesto*

1924
Insecticides first used

1920 C.E. | 1922 C.E. | 1924 C.E.

1926
Franz Kafka,
The Castle

1928
Penicillin discovered

1929
Stock market crash heralds beginning of Great Depression

1927
Virginia Woolf,
To the Lighthouse

1929
Virginia Woolf, *A Room of One's Own*

1926
Langston Hughes,
The Weary Blues

1928
First scheduled television broadcasts

1925
Vicente Huidobro,
Manifestos Manifest

1929
William Faulkner,
The Sound and the Fury

1928
William Butler Yeats,
The Tower

1926 C.E. 1928 C.E. 1930 C.E.

Contexts | Texts

1931
William Faulkner, *Spotted Horses*

1932
Kushi Fusako, *Memoirs of a Declining Ryukyuan Woman*

1933
Adolf Hitler given dictatorial powers in Germany

1933
Nazis build first concentration camps

1933
Federico García Lorca, *Blood Wedding*

1934
Stalin begins purges of Communist Party in Russia

1930 C.E. 1932 C.E. 1934 C.E.

1936–1939
Spanish Civil War

1939–1945
World War II

1935
Federico García Lorca, *Lament for Ignacio Sánchez Mejías*

1937
Wallace Stevens, *The Man with the Blue Guitar*

1939
Aimé Césaire, *Notebook of a Return to the Native Land*

1935
C. P. Cavafy, *Poems*

1937
Japan invades China

1939
Germany invades Poland

1938
William Faulkner, *Barn Burning*

1936
Premchand, *The Gift of a Cow*

1938
Ch'ae Man-Sik, *My Innocent Uncle*

1936
Lao She, *An Old and Established Name*

1936 C.E. | 1938 C.E. | 1940 C.E.

Contexts | Texts

1939–1945
World War II

1941
United States and Japan enter World War II

1945
The United States drops atomic bombs on Hiroshima and Nagasaki

1940
Richard Wright, *Native Son*

1942
Albert Camus, *The Stranger*

1944
T. S. Eliot, *Four Quartets*

1943
Bertolt Brecht, *The Good Woman of Setzuan* first performed

1941
Jorge Luis Borges, *The Garden of Forking Paths*

1943
Zhang Ailing, *Sealed Off*

1940 C.E. 1942 C.E. 1944 C.E.

1946
Churchill's "Iron Curtain" speech marks beginning of Cold War

1948
Creation of the state of Israel

1945
United Nations, Arab League founded

1947
Paul Celan, *Deathfugue*

1949
People's Republic of China established

1948
Founding of the Organization of American States

1945
Léopold Sédar Senghor, *Chants d'ombre*

1947
Partition of India and Pakistan into independent states

1946
Tadeusz Borowski, *Ladies and Gentlemen, to the Gas Chamber*

1946
Pan-African Federation formed

1949
Apartheid instituted in South Africa

1947
Transistor invented

1946
Julio Cortázar, *House Taken Over*

1946 C.E. | 1948 C.E. | 1950 C.E.

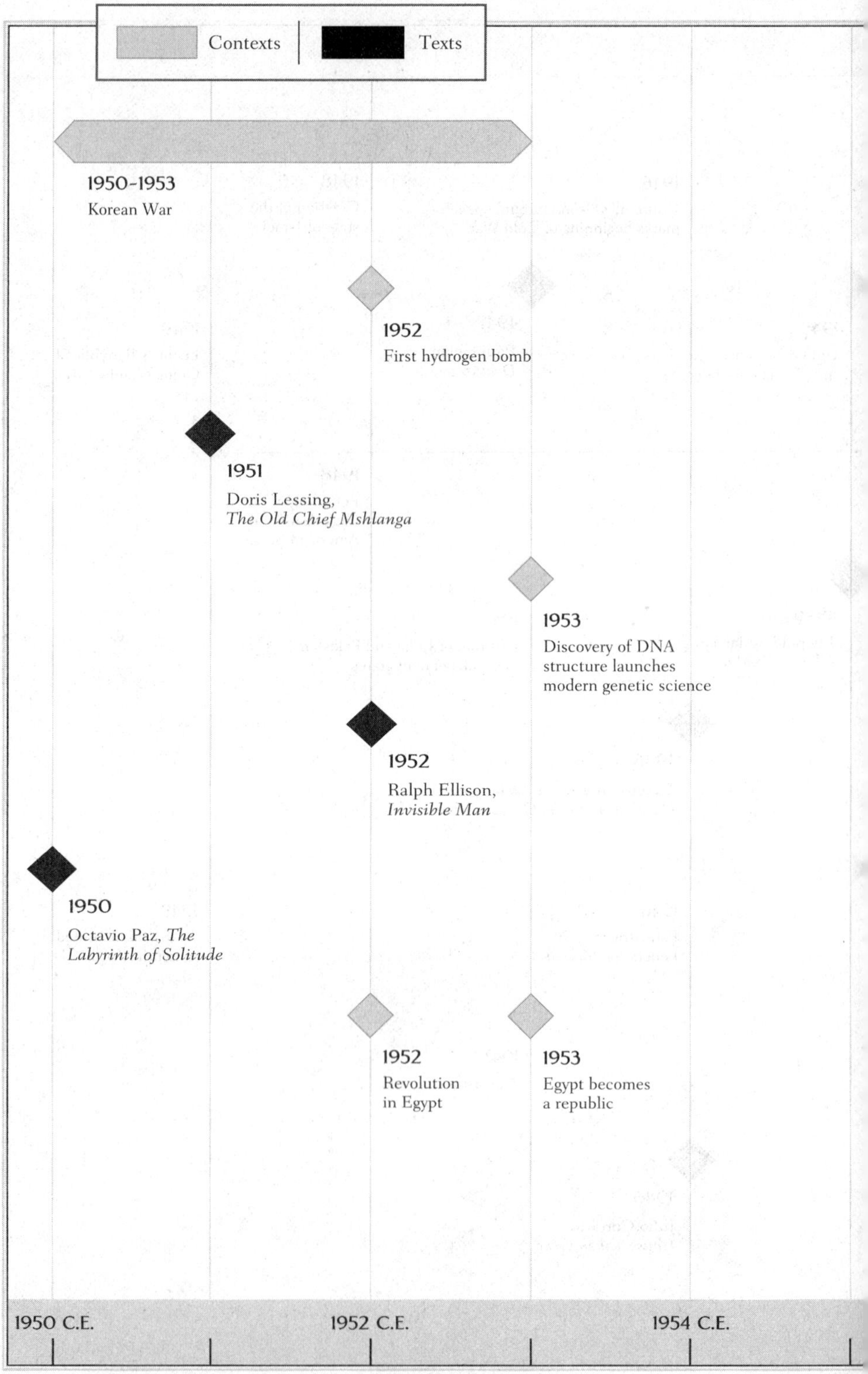
Contexts
Texts
1950–1953
Korean War
1952
First hydrogen bomb
1951
Doris Lessing, *The Old Chief Mshlanga*
1953
Discovery of DNA structure launches modern genetic science
1952
Ralph Ellison, *Invisible Man*
1950
Octavio Paz, *The Labyrinth of Solitude*
1952
Revolution in Egypt
1953
Egypt becomes a republic
1950 C.E.
1952 C.E.
1954 C.E.

1955
Saadat Hasan Manto, *Toba Tek Singh*

1955
James Baldwin, *Notes of a Native Son*

1956
First Congress of Black Writers meets in Paris

1956
Hungarian revolt against Communism crushed by Soviet Union

1956–1957
Naguib Mahfouz, *The Cairo Trilogy*

1957
Samuel Beckett, *Endgame*

1957
Albert Camus, *Exile and the Kingdom*

1958
European Common Market established

1958
Chinua Achebe, *Things Fall Apart*

1958–1962
Algerian War of Independence

1959
Vladimir Nabokov, *The Vane Sisters*

1959
Tawfiq al-Hakim, *The Sultan's Dilemma*

1956 C.E. | 1958 C.E. | 1960 C.E.

Contexts | Texts

1960–1962
Independence for Senegal, Nigeria, Algeria, and other African nations

1964
Civil Rights Act ends legal segregation in the United States

1960
Tayeb Salih, *The Doum Tree of Wad Hamid*

1962
Doris Lessing, *The Golden Notebook*

1961
Soviet astronaut orbits earth

1962
Carlos Fuentes, *Aura*

1964
Mahmoud Darwish, *Identity Card*

1960
Contraceptive pill introduced

1963
Naguib Mahfouz, *Zaabalawi*

1960
Chinua Achebe, *Chike's School Days*

1963
Alexander Solzhenitsyn, *Matryona's Home*

1960
Clarice Lispector, *The Daydreams of a Drunk Woman*

1962–1973
United States engaged in Vietnam War

1963
Anna Akhmatova, *Requiem*

1958–1962
Algerian War of Independence

1963
Julio Cortázar, *Hopscotch*

1960 C.E. | 1962 C.E. | 1964 C.E.

1965
Recorded performance by Andrew Peynetsa of *The Boy and the Deer*

1969
Stonewall Riots mark beginning of Gay Rights Movement

1967
Gabriel García Márquez, *One Hundred Years of Solitude*

1966
First Dakar Arts Festival provides showcase for African culture

1969
American astronaut is first human on moon

1966
Mao Tse-tung's Cultural Revolution attacks Confucian tradition and intellectuals in China

1968
Yehuda Amichai, *Not of This Time, Not of This Place*

1968
Valerie Solanas, *SCUM Manifesto*

1966
Black Panther Platform

1968
Alice Munro, *Walker Brothers Cowboy*

1966
Seamus Heaney, *Death of a Naturalist*

1968
Protests against Communism in Prague, against capitalism in Paris, and against the Vietnam War throughout the United States

1966 C.E. 1968 C.E. 1970 C.E.

Contexts | Texts

1972
U.S. Congress passes Equal Rights Amendment

1970
García Márquez, *Death Constant Beyond Love*

1974
The term "Internet" is coined

1972
Unarmed Catholic protesters killed by British armed forces in Northern Ireland in Bloody Sunday massacre

1971
V. S. Naipaul, *One Out of Many*

1974
Leslie Marmon Silko, *Yellow Woman*

1962–1973
United States engaged in Vietnam War

1973
Arab oil producers cut off shipments to nations supporting Israel; ensuing energy crisis reshapes global economy

1970
Ama Ata Aidoo, *Two Sisters*

1970 C.E. 1972 C.E. 1974 C.E.

1976
North and South Vietnam reunited as a single country

1977
Bessie Head, *Deep River*

1975
Wole Soyinka, *Death and the King's Horseman*

1979
Soviet invasion of Afghanistan

1975
Ngugi wa Thiong'o, *Wedding at the Cross*

1978
First "test tube baby" born in England

1976 C.E. 1978 C.E. 1980 C.E.

Contexts | Texts

1980
Salman Rushdie,
Midnight's Children

1980
Nawal El Saadawi,
In Camera

1980
Jamaica Kincaid,
Girl

1980
Ōe Kenzaburō,
The Clever Rain Tree

1981
Aquired Immune Deficiency Syndrome (AIDS) first diagnosed

1982
Mahasweta Devi,
Giribala

1982
U.S. Equal Rights Amendment fails to be ratified by states, never comes into effect

1983
Hanan Al-Shaykh,
The Women's Swimming Pool

1983
Niyi Osundare,
Poems of the Marketplace

1983–1984
Ethnic and religious riots throughout India

1983–1984
Famine in Ethiopia

1983
Toni Morrison,
Recitatif

1980 C.E. | 1982 C.E. | 1984 C.E.

1985
Mo Yan,
The Old Gun

1987
Floods destroy homes of millions in Bangladesh

1989
Berlin Wall demolished

1987
Toni Morrison,
Beloved

1986
Meltdown in Chernobyl nuclear plant spreads radiation contamination throughout Europe

1989
Isabel Allende,
And of Clay Are We Created

1986
Nuclear arms agreement between United States and Soviet Union

1989
Chinese government shoots thousands of protesters gathered in Tiananmen Square

1987
Nguyen Huy Thiep,
The General Retires

1989
Mikhail Gorbachev restructures the Soviet Union

1986 C.E. | 1988 C.E. | 1990 C.E.

Contexts | Texts

1990
East and West Germany united

1990
Derek Walcott, *Omeros*

1991
United States and USSR agree to arms reduction

1991
Economic chaos and nationalist unrest bring end of Soviet Union

1991
First Persian Gulf War begins as United States invades Iraq in response to Iraqi invasion of Kuwait in 1990

1993
World Wide Web established

1993
Maastricht Treaty forms European Union

1994
Zhu Tianxin, *Man of La Mancha*

1994
Nelson Mandela becomes president of South Africa after first multiracial elections

1994
Israel and PLO sign peace agreement establishing a Palestinian government

1990 C.E. — 1992 C.E. — 1994 C.E.

1998
Google search engine founded

1997
Roberto Bolaño, *Sensini*

1999
A European common currency, the "euro," is issued

1996
Junot Díaz, *Drown*

1999
Orhan Pamuk, *To Look Out the Window*

1997
Scientists in Scotland create Dolly, the clone of an adult sheep

1999
J. M. Coetzee, *The Novel in Africa*

1996 C.E. | 1998 C.E. | 2000 C.E.

Contexts | Texts

2001
Terrorists hijack jets and fly them into the World Trade Center and the Pentagon on September 11

2001
American- and British-led war in Afghanistan begins

2003
Second Gulf War begins with invasion of Iraq by American-led forces

2004
Indian Ocean tsunami kills over 200,000

2003
J. M. Coetzee, *Elizabeth Costello*

2002
African Union founded

2003
Human Genome Project completes sequencing of human DNA

2000 C.E. 2002 C.E. 2004 C.E.

2008
Worldwide financial recession

2008
Earthquake in China kills over 60,000

2007
Niyi Osundare, *Days*

2006 C.E. 2008 C.E. 2010 C.E.

Permissions Acknowledgments

Chinua Achebe: "Chike's School Days" from GIRLS AT WAR AND OTHER STORIES by Chinua Achebe, copyright © 1972, 1973 by Chinua Achebe. Used by permission of Doubleday, an imprint of the Knopf Doubleday Publishing Group, a division of Penguin Random House LLC. All rights reserved. Any third party use of this material, outside of this publication, is prohibited. Interested parties must apply directly to Penguin Random House LLC for permission. Rights in Canada by permission of The Wylie Agency LLC.

Chimamanda Ngozi Adichie: "The Headstrong Historian" from THE THING AROUND YOUR NECK. Copyright © 2009 by Chimamanda Ngozi Adichie, used by permission of The Wylie Agency LLC.

Anna Akhmatova: "Requiem" from COMPLETE POEMS OF ANNA AKHMATOVA, trans. by Judith Hemschemeyer, edited with an introduction by Roberta Reeder. Copyright © 1989, 1992, 1997 by Judith Hemschemeyer. Reprinted with the permission of Zephyr Press, www.zephyrpress.org.

Akutagawa Ryūnosuke: "In a Bamboo Grove" from RASHOMON AND SEVENTEEN OTHER STORIES by RYŪNOSUKE Akutagawa, trans. by Jay Rubin with an introduction by Haruki Murakami. Translation copyright © 2006 by Jay Rubin. Used by permission of Penguin Books, an imprint of Penguin Publishing Group, a division of Penguin Random House LLC. All rights reserved. Any third party use of this material, outside of this publication, is prohibited. Interested parties must apply directly to Penguin Random House LLC for permission. Rights in Canada by permission of Penguin Books Ltd.

Isabel Allende: "And of Clay Are We Created" is reprinted with the permission of Scribner, a division of Simon & Schuster, Inc. from THE STORIES OF EVA LUNA by Isabel Allende, trans. from the Spanish by Margaret Sayers Peden. Copyright © 1989 by Isabel Allende. English translation copyright © 1991 by Macmillan Publishing Company. All rights reserved.

Ama Ata Aidoo: "Two Sisters" from NO SWEETNESS HERE AND OTHER STORIES. Copyright © 1970 by Ama Ata Aidoo. Reprinted with the permission of The Permissions Company, Inc. on behalf of The Feminist Press at the City University of New York, www.feministpress.org. All rights reserved.

Yehuda Amichai: "God Has Pity on Kindergarten Children," and "Jerusalem" trans. by Stephen Mitchell; "An Arab Shepherd Is Searching for His Goat on Mount Zion," trans. by Chana Bloch, from THE SELECTED POETRY OF YEHUDA AMICHAI, trans. by Chana Bloch and Stephen Mitchell. Copyright © 1986 by Chana Bloch and Stephen Mitchell. Reprinted by permission of the University of California Press via the Copyright Clearance Center. "If I Forget Thee, Jerusalem," trans. by Assia Gutmann, "Sleep in Jerusalem," trans. by Harold Schimmel from POEMS OF JERUSALEM and LOVE POEMS [in one vol.] by Yehuda Amichai, copyright © 1981, 1988 by Yehuda Amichai. Reprinted by permission of The Sheep Meadow Press and the Estate of Yehuda Amichai.

James Baldwin: From NOTES OF A NATIVE SON by James Baldwin. Copyright © 1955, renewed 1983 by James Baldwin. Reprinted by permission of Beacon Press via the Copyright Clearance Center.

Samuel Beckett: "Endgame" from ENDGAME AND ACT WITHOUT WORDS I, copyright © 1958 by Grove Press, Inc. Used by permission of Grove/Atlantic, Inc.

Black Panther Manifesto: From BAMN (BY ANY MEANS NECESSARY): OUTLAW MANIFESTOS AND EPHEMERA 1965–1970, ed. Peter Stansill and David Zane Mairowitz, reprinted by permission of The Dr. Huey P. Newton Foundation.

Roberto Bolaño: "Sensini" from LAST EVENINGS ON EARTH, copyright © 2002 by Editorial Anagrama. Translation copyright © 2006 by Chris Andrews. Reprinted by permission of New Directions Publishing Corp.

Jorge Luis Borges: "The Garden of Forking Paths," trans. by Donald A. Yates, from LABYRINTHS, copyright © 1962, 1964 by New Directions Publishing Corp. "The Library of Babel," trans. by James E. Irby from LABYRINTHS. Copyright © 1962, 1964 by New Directions Publishing Corp. Reprinted by permission of New Directions Publishing Corp.

Tadeusz Borowski: "This Way for the Gas, Ladies and Gentlemen," from THIS WAY FOR THE GAS, LADIES AND GENTLEMEN, trans. by Barbara Vedder, translation copyright © 1967 by Penguin Books Ltd., copyright © 1959 by Maria Borowski. Used by permission of Viking Penguin, an imprint of Penguin Publishing Group, a division of Penguin Random House LLC. All rights reserved. Any third party use of this material, outside of this publication, is prohibited. Interested parties must apply directly to Penguin Random House LLC for permission. Rights in Canada by permission of Penguin Books Ltd.

Bertolt Brecht: "The Good Woman of Setzuan," English version by Eric Bentley from PARABLES FOR THE THEATRE: TWO PLAYS BY BERTOLT BRECHT. Copyright © 1947 as an unpublished ms. Copyright © 1948, 1956, 1961, 1983 by Eric Bentley. Reprinted by permission of The University of Minnesota Press.

André Breton: From MANIFESTOS OF SURREALISM, trans. by Richard Seaver and Helen Lane. Copyright © 1969 by The University of Michigan. Reprinted by permission of the University of Michigan Press via the Copyright Clearance Center.

Albert Camus: "The Guest" from EXILE AND THE KINGDOM by Albert Camus, trans. by Justin O'Brien, copyright © 1957, 1958 by Alfred A. Knopf, a division of Penguin Random House LLC. Used by permission of Alfred A. Knopf, an imprint of the Knopf Doubleday Publishing Group, a division of Penguin Random House LLC. All rights reserved. Any third party use of this material, outside of this publication, is prohibited. Interested parties must apply directly to Penguin Random House LLC for permission.

Chu T'ien-hsin: "Man of La Mancha" from THE OLD CAPITAL: A NOVEL OF TAIPEI by Chu T'ien-hsin, trans. by Howard Goldblatt. Copyright © 2007 by Columbia University Press. Reprinted by permission of the publisher.

Constantine Cavafy: "Waiting for the Barbarians," "The City," "A Sculptor from Tyana," "Ithaka," "Evening," "Kaisarion," "The Next Table," "A Craftsman of Wine Bowls" from THE COLLECTED POEMS OF C. P. CAVAFY: A NEW TRANSLATION, trans. by Aliki Barnstone. Copyright © 2006 by Aliki Barnstone. Used by permission of W. W. Norton & Company, Inc.

Paul Celan: "Zurich, at the Stork," originally published in German as "Zurich, zum Storchen" in NIEMANDSROSE, copyright © 1963 S. Fischer Verlag GmbH, Frankfurt am Main. Underlying rights by permission of Regal Hoffmann & Associates LLC as agent for S. Fischer Verlag. "Deathfugue" originally published in German as "Todesfuge" in MOHN UND GEDACHTNIS. Copyright © 1952 Deutsche Verlags-Anstalt, Munich, a division of Verlagsgruppe Random House. Underlying rights by permission of Verlagsgruppe Random House. English translations from SELECTED POEMS AND PROSE OF PAUL CELAN, trans. by John Felstiner. Copyright © 2001 by John Felstiner. Used by permission of W. W. Norton & Company, Inc.

Aimé Césaire: "Notebook of a Return to the Native Land" from THE COLLECTED POETRY by Aimé Césaire, trans. by Clayton Eshleman and Annette Smith. Copyright © 1983 by the Regents of the University of California. Reprinted by permission of the University of California Press.

Ch'ae Man-sik: "My Innocent Uncle," trans. by Bruce Fulton and Ju-Chan Fulton from MODERN KOREAN FICTION: AN ANTHOLOGY, edited by Bruce Fulton and Youngmin Kwon. Copyright © 2005 by Columbia University Press. Reprinted by permission of the publisher.

Chen Duxiu: "On Literary Revolution," trans. by Timothy Wong from MODERN CHINESE LITERARY THOUGHT, ed. Kirk A. Denton. Copyright © 1996 by the Board of Trustees of the Leland Stanford Jr. University. All rights reserved. Used with the permission of Stanford University Press, www.sup.org.

Julio Cortázar: "House Taken Over," from END OF THE GAME AND OTHER STORIES by Julio Cortázar, trans. by Paul Blackburn, copyright © 1967 by Random House, Inc. Used by permission of Pantheon Books, an imprint of the Knopf Doubleday Publishing Group, a division of Penguin Random House LLC. All rights reserved. Any third party use of this material, outside of this publication, is prohibited. Interested parties must apply directly to Penguin Random House LLC for permission.

Junot Díaz: "Drown" from DROWN, copyright © 1996 by Junot Díaz. Used by permission of Riverhead, an imprint of Penguin Publishing Group, a division of Penguin Random House LLC. All rights reserved. Any third party use of this material, outside of this publication, is prohibited. Interested parties must apply directly to Penguin Random House LLC for permission.

T. S. Eliot: "The Love Song of J. Alfred Prufrock" and "The Waste Land" from COLLECTED POEMS 1909–1962. Reprinted by permission of Faber & Faber Ltd.

William Faulkner: "Spotted Horses" and "Barn Burning" from THE COLLECTED SHORT STORIES OF WILLIAM FAULKNER. Copyright © 1950 by Random House, Inc. Copyright renewed 1977 by Jill Faulkner Summers. Reprinted by permission.

Carlos Fuentes: AURA, trans. by Lysander Kemp. Copyright © 1965 by Carlos Fuentes. Reprinted by permission of Farrar, Straus and Giroux.

Federico García Lorca: "Llanto por Ignacio Sánchez Mejías" ("Lament for Ignacio Sanchez Mejias") trans. by Pablo Medina. Copyright © Herederos de Federico Garcia Lorca. Reprinted by permission of Casnovas & Lynch Agencia Literaria S. L. and the translator c/o ARAGI Inc.

Gabriel García Márquez: "Death Constant Beyond Love" from INNOCENT ERENDIRA AND OTHER STORIES by Gabriel García Márquez, translated from the Spanish by Gregory Rabassa. English translation copyright © 1978 by Harper & Row, Publishers, Inc. Reprinted by permission of HarperCollins Publishers.

Hanan al-Shaykh: "The Women's Swimming Pool," trans. by Denys Johnson-Davies, from MODERN

ARABIC FICTION, ed. by Salma Khadri Jayyusi. Copyright © 2005 by Columbia University Press. Reprinted by permission of the publisher.

Bessie Head: "The Deep River" from THE COLLECTOR OF TREASURES AND OTHER BOTSWANA VILLAGE TALES (Long Grove, IL: Waveland Press, Inc.). Copyright © 1977 by The Estate of Bessie Head. Reissued in 2014. All rights reserved. Reproduced with permission of Waveland Press, Inc.

Seamus Heaney: "Digging," "Punishment," and "The Tollund Man" from OPENED GROUND: SELECTED POEMS 1966–1996. Copyright © 1996 by Seamus Heaney. Reprinted by permission of Farrar, Straus and Giroux and Faber & Faber Ltd.

Franz Kafka: "Metamorphosis" from METAMORPHOSIS: A NEW TRANSLATION, trans. by Susan Bernofsky. Copyright © 2014 by Susan Bernofsky. Used by permission of W. W. Norton & Company, Inc.

Jamaica Kincaid: "Girl" from AT THE BOTTOM OF THE RIVER. Copyright © 1983 by Jamaica Kincaid. Reprinted by permission of Farrar, Straus and Giroux.

Kushi Fusako: "Memoirs of a Declining Ryukyuan Woman" and "In Defense of 'Memoirs of a Declining Ryukyuan Woman'" from SOUTHERN EXPOSURE: MODERN JAPANESE LITERATURE FROM OKINAWA, trans. by Kimiko Miyagi, ed. by Michael Molasky and Steve Rabson. Copyright © 2000 University of Hawaii Press. Reprinted by permission.

Lao She: "An Old Established Name," trans. by William A. Lyell, from BLADES OF GRASS: THE STORIES OF LAO SHE, ed. by Howard Goldblatt, trans. by William A. Lyell and Sarah Wei-ming Chen. Copyright © 1999 by the University of Hawaii Press. Reprinted with permission of the publisher.

Doris Lessing: "The Old Chief Mshlanga" from AFRICAN STORIES by Doris Lessing is reprinted by permission of Simon & Schuster, Inc. and Jonathan Clowes Ltd. Copyright © 1951, 1953, 1954, 1957, 1958, 1962, 1963, 1964, 1965, 1972, 1981 by Doris Lessing. All rights reserved.

Clarice Lispector: "The Daydreams of a Drunk Woman" from FAMILY TIES by Clarice Lispector, trans. by Giovanni Pontiero. Copyright © 1972 by Clarice Lispector. Reprinted by permission of the University of Texas Press.

Lu Xun: "Ah Q-The Real Story" and "Diary of a Madman" from DIARY OF A MADMAN AND OTHER STORIES, trans. by William A. Lyell. Copyright © 1990 by the University of Hawaii Press. Reprinted with permission from University of Hawai'i Press, http://www.uhpress.hawaii.edu/

Naguib Mahfouz: "Zaabalawi" from MODERN ARABIC SHORT STORIES, trans. by Denys Johnson-Davies. Translation copyright © 1967 by Denys Johnson-Davies. Reprinted by permission of the translator.

Thomas Mann: From DEATH IN VENICE: A NORTON CRITICAL EDITION, trans. by Clayton Koelb. Copyright © 1994 by W. W. Norton & Company, Inc. Used by permission of W. W. Norton & Company, Inc.

F. T. Marinetti: "Foundation and Manifesto of Futurism" from CRITICAL WRITINGS by F. T. Marinetti, ed. by Günter Berghaus, trans. by Doug Thompson. Copyright © 2006 by Luce Marinetti, Vittoria Marinetti Piazzoni, and Ala Marinetti Clerici. Translation, compilation, editorial work, foreword, preface, and introduction copyright © 2006 by Farrar, Straus, and Giroux. Reprinted by permission of Farrar, Straus and Giroux.

Mo Yan: "The Old Gun" first published in EXPLOSIONS AND OTHER STORIES by Mo Yan, trans. Duncan Hewitt, ed. Janice Wickeri, p. 59–75. Copyright © 1991. Reprinted by permission of the Research Centre for Translation, The Chinese University of Hong Kong.

Toni Morrison: "Recitatif," copyright © 1983 by Toni Morrison. Used by permission. All rights reserved.

Vladimir Nabokov: "The Vane Sisters" from THE STORIES OF VLADIMIR NABOKOV by Vladimir Nabokov, copyright © 1995 by Dmitri Nabokov. Used by permission of Alfred A. Knopf, an imprint of the Knopf Doubleday Publishing Group, a division of Penguin Random House LLC. All rights reserved. Any third party use of this material, outside of this publication, is prohibited. Interested parties must apply directly to Penguin Random House LLC for permission.

Pablo Neruda: From Canto II. "The Heights of Macchu Picchu," from CANTO GENERAL: FIFTH ANNIVERSARY EDITION, trans. by Jack Schmitt. Copyright © 1991 by the Fundacion Pablo Neruda and the Regents of the University of California. Reprinted by permission of the University of California Press. "Tonight I Can Write" and "Walking Around," trans. by W.S. Merwin, "I'm Explaining a Few Things" and "Ode to the Tomato," trans. by Nathaniel Tarn, from SELECTED POEMS by Pablo Neruda, ed. and with a foreword by Nathaniel Tarn, published by Jonathan Cape. Reprinted by permission of The Random House Group Limited.

Ōe Kenzaburō: "The Clever Rain Tree," trans. by Brett de Bary and Carolyn Haynes from THE SHOWA ANTHOLOGY, ed. Van C. Gessel and Tomone Matsumoto. Copyright © 1980 by Kenzaburô Ōe. Anthology copyright © 1985, 1989, 1992 by Kodansha International Ltd. Reprinted by permission of the publisher.

Orhan Pamuk: "To Look Out the Window" from OTHER COLORS: ESSAYS AND A STORY by Orhan Pamuk, trans. by Maureen Freely, translation copyright © 2007 by Maureen Freely. Used by permission of Alfred A. Knopf, an imprint of the Knopf Doubleday Publishing Group, a division of Penguin Random House LLC. All rights reserved. Any third party use of this material, outside of this publication, is prohibited. Interested parties must apply directly to Penguin Random House LLC for permission. Rights in Canada by permission of Vintage/Canada/Alfred A. Knopf Canada, a division of Penguin Random House Canada Limited. Copyright © 2007 by Orhan Pamuk.

Park Wansuh: "Mother's Hitching Post, Part 2" published in MODERN KOREAN FICTION, ed. by Bruce Fulton and Youngmin Kwon, as "Mother's Hitching Post" by Pak Wanso, trans. by Kim Miza and Suzanne Crowder-Han. Copyright © 2005. Reprinted by permission of Suzanne Crowder-Han and Youngmin Kwon.

Octavio Paz: "I Speak of the City" from COLLECTED POEMS 1957–1987, trans. by Eliot Weinberger, copyright © 1984 by Octavio Paz and Eliot Weinberger. "Central Park", trans. by Eliot Weinberger, copyright © 1986 by Octavio Paz and Eliot Weinberger. Reprinted by permission of New Directions Publishing Corp. "Small Variation," trans. by Mark Strand, first published in *The New Yorker*, April 1979, is reprinted by permission of the author.

Luigi Pirandello: "Six Characters in Search of an Author," trans. by Eric Bentley, copyright © 1970 by Eric Bentley, from PIRANDELLO'S MAJOR PLAYS, trans. by Eric Bentley. Reprinted by permission of Northwestern University Press.

Marcel Proust: "Part 1: Combray" from SWANN'S WAY, trans. by Lydia Davis. Copyright © 2002 by Lydia Davis. Used by permission of Viking Penguin, an imprint of Penguin Publishing Group, a division of Penguin Random House LLC. All rights reserved. Any third party use of this material, outside of this publication, is prohibited. Interested parties must apply directly to Penguin Random House LLC for permission. Rights in Canada licensed by Penguin UK from IN SEARCH OF LOST TIME: Vol. 1: "The Way by Swann's: Overture." Translation and editorial matter copyright © 2002 by Lydia Davis. General Editor's Preface copyright © 2002 by Christopher Prendergast. (Allen Lane, The Penguin Press, 2002). Reproduced by permission of Penguin Books Ltd.

Rainer Maria Rilke: "Archaic Torso of Apollo," "The Panther," "The Swan," and "Spanish Dancer," from TRANSLATIONS FROM THE POETRY OF RAINER MARIA RILKE, trans. by M. D. Herter Norton. Copyright 1938 by W. W. Norton & Company, Inc. renewed © 1966 by M. D. Herter Norton. Used by permission of W. W. Norton & Company, Inc.

Salman Rushdie: "The Perforated Sheet" from MIDNIGHT'S CHILDREN is used by permission of The Wylie Agency LLC. Copyright © 1980 by Salman Rushdie.

Nawal el Saadawi: "In Camera" from DEATH OF AN EX-MINISTER, trans. by Shirley Eber. First published by Methuen in 1987. Copyright © 1987. Reprinted by permission of the author.

Leslie Marmon Silko: "Yellow Woman" from STORYTELLER. Copyright © 1981 by Leslie Marmon Silko. Used with permission of Viking Books, an imprint of Penguin Publishing Group, a division of Penguin Random House LLC. All rights reserved. Any third party use of this material, outside of this publication, is prohibited. Interested parties must apply directly to Penguin Random House LLC for permission.

Valerie Solanas: From SCUM MANIFESTO (1968). Reprinted by permission of Verso.

Alexander Solzhenitsyn: "Matryona's Home" trans. by Michael Glenny from STORIES AND PROSE POEMS. Translation © copyright 1971 by Michael Glenny. Copyright © Alexandre Soljenitsyne pour la langue russe. Copyright 2007 by Librairie Aetheme Fayard. Reprinted by permission of Farrar, Straus and Giroux and Librairie Artheme Fayard.

Wole Soyinka: DEATH AND THE KING'S HORSEMAN by Wole Soyinka. Copyright © 1975 by Wole Soyinka. Used by permission of W.W. Norton & Company, Inc. and Melanie Jackson Agency, LLC. Copyright © 1975, 2003 by Wole Soyinka.

Nguyen Huy Thiep: "The General Retires," trans. by Linh Dinh, from CROSSING THE RIVER: SHORT FICTION by Nguyen Huy Thiep, ed. by Nguyen Nguyet Cam and Dana Sachs. Introduction © 2003 by Nguyen Cam and Dana Sachs. Translations copyright © 2003 by the respective translators. Reprinted by permission of Northwestern University Press.

Ngugi wa Thiong'o: "Wedding at the Cross" from SECRET LIVES AND OTHER STORIES. Copyright © 1975 by Ngugi wa Thiong'o. Reprinted by permission of the author and the Watkins/Loomis Agency.

Tristan Tzara: From DADA MANIFESTO 1918, trans. by Mary Ann Caws. Reprinted by permission of the translator.

Derek Walcott: "The Almond Trees" from CASTAWAY. Copyright © 1965 by Derek Walcott. "As John to Patmos," "Crusoe's Journal," "Ruins of a Great House," "Sea Grapes," "The Sea Is History," and "Verandah" from THE POETRY OF DEREK WALCOTT 1948–2013, selected by Glynn Maxwell. Copyright © 2014 by Derek Walcott. "Chapter I" from Book I and "Chapter LXIV" from Book VII from OMEROS. Copyright © 1990 by Derek Walcott. Reprinted by permission of Farrar, Straus and Giroux.

Virginia Woolf: Excerpts from A ROOM OF ONE'S OWN by Virginia Woolf, copyright 1929 by Houghton Mifflin Harcourt Publishing Company. Copyright © renewed 1957 by Leonard Woolf. Reprinted by permission of Houghton Mifflin Harcourt Publishing Company. All rights reserved.

Yasunari Kawabata: "The Dancing Girl of Izu" from THE DANCING GIRL OF IZU AND OTHER STORIES, trans. by J. Martin Holman. Copyright © 1997 by Hite Kawabata. English translation copyright © 1997 by J. Martin Holman. Reprinted by permission of Counterpoint.

W. B. Yeats: "Leda and the Swan," "Sailing to Byzantium," and "Among School Children," copyright © 1928 by The Macmillan Company, renewed 1956 by Georgie Yeats. All rights reserved. "Byzantium," copyright © 1933 by The MacMillan Company, renewed 1961 by Bertha Georgie Yeats. All rights reserved. "Lapis Lazuli" and "The Circus Animals' Desertion," copyright © 1940 by Georgie Yeats, renewed 1968 by Bertha Georgie Yeats, Michael Butler Yeats, and Anne Yeats. All rights reserved. Reprinted with permission of Scribner, a division of Simon & Schuster, Inc. from THE COLLECTED WORKS OF W. B. YEATS, vol. 1: THE POEMS: REVISED, ed. by Richard J. Finneran.

Yu Hua: "On the Road at Eighteen," trans. by Andrew F. Jones, from THE PAST AND THE PUNISHMENT: EIGHT STORIES, ed. by Howard Goldblatt (1996). Reprinted with permission from the University of Hawai'i Press, http:///www.uhpress.hawaii.edu.

Zhang Ailing (Eileen Chang): "Sealed Off," trans. by Karen Kingsbury from THE COLUMBIA ANTHOLOGY OF MODERN CHINESE LITERATURE, ed. by Joseph M. Lau and Howard Goldblatt. Copyright © 1995 by Columbia University Press. Reprinted by permission of the publisher.

IMAGES

2–3 Rodchenko, Alexander (1891–1956) © VAGA, NY Advertisement: "Books!", 1925. Scala/Art Resource, NY. Art. © Estate of Alexander Rodchenko/RAO, Moscow/VAGA, New York; **4** Wikimedia, public domain; **5** Bettmann/Getty Images; **8** United States Holocaust Memorial Museum; **10** Picasso, Pablo (1881–1973) Guernica. 1937. Photo: John Bigelow Taylor/Art Resource, NY. © 2017 Estate of Pablo Picasso/Artists Rights Society (ARS), New York; **12** Digital Image © 2017 Museum Associates/ LACMA./Licensed by Art Resource, NY. © 2017 Artists Rights Society (ARS), New York/ADAGP, Paris; **534–535** © National Trust Images/The Society of Authors; **660** Wikimedia, public domain; **686–687** Margaret Bourke-White/The LIFE Picture Collection/Getty Images; **689** Photo by Loomis Dean/The LIFE Picture Collection/Getty Images; **690** © Bettmann/Getty Images; **874–875** Marc Riboud/Magnum Photos; **876** Jean-Claude LABBE/Gamma-Rapho via Getty Images; **877** Gallo Images/Oryx Media Archive/Getty Images; **880** Shirin Neshat

VOLUME F COLOR INSERT

C1 Alinari/Art Resource, NY; **C2** © CNAC/MNAM/Dist. RMN-Grand Palais/Art Resource, NY. © ARS, NY.; **C3** © British Library Board/Robana/Art Resource, NY; **C4** © Lorenzo Ciniglio/CORBIS/ Corbis via Getty Images; **C5** The New York Public Library/Art Resource, NY; **C6** HIP/Art Resource, NY; **C6** Eliot Elisofon/The LIFE Picture Collection/Getty Images; **C7** Imaginechina via AP Images; **C8** © The Touch Press

Index